The

VARIORUM EDITION

of the

Poetry of

JOHN DONNE

VOLUME 7

PART I

THE

VARIORUM EDITION

of the

Poetry of

JOHN DONNE

VOLUME 7, PART I

GENERAL EDITOR

Gary A. Stringer

CHIEF EDITOR OF THE COMMENTARY

Paul A. Parrish

ADVISORY BOARD

Dennis Flynn

Dayton Haskin

M. Thomas Hester

Albert C. Labriola

Paul A. Parrish

Ted-Larry Pebworth

John R. Roberts

Jeanne Shami

Ernest W. Sullivan, II

COMMENTARY

PAUL A. PARRISH
Volume Commentary Editor

HELEN B. BROOKS
Contributing Editor

ROBERT T. FALLON
Contributing Editor

P. G. STANWOOD
Contributing Editor

TEXTS

GARY A. STRINGER
Senior Textual Editor

with assistance from

DENNIS FLYNN
Assistant Textual Editor

TED-LARRY PEBWORTH
Senior Textual Editor

THEODORE J. SHERMAN
Assistant Textual Editor

ERNEST W. SULLIVAN, II
Senior Textual Editor

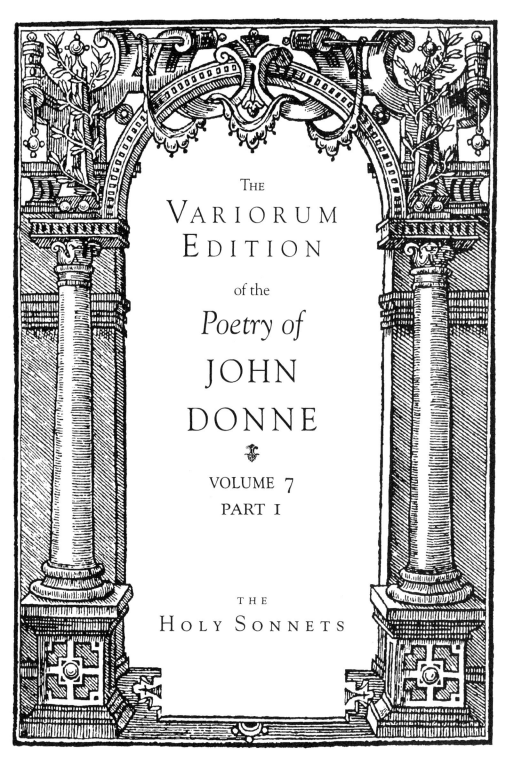

THE
VARIORUM
EDITION

of the

Poetry of

JOHN

DONNE

❧

VOLUME 7
PART I

THE
HOLY SONNETS

Gary A. Stringer, *General Editor*

Indiana University Press   Bloomington and Indianapolis

The preparation of this volume was made possible in part by grants from the Program for Collaborative Research of the National Endowment for the Humanities, an independent federal agency. Any views, findings, or recommendations expressed in this publication do not necessarily reflect those of the National Endowment for the Humanities. Work on this volume was also supported by funds from the University of Southern Mississippi Foundation.

This paper meets the requirements of the American National Standard for Information Sciences— Permanence of Paper for Printed Library Materials, ANSI Z39.48–1984.

COMMITTEE ON
SCHOLARLY EDITIONS

AN APPROVED EDITION

MODERN LANGUAGE
ASSOCIATION OF AMERICA

The Committee's emblem indicates that this volume is based on an examination of all available relevant textual sources, that it is edited according to principles articulated in the volume, that the source texts and the edited text's deviations from them are fully described, that the editorial principles and the text and apparatus have undergone a peer review, that a rigorous schedule of verification and proofreading was followed to insure a high degree of accuracy in the presentation of the edition, and that the text is accompanied by appropriate textual and other historical contextual information.

Cataloging information is available from the Library of Congress.

ISBN 0-253-34701-7 (cl. : alk. paper)

1 2 3 4 5 10 09 08 07 06 05

For

ALEX

CLAUDE

DICK

DOROTHY

ELEANOR

KAREN, KATHRYN, NATHANIEL, NAOMI, *and* SERAPHIM

and

MAC, WILSON, BEN, LIBBY, *and* STELLA

CONTENTS

Texts and Apparatuses

THE HOLY SONNETS

Commentary

THE HOLY SONNETS

Acknowledgments

A great many people and institutions have generously supported the Donne Variorum project since its inception in 1981, not only by providing specific services and financial aid, but also by offering encouragement, advice, and other forms of intangible support. We wish to acknowledge here those friends, colleagues, university administrators, library staffs, research assistants, and granting agencies and foundations that have made the work on this volume possible; and we look forward to recording similar debts as successive volumes proceed to publication.

University Administrators and Programs

We are grateful to the following university administrators and programs for providing financial support, adjusted teaching schedules, equipment and supplies, and staff assistance:

Bentley College: Robert D. Galliers, Provost and Vice President for Academic Affairs; Catherine A. Davy, Dean of Arts and Sciences; Bruce Herzberg, Chairperson of the English Department.

University of British Columbia: Hampton Research Fund.

LaSalle University: research grants program.

Middle Tennessee State University: William Connelly, Chair of the Department of English; John McDaniel, Dean of the College of Liberal Arts; Faculty Research and Creative Activity Committee; Donald Curry, former Vice Provost for Research and Dean of the College of Graduate Studies.

The University of Southern Mississippi: Cecil D. Burge, Vice President for Research; USM Foundation; Michael N. Salda, former Chair of the Department of English; Office of Sponsored Programs Administration, Connie Wyldmon, Director.

Stanford University: John W. Etchemendy, Provost and former Associate Dean, School of Humanities and Sciences; Department of English; Interdisciplinary Studies in Humanities Program.

Texas A&M University: Charles A. Johnson, Dean, College of Liberal Arts; Ben M. Crouch, Executive Associate Dean, College of Liberal Arts; C. Colleen Cook, Dean of University Libraries; Steven E. Smith, Director and Associate Dean, Cushing Library; J. Lawrence Mitchell, former Head, Department of English.

Virginia Polytechnic Institute and State University: The Edward S. Diggs Foundation; the Center for Applied Technologies in the Humanities; the Faculty Research Leave Program.

LIBRARIES AND ARCHIVES

We also wish to thank the administrators and staffs of the following libraries and repositories, who have provided indispensable aid and ready access to materials: Aberdeen University Library; Universiteitsbibliotheek, Amsterdam; Bedfordshire Record Office; Bodleian Library; Bradford District Archives; University of British Columbia Library; British Library; Cambridge University Library; Chetham's Library, Manchester; William Andrews Clark Memorial Library; Cook Memorial Library, University of Southern Mississippi; Derbyshire Record Office; East Sussex Record Office; Edinburgh University Library; Ellis Library, University of Missouri; Emmanuel College Library, Cambridge; Fitzwilliam Museum; Cecil H. Green Library, Stanford University; Grosvenor Estate Office; Guildhall Library; Harvard University Libraries; Hertfordshire Record Office; University of Illinois Library; University of Kentucky Library; Leeds Archives Department; Leicestershire Record Office; Lincoln's Inn Library; University of London Library; London Public Record Office; University of Michigan Libraries, Ann Arbor and Dearborn; National Art Library, Victoria and Albert Museum; National Library of Scotland; National Library of Wales; Library of the University of Newcastle upon Tyne; New York Public Library; University of Nottingham Library; University of Pennsylvania Library; Pierpont Morgan Library; Princeton University Library; Rosenbach Museum and Library; Rutgers University Library; John Rylands Library, University of Manchester; St. John's College Library, Cambridge; St. John's College Library, Oxford; St. Paul's Cathedral Library; South African Public Library; University of Texas Library; Texas A&M University Library; Texas Tech University Library; Trinity College Library, Cambridge; Trinity College Library, Dublin; United States Air Force Academy Library; University Research Library, University of California at Los Angeles; Wayne State University Library; Westminster Abbey Library; Library of the University College of North Wales; Yale University Library; University of York (UK) Library.

We wish to call special attention to the bibliographical contributions of John

Baky, LaSalle University Library; Bernard Meehan, Trinity College Library, Dublin; and Jayne Ringrose, Cambridge University Library.

FOUNDATIONS AND GRANTING AGENCIES

Although the National Endowment for the Humanities is acknowledged elsewhere in these pages, we wish to reiterate our profound gratitude for the support we have received through the agency's programs for collaborative research and scholarly editions. And we appreciate the work of the many anonymous reviewers and panelists who, in reviewing our grant applications over the years, have provided an invaluable critique of our efforts. Without NEH support we could neither have continued this project nor have completed this volume.

RESEARCH ASSISTANTS

Our gratitude also goes to the following research assistants who have aided us in the preparation of this volume: Mark Barnett, Margaret Carstarphen, Jaemin Choi, Cheryl Clark, James Coleman, Emily Cooley, Cody Dolan, Philip George, Victor Haseman, Jacob A. Heil, Mary E. Henley, C. David Jago, Tae-Hoon Kim, Joanna Klein, Seunghee Lee, Sonia H. Moss, Margaret Oakes, Kimberly Parsley, Chris Riels, Ryan Sanders, Cephas Sekhar, Larry Van Meter, and Linda M. Zimmerman.

We would particularly like to draw attention to the many and variegated contributions made to this volume, including its typesetting, by J. Syd Conner, Editorial Assistant to the Donne Variorum project.

FRIENDS AND COLLEAGUES

For supplying translations and other help with items in foreign languages we are grateful to Nicholas Angerosa, Bernhardt Blumenthal, William Richard Brooks, Klara Elteto, Judy Ann Gilleland, Christopher B. Hrut, Lucja M. Kwasniak, Tino Markworth, Christina Mesa, John R. Roberts, and Leo Rudnytzky.

The commentary editors wish also to thank Dennis Flynn, Ernest W. Sullivan, II, and Claude Summers, who provided helpful critiques of various portions of the commentary, and Theodore J. Sherman, who provided annotations from Zay Rusk Sullens's 1964 article on Donne's neologisms.

The textual editors express their appreciation to Dayton Haskin, Michael Salda, and Richard Todd for their careful reading of our discussion of the texts, both in the General Textual Introduction and in the textual introductions to the individual poems.

As always, this project owes more to the support of Mary Ann Stringer than can be recounted or repaid.

CONSULTANTS

Three consultants have contributed immeasurably to our work by providing specialized assistance and expertise. We should like to thank Peter Beal, who has provided continuing aid in identifying and facilitating access to manuscripts and other hard-to-locate bibliographical materials; Yoshihisa Aizawa, who has continued in his role as general consultant for items of commentary in Japanese; and John R. Roberts, who has continued to serve as the project's principal bibliographer.

Short Forms of Reference for Donne's Works

(In the interests of convenience and economy, we have used the following short forms throughout the *Variorum* commentary and the textual introductions. These forms are based on traditional headings or numberings except in cases where traditional designations are confusing, imprecise, or nonexistent. Spelling, capitalization, font, and pointing in this list are regularized, and none of these details should be accorded bibliographical or textual significance.)

Poems

Air	Air and Angels ["Twice or thrice had I loved"]
AltVic	A Letter Written by Sir H. G. and J. D. Alternis Vicibus ["Since every tree begins"]
Amic	Amicissimo et Meritissimo Ben Jonson ["Quod arte ausus es hic tua"]
Anniv	The Anniversary ["All kings and all their favorites"]
Annun	Upon the Annunciation and Passion ["Tamely frail body"]
Antiq	Antiquary ["If in his study"]
Apoth	Apotheosis Ignatij Loyolae ["Qui sacer antefuit"]
Appar	The Apparition ["When by thy scorn"]
AutHook	Ad Autorem ["Non eget Hookerus"]
AutJos	Ad Autorem ["Emendare cupis Joseph"]
Bait	The Bait ["Come live with me"]
BB	To Mr. B.B. ["Is not thy sacred hunger"]
BedfCab	Epitaph on Himself: To the Countess of Bedford ["That I might make your cabinet"]
BedfDead	To the Countess of Bedford: Begun in France ["Though I be dead and buried"]
BedfHon	To the Countess of Bedford ["Honor is so sublime"]
BedfReas	To the Countess of Bedford ["Reason is our soul's left hand"]
BedfRef	To the Countess of Bedford ["You have refined me"]

BedfShe	Elegy to the Lady Bedford ["You that are she"]
BedfTwi	To the Countess of Bedford: On New-Year's Day ["This twilight of two years"]
BedfWrit	To the Countess of Bedford ["To have written then"]
Beggar	A Lame Beggar ["I am unable, yonder beggar cries"]
Blos	The Blossom ["Little thinkest thou"]
BoulNar	Elegy upon the Death of Mrs. Boulstrode ["Language thou art too narrow"]
BoulRec	Elegy on Mrs. Boulstrode ["Death, I recant"]
Break	Break of Day ["'Tis true, 'tis day"]
Broken	The Broken Heart ["He is stark mad"]
Cales	Cales and Guiana ["If you from spoil"]
Calm	The Calm ["Our storm is past"]
Canon	The Canonization ["For God's sake hold your tongue"]
Carey	A Letter to the Lady Carey and Mrs. Essex Rich ["Here where by all"]
CB	To Mr. C. B. ["Thy friend whom thy deserts"]
Christ	A Hymn to Christ at the Author's Last Going into Germany ["In what torn ship soever"]
Citizen	A Tale of a Citizen and his Wife (noncanonical) ["I sing no harme, goodsooth"]
Commun	Community ["Good we must love"]
Compu	The Computation ["For the first twenty years"]
ConfL	Confined Love ["Some man unworthy"]
Corona	La Corona
Cor1	"Deign at my hands"
Cor2	Annunciation ["Salvation to all that will is nigh"]
Cor3	Nativity ["Immensity cloistered in thy dear womb"]
Cor4	Temple ["With his kind mother who partakes thy woe"]
Cor5	Crucifying ["By miracles exceeding power of man"]
Cor6	Resurrection ["Moist with one drop of thy blood"]
Cor7	Ascension ["Salute the last and everlasting day"]
Coryat	Upon Mr. Thomas Coryat's Crudities ["Oh to what height"]
Cross	The Cross ["Since Christ embraced"]
Curse	The Curse ["Whoever guesses, thinks, or dreams"]
Damp	The Damp ["When I am dead"]
Disinher	Disinherited ["Thy father all from thee"]
Dissol	The Dissolution ["She is dead"]
Dream	The Dream ["Dear love, for nothing less"]
Eclog	Eclogue at the Marriage of the Earl of Somerset ["Unseasonable man, statue of ice"]
Ecst	The Ecstasy ["Where, like a pillow on a bed"]
ED	To E. of D. with Six Holy Sonnets ["See, Sir, how as the sun's"]
EdHerb	To Sir Edward Herbert ["Man is a lump"]
EG	To Mr. E. G. ["Even as lame things"]

EgDD	Epigraph from *Death's Duel* ["Corporis haec animae"]

Elegies:

ElAnag	The Anagram ["Marry and love thy Flavia"]
ElAut	The Autumnal ["No spring nor summer beauty"]
ElBed	Going to Bed ["Come, Madam, come"]
ElBrac	The Bracelet ["Not that in color it was like thy hair"]
ElChange	Change ["Although thy hand and faith"]
ElComp	The Comparison ["As the sweet sweat of roses in a still"]
ElExpost	The Expostulation ["To make the doubt clear"]
ElFatal	On His Mistress ["By our first strange and fatal interview"]
ElJeal	Jealousy ["Fond woman which would'st have thy husband die"]
ElNat	"Nature's lay idiot"
ElPart	His Parting From Her ["Since she must go"]
ElPerf	The Perfume ["Once and but once found in thy company"]
ElPict	His Picture ["Here take my picture"]
ElProg	Love's Progress ["Whoever loves, if he do not propose"]
ElServe	"Oh, let not me serve so"
ElVar	Variety ["The heavens rejoice in motion"]
ElWar	Love's War ["Till I have peace with thee"]
EpEliz	Epithalamion upon ... the Lady Elizabeth ["Hail, Bishop Valentine"]
EpLin	Epithalamion Made at Lincoln's Inn ["The sunbeams in the east"]
EtAD	Epitaph for Ann Donne ["Annae / Georgii More de filiae"]
EtED	Epitaph for Elizabeth Drury ["Quo pergas, viator"]
EtRD	Epitaph for Robert and Anne Drury ["Roberti Druri / quo vix alter"]
EtSP	John Donne's Epitaph ... in St. Paul's Cathedral ["Iohannes Donne / Sac: Theol: Profess:"]
Expir	The Expiration ["So, so, break off"]
Fare	Farewell to Love ["Whilst yet to prove"]
Father	A Hymn to God the Father ["Wilt thou forgive"]
Faust	Faustinus ["Faustinus keeps his sister"]
Fever	A Fever ["Oh do not die"]
FirAn	The First Anniversary. An Anatomy of the World ["When that rich soul"]
Flea	The Flea ["Mark but this flea"]
Fun	The Funeral ["Whoever comes to shroud me"]
FunEl	A Funeral Elegy ["'Tis lost to trust a tomb"]
Gaz	Translated out of Gazaeus ["God grant thee thine own wish"]
GHerb	To Mr. George Herbert with One of My Seals ["Qui prius assuetus serpentum"]
Goodf	Goodfriday, 1613. Riding Westward ["Let man's soul be a sphere"]
GoodM	The Good Morrow ["I wonder by my troth"]
Ham	An Hymn to the Saints and to the Marquis Hamilton ["Whether that soul which now comes"]

Har	Obsequies upon the Lord Harrington ["Fair soul, which wast not only"]
Harb	The Harbinger to the Progress (by Joseph Hall) ["Two souls move here"]
Heart	"When my heart was mine own"
Henry	Elegy on the Untimely Death of . . . Prince Henry ["Look to me, Faith"]
Hero	Hero and Leander ["Both robbed of air"]
HG	To Sr. Henry Goodyere ["Who makes the past a pattern"]

Holy Sonnets:

HSBatter	"Batter my heart"
HSBlack	"O my black soul"
HSDeath	"Death be not proud"
HSDue	"As due by many titles"
HSLittle	"I am a little world"
HSMade	"Thou hast made me"
HSMin	"If poisonous minerals"
HSPart	"Father part of his double interest"
HSRound	"At the round earth's imagined corners"
HSScene	"This is my play's last scene"
HSShe	"Since she whom I loved"
HSShow	"Show me dear Christ"
HSSighs	"O might those sighs"
HSSouls	"If faithful souls"
HSSpit	"Spit in my face"
HSVex	"O to vex me"
HSWhat	"What if this present"
HSWhy	"Why are we by all creatures"
HSWilt	"Wilt thou love God"
HuntMan	To the Countess of Huntingdon ["Man to God's image"]
HuntUn	To the Countess of Huntingdon ["That unripe side of earth"]
HWHiber	H. W. in Hibernia Belligeranti ["Went you to conquer?"]
HWKiss	To Sir Henry Wotton ["Sir, more than kisses"]
HWNews	To Sir Henry Wotton ["Here's no more news"]
HWVenice	To Sir H. W. at His Going Ambassador to Venice ["After those reverend papers"]

Ignatius, verse from:

IgAver	"Aversa facie Janum referre"
IgFeath	"Feathers or straws swim on the water's face"
IgFlow	"As a flower wet with last night's dew"
IgLark	"The lark by busy and laborious ways"
IgNoise	"With so great noise and horror"
IgOper	"Operoso tramite scandent"

IgPiece	"That the least piece which thence doth fall"
IgPlum	"Aut plumam, aut paleam"
IgQual	"Qualis hesterno madefacta rore"
IgResemb	"Resemble Janus with a diverse face"
IgSport	"My little wandering sportful soul"
IgTanto	"Tanto fragore boatuque"
ILBlest	To Mr. I.L. ["Blest are your north parts"]
ILRoll	To Mr. I.L. ["Of that short roll"]
Image	"Image of her whom I love"
InAA	Inscription in the *Album Amicorum* of Michael Corvinus ["In propria venit"]
Ind	The Indifferent ["I can love both fair and brown"]
InLI	Inscription in a Bible Presented to Lincoln's Inn ["In Bibliotheca Hospitii"]
Jet	A Jet Ring Sent ["Thou art not so black"]
Jug	The Juggler ["Thou callest me effeminate"]
Julia	Julia (noncanonical) ["Hearke newes, ô Enuy"]
Klock	Klockius ["Klockius so deeply hath sworn"]
Lam	The Lamentations of Jeremy ["How sits this city"]
Lect	A Lecture upon the Shadow ["Stand still and I will read"]
Leg	The Legacy ["When I died last"]
Liar	The Liar ["Thou in the fields walkest"]
Libro	De Libro Cum Mutuaretur ["Doctissimo Amicissimoque v. D. D. Andrews"]
Licent	A Licentious Person ["Thy sins and hairs"]
Lit	A Litany ["Father of heaven and him"]
LovAlch	Love's Alchemy ["Some that have deeper digged"]
LovDeity	Love's Deity ["I long to talk with some old"]
LovDiet	Love's Diet ["To what a cumbersome unwieldiness"]
LovExch	Love's Exchange ["Love, any devil else but you"]
LovGrow	Love's Growth ["I scarce believe my love to be so pure"]
LovInf	Lovers' Infiniteness ["If yet I have not all thy love"]
LovUsury	Love's Usury ["For every hour that thou wilt spare me"]
Macaron	In Eundem Macaronicon ["Quot, dos, haec, linguists"]
Mark	Elegy on the Lady Markham ["Man is the world"]
Martial	Raderus ["Why this man gelded Martial"]
Merc	Mercurius Gallo-Belgicus ["Like Aesop's fellow slaves"]
Mess	The Message ["Send home my long strayed eyes"]
Metem	Metempsychosis ["I sing the progress of a deathless soul"]
MHMary	To the Lady Magdalen Herbert, of St. Mary Magdalen ["Her of your name"]
MHPaper	To Mrs. M. H. ["Mad paper stay"]
NegLov	Negative Love ["I never stooped so low"]
Niobe	Niobe ["By children's birth and death"]
Noct	A Nocturnal upon St. Lucy's Day ["'Tis the year's midnight"]

Para	The Paradox ["No lover saith, I love"]
Philo	An Obscure Writer ["Philo with twelve years' study"]
Phrine	Phrine ["Thy flattering picture, Phrine"]
Praise	To the Praise of the Dead and the Anatomy (by Joseph Hall) ["Well died the world"]
Prim	The Primrose ["Upon this primrose hill"]
Prohib	The Prohibition ["Take heed of loving me"]
Pyr	Pyramus and Thisbe ["Two by themselves each other"]
Ralph	Ralphius ["Compassion in the world again is bred"]
Relic	The Relic ["When my grave is broke up again"]
Res	Resurrection Imperfect ["Sleep, sleep, old sun"]
RWEnvy	To Mr. R. W. ["Kindly I envy thy song's"]
RWMind	To Mr. R. W. ["Muse not that by thy mind"]
RWSlumb	To Mr. R. W. ["If as mine is thy life a slumber be"]
RWThird	To Mr. R. W. ["Like one who in her third widowhood"]
RWZeal	To Mr. R. W. ["Zealously my muse"]
Sal	To the Countess of Salisbury ["Fair, great, and good"]
Sappho	Sappho to Philaenis ["Where is that holy fire"]

Satires:

Sat1	"Away thou fondling motley humorist"
Sat2	"Sir, though (I thank God for it) I do hate"
Sat3	"Kind pity chokes my spleen"
Sat4	"Well, I may now receive and die"
Sat5	"Thou shalt not laugh in this leaf, Muse"
SB	To Mr. S. B. ["O thou which to search"]
SecAn	The Second Anniversary. Of the Progress of the Soul ["Nothing could make me sooner"]
SelfAc	A Self Accuser ["Your mistress, that you follow whores"]
SelfL	Self Love ["He that cannot choose but love"]
SGo	Song ["Go, and catch a falling star"]
Sheaf	A Sheaf of Miscellany Epigrams
Sheaf1–61: individual poems within *Sheaf*	
Ship	A Burnt Ship ["Out of a fired ship"]
Sickness	A Hymn to God My God, in My Sickness ["Since I am coming"]
Sidney	Upon the Translation of the Psalms by Sir Philip Sidney ["Eternal God, (for whom who ever dare . . .)"]
Sorrow	Elegia ["Sorrow, who to this house"]
SSweet	Song ["Sweetest love, I do not go"]
Stat	Stationes from *Devotions* ["Insultus morbi primus"]
Storm	The Storm ["Thou which art I"]
SunRis	The Sun Rising ["Busy old fool, unruly sun"]
Tilman	To Mr. Tilman after He Had Taken Orders ["Thou whose diviner soul"]
Token	Sonnet. The Token ["Send me some token"]

Triple	The Triple Fool ["I am two fools, I know"]
TWHail	To Mr. T. W. ["All hail sweet poet"]
TWHarsh	To Mr. T. W. ["Haste thee harsh verse"]
TWHence	To Mr. T. W. ["At once from hence"]
TWPreg	To Mr. T. W. ["Pregnant again"]
Twick	Twickenham Garden ["Blasted with sighs and surrounded with tears"]
Under	The Undertaking ["I have done one braver thing"]
ValBook	A Valediction of the Book ["I'll tell thee now"]
ValMourn	A Valediction Forbidding Mourning ["As virtuous men pass mildly away"]
ValName	A Valediction of My Name in the Window ["My name engraved herein"]
ValWeep	A Valediction of Weeping ["Let me pour forth"]
Wall	Fall of a Wall ["Under an undermined and shot-bruised wall"]
Will	The Will ["Before I sigh my last gasp"]
Wing	Sir John Wingfield ["Beyond th'old pillars"]
Witch	Witchcraft by a Picture ["I fix mine eye on thine"]
WomCon	Woman's Constancy ["Now thou has loved me one whole day"]

PROSE WORKS

Biathanatos	*Biathanatos*, ed. Ernest W. Sullivan, II. Newark: U of Delaware P, 1984.
Devotions	*Devotions upon Emergent Occasions*, ed. Anthony Raspa. Montreal: McGill-Queen's UP, 1975.
Essays	*Essays in Divinity*, ed. Evelyn M. Simpson. Oxford: Clarendon, 1952.
Ignatius	*Ignatius His Conclave*, ed. T. S. Healy, S.J. Oxford: Clarendon, 1969.
Letters	*Letters to Severall Persons of Honour (1651)*. A Facsimile Reproduction with an Introduction by M. Thomas Hester. Delmar, N. Y.: Scholars' Facsimiles & Reprints, 1977.
Paradoxes	*Paradoxes and Problems*, ed. Helen Peters. Oxford: Clarendon, 1980.
Sermons	*The Sermons of John Donne*, ed. George R. Potter and Evelyn M. Simpson. 10 vols. Berkeley: U of California P, 1953–62.

ABBREVIATIONS USED
IN THE COMMENTARY

EIGHTEENTH- AND NINETEENTH-CENTURY PERIODICALS

Ac	*The Academy*. London, 1869–1916.
AR	*The Andover Review*. Boston, 1884–93.
Art	*Artist and Journal of Home Culture*. London, 1880–1902.
Ath	*The Athenaeum*. London, 1828–1921.
Bo	*The Bookman*. London, 1891–1934.
BookR	*Book Reviews*, 1893–1901.
Cit	*The Citizen*. (American Society for Extension of University Teaching) Philadelphia, 1895–98.
EdRev	*The Edinburgh Review*, 1802–1929.
FR	*The Fortnightly Review*. London, 1865–1954.
LEM	*Lowe's Edinburgh Magazine*. Edinburgh, 1846–48.
LitG	*The Literary Gazette*, 1817–62.
LLA	*Littell's Living Age*. Boston, 1844–96.
MPS	*Miscellanies of the Philobiblion Society*, 1856–57.
MR	*The Monthly Review*. London, 1749–1844.
N&Ath	*Nation [and Athenaeum]*. London, 1828–1921.
NewR	*The New Review*, 1889–97.
NMM	*The New Monthly Magazine*. London, 1814–84.
NMMC	*The National Magazine and Monthly Critic*, 1837–38.
NQR	*Notes and Queries for readers and writers, collectors and librarians*. London, 1849–1924.
NR	*The National Review*. London, 1855–64; 1883–1950.
QR	*The Quarterly Review*. London, 1809–1967.
RR	*The Retrospective Review*. London, 1820–28, 1852–54.
SN	*Studies and Notes in Philology and Literature*. Cambridge, MA, 1892–1907.

Modern Journals

ABR	American Benedictine Review
Acc	Accent
AION-SG	Annali Istituto Universitario Orientale, Napoli, Sezione Germanica (Naples, Italy)
AL	American Literature
Anglia	Anglia: Zeitschrift für Englische Philologie
ANQ	ANQ: A Quarterly Journal of Short Articles, Notes, and Reviews; formerly American Notes and Queries
Ant	Antaios
Arcadia	Arcadia: Zeitschrift für Vergleichende Literaturwissenschaft
ArielE	ARIEL: A Review of International English Literature (Calgary, Canada)
ATR	Anglican Theological Review
BNYPL	Bulletin of the New York Public Library
BookM	The Bookman (New York)
BSEAA	Bulletin de la Société d'Etudes Anglo-Américaines des XVIIe et XVIIIe Siècles
BSUF	Ball State University Forum
BuR	Bucknell Review: A Scholarly Journal of Letters, Arts and Sciences
BUSE	Boston University Studies in English
CE	College English
Centrum	Centrum: Working Papers of the Minnesota Center for Advanced Studies in Language, Style, and Literary Theory
ChQ	Church Quarterly
CIEFLB	Central Institute of English and Foreign Languages Bulletin
CL	Comparative Literature (Eugene, OR)
CLS	Comparative Literature Studies
CM	The Cornhill Magazine
ContempR	Contemporary Review
CP	Concerning Poetry
CQ	The Cambridge Quarterly
CR	Critical Review
Cresset	Cresset (Valparaiso, IN)
Criticism	Criticism: A Quarterly for Literature and the Arts (Detroit, MI)
CritQ	Critical Quarterly
CrSurv	Critical Survey
CS	Cahiers du Sud
DM	The Dublin Magazine
DownR	Downside Review: A Quarterly of Catholic Thought
DR	The Dalhousie Review
DUS	Dacca University Studies
DWB	Dietsche Warande en Belfort
EA	Etudes Anglaises: Grande-Bretagne, Etats-Unis

E&S	*Essays and Studies* (London)
EIC	*Essays in Criticism: A Quarterly Journal of Literary Criticism* (Oxford)
EIRC	*Explorations in Renaissance Culture*
ELH	*ELH* (formerly *Journal of English Literary History*)
ELLS	*English Literature and Language* (Tokyo)
ELN	*English Language Notes* (Boulder, CO)
ELR	*English Literary Renaissance*
EM	*English Miscellany: A Symposium of History, Literature and the Arts*
EMS	*English Manuscript Studies 1100–1700*
EncL	*Encounter* (London)
EnglRev	*English Review* (Oxford)
EnglStud	*Englishe Studien*
ES	*English Studies: A Journal of English Language and Literature* (Lisse, Netherlands)
EsFI	*Estudios di filologia inglese*
Expl	*The Explicator*
GHJ	*George Herbert Journal*
GRM	*Germanisch-Romanishce Monatsschrift*
HAB	*Humanities Association Review / La Revue de l'Association des Humanités* (formerly *Humanities Association Bulletin*)
Hermathena	*Hermathena: A Dublin University Review*
HLQ	*The Huntington Library Quarterly: A Journal for the History and Interpretation of English and American Civilization*
HudR	*Hudson Review*
IJES	*Indian Journal of English Studies* (Calcutta)
Ins	*Insula* (Supplemento) (Madrid)
Is	*Isis*
ISJR	*Iowa State Journal of Research*
JCP	*Journal of Canadian Poetry*
JDJ	*John Donne Journal: Studies in the Age of Donne*
JEGP	*JEGP: Journal of English and Germanic Philology*
JHI	*Journal of the History of Ideas*
JQ	*Jewish Quarterly*
JRMMRA	*Journal of the Rocky Mountain Medieval and Renaissance Association*
Káñina	*Káñina: Revista de Artes y Letras de la Universidad de Costa Rica*
KR	*Kenyon Review*
KVKEK	*Kroniek van Kunst en Kultur*
L&M	*Literature and Medicine*
Lang&S	*Language and Style: An International Journal*
LeS	*Lingua e Stile: Timestrale di Linguistica e Critica Letteraria* (Bologna)
Lis	*The Listener*
LIT	*Lit: Literature Interpretation Theory*

LitRev	The Literary Review (London)
LMer	The London Mercury
LWU	Literatur in Wissenschaft und Unterricht (Kiel, Germany)
MedHist	Medical History
MLN	MLN (formerly Modern Language Notes)
MLNew	The Malcom Lowry Review (formerly Malcom Lowry Newsletter)
MLR	The Modern Language Review
MLS	Modern Language Studies
MP	Modern Philology: A Journal Devoted to Research in Medieval and Modern Literature
MR	The Massachusetts Review: A Quarterly of Literature, Arts and Public Affairs
N&Q	Notes and Queries
Neophil	Neophilologus
NewQ	The New Quarterly
NewW	The New World
NM	Neuphilologische Mitteilungen: Bulletin de la Société Néophilologique / Bulletin of the Modern Language Society
NStat	New Statesman
NWR	Northwest Review
NYRB	The New York Review of Books
OnsE	Ons Erfdeel: Algemeen-Nederlands Tweemaandelijks Cultureel Tijdschrift
Paragone	Rivista Mensile di Arte Figurativa e Letteratura
PBA	Proceedings of the British Academy
PBSA	Papers of the Bibliographical Society of America
Person	Personalist
PLL	Papers on Language and Literature: A Journal for Scholars and Critics of Language and Literature
PLPLS	Proceedings of the Leeds Philosophical and Literary Society
PMLA	PMLA: Publications of the Modern Language Association of America
PoetryR	Poetry Review (London)
PoT	Poetics Today
PQ	Philological Quarterly (Iowa City, IA)
PURBA	Panjab University Research Bulletin (Arts)
Ren&R	Renaissance and Reformation / Renaissance et Réforme
RES	Review of English Studies: A Quarterly Journal of English Literature and the English Language
Rev	Review (Blacksburg, VA)
RevUnB	Revue de l'Université de Bruxelles
RMS	Renaissance and Modern Studies
RN	Renaissance News
RSH	Revue des Sciences Humaines
RSLR	Rivista di Storia e Letteratura Religiosa

SAQ	*South Atlantic Quarterly*
SatRLit	*Saturday Review of Literature*
SB	*Studies in Bibliography: Papers of the Bibliographical Society of the University of Virginia*
SCB	*The South Central Bulletin*
SCN	*Seventeenth-Century News*
SCRev	*South Central Review: The Journal of the South Central Modern Language Association*
SEL	*Studies in English Literature, 1500–1900*
SELit	*Studies in English Literature* (Tokyo)
SIcon	*Studies in Iconography*
SLitI	*Studies in Literary Imagination*
SMy	*Studia Mystica*
SoQ	*The Southern Quarterly: A Journal of the Arts in the South* (Hattiesburg, MS)
SSEng	*Sydney Studies in English*
SP	*Studies in Philology*
SPWVSRA	*Shakespeare and Renaissance Association of West Virginia—Selected Papers* (also known as *Selected Papers from the West Virginia Shakespeare and Renaissance Association*)
SR	*Sewanee Review*
SUSFL	*Studi Urbinati di Storia, Filosofia, e Letteratura*
TEXTiats	*TEXT: An Interdisciplinary Annual of Textual Studies*
Th	*Theology*
TLS	[London] *Times Literary Supplement*
TNTL	*Tijdschrift voor Nederlandse Taal-en Letterkunde* (Leiden, Netherlands)
Trivium	*Trivium* (Dyfed, Wales)
TSLL	*Texas Studies in Literature and Language: A Journal of the Humanities*
UCPES	*University of California Publications in English Studies*
UR	*The University Review* (Kansas City, MO)
UTQ	*University of Toronto Quarterly*
WascanaR	*Wascana Review*
XUS	*Xavier University Studies: A Journal of Critical and Creative Scholarship* (New Orleans), now called *Xavier Review*
YES	*The Yearbook of English Studies*
YJC	*The Yale Journal of Criticism: Interpretation in the Humanities*

HEBREW BIBLE

Gen.	Genesis
Exod.	Exodus
Num.	Numbers

Deut.	Deuteronomy
Josh.	Joshua
Judg.	Judges
1 Sam.	1 Samuel
2 Sam.	2 Samuel
1 Chron.	1 Chronicles
Esth.	Esther
Ps.	Psalms
Prov.	Proverbs
Eccles.	Ecclesiastes
Cant.	Canticles (Song of Solomon)
Isa.	Isaiah
Jer.	Jeremiah
Ezek.	Ezekiel
Dan.	Daniel
Hos.	Hosea
Mal.	Malachi
Zech.	Zechariah

New Testament

Matt.	Matthew
Rom.	Romans
1 Cor.	1 Corinthians
2 Cor.	2 Corinthians
Gal.	Galatians
Col.	Colossians
Phil.	Philippians
1 Tim.	1 Timothy
Heb.	Hebrews
1 Pet.	1 Peter
2 Pet.	2 Peter
Rev.	Revelation (Apocalypse)

Shakespeare's Works

Ant.	*Antony and Cleopatra*
AWW	*All's Well That Ends Well*
AYL	*As You Like It*
Cor.	*Coriolanus*
Cym.	*Cymbeline*
Err.	*The Comedy of Errors*
Ham.	*Hamlet*

1H4	*Henry IV, Part 1*
2H4	*Henry IV, Part 2*
JC	*Julius Caesar*
Jn.	*King John*
LLL	*Love's Labour's Lost*
Lr.	*King Lear*
Mac.	*Macbeth*
MM	*Measure for Measure*
MND	*A Midsummer Night's Dream*
Oth.	*Othello*
PhT	*The Phoenix and the Turtle*
R2	*Richard II*
Rom.	*Romeo and Juliet*
TGV	*The Two Gentlemen of Verona*
Tmp.	*The Tempest*
TN	*Twelfth Night*
Tro.	*Troilus and Cressida*
Wiv.	*The Merry Wives of Windsor*
WT	*The Winter's Tale*

OTHER WORKS

AV	Authorized Version
CYT	The Canon's Yeoman's Tale (*The Canterbury Tales*)
DNB	*Dictionary of National Biography*
FQ	*The Faerie Queene*
Loeb	The Loeb Classical Library, founded by James Loeb
OED	*Oxford English Dictionary*
P.G.	*Patrologia Graeca*, ed. J. P. Migne
P.L.	*Patrologia Latina*, ed. J. P. Migne
Summa	*Summa Theologica* (St. Thomas Aquinas)

Sigla for Textual Sources

Manuscript Sources

(Entries listed as "Beal, *Index*" refer to citations in Peter Beal, comp., *Index of English Literary Manuscripts*.)

AF   United States Air Force Academy, Colorado
AF1   H. Mapletoft volume (ms. emendations and transcriptions in a copy of A)

AU   Aberdeen University Library
AU1   Aberdeen ms. 29

B   British Library
B1   Add. 5956; B2   Add. 10309; B3   Add. 10337 (Elizabeth Rogers's Virginal Book); B4   Add. 15226; B5   Add. 15227; B6   Add. 18044; B7   Add. 18647 (Denbigh ms.); B8   Add. 19268; B9   Add. 21433; B10   Add. 22118; B11   Add. 23229 (Conway Papers); B12   Add. 25303; B13   Add. 25707 (Skipwith ms.); B14   Add. 27407; B15   Add. 28000; B16   Add. 30982 (Leare ms.); B17   Add. 32463; B18   Add. 34324 (Sir Julius Caesar's Papers); B19   Add. 34744 (West Papers XVIII); B20   Add. 44963; B21   Egerton 923; B22   Egerton 2013; B23   Egerton 2230 (Glover ms.); B24   Egerton 2421; B25   Egerton 2725; B26   Harley 3511 (Capell ms.); B27   Harley 3910; B28   Harley 3991 (Rawlinson ms.); B29   Harley 3998; B30   Harley 4064 (Harley Noel ms.); B31   Harley 4888; B32   Harley 4955 (Newcastle ms.); B33   Harley 5110; B34   Harley 5353; B35   Harley 6057; B36   Harley 6383; B37   Harley 6396; B38   Harley 6918; B39   Harley 6931; B40   Lansdowne 740; B41   Lansdowne 878; B42   Lansdowne 984; B43   Sloane 542; B44   Sloane 1792; B45   Sloane 1867; B46   Stowe 961; B47   Stowe 962; B48   *entry canceled*; B49   *entry canceled*; B50   Harley 791; B51   ms. Evelyn JE E3 (formerly siglum OX3)

BD   Bradford District Archives
BD1   Hopkinson's M.S.S., Vol. 17; BD2   Hopkinson's M.S.S., Vol. 34; BD3   Spencer-Stanhope Calendar No. 2795 (Bundle 10, No. 34)

BR Bedfordshire Record Office
  BR1 J1583 (St. John ms.)

C Cambridge University Library
  C1 Add. ms. 29 (Edward Smyth ms.); C2 Add. ms. 5778(c) (Cambridge Balam ms.); C3 Add. ms. 8460 (Mary Browne Commonplace Book); C4 Add. ms. 8470 (Edward Hyde ms.); C5 Ee. 4. 14 (Moore ms.); C6 Ee. 5. 23; C7 Iosephi Scaligeri [Joseph Scaliger], *OPVS NOVVM DE EMENDATIONE TEMPORVM* (1583), holograph epigram; C8 Add. ms. 8467 (Leconfield ms.); C9 Add. ms. 8468 (Narcissus Luttrell ms.); C10 Giles Oldisworth volume (ms. emendations in a copy of C); C11 Add. ms. 8466, Michael Corvinus, "Album Amicorum," holograph inscription; C12 Add. ms. 9221

CE Cambridge University, Emmanuel College Library
  CE1 I.3.16 (James 68)

CH Chester City Record Office
  CH1 CR63/2/692/219

CJ Cambridge University, St. John's College Library
  CJ1 S.32 (James 423); CJ2 U.26 (James 548)

CT Cambridge University, Trinity College Library
  CT1 R.3.12 (James 592; Puckering ms.)

DR Derbyshire Record Office
  DR1 D258/28/5i; DR2 D258/31/16; DR3 D258/60/26a

DT Trinity College Library, Dublin
  DT1 877 (formerly G.2.21); DT2 877 (formerly G.2.21, second collection)

EE Eaton Estate Office, Eccleston
  EE1 Personal Papers 2/54

ES East Sussex Record Office
  ES1 RAF/F/13/1

EU Edinburgh University Library
  EU1 D.c.1.69; EU2 Laing III.436; EU3 Laing III.493; EU4 ms. 401 (Halliwell-Phillips Collection)

F Folger Shakespeare Library
  F1 L.b.541 (Loseley); F2 V.a.96; F3 V.a.97; F4 V.a.103 (Thomas Smyth ms.); F5 V.a.124; F6 V.a.125; F7 V.a.162 (Welden ms.); F8 V.a.169; F9 V.a.170; F10 V.a.241 (Gosse ms.); F11 V.a.245; F12 V.a.262; F13 V.a.276; F14 V.a.319; F15 V.a.322; F16 V.a.339; F17 V.a.345 (Curteis ms.); F18 V.b.43; F19 V.b.110; F20 W.a.118

FM Fitzwilliam Museum, Cambridge
FM1 Fitzwilliam Virginal Book

H Harvard University Library
H1 ms. Eng. 626; H2 ms. Eng. 686; H3 ms. Eng. 966.1 (Norton ms. 4502, Carnaby ms.); H4 ms. Eng. 966.3 (Norton ms. 4503); H5 ms. Eng. 966.4 (Norton ms. 4506, Dobell ms.); H6 ms. Eng. 966.5 (Norton ms. 4504, O'Flahertie ms.); H7 ms. Eng. 966.6 (Norton ms. 4500, Stephens ms.); H8 ms. Eng. 966.7 (Norton ms. 4620, Utterson ms.); H9 ms. Eng. 1107(15) (Gell Commonplace Book); H10 William Covell, *A IUST AND TEMPERATE DEFENCE OF THE FIVE BOOKS OF ECCLESIASTICALL POLICIE* . . . (1603), holograph epigram

HH Henry E. Huntington Library
HH1 EL 6893 (Bridgewater ms.); HH2 HM 116; HH3 HM 172; HH4 HM 198 (Book I, Haslewood-Kingsborough ms.); HH5 HM 198 (Book II, Haslewood-Kingsborough ms.); HH6 HM 41536; HH7 HM 46323

HR Hertfordshire Record Office
HR1 ms. 19061

IU University of Illinois Library
IU1 William Leigh Commonplace Book; IU2 ms. 821.08/c737/17 (Joseph Butler Commonplace Book)

LA Leeds Archives Department
LA1 MX237

LL Lincoln's Inn Library, London
LL1 Douai Bible, Vol. 1, holograph inscription

LP London Public Record Office
LP1 State Papers Miscellaneous S.P. 9/51

LR Leicestershire Record Office
LR1 DG7/Lit.2 (Burley ms.); LR2 DG9/2796

LU University of London Library
LU1 Cornelius Schrevelius, *M. VALERII MARTIALIS EPIGRAMMATA* . . . (1661), Sir James Astry copy, ms. transcription

MC Chetham's Library, Manchester
MC1 Farmer-Chetham ms. 8012, A.4.15

NP University of Nottingham Library
NP1 Portland ms. Pw V 37 (Welbeck ms.); NP2 Portland ms. Pw V 191; NP3 Portand ms. Pw V 6

NT   University of Newcastle upon Tyne Library
   NT1   Bell/White 25

NY   New York Public Library
   NY1   Arents Collection, Cat. No. S191 (John Cave ms.); NY2   Arents
   Collection, Cat. No. S288 (Hugh Barrow ms.); NY3   Berg Collection,
   Westmoreland ms.

O   Bodleian Library, Oxford
   O1   Add. B.97; O2   Ashmole 36, 37; O3   Ashmole 38; O4   Ashmole 47;
   O5   Ashmole 51; O6   Aubrey 6; O7   Aubrey 8; O8   Don.b.9;
   O9   Don.c.54; O10   Don.d.58; O11   Douce f.5; O12   Eng. poet. c.9;
   O13   Eng. poet. c.50; O14   Eng. poet. c.53; O15   Eng. poet. d.197;
   O16   Eng. poet. e.14 (Lawson ms.); O17   Eng. poet. e.37; O18   Eng. poet.
   e.40; O19   Eng. poet. e.97; O20   Eng. poet. e.99 (Dowden ms.); O21   Eng.
   poet. f.9 (Phillipps ms.); O22   Eng. poet. f.25; O23   Eng. poet. f.27;
   O24   Malone 16; O25   Malone 19; O26   Malone 23; O27   Music d.238;
   O28   Music f.575; O29   Rawlinson poet. 26; O30   Rawlinson poet. 31;
   O31   Rawlinson poet. 84; O32   Rawlinson poet. 90; O33   Rawlinson poet.
   116; O34   Rawlinson poet. 117 (Wase ms.); O35   Rawlinson poet. 142;
   O36   Rawlinson poet. 160; O37   Rawlinson poet. 172; O38   Rawlinson poet.
   199; O39   Rawlinson poet. 212; O40   Rawlinson poet. 214; O41   Sancroft
   53; O42   Tanner 465; O43   Tanner 466; O44   Tanner 876 (ms. emendations
   in a copy of C); O45   ms. 1018 (St. Michael's College Library, Tenbury
   Wells); O46   ms. 1019 (St. Michael's College Library, Tenbury Wells)

OC   Oxford University, Corpus Christi College Library
   OC1   ms. 327 (Fulman ms.); OC2   ms. 328

OJ   Oxford University, St. John's College Library
   OJ1   Nathaniel Crynes volume (ms. emendations in a copy of A)

OQ   Oxford University, Queen's College Library
   OQ1   ms. 216

OX   Oxford University, Christ Church Library
   OX1   ms. Music 350; OX2   mss. 736–738; OX3   ms. Evelyn 254 (in
   Variorum vols. 2, 6, and 8; identified in subsequently published vols. as B51)

P   Private hands
   P1   ms. Bedford 26 (Woburn ms. HMC. No. 26), Bedford Estates, London;
   P2   Beal, *Index*, DnJ 1430; P3   Heneage ms.; P4   Frendraught ms. (Thomas
   Fraser Duff ms.); P5   Abel Berland volume (ms. emendations in a copy of A,
   plus ms.); P6   Sparrow ms.; P7   Hall ms.

PM   Pierpont Morgan Library, New York
   PM1   MA1057 (Holgate ms.)

PT Princeton University Library, Robert H. Taylor Collection
PT1   ms. transcriptions in a copy of 22c; PT2   Beal, *Index*, DnJ 1431

R Rosenbach Museum and Library, Philadelphia
R1   239/16; R2   239/18; R3   239/22; R4   239/23; R5   239/27; R6   240/2;
R7   243/4; R8   1083/15; R9   1083/16 (Bishop ms.); R10   1083/17

RU Rutgers University Library
RU1   FPR 2247, E37

SA South African Public Library, Capetown
SA1   Grey 7 a 29 (formerly 2.a.II)

SN National Library of Scotland
SN1   Advocates' ms. 19.3.4; SN2   2060 (Hawthornden ms. VIII); SN3   2067
(Hawthornden ms. XV); SN4   6504 (Wedderburn ms.); SN5   Advocates' ms.
33.3.19

SP St. Paul's Cathedral Library
SP1   49.B.43; SP2   52.D.14

TA Texas A&M University Library
TA1   Henry White/Alan Haughton volume (ms. emendations in a copy of A)

TM Meisei University, Tokyo
TM1   Crewe ms. (formerly Monckton Milnes ms.)

TT Texas Tech University Library
TT1   PR 1171 D14 (Dalhousie I); TT2   PR 1171 S4 (Dalhousie II);
TT3   St. John Brodrick volume (ms. emendations in a copy of A)

VA Victoria and Albert Museum, Dyce Collection
VA1   Cat. No. 17, ms. 25.F.16 (Neve ms.); VA2   Cat. No. 18, ms. 25.F.17
(Nedham ms.); VA3   Cat. No. 44, ms. 25.F.39 (Todd ms.)

WA Westminster Abbey Library
WA1   ms. 41 (Morley ms.)

WB Library of the University College of North Wales
WB1   ms. 422 (Bangor ms.)

WC William Andrews Clark Memorial Library, Los Angeles
WC1   S4975M1

WN National Library of Wales
WN1   Dolau Cothi ms. 6748; WN2   Peniarth 500B; WN3   NLW ms.

5308E (Herbert ms.); WN4   NLW ms. 5390D; WN5   NLW ms. 12443A, Part ii; WN6   NLW ms. 16852D

Y   Yale University Library, James Osborn Collection
Y1   b62; Y2   b114 (Raphael King ms.); Y3   b148 (Osborn ms.); Y4   b150; Y5   b197; Y6   b200; Y7   b205; Y8   f b66; Y9   f b88

Printed Sources

(Citations in parentheses following seventeenth-century publications below are STC numbers from A. W. Pollard and G. R. Redgrave, eds., *Short-Title Catalogue of Books Printed in England . . . 1475–1640*, and from Donald Wing et al., eds., *Short-Title Catalogue of Books Printed in England . . . 1641–1700*. Items listed ambiguously in the STC are further identified by location and shelfmark. Locations of printed sources are as follows:

AUB	Universiteits-Bibliotheek, Amsterdam
C	Cambridge University Library, Cambridge
CLU–C	William Andrews Clark Memorial Library, Los Angeles, CA
CSmH	Huntington Library, San Marino, CA
CT	Trinity College, Cambridge
CtY	Yale University Library, New Haven, CT
DFo	Folger Shakespeare Library, Washington, DC
ICN	Newberry Library, Chicago, IL
InU	University of Indiana Library, Bloomington, IN
IU	University of Illinois Library, Urbana, IL
KyU	University of Kentucky Library, Lexington, KY
L	British Library, London
LG	Guildhall Library, London
LU	London University Library
M	John Rylands Library, University of Manchester
MC	Chetham's Library, Manchester
MH	Harvard University Library, Boston, MA
MiU	University of Michigan Library, Ann Arbor, MI
NjP	Princeton University Library, Princeton, NJ
O	Bodleian Library, Oxford
OCh	Christ Church, Oxford
OWa	Wadham College Library, Oxford
TxAM	Texas A&M University Library, College Station, TX
TxLT	Texas Tech University Library, Lubbock, TX
TxU	University of Texas Library, Austin, TX.)

Seventeenth-Century Collected Editions/Issues:

A	1633	*POEMS* (STC 7045)
B	1635	*POEMS* (STC 7046)

C	1639 POEMS (STC 7047)
D	1649 POEMS (STC D1868)
E	1650 POEMS (STC D1869)
F	1654 POEMS (STC D1870)
G	1669 POEMS (STC D1871)

Selected Modern Editions:

H	1719 Jacob Tonson, ed., *Poems on Several Occasions, Written by the Reverend John Donne, D. D.*
I	1779 John Bell, ed., *The Poetical Works of Dr. John Donne.* Vols. 23–25 of *Bell's Edition: The Poets of Great Britain Complete from Chaucer to Churchill*
J	1793 Robert Anderson, ed., *The Poetical Works of Dr. John Donne.* In vol. 4 of *A Complete Edition of the Poets of Great Britain*
K	1810 Alexander Chalmers, ed., *The Poems of John Donne, D. D.* Vol. 5 of *The Works of the English Poets, from Chaucer to Cowper*
L	1839 Henry Alford, ed., *The Works of John Donne, D. D.*, vol. 6
M	1855 James Russell Lowell, ed., rev. by James Russell Lowell. *The Poetical Works of Dr. John Donne*
N	1872–73 Alexander B. Grosart, ed., *The Complete Poems of John Donne,* 2 vols.
O	1895 [Charles Eliot Norton, ed.], *The Poems of John Donne,* rev. by James Russell Lowell, 2 vols. [The Grolier Club Edition]
P	1896 E. K. Chambers, ed., *The Poems of John Donne,* 2 vols.
Q	1912 H. J. C. Grierson, ed., *The Poems of John Donne,* 2 vols.
R	1923 John Sparrow, ed., with bibliographical note by Geoffrey Keynes, *Devotions upon Emergent Occasions by John Donne*
S	1929 John Hayward, ed., *John Donne, Dean of St. Paul's: Complete Poetry and Selected Prose*
T	1942 Roger Bennett, ed., *The Complete Poems of John Donne*
U	1952 Helen Gardner, ed., *John Donne: The Divine Poems*
V	1956 Theodore Redpath, ed., *The Songs and Sonets of John Donne*
W	1963 Frank Manley, ed., *John Donne: The Anniversaries*
X	1965 Helen Gardner, ed., *John Donne: The Elegies and The Songs and Sonnets*
Y	1967 Wesley Milgate, ed., *John Donne: The Satires, Epigrams, and Verse Letters*
Z	1967 John T. Shawcross, ed., *The Complete Poetry of John Donne*
AA	1971 A. J. Smith, ed., *John Donne: The Complete English Poems*
BB	1978 Wesley Milgate, ed., *John Donne: The Epithalamions, Anniversaries, and Epicedes*
CC	1983 Theodore Redpath, ed., *The Songs and Sonets of John Donne,* 2nd ed.
DD	1985 C. A. Patrides, ed., *The Complete English Poems of John Donne*

Other Seventeenth-Century Sources and Locations:

1	1607	Thomas Dekker, *A KNIGHTS Coniuring* (STC 6508)
2	1607	Thomas Deloney, *Strange Histories* (STC 6567)
3	1607	Ben Jonson, *BEN: IONSON his VOLPONE Or THE FOXE* (STC 14783)
4	1609	Alfonso Ferrabosco, *AYRES* (STC 10827)
5	1609	Joseph Wybarne, *THE NEW AGE OF OLD NAMES* (STC 26055)
6	1611	Thomas Coryat, CORYATS *Crudities* (STC 5808)
7	1611	Thomas Coryat, *THE ODCOMBIAN BANQVET* (STC 5810)
8a	1611	John Donne, *Conclaue Ignati* (STC 7026); b 1611, Continental ed. (L C.110.f.46.); c 1681, in Thomas Barlow, *PAPISMUS* (STC B836); d 1682, in *PAPISMUS* (STC B837)
9a	1611	John Donne, *Ignatius his Conclaue* (STC 7027); b 1626 (STC 7028); c 1634 (STC 7029); d 1635 (STC 7030); e 1652, in *PARADOXES, PROBLEMS, ESSAYES, CHARACTERS* (STC D1866); f 1652, in *PARADOXES, PROBLEMES, ESSAYES, CHARACTERS* (STC D1867)
10	1611	John Donne, Elizabeth Drury Inscription (Hawstead)
11	1612	William Corkine, *THE SECOND BOOKE OF AYRES* (STC 5769)
12a	1613	Josuah Sylvester, *Lachrymæ Lachrymarū* (STC 23578; LU [D.– L.L.] (XVII) Bc [Sylvester] S.R.); b 1613 (STC 23578; DFo STC 23578.2); c 1613 (STC 23578; ICN CASE Y 185. S 9993); d 1613 (STC 23577.5; CtY Ig Sy57 612Ld); e 1613 (STC 23577.5; MC J.1.39); f 1613 (STC 23578; CtY Ig Sy57 612Lc); g 1613 (STC 23578; DFo STC 23578 copy 4); h 1613 (STC 23578; DFo STC 23578 copy 1); i 1613 (STC 23577.5; MH STC 21652 [14455.3517*]); j 1613 (STC 23577.5; M R37802)
13a	1614	Michael Scott, *THE PHILOSOPHERS BANQVET* (STC 22062); b 1633 (STC 22063)
14a	1616	Ben Jonson, *THE WORKES OF Beniamin Jonson* (STC 14751; CSmH 62101); b 1616 (STC 14751; CSmH 62104); c 1616 (STC 14751; TxU Ah J738 +B616a); d 1616 (STC 14752); e 1640 (STC 14753); f 1640 (STC 14754); g 1692 (STC J1006)
15	1617	John Donne, Robert Drury Inscription (Hawstead)
16	1617	Henry Fitzgeffrey, *SATYRES: AND SATYRICALL EPIGRAM'S* (STC 10945)
17a	1618	Henry Fitzgeffrey, *CERTAIN ELEGIES, DONE BY SVNDRIE Excellent Wits* (STC 10945.3); b 1620 (STC 10945.6)
18a	1619	William Basse, *A HELPE TO DISCOVRSE* (STC 1547); b 1620 (STC 1548); c 1621 (STC 1549); d 1623 (STC

1549.5); e   1627 (STC 1550); f   1628 (STC 1551);
g   1629 (STC 1551.3); h   1630 (STC 1551.5); i   1631
(STC 1551.7); j   1635 (STC 1552); k   1636 (STC 1553);
l   1638 (STC 1554); m   1640 (STC 1554.5); n   1648
(STC E23); o   1654 (STC E24); p   1663 (STC E25);
q   1667 (STC E25A); r   1682 (STC E25B)

19a   1621 William Basse, *A HELPE TO MEMORIE AND
DISCOVRSE* (STC 13051); b   1630 (STC 13051.3)

20a   1624 John Donne, *DEVOTIONS VPON Emergent Occasions*
(STC 7033a); b   1624 (STC 7033); c   1624 (STC 7034);
d   1626 (STC 7035); e   1627 (STC 7035a); f   1634 (STC
7036); g   1638 (STC 7037)

21   1631 John Donne, Epitaph (St. Paul's Cathedral)

22a   1632 John Donne, *DEATHS DVELL* (STC 7031); b   1633 (STC
7032); c   1633 (STC 7032a; C Keynes B.5.24); d   1633
(STC 7032a; C Keynes B.5.29)

23a   1633 Henry Holland, *ECCLESIA SANCTI PAVLI ILLVSTRATA*
(STC 13584; *L* 577.c.4.[2].); b   1633 (STC 13584; *LG*
A.7.6. no. 2 in 32); c   1634 (STC 13585)

24a   1633 John Stow, *THE SURVEY OF LONDON* (STC 23345);
b   1640 [or later] (STC 23345.5)

25a   1635 John Swan, *SPECVLVM MUNDI* (STC 23516); b   1643
(STC S6238); c   1643 (STC S6238A); d   1665 (STC
S6239); e   1670 (STC S6240); f   1698 (STC S6240A)

26   1635 Katherine Thimelby, *TIXALL LETTERS*, ed. Arthur Clifford
[prints from lost seventeenth-century ms. dated 1635 by
Keynes]

27   1640 [John Mennes?], *Wits RECREATIONS* (STC 25870)

28a   1640 Izaak Walton, *THE LIFE AND DEATH OF Dᵣ DONNE*, in
John Donne, *LXXX SERMONS* (STC 7038); b   1658 (STC
W668)

29a   1645 John Gough, *THE ACADEMY OF Complements* (STC
G1401A); b   1646 (STC G1401B); c   1650 (STC
G1401C); d   1650 (STC G1402); e   1654 (STC G1403);
f   1658 (STC G1404); g   1663 (STC G1405); h   1670,
THE Academy OF COMPLEMENTS Newly Refin'd (STC
G1405B); i   1684 (STC 1406; *IU* Hill 31 Mr.43 Gen. res.);
j   1684 (STC 1406; *O* Vet. A3 f. 313)

30   1650 *THE MIRROUR OF Complements* (STC M2223)

31a   1651 Lucius Cary [Viscount of Falkland], *Discourse of
INFALLIBILITY* (STC F317); b   1660 (STC F318)

32a   1653 Francis Beaumont, *POEMS* (STC B1602); b   1653 (STC
B1603); c   1660, Francis Beaumont and John Fletcher,
POEMS (STC B1604)

33a   1653 Samuel Sheppard, *MERLINVS ANONYMVS* (STC A1588;

DFo A1588); b   1653 (STC A1588; L E.1348.[1.]); c   1654 (STC A1589)

34a   1653 Izaak Walton, *The Compleat Angler* (STC W661); b   1655 (STC W662); c   1661 (STC W663); d   1664 (STC W664); e   1668 (STC W665); f   1676 (STC W666); g   1676, Izaak Walton, Charles Cotton, and Robert Venables, *THE UNIVERSAL ANGLER* (STC W674; L C.31.a.7); h   1676, Izaak Walton, Charles Cotton, and Robert Venables, *THE UNIVERSAL ANGLER* (STC W674; CSmH 138284)

35   1654 [Robert Chamberlain?], *THE HARMONY OF THE MUSES* (STC C105)

36a   1654 Edmund Gayton, *PLEASANT NOTES UPON Don Quixot* (STC G415; CSmH 148580); b   1654 (STC G415; CSmH 148581)

37a   1654 Izaak Walton, *THE LIFE OF Sir Henry Wotton, in Henry Wotton, Reliquiæ Wottonianæ* (STC W3649); b   1672 (STC W3650); c   1685 (STC W3651)

38   1654 Richard Whitlock, *ΖΩOTOMIA* (STC W2030)

39a   1655 John Cotgrave, *WITS INTERPRETER* (STC C6370); b   1662 (STC C6371); c   1671 (STC C6372)

40   1655 Johann Grindal, *Aendachtige BEDENCKINGEN* (AUB 2328 F28)

41   1655 Samuel Sheppard, *THE MARROVV OF COMPLEMENTS* (STC M719)

42a   1656 John Mennes, *WIT AND DROLLERY* (STC W3131); b   1661 (STC W3132)

43   1656 Abraham Wright, *Parnassus Biceps* (STC W3686)

44a   1657 Joshua Poole, *The English PARNASSUS* (STC P2814; ICN CASE X 997.69); b   1657 (STC P2814; CSmH 12886); c   1677 (STC P2815); d   1678 (STC P2816)

45   1658 William Dugdale, *THE HISTORY OF St. PAULS CATHEDRAL IN LONDON* (STC D2482)

46   1658 Henry Stubbs, *DELICIÆ Poetarum Anglicanorum IN GRÆCVM VERSÆ* (STC S6040)

47   1659 John Suckling, *THE LAST REMAINS OF Sr JOHN SVCKLING* (STC S6130)

48a   1660 William Winstanley, *England's WORTHIES* (STC W3058); b   1684 (STC W3059)

49   1661 Thomas Forde, *A THEATRE OF WITS* (STC F1548A)

50a   1661 Thomas Forde, *Virtus Rediviva* (STC F1550); b   1661 (STC F1550A)

51   1662 Margaret Cavendish [Duchess of Newcastle], *PLAYES* (STC N868)

52a   1670 Izaak Walton, *THE LIFE OF Mr. GEORGE HERBERT* (STC W669); b   1674, in George Herbert, *The Temple* (STC

H1521); c   1678, in *The Temple* (STC H1522); d   1679, in
The Temple (STC H1523); e   1695, in *The Temple* (STC
H1524)

53a   1670 Izaak Walton, *THE LIVES Of D^r. John Donne, Sir Henry
Wotton, M^r. Richard Hooker, M^r. George Herbert* (STC W671);
b   1675 (STC W672)

54a   1673 Andrew Marvell, *THE REHEARSALL TRANSPROS'D: The
SECOND PART* (STC M882); b   1673 (STC M882A);
c   1674 (STC M883)

55   1677 William Winstanley, *Poor ROBIN'S VISIONS* (STC H1598)

56a   1678 S. N., *THE LOYAL GARLAND* (O Douce H. 80 [2].);
b   1686 (O Douce S 23)

57a   1680 Nathaniel Lee, *THEODOSIUS* (STC L877); b   1684 (STC
L878); c   1692 (STC L879); d   1697 (STC L880)

58   1681 *A PARADOX Against LIFE* (STC P331)

59   1683 John Shirley, *The Compleat Courtier* (STC S3503)

60a   1684 Payne Fisher, *THE Tombes, Monuments, And Sepulchral
Inscriptions, Lately Visible in St. Pauls Cathedral* (STC F1041);
b   1684 (STC F1042)

61   1687 William Winstanley, *THE LIVES Of the most Famous English
Poets* (STC W3065)

62   1688 Jane Barker, *POETICAL RECREATIONS* (STC B770)

63   1688 Henry Playford, ed., *Harmonia Sacra* (STC P2436)

64a   1691 John Dryden, *Eleonora*, in *THE WORKS* (STC D2207);
b   1692 *Eleonora* (STC D2270); c   1693, in *THE WORKS*
(STC D2208); d   1694, in *THE WORKS* (STC D2209);
e   1695, in *THE WORKS* (STC D2210)

65   1696 Mary de la Rivière Manley, *LETTERS* (STC M434)

Modern First Printings:

66   1784 Sir John Cullum, *The History and Antiquities of Hawstead, in
the County of Suffolk.*

67   1802 F. G. Waldron, *A Collection of Miscellaneous Poetry*

68   1802 F. G. Waldron, *The Shakespearean Miscellany*

69   1852 T. E. Tomlins, *The Life of John Donne, D. D. Late Dean of St.
Paul's Church, London. By Izaak Walton. With Some Original
Notes, By An Antiquary.*

70   1856 John Simeon, *MISCELLANIES OF THE Philobiblon Society*

71   1893 Sir Edmund Gosse, "The Poetry of John Donne," *NewR*, 236–
47.

72   1899 Sir Edmund Gosse, *The Life and Letters of John Donne,* vol. 2

73   1958 Sir Geoffrey Keynes, "Dr. Donne and Scaliger," *TLS,* 21
February: 93, 108.

74   1967 John T. Shawcross, "John Donne and Drummond's
Manuscripts," *American Notes & Queries* 5:104–05.

MANUSCRIPTS LISTED BY TRADITIONAL CLASSIFICATION

Varioum siglum	Traditional siglum	Beal siglum	Shelfmark/ call number	Manuscript name
Group I				
B30	H40	Δ 2	Harley 4064	Harley Noel
B32	H49	Δ 3	Harley 4955	Newcastle
C2	C57	Δ 4	Add. 5778(c)	Cambridge Balam
C8	Lec	Δ 5	Add. 8467	Leconfield
O20	D	Δ 1	Eng. poet. e.99	Dowden
SP1	SP	Δ 6	49.B.43	St. Paul's
Group II				
B7	A18	Δ 7	Add. 18647	Denbigh
CT1	TCC	Δ 13	R.3.12	Puckering
DT1	TCD	Δ 14	877	Dublin (I)
H4	N	Δ 9	Eng. 966.3	Norton
B40	L74	Δ 8	Lansdowne 740	Lansdowne
TT1	none	Δ 11	PR 1171 D14	Dalhousie I
TT2	none	Δ 12	PR 1171 S4	Dalhousie II
WN1	DC	Δ 10	Dolau Cothi 6748	Dolau Cothi
Group III				
B46	S96	Δ 15	Stowe 961	Stowe I
H5	Dob	Δ 16	Eng. 966.4	Dobell
C9	Lut	Δ 18	Add. 8468	Luttrell
H6	O'F	Δ 17	Eng. 966.5	O'Flahertie
Group IV				
NY3	W	Δ 19	Berg Collection	Westmoreland
Associated with Group III (except HH4, these are listed as Group V in X and BB)				
B13	A25	Δ 21	Add. 25707	Skipwith
H3	Cy	Δ 22	Eng. 966.1	Carnaby
H7	S	Δ 23	Eng. 966.6	Stephens
HH1	B	Δ 24	EL 6893	Bridgewater
HH4	HK1	Δ 25	HM 198, Pt. I	Haslewood-Kingsborough (I)
HH5	HK2	Δ 26	HM 198, Pt. II	Haslewood-Kingsborough (II)
Y2	K or O1	Δ 29	b 114	King
NY1	JC	Δ 27	Cat. No. S 191	John Cave
VA2	D17	Δ 28	Cat. No. 18 [25.F.17]	Nedham
O21	P	Δ 20	Eng. poet. f.9	Phillipps
Y3	O or O2	Δ 30	b 148	Osborn

Symbols and Abbreviations Used in the Textual Apparatus

(used singly or in combination)

~	base word
∧	punctuation mark omitted
→	changed to: A → B = A changed to B
*	obscured letter (the number of asterisks approximating the number of letters obscured)
[...]	conjectured reading
/	line break
|	scribal mark indicating the end of a sentence or section
›...‹	alteration/insertion in the scribal hand
»...«	alteration/insertion in a second hand
app, apps	appearance(s)
cor	corrected state of a press variant
del	deleted
err	reading from errata list
HE	heading
ind	indented, indentation
Keynes	Geoffrey Keynes, A *Bibliography of* . . . *Donne*, 4th ed.
M	margin, marginal
missing	missing because of damage to the artifact
om	omitted
rev.	reversed
SS	subscription
st, sts	stanza(s)
unc	uncorrected state of a press variant
var	variant reading(s)
Σ	all other collated sources
1st	first
2nd	second
3rd	third
4th	fourth

GENERAL INTRODUCTION

ORIGIN AND PLAN OF THE EDITION

Modern interest in Donne's poetry is amply demonstrated by the appearance of some fourteen major editions of the whole or of parts of the canon in the twentieth century and by the flood of critical and scholarly commentary catalogued in various periodic checklists (including the annual bibliographies published by the Modern Language Association of America, *Studies in Philology*, and the Modern Humanities Research Association) and in a number of specialized reference works. Among these are the four editions of Geoffrey Keynes, *Bibliography of the Works of Dr. John Donne*; Theodore Spencer and Mark Van Doren, *Studies in Metaphysical Poetry: Two Essays and a Bibliography*; Lloyd E. Berry, *A Bibliography of Studies in Metaphysical Poetry, 1939–60*; John R. Roberts, *John Donne: An Annotated Bibliography of Modern Criticism, 1912–67*; A. J. Smith, *John Donne: the Critical Heritage*; and John R. Roberts, *John Donne: An Annotated Bibliography of Modern Criticism, 1968–1978*. In response to the accumulated bulk and the continuing vitality of the critical activity reflected in these works and to a growing conviction within the community of Donne scholars that Donne's text needed to be reedited—a conviction strongly buttressed by the publication in 1980 of Peter Beal's *Index of English Literary Manuscripts*, which identified important manuscript material that none of Donne's editors had ever incorporated—the project to produce this variorum edition was conceived.

After considerable prior discussion about the feasibility and usefulness of such a work, the effort was formally organized in the fall of 1981 when a group of scholars was invited to meet on the Gulf Park campus of the University of Southern Mississippi to define the nature of the task and outline procedures for carrying it out. At that meeting Gary A. Stringer of the University of Southern Mississippi was designated General Editor, and an advisory board comprising the following members was established: William B. Hunter, Jr., University of Houston (Emeritus); Albert C. Labriola, Duquesne University; Paul A. Parrish, Texas A&M University; Ted-Larry Pebworth, University of Michigan-Dearborn; John R. Roberts, University of Missouri; John T. Shawcross, University of Kentucky; and Ernest W. Sullivan, II, Texas Tech University. Later this group was expanded to include M. Thomas Hester, North Carolina State University, and C. A. Patrides, University of Michigan, who sat on the Advisory Board until his death in 1986. In response to evolving organizational and individual purposes, the makeup of the Advisory Board has inevitably changed over the years, but it has been an abiding principle that members would not only help to steer the project, but also actively engage in the editorial work; and the respective contributions of Advisory Board members are noted in the various volumes of the edition, along with those of the other scholars who have participated in various ways. The project has also received widespread support from other individuals and institutions throughout the academic community and from a number of foundations and granting agencies. The contributions of all these supporters are gratefully and specifically acknowledged in the pages of the various volumes.

In accordance with the traditional ways of grouping Donne's works, the edition is organized into volumes, some of multiple parts, as follows:

Volume 1: General Commentary: the Historical Reception of Donne's Poetry
from the Beginnings to the Present
General Textual Introduction and Appendices
Volume 2: Elegies
Volume 3: Satyres, Metempsychosis
Volume 4: Songs and Sonets
Volume 5: Verse Letters
Volume 6: Anniversaries, Epicedes and Obsequies
Volume 7: Divine Poems
Volume 8: Epigrams, Epithalamions, Epitaphs, Inscriptions, Miscellaneous Poems

As this outline indicates, all volumes except the first contain texts and commentary for a set of generically or thematically related poems, and the volumes are numbered in a rough approximation of the order in which the poems were composed. Although this system of numbering may entail a certain amount of bibliographical confusion while the edition is in progress, we trust that upon completion of the entire project this method of ordering the parts will appear rational to bibliographers and critics alike.

THE COMMENTARY

Purpose and Scope

Although the material here presented will undoubtedly lend itself to other uses as well, our fundamental motive in compiling this variorum commentary is to facilitate further understanding of Donne's poems by situating them squarely within the tradition of critical and scholarly discussion that has grown up around them from the poet's own time to the present. This purpose, in turn, has required that we identify and examine all items that properly belong within that tradition. As existing bibliographical aids indicate, the body of commentary on Donne is not only vast, but widely scattered. In his 458-page synopsis of comments on Donne in the Critical Heritage series, for instance, A. J. Smith locates and excerpts 222 items published between 1598 and 1889; and John R. Roberts, in his bibliographies of twentieth-century criticism, lists and annotates well over 2,400 items written on Donne between 1912 and 1978, the second of these registering a trend that now sees the publication of approximately 100 books, articles, and notes on Donne every year. In addition to sheer bulk, as suggested above, the corpus of Donne commentary exhibits two further features that make it difficult to master: much of the material, both that identified in existing bibliographies and that which we have discovered, is dispersed throughout the pages of obscure or inaccessible editions and periodicals, and a good bit of it is written in foreign languages. The result of these circumstances is that scholarly or critical works of our own time frequently fail to align themselves distinctly within the critical tradition, and the continuing interpretive enterprise is marked by repetition and fragmentation.

There has been no previous attempt of this kind. None of the existing editions marshals more than a minute part of the available material, and the bibliographical volumes produced by Smith and Roberts have neither the scope nor the design of a variorum commentary, in addition to leaving entirely uncovered the periods 1890–1911 and 1979–present.[1] This variorum commentary, therefore, will fill a conspicuous gap in the field of Donne studies. In the effort to meet this need, we have defined our task in the broadest chronological and geographical terms. Although bibliographical considerations have dictated that we attempt coverage in each volume only to within three years of the completion of the typescript—and sometimes the gap between cut-off and publication dates is even greater—we have otherwise sought to bring together and synthesize all relevant items from the seventeenth through the twentieth centuries, and we have included material written not only in English, but also in French, German, Dutch, Italian, Spanish, Portuguese, Polish, Czech, and Japanese. Displaying the poems against this evolving, variegated background of critical discourse will, we believe, not only enable a better appreciation of individual works and of Donne's overall poetic achievement, but also provide materials toward an enhanced understanding of the aesthetic and intellectual history of the modern period. In short, the material here gathered will point the way to further research in a number of areas and facilitate the ongoing critical dialogue.

An undertaking like this, of course, is by its very nature conservative, bespeaking respect not only for what Donne has left us, but also for the contributions of those prior critics who have made possible our present understanding. Like those of contemporary critics, of course, the judgments of previous commentators are inevitably conditioned by cultural and personal assumptions about what poetry is (or should be), about how it functions in the world, and about the nature of criticism itself; and the validity of such assumptions tends to appear self-evident to those who hold them, with the frequent result that they are never explicitly stated. While the clarification of such preconceptions is itself a legitimate scholarly aim, we have not attempted in these pages to interpret the criticism nor to examine the various epistemological

[1]Since this introduction was first written, Catherine Phillips has extended Smith's work in *John Donne II: The Critical Heritage* (1996), which adds items up through 1923; and Roberts's *John Donne: An Annotated Bibliography of Modern Criticism, 1979–1995* appeared in 2004.

constructs that have shaped it, but have chosen rather to let each item of commentary speak for itself as best it can in the reduced form that it must necessarily take in these volumes. We recognize, of course, that no summary, however carefully prepared, can fully replace the original upon which it is based; indeed, the longer and more complex a given argument is, the less satisfactorily it submits to condensation. The compilation of commentary here offered is thus intended as a guide to, not as a substitute for, the primary works of scholarship that make up the tradition.

Editorial Stance

In attempting this consolidation of the critical heritage we have striven for both completeness and objectivity. Within the historical and linguistic limits noted above, we have sought to gather all published items of commentary and to represent each as accurately and extensively as our format permits. We have, furthermore, presented all these materials without interjecting editorial opinion on their validity or ultimate significance, though we have reduced redundancy in the presentation by fully reporting ideas only upon their first appearance, in some cases briefly tracing the progress of a given observation or line of argument by means of a system of internal cross-referencing. We have added neither glosses nor more general interpretations of our own, and have restricted instances of editorial intrusion (denoted by the abbreviation *ed.* in the text) to the correction of obvious factual error.

Organization of the Material within Volumes

As is customary in a variorum commentary, all material included here is organized chronologically and, when necessary within a given year, alphabetically by author's surname; and each item is aligned as precisely as possible with whichever aspects of the poetry it bears on. Thus, as noted above, Volume 1 traces in general terms the reception of Donne's poetry over the centuries, while the remaining volumes focus on individual genres and groups of poems. We have arranged the commentary in each genre-based volume along a continuum of particularity, beginning with the most general and proceeding to commentary on subsets of poems (where appropriate), commentary on particular poems, and line-by-line notes and glosses.[2] The material at all levels except glosses, moreover, is further organized into topical subunits whenever a common theme or critical concern runs through a number of items. In cases where an individual item of commentary depends specifically upon a previous version of Donne's text, we have included the relevant readings from that version.

Style of Presentation

We have attempted to present the commentary as efficiently and readably as possible. At all levels of organization above Notes and Glosses, the material is invariably

---

[2] In glosses keyed to specific lines or words, of course, commentators frequently annotate items in surrounding lines as well, and it is not always possible to subdivide such manifold glosses into their component elements without destroying the author's sense. Especially in Notes and Glosses sections of the commentary, therefore, users are advised to examine each entry in the context of those that come before and after in order to ensure full coverage of what has been reported about a particular point.

summarized in narrative form, as the user is guided through the content by the editor's controlling voice, and the normal conventions of interpreting prose summary apply. In Notes and Glosses, however, which derive variously both from specific observations abstracted from longer discursive comments and from the brief, telegraphic annotations often employed by editors, we have alternated between the narrative and the dramatic styles as necessary in an attempt to present each bit of material as economically as possible (though we have not intermixed the two modes within the entry for a single author). Following any lemma in the Notes and Glosses, therefore, one commentator's remarks may be rendered dramatically, as though the original author were speaking in his or her own voice, while those of the next may be paraphrased in the editor's voice. The dramatic mode, whether or not any words or phrases in the entry appear in quotation marks, is signaled mechanically by a colon after the bibliographical citation in parentheses, the narrative mode by the absence of a colon. Editorial insertions thus appear in brackets in the dramatic mode and in parentheses in the narrative mode.

Bibliographical Conventions in the Commentary

Works mentioned in the Commentary are cited parenthetically by author and date, and these citations are keyed to a master list of Works Cited in each volume. Since the commentary throughout the *Variorum* is ordered according to a multi-leveled taxonomic system, the author index included in each volume, used in conjunction with the master list of works cited, will provide the further information needed to index the content of the volume.[3] We have used standard nonverbal symbols and short forms of reference insofar as possible, and have derived common scholarly abbreviations, including those for such items as the titles of Shakespeare's plays and books of the Bible, from the current *MLA Style Manual*. For titles of current journals we have used the abbreviations given in the *MLA International Bibliography*, and for early books we have appropriated the short forms of reference standardized by Pollard and Redgrave and by Wing in the *STC*. Lists of abbreviated references to all works cited in the commentary and to Donne's poems and prose works are provided in each volume, and we have standardized all citations of Donne's prose works in the commentary in accordance with the editions specified in the list of Short Forms. Unless otherwise indicated, cross-references pertain to the section of commentary within which they appear.

THE TEXT

Materials and Theory

Ideally stated, the goal of our work on the text is to recover and present exactly what Donne wrote. It is important, however, that we be clear about certain practical

---

[3]Beginning with our volume on Donne's elegies in 2000, we have added two further indexes: (1) an index of writers and historical figures mentioned in the commentary and (2) an index of all references to Donne's works in the commentary.

and theoretical limits that are imposed upon this goal by the available materials. Apart from about forty prose letters and certain occasional jottings, four inscriptions in the books of friends or acquaintances, and an epitaph on his wife, only a single poem—a verse epistle addressed to the Lady Carey and Mrs. Essex Riche—is known to survive in Donne's hand. Of the relatively few poems published before his death in 1631, only for the Anniversaries, in the edition of 1612, and in the first Latin and English editions of *Ignatius* is there any evidence to suggest that the author may have proofread and corrected copy. The remainder of the poems survive only in nonauthorial copies (which amount to well over 5,000 separate transcriptions of individual poems), at indeterminate degrees of remove from holograph and therefore of indeterminate authority. During and immediately following Donne's lifetime these poems, circulating individually or in groups of various sizes and composition, were copied into diaries, commonplace books, miscellanies, and poetic collections that form several distinct strands of scribal transmission; and these strands, in ways impossible to determine exactly, lie behind the print tradition that begins for most of the poems with the publication in 1633 of *Poems, by J. D. with Elegies on the Authors Death* and continues in six additional seventeenth-century collected editions and issues.

The almost total absence of holograph materials or of authorially approved printings renders impossible any attempt to locate textual authority in the author's intentions, as that concept is generally applied in scholarly editing. Indeed, the only "intention" Donne seems to have had for most of his poems in this regard was that they *not be printed at all*. Commenting on the publication of the Anniversaries in a letter to George Garrard from Paris on April 14, 1612, Donne wrote, "I . . . do not pardon my self" for having "descended to print any thing in verse" (*Letters* 238), and when in 1614 he thought himself "brought to a necessity of printing" (*Letters* 196) the poems as a "valediction to the world" before taking holy orders (a necessity he apparently escaped), he sought to borrow from his friend Henry Goodyer an "old book" (*Letters* 197) containing copies of them, thus suggesting that—at least for some of the poems—he had failed even to retain manuscript copies for his own use or reference.

If virtually none of them bears the author's imprimatur, the surviving materials for constructing a text of Donne's poems are nonetheless numerous and diverse. In addition to the seven collected printings issued between 1633 and 1669, they include 239 manuscript sources (nearly 100 of which have been unknown to any of Donne's previous editors); 3 inscriptions on monuments; over 200 seventeenth-century books that collectively contain over 700 copies of individual Donne poems or excerpts (approximately 500 of which have been unknown to Donne's previous editors); and over 20 historically significant editions of all or of parts of the canon from the eighteenth century to the present. No one would argue, of course, that all of this material is equally valuable for establishing the text, but all of it, including both corrected and uncorrected states of the seventeenth-century editions (among which we have identified many previously unrecorded press variants), is part of the bibliographical tradition that provides what we currently know of Donne's poems and their textual history. A full description of these textual artifacts and the relations among them is provided in volume 1 of the edition.

The nature of the material described above severely complicates the question of textual authority—not only with respect to the presentation of the individual poems, but also in the matters of how to order the poems within an edition and, to a lesser extent, what works to admit to the canon. No scribal artifact and no pre-twentieth-century edition includes the full complement of what are now generally recognized as authentic poems. While it preserves a general continuity in the texts of individual poems, the tradition represented by the seventeenth-century collected editions shows a gradual expansion and, especially in 1635, rearrangement of the canon, as printers sought to publish increasingly comprehensive and generically rationalized editions; and not until Grosart's edition of 1872–73 do we find a modern editor basing his work extensively on manuscript sources rather than on the print tradition. From Grierson (1912) onward, most of Donne's twentieth-century editors have adopted as copy-text for each poem an early seventeenth-century printing, sometimes emending its details (especially verbal variants) toward manuscript readings, and virtually all modern editions order their contents according to the broad generic divisions introduced in the edition of 1635.

As noted above, we also have adopted the traditional generic divisions as an ordering principle. We have not, however, necessarily followed the majority practice of locating primary textual authority for each poem in an early printing, and we have not practiced the eclecticism that has frequently accompanied such a choice. In accordance with the considerations outlined below, we have selected copy-texts variously from among all the available artifacts, and we have presented them with a minimum of editorial intervention. Both practices require explanation.

We have chosen manuscript copy-texts for many of the poems simply because they seem in fact and in theory more likely to represent the lost originals accurately than do the early printings. As noted above, the exact textual genesis of the early collected editions cannot be ascertained. Although individual poems in some of these editions *may* have been set from holograph, it is extremely unlikely that even the printer in 1633 possessed authorial copies of more than a few of the poems—and perhaps of none at all. Given the occasional composition, the piecemeal distribution, and the wide circulation of the poems in manuscript—and especially the author's apparent failure to maintain a comprehensive personal archive—it is very hard to imagine that an extensive holograph collection of Donne's poems ever existed, even in the seventeenth century. Indeed, the phrasing of Donne's request for Goodyer's "old book" may suggest that the author himself expected to retrieve transcriptions rather than original copies. Most probable is that the original holographs gradually dropped out of circulation as the poems made the rounds of transmission, and there is thus the virtual certainty that even the earliest editions were set from derivative manuscript collections very much like those that survive.

Whatever their origins, moreover, comparison of the early printings with the surviving scribal manuscripts—or even with the extant holograph verse letter—shows clearly that as texts underwent translation from manuscript to print in the publishing house, they not only suffered some measure of verbal corruption, but also were subjected to institutional conventions of punctuation, spelling, capitalization, and so forth—even in instances when the printer may have been setting from holographs.

In thus reflecting the intersection of private scribal or authorial practices with the social norms of commercial printing, the printed text inevitably became a collaborative product that differed in a number of important ways from what Donne had originally set down.[4]

The data clearly show, of course, that the poems were similarly vulnerable to change in the course of scribal transmission. Undoubtedly, many scribes automatically restyled the poems to accord with their own habits of formatting, spelling, capitalization, and punctuation; and some no doubt made conscious verbal "improvements." As they transcribed poems into private collections for their own use or that of patrons, however, the early copyists did not necessarily share the printer's programmatic determination to groom the text into a publicly negotiable, regularized form; and most of the substantive changes they introduced into the text are more likely attributable to carelessness, ignorance, and the general entropy of the transmissional system.

Most of the manuscripts antedate the printed editions, of course, and thus are chronologically closer to the hand of the author. A number of factors, however, seriously restrict any attempt to determine their dates of compilation and thus to construct a comprehensive genealogy of manuscripts. For one thing, many of the manuscripts cannot be dated except in very approximate terms; moreover, an indeterminate number of manuscripts are evidently missing. The greatest limitation on developing a reliable stemma of manuscripts, however, is that virtually all the major manuscript collections, like the printed editions, are composite artifacts containing texts of individual poems drawn from multiple sources, and a given manuscript may thus preserve an early state of one text and a late state of another side by side. In some cases, of course, particular features of content, format, and scribal style point to family relationships among manuscripts and sometimes even reveal direct lines of descent within families. Generally speaking, however, the effort to locate textual authority in a genealogy of manuscripts is doomed to fail.

Given the situation described above, the only remaining alternative is to approach Donne's text on a poem-by-poem basis, examining all copies of each poem and determining insofar as possible its individual history of transmission. As with whole manuscripts, the possibility of missing copies and the intractability of the surviving evidence also make it impossible to construct a complete genealogy for many of the poems. With varying degrees of precision, however, it is possible to identify patterns of variation that lead back to the least corrupted surviving version(s) of a poem and to chart the transmission of its text in a schema of textual relationships. As this procedure implies, of course, the effort to recover Donne's poems necessarily rests partly in the editor's evaluation of the relative semiological integrity of the surviving copies of individual poems. Once this determination has been made, the question then becomes one of how those individual copies shall be edited.

As noted above, most of Donne's twentieth-century editors have created synthetic

---

[4]Between the holograph of the 63-line verse letter and the text printed in 1633, for instance, there are 56 differences in punctuation, 63 differences in capitalization, 120 differences in spelling, and 3 differences in wording.

or eclectic texts, adopting a seventeenth-century printing of each poem as copy-text and generally following that printing's accidentals, while sometimes emending its substantives toward manuscript readings. There are, however, a number of problems with this approach. A major one, in our view, as Charles Moorman has argued in discussing a similar case, is that the practice involves the highly questionable assumption that any modern editor—even one very sensitive, learned, and wise—can reach back over hundreds of years and somehow ascertain what must have been in Donne's mind, root out instances of corruption, and synthetically reconstruct a text reflecting what he actually wrote. Indeed, as Fredson Bowers has pointed out, Greg's rationale of copy-text, the classic formulation of the synthetic principle, was intended to apply in cases in which the variant forms of a work could be assumed to form a single ancestral sequence reaching back to the author's holographs. Clearly, in the case of Donne, whose poems survive in many genealogical strands of indeterminate proximity to each other and to the manuscript originals, an eclectic approach that privileges the early printings offers only a qualified hope of recovering the author's exact words—and even less of recovering his accidentals. Additionally, of course, in cases where an author has revised a work (as Donne did in some instances), an eclectic approach entails the risk of conflating earlier and later states of the text.

Any editor of Donne must, of course, exercise judgment; but there are legitimate differences of opinion about where, how often, and especially at what stage of the editorial process that judgment can most defensibly be exercised. In light of the circumstances described above, we have attempted to identify—by combining bibliographical analysis with such logical criteria as completeness and general semantic coherence—the earliest, least corrupted state of each poem from among the surviving seventeenth-century artifacts or, in the case of poems surviving in multiple authorial versions, the least corrupted state of each version; and once that judgment has been reached, we have edited the text in the conservative manner explained below. The theory underlying our work is thus fundamentally historicist, but balanced by a respect for what we have called the semiological integrity of the individual poem as preserved in an early artifact. We recognize that, except by extreme good fortune, we are not likely to present any nonholographic poem exactly as Donne wrote it, but this approach does allow us to present a text of every poem essentially free of conjecture and anachronistic intervention.

This, then, is the sense in which we mean that we have sought to recover and present exactly what Donne wrote. Our text is a representation of the poem that stands in a metonymic relationship to the lost original, different both in that it may not have the exact wording and pointing of that original and—for texts based on manuscript originals—in that it will be a print exemplum of the copy from which it derives. It is, however, a text that somebody in Donne's own time—the one who had the copy closest to his hand and transcribed it most accurately, if we are lucky—set down as what the author had written. Because it provides an illuminating background for our work and because it is a legitimate scholarly concern in its own right, we have further undertaken to outline the textual history of each poem as fully and as accurately as possible.

Procedures for Choosing and Emending Copy-text

To the ends specified above we have adopted the following procedures for choosing and emending copy-texts and constructing the textual apparatus. First, since most of the texts survive only in nonauthorial copies, we have necessarily examined every surviving seventeenth-century manuscript and multiple copies of seventeenth-century printings.[5] In order to do this, we have entered the texts of all manuscript and early print copies of the poems into computer files and compared the files for each poem by means of the Donne Variorum Collation Program.[6] On the basis of these collations, we have constructed for each poem a schema of textual relationships that accounts, insofar as the evidence permits, for all permutations of the texts in the early artifacts. In order to corroborate the evidence of this analysis, as suggested above, we have independently assessed the evidentiary value of each artifact by determining insofar as possible its date, provenance, and process of compilation and by evaluating all this bibliographical detail in the context of what is known about manuscript transcription and practices of typesetting in the late sixteenth and earlier seventeenth centuries. The copy-text finally chosen is what seems to be the earliest, least-corrupted state of the text as preserved in the best witness among the artifacts in which it appears. Having made this identification, we have corrected obvious errors in the copy-text, emended punctuation when absolutely necessary to prevent misreading, and applied certain print conventions to manuscript copy-texts, but we have not conflated readings from multiple sources. In cases where one or more artifacts preserve a poem in a state so extensively revised or changed as to constitute a new version, we present the successive versions in full and, whenever it seems useful to do so, provide a separate historical collation for each.

In accordance with our determination to represent the copy-text authentically and accurately, we have retained in the *Variorum* texts a number of seventeenth-century orthographical and typographical features and, except for the silent changes specified below, have noted in the apparatus accompanying each poem all emendations to the copy-text. The *Variorum* texts preserve the distinct forms of "i" and "j" and "u" and "v," the ligatured vowels "æ" and "œ," and the fonts of words as they appear in the copy-text. We have, however, expanded brevigraphs, regularized "VV" to "W" and "ff" to "F," and imposed on manuscript copy-texts such print conventions as the consistent capitalization of the first word of each line of poetry. All such emendations, as well as the few editorial corrections deemed necessary, are noted in the lists of emendations. Our only silent emendations of the copy-text are typo-

---

[5]When a seventeenth-century printing is used as copy-text, we have collated at least five copies (or all copies, if fewer than five copies survive); when the copy-text is a manuscript, we have collated at least three copies of all seventeenth-century printings of the poems, except that we have generally collated only one copy if a print source contains only an excerpt from a poem.

[6]We have verified all data files used in the preparation of these texts against original sources, and have compared multiple copies of printed artifacts not only by sight, but also, when it has been possible to bring the requisite materials together, by means of the Lindstrand Comparator or the Hinman Collator. At all stages of transcription and data entry, at least three editors have proofread the work independently, resolving any problems or differences of interpretation in conference. At each stage of production we have taken similar care to verify the accuracy of both text and apparatus.

graphical and affect neither spelling nor meaning: we have reduced the long "ʃ" to "s," separated such ornamental ligatured consonants as "ſt" and "ct," and regularized inconsistencies of font and the spacing of punctuation.

Because Donne's syntax is often knotty, punctuation itself is frequently interpretive. Recognizing this, we have emended the punctuation of the copy-text very conservatively, and this principle has resulted in an actual, though not a theoretical, inconsistency. Since printers of the earlier seventeenth century tended to punctuate heavily and grammatically, while many scribes of that period punctuated lightly and rhetorically (sometimes even to the point of regarding the line end as sufficient punctuation in itself), the *Variorum* texts based on printed copy-texts and those based on manuscript copy-texts show markedly different degrees of punctuation. But we think it better to present texts that, in each case, accurately reflect a bibliographically defensible choice of copy-text than to impose consistency of punctuation and with it the possibility of editorial interpretation. Variant seventeenth-century pointing that may affect the sense of a given passage is recorded in the historical collation.

Introductions and Apparatuses

Each poem is provided with a brief textual introduction, and groups of related poems are introduced collectively when it is useful to do so. The introduction to each poem briefly locates the poem in the context of Donne's life or poetic development (when possible) and outlines the seventeenth-century textual history of the poem by grouping the artifacts into families and describing insofar as possible the relationships of those families, as well as noting readings of particular bibliographical or critical interest. It then sketches the treatment of the poem by modern editors and briefly discusses the choice and emendation of the copy-text.

For complete textual information on any poem, of course, readers must consult both the textual introductions and the various parts of the textual apparatus. As suggested above, the textual apparatus may include data drawn from five different classes of material: (1) manuscripts, (2) independent seventeenth-century editions of Donne's poetical works (including seventeenth-century editions of the Anniversaries and collected editions or issues), (3) uncollected seventeenth-century printings of individual poems and excerpts of two or more lines, (4) modern first printings of individual poems, and (5) selected modern editions of Donne's poetical works. In general, the apparatus lists the sigla of source materials in the demonstrable or probable order of the transmission of the text, ordering items within classes alphabetically or numerically as appropriate.

The following categories of information are included in the textual apparatus for each poem, except that in cases where there is nothing to report, the category is omitted:

1. Copy-text and Sources Collated. Lists by sigla the copy-text and the copies and excerpts collated, specifying the folio or page numbers on which the poem or excerpt appears in each artifact, and, in the case of deliberate excerpts, which lines are excerpted.

2. Emendations of the Copy-text. Specifies differences between the copy-text and the *Variorum* text.

3. Historical Collation.

    a. Format. Details noteworthy features of the artifacts or transcriptions, including typefaces, paragraphing, patterns of indentation (though not occasional deviations) in stanzaic verse, scribal eccentricities, lines missing in damaged artifacts, and other information affecting text or indicating authorship or provenance.

    b. Headings. Lists variant headings (not called "titles," since their authority is uncertain) in seventeenth-century artifacts.

    c. Line-by-line collation. Lists all substantive and selected semisubstantive variants (specified below) in seventeenth-century sources, as well as any omissions of words or lines in copies intended to be complete.

    d. Subscriptions. Lists all subscriptions in seventeenth-century artifacts.

4. Verbal Variants in Selected Modern Editions. Lists verbal variants in twenty-three historically or bibliographically significant editions from the eighteenth century to the present.

5. Stemma or Schema of Textual Relationships. Charts in schematic form the genealogy of each poem and the relationships of the textual artifacts, denoting definite lines of transmission with arrows, definite associations and family linkages with solid lines, and conjectural lines of relationship with dotted lines.

6. Analyses of Early Printed Copies. Lists copies collated, describes the physical makeup of each, and details press variants.

Reportage of Variants

We have tried to make the list of variants useful to many kinds of readers, from textual scholars and literary historians to critics and metricians. In order to do so, we have reported the following kinds of substantive and semisubstantive variants:

    1. All verbal variants in seventeenth-century artifacts, including variant spellings that may be read as different words in context.

    2. All nonverbal substantive variants from all seventeenth-century sources, including differences in punctuation that materially affect meaning.[7]

    3. All semisubstantive variants from all seventeenth-century sources that may affect either meaning or meter. Included in this category are the capitalization of such words as "Fate," "Nature," and "Heaven"; elided and nonelided vowels and marks of syncope that may affect the number of syllables in a line and therefore meter; and variants of spelling that, in context, may suggest different words or orthographic puns.

    4. Variants that illuminate a poem's textual history. This is the broadest and most discretionary category, but an important one nonetheless in that the details it includes clarify the transmission and history of the text. Under this heading are reported verbal variants in modern editions, which are listed separately at the end of the historical collation for each poem.

---

[7]Lists in the historical collations do not record inconsequential variants of punctuation—such as commas separating items in simple compound constructions; neither do they record the absence of nonsubstantive punctuation in corollary copies in cases where the copy-text contains the punctuation necessary for understanding.

In reporting the kinds of variants here specified, we intend to provide users with the data necessary to reconstruct in all essential respects any version of the text of any poem.[8]

Bibliographical Conventions in the Apparatus

The format for entries in the Historical Collation generally follows standard practices of bibliographical notation. Each word or item in the *Variorum* text for which variant readings are reported is presented as a lemma to the left of a right bracket (lemma]) and followed by the variant and a list of sigla for the sources in which the variant appears. Multiple variants and sigla for a given item are presented seriatim and separated by semicolons. When a variant appears in a great number of sources across the spectrum of family groups (and thus conveys no genealogical information about the texts), these sources are collectively denoted by the symbol Σ, and the sigla for artifacts containing the lemmatic reading are listed immediately after the bracket. In the Historical Collation for *ElPerf* 5, for example, the first item appears as follows:

> I,] B32 C2 C8 DT1 H4 NY3 O20 SN4 A–G; ~∧ Σ.

This entry indicates that the sources B32 through G give the lemmatic reading ("I,"), while the variant ("I" without the following comma) appears in all other sources.

As is shown in the preceding example, a swung dash (~) is used after the bracket to stand for a word in the lemma, and a caret (∧) preceding or following a word or swung dash to the right of the bracket indicates omitted punctuation. When the lemma is a single word and only variants of punctuation are to be reported, the swung dash will thus appear in combination with marks of punctuation and/or carets. For lemmas consisting of multiple words, individual swung dashes are used to the right of the bracket to represent corresponding words in the lemma when the multiword variant can be accurately and economically reported by so doing. Depending on the details of the individual instance, therefore, variants to a multiword lemma may be reported either as a series of swung dashes interspersed with appropriate carets or marks of punctuation or as a combination of words, swung dashes, and punctuation marks. In the Historical Collation for *ElAut*, for instance, the first item reported for line 15 appears as follows:

> Yet lyes not Loue] And her inshrined   CE1; And (heare inshrined)
> O34; ~ is ~ ~   P4; ~ lyeth ~ ~   WN3.

This entry indicates that CE1 and O34 substitute three (differently punctuated) words of their own for those of the lemma, while P4 and WN3 match the lemma except

---

[8]It should be noted that obvious errors in printed editions, such as "effential" for "essential" and "Beddded" for "Bedded," are not reported in the historical collations except when they result in verbal variants, such as the erroneous "patts" for "parts" (1621 ed. of *SecAn* 233) and the erroneous "close-weaning" for "close-weauing" (1611–25 eds. of *FirAn* 153) or later become the source of error, such as the misprint "*ealth*" for *health* (1625 ed. of *FirAn* 91M), which leads to the mistaken emendation "*earth*" in the subsequent edition of 1633. It should further be noted that in the case of severely damaged or mutilated manuscripts (always so designated in the Format section of the Historical Collation), only fully discernible variants and features that aid in the filiation of manuscripts are reported; no attempt is made to itemize each missing word or feature.

that they substitute respectively "is" and "lyeth" for "lyes." Similarly, the collation for *ElAut* 16 includes the following entry:

> like an] ~ to ~   B25 C9 CE1 DT2 F3 H6 TM1 Y3; ~ ~ old   C4;
> ~ a chast   F4 NP1; ~ as ~   H8 HH5 Y2 35; as to ~   O21; (as to ~   O34;
> ~ a sworne   O36.

This entry indicates that the sources B25 through Y3 read "like to an"; that C4 reads "like an old"; that F4 and NP1 read "like a chast"; that H8 through 35 read "like as an"; that O21 reads "as to an"; that O34 matches O21, except that it gives a left parenthesis before "as"; and that O36 reads "like a sworne." As these examples show, the swung dash is used only when the lemma and the variant are essentially isomorphic and the correspondences between their respective parts are clear; when this correlation is not clear, multiword verbal variants are written out in full.

It should be noted that the swung dash does not imply exact identity of spelling, capitalization, or font between the word it represents and the corresponding word in the lemma (although the two may in fact be identical), but only that the two are forms of the same word. For example, the final word of line 8 in "*ELEGIE* on the untimely Death of the *incomparable Prince*, HENRY" reads as follows in the artifacts: "*Circumference:*" in 12a–j; "Circumference." in B14, C9, H3, and H6; "Circumference" in DT1; "Cyrcumference" in H4; "circumference." in O29, WN1, and A; and "circumference:" in B through G. Since differences of spelling, font, and capitalization are not substantive in this case and are thus not reported, these variants are collapsed into the following synthetic entry in the historical collation:

> Circumference:] ~.   B14 C9 H3 H6 O29 WN1 A; ~$_\wedge$ DT1 H4.

When the artifacts generally agree in a lengthy variation, but contain minor differences that need to be reported, we have minimized clutter in the apparatus by recording such subvariations parenthetically immediately after the siglum of the source from which they derive. For example, 13a and 13b preserve the variant readings "Wheres now the" and "Where's now the" in the first half of *FirAn* 127. These variant readings, which differ only in the use of the apostrophe, are reported in the historical collation as follows:

> Where is this] Wheres now the   13a 13b(Where's).

In cases where a reading right of the bracket expresses as a single, synthetic entry variations of spelling, font, or capitalization that do not affect meaning or meter (and thus are not reported explicitly), the accidentals of any word that may appear in the entry are those of the artifact reported first in the sequence unless otherwise indicated.

Hyphenated constructions within the body of variant readings sometimes pose particular difficulties of representation. Any hyphenated compound in the reading text for which variants must be reported invariably appears in the textual apparatus as a single-item lemma; but hyphenated constructions that appear as variants to non-hyphenated collocations in the reading text may be divided at the hyphen in order to promote clarity in the Historical Collation. In a simple sequence of discrete words, for instance, the *Variorum* text reads *ElPerf* 31 as "The grimm eight foot high Iron bound Seruing man." Such a diverse array of hyphenated forms appears among the corollary texts of this line, however, that to keep all such compounds together in the list of variants would require establishing a single lemma comprising every word in the line except "The." In order to avoid the plethora of multiword variants that would thus be produced in the apparatus, we have divided the line into a number of simpler lemmas and broken compound variants at appropriate points of hyphenation. For instance, the first textual note to the line reads thus:

> grimm] ~- B28 B32 B47 C2 C8 CE1 H3 H5 H7 H8 NY1 O16 O20
> O21 O34 OC1 SP1 VA2 WN1 A–G.

This entry indicates that while the copy-text gives no hyphen between "grimm" and the following word, the sources B28 through G all read "grimm" and the following word as a hyphenated compound. Unless otherwise noted, the appearance of a hyphen after any variant word in the apparatus thus signals the connection of that word to the one that follows in the source.

As noted above, the Stemma or Schema of Textual Relationships accompanying each poem is designed to outline in broad terms what can be determined of the poem's genealogy. When the evidence is sufficient, we present a traditional stemma outlining in skeletal form the step-by-step transmissional history of the text; in other cases we provide a schema that displays, within the context of full lines, the variants that permit separation of the artifacts into family groups. Accidentals in lines selected for the schema are those of a representative member of the family, and the defining variants are shown in boldface type. Significant intra-family variations are reported parenthetically at the end of each line. Detail reported in the schema is necessarily limited; information enabling the establishment of further genealogical links among copies of the text can be derived from the Historical Collation.

The Editors

Introduction to Volume 7.1

General Textual Introduction

In comparison to such popular genres as the Songs and Sonnets, the love elegies, and even the Epigrams, Donne's Holy Sonnets had only a limited circulation in the seventeenth century. As Figure 1 shows, 200 individual copies of these poems survive in the manuscript record, and 9 of these—those in AF1, B6, and H11—derive from the printed editions. A sequence of 12 sonnets was included in the first collected edition of Donne's POEMS in 1633 (A), and the edition of 1635 (B) two years later incorporated 4 others into this group. Whether explicitly merged with the 7 poems of "La Corona" (*Corona*) or not, this sequence of 16 Holy Sonnets then descended through the remaining seventeenth-century editions (C–G) and, further, to all those of the eighteenth and nineteenth centuries as well, the exception being Alford's reversion in 1839 (siglum L) to the 12-poem sequence of A. In the 1890s, however, Edmund Gosse brought forward for the first time 3 poems unique to the Westmoreland ms. (NY3)—"Since she whom I loved" (*HSShe*), "Show me, dear Christ" (*HSShow*), and "Oh, to vex me" (*HSVex*)—and twentieth-century editors from Grierson (Q) onward have confronted an expanded canon of 19 Holy Sonnets. Dating and ordering the poems—and especially ascertaining whether there are multiple authorial arrangements—are the paramount problems that an editor faces, and attempting to solve them entails an analysis not only of the early transmissional history of the sonnets themselves, but also of their relationships to *Corona*, to the verse epistle "To E. of D., with Six Holy Sonnets" (*ED*), and to various other poems with which they have sometimes been linked. Since the questions of dating and sequence have been central to the critical reception of the poems in (especially) the twentieth century, the discussion below will not only present our conclusions on these issues, but also detail the evolving treatment of these matters in the late-nineteenth- and twentieth-century editions in which critics have encountered the poems.

The Holy Sonnets in the Manuscripts

A signal feature of the manuscript transmission of the Holy Sonnets is that none of the poems has a history of individual circulation. However ordered, these sonnets invariably traveled in groups, a fact suggesting that the concept of sequence was

Figure 1: Copies of Holy Sonnets in Seventeenth-Century Artifacts

Source \ Poem	HSMade	HSDue	HSSighs	HSPart	HSBlack	HSScene	HSLittle	HSRound	HSMin	HSSouls	HSDeath	HSWilt	HSSpit	HSWhy	HSWhat	HSBatter	HSShe	HSShow	HSVex
AF1	●		●			●				●									
B6	●																		
B7		●		●	●	●		●	●		●	●	●	●	●	●	●		
B32		●		●	●	●		●	●		●	●	●	●	●	●	●		
B46	●	●	●	●	●	●	●	●	●	●	●	●							
C2		●		●	●	●		●	●		●	●	●	●	●	●	●		
C9	●	●	●	●	●	●	●	●	●	●	●	●	●	●	●	●	●		
CT1		●		●	●	●		●	●		●	●	●	●	●	●	●		
DT1		●		●	●	●		●	●		●	●	●	●	●	●	●		
H4		●		●	●	●		●	●		●	●	●	●	●	●	●		
H5	●	●	●	●	●	●	●	●	●	●	●	●							
H6	●	●	●	●	●	●	●	●	●	●	●	●	●	●	●	●	●		
H11	●		●			●				●									
HH1	●	●	●	●	●	●	●	●	●	●	●	●							
NY3	●	●	●	●	●	●	●	●	●	●	●	●	●	●	●	●	●	●	●
O20		●		●	●	●		●	●		●	●	●	●	●	●	●		
SP1		●		●	●	●		●	●		●	●	●	●	●	●	●		
WN1		●			●	●		●	●		●		●	●					
A		●		●	●	●		●	●		●	●	●	●	●	●	●		
B–G	●	●	●	●	●	●	●	●	●	●	●	●	●	●	●	●	●		
30	●	●																	

integral to Donne's understanding of the genre from the very beginning. Fortunately, as will be demonstrated below, the validity of this implication does not rest on mere inference, for the details of Donne's handling of individual texts as they move forward in the stream of transmission confirm that the ordering of the sonnets was a matter of continuing authorial attention. Data supporting this assertion are presented schematically in Figures 2 and 3, the first of which simply lists the successive arrangements of the poems in the seventeenth-century artifacts, while the latter portrays the relationships among the artifacts more precisely by outlining the genealogy of the poems in a traditional stemma.

The early transmissional history of these poems may be described summarily as follows. Donne's first collection of religious sonnets, as shown in the leftmost columns of Figure 2, is that preserved in B46, H5, HH1, and the C9-H6 pair—4 arti-

FIGURE 2: SEQUENCES OF HOLY SONNETS IN THE SEVENTEENTH-CENTURY ARTIFACTS

Group III — B46 H5 HH1

Diuine Meditations
1. (HSMade)
2. (HSDue)
3. (HSSighs)
4. (HSPart)
5. (HSBlack)
6. (HSScene)
7. (HSLittle)
8. (HSRound)
9. (HSMin)
10. (HSSouls)
11. (HSDeath)
12. (HSWilt)

Group III — C9-H6

Diuine Meditations
1. (HSMade)
2. (HSDue)
3. (HSSighs)
4. (HSPart)
5. (HSBlack)
6. (HSScene)
7. (HSLittle)
8. (HSRound)
9. (HSMin)
10. (HSSouls)
11. (HSDeath)
12. (HSWilt)
Other Meditations
[13] (HSSpit)
[14] (HSWhy)
[15] (HSWhat)
[16] (HSBatter)

Group IV — NY3

Holy Sonnets
1. (HSMade)
2. (HSDue)
3. (HSSighs)
4. (HSPart)
5. (HSBlack)
6. (HSScene)
7. (HSLittle)
8. (HSRound)
9. (HSMin)
10. (HSSouls)
11. (HSDeath)
12. (HSWilt)
13. (HSSpit)
14. (HSWhy)
15. (HSWhat)
16. (HSBatter)
17. (HSShe)
18. (HSShow)
19. (HSVex)

Group I — B32 C2 O20 SP1

Holy Sonnets
om
1. (HSDue)
om
2. (HSBlack)
3. (HSScene)
om
4. (HSRound)
5. (HSMin)
om
6. (HSDeath)
7. (HSSpit)
8. (HSWhy)
9. (HSWhat)
10. (HSBatter)
11. (HSWilt)
12. (HSPart)

Group II — B7 CT1 DT1 H4 WN1[1]

none
om
1. (HSDue)
om
2. (HSBlack)
3. (HSScene)
om
4. (HSRound)
5. (HSMin)
om
6. (HSDeath)
7. (HSSpit)
8. (HSWhy)
9. (HSWhat)
10. (HSBatter)
11. (HSWilt)
12. (HSPart)

1633 ed. — A

Holy Sonnets
om
1. (HSDue)
om
2. (HSBlack)
3. (HSScene)
om
4. (HSRound)
5. (HSMin)
om
6. (HSDeath)
7. (HSSpit)
8. (HSWhy)
9. (HSWhat)
10. (HSBatter)
11. (HSWilt)
12. (HSPart)

1635-69 eds. — B-G

Holy Sonnets
I. (HSMade)
II. (HSDue)
III. (HSSighs)
IV. (HSBlack)
V. (HSLittle)
VI. (HSScene)
VII. (HSRound)
VIII. (HSSouls)
IX. (HSMin)
X. (HSDeath)
XI. (HSSpit)
XII. (HSWhy)
XIII. (HSWhat)
XIV. (HSBatter)
XV. (HSWilt)
XVI. (HSPart)

[1]Lacks poems 9-12

facts traditionally belonging to Group III (B46, H5, C9, H6) and 1 (HH1) Associated with Group III. Headed "Diuine Meditations," these are presented in this family of artifacts as a numbered sequence of 12 that begins with "Thou hast made me" (HSMade) and concludes with "Wilt thou love God as he thee?" (HSWilt). (As is implied by the secondary heading "Other Meditations" in C9 and H6, the 4 additional sonnets "Spit in my face" [HSSpit] through "Batter my heart" [HSBatter] were copied into the C9-H6 progenitor [γ¹ on Figure 3] at some point after the initial collection was entered.) Bearing the revised heading "Holy Sonnets," this Group-III sequence next appears at the head of the numbered series of 19 poems in NY3, the lone Group-IV manuscript, and to it have been added HSSpit, "Why are we by all creatures waited on?" (HSWhy), "What if this present were the world's last night?" (HSWhat), and HSBatter, as well as the above-mentioned HSShe, HSShow, and HSVex. Listed to the right of NY3 on Figure 2, the Group-I manuscripts B32, C2, O20, and SP1 revert to a 12-poem sequence of Holy Sonnets that incorporates 8 of the Group-III poems, but discards the 1st, 3rd, 7th, and 10th (HSMade, HSSighs, HSLittle, and HSSouls), moves HSPart to the concluding position at the very end of the sequence, and inserts HSSpit, HSWhy, HSWhat, and HSBatter into positions 7–10 of the new arrangement.¹ Thus differently constituted and reorganized, the Group-I sequence carries forward to the later Group IIs (B7, CT1, DT1, H4, and WN1) and enters print in A, set into type primarily from a Group-I manuscript. Two years later, however, as part of a general augmentation and reorganization of the canon, B's editor reclaims from a Group-III manuscript the previously dropped HSMade, HSSighs, HSLittle, and HSSouls and inserts them into his generic section of Holy Sonnets. This expanded collection of 16 poems, as noted above, defined the genre until Gosse added the final 3 from NY3 in the late nineteenth century.

Editors have not generally recognized the authenticity of the early, Group-III collection, and this *Variorum* is the first edition ever to present it as a distinct sequence. Indeed, not until Grierson systematically studied the manuscripts in preparing his edition of 1912 (Q) was identification of a Group-III tradition for the Holy Sonnets even possible; and Grierson, failing to "find a definite significance in any order" (2:231), retains the custom-sanctioned arrangement of B, appending the newly discovered Westmoreland sonnets at the end. Gardner (1952; siglum U), the next editor seriously to confront the question of sequence, concludes that "the order of the Group III set is without significance and has arisen through accident," elaborating a theory that the 4 sonnets particular to Group III—HSMade, HSSighs, HSLittle, and HSSouls—originated as a discrete, thematically unified set and were "in error . . . interpolated into" the 6-item group (on the "Last Things") with which the collections in Groups I and II and A begin (xlii).² Accordingly, Gardner prints 3 separately numbered sequences of sonnets: the 12-item sequence of A, a 4-poem set of "penitential" (xli) sonnets made up of those that she thinks were mistakenly inserted

---

¹As Patrick F. O'Connell (1981) notes, Donne's inclusion of 12 poems in both the original and the reconstituted sequences suggests that he attached some significance to this number. See O'Connell's discussion of this matter in the Dating and Order section of the Commentary below.

²Gardner supposes that HSWilt and HSFather "must have been Donne's original pendant to his six sonnets on the Last Things" (xlii), bringing the original total to eight.

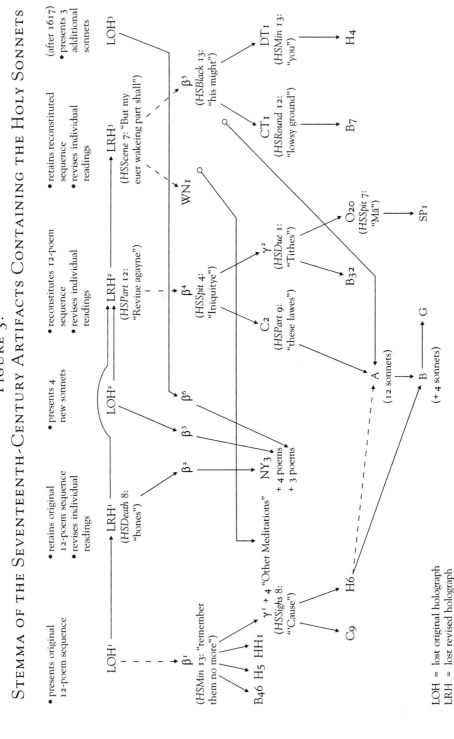

FIGURE 3:
STEMMA OF THE SEVENTEENTH-CENTURY ARTIFACTS CONTAINING THE HOLY SONNETS

- presents original 12-poem sequence

- retains original 12-poem sequence
- revises individual readings

- presents 4 new sonnets

- reconstitutes 12-poem sequence
- revises individual readings

- retains reconstituted sequence
- revises individual readings

- (after 1617)
- presents 3 additional sonnets

LOH¹

LRH¹
(*HSDeath* 8: "bones")

LOH²

LRH²
(*HSPart* 12: "Reuiue agayne")

LRH³
(*HSScene* 7: "But my euer wakeing part shall")

LOH³

β¹
(*HSMin* 13: "remember them no more")

β²

β³

β⁶

β⁴
(*HSSpit* 4: "Iniquitye")

β⁵
(*HSBlack* 13: "his might")

γ¹ + 4 "Other Meditations"
(*HSSighs* 8: "Cause")

NY3
+ 4 poems
+ 3 poems

WN1

C2
(*HSPart* 9: "these lawes")

γ²
(*HSDue* 1: "Tithes")

DT1
(*HSMin* 13: "you")

CT1
(*HSRound* 12: "lowsy ground")

B46 H5 HH1

C9

H6

A
(12 sonnets)

B32

O2o
(*HSSpit* 7: "Mā")

H4

B7

B
(+ 4 sonnets)

G

SP1

LOH = lost original holograph
LRH = lost revised holograph

Figure 4: Major Variants in the Twelve Sonnets of Group III in the Seventeenth-Century Artifacts

~ = agrees with Group-III reading   ⊰ = agrees with nearest corresponding reading on left   NIS = not included in sequence

Poem, line	Group III B46 H5 HH1 C9-H6	Group IV NY3	Group I B32 C2 O20 SP1	Group II B7 CT1 DT1 H4 WN1	1633 ed. A	1635 ed. B	1639-69 eds. C–G
Section HE	Diuine Meditations	Holy Sonnets	⊰ ⊰	*none*	Holy Sonnets	⊰ ⊰	⊰ ⊰
HSMade 7	feebled	~	NIS	NIS	NIS	feeble	⊰
8	it towards	om ~	NIS	NIS	NIS	~ ~	~ ~
12	I can my selfe (C9-H6: my selfe I can)	~ ~ ~ ~	NIS	NIS	NIS	my selfe I can	⊰ ⊰ ⊰ ⊰
HSDue 2	was I	I was	⊰ ⊰	⊰ ⊰	⊰ ⊰	⊰ ⊰	⊰ ⊰
7	thy Image	thyne ~	⊰ ~	⊰ ~	⊰ ~	⊰ ~	⊰ ~
9	thus vsurpe in	then ~ ~	⊰ ~ on	⊰ ~ ~	⊰ ~ on	⊰ ~ ⊰	⊰ ~ ⊰
12	shall see	do ~	⊰ ~	⊰ ~	⊰ ~	~ ~	~ ~
HSSighs 5	my Idolatrie (C9-H6: mine ~)	~ ~	NIS	NIS	NIS	mine ~	⊰ ~
7	sinne I now (H5-HH1: ~, now I)	~, now I	NIS	NIS	NIS	~ ~ ~	~ ~ ~
8	Because (C9-H6: 'Cause)	~	NIS	NIS	NIS	'Cause	⊰
HSPart 4	gives me (C9-H6: ~ to ~)	~ ~	~ ~	~ ~	~ to ~	~ ⊰ ~	~ ⊰ ~
7	he with	w^ch ~	⊰ ~	⊰ ~	⊰ ~	⊰ ~	⊰ ~
9	thy Lawes	~ ~	those ~ (C2: these ~)	⊰ ~	these ~	⊰ ~	⊰ ~
11	thy all-healing	om ~	om ~	om ~	~ ~	~ ~	~ ~
12	and quicken	~ ~	om againe	om ⊰	om ⊰	om ⊰	om ⊰
14	thy last	y^t ~	⊰ ~	⊰ ~	this ~	⊰ ~	⊰ ~
HSBlack 3	Thou, like a	Thou'art om ~	⊰ ~ ~	⊰ ~ ~	⊰ ~ ~	⊰ ~ ~	⊰ ~ ~
4	from whence	to ~	⊰ ~	⊰ ~	⊰ ~	⊰ ~	⊰ ~
5	or as	~ ~	~ like	~ ⊰	~ ⊰	~ ⊰	~ ⊰
13	this might	~ ~	~ ~	his ~ (WN1: ~ ~)	~ ~	~ ~	~ ~
HSScene 2	pilgrimages	~	Pilgrimage	~	~	~	~
4	latest	last	⊰	⊰	~	~	~
6	my Soule (C9-H6: om ~)	om ~	om ~	om ~	~ ~	om ~	om ~
7	or presently (I know not)	~ ~ ~ ~ ~	~ ~ ~ ~ ~	But my euer wakeing part shall (WN1: everlastinge)	⊰ ⊰ ⊰ ⊰ ⊰ ⊰	⊰ ⊰ ⊰ ⊰ ⊰ ⊰	⊰ ⊰ ⊰ ⊰ ⊰ ⊰
8	me euery	my ~	⊰ ~ (C2: ~ ~)	⊰ ~	⊰ ~	⊰ ~	⊰ ~
14	and deuill	~ ~	~ ~	~ ~	the ~	⊰ ~	⊰ ~
HSLittle 6	lands (C9-H6: land)	~	NIS	NIS	NIS	land	⊰
11	haue burnt (C9-H6: hath ~)	~ ~	NIS	NIS	NIS	om ~	om ~
12	theire flames	those ~	NIS	NIS	NIS	~ ~	~ ~
13	O Lord	~ God	NIS	NIS	NIS	~ ~	~ ~
HSRound 6	Death	dearth	~	~	~	~	~
HSMin 1	or if the	& ~ that	⊰ ~ ⊰	⊰ ~ ⊰	⊰ ~ ⊰	⊰ ~ ⊰	⊰ ~ ⊰
5	and reason	or ~	⊰ ~	⊰ ~	⊰ ~	⊰ ~	⊰ ~
9	dare	~	~	dares	~	~	~
10	thy (C9: thine)	thyne	⊰	⊰	⊰	⊰	⊰
13	no more	Some clayme	⊰ ⊰	⊰ ⊰	⊰ ⊰	⊰ ⊰	⊰ ⊰
HSSouls 8	to them (C9-H6: by ~)	~ ~	NIS	NIS	NIS	by ~	⊰ ~
10	vilde	vile	NIS	NIS	NIS	stile	⊰
14	griefe	true ~	NIS	NIS	NIS	~	⊰
HSDeath 1	haue	~	~	hath (H4, WN1: ~)	~	~	~
8	bodyes (C9-H6: bodye)	bones	⊰	⊰	⊰	⊰	⊰
10	dost	~	~	~	doth	~	~
12	easier	~	better	⊰	⊰	⊰	⊰
13	Liue	~	wake	⊰	⊰	⊰	⊰
HSWilt 10	steede	stuffe	⊰	⊰	⊰	⊰	⊰
12	stole (H5: stolne)	~	stolne	⊰	⊰	~	~

into Group III, and the 3 poems unique to NY3. As the details charted on Figure 4 indicate, however, Donne himself, not accident, is responsible for the composition and arrangement of the Group-III sequence—and for that of the other groups as well. Columns 2–5 of Figure 4 list numerous variants in the texts of individual sonnets, and some of these changes are certainly authorial. Since all of these revisions subsist in the context not only of the individual poem, but also of a group of poems, the very fact of their existence necessarily implies Donne's conscious decision either to maintain or to modify the organization of the larger unit at given points in time. That he retains the Group-III order in revising the text for Group IV, therefore, validates the authenticity of the Group-III arrangement, while his maintenance of the Group-I order as he effects the Group-II revisions both confirms his continued endorsement of that arrangement and shows that the structural changes introduced in the transition from the Group-IV sequence to that in Group I are deliberate.[3]

Dispersed throughout the 12-poem set are a number of distinctive readings that define the Group-III artifacts as a separate family. Listed on Figure 4, these include not only the aforementioned generic heading "Diuine Meditations," but also—among others— "thus [for *then*] vsurpe in" in *HSDue* 9, "shall see" (for "do see") in *HSDue* 12, "he with" (for "wch w^{t}") in *HSPart* 7, "thy [for y^t] last will" in *HSPart* 14, "from whence" (for "to whence") in *HSBlack* 4, "latest [for *last*] pointe" in *HSScene* 4, "Shakes me [for *my*] euery ioynte" in *HSScene* 8, "O Lord" (for "O God") in *HSLittle* 13, "or if the [for *& if that*] Tree" in *HSMin* 1, "no more [for *Some clayme*] as debt" in *HSMin* 13, "Thy griefe . . . into" (for "Thy true griefe . . . in") in *HSSouls* 14, "bodyes" (for "bones") in *HSDeath* 8, and "steede" (for "stuffe") in *HSWilt* 10. There can be little doubt that such of these lections as "thus vsurpe" and "shall see" in *HSDue*, "he with" and "thy last will" in *HSPart*, "latest pointe" in *HSScene*, "O Lord" in *HSLittle*, "or if the" in *HSMin*, "griefe" in *HSSouls*, and "bodyes" in *HSDeath* are authentic, representing the first heat of Donne's inspiration. Others—such as "remember them no more as debt" (*HSMin* 13) and "steede" (*HSWilt* 10)—more likely represent carelessness or misunderstanding on the part of one or more copyists. Since these errors cannot have existed in the lost original holograph (LOH), the stemma presented in Figure 3 necessarily posits the quondam existence of the ancestral β^1 in order to explain the descent of these errors to B46, H5, HH1, and γ^1. Discussion of the likely origins of particular variants is provided in the textual introductions to the various sonnets elsewhere in this volume.[4]

---

[3]In discussing the Group-III reading "steede" (for the alternative "stuffe") in *HSWilt* 10, Gardner concedes that we must "regard the text of the . . . Holy Sonnets in W [NY3] as an authentic variation of the Group III version, containing some improvements which Donne retained in the general revision that gives the Group I text, and a few others which he seems to have made as he wrote out the particular copy which W followed" (lxxx–lxxxi). Curiously, this recognition of "authentic variation" in the texts of individual poems as the series was copied out at different points in time does not prompt Gardner to reevaluate her "interpolation" theory of the origins of the Group-III order. In the 1978 update of her edition, Gardner depreciates the "improvements" she had formerly discerned in NY3's text, attributing the "coincidence in order" to the fact that the Group-III manuscripts descend "from a corrupt copy" of NY3 (lxxx).

[4]Because of their relatively limited circulation, the texts of the Holy Sonnets do not enable elaboration of a stemma for Group III beyond what is depicted on Figure 3. Although it is

The second stage in the evolution of these poems, shown in Figure 3 to the right of the Group-III line of descent, is embodied in NY3. Written in the hand of Donne's friend Rowland Woodward and resident until the latter nineteenth century in the library of the earls of Westmoreland (to the first of whom Woodward was for a time secretary), this manuscript preserves mostly early poems, including two verse epistles addressed "To "M^r. H[enry] W[otton]"" (*HWNews* and *HWKiss*) that must antedate Wotton's being knighted in 1603, when "Sir" became his proper title.[5] The authoritative pedigree of this artifact, moreover, is matched in the quality of its texts (of all manuscript copyists, e.g., Woodward alone has "dearth" rather than the erroneous "death" in *HSRound* 6), lending its handling of the "Holy Sonnets" (which it is the first so to label) the presumption of great authority. As noted above, NY3's collection of these poems opens with the original, Group-III sequence, but the text evinces a number of revisions. Several of these have been cited above, including "then [for *thus*] vsurpe in" in *HSDue* 9, "do see" (for "shall see") in *HSDue* 12, "wch w^t [for *he with*] the Legacee" in *HSPart* 7, "y^t [for *thy*] last Will" in *HSPart* 14, "Minutes last [for *latest*] pointe" in *HSScene* 4, "O God" (for "O Lord") in *HSLittle* 13, "& if that tree" (for "or if the Tree") in *HSMin* 1, "true griefe" (for "griefe") in *HSSouls* 14, and "bones" (for "bodyes") in *HSDeath* 8. And all of these revisions except those in *HSLittle* and *HSSouls*, poems not retained in the later sequence, carry forward in the stream of transmission. Following the early sequence then appear *HSSpit*, *HSWhy*, *HSWhat*, and *HSBatter*—labeled "replacement sonnets" in Figure 5—and *HSShe*, *HSShow*, and *HSVex* round out the collection. The presence of this numbered series of 19 sonnets in an artifact of such high extrinsic authority might well prompt the question whether NY3's arrangement does not represent a distinct, if perhaps transient, moment in Donne's evolving intentions for the sequence as a whole. The answer to this question lies in a physical analysis of the manuscript and of the material features of the inscription of the Holy Sonnets.

Details significant to this analysis have already been discovered by Patrick O'Connell (1981; see the Dating and Order section in the Commentary), who notes two particulars that work powerfully to delegitimate the structural integrity of NY3's 19-item sequence. First, *HSSpit*—the 13th poem in the series and the first of the 4 replacement sonnets—exhibits an alternate-line indentation pattern that is uniquely

---

impossible to know exactly how far removed β¹ may be from the original holograph, at least one instance of what we take to be error in Group III is most readily explainable as the product of incremental deterioration; and our sense that a number of now-lost manuscripts must once have bridged the gap between β¹ and LOH¹ is denoted by the hatched line connecting the two on Figure 3. (To compare a fuller genealogy of this lineage of artifacts, see the detailed stemma for *ElBrac* in volume 2 [p. 45] of this *Variorum*). We shall elsewhere argue against the legtimacy of the above-cited readings in *HSMin* 13 and *HSWilt* 10, but we should also point out that the β¹ text seems otherwise to have been sound. Indeed, even though each of the Group-III copyists introduces the occasional mistake—including, in the case of the γ¹ scribe, several instances of deliberate sophistication—no β¹ reading except "death" (for "dearth") in *HSRound* 6 would command universal identification as an error rather than as an alternative authorial reading. Similarly, it is not clear whether such accidental features as the relative prevalence of parentheses in Group III (9 occurrences as opposed to 3 in Group IV [NY3] and only 1 in Groups I and II) reflect the personal taste of the β¹ (or an earlier) scribe or an original authorial preference.

[5]*HWNews* (on f. 25) bears the additional subtitle "20 Iuly. 1598. At Court."

FIGURE 5: MAJOR VARIANTS IN THE REPLACEMENT SONNETS IN THE SEVENTEENTH-CENTURY ARTIFACTS

~ = agrees with NY3 reading
NIS = not included in sequence
◄ = agrees with nearest corresponding reading on left
Note: there are no variants to report for *HSBatter*

Poem, line	Group III B46 H5 HH1	Group IV NY3	Group I B32 C2 O20 SP1	Group II B7 CT1 DT1 H4 WN1*	C9-H6	1633 ed. A	1635 ed. B	1639-69 eds. C-G
Section HE	NIS	none	none	none	Other Meditations	none	none	none
HSSpit 1	NIS	ye	you	~	~	you	◄	◄
3	NIS	humbly	only	◄	◄	◄	◄	◄
4	NIS	Wch	Who	◄	◄	◄	◄	◄
4	NIS	no	none	◄	~	~	~	~
6	NIS	impietee	Iniquitye	~	~	~	~	~
7	NIS	inglorious	~ man	~ ◄	~ ◄	~ ◄	~ ◄	~ ◄
HSWhy 1	NIS	ame I	are we	◄ ◄	◄ ◄	◄ ◄	◄ ◄	◄ ◄
4	NIS	Simple	~	Simpler (B7-CT1: Simples)	◄	~	Simpler	◄
9	NIS	Alas I'ame weaker	Weaker I am	◄ ◄ ◄	◄ ◄ ◄	◄ ◄ ◄	◄ ◄ ◄	◄ ◄ ◄
11	NIS	greater wonder	~ ~	~ ~ (H4, WN1: great ~)	great ~	~ ~	~ om	~ om
HSWhat 2	NIS	Looke	Marke	◄	◄	◄	◄	◄
4	NIS	yt countenance	his ~	~ ~	~ ~	his ~	◄ ~	◄ ~
7	NIS	vnto hell	to ~	~ ~	~ ~	~ ~	~ ~	~ ~
8	NIS	ranck	fierce	◄	◄	◄	◄	◄
9	NIS	myne idolatree	my ~	◄ ~	◄ ~ (C9: mine ~)	◄ ~	◄ ~	◄ ~
13	NIS	Sprights	spiritts	◄ (B7-CT1: ~)	~	spirits	◄	◄
14	NIS	assures	~	~	~	assumes	◄	◄

*Lacks *HSWhat*

incongruous with Woodward's usual envelope pattern[6]; second, the slash mark that appears under the ordinal 17 (17.) beside *HSShe* is anomalous, otherwise appearing in this section of religious poems only under the generic heading at the first of the series—"Holy Sonnets .1." Both these irregularities hint at some discontinuity either in Woodward's schedule of copying or in his supply of material and invite speculation on the process by which NY3 came into being.

Though it lacks the formal elegance that might have been expected from a professional scrivener, Woodward's artifact is nonetheless an intelligently planned and artfully inscribed volume. Before ever putting pen to paper, he folded each folio leaf lengthwise into fourths, producing vertical creases on which the written left margins are carefully aligned; and the spacing between the rows of his small, italic scrawl is generous and regular, making each line of script distinct and easy to follow. The volume is tightly organized into generic sections, containing (in order) the 5 satires

[6]The envelope pattern is in fact consistent only within the octave; in the sestet Woodward vacillates between indenting lines 10 and 12 only and lines 10–11 and 13–14.

(ff. 2–10); 13 elegies (12 love poems plus the funereal *Sorrow*) (ff. 11–21v); a single epithalamion (the early *EpLin*) (ff. 22–23); 19 verse epistles to male friends and acquaintances, plus 1 ("Thou sendst me prose & rimes") addressed *to* Donne (ff. 24–32); the 19 Holy Sonnets (ff. 33–37v); the 7 sonnets of *Corona* (ff. 38–39v); 10 prose paradoxes (ff. 40–45); 20 English epigrams (f. 46r–v); and—finally—the single lyric "A Jet Ring Sent" (f. 47). Although the conclusion of a poem in mid page occasionally results in a partially blank leaf, moreover, the material is generally entered with great economy: the only fully blank pages are folios 10v, 23v, 32v, and 45v, each of which precedes the beginning of a new generic section. The calligraphy and penstroke are uniform throughout the artifact; and in only a single instance—the last in the volume, where the epigrams begin on the first page of the final gathering—does the beginning of a poem coincide with the beginning of a physical section of the manuscript, the gaps between gatherings being otherwise bridged by the carryover of individual poems from one gathering to the next. These and other physical attributes—such as Woodward's consistent handling of poem titles by writing them into the left margins rather than centering them above the text—not only indicate that NY3 is a fair-copy manuscript book of such materials as Woodward already had in hand, but also suggest that it was prepared in a brief period of concentrated work during which he was able to maintain a firm grasp on his principles of inscription as well as on the mechanical skills necessary to implement them consistently.

As noted above, almost all the works in the volume—the satires, the elegies, *EpLin*, the verse letters to male acquaintances, the prose paradoxes, and the epigrams—are early, written before or soon after 1600. And the bulk of the Holy Sonnets and *Corona* (whose dates will be discussed in more detail below) may be early as well. *HSShe*, however, cannot have been written before the death of Anne Donne in August of 1617, and the actual inscription of the artifact must necessarily postdate that event. Though it is not possible to determine exactly when Woodward received his copies of the various groups of poems, that he has earlier versions of most of them (see, e.g., the respective discussions of the Elegies and the Epigrams in volumes 2 and 8 of this *Variorum*), that his verse epistles spring exclusively from Donne's experiences as a young man about London in the 1590s, and that he has (excepting *Jet*) none of the Songs and Sonnets or the later religious lyrics suggest that he accumulated most of the items sometime around 1600, thereafter acquiring *Corona* and the Holy Sonnets in three or four separate groups over the next 15 or 20 years. Whether or not he intended NY3 specifically as a gift for Westmoreland's library, at some point after 1617 (Beal dates the artifact "c. 1620" [*Index* 252]) Woodward obviously decided to prepare a finished volume of the Donne materials in his possession, organizing and inscribing the contents in the manner described above. The previously mentioned anomalous features of *HSSpit* and *HSShe* are almost certainly due to the modular nature of the materials from which Woodward was working, indicating that after he had written the 12 Group-III sonnets into the artifact, he picked up and entered as an extension of the same numbered sequence a second (*HSSpit*, *HSWhy*, *HSWhat*, *HSBatter*) and then a third (*HSShe*, *HSShow*, *HSVex*) small set of poems that he had obtained successively from Donne over the years. The alternate-line indentation of *HSSpit* and the underlining of *HSShe*'s title thus testify either to two separate interruptions in Woodward's schedule of inscription or—perhaps more likely—to his failure to regularize certain minor physical characteristics of his original drafts as he moved from one to the other in writing out the final copy. In accordance with this analysis, the stemma in Figure 3 presents NY3's 19-poem sequence as a scribal conflation of the 3 groups separately embodied in β^2, β^3, and β^6.[7] Both because it contains a complete set of Donne's Holy Sonnets, thus enabling us to key all the textual apparatuses below to a single base text, and because it contains distinctive authorial versions of individual poems, we have printed the Westmoreland sequence in its entirety below. The sequence *per se*, however, cannot be regarded as authorial.[8]

The third major stage in the evolution of the Holy Sonnets—and the first to embody an actual change in the structure of the sequence—is that represented on Figure 3 by the LRH[2] lineage. This line of descent projects itself downward through β^4 to—on the one hand—B32 and O20 (parent of SP1) and—on the other—C2 and the eventual printing of the poems in A. As noted above, the earliest versions of the sonnets that appear as items 7–10 in this final, Group-I/II sequence had originally been appended to NY3's initial 12-poem series as items 13–16; and Figure 5 shows that the texts of 3 of these—*HSSpit*, *HSWhy*, and *HSWhat*—underwent revision before resurfacing as part of the later arrangement. Subsequently altered NY3 readings among these poems include "humbly" (for the later "only") in *HSSpit* 3, "w^{ch}" (for the later "who") and "no" (for the later "none") in *HSSpit* 4, "ame I" (for the later "are we") in *HSWhy* 1, "Alas I'ame weaker" (for the later "Weaker I am") in *HSWhy* 9, "Looke" (for the later "Marke") in *HSWhat* 2, and "ranck" (for the

---

[7] The exact nature of these missing artifacts is impossible to know. The discussion above assumes that they were discrete packets in a cache of material that Woodward accumulated over the years, but they may have existed as separate sections in a commonplace book or earlier poetical manuscript. If the latter, they would of course have been written in Woodward's hand; if the former, they might even have been holographic copies that Donne had sent to Woodward at various times. In any case, they must have descended more or less immediately from Donne's original, a fact putting the fair copy in NY3 also quite close to the author.

[8] As does this edition, O'Connell also champions the authenticity of both the early (Group-III) and later (Group-I and -II) orders, but worries that the legitimacy of both would be undermined if Woodward had in fact written the 19 sonnets of NY3 into the artifact in a single period of inscription after Anne Donne's death in 1617. By such a late date, O'Connell reasons, Woodward—"intimate enough with Donne to receive the three additional sonnets"—would "certainly" have been aware of the "definitive" Group-I/II arrangement and would have inscribed the poems in that order had he not already entered the Group-III sequence into his manuscript before he made the discovery. To support this theory, O'Connell analyzes the physical makeup of the artifact's fourth gathering, demonstrating that if Woodward had initially entered the first 12 of his Holy Sonnets and followed them with *Corona*, leaving some blank leaves at the end of the gathering, he could have reversed the fold of the inner sheets in such a way as to create space for the 4 replacement sonnets (nos. 13–16) and the final 3 (nos. 17–19) when he received them at a later time (see the fuller discusion of O'Connell in the Commentary). In "fortunate, indeed almost miraculous, confirmation" of this proposal, O'Connell notes two wrinkles that, were his theory about the refolding correct, would originally have appeared one on top of the other in the gutters of the manuscript. The lower, he asserts, "could only have been made" by the upper (334).

Brilliant as it is, this analysis does not finally hold up, for O'Connell's description of the two wrinkles is incomplete and his conclusion consequently invalid. On the verso of each of the sheets in question, the wrinkle takes a crow's-foot shape that differs distinctively from the single-strand shape it evinces on the recto. Had the sheets originally rested one atop the other so that the wrinkle in the upper had impressed itself on the page beneath, the crow's-foot shape on the verso (bottom) of sheet

later "fierce") in *HSWhat* 8. Moreover, these revisions are accompanied, as a glance at Figure 4 shows, by a further handful of authorial changes in the 8 Group-III sonnets that Donne retained in the Group-I/II set, changes including "those [for the earlier *thy*] lawes" in *HSPart* 9, "again" (for the earlier "and quicken") in *HSPart* 12, "or like" (for the earlier "or as") in *HSBlack* 5, and "better" (for "easier") and "wake" (for "Liue") in *HSDeath* 12 and 13, respectively. Other Group-I variants shown on Figures 4 and 5—"vsurpe on [for *in*]" in *HSDue* 9, "Pilgrimage" (for "pilgrimages") in *HSScene* 2, "you" (for "ye") in *HSSpit* 1, "Iniquitye" (for "impietee") in *HSSpit* 6, "hys [for y^t] Countenance" in *HSWhat* 4, "to [for *vnto*] hell" in *HSWhat* 7, and "spiritts" (for "Sprights") in *HSWhat* 13—are scribal sophistications or slips of the pen and do not perpetuate themselves into the Group-II text.

Retaining Group I's new 12-poem arrangement, the Group-II manuscripts B7, CT1, DT1, H4, and WN1 embody Donne's final adjustment of the text of the Holy Sonnets. As Figure 3 shows, these artifacts descend in two separate strands from LRH³, WN1 constituting the sole surviving member of one strand, while the parent-child pairs CT1-B7 and DT1-H4 descend through β⁵ to constitute the other. When he came to write out the ancestral LRH³, Donne had, at one stage or another, already revised the text of at least 9 of the sequence's 12 poems and—with a single exception—was apparently satisfied with the results.[9] LRH³ records distinctive variants in *HSDue* 5 ("Sunne" [for the earlier "Sonne"]), *HSMin* 9 ("dares" [for the earlier "dare"]), and *HSWhy* 4 ("Simpler [CT1-B7: *simples*]" [for the earlier "Simple"]); but each of these seems to trivialize what had originally been a stronger reading, and, collectively, they perhaps reflect Donne's inadvertence in copying out a text with which he was no longer creatively engaged. The one indisputably authorial change in Group II, which Gardner uses as the cornerstone of an effort to date the poems, is the revision of the original "Or presently, I know not, see y^t face" to "But my euer wakeing part shall see that face" in *HSScene* 7; and were it not for this reading, Figure 3 could be redrawn to depict the Group-II lineage as a second offshoot of LRH², parallel in structure and authority to the Group-I descendants of β⁴.[10]

one would have registered on the recto (top) of sheet two. In fact, however, the impressions on the rectos of each sheet exactly match as do those on the versos, indicating that rather than being caused one by the other, both wrinkles were instead caused by the same third thing—some flaw in the paper-making equipment or process that produced two sheets containing similar minor defects.

Apparently based on the assumption that Woodward must have culled his copies of *HSSpit*, *HSWhy*, *HSWhat*, and *HSBatter* (the 4 replacement sonnets) from a full Group-I/II set, O'Connell's belief that by 1617 Woodward would necessarily have known what "definitive arrangement" Donne finally intended is similarly open to question. For one thing, NY3's texts of the replacement sonnets contain unique verbal variants, a fact suggesting that Woodward received them as a discrete, free-standing set rather than after they had been integrated into a larger 12-poem group. For another, NY3's lack of such major parts of the canon as, for example, the love lyrics indicates that after about 1600 Woodward remained essentially oblivious to Donne's work for long periods of time and suggests that he never made a concerted attempt to assemble a complete collection of the poems. While we concur in O'Connell's judgment that NY3's sequence is inauthentic, in sum, we see no reason to resist the conclusion to which all the evidence points—that the artifact was put together sometime around 1620.

[9]Revisions identified in the textual introductions to individual sonnets below include those in *HSDue* 9 and 12; *HSPart* 7, 9, and 12; *HSBlack* 5; *HSScene* 4; *HSMin* 1; *HSDeath* 8, 12, and 13; *HSSpit* 3 and 4; *HSWhy* 1 and 9; and *HSWhat* 2 and 8.

[10]As indicated on Figure 3 and in the discussion above, γ¹'s copies of the four Replacement

The Seventeenth-Century Prints

Set into type in the revised arrangement, the Holy Sonnets first entered print in John Marriot's 1633 edition of Donne's collected *Poems* (A). Between the opening "THE PROGRESSE OF THE SOULE" (*Metem*) (pp. 1–27) and the "EPIGRAMS" (pp. 40–43), Marriot prints on pages 28–40 a general section of "HOLY SONNETS" that includes, first, the 7 sonnets of *Corona* (under the subheading "*La Corona*") and follows them (under the additional subheading "*Holy Sonnets*") with the 12 Holy Sonnets proper in a numbered series. Several features identify A's primary setting text as a descendant of LRH² and, more precisely, as a scion of β⁴'s C2 branch, the genealogy reflected in Figure 3. Among A's β⁴/Group-I readings are "usurpe on [for the normative *in*]" in HSDue 9, "you [for the otherwise universal *yee*] Jewes" in HSSpit 1, "Simple" (for the two-syllable "Simpler") in HSWhy 4, and "his [for *that*] countenance" in HSWhat 4. The lection that specifically links A to C2 is "these laws" in HSPart 9, where all other Group-I and -II manuscripts give "those lawes" (and Groups III and IV give "thy lawes"). And the relationship implied in this verbal similarity is confirmed by two bibliographical features unique to these artifacts: both C2 and A open with the *Metem-Corona*-Holy Sonnets sequence of material, and both deploy the "HOLY SONNETS"-"*La Corona*"-"*Holy Sonnets*" sequence of rubrics in exactly the same way (though C2 reverses the wording of the last of these to "Sonnetts. Holy.").[11]

As we pointed out in discussing the elegies in volume 2 of this edition (see especially pp. lxxvi–lxxix of the General Textual Introduction to that volume), A was carefully edited by someone attentive to matters of both meter and sense. In addition to eliding many of Donne's hypermetric collocations, this editor routinely intervened to correct outright verbal error, and he also compared multiple sources of several of the poems, sometimes preferring readings in other manuscripts to those in his base text. These interests are also evident in his work on the Holy Sonnets. In his concern with scansion, to cite a single example, A's editor elides HSBatter in over half-a-dozen instances, changing "overthrowe mee, &" to "o'erthrow mee,'and"

Sonnets (the "Other Meditations" of C9 and H6) derive from the Group-II lineage. This kinship is evidenced formally by a shared even-line indentation pattern, a feature distinguishing the "Other Meditations" from the first 12 sonnets in C9 and H6 and the entire set of Group-II sonnets from those in all other groups; and such readings as "yee" (for Group I's "you") in HSSpit 1, "Simpler" (for Group I's "Symple") in HSWhy 4, "vnto [for Group I's *to*] hell" in HSWhat 7, and "vsurpd [with a *d*]" (for Group I's "vsurp't [with a *t*]") in HSBatter 5 confirm the relationship. More specifically, the C9-H6 pair share the DT1-H4-WN1 readings "Simpler" and "farther" (as against the CT1-B7 "Simples" and "further") in HSWhy 4, and the C9-H6 spelling of "timerous" (with an *e*) in HSWhy 10 appears only in B7 and WN1 within the LRH³ lineage. Further, although WN1 is now missing the last 4 poems of the sequence and could not, in its current state, have supplied γ¹ with either HSWhat or HSBatter, its "great [for *greater*] wonder" in HSWhy 11 is the only extant source for that reading in C9-H6. The "Other Meditations" thus clearly belong to the WN1 branch of transmission and are so placed on the stemma.

[11]It is possible, of course, that the artifact actually used by A's typesetter was a cognate rather than C2 itself, but nothing in our analysis of this relationship suggests that this is so. We have postulated missing manuscripts when their quondam existence is required to account for the surviving bibliographical data—see, e.g., the stemma for *ElBrac* and *ElPart* in vol. 2 of this edition (pp. 45–46 and 365, respectively)—but to raise the spectre of such artifacts unnecessarily, out of mere doctrinaire skepticism, is to destabilize the material base of fact that makes historical scholarship possible.

in line 3, "to another" to "to'another" in line 5, "to admitt" to "to'admit" in line 6, "dearely I love you, & would bee loved" to "dearely'I love you',and would be lov'd" in line 9, "Divorce mee, vntye" to "Divorce mee,'untie" in line 11, and "you inthrall" to "you'enthrall" in line 13. And his concern for meaning is equally apparent. He rejects, for example, such obvious β4 blunders as "Pilgrimage" (for "pilgrimages") in HSScene 2, "falls [for *fall*] my sinns" in HSScene 11, "apace" (for "a space") in HSRound 9, "Iniquitye" (for "impietie") in HSSpit 6, and "to [for *vnto*] hell" in HSWhat 7, in each case favoring the normative alternative; and he further introduces "lose" (for "loose") in HSDue 14, "my soule" (for "soule") in HSScene 6, "the [for *and*] Deuill" in HSScene 14, "assumes [for *assures*] a pitious mind" in HSWhat 14, "doe [for *doth*] . . . invest" in HSPart 8, and "this last [for *that last*] Will" in HSPart 14. All of these changes, of course, reflect this editor's attempt to ensure grammatical, logical, or rhythmical correctness; and for some of them—such as "the Deuill" in HSScene 14, "assumes" in HSWhat 14, "doe . . . invest" in HSPart 8, and "this last" in HSPart 14—there is no manuscript authority.[12] He must, however, have derived "a space" in HSRound 9 and "impietie" in HSSpit 6 from another manuscript, perhaps the same Group-II source that supplied him with the revised "But my'ever-waking part shall" in HSScene 7. Four additional deviations from his Group-I exemplar, moreover, suggest that A's editor may have compared yet a third manuscript as he finalized his text—"minutes latest [for *last*] point" in HSScene 4, "no [for *none*] iniquitie" in HSSpit 4, "gives to [for *gives*] me" in HSPart 4, and "thy all-healing [for *All healing*] grace" in HSPart 11. If A's editor is capable of having modernized "none iniquitie" to "no iniquitie" and metrically smoothing "gives me" to "gives to me" on his own, that he would independently have altered "last point" to "latest point" and "All healing" to "thy all-healing" seems less likely. In any case, these four emendations were all available to him in H6, which he used heavily in the second collected edition of the *Poems* two years later (B), and they may reflect his first examination of it.[13]

In the expanded and reorganized *Poems* of 1635 (B), A's entire HOLY SONNETS unit (comprising *La Corona* plus the *Holy Sonnets* proper, under those rubrics) is moved intact to the beginning of the section of *Divine Poems* that occupies pages 327–87 far back in the volume. For this edition, however, Marriot had access to a Group-III manuscript—H6, as the evidence shows—and from it added the four sonnets that Donne had abandoned in confecting the revised, Group-I/II sequence. Rather than merely appending them to the end of the set carried over from the previous edition, moreover, B's editor attempted (with only partial success) to slot these new poems into the positions they had originally occupied in Group III, correctly inserting HSMade as the first and HSSighs as the third, but erroneously placing HSLittle fifth (before, rather than after, HSScene) and HSSouls eighth (before, rather than after, HSMin) (see Figure 2). Among the Group-III artifacts, B's readings "'Cause" (for "Because") in HSSighs 8, "land" (for "lands") in HSLittle 6, and "by them" (for "to them") in HSSouls 8 appear only in C9 and H6; and within this pair B's paren-

[12]Unfortunately, A also contributes an error of its own in printing "Thou . . . doth [for *dost*] . . . dwell" in HSDeath 10.

[13]For a discussion of the likelihood that H6 exerted a similar slight influence on the text of A's elegies, see vol. 2, pp. lxxviii–lxxix, of this edition.

thetical "(poore)" (for "poore") in *HSSighs* 12 was available only in H6. Having derived these additional sonnets from H6, moreover, B's editor apparently followed this manuscript in emending the texts of his original 12 poems in a further few instances. The change of A's "doe see" to "shall see" in *HSDue* 12 and of "stolne" to "stole" in *HSWilt* 12 are signal examples, and the replacement of A's "my soule" with "soule" in *HSScene* 6 and of A's "Simple" with "Simpler" in *HSWhy* 4 may also reflect H6's influence. A handful of other variants, as we saw in the case of A, testify to the editor's continuing willingness to correct grammar or scansion on his own.[14] In *HSDeath* 10, for example, he replaces A's ungrammatical "doth" with "dost," and in three cases imposes metrical regularity by dropping entire words: from H6's "the fire / Of lust and Enuy hath burnt it heretofore" in *HSLittle* 10–11 he omits "hath"; from A's "But wonder at a greater wonder, for to us" in *HSWhy* 11 he omits the second "wonder"; and from A's "the Legacie / Of his and thy kingdome, doe thy Sonnes invest" in *HSPart* 7–8 he omits "doe." Sporting these metrical patches and adding the trivialized "feeble flesh" (for H6's "feebled flesh") in *HSMade* 7 and "picture" (for "pictures") in *HSDeath* 5 and the incomprehensible "stile [for the manuscript's *vild*] blasphemous Conjurers" in *HSSouls* 10 to such spurious carry-overs from A as "the Deuill" (in *HSScene* 14), "assumes a pitious mind" (in *HSWhat* 14), and "this last" (in *HSPart* 14), the much-emended text of the Holy Sonnets, in the newly concocted 16-item sequence, passed on to the subsequent seventeenth-century editions.

Set into type successively from B and retaining their relative position within the volume, the Holy Sonnets in the 1639, 1649, 1650, 1654, and 1669 issues of the *Poems* (C–G) manifest little further change. C, a page-for-page resetting of B, introduces only a single verbal variant—the blunder "poysons [for the normative *poysonous*] minerals" in *HSMin* 1—and the fourth edition (D plus its reissues E and F), though it perpetuates the erroneous "poysons," introduces no variants of its own. G, whose editor extensively revises such genres as the elegies, gives little evidence that much attention was paid to the Holy Sonnets. As generally with the text inherited from F, G modernizes the spelling of these poems; and it admits the verbal changes "holy ground" (for "lowly ground") in *HSRound* 12, "we [for *me*] should defend" in *HSBatter* 7, "he might" (for "I might") in *HSLittle* 7, and "my blood" (for "thy blood") in *HSRound* 14—the first and second being trivializations, the others nonsensical blunders. Curiously, though the editor does recover from a source other than F the authentic "poysonous" for *HSMin* 1, he fails to make further use of available materials that could have enabled him to develop a more reliable text.[15]

The First Moderns: the Eighteenth- and Nineteenth-Century Editions

For the Holy Sonnets as for other genres, the succession of modern editions from Tonson (H) through Bell (I) and Anderson (J) to Chalmers (K) constitutes a tex-

---

[14]The identity of this editor—whether Marriot himself (whose literary abilities apparently extended at least to the composition of the *Hexastichon Bibliopolæ* at the front of the volume), the printer Miles Fletcher (who contributed the prefatory "The Printer to the Understanders"), or yet some third person—remains uncertain. The similarity of the editorial agendas pursued in A and B, however, suggests that the same individual was responsible for both.

[15]For a discussion of G's access to various manuscripts, including either C9 or H6, see vol. 2, pp. lxxxi–lxxxii, of this *Variorum*.

tual tradition based on G, and a number of readings in Lowell's edition of 1855 (M) place it in this line as well. H–K evince such readings specific to the seventeenth-century prints as "feeble" (for "feebled") in HSMade 7, "dies" (for "dyes") in HSBlack 14, "fire / Of . . . envy burnt it" (for "fire / Of . . . envie hath burnt it") in HSLittle 11, "the [for and] devil" in HSScene 14, "stile [for vile] blasphemous Conjurers" in HSSouls 10, "picture" (for "pictures") in HSDeath 5, "a greater, for to us" (for "a greater wonder, for to us") in HSWhy 11, "assumes [for assures] a pitious mind" in HSWhat 14, "his and thy Kingdom, thy Sons invest" (for "his and thy kingdome, doe thy Sonnes invest") in HSPart 8, and "this last Will" (for "thy/that last will") in HSPart 14. Of the four compositorial blunders unique to G ("that so he [for I] might" in HSLittle 7, "my [for thy] blood" in HSRound 14, "holy [for lowly] ground" in HSRound 12, and "we [for me] should defend" in HSBatter 7), however, H–K record only "holy ground" and "we should," restoring the normative "I might" and "thy blood" in the former two instances. That H–K exactly agree in their handling of these errors, of course, points to H (rather than G) as the immediate ancestor of I, J, and K, and this gene-alogy is confirmed in their common inclusion of four lections not recorded in the seventeenth century—"these [for those] sighs" in HSSighs 1, "hawl'd [for hal'd] to execution" in HSBlack 7, "ague's tyrannies" (for "agues, tyrannies") in HSRound 6, and "do you" (for "dost thou") in HSWhy 6. Whether or not Tonson consulted one of the earlier editions for such repairs as "I might" in HSLittle 7 and "thy blood" in HSRound 14 (as we showed in volume 2 of this edition, he corrected G's texts of the Elegies against either B or C in certain instances), that he retains such readings as "holy ground" and "we should defend" indicates that he did not undertake a thor-ough collation. The evidence suggests rather that he scanned his source text for obvious error or ambiguity, targeting for emendation only what struck him as un-clear—his "ague's tyrannies," for example, is an intelligent emendation of G's commaless "agues tyrannies"; and his "hawl'd [for hal'd] to execution" modernizes a locution that he may have found archaic. That J derives specifically from I is indi-cated by their identical (and unique) labeling and organization of generic groups within the volume (both present the Holy Sonnets as a distinct generic unit, sepa-rated from the remaining Divine Poems by a section of "Poems, Songs, and Son-nets"—see Figure 6); and that Chalmers (K) leapfrogs J and I to base his text on H is shown not only by his restoration of H's overall organization, but also by his avoid-ance of J's unique "break that note [for the normative knot] again" in HSBatter 11. The selection of poetry included in Alford (L) opens with the rubric "HOLY SON-NETS," under that head presenting Corona and the 12 sonnets of the revised ar-rangement as a continuously numbered sequence of 19 poems (see Figure 6). In his "Editor's Preface" (1:vi) Alford refers to "the old edition" of which he has made use, and several features show that edition to have been A. These include not only the composition and ordering of this series of poems and his listing of a category of "Poems not in the Edition of 1633" in his Table of Contents, but also such lections specific to A as "I do [for the later shall] see" in HSDue 12, "Simple" (for the later "Simpler") in HSWhy 4, "wonder at a greater wonder" (for the later "wonder at a greater") in HSWhy 11, "Satan stolen [for the later stole]" in HSWilt 12, and "do thy sons invest" (for the later "thy sons invest") in HSPart 8. Although notes scattered

FIGURE 6:
SEQUENCES OF HOLY SONNETS IN THE MODERN EDITIONS

Poem \ Siglum	G (1669)	H (TONSON)	I¹ (BELL)	J (ANDERSON)	K (CHALMERS)	L (ALFORD)	M (LOWELL)	N (GROSART)	O (GROLIER)	P (CHAMBERS)	Q (GRIERSON)	S (HAYWARD)	T (BENNETT)	U (GARDNER)	Z (SHAWCROSS)	AA (SMITH)	DD (PATRIDES)
ED	VL	VL	VL	VL	VL	VL	VL	i	VL	i	i	i	ii	iii	iii	i	VL
MHMary	om	om	om	om	om	om	om	ii²	om	iii	ii	ii	i	i	i	ii	VL
Corona	i	i	DP	DP	i	i³	i³	iii	i	ii	iii	iii	iii	ii	ii	iii	i
HSMade	1	1	1	1	1	om	1	1	1	1	1	1	1⁶	13(1)⁷	13	1	1
HSDue	2	2	2	2	2	1	2	2	2	2	2	2	2	1	1	2	2
HSSighs	3	3	3	3	3	om	3	3	3	3	3	3	3	15(3)	15	3	3
HSBlack	4	4	4	4	4	2	4	4	4	4	4	4	4	2	2	4	4
HSLittle	5	5	5	5	5	om	5	5	5	5	5	5	5	14(2)	14	5	5
HSScene	6	6	6	6	6	3	6	6	6	6	6	6	6	3	3	6	6
HSRound	7	7	7	7	7	4	7	7	7	7	7	7	7	4	4	7	7
HSSouls	8	8	8	8	8	om	8	8	8	8	8	8	8	16(4)	16	8	8
HSMin	9	9	9	9	9	5	9	9	9	9	9	9	9	5	5	9	9
HSDeath	10	10	10	10	10	6	10	10	10	10	10	10	10	6	6	10	10
HSSpit	11	11	11	11	11	7	11	11	11	11	11	11	11	7	7	11	11
HSWhy	12	12	12	12	12	8	12	12	12	12	12	12	12	8	8	12	12
HSWhat	13	13	13	13	13	9	13	13	13	13	13	13	13	9	9	13	13
HSBatter	14	14	14	14	14	10	14	14	14	14	14	14	14	10	10	14	14
HSWilt	15	15	15	15	15	11	15	15	15	15	15	15	15	11	11	15	15
HSPart	16	16	16	16	16	12	16	16	16	16	16	16	16	12	12	16	16
HSShe	om	om	om	om	om	om	om	om	om	om	17⁴	17	17	17[1]⁸	17	17	17
HSShow	om	om	om	om	om	om	om	om	om	om	18⁵	18	18	18[2]	18	18	18
HSVex	om	om	om	om	om	om	om	om	om	om	19⁵	19	19	19[3]	19	19	19

VL = printed among the Verse Letters
DP = printed in a section of Divine Poems exclusive of the Holy Sonnets
i, ii, iii, 1-19 = ordinal series showing the physical sequencing of items

[1]Bell prints the Holy Sonnets in Vol. 23, other Divine Poems in Vol. 24, and Verse Letters in Vol. 25.
[2]Imported from Walton's *Life of . . . Herbert*.
[3]*Cor1-7* and Holy Sonnets numbered consecutively as a single series of Holy Sonnets.
[4]First printed in Gosse, "The Poetry of John Donne" (1893; siglum 71).
[5]First printed in Gosse, *The Life and Letters of John Donne* (1899; siglum 72).
[6]*Cross, Res, Annun, Lit,* and *Goodf* intervene between *Corona* and the Holy Sonnets proper.
[7]Sonnets 13-16 printed and numbered as a separate 4-item set.
[8]Sonnets 17-19 printed and numbered as a separate 3-item set.

throughout the remainder of the collection indicate that Alford occasionally compared J, he cites no variants from J for the Holy Sonnets; and his only deviations from the text of A—"loose" (for "lose") in *HSDue* 14, "your [for *you*] numberless infinities" in *HSRound* 3, "It is" (for "'Tis") in *HSRound* 11, "Cannot he [for the normative *be*] damn'd" in *HSMin* 4, and "drown it in" (for "drown in it") in *HSMin* 12—are careless mistakes.

As noted above, Lowell's 1855 Boston edition (M) also belongs with H–K in the tradition of early texts based on G; and M's inclusion of the abbreviated *Life of . . . Donne* that had appeared in H, as well as its perpetuation of such Tonsonian innovations as "these [for the normative *those*] sighs" in *HSSighs* 1, "hauled [a further modernization of H's *hawl'd*] to execution" in *HSBlack* 7, "ague's tyrannies" (for "agues, tyrannies") in *HSRound* 6, and "do you" (for the original "dost thou") in *HSWhy* 6 mark it more specifically as the descendant of H. M does not admit, however, H's "holy [for *lowly*] ground" in *HSRound* 12, "picture" (for "pictures") in *HSDeath* 5, or "we [for *me*] should defend" in *HSBatter* 7, having obtained the normative lections from one or more other sources. Our previous work on the Elegies indicates that Lowell occasionally compared B in resolving textual difficulties in H, and a pair of corrective readings in his text of *ElServe* derive from Alford (see volume 2, page lxxxiii of this *Variorum*). Similarly, that in numbering *Corona* and the Holy Sonnets as a single series of poems he apparently imitates Alford (see Figure 6) raises the possibility of A's influence here, and his printing of A's "dyes" in *HSBlack* 14 (where B introduces "dies") may be a specific instance. That M evinces none of A's other distinctive readings, however, and that it replaces none of the four Tonsonian innovations suggest that for the Holy Sonnets Lowell's comparison of H against previous sources was at best hit-or-miss. Indeed, M's introduction of the sports "a [for the normative *an*] usurpt town" and "victory" (for "viceroy") in *HSBatter* 5 and 7, respectively, hints at a general lapse of editorial attention in this part of the volume.

As is shown in Figure 6, Grosart (N) is the first editor ever to preface his collection of Holy Sonnets (which includes *Corona*) with not only *ED* ("See, Sir, how as the sun's hot masculine flame"), but also *MHMary* ("Her of your name"). This removal of *ED* from among the verse letters arises from Grosart's understanding of the poem's reference to "the sending of six only [of a possible seven 'holy sonnets']" as a specific reference to *Corona*, a belief that further leads him to reject the example of L and M (which present *Corona* and the Holy Sonnets as a continuous series) and to print the two groups as separately numbered sets—"as in the edition of 1669." He imports *MHMary* from Walton's *Life of . . . Herbert* and positions it immediately after *ED*, as a proem to the entire genre of Divine Poems, explicitly dissenting from Walton's belief that the "Holy Hymns and Sonnets" originally introduced by *MHMary* (and mentioned in the cover letter that Walton dates July 11, 1607) are "now lost" (1670 [siglum 52a], 26). "[N]o doubt," avers Grosart, "the present 'Divine Poems' preserve all [the hymns] sent to Lady Herbert" (2:280). As the principal source of his text Grosart cites B7, but claims also to have collated other manuscripts and the printed editions. The resulting text is as eclectic as the process of its construction is unimaginable. Since they are absent from the revised sequence found in Groups I and II, Grosart must necessarily have taken *HSMade*, *HSSighs*, *HSLittle*, and *HSSouls* from a source other than B7; and the poems that do appear in B7 frequently exhibit print readings instead of the manuscript alternatives. In every instance of substantive variation in *HSPart*, for instance, N prefers the reading of the prints to that of B7, evincing "gives to me" (for "gives mee") in line 4, "thy sons invest" (for "doth thy Sonns invest") in line 8, "these [for *those*] laws" in line 9, "thy all-healing grace" (for "all healing grace") in line 11, and "this last will" (for "that last will") in line 14. And N further abandons B7 in *HSDue* 9, *HSBlack* 3, *HSScene* 4, *HSScene* 14, *HSWilt* 12, *HSWhy* 11, *HSWhat* 14, and elsewhere. In other instances, however, Grosart strains to incorporate readings from B7, including "above all those [for the normative *these*]" in *HSRound* 10, "none [for *no*] iniquity" in *HSSpit* 4, "do with thee [for the normative *with thee do*] go" in *HSDeath* 7, "more purer" (for "more pure") in *HSWhy* 3, and "say I [for *I say*] to thee" in *HSWhat* 12, the last three being extant only in that manuscript. N's unique perpetuation of G's "he [for the normative *I*] might" in *HSLittle* 7 and "my [for the normative *thy*] blood" in *HSBatter* 14 indicates that among the seventeenth-century prints Grosart relies most heavily (and perhaps exclusively) on the 1669 edition. And his replication of Lowell's "a [for the normative *an*] usurpt town" in *HSBatter* 5, as well as his glossarial reference to Lowell's "hauled" in a note on "haled" in *HSBlack* 7, indicates at least a sporadic examination of M's text, from which he almost certainly derives the Tonsonian readings "these [for the normative *those*] sighs" in *HSSighs* 1 and "do you" (for the normative "dost thou") in *HSWhy* 6. However careless or misguided Grosart's editorial practice may frequently seem, his unique reversal of the received "war, death" to "DEATH, WARR" in *HSRound* 6 indicates that basic intelligibility was one of his goals. "Probably," he reasons, "'death' was intended to present the wide thing and word, and the after 'warr, age' etc. the various forms or modes. Accordingly, I have ventured to place 'death' before 'warr'" (2:290–91). The problem he thus noted would await satisfactory solution until Gosse found "dearth" in the Westmoreland manuscript 26 years later.

According to C. E. Norton's preface in O, the Grolier editors (Norton himself and Mrs. Mabel Burnett, James Russell Lowell's daughter) based their text on A, supplementing A's canon with "some poems which first appeared in subsequent editions" (1:viii); and—at least as regards the text's verbal composition—their treatment of the Holy Sonnets bears out this claim.[16] Individually attributing the texts of *HSMade*, *HSSighs*, *HSLittle*, and *HSSouls* to "1635," O in fact presents the expanded, 16-sonnet arrangement first printed in B (see Figure 6); but for the 12 sonnets that first appeared in A, O meticulously follows the text of that edition. O thus rejects the changes that B introduces into the print tradition, preferring A's "do see" (to the later "shall see") in *HSDue* 12, "My body and my soul" (to the later "My body, and soule") in *HSScene* 6, "Simple" (to the later "Simpler") in *HSWhy* 4, "a greater wonder" (to the later "a greater") in *HSWhy* 11, "stolen" (to the later "stole") in *HSWilt* 12, and "do

[16]Dayton Haskin (2002) has now provided a detailed account of the genesis of O: out of respect for Lowell and the intermittent editorial work he had devoted to Donne over a period of nearly 40 years, Norton used M (as supplemented by Lowell's handwritten notes in his personal copy of it) as the actual copy-text for O, but—prompted by Mrs. Burnett's collations of her father's work against the seventeenth-century editions—eventually decided "to use the earliest printed version from a complete edition of Donne's poems as the verbal norm . . ." (205).

thy sons invest" (to the later "thy sonnes invest") in *HSPart* 8. That these are prin-
cipled choices is confirmed by O's citation of the alternative readings in footnotes;
that the principle is not followed blindly is indicated by the editors' (also footnoted)
correction of A's ungrammatical "[Thou] . . . doth" in *HSDeath* 10 to "[Thou] . . .
dost."[17] As Figure 6 shows, O's editors remain unconvinced by Grosart's arguments
for printing *ED* and *MHMary* with the Holy Sonnets, though O avers in a note that
the "*Holy Sonnets* sent" along with *ED* "were probably" those of *Corona* (2:257).

Although Chambers (P) shows no awareness of O, his general presentation of the
Holy Sonnets is heavy with debt to Grosart, whom he fails to acknowledge and partly
misconstrues. Most specifically, he follows Grosart in importing *ED* and *MHMary*
into his section of "DIVINE POEMS," opening that generic grouping with the se-
quence *ED, Corona, MHMary*, and the Holy Sonnets proper, which he numbers I–
XVI and prints in 1635 order (see Figure 6). This arrangement underscores his
endorsement of Grosart's notions that *ED* is specifically meant to introduce *Corona*
and that *MHMary* forms an appropriate "preface to the rest of Donne's religious verse"
(including the Holy Sonnets), though Chambers is less certain than Grosart whether
the surviving hymns or Holy Sonnets are those to which Walton refers (1:243, 245).
Textually, Chambers is a self-declared eclecticist who bases his edition on A, B, E,
G, and "[h]ere and there" one of the "innumerable MS. copies" (1:v). Though he
footnotes two readings from H7 in his presentation of *Corona* and claims to have
appropriated that manuscript's title for *ED* (1:154–55, 243)[18], Chambers constructs
his text of the Holy Sonnets exclusively from print; and his marginal citation of vari-
ants—including such of G's solecisms as "he [for I] might" in *HSLittle* 7, "my [for *thy*]
blood" in *HSRound* 14, and "we [for *me*] should defend" in *HSBatter* 7, as well as the
C–F "poysons [for *poysonous*] minerals" in *HSMin* 1—indicates that he collated the
four editions with some care. His choice of readings at points of variance, however,
seems purely random. He thus gives B's "shall see" (for A's "doe see") in *HSDue* 12;
A's "dyes [for the later *dies*] red souls" in *HSBlack* 14; B's "My body and soul" (for A's
"My body, and my soule") in *HSScene* 6; B's "thy picture" (for A's "thy pictures") in
HSDeath 5; B's "Simpler" (for A's "Simple") and "wonder at a greater" (for A's "won-
der at a greater wonder") in *HSWhy* 4 and 11, respectively; B's "Sun" (for A's "Sonne")
and "Satan stole" (for A's "Satan stolne") in *HSWilt* 11 and 12; and A's "do thy sons
invest" (for B's "thy Sonnes invest") in *HSPart* 8.

The Twentieth-Century Editions
Although Edmund Gosse, who owned NY3 at the time, had previously printed
HSShe, HSShow, and *HSVex* in the 1890s[19], Grierson (Q) is the first to include the 3

[17]The Grolier editors' one notable deviation from A occurs in *HSBlack* 14, where they replace
A's "dyes" with the later "dies." Since "dyes" had been Lowell's reading in M, this is likely a simple
oversight resulting from their policy of "practically moderniz[ing]" A's spelling (1:ix).

[18]Chambers's note on *ED* contains two misstatements: that the heading of *ED* in A–G is merely
"To E. of D." and that he obtained "the full title" from H7. In fact, (1) the subtitle "with six holy
Sonnets" appears in all the seventeenth-century editions, and (2) H7 contains no copy of *ED*.
Chambers is apparently misled by Grosart's note explaining that his text of *Corona* and "all in this
portion not otherwise noted" derive from H7 (2:276).

[19]Gosse printed *HSShe* "for the first time" on 2 separate occasions: in 1893 in an essay on Donne's

in a collected edition, appending them to the 16 poems of the 1635 arrangement as items 17–19 (see Figure 6). For Grierson, as for Gosse before him, HSShe's reference to the death of Anne Donne constitutes proof that all 19 Holy Sonnets date from 1617 or later, and Grierson endorses Grosart's reading of the relationship between ED and Corona. Grierson also follows Grosart and Chambers (without acknowledging the former) in importing MHMary from Walton's Life; but since the 1607 date that Walton assigns to MHMary conflicts with the newly posited date of the Holy Sonnets, Grierson necessarily discounts Chambers's "suggestion" (2:229) that the existing Holy Sonnets were among the poems originally sent to Mrs. Herbert. In an argument to be detailed below, he thus conjectures that both ED and MHMary were written to introduce Corona and, accordingly, reprints—though intending quite a different significance—the Grosartian sequence ED, MHMary, Corona, the Holy Sonnets. Grierson's general policy, as we have noted in prior volumes of this Variorum (see, e.g., 2: lxxxvii–lxxxviii), is to base his text of each poem on the earliest seventeenth-century printing; but he believes that the manuscripts can provide guidance at points of crux (his method entails "establishing what one might call the agreement of the manuscripts whether universal or partial, noting in the latter case the comparative value of the different groups") and that in "some cases the manuscripts alone give us what is obviously the correct reading" (2:cxvii, cxix). He thus sets 12 of the Holy Sonnets from A and 4 from B (and the final 3 from NY3), but—as Figure 7 shows—departs from his declared copy-text in some 12 instances, printing "sinne; now I repent" (for B's "sinne I now repent") in HSSighs 7, "new lands" (for B's "new land") in HSLittle 6, "the fire / Of lust and envie have burnt" (for B's ". . . lust and envie burnt") in HSLittle 10–11, "My body, and soule" (for A's ". . . and my soule") in HSScene 6, "warre, dearth [for A's death], age" in HSRound 6, "vile [for B's stile] blasphemous Conjurers" in HSSouls 10, "Thy true griefe, for he put it in my breast" (for B's "Thy griefe, for he put it into my brest") in HSSouls 14, "dost [for A's doth] . . . dwell" in HSDeath 10, "that [for A's his] countenance" in HSWhat 4, "assures [for A's assumes] a pitious minde" in HSWhat 14, "thy [for A's these] laws" in HSPart 9, and "all-healing [for A's thy all-healing] grace" in HSPart 11. Compared to the manuscript alternatives, such of these lections as "death" (HSRound 6), "stile" (HSSouls 10), "dost" (HSDeath10), and "assumes"(HSWhat 14) stand out as blunders that clearly need correction; others, however, are not obviously erroneous, and the reasons for Grierson's emendations frequently remain obscure. His adoption of NY3's "Thy true griefe, for he put it in my breast" in HSSouls 14, for example, entails discounting the evidence of every other manuscript and print artifact, yet such other unique NY3 readings as "O God" (for "O Lord") in HSLittle 13 and "ranck [for

poetry in NewR (siglum 71)—and this article was reprinted that same year in LLA (199:429–36)—and again the following year in The Jacobean Poets. All 3 of the sonnets appeared as part of the full Westmoreland sequence in his Life and Letters (siglum 72). Although recognizing that NY3's series of Holy Sonnets "offers . . . many important differences of arrangement and new readings" (Life and Letters 2:364), Gosse botched the presentation badly, not only overtly emending the text toward print readings in three instances, but silently emending (or simply misreading or misprinting) it in over 20 others. Perhaps the four most glaring errors are "itchy lecter [for Leacher]" in HSSighs 10, "span's last mile [for inche]" in HSBlack 5, "into heaven vanished [for rauished]" in HSShe 3, and "robb'd and lore [for tore]" in HSShow 3.

fierce] spight" in *HSWhat* 8 are bypassed without comment. The lack of system inherent in Grierson's procedure is succinctly evident in his handling of the 5 independent changes introduced by the editor of A—"the [for *and*] devil" in *HSScene* 14, "doth . . . dwell" (for "dost . . . dwell") in *HSDeath* 10, "assumes" (for "assures") in *HSWhat* 14, "doe invest" (for "invest") in *HSPart* 8, and "this [for *thy* or *that*] last will" in *HSPart* 14. Each of these is an instance in which the manuscripts "*alone* give us what is obviously the correct reading," yet Grierson retains the print reading in every case except *HSDeath* 10 (where A has conspicuously mangled the grammar) and *HSWhat* 14. Given that he is the first to have access to them for a scholarly edition—and that Gosse had bungled his presentation so badly—Grierson's handling of the sonnets unique to NY3 seems especially unfortunate: he not only overlooks the elisions in *HSShow* 6 and 7 and mistranscribes "cleare" as "clear" (in *HSShow* 1) and "Wholy" as "Wholly" (in *HSShe* 4), but also perpetuates Gosse's misreading of "in heavenly things" as "on heavenly things" in *HSShe* 4 and of "ye head" as "their head" in *HSShe* 6. Additionally, Grierson inserts an exclamation point after "What" in *HSShow* 2, adds commas at the ends of *HSShe* 2 and 12, replaces the manuscript's comma with a semicolon at the end of *HSShe* 6, and respells the manuscript's "woe" as "wooe" in *HSShe* 10, reporting each of these as a conscious emendation.

Hayward (S) cites Grierson as his great forerunner and replicates Grierson's practice in every particular, including (though he has independently obtained "Sir Edmund Gosse's permission" [274] to print the unique NY3 sonnets from that manuscript) his predecessor's misreadings in *HSShe* 4 and 6.

Believing that the Holy Sonnets date from after Donne entered the priesthood (see p. xxix), Bennett (T) interpolates *Cross, Res, Annun, Lit,* and *Goodf* between them and the *MHMary-ED-Corona* sequence with which he opens his section of Divine Poems (see Figure 6). And his positioning of the overarching heading "La Corona" to include *MHMary* and *ED* with the seven poems of *Corona* proper indicates his adoption of the Griersonian notion that both these presentational sonnets are intended for *Corona*. Following Grierson and Hayward, Bennett prints the Holy Sonnets as a numbered series in 1635 order, appending the NY3 poems as items 17–19 at the end; and a footnote indicates that he has taken the text of each of the first 16 sonnets from the earliest printing—except the last (*HSPart*), which he bases on H6 in apparent accordance with the notion that since "there is no single authoritative text of any kind available to us," it is "advisable to base each poem on whatever accessible text has the fewest obvious errors" (xxv). Bennett's belief in the necessity of an interventionist approach to his editorial task leads him to abandon his declared source among the prints in 10 instances (see Figure 7). Like his predecessors from Gosse onward, Bennett gives NY3's solely correct "dearth" (for "death") in *HSRound* 6, and in a further 6 places substitutes a manuscript reading for one that his examination of Grierson's apparatus may have revealed to be compositorial in origin, printing "feebled" (for B's "feeble") in *HSMade* 7; "envy'ath burnt" (for B's "envie burnt") in *HSLittle* 11; "and devil" (for A's "the Deuill") in *HSScene* 1; "vile [for B's *stile*] blasphemous conjurers" in *HSSouls* 10; "dost . . . dwell" (for A's "doth . . . dwell") in *HSDeath* 10, and "assures [for A's *assumes*] a pitious minde" in *HSWhat* 14. Also occurring in *HSWhat*, however, Bennett's further 3 verbal emendations point

FIGURE 7: SUBSTANTIVE EMENDATIONS OF THE HOLY SONNETS IN THE TWENTIETH-CENTURY EDITIONS

→ = changed to   ~ = matches corresponding word on the left
om = omitted

Poem (first printing)	Grierson Q	Hayward S	Bennett T	Gardner U	Shawcross Z	Smith AA	Patrides DD
HSMade (B)							
7: feeble flesh → feebled ~			•	•	•		
12: my selfe I can → I can my selfe				•	•	•	
HSDue (A)							
9: usurpe on → ~ in				•	•		
HSSighs (B)							
5: mine Idolatry → my ~					•		
7: sinne I now repent → ~;* now I ~	•	•			•	•	
8: 'Cause → Because					•	•	
HSLittle (B)							
6: new land → ~ lands	•	•		•	•		•
11: lust and envie burnt → ~ ~ ~ ~ have** ~	•	•	•	•	•		•
HSScene (A)							
4: latest point → last ~					•		
6: body, and my soule → ~ ~ ~ om ~	•			•	•	•	•
14: the Deuill → and ~			•	•	•	•	
HSRound (A)							
6: warre, death → ~, dearth	•	•		•			
HSSouls (B)							
8: by them be try'd → to ~ ~ ~					•		
10: stile . . . Conjurers → vile . . . ~	•	•	•	•	•		•
14: griefe . . . into → true ~ . . . in	•	•		•		•	
HSDeath (A)							
10: doth . . . dwell → dost . . . ~	•	•	•	•	•		•
HSSpit (A)							
1: you Jewes → yee ~				•	•	•	
HSWhat (A)							
4: his countenance → that ~	•	•	•	•		•	
9: my idolatry → mine ~				•			
13: spirits → sprites				•			
14: assumes . . . minde → assures . . . ~	•	•	•	•		•	
HSPart (A)***							
4: gives to me → ~ om ~				•		•	
9: these laws → thy ~	•	•	•			•	
9: these laws → those ~				•	•		
11: thy all-healing grace → om ~-~ ~	•	•		•			
14: this last will → that ~ ~				•	•	•	
14: this last will → thy ~ ~			•				

*U, Z, and AA punctuate here with a comma
**T prints "'ath"
***T follows H6 as copy-text for this poem

to an essentially impressionistic strain at the heart of his method: he reads "that [for A's *his*] countenance" in line 4, "mine [for A's *my*] idolatry" in line 9, and "sprites" (for A's "spirits") in line 13, crediting the last two of these changes to NY3, but bypassing without acknowledgment that artifact's unique "Looke" (for "Mark") in line 2 and "ranck" (for "fierce") in line 8. The most extreme manifestation of Bennett's eclecticism, of course, is the reversion to a manuscript copy-text for *HSPart*, a decision apparently dictated not so much by actual defects in the text of the first edition (A's editor had already repaired the meter of line 4 and regularized the grammar of the "which" clause in lines 7–8) as by his personal preference for such of H6's Group-III readings as "He with" (for "wch wth") in line 7 and "thy [for *that*] last will" in line 14. Though he overlooks the manuscript's elisions of "now'outwore" and "she,'and" in *HSShow* 6 and 7, respectively, and reduces the source's "trauaile" to "travel" in *HSShow* 10, Bennett generally presents an accurate text of the NY3 sonnets; and his repunctuation of the manuscript's "Dost woe my Soule for hers; offring all thine" to "Dost woo my soul, for hers off'ring all thine" in *HSShe* 10 effects an emendation of such appeal that both Gardner and Shawcross subsequently adopt it, as do we in this edition.

Helen Gardner's 1952 edition of the Divine Poems (U) provides the Holy Sonnets what was at the time the most thorough bibliographical analysis in their history, and Gardner's remains the most important and influential work on these poems to date. Except for Alford and Gosse (each a special case), Gardner is the first editor since 1635 to reject B's ordering of the poems, arguing instead that only the Group-I/II order replicated in A embodies Donne's intentions for a major sequence of Holy Sonnets; and she significantly extends the proto-genealogical method first employed by Grierson in assessing the authority of variants. Under the section heading HOLY SONNETS she presents *MHMary*, *Corona*, and *ED* (which—as noted above—she views as introductory to the 6 sonnets on the "Last Things" that open the sequence in A) and follows these—as Figure 6 shows— with the Holy Sonnets proper in 3 separately numbered groups: the 12 of 1633, the 4 "added in 1635" (with the order of *HSLittle* and *HSSighs* reversed to enhance appreciation of the "penitential" theme of the group [see U:75]), and, finally, the 3 unique to NY3. To both the 1633 and the 1635 sequences, moreover, she affixes not only the later generic heading "Holy Sonnets," but also the earlier Group-III designation "Divine Meditations," finding the latter "much better" than the "vague" description that replaced it (see U:65; see also Figure 2).

Although she recognizes that in A the text of these poems is already an amalgam of discrete genealogical strains—she cites in particular the patching of the Group-II lection "But my'ever-waking part shall" (*HSScene* 7) into the fundamentally Group-I base—Gardner remains persuaded that the section of the edition containing the Holy Sonnets preserves "the best extant text of Donne's final version of these poems" (xcii); and she further opines that "we do not improve matters" by reverting to a manuscript for the poems added in 1635 (xciii).[20] Gardner thus uses their respec-

[20]Although more skeptical of the text of A than she had been in 1952, in her 1978 reissue Gardner reiterates the conviction that "[t]he edition of 1633 provides the only possible basis for a critical edition" (xci) and that that of 1635 "can serve as a copy text" (xcii) for the poems that it introduces.

tive first printings as copy-text for the first 16 poems, but emends when she concludes that the compositor or editor has blundered, attempted deliberate repair or improvement, or followed his setting text in error. And, as noted above, she spells out precise rules of thumb for evaluating individual instances of variation: (1) we should adopt the manuscript reading when "all three groups agree against 1633"; (2) we should "usually . . . adopt the reading of Groups II and III, when they agree against 1633 and Group I" (the assumption being that "the Group I reading is a slip"); (3) we must individually assess instances in which 1633 has the support of "Group III only," but remember that the reading of Groups I and II is likely to be "preferable"; (4) we should never adopt the "reading of a single manuscript" unless the artifact is of "high authority" and the reading "unquestionably superior." Noting that the 4 sonnets added in 1635 derive from H6, Gardner adds the further caveat that (5) this artifact "tends to 'clean up' its text" and advises that we should seek "to discover the general manuscript tradition" (U:xcii–xciii). Implementing this approach entails altering the 12 poems of 1633 in some 13 places and the 4 of 1635 in a further 10 (see Figure 7). Among the sonnets of 1633, Gardner's correction of independent compositorial mistakes or sophistications includes changing "latest point" to "last point" in *HSScene* 4, "and my soule" to "and soule" in *HSScene* 6, "the devil" to "and devil" in *HSScene* 14, "doth dwell" to "dost dwell" in *HSDeath* 10, "assumes" to "assures" in *HSWhat* 14, "gives to mee" to "gives mee" in *HSPart* 4, "thy all-healing" to "all-healing" in *HSPart* 11, and "this last will" to "that last will" in *HSPart* 14. Identified as misreadings that A derives from its Group-I manuscript source (probably, she thinks, a lost cognate of C2) are "usurpe on" (for "usurpe in") in *HSDue* 9, "you [for *yee*] Jewes" in *HSSpit* 1, "his [for *that*] countenance" in *HSWhat* 4, and "these [for *those*] laws" in *HSPart* 9; and in each instance Gardner restores the normative alternative. Because of the authority of the artifact and the superiority of the reading, she also accepts NY3's unique "dearth" in *HSRound* 6. In the 4 sonnets added in B, Gardner not only corrects the compositorial "feeble" to "feebled" in *HSMade* 7, "lust and envie burnt" to ". . . have burnt" in *HSLittle* 11, and "stile" to "vile" in *HSSouls* 10, but also identifies 6 additional instances in which she believes the edition has taken corruption from its manuscript source. These include "my selfe I can sustaine" (for "I can my selfe . . .") in *HSMade* 12; "new land" (for "new lands") in *HSLittle* 6; "mine [for *my*] Idolatry," "sinne I now repent" (for "Sin, now I repent"), and "'Cause" (for "Because") in *HSSighs* 5, 7, and 8, respectively; and "by [for *to*] them be try'd" in *HSSouls* 8. Gardner views each of these as an "improvement" initiated by the H6 scribe, and she restores what she takes to be the normative Group-III reading (here given parenthetically) in each case.

The major goal of Gardner's editorial work, as the aforementioned list of "corrections" makes clear, is to reconstruct the ideal text by eradicating error. In some few instances, it is true, she reveals an awareness that variation is not always a simple matter of "right" versus "wrong"—for example, in her remark about A's preserving the "final version" of the Holy Sonnets—but she fails to flesh out a full genealogy for the poems, and her editorial theory lacks adequate provisions for dealing with authorial revision. These shortcomings are apparent in her final substantive departure from B, where she follows Grierson in replacing the edition's "griefe, for he put it into my brest" in HSSouls 14 with NY3's "true griefe, for he put it in my brest." In justification of this change she offers the speculation "that the archetype of Group III omitted 'true' in error, and that this was patched by the alteration of 'in' to 'into'" (77). It is far from certain, however, that Group III's rendition is an error rather than the author's original version of the line. In fact, this crux is bibliographically identical to three others that also appear among the sonnets added in 1635—in HSMade 8, where Group III gives "it towards" rather than NY3's "towards"; in HSLittle 12, where Group III gives "theyr flames" rather than NY3's "those flames"; and in HSLittle 13, where Group III gives "ô Lord" rather than NY3's "O God." As we have argued above, some—and perhaps all—of these seem to represent valid, authorial alternatives; yet in each of these instances Gardner retains the Group-III reading without comment. The methodological weakness here manifest is especially evident in Gardner's handling of the four replacement sonnets (see Figure 5). In a note on HSSpit she acknowledges that "a few readings" in NY3 *may* [emphasis added] represent an earlier stage of the text than that represented in Groups I and II" (70), and she cites most of the important ones in her apparatus. Despite the fact that she finds several of these strongly attractive, however, she admits none of them into her text and in some cases seems reluctant to credit them directly to Donne.[21] Except for missing the elision mark in HSShe 7 ("I haue found thee,'& thou my thirst hast fed") and regularizing Woodward's capitalization throughout, Gardner's transcriptions of the sonnets unique to NY3 match those presented in this edition; and she prints them with little emendation. Apparently in order to remove any possible ambiguity she follows Grierson in respelling the manuscript's "woe" in HSShe 10 as "wooe," and she adds commas in HSShe 2 and 12 and in HSShow 2. Her major alteration, however, occurs in the punctuation of HSShe 10, where—as noted above—she adopts Bennett's repunctuation of "Dost wooe my soule for hers; offring all thine" to "Dost wooe my soule, for hers offring all thine."

With respect to the larger organizational features, Shawcross (Z) essentially reproduces Gardner's presentation of the Holy Sonnets. Though the poems actually bear the numerical sigla 162 through 180 in his volume (and each is headed simply "Holy Sonnet"), their arrangement exactly matches that in Gardner (including the shuffled order of HSLittle and HSSighs); and the generic group is preceded by the same three-item sequence that Gardner establishes: MHMary, Corona, and ED (see Figure 6). Like most of his twentieth-century predecessors, Shawcross bases the text of each of the first 16 sonnets on their respective first printings and that of the final 3 on NY3, but—as Figure 7 shows—substantively emends those deriving from A in some 10 instances and those deriving from B in 6 others. His alterations of A in-

---

[21]E.g., in her notes to HSWhy Gardner says of line 1, "'Why ame I' (W [NY3]) is a more vivid opening [than the later 'Why are wee'], and is consistent with the use of the singular down to l. 10. The change to the plural may have been made, in order that the transition to the plural in l. 11 should seem less abrupt." Of line 9 she avers that NY3's "Alas I'ame weaker, wo'is me" (for the later "Weaker I am, woe is mee") is "[t]he finer line." In both cases, she says, "one regrets the change to the final reading" (70). These notes also illustrate two of the chief ways in which Gardner contrives to avoid crediting alternatives to Donne—the use of the passive voice (the change "may have been made") and the construction of sentences that simply skirt the question of agency altogether ("one regrets the change to the final reading").

clude changing "usurpe on" to "usurpe in" in *HSDue* 9, "you Jewes" to "yee Jewes" in *HSSpit* 1, "his countenance" to "that countenance" in *HSWhat* 4, "these laws" to "those laws" in *HSPart* 9, "and my soule" to "and soule" in *HSScene* 6, "the Deuill" to "and Deuill" in *HSScene* 14, "doth . . . dwell" to "dost . . . dwell" in *HSDeath* 10, "assumes" to "assures" in *HSWhat* 14, "this last will" to "that last will" in *HSPart* 14, and "death" to "dearth" in *HSRound* 6. Among the sonnets based on B Shawcross substitutes "feebled" for "feeble" in *HSMade* 7, "have burnt" for "burnt" in *HSLittle* 11, "vile" for "stile" in *HSSouls* 10, "I can my selfe" for "my selfe I can" in *HSMade* 12, "sinne, now I repent" for "sinne I now repent" in *HSSighs* 7, and "lands" for "land" in *HSLittle* 6. Whereas Gardner had marked each of these print readings for emendation on bibliographical grounds, categorizing them either as (a) compositorial blunders or "repairs" or as (b) nonnormative readings deriving from the source manuscript, Shawcross's less differentiated approach entails emendation when the reading of "a later [printed] version" or of "a consensus of manuscripts" appears to be "closer to Donne's 'original'" (xxi). And apart from the "sinne I now repent"/"sinne, now I repent" crux in *HSSighs* 7, where the evidence is evenly divided, each of his alterations passes the "consensus of manuscripts" test. Of the seven additional changes adopted by Gardner, however, changes that Shawcross refuses, all but that in *HSSouls* 14 pass the same test.[22] This discrepancy, plus the fact that although he cites NY3 as the source for 13 of his 16 changes (and could have cited it for 2 others), Shawcross bypasses without comment nearly as many other distinctive NY3 readings—including, for example, "Revive & quicken" (for "Revive againe") in *HSPart* 12, "O God" (for "ô Lord") in *HSLittle* 13, "live [for *wake*] eternally" in *HSDeath* 13, and "humbly" (for "only") in *HSSpit* 3 (see Figures 4 and 5)—shows that for him methodological consistency must finally defer to personal taste. Except that he does not regularize Woodward's sporadic capitalization, Shawcross's handling of the NY3 sonnets is also much like Gardner's: he refuses the comma that she inserts at the end of *HSShe* 2 and rejects her respelling of Woodward's "woe" as "wooe," as well as independently eliding the phrase "To morrow'I quake" in *HSVex* 11; but he accepts the commas she inserts in *HSShow* 2 and 12 and follows her in failing to record the elision of "found thee,'and" in *HSShe* 7. Perhaps most significantly, as noted above, Shawcross also accepts Bennett's repunctuation of "soule for hers; offring" to "soule, for hers offring" in *HSShe* 10.

In its handling of the Holy Sonnets, as of genres presented in previous volumes of this *Variorum*, Smith's (siglum AA) is a modernized, eclectic edition based principally upon the seventeenth-century prints, but owing heavy debts to its twentieth-century predecessors, especially Q and U. As is shown on Figure 6, Smith reverts to the Griersonian sequence *ED*, *MHMary*, *Corona*, and the Holy Sonnets, which

---

[22]Shawcross lists his differences from Gardner in *HSSighs* 5 and *HSSouls* 8 without comment, but those in *HSighs* 8, *HSScene* 4, and *HSPart* 4 and 11 he justifies variously on metrical and thematic grounds: "'Cause" in *HSSighs* 8 prevents the line's being "hypermetric" and averts "metrical awkwardness and misplacement of stresses"; "latest" in *HSScene* 4, which occurs in "print and other MSS, contrasts with 'last,' avoids a defective line, and is more appropriate to time"; "to" in *HSPart* 4 is the "reading of some MSS" and "[a]voids defective line"; and "thy" in *HSPart* 11 "[a]voids defective and metrically awkward line" and is the "reading of some MSS" (497).

are printed as a numbered, 19-item sequence in the manner of Grierson. Smith also follows Grierson in inserting A's section heading "HOLY SONNETS" after *MHMary*, where it serves to introduce both "*La Corona*" (which is so labeled) and the Holy Sonnets proper (which, as previously in Gardner, are specifically called "*Divine Meditations*").[23] Of the 26 emendations cited on Figure 7, Smith accepts 17, but his choices seem purely subjective. Obvious blunders aside, for example, among readings originating with A's editor/compositor Smith retains "latest point" in *HSScene* 4 and "thy all-healing grace" in *HSPart* 11, while emending similar editorial innovations in *HSScene* 6 and 14 and in *HSPart* 4 and 14; and in the poems based on B he alters "lust and envie burnt" in *HSLittle* 11, but retains the compositorial "feeble flesh" in *HSMade* 7. Other than Hayward, moreover, he is the only twentieth-century editor to follow Grierson in emending A's "these laws" in *HSPart* 9 to the earlier "thy laws" rather than to the normative Group-I/II "those laws"; and he also aligns himself with Grierson and Gardner in accepting NY3's unique "Thy true griefe, for he put it in my brest" in *HSSouls* 14. Smith's note on this reading typifies the inadequacy of his edition for serious study of the text: against the lemma "Thy true grief" he reports that "*1635–69 and severall MSS*" read "Thy grief," and against "in" he reports the same (629). Obscured in this note are the facts that (a) only one manuscript contains the reading of the lemma and (b) that that manuscript is the authoritative NY3. In this and similar notes that attribute variants to "MS," "*some MSS*," and "*most MSS*," Smith flattens the hierarchy of sources developed by his predecessors and reduces authority to mere frequency of occurrence. In his handling of the final three sonnets, Smith fails to report NY3's elision of "now'outwore" in *HSShow* 6 and of "thee,'and" in *HSShe* 7, and he omits the manuscript's comma after "lovd" ("lovd,") in *HSShe* 1; moreover—like Grierson, Gardner, and Shawcross before him—he adds commas at the end of lines 2 and 12 of that poem. His justification for reverting to NY3's original punctuation in *HSShe* 10—"Dost woo my soul for hers; offering all thine"—is summarized in the Commentary.

Uniquely among editors since Chambers, Patrides (DD) assigns *ED* and *MHMary* to a place among the Verse Letters and opens his section of "Divine Poems" with *La Corona* and the Holy Sonnets proper, presenting the latter—as had all his twentieth-century predecessors except Gardner and Shawcross—as a 19-item sequence in 1635-as-supplemented-by-NY3 order (see Figure 6). Like Grierson, he follows A in numbering the sonnets in Roman and in introducing both them and "*La Corona*" under the overarching generic heading "HOLY SONNETS," and he manifests the influence of Gardner in specifically labeling the poems both "*Holy Sonnets*" and "*Divine Meditations*." Patrides's avowed policy is to base each text on its earliest printing, and he accordingly sets 12 of the poems from A, 4 others from B, and—as will be explained below—the final 3 apparently from Q. He declares himself willing to emend when he finds the received versions "self-evidently inadequate" (3), however; and among the 16 sonnets included in B this principle leads him to abandon his copy-text in 6 instances (see Figure 7). That this is far fewer emendations than

---

[23]Smith's note on these headings (p. 620) misleadingly implies that the poems had been designated *Divine Meditations* in A–G.

had been deemed necessary by any editor since Grierson, of course, reminds us of how variably the "self-evidently inadequate" standard may be applied; and Patrides's few alterations seem more whimsical than principled. He emends the compositorial "lust and envie burnt" to ". . . have burnt" in HSLittle 11, for example, and repairs the blunder "stile [for *vile*] blasphemous Conjurers" in HSSouls 10, yet retains A's innovative "the [for *and*] Deuill" in HSScene 14, "this [for *that*] last will" in HSPart 14, and—uniquely among twentieth-century editors—"assumes [for *assures*] a pitious minde" in HSWhat 14. Like those of Smith before him, moreover, his notes attribute reported variants vaguely to "some," "several," or "most" manuscripts, and even NY3's unique "dearth" in HSRound 6 is credited merely to an unnamed "single MS." With respect to his presentation of HSShe, HSShow, and HSVex Patrides creates a virtual replica of Q—even including Grierson's misreadings of "on [for NY3's *in*] heavenly things" in HSShe 4 and "their [for NY3's y^e] head" in HSShe 6. Combined with his repetition of Grierson's misleading note that all three of these poems had been first published in 1899 and the further misstatement that the numbering of the poems as items 17–19 "is conjectural" (445), this similarity suggests that Patrides's knowledge of NY3 derives exclusively from Grierson.

The Dates of the Holy Sonnets and their Relationships to Other Poems

Perhaps because Walton's assignment of the "divine Sonnets" to the "penitential" years of Donne's "declining age" fit so smoothly into the bifurcated portrait of Donne he drew in the 1640 *Life*, the dating of the Holy Sonnets did not emerge as a topic of specific scholarly concern until late in the nineteenth century (see the General Commentary below). The seeds of modern efforts to address this concern lie in two previously discussed editorial decisions implemented by Grosart in 1873, both intended to restore something of the conditions under which these poems were distributed to their original audiences. Based on the mention of "the sending of six only, as the seventh was still 'maim'd'" (2:280) in the poem traditionally entitled "To E. of D. with six holy Sonnets" (*ED*), the first decision involved detaching *Corona* from the continuously numbered single series into which Alford and Lowell had combined it with the Holy Sonnets and retrieving *ED* from among the verse letters to serve as a specific introduction to the seven-item "crown" of sonnets. The second decision entailed similarly importing *MHMary* from Walton's *Life of . . . Herbert* and installing it alongside *ED* at the head of his section of Divine Poems. Though the justice of including these verse letters among the Divine Poems quickly came to seem self-evident—of all Grosart's successors listed on Figure 6 only the Grolier editors and Patrides fail to follow his lead—the question of where, exactly, they should be placed with respect to *Corona* and the Holy Sonnets proper proved susceptible of various answers; and the restoration of these verse letters to their putative original positions also raised a number of historical questions that bear on the matter of dating. One such question concerns the meaning of the phrase "To E. of D." and the identity of the person so addressed. If we can extrapolate the full words for which "E" and "D" stand and if we can link those words to a historical person, the thinking goes, then we may be able to adduce biographical fact in dating the "six" poems to which *ED* alludes. Other questions are prompted by *MHMary* and certain details embedded in its original Waltonian context. The Donne prose letter with which Walton prefaces *MHMary* alludes to "holy hymns and sonnets," and *MHMary* specifically mentions the sending of "hymns" to Lady Herbert (see the section Dating and Order in the Commentary below). Which are the poems here referred to? Do they subsist among the surviving Divine Poems, or are they now "lost," as Walton asserts? And does Walton mean to say that all the poems sent to Lady Herbert are lost, or just the "hymns"? Is the July 11, 1607, date that Walton affixes to the prose letter accurate? And, if so, what are its implications for dating surviving poems? These are among the issues raised by Grosart's relocation of *ED* and *MHMary*, and much of the succeeding discussion of the dates of the Holy Sonnets is framed in response to them.

Grosart's own answers to these questions are not altogether clear. Though he argues on thematic grounds that "*the principal 'Divine Poems'*" are early, written while Donne "*was still a Roman Catholic*" (2: x), he nowhere postulates an inclusive schedule of dates for these poems; and determining exactly which poems he thinks covered by the date on the prose letter cited by Walton is impossible. He denies Walton's assertion that the "hymns" mentioned in *MHMary* are lost—"no doubt, the present 'Divine Poems' preserve all sent to Lady Herbert" (2: 275)—and, interpreting Walton's comment to include the "Holy Sonnets," counters that "we have in the present section these identical Sonnets" (2: 280). But whether he means only *Corona*, only the Holy Sonnets, or both is impossible to tell; and his sequencing of items— *ED, MHMary, Corona,* Holy Sonnets, other Divine Poems—does not clarify the matter. Indeed, placing *MHMary* between *ED* and *Corona* separates *ED* from the very poems Grosart thinks it specifically meant to introduce and appears to provide *Corona* with two prefatory sonnets, while failing to indicate how broadly *MHMary's* introductory function is intended to extend. In his title to *ED*, moreover, Grosart designates the recipient as "Viscount Doncaster," thus correcting Lowell's "Earl of Doncaster . . .,"[24] but he does not comment on the discrepancy between the (ostensibly early) date of the poem and that of Lord Hay's creation as Viscount. Finally, Grosart is the first to identify *BoulRec's* opening "Death I recant" as a "reference" to *HSDeath's* "Death be not proud" (2: 137)—a connection that subsequently figures prominently in Gardner's effort to date these poems.

Adopting Lowell's identification of the recipient as the "Earl of Doncaster," the Grolier editors leave "TO THE E. OF D. WITH SIX HOLY SONNETS." in its traditional place among the verse letters, omit *MHMary* altogether, and make no attempt to date the Holy Sonnets. Indeed, their only nod toward Grosart's treatment of these matters appears in a note to *ED*, which allows—without acknowledging Grosart— that the "Holy Sonnets sent to the Earl were probably" those of *Corona* (2: 257). Chambers, on the other hand, also without crediting his predecessor, appropriates Grosart's handling of these poems in virtually every detail. Conceding that his heading "TO THE E[ARL] OF D[ONCASTER] . . ." is "not quite correct, for there was no Earl of Doncaster," Chambers agrees that *ED* is intended as an introduction to *Corona;*

---

[24]Lowell had apparently derived his identification from a footnote in Alford. Grosart alters "Earl" to "Viscount" on grounds that "[t]here was, properly speaking, no Earl of Doncaster at the period of these lines" and briefly summarizes James Hay's career, pointing out that "[o]n 5th July 1618 he was created Viscount *Doncaster*; and finally 13th September 1622, Earl of Carlisle" (2:273–74).

and—though uncertain whether the surviving Holy Sonnets or "some later ones" or, indeed, "some lost hymns, as distinguished from the sonnets" are the poems Walton thought "lost"—he pronounces MHMary an appropriate "preface to the rest of Donne's religious verse" (1:245) and opens his section of Divine Poems with the sequence ED, Corona, MHMary, the Holy Sonnets. To what is implied by this arrangement of items, moreover, Chambers adds the explicit opinion that—although the Divine Poems are generally Donne's "latest group"—"[s]ome at least of the Sonnets were probably written before 1607" (1:243). This observation may be primarily rooted in the date on the prose letter quoted by Walton, but Chambers adduces a further bibliographical fact that seems to lend it support: "[i]n Harl. 4955 [B32]," he notes, "the divine sonnets (Holy Sonnets and La Corona) are said to have been 'made 20 years since,'" and that manuscript "includes a poem dated 1629" (1:245). This detail in B32, as well as Chambers's construction of its significance, assumes considerable importance in subsequent discussions of the dating of these poems, as does his perpetuation of the (unacknowledged) Grosartean notion that HSDeath "is probably earlier" than BoulRec (1:246).

A final nineteenth-century development that figures prominently in subsequent efforts to date the Holy Sonnets is, of course, the discovery in the 1890s of the Westmoreland manuscript, which had recently come into the possession of Edmund Gosse. In his 1893 essay "The Poetry of John Donne," Gosse prints HSShe for the first time and—amid a series of remarks whose bizarreness must be partly dictated by his uncritical conclusion on the poems' dates—opines that all the Holy Sonnets "probably belong to 1617, or the period immediately following the death of Donne's wife" (NewR 9:241). By the time the Life and Letters appeared six years later (in 1899), probability had hardened into certitude: the discovery of HSShe, Gosse averred, "settles any doubt as to the Holy Sonnets being subsequent to August 1617" (2:106).

With the appearance of Grierson's edition in 1912 Gosse's suggestion is elevated to the status of received truth: "the Holy Sonnets were composed, we know now from Sonnet XVII [HSShe], first published by Mr. Gosse, after the death of Donne's wife in 1617" (2:225). Accordingly, Grierson focuses on "[t]he more difficult question" of the dating of Corona, which—in contradistinction to the "usual" assignment of it to "the later period of Donne's ministry" (he perhaps has Chambers and Gosse in mind here)—he believes to have been written "at Mitcham in or before 1609" (2: 226). In support of this proposition he advances two lines of argument, each of which traces its origin to one of the verse letter-Holy Sonnets connections posited by Grosart 40 years previously. In the first, Grierson agrees that ED must have been sent with a copy of "six of these sonnets [of Corona]," but disputes the traditional identification of the intended recipient of the verse letter as Doncaster. In print and in the O'Flahertie manuscript (H6), he notes, the poem is headed "To E. of D. with six holy Sonnets"; in NY3, however—where it "belongs to" an exchange of youthful verse letters on poetical subjects that were "written apparently between 1597 and 1609–10"—it is headed simply "To L. of D." And—given the chronology of his career—neither of these headings would ever have constituted an appropriate form of address for James Hay. If the heading "To E. of D." is legitimate, it cannot refer to Hay because—as Donne knew and Grosart had previously pointed out—Hay was

Viscount, not Earl, of Doncaster. Correspondingly, "L. of D." (for "Lord of Doncaster") is unsuitable because during the pre-1610 years to which the letter's position in NY3 points Donne would have styled Hay "Lord Hay" and would likely have addressed the poem "To the L. Hay" or "To the L. H." (2: 226). And unlike the man praised in the poem for his poetic powers, Grierson further observes, "we nowhere hear that Lord Hay wrote verses" (2:227). Grierson's nominee for the vacancy he has thus created—a man who he thinks "may well have written verses" (2: 228)—is Richard Sackville, who on February 25, 1608/9, entered Donne's circle by marrying the niece of Lucy, Countess of Bedford, and two days later "succeeded as third Earl of Dorset" (2:26). After—but not before—this date a verse letter could properly have been addressed to him as either "L[ord]" or "E[arl]" of "D[orset]" and fit exactly into the time slot Grierson proposes for its composition. Almost miraculously, Grierson finds bibliographical support for this chronology in the details in B32 to which Chambers had previously pointed—the rubric "Holy Sonnets: written 20 yeares since," which precedes the inscription of *Corona* and the following sonnets, and the manuscript's inclusion of a Richard Andrews poem dating from 1629. Subtracting 20 from 1629 brings us to the year of Dorset's accession, Grierson reasons, and although the rubric cannot apply to the sonnets "written later" (i.e., after 1617), it may well apply to those of *Corona* and help to fix their dates.

Grierson's second major argument for assigning *Corona* to the years 1607–09 is rooted in his interpretation of *MHMary* and the accompanying prose letter to Magdalen Herbert that Walton cites. He credits the 1607 date on the prose letter on grounds that, under the Julian Calendar then in use, July 11 would have been St. Mary Magdalen's day and reads Donne's description of it as "this good day" as a kind of suppressed pun associating the feast date with the recipient. And despite Walton's assertion that they are lost, Grierson believes the hymns mentioned in *MHMary* 14 are the very sonnets of *Corona*: "'Hymns, to his dear name addrest' is an exact description of the *La Corona* sonnets" (2: 228–29). Having developed this argument, Grierson proceeds to suggest that Donne in fact sent *Corona* to two different patrons at separate times—first, in July of 1607, to Magdalen Herbert; later, perhaps in 1609, to Dorset, holding back "for correction" one of them that "seems to have been criticized." Why hypothesizing this particular sequence of events does not lead Grierson to print *MHMary* before, rather than after, *ED* is unexplained (see Figure 6). Grierson admits that this reconstruction of *Corona*'s original transmissional history "is conjectural," but finds the notion that the sequence was "written about 1617 and sent to Lord Doncaster . . . equally so." And he concludes with an argument from style: these poems are "more in the intellectual, tormented, wire-drawn style" of Donne's "earlier religious verse . . . than the passionate and plangent sonnets and hymns of the years which followed the death of his wife" (2: 229).

Basing her effort to date the Holy Sonnets on a "hypothetical reconstruction" of their genealogy, Helen Gardner begins by discounting the Gossean notion that all the poems were written late, after the death of Donne's wife, and seeks to identify among them those that were composed earliest. According to her analysis, as noted above, these are a set of "six sonnets on the Last Things" that opens the sequence in Groups I and II and—though four "penitential" sonnets have been mistakenly interpolated into it—also constitutes the "core" of the Group-III arrangement (xlii; see Figure 2). Three strands of argument converge to convince Gardner that these six poems were written in "the earlier part of 1609" (xliii). The first strand involves an alleged change in Donne's view on "precisely what happens to the soul at the moment of death" (xliii), a change that Gardner identifies in the revision of Group I's "Or presently, I know not, see y^t Face" to Group II's "But my euer wakeing part shall see that face" in *HSScene* 7. When Donne wrote the former version, Gardner asserts, he had no fixed opinion on the soul's fate at death; by the time he wrote the latter, he had. And in 1612 his new-found conviction is reflected in *SecAn's* expression of the "belief that at death the righteous soul is immediately in heaven" (xlvi). The work revealing Donne's investigation and adoption of this idea, Gardner thinks, is *Pseudo-Martyr*, written in the "latter half of 1609"; thus the sonnets on the Last Things, evincing the early version of *HSScene* 7, "cannot have been written later than the first half of that year" (xlvii). Based on a resurrection of Grosart's observation—which she attributes to Chambers—that *HSDeath* (beginning "Death be not proud") must precede *BoulRec* (beginning "Death I recant"), Gardner's second argument also supports a first-half-of-1609 date for the sonnets on the Last Things. *BoulRec* ("An Elegie vpon the death of M^{rs}. Bulstrod."), she notes, stems from the period immediately after the death of Cecilia Boulstrode on August 4, 1609, as apparently also does the elegy beginning "Death bee not proude, thy hand gaue not this blowe" that Grierson and others have plausibly attributed to the Countess of Bedford (see the texts of and commentary on these poems in volume 6 of this *Variorum*). Both Donne's elegy and the other, Gardner avers, "would be apposite only if Donne had fairly recently written . . . [the] defiance of death" (xlviii) embodied in the Holy Sonnet; the sonnets on the Last Things, therefore, must have been written shortly before August 1609. In her third line of argument Gardner posits a *terminus a quo* for the "Last-Things" sonnets, endorsing Grierson's suggestion that *ED* is addressed to Sackville as Earl of Dorset, but for reasons involving both esthetics and tact disbelieving that it heralds Donne's sending of six of the *Corona* sonnets to a second recipient. The poems Gardner thinks *ED* written to introduce are the six on the Last Things, which—though "beautiful and complete enough as a set to be sent to a patron"—lack the "proper religious climax" of a seventh "on the joys of heaven" (hence "I send as yet / But six, they say the seventh hath still some maime"). Gardner thus dates these six sonnets "between February 1609, when Dorset succeeded to the title, and August 1609, when Mrs. Bulstrode died" (xlix). The other six Group I/II sonnets Gardner presumes "to have been written soon afterwards," the "four penitential sonnets . . . between the second half of 1609 and the writing of *The First Anniversary*" in 1611 (xlix–l), and the Westmoreland sonnets "after . . . [Donne's] ordination" (76; see the Commentary). In her notes on *Corona* Gardner cites B32's heading "Holy Sonnets written 20 yeares since" and "the date 1629" that appears among poems preceding the Donne collection, but thinks these details support us only "in putting 'La Corona' (and possibly the 'Holy Sonnets') rather before 1610 . . ." (57). In accordance with the argument outlined above, as Figure 6 shows, Gardner's edition presents the sequence *MHMary, Corona, ED,* the Holy Sonnets.

None of Gardner's editorial successors seriously challenges her views on dating;

and—with the notable exception of Flynn (1988)[25]—most subsequent critics and scholars have accepted Gardner's as the last word on the matter (see the section Dating and Order in the Commentary below). As the above account shows, however, Gardner's theory represents merely the final stage of a cumulative discussion that had evolved over a period of some 80 years and, regrettably, incorporates a number of bibliographically indefensible and interpretively questionable assertions. We may examine these one by one.

1) *That Donne wrote a set of "six sonnets on the Last Things"* (Gardner). As we have demonstrated above, there is no bibliographical support for this notion. In both the Group-III sequence and NY3's revised version of it, what Gardner labels the sonnets on the Last Things subsist as poems 2, 5, 6, 8, 9, and 11 of a 12-poem sequence (see Figure 2); and when these poems come together as items 1–6 in the reconfigured Group-I/II sequence, they remain an integral part of a larger (though different) 12-poem structure. These bibliographically undeniable circumstances entail at least the following three consequences: (a) dating the "sonnets on the Last Things" as distinct from the other 6 Group-III/IV poems is not possible; (b) there are no grounds for supposing that Donne ever sent "six sonnets on the Last Things" as a distinct group to a patron; (c) HSDeath ("Death be not proud") never stood as the resounding "denigration of death" (U:xlviii) at the end of a sequence of Donne sonnets.

2) *That Donne wrote a separate four-poem set of "penitential" sonnets* (Gardner). We have also demonstrated above the complete absence of bibliographical evidence for this idea. As Figure 2 shows, the 4 poems in question exist as items 1, 3, 7, and 10 of the early, Group-III sequence, but are discarded in the general revision that leads to the Group-I/II set. As part of the original, 12-sonnet sequence, of course, the "penitential" sonnets share the date of the other 8.

3) *That B32's heading "Holy Sonnetts . written . 20 . yeares since," coupled with the 1629 date on one of the other poems in the artifact, can be used to date the poems* (Chambers, Grierson, Gardner). First noticed by Chambers, these details assumed major importance in Grierson's identification of "E. of D.," and Gardner found in them support for dating Corona and "possibly the 'Holy Sonnets' rather before 1610" (57). Curiously, these artifactual features have never been fully described nor analyzed, and their implications for the question of dating have not been accurately understood. One of the five principal Group-I manuscripts, B32 (British Library ms. Harley 4955) is a composite poetical miscellany compiled—as Hilton Kelliher (1993) has shown—between about 1629 and 1634 under the aegis of William Cavendish, Earl and later first Duke of Newcastle. As Kelliher has further demonstrated, the manuscript is written throughout in the hand of Newcastle's secretary John Rolleston, who over the years entered successive batches of material not only by Donne, but also by Ben Jonson, Richard Andrews (the London physician to whom Donne addressed

---

[25]Not only through his article, but also in additional private conversation, Dennis Flynn has contributed hugely to the remarks that follow, being the first to examine methodically the evidence and reasoning involved in, especially, Gardner's efforts to date these poems. Had Flynn had access to the bibliographical information now available, his conclusions would doubtless have closely resembled those presented below.

Libro), and others. While various groups of Jonson and Andrews poems appear spo-radically throughout the manuscript, the Donne poems constitute a single discrete section (ff. 88r–144v) deriving, through at least one intermediary, from the Group-I archetype (see Figure 3). Folio 138v begins with the final three lines of *Lit*, after which appear the following: (a) the phrase "Holy Sonnetts . written . 20 . yeares since." (aligned at the right margin); (b) the phrase "Deigne at my handes" (aligned at the right margin); (c) the heading "La:· Corona .1." (rubricated and centered be-tween two horizontal rules); (d) the first sonnet of *Corona* (beginning "Deign at my handes"); (e) the remaining 6 sonnets of *Corona*, each headed by a centered arabic numeral (2–7); (f) the centered heading "1. Sonnett," followed by *HSDue*; (g) the remaining 11 sonnets of the Group-I/II arrangement, each headed by a centered ara-bic numeral (2–12); (h) the heading "To the Countesse of Salisbury / Aug: 1614," followed by the poem; (i) *Har* (properly titled "Obsequies to the Ld Harrington, Brother to / the Countesse of Bedford.│"), the last Donne poem in the artifact. The date from which Donne's editors have wished to subtract 20 years appears at the end of a poem on folio 86v in the preceding section: "London August 14 / 1629."

Obviously, these details cannot lead to a precise date for the "Holy Sonnets"—whether that term is understood to apply solely to *Corona* or (as seems more likely) to the following 12 poems as well. For one thing, the phrase "Holy Sonnetts . writ-ten . 20 . yeares since." combines a generic section heading with an explanatory an-notation in a manner not otherwise seen among the Donne poems in B32, and there is no reason to suspect that Newcastle's amanuensis would have possessed personal knowledge of when these—or any other—Donne poems were written or that he would have interpolated such information if he had. The explanatory "written . 20 . yeares since." almost certainly results from his copying literally what he saw before him; and that he was momentarily distracted from his task, transcribing mechanically, is suggested by his mishandling of both this heading (which he uncharacteristically fails either to center or to engross)[26] and that for *Corona* (which he confusingly precedes, as though mindlessly copying a catchword from his source document, with the right-aligned phrase "Deigne at my handes"). Indeed, even had Rolleston known when the Holy Sonnets were written and had he inserted "20 yeares since" with the intention of dating them, he surely would not have expected his readers to revert to a date subscribed to one of the Andrews poems in the previous section as a point of refer-ence for interpreting this note. The virtual certainty, of course, is that "written 20 yeares since" is the annotation of the source manuscript's owner or of some prior borrower; and, though there is no way of knowing when it was added, it may well point to an even earlier dating of the Holy Sonnets than that advocated by Gardner or Grierson. The Group-I manuscripts derive from an archetype apparently compiled about 1615, and B32's fellow group members are speculatively dated "c. 1620–33"

---

[26]In accordance with Rolleston's usual procedure, the heading "Holy Sonnetts" is centered on the page and followed by a period; the annotational "written . 20 . yeares since." then follows, extending the string of words to the right margin. This configuration of detail suggests that the actual heading that Rolleston saw and copied from the source was "Holy Sonnetts" and that "written . 20 . yeares since" was a marginal or interlinear note, which he subsequently noticed and appended to what he had already written.

(Beal 250). If B32's parent was contemporaneous with these, the "20 yeares since" note could imply a date closer to 1600 than to 1610 for the composition of the Holy Sonnets.

4) *That ED was written to introduce a set of Holy Sonnets* (Grosart, Chambers, Grierson, Gardner, et al.; see Figure 6). From its appearance in 1633 as "To E. of D. with six holy Sonnets" forward, the subtitle "with six holy sonnets" has invariably appeared in this poem's heading; yet there are both thematic and bibliographical reasons to doubt its authenticity. Indeed, even though he accepts without question that the poem must originally have accompanied some Holy Sonnets, Grierson registers perplexity over "the content" of *ED*, which he finds to be "in the same strain" as the surrounding "poetical epistles" to Donne's youthful correspondents (2: 227); and Flynn asserts this concern more strongly, averring that *ED*'s references to "strange creatures" and "lusty Rhyme" are "inappropriate to the Holy Sonnets" (42).[27] At least with respect to *Corona*, we may add, this judgment seems irreproachable, since *ED*'s characterization of the accompanying "Songs" as "the fruit" of the addressee's inspiring verse explicitly undercuts the hope expressed in *Cor7* 13 that "thy holy Spirit my muse did raise." More powerful than this tonal incongruity, however, is the bibliographical evidence against linking *ED* with the Holy Sonnets; and the nearest argument arises from the variation in form that the heading of the verse letter assumes in manuscript. WN1 and H6, the first of which apparently supplied the text for the poem's entry into print in 1633,[28] record the title "To . the . E . of D. with six holy Sonnetts." (H6 omitting "the"); the earlier NY3 and B11, on the other hand, entitle the poem simply "To L. of D." (B11 omitting "To"). That the heading in B11 is essentially identical to that in NY3 has not previously been recognized— of all prior editors, only Shawcross collates B11, and he misreads its heading as "E: of D."—nor has the fact that these artifacts contain a genealogically distinct version of the poem (reading, e.g., "these Songs are the fruit [for the alternative *their fruits*]" in line 4 and "I chose [for the alternative *choose*] your iudgment" in line 9). More significant than these similarites of text, however, is that in both these manuscripts

---

[27]Though he lacks the material to ground his case bibliographically, Flynn goes so far as to suggest that "perhaps we should regard reference to the Holy Sonnets in . . . [H6 and WN1] as mistaken" (42).

[28]Detail at both the macro and the micro levels points to WN1 as A's source for the poem: A and WN1 uniquely share the sequence *RWSlumb, ILRoll, ILBlest,* and *ED*; and although A's editor would have found the first three of these in sequence in his other Group-II manuscript, his primary reliance on WN1 in this section of the volume is evidenced by his addressing *ILBlest* "To M. I. P."—the "P" (for the normative "L") being available only in WN1 (detailed information on A's handling of these texts will be presented in this *Variorum*'s forthcoming volume on the Verse Letters). Bibliographical analysis indicates a further—and previously unrecognized—fact: that WN1 is the sole authoritative manuscript for the later version of *ED*, H6 having derived its copy of the poem from A. From the opening of its section of "Letters to Seuerall Personages" on page 189 down through *MHPaper* on pages 238–40, H6 contains a run of 34 verse epistles (5 of which are spurious) that exactly matches the contents of its sibling C9. In a noticeably more compact hand, the scribe of H6 (though not that of C9) then continues with *ED* (p. 240), *BedfDead* (pp. 240–41), and the final 24 lines of *Sal* (pp. 241–42), these latter completing a partial copy of the poem entered earlier in the artifact (C9's copy is similarly incomplete). The bottom half of page 242 and all of pages 243 and 244 are blank, and the artifact's collection of "Sonnets and Songs" begins on page 245. Up through *MHPaper*— including the fragmentary copy of *Sal*—these manuscripts embody a distinct Group-III tradition in

ED appears at the head of the same six-item sequence of verse letters that, throughout, embodies an independent textual tradition for these poems (indeed, of two of the poems in the sequence—*RWZeal* and *RWMind*—B11 and NY3 contain the only surviving copies).[29] In NY3 this sequence appears on folios 28v–29v, merged into the section of early verse letters that follows *EpLin* in the artifact (see p. lxix above); in B11, however, it constitutes the sole content of a single sheet (f. 132r–v) that is written front and back in a single hand and pasted into the volume amid sheets of varying sizes containing the works of other poets and penned by other scribes, and this is the form in which it must have come into the repository of papers out of which B11 was assembled (see Beal 247–48).[30] For the present discussion, of course, the importance of this sheet can scarcely be overstated, for its existence enables us to identify as a discrete group the six-poem sequence of which *ED* is the introductory, first member.[31] This recognition, in turn, prompts the conclusion that, *pace* Gardner, in NY3 *ED* is not detached from the "Holy Sonnets it was written to introduce" (lxxx), but remains exactly where Donne placed it and that the subtitle "with six holy sonnets" is the spurious addition of a later copyist.[32]

In light of the bibliographical circumstances here set forth, such an expansion of this title is not difficult to imagine, for it rests on the same inference that underlay

their texts of the verse letters (reading, e.g., "barke [for *booke*] of creatures" in *Sal* 8 and "dare to [for the normative *not*] pardon" in *MHPaper* 12); but H6's copies of *ED* and *BedfDead*, both of whose only other manuscript appearances occur in WN1, closely reproduce the Group-II text of WN1 and A, and the headings of these two poems—where H6 matches A in omitting "the" from WN1's "To the E. of. D. . . ." (giving "To E. of D.") and in expanding WN1's abbreviated "B." to "Bedford" in *BedfDead*—align H6 more closely with A than with WN1. Evidence confirming that H6's kinship is precisely with A appears in the lines appended to complete *Sal*, where a constellation of readings in lines 69, 74, 77, and 78 sets the two apart from all other manuscript sources. That this segment of H6's copy of *Sal* is of a different lineage from the earlier portion, whereas A's text of the poem is genealogically consistent throughout, indicates that A-to-H6 (rather than vice versa) is the direction of flow for these lines; and this fact, supported by the argument from sequence presented above and by the similarities in their texts of *ED* and *BedfDead*, proves beyond reasonable doubt that these additions to H6's original collection of verse letters derive from the printed edition.

[29]In order, the six poems are *ED*, *TWPreg*, *TWHence*, *RWZeal*, *RWMind*, and *CB*.

[30]Milgate (Y:lxv) opines that this sheet constitutes all that remains of what must once have been a fuller "duplicate" of NY3; such discrepancies as those in *TWPreg* 4, where B11 records the normative "oᶠ streetes" (while NY3 gives the trivialized "yᵉ Streets") and *CB* 6, where B11 reads the normative "by this division" (while NY3 omits "this"), however, show that B11 cannot have been copied from NY3 but must instead derive from a common source.

[31]Whether Donne ever actually intended a seventh poem as part of this series is impossible to know with certainty. By the late 1590s, however, his reputation as a poetic master was already well established (see Flynn 39), and it is difficult to take literally his disclaimer of a "maim[ed]" poem censured by some unspecified "they." More likely is that mention of the "seventh" poem is an effect of his exercise of *inventio*, dictated by the exotic fertility-of-the-Nile conceit. A full treatment of this group of poems will be provided in the forthcoming volume on the Verse Letters in this *Variorum*.

[32]Among the verse letters intended for the person designated "L. of D.," Rowland Woodward presumably already possessed copies of those that had originally been addressed to him (*RWZeal* and *RWMind*)—and perhaps of some of the others as well—when he received the organized set of poems that Donne had assembled to send to the recipient. When he eventually undertook to write out his final collection of Donne's poetry, he apparently decided to preserve the group as a unit within it, though whether he constructed the sequence from copies he originally had in hand or merely adopted the text of the set as he had finally received it is impossible to know.

Grosart's repositioning of the poem two-and-a-half centuries later: a reader at least generally acquainted with Donne's poetic canon and attentive to *ED*'s content interpreted "I send as yet / But six, they say the seventh hath still some maime" as a reference to the seven-part *Corona* and incorporated his insight into the heading as a gloss. As is implied above, the surviving evidence suggests that the person responsible for this modification—and for the alteration of "L" to "E" as well—was the scribe of WN1.[33] The scenario here presented does not depend on his having special knowledge of Donne's intentions or even a greater familiarity with the poems than he could have gained in the process of compilation, for he would have confronted the seven-sonnet *Corona*, the first item entered in his manuscript, each time he opened the volume to record new material (that *ED* appears with other verse letters toward the end of the manuscript rather than immediately before *Corona*—where the subheading would have been unnecessary—indicates either that the scribe did not make the connection between the two poems before beginning to write out the manuscript or that he did not have the verse letter in hand when he began that process). Further, corroboration of this scribe's willingness to adjust a title in the direction of greater historical precision appears in his heading for *HWKiss*, where he uniquely expands the normative "To S^r [or M^r] H W" to "To S^r H W many years since." The transmissional history of *ED* described here, of course, nullifies the disputed question of which religious sonnets the verse letter was specifically meant to introduce and renders both the meaning of the abbreviated title and the identity of the person to whom it refers irrelevant to the problem of dating the Holy Sonnets.

5) *That in alluding to the opening of* HSDeath (*"Death be not proud"*), BoulRec (*"Death I recant, and say, unsaid by mee / What ere hath slipt, that might diminish thee"*) *provides a point of historical reference useful in dating the Holy Sonnets* (Grosart, Chambers, Gardner, et al.; see the Commentary). Grosart and Chambers developed this idea no further than to aver that *BoulRec*—occasioned by the death of Cecilia Bulstrode at Twickenham Park on August 4, 1609—must postdate *HSDeath*, and it dropped from sight after Gosse promulgated the view that the presence of *HSShe* in NY3 indicated a post-1617 date for the entire collection. In 1952, however, this notion was resuscitated by Gardner in her aforementioned effort to date the "sonnets on the Last Things" in "the earlier part of 1609" (xliii). Noting that not only *BoulRec*, but also Lady Bedford's "Death bee not proude" constitutes an elegiac response to Mrs. Bulstrode's death, Gardner sees in the opening of Donne's poem a recantation of the "defiance of death" sounded by *HSDeath* at the end of the "Last-Things" sequence, an admission "that death's power was real and terrible"; and she reads the Countess's elegy as a chastening response to Donne's own, one that "rebuk[es] him with words out of his own mouth" for having conceded so much to death's power. And both these references to the sonnet, she asserts, "would be apposite" only if Donne had written it "fairly recently" (xlviii). Clearly, both the intertextual dynamic that Gardner perceives among these three poems and her conviction that the sonnet must be of recent composition are driven by the notion that *HSDeath*

---

[33] Whether this change of "L" to "E" reflects a misreading or the WN1 scribe's knowledge that the person originally labeled "L" had in later life gone on to become "E" is impossible to say.

resoundingly denounces death from a climactic place at the end of a sequence of sonnets on the Last Things, a notion shown above to be untenable. Read in either of its proper bibliographic contexts—and especially as the sixth poem in the Group-I/II sequence—*HSDeath* strikes a less obviously definitive blow than Gardner imagines (indeed, to some it has seemed hollow and ineffectual; see the Commentary). Further, although the opening of *BoulRec* may well have the sonnet at least partly in view, Donne surely also intends reference to the recently composed "An Elegie vpon the death of the Ladie Marckham" (*Mark*), written to commemorate the demise (on May 4, 1609) of another of Lady Bedford's friends at Twickenham Park. In this poem, whose opening conceit strikingly declares that "Man is the world, and Death the Ocean" (l. 1), Donne not only categorically denies death's power ("In her, this sea of Death hath made noe breach" [l. 17]), but even asserts that Lady Markham had "buried both" the "younger" death, which "[v]surpe[s] the bodie," and "th'elder," to which "our Soule . . . subiect is" (ll. 30–34). And even though Lady Bedford begins her elegy with a direct quotation from the sonnet, *Mark*—as well, perhaps, as *BoulRec*—cannot have been absent from her mind as she wrote.[34] In the atmosphere of combined sorrow and excitement that must have accompanied the poetic exchanges swirling about Twickenham Park in the summer of 1609, the point is, the sonnet *HSDeath* can have formed only a constituent—but not the sole or even a necessarily pre-eminent—part. And the notion that its "apposite[ness]" could ever have depended on chronological proximity seems similarly misguided. Indeed, after "For whom the bell tolls" and "No man is an island," it is hard to think of a Donne phrase that is more instantly and permanently unforgettable (see Flynn 44). That Lady Bedford repeats it in her poem proves that it existed first,[35] but says nothing of how long she had known it.

6) *That a change in Donne's view on "precisely what happens to the soul at the moment of death" can be used to date the poems* (Gardner). Deriving from Gardner's understanding of the overall transmissional history of the Holy Sonnets, this argument, too, focuses specifically on the so-called sonnets on the Last Things. As noted above, the linchpin of the argument is Donne's revision of the earlier "Or presently, I know not, see y^t Face" in *HSScene* 7 to the later "But my euer wakeing part shall see that face," a change Gardner locates in the lucubrations in which Donne was involved while composing *Pseudo-Martyr* in the latter part of 1609. Citing *HSRound*'s call to the "numberles infinities/ Of Soules" to "arise/ From Death" (ll. 2–4) and alleging that *HSDeath* lacks any "suggestion that the soul does not sleep like the body" (xlvi), as well as noting the apparent contradiction between the equivocal "Or presently, I know not see y^t Face" version of *HSScene* 7 and line 9's depiction of the soul's im-

---

[34] A number of images and ideas in the Countess's epicede seem to echo Donne's on Lady Markham, among them images of the deceased's "Christall" purity (l. 42, Donne; l. 7, Bedford) and of death as a "sea" (ll. 1 and throughout, Donne; l. 40, Bedford), a concern with Death's power in destroying "the Iust" (l. 33, Donne; l. 4, Bedford), and a declaration that death's "doome" is somehow sealed in the demise of the deceased (l. 35, Donne; l. 28, Bedford).

[35] Though no one would wish to deprive Donne of the phrase, we should also note that no evidence negates the (at least theoretical) possibility that the Countess herself coined "Death bee not proude" and passed it on to Donne, rather than vice versa.

mediate flight "to'heauen her first Seate," Gardner concludes that "when he wrote these sonnets Donne had given no serious thought to the matter [of the soul's fate at death] at all" (xlvi). Certified in *SecAn* in 1612, however, the position Donne arrived at in the writing of *Pseudo-Martyr* is reflected in the revision of *HSScene* 7— "My euer wakeing part shall see that face, / Whose fear already shakes my euery ioynte." According to this reasoning the earlier version of *HSScene*—and, by extension, the remaining five members of the "Last Things" sequence—must therefore have been composed no later than the earlier part of 1609, before Donne made up his mind on this issue. A number of objections to this argument present themselves. The most immediate centers on the conceptual inconsistency in *HSScene* to which Gardner herself points, prompting the suspicion that the revision of line 7 rather reflects Donne's concern for the internal coherence of the poem than for the up-to-dateness of its theology. And this suspicion is considerably strengthened by the fact that he apparently never felt the need to adjust the language of *HSRound* and *HSDeath*—the other two sonnets that allegedly entertain the notion of soul-sleeping. Indeed, although Gardner is surely right that "poetry need not be as precise in its expressions as theology" (xlvi), it is by no means clear that Donne intended these sonnets to engage the theological dispute over mortalism at all: *HSRound*'s call for souls to "Arise / From Death" (ll. 2–3) no more takes a position on the previous location of those souls than does *Relic*'s vision of "soules, at the last busie day, / Meet[ing] at this grave" (ll. 10–11); moreover, while line 13 of *HSRound* ("One short sleepe past, wee wake æternallye") may contain no "suggestion that the soul does not sleep like the body," the poem earlier proclaims that in death "our best men" experience "Rest of their bones, and Soules deliuery" (ll. 7–8). A further weakness in Gardner's argument, obscured by the spurious concept of a 6-poem "sequence on the Last Things," is that in *HSSouls*, the 10th in the early 12-sonnet sequence of which the 6 on the Last Things are a part (see Figure 2), Donne vividly envisions the possibility that his "fathers Soule" may be "alike glorified / As Angels" and from that vantage point may see "That valiantly'I hells wide mouth orestride" (ll. 2–4). Finally, we might note, all three of the epicedes that Donne wrote on noble ladies in the summer of 1609 (*Mark*, *BoulRec*, and *BoulNar*) aver explicitly that the soul of the deceased is "alreadie in heau'n" (*Mark* 51; see also *BoulRec* 46 and *BoulNar* 42). In sum, both in poems demonstrably written before the composition of *Pseudo-Martyr* and in some—including *SecAn*—certainly written after, Donne seems always to have found richer imaginative possibilities in the idea of the ascendant—rather than the dormant—soul; thus the attempt to date the Holy Sonnets by tracking his views on the theological issue of "precisely what happens to the soul at the moment of death" is fruitless.

A final source of potential guidance in this matter of dating concerns the physical relationships that obtain between the Holy Sonnets and other poems in the various artifacts. And *Corona* is a particular focal point in this regard both (a) because—except in those of Bell (I), Anderson (J), and Bennett (T)—it has closely preceded the Holy Sonnets proper in every major edition since 1633 (see Figure 6) and (b) because editors from Grierson onward have understood a reference to *Corona* in *MHMary*'s mention of "hymns to his dear name addressed" and, correspondingly, have tended to accept the 1607 date affixed to the prose letter that accompanies *MHMary* in Walton as the (at least approximate) date of the crown of sonnets.[36] Especially since 1952, when Gardner decredited the notion that all the sonnets necessarily dated from after 1617, the combined effect of these associations has been, willy nilly, to locate the Holy Sonnets chronologically somewhere between 1607 and 1609 as well. Yet the physical contiguity of *Corona* and the Holy Sonnets is not bibliographically inevitable; consequently, neither is this dating. The conventional arrangement of *Corona* and the Holy Sonnets in sequence ultimately derives from C2, the Group-I manuscript used as the setting text for A, and this artifact—like its fellow group members—also presents both sets of poems under the umbrella rubric "HOLY SONNETS" (see the discussion on p. lxxii above). And although the designation "Holy Sonnets" does not carry over into the (later) Group-II manuscripts, the two sets of poems again appear in sequence in these artifacts. In the earlier, Group-III manuscripts, however, *Corona* and the Holy Sonnets are not linked by name (the former is entitled *The Crowne*, while the latter are labeled "Diuine Meditations"), and of the five artifacts in the family only H5 presents the two sets of poems in tandem.[37] Like B46 and HH1 in the prior group, moreover, the lone Group-IV manuscript (NY3) locates its Holy Sonnets before *Corona*, a fact suggesting—though it does not prove certainly—that Woodward received at least the first set of 12 before *Corona* came into his hands. A final indication of the independence of *Corona* from the Holy Sonnets in (at least) their earliest periods of circulation lies in the fact that the former appears in three manuscripts—H7, H8, and Y2—that do not contain the latter at all. In short, as this survey of the data shows, the institutionalization of the *Corona*-Holy Sonnets sequence appears to have originated with the Group-I archetype, and we cannot be sure that it reflects even the order in which the two sets of poems were composed, much less any intention that Donne may have had for their presentation. Their customary connection, therefore, provides no help on the matter of dating.

In conclusion, after examining the evidence anew and sifting the arguments of prior editors, we are left with little upon which to base a theory about when the majority of the Holy Sonnets were written. Generally supported by B32's annotation "written . 20 . yeares since," Lady Bedford's quotation of "Death bee not proude" (if, indeed, it is a quotation and not the original) suggests that the earlier, Group-III sequence antedates the summer of 1609, but whether by several years or only by a

---

[36]After surveying Grierson's treatment of the matter, David Novarr (1957) convincingly demonstrates that the date Walton gives for the prose letter "is worthless" (264). Alleging affinities of style and motive between *Corona* and *Annun* (written in 1608), he resurrects the argument that Grierson based on B32's "20 . yeares since" to date *Corona* "shortly before the *Holy Sonnets*, that is, late in 1608 or early in 1609" (265). In her 1978 revision, Gardner generally accepts Novarr's reasoning, but thinks 1608 "more probable" than 1609 as *Corona*'s date of composition (152).

[37]H5 opens with three Donne sermons, after which follow *Corona*, the 12 "Devine Meditations," and a series of 7 additional religious poems; B46 gives the sequence "Diuine Meditations," *Goodf*, the noncanonical "On the Blessed Virgin, Marie," *Corona*, other religious poems; H6 and C9 interpolate *Father* (usually dated 1623) between "*The Crowne*" and the "Diuine Meditations"; and HH1 evinces the series *Lam*, "Devine Meditations," *Annun*, the spurious "On the Blessed Virgin Mary," *Lit*, *Goodf*, *Corona*, *Christ*.

few weeks is impossible to tell. And while the history of their transmission shows that Donne worked on the main body of Holy Sonnets in at least three major stages (as reflected in the Group-III, Group-IV, and Group-I/II manuscripts), we currently have no way of knowing whether the development of his sonnet cycle was the project of days, of weeks, of months, or even—as his composition of the three late poems unique to NY3 might suggest—of years. Until further bibliographical or historical evidence comes to light, these will necessarily remain matters of critical speculation.

Copy-texts Used in this Edition

In accordance with our demonstration above that Donne not only revised the texts of individual sonnets, but also reconfigured his original sequence by replacing four of its members with new poems and reorganizing the whole, we below present separate texts of each of these authorially sanctioned groups. Because its text represents an important, transitional stage in the evolution of the original, Group-III poems; because it contains the earliest versions of the four replacement sonnets; and because it contains the sole manuscript copies of three of the Holy Sonnets, we also print the NY3 (Group-IV) sequence, placing it in its proper evolutionary position between the earlier Group-III text and the later one found in Groups I and II. Further, because it embodies the arrangement in which readers have encountered these poems during almost all of their history as print artifacts, we also present in an appendix the editorially confected sequence of 1635. Printed without emendation, this latter is rendered as a typographical facsimile. The texts in the other sequences, however, have been regularized in order to bring the manuscript renditions into conformity with the conventions of print; and we have also (a) corrected obvious scribal blunders (such as the H5 copyist's inscription of "hat" [for "hath"] in HSScene 3); (b) substituted, in both the original and the revised sequences, the typical reading in places where the chosen exemplar deviates from the group norm; and (c) modified punctuation as minimally necessary to ensure the readability of the text preserved in each of the manuscript traditions. As is stressed above, this procedure differs fundamentally from the attempt to confect a single "true" text out of the welter of disparate, equally authoritative materials; and this eschewal of eclecticism entails the retention of a number of readings in (especially) the two authorial manuscript sequences that may well be scribal in origin. All such instances are discussed in the following paragraphs and in the textual introductions to the individual sonnets. An explanation of our handling of indentation in all three sequences appears below in the concluding paragraph of this section.

The manuscript chosen as copy-text for the original sequence is H5, one of three extant artifacts shown in Figure 3 as direct descendants of the group prototype β^1 (for a comparative view of the genealogical relationship of these manuscripts, see the more detailed stemma for *ElBrac* in volume 2, page 45, of this *Variorum*). Containing three of Donne's sermons, two "characters," his *Paradoxes and Problems*, and 119 poems, all written in a single hand, this manuscript belonged in the seventeenth century to Dr. William Balam (1651–1726) of Ely, Cambridgeshire (Beal 251–52). As noted above, such erroneous family readings as "no more [for *some clayme*] as debt" in *HSMin* 13 suggest that β^1 must have descended from Donne's original

(LOH[1]) through a series of incrementally deteriorating manuscripts, since it seems unlikely—though it is not impossible—that a scribe copying from the author's own papers would have introduced such a radical change in a single act of mistranscription. Similarly, the quantity of substantive error in B46, H5, and (especially) HH1 hints that none of these stems immediately from β[1]. Whatever the case, H5 is marginally the least corrupt of the three, though its punctuation has required modification in nearly a dozen instances (see the list of emendations given below), and its substantives in a further seven. Among these substantive anomalies, one apparently represents a conscious attempt to eliminate ambiguity (rewriting the normative Group-III "would presse me to hell" in *HSScene* 12 as "would presse me, Hell"), and the remainder are errors of inadvertency or misreading. These include "let" (for the normative "but") in *HSPart* 11, "hath" (for the Group-III lection "had") in *HSBlack* 3, the above-cited "hat" (for the correct "hath") in *HSScene* 3, "I might" (for the normative "so I might") in *HSLittle* 7, "creepe" (for the normative "weepe") in *HSSouls* 9, and "stolne" (for Group-III lection "stole") in *HSWilt* 12. And in all these instances we have restored the normative or group reading.

A full bibliographical description of NY3, whose 19 Holy Sonnets immediately follow the original sequence in the presentation below, is given on pages lxvii–lxxi above and need not be repeated here. In keeping with the general quality of the texts in this manuscript, Woodward's copies of the Holy Sonnets are remarkably clean. For 9 of the poems we have imposed no emendation beyond the regularization of manuscript features, and to produce a readable text of the remaining 10 has generally required only minor additions to or adjustments of punctuation (see the list of emendations in the apparatus below). Our three substantive emendations appear in *HSBlack* 3, where Woodward inadvertently omits "like" from the intended simile, in *HSScene* 12, where Woodward mistakenly writes "tell" for the correct "hell," and in *HSShe* 10, where—not entirely without misgivings—we adopt Bennett's repunctuation of "Dost woe my Soule for hers; offring all thine" to "Dost woe my Soule, for hers offring all thine," believing that the sense of the poem requires this change. In *HSDue* 13, finally, we have respelled Woodward's "chose" as "choose," believing the latter to represent his intention. As others—including Gardner (see U:77)—have noted, Woodward's use of majuscule letters seems virtually random (indeed, it is frequently impossible to distinguish between the capital and lower-case forms of his *l*s, *m*s, *n*s, *o*s, *s*s, and *w*s with any confidence); nevertheless, we have attempted to preserve these forms as they appear in the manuscript, listing all instances of regularization in the textual apparatus.

The copy-text for the revised sequence is DT1, generally the most reliable of the Group-II manuscripts and one that has supplied copy-texts for poems in previous volumes of this edition. Transcribed *circa* 1623–25 (Beal 251), this artifact contains 143 Donne poems, all except the two on folio 104r–v (each of which is in a different hand) entered in a single hand; and—as explained above—its copies embody Donne's final intentions for the Holy Sonnets, including not only the reconstitution and rearrangement of the sequence, but also the revisions introduced at the Group-I stage (discussed on pp. lxx–lxxi above) and Group II's unique "But my euer wakeing part shall" (for the earlier "Or presently, I know not") in *HSScene* 7. As

Figure 3 shows, however, DT1 is at least two steps removed from Donne's last holograph (LOH³); and this distance—as well, perhaps, as the remoteness of these poems from the first heat of the author's original inspiration—has resulted in a substantial amount of textual deterioration. As suggested above, LOH³ readings that are quite probably erroneous include "Sun" (for the earlier "Sonne") in *HSDue* 5, "dares" (for the earlier "dare") in *HSMin* 9, and "Simpler" (for the earlier "Simple") in *HSWhy* 4; the anomalous lections "his" (for "this") in *HSBlack* 13, "death" (for "dearth") in *HSRound* 6, and "hath" (for "haue") in *HSDeath* 1 are traceable to the β⁵ scribe. All these we have left unchanged, as being characteristic of the transmissional strain within which DT1 exists. This desire to render DT1 congruous with the other members of its family in fact accounts for our one verbal emendation, which occurs in *HSMin* 2 and entails changing DT1's anomalous "you" to the "thou" found in all other artifacts (except DT1's offspring H4). Finally, in order to prevent misreading, we have altered the variant spelling "breath" to "breathe" in *HSBatter* 2 and "by" to "buy" in *HSWilt* 10, and—as detailed in the list of emendations below—we have adjusted the punctuation in numerous instances throughout the sequence.

The handling of indentation in the printing of these poems requires special comment, particularly that followed for the H5 and the NY3 groups. As is evident in the presentation below, the first 8 poems in the H5 sequence exhibit one pattern (indenting lines 2, 3, 6, 7, 10, and 12), while sonnets 9 through 12 exhibit another (indenting lines 2, 3, 6, 7, 10, 11, 13, and 14). Since sonnet 9 (*HSMin*) begins at the top of a sheet (f. 84) in the artifact, we might normally imagine that the copyist altered the pattern inadvertently as he moved to the top of a new page and then decided to retain the innovation rather than reverting to the original plan for sonnets 10 through 12. Such an understanding would then dictate regularizing indentation throughout the cycle as the poems were set into type. What marks this shift as Donne's change rather than a scribe's mistake, however, is that NY3—whose texts, as we have argued above, evince several instances of authorial revision—exhibits indentation for these 12 sonnets identical to that of H5, including the shift in pattern at *HSMin*.[38] In the belief that users will be interested in this authorial feature, we have therefore retained the indentation of H5 and NY3 in the presentation below. Since the DT1 scribe is inconsistent—and frequently indistinct—in his handling of indentation, however, and since his treatment of the matter carries no apparent authority, in the printing below we have imposed his most frequently employed pattern (the indentation of all even-numbered lines) throughout the sequence.

THE CRITICAL TRADITION

In The General Textual Introduction, we comment on a number of issues that have been germane to the critical tradition as well, particularly concerns about dating the Holy Sonnets and efforts to determine a preferred (authorial?) sequence for the poems. In the commentary that follows, we represent these concerns through

---

[38]That the Holy Sonnets in Group I generally replicate the indentation of their counterparts in the earlier Groups III and IV constitutes further proof that this indentation is Donne's.

the critical observations of the many scholars who have dealt with such issues (especially in the section on Dating and Order), and we have attempted, as well, to group other items of commentary in logical and instructive ways.

The comparatively limited circulation of the Holy Sonnets in the seventeenth century suggests that they generated less interest than some other of Donne's poems, such as the Elegies and Songs and Sonets, but from the beginning Donne was recognized as a religious poet, as well as a secular one. Walton (1640) claims that, though in his "penitentiall" years Donne regretted the poetry he wrote in his youth, his "many divine Sonnets" confirm his late allegiance to "heavenly Poetry," a view that appears to have been largely accepted until the twentieth century. And even as scholars challenged his simplistic emphasis on an earlier secular Jack Donne and a later sacred Dean, Walton's awareness of the tension between the secular and the sacred is mirrored in many commentaries on the Holy Sonnets, as the following pages attest.

General Commentary on the Holy Sonnets is wide-ranging, with earlier critics, especially, finding moments of brilliance in the midst of disturbing imagery or irregular rhythmic patterns. As one moves into and through the twentieth century, however, critics are more apt to praise Donne's effort, Helen Gardner (1952), for example, observing that, except for the Hymns, the Holy Sonnets are Donne's "greatest divine poems." Beyond such assertions (or instances of qualified praise), much of the more recent commentary on the Holy Sonnets is aimed at assessing their place within the whole of Donne's achievement, or at speculating on the relationship between the Holy Sonnets and Donne's life, or at identifying images, themes, and perspectives that can be found in one or more of the poems.

As commentary of the late nineteenth and twentieth century became more extensive and more specific, greater attention was given to the role and perspective of the persona and, for those who identify Donne with his speaker, the poet himself. Many critics, identified especially in the section The Poet/Persona, have focused in one way or another on the speaker's inner struggles—what Grierson (1929), for example, describes as "the sense of conflict of soul, of faith and hope snatched and held desperately, of harmony evoked from harsh conditions," what Potter (1934) calls the "painfully fierce self-searchings" in the poems, and what Rollin (1986) identifies as a kind of "spiritual malaise meant to be exemplary to disease-prone readers." Each of these readers, as well as many others, notes especially the instances of un-ease in the Holy Sonnets, the tension between the speaker's expectation and his sense of personal fulfillment or between his aspiration to be at one with God and his struggle to reach such a state. In different ways and through different critical lenses, scholars have seen in the Holy Sonnets evidence of the speaker's loneliness, his near-obsession with death, or, for some, his struggle to reconcile his Catholic upbringing and his conversion to Protestantism.

Two of the scholars who most strongly influenced views of Donne's religious poetry throughout the latter half of the twentieth century are Helen Gardner, especially through her edition of the Divine Poems (1952, 1978) and Louis Martz, especially in his seminal *The Poetry of Meditation*. As the previous discussion of the texts and textual history of the Holy Sonnets confirms, Gardner's views of the dating, order, and textual histories of the Holy Sonnets have been confirmed, challenged, and denied, but they remain to the present day views that cannot be ignored. Moreover, both she and Martz, arriving at similar conclusions independently, provide evidence of the influence of the meditative tradition on the themes and structure of the Holy Sonnets. Indeed, much of the commentary grouped in this volume under Genre and Traditions pertains to one of two concerns: the influence of the tradition of meditation or the position of the Holy Sonnets within the sonnet tradition. Within the latter discussions, especially, there are a number of observations not only on the relationship between the Holy Sonnets and the sonnet tradition that precedes them, but also on the relationship between Donne's poems and those of sonneteers who follow him, most especially Gerard Manley Hopkins.

As with much of Donne's verse, matters of language, style, and prosody are of interest to commentators on the Holy Sonnets, with earlier observations by commentators who are typically unimpressed by Donne's manner increasingly giving way to more positive assessments of his distinctive but not ineffective style or to more specific studies of such elements as paradox (Faerber 1950, Warnke 1972), repetition (Martinet 1982, Austin 1992), or mixed rhetorical strategies (Frontain 1992).

Beginning with Walton's distinction (1640) between Donne's youthful verse and his later "heavenly Poetry" (and, indeed, with Donne's own comments about his two personas as Jack and the Dean), critics have written much about the intermingling of secular and sacred (or as we term them here, the Sacred and Profane) in Donne. The commentary on this topic is itself quite diverse, with some readers identifying important connections between the secular and the sacred (Fausset 1924, Hardy 1942, Cox 1956b, Parfitt 1989, Gill 1990) and others noting within the continuities important differences between the two modes (Hopkins 1962, Marotti 1986, Pallotti 1993). A significant concern in much of this commentary is with the varied but related roles of the speaker as suitor of both women and God.

In addition to the focus on the sacred and the profane that has accompanied interest in the Holy Sonnets almost from the beginning, other prominent themes have been identified, either in the poems as a whole or in individual sonnets. Not surprisingly, the commentary in the section on Themes complements much of what is found in the commentary on The Poet/Persona. That is, much as some critics have seen the speaker as lonely, or self-concerned, or struggling in his relationship with God, so commentators have identified such evident themes as death, sin, fear, violence, or insecurity. Whether, as Zunder (1982) and others speculate, the Holy Sonnets were written during a period of "spiritual crisis" for Donne, the poems, in the eyes of many, reveal a speaker who struggles with continuing uncertainty and doubt about his own salvation and his relationship to God. Others, notably Martz (1954, 1985), see the poems moving toward some affirmation, what Martz describes (1985) as a "mode of rectified devotion."

Finally, the Holy Sonnets have provoked comparisons with a number of other works and writers, and we thus highlight those connections in the section on The Holy Sonnets and Other Works. Among the writings to which the Holy Sonnets have been related are the Bible (especially the Psalms) and works of Milton, Michelangelo, Ronsard, St. John of the Cross, Shakespeare, Emily Dickinson, T. S. Eliot,

Benjamin Britten, and Gwendolyn Brooks, among others. Many readers have noted and commented on the association of the Holy Sonnets with the poems of two other writers: Donne's contemporary George Herbert and the nineteenth-century poet and priest Gerard Manley Hopkins.

Our arrangement of the commentary on the Holy Sonnets as a whole is repeated in the commentary on individual poems, thus enabling users of this volume both to appreciate the coherence within individual sections of commentary and also to connect sections of commentary that are widely separated in the volume (e.g., the several sections devoted to The Poet/Persona or Language and Style or Sacred and Profane). As has been our aim with previous volumes in this series, we hope that our presentation of the rich history of critical commentary on Donne's poems will provide readers with an understanding of what has been thought and said while stimulating further inquiries and insights.

§

This, the fourth published volume of *The Variorum Edition of the Poetry of John Donne*, results from the collaborative labors of the many scholars who are named on the title page, in the Acknowledgments, and elsewhere in these pages. Gary A. Stringer was the original Volume Commentary Editor and in that capacity was principally responsible for compiling the initial bibliography of relevant items of commentary, and Stringer annotated a considerable number of pre-1900 books and articles as well. Eventually, however, when the growing demands of his work as General Editor and Senior Textual Editor forced Stringer to relinquish the position of Volume Commentary Editor, Paul A. Parrish agreed to assume that role, retaining as well his broader responsibilities as Chief Editor of the Commentary for the entire *Variorum* project. In addition to overseeing the integration and final editing of all the commentary in the volume and preparing the list of Works Cited (and the three indexes that follow it), Parrish took on specific responsibility for all commentary published before 1900. Parrish also wrote the section headed The Critical Tradition in this introduction to the volume. The task of reading and annotating the commentary of the twentieth century was carried out by three Contributing Editors, who divided their task chronologically as follows: Robert T. Fallon covered the period 1900–59; P. G. Stanwood, the period 1960–78; and Helen B. Brooks, the period 1979–95, 1995 being the last year for which commentary is reported in the volume.

Like the commentary, the texts and apparatuses in this volume represent the collective, incremental efforts of a number of scholars. The first textual work on the Holy Sonnets to take place within the precincts of this *Variorum* project is presented in Theodore J. Sherman's 1993 University of Southern Mississippi doctoral dissertation "A Critical Edition of the Holy Sonnets of John Donne," a work for which the edition's senior textual editors served, respectively, as director (Gary A. Stringer) and readers (Ted-Larry Pebworth and Ernest W. Sullivan, II). While the present volume expands the scope of this work considerably beyond that contemplated by Sherman and in many instances reaches different conclusions, we wish to acknowledge here the importance of his pioneering foray into the field and its influence upon the present volume. The subsequent history of our work on these texts has witnessed the continued participation of Pebworth and Sullivan as occasional proofreaders and vettors; and Dennis Flynn, Dayton Haskin, Michael Salda, Audell Shelburne, Theodore Sherman, and Richard Todd have contributed significantly in various ways. As the principal textual editor for the volume, Gary Stringer is ultimately responsible for the presentation and analysis of the texts and apparatuses, as well as for the General Textual Introduction and the textual introductions to the individual Holy Sonnets. In his role as General Editor, Stringer also had charge of the organization and final assembly of the volume, as well as of overseeing the labors of the typesetter, J. Syd Conner.

PAUL A. PARRISH

Chief Editor of the Commentary
and
Volume Commentary Editor

GARY A. STRINGER

General Editor
and
Senior Textual Editor

TEXTS
and
APPARATUSES

THE
HOLY SONNETS

Devine Meditations.

1.

Thou hast made me, and shall thy worke decay?
    Repaire me nowe, for nowe mine end doth hast,
    I runne to Death, and Death meets me as fast,
And all my pleasures are like yesterday.
I dare not moue my dimme eyes any way,   5
    Despaire behind, and Death before doth cast
    Such terrour, and my feebled flesh doth wast
By sinne in it, which it t'wards Hell doth weigh;
Only thou art aboue, and when t'wards thee
    By thy leaue I can looke, I rise againe: 10
But our old suttle foe soe tempteth me,
    That not one houre I can my selfe sustaine.
Thy grace may winge me to prevent his Art,
And thou, like Adamant, drawe mine yron hart.

2.

As due by many titles I resigne
    My selfe to thee (o god): first was I made
    By thee, and for thee, and when I was decay'de,
Thy bloud bought that, the which before was thine:
I am thy sonne, made with thy selfe to shine,   5
    Thy servant, whose paines thou hast still repayd,
    Thy sheepe, thy Image, and (till I betray'd
My selfe) a Temple of thy spirit Devine.
Why doth the Deuill thus vsurpe in me?
    Why doth he steale, nay ravish thats thy right?   10
Except thou rise, and for thine owne worke fight
    Oh, I shall soone despaire, when I shall see
That thou lou'st Mankind well, yet wilt not chuse me,
And Satan hates me, yet is loth to loose me.

3.

O might those sighes and teares returne againe
    Into my brest and eyes, which I haue spent
    That I might in this holy discontent
Mourne with some fruite, as I haue mourn'd in vaine.
In my Idolatry, what shoures of rayne   5
    Mine eyes did wast? what greifs my hart did rent?
    That sufferance was my sinne, nowe I repent,
Because I did suffer, I must suffer paine.
Th' Hydroptique Drunkard, and night-scoutinge Theife
    The itchy Letcher, and selfe-tickling proud   10
Haue the remembrance of past ioyes for releife
    Of comminge ills: to poore me is allow'd
Noe ease, for longe, yet vehement greife hath byn
Th' effect and cause, the punishment and sinne.

4.

Father, part of his double Interest
    Vnto thy kingdome, thy sonne giues to me;
    His ioynture in the knotty Trinity
He keepes, and giues me his Death's conquest.
This lambe, whose Death with life the world hath blest   5
    Was from the worlds beginninge slayne, and he
    Hath made two Wills; he with the Legacy
Of his and thy kingdome doth thy sonnes invest.
Yet such are thy lawes, that men argue yet
    Whether a man those statuts can fullfill.   10
None doth: but thy all-healing grace and spirit
    Reviue and quicken, What lawe and letter kill.
Thy lawes abridgement, and thy last command
Is all but Loue, Oh let thy last will stand!

5.

O my blacke Soule, nowe thou art summoned
    By sicknes, Deaths herauld and Champion,
    Thou like a pilgrimme which abroad had done
Treason, and durst not turne from whence hee's fled;
Or as a Theife, which till Deaths doome be read   5
    Wisheth himselfe deliuered from prison,
    But damn'd, and hal'd to Execution
Wisheth that still he might b' imprisoned.
Yet grace yf thou repent, thou canst not lacke,
    But who shall giue thee that grace to beginne?   10
O make thy selfe with holy mourninge blacke,
    And red with blushinge as thou art with sinne;
Or wash thee in Christs bloud, which hath this might,
That being red, it dyes red soules to white.

6.

This is my Playes last scene, here heav'ns appoint
    My Pilgrimages last mile, and my race
    Idly, yet quickly runne, hath this last pace,
My spans last inch, my minuts latest point,
And gluttonous Death will instantly vnioynt   5
    My body and my soule, and I shall sleepe a space,
    Or presently (I knowe not) see that face,
Whose feare already shakes me euery ioynt.
Then, as my soule to Heav'n (her first seate) taks flight,
    And earth-borne body in the Earth shall dwell   10
Soe fall my sinnes, that all may haue their right
    To where they are bred, and would presse me, to Hell.
Impute me righteous, thus purg'd of euill,
For thus I leaue the World, the flesh, and Deuill.

7.

I am a litle World, made cunningly
    Of Elements, and an Angelicke spright
    But blacke sinne hath betrayd to endles night
My worlds both parts, and (oh) both parts must dye.
You, which beyond that heav'n which was most high   5
    Haue found newe spheares, and of newe lands can write
    Powre newe seas in mine eyes, that so I might
Drowne my world with my weepinge earnestly,
Or washe it, yf it must be drown'd no more.
    But oh! it must be burnt: alas the fire   10
Of lust and envy haue burnt it heeretofore
    And made it fowler: let theire flames retire
And burne me, o Lord, with a firy zeale
Of thee and thy house, which doth, in eatinge, heale.

8.

At the round Earths Imagin'd corners blowe
    Your Trumpetts, Angells, and arise, arise
    From Death you numberles Infinities
Of soules, and to your scattered bodies goe,
All whome the floud did, and fire shall o're-throwe   5
    All whome Warre, death, age, agues, Tyrannies,
    Despaire, Lawe, Chaunce, hath slayne, and you whose eyes
Shall behold God, and neuer tast Deaths woe:
But let them sleepe, Lord, and me mourne a space
    For yf aboue all these my sinnes abound,   10
'Tis late to aske abundance of thy grace,
    When we are there; here on this lowly ground
Teach me howe to repent, for thats as good
As yf th' hadst seal'd my pardon with thy bloud.

9.

Yf poysonous Mineralls, or yf the Tree
    Whose fruite threwe death on (els immortall) vs,
    Yf letcherous Goates, yf serpents envious
Cannot be damn'd, alas, why should I be?
Why should intent and reason borne in me,   5
    Make sinnes (els equall) in me more haynous?
    And mercy being easy and glorious
To God, in his sterne wrath why threatens he?
But who am I, that dare dispute with thee?
    O God, o of thy only worthy bloud   10
    And my teares make a heav'nly Lethean floud
And drowne in it my sinnes blacke memory
    That thou remember them no more as debt,
    I thinke it mercy, yf thou wilt forgett.

10.

Yf faithfull Soules be alike glorify'd
    As angells, then my Fathers soule doth see
    And adds this ev'n to full felicity,
That valiantly I Hells wide mouth ore-stride.
But yf our mindes to these soules be descry'd   5
    By circumstances, and by signes that be
    Apparent in vs, not Immediately,
Howe shall my mindes white truth to them be try'de?
They see Idolatrous Lovers weepe and mourne
    And vile blasphemous coniurers to call   10
    On Iesus name; and Pharisaicall
Dissemblers faine devotion: then turne
    (O pensiue soule) to God, for he knowes best
    Thy greife, for he put it into my brest.

11.

Death be not proud, though some haue called thee
    Mighty and dreadfull, for thou art not soe.
    For those whome thou thinkst thou dost ouerthrowe
Dye not (poore Death) nor yet canst thou kill me.
From rest and sleepe, which but thy pictures be,   5
    Much pleasure, then from thee much more must flowe
    And soonest our best men with thee doe goe,
Rest of their bodyes, and Soules deliuery.
Th' art slaue to fate, Chaunce, Kings, and desperate men,
    And dost with poyson, warre, and sicknes dwell   10
    And poppy or charmes can make vs sleepe as well
And easyer then thy stroke: why swell'st thou then?
    One short sleepe past, we liue eternally
    And Death shalbe no more: Death thou shalt dye.

12.

Wilt thou loue God, as he thee? then digest
    My soule, this wholesome meditation,
    Howe God the spirit by Angells waited on
In heav'n, doth make his Temple in thy brest.
The Father having begotten a sonne most blest,   5
    And still begettinge, (for he nere begunne)
    Hath daign'd to chuse thee by adoption
Coheire to his glory and Sabbaoths endles rest:
And as a rob'd man, which by search doth find
    His stolne steede sold, must loose, or buy't againe,   10
    The sonne of glory came downe, and was slayne,
Vs whome h' had made, and Satan stole, t' vnbind.
    'Twas much that man was made like God before,
    But that God should be made like man, much more.

Holy Sonnets.

1.

Thou hast made me, and shall thy worke decay?
    Repaire me now, for now myne end do'th hast.
    I run to death, and death meets me as fast,
And all my pleasures are like yesterday.
I dare not moue my dimme eyes any way,   5
    Dispaire behind, and death before doth cast
    Such terror, and my febled fleshe doth wast
By Sin in it, which towards hell doth weigh.
Only thou art above; and when towards thee
    By thy leaue I can looke, I rise agayne.   10
But our old subtile foe so tempteth mee
    That not one hower I can my selfe sustayne.
Thy grace may winge me, to preuent his art
And thou like Adamant, draw myne Iron hart.

2.

As due by many titles I resigne
    My selfe to thee (O God): first I was made
    By thee, and for thee, and when I was decayde
Thy blood bought that, the which before was thyne.
I ame thy Sonne made with thy selfe to shyne,   5
    Thy Servant, whose paines thou hast still repayde,
    Thy Sheepe, thyne Image; and (till I betrayde
My selfe) a Temple of thy Spirit divine.
Why dothe the deuill then vsurpe in mee?
    Why doth he steale, nay ravish that's thy right?   10
Except thou rise, and for thyne owne worke fight
    O I shall soone dispayre, when I do see
That thou lov'st Mankind well, yet wilt not choose mee,
And Satan hates me yet is loth to loose mee.

3.

O might those sighes and teares returne againe
    Into my brest and eyes, which I have spent;
    That I might in this holy discontent
Mourne with some fruite, as I haue mournd in vaine.
In my Idolatry what showrs of raine   5
    Myne eyes did wast? what griefes my hart did rent?
    That sufferance was my Sin, now I repent;
Because I did suffer, I must suffer paine.
Th'Hydroptique dronkerd, and night-scowting theefe,
    The itchy Leacher, and selfe-tickling proud,   10
Haue the remembrance of past ioyes for reliefe
    Of comming ills; to poore me is allowd
No ease; for long yet vehement griefe hath beene
The effect and cause; the punishment and Sinne.

4.

Father, part of his double interest
    Vnto thy kingdome thy Sonne giues to mee;
    His ioynture in the knotty trinitee
He keepes, and giues me his deaths Conquest.
This Lambe whose death with life the world hath blest   5
    Was from the Worlds beginning slayne, and hee
    Hath made two Wills, which with the Legacee
Of his, and thy kingdome, doth thy Sonnes invest.
Yet such are thy Laws, that Men argue yett
    Whether a man those Statutes can fullfill.   10
None doth; but all-healing Grace and Spiritt
    Revive and quicken what Law and Letter kill.
Thy Lawes abridgment, and thy last Command
Is all but Love; Oh let that last Will stand.

5.

Oh my black Soule, now thou art summoned
    By Sicknes, Deaths Harold and Champion;
    Thou'art like a Pilgrim, which abroad had don
Treason, and darst not turne to whence he'is fled,
Or as a thiefe which till death's doome be red   5
    Wisheth himselfe deliuered from prison
    But damn'd and haled to execution
Wisheth that still he might be'imprisoned.
Yet grace, if thou repent thou canst not lacke.
    But who shall giue thee that grace to begin?   10
Oh make thy selfe with holy mourning blacke,
    And red with blushinge as thou art with Sin.
Or washe thee in Christs blood, which hath this might
That beeing red, it dyes red Soules to whight.

6.

This is my Playes last Scene, here heauens appoint
    My Pilgrimages last Mile, and my race,
    Idely, yet quickly run, hath this last pace
My Spanns last inche; my Minutes last pointe.
And gluttonous death will instantly vnioynt   5
    My body and Soule, and I shall sleepe a space,
    Or presently, I know not, see that face
Whose feare allredy shakes my euery ioynt.
Then as my Soule, to' heauen her first Seate takes flight,
    And earthborne body in the earth shall dwell,   10
So fall my Sins, that all may haue their right,
    To where they'are bred, and would presse me, to hell;
Impute me righteous thus purg'd of euill,
For thus I leaue the world, the fleshe, and deuill.

7.

I ame a litle World, made cunningly
    Of Elements and an Angelique Spright,
    But blacke Sin hath betrayd to endles night
My Worlds both parts, and Oh both parts must dy.
You, which beyond that heauen, which was most high   5
    Haue found new Sphears, and of new Lands can wright
    Powre new Seas in myne eyes, that so I might
Drowne my World, with my weeping ernestly.
Or washe it: if it must be drown'd no more:
    But Oh it must be burn'd; alas the fyer   10
Of Lust and Envy haue burnt it hertofore
    And made it fouler; Let those flames retyre,
And burne me O God with a fiery Zeale
Of thee,' and thy house, which doth in eating heale.

8.

At the round Earths imagind corners blow
    Your trumpets Angels, and Arise Arise
    From Death you numberles infinities
Of Soules and to your scattered bodyes go,
All whom the Flood did and fyre shall overthrow   5
    All whom Warr, dearth, age, agues, tyrannyes,
    Dispayre, Law, Chance, hath slayne, and you whose eyes
Shall behold God, and never tast deaths wo.
But let them sleepe, Lord, and me mourne a space,
    For if above all these my Sins abound   10
Tis late to aske abundance of thy grace
    When we are there: Here on this lowly ground
Teach me how to repent, for that's as good
As if thou hadst Seald my pardon with thy blood.

9.

If poysonous Minerals, and if that tree
    Whose fruite threw death on els immortall vs,
    If Lecherous gotes, if Serpents envious
Cannot be damn'd, alas why should I bee?
Why should intent, or reason, borne in me   5
    Make Sins els equall, in me more hainous?
    And mercy beeing easy, and glorious
To God, in his sterne wrath why threatens hee?
But who am I that dare dispute with thee
    O God? O of thyne only worthy blood   10
    And my teares make a heauenly Lethean flood
And drowne in it, my Sins blacke memoree.
    That thou remember them, Some clayme as dett,
    I thinke it Mercy if thou wilt forgett.

10.

If faythfull Soules be alike glorified
    As Angels, then my fathers Soule doth see
    And ads this even to full felicitee
That valiantly'I hells wide mouth orestride.
But if our Minds to these Soules be discride   5
    By Circumstances, and by Signes that bee
    Apparant in vs, not immediatlee
How shall my Minds whight truthe to them be tride?
They see Idolatrous Lovers weepe and mourne
    And vile blasphemous Coniurers to call   10
    On Iesus Name, and pharasaicall
Dissemblers feigne devotion: then turne
    O pensive Soule to God; for he knowes best
    Thy true griefe, for he put it in my brest.

11.

Death be not proud, though some haue called thee
    Mighty and dreadfull, for thou art not so.
    For those whom thou thinkst thou dost overthrow
Dy not poore death, nor yet canst thou kill mee.
From rest and sleepe which but thy pictures bee,   5
    Much pleasure; then from thee much more must flow,
    And soonest our best men with thee do go,
Rest of ther bones, and Soules deliueree.
Thou art Slaue to Fate, Chance, kings, and desperat men,
    And dost with poyson, warr, and sicknesse dwell;   10
    And Poppy or Charmes can make vs sleepe as well,
And easier then thy stroke, why swellst thou then?
    One short sleepe past, we live eternally
    And Death shalbe no more, Death thou shallt dy.

12.

Wilt thou love God, as he, thee? then digest
    My Soule, this holsome meditation:
    How God the Spirit by Angels wayted on
In heauen; doth make his temple in thy brest.
The father hauing begott a Sonne most blest,   5
    And still begetting, (for he nere begonne)
    Hath daignd to chuse thee by adoption
Coheir to his glory'and Saboths endles rest.
And as a robd Man, which by search doth find
    His stolne stuffe sold, must loose or buy'it againe;   10
    The Sonne of glory came downe and was slaine
Vs, whom he'had made, and Satan stole, to'vnbind.
    'Twas much that Man was made like God before,
    But that God should be made like Man much more.

13.

Spitt in my face ye Iewes, and pierce my side,
  Buffet, and scoffe, scourge, and crucify mee:
For I haue sin'd, and sin'd: and humbly hee
  Which could do no iniquity hath dyde.
But by my death cannot be satisfy'de   5
  My sins; which passe the Iewes impietee:
They killd once an inglorious, but I
  Crucify him dayly, beeing now glorifyde.
Oh let me then his strange love still admyre:
  Kings pardon, but he bore our punishment.   10
And Iacob came clothd in vile harsh attyre
  But to supplant and with gainfull intent:
God cloth'd himselfe in vile Mans flesh, that so
He might be weake inough to suffer wo.

14.

Why ame I by all Creatures wayted on?
  Why do the prodigall Elements supply
  Life and foode to mee, beeing more pure then I,
Simple, and farther from corruption?
Why brookst thou ignorant horse subiection?   5
  Why dost thou Bull and bore, so selily
  Dissemble weaknes, and by one Mans stroke dy
Whose whole kind you might swallow and feed vpon?
Alas I'ame weaker, wo'is me, and worse then you,
  You haue not sin'd, nor neede be timorous.   10
  But wonder at a greater wonder; for to vs
Created Nature doth these things subdue,
  But their Creator, whom Sin nor Nature tyed,
  For vs his creatures and his foes hath dyed.

15.

What yf this present were the worlds last night?
    Looke in my Hart, O Soule, where thou dost dwell
    The picture of Christ crucifyde and tell
Whether that countenance can thee affright?
Teares in his eyes quench the amazing Light,   5
    Blood fills his frowns which from his pierc'd head fell.
    And can that toung adiudge thee vnto hell
Which prayed forgiuenes for his foes ranck spight?
No, No; but as in myne idolatree
    I sayd to all my prophane Mistressis   10
    Bewty of pity, foulnes only is
A Signe of rigor; So I say to thee
    To wicked Sprights are horrid Shapes assignd,
    This bewteous forme assures a piteous mind.

16.

Batter my hart, three-persond God, for you
    As yet but knock, breathe, shine, and seeke to mend;
    That I may rise, and stand, orethrow me; and bend
Your force to breake, blow, burne, and make me new.
I like an vsurp'd towne to'another dew   5
    Labor to'admit you, but Oh to no end.
    Reason your viceroy in me, me should defend,
But is captiv'd and proves weake or vntrew.
Yet dearly I love you, and would be loved faine:
    But ame betroth'd vnto your enemy: 10
Diuorce me, vnty or breake that knott agayne,
    Take me to you, emprison me, for I
Except you enthrall me neuer shalbe free,
Nor euer chast except you rauishe mee.

17.

Since She whome I lovd, hath payd her last debt
    To Nature, and to hers, and my good is dead
    And her Soule early into heauen rauished,
Wholy in heauenly things my Mind is sett.
Here the admyring her my Mind did whett   5
    To seeke thee God; so streames do shew the head,
    But though I haue found thee,'and thou my thirst hast fed,
A holy thirsty dropsy melts mee yett.
But why should I begg more Love, when as thou
    Dost woe my Soule, for hers offring all thine: 10
And dost not only feare least I allow
    My Love to Saints and Angels, things diuine,
But in thy tender iealosy dost doubt
Least the World, fleshe, yea Deuill putt thee out.

18.

Show me deare Christ, thy Spouse, so bright and cleare.
    What is it She, which on the other Shore
    Goes richly painted? Or which rob'd and tore
Laments and mournes in Germany and here?
Sleepes She a thousand, then peepes vp one yeare?   5
    Is She selfe truth and errs? now new, now'outwore?
    Doth She,'and did She, and shall She evermore
On one, on Seauen, or on no hill appeare?
Dwells She with vs, or like adventuring knights
    First trauaile we to seeke and then make Love?   10
Betray kind husband thy Spouse to our Sights,
    And let myne amorous Soule court thy mild Dove,
Who is most trew, and pleasing to thee, then
When She'is embrac'd and open to most Men.

19.

Oh, to vex me, contraryes meete in one:
    Inconstancy vnnaturally hath begott
    A constant habit; that when I would not
I change in vowes, and in devotione.
As humorous is my contritione   5
    As my prophane love, and as soone forgott:
    As ridlingly distemperd, cold and hott,
As praying, as mute; as infinite, as none.
I durst not view heauen yesterday; and to day
    In prayers, and flattering Speaches I court God: 10
    To morrow I quake with true feare of his rod.
So my deuout fitts come and go away
    Like a fantastique Ague: Save that here
    Those are my best dayes, when I shake with feare.

Revised Sequence

1.

As due by many titles I resigne
  My self to thee ô God; first I was made
By thee, and for thee, and when I was decay'de
  Thy bloud bought that the which before was thine.
I am thy Sun, made with thy self to shine,   5
  Thy seruant, whose paines thou hast still repaid
Thy sheepe, thine Image, And till I betray'd
  My self a Temple of thy spiritt Divine.
Why doth the Deuill then vsurpe in mee?
  Why doth hee steale, nay ravish that's thy right?   10
Except thou rise, and for thine owne worke fight
  Oh I shall soone despaire, when I doe see
That thou lou'st Mankind well, yet wilt not chuse mee
  And Satan hates mee, yet is loath to loose mee.

2.

Oh my black Soule, nowe thou art summoned
  By Sickness, Deaths Herald, and Champion,
Thou'art like a Pilgrim which abroad had done
  Treason, and durst not turne, to whence hee is fled
Or like a Theife which till Deathes doome bee read   5
  Wisheth himself deliuered from prison,
But damn'd, and hal'd to execution
  Wisheth that still hee might bee'imprisoned.
Yet Grace, if thou repent, thou canst not lack.
  But whoe shall giue thee that Grace to beginne?   10
Oh make thy self with holy mourning black
  And red with blushing as thou art with sinne
Or wash thee in Christs bloud, which hath his might
  That being Red, it dyes red soules to white.

3.

This is my Playes last Scene, Here heau'ns appointe
   My Pilgrimages last mile; And my race
Idly, yet quickly run, hath this last pace,
   My spanns last Inch, my minutes last point.
And gluttonous Death will instantly vnioynt   5
   My Bodie, and Soule; And I shall sleepe a space
But my euer wakeing part shall see that face
   Whose feare already shakes my euery ioynt.
Then as my soule, to heau'n her first seat, takes flight
   And earth-borne body, in the earth shall dwell,   10
Soe fall my sinnes, that all may haue their right
   To where they'are bred, and would press mee, to Hell.
Impute mee righteous thus purg'd of evill.
   For thus I leaue, the world, the fleash, and Deuill.

4.

At the round Earths imagin'd corners blowe
   Your Trumpetts Angells: and arise, arise
From Death, you nomberless infinities
   Of Soules, and to your scattred Bodies goe,
All whom the floud did, and fire shall overthrowe   5
   All whom Warr, Death, Age, Agues, Tyrannies
Despaire, Lawe, Chaunce hath slaine, and you whose eyes
   Shall behold God, and neuer tast Deaths woe,
But lett them sleepe Lord, and mee mourne a space
   For if aboue all these, my sinnes abound   10
'Tis late to aske aboundance of thy grace
   When wee are there; here on this lowly ground
Teach mee howe to repent, for thats as good
   As if thou'hadst seal'd my Pardon with thy bloud.

5.

If poysonous mineralls, and if that tree
    Whose fruit threwe death on, ellse immortall, vs,
If Leacherous Goates, if Serpents Envious
    Cannot bee damn'd, Alass why should I bee?
Why should intent, or reason borne in mee   5
    Make sinnes, ells equall, in mee more heynous?
And mercy being easie, and glorious
    To God, in his sterne wrath, why threatens hee?
But whoe am I, that dares dispute with thee?
    O God, oh of thine only worthy bloud   10
And my teares make a Heauenly Lethean floud,
    And drowne in it my sinnes black memory.
That thou remember them, some clayme as debt,
    I think it mercy, if thou wilt forgett.

6.

Death bee not proude, though some hath called thee
    Mighty and Dreadfull, for thou art not soe
For those whom thou thinck'st thou dost overthrowe
    Dye not poore Death, nor yet canst thou kill mee.
From rest, and sleepe, which but thy pictures bee,   5
    Much pleasure, then from thee, much more must flowe
And soonest our best men with thee doe goe,
    Rest of their bones, and Soules deliuerie.
Thou art slaue to Fate, Chance, Kings, and desperate men,
    And dost with poyson, warr, and sicknes dwell   10
And Poppie or Charmes, can make vs sleepe as well
    And better then thy stroak, why swell'st thou then?
One short sleepe past, wee wake æternallye
    And Death shall bee noe more. Death, thou shalt dye.

7.

Spitt in my face yee Iewes, and peirce my side,
    Buffett, and scoff, scourge, and crucifie mee,
For I haue sinn'd, and sinn'd, and only hee
    Who could doe none iniquitie hath dyed.
But by my Death cannot bee satisfied   5
    My sinnes which pass the Iewes impietie;
They kill'd once an inglorious man, but I
    Crucifie him daily, being nowe glorified.
Oh lett mee then his strange loue still admire,
    Kings pardon, but hee bore our punnishment;   10
And Iacob came cloathed in vile harsh attire,
    But to supplant, and with gainfull intent;
God cloath'd himself in vile mans fleash that soe
    Hee might bee weake enough to suffer woe.

8.

Why are wee by all Creatures waited on?
    Why doe the prodigall Elements supplye
Life, and foode to mee, being more pure then I,
    Simpler, and farther from corruption?
Why brook'st thou ignorant horse, subiection?   5
    Why dost thou Bull, and Bore soe sillilye
Dissemble weaknes, and by one mans stroke dye,
    Whose whole kinde you might swallowe, and feed vpon?
Weaker I am, woe is mee, and worse then you.
    You haue not sinn'd, nor neede bee timorous;   10
But wonder at a greater wonder, for to vs
    Created Nature doth these things subdue.
But their Creatour, whom sinne, nor nature tied
    For vs his Creatures, and his foes hath died.

9.

What if this present were the worlds last night?
   Mark in my hart Ô Soule where thou dost dwell
The Picture of Christ crucified, and tell,
   Whether that countenance can thee affright.
Teares in his eyes quench the amazeing light,   5
   Bloud fills his frownes which from his pierc'd head fell
And can that tongue adiudge thee vnto hell
   Which prayed forgiuenes for his foes fierce spight?
Noe, noe, but as in my Idolatrie
   I said to all my Prophane Mistresses,   10
Beauty of pitty; foulness only is
   A signe of Rigor; soe I say to thee
To wicked spiritts are horrid shapes assign'd,
   This beauteous forme assures a piteous minde.

10.

Batter my heart, three person'd God; for you
   As yet, but knock, breathe, shine, and seeke to mend,
That I may rise and stand, orethrowe mee, and bend
   Your force to break, blowe, burne, and make mee newe.
I, like an vsurp'd towne, to another due,   5
   Labour to'admitt you; but oh to noe end,
Reason, your Vice-roye in mee, mee should defend,
   But is captiu'd, and proues weake or vntrue,
Yet dearly I loue you, and would bee loued faine
   But am betroath'd vnto your enemye.   10
Divorce mee,'vntye, or breake that knott againe;
   Take mee to you, imprison mee, for I,
Except you inthrall mee, neuer shalbee free
   Nor euer chast except you ravish mee.

11.

Wilt thou loue God as hee thee, then digest
  My soule, this wholsome meditation,
Howe God the Spirit by Angells wayted on
  In heauen, doth make his Temple in thy breast.
The Father having begott a Sonne most blest   5
  And still begetting, (for hee nere begunne)
Hath daign'd to chuse thee by adoption
  Coheire to his Glorie, and Sabaaths endless rest;
And as a robb'd man, which by search doth finde
  His stollen stuff sold, must loose, or buy'it againe   10
The sonne of glory came downe, and was slayne
  Vs, whom hee had made, and Satan stolne, to vnbind.
'Twas much that man was made like God before
  But that God should bee made like man, much more.

12.

Father, part of his double interest
  Vnto thy kingdome, thy Sonne giues to mee,
His Ioincture in the knotty Trinity
  Hee keeps, and giues mee his Deaths Conquest.
This Lambe, whose Death with life the world hath blest   5
  Was from the worlds beginning slayne: and hee
Hath made twoe wills, which with the Legacie
  Of his, and thy kingdome, doth thy sonnes invest.
Yet such are those lawes, that men argue yet
  Whether a man those statutes can fulfill;   10
None doth; but all healing grace, and spiritt
  Reviue againe, what lawe and letter kill.
Thy Lawes Abridgment, and thy last command
  Is all but Loue, Oh lett that last will stand.
                         Finis

COPY-TEXTS FOR THE THREE SEQUENCES
AND LIST OF EMENDATIONS

Original Sequence

Copy-text: H5.   **Emendations of the copy-text:** General heading: *italics supplied*   **HSMade:** Heading: 1.] ~∧   Line 2 Repaire] repaire
4 And] and   5 dimme] dīme   way,] ~∧   6 Despaire] despaire
7 Such] such   8 By] by   which] wᶜʰ   9 Only] only   10 By] by
11 But] but   12 That] that   14 And] and   **HSDue:** Heading: 2.]
~∧   Line 2 My] my   god):] ~)∧   3 By] by   4 Thy] thy   which]
wᶜʰ   6 Thy] thy   7 Thy] thy   betray'd] betra'yd   8 My] my
9 Why] why   10 Why] why   12 Oh] oh   13 Mankind] Man kind
14 And] and   **HSSighs:** Heading: 3.] ~∧   Line 2 Into] into   which]
wᶜʰ   3 That] that   4 Mourne] mourne   vaine.] ~∧   5 In] in
6 Mine] mine   7 That] that   repent,] ~∧   8 Because] because
9 Th'] th'   10 The] the   11 Haue] haue   12 Of] of   comminge]
comīnge   13 Noe] noe   14 Th'] th'   **HSPart:** Heading: 4.] ~∧
Line 1 Father] ffather   2 Vnto] vnto   3 His] his   5 the] yᵉ
6 Was] was   7 Hath] hath   8 Of] of   9 Yet] yet   10 Whether]
whether   11 but] let   12 Reviue] reviue   13 command] comānd
HSBlack: Heading: 5.] ~∧   Line 1 summoned] sumōned   2 By] by
3 Thou] thou   pilgrimme] pilgrīme   which] wᶜʰ   had] hath
4 from] frō   5 Or] or   which] wᶜʰ   6 Wisheth] wisheth   7 But]
but   hal'd] hald'   8 Wisheth] wisheth   9 Yet] yet   10 But] but
12 And] and   13 which] wᶜʰ   14 That] that   **HSScene:** Heading:
6.] ~∧   Line 1 heav'ns] heavn's   2 My] my   3 Idly] idly   hath]
hat   pace,] ~∧   4 My] my   5 And] and   6 My] my   7 Or] or
8 Whose] whose   10 And] and   12 To] to,   presse] pʳᵉsse   to]
om   14 For] for   **HSLittle:** Heading: 7.] ~∧   Line 2 Of] of
3 But] but   4 My] my   5 You] you   which] wᶜʰ   which] wᶜʰ
6 Haue] haue   7 Powre] powre   so] om   8 Drowne] drowne
9 Or] or   10 But] but   11 Of] of   12 And] and   13 And] and
14 Of] of   which] wᶜʰ   **HSRound:** Heading: 8.] ~∧   Line 1
Imagin'd] Imagind'   2 Your] your   3 From] frō   4 Of] of   goe,]
~.   5 All] all   o're-throwe] or'e-throwe   6 All] all   7 Despaire]
despaire   and] &   8 Shall] shall   9 But] but   10 For] for
11 'Tis] t'is   12 When] when   14 As] as   seal'd] seald'
HSMin: Heading: 9.] ~∧   Line 1 Yf] yf   2 Whose] whose
immortall] imōrtall   3 Yf] yf   4 damn'd] damnd'   5 Why] why
6 Make] make   7 And] and   9 But] but   11 And] and
12 And] and   13 That] that   them] thē   **HSSouls:** Heading: 10.]
~∧   Line 1 Yf] yf   2 As] as   Fathers] ffathers   3 And] and
4 That] that   5 But] but   6 By] by   7 Apparent] apparent

Immediately] Im̄ediately   8 them] thē   9 They] they   weepe] creepe
10 And] and   11 On] on   12 Dissemblers] dissemblers   14 Thy]
thy   **HSDeath:** Heading: 11.] ~∧   Line 2 Mighty] mighty   3 For]
for   ouerthrowe] ou^{er}throwe   5 From] ffrom   which] wch be,] ~∧
6 Much] much   from] frō   7 And] and   our] o^r goe,] ~.
8 Rest] rest   deliuery.] ~∧   9 Th'] th'   and] &   desperate] despate
10 And] and   11 And] and   12 And] and   then?] ~.   13 One]
one   14 And] and   **HSWilt:** Heading: 12.] ~∧   Line 2 My] my
3 Howe] howe   5 Father] ffather   6 And] and   7 Hath] hath
8 Coheire] coheire   9 And] and   rob'd] ro'bd   which] w^{ch}
10 His] his   11 The] the   12 Vs] vs   stole] stolne   13 'Twas]
t'was   14 But] but

Westmoreland Sequence

Copy-text: NY3.   **Emendations of the copy-text:** General heading: *Holy*
Sonnets] Holy Sonnets   **HSMade:** Heading: 1] 1   Line 1 and] &
3 and] &   5 way,] ~.   6 and] &   7 and] &   8 which] w^{ch}
9 and] &   11 our] o^r **HSDue:** Heading: 2] .~   Line 2 God):]
~)∧   3 and] &   and] &   4 which] wch 5 with] w^t shyne,] ~.
6 repayde,] ~.   7 and] &   11 and] &   13 choose] chose   mee,]
me[e][,]   **HSSighs:** Heading: 3] .~   Line 1 and] &   2 and] &
which] wch 4 with] w^t 9 and] &   10 and] &   11 the] y^e
12 comming] cōming   14 and] &   and] &   **HSPart:** Heading: 4]
.~   Line 4 and] &   5 with] w^t the] ye 6 from] frō   and] &
7 which] wch with] w^t 8 and] &   9 that] y^t 11 and] &
12 and] &   and] &   13 and] &   Command] Cōmand   14 that]
y^t **HSBlack:** Heading: 5] .~   Line 1 summoned] sum̄oned   2 and]
&   3 like] *om*   which] wch 4 and] &   fled,] ~.   5 which] w^{ch}
6 from] frō   7 and] &   8 that] y^t 10 that] y^t 11 with] w^t
12 with] w^t with] w^t 13 which] w^{ch} **HSScene:** Heading: 6] .~
Line 6 and] &   and] &   7 that] y^t 11 that] y^t 12 and] &
hell] tell   14 and] &   **HSLittle:** Heading: 7] .~   Line 1 cunningly]
cūningly   2 and] &   4 and] &   5 which] wch that] y^t
which] wch 6 and] &   7 that] y^t 8 with] w^t 10 the] y^e
11 and] &   13 with] wth 14 and] &   which] w^{ch} **HSRound:**
Heading: 8] .~   Line 1 the] ye 2 Your] Y^r 4 and] &   go,] ~.
7 and] &   8 and] &   9 and] &   10 For] for   12 When] when
14 with] w^t **HSMin:** Heading: 9] .~   Line 1 and] &   8 God,] ~∧
9 that] y^t with] w^t 13 them] thē   dett,] ~∧   **HSSouls:** Heading:
10] .~   Line 5 our] o^r 6 and] &   that] y^t 9 and] &
HSDeath: Heading: 11] .~   Line 3 For] for   5 From] Frō   and] &
which] wch bee,] ~∧   6 from] frō   7 our] o^r with] w^t 8 and]

&   9 and] &   10 with] w^t   and] &   **HSWilt:** Heading: 12] .~
Line 9 which] w^ch   13 'Twas] T'was   that] y^t   14 that] y^t
HSSpit: Heading: 13] .~   Line 1 and] &   2 and] &   and] &
3 and] &   and] &   4 Which] W^ch   6 which] w^ch   the] y^e
10 our] o^r   12 with] w^th   13 that] y^t   **HSWhy:** Heading: 14] .~
Line 3 and] &   4 and] &   from] frō   6 and] &   7 and] &
8 and] &   9 and] &   14 and] &   **HSWhat:** Heading: 15] .~
Line 1 the] y^e   4 that] y^t   5 Light,] ~_∧   6 which] w^ch   from] frō
7 that] y^t   8 Which] W^ch   **HSBatter:** Heading: 16] .~   Line 2
and] &   3 1st and] &   4 and] &   9 I love] Ilove   and] &
would be] wouldbe   11 that] y^t   **HSShe:** Heading: 17] .17.   Line 2
and] &   6 the] y^e   7 and] &   10 Soule,] ~_∧   hers] ~;
12 Angels,] ~_∧   diuine,] ~_∧   14 the] y^e   **HSShow:** Heading: 18]
.~   Line 1 and] &   2 which] w^ch   3 which] w^ch   and] &
4 and] &   and] &   6 and] &   7 2nd and] &   9 with] w^t
10 First] first   and] &   11 our] o^r   12 Dove,] ~[,]   13 and] &
14 and] &   **HSVex:** Heading: 19] .~   Line 3 that] y^t   4 and] &
6 and] &   7 and] &   9 and] &   10 and] &   11 with] w^t
13 that] y^t   14 with] w^t

Revised Sequence

Copy-text: DT1.   **Emendations of the copy-text: HSDue:** Line 3 and] &
4 that] y^t   which] w^ch   thine.] ~_∧   5 with] w^th   7 betray'd] ~,
12 see] ~.   **HSBlack:** *Ind pattern regularized*   Line 2 and] &
Champion,] ~_∧   3 which] w^ch   4 and] &   5 which] w^ch
6 prison,] ~.   8 imprisoned.] ~_∧   10 that] y^t   beginne?] ~_∧
11 with] w^th   12 with] w^th   with] w^th   13 which] w^ch   **HSScene:**
Ind pattern regularized   Line 3 pace,] ~_∧   11 that] y^t   12 and] &
mee,] ~_∧   14 For] ffor   the] y^e   and] &   **HSRound:** *Ind pattern
regularized*   Line 3 From] ffrom   4 your] yor   goe,] ~_∧   5 and] &
7 and] &   you] yo^u   8 and] &   10 For] ffor   11 'Tis] Ti's
grace] ~.   14 with] w^th   **HSMin:** *Ind pattern regularized*   Line 9
with] w^th   12 memory.] ~_∧   13 thou] you   **HSDeath:** *Ind pattern
regularized*   Line 3 For] ffor   4 mee.] ~_∧   5 From] ffrom   which]
w^ch   bee,] ~_∧   6 pleasure,] ~_∧   7 with] w^th   8 deliuerie.] ~_∧
9 Fate] ffate   and] &   men,] ~.   10 with] w^th   **HSSpit:** Line 1
side,] ~_∧   2 and] &   3 For] ffor   and] &   6 which] w^ch
9 admire,] ~_∧   12 and] &   with] w^th   intent;] ~_∧   13 that] y^t
HSWhy: Heading: 8.] ~_∧   Line 3 I,] ~?   4 and] &   7 and] &
dye,] ~?   8 and] &   vpon?] ~_∧   14 For] ffor   **HSWhat:** Line 1
the] y^e   6 which] w^ch   7 that] y^t   8 Which] W^ch   9 Idolatrie] ~.
13 assign'd,] ~_∧   **HSBatter:** *Ind pattern regularized*   Line 2 breathe]

breath   and] &   mend,] ~_∧   3 and] &   4 Your] Yo^r   and] &
newe.] ~,   6 end,] ~_∧   7 your] yor   8 and] &   9 you] yo^u
10 enemye.] ~_∧   11 mee,] ~_∧   12 you] yo^u   13 you] yo^u
14 you] yo^u   mee.] ~_∧   **HSWilt:** Line 2 meditation,] ~.   4 heauen,]
~_∧   breast.] ~_∧   5 Father] ffather   8 and] &   rest;] ~_∧
9 which] w^{ch}   10 buy] by   12 and] &   stolne,] ~;   vnbind.] ~_∧
13 'Twas] T'was   that] y^t   14 that] y^t   more.] ~_∧   **HSPart:**
Line 1 Father] ffather   2 mee,] ~_∧   4 Conquest.] ~_∧   5 with] wth
6 the] y^e   7 which] w^{ch}   8 and] &   invest.] ~_∧   9 that] y^t
11 spiritt] ~.   Subscription: Finis] ffinis

Textual Introductions and Apparatuses for Individual Holy Sonnets

(The Textual Introductions and Apparatuses presented here are arranged alphabetically by *Donne Variorum* short forms.)

HSBatter

Textual Introduction

As is shown on Figure 2 in the General Textual Introduction (p. lxii), *HSBatter* is the sixteenth item in NY3's collection of "Holy Sonnets," the fourth of the replacement sonnets that NY3 appends to its replication of Group III's earlier sequence of "Diuine Meditations."[1] In the restructuring that gives rise to the subsequent Group-I/II arrangement, however, the poem moves to the tenth position in the sequence and appears there in its first print appearance in A. In B, when the four discarded Group-III sonnets are recovered from H6 and reinstalled in the sequence, *HSWhat* is relocated to fourteenth place and remains so positioned in all subsequent editions save those of Alford (L), who reproduces the 1633 sequence; Lowell (M), who combines the Holy Sonnets with *Corona* in a continuously numbered series; Gardner (U), who prints the 1633 sequence; and Shawcross (Z), who essentially follows Gardner (see Figure 6 on p. lxxvi).

Manifesting no substantive variation within the body of seventeenth-century artifacts other than a handful of isolated copyists' blunders, *HSBatter* is apparently the sole poem among the replacement sonnets that Donne never felt the need to revise. Among the Group-I manuscripts B32 misrecords "you [for the correct *your*] Enemye" in line 10, and C2—the usual setting text for A—evinces a pair of misreadings: "Better [for *Batter*] my Hart" in line 1 and the plural "Enemyes" (for "Enemye") in line 10. Within the later Group II, however, only a single sport ap-

---

[1]As is shown on Figure 3 (p. lxiv) and noted in the General Textual Introduction (p. lxiii), γ¹'s "Other Meditations"—of which *HSBatter* is the fourth—were obtained from a Group-II source at some point after the original collection was entered into the artifact.

pears—H4's "or [for *and*] proves" in line 8. All manuscripts except NY3, it might be noted, give the older spelling "breath" (for "breathe") in line 2; but this was still an acceptable form in Donne's time, and there can be no doubt that the verb is intended. (In order to dispell this ambiguity for modern readers we have emended DT1's "breath" to "breathe" in the text of the Revised Sequence presented above.)

In setting the text into print in 1633, A's editor not only imposes the modern spelling "breathe" in line 2, but also among the other manuscripts in his possession finds corrections for the above-noted errors in C2 (see the General Textual Introduction, pp. lxxii–lxxiii). He also works very hard to regularize the poem's meter, eliding collocations in lines 3, 5, 6, 9 (two separate instances), 11, and 13. Most of these adjustments carry over into the subsequent seventeenth-century editions (B–G); and the only outright error introduced among these is G's "we [for the normative *me*] should defend" in line 7 (why G reverts to the manuscripts' "breath" in line 2 is unclear).

As in the seventeenth century, the text of *HSBatter* exhibits little variation among the modern editions. Tonson (H) picks up G's anomalous "we" in line 7 and passes it on to I, J, and K; and J prints the blunder "note" (for "knott") in line 11. The only other deviations found among the postseventeenth-century editions, however, are Lowell's (M's) "a [for *an*] usurpt" in line 5—a modernization perpetuated in N— and his inadvertent "victory" (for "viceroy") in line 7.

Textual Apparatus

Copy-text: NY3.   **Texts collated:** B7 (f. 106v); B32 (f. 141); C2 (f. 15); C9 (f. 97v); CT1 (p. 232); DT1 (f. 120); H4 (f. 99); H6 (p. 32); IU2 (*ll. 12–14 only*, f. 50v); NY3 (f. [36v]); O20 (ff. 45v–46); SP1 (f. [60]); A (p. 38); B (p. 340); C (p. 340); D (p. 323); E (p. 323); F (p. 323); G (p. 320).
Emendations of the copy-text: Heading: 16.] .~.   Line 2 and] &   3 and] & 4 and] &   9 I love] Ilove   and] &   would be] wouldbe 11 that] y^t

HISTORICAL COLLATION

Format:
    Indentations: *even numbered lines ind* B7 CT1 DT1(*plus 13*) H4(*plus 13*);
        ll. 2, 3, 6, 7, 10, 12 ind B32 C2 NY3 O20 SP1; *ll. 2, 4, 6, 7, 10, 12*
        ind C9 H6; *no ind* A–G.
    Miscellaneous: *poem is last of four sonnets entered under the general HE* Other
        Meditations. C9 H6; »P.« *above l. 1* H6; »p. 320.« *left of HE* O20.
Headings: 10 B32 C2(~.) DT1(~.) H4(~:) O20(~.) SP1(~.).   .16. NY3.
    X. A.   XIV. B–G.   *om* B7 C9 CT1 H6 IU2.

    1 Batter] Better C2.   hart,] ~$_\wedge$ B7 CT1 SP1; heart, C9 DT1 H6 A–G;

heart$_\wedge$ H4.   three-persond] C9 H6 NY3; ~$_\wedge$ ~ Σ.   God,] ~$_\wedge$ B7; ~; B32
C2 DT1 H4 O20 A–G.   for] ~, A–G.

2 yet] ~, B32 C2 DT1 O20.   knock,] ~$_\wedge$ H6.   breathe,] breath$_\wedge$ B7
H4 H6; breath, B32 C2 C9 CT1 DT1 O20 SP1 G.   shine,] ~$_\wedge$ H6.
mend;] NY3 A–G; ~, CT1 O20; ~$_\wedge$ Σ.

3 rise,] ~$_\wedge$ C9 DT1 H6.   orethrow] ore throw B32 H6; overthrowe C2.
me; and] NY3; ~$_\wedge$ ~ C9 SP1; ~,'~ A–G; ~, ~ Σ.   bend] ~, C2.

4 force] ~, A–G.   breake,] ~$_\wedge$ H6.   blow,] ~$_\wedge$ H6.   burne,] ~$_\wedge$ A.
new.] ~, B7 B32 DT1 O20; ~$_\wedge$ CT1 H4 H6 SP1.

5 I] B7 C2 CT1 H4 NY3; ~, Σ.   vsurp'd] vsurped B7 CT1.   towne]
C9 H6 NY3; ~, Σ.   to'another] NY3 A B; ~$_\wedge$ ~ Σ.   dew] NY3; due C9
H6; due, Σ.

6 to'admit] DT1 NY3; ~$_\wedge$ ~ Σ.   you,] ~; B7 CT1 DT1 SP1.   but Oh]
~ ~; B7; ~ ~, CT1 A–G; ~' ~ H4.   end.] NY3 O20 C–G; ~, A B;
~$_\wedge$ Σ.

7 Reason] ~, DT1.   viceroy] vice-roy B7 C9 CT1 DT1.   me,] ~$_\wedge$ C9
H6.   me] we G.   defend,] ~$_\wedge$ B7 C9 CT1 H4 H6 SP1.

8 captiv'd] C9 H6 NY3; ~, Σ.   and] or H4.   proves] ~, B7.
weake] ~, B7 B32 CT1 H4 O20.   vntrew.] NY3; ~$_\wedge$ B7 C9 H4 H6; ~, Σ.

9 dearly I love] dearly Ilove NY3; ~'~ ~ A–G.   you, and] ~',~ A–F;
~'$_\wedge$~ G.   would be] wouldbe NY3.   loved] lov'd H4(loued') A–G.
faine:] NY3; ~, B32 C2 O20 SP1 A–G; ~$_\wedge$ Σ.

10 your] you B32.   enemy:] NY3; ~$_\wedge$ B7 C9 CT1 DT1 H6; Enemyes,
C2; ~, Σ.

11 me, vnty] C9 NY3; ~$_\wedge$'~, DT1; ~,'~, A–G; ~, ~, Σ.   agayne,] ~$_\wedge$
B7 C9 CT1 H4 H6; ~; DT1.

12 you,] ~,, C9; ~; H4; ~$_\wedge$ IU2 SP1.   me,] ~$_\wedge$ IU2.   I] ~, DT1.

13 you enthrall] ~ in thrall H4; ~'~ A–G.   me] C9 H6 IU2 NY3; ~, Σ.
shalbe] B7 B32 DT1 NY3 SP1; shall be Σ.   free,] NY3 O20 A–G; ~$_\wedge$ Σ.

14 chast] ~, B32 C2 H4 O20 A–G.   mee.] ~$_\wedge$ B7 CT1 DT1; ~.| C2 H6
SP1.

Subscriptions: *none.*

Verbal Variants in Selected Modern Editions

Editions Collated: H I J K L M N O P Q S T U Z AA DD 72.
Format:

Indentations: *ll. 2, 3, 6, 7, 10, 12 ind* N; *no ind* H–M O–Q S–U Z AA DD 72.

Headings: XIV. H–K N–Q S DD. XVII. L. XXI. M. 14 T AA. 10 (*first group*) U. 171 *Holy Sonnet.* Z. XVI 72.

5 an] a M N.

7 viceroy] victory M. *second* me] we H–K.

11 knott] note J.

HSBlack

Textual Introduction

As is shown on Figure 2 in the General Textual Introduction (p. lxii), *HSBlack* is the fifth poem in both the earlier, Group-III sequence of "Diuine Meditations" and in NY3's later replication of that sequence at the beginning of its collection of "Holy Sonnets." In the restructuring that gives rise to the subsequent Group-I/II arrangement, however, the poem moves to the second position, following *HSDue*, and remains there in its first print appearance in A. In B, when the four discarded Group-III sonnets are recovered from H6 and reinstalled in the sequence, *HSPart* having been moved to the end of the group, *HSBlack* is relocated to fourth place and remains in that position in all subsequent editions except those of Alford (L), who reproduces the 1633 sequence; Lowell (M), who combines the Holy Sonnets with *Corona* in a continuously numbered series; Gardner (U), who prints the 1633 sequence; and Shawcross (Z), who essentially follows Gardner (see Figure 6 on p. lxxvi).

As is shown in the historical collation below and on Figure 4 in the General Textual Introduction (p. lxv), the manuscripts of *HSBlack* vary significantly in lines 1, 3, 4, 5, 13, and 14; and some of these changes are undoubtedly authorial. The CT1-B7 reading "thou now" (for "now thou") in line 1 is scribal, as are the line-13 "his [for the normative *this*] might" in B7, CT1, DT1, and H4 and the line-14 "dies" (for the normative "dyes") in H4, HH1, SP1, and WN1. The variants appearing in lines 3, 4, and 5, however, are more problematic, and may point to unresolved difficulties in Donne's own early copies of the poem. As embodied in the Group-I and -II manuscripts, Donne's final version of the similes spanning lines 3–8 is clear: of his "black Soule" he proclaims, "Thou'art like a Pilgrim . . . Or like a Theife . . ." (see the text in the Revised Sequence above). Whether this is how he always intended these lines to read is less clear. The early, Group-III text has no verb after "Thou" in line 3 ("Thou like a pilgrimme . . .") and in line 5 introduces the second simile with "as" rather than "like" ("Or as a Theife . . .") (see the text in the Original Sequence above). That Group III's version of line 3 is metrically regular, however, may suggest that Donne initially meant the construction in these lines as an elliptical clause. If so, that intention was apparently short-lived, for at the next stage of the text's evolution—recorded in NY3—the verb has been inserted ("Thou'art a Pilgrim, wch abroad had don"). Unfortunately, it lacks the preposition ("like") that had appeared in Group III, and the elision of "Thou'art" renders the line submetrical. Since a metaphor seems less suitable here than a simile and since the elision implies the need to reduce the syllable count, we infer that "like" was inadvertently dropped in the transcription of NY3 and have emended the line accordingly. That NY3 follows Group III in opening the simile in line 5 with "as" suggests that this was the word Donne originally wrote, but that he did not use "like" to introduce both the similes in these lines hints either that his original conception of these lines was considerably different from what he eventually settled on or that both the β¹ scribe and Rowland Woodward (the scribe of NY3) mishandled the text in some way. Further questions about the content of these lines involve the "had/hath/hast done" variant in the latter half of line 3 and the "turne from/to whence" crux in line 4. That "had" appears in the majority of the Group IIIs and in NY3 suggests that Donne originally intended the preterite, but the "hath" of Group I and the more reliable Group IIs (DT1 and H4) must reflect his final choice. Whether the Group-III "turne from" is Donne's original reading or a scribal blunder is unclear, but the "turne to" of all later artifacts is clearly authorial.

Following the copy in C2, A sets the Group-I/II text into print without substantive change, and B's only significant difference from A is the alteration of "dyes" to "dies" in line 14. Except that G modernizes the spelling of a few words, the remaining seventeenth-century editions impose no further changes. Indeed, except for some divergence of opinion over the "dyes/dies" crux in line 14, the only noteworthy variant in the entire body of moderns is Tonson's "hawl'd" (for "hal'd") in line 7, a mistake he passes on to I, J, K, and M (see the apparatus below).

Textual Apparatus

Copy-text: NY3.   **Texts collated:** B7 (f. 104v); B32 (ff. 139v–40); B46 (f. 98); C2 (f. 13v); C9 (f. 95); CT1 (p. 228); DT1 (f. 118); H4 (f. 97); H5 (f. 83); H6 (p. 27); HH1 (f. 127r–v); NY3 (f. [34]); O20 (f. 43v); SP1 (f. [57r–v]); WN1 (p. 5); A (p. 33); B (pp. 333–34); C (pp. 333–34); D (p. 318); E (p. 318); F (p. 318); G (pp. 315–16).

Emendations of the copy-text: Heading: 5.] .~.   Line 1 summoned] suṁoned   2 and] &   3 like] *om*   which] wᶜʰ   4 and] &   fled,] ~.   5 which] wᶜʰ   6 from] frō   7 and] &   8 that] yᵗ   10 that] yᵗ   11 with] wᵗ   12 with] wᵗ   with] wᵗ   13 which] wᶜʰ

HISTORICAL COLLATION

Format:

Indentations: *ll. 2, 4, 6, 8, 10, 12, 13, 14 ind*   B7 CT1; *ll. 2, 3, 6, 7, 10, 12 ind*   B32 B46 C2 C9 H5 H6 NY3 O20 SP1 WN1; *ll. 2, 4, 6, 8, 10, 11, 13, 14 ind*   DT1; *even numbered lines ind*   H4; *ll. 3, 4, 7, 10, 12 ind* HH1; *no ind*   A–G.

Miscellaneous: »P« *left of HE*   H6; »p.315.« *left of HE and* »333« *right of HE*   O20.

Headings: .2| B32 C2(ₐ~.) DT1(ₐ~.) H4(ₐ~:) O20(ₐ~.) SP1(ₐ~ₐ) WN1(ₐ~ₐ).   5   C9 H5 H6 HH1 NY3(.~.).   I I.   A.   I V.   B–G.   *om*   B7 B46 CT1.

1 Soule,] ~∧   C9 WN1 B–G; ~!   A.   now thou] thou now   B7 CT1.
summoned] ~,   B32.

2 Sicknes,] ~∧   C9 H6 HH1 D–F.   Deaths] ~,   B32.   Harold] ~,   B7
B32 C2 CT1 DT1 H4 O20 SP1 WN1 A.   Champion;] ~∧   B7 B46 C9 CT1
DT1 H4 H6 O20 SP1 WN1; ~,   B32 C2 H5 HH1.

3 Thou'art] ~∧ ~   B7 B32 C2 CT1 H4 O20 SP1 WN1 A–G; Thou,   B46;
Thou   C9 H5 H6(~ ›art‹) HH1.   like a] ~'~   C2; Wᶜʰ(M *var*: »~«) ~   HH1;
om a   NY3.   Pilgrim,] ~∧   DT1 H4 H5 WN1.   had don] hast ~,   B7;
hath ~,   B32; hath ~   C2 H5 SP1 A–G; hast ~   CT1 HH1; ~ → ›hath‹ ~   H6;
hath'~   O20.

4 darst] NY3; durst   Σ.   turne] ~,   B7 CT1 DT1.   to] from   B46 C9
H5 H6(*var*: ›to‹) HH1; ~ whom to   SP1.   he'is] ~∧ ~   B7 C2 CT1 DT1 H4
WN1 A–G; he   C9.   fled,] ~∧   B7 B46 C9 CT1 DT1 H4 HH1 SP1; ~;   B32
H5 H6; ~.   NY3.

5 as] B46 C9 H5 H6 HH1 NY3; like   Σ.   thiefe] ~,   B32 B46 C2 H5 O20
SP1 WN1 A–G.   death's] Deaths   B32 C2 CT1 DT1 H5 O20.   red] NY3;
reade, B32 A–G; redd,   C2; read   Σ.

6 himselfe] him selfe   WN1.   deliuered] deliver'd   C2 C9 H6 O20.
prison] ~ | B7; ~;   C2 A–G; ~.   DT1; ~,   H5 H6.

7 But] ~,   H6.   damn'd] ~,   B32 DT1 H4 H5 O20 SP1.   haled] hald
C9 DT1 H4 H5 H6 HH1 A–G.   execution] ~,   B32 C2 H6 O20 SP1 A–G.

8 be'imprisoned.] ~∧ ~;   B7 B32 H4 A–G; ~∧ ~.   B46 C9 H6; ~∧ ~,   C2
CT1 O20; ~'~∧   DT1; ~∧ ~∧   HH1 SP1 WN1.

9 grace,] ~∧   B7 B46 C9 CT1 H5 H6 HH1 WN1 B C.   if] (~   C9 H6
HH1.   repent] ~,   B32 C2 DT1 H4 H5 O20 SP1 WN1 A–G; ~)   C9 H6
HH1.   lacke.] ~∧   B7 C9 CT1 H6 HH1 SP1 WN1; ~,   B32 H5 O20; ~;   C2
H4 A–G.

10 begin?] ~∧   DT1 SP1; ~;   H4.

11 Oh] Or   B7; ~,   B46.   thy selfe] ~ ~,   B32; thyselfe   C9 O20.
blacke,] C2 H5 NY3 A–G; ~∧   Σ.

12 red] ~,   WN1.   blushinge] ~,   B32 C2 O20 SP1 WN1 A–F.   Sin.]
B46 NY3; ~,   B32 C2; ~;   H5 A–G; Sinns∧   H6; ~?   SP1; ~∧   Σ.

13 in] with   WN1.   blood,] ~∧   B7 C9 CT1 HH1.   this] his   B7 CT1
DT1 H4.   might] ~,   H5 WN1

14 red,] ~$_\wedge$ B46 C9 H6.   dyes] dies   H4 HH1 SP1 WN1 B–G.   whight.]
NY3 O20; white$_\wedge$ B7 H6 HH1; ~$_\wedge$ B32; whyte.⏐ C2 SP1; white. Σ.

Subscriptions: *none.*

Verbal Variants in Selected Modern Editions

Editions Collated: H I J K L M N O P Q S T U Z AA DD 72.
Format:
  Indentations: *ll. 2, 3, 5, 8, 10, 12 ind*   N; *no ind*   H–M O–Q S–U Z AA
    DD 72.
Headings: IV.   H–K N–Q S DD.   IX. L.   XI. M.   4 T AA.
  2 (*first group*) U.   163 *Holy Sonnet.* Z.   V 72.

3 had] hath   Σ.

5 as] like   Σ.

7 haled] hawl'd   H–K; hauled   M.

14 dyes] dies   H–K O.

HSDeath

Textual Introduction

As is shown on Figure 2 in the General Textual Introduction (p. lxii), *HSDeath* is the eleventh poem in both the earlier, Group-III sequence of "Diuine Meditations" and in NY3's later replication of that sequence at the beginning of its collection of "Holy Sonnets." In the restructuring that gives rise to the subsequent Group-I/II arrangement, however, the poem moves to the sixth position, following *HSMin*, and remains there in its first print appearance in A. In B, when the four discarded Group-III sonnets are recovered from H6 and reinstalled in the sequence, *HSPart* having been moved to the end of the group, *HSDeath* is relocated to tenth place and remains in that position in all subsequent editions except those of Alford (L), who reproduces the 1633 sequence; Lowell (M), who combines the Holy Sonnets with *Corona* in a continuously numbered series; Gardner (U), who prints the 1633 sequence; and Shawcross (Z), who essentially follows Gardner (see Figure 6 on p. lxxvi).

As is shown in the Historical Collation below and on Figure 4 in the General Textual Introduction (p. lxv), the text of *HSDeath* evinces a certain amount of substantive change as it passes from the earlier, Group-III artifacts through Group IV (NY3) and on into the later Groups I and II. The Group-II "some hath [for the normative *haue*] called" (except H4 and WN1) in line 1 reflects a misunderstanding on the part of the β5 scribe, and such readings as B32's "most [for *more must*] flowe" in line 6, C9's "must more" (for "much more") in line 6, and B7's "doe wth thee" (for "with thee do") in line 7 are the isolated blunders of individual copyists. Other variants show, however, that as he copied the Group-III text into the NY3 arrangement and subsequently imported the NY3 text into the reconfigured Group I/II sequence, Donne himself revised the text at each successive stage. Since we cannot be sure whether the parentheses enclosing "poor Death" in the Group-III rendition of line 4 are authorial or scribal (see note 4 on pp. lxvi–lxvii above), we cannot know whether their disappearance in NY3 represents Donne's change of mind (the line-5 parentheses in C9 and H6 stem from a scribal sophistication in γ1); but NY3's substitution of "bones" for the earlier "bodyes" in line 8 is clearly Donne's. This revision carries over into the final Group-I/II text, and two further authorial changes are introduced at the Group-I stage—the replacement of "easier" with "better" in line 12 and of "Liue" with "wake" in line 13.

Set into type in A from the editor's usual Group-I manuscript (C2), this twice-revised text undergoes little further change among the seventeenth-century prints, and—with the exceptions noted below—all modern editors have printed this final version. A considerably strengthens the manuscript's punctuation—especially in lines 2, 3, and 4—but alters its verbals only in misreading "doth" (for the correct "dost") in line 10, an error that is immediately repaired in B. On no manuscript authority, however, B incorporates a verbal change of its own, dropping the "s" from "pictures" in line 5 (leaving "picture"); and this mistake persists not only throughout the rest of the century (in C–G), but also—through the influence of G—into H–K and P. The few changes to A's punctuation effected in B–G are reported in the Historical Collation, as is the somewhat puzzling absence in all but five seventeenth-century artifacts of terminal punctuation in line 8.

Other than N's adoption of B7's "doe wth thee" (for "with thee do") in line 7 and DD's typographical blunder "are" (for "art") in line 2, no further changes are recorded in the moderns.

Textual Apparatus

Copy-text: NY3.　　**Texts collated:** B7 (f. 105v); B32 (f. 140v); B46 (f. 99v); C2 (f. 14); C9 (f. 96v); CT1 (p. 230); DT1 (f. 119); H4 (f. 98); H5 (f. 84v); H6 (p. 30); HH1 (f. 129r–v); NY3 (f. [35v]); O20 (ff. 44v–45); SP1 (ff. [58v–59]); WN1 (p. 7); A (pp. 35–36); B (pp. 337–38); C (pp. 337–38); D (p. 321); E (p. 321); F (p. 321); G (p. 318).

Emendations of the copy-text: Heading: 11.] .~.　　Line 3 For] for　　5 From] Frō　　and] &　　which] w^ch　　bee,] ~_∧　　6 from] frō　　7 our] o^r with] w^t　　8 and] &　　9 and] &　　10 with] w^t　　and] &

HISTORICAL COLLATION

Format:

Indentations: *even numbered lines ind*　B7 CT1 DT1(*plus* 13) H4(*plus* 13) WN1; *ll. 2, 3, 6, 7, 10, 11, 13, 14 ind*　B32 B46 C2 C9 H5 H6 NY3 O20 SP1; *ll. 2, 3, 6, 7, 13, 14 ind*　HH1; *no ind*　A–G.

Miscellaneous: »P.« *left of HE*　H6; »p. 318« *left of HE*　O20.

Headings: 6.　B32 C2 DT1 H4(~_∧) O20 SP1 WN1(~_∧).　　11　C9 H5 H6 HH1 NY3(.~.).　　V I.　A.　　X.　B–G.　　*om*　B7 B46 CT1.

1 Death] ~,　C9 H4.　　proud,] ~_∧　H6 HH1.　　some] wee　HH1.　　haue] hath　B7 CT1 DT1; ~,　WN1.　　called] call'd　CT1 WN1.　　thee] ~　HH1.

2 Mighty] ~,　B7 B32 C2 CT1 H4 O20 WN1.　　dreadfull,] ~_∧　B46; ~;　H4. for] ~,　A–G.　　so.] H5 NY3; ~;　B7 CT1 H4; ~,　B32 O20 A–G; ~:　HH1 WN1; ~_∧　Σ.

3 For] ~,　A–G.　　those] ~,　A–G.　　thinkst] ~,　B7 H4 A; thinkest HH1 SP1.　　dost] doest　HH1.　　overthrow] over throw　H6; ~,　WN1 A–G.

4 not] ~,　B32 C2 O20 SP1 WN1 A–G.　　poore] (~　B46 C9 H5 H6 HH1. death,] Death;　B7 CT1 H4; Deathe)　B46 H5; Death,　C2 DT1 O20; ~)　C9 H6 HH1.　　mee.] ~_∧　B7 CT1 DT1 H6 HH1 SP1; ~,　H4; ~:　WN1; ~;　A.

5 rest] ~,   B7 B32 CT1 DT1 H4 H6 O20 SP1 WN1.   sleepe] ~,   B32 B46
C2 DT1 H4 H5 O20 SP1 A–G.   which] (~   C9 H6.   pictures] picture
B–G.   bee,] C2 A–C; ~)   C9 H6; ~:   D–G; ~∧   Σ.

6 pleasure;] B46 NY3; ~∧   B7 CT1 DT1 H4 HH1 C–G; ~,   Σ.   then] ~,
C9 H6.   thee] ~;   B7 CT1; ~,   C2 C9 DT1 H4 H6 WN1 A–G.   much]
must   C9; and   H4(*var*: »~«).   more] *om* B32; ~,   C9.   must] most
B32.   flow,] ~∧   B7 B46 CT1 DT1 H5 H6 HH1 WN1; ~.   C9.

7 men] ~,   B32 O20.   with thee do] doe wth thee   B7; ~ ~ doth   C2;
~ |~| ~   C9 H6.   go,] ~∧   B7 C9 H6 HH1; ~;   B32 O20 SP1; ~.   B46 H5.

8 Rest] And   HH1(→ »~«).   ther] thy   B7.   bones,] bodyes,   B46 H5;
bodye,   C9; bodye∧   H6(*var*: ›~∧‹); bodies∧   HH1.   deliueree.] C9 H6 NY3;
~;   B7; ~,   B32; ~∧   Σ.

9 Thou art] Th'~   B46 C9 H5 H6; ~ ~;   HH1.   kings,] ~∧   B7 WN1.
men,] ~∧   B46 C9 H6 O20 SP1 WN1; ~.   CT1 DT1; ~:   H4.

10 dost] doest   HH1; doth   A.   poyson,] ~∧   C9 H6 HH1.   warr,] ~∧
C9 H6 HH1 G.   dwell;] NY3; ~,   B32 H4 WN1 B–G; ~.   C2 A; ~:   C9;
~∧   Σ.

11 Poppy] DT1 H5 HH1 NY3; ~,   Σ.   Charmes] ~,   B7 C9 CT1 DT1.
as well,] aswell∧   B7 CT1; ~ ~∧   B46 C2 C9 DT1 H5 H6 HH1 WN1; ~ ~.   O20
SP1.

12 easier] B46 C9 H5 H6 HH1 NY3; better   Σ.   stroke,] ~;   B7 B32 C2
CT1 H4 O20 SP1 A–G; ~.   B46 C9 H6; ~:   H5.   then?] ~∧   B7 CT1 WN1;
~.   H5; ~,   B C.

13 past,] ~∧   HH1 WN1.   live] B46 C9 H5 H6(→ ›wake‹) HH1 NY3; wake
Σ.   eternally] ~,   B32 C2 HH1 O20 WN1 A–G.

14 shalbe] shall be   B32 C9 DT1 H4 H6 WN1 A–G.   more,] ~;   B46 C9
H6 HH1; ~.   DT1; ~∧   H4; ~:   H5.   Death] ~,   B46 C9 DT1 H4 HH1.
dy.] ~∧   B7 HH1; ~.| B32 C2 SP1; ~!   CT1; ~[*missing*]   WN1.

Subscriptions: *none.*

Verbal Variants in Selected Modern Editions

Editions Collated: H I J K L M N O P Q S T U Z AA DD 72.
Format:
    Indentations: *ll. 2, 3, 6, 7, 10, 11 ind*   N; *no ind*   H–M O–Q S–U Z AA
        DD 72.

Headings: X. H–K N–Q S DD.   XIII. L.   XVII. M.   10   T AA.
   6 (*first group*) U.   167 *Holy Sonnet.* Z.   XI   72.

   2 art] are   DD.

   5 pictures] picture   H–K P; ~ (M *var:* picture)   O.

   7 with thee do] doe with thee   N.

   12 easier] 72; better   Σ.

   13 live] 72; wake   Σ.

HSD*ue*

Textual Introduction

As is shown on Figure 2 in the General Textual Introduction (p. lxii), HSD*ue* is the second poem in both the earlier, Group-III sequence of "Diuine Meditations" and in NY3's later replication of that sequence at the beginning of its collection of "Holy Sonnets." In the restructuring that gives rise to the subsequent Group-I/II arrangement, however, the moves to the first position in the sequence and appears there in its first print appearance in A. In B, when the four discarded Group-III sonnets are recovered from H6 and reinstalled in the sequence, HSD*ue* is relocated and again appears in position two, where it remains in all subsequent editions save those of Alford (L), who reproduces the 1633 sequence; Lowell (M), who combines the Holy Sonnets with *Corona* in a continuously numbered series; Gardner (U), who prints the 1633 sequence; and Shawcross (Z), who essentially follows Gardner (see Figure 6 on p. lxxvi).

As the Historical Collation shows, the manuscripts of the poem exhibit a considerable amount of variation. The earlier Group-III text has four readings—"was I" in line 2, "thy Image" in line 7, "thus usurpe" in line 9, and "shall see" in line 12—that are altered, respectively, to "I was," "thyne Image," "then vsurpe," and "do see" as the text passes on to NY3 (Group IV); and that these are carried forward into Group I and, later, Group II marks them as deliberate authorial changes. Three members of Group I (B32, O20, and SP1) exhibit the sports "tithes" (for "titles") in line 1 and "works" (for "worke") in line 11; and the entire group gives "vsurpe on [for the normative *in*]" in line 9. Within Group II the parent-child pair CT1 and B7 evince "this [for *thy*] Spiritt" in line 8, and three Group IIs—DT1, H4, and WN1—trivialize "Sonne" to "Sunne" in line 5. Other variants are recorded in the apparatus below.

A sets HSD*ue* into print from C2 (see p. lxxii above) and thus includes the authorial revisions introduced in NY3 and the scribal "usurpe on" in line 9, as well as respelling the manuscripts' "loose" as "lose" in line 14. Into the text received from A, B introduces a full stop after "ô God" in line 2 and—following H6—alters "do see" to "shall see" in line 12. C reprints B's text without change, and D–F's only changes to C involve strengthening commas to semicolons in lines 2 and 3 and adding a medial comma in line 10. G modernizes the spelling of a few words—most notably "chuse" to "choose" in line 13—but otherwise reprints the D–F text exactly. 30, presenting the poem in tandem with HSM*ade* and entitling it *The Conclusion*, derives its text from B or C (see the Textual Introduction to HSM*ade*).

That most modern editions position the poem as in B is noted above, and all base their texts on the seventeenth-century prints as well. As is recorded in the list of verbal variants in the moderns below, every editor other than Gosse (72), Gardner

(U), and Shawcross (Z) prints the scribal "usurpe on" that had entered print in A. And the influence of B–G is reflected in the fact that all eighteenth- and nineteenth-century editions except L, N, and O give "shall see" in line 12; beginning with Grierson, however, every twentieth-century editor reverts to the "doe see" of A. In two apparently independent instances of modernization, both Grosart and Gosse change "wilt" to "will" in line 13; the imposition of the manuscript reading "loose" (for the prints' "lose") in line 14 may represent conscious archaizing on the part of both Alford and Grosart.

Textual Apparatus

Copy-text: NY3.　　**Texts Collated:** B7 (f. 104r-v); B32 (f. 139v); B46 (f. 97); C2 (f. 13v); C9 (f. 94); CT1 (pp. 227–28); DT1 (f. 117v); H4 (f. 96v); H5 (f. 82); H6 (p. 25); HH1 (f. 126r-v); NY3 (f. [33]); O20 (f. 43r-v); SP1 (f. [57]); WN1 (p. 5); A (p. 32); B (p. 332); C (p. 332); D (p. 317); E (p. 317); F (p. 317); G (pp. 314–15); 30 (pp. 163–64).

Emendations of the copy-text: Heading: 2.] .~.　　Line 2 God):] ~)∧　　3 and] & 　　and] & 　　4 which] wᶜʰ 　　5 with] wᵗ 　　shyne,] ~.　　6 repayde,] ~.　　7 and] & 　　11 and] & 　　13 choose] chose 　　mee,] me[e][,]

HISTORICAL COLLATION

Format:

Indentations: *even numbered lines ind*　B7 CT1 DT1 H4; *ll. 2, 3, 6, 7, 10, 11, 13, 14 ind*　B32 C2 O20 SP1 WN1; *ll. 2, 3, 6, 7, 10, 12 ind*　B46 C9 H5 H6 NY3; *ll. 10, 12 ind*　HH1; *no ind*　A–G 30.

Miscellaneous: *Holy Sonnets follow Corona immediately*　B7 B32 C2 CT1 DT1 H4 O20 SP1 WN1; *general HE Diuine Poems precedes Corona-Holy Sonnets group, with no subheading for Holy Sonnets*　B7 CT1 DT1 H4 WN1; *general HE Holy Sonnetts. written. 20. yeares since. precedes Corona-Holy Sonnets group*　B32; *general HE Holy Sonnets. precedes Corona-Holy Sonnets group*　C2 O20 SP1; »P« *left of HE*　H6; »p. 314.« *left of HE*　O20.

Headings: 1. Sonnett.　B32.　　Sonnett. I.　O20 SP1(~∧ 1∧).　　1. Sonnetts. Holy.　C2.　　2　C9 H5 H6 HH1 NY3(.~.).　　1.　DT1 H4(~∧) WN1(~∧).　　*Holy Sonnets. [section HE]* I.　A.　　II.　B–G.　　*The Conclusion.*　30.　　*om*　B7 B46 CT1.

1 due] ~,　B46.　　titles] Tithes,　B32 SP1; ~,　HH1 30; Titles → ›Tithes‹, O20.　　resigne] ~,　HH1.

2 My selfe] myself　H4.　　thee] ~,　B32 C2 C9 A–G 30; ~;　O20 SP1. (O] H5 NY3; ∧~　Σ.　　God):] ~,　B7 C2 CT1 O20 SP1 A; ~;　B32 C9 DT1

H4 HH1 WN1; ~∧ B46 30; ~. H6 B–G; ~) NY3.   first] I ~ 30.   I was]
was I   B46 C9 H5 H6 HH1.

3 thee,] ~∧   B46 H6 30; ~;   B C.   thee,] ~;   WN1 D–G; ~: 30.   and]
om 30.   decayde] ~, B32 C2 H5 D–G 30; decayed,   HH1; decayed   SP1.

4 Thy] The   30.   that,] ~∧   B7 B46 C9 CT1 DT1 H6 HH1 G 30.   the]
om HH1.   thyne.] ~∧   B7 B46 C9 DT1 H4 H6 SP1 WN1; ~,   B32 C2 CT1
HH1 O20 A–C 30; ~:   H5; ~;   D–G.

5 Sonne] ~,   B32 B46 C2 C9 H5 H6 HH1 O20 SP1 A–G; Sunne,   CT1 DT1
WN1; Sun   H4.   thy selfe] thee → »thy« »felfe«   HH1; Thyselfe   O20.
shyne,] ~∧   B7 B46 H4 HH1 WN1; ~;   B32 O20 SP1; ~.   NY3.

6 Servant,] ~∧   B7 B32 CT1 H4 O20 SP1 30.   repayde,] ~∧   B7 B46 C9
CT1 DT1 H4 H6 HH1 O20 SP1 WN1; ~.   NY3.

7 Sheepe,] ›Thy‹ ~,   H6; ~∧   WN1.   thyne] thy   B46 C9 H5 H6 HH1
30.   Image;] NY3; ~,   Σ.   and] ~,   B32 O20.   (till] ∧~   B7 B32 C2
CT1 DT1 H4 O20 SP1 WN1 A–G 30.   betrayde] ~,   DT1.

8 My selfe)] ~ ~,   B7 B32 C2 CT1 H4 WN1 A–G 30; Myselfe)   C9; ~ ~∧
DT1 SP1; Myselfe,   O20.   thy] this   B7 CT1; they   30.   divine.] ~∧   B7
B46 C9 CT1 O20 SP1; ~,   B32; ~;   C2 A–G.

9 then] thus   B46 C9 H5 H6 HH1.   in] on   B32 C2 O20 SP1 A–G 30;
~ → ›on‹   H6.   mee?] ~∧   B7 C9 CT1 H6.

10 steale,] ~∧   C9 A–C.   nay] ~,   30.   that's] whats   B7(whates) CT1.
right?] ~,   C2.

11 rise,] ~∧   C9 H6 A–F.   thyne] thy   HH1 30.   owne] one   HH1.
worke] works   B32 O20 SP1.   fight] ~,   B32 HH1 O20 A–G; ~.   WN1;
~;   30.

12 O] ~;   B7; ~,   B32 H5; ~!   30.   dispayre,] ~∧   B46 C9 H6 HH1 WN1;
~;   C2.   do] shall   B46 C9 H5 H6 HH1 B–G 30.   see] ~,   HH1.

13 lov'st] lovest   C2 SP1.   Mankind] man kinde   B46 H5.   well,] ~∧
B46 C9 H4 H6.   wilt not] will ~   B7 B32 WN1; ~'~   A–F.   choose] B7
B46 C9 CT1 H6 G 30; chose   NY3; chuse   Σ.   mee,] ~∧   B7 B46 C9 CT1
DT1 H4 H6 SP1 WN1; ~.   C2 A; m[e][,]   NY3.

14 me] NY3 SP1; ~,   Σ.   loose] lose   A–G 30.   mee.] ~| B7; ~.| B32
B46 C2 SP1; ~∧   CT1.

Subscriptions: *none.*

VERBAL VARIANTS IN SELECTED MODERN EDITIONS

Editions Collated: H I J K L M N O P Q S T U Z AA DD 72.
Format:
> Indentation: *ll. 2, 3, 6, 7, 10, 11 ind*   N; *no ind*   H–M O–Q S–U Z AA DD 72.

Headings: II.   H–K N–Q S DD 72.   VIII.   L.   IX.   M.   2   T AA.
> 1 (*first group*)   U.   162 *Holy Sonnet.*   Z.

9 in] on   H–Q S T AA DD.

12 do] shall   H–K M(M *var:* do) P; ~ (M *var:* shall)   O.

13 wilt] will   N 72.

14 loose] lose   H–K M O–Q S–U Z AA DD 72.

HSLittle

Textual Introduction

As is shown on Figure 2 in the General Textual Introduction (p. lxii), *HSLittle* is the seventh poem in both the earlier, Group-III sequence of "Diuine Meditations" and in NY3's later replication of that sequence at the beginning of its collection of "Holy Sonnets." The poem is discarded in the restructuring that gives rise to the subsequent Group-I/II sequence, however, and thus does not appear in A in 1633. In the editorially constructed sequence of 1635 (B), the poem is recovered from H6 and—in an apparently botched attempt to restore it to it to its original position— inserted in fifth position (before, rather than after, *HSScene*), where it remains in all subsequent editions save those of Alford, who reproduces the 1633 sequence; Lowell (M), who combines the Holy Sonnets with *Corona* in a continuously numbered se- ries; Gardner, who prints it as the second of the "penitential" sonnets "added in 1635"; and Shawcross, who essentially follows Gardner (see Figure 6 on p. lxxvi).

Within Group III the C9-H6 pair differs from B46, H5, and HH1 in two impor- tant instances, giving "land" (for the alternative "lands") in line 6 and "fire / Of Lust and Enuy hath [for the alternative *haue*] burnt" in line 11. Both likely reflect the γ¹ scribe's conscious attempt at improvement or correction, though NY3's later reitera- tion of "haue" in line 11 suggests that "haue" is not a mistake, but that Donne in- tended the verb to be governed by the plurality of "Lust and Enuy." Besides failing to punctuate "Oh" as parenthetical in line 4 (all Group IIIs except HH1 do so), the NY3 (Group-IV) text diverges from Group III in two other signal instances—in line 12, where it alters Group III's "their flames" to "those flames," and in line 13, where it uniquely reads "O God" rather than "O Lord." How, if at all, Donne intended "Oh" to be punctuated is unclear (the Group-III parentheses may well have origi- nated with the β¹ scribe), but the changes from "their" to "those" and "O Lord" to "O God" are very likely authorial. Unfortunately, these revisions exerted no influ- ence on the subsequent history of the text, as NY3 remained unknown until Gosse's work in the 1890s, and neither was ever adopted by a subsequent editor.

B sets the H6 text into print, including the parenthesized "Oh" in line 4 and the singular "land" in line 6. But B finesses the "haue/hath" problem in line 11 by drop- ping the word altogether, perhaps primarily in order to regularize the meter, and changes the spelling "dye" in line 4 to "die." This text of B passes on to the remain- ing seventeenth-century prints, and is modified by D's addition of a comma at the end of line 5 and by G's inexplicable change of "I might" to "he might" in line 7. The AF1 text, which contains the erroneous "he" in line 7, is copied from G, and B11 apparently derives from B (see the Textual Introduction to *HSMade*).

That most modern editions position the poem as in B is noted above, and most follow the text of the seventeenth-century prints as well. Tonson (I) corrects G's erroneous "he" in line 7, and of subsequent editors only Grosart (N) resurrects the mistake. All editors up through Chambers in 1896 read the editorial "land" in line 6; and Gosse (72) in 1899 joins these in omitting "haue" in line 11. Except for Bennett (T)—who keeps the singular "land" in line 6 and gives "'ath" in line 11—all twentieth-century editors return to the manuscript readings "lands" and "haue burnt."

Textual Apparatus

Copy-text: NY3.   **Texts collated:** AF1 (pp. [407–08]); B46 (f. 98v); C9 (f. 95v); H5 (f. 83v); H6 (p. 28); H11 (p. 71); HH1 (f. 128); NY3 (f. [34v]); B (p. 334); C (p. 334); D (pp. 318–19); E (pp. 318–19); F (pp. 318–19); G (p. 316).

Emendations of the copy-text: Heading: 7.] .~.   Line 1 cunningly] cūningly
  2 and] &   4 and] &   5 which] w^ch   that] y^t   which] w^ch
  6 and] &   7 that] y^t   8 with] w^t   10 the] y^e   11 and] &
  13 with] w^th   14 and] &   which] w^ch

HISTORICAL COLLATION

Format:

  Indentations: *ll. 2, 3, 6, 7, 10, 12 ind*   B46 C9 H5 H6 NY3; *ll. 3, 6, 7, 10, 13, 14 ind*   HH1; *no ind*   AF1 H11 B–G.

  Miscellaneous: ibid: *beside HE (refers to the citation page. 33. beside the HE of HSSighs)*   AF1; »P« *left of HE*   H6.

Headings: V. AF1 B–G.   7 C9 H5 H6 HH1 NY3(.~.).   Sonnet. 5 H11.   *om* B46.

  1 World,] B46 H5 NY3; ~_∧ Σ.

  2 Elements] ~,   AF1 B46 H5 H6 HH1 B–G.   Spright,] ~_∧ B46 C9 H5 H6; Spirit, HH1.

  3 Sin] B46 H6 NY3; sin Σ.   betrayd] betrayed HH1.   to] me ~ B46 HH1.   endles] darke B46.   night] ~; HH1.

  4 and] *om* HH1.   Oh] AF1 NY3; /~/ C9 H6; ~, HH1; (~) Σ.   dy.] ~_∧ B46 C9; ~, HH1.

  5 You,] ~_∧ AF1 C9 H6 H11 B–G.   heauen,] NY3; heav'n_∧ H5; ~_∧ Σ.   high] ~, D–G.

  6 Lands] land AF1 C9 H6 B–G.   wright] NY3; write, AF1 HH1 B–G; write Σ.

7 mine] my H11. so] *om* H5. I] he AF1 G.

8 World,] NY3; ~∧ Σ. ernestly.] NY3; ~∧ B46; To ~, H11; ~, Σ.

9 it:] ~, AF1 C9 H5 H6 HH1; ~∧ B46 H11 B–G. more:] ~, B46; ~. C9 H5 H6; ~∧ HH1.

10 Oh] (~) B46 H11; ~! H5. burn'd;] NY3; burnt: H5; burnt∧ HH1; burnt, Σ. alas] (~) HH1. the] with HH1. fyer] ~: HH1.

11 Of] Oh HH1. Lust] ~, HH1. Envy] ~, HH1. haue] *om* AF1 H11 B–G; hath C9 H6. hertofore] ~, AF1 HH1 B–G.

12 fouler;] B46 NY3; ~: H5; ~. H11; ~, Σ. those] NY3; their Σ. retyre,] ~∧ B46 C9 H5 H6 H11.

13 me] ~, H5. O] (~ HH1. God] NY3; Lord C9 H11; Lord, Σ. fiery] firy H5. Zeale] ~, HH1.

14 thee,' and] NY3; ~,∧ ~ AF1 HH1; ~∧∧ ~ Σ. thy] of thine AF1. doth] ~, H5. in] (~ B46. eating] ~) B46; ~, H5; ~[*missing*] H6. heale.] ~∧ H6.

Subscriptions: *none.*

Verbal Variants in Selected Modern Editions

Editions Collated: H I J K M N O P Q S T U Z AA DD 72.
Format:
    Indentations: *ll. 2, 3, 6, 7, 10, 12 ind* N; *no ind* H–K M O–Q S–U Z AA DD 72.
Headings: V. H–K N–Q S DD. XII. M. 5 T AΛ. 2 (*second group*) U. 175 *Holy Sonnet.* Z. VII 72.

6 lands] land H–K M–P T.

7 myne] my P 72. I] He N.

11 haue] *om* H–K M–P 72; 'ath T.

12 those] 72; their Σ.

13 God] 72; Lord Σ.

HSMade

Textual Introduction

As is shown on Figure 2 in the General Textual Introduction (p. lxii), *HSMade* is the introductory poem in both the earlier, Group-III sequence of "Diuine Medita-tions" and in NY3's later replication of that sequence at the beginning of its collec-tion of "Holy Sonnets." The poem is discarded in the restructuring that gives rise to the subsequent Group-I/II sequence, however, and thus does not appear in A in 1633. In the editorially constructed sequence of 1635 (B), the poem is recovered from H6 and restored to its original place at the head of the set, a position it occupies in all subsequent editions save those of Alford, who reproduces the 1633 sequence; Lowell (M), who combines the Holy Sonnets with *Corona* in a continuously numbered series; Gardner, who prints it as the first of the "penitential" sonnets "added in 1635"; and Shawcross, who essentially follows Gardner (see Figure 6 on p. lxxvi).

The primary manuscript texts exhibit little substantive variation and none that is unquestionably authorial. Within Group III the Historical Collation reports HH1's "my" (for the normative "myne") in line 2 and a split between "I can my selfe" (B46, H5, HH1) and the very likely scribal "my selfe I can" (C9, H6) in line 12; and the second-stage text of NY3 differs from its predecessors only in giving "towards [for *it t'wards*] hell" in line 8. Since NY3 never entered the contemporary stream of tex-tual transmission, however, and since—save Shawcross (Z), who lists the variant in his apparatus—no editor (including Gosse) has even noted the absence of "it" in NY3's rendition, the reading has practically been lost until now. "[T]owards hell" conveys essentially the same idea as Group III's "it towards [or *t'wards*] hell," how-ever, and may represent Donne's attempt to unclutter the line and clarify its meter.

Introducing the editorial "feeble" (for the manuscripts' "feebled") in line 7, B sets the H6 text into print, and the poem subsequently appears in C–G without further change. The texts in the remaining seventeenth-century sources derive, respectively, from one or another of these collected editions. As the inscriber's marginal note indicates (see the Format section of the Historical Collation below), the text in AF1 is taken from G. Although evidence within *HSMade* per se is lacking, the fact that among its Donne entries B6 includes the spurious "On the Sacrament" (first printed as Donne's in the 1635 *Poems* [B]) combines with a number of readings in *SecAn*—in line 96 (where B6 avoids B's erroneous "patch'd" [for the correct *parch'd*]), in line 103 (where B6 avoids G's erroneous "trust" [for the correct *thrust*]), and in line 350 (where B6 matches C's unique lowercasing of "suns" [where B and D–G capitalize the word])—to suggest that B6's copies of all its Donne texts, including *HSMade*, derive from C. H11 consists of handwritten additions to a copy of A that is now in the Harvard library, and the cataloguer's assertion that these stem "largely from the

1635 edition" is supported by a number of readings among the Holy Sonnets—including "feeble" (for "feebled") in *HSMade* 7—that exist only in the seventeenth-century prints; and H11's capitalized version of "Adamant" in *HSMade* 14 appears only in B and C. In a somewhat careless and deliberately emended printing, the 1650 *Mirrour of Complements* (siglum 30) includes not only *HSMade* (entitled *A holy Prayer*), but—following immediately—*HSDue* (entitled *The Conclusion*). Since readings among the epigrams indicate that the Donne texts in 30 derive from A, B, or C (see vol. 8, p. 24, of this *Variorum*), and since *HSMade* first appears in B, B or C must be the source of 30's Holy Sonnets.

That most modern editions position the poem as in B is noted above, and most follow the text of the seventeenth-century prints as well, the exceptions being that T, U, and Z give the manuscripts' "feebled" (for B's "feeble") in line 7 and that U, Z, and DD reject B's "my selfe I can" in line 12 in favor of the "I can my selfe" found in B46, H5, HH1, and NY3.

Textual Apparatus

Copy-text: NY3.   **Texts Collated:** AF1 (p. [407]); B6 (ff. 158v–59); B46 (f. 97); C9 (f. 94); H5 (f. 82); H6 (p. 25); H11 (p. 323); HH1 (f. 126); NY3 (f. [33]); B (pp. 331–32); C (pp. 331–32); D (pp. 316–17); E (pp. 316–17); F (pp. 316–17); G (p. 314); 30 (pp. 162–63).
Emendations of the copy-text: Heading: 1.] 1.   Line 1 and] &   3 and] &   5 way,] ~.   6 and] &   7 and] &   8 which] wch 9 and] &   11 our] o^r

Historical Collation

Format:
> Indentations: *ll. 2, 3, 6, 7, 10, 12 ind*   B46 C9 H5 H6 NY3; *ll. 6, 7, 11, 12 ind*   HH1; *no ind*   AF1 B6 H11 B–G 30.
> Miscellaneous: Additions to Dr Donne in y^e Edition 1669. 8vo | In the Holy Sonnets to be inserted, pag: 32. *written at top of p. [407]*   AF1; »P.« *left of HE*   H6.

Headings: 1   AF1.   Holly Sonnets   B6.   Diuine Meditations: [*section HE*] B46 HH1(~ ~$_\wedge$).   Diuine Meditations. [*section HE*] / 1.   C9 H5(1$_\wedge$) H6(1$_\wedge$).   A holy Sonnet. 1   H11.   Holy Sonnets. [*section HE*] 1. NY3 B–G.   A holy Prayer.   30.

1   Thou] LOrd ~   30.   me,] ~$_\wedge$ B6.   and] *om*   30.   worke] works B6.   decay?] ~$_\wedge$ B6; ~,   HH1 B.

2   me] ~,   H11.   now,] ~$_\wedge$ B6 H11.   myne] my   HH1 30.   hast.] ~, AF1 H5 H11 HH1 B–G 30; ~$_\wedge$ B6 B46 C9 H6.

3 death,] Death, AF1 B46 H5 H11; ~ʌ B6 C9.   death] Death AF1 B46
H5.   fast,] ~ʌ B6 B46 C9 H6 HH1.

4 pleasures] ~, HH1.   like] as 30.   yesterday.] ~: AF1; ~ʌ B6 C9
H6; ~, H11 HH1 B–G.

5 dimme] dark 30.   way,] ~ʌ B6 B46 C9 H5 H6; ~. NY3; ~; D–G.

6 behind,] ~ʌ B6.   death] Death AF1 B46 H5.   cast] ~, HH1.

7 terror,] ~ʌ B6.   febled] feeble AF1 B6 H11 B–G 30.   wast] ~. H6;
~, HH1 30.

8 Sin] sin AF1 B6 C9 H5 H11 HH1 B–G 30.   it,] ~ʌ B6 30.
which towards] ~ it t'wards AF1 C9 H5 H6 H11 B–G 30; ~ it ~ B6 B46 HH1.
doth] doeth 30.   weigh.] ~; AF1 H5 H11 HH1 B–G; ~ʌ B6 B46 C9 H6;
~, 30.

9 above;] ~, AF1 B46 C9 H5 H6 H11 HH1 B–G 30; ~ʌ B6.   towards]
t'wards H5 30.   thee] ~, HH1.   looke,] ~ʌ B6.

10 agayne.] ~; AF1 H11 HH1 B–G; ~ʌ B6 B46 C9 H6; ~: H5; ~, 30.

11 foe] ~, B46.   mee] ~, AF1 H5 H11 HH1 B–G 30.

12 I can my selfe] my selfe I can B6 C9 H6 H11 B–G.   sustayne.] ~: AF1;
~ʌ B6 B46 C9 H6 H11; ~, HH1 B–F 30; ~; G.

13 me,] NY3; ~ʌ Σ.   art] ~, AF1 H5 HH1 D–G 30; ~. H6.

14 thou] ~, H5.   Adamant,] H5 NY3; ~ʌ Σ.   myne] my 30.
hart.] H5 H11 NY3; ~ | B46; ~ʌ H6; heart. Σ.

Subscriptions: *none.*

Verbal Variants in Selected Modern Editions

Editions Collated: H I J K M N O P Q S T U Z AA DD 72.
Format:
>   Indentations: *ll. 2, 3, 6, 7, 10, 12 ind* N; *no ind* H–K M O–Q S–U Z AA
>   DD 72.
>   Miscellaneous: *immediately preceded by general HE* Holy Sonnets H I J N O–
>   Q S T 72; *preceded by general HE* Holy Sonnets / (added in 1635) /
>   Divine Meditations U; *preceded by general HE* Divine Meditations
>   AA; *preceded by general HE* Holy Sonnets / Divine Meditations DD;
>   *general HE om* K Z.

Headings: I.   H–K N–Q S DD 72.   VIII.   M.   1   T AA.   1 *(second group)*   U.   174 *Holy Sonnet.*   Z.

7 febled] feeble   H–K M–Q S AA DD.

8 towards] it ~   Σ.

12 I can my selfe] my self I can   H–K M–Q S T DD.

HSMin

Textual Introduction

As is shown on Figure 2 in the General Textual Introduction (p. lxii), *HSMin* is the ninth poem in both the earlier, Group-III sequence of "Diuine Meditations" and in NY3's later replication of that sequence at the beginning of its collection of "Holy Sonnets." In the restructuring that gives rise to the subsequent Group-I/II arrangement, however, the poem moves to the fifth position, following *HSRound*, and remains there in its first print appearance in A. In B, when the four discarded Group-III sonnets are recovered from H6 and reinstalled in the sequence, *HSPart* having been moved to the end of the group, *HSMin* is relocated and again occupies ninth place, remaining in that position in all subsequent editions except those of Alford (L), who reproduces the 1633 sequence; Lowell (M), who combines the Holy Sonnets with *Corona* in a continuously numbered series; Gardner (U), who prints the 1633 sequence; and Shawcross (Z), who essentially follows Gardner (see Figure 6 on p. lxxvi).

As is shown in the Historical Collation below and on Figure 4 in the General Textual Introduction (p. lxv), the manuscripts of *HSMin* exhibit a fair amount of variation; and most of it emerges as the text moves from the earlier, Group-III stage to its subsequent manifestation in NY3/Group IV. Distinctive Group-III readings include "or if the [for *and if that*] tree" in line 1, "and [for *or*] reason" in line 5, "thy [for *thine*] only worthy Blood" in line 10 (except for C9), and "remember them no more as debt" (for "remember them, Some clayme as debt") in line 13. The β¹ scribe also encloses "else immortall" (l. 2) and "else equall" (l. 6) in parentheses, a feature dropped in Groups IV, I, and II. While several manuscripts evince individual misreadings—e.g., WN1 gives "once els" (for "on els") in line 2, and the B7-CT1 pair omit "them" from the phrase "remember them" in line 13—the only family variant to emerge in the later stages of the text's evolution is Group II's trivialization of "dare" to "dares" in line 9. The text that appears in NY3 thus apparently embodies Donne's final intentions for the poem.[1]

Whether the parentheses in lines 2 and 6 are scribal or ultimately authorial,

---

[1]NY3's configuration of the syntax of lines 9 and 10 probably constitutes an exception to this statement. Like three members of Group III (the C9-H6 siblings and HH1) and one of Group II (WN1), NY3 fails to punctuate the end of line 9 as the end of a sentence, instead attaching the vocative at the beginning of line 10: "But who am I that dare dispute with thee / O God?" All other sources end the sentence with the line, pushing the vocative to the beginning of the subsequent sentence: ". . . dispute wᵗʰ thee? / Oh God, oh, of thine only worthy . . . ." That Group III is evenly divided between these alternatives (weighing γ¹'s offspring [C9 and H6] as a single instance) shows how vulnerable to scribal preference this reading was as well as making it impossible to determine whether NY3's version shows Donne changing his mind or reaffirming his former choice. In any case, Groups I and II (WN1 excepted) embody the second version, which is apparently what he finally settled on.

moreover, it seems likely that at least some of the distinctive Group-III verbals noted above embody Donne's earlier intentions. As noted in the General Textual Introduction above (see note 4, pp. lxvi–lxvii, above) for the Holy Sonnets the Group-III text is generally sound, and the β¹ scribe seems neither careless nor prone to alter his source deliberately. Thus "or if the" in line 1 and "intent and reason" in line 5 are probably early authorial choices; the evidence on whether "thy" in line 10 is also likely to be Donne's is inconclusive.[2]

Clearly, the most puzzling (and important) manuscript variant involves the "no more / Some clayme" crux in line 13. The latter clearly satisfies the criteria listed in Appendix 2 for indentifying authorial (as opposed to scribal) readings and is certainly Donne's. Opinions may differ, however, on whether Group III's "no more" also satisfies these criteria and represents the author's original conception or whether it reflects the misunderstanding of one or more scribes along the β¹ line of transmission. Regrettably, there is no purely bibliographical answer to this question. One approach to the problem is to recognize that if the later version of the line did not exist, Donne's authorship of "And drowne in it my sinnes blacke memory / That thou remember them no more as debt" would never be questioned. It is only in comparison to the "Some clayme" reading that the earlier version may seem repetitious, devoid of conceptual density, and unlikely to be authorial. Following Gardner's prior suggestion (p. 69), for instance, Stringer (2002) urges the probability that "no more" is a scribal trivialization in which the comparatively complex "Some clayme" version of these lines is overwritten by the simpler and "virtually self-inscribing" Biblical phrase "And their sinnes and iniquities will I remember no more" (Heb. 10.17 and 8.12) (p. 137).[3] But this conclusion is interpretively, not bibliographically, based and is by no means inevitable. Once readers become aware of the legitimacy of the early, Group-III sequence of Holy Sonnets, the claims to authenticity of its distinctive readings—including "remember them no more as debt"—will surely find their defenders.

In setting into type the revised version of HSMin from his usual Group-I manuscript, the editor of 1633 (A) essentially fixed its text for the next three-and-three-quarters centuries. Except for the line-1 typesetting blunder "poysons" (for "poysonous") that enters the stream of transmission in C (and remains until corrected 30 years later in G), the only changes introduced in B–G are a few instances

---

[2]The 12 sonnets of the early sequence contain 7 collocations in which the possessive pronouns "my/mine" or "thy/thine" precede a noun or adjective beginning with a vowel—in HSMade 2 and 14, HSDue 7 and 11, HSSighs 5, HSLittle 7, and HSMin 10. With the single exception of HSSighs 5 ("my Idolatry"), NY3 invariably uses the archaic "-ne" form, as do Groups I and II in those instances in which they contain the poem. Group III, however, is less consistent, reading "mine end" in HSMade 2, "mine iron heart" in HSMade 14, "thine owne worke" in HSDue 11 (HH1 misreads this as "thy one work"), and "myne eyes" in HSLittle 7—but "thy Image" in HSDue 7, "my Idolatrie" in HSSighs 5 (γ¹ [C9-H6] sophisticates to "mine Idolatry"), and "thy only worthy" here (except C9, which independently sophisticates to "thine").

[3]If this argument is valid, it perhaps implies—as we have suggested in the General Textual Introduction above (pp. ci–cii)—that the change from the original "Some clayme" to the corrupt "no more" occurred in an incremental series of missteps, since a scribe knowingly copying directly from Donne's papers might be expected to exercise particular care in following his source. In contradistinction to this view, however, Gardner seems to view the change as the work of a single

of altered punctuation and a gradual modernization of the spelling.[4] Among the moderns, only Alford (L)—who carelessly prints "he" (for "be") in line 4 and "it in" (for "in it") in line 12—and Grosart (N)—who in line 9 derives "dares" (for the standard "dare") from B7—exhibit any variation.

Textual Apparatus

Copy-text: NY3.   **Texts collated:** B7 (f. 105r–v); B32 (f. 140r–v); B46 (f. 99); C2 (f. 14); C9 (f. 96); CT1 (pp. 229–30); DT1 (f. 118v); H4 (f. 97v); H5 (f. 84); H6 (p. 29); HH1 (f. 128v); NY3 (f. [35]); O20 (f. 44v); SP1 (f. [58r–v]); WN1 (p. 7); A (p. 35); B (p. 337); C (p. 337); D (pp. 320–21); E (pp. 320–21); F (pp. 320–21); G (p. 318).

Emendations of the copy-text: Heading: 9.] .~.   Line 1 and] &   8 God,] ~∧   9 that] y^t with] w^t 13 them] thē   dett,] ~∧

Historical Collation

Format:

Indentations: *even numbered lines ind*   B7(*except 6*) CT1(*except 6*) DT1(*plus 9, 11, 13*) H4 WN1; *ll. 2, 3, 6, 7, 10, 11, 13, 14 ind*   B32 B46 C2 C9 H5 H6(*except 10*) HH1(*except 13*) NY3 O20 SP1; *no ind*   A–G.

Miscellaneous: »P.« *left of HE*   H6; »p. 318« *left of HE*   O20.

Headings: 5   B32 C2(~.) DT1(~.) H4 O20(~.) SP1(~.) WN1.   9   C9 H5 H6(.~.) HH1 NY3(.~.).   V.   A.   I X.   B–G.   *om*   B7 B46 CT1.

1 poysonous] poysons   C–F.   and if that] or if the   B46 C9 H5 H6 HH1. tree] Tree   B7 B32 B46 C2 C9 H5 H6 HH1(~ → »Tree«) O20; ~,   A–G.

2 death] ~,   B32 O20 SP1; Death,   C2; Death   CT1.   on] ~,   DT1 H4; (or   HH1; once   WN1.   els] (~   B46 C9 H5 H6 B–G.   immortall] ~) B46 C9 H5 H6 HH1 B–G; ~,   DT1 H4.   vs,] ~∧   B7 B32 B46 C2 C9 H4 H6 WN1 G; *s → »~∧«   HH1.

3 Serpents] serpents   B32 H5 SP1 A–F; Serpent   HH1; serpent   WN1. envious] ~,   B32.

4 damn'd,] ~;   C2 O20 SP1 A; damned,   HH1; ~∧   WN1.   alas] ~,   C2 H5 B–G; ~;   A.   bee?] ~∧   B7 C2; ~:   HH1.

5 intent,] ~∧   B7 B46 C2 C9 H5 H6 HH1 WN1 A–G.   or] and   B46 C9 H5 H6 HH1.   reason,] ~∧   B7 B46 C9 DT1 H4 H5 H6 HH1 SP1 WN1;

scribe, who carried "too many words in his head" and substituted the "obvious" for the author's more difficult reading (p. 69).

[4]Whether G's "born" in line 5 (for the previous "borne") is meant as a more up-to-date spelling or a different word is unclear.

Reason, C2.   borne] born HH1 G.   in] to HH1(M *var:* »~«).   me]
~, H5 A–G.

6 Sins] B46 C9 H5 H6 HH1 NY3 WN1; ~, Σ.   els equall,] (~ ~) B46
C9 H5 H6 HH1.   me] ~, C2 A.   hainous?] ~∧ B46 HH1 SP1.

7 mercy] ~, B7.   easy,] ~∧ B7 B46 C9 CT1 H5 H6 HH1 WN1 G.
glorious] ~, B32 HH1.

8 God,] ~∧ B7 B32 CT1 HH1 NY3; ~; B–G.   wrath] ~, B7 B32 B46
C2 CT1 DT1 HH1 O20 SP1 A–G.   hee?] ~∧ SP1.

9 I] ~, B32 C2 DT1 H5 O20 SP1 A–C.   dare] dares B7 CT1 DT1 H4
WN1.   thee] C9 H6 HH1 NY3 WN1; ~? Σ.

10 O] ~, B7.   God?] C9 H6 NY3 WN1; ~; B32 O20 SP1; ~, Σ.   O]
~, B46 C2 CT1; ~! A–G.   thyne] thy B46 H5 H6 HH1.   blood] ~,
C2 HH1 WN1 A–G.

11 teares] ~, B46 C2 C9 WN1 A–G.   a] an C9.   heauenly] heau'nly
CT1 H4 H5; heavenly HH1.   flood] ~, B32 DT1 O20 SP1 A–G; ~. C2.

12 in it,] NY3; it in∧ B7; ~ ~∧ Σ.   memoree.] ~∧ B7 B46 C9 DT1 H4
H5 H6 HH1 SP1 WN1; ~; B32 O20 B–G; ~, C2 CT1 A.

13 thou] you DT1 H4.   remember] ~, B7 CT1.   them,] *om* B7 CT1;
~∧ B46 C9 H5 H6 HH1.   Some clayme] no more B46 C9 H5 H6 HH1;
~ ~, H4.   dett,] ~∧ B7 B46 C9 CT1 H4 H6 HH1 NY3 SP1 WN1.

14 Mercy] ~, B32 C2 DT1 H4 H5 O20 SP1 A.   wilt] doe B7; will B32.
forgett.] ~∧ B7 B46 C9 CT1 H6 HH1; ~.| C2; ~, A.

Subscriptions: *none.*

Verbal Variants in Selected Modern Editions

Editions Collated: H I J K L M N O P Q S T U Z AA DD 72.
Format:
Indentations: *ll.* 2, 3, 6, 7, 10, 11 *ind* N; *no ind* H–M O–Q S–U Z AA
DD 72.
Headings: IX. H–K N–Q S DD 72.   XII. L.   XVI. M.   9 T AA.
5 (*first group*) U.   166 *Holy Sonnet.* Z.

4 be] he L.

9 dare] dares N.

12 in it] it in L.

HSPart

Textual Introduction

As is shown on Figure 2 in the General Textual Introduction (p. lxii), *HSPart* is the fourth poem in both the earlier, Group-III sequence of "Diuine Meditations" and in NY3's later replication of that sequence at the beginning of its collection of "Holy Sonnets." In the restructuring that gives rise to the subsequent Group-I/II arrangement, however, the poem is moved to twelfth position at the very end of the sequence and appears there in its first print appearance in A. In B, when the four discarded Group-III sonnets are recovered from H6 and reinstalled in the sequence, *HSPart* retains its place as the final (but now sixteenth) poem in the group and remains in that relative position in all subsequent editions except those of Gardner (U) (who prints three separate sets of Holy Sonnets) and Shawcross (Z) (who essentially follows Gardner, even though he numbers all the sonnets in a continuous series) (see Figure 6 on p. lxxvi).

As is shown in the Historical Collation below and on Figure 4 in the General Textual Introduction (p. lxv), the text of *HSPart* underwent authorial revision at both the Group-IV and the Group-I stages of its manuscript evolution and was subjected to further alteration at the hands of the editor in both 1633 (A) and 1635 (B). Group-IV (NY3) revisions of the early, Group-III text include changing (1) "made two Wills; he with the Legacie / Of his and thy kingdome doth thy Sonnes invest" to "made two Wills, which with . . . doth thy Sonnes invest" in lines 7–8; (2) "thy all healinge Grace" to "all-healing Grace" in line 11; and (3) "thy last will" to "that last Will" in line 14. Thus altered, NY3's version of the poem is further revised at the subsequent (Group-I) stage, evincing "those [C2: these] lawes" (for the earlier "thy Laws") in line 9 and "Reviue agayne" (for the earlier "Revive and quicken") in line 12. A sets this twice-revised text into print, its "these laws" in line 9 representing the conclusive link between it and C2, but the editor alters his Group-I/II text in four places. Though the full effect of H6 was not to be felt until the second edition of 1635 (B), there is some evidence that H6 affected a few readings in A (see, e.g., vol. 2, p. lxxvii, of this *Variorum*); and the change of C2's "gives me" to "gives to me" in line 4 and "All healinge Grace" to "thy all-healing grace" in line 11 may be further examples. A's institution of "this [for C2's *that* or H6's *thy*] last will" in line 14, on the other hand, is independent of any manuscript authority; and A's alteration of "doth" to "doe" in line 8 is apparently intended to repair a grammatical error inadvertently created when the revision of lines 7–8 replaced the singular "he" with the plural "wills" as the governor of the verb. B takes this resolution of the problem a step further, dropping the verb entirely in a move apparently calculated both to preserve the grammatical repair and to regularize the meter of the line. Thus modified, B's text passes on to C–G without further substantive change.

As is noted above, most modern editors position the poem as in B. Most also base their texts on the seventeenth-century prints, though some occasionally adopt manuscript readings, and Bennett (T) selects a manuscript (H6) as copy-text. Bennett is thus the sole modern editor to print "he with" (for "which with") in line 7 and "thy" (for "that" or "this") in line 14; and apart from Gosse (72)—who presents the text of NY3—Bennett is also the only modern editor to print "doth . . . invest" in line 8 and "and quicken" in line 12. All modern editors except Gardner (U) and Smith (AA) give A's emended "gives to me" (for "gives mee") in line 4, and all except Grierson (Q), Hayward (S), and Gardner accept A's emended "thy all-healing" (for "All healinge") in line 11. Deriving most directly from G, the eighteenth- and nineteenth-century editions H–K, M, and N accept B's omission of "doth" in line 8, but Alford (L) restores A's "doe" in that line and is followed by O, P, and all twentieth-century editions except T. Each of the alternatives at the "thy/these/those" crux in line 9 attracts adherents: Q, S, T, and AA prefer the Group-III/IV "thy"; N, U, and Z adopt the Group-I/II "those"; and the remainder accept the scribal "these" derived from C2 through A. The editorial "this" in line 14 makes its way into all modern editions except T (which follows H6's "thy") and N, U, Z, and AA (which adopt the Group-I/II "that").

Textual Apparatus

Copy-text: NY3.   **Texts collated:** B7 (f. 107); B32 (f. 141v); B46 (f. 97v); C2 (f. 15); C9 (f. 94v); CT1 (p. 233); DT1 (f. 120v); H4 (f. 99v); H5 (f. 82v); H6 (p. 26); HH1 (f. 127); IU2 (*ll. 13–14 only*, f. 59); NY3 (f. [33v]); O20 (f. 46r–v); SP1 (f. [60v]); A (pp. 39–40); B (pp. 341–42); C (pp. 341–42); D (p. 324); E (p. 324); F (p. 324); G (p. 321).

Emendations of the copy-text: Heading: 4.] .~.   Line 4 and] &   5 with] w^t the] ye 6 from] frō   and] &   7 which] wch with] w^t 8 and] &   9 that] y^t 11 and] &   12 and] &   and] &   13 and] &   Command] Cōmand   14 that] y^t

HISTORICAL COLLATION

Format:
Indentations: *even numbered lines ind*   B7 CT1 DT1 H4; *ll. 2, 3, 6, 7, 10, 12 ind*   B32 B46 C2 C9 H5 H6 NY3 O20 SP1; *ll. 3, 6, 7, 10, 13, 14 ind*   HH1; *no ind*   A–G.
Miscellaneous: »P.« *left of HE*, »Q.º *omitted« right of HE*   H6; *appears with other snippets under the collective HE* Pious things   IU2; »p. 321.« *left of* HE   O20.

Headings: 12.   B32 C2 DT1 H4(~$_\wedge$) O20 SP1.   4   C9 H5 H6 HH1   NY3(.~.).   X I I.   A.   X V I.   B–G.   *om*   B7 B46 CT1.

1 Father,] ~; H6; ~? HH1.   part] (~ B46.   interest] ~) B46;
~, HH1.

2 kingdome] B46 C9 H6 NY3; ~, Σ.   mee;] ~∧ B7 B32 CT1 DT1 H4;
~, B46 C2 O2o SP1 A–G; ~. C9 H6.

3 ioynture] ~, C2.   knotty] holy C9.   trinitee] ~, B32 C2 SP1 A.

4 keepes,] ~∧ C2 O2o SP1; ~; H6.   me] to ~ C9 H4(»to«) H6 A–G.
deaths] Death's B32 B46 C2 DT1 H4 H5 O2o.   Conquest.] ~∧ B7 CT1
DT1 H4 SP1; ~, B32 C2 O2o; ~: H6 HH1.

5 Lambe] B7 CT1 NY3; ~, Σ.   whose] (~ C9 H6.   death] C9 DT1
H4 H5 H6 NY3; ~, Σ.   life] ~, B7 B46 H4.   blest] ~, B32 C2 HH1
O2o SP1 A–G; ~) C9; ~,) H6.

6 slayne,] ~: B7 CT1 DT1; ~; B32 H4 HH1 O2o; ~∧ D–G.

7 Wills,] ~∧ B7; ~; B46 H5; ~. C9 H6.   which] he B46 C9 H5 H6(→
›~‹) HH1.

8 his,] ~∧ B46 C2 C9 H5 H6 HH1 SP1 A–G.   kingdome,] ~∧ B46 C9
H5 H6 HH1.   doth] ~ (M var: »doe«) H6; doe A; om B–G.   invest.]
~∧ B7 B46 CT1 DT1 H4; ~, B32 C2 O2o SP1 A–C; in vest∧ C9; in vest.
H6; ~; HH1; ~: D–G.

9 thy] those B7 B32 CT1 DT1 H4 O2o SP1; these C2 A–G.   Laws,] ~;
B7; ~∧ C9 H6.   men] we B46.   yett] ~, HH1.

10 Whether] whither B46 H4.   fullfill.] ~; B7 C2 CT1 DT1 A–G; ~,
B32 HH1 O2o SP1; ~∧ B46 C9 H6; ~: H4.

11 doth;] ~, B46 C2 C9 H6 A; ~: H5.   but] let H5.   all-healing]
~∧~ B7 C2 CT1 DT1; thy ~∧~ B46 H4(»thy« ~∧~) H6 HH1; thy ~–~ C9
H5 A–G.   Grace] ~, B32 DT1 H4 O2o SP1.   Spiritt] ~. DT1; ~, HH1
A.

12 Revive] ~, B46; Renew HH1.   and quicken] againe B7 B32 C2 CT1
O2o SP1 A–G; againe, DT1 H4; ~ ~, H5 HH1.   Law] ~, B7 CT1 H4.
kill.] ~∧ B7 B46 C9 CT1 H6; ~, B32 C2 O2o SP1 A.

13 abridgment,] ~∧ B46 C9 H6 HH1 IU2.   Command] ~, B32.

14 Is] Was IU2.   Love;] ~, B7 B32 C9 CT1 DT1 H5 O2o SP1; ~∧ IU2.
that] thy B46 C9 H5 H6 HH1; the IU2; this A–G.   stand.] ~∧ B7 C9
H6 IU2; ~.| B32 C2 HH1; ~: H4; ~! H5 A–G; ~| SP1.

Subscriptions: ffinis| B7; <u>ffinis</u> CT1 DT1 H4; om Σ.

Verbal Variants in Selected Modern Editions

Editions Collated: H I J K L M N O P Q S T U Z AA DD 72.

Format:
> Indentations: *ll.* 2, 3, 6, 7, 10, 12 *ind* N; *no ind* H–M O–Q S–U Z AA DD 72.

Headings: XVI. H–K N–Q S DD.   XIX. L.   XXIII. M.   16 T AA. 12 (*first group*) U.   173 *Holy Sonnet.* Z.   IV 72.

4 me] to ~   H–Q S T Z DD 72([to] ~).

7 which with] he with   T.

8 doth] *om*   H–K M N; do   L O(M *var: om*)–Q S U Z AA DD.

9 thy] these   H–M O P DD; those   N U Z.

11 all-healing] thy all-healing   H–P T Z AA DD 72([Thy] ~-~).

12 and quicken] again   H–Q S U Z AA DD.

14 that] this   H–M O P Q S DD; thy   T.

HSRound

Textual Introduction

As is shown on Figure 2 in the General Textual Introduction (p. lxii), *HSRound* is the eighth poem in both the earlier, Group-III sequence of "Diuine Meditations" and in NY3's later replication of that sequence at the beginning of its collection of "Holy Sonnets." In the restructuring that gives rise to the subsequent Group-I/II arrangement, however, the poem moves to the fourth position, following *HSScene*, and remains there in its first print appearance in A. In B, when the four discarded Group-III sonnets are recovered from H6 and reinstalled in the sequence, *HSPart* having been moved to the end of the group, *HSRound* is relocated to seventh place and remains in that position in all subsequent editions except those of Alford (L), who reproduces the 1633 sequence; Lowell (M), who combines the Holy Sonnets with *Corona* in a continuously numbered series; Gardner (U), who prints the 1633 sequence; and Shawcross (Z), who essentially follows Gardner (see Figure 6 on p. lxxvi).

As is shown in the Historical Collation below and on Figure 4 in the General Textual Introduction (p. lxv), the manuscripts of *HSRound* evince few variants, and all of them are scribally initiated sports that—with one notable exception—exert no influence on the subsequent history of the text: such variants include WN1's "memberles" (for "numberles") in line 3 and B7's "infirmities" (for "infinities") in that same line, WN1's "Agues tiranies" (for "agues, tyrannyes") in line 6, the Group-I "apace" (for the normative "a space") in line 9, and the B7-CT1 pair's "lousy [for *lowly*] ground" in line 12. The one variant of consequence appears in line 6, where—in every manuscript except NY3—"death" (for the authorial "dearth") is catalogued with "warr," "age," "agues," and "tyrannies" as a cause of the "Death" (l. 2) from which the "numberles infinities / Of Soules" are enjoined to "Arise." And, since NY3 remained unknown until the 1890s, the printed editions from 1633 (A) down to 1899, when Gosse's *Life and Letters* (72) appeared, invariably printed "death" as well.[1] The evidence thus indicates—unless WN1 and β⁵ derived the error from a parent artifact that should be added between them and LRH³ on the stemma shown in Figure 3 (see p. lxiv above)—that at least four scribes (those of β¹ and β⁴ in addition to those of WN1 and β⁵) misread "dearth" as "death" in transcribing the poem. Especially in light of the fact that "dearth" proved to be nowhere near so susceptible to misunderstanding in Donne's other uses[2], this is a troubling percentage of error.

---

[1] As noted above (p. lxxviii), Grosart (N) attempted to make sense of this line by placing "DEATH" first in the catalogue.

[2] Donne uses "dearth" or "dearths" in four other poems: in *Sat3* 19 ("To leaders rage, to stormes, to shot, to dearth?") 10 of 28 manuscripts misread "dearth" as "death"; but in *Sat2* 6 ("As I think that brings dearths, and Spaniards in") only 2 of about 30 manuscripts misread "dearths" as "death"; and

The alternatives—that "dearth" is a scribal sophistication or that both "death" and "dearth" reflected Donne's choice at various times—finally seem even less acceptable, however, and we must look to the thematic context for an explanation of the prevalence of the mistake in this particular instance.

Evincing the erroneous "death" in line 6, *HSRound* enters print in A, and the similarity of their punctuation in lines 7 (both give a comma after "chance"), 8 (both give a comma after "woe"), 10 (both give a comma after "these") and elsewhere suggests that A's compositor based his text—as usual—on C2. That he avoids such of C2's misreadings as "tasts" (for "tast") in line 8 and, especially, "apace" (for "a space") in line 9, however, indicates that he corrected the C2 text against another manuscript (see pp. lxxii–lxxiii above). Other changes—such as the addition of commas after the first "arise" in line 2 and "For" in line 10, as well as his elisions of "overthrowe" to "o'erthrow" in line 5 and "thou had'st" to "thou'hadst" in line 14— further bespeak the editor's characteristic concerns with sense and meter. From A, the text moves successively through B–F with little further change. G, however, introduces "agues tyrannies" (for "agues, tyrannies") in line 6, "holy (for *lowly*) ground" in line 12, and "my blood" (for "thy blood") in line 14. The eighteenth- and earlier nineteenth-century editions H–K and M adopt G's alteration in line 6 (reading "ague's tyrannies"), and H–K adopt "holy" in line 12 as well. G's "my blood," however, subsequently appears only in Grosart (N), who also prints "those" (for "these") in line 10 and—as noted above—reverses "warr" and "death" in line 6. Except for universally accepting NY3's "dearth" in line 6, the late nineteenth- and twentieth-century editors essentially print the text as given in A.

Textual Apparatus

Copy-text: NY3.   **Texts collated:** B7 (f. 105); B32 (f. 140); B46 (f. 98v); C2 (f. 14); C9 (f. 95v); CT1 (p. 229); DT1 (f. 118v); H4 (f. 97v); H5 (f. 83v); H6 (p. 28); HH1 (f. 128r–v); NY3 (f. [34v]); O20 (f. 44r–v); SP1 (f. [58]); WN1 (p. 6); A (p. 34); B (pp. 335–36); C (pp. 335–36); D (pp. 319–20); E (pp. 319–20); F (pp. 319–20); G (p. 317).

Emendations of the copy-text: Heading: 8.] .~.   Line 1 the] yᵉ   2 Your] Yʳ   4 and] &   go,] ~.   7 and] &   8 and] &   9 and] &   10 For] for   12 When] when   14 with] wᵗ

HISTORICAL COLLATION

Format:

Indentations: *even numbered lines ind* B7 CT1 DT1 H4; *ll. 2, 3, 6, 7, 10, 12 ind* B32 B46 C2 C9 H5 H6 NY3 O20 SP1 WN1; *ll. 2, 4, 6, 7, 10 ind* HH1; *no ind* A–G.

in *ElAnag* 19 ("In that leane dearth of Words, what could we say?") only 4 of 62 manuscripts wrongly record "death." In *EG* 7 ("Now pleasures dirth our City doth posses") the lone exemplar (NY3) correctly reads "dirth."

Miscellaneous: »P« *left of HE*   H6; »p. 317.« *left of HE*   O20.

Headings: 4.   B32 C2 DT1 H4(~:) O20 SP1(~ₐ) WN1(~ₐ).   8   C9 H5 H6 HH1 NY3(.~.).   I V.   A.   V I I.   B–G.   *om*   B7 B46 CT1.

1 At] As   C2 O20 SP1.   imagind] imagined   WN1.   corners] ~,   B32 C2 O20 SP1 A–G.

2 trumpets] ~,   B32 C2 C9 H5 O20 SP1 A–G.   Angels,] ~;   B7 C9 CT1; ~:   DT1; ~ₐ   H6.   and] ~,   H6.   Arise] B46 C2 NY3; ~,   Σ.   Arise] ~,   B46 C9.

3 Death] death   B7 C9 CT1 H6 SP1 WN1; death,   B32 H4 HH1 A–G; ~,   C2 DT1 O20.   you] yoʳ   B7.   numberles] memberles   WN1.   infinities] infirmities   B7; infinites   HH1.

4 Soules] NY3; ~,   Σ.   scattered] scattred   B32 C2 C9 CT1 DT1 H4 H6 O20 SP1 A B.   go,] ~ I   B7; ~ₐ   B32 CT1 DT1 H4 H6 O20 SP1 WN1; ~;   B46; ~.   C9 H5 NY3.

5 Flood] B7 NY3; flood   Σ.   did] B7 CT1 H6 NY3; ~,   Σ.   fyre] Fyre O20.   shall] ~,   HH1.   overthrow] ore'throwe   B46 C9; or'e-throwe   H5; or'e throw   H6; ~,   O20 SP1 G; o'erthrow,   A–F.

6 All] ~,   B46.   whom] ~,   C2.   Warr,] warr,   B7 CT1 H4 HH1 SP1 A–G; ~ I ,   H6.   dearth] death   B7 CT1 H4 H5 HH1 SP1 A–G; Death   B32 B46 C2 C9 DT1 H6 O20 WN1.   age,] Age,   B32 B46 C2 C9 DT1 O20 SP1 WN1; Age I   H6.   agues,] Agues,   B32 B46 C2 C9 DT1 H4 H6 O20 SP1; Aguesₐ   WN1; ~ₐ   G.   tyrannyes,] ~ₐ   B7 CT1 HH1 WN1; Tyrannies,ₐ B32 B46 C2 C9 DT1 H4 O20 SP1; Tyrannies,   H5 H6.

7 Law,] love,   B7; law,   C2 CT1 HH1 WN1 A–G.   Chance,] ~ₐ   B7 B46 DT1 H4 H6; chance,   C2 HH1 A; chanceₐ   CT1 WN1 B–G.   slayne,] ~; B7 CT1; ~.   C9 H6; ~ₐ   HH1.   and] And   C9 H6 WN1.   you] ~,   B C. eyes] ~,   B32 C2 A B; ~.   WN1.

8 tast] tasts   C2 O20; last   WN1.   deaths] Deaths   B32 B46 C2 DT1 H4 H5 O20 D–F.   wo.] ~ₐ   B7 B46 O20; ~,   B32 C2 CT1 DT1 SP1 WN1 A–F; ~:   H5; ~;   HH1 G.

9 sleepe,] ~ₐ   B7 B32 B46 C9 CT1 DT1 H6 HH1 O20 SP1 WN1.   Lord,] (~),   H6.   me] wee   HH1.   a space,] ~ ~ₐ   B7 B46 C9 DT1 H4 H5 H6 HH1; ~ pace;   B32; apace,   C2; apace;   O20 SP1.

10 For] ~,   A–G.   if] ~,   H4.   these] those   B7 CT1; ~,   C2 DT1 H4 A B.   abound] ~,   B32 C2 H5 HH1 A–G.

11 grace] Grace,   B32; Grace   B46 C2 O20; ~.   DT1; ~,   H5 A–G.

12 there:] ~;   B7 B32 B46 C2 CT1 DT1 H5 HH1 O20 A; ~,   C9 SP1 WN1;

~.   H6 B–G.   Here] ~,   B32 C2 O20 SP1.   this] yᵉ HH1.   lowly] lousy
B7 CT1; holy   G.   ground] ~,   C2 A–G.

13 repent,] ~;   B32 C2 HH1 O20 SP1 A–G; ~ₐ B46.   that's] that   B46.
good] ~,   HH1.

14 thou hadst] th'hadst   B46 C9 H5 H6; ~'~   DT1 A.   Seald] ~,   HH1.
pardon] ~,   B32 C2 O20 SP1 A–G.   thy] my   G.   blood.] ~ₐ   B7 CT1
H6; ~. | C2; ~:   H4; ~. | SP1.

Subscriptions: *none.*

Verbal Variants in Selected Modern Editions

Editions Collated: H I J K L M N O P Q S T U Z AA DD 72.
Format:
   Indentations: *ll. 2, 3, 6, 7, 10, 12 ind*   N; *no ind*   H–M O–Q S–U Z AA
      DD 72.
Headings: VII. H–K N–Q S DD.   XI. L.   XIV. M.   7 T AA.
      4 (*first group*) U.   165 *Holy Sonnet.* Z.   VIII 72.

   3 you] your   L.

   6 Warr, dearth] ~, death   H–M O P; DEATH, warr   N.   agues, tyrannyes]
ague's ~   H–K M.

   10 these] those   N.

   12 lowly] holy   H–K.

   14 thy] my   N.

HSScene

Textual Introduction

As is shown on Figure 2 in the General Textual Introduction (p. lxii), *HSScene* is the sixth poem in both the earlier, Group-III sequence of "Diuine Meditations" and in NY3's later replication of that sequence at the beginning of its collection of "Holy Sonnets." In the restructuring that gives rise to the subsequent Group-I/II arrangement, however, the poem moves to the third position, following *HSBlack*, and remains there in its first print appearance in A. In B, when the four discarded Group-III sonnets are recovered from H6 and reinstalled in the sequence, *HSPart* having been moved to the end of the group, *HSScene* assumes sixth place and remains in that position in all subsequent editions except those of Alford (L), who reproduces the 1633 sequence; Lowell (M), who combines the Holy Sonnets with *Corona* in a continuously numbered series; Gardner (U), who prints the 1633 sequence; and Shawcross (Z), who essentially follows Gardner (see Figure 6 on p. lxxvi).

As is shown in the Historical Collation below and on Figure 4 in the General Textual Introduction (p. lxv), the manuscript texts of *HSScene* are rife with variation. A number of these variants are isolated sports that exert no influence on the subsequent transmission of the text: for example, B46's "a part" (for "appoint") in line 1; HH1's "place" (for "pace") in line 3; C2, B7, and HH1's "pace" (for "space") in line 6; SP1's "was [for *as*] my soule" in line 9; C2's "state" (for "seate") in line 9 (an error that also appeared initially in C9, H6, and HH1); WN1's "full" (for "fall") in line 11; and H5's "Hell" (for "to hell") in line 12. Even such family readings as Group I's "Pilgrimage" (for the normative "Pilgrimages") in line 2 and "falls [for *fall*] my sinns" in line 11 are readily identifiable as scribal errors. Other variants, however, appear to be authorial, showing that as the text evolved from the original form recorded in the Group-III artifacts to its final state in Group II, Donne intervened to revise it on two separate occasions—first, in the transition from its early, Group-III state to the intermediate state embodied in NY3 (Group IV); second, in the transition from Group I to its final form in Group II. The original (Group-III) text evinces a trio of readings that differentiate it from its successors: "latest [for the subsequent *last*] pointe" in line 4, "and my Soule" (for "and Soule") in line 6, and "shakes me [for *my*] euery ioynt" in line 8.[1] That the bracketed alternatives to these three readings appear at every succeeding manuscript stage of evolution leaves no doubt as to Donne's final preferences; and if we are not to regard the alternatives as revisions, we must regard the Group-III readings as scribal mistakes—not an impossible explanation, to be sure, but also not self-evidently a necessary one. Indeed, to take the

---

[1]The text in the Group-III siblings C9 and H6 has been scribally edited, recording "soule" [for "my soule"] in line 6, "thus purged" (for "purged thus") in line 13, and "so [for *thus*] I leaue" in line 14.

most salient example, the conviction that "last [not *latest*] pointe" was the spurious reading led A's editor to emend his Group-I setting text (C2) to "latest," and not until the publication of Gardner's *Divine Poems* (U) in 1952 was the existence of "last" even acknowledged by an editor.

Exhibiting the revisions "last pointe," "and Soule," and "shakes my euery ioynt," *HSScene* next appears in NY3, and passes on to Group I without substantive change. The later Group-II artifacts, however, record a final authorial revision in line 7, the original "Or presently, I know not, see y^t face" becoming "But my euer wakeing part shall see that face." (For the possible significance of this change see the Commentary and pp. xcviii–xcix in the General Textual Introduction above.) Bearing this revision, the text enters print in A; and the editor's avoidance of the errors "Pilgrimage" (for the normative "pilgrimages") in line 2, "pace" (for the correct "space") in line 6, "me" (for "my") in line 8, "state" (for "seate") in line 9, and "falls" (for "fall") in line 11 indicates either that he heavily emended his usual setting text (C2) or that he abandoned it altogether in favor of the Group-II source containing the revised line 7. In addition, A evinces two changes—"latest [for *last*] point" in line 4 and "my soule" (for "Soule") in line 6—that were available in neither Group I nor Group II and one—"the [for *and*] devill" in line 14—that appears in no manuscript at all. If the first of these could reflect the influence of H6 (see the Textual Introduction to *HSPart*), sole responsibility for the second and third must be laid at the foot of the editor. That "the devill" persists in B (and, indeed, in C–G) indicates that the editor remained satisfied with this change, but his reversion to "soule" (from "my soule") in B suggests that A's version of line 6 may have been a mistake.

Modified by the omission of "my" in line 6, the text of *HSScene* passes on to C–G without change, and even the postseventeenth-century editions exhibit little variation. As is shown in the apparatus below, A's "latest" in line 4 appears in every edition except that of Gardner (U); and B's deletion of "my" in line 6 carries forward to all subsequent editions except L, O, and T—including several that declare A (which has "my") as their copy-text. Though it was included in Gosse's presentation of the text of NY3 in the *Life and Letters* (72), the original version of line 7 ("Or presently, I know not") has never appeared outside the apparatus in an edition of Donne's poetry; and of all modern editors only Bennett (T), Gardner (U), Shawcross (Z), and Smith (AA) abandon the editorial "the devill" in line 14 in favor of Donne's "and deuill."

Textual Apparatus

Copy-text: NY3.   **Texts collated:** B7 (ff. 104v–05); B32 (f. 140); B46 (f. 98); C2 (f. 13v); C9 (f. 95); CT1 (pp. 228–29); DT1 (f. 118); H4 (f. 97); H5 (f. 83); H6 (p. 27); HH1 (ff. 127v–28); NY3 (f. [34]); O20 (f. 44); SP1 (ff. [57v–58]); WN1 (p. 6); A (pp. 33–34); B (p. 335); C (p. 335); D (p. 319); E (p. 319); F (p. 319); G (pp. 316–17).
Emendations of the copy-text: Heading: 6.] .~.   Line 6 and] &   and] &   7 that] y^t 11 that] y^t 12 and] &   hell] tell   14 and] &

HISTORICAL COLLATION

Format:

Indentations: *even numbered lines ind* B7(*except 2*) CT1 DT1(*plus 13*) H4; *ll. 2, 3, 6, 7, 10, 12 ind* B32 B46 C2 C9 H5 H6 NY3 O20 SP1 WN1; *ll. 2, 4, 6, 7, 10 ind* HH1; *no ind* A–G.

Miscellaneous: »P.« *left of HE* H6; »p. 316.« *left of HE* O20.

Headings: 3.| B32 C2(~.) DT1(~.) H4(~:) O20(~.) SP1(~‸) WN1(~‸). 6 C9 H5 H6 HH1 NY3(.~.). I I I. A. V I. B–G. *om* B7 B46 CT1.

1 Scene,] ~; B46; ~: H4; ~. H6; ~‸ WN1. heauens] heau'ns B7 CT1 DT1 H5; heauen's B46. appoint] a part B46; ~, → ›~‸‹ H6.

2 Pilgrimages] Pilgrimage B32(Pilligrimage) C2 O20 SP1. Mile,] ~; B7 B32 C2 CT1 DT1 H4 H6 O20 SP1 A–G. race,] B7 CT1 NY3; ~‸ Σ.

3 Idely,] ~‸ B7 B46 SP1 WN1; (~, C9 H6. quickly] ~, H6. run,] ~) C9 H6; ~‸ H4. hath] hat H5. pace] ~, B32(space → ›~‹,) C2 CT1 H6 O20 SP1 A–G; place HH1.

4 inche;] NY3; ~, Σ. last] latest B46 C9 H5 H6 HH1 A–G. pointe.] ~‸ B7 B46 C2 H4 HH1 O20 SP1 WN1; ~, B32 C9 H5 H6 A–G.

5 death] ~, B32 O20 SP1 A; Death, C2; Death C9 DT1 H4 H5.

6 body] ~, B32 C2 CT1 DT1 H4 O20 WN1 A. Soule,] my ~; B46; ~‸ C9; ~; DT1; my ~, H5 HH1 A. space,] pace‸ B7 C2 CT1(→ ›~‹‸) H6(→ ›~‹‸) HH1; ~‸ B32 B46 C9 DT1 H4 O20 SP1 WN1.

7 Or presently, I know not,] But my everwakinge part shall B7 CT1(euer wakeing) DT1(euer wakeing) H4(euer=waking) WN1(everlastinge) A–F(my'ever-waking) G(ever-waking); ~ ~‸ (~ ~ ~) B46 C9 H5 H6 HH1. face] ~, B32 C2 H5 A–G.

8 my] me B46 C2 C9 H5 H6 HH1. ioynt.] ~‸ B7 B32 B46 CT1 H4 HH1 O20 SP1 WN1; ~: A–G.

9 Then] ~, C9 H5 H6 A B D–G. as] was SP1. Soule,] ~‸ B7 B46 C9 CT1 H5 H6 HH1 WN1. to' heauen] ~‸ ~, B7 CT1 WN1; ~‸ ~ B32 B46 C2 C9 H6 O20 SP1 B–G; ~‸ heau'n DT1 H5 HH1; ~‸ heaue'n, H4. her] (~ B46 C9 H5 H6 HH1. Seate] ~, B32 DT1 H4 O20 SP1 A–G; ~) B46 H5; state, C2; state → ›~‹ C9 H6; state HH1(→ »~«). takes] take B7 C9 CT1. flight,] H5 NY3 A–G; ~: C2; ~‸ Σ.

10 earthborne] Earth borne B7 B32 O20 SP1 WN1 A; earthe=borne B46 C9 CT1 DT1 H4 H5 H6 HH1 B–G. body] ~, B32 C2 DT1 O20 SP1 A B. dwell,] ~‸ B7 B46 C9 H4 H5 H6 HH1 SP1 WN1; ~. C2.

68 ❦ TEXTS AND APPARATUSES

11 So] ~, A–G.   fall] falls   B32 C2 O2o SP1; full   WN1.   Sins,] ~₍∧₎
WN1.   that] (~   H6.   their] there   CT1.   right,] B32 NY3 A–G;
~) H6; ~₍∧₎ Σ.

12 To] ~,   H5.   they'are] ~₍∧₎~   B7 B32 C2 CT1 H5 O2o SP1 WN1; th'~
B46 C9 H6 HH1.   bred,] ~₍∧₎   C9 HH1; ~;   O2o WN1.   me,] ~₍∧₎   B7
B46 C2 CT1 DT1 H4 HH1 WN1 C–G; ~;   H6.   to] *om*   H5.   hell;] B32
O2o SP1; ~₍∧₎   B7 CT1 WN1; ~,   C9; tell;   NY3; ~.   Σ.

13 righteous] ~,   B46 H4 H5 HH1 A–G.   thus purg'd] ~ purged   B32 C2
O2o; purged thus   C9 H6.   euill,] H5 NY3 A–G; ~.   DT1; ~₍∧₎   Σ.

14 thus] that   B7 CT1; so   C9 H6.   leaue] ~,   B32 DT1 O2o SP1.
fleshe,] ~;   H6; ~₍∧₎   HH1 SP1 A.   and] the   A–G.   deuill.] ~.| B7 C2
SP1; ~₍∧₎   CT1 H6 HH1 WN1.

Subscriptions: *none.*

Verbal Variants in Selected Modern Editions

Editions Collated: H I J K L M N O P Q S T U Z AA DD 72.
Format:
> Indentations: *ll. 2, 3, 6, 7, 10, 12 ind*   N; *no ind*   H–M O–Q S–U Z AA
> DD 72.

Headings: VI.   H–K N–Q S DD 72.   X.   L.   XIII.   M.   6   T AA.
> 3 *(first group)*   U.   164 *Holy Sonnet.*   Z.

4 *second* last] U; latest   Σ.

6 *first* and] and my   L O T.

7 Or presently, I know not] 72; But my 'ever-waking part shall   Σ.

14 and] the   H–Q S DD 72.

HSShe

Textual Introduction

As is indicated on Figure 2 in the General Textual Introduction (p. lxii), that in NY3 is the sole manuscript copy of *HSShe,* and the poem never appeared among the seventeenth-century editions. Indeed, the very existence of this sonnet remained generally unknown until Edmund Gosse published it—and eventually the entire NY3 sequence—in the 1890s (see the General Textual Introduction, pp. lxxix–lxxx [fn. 19] and xc). Having been brought to light, of course, the poem has appeared in all subsequent editions, always appended at the end of the previous 16 Holy Sonnets (however arranged) as the first of the 3 sonnets unique to the Westmoreland manuscript (see Figure 6 on p. lxxvi).

A prolific editor, Gosse took a considerably looser approach to his task than have most of his successors, and—as is shown in the Historical Collation—some details in his three printings of *HSShe* vary not only from the manuscript, but also from one another. At the end of line 3, for example, where NY3 reads "rauished," (so spelled and punctuated), Gosse reports "vanished"; moreover, he punctuates here in three different ways, using a dash in 71 (—), a period and a dash in *Jac* (.—), and a comma and a dash in 72 (,—). Gosse's unvarying substitution of "vanished" for "rauished" may be a deliberate bowdlerization, and other divergences from the manuscript—such as his "on [for NY3's *in*] heavenly things" in line 4 and "their [for NY3's *the*] head" in line 6—perhaps represent conscious "improvements." Such anomalies as *Jac*'s "Does" (for Dost") in line 10 and "this [for *the*] World" in line 14, however, can only be attributed to carelessness. Although Gosse follows the manuscript's pattern of indentation in both 71 and *Jac,* in 72, as part of a regularized presentation of the entire NY3 sequence, the poem appears without indentation.

All twentieth-century editions also print the poem without indentation, instead imposing the flush-left style that they follow for the first 16 sonnets. Grierson (Q) and, following him, Hayward (S) and Patrides (DD), moreover, all print Gosse's "on" (for "in") in line 4 and his "their" (for "the") in line 6. As is noted in the General Textual Introduction (see pp. lxxxiii and cii), a major crux involving punctuation appears in line 10, where the manuscript gives "Dost woe my Soule for hers; offring all thine . . . ." Though he reduces the semicolon to a comma, Gosse preserves the syntax of the line as it exists in the manuscript; and Grierson (who reinstitutes the semicolon), Hayward, Smith (AA), and Patrides follow him in this. Finding the manuscript's version of the line unintelligible, however, Bennett (T) removes the punctuation after "hers" and inserts a comma after "Soule"; and his emended "Dost woo my soul, for hers off'ring all thine" is adopted in all subsequent editions—including the present one—save those of Smith and Patrides.

Textual Apparatus

Copy-text: NY3.   Texts collated: NY3 (f. [37]); 71 (p. 242); *Jac* (p. 59); 72 (pp. 370–71).

Emendations of the copy-text: Heading: 17.] .17.   Line 2 and] &   6 the] y^e 7 and] &   10 Soule,] ~$_\wedge$ hers] ~;   12 Angels,] ~$_\wedge$ diuine,] ~$_\wedge$ 14 the] y^e

HISTORICAL COLLATION

Format:

Indentations: *ll.* 2, 3, 6, 7, 10, 12 *ind*   NY3 71 *Jac; no ind*   72.
Headings: .17.   NY3.   *om*   71 *Jac* 72.

1 She] NY3; she   Σ.   lovd,] NY3; loved$_\wedge$ Σ.

2 hers,] ~$_\wedge$ 71 *Jac*; her's,   72.   dead] NY3; ~,   Σ.

3 Soule] NY3; soul   Σ.   rauished,] vanished—   71; vanished.—   *Jac*; vanished,—   72.

4 in] NY3; on   Σ.

6 thee] NY3; ~,   Σ.   shew] NY3; show   Σ.   the] NY3; their   Σ. head,] ~;   71.

7 thee,'and] NY3; ~,$_\wedge$ ~   Σ.

9 when as] whenas   71 72.

10 Dost] Does   *Jac.*   woe] NY3; woo   Σ.   Soule,] ~$_\wedge$ Σ.   hers] ~; NY3; ~,   Σ.   thine:] ~;   71 72.

11 least] NY3; lest   Σ.

12 Angels,] ~$_\wedge$ NY3.   diuine,] ~$_\wedge$ NY3.

14 least] NY3; lest   Σ.   the] this   71 *Jac.*   Deuill] ~,   71 72.   out.] NY3; ~?   Σ.

Subscriptions: *none.*

VERBAL VARIANTS IN SELECTED MODERN EDITIONS

Editions Collated: Q S T U Z AA DD.
Format:

Indentations: *no ind*   Q S–U Z AA DD.

Headings: XVII. Q S DD.   17 T AA.   1 (*third group*) U.   178 *Holy Sonnet.* Z.

4 in] on   Q S DD.

6 the] their   Q S DD.

10 Soule,] ~∧   Q S AA DD.   hers] ~;   Q S AA DD.

HSShow

Textual Introduction

As is indicated on Figure 2 in the General Textual Introduction (p. lxii), that in NY3 is the sole manuscript copy of *HSShow*, and the poem never appeared among the seventeenth-century editions. Indeed, the very existence of this sonnet remained generally unknown until Edmund Gosse published it as part of his presentation of the entire NY3 sequence in 1899 (see the General Textual Introduction, pp. lxxix–lxxx [fn. 19] and xc). Having been brought to light, of course, the poem has appeared in all subsequent editions, always appended at the end of the previous 16 Holy Sonnets (however arranged) as the second of the 3 sonnets unique to the Westmoreland manuscript (see Figure 6 on p. lxxvi).

A prolific editor, Gosse took a considerably looser approach to his task than have most of his successors, and—as is shown in the Historical Collation—his printing of *HSShe* in 72 is unfaithful to the manuscript at numerous points. He alters the punctuation of his source in some 13 instances, observes none of the manuscript's elisions, and—apparently in the interests of stylistic improvement—changes Donne's "w^{ch}" to "who" in both lines 2 and 3. His "lore" (for "tore") at the end of line 3 is apparently a careless mistake. Finally, perhaps because he wishes to regularize the physical appearance of all the sonnets in the sequence, he abandons the manuscript's indentation pattern and prints all lines in the poem flush left.

All twentieth-century editions also print the poem without indentation, instead imposing the left-aligned style that they follow for the first 16 sonnets. No twentieth-century editor, however, reproduces Gosse's verbal alterations of the poem, and Bennett's trivialization of "trauaile" to "travel" in line 10 is the only verbal variant reported in the apparatus. Other than expanding abbreviations and otherwise aligning the manuscript text with the conventions of print, our only emendation involves reifying an only-partly-visible comma at the end of line 12.

Textual Apparatus

Copy-text: NY3.   **Texts collated:** NY3 (f. [37]); 72 (p. 371).
Emendations of the copy-text: Heading: 18.] .~.   Line 1 and] &   2 which] wch 3 which] wch and] &   4 and] &   and] &   6 and] &   7 *2nd* and] &   9 with] w^t 10 First] first   and] &   11 our] o^r 13 and] &   14 and] &

HISTORICAL COLLATION

Format:
    Indentations: *ll. 2, 3, 6, 7, 10, 12 ind*   NY3; *no ind*   72.

Headings: .18. NY3.   XVIII   72.

1 me] ~,   72.   Spouse,] ~ₐ   72.

2 What] ~?   72.   which] who   72.

3 Or] ~,   72.   which] who,   72.   rob'd] robb'd   72.   tore] lore,   72.

6 selfe truth] ~‑~,   72.   now'outwore?] ~ₐ ~?   72.

7 She,' and] ~ₐₐ ~   72.   She,] ~ₐ   72.

10 seeke] ~,   72.

11 Betray] ~,   72.   husband] ~,   72.   Sights,] ~ₐ   72.

13 trew] true   72.

14 She'is] ~ₐ ~   72.

Subscriptions: *none.*

Verbal Variants in Selected Modern Editions

Editions Collated: Q S T U Z AA DD.
Format:
   Indentations: *no ind* Σ.
Headings: XVIII.   Q S DD.   18   T AA.   2 *(third group)*   U.
   1 79 *Holy Sonnet.*   Z.

10 trauaile] travel   T.

HSSighs

Textual Introduction

As is shown on Figure 2 in the General Textual Introduction (p. lxii), *HSSighs* is the third poem in both the earlier, Group-III sequence of "Diuine Meditations" and in NY3's later replication of that sequence at the beginning of its collection of "Holy Sonnets." The poem is discarded in the restructuring that gives rise to the subsequent Group I/II sequence, however, and thus does not appear in A in 1633. In the editorially constructed sequence of 1635 (B), the poem is recovered from H6 and restored to its original place in third position, where it remains in all subsequent editions save those of Alford, who reproduces the 1633 sequence; Lowell (M), who combines the Holy Sonnets with *Corona* in a continuously numbered series; Gardner, who prints it as the third of the "penitential" sonnets "added in 1635"; and Shawcross, who essentially follows Gardner (see Figure 6 on p. lxxvi).

The Group-III manuscripts vary importantly in lines 5, 7, and 8; and all three changes are the work of the γ¹ scribe, whose alterations are passed on to the siblings C9 and H6. This scribe sophisticates "my Idolatry" to "mine Idolatry" in line 5 and "Because" to "'Cause" in line 8, additionally changing the syntax of the original "That sufferance was my Sin, now I [B46: *I now*] repent" in line 7 to "That sufferance was my sinne I now repent" by dropping the internal comma. NY3 (Group IV) carries forward the B46-H5-HH1 version of the Group-III text without substantive alteration.

B sets the H6 text into print, and the poem subsequently appears in C–G without further change. The manuscript copy in AF1 is taken from G and, apparently, that in H11 from B (see the Textual Introduction to *HSMade*).

That most modern editions position the poem as in B is noted above, and most follow the text of the seventeenth-century prints as well, the exceptions being that Tonson (H) introduces "these" (for "those") in line 1 and is followed in this reading by I–K, M, and N; that U reject's B's "mine" in favor of the manuscripts' "my" in line 5; that U and AA refuse B's "'Cause" for the manuscripts' "Because"; and that a number of these editions choose the manuscripts' "now I" over B's "I now" in line 7 (see the section Verbal Variants in Selected Modern Editions below). Although a majority of the moderns also reproduce B's syntax in line 7, half-a-dozen restore the manuscript original: P, U, Z, and AA punctuate the line with a comma after "Sin," while Q and S supply a semicolon.

Textual Apparatus

Copy-text: NY3.   **Texts collated:** AF1 (p. [407]); B46 (f. 97v); C9 (f. 94v); H5 (f. 82v); H6 (p. 26); H11 (pp. 323–24); HH1 (ff. 126v–27); NY3

(f. [33v]); B (p. 333); C (p. 333); D (pp. 317–18); E (pp. 317–18); F
(pp. 317–18); G (p. 315).

Emendations of the copy-text: Heading: 3.] .~.   Line 1 and] &   2 and] &
which] w^ch   4 with] w^t   9 and] &   10 and] &   11 the] y^e
12 comming] cōming   14 and] &   and] &

HISTORICAL COLLATION

Format:

> Indentations: *ll. 2, 3, 6, 7, 10, 12 ind* B46 C9 H5 H6 NY3; *ll. 3, 5, 6, 7,
> 11 ind* HH1; *no ind* AF1 H11 B–G.
>
> Miscellaneous: *page. 33. to right of HE (indicating where poem is to be inserted
> earlier in the volume)* AF1; »P.« *left of HE* H6.

Headings: III. AF1.   3 C9 H5 H6 HH1 NY3(.~.).   Sonnet 3 H11.
    I I I. B–G.   *om* B46.

1 againe] ~, HH1.

2 eyes,] ~_∧ B46 C9 H11 HH1.   spent;] ~, AF1 H6 H11 B–G; ~_∧ B46
C9 H5.

3 discontent] ~, HH1.

4 Mourne] ~, C9 H6.   vaine.] ~: AF1; ~_∧ B46 H5 HH1; ~, H6
E(CtY); ~; H11 B–G.

5 my] mine C9 H6 H11 B–G.   Idolatry] ~, H5; ~. H6.   what]
with HH1.   raine] ~; HH1.

6 wast?] ~_∧ HH1.   what] with HH1.   griefes] greefe C9 H11; greef,
HH1.   my] mine AF1 C9.   hart] heart AF1 C9 HH1 B–G.   rent?]
~_∧ HH1.

7 Sin,] ~_∧ AF1 C9 H6 H11 HH1 B–G.   now I] I now AF1 B46 C9 H6
H11 B–G.   repent;] ~, AF1 C9 H6 H11 B–G; ~_∧ B46 H5.

8 Because] 'Cause AF1 C9 H6 H11 B–G.   suffer,] ~_∧ AF1 C9 H6 B–G.
paine.] ~., HH1.

9 dronkerd,] ~_∧ C9.   night-scowting] ~_∧~ H6 HH1.   theefe,] ~_∧
B46 C9 H5 H6 H11 HH1.

10 itchy] Itching HH1.   selfe-tickling] ~_∧~ C9 H11 HH1 B–F.   proud,]
NY3; ~_∧ Σ.

11 ioyes] ~, H6 B–G.   reliefe] the ~ AF1.

12 comming] com̄on C9.   ills;] ~, AF1; ~: B46 H5 H11 HH1; ~. C9
H6 B–G.   poore] (~) H6 HH1 B–G.

13 ease;] ~,   AF1 B46 C9 H5 H6 G; ~:   HH1.   for] ~,   B.   long] ~,
AF1 H5 H11 B–G.   beene] ~,   HH1.

14 The Effect] B46 HH1 NY3; Th'effect,   AF1; Th'effect   Σ.   cause;] NY3;
~,   Σ.   punishment] ~,   AF1 B46.   and] of   HH1.   Sinne.] ~_∧   H6.

Subscriptions: *none.*

Verbal Variants in Selected Modern Editions

Editions Collated: H I J K M N O P Q S T U Z AA DD 72.
Format:
   Indentations: *ll. 2, 3, 6, 7, 10, 12 ind*   N; *no ind*   H–K M O–Q S–U Z AA
   DD 72.
Headings: III.   H–K N–Q S DD 72.   X.   M.   3   T U(*second group*) AA.
   176 *Holy Sonnet.*   Z.

   1 those] these   H–K M N.

   5 my] mine   H–K M–Q S T Z AA DD.

   7 now I] I now   H–K M–P T DD.

   8 Because] 'Cause   H–K M–Q S T Z DD.

   9 night-scowting] night-scouring   M.

   10 Leacher] lecter   72.

HSSouls

Textual Introduction

As is shown on Figure 2 in the General Textual Introduction (p. lxii), *HSSouls* is the tenth poem in both the earlier, Group-III sequence of "Diuine Meditations" and in NY3's later replication of that sequence at the beginning of its collection of "Holy Sonnets." The poem is discarded in the restructuring that gives rise to the subsequent Group-I/II sequence, however, and thus does not appear in A in 1633. In the editorially constructed sequence of 1635 (B), the poem is recovered from H6 and—in an apparently botched attempt to restore it to its original position—inserted in eighth position (before, rather than after, *HSMin*), where it remains in all subsequent editions save those of Alford, who reproduces the 1633 sequence; Lowell (M), who combines the Holy Sonnets with *Corona* in a continuously numbered series; Gardner, who prints it as the fourth of the "penitential" sonnets "added in 1635"; and Shawcross, who essentially follows Gardner (see Figure 6 on p. lxxvi).

As the Historical Collation shows, the text of the poem varies little in manuscript. Individual members of (the earlier) Group III exhibit the occasional sport—e.g., B46 reads "blasphemers" in line 10 (where the other group members have "blasphemous"); H5 corrupts "weepe" to "creepe" in line 9; and both B46 and HH1 give "thy [for the normative *my*] brest" in line 14—but the only variant of consequence occurs in line 8, where the siblings C9 and H6 evince "by [for the alternative *to*] them be tryd." The later text of NY3/Group IV also records a comma after "vs" in line 7, which significantly aids interpretation of the line, and it uniquely elides "valiantly'I" in line 4 in an apparent attempt to clarify the meter. NY3's most important variant, however, appears in line 14, where it replaces Group III's "Thy grief, for he put it into my brest" with "Thy true griefe, for he put it in my brest." Our reasons for viewing this as an authorial revision are set out below.

B sets the H6 text into print, including the scribal "by them" (for "to them") in line 8, but in line 10 introduces the unintelligible "stile [for *vile/vild*] blasphemous Conjurers." C–G perpetuate B's text without significant alteration. Copied from G (see the Textual Introduction to *HSMade*), AF1 rewrites line 10's "stile" as "still," while H11 (copied from B) offers "sly" in the same place. (Curiously, a copy of E once belonging to Izaak Walton and now in the Harvard Library [shelfmark EC D7187 633pe (B)] proposes "slie" in a marginal note.)

That most modern editions position the poem as in B is noted above, and most follow the text of the seventeenth-century prints as well. Up through that of Chambers (P) in 1896, every postseventeenth-century edition reads the erroneous "stile" in line 10 (O proposing "still" in a marginal note), but after Gosse (72) brought

NY3 forward in 1899, all subsequent editors have printed "vile." Uniquely in the print history of the poem, Gardner (U) reads "to [for *by*] them" in line 8, and she is one of only four editors—the others being Grierson (Q), Hayward (S), and Smith (AA)—to adopt NY3's "true griefe . . . in" in line 14. Though the other three print NY3's rendition of the line without comment, Gardner explains that she finds it "likely that the archetype of Group III omitted 'true' in error, and that this was patched by the alteration of 'in' to 'into'" (p. 77). This rationale, however, is questionable on both esthetic and procedural grounds: first, NY3's "true grief . . . in" is not so incontestably superior to Group III's "griefe . . . into" that Donne could not imaginably have written the latter at a particular stage in the sonnet's development. Indeed, until Gosse printed the NY3 sonnets in 1899, readers apparently found the Group-III text unexceptionable; and among Gosse's editorial successors, Bennett (T), Shawcross (Z), and Patrides (DD) refuse the NY3 reading. Procedurally, Gardner's explanation requires either that the same scribe both omitted "true" and expanded "to" to "into" or that the deterioration occurred incrementally, as an initial copyist omitted "true" and a successor, noticing the metrical deficiency, added another syllable. Imagining that a particular scribe would evince both the carelessness and the metrical sensitivity required by the single-act scenario strains credibility; and although the multiple-stages scenario is somewhat more plausible, the Group-III texts of these poems exhibit enough examples of metrical irregularity to show that neither the β¹ scribe nor any of his predecessors made it his business to impose rhythmical correctness on every line—a fact highlighted in several cases by the contrary practice of the γ¹ scribe, whose regularizations of meter appear in C9 and H6. In *HSSighs* 8, for instance, B46, H5, and HH1 derive from β¹ the hypermetrical "because I did suffer, I must suffer paine" (γ¹ reduces this to "'Cause I did suffer . . ."). And *HSPart* contains two similar examples: in line 4 β¹ records the submetrical "He keepes, and giues me his Deaths Conquest" (while γ¹ adds "to" to produce 10 syllables ["giues to me"]); and in line 11 all Group-III manuscripts read the 11-syllable "None doth, but thy all healinge Grace and Spiritt," whereas Groups IV, I, and II omit "thy" and thus record a 10-syllable line. In the upshot, a simpler—and, we are convinced, the right—explanation for the discrepancy between the texts of Group III and NY3 in *HSSouls* 14 is that among NY3's authorial revisions of the Group-III text, "true griefe . . . in" is one. Since *HSSouls* was discarded at the next stage of the Holy Sonnets' evolution, however, we cannot tell whether this was a revision with which Donne remained satisfied.

Textual Apparatus

Copy-text: NY3.   Texts collated: AF1 (p. [408]); B46 (f. 99); C9 (f. 96); H5 (f. 84); H6 (p. 29); H11 (p. 68); HH1 (f. 129); NY3 (f. [35]); B (p. 336); C (p. 336); D (p. 320); E (p. 320); F (p. 320); G (pp. 317–18).
Emendations of the copy-text: Heading: 10.] .~.   Line 5 our] oᶜ   6 and] & that] yᵗ   9 and] &

Format:

Indentation: *ll. 2, 3, 6, 7, 10, 11, 13, 14 ind* B46 C9 H5 H6 HH1(*except 13*) NY3; *no ind* AF1 H11 B–G.

Miscellaneous: »page 35.« *entered to right of HE (indicating where poem is to be inserted earlier in the volume)* AF1; »P.« *left of HE* H6; *slie written as M var to style in MH copy of E (shelfmark EC D7187 633pe [B]).*

Headings: VIII. AF1 B–G.   10 C9 H5 H6 HH1 NY3(.~.).   Sonnet 8. H11.   *om* B46.

1 glorified] HH1 NY3; glorifid Σ.

2 Angels,] ~; H11.   see] ~, AF1 H11 B–G.

3 even] ev'n H5 HH1.   felicitee] ~, AF1 H5 H11 B–G.

4 valiantly'I] NY3; ~$_\wedge$ ~ Σ.   orestride.] ~: AF1 B–G; ~$_\wedge$ B46 C9; ore-stride. H5; or'e stride$_\wedge$ H6 HH1; ~; H11.

5 be] are AF1.   discride] ~, AF1 D–G; descryed C9.

6 Circumstances,] ~$_\wedge$ B46 C9 H6 H11 HH1 D–G.

7 vs,] ~$_\wedge$ AF1 H6 H11 B–G.   immediatlee] ~, AF1 H5 H11 B–G; ~. B46.

8 to] by AF1 C9 H6 H11 B–G.   them] y^{rs} HH1(M *var:* »~«).   tride?] tried$_\wedge$ HH1.

9 weepe] creepe H5.   mourne] ~, AF1 B–G.

10 vile] still AF1; vilde B46 H6 HH1; sly H11; stile B–G.   blasphemous] blasphemers, B46.   to] do AF1.

11 Name,] ~; H5 HH1.

12 feigne] faine C9(M *var:* ›~‹) H5 H6 HH1; fein G.   devotion:] H5 NY3; ~; HH1; ~. Σ.   turne] ~, AF1; ~: H6.

13 O] (~ H5 HH1.   Soule] ~) H5 HH1; ~, H6 B–G.   God;] NY3; ~. B46; ~) HH1; ~, Σ.

14 true] NY3; *om* Σ.   griefe,] ~$_\wedge$ B46 G.   put] putts HH1.   in] NY3; into Σ.   my] thy B46 HH1.   brest.] ~.| B46; ~$_\wedge$ H6.

Subscriptions: *none.*

VERBAL VARIANTS IN SELECTED MODERN EDITIONS

Editions Collated: H I J K M N O P Q S T U Z AA DD 72.
Format:
> Indentation: *ll. 2, 3, 6, 7, 10, 11 ind* N; *no ind* H–K M O–Q S–U Z AA
> DD 72.

Headings: VIII. H–K N–Q S DD. XV. M. 8 T AA. 4 *(second*
> *group)* U. 177 *Holy Sonnet.* Z. X 72.

  8 to] U 72; by Σ.

 10 vile] stile H–K M N O(*var:* still (?)) P.

 11 Iesus] Jesu's P 72.

 14 true] *om* H–K M–P T Z DD. in] into H–K M–P T Z DD.

HSSpit

Textual Introduction

As is shown on Figure 2 in the General Textual Introduction (p. lxii), *HSSpit* is the thirteenth item in NY3's collection of "Holy Sonnets," the first of the replacement sonnets that NY3 appends to its replication of Group III's earlier sequence of "Diuine Meditations."[1] In the restructuring that gives rise to the subsequent Group-I/II arrangement, however, the poem moves to the seventh position in the sequence and appears there in its first print appearance in A. In B, when the four discarded Group-III sonnets are recovered from H6 and reinstalled in the sequence, *HSSpit* is relocated to eleventh place and remains so positioned in all subsequent editions save those of Alford (L), who reproduces the 1633 sequence; Lowell (M), who combines the Holy Sonnets with *Corona* in a continuously numbered series; Gardner (U), who prints the 1633 sequence; and Shawcross (Z), who essentially follows Gardner (see Figure 6 on p. lxxvi).

The original, NY3 version of *HSSpit* contains four readings that do not survive the transition to the later Group-I/II state of the text—"humbly [for the later *only*] hee" in line 3, "W^{ch} [for *Who*] could do" in line 4, "no iniquity" (for "none iniquity") in line 4, and "inglorious" (for "inglorious man") in line 7. There is no reason to doubt that "humbly," "W^{ch}," and "no" are authorial[2], and perhaps "inglorious" is as well. "[I]nglorious" (without "man") gives a metrically regular line, and Donne may have coined the usage by analogy to "glorioso," defined in the *OED* as "a boaster, a braggart" and illustrated by a citation from 1589. Further, his use of similar locutions elsewhere (e.g., in *Calm* 44: "A desperate may live") markedly strengthens this possibility. If "inglorious" was Donne's initial choice, however, he apparently later opted for greater clarity at the expense of rendering the line hypermetrical.

Bearing the revisions "only hee," "Who could doe," "none iniquitie," and "inglorious man," the poem next appears in the Group-I artifacts, where it also evinces two scribal innovations—the modernized "you" (for the "yee" found in all other manuscripts) in line 1 and the blunder "Iniquitye" (for "impietee") in line 6. The subsequent Group-II text not only retains the Group-I revisions mentioned above, but also restores the correct "yee" and "impietie" in lines 1 and 6, the only anomalies being H4's "noe" (for "none") in line 4 and B7's "white [for *vile*] harsh attire" in line 11.

As the Historical Collation shows, the snippet of the sonnet in IU2 (ll. 11–14)

---

[1] As is shown on Figure 3 and noted in the General Textual Introduction (pp. lxiv, lxiii), γ¹'s "Other Meditations"—of which *HSSpit* is the first—were obtained from a Group-II source at some point after the original collection was entered into the artifact.

[2] H4's "noe" bespeaks the scribe's failure to reproduce the "none" in DT1 (see Figure 3), and the "no" in C9 and H6 almost certainly reflects the γ¹ scribe's modernization of his Group-II source text.

has been scribally recast as a stand-alone quatrain, and the origins of the excerpt cannot be determined from the surviving evidence. Our previous work with this manuscript, however, has shown its texts to derive from B–F (see the Textual Introduction to *ElComp* in vol. 2, p. 58, of this *Variorum*).

The text of *HSSpit* evinces remarkable stability throughout its history in print. Although apparently following C2 as his primary source (as is suggested by the Group-I "you" in line 1), A's editor prints "no" for C2's "none" in line 4 and corrects C2's erroneous "Iniquitye" to "impiety" in line 6;[3] apart from a few adjustments of punctuation, however, B–G introduce no further changes. From the text developed within the seventeenth-century print tradition, moreover, the modern editions vary little: apparently following B7, Grosart (N) alone prints Donne's revised "none [for *no*] iniquity" in line 4; and only Gardner (U), Shawcross (Z), and Smith (AA) give the solely authorial "yee" in line 1.

Textual Apparatus

Copy-text: NY3.   **Texts collated:** B7 (ff. 105v–06); B32 (f. 140v); C2
(f. 14v); C9 (f. 97); CT1 (pp. 230–31); DT1 (f. 119); H4 (f. 98); H6 (p. 31);
IU2 (*ll. 11–14 only*, f. 59); NY3 (f. [36]); O20 (f. 45); SP1 (f. [59]); WN1
(p. 8); A (p. 36); B (p. 338); C (p. 338); D (pp. 321–22); E (pp. 321–22); F
(pp. 321–22); G (p. 319).

Emendations of the copy-text: Heading: 13.] .~.   Line 1 and] &   2 and]
&   and] &   3 and] &   and] &   4 Which] W^{ch} 6 which]
wch the] ye 10 our] o^r 12 with] wth 13 that] y^t

HISTORICAL COLLATION

Format:

Indentations: *even numbered lines ind*   B7 C9 CT1 DT1 H4 H6 NY3(*except*
14) WN1; *ll. 2, 3, 6, 7, 10, 12 ind*   B32 C2 O20 SP1; *no ind*   A–G.

Miscellaneous: *poem is 1st of four sonnets entered under the general HE* <u>Other
Meditations.</u> C9 H6; »P.« *left of HE* H6; »p. 319.« *left of HE* O20.

Headings: 7.   B32 C2 DT1 H4(~$_\wedge$) O20 SP1(~$_\wedge$) WN1(~$_\wedge$).   .13.   NY3.
V I I.   A.   X I.   B–G.   *om*   B7 C9 CT1 H6 IU2.

1 face] ~,   B7 CT1.   ye] you   B32 C2 O20 SP1 A–G.   Iewes,] ~$_\wedge$ C9
WN1.   side,] B32 C2 NY3 A–G; ~$_\wedge$ Σ.

2 Buffet,] ~$_\wedge$ B7 C9 H6 O20 SP1.   scoffe,] ~$_\wedge$ B32.   scourge,] ~$_\wedge$ C9
H6 WN1.   mee:] NY3; ~$_\wedge$ C9 H6 SP1 WN1; ~;   H4; ~,   Σ.

---

[3]The editor may have modernized "none" on his own, but he must have obtained "impiety" from either his Group-II manuscript or—as the spelling ending in "-ty" might indicate—from H6. See the General Textual Introduction, p. lxxiii, for a discussion of the possibile influence of H6 on the text of A.

3 sin'd,] ~ˌ C9 H6.   sin'd:] NY3; ~ˌ B7 SP1; ~, Σ.   humbly] NY3; only Σ.   heel] ~, A–G.

4 Which] NY3; Who Σ.   no] C9 H4 H6 NY3 A–G; none Σ.

iniquity] ~, B32 C9 H6 O20 SP1 A–G.   dyde.] dyed ˌ B7; dyed, B32 C2 CT1 O20; dyed. DT1 SP1; ~ˌ H4 H6; died; WN1; dyed: A–G.

5 by my] ~'~ SP1.   cannot] can not A–G.   satisfy'de] satisfied B7 CT1 DT1 WN1 A–G; satisfyed, B32 C2; satisfyed. O20 SP1.

6 sins;] NY3; ~, B32 A–G; ~ˌ Σ.   impietee:] ~ˌ B7 C9 CT1 H4 H6; Iniquityeˌ B32 C2 SP1; ~; DT1; Iniquitye, O20; ~, WN1.

7 killd] killed CT1 WN1.   inglorious,] NY3; in=glorious man; H4; ~ˌ man, Σ.   I] ~, B32.

8 dayly,] ~ˌ C9 H6 WN1 C–G; ~; H4.   glorifyde.] glorified ˌ B7 CT1; Gloryfyed. B32 DT1 B–G; ~ˌ C2 H6; glorified: H4; gloryfyed, O20 SP1 WN1; glorified; A.

9 Oh] ~: B7.   then] ~, C2 A.   admyre:] ~ˌ B7 CT1 DT1 H6 SP1 WN1; ~, B32 C2 C9 O20; ~. H4.

10 punishment.] ~, B7 B32 O20 SP1 WN1; ~ˌ C9 H4 H6; ~; CT1 DT1.

11 And] om IU2.   clothd] cloathed CT1 DT1 H4 SP1 WN1.   vile] white B7.   harsh attyre] ~ ~, B7 B32 CT1 DT1 SP1 B–G; & ~ ~ IU2; ~ˌ~, O20.

12 supplant] IU2 NY3; ~, Σ.   gainfull] a false IU2.   intent:] ~ˌ B7 CT1 DT1 IU2 A; ~, B32 H4 O20 SP1 WN1; ~. C2 C9 H6.

13 cloth'd] cloath IU2; clothed SP1.   himselfe] ~, B7 SP1; him self IU2.   flesh,] ~ˌ B7 C9 DT1 IU2 WN1.

14 wo.] ~| B7; ~.| B32 C2 SP1; ~|. H4; ~ˌ H6 IU2; ~,. WN1.

Subscriptions: *none.*

Verbal Variants in Selected Modern Editions

Editions Collated: H I J K L M N O P Q S T U Z AA DD 72.
Format:
   Indentations: *ll. 2, 3, 6, 7, 10, 12 ind* N; *no ind* H–M O–Q S–U Z AA DD 72.

Headings: XI.   H–K N–Q S DD.   XIV.   L.   XVIII.   M.   11   T AA.
 7 *(first group)*   U.   168 *Holy Sonnet.*   Z.   XIII   72.

1 ye] you   H–Q S T DD.

3 humbly] 72; only   Σ.

4 Which] Who   Σ.   no] none   N.

7 inglorious] ~ [man]   72; ~ man   Σ.

HSVex

Textual Introduction

As is indicated on Figure 2 in the General Textual Introduction (p. lxii), that in NY3 is the sole manuscript copy of *HSVex*, and the poem never appeared among the seventeenth-century editions. Indeed, the very existence of this sonnet remained generally unknown until Edmund Gosse published it as part of his presentation of the entire NY3 sequence in 1899 (see the General Textual Introduction, pp. lxxix–lxxx [fn. 19] and xc). Having been brought to light, of course, the poem has appeared in all subsequent editions, always appended at the end of the previous 16 Holy Sonnets (however arranged) as the third of the 3 sonnets unique to the Westmoreland manuscript (see Figure 6 on p. lxxvi).

A prolific editor, Gosse took a considerably looser approach to his task than have most of his successors, and—as is shown in the Historical Collation—his printing of *HSVex* in 72 is unfaithful to the manuscript at numerous points, particularly with respect to punctuation. Indeed, he alters NY3's punctuation in some 16 instances, and the apparatus reports at least one change for every line in the poem except the second and fifth. Perhaps because he wishes to regularize the physical appearance of all the sonnets in the sequence, Gosse also abandons the manuscript's indentation pattern and prints all lines in the poem flush left.

All twentieth-century editors also abandon the manuscript's indentation of the poem in favor of the left-aligned style that they follow for the first 16 sonnets, but no variation in the wording of the text appears among their editions.

Textual Apparatus

Copy-text: NY3.   **Texts collated:** NY3 (f. [37v]); 72 (p. 371).
Emendations of the copy-text: Heading: 19.] .~.   Line 3 that] y^t   4 and]
&   6 and] &   7 and] &   9 and] &   10 and] &   11 with] w^t
13 that] y^t   14 with] w^t

Historical Collation

Format:
     Indentations: *ll.* 2, 3, 6, 7, 10, 11, 13, 14 *ind*   NY3; *no ind*   72.
Headings: .19. NY3.   XIX 72.

     1 one:] ~;   72.

3 that] ~, 72.   not] ~, 72.

4 vowes,] ~∧ 72.

6 forgott:] ~, 72.

7 hott,] ~; 72.

8 praying,] ~∧ 72.   infinite,] ~∧ 72.

9 heauen] Heaven 72.   and] ~, 72.   to day] ~-~, 72.

10 prayers,] ~∧ 72.   Speaches] ~, 72.   God:] ~; 72.

11 To morrow] ~-~ 72.

12 away] ~, 72.

13 Ague:] ~, 72.

14 dayes,] ~∧ 72.

Subscriptions: *none.*

Verbal Variants in Selected Modern Editions

Editions Collated: Q S T U Z AA DD.
Format:
     Indentations: *no ind* Σ.
Headings: XIX Q S DD.   19 T AA.   3 (*third group*) U.   180 *Holy Sonnet.* Z.

HSWhat

Textual Introduction

As is shown on Figure 2 in the General Textual Introduction (p. lxii), *HSWhat* is the fifteenth item in NY3's collection of "Holy Sonnets," the third of the replacement sonnets that NY3 appends to its replication of Group III's earlier sequence of "Diuine Meditations."[1] In the restructuring that gives rise to the subsequent Group-I/II arrangement, however, the poem moves to the ninth position in the sequence and appears there in its first print appearance in A. In B, when the four discarded Group-III sonnets are recovered from H6 and reinstalled in the sequence, *HSWhat* is relocated to thirteenth place and remains so positioned in all subsequent editions save those of Alford (L), who reproduces the 1633 sequence; Lowell (M), who combines the Holy Sonnets with *Corona* in a continuously numbered series; Gardner (U), who prints the 1633 sequence; and Shawcross (Z), who essentially follows Gardner (see Figure 6 on p. lxxvi).

The earlier, NY3 version of *HSWhy* contains two readings that Donne revises before transporting the poem into the subsequent Group-I sequence—"Looke" (for the later "Marke") in line 2 and "ranck" (for the later "fierce") in line 8—and the changes of "myne idolatree" to "my Idolatree" in line 9 and of "Sprights" to "Spirrits" in line 13 may be authorial as well.[2] In addition to these revisions, moreover, the

---

[1]As is shown on Figure 3 and noted in the General Textual Introduction (pp. lxiv, lxiii), γ¹'s "Other Meditations"—of which *HSWhat* is the third—were obtained from a Group-II source at some point after the original collection was entered into the artifact.

[2]As is noted in the Textual Introduction to *HSMin* (fn. 2), Rowland Woodward, who wrote NY3, employs the older form of "my" and "thy" (with the "-ne" suffix) before words beginning with vowels on six of a possible seven occasions in the Group-III/IV sonnets, and he does so at both of the two opportunities that exist in his seven additional sonnets (here, in *HSWhat* 9, and in *HSShow* 12). Unfortunately, his one failure to use the "-ne" form (in *HSSighs* 5) involves the very phrase "my Idolatry," and it is impossible to know whether the inconsistency between that usage and this in *HSWhat* is his or Donne's. Similarly, although the Groups-I and -II manuscripts use the older form ("thine") at each of their three opportunities among the Group-III sonnets, they here record "my Idolatrie" (since they lack *HSSighs*, we cannot compare their handling of this phrase in that poem). If this divergence from their usual practice suggests that they here derive "my" from the LRH² and LRH³, respectively, we still cannot be certain whether NY3's "myne" stems from the LOH² or simply represents Woodward's preference. Thus whether this change from "myne" to "my" represents an authorial revision remains indeterminate.

A similar ambiguity surrounds the "Sprights"/"Spirrits" variant in line 13. The Holy Sonnets contain five occurrences of "Spright" or "Spirit"—in *HSDue* 8 ("thy Spirit Divine"), *HSPart* 11 ("all-healing Grace and Spiritt"), *HSLittle* 2 ("Angelique Spright"), *HSWilt* 3 ("God the Spirit"), and this in *HSWhat* 13 ("wicked Sprights"/"Spirrits"); and only in this last instance is there any disagreement among the manuscripts. In none of the other four instances is the alternative word possible, and collectively they show that Donne regarded both words as available for poetic use. It seems likely that NY3's "Sprights" here is Donne's, but the divergence within the later Groups I and II—for which, see the Historical Collation—makes it impossible to know whether he ever revised it to "Spirrits."

Group-I text exhibits two corruptions—"his [for NY3's y^t] Countenance" in line 4 and "adiudge thee to [for *vnto*] hell" in line 7—that are due to the carelessness of the β4 scribe, and neither is perpetuated into the Group-II text. Indeed, although the Group-II manuscripts incorporate Group I's "Mark" (l. 2), "fierce" (l. 8), "my" (l. 9), and—except the CT1-B7 and C9-H6 pairs—"spiritts" (l. 13), they evince no further changes except for such isolated sports as C9's "mine" in line 9, B7's "saye I" (for "I say") in line 12, and B32's "Soe" (for "To") in line 13.

That A prints the anomalous "his [for *that*] countenance" in line 4 shows that the editor used his Group-I manuscript (C2) as his primary setting text; that he regularizes the meter of line 7 by expanding "to" to "unto" shows that he does not follow his source slavishly. This attention to detail, however, does not save A's editor from perhaps his most notable blunder among the Holy Sonnets—the misreading of "assures a piteous mind" in line 14 as "assumes a piteous mind." And this error, which persists in every subsequent edition up though the end of the nineteenth century (and in one in the twentieth), is all the more curious in that "assumes" appears in neither of the other manuscripts that A's editor sometimes compares (see the General Textual Introduction, pp. lxxii–lxxiii). Indeed, it appears in no manuscript at all.

Evincing Group I's "his" in line 4 and the editor's "assumes" in line 14, as well as the corrected "unto" in line 7, A's text of *HSWhat* passes on to B and the succeeding seventeenth-century editions without substantive change. Indeed, except for Grosart's (N's) adoption of B7's "saye I" (for the normative "I say") in line 12, no editor up through Chambers (P) in 1896 deviates substantively from the text established in A. Beginning with Grierson (Q), however, all twentieth-century editors except Patrides (DD) replace A's "his" in line 4 with "that" and reintroduce "assures" in line 14.

Textual Apparatus

Copy-text: NY3.   **Texts collated:** B7 (f. 106r–v); B32 (f. 141); C2 (f. 14v); C9 (f. 97v); CT1 (pp. 231–32); DT1 (f. 119v); H4 (f. 98v); H6 (p. 32); NY3 (f. [36v]); O20 (f. 45v); SP1 (ff. [59v–60]); A (pp. 37–38); B (pp. 339–40); C (pp. 339–40); D (pp. 322–23); E (pp. 322–23); F (pp. 322–23); G (p. 320).

Emendations of the copy-text: Heading: 15.] .~.   Line 1 the] y^e 4 that] y^t 5 Light,] ~$_\wedge$ 6 which] wch from] frō   7 that] y^t 8 Which] W^{ch}

HISTORICAL COLLATION

Format:
  Indentations: *even numbered lines ind*   B7(*except 6*) C9 CT1 DT1 H4(*except 14*)   H6; *ll. 2, 3, 6, 7, 10, 11, 13, 14 ind*   B32 C2(*except 11*) NY3 O20 SP1; *no ind*   A–G.

Miscellaneous: *poem is 3rd of four sonnets entered under the general HE* <u>Other</u>
<u>Meditations.</u> C9 H6; »P.« *above l. 1* H6; »p. 320« *left of HE* O20.
Headings: 9 B32 C2(~.) DT1(~.) H4(~:) O20(~.) SP1. .15. NY3. I X.
A. X I I I. B–G. *om* B7 C9 CT1 H6.

1 present] ~, B32 C2 O20. night?] ~‸ B7.

2 Looke] NY3; Marke Σ. my] thy C9. Hart,] ~‸ B7 C2 CT1 DT1
SP1; Heart‸ C9 H4 H6; heart, A–G. Soule,] ~‸ C9 DT1 H4 H6.
dwell] ~, C2 A–G.

3 crucifyde] crucified, B7 B32 C2 CT1 DT1 O20 A; ~, C9 H6 B–G;
crusified SP1. tell] ~, B32 DT1.

4 that] hys B32 C2 O20 SP1 A–G. affright?] NY3; ~‸ B7 C2 SP1;
~, B32 O20 A–G; ~. Σ.

5 Light,] B32 CT1 DT1 A–G; ~‸ Σ.

6 frowns] C9 DT1 NY3 SP1; vaynes → ›~‹ H6; ~, Σ. pierc'd] pierced
C2 O20 SP1. fell.] ~‸ B7 C9 DT1 H4 H6 SP1 A B; ~, B32 C2 CT1 O20.

7 vnto] to B32 C2 O20 SP1. hell] ~, B32 H4 O20 A–G; ~; CT1
SP1.

8 prayed] prayd C9 CT1 H4 H6 A–G. ranck] NY3; fierce Σ.
spight?] ~‸ B7 SP1; spite? C9.

9 No,] ~; C2. No;] ~, B7 C9 CT1 DT1 H4 H6. myne] C9 NY3;
my Σ. idolatree] ~, B32 CT1; ~. DT1.

10 Mistressis] NY3; Mistresses B7 C2 C9 H6 SP1; Mistresses: H4; Mistresses,
Σ.

11 Bewty] NY3; Beauty, A–G; Beauty Σ. pity,] ~; B7 CT1 DT1 H4.

12 rigor;] ~‸ B7; ~: C2 A–G; ~, CT1 H4 O20 SP1. I say] saye I B7.
thee] ~, B32 O20 A–G; ~. C2.

13 To] Soe B32. Sprights] ~, B7 CT1; spiritts, B32 C2 O20 SP1;
spiritts DT1 H4 A–G. assignd,] assigned‸ B7 SP1; ~‸ B32 C9 CT1 DT1
H4 H6.

14 bewteous] NY3; beauteous Σ. forme] ~, C2 O20 SP1. assures]
assumes A–G. mind.] ~| B7; ~.| B32 C2 SP1; ~‸ CT1; ~: H4.

Subscriptions: *none.*

VERBAL VARIANTS IN SELECTED MODERN EDITIONS

Editions Collated: H I J K L M N O P Q S T U Z AA DD 72.
Format:
Indentations: *ll.* 2, 3, 6, 7, 10, 11 *ind* N; *no ind* H–M O–Q S–U Z AA
DD 72.
Headings: XIII. H–K N–Q S DD.   XVI. L.   XX. M.   13 T AA.
9 (*first group*) U.   170 *Holy Sonnet.* Z.   XV 72.

2 Looke] 72; Mark Σ.

4 that] his H–P DD.

8 ranck] 72; fierce Σ.

9 myne] 72; my Σ.

12 I say] saye I N.

13 Sprights] spirits Σ.

14 assures] assumes H–P DD.

HSWhy

Textual Introduction

As is shown on Figure 2 in the General Textual Introduction (p. lxii), *HSWhy* is the fourteenth item in NY3's collection of "Holy Sonnets," the second of the replacement sonnets that NY3 appends to its replication of Group III's earlier sequence of "Diuine Meditations."[1] In the restructuring that gives rise to the subsequent Group I/II arrangement, however, the poem moves to the eighth position in the sequence and appears there in its first print appearance in A. In B, when the four discarded Group-III sonnets are recovered from H6 and reinstalled in the sequence, *HSWhy* is relocated to twelfth place and remains so positioned in all subsequent editions save those of Alford (L), who reproduces the 1633 sequence; Lowell (M), who combines the Holy Sonnets with *Corona* in a continuously numbered series; Gardner (U), who prints the 1633 sequence; and Shawcross (Z), who essentially follows Gardner (see Figure 6 on p. lxxvi).

The earlier, NY3 version of *HSWhy* contains two readings that do not survive the transition to the subsequent Group-I state of the text—"ame I" (for the later "are we") in line 1 and "Alas I'ame weaker, wo'is" (for the later "Weaker I am, woe is" in line 9—and no clearer examples of original and revised authorial lections exist among the Holy Sonnets. Excepting these two adjustments, however, Donne apparently remained satisfied with the text of this poem, and subsequent manuscript variations—all of which appear among the Group-II artifacts—are scribal in origin. These include B7's "more purer" (for "more pure") in line 3, B7 and CT1's "further" (for "farther") in line 4, C9 and H6's "Beare" (for "bore") in line 6, and the C9-H6-WN1 reading "great wonder" (for "greater wonder") in line 11. The Group-II manuscripts (including C9 and H6) also record the more modern spelling "sillilye" (for "seelylye") in line 6, C2 diverging from its Group-I fellows to join them.

The remaining Group-II change—that of "simple" to "simpler" in line 4 (B7 and CT1 misread as "simples")—is more difficult to explain. Bearing every earmark of a trivialization, this almost certainly does not represent a third authorial revision, even though on the stemma depicted in Figure 3 its origin would have to be located in the LRH[3] and thus attributed to the author. A possible explanation is that the stemma is inadequately detailed, that the error was introduced in a lost scribal manuscript that once existed below LRH[3] on the genealogical tree and was the parent of WN1 and β[5]. If such an artifact was once extant, however, it is somewhat surprising that the manuscripts contain nothing beyond this single variant that implies its

---

[1]As is shown on Figure 3 and noted in the General Textual Introduction (pp. lxiv, lxiii), γ[1]'s "Other Meditations"—of which *HSWhy* is the second—were obtained from a Group-II source at some point after the original collection was entered into the artifact.

existence. An equally plausible alternative is that Donne himself introduced the reading into LRH³ by mistake, as he copied out a familiar text with which he was no longer creatively engaged.

As is implied by the line-4 reading "Simple" (where the later Group IIs give "Simpler"), A sets the sonnet into type from the editor's Group-I manuscript (C2). In the process, however, A's editor independently alters his source's "farder" in line 4 to "further" and its "sillylye" in line 6 to "seelily," as well as adjusting the punctuation in several places and eliding the manuscript's "by one" to "by'one" in line 7 in an attempt to regularize the meter. Perpetuating A's "further" and "seelily," B modernizes A's "then" to "than" in line 9, institutes the additional elision "Creator,'whom" in line 13 (although inexplicably dropping the elision A had imposed in line 7), and introduces two further verbal changes, substituting "Simpler" for A's "Simple" in line 4 and dropping the second "wonder" from line 11 altogether (leaving "wonder at a greater"). H6 is almost certainly the source of the line-4 trivialization and—in exhibiting the alternative "great wonder"—may have encouraged the editor to go the whole way in regularizing the meter of line 11. Whatever motivated this emendation, it, as well as the other editorial alterations introduced into the prints by the editor(s) of A and B, is passed on to the subsequent seventeenth-century editions, which reproduce B's text without further substantive change.

As is explained above in the General Textual Introduction (pp. lxxiv–lxxix), the modern editors up through Chambers (P) characteristically present a text based on B–G, the exceptions being Alford (L) and the Grolier editors (O), who follow A as their copy-text (Lowell [M] obtains a few of A's readings through Alford). Beginning with Grierson (Q), however, A—or the first printing—is ordinarily the copy-text of choice, even with editors who are willing to consult manuscript readings. And this general pattern holds with respect to HSWhy. Apart from Gosse's printing of the Westmoreland sequence in the *Life and Letters* (siglum 72), the NY3 readings "Why ame I" (l. 1) and "Alas I'ame weaker" (l. 9) have never before appeared outside the apparatus in a modern edition, and no prior editor from 1633 onward has ever printed the authorial "farther" in line 4. L and O excepted, the life of B's two primary alterations of the text of A—"Simpler" in line 3 and "wonder at a greater" in line 11—extends all the way through Chambers (P), but in the twentieth century A's "Simple" and "wonder at a greater wonder" are invariably restored. The only other variants to report among the moderns are Grosart's (N's) adoption of B7's line-3 anomaly "more purer" and the substitution in H, I, J, K, M, and N of "do you [for the authorial *dost thou*] Bull and bore" in line 6—no doubt a change instituted by Tonson in the interests of improving Donne's grammar.

Textual Apparatus

Copy-text: NY3.   **Texts collated:** B7 (f. 106); B32 (ff. 140v–41); C2 (f. 14v); C9 (f. 97); CT1 (p. 231); DT1 (f. 119v); H4 (f. 98v); H6 (p. 31); NY3 (f. [36]); O20 (f. 45r–v); SP1 (f. [59r–v]); WN1 (p. 8); A (p. 37); B (p. 339); C (p. 339); D (p. 322); E (p. 322); F (p. 322); G (p. 319).

Emendations of the copy-text: Heading: 14.] .~.   Line 3 and] &   4 and]
&   from] frō   6 and] &   7 and] &   8 and] &   9 and] &
14 and] &

Historical Collation

Format:

Indentations: *even numbered lines ind* B7 C9 CT1 DT1 H4 H6 WN1; *ll. 2,
3, 6, 7, 10, 11, 13, 14 ind* B32 C2 NY3 O20 SP1; *no ind* A–G.

Miscellaneous: *poem is the 2nd of two sonnets entered under the general HE*
<u>Other Meditations.</u> C9 H6; »P.« *above l. 1* H6; »p. 319.« *left of HE*
O20.

Headings: 8 B32 C2(~.) DT1(~.) H4(~:) O20(~.) SP1 WN1.   .14. NY3.
V I I I. A.   X I I. B–G.   *om* B7 C9 CT1 H6.

1 ame I] NY3; are wee Σ.   by] *om* B7.

3 Life] ~, B32 CT1 DT1 H4.   mee,] ~; B32 O20; ~∧ H6.   pure]
purer B7.   I,] ~∧ B7 C9 CT1 H4 H6 SP1; ~? B32 C2 DT1 O20.

4 Simple,] Simples, B7 CT1; ~∧ B32 O20 SP1; Simpler∧ C9 H6 B–F;
Simpler, DT1 H4 WN1 G.   farther] further B7 CT1 A–G.   corruption?]
~, B32 O20; ~∧ SP1.

5 thou] ~, C9 H4 H6 A.   horse] B7 B32 C2 NY3 WN1; ~, Σ.
subiection?] ~∧ B32; ~, C2.

6 thou] ~, SP1.   Bull] B7 C9 H6 NY3; ~, Σ.   and] or, B7.
bore,] B7 NY3 WN1; Beare∧ C9 H6; ~∧ Σ.   selily] sillilie B7 C2 C9 CT1
DT1 H4 H6 WN1.

7 weaknes,] ~∧ H6.   by one] ~'~ A.   stroke] stoke WN1.   dy] ~?
B7 C2 CT1 DT1 H4; ~, B32 O20 SP1 A–G; ~. WN1.

8 kind] ~, B32 C2 O20 SP1 A B.   swallow] ~, B7 B32 C2 CT1 DT1
H4 O20 SP1.   vpon?] ~∧ B7 CT1 DT1 WN1; ~; B32 O20 SP1; ~. C2.

9 Alas I'ame weaker,] NY3; Weaker I am H6; Weaker I am, Σ.   wo'is]
NY3; ~∧ ~ Σ.   you,] ~∧ B7 C9 CT1 H6; ~. B32 DT1 O20 SP1; ~; H4.

10 sin'd,] ~∧ C9.   timorous.] ~∧ B7 C2 C9 WN1; ~; B32 CT1 DT1 O20
SP1; ~, A–G.

11 greater wonder;] ~ ~, B32 C2 DT1 O20 SP1 A; great ~, C9 H6 WN1;
greater, *om*∧ B–G.

12 Nature] nature   C9 H4 SP1 A–G.   subdue,] ~.   DT1; ~∧   H4 H6 WN1
C.

13 Creator, whom] ~∧ ~   B32 C9 H6 O20 SP1; ~,'~   B–G.   Sin] sinn,   B7
CT1 DT1 H4 A–G; sinn   B32 H6 SP1 WN1; ~,   C2.   Nature] nature   B7
DT1 H4 SP1 WN1 A–G.   tyed,] ~∧   B7 DT1 WN1; ty'd∧   C9 CT1 H4 H6;
~;   O20 SP1 D–G.

14 vs] ~,   B32 H4 O20 A–G.   creatures] C9 H6 NY3; ~;   SP1; ~,   Σ.
foes] ~,   A–G.   dyed.] ~∧   B7; ~.| C2; dy'd.   C9 H4; dyd∧   H6; ~,   D–F.

Subscriptions: *none.*

VERBAL VARIANTS IN SELECTED MODERN EDITIONS

Editions Collated: H I J K L M N O P Q S T U Z AA DD 72.
Format:
    Indentations: *ll.* 2, 3, 6, 7, 10, 11 ind   N; *no ind*   H–M O–Q S–U Z AA
        DD 72.
Headings: XII.   H–K N–Q S DD.   XV.   L.   XIX.   M.   12   T AA.
    8 (*first group*)   U.   169 *Holy Sonnet.*   Z.   XIV   72.

1 ame I] 72; are we   Σ.

3 pure] purer   N.

4 Simple] Simpler   H–K M N P; ~ (M *var:* Simpler)   O.   farther] further
Σ.

6 dost thou] do you   H–K M N.

9 Alas I'ame weaker] 72; Weaker I am   Σ.

11 *second* wonder] *om*   H–K M N P; ~ (M *var: om*)   O.

HSWilt

Textual Introduction

As is shown on Figure 2 in the General Textual Introduction (p. lxii), *HSWilt* is the twelfth poem in both the earlier, Group-III sequence of "Diuine Meditations" and in NY3's later replication of that sequence at the beginning of its collection of "Holy Sonnets." In the reconstituted Group-I/II arrangement, which replaces four poems (*HSMade*, *HSSighs*, *HSLittle*, and *HSSouls*) with four others (*HSSpit*, *HSWhy*, *HSWhat*, and *HSBatter*) and removes *HSPart* to the very end of the group, *HSWilt* moves to eleventh place and occupies that position in its first print appearance in A. In B, when the four discarded Group-III sonnets are recovered from H6 and reinstalled in the sequence, *HSWilt* is relocated to fifteenth place and remains in that position in all subsequent editions except those of Alford (L), who reproduces the 1633 sequence; Lowell (M), who combines the Holy Sonnets with *Corona* in a continuously numbered series; Gardner (U), who prints the 1633 sequence; and Shawcross (Z), who essentially follows Gardner (see Figure 6 on p. lxxvi).

As is shown in the Historical Collation below and on Figure 4 in the General Textual Introduction (p. lxv), the text of *HSWilt* evinces little substantive change as it passes from the earlier, Group-III manuscripts through Group IV (NY3) and on into the later Groups I and II, and—in our view—none that is without doubt authorial. Distinctive Group-III readings include only "begotten" (for "begot") in line 5 (if, as seems likely, the C9-H6 "begot" reflects γ¹'s attempt to regularize the line's meter) and "steede" (for "stuff") in line 10; and neither of these migrates into the text of NY3. Indeed, apart from individual sports such as SP1's "holy [for *whole-some*] meditācōn" in line 2 and B7's "of Angells" (for "by Angels") in line 3, the only substantive variants manifest in the later, Group I/II manuscripts of this poem are the β⁴ "sun [for the normative *sonne*] of Glorye" in line 11 (B32 independently reverts to "Sonne") and "stolne" (for the earlier "stole") in line 12, which was apparently the reading of LRH² and may be—though not certainly is—an authorial change.[1]

Other than the "stole"/"stolne" variant in line 12, only the "steede"-to-"stuffe" change in line 10 is possibly authorial—the argument having been advanced by Gardner in 1952. As is reported more fully in the Commentary, Gardner believes that "'[s]tuffe' and 'steede' are not easily read for each other" and concludes that Group

[1]H5's "stolne" in line 12 is anomalous within Group III and may bespeak the lingering influence of line 10, where all artifacts except DT1 (which has "stollen") read "stolne" before either "steede" or "stuffe." Since "stolne" is not demonstrably wrong, however, in the clear text presented above we have not emended H5 toward the group reading. Although H6 now records a scribally canceled letter after the "l" in this same word (leaving "stol*e"), it probably also initially read "stolne" and, similarly, may have been influenced by the line-10 reading.

III's "steede . . . can hardly be a copyist's error," further citing sixteenth-century law that she says makes "steede" more thematically appropriate to the poem's content and suggesting that although Donne may initially have preferred "steede" over the obvious "horse" for its sonic qualities, he later "altered it to 'stuffe' to avoid a too poetical word" (p. 72).[2] As finally developed, of course, this argument is primarily esthetic, but it begins in the bibliographical opinion that no scribe would likely read "stuffe" as "steede." In our view, however, such confusion is entirely possible, especially if one or more scribes in the β^1 line of transmission wrote a rather slipshod hand. The overall shapes of these words are remarkably similar: each has—or can have—the same number of letters; the first two letters ("st") of each are the same, as is the last if the words are spelled with terminal "e's"; the fifth letter ("f" or "d") is in each case formed with a prominent ascender; and a "u," with its two parallel upright sides, might well in some hands look like a pair of closed-loop "e's". The plausibility of this scenario, in turn, raises doubts about Gardner's justifications for the alleged change: if Donne in fact found the legalities of buying back stolen horses (as opposed to other goods) particularly analogous to "the old Ransom theory of Atonement" (p. 72), would he be likely to give up the analogy because "steed" at some point came to seem "too poetical"? Would an author who found "horse sold" harsh to the ear find "stuff sold" any more pleasant? In short, we believe that rather than preserving the author's original reading, "steede" is a scribal corruption of the only word Donne ever intended for this location—"stuffe."

In setting the C2 text of *HSWilt* into type, A alters the manuscript's punctuation in a few places and adds elision marks in lines 8, 10, and 12 (see the Historical Collation); but the edition changes the manuscript's verbals only in line 10 (spelling C2's "Loose" as "lose") and 11 (printing "Sonne" for C2's "sun"). Retaining A's "lose" in line 10, B changes A's line-11 "Sonne" to "Sunne" and A's line-12 "stolne" to "stole." If this latter change reflects the influence of H6 (as is often the case with B's alterations of A), the "Sonne"-to-"Sunne" change is more difficult to explain, since the corrected "Sonne" that H6 ends up with (see the Historical Collation) would have been clearly legible to B's compositor. In any case, the subsequent seventeenth-century editions evince no further verbal changes and only a single change of punctuation—D's replacement of C's exclamation point in line 1 with a question mark.[3]

Verbal variation in the modern editions is also minimal, and all of it involves the above-mentioned cruxes in lines 10, 11, and 12. Perhaps following B7, Grosart (N) gives the manuscripts' "loose" in line 10; all other modern editors take "lose" from the editions (A–G). On the "Sunne"/"Sonne" variant in line 11 the moderns are split, most of the pretwentieth-century editors preferring the Group-I/B–G "u" version and all of the twentieth-century editors plus Alford (L) and Chambers (P)

---

[2]In the 1978 update of her edition, Gardner softens "can hardly be a copyist's error" to "is arguably not a copyist's error" and concedes—against her new-found conviction that Group-III represents a corruption of the text in NY3 (rather than an earlier version)—that "[t]his is the one example of a reading in Group III which cannot easily be taken as an error made in copying the text in W [NY3], but points to the text in Group III being independent" (p. 72).

[3]It is worth pointing out that line 6's "(for he nere begonne)" is the sole instance among the Holy Sonnets in which every seventeenth-century source (excepting only HH1) employs parentheses.

HSWilt ❦ 97

preferring the "o" version found in Groups III, IV, II, and A. With respect to the "stole"/"stolne(en)" variant in line 12 the moderns group themselves in exactly this same way, the pretwentieth-century editors printing "stole" (the Groups III and IV and B–G reading), while their successors (plus L and P) choose a spelling that includes "n."

Textual Apparatus

Copy-text: NY3.   **Texts collated:** B7 (ff. 106v–07); B32 (f. 141r–v); B46 (f. 99v); C2 (f. 15); C9 (f. 96v); CT1 (pp. 232–33); DT1 (f. 120); H4 (f. 99); H5 (f. 84v); H6 (p. 30); HH1 (f. 129v); IU2 (*ll. 13–14 only*, f. 59); NY3 (f. [35v]); O2o (f. 46); SP1 (f. [6or–v]); A (p. 39); B (p. 341); C (p. 341); D (pp. 323–24); E (pp. 323–24); F (pp. 323–24); G (p. 321).
Emendations of the copy-text: Heading: 12.] .~.   Line 9 which] w^ch   13 'Twas] T'was   that] y^t   14 that] y^t

HISTORICAL COLLATION

Format:

Indentations: *even numbered lines ind*   B7 CT1 DT1 H4; *ll. 2, 3, 6, 7, 10, 11, 13, 14 ind*   B32 B46 C9 H5 H6 HH1 (*except 13*) NY3 O2o SP1; *ll. 2, 3, 6, 9, 10, 12 ind*   C2; *no ind*   A–G.

Miscellaneous: »P.« *left of HE*   H6;   *appears with other snippets under the collective HE* Pious things   IU2; »p. 321.« *left of HE*   O2o.

Headings: 11.   B32 C2 DT1 H4(~_∧) O2o SP1(~_∧).   12   C9 H5 H6 HH1 NY3(.~.).   XI.   A.   X V.   B–G.   *om*   B7 B46 CT1 IU2.

1 God,] ~_∧   B46 C9 DT1 B–G.   he,] C2 H4 NY3; ~_∧   Σ.   thee?] ~, B7 B32 C2 CT1 DT1 HH1 O2o SP1; ~!   A–C.   digest] ~,   H4 A–G.

2 My] (~   B46.   Soule,] ~_∧   B32 C2 H6 HH1 O2o SP1; ~)   B46. holsome] holy   SP1.   meditation:] NY3; ~,   B32 C2 H5 O2o SP1 A–G; ~.   DT1; ~_∧   Σ.

3 God] ~,   H5.   the] (~   C9 H6.   Spirit] ~,   B32 C2 HH1 O2o SP1 A–G.   by] of   B7; (~   HH1.

4 heauen;] NY3; ~_∧   B7 DT1; ~)   C9 H6 HH1; heau'n_∧   CT1; heav'n,   H5; ~,   Σ.   brest.] B46 H5 NY3; ~,   B32 C2 O2o A–G; ~_∧   Σ.

5 begott] begotten   B46 H5 HH1.   Sonne] ~,   HH1.   blest,] ~| B7; ~.   B46; ~_∧   C2 C9 CT1 DT1 H4 H6.

6 begetting,] ~_∧   B7 B46 C2 C9 H4 H6 O2o SP1; ~:   HH1.   (for] _∧~ HH1.   begonne)] B32 C2 NY3 O2o A; ~_∧   HH1; begunne)   Σ.

7 daignd] deigned   H4 HH1.   chuse] choose   B7 B46 C9 CT1 H4 H6;
chose HH1.   thee] ~, B46.   adoption] ~,   B32 C2 HH1 O20 SP1 A–G.

8 Coheir] Co-heire   C9.   to his] ~ 's   B46; ~'~   A G.   glory'and]
NY3; ~_∧ ~   H5; ~, '~   A–G; ~, ~   Σ.   rest.] ~_∧   B7 C9 CT1 DT1 H4 H6;
~,   B32 O20 SP1; ~:   B46 H5 HH1; ~;   C2 A.

9 Man,] ~_∧   B46 C9 H4 H6.

10 stolne] stollen   DT1.   stuffe] steede   B46 C9 H5 H6(var: ›~‹) HH1.
loose] ~,   B7 B32 C9 CT1 DT1 H4 H5 H6 O20; lose,   B46; lose   A–G.
buy'it] ~_∧ ~   B7 B32 C2 CT1 HH1 O20 SP1; ~'t,   B46.   againe;] ~_∧   B7
B46 C9 CT1 DT1 H6 HH1; ~,   B32 H5 O20 SP1; ~.   H4; ~:   A–G.

11 Sonne] sun   C2 H6(→ ›~‹) O20 SP1 B–G.   downe] ~,   B32 B46 C2
CT1 DT1 H5 O20 A–G.   slaine] ~| B7; ~,   B32 C2 H5 O20 SP1 A–G.

12 Vs,] ~_∧   B46 C9 H5 HH1 SP1 A–G.   he'had] H5 NY3 A–G; ~_∧ ~   Σ.
made,] ~_∧   B46 HH1.   stole,] stolne_∧   B7 CT1; stolne,   B32 C2 H4 H5 H6
O20 SP1 A; ~_∧   B46 C9 HH1; stolne;   DT1; stol*e,   H6.   to'vnbind.] ~_∧ ~_∧
B7 CT1 DT1 H4 H6 HH1; ~_∧ ~,   B32 O20 SP1; ~'~_∧   B46 C9; ~_∧ ~.   C2 A–G.

13 much] ~,   C2 A–G.   before,] ~| B7; ~_∧   B46 C9 CT1 DT1 H4 H6
HH1; befor[trimmed]   IU2.

14 But] ~,   A–G.   Man] B32 IU2 NY3 SP1; ~,   Σ.   more.] ~| B7 B46;
~.| C2 SP1; ~_∧   DT1 H6 HH1; m*r[trimmed]   IU2.

Subscriptions: *none.*

Verbal Variants in Selected Modern Editions

Editions Collated: H I J K L M N O P Q S T U Z AA DD 72.
Format:
>Indentation: *ll.* 2, 3, 6, 7, 10, 11 *ind*   N; *no ind*   H–M O–Q S–U Z AA
>>DD 72.

Headings: XV.   H–K N–Q S DD.   XVIII.   L.   XXII.   M.   15   T AA.
>11 (*first group*)   U.   172 *Holy Sonnet.*   Z.   XII   72.

10 loose] N; lose   Σ.

11 Sonne] Sun   H–K M N P 72; ~ (*var:* sun)   O.

12 stole] stolen   L O(*var:* stole) Q S–U Z AA DD.

Analyses of Early Printed Copies

(Since the Holy Sonnets appear as a continuous series of poems in all seventeenth-century editions and issues, they are treated in this analysis as a single bibliographical unit.)

Poems, by J. D., 4to, 1633 (siglum A)

Copies collated: CtY, DFo, L (G.11415), M, MH, TxAM.
Relevant section: E4v–F4v; pp. 32–40.
Press variants: *none.*
Miscatchings: *none.*

§

Poems, by J. D., 8vo, 1635 (siglum B)

Copies collated: C¹ (Keynes B.4.4.; *HSMade, HSLittle, HSSighs, HSSouls* only), C² (Syn. 8.63.95; *HSMade, HSLittle, HSSighs, HSSouls* only), CtY, DFo¹ (STC 7046 Copy 1 [Arnold copy]), DFo² (STC 7046 Copy 2 [Harmsworth copy]), MH.
Relevant section: Y4–Z1v; pp. 331–42.
Press variants: *none.*
Miscatchings: *none.*

§

Poems, by J. D., 8vo, 1639 (siglum C)

Copies collated: C¹ (Keynes B.4.7), C² (Keynes B.4.8), CtY, MH.
Relevant Section: Y4–Z1v; pp. 331–42.
Press variants: *none.*

Miscatchings:

	Catchword:		Initial Word:	Affects:
Y6	Shall,	Y6v	Shall‸	HSRound 8
Y7v	X.I.	Y8	XII.	HSWhy heading

Note: In the section containing the Holy Sonnets, this edition is a page-for-page resetting of the text of B.

§

Poems, by J. D., 8vo, 1649, 1650, 1654 (sigla D, E, F)

Copies collated: 1649: CtY, MH.   1650: CtY, MH.   1654: CtY, CSmH, MH.

Relevant section: X6v–Y2v; pp. 316–24.
Press variants: *none.*
Miscatchings: *none.*

Notes: 1) Examination of multiple copies on the Lindstrand Comparator shows that the sections of D, E, and F containing the Holy Sonnets are printed from a single typesetting, E and F being reissues of the sheets of D.

§

Poems, by J. D., 8vo, 1669 (siglum G)

Copies collated: *CtY, L, MH.*
Relevant section: X4v–X8; pp. 314–21.
Press variants: *none.*

Miscatchings:

	Catchword:		Initial Word:		Affects:
X7	VIII.	X7v	XIII.		*HSWhat* heading

Appendix 1

The following sequence of 16 Holy Sonnets was first printed in the collected *Poems* of 1635 (pp. 331–42), when the editor extracted *HSMade*, *HSSighs*, *HSLittle*, and *HSSouls* from H6 and inserted them into the 12-poem set carried over from the prior *Poems* of 1633. Though without manuscript authority, this 16-poem sequence was reproduced in all the remaining seventeenth-century editions and—except for those of Alford (L), Gardner (U), and Shawcross (Z)—has appeared in all subsequent editions up through that of Patrides (DD) (see Figure 6, p. lxxvi above). Because of its historical significance, we include this editorially constructed sequence here, presenting the 1635 text as a typographical facsimile.

THE 1635 SEQUENCE

Holy Sonnets.

I.

THou hast made me, And shall thy worke decay,
Repaire me now, for now mine end doth haste,
I runne to death, and death meets me as fast,
And all my pleasures are like yesterday,
I dare not move my dimme eyes any way,   5
Despaire behind, and death before doth cast
Such terrour, and my feeble flesh doth waste
By sinne in it, which it t'wards hell doth weigh;
Onely thou art above, and when towards thee
By thy leave I can looke, I rise againe;   10
But our old subtle foe so tempteth me,
That not one houre my selfe I can sustaine,
Thy Grace may wing me to prevent his art
And thou like Adamant draw mine iron heart.

I I.

AS due by many titles I resigne
My selfe to thee, ô God. First I was made
By thee; and for thee, and when I was decay'd
Thy blood bought that, the which before was thine,
I am thy Sonne, made with thy selfe to shine,   5
Thy servant, whose paines thou hast still repaid,
Thy sheepe, thine Image, and till I betray'd
My selfe, a temple of thy Spirit divine;
Why doth the devill then usurpe on me?
Why doth hee steale nay ravish that's thy right?   10
Except thou rise and for thine owne worke fight,
Oh I shall soone despaire, when I shall see
That thou lov'st mankinde well, yet wilt'not chuse me,
And Satan hates me, yet is loath to lose me.

I I I.

O Might those sighes and teares returne againe
　　Into my breast and eyes, which I have spent,
That I might in this holy discontent
Mourne with some fruit, as I have mourn'd in vaine;
In mine Idolatry what showres of raine　　　　　　5
Mine eyes did waste? what griefs my heart did rent?
That sufferance was my sinne I now repent,
'Cause I did suffer I must suffer paine.
Th'hydroptique drunkard, & night-scouting thiefe,
The itchy Lecher, and selfe tickling proud　　　　　10
Have the remembrance of past joyes, for reliefe
Of comming ills. To (poore) me is allow'd
No ease; for, long, yet vehement griefe hath beene
Th'effect and cause, the punishment and sinne.

I V.

O H my black Soule now thou art summoned
　　By sicknesse, deaths herald and champion;
Thou art like a pilgrim, which abroad hath done
Treason, and durst not turne to whence he is fled,
Or like a thiefe, which till deaths doome be read,　　5
Wisheth himselfe delivered from prison;
But damn'd and hal'd to execution,
Wisheth that still he might bee imprisoned;
Yet grace if thou repent, thou canst not lacke;
But who shall give thee that grace to begin?　　　　10
Oh make thy selfe with holy mourning black,
And red with blushing, as thou art with sinne;
Or wash thee in Christs blood, which hath this might
That being red, it dies red soules to white.

V.

I Am a little world made cunningly
  Of Elements, and an Angelike spright,
But black sinne hath betraid to endlesse night
My worlds both parts, and (oh) both parts must die.
You which beyond that heavē which was most high   5
Have found new sphears, and of new land can write,
Powre new seas in mine eyes, that so I might
Drowne my world with my weeping earnestly,
Or wash it if it must be drown'd no more:
But oh it must be burnt, alas the fire   10
Of lust and envie burnt it heretofore,
And made it fouler, Let their flames retire,
And burne me ô Lord, with a fiery zeale
Of thee and thy house, which doth in eating heale.

V I.

This is my playes last scene, here heavens appoint
  My pilgrimages last mile; and my race
Idly, yet quickly runne, hath this last pace,
My spans last inch, my minutes latest point,
And gluttonous death will instantly unjoynt   5
My body and soule, and I shall sleepe a space,
But my'ever-waking part shall see that face,
Whose feare already shakes my every joynt:
Then, as my soule, to heaven her first seat, takes flight,
And earth-borne body, in the earth shall dwell,   10
So, fall my sinnes, that all may have their right,
To where they'are bred, & would presse me, to hell.
Impute me righteous, thus purg'd of evill,
For thus I leave the world, the flesh, the devill.

V I I.

AT the round earths imagin'd corners, blow
    Your trumpets, Angels, and arise, arise
From death, you numberlesse infinities
Of soules, and to your scattred bodies goe,
All whom the flood did, and fire shall o'rthrow,   5
All whom warre, death, age, agues, tyrannies,
Despaire, law, chance hath slain, and you, whose eies,
Shall behold God, and never taste deaths woe,
But let them sleepe, Lord, and me mourne a space,
For, if above all these, my sinnes abound,   10
'Tis late to aske abundance of thy grace,
When we are there. Here on this lowly ground,
Teach me how to repent; for that's as good
As if thou had'st seal'd my pardon, with thy blood.

VIII.

IF faithfull soules be alike glorifi'd
    As Angels, then my fathers soule doth see,
And adds this even to full felicitie,
That valiantly I hels wide mouth o'rstride:
But if our mindes to these soules be descry'd   5
By circumstances, and by signes that be
Apparent in us not immediately,
How shall my mindes white truth by them be try'd?
They see idolatrous lovers weepe and mourne,
And stile blasphemous Conjurers to call   10
On Iesus name, and Pharisaicall
Dissemblers feigne devotion. Then turne
O pensive soule, to God, for he knowes best
Thy griefe, for he put it into my breast.

I X.

If poysonous minerals, and if that tree,
   Whose fruit threw death on (else immortall) us,
If lecherous goats, if serpents envious
Cannot be damn'd, alas, why should I be?
Why should intent or reason, borne in mee,   5
Make sinnes, else equall, in me more hainous?
And mercy being easie, and glorious
To God; in his sterne wrath, why threatens hee?
But who am I, that dare dispute with thee?
O God, oh! of thine onely worthy blood,   10
And my teares, make a heavenly Lethean flood,
And drowne in it my sinnes black memorie;
That thou remember them, some claime as debt,
I thinke it mercy if thou wilt forget.

X.

DEath be not proud, though some have called thee
   Mighty and dreadfull, for, thou art not so,
For, those, whom thou think'st thou dost overthrow,
Die not, poore death, nor yet canst thou kill me.
From rest and sleepe, which but thy picture be,   5
Much pleasure, thē from thee, much more must flow,
And soonest our best men with thee doe goe,
Rest of their bones, and soules deliverie
Thou art slave to Fate, chance, kings, and desperate men,
And dost with poyson, warre, and sicknesse dwell,   10
And poppy, or charmes can make us sleepe as well,
And better than thy stroke; why swell'st thou then,
One short sleep past, wee wake eternally,
And death shall be no more, death thou shalt die.

X I.

S Pit in my face you Iewes, and pierce my side,
  Buffet, and scoffe, scourge, and crucifie mee;
For I have sinn'd, and sinn'd, and onely he,
Who could doe no iniquity, hath dyed:
But by my death can not be satisfied   5
My sinnes, which passe the Iewes impietie:
They kill'd once an inglorious man, but I
Crucifie him daily, being now glorified.
O let me then his strange love still admire:
Kings pardon, but he bore our punishment.   10
And *Iacob* came cloath'd in vile harsh attire,
But to supplant, and with gainfull intent:
God cloath'd himselfe in vile mans flesh, that so
Hee might be weake enough to suffer woe.

X I I.

W Hy are we by all creatures waited on?
  Why doe the prodigall elements supply
Life and food to me, being more pure than I,
Simpler and further from corruption?
Why brook'st thou ignorant horse, subjection?   5
Why dost thou bull, and bore so seelily
Dissemble weaknesse, and by one mans stroke die,
Whose whole kinde, you might swallow and feed upõ?
Weaker I am, woe is me, and worse than you,
You have not sinn'd, nor need bee timorous,   10
But wonder at a greater, for to us
Created nature doth these things subdue,
But their Creator, 'whom sinne, nor nature tyed,
For us, his Creatures, and his foes, hath dyed.

XIII.

WHat if this present were the worlds last night?
　　Marke in my heart, ô Soule, where thou dost dwell,
The picture of Christ crucifi'd, and tell
Whether his countenance can thee affright,
Teares in his eyes quench the amazing light,　　　　　　　　5
Blood fils his frownes, which from his pierc'd head fell
And can that tongue adjudge thee unto hell,
Which pray'd forgivenesse for his foes fierce spight?
No, no; but as in my idolatrie
I said to all my profane mistresses,　　　　　　　　　　10
Beauty, of pitie, foulnesse onely is
A signe of rigour: so I say to thee,
To wicked spirits are horrid shapes assign'd,
This beauteous forme assumes a piteous minde.

XIV.

BAtter my heart, three person'd God; for, you
　　As yet but knock, breathe, shine, & seek to mend;
That I may rise, and stand, o'rthrow me,'and bend
Your force, to break, blow, burn, & make me new.
I, like an usurpt towne, to'another due,　　　　　　　　5
Labour to admit you, but oh, to no end,
Reason your Viceroy in me, me should defend,
But is captiv'd, and proves weake or untrue,
Yet dearly'I love you', and would be lov'd faine,
But am betroth'd unto your enemy,　　　　　　　　　10
Divorce me, 'untie, or breake that knot againe,
Take me to you, imprison me, for I
Except you'enthrall me, never shall be free,
Nor ever chaste, except you ravish me.

X V.

WIlt thou love God as he thee! then digest,
　　My Soule, this wholesome meditation,
How God the Spirit, by Angels waited on
In heaven, doth make his Temple in thy brest,
The Father having begot a Sonne most blest,　　　　　　5
And still begetting, (for he ne'r begun)
Hath deign'd to chuse thee by adoption,
Coheire to'his glory,'and Sabbaths endlesse rest.
And as a robb'd man, which by search doth finde
His stolne stuffe sold, must lose or buy'it againe:　　　　10
The Sunne of glory came downe, and was slaine,
Vs whom he'had made, and Satan stole, to unbinde.
'Twas much, that man was made like God before,
But, that God should be made like man, much more.

X V I.

FAther, part of his double interest
　　Vnto thy kingdome, thy Sonne gives to me,
His joynture in the knottie Trinitie
He keeps, and gives to me his deaths conquest.
This Lambe, whose death, with life the world hath blest,　　5
Was from the worlds beginning slaine, and he
Hath made two Wils, which with the Legacie
Of his and thy kingdome, thy Sonnes invest,
Yet such are these lawes, that men argue yet
Whether a man those statutes can fulfill;　　　　　　10
None doth; but thy all-healing grace and Spirit
Revive againe what law and letter kill.
Thy lawes abridgement, and thy last command
Is all but love; O let this last Will stand!

Appendix 2

A Note on Identifying Authorial Revisions Among Manuscript Variants

(Excerpted and adapted from Gary A. Stringer, "Discovering Authorial Intention in the Manuscript Sequences of Donne's Holy Sonnets," *Renaissance Papers 2002* [Southeastern Renaissance Conference: Camden House, 2003], pp. 127–44. Reprinted by permission.)

Finding the needle of authorial revision in the haystack of variation that arose as Donne's poems passed from copyist to copyist in a manuscript culture is a tricky business, and the editor who claims to have succeeded in this task may well be regarded with skepticism. Indeed, the very idea that such a needle exists is by no means commonplace among Donne scholars, not only because we lack the holograph artifacts that might provide ocular proof, but also because in one of the more widely known references that he makes to his role as a poet—the letter to Henry Goodyere of 20 December 1614—Donne depicts himself as one who tended to write a poem, present it to the intended audience, and be done with it.[1] As I have suggested above with respect to the Holy Sonnets, however (and as we have shown with respect to other poems in previous volumes of the *Variorum*), abundant manuscript evidence counters this portrait of Donne as a neglectful custodian of his own work, revealing instead an artist who very much cared about his poems and who continued to fine-tune or revise individual items, sometimes in multiple stages, even after distributing the original versions. The question is, How do we discriminate such instances of change from those that are merely adventitious?

In working with the Donne materials over the years, I have developed a set of four criteria in terms of which to evaluate a given variant's claim to authenticity. The questions to be asked are these:

(a) Does the reading represent a "genuine alternative"?[2] A positive answer to this question entails the judgment that the variant in question cannot be dis-

[1] In the letter Donne says he is "brought to a necessity of printing . . . [his] Poems" and speaks of needing to retrieve copies of some of them from Goodyere's "old book," averring that it has "cost . . . [him] more deligence to seek [his poems] . . ., than it did to make them" (*Letters to Severall Persons of Honour*, ed. M. Thomas Hester [New York: Scholar's Facsimiles, 1977], pp. 196–97).

[2] The phrase is Gardner's (1958:124), used to describe certain powerfully appealing readings that she is not willing to set down as "revisions."

missed as a scribal effort at improvement or clarification (i.e., "sophistication"or "trivialization") and that its aptness of sound and/or sense is essentially equivalent to that of the alternative.

(b) Is the reading readily explicable as a scribal misreading or slip of the pen? Application of this rubric requires familiarity with the diversity of forms, some of them quite idiosyncratic, found in the handwriting of Donne's contemporaries.

(c) Is the reading appropriately located in the poem's transmissional history? Generally speaking, only a position at the head of a line of transmission, where scribal corruptions are least likely to appear, qualifies as "appropriate" under this rubric. To ascertain whether a variant is so placed, of course, requires development of a stemma or schema of the relationships among a poem's various sources, and the failure to carry out such filiation will doom one's efforts to separate authorial from scribal changes.

(d) Are there extrinsic considerations touching individual scribes, artifacts, or transcriptions that affect confidence in the legitimacy of particular readings? With the exception of Rowland Woodward (who penned the Westmoreland manuscript [NY3]) and a couple of others, the personal identity of Donne's copyists is unknown and thus speaks neither for nor against the likelihood of their accuracy. In working through (especially) the major manuscript collections of Donne's poetry, however, even though their scribes remain anonymous, one eventually acquires a general sense of the reliability of each and can bring that experience to bear in evaluating specific readings.

In practice, the answer to any one of these guiding questions may be far from clear-cut, and they may thus not lead to certainty in every particular instance. Collectively, however, they provide a means of minimizing the element of subjective taste in the task of discrimination and put the enterprise upon a systematic, if not quite scientific, footing. Any variant that passes muster with all of these questions is quite likely authorial, and the case is virtually airtight if the change is incorporated into a subsequent stage of development that itself exhibits further revision.

COMMENTARY

THE
HOLY SONNETS

General Commentary on the Holy Sonnets

Walton (1640) says that in Donne's later, "penitentiall" years he regretted the poetry of his youth, but that "he was not so falne out with heavenly Poetry, as to forsake it, no not in his declining age, witnessed then by many divine Sonnets, and other high, holy, and harmonious composures" (B4^r).

G[iles] O[ldisworth] (c. 1650) marks on a copy of the 1639 *Poems* (C) and prefaces the Holy Sonnets and *Corona* with his own couplet:

> Marke his Soules Progresse! Hee wch sang of ^{fleas}
> At first, at last sings Halleluiahs!

Oldisworth is identified in Sampson (1921).

Cattermole (1841, 2:86), including *HSScene*, *HSRound*, *HSDeath*, and *HSMade* among his *Gems of Sacred Poetry*, comments that, though not "in the strictest sense of the word a sacred poet," Donne shows a "reverence of religion with the warmth and sincerity of genuine feeling."

Gilfillan (1860, 1:203–04) includes all of the Holy Sonnets from 1633 and 1635, along with *Metem*, in his anthology, though he also notes the "spilt treasure" of Donne's verse. For Gilfillan, "[e]very second line . . . is either bad, or unintelligible, or twisted into unnatural distortion, but even the worst passages discover a great, though trammelled and tasteless mind." Acknowledging the justice of some of Johnson's strictures against Donne and others in his *Life of Cowley* (1779), Gilfillan nonetheless points favorably to Donne's "rich fancy," "sublime intuition," and "lofty spirituality."

An anonymous author in *QR* (1862–63, 85) comments on the "occasional points of similitude in the lives, as well as in the exquisite sonnets, of Donne and of Drummond."

Kok (1863, 157–60) prints *HSMade*, *HSDue*, *HSDeath*, *HSWhy*, and *HSWilt* and observes that Donne's Holy Sonnets "were once highly praised" (157).

Hunt (1867, 78, 117) explains the absence of Donne from his *The Book of the Sonnet* by observing that, though Donne's sonnets are of a "legitimate order" and though he is unusual in writing "a Crown of Sonnets" with "fine passages" (*Corona*), Donne's "piety, though sincere, was not healthy" (78). He adds that Donne's religious temper "does not do justice to the Divine Goodness" (78). Later, commenting on the poems of Jones Very, Hunt says that the "old metaphysical rhapsodists," including Donne, are Very's poetic models, but he finds this unfortunate, noting that

Very "has reproduced their style, more in its faults . . . than in its excellences" and that, in choosing Donne as "his favorite," Very "could not, in many respects, have chosen a worse master" (117). Hunt concludes that Very's "great fault" is a "vague mysticism of reflection, encouraged by, if not absolutely derived from his too familiar acquaintance" with poets such as Donne, Herbert, and Vaughan (117).

MacDonald (1868, 121), commenting broadly on the Holy Sonnets, says that each one "possesses something remarkable."

Ward (1869, 324–25) notes the "two distinctly marked divisions" of Donne's poetry, the "profane and religious," commenting that the Funeral elegies "show the transition to sacred poetry" and that on those poems and the Holy Sonnets "rests Donne's claim to be called a metaphysical poet."

Deshler (1879, 123–26) discusses a number of poets, using the form of a dialogue between a professor and a student. The "professor" judges Donne's poems generally quite harshly, finding most of them to be "repellent by reason of their sombreness, quaintness, and prosaic cast" (123). Leading into a long paragraph on the Holy Sonnets, he notes that when Donne's poems "are not complimentary, elegiac, or satirical, they take the form of dogmatic teaching, or of philosophical or religious reasoning." The Holy Sonnets, he observes, "share the prevailing tone of his other poems; none of them are amatory or fanciful, and they are generally couched in a strain of religious sentimentalism, with an undertone of melancholy which is tempered by faith and enlivened by Christian hope" (124). He further finds the Holy Sonnets "severely, and at times impressively introspective," though he also acknowledges that they have different subjects and emphases. Along with "these confessions, lamentations, and pleadings," he says, are "strange metaphysical speculations on the nature of man's being, as to the influences of the animate and inanimate creation upon the soul, and concerning the power and attributes of God," and he argues that "notwithstanding the tremendous greatness of his subjects," Donne "fails to reach the heights of true sublimity in his poetry" (125). The "professor" then concludes by citing HSRound and HSDeath as "characteristic" of Donne (125).

Noble (1880, 455), in an essay that is essentially a review of Main (1880), places Donne among the "minor singers" of the Elizabethan and Jacobean period, and remarks of him, Raleigh, Chapman, Greene, Drayton, and W. Browne that there is "little in their contributions to sonnet literature to repay the study of anyone but an editor or a specialist."

Schelling (1895, xviii) counts Donne among several poets who used the sonnet form for the "expression of religious emotion in sequences of 'Divine Sonnets.'"

Gosse (1899, 2:106–10) offers a number of comments about individual Holy Sonnets, treating them as a kind of continuing series, and sets the whole group in the context of Donne's life, a life, he says, that was at the time "a shining light among his old friends" (106). Gosse finds "the voice of personal emotion" more evident in the Holy Sonnets than anywhere else in Donne's religious verse, and sees in them a preoccupation with the passing of time and with the nearness of death, that leaves Donne barely daring "to hope that he may yet work for God" (106–07). But, says Gosse, Donne still "pours himself out in prayer" for more time to serve God (106–07).

Symons (1899, 743) says that the Holy Sonnets "are a kind of argument with God" and comments that they "tell over, and discuss, and resolve" the "perplexities of faith and reason" that would occur to "a speculative brain like his." Often, Symons suggests, "[t]hought crowds in upon thought" in "tightly-packed lines." He finds that lines 1–4 of HSBatter typify the exactness and minuteness that make Donne hate "to leave anything out." Donne, he says, dreads "diffuseness" and "the tame sweetness of an easy melody"; thus, he uses "only the smallest possible number of words to render his thought." Consequently, Symons concludes, Donne is "too often ingenious rather than felicitous, forgetting that to the poet poetry comes first, and all the rest afterwards."

Grierson (1912, 2:li, liii) does not hear in the Holy Sonnets that note of "high and passionate joy" to be found in works like Anniv. Rather, he says, "effort" is the predominant note, "the effort to realize the majesty of God, the heinousness of sin, the terrors of Hell, the mercy of Christ" (li). Grierson detects in the sonnets a "passionate penitence," a desire to break through human limitations "to a fuller apprehension of the mercy and love of God." But Donne's was a soul, Grierson continues, that knew well "how to be subtle to plague itself" and so could conjure up the image of divine wrath "more easily than the beatific vision" of divine love. He sought and came as close to the latter as the "self-tormented mind" of a seventeenth-century theologian could, but only in brief moments when "love and ecstasy" were able to gain ascendance over "fear and penitence," and then only in the sermons (liii).

Fausset (1924, 238) suggests that Corona and the Holy Sonnets "were a tribute of regret and resolution to his dead wife."

Addleshaw (1931, 53) observes that the Holy Sonnets occupy a high place among the small number of great religious poems in English.

Fausset (1938, xiv) finds that Donne's "determination to fight his spiritual battle through to victory or defeat" gives the Holy Sonnets a compelling reality.

Moloney (1944, 132), who comments that the Holy Sonnets are "none too happy an achievement in their entirety," nonetheless finds that they "contain numerous examples of high poetic accomplishment." In illustration, he quotes HSMade 13–14, HSBatter 1, HSRound 1–2, and HSMin.

Turnell (1950, 273) finds the Holy Sonnets the most successful of the divine poems.

Gardner (1952, xxix), though doubting that the Holy Sonnets "spring from a deeper religious experience" than that which lies behind a poem like Lit, nonetheless declares that, other than perhaps the Hymns, the Holy Sonnets are Donne's "greatest divine poems."

Gransden (1954, 127–38) finds that Donne's "greatness as a religious poet" resides in his "truthfulness," in the "personal record" found in the Holy Sonnets of "a brilliant mind struggling towards God" (132). For the poet, he says, the goal is "never in doubt" (132). Throughout the Holy Sonnets, he suggests, even the "black soul" that is "trapped like a terrified criminal in a dark alley between despair and death" experiences the love of God as "eternally available to effect a rescue" (133). In the sonnets, Gransden asserts, Donne does not speak "professionally or doctrinally" but meditates "privately upon that 'little world made cunningly of elements' [*HSLittle* 1–2], the human soul" (136).

Daiches (1960, 357, 359, 368) suggests that Ben Jonson and Donne "represented," though differently, a "revolt against or at least a turning away from the Spenserian tradition, and the result was decisive for English poetry" (357). Against Spenser's "highly stylized artfulness," Daiches says, Donne "set a poetry which combined violence of personal passion with intellectual ingenuity and an imagery both starkly realistic and startlingly cunning" (359). Daiches cites *HSBatter, HSDeath, HSRound,* and *HSWhat* as examples of the "peculiar blend of thought and passion" found also in the Songs and Sonnets. In these Holy Sonnets, he says, passion is "that mixture of hope and anguish that characterizes the religious man searching for the right relationship with God, aware both of his own unworthiness and of God's infinite greatness" (368). Daiches observes that Donne's style in the Holy Sonnets is perhaps less novel than in his secular poems, for the metaphysical mode requires paradox, which is always "at the heart of religious experience" (368).

Ellrodt (1960, 1,i:83, 147, 173, 183, 216, 222, 254; 1:ii, 291, 295, 381, 419, 439) considers Donne's poetry to be a work of "présence" in time and in space (83), commenting further that fear of hell made the poet shudder, but his fear of death is not quite so obvious (147). He finds repeated expression of repentance in the Holy Sonnets (173) wherein the sinner feels so ridiculous before his own conscience that he does not shrink before the Creator (183). Yet the idea of the resurrection of the body haunts the author of the Holy Sonnets (216), Ellrodt thinks, for death is a violent uprooting, a tearing apart of the human person (381). Nevertheless, he says, Donne presents the resurrection of the flesh as the resurrection of the entire person in *HSDeath*. Ellrodt believes that Donne is convinced of the existence of the God whom he implores, but he never convinces us that this God is for him a concrete presence, a center of interest and of affection, a "thou" ("toi"); He is an object of meditation, of fear, of adoration (295).

According to Ellrodt, sensitive contemplation is less frequent than intellectual meditation in the Holy Sonnets (439). Thus we meet the terror of a man confronting his fate, who is suspended in the judgment of an angry God (*HSDeath* 12, *HSDue* 5–8, *HSMin* 10–11, *HSRound* 1–8); we observe religious melancholy, notably in *HSBlack, HSDeath, HSDue, HSMin, HSPart, HSRound, HSSpit,* and *HSWhat* (160); we discern an insistence on grace in *HSDue* 1, *HSRound* 10, *HSSouls* 11, and *HSSpit* 11 (419); and we must worry over the strangeness of Christ who "buys" ("racheté") with his death what he already possesses (*HSDue*) (222). Ellrodt believes that Donne—a former libertine and a former Catholic—principally reflects in his religious life a tension between the appetite of the flesh and the desire for chastity (254); but Donne is too fascinated by the present ever to give us a mere recital of his life (291).

Oras (1960, 19) discusses Donne's poetry against the backdrop of the Spenserian tradition, arguing that while Donne's earlier poetry is in many respects clearly anti-Spenserian, the "picture changes" in Donne's later verse, especially the Holy Sonnets, which "revert to a type of firm design, with iambic peaks, in some instances reminiscent of Spenser."

Zimmerman (1960, 25–26) calls the Holy Sonnets the "prayers of one who has discovered the truth of his own being and the certainty of God's," but he also notes that the poems "reveal little of the serenity usually associated with such certitude, for Donne knows the weaknesses of humanity and the dangers of its complacency."

Warnke (1961, 8), writing broadly about a European metaphysical tradition, says that Donne's religious poetry, including the "passionately individual utterances" of the Holy Sonnets, represents as much of a departure from existing conventions as does his love poetry.

Adams (1962, 784n1, 784n2) observes that Donne's religion "was never a secure or comfortable experience" and that we see in the Holy Sonnets "anguished despair" mingled with "no less anguished hope" (784n1). Adams sees in many of the Holy Sonnets "a combination of strong imperatives and protestations of abject helplessness which determines the tone of Donne's religious feeling" (784n2).

Poisson (1962, 14–16), noting that in his religious poetry, including the Holy Sonnets, Donne speaks of the same concerns as in his sermons, presents paraphrases (in French) of the ideas found in several Holy Sonnets. Throughout this writing, he says, Donne celebrates God's generous love for all humankind.

Silhol (1962, 341), focusing on *Lit*, considers that the progress of its attitude and interest, from pious zeal to one that is more self-oriented, is similar to the thought process that lies behind the Holy Sonnets.

Cohen (1963, 167) finds that, unlike some other writers of religious poems, Donne "presented himself entire" in the Holy Sonnets, confronting physical and sacred love, scientific learning, death, and "his tortured wish," after Anne's death, "to devote himself entirely to religion." As "poet, lover, and searcher after divinity," Cohen asserts, Donne was "totally committed."

Girri (1963, 93) maintains that in the Holy Sonnets Donne was writing not as a priest, but as a man.

Buckley (1965, 19, 29–30) argues that the enduring quality of Donne's shorter poems lies in their passion, which he defines as "a kind of action, of acting out the personality's deepest powers in terms of explicit feeling" (19). In this context, he says that the Holy Sonnets, though "occasionally magnificent productions," have variously "a certain hollowness of accent or a certain wilfulness of imagery" (29). He echoes Gardner (1952) in finding in the Holy Sonnets a nearly "histrionic note" and a "deliberate stimulation of emotion"; for these reasons, he believes, the Holy Sonnets, though in important respects "resoundingly impressive," are "not quite so distinctive as one might have expected, and not entirely satisfactory in suggesting the super-natural dimensions of the dialogue" (29). Buckley adds that "God is a dangerous interlocutor for poetry, even when it is Donne who addresses Him" (29).

Alvarez (1966, 131–35) says that the Holy Sonnets "have nothing to do with the certainties of faith" but are about the "lack of faith, about guilt, hesitation, uncertainty and spiritual failure" (132). Moreover, he argues that the poems are "inner debates" with uncertain outcomes that include much "intricate theological argument" (132). For Alvarez there remains in the poems a "distinct and unresolved clash between the private, the spiritual, and the worldly" (132). Finding that in the Holy Sonnets Donne's "logical compression sometimes jams up," Alvarez declares that Donne's religious verse appears "less convinced and convincing" than his secular poetry (133), and he notes that the drama of the sonnets makes them similar to the sermons. Alvarez concludes that in the Holy Sonnets Donne "debates with himself and with God, whose presence and reactions, even if they could possibly be presumed, certainly could not be predicted," and thus Donne "created the drama and the audience by assault" (135).

Gardner (1966b, 198) supposes that Donne gave the Holy Sonnets "no general title."

Warnke (1967, xxxi) thinks that in the Holy Sonnets Donne's poetic gift is in the service of a "tortuous and passionate quest through paradox and contradiction," a quest that, he asserts, "has as its object the same principle of transcendence and permanence which the young poet had sought beneath the multiple disguises of physical passion."

Honig and Williams (1968, 9–11) maintain that Donne puts "much passionate humanity" into his Holy Sonnets in order to realize God (9).

Miner (1969, 174–82) sees in the Divine Poems, including specific Holy Sonnets, a shift from the focus of the secular poems, which attacked the world as "culpable, inferior, and often wrong" (174), to an attention to the "culpability, inferiority, and wrong" in the speaker. Holy Sonnets such as *HSMin*, *HSSpit*, *HSBatter*, and *HSLittle* point to the "inadequacy" of the speaker and an accompanying "violence" and "direction" that mark the Holy Sonnets as different from the secular poetry. Miner notes another "thematic reversal" as we move from the secular poetry to the religious verse, especially the Holy Sonnets, as "imagery from the customary world" is viewed as "imagery of normality or even of value," while there is at the same time a "certain harrying of God" (181), an "inclination to tell God what to do" (182).

Nelly (1969, 135–36) states that the Holy Sonnets, along with Donne's other poetry, show that he is "more interested in analysing and presenting the truth of his own experience" than in offering "neat conclusions" from which all the contradictions and "attractive sensibilities" of his nature had been drained.

Roy and Kapoor (1969, 107–128) argue that Donne's concern with religion was a crucial matter for him all his life, not just a passing phase or an issue limited to his later years, and that he was always trying to seek truth or reality (111). They further contend that Donne's religious verse "was not propaganda for or an expression of isolated Anglican faith." On the contrary, they state, Donne "speaks to his God, not for or against any religious order" (114–15). They also find that "honest doubt" was rarely absent from Donne's mind and that he constantly doubted his integration with religion. In all of Donne's religious poems, and most obviously in the Holy Sonnets, Roy and Kapoor claim, the individual is more important to him than the group.

Bald (1970b, 233–36) urges that in the Holy Sonnets Donne is preoccupied with despair and afflicted by distrust in God and His mercy (234). Quoting from *HSDue* and *HSMade*, Bald illustrates how Donne doubts his salvation, fearing death and recollecting his sin. In *HSWhy*, Bald further notes, Donne looks enviously on dumb animals, "and even on the tree that bore the forbidden fruit," for they cannot be damned. At the time of the writing of the Holy Sonnets, Bald thinks, Donne "had no vocation and felt keenly that he had no place in the divinely ordered scheme" (236).

French (1970, 111–12, 123–24) claims that what strikes a reader first about the

Holy Sonnets are the frequent "feelings of fear pushed to the point of terror," noting that "however convinced Donne may have been intellectually that he was going to be saved, he was really very worried about being damned" and that however much he wanted to believe that his God was a "God of love," he nonetheless "found it emotionally hard to reconcile this God of love with the fact, or anyway possibility, of perdition" (111). Over and over again in the Holy Sonnets, French asserts, Donne confronts a "dispensation that seems either cruel or completely incomprehensible," and he evades a crisis of conscience that would result from this "by taking refuge in a quasi-logic which is either suspect or patently false" (112). French believes that one of the basic troubles with the Holy Sonnets is that they "continually reflect theological impasses without allowing themselves to be fully conscious of them *as impasses*" (123). Since the Holy Sonnets antedate Donne's ordination by five or six years, he says, it would be "quite natural" to find Donne struggling "painfully" in these poems to clarify his ideas; and it would be understandable if, in the midst of the "bitter controversy between people who held absolutely irreconcilable theological positions," Donne might have "wavered and been worried and confused" (123). Furthermore, French claims, since the relationship between humankind and God may appear one-sided, God can seem a "bullying tyrant" or a "desired mistress," but since one cannot actually say such things, the "language of adoration" becomes "strangely and inexplicably contaminated," as if one were obliged to worship God more for the very qualities that provoke one's hostility. This process, he suggests, is at work in the Holy Sonnets (124).

Martz (1970, 105–08), writing of Donne's Hymns and Holy Sonnets (and in particular HSMin and HSShe), cautions against overestimating the influence of Donne upon the course of devotional poetry in the seventeenth century. Donne's religious consciousness, he says, is peculiar to him. See more under Commentary and Notes and Glosses on HSMin and HSShe.

Smith (1970, 161–63) states that the Holy Sonnets "were no more produced in a single impulse than were the Songs and Sonets," observing that they are likely aligned with his devotional practices "over a number of years." Citing numerous Divine Poems and particularly the Holy Sonnets, Smith asserts that Donne employs a "declamatory rhetoric" in his religious verse and that this rhetoric "is not an obvious mark of inward sincerity." Donne's writing, Smith contends, "invests our human affairs with a dignity that befits man's standing, at the centre of a cosmic drama," and thus there is "no question" of "inward conflict" or "personal anguish." Smith calls Donne's rhetoric an "affirmation"; that is, "it proclaims the possibility of a heroic triumph snatched from likely defeat" (161). Smith argues that the substance of the Holy Sonnets is one man's struggle "to recognize himself by first coming to terms with the way things inevitably are," and the poems, Smith continues, present themselves not simply as a "record of the struggle" but as "dynamic enactments" of it. Smith argues that in these texts Donne represents his understanding of the truth of the human condition, in which "men must fall into sin and merit death, yet cannot avail themselves of Christ's love and atoning blood without God's grace" (162), and thus the Holy Sonnets ultimately function as intermediaries between the "vast conflicting forces" of this world (163). Donne's Divine Poems are "inherently dramatic," Smith says, because Donne sees the issue of attaining salvation as a drama (163).

Winny (1970, 34–35, 140–43) comments that while in the Holy Sonnets Donne's youthful intemperate writing persists, his object is no longer to overwhelm his mistresses' objections but to compel God to acknowledge him. The thought of the Last Judgment, Winny asserts, becomes a "haunting preoccupation" which "rises up to strike at Donne without warning" (35). Winny believes that an unrevealed sin oppressed Donne so greatly that "the self-assured lover" of the Songs and Sonets vanished completely, to be replaced by a figure "haggard with anxiety, whose yearning to be united with God is continually frustrated by the sins which he cannot expiate or forget" (35). Arguing that Donne wrote the Holy Sonnets after his wife's death in 1617, Winny says that the poems reflect a "deep disturbance of spirit," that having lost the security of his wife's love, Donne seeks for such assurance from God (140). However, Winny continues, Donne seems unable to persuade himself either that he deserves or that he can expect divine forgiveness. Winny says that Donne's "spiritual anxiety" is felt in the "choked utterance" of the poems, which "wrench language and metre into strained phrases, to represent Donne's agitation directly." As Donne tries to reason himself into a state of spiritual calm, his arguments in the poems fail to follow a logical progression (141). Winny notes that Donne counters the "emotional explosiveness" of the poems with structural formality and that what distinguishes Donne's devotional poetry from that of later metaphysical poets is its argument: it is directed by a "hard, stubbornly persistent core of dialectic whose purposes dictate the poem's general form and the particular nature of its images" (143).

Gardner (1971, 189–91) observes that the Holy Sonnets have "the dramatic immediacy of the present tense" which George Herbert "tends to avoid." Acknowledging that some readers regard the Holy Sonnets as "over-dramatic and too self-concerned," Gardner finds nonetheless a "range of theological reference" and a "width of reference in the imagery" that push them toward universal feelings. The sonnets are not "claustrophobic," she notes, in spite of "their intensity of personal feeling" (189), and she thinks that they express what is never said in Donne's love poetry: "a sense of human need" (191).

Hebaisha (1971, 59) calls the Holy Sonnets and the three Hymns the "most typical" and also the "best" of Donne's religious poetry.

Partridge (1971, 231) associating the theology of Donne's sermons with the "speculations" of the Holy Sonnets, says that in spite of "the naturalism of expression," Donne's "mystical side" is "near the surface" and is "revealed in his belief that knowledge of God cannot be attained through the intellect." Partridge disagrees with Bald's effort (1970b) to play down "Catholic mysticism" in Donne, finding evidence of it in Christ and several Holy Sonnets. See also Flynn (1976).

Sanders (1971, 111–12, 120–26) contends that the Holy Sonnets leave readers with a "vague dissatisfaction" connected with a "shallow assurance which is the very opposite of wonder" (111). In his worst religious verse, Sanders asserts, Donne exhorts us to a "vacuous kind of "wonder," a "sanctimonious mummery" (112). There is an irritant in the sonnets, Sanders argues, "an annoying contradiction of feeling" (120): on the one hand they are "jeux," and on the other they dispense "more than a little" gloom (120–21). Sanders states that the "sober and energetic" steadiness and self-scrutiny present in *Lit* are not much evident in the Holy Sonnets (123), finding instead a "repressive violence" that springs from an old dualism: the division within the personality between the consenting and therefore "higher" faculties of perception and the rebellious, "lower" faculties (124). Donne is reaching for simplicities no longer available to him, Sanders claims, and the Holy Sonnets consequently read as paraphrase of scripture and nothing more (125). When Donne attempts to persuade in the Holy Sonnets, Sanders asserts, one is "very conscious" of a rhetorical strain. Donne relies on a kind of verbal assault, which he uses as a weapon to subdue the reader (126).

Sicherman (1971, 69–88) argues that Donne's greatest poems, including the twelve Holy Sonnets printed in 1633, manifest a common developmental pattern: "after a confident or at least decisive opening, the speaker moves from initial certainties to new perceptions and emerges finally to an assured conclusion, making discoveries about himself which neither he nor his readers have fully anticipated" (69). She states that the central question in the sequence of twelve sonnets is the state of the speaker's soul (84) and that, while none of the individual sonnets completes the record of Donne's discoveries, the total sequence of twelve does form such a record.

Nye (1972, 357) finds it a "merit" of the Holy Sonnets that they are the work of a man "in whom we do not feel the action of a great natural sanctity or even spirituality." Though Donne's mind is "remarkable," Nye observes, his "holiness is not." Donne writes not as a saint or a mystic but as an ordinary man down on his knees before God," Nye suggests, commenting further that we ought to appreciate the Holy Sonnets for their "plainness"—an effect that Donne must have achieved only with great effort.

White and Rosen (1972, 13, 51) state that the sonnets are intense, tormented, and as personal as Donne's earlier love poetry when, "as a young man, he had addressed a mistress rather than God" (13). The poems, White and Rosen remark, are "passionate and intense to the verge of hysteria" and "intellectual, witty, ingenious, and paradoxical" (51).

Altizer (1973, 83–88) says that in the Holy Sonnets Donne attempts to identify with the first Adam "fully and experientially, and thus to experience the new life embodied in Christ" (83). Altizer claims that the Holy Sonnets do not succeed in this project, although, she concedes, "rhetorically and dramatically they are powerful and often moving" (83). Their religious or spiritual failure, Altizer maintains, is directly related to the lack of a positive "concetto" unified enough to obliterate the two conflicts "that for years kept Donne imprisoned within himself": (1) that between "the willful self-control required by reason and the loss of self and will required by faith," and (2) that between "a conception of Christ as Lord and Judge and a conception of Him as suffering Man and merciful Redeemer" (83). The problem of truly identifying with the first Adam, Altizer contends, is further complicated by a confused image of the second Adam. Throughout the Holy Sonnets, Altizer writes, we discover a tendency to associate repentance on the one hand with forgiveness and mercy and on the other with judgment and punishment, and thus the tone of the poems ranges from indignation to desired fear and chastisement (84).

Altizer concludes that during the period in which the Holy Sonnets were written, Donne seems to have needed to "understand logically the mysteries of Christian faith" (86), but was unable to "lay hold of the mystery of Christ" and thus his sense of "self-imprisonment" intensified (86).

Oppel and Schluter (1973, 238–45) remark that even though religious poetry had been written before Donne, he created the first really significant poetry of this kind. The nineteen Holy Sonnets take us back to Petrarch in their metrical form, they note, and the poems reflect very deep emotion. Tormented by his conscious sins, they conclude, Donne seems unable to find the assurance of God's forgiveness.

Ansari (1974, 142–43) writes that the Holy Sonnets possess a "dramatic brisk-ness and an intensity of passion" similar to that of the Songs and Sonets (142), point-ing out that they are marked by dramatic openings but reveal the "stamp of a process of meditation" (143). He argues that the poems are motivated by a "personal ur-gency," characterized by "immediacy, spontaneity and informality," and centered on the themes of a "sense of fear" and a "sense of intellectual pride" (143). Ansari sug-gests two ways of assessing the structure of the Holy Sonnets: first, by seeing in the octave "an intensification of sin or shame" and in the sestet a "prayer for mercy and for moral and spiritual rehabilitation," or, alternatively, seeing in the octave "the impatient and rebellious questioning of the ways of divinity" and in the sestet "a reticence and a submission which closes all" (143).

Blanch (1974, 477), identifying fear as the "overriding tone" of the Holy Son-nets, finds that the poems bear the imprint of a "sick soul," of a man so tortured by doubts that he welcomed fear. Indeed, he thinks, Donne deliberately evoked fear in order to drive himself to God. Blanch sees a relationship between fear and the love of God, noting that "in those sonnets evincing fear, there is an underlying impulse towards love of God; and in those sonnets portraying God's mercy, there is a corre-sponding recognition of the potency of fear."

Grant (1974, 42–43) argues that the Holy Sonnets exhibit a "synthesis" of "tra-ditional Augustinianism" and a "characteristically seventeenth-century latitudinar-ian desire to repudiate the harsh doctrinal derivations from Augustine" (42). Reading St. Augustine as supporting a "guilt culture" (43) and the Neoplatonic latitudinar-ian position as enlightened, Grant argues that in the Holy Sonnets Donne struggles to identify "a middle way" between these two positions.

Porter and Thwaite (1974, 107) argue that Donne's "baroque" religious poems are "full of the hysteria" associated with the resurgence of the Counter Reformation. The Holy Sonnets are "perhaps the most remarkable" of Donne's religious poems, they assert, adding that Donne reveals in them how love is "the mainspring of hu-man life and of poetical creation."

Sellin (1974, 191–94) interprets the Holy Sonnets in the context of the Refor-mation, arguing that too much critical emphasis has been placed on Donne's "affin-ity with the Anglo-Catholic tradition" (191) and that this has obscured the degree to which his poetry is seen as being influenced by Reformation traditions.

Cathcart (1975, 157–58) says that Donne is confrontational in his religious po-etry just as he is in his secular verse, noting that HSBatter, HSMade, and HSMin gen-erally display arguments in dialogue, a form that also occurs in the Songs and Sonets.

Dittmar (1975, 95–96) observes that the Holy Sonnets develop in intellectual realism from poem to poem, pointing out that the dialogue with God becomes increasingly intense as He is portrayed as a partner of the poet who, through self-willed linguistic and metrical means, imagines himself upon a stage.

Granqvist (1975, 125–28) surveys the publication of Donne's poetry in 18th- and 19th-century anthologies, noting the general neglect of his sacred verse until the first quarter of the 19th century. He further describes the various appearances of the Holy Sonnets in anthologies published especially between 1831 and 1868. Noting the printing of most of the Holy Sonnets in Robert Southey's *Select Works of the British Poets, from Chaucer to Jonson* (1831) and in Alford's edition (1839), he comments that the audiences for these works were "limited" and that knowledge of Donne as an author of Holy Sonnets was "still lacking" during this time (126). Granqvist detects, however, a "gradual awakening" of interest in these poems from the 1830s onward (126).

For Parker (1975, 55) the Holy Sonnets, as well as *Lit* and *Corona*, give evidence that "sobriety predominated in Donne's inner life" in 1610 and early 1611; and he further suggests that the Holy Sonnets reveal Donne to have been in despair at this time, noting that both despair and fear of death "weighed with him against entering the Church."

Smith (1975, 434) notes that, though Palgrave included three of the Holy Sonnets in his *The Treasury of Sacred Song*, he did not include Donne in the *Golden Treasury* and made various ticks and circles next to a number of Holy Sonnets in Grosart's edition (1872–73).

Flynn (1976, 186–91), writing especially *contra* Bald (1970b), says that the years between Donne's marriage in 1601 and his ordination in 1615 reveal the continuing influence of Catholicism on his life and thought. Donne, he asserts, "could not fully accept Anglicanism as long as he felt a deep division between his private religious feelings and the institutional religion to which he subscribed" (186). With particular attention to the Holy Sonnets and other devotional verse written during these years, Flynn sees Donne emphasizing "the value of private devotion," and in that, he says, "the tone of this devotion was essentially Catholic" (188). The Holy Sonnets, Flynn says, are largely devoid of a sense of institutional religion and thus reveal a "deeper spiritual malaise" than we see in such poems as *Cor* and *Lit* (190). Flynn finds the poems to be "primarily concerned" with dramatizing "the isolation of an individual soul aware of the odds against salvation without institutional support" (190). Analyzing HSSouls, Flynn finds in that poem, and indeed "throughout" the Holy Sonnets, the individual soul "haled before the divine judgement totally isolated, overstriding hell in a harsh blackness" (191).

Huebert (1977, 15–16, 134) argues that spiritual agitation "writhes" through the Holy Sonnets, and that as metaphysical poetry they display a tone of intellectual skepticism, filled with "harsh imagery" (15). He further notes that Donne's "agitated frenzies" (15) fail to satisfy the needs of his frustrated poetic characters and that Donne "equivocates" between the concrete and the abstract in the Holy Sonnets (134).

Skelton (1978, 67–68), writing about the relationship between a poet's beliefs and those of his readers, observes that in the Holy Sonnets "the personal involve-ment of the speaker in his beliefs is so clearly indicated that our possible disagree-ment with those beliefs cannot affect the intensity of our perception of a man wrestling with them" (67). Citing as a particular example *HSRound* and belief in the Last Judgment, he says that "expressed beliefs" should be viewed as "symptomatic of all beliefs of a certain kind" (68).

Allain (1980, 18, 21–22) observes that although Donne's secular poems are marked by discontinuity in time, when he "fixed his attention on a steadfast woman and an unchangeable God, he gained a sense of personal continuity" (21). Allain finds this "new continuity" (after Donne's marriage) reflected in the Holy Sonnets. For Allain, the "surface busyness, the dislocations, the fluctuations of the secular poems" have yielded to "a certain unity of mood and tone," and yet, Allain adds, "the new-found evenness was not without its trials." The first of the Holy Sonnets, in Allain's view, "are filled with self-abasement and despair" (22).

Carey (1981, 48, 57–58) claims that the Holy Sonnets are "the fruit" of Donne's "apostasy" and that if Donne had not abandoned the Catholic for the Protestant church, and thus "entered the realm of doubt," the Holy Sonnets could never have been written (57). For example, *HSBatter* gives us Donne's "Protestant religious pain," according to Carey, in that he acknowledges "that God must act first, and that his own efforts are futile" (57). Carey adds that the anxiety Donne experiences about woman's constancy in the love poems, which Carey sees as "a profound anxiety about his own ability to attract or merit stable affection," is "transposed to the religious sphere" (58). Carey further claims that Donne is afflicted by "the unfitness of what he can find to say to God," so that he even "sneers" in such poems as *HSVex* at his own attempts: "In prayers, and flattering speaches I court God" (l. 10) (48).

Marotti (1981, 227) finds that Donne used the religious poems written before his ordination "to good advantage in his social life," pointing specifically to the "Holy Hymns and Sonnets" sent to Magdalen Herbert and to the "same complimentary gesture" of giving six Holy Sonnets to the "extravagant new Earl of Dorset."

Mroczkowski (1981, 217–19) describes Donne as a writer seeking a truly contrarian expression: provocatively violating assumptions about rhythm and also reaching for the strangest associations. But on the other hand, Mroczowski finds that, particu-larly in the later religious lyrics, Donne could be equally surprising in being simple and accurate, citing lines from *HSMade* and *HSLittle* as examples.

Den Boer (1982, 31, 73, 75, 139, 149–56) finds many instances of melancholy, doubt, and despair in the Holy Sonnets (31), noting also that Donne's fear of hu-man unworthiness in the face of God's divinity sometimes borders on doubt and despair (73). Citing Esch (1955), Den Boer avers that the Holy Sonnets are the first major religious sonnets in England (75), and he reviews a number of twentieth-cen-tury translations of the Holy Sonnets into Dutch (139, 149–56).

Donker and Muldrow (1982, 208) state that Donne probably thought of the twelve Holy Sonnets of 1633 as "a kind of meditative sequence on death and God's love for sinful man."

B. King (1982, 46–47) views the Holy Sonnets as "dramati[zing] Donne's sense of unworthiness in contrast to divine power and mercy" (46). King claims that the sonnets' "intense immediacy is influenced by Ignatian meditation" (46), and of the twelve sonnets of 1633 he finds that six "focus on Last Things" and six are "colloquies on divine love" (46). King proposes that the twelve sonnets can be understood as a "linked sequence" beginning with the opening of *HSDue* and concluding with the "reconciliation" in *HSPart* 13–14 (46). King adds that the other sonnets include "four penitential meditations" and "some miscellaneous pieces including the resigned poem on the death of his wife" (*HSShe*) (46–47). King concludes that although Donne's religious poems confirm the early seventeenth-century effort "to use secular verse forms for spiritual purposes," they remain "less inventive" stanzaically than Herbert's poems or Donne's secular poetry (47).

J. King (1982, 159) finds that the Holy Sonnets "recount the Christian warfare against 'the world, the flesh, the devill.'"

Yearwood (1982, 210, 216), following Gardner's 1952 ordering, finds that the twelve Holy Sonnets of 1633 trace a conversion process that "begins in pride, proceeds to confession and despair, and culminates in a humble joy and confidence" (210). Among these, Yearwood says, *HSSpit*, *HSWhy*, *HSWhat*, and *HSBatter* reveal the speaker's "profound despair at his sinfulness, still unable to accept his forgiveness" (216). *HSSpit*, according to Yearwood, reveals the speaker's unsuccessful attempt to understand the Incarnation through logical means, and this effort leads to the "overwhelming fear" we see in *HSBatter* (216).

Sherwood (1984, 16–17, 94, 143) claims that Donne's "basic epistemology" stems from the "sense that knowledge begins with immediate, palpable bodily experience," a view that undergirds both the secular and divine poetry (16). He asserts that the "dramatically realized Christ" of the Holy Sonnets, *Goodf*, and the sermons is "presented in physical as well as spiritual terms" and is "a tangible model of bodily and spiritual continuity" (94). Thus, for Sherwood, "to assess the composite of body and soul is to explore its condition of suffering" (17), and he notes that in the Holy Sonnets, as much as in lyrics like *ValWeep*, "suffering is the measure of love" (143).

To Parfitt (1985, 42–43), Donne's religious poetry, including the Holy Sonnets, "is certainly a record of belief"—that is, God "not only exists for Donne, but exists with an immediacy and intensity which are startling" (42–43). But, Parfitt adds, God is "characterized by force and sternness rather than by love and serenity," and thus Donne possesses doubts and fears about the nature of God and even has "great difficulty in trusting the God in whom he must believe" (43).

Parry (1985, 67–68) finds Donne, in his "middle years" and in the Holy Sonnets in particular, turning "with increasing anxiety to the last scene of his life and the world's" (67). Donne's preoccupation with his sinfulness and need for grace inspired him to employ the techniques of Ignatian meditation, which, according to Parry, underlie the "structure of most of the *Holy Sonnets*, just as it is frequently used to secular ends in the love poems" (68). Parry adds that the religious poems not only served Donne's "spiritual discipline," but they also had "a social function" in that he circulated them among his friends (many of whom shared his "religious condition") so that the poems could "serve the needs of others" (68).

Patrides (1985a, 44) says that "the summit of [Donne's] art is in the Holy Sonnets."

Gaster (1986, 5–6, 9) attributes the "mood of despair" prevalent in some of the

Holy Sonnets especially to the "ruination" of all Donne's "worldly ambitions" following his secret marriage to Anne More, as well as to "the uneasy consciousness of his defection from the Catholic Faith" (5). Gaster describes Donne's despair as, at worst, "the Faustian despair of a man in the act of succumbing to the temptations of Satan" and, at best, as "the despair of a frail human who was unable to concentrate on willing himself towards a closer relationship with God" (6). In Gaster's view, most of the Holy Sonnets—like other Donne poems—were intended for private circulation, and "though they adumbrate much that was to be expanded in the Sermons, they are essentially the personal and often dramatic revelations of a man in turmoil" (9).

Rollin (1986, 141–42), finding mood swings to be characteristic of the Holy Sonnets, addresses one possible argument against that view, namely, that "bipolarity or mood swings are characteristic of the sonnet form itself, its traditionally reflexive structure, with sestets reversing octets, couplets turning upon quatrains" (141). But Rollin argues that this view is challenged by several Holy Sonnets that "exhibit a high degree of internal consistency in mood and theme": HSScene, HSSpit, HSWhat, HSWhy, HSWilt, and HSPart (141–42).

Van Emden (1986, 29, 51–53) finds Donne's religious poetry suffused with the fear of a despair resulting from his departure from the Roman Catholic Church. Van Emden sees this state of mind—even "a sense of panic at the possibility"—particularly in HSMade, HSRound, and HSBatter (29). Van Emden claims further that Donne's "sense of guilt and fear of ultimate despair sometimes make him more aggressive and demanding towards God than he had been towards women in his younger days" (51). She notes that in the Holy Sonnets "the problem is thought through during the poem itself, rather than reflected on with hindsight, and with the considerable use of the personal pronoun, there is at times 'a sense of sheer terror' evident in the writer" (53).

Zemplényi (1986, 157), writing of the twelve Holy Sonnets of 1633 (and Gardner's 1952 arrangement), finds "structural parallels between the individual sonnets," noting, for example, that the first and last (HSDue and HSPart) "rhyme together with their invocation to God," that the second and next to last (HSBlack and HSWilt) "are both directed to the soul," that the fourth and the fourth from the last (HSRound and HSWhat) "both begin with the Last Judgement," that the fifth and the eighth (HSMin and HSWhy) "are both concerned with the calling of mankind," and that "there are, of course, also many correspondences in detail."

McNees (1987, 94–97, 100–04, 110–12) writes in opposition to the usual emphasis on Roman Catholic or Calvinist models of meditation, attending rather to Donne's "allegiance to the Anglican doctrine of the Eucharist and the effect of this doctrine on his poetry" (94). Noting that Donne's divine poetry, including the Holy Sonnets, avoids the direct debate over the Real Presence in the Eucharist, she nonetheless finds that the later writings, specifically Death's Duell and the Holy Sonnets, focus on the "necessity of personal sacrifice" and establish a connection between "self-sacrifice and eucharistic fulfillment" (100). In other words, according to McNees, participation in the Eucharist involves a giving of oneself, a "symbolic sacrifice," that "prefigures one's actual death and resurrection on Judgment Day" (101). She believes that poems such as Goodf and the Holy Sonnets, especially HSBlack and

HSRound, "continually seek affliction" as a way of "realizing Christ's presence"—i.e., in "alluding to the crucifixion and its representation in the Eucharist," the poems also "beg for purgations—washing, drowning, burning—as mandatory conditions of full eucharistic participation" (110).

Warnke (1987, 104–05) concurs with the view of Martz (1954) and others that the Holy Sonnets are greatly influenced by the practice of meditation, with the typical sonnet reflecting "the third stage of the meditation, the colloquy" (104). He cites HSMade as an example and also notes that this poem captures the sensibility evident in the majority of Donne's Holy Sonnets, namely, a "tone of desperation." Warnke contends that, from an "orthodox Christian point of view," the Holy Sonnets are not "edifying" (as are, for example, the poems of George Herbert); rather, he finds that what one encounters in the Holy Sonnets is "naked fear: the speaker desperately wishes to go to Heaven and—even more markedly—to escape Hell." Moreover, Warnke adds, "the concentration on the self is extreme, and the terrified eloquence of that self, unforgettable" (105).

Larson (1989, 111) explores the "boost" New Criticism gave to the study of Donne, arguing that perhaps its greatest contribution was to remove Donne's poetry, "at least temporarily, from biographical studies." As a consequence, she says, the Holy Sonnets could be viewed as "artifacts rather than personal testimonies of religious doubt or faith."

Martz (1989, 48–49) contends that in the Holy Sonnets Donne "seems to be pondering, with fearful anxiety, how he might come to terms with Calvinist orthodoxy, while using essentially Jesuit methods of meditation as part of his quest for a solution" (48–49). But, Martz adds, in his late sermons, which are preached before King Charles in 1629, Donne "had clearly adopted an Arminian, anti-Calvinist position" (49).

In his analysis of the Holy Sonnets, Strier (1989, 357–58, 361–62, 367) focuses on the process of coining and sealing, that is, "making an impression," because "the image of re-imprinting a coin seems to have had special meaning" to Donne "as a figure for incomplete transformation" (357). Strier suggests that Donne's Roman Catholic upbringing remains a presence in his subsequent change of faith and that in many of the Holy Sonnets of 1608–10 we see Donne "awry and squint," for "the Protestant imprint is clear enough, but the underlying matter does not fully 'take' the print" (358). Strier believes that the "psychological states" evident in the Holy Sonnets are "biographically anchored and informative" (358), and he contends that Carey (1981), Stachniewski (1981), and others are wrong in seeing the Holy Sonnets as "consistently Calvinist in theology" (361). Strier argues that the "pain and confusion" in a number of the Holy Sonnets is "not that of the convinced Calvinist but rather that of a person who would like to be a convinced Calvinist but who is both unable to be so and unable to admit that he is unable to be so" (361). Strier contrasts the view of White (1936) that justification by faith was a doctrine "of release, of consolation and reassurance" with that of Carey, who finds it a "recipe for anguish" (361). Strier concludes that the Holy Sonnets and Corona reveal Donne's "difficulties with and occasional successes at imprinting Calvinism" on a soul that had, as Donne says in Pseudo-Martyr, "first to blot out, certaine impressions of the Romane religion" (367).

Carey (1990b, xxvii–xxviii), citing the linguistic echoes in *BoulRec*, *HSDeath*, and the Countess of Bedford's epicede "Death I recant" (printed in vol. 6 of this *Variorum*), suggests that the Holy Sonnets may develop from Donne's "relationship with the Countess, and were perhaps written for her" (xxvii–xxviii). Carey thinks that it was through the Countess that Donne became acquainted with the Earl of Dorset, to whom he sent six of the Holy Sonnets (xxviii). The Calvinist features of the Holy Sonnets—"the incipient despair, the terror of damnation, the total dependence on God's election"—are not too surprising, in Carey's view, given the Countess's Calvinism (xxviii). Furthermore, according to Carey, the expression of rejection in the poems and their "plea for recognition" move to "a religious plane" characteristics that grounded Donne's relationship with the Countess—"the feelings of failure and exclusion, the supplications for help, and the trepidation about giving offence" (xxviii). Carey concludes that the Holy Sonnets may thus "be 'about' her as well as about God" (xviii).

Dubrow (1990, 164) points to Donne's "tendency to map relationships in terms of domination and submission" in the Holy Sonnets.

Labriola (1990, 64) comments on Donne's practice of paradoxically harmonizing Christ's "divine attributes with human nature, as in *Cor2*: "Immensity cloystered in thy deare wombe." *HSSpit* and *HSWhy*, according to Labriola, contain similar imagery.

Mackenzie (1990, 76–77) notes how often the religious poems, and especially the Holy Sonnets, are treated as if they were "all of a piece" (76). And yet, Mackenzie says, the Holy Sonnets vary notably "in procedure and in success" (76). Mackenzie finds *HSWilt* to be "the least successful" of the Holy Sonnets and identifies at the "opposite extreme" poems such as *HSBlack* and *HSScene*, which "create a pivotal drama of salvation" (76). Mackenzie locates the pivotal nature of the drama in the octave, which evokes the "plight of the sin-stricken soul, galvanised by sickness, death, and the prospect of judgement," while the sestet "offers the salvation which will answer that plight" (76). Mackenzie identifies the Petrarchan sonnet form and the dramatic possibilities afforded by meditation as resources Donne appropriates to achieve poetry that is "at once comprehensive and intense" (76). For Mackenzie, some sonnets fall short of their potential, because "the dramatising of terror outweighs the salvation that should swallow it up," making them either "contrived" or "limp" (76). Mackenzie contends that the Holy Sonnets that "wear best on continued reading" are those that allow us to see Donne accepting the "fluctuating devotion, the incongruities of his spiritual life, without trying for a dramatic resolution" (76–77), the "finest" of such poems, in Mackenzie's view, being *HSMade* (77). For Mackenzie, the Holy Sonnets are the "core" of Donne's religious verse, given "the variety of directions in which they jet," but they are not the "climax," which Mackenzie reserves for "the freer movements" of *Lit* and the Hymns (77).

Ray (1990b, 162–63 and *passim*) offers a "companion" to Donne and includes a discussion of the Holy Sonnets generally and ten of the poems separately: *HSDue*, *HSRound*, *HSBatter*, *HSDeath*, *HSLittle*, *HSShow*, *HSShe*, *HSScene*, *HSMade*, and *HSWhat*. He summarizes issues pertaining to the sequencing of the poems and offers interpretive paraphrases of the ten identified here.

Hester (1991a, 175–77) cites a passage from Donne's letter to Henry Goodyer, written during the Mitcham period, in which he states that "words which are our subtillest and delicatest creatures . . . are so muddie, so thick, that our thoughts are so, because (except at the first rising) they are ever leavened with passions and affections" and adds "I scarce think any effectual prayer free from both sin, and the punishment of sin" (*Letters*, pp. 110–11) (175). Hester regards the passage as central to the Holy Sonnets and "their vigorous explorations of man's attempts to re-sign his self *in imagines dei*," and, in Hester's view, their primarily "ineffectual" efforts to "affirm any enduring sense of assurance" (175). Hester examines two Holy Sonnets (*HSBlack* and *HSScene*) that he views as representative of the Holy Sonnets as a whole, that is, of the "moral interrogation of the central issues of the English (Counter) Reformation debate about justification" (177). Hester finds that the poetic meditations "affirm man's limited powers of recreation" (familiar in both Catholic and Protestant thought), thus displaying the "tensions inherent to, and the psychic questions raised by, the Protestant doctrine of imputation to the human condition" (177). See more under *HSBlack*: The Poet/Persona and *HSScene*: The Poet/Persona.

Gorbunov (1993, 122) considers the Holy Sonnets to be Donne's best poetic achievements.

Ousby (1993, 266) states that the Holy Sonnets variously convey "spiritual struggle" and "near despair" but also the "hard-won triumph of the famous" *HSDeath*.

Malpezzi (1995, 142–46, 151) finds that the work of Mircea Eliade is particularly helpful in understanding Donne's religious imagination, both in the Holy Sonnets and elsewhere, for, in Malpezzi's view, even a "cursory" review of Donne's work suggests its association with Eliade's definition of "*homo religiosus*, the religious human" (cf. *The Sacred and the Profane: The Nature of Religion*, trans. Willard R. Trask. [New York: Harcourt, Brace and World, 1959, 202]) (142). Eliade, according to Malpezzi, views "the transcendent reality of the sacred" as manifested in and sanctifying the world; hence "sacred history can and must be reactualized," and this view is "the core of Donne's religious art" (142). Malpezzi argues that Donne both "perceived the world as imbued by the sacred" and also "clearly believed the principal events of sacred experience, those preserved in Scripture, are repeatable and accessible to humanity" (142). Moreover, according to Malpezzi, "this abstraction assumes concrete form in those divine poems which become hierophanies, manifestations of the sacred, their very time and space transformed to the eternal and cosmic" (143). Malpezzi points to the speaker in *HSLittle*, who sees himself as a microcosm of the macrocosm (145), and the speaker in *HSBlack*, who realizes that "even the colors of the spectrum" embody the "spiritual realities of sin, contrition, and redemption through Christ's salvific blood" (146). Malpezzi cites still other Holy Sonnets, including *HSShe*, *HSSpit*, and *HSMade*, which, in their different ways, provide examples of the "sacralization of the profane by paralleling worldly experience to that of sacred history" (151).

Rollin (1995, 147) designates Donne as "the most notable" of the seventeenth-century poets who use "the element of game" in their conception of wit. Rollin adds that, "like Herrick," Donne can play the game of representing contradictory views on love and women (in the Songs and Sonets) and on religion (in the Holy Sonnets), "leaving his readers to wonder when the real John Donne will stand up" (147).

For the present editors' views on the matters of ordering and dating these poems, see the General Textual Introduction above.

Walton (1670, 17–18) reproduces a letter from Donne to Magdalen Herbert in which Donne refers to "inclosed Holy Hymns and Sonnets," and he prints the whole of MHMary, which refers to "these Hymns." Walton comments that the "Hymns" identified "are now lost to us; but doubtless they were such, as they two [Donne and Magdalen Herbert] now sing in *Heaven*."

Gosse (1893, 429–36) points to a "large number" of Holy Sonnets that Walton (1670) thought had been lost and remarks that they all "probably belong to 1617, or the period immediately following the death of Donne's wife" (432–33). Reflecting on this date, Gosse observes that the sonnets "are very interesting for the light they throw on Donne's prolonged sympathy with the Roman Church, over which his biographers have been wont to slur" (432), but he also agrees with Walton's view that, "though Donne inquired early in life into the differences between Protestantism and Catholicism, yet he lived until the death of his wife without religion" (although Walton does indeed remark on Donne's investigations of Catholicism and Protestantism, he does not appear to have suggested that Donne lived without religion until the death of his wife—ed.) (433).

Schelling (1895, xvii) says simply that the Holy Sonnets "remain of uncertain date."

Chambers (1896, 1:243–45) says of the Divine Poems generally that they are the "latest group" of Donne's poems, though some may have been written before 1607 (243). He cites Walton's remarks (1670) about lost hymns and suggests that the poems referred to may have been "later" Holy Sonnets or that Walton may be referring to some other poems "as distinguished from the sonnets" (245). MHMary, he adds, can serve as a kind of "preface to the rest of Donne's religious verse" (245). Chambers also points to notes in a manuscript (B32) of the Holy Sonnets and Corona that observes that the poems were "made 20 years since" and adds that the manuscript includes a poem dated 1629 (245).

Gosse (1899, 2:106), commenting on the usual uncertainty about dating the Holy Sonnets, cites Donne's letter to Magdalen Herbert (11 July 1607) referring to "enclosed holy hymns and sonnets," but notes Walton's observation (1670) that the poems mentioned are lost. He also cites Chambers's comment (1896) regarding the manuscript copy of Corona and the Holy Sonnets, but says that since the date of the manuscript is unknown the note is of little help. More conclusively, he points to HSShe, which, he says, "settles any doubt" about the Holy Sonnets being "subsequent to August 1617." For Gosse, "[i]nternal evidence" suggests that 1617 ("or 1618 at latest") is the year of composition. Gosse also notes that he is making available the first printing of all nineteen Holy Sonnets in his volume, and he follows the text and order of the poems in the Westmoreland ms. (NY3)—an order, he says, that is "much . . . to the advantage of their intelligibility" (106). Many critics follow Gosse in dating the composition of the Holy Sonnets in 1617–18, and they often explicitly derive that date from the date of Anne Donne's death. See Grierson (1912),

Aronstein (1920, 82), Grierson (1921), Fausset (1924, 238, 241), Bredvold (1925, 213), Praz (1925), Payne (1926, 138), Judson (1927), Grierson (1929), Hayward (1929), Fausset (1931a, xxi), Schirmer (1937, 299), Fausset (1938), Anonymous (1938, 814), Feist (1945, 576), Moloney (1944), Bush (1945, 133), Leishman (1951), Willey (1954, 386), Nicolson (1956, 55), Girri (1963, 93), Honig and Williams (1968, 39), Winny (1970), and Partridge (1971).

Garnett and Gosse (1903, 294) suggest that the Holy Sonnets were composed in 1610–11, at about the same time as *Pseudo-Martyr* and *Ignatius*.

Grierson (1909, 249) says that the Holy Sonnets belong "to the years of his ministry."

Schelling (1910, 133) observes that *Corona* and the Holy Sonnets are collections "of questionable date."

Grierson (1912, 2:xlix, lii, 225–29, 231) accepts Gosse's position that since *HSShe* can be confidently dated, all of the Holy Sonnets were composed after the death of Donne's wife (xlix, lii, 225). Grierson then argues that the poems cited in and accompanied by *ED* and *MHMary* are those of the *Corona* sequence, which can be dated in or before 1609. Grierson further contends that the inscription in B32, "Holy Sonnets: written 20 yeares since," applies only to *Corona* and that it is "certainly wrong" to believe that the implied date of 1609 refers as well to the twelve Holy Sonnets that follow *Corona* in the manuscript (227). The "Hymns" mentioned in *MHMary* 14, Grierson asserts, are therefore not "lost," as Walton (1670) believed, nor are they Holy Sonnets, as Chambers tentatively suggests (1895), but are in fact the poems of *Corona*. In Grierson's reading, lines 13–14 of *MHMary* indicate that the accompanying poems are addressed to Christ, as are the *Corona* poems, a claim which can be made of only one of the Holy Sonnets (*HSShow*) (228–29). Grierson adopts the order of the 1635–1669 editions, appending the three found in NY3. Since Grierson finds no significance in any of the manuscript or print orders, he regards each poem as a "separate meditation or ejaculation" (231).

Guiney (1920, 14) suggests that some of the Holy Sonnets, such as *HSBatter* and *HSMade*, could well have been written very early, in Donne's "yeasting youth," when he was struggling with sinful passions but still sensitive to the appeal of grace. Guiney implies that the note of spiritual conflict arises from Donne's leaving the Catholic Church.

Grierson (1921, 228) observes that all of the Donne religious poems included in his collection of metaphysical poems—among which are *HSMade*, *HSScene*, *HSRound*, *HSDeath*, *HSWhat*, *HSBatter*, and *HSShow*—"were written after the death of his wife in 1617, and are eloquent of sorrow and remorse."

Hutton (1924, 152) believes that the Holy Sonnets were written after the composition of *Pseudo-Martyr* but before Donne's ordination.

Simpson (1924, 231) says that the Holy Sonnets "were written a few years earlier" than the *Devotions*.

Praz (1925, 66) thinks that Donne's sacred poetry, including the Holy Sonnets, was occasioned by the death of his wife, after which he went into seclusion and became in Walton's description [1658, 52–53] dead to the world as sorrow took over his heart, a state reminiscent of Job suffering in his solitude.

Judson (1927, 245) observes that though Donne wrote most of his religious poetry before he took orders, the Holy Sonnets, "the noblest of his sacred poems," appear to have been written after the death of his wife.

Grierson (1929, xli–xlii) asserts that the finest of Donne's divine poems, including the Holy Sonnets, were written between the death of his wife and the sicknesses that brought on his death.

Hayward (1929, 274) observes that the Holy Sonnets were composed after the death of Donne's wife in 1617. Hayward is convinced that the poet's love for and faith in her were sublimated into a love of God, producing "a sensuousness of feeling comparable to the ecstasies of Crashaw derived from that sublimation." See Hayward (1950).

Fausset (1938, ix) doubts that Donne experienced a religious conversion prior to his wife's death in 1617. The first fruits of his conversion, Fausset believes, were the Holy Sonnets, which were written in the months following.

Bennett (1942, xxix) suggests that the Holy Sonnets were composed after Donne's entry into the priesthood.

Moloney (1944, 42–43) asserts that the Holy Sonnets were composed early in the period 1617–1621, and he adds, citing Gosse (1899), that *HSShe*, *HSShow*, and *HSVex* "were suppressed by the editors of 1633 and 1635" because they "betrayed certain Romish doctrines" (43).

Raine (1945, 390) identifies the Holy Sonnets as "the last poems that . . . [Donne] wrote."

Hayward (1950, 14, 22) acknowledges "the valuable criticism and advice" of Gardner (14) and revises his previous dating of the Holy Sonnets (see Hayward [1929]), noting that the dates of composition are "uncertain" and hinting that the sixteen poems printed in 1635 may have been written before 1615 (22).

Mahood (1950, 124), assuming that the Holy Sonnets were written late, finds that "the violent *contemptus mundi* which marred much of the writing of his middle years" is no longer present in them.

Leishman (1951, 251, 258–59), citing Gosse, states that the Holy Sonnets were written after the death of Anne in 1617. In a revised edition (1954, 251, 263–64), he agrees with Gardner that Donne composed the first six of the 1633 Holy Sonnets in 1609 and those from the Westmoreland ms. (NY3) after his ordination. See also Leishman (1954).

Gardner (1952, xxxvii–l, 75, 77–78) rejects Walton's dating of the Holy Sonnets as having been written in Donne's "declining age" and Gosse's reasoning that all the sonnets were written after the death of Anne Donne (xxxviii). She precedes her own dating of the sonnets by first pointing out the order of twelve sonnets that appear in the Group I and Group II manuscripts and in the 1633 edition (*HSDue*, *HSBlack*, *HSScene*, *HSRound*, *HSMin*, *HSDeath*, *HSSpit*, *HSWhy*, *HSWhat*, *HSBatter*, *HSWilt*, and *HSPart*). Following these twelve, Gardner groups four more sonnets (*HSMade*, *HSLittle*, *HSSighs*, and *HSSouls*) that appeared in the 1635 edition, except that she reverses the order of the middle two (printing them in the order indicated) because, as she explains, *HSLittle* is "a general meditation," while *HSSighs* "considers a particular sin and leads on to" *HSSouls* (xxxviii–xliii and 75).

Gardner argues that these sixteen sonnets can be dated according to the two distinct groups into which they fall. The first six sonnets, Gardner suggests, constitute a sequence of meditations on the Last Things (xl). Because among these six are three that she argues cannot have been written after August 1609, Gardner reasons that the whole group of six sonnets on the Last Things must antedate August 1609. Citing HSRound 1–4, HSScene 5–8 and HSDeath, she observes that these poems express something like the heresy of mortalism, or soul-sleeping, a theological view Donne had decidedly rejected by the time he finished Pseudo-Martyr late in 1609. Moreover (as pointed out by Chambers [1895—see HSDeath: Dating and Order]), HSDeath must have preceded BoulRec (written on the death of Cecilia Bulstrode, who died 4 August 1609), which alludes to HSDeath (xliii–xlviii). Gardner presumes further that a second group of six sonnets, those following the first six in Groups I and II and in 1633, not only have thematic unity as meditations on God's love for man and man's love for God, but "are so closely linked to the first set in inspiration" that they may therefore have been written just after the first six, "between February and August 1609" (xl, xlix–l). As for the four sonnets added in the 1635 edition, Gardner "tentatively" concludes that they were written "between the second half of 1609" and the writing of FirAn in 1611 (l).

Proposing the period 1609–1611 as a *terminus ad quem* for the composition of sixteen of the sonnets, Gardner turns to a theory of their *terminus a quo*, which she bases on the assumption that six of them (those she labels the sonnets on the Last Things) must have been enclosed with ED, Donne's verse letter headed in 1633 "To E. of D. with six holy Sonnets." Believing, with Grierson, that "E. of D." was Richard Sackville, third Earl of Dorset, and noting that Dorset succeeded to his earldom in February 1609, Gardner reasons that the six sonnets on the Last Things, the earliest of the sonnets in her view, must have been written after that date (xlviii–xlvix).

Finally, Gardner dates the remaining three of the nineteen Holy Sonnets as follows: Donne must have written HSShow and HSVex after his ordination in 1615 and withheld them from circulation, because they do not appear to have circulated in manuscript. The final sonnet, HSShe, on the death of Anne Donne, cannot have been written before 1617, and its "tone of resignation," according to Gardner, relates its composition to that of Christ, before May 1619 (77–78). A number of critics respond to, and often endorse, Gardner's comments on dating and order, including Simon (1952), Gransden (1954), Leishman (1954), Martz (1954), Esch (1955), Peterson (1967), Shawcross (1967), Hebaisha (1971), Smith (1971), Hollander and Kermode (1973), Lewalski and Sabol (1973), Kermode (1974), Milward (1979), O'Connell (1981), Barańczak (1984), Shawcross (1986a), Zemplényi (1986), Flynn (1988), Mohanty (1988), Carey (1990), Gorbunov (1993), and Low (1993).

Simon (1952, 201–02) agrees with Gardner (1952) on dating and questions why critics continue to infer from the date of one sonnet, HSShe, that all of them must have been composed in Donne's later life. She agrees with Gardner's order as well, accepting the twelve 1633 sonnets as spiritual exercises in the Ignatian method, the four 1635 poems as linked by the theme of "sin and tears for sin," and the three NY3 sonnets as "separate ejaculations."

Gransden (1954, 127–28), acknowledging that dating the Holy Sonnets is a "complex, largely theological" problem, follows Gardner (1952) in dating the NY3 sonnets after 1617, and the other Holy Sonnets, "it seems likely," in the years of doubt and uncertainty that preceded Donne's ordination, with a few, because of their "occasional roughness of meter and phraseology," possibly before Corona (1609). The majority, Gransden concludes, were written in the years 1609–1617 (127). According to Gransden, HSBlack, HSMade, and HSScene probably refer to Donne's illness in 1608, not that in 1623 (128).

Leishman (1954, 76–78) agrees with Gardner (1952) that the first six of the 1633 sonnets, those on the Last Things, were composed in early 1609 (76). He disagrees, however, with her suggestion that ED refers to these six rather than to Corona (77–78).

Martz (1954, 216–20) questions Gosse's procedure of dating (1899) all nineteen Holy Sonnets after 1617 on the basis that one of them is a response to the death of Donne's wife. Martz argues that the stylistic distinctions between Corona and the Holy Sonnets may be attributed to Donne's use of different meditative traditions rather than to the composition of the two groups at different periods, as Grierson (1912) claims. Further, he rejects Grierson's conclusion that the inscription in B32, "Holy Sonnets: written 20 yeares since," applies only to the sonnets of Corona. Citing Grierson's remark that "each sonnet is a separate meditation or ejaculation," Martz concludes that the Holy Sonnets "were not necessarily all written in the same period." To illustrate, he observes that BoulRec is a "recantation" of HSDeath, and that since Mrs. Bulstrode died on 4 August 1609, the sonnet must have been written before that date, and the same may be true of others (216–18). Martz finds Gardner's dating (1952) "absolutely convincing" and her ordering of the sonnets into groups of twelve, four, and three "surely the right way to present them" (216–18). Martz sees in many of the Holy Sonnets evidence of Donne's anxiety over the question of his vocation. Some of the sonnets, and the Anniversaries, follow the pattern of Jesuit meditation as efforts to resolve the problem of "election," a crucial juncture in the second week of St. Ignatius Loyola's Spiritual Exercises, in which the meditant is urged to focus on God's love, death, and the Day of Judgment. Martz argues that Donne underwent a process of "fervent and painful self-analysis" in pursuing the issue from 1601 to 1615, arriving at a tentative resolution in 1612; hence, Martz concludes, individual Holy Sonnets could have been written in any of those years (219–20).

Umbach (1954, 19) observes that Donne's Divine Poems were all written after 1610.

Cox (1956a, 109), noting his disagreement with Gardner (1952), suggests that the Holy Sonnets "and the rest of the Divine Poems" were composed between 1615 and 1621.

Gardner (1957a, 52–56) includes in her edition HSDue, HSBlack, HSScene, HSRound, HSMin, and HSDeath, noting that the sequence was probably written in 1609. She also includes HSBatter, composed, she thinks, at about the same time and HSShe, noting that Anne Donne died in 1617.

Peterson (1959, 518) argues that although the Holy Sonnets have a "unity of theme and purpose" in their expression of the Anglican doctrine of sorrowful contrition, such unity does not necessarily mean that they were written within a fixed period of time, as suggested by Grierson (1912) and Gardner (1952); nor does it mean that the sonnets of the 1633 and 1635 editions were composed in the order in which they appear there.

Adams (1962, 758–59), including HSMade, HSLittle, HSRound, HSDeath, HSBatter, and HSShow in The Norton Anthology of English Literature, remarks that as for dates of composition, each "might be assigned a question mark" (758). Adams suggests that we must guess at their dates of composition from the "scanty marks of internal evidence" (758), and he challenges the view that all the Songs and Sonets were written by the "young Jack Donne," all the devotional poems by the "godly divine." Adams believes that exact dates of composition are finally not important, since in the poetry "it is one mind throughout, whatever different facet happens to be showing" (883). In the revised edition (1968, 908n1), Adams sets the composition date of most of the Holy Sonnets (with the specific exception of HSShe and HSShow) as 1609–10.

Ricks (1966, 187–95) relies heavily on the ordering of the Holy Sonnets in NY3, which, he says, has "very good textual authority" (187). He takes issue with Gardner's ordering (1952) of the Holy Sonnets, saying that her pursuit "of the relationship between the formal meditation and the sequence involves so many qualifications that it is rather easy to suspect Ignatius does not explain Donne's structure at all" (188). For Ricks, the Holy Sonnets might better be read "as an adaptation of the structural techniques of the Elizabethan love sonnet sequence to the purposes of religious poetry" (187), and he identifies four groups of poems based on the order of NY3: 1–4 (HSMade, HSDue, HSSighes, HSPart) form a proem that "reveals the poet's uncertainty and suggests the main themes to be developed in the sequence" (189); 5–11 (HSBlack, HSScene, HSLittle, HSRound, HSMin, HSSouls, HSDeath) form "a meditation by means of which the poet arrives at a realization of the relevance of redemption to him personally" (190); 12–15 (HSWilt, HSSpit, HSWhy, HSWhat) present a "celebration by which redemption is effected" (190); 16–19 (HSBatter, HSShe, HSShow, HSVex) include a "prayer" (HSBatter) "affirming the poet's new-found religious confidence" and three poems that form a "personal epilogue in which the poet, enjoying the peace of mind following from the successful meditation, assumes a less serious attitude to Christ and to his own fervent meditative endeavors" (190). The "prayer-like climax" of HSBatter, Ricks suggests, "brilliantly recapitulates both the negative and positive sections of the sequence" (192). With respect to the question of the order of the Holy Sonnets, Ricks, though preferring the order preserved in NY3, concludes that we have no certain evidence that Donne intended the poems to "form a sequence," nor, if he did, which of the surviving manuscripts, if any, preserve the "intended ordering" (195).

Peterson (1967, 335, 348) believes that Gardner's sequencing of the Holy Sonnets (1952) helps to reveal "the devout Anglican's quest for 'saving sorrow'" (335) and, in their unity of purpose, "the Anglican experience of contrition" (348).

Shawcross (1967, 338–51) follows Gardner's arrangement (1952) of the Holy Sonnets into three groups. See also Shawcross (1986).

Donne wrote the Holy Sonnets during an anxious and disturbed time of his life, Bald (1970b, 236) asserts, in the years 1607–10, before his "conversion" when he would become "secure in the conviction of God's ever-present mercy."

Smith (1970, 161) states that the Holy Sonnets "were no more produced in a single impulse than were the Songs and Sonnets," adding that they may represent Donne's "devotional exercises over a number of years."

Winny (1970, 140) contends that Donne wrote the Holy Sonnets after 1617, "a later and darker period of his life, when the death of his wife robbed him of his greatest comfort, and profoundly changed his personal outlook."

Hebaisha (1971, 59–61) accepts in principle Gardner's arguments (1952) about the dating and order of the first six sonnets from 1633 (HSDue, HSBlack, HSScene, HSRound, HSMin, and HSDeath) and their meditation on Last Things, but generally finds Donne following a "pattern freer from the Ignation meditations" than Gardner's analysis suggests. For Hebaisha, HSDue is not so much a "preparatory prayer" as a "statement of a theme—a statement of a dilemma" (60) concerning humanity's relationship to God—and the four poems following represent different ways the poet finds a "reassurance of Christ's interference on his behalf" (61). Thus, Hebaisha asserts, the sixth sonnet in the sequence (HSDeath) is a "natural outcome of this repeated pattern of re-assurance": with the certainty of Christ's help, the poet "need not fear death" (61).

Partridge (1971, 252) thinks that Donne composed "most" of the Holy Sonnets after his wife's death in 1617.

Smith (1971, 623–25) alludes to Walton's claim that Donne wrote his religious verse after he was ordained in 1615, a view held by some other readers, but says that "there is nothing to suggest" that the Holy Sonnets "make up a single body of work written over a short period of time" (623). He points to the editorial and textual work of Gardner (1952) but finds her groupings of the poems, and her argument that the 1633 order represents Donne's order, insufficiently convincing to determine the order in his edition. "To congeal such writings in a set mould," Smith says, might "prejudge" a reading of a particular poem, and he therefore adopts the order of the 1635 edition, with the three poems in the Westmoreland ms. (NY3) at the end. Such a "neutral" order, he says, is "preferable" (624).

Grant (1973, 39–42) believes that the Holy Sonnets were written in 1609, asserting that between 1608 and 1615 Donne was demonstrably interested in the Heptaphus of Pico (1489) and suggesting that book 5, chapters 6–7 of that work might be a direct source for HSWhy (39). See the section HSWhy and Other Works below.

Hollander and Kermode (1973, 1:1050–53) date all the Holy Sonnets except the three in NY3 (HSShe, HSShow, HSVex) in 1609–11. They place HSShe in 1617 following the death of Anne Donne and HSShow in 1620 after the defeat of the protestants in the battle of the White Mountain, giving HSVex an uncertain, but presumably late, date (1050). They believe that the twelve sonnets appearing in the 1633 edition originated as two sequences of six and agree with Gardner (1952) that their order in that edition is the correct one, noting that the four remaining sonnets are "additional" to the twelve of 1633 (1050). Hollander and Kermode also echo

Gardner in finding the first six sonnets in 1633 to be meditations on the Last Judgment, while the second six meditate on the Atonement and on the love that humans owe to God and to one another as they also plead for God's intervention in human lives.

Lewalski and Sabol (1973, 13–14, 150–61) concur in Gardner's (1952) ordering of the sixteen Holy Sonnets of 1633 and 1635 (13), noting that the three sonnets from the Westmoreland ms. (NY3) are "unrelated, nonmeditative poems" (151). Lewalski and Sabol, however, do not follow Gardner in reversing the order that HSLittle and HSSouls evinced in 1635, maintaining that "as a sequence on sin and repentance" the 1635 order offers a "progression from tears and grief" (HSMade, HSSighs, most of HSLittle) to an "affirmation of 'fiery zeale'" (HSLittle 10–14) to a "concern with false and true varieties of both tears and zeal" (HSSouls 9–12) (157). Lewalski and Sabol believe that the NY3 sonnets were probably written after Donne's ordination, "when he was not eager to be known as a poet, and thus they had limited circulation" (159).

Kermode (1974, 90–91) says that all of the Holy Sonnets, except for HSShe, HSShow, and HSVex, were written in the years 1609–1611, and he asserts that the appearance of the twelve poems, in two groups of six (cf. Gardner [1952]), in 1633 is the "correct order" (91).

Parker (1975, 55, 95) argues that the Holy Sonnets as well as Lit and Corona give evidence that "sobriety predominated in Donne's inner life" (55) in 1610 and early 1611. Parker also states that the Holy Sonnets show that Donne at this time was in despair, further noting that this state "weighed with him against entering the church" (55). Parker also believes that in 1623 Donne's illness prompted him to write Father, Sickness, and HSVex (95).

Lewalski (1979, 264–65) refers to various schemes that have been offered for grouping the Holy Sonnets thematically, most notably those of Martz (1954), who employed the "topics and structure" of Ignatian meditation, and Gardner (1952), who referred to the "Last Things" and to "penitence"; but Lewalski prefers "the Protestant paradigm of salvation in its stark, dramatic, Pauline terms," which she finds "akin to but transcending" other paradigms (264–65). Lewalski suggests that Donne may not have intended the sonnets to constitute a sequential arrangement, for, as is clear from "the Protestant emblem books and lyric collections," the "various states" are on the whole "not so much sequential as concomitant," as is indicated by Calvin's assertion that God's graces "come not singly but together" (Calvin, Institutes, III.xi.6) (265). Lewalski finds the sonnets as arranged in the 1635 edition to be "an expansion of the fundamental terms and direction of the twelve-sonnet group" (of 1633) and concludes that whoever organized the 1635 sonnets saw the "essential thematic concern of the twelve to be the analysis of states of soul attendant upon Christian regeneration, and inserted the four additional sonnets precisely where they would be thematically most suitable" (265).

Milward (1979 [1988, 86, 99–100]) notes that the four sonnets added in 1635 are "scattered" among the other Holy Sonnets and that, especially like the first six, they are of a "penitential nature," though less directly linked to Ignatius's Spiritual Exercises (86). As to the three sonnets in NY3 but not in 1633 or 1635, Milward agrees with Gardner's conjecture (1952) that they were composed after Donne's ordination; he judges them to be of "a more private nature" than *Christ* and *Father*—hymns Donne also wrote after his ordination—and suggests that Donne may have regarded them as less "appropriate to his sacred calling," though they are, Milward adds, "by no means profane" (100).

Novarr (1980, 117–20) examines the debate surrounding the dating of NY3 and suggests that Grierson's (1912) view that the manuscript may have been transcribed as late as 1625 as well as Gardner's (1967) view that it could not have been written before 1617 rests on the assumption—put forth by Gosse (1899) and never challenged—that *HSShe* refers to the death of Anne Donne in 1617 (117–18). Novarr also questions the strength of the evidence that the three sonnets unique to NY3 (*HSShe, HSShow,* and *HSVex*) were written after Donne's ordination (118). Novarr points out that the "she" of *HSShe* "may refer to any one of Donne's real or imagined 'prophane' loves, possibly to Cecilia Bulstrode, "who died on August 4, 1609, and whose death Donne and many others noticed in verse" (118). Novarr acknowledges the merit of Gardner's (1952) view that the sonnet's image of the woman who "rob'd and tore / Laments and mournes in Germany and here" (ll. 3–4) reflects "the captivity of Israel and the collapse of the Protestants after the defeat of the Elector in the battle of Weisser Berg on November 8, 1620," but he adds that Donne was concerned about "the condition of Protestantism abroad, and particularly in Germany, long before 1621" (119). With respect to *HSVex*, Novarr claims that there is even less evidence that it was written after Donne took orders (119). The only evidence, in Novarr's view, is that the sonnet appears in NY3 along with the other two sonnets that may have been written after Donne's ordination (119). If the three sonnets are late, which Novarr acknowledges as a possibility, then "they are the most personal, the most intimately self-expressive poems Donne wrote after his ordination" (120).

Cain (1981, 312) includes the twelve sonnets from 1633 and *HSShe* in his anthology of Jacobean and Caroline poetry, noting that the 1633 ordering of the sonnets most likely was Donne's and pointing to "a coherent meditative sequence designed to lead to that state of contrition that is a necessary precondition of grace."

O'Connell (1981, 324, 326, 328–29, 334, 337–38) supports Gardner's (1952) presentation of the first twelve of the Holy Sonnets according to the 1633 order, adding that Gardner is "reproducing as well the order of the two most reliable groups of manuscripts" (324). But O'Connell finds Gardner's comments on the four sonnets added in 1635 (and "not found in these manuscript groups") to be "much less satisfactory" and "completely dependent on her own critical presuppositions" (324). O'Connell points out that, on the basis of manuscript appearances, there are three possible arrangements for the Holy Sonnets: the twelve poems found in Groups I and II (and 1633), the twelve found in Group III, and the nineteen ("or sixteen if the last three sonnets are considered as separate") found in NY3 (326). Referring to differences between the Westmoreland manuscript's texts of *HSSpit, HSWhy, HSWhat,* and *HSBatter* and the texts in the Groups I and II manuscripts and 1633, O'Connell avers that Gardner's "whole argument tacitly presupposes" (328) that the Group-III order must be the work of Rowland Woodward, the Westmoreland scribe. O'Connell finds contradictions in this conclusion that he says would make the "authenticity" of the 1633 order "dubious" (328). O'Connell's detailed analysis of the manuscripts finally leads him to support Gardner's belief that the arrangement of Groups I and II (and 1633) is Donne's "definitive ordering"; but he rejects her view that the four sonnets added in 1635 are a "related group," arguing instead that they are "left over" from the earlier Group-III arrangement, which is also authorial (334). O'Connell next considers another of Gardner's theories, namely, the existence of a group of six Holy Sonnets possibly sent to the Earl of Dorset with *ED*, but he supports Grierson's (1912) view that *ED* refers to *Corona* (334). Finally, O'Connell explores the question of why Donne didn't "simply create an expanded sequence of sixteen sonnets [for Group I and II mss.], instead of substituting four new sonnets for four of the original set." (337). Although O'Connell acknowledges that any answer must be speculative, he believes that for Donne the number twelve (like the seven of *Corona*) had a "certain symbolic force" lacking in the number sixteen (337). O'Connell also suggests that Donne may have had in mind *The Steps of Humility and Pride*, by St. Bernard, which "parallels the twelve degrees of humility set forth by St. Benedict in Chapter 7 of his *Rule*, with twelve descending steps of pride" (338). For O'Connell, the evidence thus confirms the view that Donne restricted the number of Holy Sonnets to a symbolic twelve, beginning with "an original sequence preserved in Group III manuscripts" and culminating in "a revised version found in Groups I and II and in the first printed edition of 1633" (338).

Noting that the dating of these poems is uncertain, Rissanen (1983, 43–44) thinks 1610–20 is "as close as we can possibly date them," with the "obvious exceptions" of *HSShe* and *HSShow*.

Barańczak (1984, 161) observes that the most recent biographical research indicates that Donne probably wrote the sixteen sonnets of 1635 between 1609 and 1611 before becoming a clergyman and that of the three in NY3, at least *HSShe* must have been written after Donne's ordination, as it refers to his wife's death.

Shawcross (1986a, 122, 134–35, 146–48) presents evidence for arranging and ordering Donne's poems by genre (122). Shawcross notes that the Holy Sonnets "present a special problem of ordering," for 1633 "prints twelve sonnets which are given in the same order in Group I and Group II," and 1635 "adds four more [HSMade, HSSighs, HSLittle, and HSSouls] which it intersperses among the former ones" (134). Shawcross compares the two editions with the various manuscripts of Donne's poems, and agrees with Gardner's (1952) contention that the nineteen sonnets fall into four groups. Shawcross suggests that the interspersing of the four new poems in 1635 may derive from a manuscript such as HH1, "whose order for other subgenres can be seen frequently to be haphazard and in opposition to evidence of ordering in other manuscripts" (134). Shawcross concludes that *HSMade*, *HSSighs*, *HSLittle*, and *HSSouls* "should probably be considered in that order," although he had followed Gardner (1952) in his edition (1967) by reversing the positions of the middle two (134–35). Gardner's argument for reversing the order, Shawcross observes, "rests on content interpretation" (135). Shawcross defends his view that a generic approach to the sonnets is "advantageous," suggesting that each be viewed "as an example of the form, structure, and characteristics of the genre to which it is assigned, determining what is drawn from the standard and how, if at all, it is altered from the standard, all with a view toward levels of meaning" (146). He examines, for example, Gardner's ordering of the four penitential sonnets added in 1635 (*HSMade*, *HSLittle*, *HSSighs*, and *HSSouls*) and finds within the four a movement "from a statement of sinfulness and need of God's grace to prevent Satan's art, to a plea to God to bring the destruction of his world (himself)" by an act "analogous to Noah's flood" or to the "conflagration of 2 Peter 3:10, then to a prayer that his grief (sufferance) be granted visible show, now nonexistent because such show (fruit) has been used up in vain in the past, and finally to an address to his soul to turn to God rather than be seen as a weeping, mourning, idolatrous lover who conjures Jesus's name and dissembles devotion" (147). Shawcross finds that Gardner's ordering places considerable emphasis "upon sufferance as particular sin," whereas the manuscript ordering of the four sonnets (*HSMade*, *HSSighs*, *HSLittle*, and *HSSouls*) "lessens that emphasis and places a stress instead on I's [i.e., the persona's] new fiery zeal 'Of thee and thy house'" (148). Thus the manuscript ordering of the four sonnets, argues Shawcross, "adds meaning in content and interpretation through its linkages and development" (148). Shawcross finds, therefore, that "the order of poems is of major importance in establishing meaning and craft" (148).

Zemplényi (1986, 156–157) cites Gardner's (1952) observations on the probable composition dates and themes of the twelve sonnets in 1633 but points to a feature of the sonnets unnoticed by either Gardner or Martz (1954), namely, the relationship between the "schematic structure" of the first six sonnets and one of the most popular meditative works, the *Book of Prayer and Meditation* (1554) by Fray Luis de Granada (156–57). Zemplényi calls attention to the striking similarity between the pattern of Donne's first six sonnets and the sequence of seven meditations suggested by Fray Luis de Granada, adding that the seventh meditation ("the benefits of God") could be either the eleventh sonnet (*HSWilt*) or the twelfth (*HSPart*)—"probably the latter" (157). To Zemplényi this connection suggests that the cycle would originally have consisted of the first six sonnets and *HSPart*, with the later addition of *HSWilt* and even later of *HSSpit*, *HSWhy*, *HSWhat*, and *HSBatter* (157).

Flynn (1988, 35–43) claims that Gardner's (1952) theory dating the Holy Sonnets "has never been seriously challenged" (35). He points to her discussion of the six Holy Sonnets on the Last Things, among which she places three (*HSRound*, *HSScene*, and *HSDeath*) that "express something like the heresy of mortalism, or soul-sleeping," a view rejected by Donne in late 1609, when he wrote *Pseudo-Martyr* (36). Flynn concedes that Gardner establishes August 1609 as a *terminus ad quem* for at least these three poems but argues that no *terminus a quo* is evident, since Donne "may from an early age have held the kind of mortalist views" Gardner perceives in the three sonnets (36–37). Noting that Gardner further bases her dating of the sixteen Holy Sonnets published in the seventeenth century on the conjecture that six of them were sent with Donne's verse letter *ED*, as is suggested by the poem's heading in some manuscripts, Flynn explores Gardner's conjecture and in particular examines her assumption that "E. of D." was Richard Sackville, third Earl of Dorset, who succeeded to his title in February 1609. Gardner's conjecture and assumption,

Flynn points out, constitute the entire basis for her dating the six sonnets on the Last Things (along with the other six published in 1633) after February 1609 (37). However, Flynn notes, Donne's friend Rowland Woodward inscribed *ED* in the Westmoreland manuscript (NY3) not with the Holy Sonnets Gardner supposes it enclosed but along with similar verse letters Donne addressed to "Woodward and other friends of theirs when they attended Lincoln's Inn in the 1590s" (37–38). Concerning Gardner's identification of "E. of D." as Sackville, Flynn finds the content of *ED* to be inconsistent with anything that Donne might have addressed to Sackville in 1609: Donne speaks of the recipient of *ED* as an admired poet; therefore, Flynn contends, "more and better evidence" points to William Stanley, who succeeded as sixth Earl of Derby after his older brother Ferdinando died (16 April 1594) (39–40). Flynn points out that both William and Ferdinando, unlike Dorset, had repute as poets and patrons of poets; but for Flynn, the most compelling evidence that "E. of D." was William Stanley is that Stanley "was admitted to Lincoln's Inn when Donne and Woodward were students there" (40–41). If *ED* was not written to Sackville, Flynn asserts, Gardner has no basis for dating any of the sixteen Holy Sonnets after 1609, and can prove only that three of them had been written by August 1609. For the rest, she cannot show "that any of them was not written at any point in Donne's mature life" (42–43). Flynn suggests that Gardner sought to date the Holy Sonnets prior to Donne's ordination because of their apparent spiritual turmoil, but points out that the period prior to ordination was not the only time of spiritual crisis in Donne's life: the mid-to-late 1590s—the period of the satires and *Metem*—was "another such period." Flynn concludes that the "paucity" of Gardner's evidence should perhaps lead Donne scholars to be cautious about relying on Gardner for their interpretations of the Holy Sonnets. It might be the case, Flynn adds, that the Holy Sonnets, like other sonnet sequences, were composed in the 1590s (43).

Mohanty (1988, 61–62) contends that Gardner's second edition (1978) of Donne's Divine Poems does not correct "what appears, from the perspective of both textual evidence and critical analysis, to be an error [found originally in the first (1952) edition]" (61), specifically her decision to reverse the middle two of the four "penitential" sonnets first appearing in 1635 (see Gardner [1952]). Mohanty finds that the 1635 ordering (*HSMade, HSSighs, HSLittle, HSSouls*) is more logical, since Donne's "prayer" in *HSSighs* is "appropriately answered" in *HSLittle*, where the "sin of grieving" in *HSSighs* is "transformed into grieving for sin" (62). For Mohanty, the "leap" from the "stagnation of idolatrous love" in *HSSighs* directly to the "sudden possession of 'white truth'" (*HSSouls* 8) would appear "far too abrupt" (62). And, similarly, according to Mohanty, Donne's "uncharacteristically optimistic 'I hells wide mouth o'rstride'" (*HSSouls* 4) offers "too sharp a contrast" if that sonnet follows the "utter abjection" of *HSSighs* (62). Mohanty is persuaded that future editions of the Divine Poems "would benefit by taking into account these textual and thematic factors" (62).

Carey (1990b, 454), following Gardner, dates *ED* as "probably 1609" (since on that date Richard Sackville became Earl of Dorset) and suggests that the poems accompanying *ED* may have been the first six from 1633 (*HSDue, HSBlack, HSScene, HSRound, HSMin,* and *HSDeath*).

Martin (1990, 58) says that it is "generally agreed" that most of the Holy Sonnets were written around 1609–10.

Porter (1991, 11, 48–56) dates the Holy Sonnets during the first ten years of James's reign, when Donne was undergoing the withdrawal "far from court" that followed his secret marriage to Anne More (11). Porter regards the sonnets, written during the period of Donne's "eclipse," as "products of his guilt" and thus as "poems in search of faith, not statements of belief" (11).

Albrecht (1992, 23–24, 27–30) interprets the twelve Holy Sonnets of 1633 as a "fixed" sequence "based upon structuring principles similar to those of the cinema," namely, *mise en scène* and montage (23). Donne, in Albrecht's view, "has provided many of the sonnets with what amounts to stage directions, controlling images, actors," and even an indication of "the actor's voice according to a specific point of view" (23). Albrecht finds that "Donne's definitive ordering of the sonnets establishes the cinematic process," or *mise en scène*, with montage evident in the way the sonnets are situated adjacent to one another so that "new meaning is created by the dialectic between them" (23). In Albrecht's view, the twelve sonnets from 1633 "consist of two series of six each, forming something like a diptych, with each sonnet in the one half corresponding very closely to its counterpart in the other" and forming an "identity and/or opposition"(24). She believes that I (*HSDue*) pairs with XII (*HSPart*), II (*HSBlack*) with XI (*HSWilt*), III (*HSScene*) with X (*HSBatter*), IV (*HSRound*) with IX (*HSWhat*), V (*HSMin*) with VIII (*HSWhy*), and VI (*HSDeath*) with VII (*HSSpit*) (24) and cites for particular illustration the pairing of *HSScene* and *HSBatter* (27–30). See more under General Commentary on *HSBatter*.

Gorbunov (1993, 122) accepts Gardner's (1952) dating of the sonnets, namely, that most of them were composed approximately ten years before Donne took holy orders and the final three after his wife died.

Low (1993, 83) believes that the "main body" of the Holy Sonnets was "probably written about 1609," the three poems in NY3, or at least *HSShe*, after his wife's death in 1617, and *Christ* in 1619; but, according to Low, "the imagery in these various poems reveals no noticeable evolution in Donne's general attitude toward or treatment of the marriage trope." Low notes further that "at least two of these poems," and probably also *HSShow*, "were written after he joined the Anglican ministry" and that "the only other poem certainly written after Donne's ordination that makes significant religious use of sexual imagery" is *Tilman*.

Ruf (1993, 297–98), drawing on Bald's view (1970b, 235) that the "most disturbed and anxious" time for Donne was the years 1609–1611, finds that the Holy Sonnets record "a spiritual crisis in powerful terms" and dates them during that period, observing that they "present a view of his life that is intimate to a degree that few other works can rival" (298).

Davies (1994, 67), finding that Donne's Hymns admit reasonably certain dating, says that they "were composed after Donne's ordination," along with "at least two" of the Holy Sonnets—*HSShe* and *HSShow*.

Strier (1994, 235) thinks that Donne most likely wrote the Holy Sonnets in the years 1607–1610.

THE POET/PERSONA

Praz (1925, 66) describes the Donne of these poems as one who sees death as the beginning of a new life connected to the old by a chain of eternal retribution. He turns his eyes inward, Praz continues, and in the midst of the familiar aspects of life he catches sight of a shadow, unexpected, threatening, and imminent, "that knows the where and why" ("chi sa donde e perchè"), a shadow that invites him on an unknown journey, one which he is frightened to undertake, finding himself unworthy.

Payne (1926, 138) finds that the death of Donne's wife left him with "an intense loneliness," causing him to turn to God for comfort. The event precipitated his "conversion," though because of his "vast egotism" he was never able to attain a "*continual* consciousness" of the presence of God within him.

Grierson (1929, xli–xlii) comments that the Holy Sonnets give "the sense of conflict of soul, of faith and hope snatched and held desperately, of harmony evoked from harsh conditions."

Fausset (1931a, xxi) finds that in Donne's Holy Sonnets "the conventional idiom of religion never intrudes upon the drama of his own imperfect conversion, with 'Despair behind' and 'Death before,' of which they are the concentrated expression."

Elton (1933, 211–12) cites HSDeath, HSMade, and HSRound in observing that Donne's religious verse is "alive with remorse and fear and expectancy and rapture," though the poet falls short of attaining "the mystical vision." Elton finds that Donne's repentance is mixed with the memory of his wanton youth; hence he is "seldom really at peace."

In the context of his emphasis on Donne's persistent search for self-knowledge, Potter (1934, 14) describes "the painfully fierce self-searchings" found in the Holy Sonnets.

White (1936, 123, 127–28, 131–32) cites the Holy Sonnets liberally in observing that there "is hardly a line that Donne wrote but bears on its face the impress of his extraordinary capacity for self-observation." She further comments that "his self-observation neither checks his fancies nor dries the springs of his passion" and that such a quality provides a witness to "the integrity of his feeling far more transparent than any simplicity or reserve." White then quotes the first two lines of HSLittle, which she says "puts the matter in a word" (123). Pointing to Donne's "restlessness," she thinks it "due to that want of concentration, that constant liability to distraction, of which he was himself so sharply aware." She finds the "root" of this distraction most likely to be Donne's "incapacity to let go of himself, to surrender that acute and pervasive self-awareness that is the secret of his genius and his fascination" (127–28). White also finds Donne possessed of a "sense of shortcoming" arising from this "consciousness of his own instability, his changeableness, his incapacity for that steady equilibirium which is one of the great ideals of the spiritual life of his age." His was a "divided consciousness," she thinks, torn between a sense of unworthiness and a desire to serve God (131–32).

Schirmer (1937, 299) observes that in contrast to Donne's earlier works on religious themes, the Holy Sonnets demonstrate a struggle "of his tormented soul and his restless spirit" ("seiner gequälten Seele und seines ruhelosen Geistes"). He notes, further, that although Donne at times reflects a certain tranquility and simplicity of language in the sonnets, he never achieved a sense of security in God and the joyous piety that comes from it.

Brooke (1948, 635) comments that the poems "show little piety and are remarkably egocentric, dealing mainly with Donne's two phobias: his sense of personal unworthiness and the terrors of Judgment Day."

Gardner (1952, xxxi) finds "a note of anguish" in the Holy Sonnets. She sees the "image of a soul in meditation" that is "working out its salvation in fear and trembling," oscillating between "faith in the mercy of God in Christ, and a sense of personal unworthiness that is very near despair."

Gransden (1954, 132–35) calls the Holy Sonnets "a personal record of a brilliant mind struggling towards God," concluding, however, that Donne does not triumph in that struggle. As a poet he "is passionate but not transcendental," and hence not a mystic, Gransden argues, and the sonnets record "the appalling difficulties of faith" for an "imperfect, temperamental man" who, beset by despair and death, believes that though the love of God is always available, it must be constantly courted like the love of a profane mistress. Gransden believes that Donne accepted "the idealistic splendour of the Catholic world-picture," but came to see Christianity as a "psychological prescription," a guide not to conduct, but to one's thought processes; it was both "a doctrine and a technique for believing in that doctrine."

Hunt (1954, 136–37) thinks that "Christian humility came hard to Donne." He is a "haughty egotist" in his early poems and in his religious verse seems "to be trying to Tell All"; hence many of the Holy Sonnets "can be agreeable only to those who are edified—or titilated—by the pathology of religious self-abasement." Hunt concludes that despite Donne's expressed "desire to be 'burnt' and 'ravished' by God and to 'know' utterly by seeing Him face to face," he does not "seem ever to have experienced anything like the Mystical Rapture or the Mystical Ecstasy."

Esch (1955, 45–46) cites the arguments of White (1936) and Gardner (1952) that the Holy Sonnets reflect the influence of the *Spiritual Exercises* of St. Ignatius Loyola and suggests that this influence explains some of the "dramatization and exaggeration, the overheating of the emotions" ("Dramatisierung und Übertreibung, das Übertemperieren der Affekte") of the poems, adding that, though there are unquestionably personal elements present, the Ignatian influence keeps us from interpreting them too autobiographically.

Groom (1955, 65) comments that the Holy Sonnets "are written from the depths."

Cox (1956b, 55) finds Donne's religious feelings to be "'devout fits' coming and going 'like a fantastic ague.'" In the Holy Sonnets, Cox thinks, "the note deepens; it is for the most part one of torment and struggle, and the style expresses this passionate conflict with dramatic vividness," as in HSMade 5–7. Cox (1956a, 113) observes that in contrast to the expression of "assured faith" in *Father*, the Holy Sonnets always contain "an element of conflict and doubt or fear."

Adams (1962, 1:784) calls the Holy Sonnets "rhythmically bold" and "powerful in their imagery," and says they are "marked by deep emotional coloring." Donne's religion, he claims, was "never a secure or comfortable experience," and the Holy

Sonnets "mingle anguished despair with no less anguished hope." Throughout the sonnets, Adams notes, there is a "combination of strong imperatives and protestations of abject helplessness," a combination, in his view, that "determines the tone of Donne's religious feeling."

Buckley (1965, 29) comments that the "voice" heard often in the Holy Sonnets is "one of highly rhetorical self-reproach" and is thus akin to a convention. He adds that the "imagined personal stance from which the voice issues" is a familiar one from other poetry, as well as sermons, homilies, and prose meditations. To Buckley, the speaker's "self-analysis and self-reproach" are undertaken on behalf of others who will recognize the "representativeness" of the process.

Herbold (1965, 292, 294) sees Donne "trying on the masks of saint and scoffer, doctor or doubter," and he concludes that in the religious verse we do not see a "zealous theist or a cynical atheist," but a "hopeful doubter" (292). Donne, says Herbold, "continued to reach when Truth exceeded his grasp," thus finding "a voice for his desires and doubts" (294).

Alvarez (1966, 131–35) believes that Donne generally in the Holy Sonnets carries on a debate with himself and with God, neither of whose presence and reactions, even if they could possibly be presumed, could be predicted. So, he concludes, Donne "created the drama and the audience by assault" (135).

Roy and Kapoor (1969, 111, 115, 118) argue that Donne's concern with religion was a crucial matter for him all his life, not just a passing phase or an issue limited to his later years. They write that he was always trying to seek truth or reality (111). In all of Donne's religious poems, Roy and Kapoor also claim, the individual is more important to him than the group. Such a sonnet as HSShow demonstrates that Donne is speaking in his own voice to his own God, they say, and not "for or against any religious order" (115). They conclude that the voice that speaks through the Holy Sonnets is that of a "lone soul that is perturbed and is full of passionate intensity" (118).

Winny (1970, 34–35, 140–43) supposes that the intemperateness of Donne's youthful writing persists in the Holy Sonnets, yet his object is no longer to overwhelm his mistresses' objections but to compel God to acknowledge him (35). The thought of the Last Judgment, Winny asserts, becomes a "haunting preoccupation" which "rises up to strike at Donne without warning" (35). An unrevealed sin oppressed Donne so greatly that "the self-assured lover" of the Songs and Sonets vanished completely, thinks Winny, to be replaced by a figure "haggard with anxiety, whose yearning to be united with God is continually frustrated by the sins which he cannot expiate or forget" (35). The poems reflect a "deep disturbance of spirit"; having lost the security of his wife's love, Donne turns to God for the assurance of love (140). However, Winny continues, Donne seems unable to persuade himself either that he deserves or that he can expect divine forgiveness. Donne's "spiritual anxiety" is felt in the "choked utterance" of the poems, which "wrench language and metre into strained phrases, to represent Donne's agitation directly" (141), and, Winny concludes, although Donne tries to reason himself into a state of spiritual calm, his arguments in the poems do not follow a logical progression (141).

Parfitt (1972, 381–86), citing a number of Holy Sonnets, notes the "emphasis upon self," the focus on the "self-figure," that seems to define the kind of religious verse Donne writes. There is, he says, a self-awareness and a self-consciousness that mark the poems, but these also give rise to a lack of assurance and confidence on the part of the speaker. Parfitt questions whether, on the whole, Donne is a "representative religious poet," noting that the Holy Sonnets and Hymns "betray little awareness of other people, except insofar as the stagings presuppose an audience" (384). Few would deny, he believes, that Donne is "better as a poet of individual faith and doubt" than as one who celebrates the "communion of Christian belief" and the "great occasions of the life of the Church" (386).

Stringer (1976, 191–94) argues that if Donne wrote his Holy Sonnets for a "didactic end" then the reader "will be required to discern a *persona* whose identity has been especially created for the occasion and whose fortunes are exhibited through the twelve episodes of a carefully structured sequence" (192). He writes that the spiritual status of the speaker is the chief concern of the Holy Sonnets and adds that the sequence relates its "story by implication, comprising twelve discrete dramatic episodes that trace the speaker's progress from something near" the "despair" that is identified at the end of *HSDue* to "confidence" (expressed in *HSWilt*) that "the Father 'Hath deign'd to chuse' him 'by adoption'" (193). He remarks that the "climax" of the Holy Sonnets is *HSBatter*, "where the speaker's prior, apparently ineffectual efforts to assure his election through various meditative gestures are swept away in an anguished call for forcible rape" (193).

H. Thomas (1976, 186, 189) writes that the Holy Sonnets appear to be "intensely personal, essentially individual" (186). She warns that "postulating a mandatory *persona* does not serve to dissipate the uncertainty, the 'tension'" of these poems (189).

Wall (1976, 189–91, 200–02) argues that the persona of the Holy Sonnets "strives for a sense of harmony with the divine" (189), but that progress is not a central feature of the Holy Sonnets: the speaker "constantly changes his strategy of approach to God," and thus "his movement is circular, not linear" (191). Consequently, Wall writes, we see in the Holy Sonnets "not a movement of the speaker toward resolution of his relationship with God, but instead an exploration of the paradoxes of the Christian life on earth" (191). In Wall's view the speaker in the Holy Sonnets strives to open himself to "God's repeating in him in microcosm the universal salvation history of mankind" (200), and thus the Holy Sonnets express both the idea of Christian history and "human history." Wall writes that as "background for the dramatic movement" found in the Holy Sonnets, the speaker "presents the entirety of creation and history in their involvement in God's plan of salvation in an attempt to locate himself within that plan" (201). He suggests that in the Holy Sonnets "the speaker's life takes place in a particular moment in time on the stage of the world at a particular intersection of the macrocosm of creation with the salvation history." This history, he observes, "must be repeated in the speaker-as-microcosm if it is to be open to him" (201–02). Wall believes that to achieve this the speaker "calls on God by assuming several roles identifiable with the five basic types of prayer" (202). In the role of a "spokesman for all mankind" the speaker is equated with thanks and praise, and as an "individual sinner" the speaker is equated with confession, petition and lamentation (202).

Brink (1977, 90, 99–108) takes a biographical and psychoanalytical approach to understanding the Holy Sonnets. Brink sees the Songs and Sonets as the expression of Donne's ego-centered "problem of attraction vying with avoidance in a power relation with women" (90), but argues that "by about 1608/1609 the erotic false solutions reflected by these poems built up to the breaking point, and Donne could sustain the idealizations and disappointments no longer" (99). By 1609, says Brink, Donne, conscious of "the repressed guilt and fear that had long been active," changed the object of his search from "living woman" to his "lost father in heaven" (101). In *HSMade* and *HSDue*, Brink says, Donne appeals to "the procreating father as well as the Father in heaven to lift the guilt of a misspent erotic life" (101), and in *HSSighs* Donne penitentially reconsiders his idolatrous worship of woman, renouncing his "suicidal thoughts to place trust in the Father above." Donne's crisis is so desperate, Brink asserts, that only the "violent purgation" of *HSMade* will control it. In *HSSpit* and *HSWhy*, Brink argues, Donne "preaches to his soul in tones of hope newly vested in the Father, who holds the son in especial esteem, as though a reconciliation of natural father and son had taken place" (102). Finally, Brink claims, *HSWilt* reveals "partially conscious vestiges" of Donne's "lost father," building them into "a theological system of hope far more ample than any belonging to his days of inconstancy in love idolatry" (102). At the center of Brink's analysis lies religion, Donne's "psychological salvation, a merciful release from bondage to compulsions within" (107).

Stachniewski (1981, 677, 683–85, 699) attributes "the dominant mood of despair" in the Holy Sonnets to a "strong Calvinist influence" on Donne's thinking (677). Stachniewski indicates that this reading of the sonnets requires that he question the arguments, including that of Gardner (1952), that the sonnets follow a sequence and reflect "a progression towards peace of mind," which, for Stachniewski, "conspire to depersonalize the poetry" (677). For Stachniewski, the Holy Sonnets "embody the strain between an intense psychic state which gave rise to them and the verbal and formal restrictions imposed on the expression of that state by verse" (684). He also points out that Donne wrote other religious poems near the probable time of composition of the Holy Sonnets that "do not convey their personal impetus," poems such as *Corona*, "with its reassuring circularity, and *Lit*, "containing a calm inventory of temptations and petitions in a format traditional to the Church" (685). But, according to Stachniewski, the Holy Sonnets suggest that Donne "experienced tormented doubt of his salvation in a way not dissimilar to [other] Calvinist despairers" (699).

Yearwood (1982, 220) resists identifying the speaker of the Holy Sonnets as Donne himself, but prefers instead to regard the "persona" as "a state of soul." For Yearwood, the sonnets function as a "sequence of spiritual postures," which readers "are urged by their rhetorical framing to 'try on.'"

Rissanen (1983, 43–44) sees in Donne's religious poetry a gradual development away from the treatment of "the objective mysteries and paradoxes of Christian faith" toward a religious perspective grounded increasingly in experience, which makes its "entry" in the Holy Sonnets (43). Rissanen finds the Holy Sonnets informed by "a heavy existential anguish" and cites *HSMade*, where "the theme of death, decay and destruction is prominent" (44). Rissanen observes further that when Donne addresses

God in the Holy Sonnets, "his words do not carry the same conviction as when he is describing his own state" (44).

Sinfield (1983, 11) finds several of the Holy Sonnets affirming Donne's acceptance, following his conversion, of the Protestant view of his "unworthiness" and of God's freely given grace as fundamental to his salvation. Sinfield cites Carey's view (1981) that Donne's religious anxiety is a consequence of his change from Catholicism but observes that "most sixteenth-century protestants had been born Catholics," and thus the "structure of Donne's anxiety" was in no way "merely personal."

Parfitt (1985, 42) finds repeated use of the first person singular pronoun throughout Donne's Holy Sonnets, noting, for example, in HSMade, the presence of fourteen first person pronouns, while at the same time "the figure projected by way of these pronouns is very much a dramatic one." The figures depict a variety of postures, according to Parfitt, including "being thirsty, derided, in need of instruction or seduction," thus expressing "a variety of emotions, but typically pleading, fear, uncertainty."

Llasera (1986, 41–51), in her discussion of the disparate elements in Donne's poetry, points to the way in which Donne cultivates "an extraordinary variety of "characters" or personae (or masks)," a practice she associates with theatre (41). Among his religious poems, Llasera finds such personae as "the sinner" (HSSpit) and "the sophist" (HSMin) (41–42). She also claims that Donne's religious poetry curiously lacks the language of "joy" and "ecstasy" that is found in his secular verse, and she notes, for example, that the "cry of frustration" found in HSBatter is not heard in the Songs and Sonets (51).

Marotti (1986, 251–61) identifies in the Holy Sonnets and other religious poetry the presence of "despair and hope, spiritual pride and humility, sin and redemption in ways that signaled specific personal, social, and political coordinates for these typical preoccupations of a devout Christian" (251). But Marotti contends that even though Donne may have written about his religious anxieties, "at least when he wrote his early Jacobean religious poems," he was "no saint and his energies and desires were directed toward worldly success" (251). Donne himself, Marotti adds, felt that his pre-ordination religious verse was "contaminated by self-interest" (251). Marotti finds that the Holy Sonnets exemplify the "contradictory attitudes of assertion and submission that were intrinsic to Donne's temperament," attitudes that were "heightened by the desperateness of his ambition in the early Jacobean period" (253), and that Donne's "presentation of the self's conflicts between assertion and submission" incorporated the "acts of witty indecorum" so evident in the Holy Sonnets (257).

Nardo (1986, 158) points out that whereas several of Donne's love poems are "mock-serious paeans to promiscuity" (ConfL), "cynical justifications for the rake's life" (Commun), or "disillusioned renunciations of love" (LovAlch), such "contradictory fears of both separation and union reappear with less distanced personae in poems about Donne's relationship to God." For example, Nardo says, the Holy Sonnets "argue God's property rights over him" (HSDue), "ask God to be the adamant to draw his iron heart" (HSMade), and "even command God to imprison, enthrall, and ravish him because he is powerless to overcome his separation from divine unity" (HSBatter).

Rollin (1986, 131–32, 134–36, 142–43, 146) regards the Holy Sonnets not so much as "private ejaculations" or "highly personalized confessional works," as "sacred poems" i.e., "public demonstrations" of a kind of "spiritual malaise meant to be exemplary to disease-prone readers," and "they succeed in creating this effect by presenting readers with a kind of composite portrait of one suffering from what Renaissance psychology classified as 'religious melancholy' (and what modern psychiatry understands as a form of 'affective disorder')" (131). Thus, whereas Gardner's study (1952) of the psychological tension of the Holy Sonnets proceeds mainly in "religious terms," according to Rollin, his study begins where her study leaves off, that is, in the terms of seventeenth- and twentieth-century psychology (132). Rollin proposes that Donne does on a smaller scale what Burton's *Anatomy of Melancholy* "attempts on the grandest possible scale": to "hold a mirror up to human psychological nature" (134). Rollins finds Donne's speaker "changeable, 'humorous,' 'distempered,' swinging wildly between hope and fear—in a word, sick: 'So my devout fitts come and go away/Like a fantastique Ague'" [*HSVex* 12–13] (135). Rollins cites *HSSouls*, *HSMin*, *HSMade*, *HSWhy*, *HSBlack*, and *HSScene* as sonnets that document "episodes of mania" followed by "episodes of major depression" (136).

Rollin further groups *HSWhy*, *HSWilt*, and *HSPart* in terms of their reflection of an observation in Burton's *Anatomy*, namely, that "religious melancholy could be 'counter-poised,' according to Burton, by 'comfortable speeches, exhortations, arguments'" (142). Rollin finds this "remedy" to be effective in the "unipolar" sonnets *HSWhy*, *HSWilt*, and *HSPart*, none of which, in his view, "is predominantly manic or depressive" (142). In all three of these "wholsome meditations" [*HSWilt* 2], according to Rollin, "there is no discernible tension between the speaker's ego and superego, and no radical shift in mood between octet and sestet," as is found elsewhere in the Holy Sonnets (142). Rollin adds that both *HSWilt* and *HSPart* are "notable for their father-son motifs," calling to mind Freud's view that "the concept of God was 'a cosmic projection of the Father of our childhood'" (*The Standard Edition of the Complete Psychological Works of Sigmund Freud*, ed. James Strachey et al., 24 vols [London: Hogarth Press, 1964], 3:128) (142–43). Rollin identifies *HSMade*, *HSLittle*, and *HSSighs* as poems that "counteract" the "wholsome meditations" of *HSWhy*, *HSWilt*, and *HSPart* (143). The consistency of *HSMade*, *HSLittle*, and *HSSighs*, in Rollin's view, "resides in their moods of almost unrelieved depression" (143). In fact, Rollin adds, the three sonnets "present this image of the superego as moral tyrant" (143). Although *HSBatter* is separated from the three sonnets in both Grierson's (1912) and Gardner's (1952) orderings, Rollins believes that it belongs among them (143). Rollin claims that "all four illustrate an ego generating anxiety in response to guilt, and in each the corollary of emotional trauma is a passivity (conveyed by a number of intransitive verbs and passive voice constructions) reminiscent of the state labeled 'psychomotor retardation' in modern psychiatry" (143). About the Holy Sonnets as a whole, Rollins concludes that it can hardly be doubted that they "constitute powerful dramatizations of how deeply rooted melancholy is in human nature and in the human condition" (146).

Ellrodt (1987, 7–10, 13) finds that in Donne's religious poetry, and most notably in *Lit* and *HSShow*, what Donne seeks with respect to the problem of truth in poetry is a common truth for all humankind in all circumstances (7). In fact, he says, the drive toward the universal is constant in Donne's poetry (7). What Ellrodt finds unique in Donne's poetry, however, is the need to persuade himself, particularly in the Holy Sonnets and in the Hymns (8). Ellrodt counters the view that Donne's fashioning of a self in his poetry works against authenticity, pointing out that Donne acknowledges in *HSVex* that he is himself subject to mood swings (9) and adding that in *HSSighs* and *HSWhat* Donne deplores the errors of his youth (10). Ellrodt concludes that the words "truth" and "true" occur again and again in Donne's poetic work and that while Donne knew doubt, he never doubted that there was a truth (13).

Young (1987, 20, 23, 26) challenges the frequently stated view that the Holy Sonnets express "the final crisis in the poet's conversion from Catholic recusancy to a Calvinist orientation consistent with Anglican orthodoxy" (20). Young contends that the persona of the Holy Sonnets seems "almost to be 'trying out' different versions of grace in order to arrive at a theologically moderate position," adding that "the emphasis on the corporate unity of the Church seems incompatible with the stress on individual election urged by Calvin" (23). For Young, Donne "clung consistently to an un-Calvinist belief in freedom of the will" (26).

Arndt (1990, 39, 47) cites Carey's (1981) biography of Donne in which he claims that there are two facts that are central to Donne: "first, that he was a Catholic and, second, that he betrayed his Faith," so that "a picture emerges of a troubled apostate haunted by guilt and the possibility of damnation" (39). The Holy Sonnets, according to Arndt, "give glimpses of this second Donne," for "in them, Donne is not pursuer but pursued, not conqueror but victim, not central actor but passive sufferer of action that is exclusively God's," and "it is he who must change (be changed), not the beloved" (39). As an example, Arndt cites *HSBatter*, in which he finds Donne reflecting "a fundamental desire to be un-done," for here and in similar poems, Donne sees "that he *must suffer God to act*, and that "what he must do is surrender"(47).

Fish (1990, 241) argues that in the Holy Sonnets Donne "occupies (or tries to occupy) the position of the creature and yields the role of the shaper to God," adding that the God of the Holy Sonnets is notably similar to the protagonist of the Elegies, a "jealous and overbearing master who brooks no rivals and will go to any lengths (even to the extent of depriving Donne of his wife) in order to secure his rights." Fish contends that "it is as if Donne could only imagine a God in his own image, and therefore a God who acts in relation to him as he acts in relation to others, as a self-aggrandizing bully." Fish acknowledges that the speaker of the Holy Sonnets, as in *HSBatter*, "rather than exerting masculine persuasive force begs to be its object," but to him this "rearrangement of roles only emphasizes the durability of the basic Donnean situation and gives it an odd and unpleasant twist: the woman is now asking for it ('enthrall me,' 'ravish me')." It seems, Fish proposes, that "the purpose of the sonnets, in Donne's mind, is retroactively to justify (by baptizing) the impulses to cruelty and violence (not to say misogyny) he displays so lavishly in his earlier poetry."

Norbrook (1990, 16), drawing on Aers and Kress (1981), comments that Donne's "lack of ease with inwardness, his sense of the imminent collapse of a private self into nothingness," can be seen in the Holy Sonnets, as well as in other poems. Norbrook suggests that in the context of a "deconstructionist perspective" one might find "laudable" Donne's "lack of any sense of a coherent self," but it may also reveal "political precariousness" (16).

Nardo (1991, 49–50) finds that Donne "defined his self in response to a radical contradiction in his inner life: simultaneous fears of separation from and possession by the beloved whether a woman or God" (49–50). She notes that whereas the Holy Sonnets "argue God's property rights to him," as in *HSDue*, "ask God to be the adamant to draw his iron heart," as in *HSMade*, or "even command God to imprison, enthrall, and ravish him because he is powerless to overcome his separation from divine unity," as in *HSBatter*, the Divine Poems more often present a speaker who "willfully runs away from love and grace abounding," as is the case in *Goodf* (50).

Sinfield (1992, 159–60, 162) contends that the "main impetus" of English Calvinism in Donne's time "derives from its attractiveness . . . as an instrument for the creation of self-consciousness, of interiority" (159). According to Sinfield, metrical "roughness," such as Donne's religious poems evince, is "not the innocent expression of spiritual anguish" but rather a "self-conscious deployment and cultivation of self-awareness," an element in the "project for actualizing interiority" (159–60), and he finds the "self-examination" and "self-consciousness" evident in a number of Holy Sonnets and associated with "protestant practice" not so much a "byproduct, or even a characteristic, but the goal; the orthodox god did not just demand self-awareness, he justified it" (160). According to Sinfield, "envisaging one's fate in the hands of the Reformation god of incomprehensible love and arbitrary damnation must have been a great provoker of self-consciousness" (160), and thus if Donne seems to be "picking a fight with God, it is because the self is constituted by being pitted against this powerful other" (164).

Low (1993, 67–69) considers the nature of Donne's speakers' relationships to God in the divine poems, observing that three significant ways Donne relates to God in his religious verse are "as king, master, and father" (68–69), and he identifies various images associated with God in several Holy Sonnets: "king, father, and property owner, as well as creator" (*HSPart* 1–2); "a great king against whom the soul has committed treason" (*HSBlack*); "a king who has left a deputy to command his city" (*HSBatter*); the "lord of a 'house,' which the poet wants to join, that is, he is head of a family, tribe, or nation" (*HSLittle*); one who "bears the 'rod' or scepter of authority, the sign of his ability to punish his subjects" (*HSVex*) (69).

Coyle (1994, 139–41, 146, 149–50) sets as his aim "to speculate about the idea of the subject in Renaissance poetry," and in particular in the Holy Sonnets and in Shakespeare's sonnet sequence (139). Coyle claims that for the subject to exist there must be "a reader who reads him/her as a subject," and that "the subject only becomes autonomous once there is a growth of private reading" (140). Coyle examines two of Donne's sonnets in this regard: *HSSpit* and *HSBatter*. He finds that what is being negotiated in the poems is more than whether Donne can separate himself from his Catholic upbringing or whether he would or would not be saved. Coyle is concerned with the poems "as texts which articulate the struggle that characterises the subject" (140–41). Coyle suggests that perhaps in the religious poetry "the speaker will never be allowed to discover himself as subject in any full sense since the very premise of religious poetry is that the speaker is always-already God's subject" (146). Coyle continues by comparing Shakespeare's sonnets with Donne's, and finds that they differ significantly with respect to their focus on subjectivity. Shakespeare's speakers, unlike those in Donne's Holy Sonnets, are aware of their own thoughts and how their analysis of those thoughts affect themselves (149). Thus, in Coyle's view, Shakespeare's sonnets are distinguished from the Holy Sonnets in their "consciousness of this process, their analysis of what goes on in the subject"; in Donne's Holy Sonnets, by contrast, we find "the crisis of the subject in its recognition of its difference from other figures" (150). Coyle feels that the two—"crisis and analysis"—are both necessary "in the shaping of the subject, though we perhaps tend to identify the subject more readily" with the analysis of Shakespeare's sonnets than with the crisis of the Holy Sonnets (150).

Davies (1994, 57, 63–65) argues that Donne's religious verse and prose are "lit up with apocalyptic horror" and finds, moreover, that the "terror of Judgment electrifies" the speaker of the Holy Sonnets, citing, as examples HSWhat and HSScene. Davies finds that Donne's "habitual melancholy" in the sonnets "assumes a Faustian emergency status," for "time is lacking" (63), and further notes that even though the Holy Sonnets "claim helpless despair," none of them appears to be "an effusion of a supine man" (64). Instead, Davies states, Donne's poems "signal their active desperation, like the Psalmist, by challenges to God," as in HSDue 9–10 (64). The persona, frequently "[s]elf-dramatizing," says Davies, is "conscious of an audience or reader," for the sonnets "give little impression of being private meditations, inward communings between the spirit and God" (65). Rather, Davies argues, they seem "designed to impress, and they do impress" (65). Still, Davies adds, the sonnets are "raw with guilt and fear," and some of the power of the poems "derives from their consciousness of their willful failure as acts of meditation" (65). Nonetheless, Davies emphasizes, the sonnets are "acts of will," for Donne, "unlike Herbert and Vaughan," is seldom "capable of the poetry of mysticism, in which the ego is mercifully absolved and dissolved into the being of the other" (65). Davies therefore claims that the "remorse" Donne experiences in the Holy Sonnets is "not only real, and realized on the page before us, but generated by the act of writing fallen meditations" (65).

Marotti (1994a, 84–85) claims that one of the ways Donne's religious verse differs from his earlier secular poetry is in its "changed attitude toward male authority" (84). In most of Donne's erotic and satiric poetry, Marotti finds fathers or other authority figures "portrayed negatively, often derisively" (84). But in HSSouls 1–4, for example, Marotti notes that Donne "imagines the father who died in his early childhood benevolently looking down from heaven on his spiritual triumphs" (84). Marotti sees Donne as capitulating "before a God who seems, in some ways, to have been for him a lost father found," and he attributes Donne's interest in fathers and a "paternal deity" to Donne's feelings of neglect and abuse "by secular authorities, including the king," thus leading to portrayals of a "paradoxically hurtful and helpful God whose power he both resisted and felt drawn to" (84–85). Marotti cites several places in the Holy Sonnets where he finds such paradoxical representation, among which is the deity in HSBatter, "whose violent punishment the speaker masochistically calls upon," and also the usually "loving and merciful" Christ (as seen in HSWhat) represented as "gruesomely frightening, his redemptive act primarily one of power," in HSBlack 13 (85). Marotti cites further examples (from HSScene 7–8 and HSWilt 2–3, 7–8) of the paradoxical representations of authority figures, evidence that "behind Donne's theological preoccupation with strength and weakness lay his experiences in the secular world" (85).

Marotti (1994b, 8) views the Divine Poems and Holy Sonnets as "coterie texts rooted in Donne's sociopolitical circumstances and social relations," observing that, with England under the rule of a King who also had written religious poetry, Donne was able in Corona "to accept the identity of poet—a role which he had earlier consistently rejected." Marotti finds in the Holy Sonnets "the enactment of a conflict between autonomy and dependence, or of assertion and submission, appropriate to Donne's situation as an ambitious but frustrated seeker of preferment."

Rollin (1994, 52) invites readers to view the Holy Sonnets and the Devotions, "not as autobiography, but as autobiographical *fictions*, as dramatizations of the Donnean 'I' that are of special interest because they may be as much fictive as factual." Rollin acknowledges that his proposition is "easier to accept" for the Holy Sonnets than for a devotional poem such as Goodf, since the Holy Sonnets generally "*discourage* an insistently autobiographical reading."

Strier (1994, 235–36) says that in the Holy Sonnets Donne "had trouble fully inhabiting the Protestant devotional stance, the stance that devalued agency and threw itself entirely on grace" (235–36). For Donne, in Strier's view, this stance was interpreted as "a form of willed (and willful) submission to violence: 'Burne me o Lord, with a fiery zeale' [HSLittle 13]; 'like Adamant draw mine iron heart' [HSMade 14]" (236).

Watson (1994, 36, 97–98, 176–77, 190, 260, 317) examines Donne's poetry, including HSDeath, HSBatter, HSShe, and HSLittle, as the expression of Donne's deep anxiety about conventional promises of immortality, an expression Watson finds evident in "the literature of consolation around the beginning of the seventeenth century" (36). HSDeath provides Watson with one vivid illustration of Donne's anxiety about death and his need to construct "a consoling fiction" (97–98), while in HSLittle Donne's fear of "parting" requires him "to practice the dreaded farewell between his spiritual and physical aspects," a practice Watson finds evident in Donne's other valedictory poems (190). Watson concludes that the problem that Donne confronts in the Holy Sonnets and Goodf is the necessity of "the zealous Protestant [to] construct a narrative of the self, yet that narrative is inevitably so deeply entwined with sin that God will, at best, erase it" (317).

Yen (1995, 214–15, 227–29) reads Ignatius and the Holy Sonnets "through the metaphor of the *pharmakon*, or 'physicke'" as explored through a "multivalency of meanings" by Jacques Derrida ("Plato's Pharmacy." In Dissemination, trans. Barbara Johnson. London: Athlone Press, 1981, pp. 63–94) in his reading of Plato's Phaedrus (214). Describing the *pharmakon* as "simultaneously both a poison and a cure," Yen finds parallels in the "strategies of verbal equivocation" Donne uses in the Holy Sonnets to "praise and court God in 'prayers, and flattering speaches'" (HSVex 10) (214–15). Yen claims that "the language of both flattery and praise that Donne uses

to articulate his hopes and disillusionment about his search for political advance-
ment" is similar to his language in the Holy Sonnets dramatizing the "difficulty of
religious belief" (228). For example, the speaker of HSVex "describes his spiritual
malaise in contradictory terms": his only "constant habit" is "inconstant devotion
and changeable contrition," according to Yen, and the speaker "knows no cure for
his religious ailment" (227). In keeping with the metaphor of *pharmakon*, or
"physicke," which Yen observes in several of the Holy Sonnets (at once "a poison
and a cure"), the speaker of HSVex finds that, "at best, his intermittent faith is pe-
riodically beset by feverish tremors: 'I shake with feare'" (l. 14) (227). Similar ten-
sion and ambivalence between doubt and assurance, between devotion to God and
being claimed by "God's enemy," she observes, can be seen in HSMade and HSBatter
(227–28). And in HSMade, according to Yen, Donne's speaker "is also terrified by
doubts about his salvation," but "the thought of God temporarily raises him from
despair and he even attempts to flatter God by professing his complete dependence
on divine mercy" (227). Thus, according to Yen, the speakers in the Holy Sonnets
ultimately "fail to find the 'profits of physicke,' or the cure for religious malaise" (229).

GENRE AND TRADITIONS

Caine (1882, 323–24) prints HSDue, HSDeath, and HSRound among poems un-
der the heading "Sonnets of Miltonic Structure" and explains that these are poems
"in which the rhyme-arrangement is structurally that adapted by Milton (whatever
the number of rhymes employed), and in which the thought has one facet only, and
is rendered continuously whether without break between octave and sestet, as in
Milton, or with an accidental metrical pause of comma, colon, or period" (323). In
Caine's scheme, this structural type is opposed to the "Shakespearean," "Contempo-
rary," or "Miscellaneous" type.

Gosse (1893, 432) says that the sonnets are "more properly quatorzains," "more
correct in form than the usual English sonnet of the age—for the octett [sic] is prop-
erly arranged and rhymed—but closing in the sestett with a couplet."

Gosse (1894, 103) largely repeats his observations of 1893, adding, in a comment
about Drummond, that Drummond's sonnets "approach more nearly to perfection of
rhyme-structure than any of those of his contemporaries, except perhaps Donne's."

Gosse (1899, 1:268–69) notes that virtually all of Donne's work in the sonnet
form is found among his religious poems, observing that he "disdained the softness
and vagueness of the Petrarchists," while avoiding Drayton's or Daniel's addresses to
a "dimly-outlined Idea or Delia." Gosse finds the form Donne adopted in his son-
nets to be "neither purely Italian, nor purely Elizabethan," and he comments that
Donne lacked Milton's "courage" in hearkening back to the "splendid fulness of the
sonnet of Petrarch" while he also shunned the "laxity of the English writers of his
age." Gosse expresses regret that Donne makes use of a final couplet (a "concession
to triviality"), but he finds the octave, with its two rhymes, to be of "perfect ar-
rangement." Gosse concludes that it is characteristic of Donne's "irremediable im-
perfection as an artist" that he both created "much noble poetry in his divine sonnets"

and produced not one "that can be considered faultless" (268). This style, Gosse concludes, was "extremely characteristic" of Donne and of "certain exotic influences of his time"—which, according to Gosse, includes Tansillo, Molza, Spenser, Galileo, Bruno, and Campanella (269).

Hagerdorn (1934, 74) observes similarities in thought between the Holy Sonnets and Luis de Granada's *Of Prayer and Meditation*. The parallels, she suggests, do not necessarily indicate influence since they might be accidental, but the similarities in imagery are noteworthy.

Hillyer (1941, xvi–xvii) points out that in Donne's youth the sonnet tradition, with such exceptions as Drayton and Shakespeare, had lost its vigor, presenting "an irresistible challenge to reform." In consequence, Hillyer observes, Donne chose to express himself, not in that tradition, but through "the complexity and stanzaic richness of the Elizabethan song." In later years, he concludes, save for "an occasional lyric masterpiece" like *HSDeath* and *Father*, his verse was more conventional, since "much of his power was diverted into his sermons."

Hardy (1942, 182) contends that as Donne grew older, the tension within him lessened and the tendency toward ambiguity in his poems diminished. Hence, the Holy Sonnets are "smoother" stylistically but no less "tortured in thought" than his early works. His expression of the desire for a perfect union with God was "too intense, too self-conscious and too personal" to have been inspired by an Italian St. Francis; Hardy concludes, rather, that he was strongly influenced by the Spanish mystics.

Gardner (1952, xxix, xxxi–xxxii, l–liv) argues that the "poetic greatness" of the Holy Sonnets is attributable in part to their integration of the tradition of meditation and the sonnet form (xxix). The "almost histrionic note" of the Holy Sonnets, she says, results partly from the "deliberate stimulation of emotion" associated with the meditative tradition, while the "plain unadorned speech" (having the "ring of a living voice") characteristic of the Holy Sonnets is realized by "exploiting to the full the potentialities of the sonnet" (xxxi–xxxii). Donne is especially adept, she says, in creating from the "formal distinction" between octave and sestet a "dramatic contrast" (xxxii). Of the sonnets' final lines Gardner observes that Donne avoids "the main danger of the couplet ending: that it may seem an afterthought, or an addition, or a mere summary," and she praises his couplets, "whether separate or running on from the preceding line," as "true rhetorical climaxes, with the weight of the poem behind them" (xxxii). Gardner discusses the divisions of the meditation as systematized by St. Ignatius Loyola in his *Exercitia Spiritualia* (1548) and their effort to evoke the "three powers of the soul": memory, reason or understanding, and will (l). To Gardner, the twelve sonnets printed in 1633 in particular reveal the influences of meditative practices, the four added in 1635 less so. She concludes that for the Holy Sonnets as a whole the "influence of the formal meditation" is not so much a "literary source" as a "way of thinking, a method of prayer" (liv).

Martz (1954, 25–56, 43–53, 125–33, 137–40) argues that the Holy Sonnets reflect the influence of the Jesuit practice of meditation as defined by St. Ignatius Loyola, Fray Luis de Granada, St. Francis de Sales, Luis de la Puente, and others. The practice was based on the "the three powers of the soul," memory, understanding, and will, which in the poetry of Southwell, Herbert, and Donne appear as "a threefold structure of composition (memory), analysis (understanding), and colloquy (affections, will)" (25–43). Donne's dramatic openings, for example, reflect the practice of "composition," wherein the memory is called upon to fix before the eyes a place or event that is to be the subject of the meditation, as in *HSBlack* 1–5, *HSScene* 1–4, *HSSpit* 1–2, *HSWhat* 1, and *HSRound* 1–2 (30–31).

Martz explains that individual Holy Sonnets may contain one or more of these three elements. A given poem may, he says, include "a portion of an exercise . . . especially the colloquy," in which the "'three powers' fuse, become incandescent," or now and then it may recapitulate the entire exercise (46). *HSWilt*, for example, dwells only on the second power, analysis (45–46), *HSDue* on the last, colloquy (48). Martz finds that some few of the sonnets would seem to include all three powers, as in *HSWhy* (44), *HSSpit* (50), *HSRound* (51), *HSMin* (52), and *HSLittle* (53). In these instances Donne's use of the traditional Petrarchan sonnet division (4-4-6) demonstrates how "poetic structure may be fertilized and developed by the meditative tradition" (49). Martz notes that three of the manuscripts of the Holy Sonnets entitle them "Devine Meditations," and concludes that the influence of the Ignatian method on the poems is "evidence for the profound impact of early Jesuit training" on Donne's later career (53). He and other poets of the period, apparently influenced by that same training, were able, Martz says, to achieve "the perfect equipoise of a carefully regulated, arduously cultivated skill" (56).

Martz argues that Donne employed the method of self-examination proposed in *Spiritual Combat*, a work attributed to Lorenzo Scupoli and widely distributed at the time. The method, Martz notes, defined spiritual exercises in which reason struggles constantly for mastery over the lower appetites, encouraging a distrust of self, a confidence in God, and the constant "exercise" of the faculties of the soul in a battle to purge vices and plant virtues (125–27). Martz finds that Donne consciously and deliberately engages in this spiritual training in poems like *HSMade* and *HSMin*, where he faces his sins squarely, chiefly those of fear and intellectual pride, examines them rationally, and then repels them "by confidence in God's grace" (132–33). Martz further observes that the Jesuit practice of meditation placed great emphasis on contemplation of the hour of death. He quotes Fray Luis de Granada's *Of Prayer, and Meditation* at some length, citing the author's emphasis on the two voyages, those of the body to the grave and the soul to judgment. Martz argues that the latter voyage occupies Donne's attention in the Holy Sonnets, as in *HSBlack* 1–2, *HSScene* 5–8 and especially *HSMade* 1–8. Martz finds Donne here, as in *Devotions* and *SecAn*, "carefully tying himself in his shroud, analyzing the outward and inward conditions of the sickbed" (140).

Esch (1955, 45–54) observes that the theme of the Holy Sonnets, the tension between sin and grace, is reflected in the structure of the poems, the traditional Italian division of octave and sestet, with the former expressing the turmoil of sinful man and the latter the calming influence of grace, as in *HSRound*, *HSWhat*, *HSSighs*, *HSMade*, and *HSSpit* (47–48). There are variants, however, as in *HSDue*, where the octave is calm and the sestet dramatic, and *HSBatter*, where the entire poem is unified in tone, uttered with a prevailing breathlessness ("Atemlosigkeit") (49–50). Other sonnets, Esch continues, delay the customary turn of the sestet until later in the lines, reducing the antithesis between the two parts. In *HSLittle*, for example, the final part ("der Abgesang") begins at line 10, in *HSWhy* and *HSShow* at line 11, in *HSSouls*, *HSWilt*, *HSDeath* at line 13 (50–52). This delay and reduction of the concluding statement, Esch suggests, makes for a more dramatic ending and conforms more closely to Donne's actual experience. In the Holy Sonnets, therefore, the Italian sonnet form converges with the Surrey-Shakespeare structure ("der Surrey-Shakespeare-Typ"), a synthesis best demonstrated in *HSScene* (52–53). Esch argues that the Holy Sonnets are superior to *Corona* because their theme, the human being caught between sin and salvation, the anger and grace of God, nature and spirit, is more appropriate to the sonnet form. The structure, he thinks, lends itself better to expressing the contrast between the spiritual life and everyday reality than to the biblical, liturgical tradition of the *Corona* poems. Esch recognizes that in varying the Italian form and delaying the turn so as to resemble the English structure ("der national-englische Struktur") Donne at times ends some sonnets with an unsatisfactory cliché, but in others, he finds, the couplet arrives at a true climax, illuminating the entire poem. Further, in varying the structure Donne exploits all of the potential of the sonnet form in which he achieves the utmost density of meaning with an economy of words. This variety of structure accounts for the success of the Holy Sonnets, Esch suggests, for each poem has its unequivocally individual note, a closed unit without reference to its position in the sequence. Donne, Esch concludes, is able to achieve a balance between thought and emotion unequaled by later poets until Hopkins's "terrible sonnets," which mark him as the earlier poet's only legitimate successor in the composition of religious sonnets (53–54).

Denonain (1956, 227) says that in dedicating the Holy Sonnets to Lady Magdalen Herbert, Donne is following a seventeenth-century poetic tradition of praise for Mary Magdalen.

Martz (1960, 329) continues his study of "meditative poetry" by stressing that the Holy Sonnets reveal the "essential process" of this form: the dependence "upon the interaction between a projected, dramatized part of the self, and the whole mind of the meditative man."

Archer (1961, 137–47) rejects the views of Gardner (1952) and Martz (1954) that Donne constructed his Holy Sonnets according to the Ignatian method of meditation. He sees, rather, a structure like that of the strophe, antistrophe, and epode of the chorus in Greek drama.

Martz (1963, xxxii), in his anthology of seventeenth-century verse, continues to link Donne's Holy Sonnets with "the meditative tradition." See Martz (1954).

Alvarez (1966, 131) writes that the Holy Sonnets are "an altogether more individual achievement" than *Corona*, but "an achievement almost in the teeth of the sonnet form." He argues that Donne "used the inherent tightness of the sonnet to reflect both personal tensions and the highly organized, compressed thinking that, with Donne, always went with emotional disturbance."

Cruttwell (1966, 28–29), acknowledging that poems such as *HSVex* and *HSBatter* may to some appear "too obviously egoistic" for divine poetry, says about the Holy Sonnets generally that there can be no denying their "technical mastery." In most of them, he observes, there is a "strict division between octave and sestet which the

Shakespearean form has to lose" and that the division is used "to tremendous effect for a long dramatic pause and a drastic change of tone" (29). He quotes *HSRound* in full to illustrate this quality.

Halewood (1970, 79–85) agrees with Martz (1954) that the Ignatian system of meditation lies behind the Holy Sonnets but thinks that, besides the deliberate stimulation of emotion, which is the function of the understanding and the will in meditation, there is in such devotional poetry as the Holy Sonnets an expression of reconciliation (79). Halewood believes that in the Holy Sonnets Donne methodically cultivates single states of emotion, a process that is encouraged in meditation. The poetry of meditation, Halewood contends, is constructed "with a view to producing what is in the language of poetics a 'resolution' (or 'reconciliation') and in the language of religion a 'consolation' (or 'reconciliation')" (83). However, he observes, it is essential to the dialectic and dramatic character of the Holy Sonnets that the poems contain some dramatized opposition, "an ostensible clash of apparent incompatibles" (83–84).

Hebaisha (1971, 65–66), though noting that Donne's choice of the sonnet form for the Holy Sonnets is unoriginal, even "conventional" (65), argues that he uses the form so "brilliantly" that a reader is "left with the impression that he invented the form and that no other form could have expressed what each particular sonnet expressed" (66).

Fuller (1972, 22–23) remarks that the history of the English sonnet in late Elizabethan times is largely one of assimilation with the Italian sonnet. He argues that Donne, like Milton, presided over the general blurring of the sonnet's musical form, and he cites as an example *HSDeath*, in which there occurs an Italian octave followed by an enclosed quatrain and couplet. See more under *HSDeath*: Language and Style.

Nye (1972, 355–57) acknowledges the influence of meditative practices on Donne's poetry, noting particularly *HSDue*, *HSBlack*, *HSDeath*, *HSShe*, and *HSVex*. Nye identifies *HSDue* as a "preparatory prayer," claiming further that the solitary reader should read the Holy Sonnets in one sitting, because the poems proceed according to the method of St. Ignatius Loyola, of meditation by stages (355). He adds that the "slow cumulative effect of Donne's pondering on Last Things is great" (355). Nye notes that it has been observed elsewhere (he is presumably referring to, without citing, Martz [1954, 1960, 1963]—ed.) that "meditative" poetry would be a more precise denomination and more general than "metaphysical" poetry.

White and Rosen (1972, 12) claim that the Holy Sonnets announce a "new chapter in the history of the sonnet." They state that until those of Hopkins, Donne's remained the greatest sonnets written in English on religious subjects. The best of them, White and Rosen argue, are "incomparable" in their union of "those diverse qualities that characterize metaphysical poetry." Donne's sonnets, they conclude, reject most of the "poetical furniture" of the time, instead employing a "muscular vocabulary, a varied and colloquial diction, a direct, harsh, abrupt versification, a new use of the old sonnet conceits and a new metaphor drawn from science and divinity."

Hollander and Kermode (1973, 1050) hold that in the Holy Sonnets Donne adapted the "form of Ignatian meditation to an Italian sonnet form." They find that there is "usually" a "clear break at the *volta*, after the eighth line, and a change of tone in the sestet, which is quieter and more reflective than the octave." This form, they say, "was admirably suited to his powers," and provided "passionate," "excited," and "devotional language and rhythms."

Lewalski (1973, 106) says that the Holy Sonnets are "meditations more nearly in the Protestant spirit than in the Ignatian," asserting that the topics are "persistently applied to, located within, the self." Poems such as HSSpit, HSDeath, HSWhat, and HSBatter, she thinks, focus on the speaker in a way that is more representative of Protestant meditative practices.

Kermode (1974, 91–93) writes of the Holy Sonnets as meditations, following the reading of Gardner (1952). The sonnet form, he suggests, is "not wholly suitable for use as a composite exercise in meditation," but Donne exploited its possibilities, especially the "strong break between the octave and the sestet," (91). Characteristically, Kermode observes, Donne's octaves are "quieter, more contemplative," and his sestets grow out of the meditation or contemplation of the opening eight lines (91). Giving particular attention to HSRound, Kermode finds the first six poems in 1633 to be more obviously meditative, but the second sequence of six to be "rather harder to describe . . . as one of meditations" (93).

Bellette (1975, 322–47) argues that the Holy Sonnets should be read on the basis of their "form and structure," as well as their "intellectual and emotional content," suggesting that the Holy Sonnets fully develop a tendency in Shakespeare's sonnets in which "form itself cannot convincingly resolve . . . the emotional and spiritual forces that have been set in motion." He asserts that in the Holy Sonnets "our expectations of form are thwarted, which brings us to the closest possible relationship with the spiritual occasion of the poems" (328), and he thinks that Donne's use of the sonnet form may be read as a "knowing violation of convention" (333).

Stull (1975, 29–44) argues that Elizabethan sonnet poets such as Barnabe Barnes, Henry Constable, and Henry Lok "both anticipate Donne's sonnet form, specifically its complex logical structure, and establish a precedent for his adoption of the secular sonnet to religious themes" (29). He notes that in all nineteen of the Holy Sonnets Donne abandoned the pattern of both the "true" Italian sestet (cdecde) and the Sicilian version (cdccdc) with its rhyme in balanced tercets, adding that Donne's "manipulation of the volta shows him to be in the mainstream of writers who continued Wyatt's experiments with two turns" (33). In HSSouls and HSBatter, he says, Donne "moves the final turn one foot back into the twelfth line to avoid a facile epigram, in the former sonnet making the word 'turne' itself the rhyme word that pivots the speaker toward a final resolution" (33). He notes that in the Holy Sonnets Donne fuses the English and Italian forms to produce a structure "that is capable of accommodating meditation, deliberation, or even forensics" (33) and adds that eleven Holy Sonnets (HSBlack, HSScene, HSRound, HSMin, HSSpit, HSWhy, HSWhat, HSBatter, HSWilt, HSMade, and HSShe) give evidence of the fourfold structure (4-4-4-2) created by Wyatt. To Stull, Surrey's influence on the Holy Sonnets was "negligible except for his having established the epigrammatic closing couplet as a typically English device" (35) and he finds Sir Philip Sidney's practice of compressing the turn in the final line absent from the Holy Sonnets. Many of Henry Constable's religious sonnets, he says, and half the secular sonnets in Constable's

Diana follow Donne's preferred rhyme scheme. He concludes that the evidence shows that Donne "was *un*original in everything but genius" (40).

Parini (1977, 304–05) writes that the Holy Sonnets adhere, individually and as a whole, to the structure of the Ignatian *Spiritual Exercises*, "where the movement of each exercise is from fear and despair to consolation and affection (praise)" (304). He writes that like the Ignatian exercises which "begin with images of purgation," the octaves of *HSSpit, HSWhy, HSWhat, HSBatter, HSWilt* and *HSPart* "dwell on sin" (305).

Low (1978, 57–58) writes that the Holy Sonnets are dominated by the Ignatian method, arguing that in the Holy Sonnets the balance between liturgical and private forms is abandoned when Donne "turns to Ignatian meditation for the structure and texture of his poetry and the [primary] method of his devotion" (57). He also states that the Holy Sonnets have more appeal to the imagination of readers than do the "mixed techniques of the earlier poems" (58), adding that "they are designed to stimulate emotion" and that "their kind of devotion is immediately accessible to unpracticed readers" (58).

Partridge (1978, 130) argues that the Holy Sonnets are interior meditations aimed at expressing confidence in God and that the sonnet form Donne adopted "is important to the nature of the impact he intended," for he wished to flout the Petrarchan smoothness of his predecessors.

Chanoff (1980, 159, 163–64) proposes that studies of Donne's religious poetry in the context of meditative techniques, including that of Martz (1954), have ignored the relationship of meditation "to the worship of the Church" (159). Chanoff points out that "Protestant use of meditative techniques" generally focused on the "personal nature of the contemplative union with God," but that in the mid to late sixteenth century the Spanish Inquisition "turned its attention to the Alumbrados, heretics whose emphasis on illuminism seemed in many ways close to Protestantism," and that there was subsequently an "attack on popular private devotions of all types" (159). Chanoff adds that "it was against this background that the Jesuits began to define the relationship between meditative devotion and the public worship of the Church" (159). Chanoff further adds that Donne "was separated from Catholicism" in his middle years, but the "Catholic commitment to order, authority and corporate worship was part of his soul" (163). Thus, in Chanoff's view, the poems of 1607–09 (including the Holy Sonnets), the letters, and "the cult of friendship all show Donne struggling to place himself, and especially his religious experience, within a social milieu" (163). According to Chanoff, "the milieu Donne was in search of could only be provided by the Church" (163). Chanoff concludes, therefore, that in the Holy Sonnets, "the concept of the spiritual marriage between man and Christ in the Church is absent," and that "the sacramental outlook of the later sermons and *Devotions*, and not the immediate approach of the sonnets, is the essential fibre of Donne's spirituality," for "these later works show Donne recovering important aspects of his Catholicism within the context of the Established Church" (164). Donne's later works, Chanoff claims, "show how far Anglicanism, from Hooker to Laud, fostered (or at least permitted) a preservation of the medieval heritage" (164). As Chanoff observes, "perhaps the most essential aspect of this framework is the instrumentality [Catholicism] assigns the Church in the sanctification of individuals" (164).

Carey (1981, 50–54) supports the view that the Holy Sonnets are indebted to the Ignatian meditative exercises, reflecting "vestiges of Catholic devotion" on the part of Donne, although Carey finds a more heightened sense of despair in the poems than one would expect to find in the exercises themselves (50). Carey adds that if Martz (1954) is correct that the sonnets "began as calmly plotted devotional exercises, intended to extirpate fear and despair, we can only say that they failed as exercises, and so succeed as poems" (54).

Martz (1982, 173) finds convincing Lewalski's discussion (1979—see Dating and Order) of the sequence of the Holy Sonnets in a "Calvinist context," suggesting that her thesis "does not invalidate the presence of the Ignatian kind of meditation within the bounds of an individual sonnet," as the speaker enacts what Lewalski calls the "Protestant drama of regeneration."

Miller (1982, 835–36) cites Gardner (1952) and Martz (1954) (see above and Dating and Order) among others who have demonstrated the influence of the Ignatian meditative exercises on Donne's poetry (835). He adds that Gardner, "by restoring the manuscript order, has been able to see in these poems a sequential meditative exercise" (835). But Miller finds that the "sensuous language" of the Holy Sonnets points to the meditative practices of St. Francis de Sales as a greater influence than St. Ignatius Loyola (835–36). Miller also cites Ricks (1966—see Dating and Order), who contends that the order of the poems in the Westmoreland ms. (NY3) suggests "an Elizabethan sonnet sequence and not a meditative exercise at all" (836).

Ferry (1983, xi, 14, 70), whose study includes attention to a number of Holy Sonnets, explores whether Donne and other early modern writers, though "without modern vocabularies for describing what we call the *real self* or the *inner life*, nevertheless conceived of inward experience in any sense to which our terminologies can intelligibly be applied" (xi). Ferry finds that only a few poets, "and those almost exclusively in sonnets," were concerned "with what a modern writer would call *the inner life* or *real self*" (14). According to Ferry's study of the sonnet tradition, Donne's innovations in the representation of the inward state in his sonnets grew out of the history of the sonnet in England, namely, from Wyatt and Sidney, who "learned individually as English innovators in the sonnet form and the sonnet sequence, what Shakespeare taught himself directly from *Astrophil and Stella*, and what Donne assimilated from the associations which the form had accumulated for him by the time he chose to work within it" (70).

Booty (1984, 200–01, 222–23) contends that the Book of Common Prayer dominated Anglican spirituality during the reigns of Elizabeth I and James I, and that, while "Ignatian, Salesian, and other forms of post-Tridentine meditation" may well have influenced English practices, the presence of "a native tradition of meditation" is "more pervasive and more influential" (200–01). Booty turns to Joseph Hall's *Arte of Divine Meditation* (1606) as an example, noting Donne's association with Hall and claiming tht Donne's religious poetry is grounded in the Book of Common Prayer, while the Holy Sonnets in particular are "clearly meditative" and seem to follow the meditative sequence of the Anglican Eucharist (222–23). Booty schematizes the sequence according to the following stages: A. "The stage is set: preparatory prayer" (*HSDue*); B. "The agony: contrition with pleading for sacramental grace" (*HSBlack*, *HSScene*, *HSRound*, *HSMin*); C. "Transition: defiant faith" (*HSDeath*); D. "The Cross of Christ: the means of grace" (*HSBatter*, *HSWilt*, *HSPart*). Booty adds that it might be too much to claim that Donne was "deliberately writing" a "meditative series of poems for use in relation to the Eucharist," but we can make a stronger claim that Herbert did exactly that (223).

Alves (1985, 31) cites Martz (1954) approvingly, noting that Martz demonstrates the importance of Ignatian meditation among Catholics "served by priests of the Jesuit mission to England" and that the Holy Sonnets should be understood in the context of Ignatian meditations.

Martz (1985, 14) once again calls attention to Donne's use in the Holy Sonnets of the methods of meditation "learned in his early years to explore the possibility of repentance under the new reformed theology of imputed righteousness." Martz adds that Donne, or someone else, has arranged the sonnets into "sequences of twelve or sixteen that move from fear to love."

Patrides (1985a, 43) explains Donne's control of "the potential hysteria" in the violent imagery of the Holy Sonnets by focusing on his use of the sonnet form. In Patrides's view, the form of the sonnet "tempers, moderates, restrains," and may even be seen to "intimate a terminal Order which the Holy Sonnets never directly assert, and sometimes even question." The sonnet also provided Donne with the opportunity to offer a "nominal division" following the Shakespeare model (4-4-4-2) and an "actual one after the Italian pattern (an octave and a sestet)." But, Patrides, observes, the "most impressive" effect of Donne's use of sonnet form is that "he appears not to use the form at all," that is, "so swift is the flow of the given movement, and so overpowering are the punctuation and the imagery, that the rhymed lines are submerged until we are, abruptly, stopped." The only other English poet, in Patrides's view, who succeeds in "obliterat[ing] the sonnet form even as he was demonstrating its immense powers" is Hopkins.

Robson (1986, 52) notes that "sonneteering in the Petrarchan mode "subsided" after the turn of the century, but "the English sonnet continued," with Donne and Milton as "the greatest masters of its form." Robson adds that Donne, however, ignored the use of the form for love poems since he perhaps "associated it with the courtly romanticism against which he was reacting" but it became "powerful religious drama" in the Holy Sonnets.

Van Emden (1986, 52–53) finds that *HSMade*, *HSDeath*, and *HSBatter* "adhere to the sonnet form of fourteen lines divided into the octet (eight) and the sestet (six), with a turning point in meaning or emphasis between the two" (52), though she calls the rhyme scheme in the three poems (abba, abba, cdcdee) "unusual." The "octet rhymes," she notes, are different from those of Shakespeare or Sidney but "similar to those of Petrarch," while the sestet differs from Petrarchan form. She further finds that Donne "uses the turning point between octet and sestet in the normal way" (52–53).

Zemplényi (1986, 155), citing Martz (1954), calls attention to a change in the nature of devotion in the late sixteenth and seventeenth centuries, noting that it became "much more personal, as humankind's "relation to God also became much more individual than before," and pointing out that the practice of meditation was "an important part of religious life" and "had profound resonances in the poetry of the age," such as the Holy Sonnets.

Tomlinson (1990, 35–37) claims that Donne's religious verse "obviously changes as he moves fully into the Anglican Church," but he also observes that we "cannot assume that his poetry gets better, and so more significant, simply for this reason" (35). Moreover, in Tomlinson's view, in the Holy Sonnets the "very neatness of the sonnet form" appears to "restrict the poet more than it helps him" (36). For example, he says, in HSScene, the "fine opening line" and the "agile patterning of rhetorical points" are "highly promising," but it is as if here, as elsewhere, the material "seems to want to burst the bounds set by the fourteen lines," and thus the final couplet seems "limp and resigned to defeat" (36). In another sonnet, HSDeath, Tomlinson finds a "strongly sensuous figure of death" evoked by the phrase "Why swell'st thou then?" (l. 12), but "the neatness of the argument in the poem as a whole seems to demand a neat ending, even at the cost of a piece of rather hollow rhetoric" (37). Tomlinson thus believes that given "more space and freedom" than the sonnet form allows, the later Donne writes both "more impressively" and "far beyond the range of either conventional belief and practices" (as, for example, in Lit) or the "formal doctrines of his profession" (37).

Shawcross (1991, 85-86, 94, 218n12) contends that the "most notable element" in a consideration of what defines the lyric as a genre is "the authorial intention toward the act of writing the poem"; that is, he suggests, the lyric "presents an authorial presence but its function is fully reader response," for it presents a "mimesis of experience for the reader to comprehend or sense" and a "calculated mimesis devised by the maker, whose concern is poetic art" (85). Shawcross adds that what is primary is not the "presentation of the emotion or idea" but rather the "creation of the literary artifact to sustain that emotion or idea" (86). Shawcross contends that his view of the lyric form is crucial also to reading Donne's Holy Sonnets (even while reading them "subgenerically" as sonnets), for those poems are often "critically misread as only documents of the poet's wrestling with self and ontological concerns" (94, 218n12).

Austin (1992, 40–41) associates the Holy Sonnets with the emblem tradition, finding, for example, that occasionally Donne's images reflect the Jesuit emblem tradition, such as that found in HSBatter, where "the poet implores God to chastise him with the various types of suffering that were illustrated in those emblems in which hearts were drawn with hands hammering them, piercing them with nails and other tortures" (41). Austin finds another instance in HSMade 3–7, which "embodies the narrative idiom present in Francis Quarles's emblems" and their depiction of the "religious adventures of Anima (the Soul)" (41).

Gorbunov (1993, 122–24) comments that the Holy Sonnets, radically changing the Italian form of the sonnet that we find in Petrarch, bring to the sonnet form simplicity, dramatism, and power of emotion (122). Gorbunov agrees with Martz (1954) that the first sixteen of the Holy Sonnets are indebted to the Ignatian meditative exercises, popular in the sixteenth and seventeenth centuries, but Gorbunov adds that Donne gave new meaning to this tradition by subjecting it to his own individuality (123). Gorbunov finds the sonnets to be infused with the feeling of spiritual conflict, inner struggle, fear, doubt and pain, which is exactly the type of feelings from which the meditations were supposed to free the meditator (123). Gorbunov thus concludes that it is not advisable to strongly stress the dependence of the Holy Sonnets on Ignatian meditation, and moreover there is no evidence that Donne in fact used the method as a young man (124). Furthermore, according to Gorbunov, poems written in the form of religious meditation existed before Loyola, such as the poetry of John Skelton (124). Gorbunov finds HSShe, HSShow, and HSVex, most probably written after 1617, also unconnected to the practice of meditation (124).

Ruf (1993, 295–303, 305) seeks to explore "the possibilities and limitations of lyric autobiography" by examining the Holy Sonnets (295). To do this, Ruf distinguishes among the three genres of narrative, lyric, and drama and in particular "the ways in which readers stand in relation to the genres' characteristic *speaking voices*" (295). Broadly speaking, Ruf finds that narrative presents "a magisterial voice which surveys people, events, and their meanings from a certain distance, as though . . . without mystery or confusion," while drama contains a "multiplicity of voices, without an overarching voice that is able to encompass persons and actions" (296). By contrast, the lyric is, in Ruf's view, "characteristically spoken without distance or survey, but personally of private moments," yielding a voice "speaking from within" (296). Ruf cites approvingly Lewalski's observation (1979, 265) that "the painstaking self-analysis that was a requirement of seventeenth-century English Calvinism found an apt literary match in the religious lyric" (298). Ruf distinguishes Donne's lyric from narrative by contrasting the octave from HSMade with a narrative passage from John Bunyan's Grace Abounding to the Chief of Sinners, focusing on the octave's greater sense of the present, its narrower range of vision, its concern with getting "inside" the poet (299–301). Lyric poetry, according to Ruf, is more revealing in its attention to the audience—whoever the audience is—for the lyric voice "beseeches, condemns, and also listens" (303). Narrative most often "presents a sequence," and, in Ruf's view, the Holy Sonnets may seem to be "sequential, and in many ways they are," but he adds that lyric poetry also "models a self that is caught up in one moment that expressly has no sequel" (305). Ruf concludes that in keeping with the features of lyric form, neither "expansiveness" nor "inclusivity" is evident in the Holy Sonnets or in the lyric generally, "so that we do indeed get the 'little world' that he liked to write about in early lyrics" (305). "The self fills nearly the entire stage in Donne's poems," according to Ruf, "which makes his notorious self-absorption not so surprising" (305).

Stanwood (1994, 105–06, 112) argues that the "one distinguishing feature" of seventeenth-century religious lyric poetry offering "some kind of praise or worship or thanksgiving to God" is that it is "always broadly liturgical" (105). For Stanwood, liturgy applies to "the public and written offices of the Church and particularly to the Eucharistic rite," and also, in it broadest sense, liturgy suggests "shape, form, repetition, order, the regulation of private feelings into normalized, public expression" (106). Stanwood calls attention to the liturgical features of the Holy Sonnets, and especially of the "penitential group" (i.e., HSMade, HSLittle, HSSighs, HSSouls), that is, the four sonnets which were added to the 1635 edition of Donne's poems (112).

LANGUAGE AND STYLE

Although praising the Holy Sonnets as often "remarkable," MacDonald (1868, 121) says that "[r]hymed after the true Petrarchian fashion, their rhythm is often as bad as it can be to be called rhythm at all." But regarding the three he chooses for his anthology (HSDeath, HSMade, HSSouls), he observes that they are "very fine."

Caine (1882, 276–77) finds that, with the exception of HSDeath, Donne's sonnets, "while distinguished by great power of fundamental conception, and (although rugged in workmanship) by occasional felicity of phrase," are more thoroughly "disfigured by metaphysical involution" and by a tendency "to degenerate into a sort of metaphysical antithesis very damaging to poetic harmony" (276–77). Caine concludes, however, that Donne's achievement is not "unequal," for his sonnets "have very balanced merit" (277).

Schelling (1895, xlvii–xlviii), discussing "Elizabethan Lyrical Measures," looks at stanzaic forms with lines of dissimilar lengths, the use of rhyme to bind together lines of similar length, and enjambment ("overflow"). He says that Shakespeare in his late lyrics, Jonson and Fletcher occasionally, and Donne "constantly," demonstrate "much freedom and art in phrasing and in the employment of the overflow" (xlviii), and he points to Fun and HSDeath as examples.

Chadwick (1900, 46), analyzing the Holy Sonnets as poems written in 1617 or after, finds them to be superior to the "hard and gritty" earlier religious poems. The conceits, Donne's "besetting sin," are less in evidence, he says, and his verse is more melodious. Chadwick quotes HSRound as an example.

Grierson (1912, 2:xlix, 229) finds that the "great sorrow that struck him down" at the death of his wife worked a change in the tone of Donne's work, giving his "subsequent sonnets and hymns a sincerer and profounder note, his imagery a more magnificent quality, his rhythms a more sonorous music" (2:xlix). The Corona sonnets, written before Anne's death, have, Grierson thinks, more of the "intellectual, tormented, wire-drawn style of his earlier religious verse," while the Holy Sonnets are more "passionate and plangent" (229).

Newbolt (1926, 288) remarks on Donne's "power of expression" which he describes as "the thoughts of the imagination made audible." The Holy Sonnets, then, attest to "the ardour, the weight, the swift subtlety of those thoughts."

Newbolt (1929, xxi) slightly amends his comment by saying that in the Holy Sonnets we experience "the imagination of his heart made audible."

Hamer (1930, 200), who praises Corona for its blend "of exquisite tenderness and amazing energy," finds the Holy Sonnets "more remarkable for energy than tenderness."

Elton (1933, 212) finds some of Donne's divine poems "near to perfection," and, citing HSDeath, HSMade, and HSRound, observes that "the words are cut to the quick, the thought goes like a weaver's shuttle." In comparison to his earlier works, Elton concludes, "the imagination is now steadier and more consistently lofty, the execution less fitful."

Moloney (1944, 163) argues that the Holy Sonnets exhibit an "overemphasis on thought and thought-processes to the detriment of the sensory elements," quoting HSDue and HSSouls in full to illustrate his point. He concludes that there are "passages here and there which throb with magnificent imagery," evidence that Donne, "a poet of genuine gifts," could occasionally "escape the toils of the poetic philosophy which unconsciously was stifling him."

Stauffer (1946, 73–74) cites HSWhat 1, HSRound 6–7, and HSBatter 3–4 to illustrate how the poet achieves intensity by ellipsis, the delay of completion of the thought to the final words, and the building of momentum by crowding compound verbs and subjects together.

Faerber (1950, 8–33, 66), in a complex study of the paradoxes of Donne's religious poetry, classifies them under several categories, among them: "Ausholen", literally a "reaching back," a process whereby a line or series of lines, by virtue of both the thought contained in them and the form they take, add intensity or give force, by comparison or contrast, to succeeding lines which use that same thought or form (9–12); "Ergreifen und Entkünftigung," his seizing upon, in both thought and language, a present union with God and a defuturization (i.e., denial) of much feared events to come, in effect rendering them harmless (13–17); his "Glaubensgewissheit," or "sure faith" (19–21); his sense of sin and self as impediments to salvation (21–22); and the paradoxes of God, Christ, and human existence (23–30).

In discussing the paradoxes of God, Faerber cites the impossibility of describing an infinite being in terms of one fixed in time and place, and the contradictions encountered in concretizing the relationship between God and Satan (24–26). In the paradoxes of Christ he argues that Donne's playful informality is usually lacking, since such paradoxes arise from a deeper level of his being. Faerber finds that in addition to the expression of something exceptional, these paradoxes contain another characteristic trait: their contradiction is not a logical but an emotional one. Donne, Faerber continues, finds something "monstrous" ("Ungeheuerliche") in Christ's death for corrupt humanity, by which he has placed himself at the bottom of the proper hierarchy. Faerber argues that in the deepest recesses of his being Donne resents this sacrifice; it is an annoyance to him even if he would never admit it. Faerber notes that Donne seldom mentions Christ in his sermons, where he is much firmer in his faith than in his poetry, and concludes that he never came fully to terms with the humiliation and senselessness of the sacrifice. Faerber contends that when Donne discusses a miracle, it is with a sense of "irritation" ("Irritiertsein"), particularly in his Christ paradoxes, with the feeling that something is not right about them, an element that offends reason and justice (26–28). In his analysis of Donne's paradoxes of human existence, Faerber contrasts the concept that we are simply thrown into the world ("Geworfenheit") without meaning and purpose with the belief that we are "children of God" ("Gotteskindschaft") (28–30). Faerber provides a list of various paradoxes in the religious and love poetry in order to provide a fuller picture of Donne the poet, including as examples HSWilt 5–6, HSBlack 13–14, HSDue 4, 13–14, HSMade 1, and HSBatter 13–14 (66).

Gardner (1952, xxx–xxxii) finds that in comparison to Donne's other religious verse the Holy Sonnets have "a note of exaggeration to them" (xxx). She attributes this "almost histrionic note" in part to the danger any writer encounters while composing in the meditative tradition "that, in stimulating feeling, . . . may falsify it, and overdramatize the spiritual life" (xxxi). Gardner further proposes that in writing the Holy Sonnets, Donne used "no art at all." In Donne's language she hears "the ring of a living voice, admonishing his own soul, expostulating with his Maker, defying death, or pouring itself out in supplication," creating "the illusion of present experience" (xxxi). His "plain unadorned speech, with its idiomatic turns, its rapid questions, its exclamatory Oh's and Ah's, wrests the movement of the sonnet to its own movement," she argues, and the individual line is "weighted with heavy monosyllables, or lengthened by heavy secondary stresses, which demand the same emphasis as the main stress takes" (xxxii).

Hunt (1954, 134–35) finds Donne's religious poetry "coldly intellectual" and "dully ingenious"; his meditative poems tend "to take the form of an intellectual fussing around with theological concepts, doctrinal paradoxes, and ambiguities on words." Further, he observes, they "seem forced or pointless twitchings of the analytic mind in a state of 'holy discontent,' and only rarely do they spring to life in passages of intellectual intensity or organized imaginative power" (134). On the other hand, Hunt acknowledges that "there are times when a cramp over sin or damnation can produce poetry of superb dramatic power, bursting on the reader with those coups de théâtre which Donne often used in the openings of his love poems." As examples, Hunt quotes HSWhat 1, HSSpit 1, and HSRound 1–4.

Samson (1963, 46–52), writing about relationships between poetry and music, identifies Donne's subtle irony, abrupt transitions from one mood to another, complex and learned imagery, sudden shifts of tone, and the rhythmic patterns of speech as challenges to the composer and concludes that these remain serious, if not impossible, obstacles for the song-writer. See also Morris (1972) and The Holy Sonnets and Other Works.

Hauser (1965, 1:36–43, 299–301) considers Donne one of "the first modern poets" (36), a typical representative of "mannerism" (43). Focusing on Donne's conceits and commenting especially on HSRound, Hauser observes that Donne finds striking images for the most well-worn ideas (299).

Peterson (1967, 285, 330–33) traces the history and development of the English lyric in its relation to the "plain and courtly traditions" (285), finding that Donne, a poet opposed to the courtly, retains the "old plain style" while also continuing the tradition of "renunciation and penitential lyric" (330), of which HSBlack and HSScene, with their technique of visualizing the moment of death, are illustrative (333).

Using a methodology of descriptive stylistics, Strzetelski (1968, 107–12) conducts a linguistic analysis of Donne's Holy Sonnets and compares Donne's syntax to that of other English sonneteers.

In Holy Sonnets such as HSDue, HSMin, and HSBlack, Nelly (1969, 141) finds absent the "tension, ambiguity, [and] stress" of Donne's love lyrics, but she sees in these sonnets "a labouring of the dialectic to simplify and to state the case rather than to grapple with it and resolve it." She says that the final couplet in many of the

Holy Sonnets states a truth in paradoxical form. Some of the couplets are memorable, others forced and melodramatic. Comparing the Holy Sonnets with George Herbert's divine colloquies, Nelly finds Donne's "assaults upon Heaven" more urgent and more ruggedly individual.

Writing on Donne's wit in the religious poems and citing several Holy Sonnets as examples, Smith (1970, 163–66) contends that Donne was aware of the possibility of being criticized for "showmanship" but that he also envisaged a "right functioning of religious wit" (163) when it has a "dramatic substance," a "pungent life and force," and, finally, a "point" (163–64). Wit, Smith says, enables us to realize "a truth that is there but not otherwise accessible to us now, and which our conventional account of things only masks" (165), and thus Donne's wit, Smith concludes, points to the ironies and paradoxes "at the heart of our reality" (166).

Morris (1972, 219–51), commenting on Benjamin Britten's setting of the Holy Sonnets, remarks that the opening phrase of HSDeath is a subtle contraction of the opening phrase of HSBlack. He states that the echo suggests that the emotion explored in the sonnet cycle "has now been governed and directed towards the central Christian realisation that the last enemy is itself no more than 'slave to Fate'" (248). By the end of HSDeath, Morris argues, Donne asserts a plain faith, but it is a plainness that Donne has "won out of real emotional complexity" (249). He commends Britten for his "restrained recitativo style" which follows the modulations of the speaking voice, calling it a "triumph of timing" and a "perfect realisation of the stress between speech rhythm and metre which gives Donne's sonnets their power and life" (249).

Nye (1972, 357) thinks that the "plainness" of the Holy Sonnets Donne achieved only with effort, given his "delight in sophistication." He suggests that Donne followed Sidney in chooding the "harder" sonnet form, perhaps believing that "the technical difficulties" would test his conscience. The many "intricate rhymes," Nye concludes, "must have acted as a hair shirt."

Warnke (1972, 133–35, 207), finding paradox "of one sort or another" to be "central to the genre of devotional poetry," says that in the Holy Sonnets the "paradoxical element is so intense and all-pervasive" that a reader is led to believe that for Donne there are "two opposed orders of truth: the earthly, founded on experience, and the heavenly, which systematically and unfailingly reverses or defies the findings of experience and logic and, in so doing, surpasses them" (133). He illustrates his argument by citing HSBatter, HSShow, HSBlack, and HSLittle.

Partridge (1978, 130–38) writes that the language of the Holy Sonnets resembles the language used in St. François de Sales's Introduction to the Devout Life (1609), which Donne had read prior to composing these poems (130), suggesting that the Holy Sonnets were interior meditations aimed at expressing confidence in God. He writes that the sonnet form Donne adopted "is important to the nature of the impact he intended" (130) and enabled him to achieve something quite different from his predecessors. He practiced, for example, a "boldly libertarian stress modulation, acceptable in verse dramatists, but not usually among conventional lyricists" (130). Partridge notes that the language in the Holy Sonnets is "plain and idiomatic," but "spirited enough to be adaptable to his moods" (131). He comments that Donne's sonnets "seem to confirm a preference for compact forms and patterns with minimal change of rhyme, so that the poet might concentrate on the conflict of thought and exceptional feelings." Partridge reads the Holy Sonnets as "meditations of a strenuous personality struggling to live up to the moral truths of religion, but falling short in real or imaginary defeat," and he asserts that these texts are not "coterie poetry," but "metaphysical in the patristic sense" (138). For Partridge, Donne's style in the Holy Sonnets "flouted the Petrarchan tradition of smoothness," as did his use of a final couplet. He describes Donne as a "pedantic syllabist practicing a boldly libertarian stress modulation, acceptable in verse dramatists but not usually among conventional lyricists" (130). He notes that Donne frequently employs "synaloepha" and reduces weak vowels "where unstressed syllables of single words end in . . . l, m, n, or r." This, he argues, produces "a subtler variety of rhythm . . . than would otherwise have been attainable" (131). See also Partridge (1971) under Holy Sonnets: General Commentary.

Martinet (1982, 23, 32) associates repetition with celebratory ends, in which it functions like an echo; with satirical use, supported by rhymes forced in between other rhymes; and, most frequently, with an effort to evoke poetic melancholy. Martinet interprets the variations of these strophic structures in the Holy Sonnets to be representations of the oscillation between anxiety of sin and of grace (23). According to Martinet, of the two preparatory sonnets (HSDue and HSBlack) in the first group of six sonnets, the first has three quatrains of "embraced rhymes" ("rimes embrassées"), the second, two such quatrains. Tension emerges in the rhymes, where the words should be prolonged, as, for example, in HSBlack ("summoned," "execution" the latter rhyming with the unstressed syllable in "prison"). But in the second movement, Martinet adds, grace ("Yet grace . . .") comes from the ninth verse, the third quatrain contrasting by alternating rhymes and by images drawn from biblical symbolism (colors drawn from Isa.1.18) (32). In the following four sonnets that relate to "The Four Last Things" (HSScene, HSRound, HSMin, and HSDeath), the first two (on "Death and Judgment") have, Martinet notes, alternating rhymes in the third quatrain. The last two sonnets in the group (HSMin and HSDeath), according to Martinet, which focus on the final outcome ("Damnation and Resurrection"), are more emphatic, employing embraced rhymes in the third quatrain. Martinet concludes that in Donne, the repetitive schemes are always in contradiction with each other, and from these tensions, which partly mask themselves, the tone of the poem is born (32).

Miller (1982, 835) claims that "the bold demand for salvation in audacious, even shocking language" representative of the Holy Sonnets contradicts the view that Donne is "a poet of religious doubt." In Miller's view, Donne's strong language suggests that he "writes from a deep-seated conviction of election."

Parfitt (1985, 42) finds that Donne's writing reflects "a strong tendency to project hypothetical situations in a syntax which may undermine the assertions being made, a syntax of appeal and condition," adding that Donne's language is marked by violence and by "erotic vocabulary."

Patrides (1985a, 44) describes the "tonal range" of Donne's Holy Sonnets as "immense," pointing to the very different opening lines of HSShe (a "moving acceptance" of Anne's death), HSLittle ("reflective amazement"), HSShow ("passionate anxiety"), HSRound ("triumphant vision"), and HSWhat ("sheer terror").

Marotti (1986, 259–60) finds Donne's Holy Sonnets in particular utilizing the "symbolic I" associated with Protestant meditation and preaching as one way of sharing his religious experience with his readers (259). But Marotti also finds that Donne "assaults" his readers through the use of violent metaphors and "strong language," all of which work to "proclaim Donne's individuality and aesthetic superiority," thus tending to undercut "communal spokesmanship" (260).

Stanwood and Asals (1986, 70–71, 125) point out that, for Donne, "tense, mood, and voice in verb structure" are vital to "an understanding of the divine Logos," for "God's judgments are conditional, God's idiom is imperative." Donne's views about grammar are closely related to his views about logic, according to Stanwood and Asals. For example, logic appears as "the 'quia' of argumentation in grammatical structure," they say, but the word "for" is crucial to Donne's views about prayer, that is, "all prayer must have a *quia* (or a 'for') to ground it in reason." They cite a number of Holy Sonnets in which Donne uses "for" at a pivotal point, as in "for I/Except you'enthrall mee" (*HSBatter* 12–13) and "For I have sinn'd'" (*HSSpit* 3) (70). Stanwood and Asals add that "how" and "why," the "dangerous monosyllables," are the "tools of sophistry that defeat us in the Devil," and he cites in particular "Why are wee by all creatures waited on?" (*HSWhy* 1) and "How shall my mindes white truth to them [faithful souls] be try'd?" (*HSSouls* 8) (70–71). In discussing Donne's use of voice and tense, and its connection to "the revelation of self," they locate its basis in the belief that "because Christ puts on manhood through His incarnation, we are able to put on the new man through the regeneration which He has thus made possible," and so in the human soul's ultimate destiny, "where human and divine can meet, we may dress ourselves in Christ's garment" (125). They find Donne describing "this 'rite of reclothing'" in *HSSpit* 11–14, "where the expectation is at once a hope and a fulfillment" (125). In our "becoming a wholly new person," according to Stanwood and Asals, we also give "prophetic voice to the changes to come and which will have been made; for life is lived in the future perfect tense where whatever is looked for is accomplished" (125).

Rogers (1987, 172–73) finds that whereas in the secular poems Donne "uses a great range of stanza forms" (including forty he invented) and rarely repeated a form, in his religious verse he is formally "more conventional" (172). But, Rogers notes, the Holy Sonnets have some of the qualities we see in the love poems, such as the "insistent imperatives" and the "development of an idea to its absolute, as seen in *HSBatter*. Observing that the Holy Sonnets are usually "less witty," Rogers suggests that perhaps the "regularity of the form and its brevity" did not provide Donne with enough "scope and variety," or possibly he thought of the Holy Sonnets as "more serious theological essays" (173).

Gill (1990, 141) sees the Holy Sonnets as being "unusually visual," citing specifically "the uncomfortably physical figure of death" in *HSScene*, the "vivid, eschatological panorama" in *HSRound*, the "harrowing picture of the crucified Christ" in *HSWhat*, and the "powerful picture" of "the soul labouring to admit God" in *HSBatter*.

Austin (1992, 23, 39–41, 44–45) comments on the nature of Donne's language in the Holy Sonnets, noting first his considerable use of monosyllables, such as in *HSSpit* and *HSShow* (23). Austin notes also that images in the Holy Sonnets and

Hymns are "usually physical," and therefore often "visual," and "emblematic," such as the globe-like image that Donne uses in *HSRound* 1 in conjunction with "the long outmoded notion of a flat world" (39–40). Austin finds that "it is the emblem tradition that allows Donne to present these two world views visually and simultaneously, one superimposed upon the other" (40). But, in Austin's view, Donne's "principal rhetorical device," other than conceits and emblems, is "repetition in all its many forms," such as the repetition, not of the word itself, but of the part of speech, evident in *HSRound* 6–7: "All whom warre, dearth, age, agues, tyrannies,/Despaire, law, chance, hath slain" (44). Austin finds that through this device "the lines gather momentum in a way that reflects the pouring forth of the dead souls" (44). And, finally, Austin points to Donne's repeated use of paradox, one form defined as *antimetabole*, in which "the whole proposition is repeated in reverse order," such as in *HSWilt* 14, and a second form as *polyptoton*, "the repetition of a word in a different form," such as that found in *HSVex*: "inconstancy" (l. 7) and "constant" (ll. 2–3), and including also the use of multiple opposites, such as "cold" and "hot" (l. 7), "praying" and "mute" (l. 8), and "infinite" and "none" (l. 8) (45).

Frontain (1992, 85, 91, 94–95, 99–100) finds in Donne's Holy Sonnets heightened anxiety instigated by the Protestant Reformation's emphasis on the absolute dependency on God for one's salvation (85). Frontain argues that Donne's speakers resort to a number of rhetorical strategies in their desperate attempt to provoke God to impute their righteousness, strategies that Frontain argues are also evident in certain Psalms in their speakers' plea for "release from captivity and exile or as the unnamed Hebrew's rescue from persecution by his anonymous enemies" (99–100). Apart from the recurring use of the imperative voice, as, for example, in *HSBatter*, Frontain cites related strategies used by the speaker of the Holy Sonnets, notably in *HSMade* and *HSMin*, to "enlist God in his cause," such as the use of "rhetorical strategic questions" aimed at engaging God in "dialogue," with the hope that God will elect the speaker and provide him "with the desperately desired prevenient grace" (95). The last rhetorical strategy Frontain discusses is the recurring "shift in tone" in the sonnets, noting, for example, "the shift in tone in *HSDue* representative of a "complexity of address that runs throughout the Holy Sonnets," as the speaker progresses from "calm resignation to near despair" in only fourteen lines (95). Frontain identifies several Holy Sonnets in which he finds comparable shifts between "self-examination or meditative reflection and outright entreaty of divine aid," including *HSMin*, *HSLittle*, *HSRound*, and *HSShe* (95).

Pallotti (1993, 168–70,179–80) finds that the dominant speaker-hearer relationship in the Holy Sonnets is grounded in the interrogative mode (168), pointing out that the 266 lines in the 19 Holy Sonnets contain 27 questions found in 11 poems, resulting in an "average frequency" of one question every 9.8 lines (169). Pallotti notes further that of these questions, 17 are content-oriented ("wh-questions") and ten are "polar, yes-no questions" (169), with most of the "Wh-questions" introduced by the adverb "why" (11 examples) (169). The interrogative mode is less evident in the secular poetry, according to Pallotti, and the majority of questions posed there are of the "yes-no" type, with "what" as the word that most often introduces Wh-questions (169). In the religious verse there is a higher occurrence of questions and a higher frequency of questions introduced by "why," questions that "tend to be addressed—directly or indirectly—to God" (170). Pallotti also finds that questions occupy "strategic positions" in the Holy Sonnets: at the *incipit* (*HSMade, HSWhy, HSWhat, HSWilt*); at the "syntactic and semantic turns" of the poems (*HSDue, HSMin, HSWhy, HSShe*); at the end of the first quatrain (*HSMin*) or at the end of the octave (*HSWhat*); and throughout the poem (*HSShow*) (171). Pallotti concludes that regardless of position, questions "always bring forth shifts of thought or feeling, expressions of conflicting views on, and bafflement at, the state of affairs presented and/or implied" (171), and she points to a passage in one of Donne's sermons (*Sermons*, 6:187–88) in which the "orthodox" preacher recognizes the danger of asking too many questions (179–80), noting that the preacher aims to state laws and articulate the "dominant opinion," while the poet voices doubts and confronts "perplexity and difficulty about authority, faith and self, *things divine*" (180).

Borkowska (1994, 29–30) points to Donne's frequent use of the word "but" in his poetry, thereby "inverting the natural course of things and directing us to the secondary meaning as more important" (29), citing specifically *HSMade* 10–12, *HSSpit* 7–8, and *HSBatter* 9–10. In the last instance, according to Borkowska, Donne speaks to God spitefully, "as if in sheer wantonness, out of pure cussedness, challenging and provoking the divine, almost notwithstanding God's infinite mercy and forbearance; he can impugn divine authority, employ ironic banter, traduce God and pun on him even when praying" (30).

Fischler (1994, 184) contends that the Holy Sonnets "provide the best illustrations of Donne's dialectic method," the "usual formula" invoking in Donne's poetry the "divine or spiritual effect of a given force—a 'thesis'—butting up against the natural, bodily, and entirely antithetical effect of the same force." Thus, he suggests, the "red blood of Christ defies natural law by dyeing 'red souls to white'" (*HSBlack* and *HSBatter*), as does "a fiery zeal for God 'which doth in eating heal'" (*HSLittle* and *HSBatter*). Similar paradoxes exist in *HSBatter*, he notes, where "rising is achieved by overthrow" and "chastity through ravishment," and in *HSShow* 14, the "fidelity of Christ's spouse (the true Church) asserts itself 'When she is embraced and open to most men.'" Furthermore, Fischler notes, though Donne begins *HSVex* by "expressing his vexation that 'contraries meet in one'" (l. 1), he moves closer to God "by this very circumstance, as sickness begets health in the 'devout fitts' which 'come and go away / Like a fantastic ague'" (ll. 12–13).

Marotti (1994a, 78–79) finds that Donne's "personal feelings connected with his search for employment and advancement in the early Jacobean period" lie behind some of the language and metaphors he used in making "conscious and unconscious connections" between the "religious and the political" (78), and he cites examples from *HSSpit, HSVex, HSRound*, and *HSDeath*.

Creswell (1995, 184–87, 196) contends that Donne's religious verse manifests "an iconoclastic skepticism about the truth of images," and thus his "rejection of truth as vision, like his rejection of individual revelation, is an insistence upon interpretation over immanent seeing, often thematized as a move toward 'hearing' the Word or turning to the 'voice,'" a shift that derives from Donne's "reconceptualization of the Word and the status of praise" (184). According to Creswell, the Holy Sonnets, like some of Donne's sermons, reveal a "mistrust of the iconic image," that is, "rather than serve as an emblem of the specular Logos, the figure of Christ within these sonnets remains resolutely verbal and opaque," and as with Christ's blood in HSBlack 13–14, the "truth or efficacy of the figure" in the Holy Sonnets lying not in its appearance (as blood) but in its interpretation ('being red/read')" (184). Creswell observes that one cannot "invoke God without imposing the distortion of one's own tropes," for "praise cannot address the very object and origin of its speech" (187). In their "revision of the poetics of praise," Creswell concludes, the Holy Sonnets imply that the "mystical union may not be a consummation that makes whole but a binding that ceaselessly rends apart," offering a "revision of epideictic rhetoric" in the attempt "to seek an address that does not appropriate—through identification or any relation of the self—the other" (196).

Frontain (1995, 17–18) finds that Donne's poetry is, more than that of most seventeenth-century poets and perhaps even more than Milton's, "heavily logocentric" (17). For Donne, according to Frontain, language is the medium "by which a highly vulnerable but deeply hopeful petitioner attempts to pass from the dissolute, fragmentary world of the profane to a realm of completeness and transcendence," and, Frontain adds, this is particularly true in the poems that are "more tonally complex"—e.g., ElBed, Goodf, and the Holy Sonnets—poems in which the speaker "uses all the powers of language available to him to engage the numinous on his own behalf that he may be 'translated' from the profane realm to the sacred" (18). Frontain cites as examples ElBed and the Holy Sonnets, poems in which a speaker "provocatively adopts the imperative mode to elicit a salvific response from an all-powerful woman or deity, not with the confidence of primitive, religious man, but precisely because the speaker lacks confidence and finds himself in such great need" (18).

Johnson (1995, 314–15) comments on the limited amount of attention devoted to the "rhetorical implications" of the Holy Sonnets as "prayerful utterances" (314), citing the previous studies of Asals (1979), Dubinski (1986), and Frontain (1992). Johnson finds that the "orthodoxy" of the "prayerful struggle" in Donne's religious poetry, which aims "to procure the assurance of salvation," both "echoes the language of the Psalms" and also "suggests a public dimension for these poems as devotional models" (315). Johnson observes that although the Holy Sonnets dramatize Donne's spiritual struggles, it is in his "religious occasional verse," especially the Hymns, that we see him resolving his struggle (315).

PROSODY

Richter (1902, 398–99) finds that in his later years Donne drew on his interior life for inspiration, hence his poetry, including the Holy Sonnets, became deeper and its form purer, exhibiting fewer lines with "hovering accent" ("schwebende Betonung").

Lang (1912, 288) notes of the Holy Sonnets that though there may be "some noble almost Miltonic passages" in them, they contain lines "that cannot be made to scan" and "hyperbolic conceits."

Bennett (1934, 46) defends Donne's meter, arguing that his "rhythm demands variety of pace." In a later edition (1953, 47–48) Bennett, citing Jonson's complaint about Donne's "accent," quotes and scans HSBatter 5–8, observing that, as in Hopkins's "sprung rhythm," in Donne's basic five-foot line he "sometimes shifts the stress from the second to the first syllable of a foot," and that he at times "introduces extra syllables, indicating that they should be slurred."

White (1936, 92) observes that like almost all "masters of singing" Donne "bent each pattern to his own ends." A "notable example" she finds among the Holy Sonnets. Recognizing the regular pattern of these sonnets, White nonetheless argues that Donne "makes the most of that liberty of variation that is the one sure note of English prosody."

Gardner (1952, 54–55) finds the versification of the Holy Sonnets to be "very bold and original," observing that Donne's "metrical base" in the poems "is a deca-syllabic line of five feet, each foot consisting of an unstressed and a stressed syllable," but that he "varies from this base with a boldness unprecedented in non-dramatic verse before Milton" (54). She finds that "in the arrangement of his stresses Donne again anticipates Milton, particularly in his fondness for using feet with level stress" (54–55).

Leishman (1954, 79) observes that although some passages in the Holy Sonnets "present a bold, deliberate, and often triumphantly successful metrical invention," at the same time they reflect an "astonishing metrical incompetence."

Oras (1960, 1, 18–19) sets out to examine verse "for its own sake," seeing it as one of the "principal elements" of Renaissance drama (1). In so doing he maintains that in his early poetry Donne uses many of the same features that Jonson and other authors did in the drama and that Donne characteristically writes opposite to that of the Spenserian school. But in the Holy Sonnets, he suggests, Donne reverts to a kind of "firm design, with iambic peaks," which sometimes recalls Spenser (19).

Adams (1962, 784n1) comments that the Holy Sonnets, though "conventional in their rhyme scheme and broad metrical pattern," are "rhythmically bold, power-ful in their imagery, and marked by deep emotional coloring."

Partridge (1964, 91–96) notes that the mss. of the Holy Sonnets contain many examples of lines that are incapable of elision and points to HSDeath and HSScene 9 as instances (91–93). Partridge believes that "not even the most ingenious devices of elision" will make certain lines of Donne's poetry fit the basic metrical pattern (96).

Beaver (1967, 310–21), building his argument on the Halle-Keyser principles of meter (see Morris Halle and Samuel J. Keyser, "Chaucer and the Study of Prosody," College English 28 [1966]: 187–219), looks in particular at the positions of stress within lines of poetry. He includes a study of ten of Shakespeare's sonnets with the "first ten" (apparently as printed in 1633—ed.) of Donne's Holy Sonnets, noting that Donne tends to put greater stress near the beginning and ending of lines, "some-what like a suspension bridge, perhaps at the expense of medial stability" (320). Another potential stylistic consideration, Beaver states, is the use and frequency of unmetrical lines. He finds only one such line in the ten sonnets of Shakespeare but four in Donne. Donne, says Beaver, "appears to seek the device which will capture attention, by departing from the usual" (320). One way of doing this, he says, is by deliberately placing "stress maxima" in "off" positions (321). He cites lines from *HSMade* and *HSBlack* in support of his contention. Donne's experiments in stress and metrical (ir)regularity, Beaver argues, lend his verse its "rough-hewn effect" (321).

Winters (1967, 74–78) cites approvingly Ben Jonson's remark that Donne "should have been hanged for his misplacing of accents" (74), noting two cases in which Donne too obviously violates the meter. Winters writes that in *HSDue* 6 the accentuation violates poetic principles, for the language must be deformed in order to fit the line into a pentameter pattern. Identifying similar problems of prosody in *HSSighs* 11, Winters suggests that Donne often violates poetic form and concludes that the high incidence of these violations shows "a relative unawareness of the nature and importance of sound" (75). Winters argues that *HSMade* is inferior to Jonson's "To Heaven" because Donne uses "stereotyped language," and because of his "simple and mechanical use of syntax and rhythm" (75). Winters, concluding that Donne's "greatest poetry and some of his worst meter can be found in the Holy Sonnets" (78), identifies the best sonnets as *HSMade*, *HSRound*, *HSWhat*, and *HSBatter*, noting that they are relatively free of metrical problems.

Linville (1984b, 69–70, 73–74, 77, 80) draws on Stein's (1942) study of Donne's use of enjambment, which, though focused primarily on the Satires, is, according to Linville, illuminating for the Holy Sonnets (69). Stein's study, Linville notes, shows how Donne "reverses the norms" promoted by Puttenham (i.e., "a model of maximum end-stopped lines") by creating greater flow from one line to the next through the use of "polysyllabic end-words to lighten the last foot of a line and to lighten rhythm; by using post-medial caesuras; and by using stress shifts" (69–70). The effect of stress shifts (that is, combining trochees and iambs) "brings unstressed syllables together," thus "creating a propulsive effect" (73). Two examples, according to Linville, can be found in *HSLittle* 7–8 and *HSBatter* 1–2, where Donne "links enjambment, radical metric disruption and apocalyptic imagery," so that "the rhythm expresses well that explosion of normal constraints that revelation entails" (74). Although Donne's "mimetic uses of line form" (77) strongly reinforce the subject matter of individual Holy Sonnets, Linville argues that Donne's poetry "absolutely depends on conventions and the expectations they generate to create tension and enrich meaning" (80). Linville claims therefore that Donne's poems "belie the notion that he elevates matter over manner" (80).

Van Emden (1986, 53) observes that Donne keeps to the iambic as his fundamental rhythmical pattern, but "changes it frequently, forcing the words to obey his dramatic intention and heightened emotion," and on occasion using "heavy stress" so as to "emphasize the meaning of the words."

SACRED AND PROFANE

An anonymous author (1900, 609) finds that Donne's Divine Poems have the same "intensity of imagination" and "fine *exordia*" as his secular verse, and he quotes *HSDeath* in full to illustrate.

Grierson (1912, 2:lii–liii) finds that after the death of his wife Donne is "alone with his soul," and that the Holy Sonnets, written after that event, reflect some of the qualities of his love poems, an "intensity of feeling, subtle turns of thought, and an occasional Miltonic splendour of phrase." Grierson identifies HSScene 1–4, HSRound 1–4, and HSWhat 1–6 as comparable to "the magnificent openings" of the love verse.

V. M. (1923, 85–89) includes HSVex, HSShe, and HSBatter in a volume of Donne's love poems as examples of works "in which earthly and heavenly love are contrasted—and compared."

Simpson (1924, 9, 65) argues that Donne's conversion did not change his "habit of mind, but provided new channels into which his passionate energy could flow." She adds that the "divine fire burned as intensely, and more purely," in Donne's Holy Sonnets as in the Songs and Sonnets "of his youth" (9). Simpson observes that readers accept the "sincerity of the agonized penitence" of the Holy Sonnets, but that they cannot "fit the passionate, cynical, sensuous figure of the poet into the ecclesiastical garments of the Dean" (65).

Fausset (1924, 244–45) contends that in the Holy Sonnets Donne woos his God "with both the fervour and the self-indulgence with which he had before addressed his mistresses," even retaining the erotic imagery. In doing so, Faussett continues, Donne suffered "all the torments of a frustrated lover to whom death only could bring alleviation, all a lover's agonized feeling of unworthiness, and all his yearning for that consummation, those ultimate bridals, which the flesh at best so tantalizingly, at worst so grossly denies."

Read (1928, 66), suggesting that Donne achieves a union of thought and emotions in his early poems, finds that by the time of the composition of the Holy Sonnets, the emotion had changed from doubt to faith and renunciation; but the union prevailed, producing images and expressions of "the same dialectical subtlety and impassioned majesty" found in the early works, as in HSRound 1–4 and HSBatter 1.

Bennett (1934, 26–27) finds that in the Holy Sonnets Donne's "desire for intellectual rest is interwoven with a need for the emotional serenity he had tasted in marriage." Bennett quotes HSBatter 12–14 and HSWhat 1–4 and 9–14 to illustrate Donne's use of images of secular love to express sacred themes.

Rugoff (1939, 86–87) identifies images of the "fusion of the holy and the erotic" in which "religious devotion becomes a sexual relationship," as in HSVex 10, HSShow 12–14, and HSBatter 9–14.

Hardy (1942, 178) observes that in the Holy Sonnets Donne addresses God in words as impassioned as those he had used to plead with his former mistresses.

Raine (1945, 390) finds in the Holy Sonnets "the very imagery of the early love poems."

Louthan (1951, 120), quoting HSWhat, HSBatter, HSShe, and HSShow in full, acknowledges that they contain "references to Christ as a delighted cockold and to God as a burly rapist and jealous lover," but he argues that the implications of the secular-sacred imagery "are under strict control."

Simon (1952, 125–26) observes that in the Holy Sonnets Donne "uses figures and devices" found in his earlier poems: scenic and dramatic presentation (HSBatter), argument (HSPart), rhetorical emphasis (HSSighs), realistic details (HSSighs), self-analysis (*HSLittle*, *HSVex*), puns (*HSDue*), conceits (*HSDeath*, *HSPart*), paradoxes (*HSDue*, *HSWilt*), and imagery from science and philosophy (*HSLittle*, *HSSouls*). She notes, however, that he does not use "dissonant images," and this because they would detract from the "organic development" of the sonnets, the essential interdependence and interaction of separate parts of the poem.

Martz (1954, 215–16) finds that Donne's poetry "moves along a Great Divide between the sacred and the profane," pointing out that in six Holy Sonnets (*HSSighs*, *HSWhat*, *HSBatter*, *HSShe*, *HSShow*, and *HSVex*) images of profane love appear in religious poems.

Evans (1955, 166) argues that Donne delighted in shocking his readers by ascribing sexual associations to traditional images, such as the besieged fort in *HSBatter* 5–6. On the other hand, he observes, such an association is appropriate for a poet "who has become religious but finds his greatest temptations in his physical nature."

Cox (1956b, 51) finds in the love poetry a "realistic force and eager play of mind," and in the religious poetry "no change of style or method." He detects in both that the "same variety and range of experience are drawn out," that the "same dramatic power expresses his mental conflicts," and he quotes *HSBatter* 1–4 as an example. In comparing the two genres, Cox (1956a, 113) determines that in the religious verse, "as in the love poetry," there is a "considerable variety of tone and method, ranging from mere casuistry and debating tricks to a profound urgency and conviction," with both sometimes apparent in the same poem.

Hart (1958, 20) notes that in the Holy Sonnets Donne's effort to "establish a relationship between himself and God reflects the moods of love: beseeching, despairing, impatient, ecstatic."

Hopkins (1962, 102) believes that Donne's sacred poetry celebrates love with a greater intensity than his secular poetry, noting that "when Donne had shown how love for a woman might be a high ecstasy, he went on to show that love for God was a higher: and it must be so." In addition, Hopkins argues that Donne brought to his subject a "secular sophistication" that Christianity "had never met with before," and he points to *HSRound* as the apogée of Donne's efforts.

Wanning (1962, 18–19), acknowledging the connections established by Gardner (1952) and Martz (1954) between the Holy Sonnets and the meditative tradition (see Genre and Traditions), nonetheless stresses that the emotion in the poems is "unmistakably Donne's," as he assumes the "posture of the devotee before God not wholly unreminiscent of the younger Donne's before his mistress."

Broadbent (1964, 66, 72) comments that "when the state took over authority from the Church, it closed the medieval duality of sacred and profane," but reopened it as an "internecine duality of soul and body," and this, he says, is the "plot" of the Holy Sonnets (66). Broadbent continues by declaring that Sidney, Drayton and Donne established a "realistic and naturalistic mode in a strictly English vernacular" and that Spenser and Donne "infused the moribund Petrarch-Ronsard tradition with Platonic and Christian spirit" (72).

Demaray (1965, 367) thinks that Donne wrote so "fearlessly and so personally about death" in the Holy Sonnets, devotions, and sermons because of his changing attitudes toward natural law in the 1601–12 period, as is evident, for example, in

Biathanatos and the Anniversaries. Donne, Demaray says, "turned his attention from ethics to theology, from man to God, and from secular life to holy death." See also Demaray (1965) in the General Commentary on the Holy Sonnets.

Blamires (1974, 116–17) discovers in the Holy Sonnets the "voice of the lover" who engages in a "tortuous dialogue" with God (116). He remarks on the continuity between the Holy Sonnets and Donne's secular poetry, writing that, in the Holy Sonnets, "the reluctance of the beloved has become the reluctance of God to sweep away the reluctance of the poet" (117).

Kerrigan (1974, 40–42) notes that the manner of Donne's presentation of "conventional metaphors of love poetry" is precisely analogous "to the way he 'unraveled' or 'opened' the sacred context of his sermons" (40). *HSBatter* is, to Kerrigan, particularly illustrative of Donne's conception of sacred metaphor, in which accommodated marriage would enfold infidelity, divorce, and even imprisonment, for in that poem "sexual rape" is understood as "a metaphor for the forcible entry of the deity into an otherwise impenetrable soul" (42).

Porter and Thwaite (1974, 102–07) claim that the one consistent attitude throughout all of Donne's writings is his casting himself in the role of a wooer, either of women or of God (102). Arguing that Donne's "baroque" religious poems "are full of the hysteria which accompanied the return to faith on the Continent" with the Counter-Reformation, they view the Holy Sonnets as the most remarkable of Donne's religious poems, for they show that love is the "mainspring" of human life and poetic creativity (107).

Granqvist (1975, 84–85) comments that Coleridge's lack of attention to the Holy Sonnets and other sacred poems is a "surprising omission" given his interest in Donne's sermons. He speculates that Coleridge "could not tolerate the juxtaposition of the religious and profane" (85).

Ferrari (1979, 43–44) finds that Donne experienced the anguish and torment of the conflict between pagan and Christian ideals (43). Citing *HSSighs* 1–7, Ferrari claims that although Donne shed tears of repentance for having written poetry about vain things, he tries to attenuate the tension between the classical and Christian worlds and to reconcile, if not to merge, the sacred with the profane (44). But Ferrari finds that *HSShow* reflects Donne's nostalgia for the Catholic Church and his continuing anguished search for the Bride of Christ, noting that although interested in science, Donne remained medieval in the way he treats doctrinal and theological issues.

Zunder (1982, 91, 94–96) locates the origin of fear, which recurs in the Holy Sonnets, in "personal inadequacy" and finds this feeling expressed explicitly in *HSScene* 3–4 (91). The "resolution of feeling," according to Zunder, involves "a rejection of the central, all-informing relationship of the love poems," most evident in the sonnets written in 1609–11, particularly in *HSSighs*, but also in *HSShe*, probably written in 1619, two years after the death of his wife, Anne (94–96).

Raspa (1983, 63) claims that Donne's "apparent confessions of lust in his sonnets were counterbalanced by sexual imagery depicting profound spiritual unions," including "basic religious relationships" between the speaker and God (*HSBatter* 13–14) and the speaker and the Church, the spouse of Christ (*HSShow* 9–10). In Raspa's view, Donne's sexual imagery may be read "in the light of its emotive origins in forms of willed experience that led men as much to God as to anything else."

Singer (1984, 202–04) finds in Donne's "synthesizing love-poetry of his youth" the view that "profane love is *itself* sacred, that love is holy wherever it appears and most obviously in sexual consummation" (202). But Singer draws a comparison with the paintings of Titian and the philosophy of love in St. John of the Cross and St. Teresa of Avila, which are "typically Catholic" (202–03). Although the Spanish mystics "draw on the language of earthly love in order to enliven our imagination to the infinitely superior values of ecstatic oneness with the divine," they, unlike Donne, "deny the possibility of merging sacred and profane" (203). Singer attributes some of Donne's youthful attitude to early Protestant thinking, specifically "Luther's ideas about God's agapē descending to earth and showing itself in ardent embraces of men and women" (203). But Singer finds a development toward a more Catholic perspective in Donne's later devotional poetry, something closer to that of Titian and St. John of the Cross, while it retains something of the passion intrinsic to his earlier poetry.

Grant (1985, ix, 84) attributes the heightened interest in reconciling the flesh and the spirit in the Renaissance to the discovery of "scientific method," which "precipitates a characteristically modern divorce between physics and metaphysics" (ix). In this context, Grant finds that Donne's interest in the heart, and in its role in reconciling the flesh and the spirit, can be found in both the love poems and the Divine Poems, with the heart's "association with love and its status as seat of the soul remain[ing] constant" (84). In Grant's view, the Holy Sonnets, being love poems converted to spiritual ends, combine these motifs. But Grant claims that, like *Ecst*, the Holy Sonnets are "not escapist," for they "continuously reassert tensions inherent in the human condition, especially expressing the anguish of faith that seeks understanding but never understands enough, so that it must fall back upon a sheer act of will, or love, a true act of the heart" (84).

Mann (1985–86, 546) finds that Donne's Holy Sonnets "explore continuities and contrasts between human and divine love in terms of repentance and contrition," noting that the sonnets "begin with a heightened sense of distance between man and God but move towards the love of God." The sonnets, according to Mann, "do not repudiate the human love" Donne celebrates in his love poems but rather repudiate "love that is not referred to divine love and is therefore 'idolatrous,' in Augustinian phrases Donne uses throughout the sermons." In Mann's view, the Holy Sonnets "dramatize the painful effort to turn from the world to the love of God," and yet "the love of God does not exclude love for creatures; it purges, harmonizes, and renders human love subordinate to divine love." Mann adds, however, that, for Donne, love remains "a natural affection, directed rightly through grace and human effort." HSShe, Mann contends, illustrates Donne's view of the ideal relationship between human love and the love of God.

Gaster (1986, 8) notes Donne's own hope that his readers would "differentiate between the 'Jack' Donne of the love poems and the 'Dr Donne' of the religious writings," but Gaster claims that "the imagery which drew its inspiration from the worlds of war, exploration, disease and philosophy recurs in the sacred verse just as the erotic poetry, with its images from the spirit world, foreshadowed the poet's later expression of his spiritual anguish." Gaster adds that in the sacred verse Donne assumes what had been his mistresses' role as "fickle lover," and, noting specifically HSVex, Gaster sees Donne, like the women of his secular verse, as "constant only in his inconstancy."

Marotti (1986, 253–54, 258–59) finds Donne's religious verse significantly different from his secular poetry in its different attitude toward male authority (253). Whereas Donne portrays fathers and other authority figures in a negative way in his erotic and satiric poetry (with the exception of Sat3), Donne's attitude is changed, in Marotti's view, in his religious poetry, and in particular in the Holy Sonnets (253–54). For example, in HSSouls, according to Marotti, Donne "imagines the father who died in his [Donne's] early childhood benevolently looking down from heaven" on his son's "spiritual triumphs" (254). In the Holy Sonnets, Marotti says, Donne typically portrays "a paternal deity with whom he wishes to come to terms and whose love he wishes to enjoy" (254). Marotti explains the difference as lodged in Donne's feeling of betrayal and abuse by the secular authorities, including the King, and thus he portrays "a paradoxically hurtful and helpful God whose power he both resisted and felt drawn to" (254). Marotti attributes Donne's use of the language of love in his Holy Sonnets to the precedents for sonnet sequences, which were basically amorous in nature, and to Donne's own love lyrics (258). But Marotti also identifies precedents in biblical passages as well as the possibility that Donne experienced a religious conversion similar to Augustine's from "the unholy amorist into the holy Christian" (258). Marotti cites HSWhat and HSBatter as examples of Donne's "eroticized spirituality" (258–59).

Mueller (1989, 148–49) focuses on the issues that she claims arose when Donne began, after 1607, to write religious lyrics and verse letters following the composition of his secular love poems. Mueller finds that the religious lyrics, specifically, and also the verse letters "in praise of prospective or actual patronesses," seemed to have "brought into question, as inappropriate or wholly inapplicable, the framework of sexual consummation between a man and a woman within which he had located virtually everything he had written about love." Mueller states that Donne retained "the highly developed subjectivity of the male speaker," but in these new genres, the speaker "had to discourse differently on love." Mueller emphasizes that in the Holy Sonnets, Donne found it continuously difficult "for the male speaking-figure to do without heterosexual love as a model for ideality." Donne "pursues his self-explorations alone," which now "leave him overwhelmed with his sins, which he sometimes expressly equates with his former active sexuality now branded as 'Idolatry'" (HSSighs 5–6, HSWhat 9). Mueller concludes that the male speaker, "deprived of the resources of human intersubjectivity," consistently "appears at a loss for ways to relate to God as the sole divine Other," a relationship that depends on a male speaker seeking "engagement with his male God" (148). Mueller notes that "the father-son model carried full biblical and theological sanction" but finds it "remarkable" that Donne only rarely and indirectly uses it (149). Instead, she says, Donne's speaker, "tenaciously figuring his maleness as adult manhood," demonstrates the "residual force of the sexualized model for love in Donne's religious poetry" (149). The effect, according to

Mueller, is a God who "expresses love through torture, rape, and bondage" in *HSBatter* and a spouse who "fulfills her role by behaving like a whore" in *HSShow* (149).

Parfitt (1989, 89–92) finds Donne's move from the secular to the religious involving "no abrupt break, but rather a refocusing," noting that if religious language is "redirected to orthodox religious subjects," so too "sexuality is now redeployed to the service of religious experience," notably in poems such as *HSBatter* and *HSShow* (89). Parfitt also finds a continuation in the religious verse of "striking, aggressive openings," "wit and paradox," and an emphasis upon first-person pronouns, especially in *HSMade* (89–90). He further notes that the "restless, shifting moods" of the secular verse find parallels in the divine poetry and that the grief and melancholy of such poems as *Twick* and *Noct* are mirrored in worries about the "apostasy of despair" in *HSBlack* 9–10 and *HSLittle* 3–4 (90). But Parfitt finally cautions against too easy a claim about similarity, especially considering some of the more famous secular poems, in which "the usual postures of the personae are aggressive and assimilative" (90–91). Parfitt acknowledges that the "same prominent sense of self" can be seen in Donne's religious verse, but he argues that "supplication is more common than assertion" and that these poems often begin with "conditional phrasing" or "questioning" (92).

Gill (1990, 129–34) emphasizes "the continuities" between Donne's religious poetry and his love poetry, noting three features the two groups of poems share: argument, egotism, and speaker-interlocutor relationship (129–33). With respect to argument, Gill cites *HSScene*, *HSRound*, and *HSBatter* as poems in which the speaker goes so far as to order God to act; similarly, *ElFatal* is "charged with *masculine persuasive force*" (129). For Gill, Donne's use of personal pronouns is a sign of the extent to which the speaker is concerned with himself, and to this end, Gill finds, for example, that in *HSScene* the word "my" occurs ten times, and "I" and "me" occur twice (130). But Gill sees an important difference between the egotism of the religious poetry and that of the love poetry: whereas the mistress in the love poetry is perceived as passive, the God of the divine poems, as in *HSBatter*, "is usually seen as, or asked to be, active" (132). Gill asks, therefore, "whether it is egotistical to seek that which is absolutely necessary for one's salvation" (132). Related to the feature of egotism in Donne's poetry, in Gill's view, is the relationship between the speaker and the interlocutor. Because Donne's God is perceived as an active presence in his religious verse, unlike, for the most part, his mistresses, Gill agrees with Gardner's (1952) view that Donne's God is "more powerfully present to the imagination in his divine poems than any mistress is in his love poems" (132).

Schoenfeldt (1990, 290), writing primarily of sexuality and spirituality in Herbert's *The Temple*, finds that in *HSShow* and *HSBatter* Donne "engages in a superficially similar sexualization of his relationship with God." But, Schoenfeldt points out, in Donne the "stunning blend of erotic and religious impulses is easily comprehended precisely because the eroticism is so explicit." In *HSShow*, according to Schoenfeldt, "the vast differences between earthly and heavenly promiscuity are underscored by the apparent contradiction of the final couplet, in which Christ's spouse, the church, is 'most new, and pleasing to thee, then / When she'is embrac'd and open to most men.'" And, similarly, in *HSBatter*, "the paradox of a rape which makes one chaste is readily understood as a form of divine rapture in erotic terms." Schoenfeldt cites approvingly Kerrigan's suggestion (1974, 355) that in Donne there is an "'awful discrimination' of heavenly and earthly love," a quality Schoenfeldt distinguishes from the "awe-inspiring" effect of the similarity between heavenly and earthly love in a poem such as Herbert's "Love (III)."

Gorbunov (1993, 122–24) says that the lyrical hero of the sonnets and God are separated by an abyss (123) and that while one may find this relationship inexplicable, and the unexpected erotic images shocking and even blasphemous, one can see in the Holy Sonnets the influence of the Song of Solomon, an allegorical hymn celebrating the marriage of Christ and the Church. According to Gorbunov, Donne inverts the allegorical hymn into sacred parody, which was popular during the Middle Ages, but even more popular during the Counter Reformation. Gorbunov cites both medieval and early modern examples, including the sacred parody of Robert Southwell, who, in Gorbunov's view, was the first to draw on the Ignatian meditative tradition. But in Donne, according to Gorbunov, there is no spirituality, nor mysticism, and he uses erotic language primarily to force the reader to understand his tormenting, spiritual crisis (124).

Discussing the relationship between God and the speaker in the Holy Sonnets, Low (1993, 69–70, 77–78) points out that though Donne has strong feelings about the "figure of the authoritative father," the "strongest emotion" in the Holy Sonnets appears to be that "between man and woman, husband and wife" (69). Low finds that these poems, "far from being pious exercises on the established conventions about love," have as their focus the "inner psychological or spiritual tensions" arising from the speaker's "sexual identity" (69–70). For Low, the poems reflect "conflicting roles," in which Donne is at once "an insistently masculine seeker after mistresses or truths" as well as the "necessarily feminine and passive recipient of God's love" (70). He further finds that in several of the sonnets from 1633 and 1635 the "individual marriage trope" is important (77). In *HSDue*, for example, the trope "is implied by the rivalry between God and the devil, who has usurped, stolen, 'nay ravish[ed]' (l. 10) what belongs to God." The marriage trope is, according to Low, "reversed" in *HSWhat*, for the "bloody face of the crucified Christ becomes a potential rival of 'all my profane mistresses'" (l. 10) and is, at least implicitly, the "feminine object of Donne's still masculine (and touchingly Petrarchan) love" (l. 14). The marriage trope "appears very tenuously" in *HSLittle*, says Low, a poem in which the speaker asks God to "burn the fires of lust and envy out of his soul" (ll. 13–14), and Low views the speaker in this poem as Donne more or less "playing the passive role of love object to the end" (78).

Pallotti (1993 ,167–69) concurs with the view that Donne's religious poetry does not reflect a sharp break with his secular poetry nor are there strong stylistic differences, but only a "refocusing" of the "language of love" toward "religious language." Pallotti, however, does see a fundamental difference in "the participants in fictional discourse." Whereas in the secular poems the participants "are identified as mistress or lover, patron or patroness," in the religious poems, the "speech partners" include "God, Jesus Christ, Angels, Soul, Self, Death." These differences, according to Pallotti, alter the "discursive roles" in the poems, leading to "changes in the selection of interpersonal options" (167). In the Holy Sonnets, Pallotti argues, Donne selected "the interrogative option" as the dominant speaker-hearer relationship, and the poems thus characteristically invite the reader to devise answers to the questions that are raised, answers that often are challenged, and ultimately, "in the clash of viewpoints, the 'authority' of the poetic subject is inevitably undermined" (169). But, in Pallotti's view, questions and doubts appear to contemporary readers as "more authenticating than any 'unified,' received truth can possibly be" (169).

Davies (1994, 51) finds that in the Divine Poems, including the Holy Sonnets, Donne moves to "a more transcendent realm of sexual paradox" than we find in the secular poems, for in the religious poems Donne, "abdicating his male gender though not the 'virile' style," could "represent himself as the female partner," as derived from the Song of Solomon. Davies, noting that "such trans-sexual identification did not call for a revision of misogynistic attitudes," finds similarities between certain of the Divine Poems, HSShow, HSBatter, and HSShe, and "the more salacious of the earlier erotica."

Marotti (1994a, 87–90) finds Donne's "presentation of the self's conflicts between assertion and submission" evident in "acts of witty indecorum," which Marotti describes as a "metacommunicative device to signal the emotional ambivalences at the heart of his religious verse," a technique that Donne used in his prose paradoxes, his love poetry, and his poetry of compliment (87–88). Although the forceful effect of such features as "the sexualization of the speaker's relationship to God" may be sought by Donne, Marotti identifies further implications, namely, those "having to do both with Donne's relationship with his coterie audience and with his attitudes toward the political establishment." For example, Marotti points to HSWhat as a sonnet that "explicitly connects his amorous wooing with his religious suitorship" (88). And HSBatter, in Marotti's view, well-illustrates Donne's "witty indecorum" in its "sexualization of the speaker's relationship to God." Marotti finds it "shocking," because the relationship "has the shape of a passive homosexual fantasy," or, in other words, it "homoerotically sexualizes salvation." Marotti connects this attitude to some aspects of the "change in sociopolitical codes from the Elizabethan to the Jacobean periods," which was applicable both to "male-male patron-client transactions generally" (as seen in Shakespeare's sonnets) and to "Jacobean courtier-King relationships specifically" (89). Marotti concludes that in these sonnets Donne "utilizes the 'symbolic I' of Protestant meditation and preaching as a way of forging a bond with an audience by means of which personal religious experience and insight, communal piety and general truths, can be joined." In both "thematic design" and "coterie 'publication,'" Marotti asserts, the Holy Sonnets were "attuned to the religious and political realities of Jacobean England" (90).

THEMES

Osmond (1919, 53–54) notes that in the Holy Sonnets Donne dwells on "the thought of sin and the less hopeful aspects of spiritual life," as in HSMade 6, where the phrase, "Despaire behind, and Death before" could "serve as a motto" for all the Divine Poems. Because of this focus, Osmond argues, Donne is not a true mystical poet. For other comments on Donne's mysticism, or lack of it, see Bennett (1934), Hardy (1942), and Turnell (1950). See also Elton (1933), Gransden (1954), and Hunt (1954) under The Poet/Persona.

Fausset (1924, 239–40) finds that in the Holy Sonnets Donne is "absorbed" by two thoughts, his "emancipation from worldly values" and a lament "for past sins." The two, he concludes, "met in the theme of Death, image alike of spiritual freedom and physical bondage."

Praz (1925, 68) contends that the dominant theme of the Holy Sonnets is Donne's fear that he will be judged before he is ready.

Judson (1927, 245) finds that the Holy Sonnets reveal Donne's "almost morbid fascination" with the thought of death.

Fausset (1931a, xxi) repeats a number of comments from 1924, also noting that in the Holy Sonnets the "conventional idiom of religion" fails to intrude upon "the drama" of Donne's "imperfect conversion."

Kortemme (1933, 44–45) finds in Donne's religious poetry a "baroque scholastic element" ("barock-scholastiche Element"), particularly in its unrest and nervousness about the relationships portrayed. The sonnets, he thinks, reflect a genuinely pessimistic baroque world view indicated by their consciousness of sin and desire for repentance and atonement. Kortemme observes that Donne's consciousness of sin in his religious poetry grows to almost immeasurable proportions and that he finds humankind immersed in sin and more impure than nature, indeed shamed in the presence of every tree and animal, because human beings resist the order of God that nature observes unconsciously. Donne, Kortemme believes, hates sin because it carries within itself its own punishment and because it offends God. Kortemme surveys the Holy Sonnets and discovers in them Donne's "sense of life without harmony" ("harmonielose Lebensgefühl"), evidenced in a desire to struggle with God and argue with him, using the full fantasy of his wit, about the contradictions in theological teachings and in God's actions. Kortemme finds the Holy Sonnets unique in their baroque feeling for life, in the inner union of content and form, and in the use of antithesis and contradiction. He believes Donne found in the church fathers, especially in St. Thomas Aquinas, a rich source for his thought regarding the opposition between the infinity and richness of God on the one hand and the misery and spiritual limitations of humankind on the other. Kortemme finds similarities between Donne's religious verse and medieval Latin poetry, the hymns of the scholastics, and contemporary German baroque poetry, suggesting a common source in the church fathers.

Bennett (1934, 36–37, 117) observes that because of Donne's long experience with sickness in his married life, "during which several of his children died, he himself was repeatedly ill, and finally his wife died," his later prose and poetry are haunted with "images from disease and dissolution," and she cites as examples the images of dropsy in HSShe 7–8 and ague in HSVex 12–14. Bennett believes that Donne, unlike poets such as Vaughan, Blake, and Francis Thompson, was not a "seer or mystic." Arguing that although the "immediate sense of God was not for him," she quotes HSShe 5–6 to indicate that, nonetheless, "he shared their desire," aware that "human love was not enough" (117).

White (1936, 129) observes that in the Holy Sonnets, as in his religious poetry generally, "the first and greatest of Donne's themes is sin."

Fausset (1938, xii) finds death "the predominant theme" of the Holy Sonnets, first stated in HSMade and climaxing in HSRound and HSDeath.

Hardy (1942, 175, 179), quoting HSShe 1–8, argues that Donne, overcome with grief at the death of his wife, "sublimated his love and epitomized his sorrow" in composing the Holy Sonnets. Hardy adds that Donne strove constantly to bridge what he saw as "the chasm lying dark and immeasurable between his soul and God." In his failure to do so, Hardy concludes, he fell short of becoming a "true mystic." Hardy quotes HSDue 11–14 and HSBlack 3–8 as illustration (179).

Bush (1945, 134) notes that over all Donne's religious poetry "hangs the lurid shadow of death." He further observes that Donne, finally, has "only one theme, his sins and his salvation, 'Despaire behind and death before' [HSMade 6]" and further that "the abysses of sin and death are more constantly vivid to his imagination than is the abyss of God's love and mercy."

Stauffer (1946, 85) argues that Donne delights in riddles and that his paradoxes "shock us into attention," with two contradictory answers to the riddles producing a deeper understanding of religious faith. To illustrate, Stauffer quotes HSBatter 12–14 and HSShow 12–14.

Spörri-Sigel (1949, 85–87) finds that in the Holy Sonnets Donne emphasizes the antithesis God-Sin rather than the God-World of his other religious verse. Sin delivers humankind to the opponent of God, creating an enemy-like relationship, splintering reality antithetically. On the one side stands God, on the other humankind, bound to Satan. This dualism, Spörri-Sigel continues, is overcome by Christ, who through his death, an act of love that provides humankind with grace, defeats sin and creates a bridge between God and the human being.

To Turnell (1950, 273) Donne is no mystic, since the Holy Sonnets are "distinctly Protestant in feeling," full of the doubts of the sinner and the "figure of an avenging God," inappropriate to a mystical vision.

Simon (1952, 114–17, 122, 125–26) summarizes the themes of the Holy Sonnets, noting that Donne "meditates on death and salvation, on his own unworthiness and his fear of judgment, and on the mercy of God," and that, no longer considering perplexing truths, he is "immersed in his own drama, intensely aware of his sins, harrowed by the sense of his own weakness and unable to comprehend the mystery of Grace." His sense of unworthiness, Simon suggests, causes Donne to question salvation but it also leads to a realization of God's mercy; for the speaker, however, Grace has to be won over and over, which he accomplishes in meditation "by dwelling on scenes that fill him with fear." Reason, Simon argues, is no aid in his urgent appeal for mercy; God's love is his only recourse, a realization that draws him to the figure of Christ as "the only support that can avail," a theme particularly prominent in HSSpit and HSWhat (114–15). Simon concludes that "mercy and justice, or sin and grace, thus constitute the real theme of the sonnets," but, she says, the apprehension of God's love is a hard ascent for him, since "his reason is never silenced" and "he must be battered, overthrown, bent, broken, blown, burnt before he can 'admit' God" (115). Donne, Simon thinks, never achieves the mystic's natural love of God but is ever "a spirit in conflict," in part because of his upbringing. Nor does he achieve "spiritual union," Simon continues; he prays for "rapture, not ecstasy," but there is no evidence in the divine poems that he "ever knew this death of the soul which alone could have given him rest" (116–17).

Simon comments on Donne's "power to suggest scenes, especially of terror," and his use of such scenes to "heighten feeling or stimulate thought," as in HSScene, HSRound, and HSWhat. In other sonnets, Simon asserts, the drama is expressed as argument (HSDeath), or close reasoning (HSDue), or by the emotional appeal of one already "torn and broken" (HSBatter). In HSSouls, she observes, confidence in salvation is expressed "without suggesting a hard fight," and thus the poem is less effective (122). Simon concludes that because Donne attempts "to feel more intensely the living God" in the Holy Sonnets, they are marked by a "depth and urgency" of emotions, and their structure resembles that of a "living organism" in which each part interacts with other parts. Simon argues that in the Holy Sonnets Donne uses many of the figures and devices he used in his earlier poems, with the exception of "dissonant images," since they "do not allow for organic development." Thus, the imagery of the Holy Sonnets differs from that of the Songs and Sonets because in the religious poems he wants to "intensify rather than to control his feelings," a quality that explains why the Holy Sonnets "stand nearer" to Shakespeare's Sonnets than do the works of any of the other metaphysical poets (125–26).

Gransden (1954, 127–38) surveys the Holy Sonnets for recurrent themes: HSMade, HSBlack, HSScene—the note of regret over the sin of despair, brought on by both physical and spiritual sickness (127–28); HSDue, HSBatter—the desire to leave the world and escape the Devil (128–29); HSShow, HSShe, HSSighs, HSWhat, HSMin, HSWhy—the "practice of putting secular passions to divine use" (130–32); HSVex— the record of "a brilliant mind struggling towards God" (132–33); HSBatter—the importance of the "psychotherapeutic" value of Christianity, as a guide to one's thought processes, in the medieval tradition; HSDeath, HSLittle, HSPart—a faith in the final triumph, achieved by the sinner's struggle to repent; and HSShe—the supremacy of the universal Church over any particular form of Christianity (137–38).

Leishman (1954, 74–75), in a review essay of Gardner's edition (1952), applauds her division of the sonnets into three (or four) groups, but questions the basis for dividing the twelve 1633 poems into two groups of six according to theme, the first on death, the second on love. He argues that each of the sonnets is "concerned with the twofold theme of love which alone can save us from eternal death" (75).

Esch (1955, 46) observes that Corona and the Holy Sonnets differ thematically, the former concerned with the Incarnation of Christ, the latter with humanity in a position between sin and grace.

Denonain (1956, 149–50, 153) argues that the Holy Sonnets are an arbitrary collection of occasional pieces whose present numbering in most editions should not mislead the reader. He points out that HSShe, HSShow, and HSVex are additions of modern editors but that common themes can be detected in others of the collection: HSSighs, HSLittle, HSScene, HSRound, and HSDeath, for example, deal with the sense of sin (149–50); and HSSpit, HSWhat, HSWhy, HSBatter, and HSWilt celebrate the "goodness" ("bonté") of God and Christ (153).

Coanda (1957, 181) argues that Donne was not a mystic, since certain elements of his poetry—e.g., "morbidity, egocentricity, self-thwarting"—are "antagonistic to mysticism." Coanda finds morbidity in the "Meditations" of the *Devotions* and the Holy Sonnets, especially *HSMin* and *HSSpit*. In Donne, Coanda concludes, there is much surprise but little wonder, and since the states of being he describes are those of ordinary experience, he "is merely a poet sometimes religious."

Peterson (1959, 506–18) agrees with Gardner's grouping of the poems (1952) but argues that her classification of the groups according to theme "violates the essential unity" of the Holy Sonnets. Rather than one group being concerned with fear, another with love, and a third with repentance, Peterson asserts, all reflect one unifying principle, the Anglican doctrine of contrition, which incorporates fear, love, and repentance, and he quotes *Sermons* 6:113 to corroborate (506). In keeping with this doctrine, Peterson continues, the fear expressed in the first six of the 1633 sonnets stimulates the love of the second six, which in turn, with the help of grace, produces the contrite sorrow of the four penitential sonnets of 1635 and the three in the Westmoreland ms. The Holy Sonnets, then, represent an effort "to experience those states of feeling that either precede or are concomitant with contrition" (508).

Peterson argues that the first in the sequence, *HSDue*, states the problem: having acknowledged sin (1–10), the penitent must seek the grace "essential to contrite sorrow" (11–14). This is done in arousing fear, in keeping with the Ignatian method of meditation, by contemplation of the Last Things in *HSBlack*, *HSScene*, and *HSRound*. *HSMin* and *HSDeath* are transitional sonnets looking forward to the next stage, "the transcendence of fear through love" (510). The next three, *HSSpit*, *HSWhy*, and *HSWhat*, Peterson continues, describe the goodness and mercy of God, and *HSBatter* is a prayer for the grace necessary for contrition. *HSWilt* and *HSPart* complete the sequence but without any assurance that the process has been successful (511–13). Of the 1635 sonnets, the first three, *HSMade*, *HSLittle*, and *HSSighs*, are indeed, Peterson asserts, expressions of contrite sorrow and *HSSouls* a summary of the success of the process. Peterson finds the Westmoreland sonnets, *HSShe*, *HSShow*, and *HSVex*, to be "comments on the experience of contrition" (518); hence they are not, he argues, unconnected with one another or with the previous sixteen, as Gardner suggests (514). Reading the poems thus in their theological context, Peterson concludes, may help revise "contemporary commonplaces about Donne's neurotic and melancholy faith" or his "overwrought religiosity" (518). Peterson argues that although the Holy Sonnets are a unified representation of the Anglican experience of contrition, this does not necessarily mean that they were written within any limited time period, either that proposed by Grierson (1912) or that suggested by Gardner; nor does it mean that they were composed in the order of the 1633 and 1635 editions (518).

Demaray (1965, 366) considers Donne's treatment of death in many of his works, including the Holy Sonnets, and says that to "understand how Donne came to write so fearlessly and so personally about death," one must examine his "varying attitudes towards natural law," especially in *Biathanatos* (c. 1608), *FirAn* (1611), and *SecAn* (1612).

Herbold (1965, 277, 279–81, 285, 291) is concerned with what he describes as "dialectics" in Donne. He defines this concept as "a critical example of hypotheses and principles, an examination by discussion, tacit if not explicit." Identifying different modes of dialectics, Herbold notes that in all modes "a question and answer form is discernible" (277). He refers to HSSpit as a "single dialectical syllogism" (279), arguing that the "keynote" of Donne's dialectics is "his search for an equilibrium between balanced polarities" (280). In the Holy Sonnets, he says, Donne's dialectics is "chiefly between Faith and Doubt," as he "accepted the dialectician's conviction that 'contraryse meete in one'" (HSVex 1) (281). Herbold asserts that Donne "tied the strings to the first term, much as a dialectician would anticipate an opponent's additions" (285), and he notes that most of Donne's poems consist of questions. For Herbold, Donne's dialectics did not so much "force a crisis" as it put off "decision," and he identifies both "scepticism" and "despair" as debaters in the Holy Sonnets (291).

Bell (1969, 15–17) opposes the view that Donne's "genius" and "characteristic ingenuity" explain why he casts God in dramatic roles in the Holy Sonnets. He argues instead that Donne uses dramatic roles for God as a conceit which he gleaned from his theological reading and that Donne's "theological conceit" consistently connotes the Atonement, which he says is the unifying motif of the Holy Sonnets (15). Donne, Bell argues, draws on the "classic" or "dramatic" theory of the atonement in which the atonement is seen as a divine conflict and victory, a view of God as one who *acts*. This is in contrast to the "satisfaction" theory of atonement, Bell states, which presents a God who is acted *upon* (15). Donne's sources, says Bell, are at least three: the writings of St. Paul, of the early church Fathers, and of Luther.

Nelly (1969, 134–50) states that the Holy Sonnets, along with Donne's other poetry, show that he "is more interested in analysing and presenting the truth of his own experience . . . than in giving us neat conclusions" from which all the contradictions and "attractive sensibilities" of his nature had been drained (135–36). In the Holy Sonnets on death, Nelly claims—citing in particular HSDue, HSMin, and HSBlack—the "tension, ambiguity, stress, and 'anguish of the marrow'" present in his great love lyrics are not evident (141). Instead, Nelly finds in these sonnets "a labouring of the dialectic to simplify and to state the case rather than to grapple with it and resolve it" (141), as, for example, the final couplet in many of the Holy Sonnets states a truth in paradoxical form. Comparing the Holy Sonnets with Herbert's divine colloquies, Nelly finds Donne's "assaults upon Heaven" to be more urgent and more ruggedly individual (141).

Grant (1971, 544, 556–58) argues that the Holy Sonnets are a synthesis, on the one hand, of a traditional Augustinianism such as informs Bonaventure's works and, on the other hand, a "characteristically seventeenth-century latitudinarian desire to repudiate the harsh doctrinal derivations from Augustine," such as they were to be found among the Reformers (544). The hallmarks of the most distinguished and mainstream tradition of devotion to Augustine in the high middle ages, Grant states, are as follows: (1) the development of affective piety evoking, through the senses, specifically Biblical themes; (2) particular interest in the cross as the central motif for devotion; (3) prepossession with the cross in relation to Adam's fallenness and original sin, as expressed in the formula *Cur Deus homo si Adam non pecasset?*; (4) an emphasis on contrition rather than penance or attrition for the forgiveness of sins; and (5) use of meditation on last things to inspire man with a sense of his fallenness, and move him towards contrition. Grant finds these features in the Holy Sonnets, and he argues that they seem not only to confirm interests well attested in Donne's other theological writings, but in the quality of the experience they offer, to be what Grant describes as traditionally Augustinian (556). Further, Grant detects in Donne's prose writings "a latitude of both spirit and language" and "a sensibility approaching . . . the Cambridge Platonists" (558). He concludes that the Holy Sonnets "reflect the tensions of the young Renaissance latitude-man, attempting to express himself in the mould of older models of devotion despite aspirations to achieve new" (558).

Hebaisha (1971, 64) believes that Donne's "expression of conflict" in the Holy Sonnets, often cited to indicate the insecurity of his faith, is typical of devotional meditations and argues, moreover, that this theme is superceded by the main one of the poems: "the belief in Christ's final intervention for man's salvation." Hebaisha further suggests that two themes are most evident throughout the Holy Sonnets: a sense of the poet's "unworthiness" and occasional "self-abnegation" and a "belief in God's mercy and love."

Kremen (1972, 81, 107–14) finds in all of Donne's poetry and sermons the theme of resurrection and shows that Donne distinguishes four types: (1) the resurrection from natural calamities; (2) the first, or spiritual, resurrection on earth from sin to grace; (3) the general resurrection of all people, living and dead, in body and soul on judgment day; and (4) the final resurrection of the saved in body and soul to the kingdom of God (81). She urges that Donne's prime concern in the divine poems is with "the doctrine of the first, or spiritual, resurrection through the simultaneous cooperation of God's grace and man's penance, which assures his final resurrection" (108). Kremen illustrates these themes by reference to *HSBatter*, *HSShow*, and *HSRound*.

Ramsaran (1973, 161–62) notes that the Holy Sonnets "play variations" on the themes of human suffering while they progress in the "meditative manner of an Ignatian 'spiritual exercise.'" Ramsaran reads *HSScene* as expressing "an unusual detachment" in which "it appears as though Donne has stepped out of his poem to see himself in a colloquy with God" (161). He points to death as an important theme of several of the Holy Sonnets and notes that in the "supreme death of God" represented in their climax, "Christian doctrine complements the ideas and imagery of the Psalms." According to Ramsaran, *HSWhy* and *HSBatter* also relate to the theme of death: in *HSWhy* the marvel of God's providence and His glory "is surpassed by the greater marvel of redemption through the suffering and death of Christ"; in *HSBatter* death is "destroyed by the love of God which makes the human soul His bride" (162).

Samarin (1973, 162–78) writes that Donne's "tragedy" consists in his development from Renaissance and humanistic forms and themes to Baroque forms and religious themes, especially embodied in the fear of death. In the 1600s, Samarin says, Donne begins to use genre concepts that arose in the late Middle Ages or early Renaissance; long poems appear which he calls "anatomies" or "spiritual poems" (using "divine" even when they are cycles of sonnets, i.e. works of a markedly Renaissance genre) (165). Samarin argues that Donne's poetry of this time, and especially *Metem*, can be considered as the indisputable expression of the crisis of the poet's Renaissance and humanistic views, and the Holy Sonnets may be understood as the work that completed Donne's poetic path, providing evidence, along with other religious poems, of the Baroque.

Blanch (1974, 477) writes that the "overriding tone" of the Holy Sonnets is fear, arguing that the whole sequence bears the imprint of a "sick soul," of a man so tortured by doubts that he welcomed fear, deliberately evoking it in order to drive himself to God. Blanch sees a relationship between fear and the love of God, noting that "in those sonnets evincing fear, there is an underlying impulse towards love of God; and in those sonnets portraying God's mercy, there is a corresponding recognition of the potency of fear."

McCanles (1975, 55–56, 69–70) argues that the Holy Sonnets are structured by a "dialectical logic" which he delineates in his study of *Ecst* and *Anniv*. Following the phenomenological analysis of Edmund Husserl, McCanles argues that in these texts "conflict is abrogated, because the fragmentation of the poem's vision into different perceptions in the noematic continuum is allowed fullest range for development" (69)—i.e., the poems reflect realities "around which no human mind can completely walk" (55). Moreover, he states that the Holy Sonnets strive to bridge an infinite gulf between God and Sinner, but the love poems are limited to abrogating the distance between separated lovers. McCanles argues that "the poles between which the dialectic in these poems moves—sin and salvation, despair and hope—interpenetrate at only the highest reaches of human intuitive experience, an experience that even more radically discounts human finiteness than do the love poems" (70).

Grant (1979, 82–83), in his study of texts that focus on the association between *caritas* and "wonder," points to two of Donne's Holy Sonnets, *HSSpit* 9 ("O let me then, his strange love still admire") and *HSWhy* 11 ("But wonder at a greater wonder . . ."), which Grant reads as exhorting "himself (and his readers)" to wonder at "God's redemptive love" (82–83).

Lewalski (1979, 104–05) finds that the Holy Sonnets possess a distinct Donnean feature, namely, "the framing of the tropes so as to show the Christian speaker subject to various kinds of holy violence and force" (104). Lewalski points to such examples as: "the sinful state as a living death" in *HSMade*; "sin as bondage: the speaker has been ravished or captured or stolen by Satan," in *HSDue*, *HSBatter*, and *HSWilt*, and "Christ must unbind him, or paradoxically, 'enthrall' him in order to free him" in *HSBatter*; "Christ the Bridegroom of the Church is urged to become a pander to his Spouse, exposing her to many lovers, since she best pleases him 'When she'is embrac'd and open to most men'" in *HSShow* 14; and, in *HSDue*, the speaker identifies a number of familiar tropes as "metaphoric 'titles' by which God could and should claim him," including "son, sheep, image, temple"; the speaker then, in response to "Satan's challenge to these titles," proceeds to employ and recast the "Christian warfare trope, asserting that not his own warfare but God's is necessary to support and defend these metaphoric claims" (104–05).

Milward (1979 [1988, 41]) follows Gardner's (1952) ordering of the Holy Sonnets from 1633, and notes that the twelve sonnets fall into two groups of six each, the first group dealing with the "general theme of the fear of sin and the punishment due to it" and the second with the "contrasting theme of the love of God and one's neighbour." Milward finds the sonnets of the first group to be "poetic meditations" on the "four last things"—death, judgment, hell and heaven—and points to sixteenth-century commentaries by Denis the Carthusian and Sir Thomas More.

Chatterjie (1980, 39) finds that some of Donne's religious poems are "vibrant with mystic fervour," noting that in the Holy Sonnets there is an appealing "note of direct and close communion, a kind of unusual intimacy."

Shaw (1981, 49) finds that the sonnets in which the speakers meditate "upon the Last Things" (HSBlack, HSScene, HSRound, HSWhat) "follow tradition by constantly portraying judgment as a present reality" (49).

Yearwood (1982, 208–11, 220) focuses her study "on the doctrinal and emotional aspects of conversion" as "a critical framework for the poems," a study which reveals, according to Yearwood, "a precise organization and sequence," as well as "a didactic or instructive character," thus inviting from their readers a "common response" (208). In Yearwood's view, the poems require "sympathetic participation from the beholders" (208). Yearwood contends that Donne's understanding of conversion was "formed during the Mitcham/London period and did not change thereafter, even through his many years in the pulpit," legitimating, therefore, the use of the sermons to clarify his views even years before the sermons were written (209). Yearwood identifies three doctrines that provide the framework of Donne's conception of conversion: "(1) that God does all, either by his preventing or his sustaining grace; (2) that human action—specifically confession—is a *sine qua non* of salvation; and (3) that there is predestination only to salvation, not to damnation, consequently that salvation is available to everyone who will confess, and to no one who will not" (210–11). Conversion thus involves accepting "responsibility for one's own overwhelming sin," and acknowledging "total dependence on divine will" (210). The conversion process in Donne's twelve Holy Sonnets of 1633, according to Yearwood, thus "begins in pride, proceeds to confession and despair, and culminates in a humble joy and confidence" (210). A cursory look at the Holy Sonnets, following Gardner's ordering (1952), shows, in Yearwood's view, the following: whereas the first sonnet begins in the confidence that the speaker can achieve salvation through his own declaration of humility, by the end of the sonnet, the speaker finds that he cannot, and thus "berates God"; in the second sonnet, "the voice of grace" instructs the speaker as to what he must do, namely, "confess"; sonnets 3 through 5 reflect the speaker "presumptuously attempting confession of his sins and finally attaining it"; the sixth sonnet "celebrates his joy"; sonnets 7 and 8 depict the speaker "wallowing in guilt and despair"; so that by the ninth sonnet, "the outside voice intervenes again," and offers "reassurance which is only superficially accepted"; the tenth sonnet "marks his achievement of true humility and, simultaneously, of utter despair"; in sonnet 11, "the voice of grace intervenes again," but "this time with imperative therapeutic counsel"; the twelfth sonnet "demonstrates the soul's final acceptance of salvation and dependence on God," manifesting a "humble faith" (211).

Zunder (1982, 89–94) sees the Holy Sonnets as being written during a period of "spiritual crisis," in that what they "primarily express is a fear of total alienation, a fear of being somehow irretrievably lost," a fear expressed "most powerfully" in the Holy Sonnets written in 1609–11 (89–90). Zunder finds that the origin of this fear, as expressed in the sonnets, is "personal inadequacy" and sees this explicitly in HSScene 3–4 (91). But the "resolution of feeling," according to Zunder, is manifest in the closing couplet of such sonnets as HSDeath and HSWilt (93–94).

Booty (1982, 33–35) examines the meaning of contrition as it appears in the writings of Hooker, Donne and Herbert. Booty begins by focusing on Donne's understanding of "the centrality of contrition for the Christian life" as it is revealed in his *Devotions* and then in his Holy Sonnets. Six of the original sonnets in 1633 are "concerned for the stimulation of fear and six concerned for the stimulation of love," with the first sonnet, HSDue, "a kind of preparatory prayer" for the following five sonnets, which are "concerned for the stimulation of fear," with HSBlack as a contemplation of that which the poet most fears: death. In HSRound, the "judgment is depicted and repentance yearned for," and the next sonnet, HSMin, "reflects upon the transcendence of fear through love," and the mercifulness of God. The final sonnet in the group of six, HSDeath, focuses on "the stimulation of fear" and is, for Booty, "a magnificent expression of defiant faith in the face of prideful death." The next group of six, which focus on the stimulation of love, begins with "meditations on the Cross of Christ in the Ignatian manner" (33). HSSpit ends with "amazement" that Christ has died (34), and HSWhat affirms Christ's forgiveness. The next sonnet, HSBatter, "reflects the struggles of one who would repent," but who requires the mercy of God to free him from his sinfulness (34). HSWilt "returns to the meditative mood to remember God's adoption of humankind," and the final sonnet, HSPart, "ends with a firm evocation of the divine Love" (34). The second set of sonnets shows that "the eyes of faith have been opened," and the speaker understands the "ultimate truth, that God is merciful" (34). The 1635 sequence of Holy Sonnets, according to Booty, "expresses contrite sorrow" as well as the "mutual love of God and the poet" (35), and he cites the first sonnet in 1635, HSMade, as the most "impressive" (35). Booty concludes that "it would not be incorrect to refer to the theology of John Donne as the theology of divine mercy" (35).

Klause (1983, 47–48) finds that Donne's interest in "the imperfections of love" extends beyond human love to "the resistance that divine love encounters as it pulses through creation." Klause claims that Donne "does not entirely regret" this resistance, and, in fact, "that violence seems for Donne almost exhilarating" (47). Klause cites HSBatter 1–4 and HSVex 14 as evidence of the appeal of the violent paradox to Donne (48). Its appeal, according to Klause, may be in the way paradox fosters a "sense of the miraculous nature of human love or divine majesty" (47–48).

Mallett (1983, 54–55), reaffirming the influence of Ignatian meditation on the Holy Sonnets, identifies two dominant themes on which Donne meditates: "personal sinfulness, and the judgement of God on sinners" (55).

Alves (1985, 31, 38–39), in noting Donne's "religiosity and thorough conversion," points out that some of the "more notable" Holy Sonnets deal "vigorously and starkly with the eschatological themes that colour a Christian's view of his last end viz death, judgement, heaven and hell" (38). Alves adds that for Donne, "death was an obsessive preoccupation; so too was sin, especially unforgiven sin" (38). He cites two sonnets that deal, respectively, with these themes: *HSDeath* and *HSBatter* (39).

Martz (1985, 15–16) traces the uncertain progression of the Holy Sonnets in the arrangement of 1635 toward "greater confidence" (15). Pointing to later sonnets in that sequence, he finds that even though *HSBatter* "cries so vehemently for the will of God to act upon him," the "indispensable ingredient of this struggle is the love expressed in the first line of the sestet" (15). Martz notes that the word "betrothed" in *HSBatter* 10 does not signify marriage, for it "can be broken, and it will be broken by the power of love," as *HSWilt* and *HSPart*, the last two poems in the sequence, confirm (15). According to Martz, *HSWilt* "speaks in a steady rational vein that offers an assurance of being chosen as part of a generous gift to all mankind," and *HSPart*, through its legal imagery, "renews with rich affirmative meaning the 'many titles' that seemed so useless" in *HSDue*, the second sonnet in the sequence (15). In the final line of *HSPart*, Martz observes, Donne stresses the power of love that is "all-healing" (l. 11). Martz concludes that "within this mode of rectified devotion," Donne "creates a spirituality that blends the Reformation with the Counter Reformation, and that blending, so tormented, so strenuous, will perhaps explain why Donne has seemed unusual, even eccentric, in the course of English poetry" (16), though he goes on to suggest that Donne "does not seem eccentric when viewed in the full European context and especially in the Spanish context, both poetical and religious" (16).

Patrides (1985a, 30–33) claims that Donne is the "foremost" English poet and prose writer of death and, moreover, that death was an "obsession" for Donne (30–31). Patrides finds that death is evident even in Donne's poetry where it "appears to have been virtually stilled into extinction" (32). Patrides points to *HSRound*, for example, which "nominally advances from the loftiness of the octave's sweeping movement to the meekness of the sestet's threnodic rhythms" (32), explaining that the "departure from the basic iambic beat in the octave induces a counter-movement," thus calling attention through the "disturbed rhythm" to the images of death in lines 5–7. Patrides identifies *HSDeath* as another example in which the same pattern emerges, where the conjoining of "three strongly-accented words" ("Fate, Chance, kings") in line 9 "calls attention to the masters not of death but of ourselves" (33).

Guibbory (1986, 90) finds that memory is central to the Holy Sonnets, wherein Donne "calls to remembrance his former sins, defining his own sinfulness in terms of biblical history," in such a way that "Donne becomes Adam, and the pattern of his life recapitulates the history of mankind from Creation through the Fall to Redemption" (90). Consequently, "memory becomes not simply something private and individual," according to Guibbory, "but rather a kind of typological memory, linking Donne with biblical history and mankind as a whole" (90).

Stein (1986, 94) situates his analysis of Donne's poetry in the well-known Renaissance metaphor that sees human life and death as resembling a "theatrical performance." But Stein finds that when in Donne's verse "fictional deaths" are cited to "illustrate death," the metaphors are "drawn within tighter lines" than when his "fictional deaths" serve to "furnish scenes of life." According to Stein, Donne tests the "soundness of the imagined action of life by stopping it and imposing a radical revision." In so doing, "the last act will be ordered to begin at once," as in *HSBlack*

1–2 or *HSScene* 1–6. Or, Stein adds, "the personal last act may be enlarged and co-ordinated with the final day of judgment," as in *HSWhat* 1 and *HSRound* 1–2. The examples Stein cites, which he also associates with Ignatian meditative practices, "represent one kind of arbitrary extreme by means of which the imagined moment of death makes room for a conclusion" that may "release the anticipated benefits of beginning with the end."

Parker (1987, 75, 79), identifying the "powerful entanglement" in Donne's lyrics of "the thread of death and the thread of life and love" (75), finds in the Holy Sonnets a "violent coincidence" of "a sense of death, arising from the poet's sinfulness," and "a discerning of life, arising from Divine Love," the conjunction giving the poems "great energy and force, and their emotion great authority" (79).

Pawar (1987, 42–44), following Gardner's ordering of the Holy Sonnets (1952), finds that the first six sonnets (*HSDue, HSBlack, HSScene, HSRound, HSMin,* and *HSDeath*) are dominated by the "terror of Hell," while the next six (*HSSpit, HSWhy, HSWhat, HSBatter, HSWilt,* and *HSPart*) "produce a shift in emphasis from fear of death and damnation to a realization of the love of God for his creatures, and the healing nature of his love" (42). Pawar states that the four sonnets that were added in 1635 (*HSMade, HSLittle, HSSighs,* and *HSSouls*) are "united by an over-riding concern with penitence" (43). But the three sonnets drawn from the Westmoreland manuscript (*HSShe, HSShow,* and *HSVex*) "show no logical or thematic connection with each other," being distinct from the previous 16 by not being cast in the "mould of the formal meditation" (43). Pawar adds that the "Christ-centered" sonnets at the end of the sequence of 16 sonnets "suggest the realisation of the redemptive power of Grace" (43). Thus, the Holy Sonnets, in Pawar's view, are "a complete expression both of the sickness of spirit and of the restoration of Grace, and their continuing co-existence in the world" (44).

A. Smith (1987, 162–65) states that "the tense urgency" of Donne's writing affirms that "the issues are fought out in every contingency," but in the Holy Sonnets Donne fixes the "critical juncture as the moment of the poem itself," epitomized, for Smith, in *HSWhat* 1. Thus, for Smith, the focus of the Holy Sonnets is "a man's struggle to recognize himself by first coming to terms with the way things inevitably are." Donne's sonnets, therefore, according to Smith, "present themselves not as a mere record of the struggle but as dynamic enactments of it," and in so doing, "the poems themselves are the initiating instruments, in that they seek in the same impulse to involve God, and to work upon the poet himself," as for example, in *HSBatter*. In Smith's view, "the resolution rests with God, but begins with the sinner himself in the submissive acceptance he displays to God" (162). Smith adds, however, that the circumstances of Donne's concern are not "exclusive or even private," for "while the critical matter for the poet is the disposition of his own soul, that consequence isn't peculiar to him or finally decided there" (163). Donne, he says, "takes station with us all on the universal stage, subject to the general circumstances that govern created nature since the Fall," and "shows us too where we stand" (163). For example, Smith observes, Donne responds to a "personal and domestic event" (the death of his wife in *HSShe*) in "the larger context of God's offer for his soul against the world, flesh, and devil" (165).

Clements (1990, 77, 260n) finds that Donne's Divine Poems, in general, are "meditative" rather than "contemplative": the poems are "purgative rather than illuminative or unitive; they are pre-mystical rather than precisely mystical . . . they do not show the true self breaking through the barriers of the false self" (77). Hence, in Clements' view, the melancholy that pervades Donne's Holy Sonnets is "a consequence of a profound belief in and desire for union with God accompanied by an equally profound sense of God's absence" (260n).

Although Gill (1990, 133–42) finds several themes common to Donne's secular and religious verse, he identifies at least three that are peculiar to Donne's religious poetry: the religious experience as "fundamentally that of yearning for an experience of God's mercy, not one of actually receiving it" (133); "the preoccupation with salvation," and specifically salvation viewed from "an eschatological or apocalyptic perspective" (134); and the attraction to paradox, which was, for Donne, at the center of human existence, and which gave him the opportunity to display "his verbal skill" (136). Gill identifies other features of Donne's poetry that may have issued from his religious life. His anxiety about faithfulness in both his love and religious poetry, Gill thinks, carries with it the implication that "someone who has been unfaithful to his religion and who has found that he can change his loyalties might become nervously aware of the capacity of other people to change their minds or appear to be faithful when they are not" (140). The visual imagery in Donne's poetry may be a product of the differences between Catholicism and Protestantism, according to Gill, who points out that Catholicism is much richer in its use of physical and verbal imagery than Anglicanism (140–41). But Gill adds that one could also argue that in the Holy Sonnets there is "a very strong sense of the individual soul before the judgment seat of God, and that is a distinctly Protestant notion" (141). Gill illustrates the tension between Catholicism and Protestantism in Donne's verse by showing that in HSRound "the octave is highly visual and essentially Catholic in its communal imagery, thought and feeling, whereas the rest of the poem (the sestet) seems quite Protestant in its emphasis upon the individual's relationship with God and the way it is visually restrained" (141–42).

Gorbunov (1990, 86) finds that the Holy Sonnets are permeated by internal conflict, fear, doubt and pain. Moreover, an inevitable rift divides God and the poetic subject of the first sixteen sonnets, and therefore, according to Gorbunov, one finds dull pain and devastation in HSSighs; feelings of desperation and alienation in HSDue; and the impropriety of erotic desires on the verge of sacrilege in HSWhat and HSBatter. But Gorbunov finds similar themes in Donne's later sonnets, written after 1617 (HSShe, HSShow, HSVex), suggesting that behind the deceptive quiet and deep concentration over the death of his wife, there is not only an oppressive fever of loss, but also the unquenched thirst for love. And in HSShow, according to Gorbunov, the poet is painfully vanquished by the sensual contrast between the heavenly church and its distance from the ideal of an earthly embodiment. Gorbunov adds that HSVex, while resting on the general mood of fear and trepidation, also discloses the contradictory nature of the poet's character, where "inconstancy unnaturally hath begot / A constant habit" (HSVex 2–3).

Pezzini (1990, 488–97) comments on the central position of the theme of Christ's passion and the cross in Donne's Christology and observes its importance in *Lit, Cross, Goodf*, and several Holy Sonnets.

Allinson (1991, 31–33, 38, 40–44), responding to Donald Ramsay Roberts's argument that there is a "death wish" in Donne ("The Death Wish of John Donne." *PMLA* 62[1947]: 958–76), studies the theme of death in Donne, drawing on post-Jungian psychology for his analysis. For "the heroic consciousness" of Jung, Allinson says, "descent into the underworld of the psyche means death, against which it must fight" (33), but Donne claims that Christ died because he chose to die, and thus did not die "naturally, nor violently, as all others do, but only voluntarily" (*Sermons*, 2:208) (38). Allinson notes that Donne says that Christ's "soule did not leave his body by force, but because he would, and when he would" (*Sermons* 2:108) (38). Consequently, according to Allinson, Donne is claiming that Christ is "a type of suicide" and that *Biathanatos* seems to support this view (38). Allinson contends that in Donne's conviction of "Christ's control over death we find the same need for ego control over death to which he himself felt attracted" (40). In light of this context, Allinson reads the Holy Sonnets as "spiritual autobiography," arguing that Donne's preoccupation with suicide and death suggests that for him an "ego death" was the "path to transformation" (41). In *HSDeath*, for example, Allinson finds that "the heroic ego's need to control and appropriate death" results in a "death sentence passed on Death," that is, "the ambivalence toward death in the poem discloses a lack of that deep assurance of faith which flows from self-transcendence" (41). Allinson reads *Goodf* as another instance of Donne's "vulnerable heroic self" (41–42) and concludes that "the more Donne's heroic ego 'thirsts' after the salvation to come" (cf. *HSShe* 8) the "more the corrosive imagery of fluids accumulate to break it down, the soul longing for the ego 'to be dissolved'" (44).

Hirsch (1991, 69, 81–82) points to the "revival of ancient atomism" in the late sixteenth and early seventeeth century and suggests that this "highly controversial theory of essence" might have allayed Donne's "persistent materialistic anxieties surrounding death and resurrection" (69). Hirsch attributes Donne's view of "the material soul's immortality" to its "atomic nature" (81), and he finds that interest manifested in several Holy Sonnets. For example, Hirsch notes, *HSLittle* indicates that the self is composed "Of elements, and an Angelike spright" (l. 2), both of which "must die because of 'black sinne' [l. 3]" (81). He also echoes Carey (1981) in positing that in *HSRound* Donne views the soul as "an object as mortal as the body, an entity which must await the Apocalypse for a re-entry into life" (81). Hirsch adds that this "unorthodox idea of the soul as a dead object resurrected simultaneously with the body" hints at Donne's association with "mortalism," a view Donne himself aligned with "Heretickes" in one of his sermons (*Sermons*, 3:115) (81). Although Hirsch grants that Donne's belief in the immortality of the soul is generally "unquestioning," he also believes that when Donne thinks about the soul's "substantial reality," he is "more than tempted to define it in material terms" (82).

Spurr (1991, 165–68) contends that the most distinctive feature of Donne's religious poetry is its "striking extremity," or "preoccupation with grace and the conviction of sinfulness" (165). For all his "professed Anglicanism," Spurr observes, Donne "was decidedly not a poet of compromise," which, for Spurr, distinguishes him from other Anglican poets such as Herbert (165). Spurr finds that in Donne's poetry "his own scourging and crucifixion are habitually desired" (166), pointing, for example, to *HSSpit*, where "never has the *imitatio Christi* been so boldly embraced" (166). In Spurr's view, Donne's poetry is mindful of "the dark night of the soul of St. John of the Cross" and looks ahead to the "desolation" of Hopkins for whom, as for Donne, the "extremity of the self-analysis . . . authenticates the experience" (167).

McNees (1992, 51, 61, 67, 190–91) finds that in his longer religious verse, Donne is "almost exclusively absorbed with the mystery of the Incarnation and Resurrection" (51). Furthermore, according to McNees, "the significance of the Eucharist as the only point of intersection of divine and temporal thus becomes a cornerstone of the divine lyrics" (51). McNees notes that Donne's Holy Sonnets compress the speaker's "struggle toward death and resurrection into pleas to God to punish him so that he will be worthy of salvation," while the longer hymns and poems "protract that struggle" (51). In the longer poems, according to McNees, Donne uses paradox and parable to articulate "the kingdom of God," and the speaker is "less agonized, the poem less intensely personal than in the sonnets" (51). The Holy Sonnets, she contends, "press for the necessity of repentance and contrition as prerequisites to union with God" and "identification with Christ's Passion as a route toward that union" (61). The sonnets "continually seek affliction as a means of realizing Christ's presence," McNees states, and they "borrow liturgical language and rhythm to lend authority to the individual drama" (61). She adds that, though most of the sonnets "discuss the sinner striving for grace," several "conclude with specifically eucharistic imagery" (61). McNees finds in the Divine Poems, including the Holy Sonnets, a representation of Anglican Real Presence in the Eucharist, noting that Donne's "method of realizing such a presence in his poems is to multiply the meanings of words by playing on their secular and spiritual definitions and contexts," and thus by incorporating terms from the only sacrament that "merges human and divine," Donne makes his poems "partial mimeses of the Anglican Eucharist" (67).

Sinfield (1992, 147, 158) questions the view of Martz (1954) that Donne's Holy Sonnets "are meditations leading to the achievement of a state of 'devotion'" (147), arguing instead that, given Donne's English Calvinism, approximately half the Holy Sonnets "end with the condition of Donne's soul in *question*—unaffected by his devotional efforts, awaiting God's mysterious judgment," for "any move towards God depends on God moving first" (147). Sinfield cites *HSBlack* and *HSBatter* as instances of this position.

Low (1993, 69) identifies several ways the speaker of the Holy Sonnets relates to God but finds, nonetheless, that the "strongest emotion" in the Holy Sonnets remains that "between man and woman, husband and wife," based on "the authority of Genesis." Low thinks, however, that Donne fails to bring together "the love of woman with the love of God without experiencing agonizing inner conflicts and difficulties, which the poems reflect."

Marotti (1994a, 84–87) finds that in the Holy Sonnets Donne "relocates in a religious framework the conflict between autonym and dependence" found in his encomiastic poetry, and thus the poems exemplify the "contradictory attitudes of assertion and submission that were basic to Donne's temperament, but that were heightened by the desperateness of his ambition in the early Jacobean period" (84). Marotti adds that the "social and political dimensions of this conflict" are accented in several characteristics of the sonnets: "the portrayal of male authority, the rhetorical elaboration of the struggle of spiritual pride and humility, the subversive indecorum of particular works, and the general transformation of a (religiously expressed) passive aggression into an aesthetically sadomasochistic relationship with his readers" (84).

Marotti finds "the conflict between assertion and submission" in the Holy Sonnets evident in, among other ways, "the thematic and rhetorical interplay of spiritual pride and humility" (85), attributable to the "familiar devotional material" that shows the individual's "resistance, then capitulation, to God's grace and love," a pattern especially evident in the twelve poems from 1633 (85). Marotti notes, for example, *HSDue*, which "seems more concerned with blaming God than with loving Him," and ultimately appears to hand God a "moral ultimatum" in lines 11–12 (85). According to Marotti, the "problem of spiritual acritude" here must be solved in poems that follow, such as *HSRound*, which "self-consciously pulls back in the sestet from the tone and tenor of the octave, in which the speaker, in effect, has usurped God's role as the initiator of the Apocalypse" (85–86). Still, in Marotti"s view, "there is something intractably boastful and self-advertising" that persists "despite the gestures of self-effacement" (86). Here, and in other poems such as *HSBlack*, *HSScene*, and *HSSpit*, Marotti finds that Donne "*overdramatizes the self*" (86). Marotti acknowledges that meditative exercises "might have sanctioned vivid imagery and emotional heightening in devotional acts of the imagination," but in these poems, he thinks, "the poetic act of intensification is as much one of self-reflective performing as of emotional scene-setting" (86–87).

THE HOLY SONNETS AND OTHER WORKS

Aronstein (1920, 82) finds the Holy Sonnets to resemble the Psalms in their strong sensitivity and intensity of religious experience. See also Ramsaran (1973), Patrides (1985a), Dubinski (1986), and Radzinowicz (1987).

Simpson (1924, 231) finds the *Devotions* the "nearest counterpart in prose" to the Holy Sonnets, noting that the poems "give expression in verse to the same intensity of spiritual conflict."

Hamer (1930, 202) observes that Milton adopted some of Donne's "technical habits" in his departures from the conventional divisions within the sonnet. See also Moloney (1950).

Williamson (1930, 104) argues that Herbert "carried on the strangely personal religious poetry" of Donne, but that the "sense of religious fear" in Donne prevented him from achieving a personal love of God; hence in the Holy Sonnets he could not express "a lover's praise" of God with Herbert's "emotional simplicity." To Williamson, Herbert sounds at times like a Petrarchan lover, with none of "the troubled accents of Donne's profound distress." For other comments on Donne and Herbert, see Faerber (1950), Martz (1954), Denonain (1956), Hebaisha (1971),

Ramsaran (1973), Benet (1984), Mazzaro (1987), Singleton (1987), Martz (1988), Schoenfeldt (1991), and Low (1993).

Praz (1931, 69–72) finds the Holy Sonnets closer to the poetry of Michelangelo than to that of anyone else, markedly in Donne's "peculiar mixture of realism and platonism," in "the dramatic turn of his genius," in "his laborious yearnings for beauty and religion," in his "double character of half-baffled, half-triumphant struggle," and in "his power of depicting the horrors of sin and death, and the terrible effects of the wrath of God" (72). Praz quotes comparable lines to show that the two share an "earnestness and intensity of religious thought," and that "faith has proved such a difficult conquest for them, that they are continually afraid of slackening in zeal" (69). See also Praz (1970).

Hamburger (1944, 159) observes that Hopkins's "syncopated rhythms" resemble Donne's irregularities, "the 'dromedary trot' of his muse." Hamburger argues that Donne achieved the same effect as the dramatists of his time, and compares *HSBatter* 1–4 to *Lr.* 3.2.1–6 as examples of lines where the stresses are adapted to the emotions they are meant to convey. On Hopkins and Donne, see also Morris (1953), Esch (1955), Coanda (1957), Duncan (1959), Stephenson (1959), Pawar (1987), and Low (1993).

Moloney (1944, 43) notes that "in conformity with general Anglican practice at the time," Donne's biblical citations in the Holy Sonnets were not from the King James Bible but from "the Douai edition of the Vulgate, printed in six volumes in 1617."

Wagner (1947, 253–54) concludes that a poet who writes such dramatic opening lines as those of *HSSpit* and *HSBatter* "clearly owes something to Marlowe."

Simpson (1948, 211–12) links the Holy Sonnets with the *Essays* in that the poems "draw on the apocalyptic imagery" of Revelation for "their background of 'the round earth's imagin'd corners,' the angels' trumpets, the rising of the dead from earth and sea, the dyeing of the souls in Christ's blood which makes them white, the description of Christ as 'the lamb slain from the foundation of the world,'" as seen in Rev. 7.1, 14; 8.2, 6–12; 20.13, 14; and 13.8. For comparison, Simpson cites *Essays*, pp. 1, 31, 61, 63, 113, and 168; and *Sermons*: 5:no. 4; 6:nos. 2 and 7; and 8:no. 1.

Boase (1949, 169–70) compares the Holy Sonnets to the *Théorèmes* of Jean de La Ceppède in their pictorial quality and the realism of images depicting the Passion.

Faerber (1950, 16–19) contrasts the poetry of Herbert and Donne, noting that Herbert has no fear of death, while Donne breaks it down into various categories, intellectualizing it in order to master it. In this way he defuturizes death and reduces his fear of it (16–17). Donne, says Faerber, employs parataxis, or the use of coordinating conjunctions, in his poetry, while Herbert omits them (18). He further suggests that Herbert rests confidently in his faith, demonstrating a pious openness to the future, while Donne is closed to it, anticipating and striving to take possession of it (19). See more under Holy Sonnets: Language and Style.

Mahood (1950, 145) comments that Donne's sermons combine the erudition of his prose with "the strong personal feeling" of the Holy Sonnets.

Moloney (1950, 238) observes that although he knows of "only one direct echo of Donne in Milton" (*HSMin* 1–2 and *Paradise Lost*, 1:1–2) it is possible that Donne may have been "one of Milton's prosodic mentors" and "an intermediary between English dramatists and Milton." Moloney cites as evidence the frequent appearance of "centroidal groupings" of words as in *HSRound* 6–7, *HSDeath* 9, and *HSPart* 1. The abruptness achieved by these groupings is "scarcely more emphatic" than by similar lines in Milton, e.g., *Paradise Lost*, 1:767; 2:11, 509; 3:581; 4:955; 5:352, 732; 6:866; 8:216; and 10:234.

Umbach (1951, 102) describes the Holy Sonnets as poems "not as intricately woven" as *Corona* but "more directly related in idea."

Morris (1953, 17–79, 85–100, 120, 130) writes about Gerard Manley Hopkins and T. S. Eliot in the context of the "Donne tradition." He argues a close affinity between the poetry of Donne, including the Holy Sonnets, and that of Hopkins, suggesting an indirect, if not a direct, influence (79). He observes that Hopkins most resembles Donne in the passionate intellectuality of the former's later sonnets, concluding that "it is difficult to imagine these poems having been written without the example" of the Holy Sonnets (22). Morris examines parallels between the Holy Sonnets and Hopkins's works in several respects: the union of thought and feeling (21–22), the use of the conceit (23–32), versification (41–55), assonance and alliteration (56–61), diction and syntax (61–72), and their "metaphysical" qualities (35, 73–79). Morris also finds similarities between the Holy Sonnets and some of the works of Eliot. "Prufrock" (ll. 65–69), he argues, has the same quality of self-questioning (85), and "Gerontion" (ll. 34–48) the "more personal tone" and impassioned thought of the Holy Sonnets (87–88); and, he adds, their works share some of the same poetic vocabulary (120) and syntax (130). Morris acknowledges that, although there is nothing in Eliot's poetry that corresponds to Donne's religious lyrics, the Holy Sonnets taken as a whole bear a resemblance to "Ash Wednesday," in that they share a strong sense of sin, death, and spiritual struggle and are marked by introspection and analysis. The works differ in some respects, he observes, Eliot expressing a tone of humility, for example, not found in the Holy Sonnets, where Donne is constantly tortured by doubt. Morris concludes that though Eliot is analytic and metaphysical in the poem, his style is completely different (98–100).

Martz (1954, 107–11, 144–47) contends that the difference between the sonnets of *Corona* and the Holy Sonnets lies not in Donne's spiritual maturity but in the fact that they were composed according to different meditative practices. *Corona*, he explains, was influenced by "English rosary pieces" which used a "corona of our Lord" in meditation on the life of Christ, and by the practice of continental secular poets, achieving thereby "a complex synthesis of methods and materials from both religious and profane poetry." Martz finds the corona of the Jesuit Sabin Chambers especially suggestive (107–10). On the other hand, Martz contends, the Holy Sonnets were composed in the tradition of St. Ignatius Loyola's *Spiritual Exercises*, structured according to the three powers of the soul, and hence may contain within a single sonnet "a powerful development from vivid composition of place, through devout analysis, to impassioned colloquy," resulting in "a powerful union and compression of forces within an individual poem." We should not expect, he concludes, "the compacted strength" of *HSRound* or *HSLittle* in a longer sequence that weaves one sonnet with another into a larger whole (110–11).

Martz further contrasts "the agony, the turbulence, the strenuosity of Donne" in a poem like *HSVex* 9–14 to "the comparative calm, assurance and mildness" in the poetry of Herbert. For example, in contemplating death Donne stresses the depravity of "feeble flesh," while Herbert has "no such revulsion" (144). In Donne's works, Martz continues, "the noise of thoughts is clamorous; the grief pours forth in anguished eruption" as in the "violence and tumult" of *HSBatter*. Martz attributes the contrast in the two poets to "the different schools of spirituality" in which the two had been trained or found affinity (144–45). Herbert, he argues, was no less subject to turmoil and inner conflict, but wrote in the tradition of St. Francis de Sales and Scupoli's *Spiritual Combat*, which urged that while the meditant should stand in fear of God, he must maintain a tranquility of mind, with his sorrow "calm and moderate," since any disquiet would displease God. The Holy Sonnets combined this fear with love of God, but, Martz argues, the Jesuit training allowed for "greater violence in both directions" than did the Salesian (146–47).

Cruttwell (1954, 11) finds that Shakespeare's sonnets on "the dark lady" (nos. 127–52) may be taken as a single poem in the same way that the Holy Sonnets are a single poem. See also Ferry (1983).

Esch (1955, 54) concludes that, because of his ability to achieve a balance between thought and emotion in his "terrible sonnets," Gerard Manley Hopkins is Donne's only legitimate successor in the composition of religious sonnets.

Coanda (1957, 186–87) finds many parallels between the works of Donne and Hopkins, in their sense of movement, note of anguish, expansion of the sonnet form, and imagery. He concludes that "at their best the two are most alike, near-mystic and quite metaphysical."

Duncan (1959, 101) suggests that the Holy Sonnets influenced some of Hopkins's late "terrible" sonnets.

Stephenson (1959, 301–310, 320) acknowledges the contributions of Gardner (1952) and Martz (1954) (see Dating and Order and Genres and Traditions) but insists that Donne, while admittedly "a poet of meditation," is not "the poet of the Spiritual Exercises," since they were "distinctly Catholic." He argues that there are similarities in the use of language between Donne and Hopkins, in that they both employ the "rhythms of living speech" and express "the very movement of consciousness" (301–02). Stephenson finds parallel phrases in *HSMade* and "The Wreck of the Deutschland," but argues that the similarities do not necessarily indicate influence, for there is no evidence that Hopkins ever read Donne (304). In analyzing rhythm he finds the "wonderfully controlled *tempo*, the grave majestic movement, the richly various and subtle music of the Holy Sonnets" much superior to Hopkins' sprung rhythm (305–07); but he goes on to say that Hopkins is superior to Donne as a religious poet "because his Christian vision is deeper and more inclusive" (309). Stephenson argues that the Holy Sonnets are "'biblical' in a rather narrowly Protestant sense," *HSScene*, for example, presenting a "rather closed world of religious experience" in contrast to Hopkins's "more open world" (310). He concludes that Donne lacks Hopkins' spirituality, his "strong sense of Christ's presence and action in history" (320).

Ellrodt (1960, 2:239–40) briefly associates Lope de Vega's *Soledades* and the Holy

Sonnets, noting that Lope de Vega may remind a reader of Donne in those poems that express the cry of the Christian conscience, but he adds that affinities between the two do not necessarily indicate that Donne, writing earlier, influenced Lope.

Satterthwaite (1960, 211–13) is concerned with Donne's sense of conflict and of violent feeling, particularly in the Holy Sonnets (211). He compares the final line of DuBellay's Sonnet 109 and the last two lines of *HSWhat* (213).

Banzer (1961, 417–19, 433) claims that Emily Dickinson, "like Donne, sought release in a poetry of paradox, argument, and unifying conceits" (417). Quoting *HSBatter*, she adds: "His orthodoxy hard-won, a middle-aged Donne demanded of God both intellectual rest and emotional satisfaction" (418). Banzer points to similarities in the technique of the two poets, the most crucial being "their use of Anglo-Saxon and Latinate words as double witnesses of the truth in one phrase"; the abandonment of "regular metrics to assist the immediacy of the speaking voice"; the development of a poem following the "thesis of its opening line or by the elaboration of a radiant conceit"; "the use of religious phraseology to express profane love"; and a "fondness for paradoxical arguments" (419). She concludes that Dickinson's "inner vision and unifying style" are links to Donne, who "argued the community of all 'that which God doth touch and own'" (433).

Cohen (1963, 166–69) discusses the Holy Sonnets alongside examples of the Baroque lyric, including poems by Bartolomé Leonardo de Argensola, Miguel de Guevara La Ceppède, and Andreas Gryphius, and finds Donne's poems characteristically engaged in "uninhibited self-examination" and thus "more intense" (166). See also Hemmerich (1965).

Samson (1963, 46–52), writing about relationships between poetry and music, notes that not all poetry is ideal for a song writer, observes that most metaphysical poetry is not appropriate for musical setting, and discusses Benjamin Britten's settings of the Holy Sonnets. She suggests that they make the already complex poetry almost impossible to follow and that the songs are therefore less satisfying in performance than the poems alone are. She notes that the Australian composer Dorian LeGallienne has also set the Holy Sonnets to music with similarly mixed results, and she concludes that Donne's poems have not yielded much in the way of successful music, pointing to such qualities as subtle irony, abrupt transitions from one mood to another, complex and learned imagery, sudden shifts of tone, and the rhythmic patterns of speech that make it difficult, if not impossible, for a song writer to achieve an effective result. See also Morris (1972), Gaston (1986), Docherty (1988), Martz (1988), and Makurenkova (1994).

Sparrow (1964, 625–53) points out John Wesley's use of the Divine Poems as hymn lyrics which, through Wesley, became known to the Moravians who finally published a hymn book containing many of these poems. The poems were altered to fit the tunes. He sees this Hymnal as an attempt to popularize, in the form of hymns for congregational singing, a not inconsiderable body of religious poetry.

Hemmerich (1965, 18–23) compares Andreas Gryphius with Donne and notes that both poets wrote over a number of years, with developing interests. Hemmerich quotes from *HSVex* and *HSMade* in order to display his belief that fear and love are the object of both poets. But in Donne, he says, contrition always provokes passion.

Honig and Williams (1968, 9–11) point to the "typical Donneian dialogue of conflict" (11) as, for example, in the Holy Sonnets and suggest that this feature connects his poetry more to that of Crashaw and Marvell than that of Vaughan and Herbert.

Bald (1970b, 234–35) suggests parallels between Donne's spiritual state and Bunyan's account of his conversion in *Grace Abounding*, quoting from Bunyan and comparing selected passages from *Grace Abounding* with *HSBlack, HSBatter, HSDue, HSScene, HSMin,* and *HSWhy.*

In his study of the parallel between literature and the visual arts, Praz (1970, 45, 97–100) compares the Holy Sonnets to the sonnets of Michelangelo. While Michelangelo is unique in the Italian tradition of Neoplatonic sonneteers, Praz argues, the Holy Sonnets offer some similarities to Michelangelo's poems. He says that both Donne and Michelangelo struggled in their faith and were continually afraid of slackening in their zeal. Both, he says, tried to overcome the aridity of their hearts, and both felt a barrier between themselves and God that only God could break down. Praz also contends that Donne's chief trait does not lie in his conceits and witticisms but in the "nervous dialectic of his impassioned mind," which finds parallels in the poetry of Maurice Scève and may be traced to Petrarch. "Donne uses the elements of the Petrarchan subject matter," Praz states, "but in a bizarre, unorthodox way that recalls the use of classical elements by Michelangelo in the anteroom of the Laurentian Library" (97). Further, says Praz, there are certain affinities of Donne with the proceedings of mannerist painters, in particular in the prominence given to an accessory detail, turning upside down what in other poets would have been the normal process (97). He observes that Donne's "tortuous line of reasoning" often takes the form of a statement, reversed by a "but" at the beginning of a line (97). He provides several examples from the Songs and Sonets and then turns to the Holy Sonnets, citing *HSMade* 11, *HSRound* 9, *HSSpit* 5–6, and *HSBatter* 8, 10 (100).

Hebaisha (1971, 62–63) finds the difference between Herbert and Donne more one of "technique" than in the "kind of faith reached." Hebaisha argues that while Herbert's poems deal with the memory of "the moment of doubt," Donne's poetry deals with "the moment of doubt, at the moment of doubt." Hebaisha concludes, though, that Donne's tone does not necessarily suggest that "his faith was any less secure than Herbert's" (63).

Morris (1972, 244–49) comments on Benjamin Britten's settings of nine of Donne's Holy Sonnets, finding that Britten's success is primarily attributable to two factors: (1) Britten "saw that the essence of drama in music is the single emotional impact of thematic material to be developed," and (2) he understood that the "rhythms of his vocal line" need not be "limited by those of the poem" (245). Morris proceeds to analyze each of the sonnets, giving particular attention to *HSBlack, HSShe* ("the centre of the cycle, its climax and one of Britten's finest achievements" [246]), and *HSDeath* ("a masterpiece of control and restraint" [248]). In his settings, Morris observes, Britten handled Donne's texts with "intelligence and transparent honesty," and, technically, he "succeeded in finding musical expression for Donne's phraseology." The musical cycle shows, Morris concludes, "how a composer who is inward with Donne's unique mode of utterance and his very personal dramatic sense can give them perfect expression" (249).

Warnke (1972, 135) observes that Constantijn Huygens's "Paeschen" ("Easter") is reminiscent of the Holy Sonnets in the "complex way" the poem "investigates the image of blood," suggesting at once "human lust," "mortal punishment," and, through Christ's blood, "redemption."

Ramsaran (1973, 159–63) notes that, whereas Donne's *Corona* is "skillfully unified in conception and execution" (160), his Holy Sonnets more directly express "spiritual conflicts" that recall the Psalms to "recharge them with the fresh currents of the new dispensation of Christian experience" (161). Ramsaran argues that the Holy Sonnets lack the tenderness of love of the *Padas* of Tulasī Dāsa or George Herbert's lyrics. He suggests that, in their tone, the Holy Sonnets recall "the severity of an inexorable Old Testament prophet" (161). Ramsaran compares Donne's Holy Sonnets with the Psalm translations of Sir Philip Sidney and the Countess of Pembroke, as well as the *Vinaya Patrikā*, calling them all "confessionals of the soul" in which the "feelings, emotions and divine aspirations" are the "means and the end of a religious poetry inspired by the bhakti" [i.e., "loving devotion to a personal God as manifested in His incarnations" (1)] (163).

Fuzier (1976, 153–71) finds in all of the Holy Sonnets parallels to the work of Ronsard, DuBellay, La Ceppède, and Lazare de Selve. See also Prescott (1978).

Prescott (1978, 115) argues that several passages in Donne's poetry "strikingly resemble" moments in the poetry of Ronsard.

Mano (1979, 10) compares the mystical orientation of the poetry of Donne and St. John of the Cross, and concludes: "though their language and imagery are similar, Donne and St. John begin from different starting blocks, different premises," for St. John "has attained and needs to express," whereas Donne "needs to express so that he—and his reader—might hope to attain" (10).

Stachniewski (1981, 683) rejects the notion that Donne's primary source of inspiration was *The Spiritual Exercises* of St. Ignatius, since these have their source in ancient exercises, arguing instead that Donne "regarded Augustine and Calvin jointly as the greatest Bible exegetes, and Calvin, the more immediate figure."

Den Boer (1982, 139, 149–56) discusses the influence of Donne on Constantijn Huygens (1596–1687) and reviews a number of twentieth-century translations of the Holy Sonnets into Dutch. See also Daley (1990b).

Stull (1982b, 130, 135) claims that Donne, Herbert and Milton, "while far excelling their Tudor predecessors," nonetheless write in "the same literary tradition" as authors such as Constable, Barnes, Lok, and Alabaster, and even decidedly minor figures such as Nicholas Breton, John Davies of Hereford, and William Drummond of Hawthornden (135). Stull suggests that this relationship with the earlier poets accounts for the appearance of Constable's sonnet "On the Blessed Virgin Mary" following Donne's *HSPart* in the 1635 edition of Donne's poems, where it is assumed to be a poem by Donne (130).

Ellrodt (1983, 19–22, 27–29) situates his study of such works as *Sat3*, *HSShow*, *HSWhat*, and *HSBatter* in the context of a larger consideration of Mannerism and the Baroque, finding not only in the poetry of the period but also in the art signs of emotional agitation, violent movements, bizarre poses, and intellectual indifference (20). This art, which Ellrodt associates with Mannerism, attempts to create an impression of instantaneousness, by grasping the intensity; it is an art of expectation, since it leaves its viewers in suspense (21). Poetry before Donne expresses the feeling, Ellrodt observes, but Donne and his authentic successors bring to life again the moment where an individual gains consciousness of an emotion and expresses it in a dramatic monologue with the shock of its beginning, as in HSWhat 1 (21). Ellrodt finds in his analysis of the work of de Vinci and Tintoretto, for example, a space rigorously closed so that infinity becomes enclosed in a tight space, eternity quivers in the true moment (22). This is the fundamental paradox, according to Ellrodt, that Donne transposes into triumphant certainties in his sacred poetry, that is, the image of the alliance that Donne creates between the sharp sense of earthly things and the haunting desire for an eruption of the transcendent into this opaque and tangible world (22). It is not surprising, for Ellrodt, that Donne may show less diversity in his religious poetry, perhaps also less truth in certain Holy Sonnets which appear too much like "spiritual exercises," which Donne may or may not have modeled on Jesuit "meditation" (27). Donne's piety, according to Ellrodt, has been called Baroque, but it appears still essentially Mannerist (27). Whereas the Baroque seeks to unite heaven and earth, to reconcile the flesh and the spirit, to confuse in erotic mysticism spirituality and sensuality, the tension of Mannerist art, in Ellrodt's view, rests on an exacerbated dualism, in which the lack of confidence and sense of abandon express anxiety and call up asceticism (27).

Ferry (1983, 219–221) points to resemblances between Donne's Holy Sonnets and Shakespeare's sonnets, suggesting the possibility that Donne may have read Shakespeare's poems, or at the least that Donne's sonnets are part of a longer sonnet tradition in England (219). In one respect, Ferry notes, Donne's sonnets are closer to those of Sidney, in that "they have only two rhymes in the octave, usually in two closed quatrains," but they are like Shakespeare's in that "they always rhyme the last two lines" (219). Ferry recalls Cruttwell's (1966) observation of a shared "introspectiveness" in a comparison of HSVex and Shakespeare's Sonnet 62, with the latter "an adaptation of Astrophil and Stella 27" (219–20). Shakespeare's Sonnet 19 and Donne's HSDeath share the device of employing "the rhetorical strategy of boastfully challenging a personified abstraction" (220). Both Shakespeare and Donne, in Ferry's view, expand the "traditional metaphor of man's body and soul as a world," Shakespeare in Sonnet 146 and Donne in HSLittle (220). And HSShe "does seem to echo Shakespeare's Sonnet 144," Ferry thinks, in that the situations in the two poems "are close enough, and bizarre enough, to suggest imitation" (220). Ferry finds that both poets "associate the speaker as poet with the same struggle to find a true language for what is in the heart that Shakespeare made the concern of his poet-lover, on the model of Astrophil" (221).

Raspa (1983, 74) finds that the grouping of Donne's religious sonnets into, first, the Corona sequence on "Christian Mysteries" and, second, the Holy Sonnets on "his personal spiritual life" might be likened to the Jesuit Francis Borgia's distinction between "'crownes' on Mysteries and those on 'the obteyning of Christian Perfection' [in The Practice of Christian Perfection]" (74). Raspa emphasizes that "this division is found in the work of no other English sonneteer except Alabaster and was the major distinction of meditative topics in the tradition of *Exercises*" (74). For another comment on *Corona* and the Holy Sonnets, see Pinnington (1987).

Benet (1984, 133–34) draws a comparison between the religious poetry of George Herbert and Donne's Holy Sonnets, claiming that "many of Herbert's poems end in a quiet dissolution of the problem or conflict they depict," whereas Donne's sonnets, with their typical focus on the speaker's "doubts and fears," usually conclude "with his unrest and turmoil unaltered" (133–34).

Martinet (1984,1–3) finds analogies between Vaughan's *Silex Scintillans* (1650–55) and prior collections: Donne's Holy Sonnets and Herbert's *The Temple* (1). Both the introductory passages of Vaughan's poem and the final "distich" ("distique") of HSBlack, which precedes a reflection on "The Last Things," have their source in the biblical passages Rev. 1.5 and Isa. 1.18, that is, on prophetic and apocalyptic times (2–3). Martinet finds another direct parallel in the evocation of Ps. 69 in Vaughan's "The Lamp" and HSBlack, both of which are on time and sin (3).

Sherwood (1984, 143, 146, 156) claims that in the Holy Sonnets, as in lyrics like ValWeep, "suffering is the measure of love," and thus "penitential mourning, guided by the affecting image of the crucified Christ, works to nullify the sinful grief of idolatry, reforming one love with another" (143). In Sherwood's view, "widespread adaptation of the Petrarchan sonnet for devotional uses lengthened further a Christian tradition that, by intersecting the vocabularies of secular and divine love, adapted easily to repentance" (146). Sherwood cites the sonnets of the French poet Antoine Favre as one example of the "commonplace tie" of Donne's Holy Sonnets to the Continental background (146). Sherwood concludes that Donne sees in "God's several faces the expressions of divine love that guide the human struggle to reform idolatrous love in accordance with divine pattern" (156).

Stull (1984, 3, 8) looks at the Holy Sonnets in the context of the writings of several other poets, including William Alabaster. He argues that Alabaster's sonnets anticipate the Holy Sonnets in their "metaphysical style and meditative tone" (3) and that, indeed, they suggest that in his poems Donne was "unoriginal in everything but genius" (3). Stull also finds Robert Southwell to be "one of the most articulate spokesmen" for divine verse in the period, and he believes that, like Sidney, Southwell "laid the theoretical groundwork" for the religious sonnets of such varied poets as Lok, Barnes, Constable, Alabaster, Donne, Herbert, and even Milton (8).

Walls (1984, 248), in his study of the setting of Renaissance poetry to music, notes that an anonymous poem, "Down, down, afflicted soul and pay thy due/To death and misery; weep, howl, and rue. . . ," reminds one of Donne's Holy Sonnets "not just in its imperatives but in the way its sense of urgency is conveyed by enjambment which propels the verse forward."

Patrides (1985a, 42–43) sees the Psalms as a key influence on the varieties of religious experience evident in the Holy Sonnets, "re-enacted in the light of the cosmic patterns of the Christian view of history" (42). But, according to Patrides, the Book of Lamentations exerted an even more decisive influence on the Holy Sonnets (42), for its "characteristic mood of black despair could not have escaped Donne, especially once he versified its passionate cries of agony" in his own *Lam* (42). Patrides finds that the "violent imagery" in *Lam* and in the Holy Sonnets "proclaims how intermittent the sense of God's favour is, and how impossible readily to attain 'the peace that passeth understanding'" (43). But, Patrides adds, Donne was able to control "the potential hysteria" by writing *Lam* in rhyme and by adopting the "mould" of the sonnet for the Holy Sonnets (43).

Dubinski (1986, 201, 203, 205–14) finds that the seven penitential Psalms (6, 32, 38, 51, 102, 130, 143 in the Authorized Version) exerted as much if not more influence on Donne's Holy Sonnets as formal meditations (201). Dubinski cites Donne's attraction to the penitential Psalms expressed in his sermons as well as in *Sidney* (203). Dubinski claims that whereas the Psalms "speak to man's spiritual condition in the language of the Old Testament," Donne "transforms this language to talk about the same condition in the language of the New Testament," what Lewalski (1979) calls the "Protestant paradigm of salvation—election, calling, justification, adoption, sanctification, glorification" (205–07). For Dubinski *HSDue* is concerned with election, *HSScene* with justification, and *HSBatter* with regeneration and sanctification (208). But according to Dubinksi, Donne finds the penitential Psalms to be most fundamentally "prayers and praises," exhibiting a mix of "lamentations, deprecations and postulations, confessions, and thanksgivings and praises" (209). Examples cited by Dubinski include lamentation in *HSBlack* and *HSDue*, with the latter sonnet most closely resembling the laments in Psalms 38 and 102 (210–11); cleansing and purification in *HSBlack* and *HSRound*, with the latter closer to that of such Psalms as 51 (212); confession and contrition in *HSScene* and *HSMin*; and thanksgiving in several poems, including *HSSpit*, *HSWhy*, *HSWhat*, *HSWilt*, and *HSPart* (213). Dubinski concludes with the suggestion that Donne may have intended the Holy Sonnets written between 1608 and 1610 as well as other poems such as *Corona* and *Lit* "to be used in the private devotions of his friends" (214).

Evett (1986, 107–08, 113) finds "more ambiguity" in the correspondences that Roston (1974) and Martin Elsky ["La Corona: Spatiality and Mannerist Painting," *MLS* 13 (1983):3–11] see in Donne's poetry and Mannerist art (107). Evett sees Donne "too centrally and actively involved to correspond with the subordinate, passive people who usually occupy the *sprecher* role—and a position at the periphery, not the center, of the painting" (107). In Evett's view, Donne's focus on the self, which he finds in *Corona*, is represented in many other religious poems, including *HSDue*, *HSMin*, *HSBatter*, *HSMade*, *HSSighs*, *HSSouls*, *HSVex*, *Goodf*, *Christ*, *Sickness*, and *Father* (107–08). Evett concedes that each of these poems does reflect "some glimpse of freedom from the toils of the world," which Roston finds in continental Mannerism, such as that of Tintoretto and El Greco, but he believes that any "transcendent" movement is always diminished by "the final frame" of Donne's poetry, which "always shows Donne entangled in the here and now" (108). Moreover, Evett contends, "nowhere outside the drama is the flavor of street and house so strong as in Donne's work" (108, 113). Evett concludes, therefore, that like Donne's "self-centeredness," the "incessant *commonness* of his writing" challenges the assertion that he is Mannerist (113).

Gaston (1986, 202, 206, 213), citing some of Donne's other writing, points out that there is sufficient evidence to show that "he enjoyed, respected, and understood music," but observes that composers contemporary with Donne "must have been hard-pressed to cope with the challenges Donne's poetry offers" (202). More recent developments in music, musical instruments, and in vocal and instrumental technique have, according to Gaston, extended the possibilities for composition. Benjamin Britten, he notes, set nine of the Holy Sonnets to music (*HSBlack*, *HSBatter*, *HSSighs*, *HSVex*, *HSWhat*, *HSShe*, *HSRound*, *HSMade*, and *HSDeath*), a composition for "high voice and piano" that is, Gaston believes, an "elegant bridge between the twentieth and seventeenth centuries" that preserves the "complexity" of Donne's poems (206). Overall, Britten's cycle, Gaston says, moves "through different and unpredictable stages in the life of faith to achieve at the last a sense of firm confidence in the soul's immortality" (213).

Rollin (1986, 142–43) points out that both *HSWilt* and *HSPart* are "notable for their father-son motifs" and call to mind Freud's view that "the concept of God was 'a cosmic projection of the Father of our childhood'" [*The Standard Edition of the Complete Psychological Works of Sigmund Freud*, ed. James Strachey et al., 24 vols (London: Hogarth Press, 1964), 3:128].

Mazzaro (1987, 241, 244–52) compares the sonnets of Donne and Herbert, emphasizing that Herbert's poems "represent challenges to the traditional style and themes of his day in order to assert sincerity" (241). Mazzaro finds that Donne appears to be "far more influenced than Herbert by the Continent and by plays of verbal wit," as seen, for example, in *Corona* and the Holy Sonnets (244). Mazzaro points out that both Donne and Herbert use two rhyme schemes—*abbaabbacdcdee* and *abbaabbacddcee*—but in the Holy Sonnets Donne adheres more fully to rhetorical convention, "letting enjambment and verbal interplay rather than opposition to form define his character and sincerity" (245). Mazzaro writes specifically about *HSVex* and *HSDeath*, noting that the last seems true to T. S. Eliot's phrase about the metaphysical poets, namely, that "the event is so precisely realized that it seems to unify and 'devour any kind of experience'" (250). See also Mazzaro under *HSDeath*: Language and Style and *HSVex*: Language and Style.

Pawar (1987, 39–40, 44, 47–51) finds that the underlying theme in the sonnets of both Donne and Hopkins is "the terror of the soul at the prospect of an estrangement from God" (40). This terror, according to Pawar, is derived in large part from the loss of established beliefs and systems of order that pervaded the time-periods of Donne and Hopkins (39–40). For Donne, Pawar thinks, the impact of the Reformation and the Copernican revolution were central to his concerns; for Hopkins, a Jesuit living in the nineteenth century, it was the heightened interest in science, which "encouraged scepticism and doubt," along with the notion of evolution, which "had done away with the grand design of Divine creation" (40). Pawar notes that although "both poets are seeking succor from God," there is in Donne "a greater emphasis on the blackness of his sins and the fear of damnation," while in Hopkins there is a corresponding emphasis on his spiritual aridity and frustration" (40). With respect to their structure, both groups of sonnets, according to Pawar, are attentive to a progression of some kind, either "leading from despair to a resolution of despair, or leading from terror circuitously back to despair" (40). But Pawar notes that it is easier to see a thematic progression in the sonnets of Hopkins because they were all written in 1885 when he may have been experiencing a "spiritual crisis" (44). Pawar points out that both poets have been described as "Modern," given "their audacity of diction, their inversions, their unexpected images and the force of their lives" (47). Both poets, according to Pawar, are "intensely dramatic;" both are "highly skilled in using unexpected and unconventional imagery" (47–48). But the two poets differ in their conceptions of God, Pawar observes: for Donne God is identified in terms of "power and will," but Hopkins's image of God is of one "who can be terrible but who is more often a source of solace" (49). Both Donne and Hopkins, in Pawar's view, "seem to be less concerned with the nature of God, and more with their relation to God" (50). And, finally, Pawar finds that the goal of the speaker in the Holy Sonnets is that God will repeat in him (as the "microcosm") the "universal salvation history of mankind," whereas Hopkins's "terrible sonnets" are quite personal, exhibiting "none of the universal scope of time and place which is so distinctive in Donne" (50–51).

Pinnington (1987, 133–34), in contrast to other critics who have found clear contrasts between "the devotional temper" of *Corona* and that of the Holy Sonnets, sees a similar "theological understanding of the relationship between man and God" informing both sets of poems, and he argues that, "beneath the surface formality" of the Holy Sonnets, the "same spiritual anxieties" seen in *Corona* are evident (133). Pinnington points, for example, to the opening sonnet of *Corona* as illustrative of the anxieties that the two groups of sonnets reflect, namely, the "denial of any human merit: all good is from God" (134).

Radzinowicz (1987, 40–41, 45, 55) identifies five of Donne's Holy Sonnets, probably written before his ordination (*HSSighs*, *HSBlack*, *HSWhat*, *HSWilt*, and *HSSouls*), as poems that directly employ a poetical device found in eight of the Psalms, namely, "the *anima mea* device, or "the dialogue of a man with his soul" (40–41). She adds that *HSShe*, most likely written after his ordination, implies the same poetical device and that such a technique helps Donne distinguish between "a speaker and the agency of his inner feeling," a distinction that later informed his preaching, namely, "the combination of believer and teacher" (41). The Psalms, Radzinowicz believes, and in particular their dialogic nature, exemplify the "combination of personal and congregational lyric voice that moves [Donne's] poetry toward his priestly vocation" (41). She adds that "the value of the device . . . lies in the distinction it permits between the protagonist as teacher and his soul as pupil" (55). Three of the sonnets written before Donne's ordination (*HSSighs*, *HSBlack*, and *HSWhat*) are, according to Radzinowicz, "fully penitential," representing "the self-examination of a man spiritual by nature but reluctant to take holy orders" (45).

Singleton (1987, 9, 207n) considers those poets who may have provided the "courtly contexts" (9) for Donne's poetry, but is "not convinced that the courtly ideal *as* an ideal—either to aspire toward, resist, reject, or reshape—exerted power over Donne as it did for Sidney, or Herbert, or Carew" (207n). Singleton acknowledges the courtly references in *HSShow* 12 and *HSVex* 10, but she contends that these two sonnets "by no means typify Donne's self-figuration in his religious poems" (207n). Singleton, cites, for example, *HSBatter*, with its "far more characteristic drama and extremity," and she adds that "Donne's various roles in the secular poetry seldom play on conflicts between courtly ideal and actuality" (207n).

G. Smith (1987, 167–69,175) associates Gwendolyn Brooks's "best work" not only with the "protest tradition" of the Harlem Renaissance, but also the "traditional and contemporary styles of European and American poetry," finding that the "precise juggling of these various and complex traditions" is the quality that "contributes to the metaphysical quality of her verse" (167). Smith contends that, like Donne, Brooks "creates a depth and range of feeling in her poetry that often overshadows her commonplace subject matter" and that she "displays a metaphysical wit that features startling and incongruent figures of speech," using "poetic diction that is a mixture of formal and colloquial speech" (167). According to Smith, Brooks's sonnet sequence, *The Children of the Poor*, has many of the "stylistic difficulties" found in the Holy Sonnets, but thematically Brooks's sequence is a "distinct departure" from Donne (169). Brooks "does not adhere to the theme of resolution," he notes, and while, like Donne, she "entertains questions of religious faith in her sonnets," Brooks "rejects religion as a viable means of resolving complex social problems" (169). Finally, while in the sonnets of both Brooks and Donne "love plays a decisive role," Brooks is "most adept at describing its absence" (169).

Thorpe (1987,138–40) compares some of the dramatic opening lines of Donne's Holy Sonnets with opening lines from Francis Bacon's *Essays* (138). Both writers, Thorpe claims, "invite us to go on and read the remainder of the sonnet or the essay," but whereas Donne's openings are "personal," those of Bacon are "impersonal" (139–40). Donne's openings, according to Thorpe, "are generally in the first or second persons; the speaker of the poem is talking in his own person about himself, or he is making a petition in the imperative, or he is addressing another or a part of himself" (140). And, Thorpe adds, because the poems are personal, "they also speak to us as fellow human beings" (140). The openings from Bacon, however, are impersonal, that is, "they are all in the third person . . . they are all assertions of opinion directed at the world at large," and "they are spoken on behalf of enunciating a truth," wherein "their appeal is intellectual" (140).

Docherty (1988, 2, 11) compares Britten's musical settings of the Holy Sonnets and Michael Tippett's setting in *The Heart's Assurance*, noting that Tippett believed that it was necessary "to destroy all the verbal music of the poetry he set and to substitute 'the music of music,'" while Britten follows a practice of "designing a musical structure compliant to his purpose while according the words the care of the poet whose art they first were" (2). She concludes that neither approach is inherently "better" as each reveals a "new range of sensibilities" an artist seeks to disclose, sensibilities "beyond the capacity of words or music individually to express" (11).

Martz (1988, 21, 23–25, 27–28, 31–34) explores at considerable length what he sees as "essential differences" between the poetry of Donne and Herbert by focusing on their "common theme of sighs and tears" (21). Martz finds an unsettled perspective, a "theological uncertainty," in poems such as *HSBlack* and *HSDue*, and he suggests that the Holy Sonnets "arise from dual causes of vehement grief—a profound personal sense of sin and a deeply troubled theological outlook that finds it difficult to resolve that vehement grief" (24). But Martz also points to *HSPart* 11–12, which he claims "resolve that vehement grief," at least "tentatively" and "optatively," in their "intricate, legal metaphors" ("all-healing grace and spirit/Revive againe what law and letter kill") (24). Donne concludes, according to Martz, "by throwing his hope upon the gospel of love revealed by St. John" and uttered at the end of HSPart, with its hope "for mercy rather than justice" (24). Martz finds this to be a "vast area of human experience" Herbert is aware of (e.g., in "The Holdfast" and "The Method") but does not explore (25). Martz points to the hope embedded in the "heroic, histrionic image" in HSSouls 1–4 but finds that such an image "marks the immense difference between the world of grief that these two poets inhabit" (27). Martz notes that in his poem "The Familie," Herbert "struggles to avoid such histrionic gestures, both in himself and in the larger family of the Christian community" (27), yielding evidence of a "basic concept of expressive control that lies at the center of Herbert's poetic and, no doubt, at the center of his conception of the Christian life" (28).

Martz points out that music is not often associated with Donne, observing that Benjamin Britten's settings of the Holy Sonnets are among his "least successful efforts" (31). Martz goes on to distinguish the "value" of Herbert's poetry from that of Donne by the manner in which Herbert's poems "dance and pirouette above the theological issues, dance above the old facts of history," liberating themselves from the "stern and warring doctrines of the time" (32). Donne, in contrast, according to Martz, experiencing the "deep anxiety" of trying to find the "one true Spouse of Christ," ends up devouring the "entire universe of controverted divinity," and in so doing, his poetry "conquers by vehement attack upon the Gordian knot," winning by asking God to "ravish him, thus merging the worlds of flesh and spirit in the only way possible to his erotic self" (33). Martz admits a reluctance to say that either poet is "better," but he acknowledges that if, "approaching a desert island upon a sinking ship, one were driven to make a choice, I would, like the poet Camoens, rescuing his manuscript from shipwreck, hold my volume of Donne above the waves" (34). Martz also examines each in relation to "European schools of spirituality" while he resists a view that either—especially Herbert—is defined within a "particular range of Protestantism" identified as "Calvinist" (33). Martz concludes that the "poetic" of Protestant writers like Donne and Herbert was "broad enough to include many different religious impulses generated on the continent" (33). According to Martz, Donne seems more closely aligned with Spain, "with the vehement grief of its bleeding statues and the strenuous, anxious art of El Greco, attempting to stride and stretch from earth to heaven," while Herbert seems more associated with the "gentler lessons of devout humanism in France and Italy, the lessons of tranquility and silent tears" (34).

Daley (1990b, 23, 26, 86–87) finds the emotional state expressed "so poignantly" in HSMade to be similar to that articulated in Goodf (26). Daley compares Constantijn Huygens's translation of Goodf with Donne's original, finding that Huygens's traveler "knew that the process of sanctification had begun and that God would recognize him and eventually glorify him in heaven," whereas Donne's traveler (and his speaker in HSMade) are both in early and middle stages of such a process. Donne's traveler, he further observes, "will implore, even demand, justification," as does the speaker in HSBatter (26). Daley goes on to cite Colie

(1959), who believes that there are "overtones" of Donne's Holy Sonnets in Huygens's religious poetry, especially in *Heilighe Daghen* (86). Daley agrees that the two poets share such features as "colloquial style, occasional rough language, and abrupt opening questions" (86). But Daley also finds some crucial differences: unlike Donne's sonnets, Huygens's sonnets "witness his unshakable faith in the grace of a forgiving God," and "the demanding voice of Donne's persona is absent," along with "his near despair and oscillating attitudes" (86–87).

Gorbunov (1990, 87) thinks that a kind of peace and simplicity in the tone of Donne's Hymns distinguishes them from the internal conflict, fear, doubt and pain of the Holy Sonnets, written earlier in his career.

Porter (1991, 11–12) contends that the Holy Sonnets are "the finest examples of baroque in English literature, the equivalent in words of Bernini's architecture and sculpture" (11), concluding that Donne is "never moderate," instead, living "always on the high ground" (12).

Schoenfeldt (1991, 130–31, 159, 239, 262–63, 320n) finds that throughout George Herbert's *The Temple* "pain mediates the relationship between divinity and humanity," but the pain that Herbert experiences "is very different from the masochism of Donne or Crashaw" (130). Donne "begs" God to "Batter my heart" (130), whereas Herbert "is not seeking the pain, but lamenting it" (131). And although Donne states in *HSVex* that "those are my best dayes, when I shake with feare," Herbert's "best" dayes, as reflected in "The Storm," are those "spent in a tempest that blends internal suffering with external aggression" (159). Focusing on the two sonnets of Herbert entitled "Love," Schoenfeldt remarks that for Herbert "the erected wit, if not directed exclusively towards God, is the product of infected will" (239), but Herbert's second sonnet on love "looks forward to the prospect of rectifying this faculty" (239). In *HSLittle*, Donne similarly juxtaposes "the fire/Of lust" to the "fiery zeale" of God, "which doth in eating heale" (320n). Furthermore, two of Donne's Holy Sonnets (*HSBatter* and *HSShow*) engage in "a superficially similar sexualization of his relationship with God" that Schoenfeldt finds in Herbert's "Love (III)" (262). But Donne's "blend of erotic and religious impulses" is explicit (262), whereas in Herbert's "Love (III)" the eroticism is "at once more delicate and more deeply engrained in the divine" (263). In *HSShow*, according to Schoenfeldt, the "vast differences between earthly and heavenly promiscuity are underscored by the apparent contradiction of the final couplet, in which Christ's spouse, the Church, is 'most new, and pleasing to thee, then / When she'is embrac'd and open to most men'" (262). And, similarly, in *HSBatter*, "the paradox of a rape which makes one chaste is readily understood as a form of divine rapture stated in erotic terms" (262). Schoenfeldt, citing Kerrigan (1974), adds that in Donne we see the "'awful discrimination' of heavenly and earthly love" (263), whereas in Herbert we see their "equally awe-inspiring similarity" (263).

Todd (1991, 114–16) finds in Carew's elegy on Donne a consciousness of the impact of the death of Donne, "the poetic and rhetorical exemplar" (114). Carew struggles, according to Todd, with "what happens when any poet remaining on earth after the subject's departure attempts to imitate Donne's inimitable poetic gifts" (114). Todd finds that the "striking metrical liberties" and "accentual cataloguings" seen in such Holy Sonnets as *HSRound* and *HSBatter* are evoked by Carew's description of the poet in lines 76–82 (114–15). Todd points out that others have "sporadically noted" many echoes of Donne's works, including the Holy Sonnets, in Carew's poem (116).

Fishelov (1992, 187–89) draws close parallels between the poetry of Amichai and Donne, without obscuring the modernism of Amichai's verse. For example, both poets "connect the domain of elevated spiritual religion with the domain of corporal mundane love" (187). In *HSVex*, for example, Donne "describes praying in terms appropriate for courting a woman," and in his *HSDeath* he "concludes his passionate prayer by asking God to 'ravish' him" (187). Fishelov adds, however, that this similarity between the two poets draws out an important difference: "Donne *accepts* the high associations involved in the religious domain and exploits them in order to build a new notion of love, a holy kind of love" (187). But when Amichai "juxtaposes high religious concepts and mundane love, the high religious terms are usually parodied and devaluated," as in "Poems for a Woman" (187–88). Fishelov notes that unlike Donne's "fundamental criterion," Amichai's "measuring rod is secular and existential" (189).

Frontain (1992, 85–87, 91–93, 96, 100) calls attention to the heightened anxiety evident in Donne's poetry, and particularly in the Elegies and Holy Sonnets, brought about by the Protestant Reformation's stress on individual faith over church rituals and on a God whose wrath toward the unsaved was not mitigated by the church or individual action. Frontain notes that Donne states in his sermons that "people can only cooperate with God's prevenient grace, they cannot instigate the process of their own salvation" (*Sermons*, 2:305) (87). In the face of such overwhelming odds, according to Frontain, Donne's speakers in the Holy Sonnets undertake a "rhetorical campaign" to be "'imputed righteous' [*HSScene* 13]" (86). In Frontain's view, the model for Donne's rhetorical strategy is similar to that seen in certain Psalms that "simultaneously implore and assure the Lord's action on the speaker's behalf" (86). But Frontain points out that, unlike the Psalms, the Holy Sonnets "give no assurance that . . . assistance [from God] was ever provided," and thus, "the reader remains as anxiously suspended as the speaker" (100). Frontain notes that the Psalms do not "betray an autonomous ego at all" but instead "narrate the process of the self in search of a partner," recording the "breaking of the imprisoning subjectivity that is the very plight of Donne's speaker in the Holy Sonnets" (96).

Skulsky (1992, 118–19, 265–66) claims that in the "serial drama" of the Holy Sonnets, Donne's "Christian soldier is another Renaissance incarnation of Thraso, the braggart soldier of Roman comedy" (118). Donne's speaker, in Skulsky's view, is a "Christian Thraso who wants his audience to imagine that his faith leaves no room for fears of death or of what comes afterward" (118). But Skulsky poses the question: "Why would a Christian poet purposely inflict a terrified word corrupter on his Christian readers?" (118). One possible answer, according to Skulsky, is that for "an incurably fissured creature, self-preservation lies in exploring the fissure" (118).

Spiller (1992, 177–80) finds Herbert's early sonnet "My God, where is that ancient heat towards thee" to be "quite remarkably transgressive" and in the spirit of Donne's mature poems (178). Spiller explains the poetic transgressions in both poets as "the dramatizing of the pressure of speech in a new way" (179). Spiller's suggestion that Donne's later verse was influential on the "very first sonnets" of Herbert rests on Donne's acquaintance with Herbert's mother between 1604 and her death in 1627, and on the likelihood that Donne was acquainted with the young Herbert when the latter was living in London (1604–09) with possible access to some of Donne's sonnets and perhaps *Corona* (179–80). But what distinguishes Donne's sonnets from those by Herbert is "violent eclipsis (omission of normally necessary words), a kind of compression which Herbert did not like," in Spiller's view, given Herbert's attraction to the "plainness of style" (180).

Carpenter (1993, 286), studying Donne's poetry in the context of T. S. Eliot's essay on the poetry of Sir John Davies (in *On Poetry and Poets*. London: Faber, 1957, pp. 132–37), writes that Eliot found Davies "speak[ing] like a man reasoning with himself in solitude," never raising his voice. In contrast, according to Carpenter, Eliot found Donne, influenced by the Latin rhetoricians, "always raising his voice from the page in secular or spiritual contexts," and in his verse ("full of theatrical posing," as in *HSSpit*) Eliot found, says Carpenter, a poetry that is "pathologically rhetorical."

Di Nola (1993, 105–49) compares and contrasts at some length the Holy Sonnets and the poetry of the Italian Dominican theologian, philosopher, and astrologer, Tommaso Campanella (1538–1639), showing how their philosophical and religioius ideas inform their lives and poetry and observing how both men are intrigued by self-analysis and by the metaphysical questions of their day. Di Nola compares their eschatological and anthropological perspectives and stresses their attention to the theme of repentance and contrition, demonstrating how each incarnates the values of Christian theology in their poetry, albeit in unique ways. Di Nola includes in his discussion comments on *HSSpit*, *HSSighs*, *HSMade*, *HSDeath*, *HSRound*, *HSWhy*, *HSVex* and *HSWhat*.

Low (1993, 85–86) contends that the "repeated failure of love" in Donne's religious verse leads to his having "far less direct influence on the devotional poets who followed him than George Herbert" (85), poets who preferred a pattern of "doubt followed by faith and questions followed by answers—not struggle followed by failure or prayer followed by silence" (85–86). But, Low adds, Donne spoke "strongly to the troubled and disillusioned sensibilities of later ages: to Gerard Manley Hopkins in the 'terrible' sonnets, to T. S. Eliot before his public conversion, to the many modern composers who have set his Holy Sonnets to music, and to many others of our century who have found God harder to reach than Donne's contemporaries" (86). Finally, Low notes, Donne perhaps speaks even more "to those who live in the absence of God and find all talk of 'relation' inconceivable in such a context" (86).

Pallotti (1993,170–71), focusing on the interrogative mode as the prevailing discourse pattern between the speaker and hearer in Donne's Holy Sonnets, emphasizes that the act of questioning has its roots within the "tradition of religion," such as in Job, the Psalms, and Jeremiah (170). But Pallotti adds that for the "biblical questioners such as Job, the recognition of the impossibility of intellectually grasping divine mystery and paradox leads them to repose confidence in God," whereas in the Holy Sonnets the "same recognition leads the speaking subject to doubt, to uncertainty, to fear" (171).

Davies (1994, 66–67) contends that readers of Donne's Holy Sonnets seldom feel that they "are witnessing a verbal process representative of the act of contrition, but rather a dizzy, dazzling reportage of the experience of life," a kind of "performance-art" (66). In Davies's view, "grace is not within reach" so long as the speaker continues to perform," as in HSBlack 9–10 ("Yet grace, if thou repent, thou canst not lacke;/ But who shall give thee that grace to beginne?") (66). For Davies, the lines echo Faustus's dialogue in Marlowe's play: "Accursed Faustus, where is mercy now?/I do repent, and yet I do despair;/Hell strives with grace for conquest in my breast" (18.70–72) (66), and he observes that, like Faustus, Donne's "struggle" is also a kind of "staged event" that he is not ready to abandon (66). Thus, Davies adds, in HSScene the speaker "expresses a Faustian sense of shock at the termination of the time allotted to his performance," and his only hope, Davies claims, is that his body "will take all the hellbent sins down into the grave with it: a nonsense" (66). But in some of the sonnets, such as HSRound 9, 13–14 and HSVex 12–13, Davies thinks, a "more tender note" is apparent (66–67).

Low and Harding (1994, 12–13) cite Ferry's (1983) observation (see Holy Sonnets: Language and Style) that in the Holy Sonnets Donne's speakers express "a kind of modern consciousness" (12), finding Ferry's perspective supportive of the view that some seventeenth-century poets anticipate Romanticism in their attention to an "inner life" and a "real self," even though, as Ferry asserts, the language of a "modern consciousness" was not available to Donne and his contemporaries (12). According to Low and Harding, Donne, like Wordsworth, "responds to crisis by a kind of reality-testing, trying to fix experience to a specific moment" (13).

Makurenkova (1994, 45) observes that with the exception of a beautifully written melody by Browning, there have not been too many attempts to revive the musical tradition of Donne's songs. But in 1945, Makurenkova notes, Benjamin Britten turned to Donne's poetry, composing music for the Holy Sonnets in which the poet's voice is woven into the chorus of twentieth-century European culture, renouncing the evil of Nazism.

Rollin (1994, 51–58) claims that Donne's Devotions can be better understood if it is viewed as a sequel to the Holy Sonnets, a view that supports Mary Papazian's contention ["Donne, Election, and the Devotions upon Emergent Occasions," HLQ 55 (1992): 617] that the Devotions are not so much a "meditative exercise on sickness" as a "dramatic account of the speaker's fall into affliction," thus sharing characteristics with Donne's "impassioned religious poetry" (51). Rollin finds the "central theme" of the Devotions to be basically the same as that of the Holy Sonnets: "the effects upon a susceptible Christian of what might be called 'spiritual malaise'" (51). Having gone "largely untreated" in the Holy Sonnets, according to Rollin, it is "considerably ameliorated if not cured" in the Devotions (51). In Rollin's view, the Devotions "constitute a positive lesson in holy dying, a typically Donnean innovation upon the tradition of ars moriendi" (53). Rollin argues that both the Holy Sonnets and Devotions confirm that seventeenth-century devotional writings are "more public than private," functioning as "vehicles for the diagnosis of spiritual malaise and as sources of remedies, as, in the end, acts of caritas more than of self-expression" (53). Acknowledging that a few Holy Sonnets (e.g., HSWhy, HSWilt, HSPart) might be described (in Burton's language) as "wholesome meditations" (56), Rollin sees the Donne persona as more likely swinging between "profound depression" and something akin to "sheer mania" (54). No matter in what order the Holy Sonnets are read, Rollin adds, readers will confront "disorder—disorder within or between or among poems" (54). In Rollin's view, the Holy Sonnets remain "deconstructed and that is the source of their power; the *Devotions* are reconstructed and that is the source of *their* power" (55). Rollin concludes that the *Devotions* are the "penultimate act of the divine comedy of John Donne," in which are "largely resolved most of the complications that lent such dramatic tension to its earlier actions," including the "act" of the Holy Sonnets (57–58).

Brooks (1995, 284–88, 299) calls attention to Martz's "seminal study" (1954) of Ignatian meditation (see Holy Sonnets: Genre and Traditions) and, in particular, Martz's interest in the "seamless flowing together" of the three stages of meditation and the three faculties of the soul (285–86). According to Brooks, there has been insufficient attention to the "mechanism" through which such "integration" of the stages and the soul's faculties occurs (285). Brooks finds that Augustine's conception of time in his *Confessions* and its relation to the faculties of the soul offers an illuminating interpretive framework for the way the meditative exercise—and meditative poems—achieves "the coalescence of the soul's faculties with its true object of desire: the timeless image of God" (286). Brooks notes that "both Augustine and Donne held to a Christocentric theology in which redemption depends on renewal of the defaced, salvific image of God within," but for both, "human existence is a life-long struggle to free oneself from the ravages of time, that is, from the transitory, worldly distractions that repeatedly fail to satisfy the soul's unmitigated longing for union with God" (286). The crucial ingredient in Augustine's psychology of time, according to Brooks, is "the mind's faculty of 'attention,' [which] alone persists in a continuous 'present' as it processes, or 'understands' both the ongoing remembrance of the past and the expectation of the future (*Conf.* XI.28)" (287–88). In a detailed analysis of the structure of Donne's *Goodf*, Brooks finds in that poem and in those Holy Sonnets shaped by the structure of the Ignatian *Exercises*, a neglected key to their cohesiveness in Augustine's psychology of time (299).

Dubrow (1995, 203–07, 226–28) finds that Donne's Holy Sonnets share in a "counterdiscourse" that Dubrow observes elsewhere in English poetry, and specifically in the deployment of Petrarchan elements (203–07). But Dubrow argues against too narrowly defining Donne's responses to Petrarchism, insisting that "if Donne participates enthusiastically in certain modes of Petrarchism, he simultaneously reacts against others" (206). Part of the challenge one confronts on this issue, according to Dubrow, is that Petrarchism "meant something very different in England in the early 1590's, when Donne first arrived at the Inns of Court, than it did only a few years later, let alone in the subsequent decade," and therefore Donne's "responses to Petrarchism include and even at times center on his reactions to his own previous involvement with that tradition" (206). Dubrow observes that in the Holy Sonnets Donne "repeatedly contrasts earthly and spiritual love," and in doing so, "frequently adduces Petrarchism as a model for the former" (226). Dubrow notes, for example, that Donne's multiple references to idolatry (e.g., *HSSouls* 9, *HSWhat*

9–10, *HSSighs* 5–6) recall Petrarch's concern that his love for Laura is "a form of idolatry," and she further comments that *HSBlack* 13–14 "more subtly evokes Petrarchism in order to rebuke it" (226). In this poem, Dubrow contends, the "verse form" prompts a comparison with Petrarchism, and the poem overall "plays the Christian iconography of red and white against its Petrarchan counterpart in which in many senses the red is not dyed out" (226). Dubrow posits that Donne's religious poems do in part "synecdochically criticize the secular world by calling into question one of its literary discourses," but she emphasizes that the relationship between the poems and Petrarchism is "more complex" (228), citing, for example, Martz's claim (1954, 49) that there is "an affinity between the structure of the Petrarchan sonnet and meditative practices" (228).

HSBatter

COMMENTARY

General Commentary

Gosse (1899, 2:109) paraphrases the poem thus: Donne "conceives himself a help-less, beleaguered city held by a hateful and tyrannic foe. The city, unarmed, cannot resist, cannot even make a sign, but with all its heart it yearns after its besieger; and so the soul, bound and betrothed to Satan, and occupied by his armed forces, dearly loves God, and would fain see His victorious army enter its gates and drive out the abhorred usurper."

Hooper and Harvey (1958, 13–15) explicate the sonnet to illustrate methods of discussing poetry, commenting on its tone, prosody, vigorous imagery, biblical echoes, dramatic form, and its reflection of personal experience.

Pointing to HSBatter, Banzer (1961, 418) suggests that Donne's orthodoxy is hard-won; as a middle-aged man, he demanded of God both intellectual rest and emotional satisfaction.

Adams (1962, 784n1) argues that in HSBatter Donne's faith "rises to a series of 'knotted paradoxes' involving coercion and submission." These paradoxes would be "revolting," he suggests, "were it not for the full and evident sincerity of the mind to which they were inevitable."

Cohen (1963, 166) identifies HSBatter as an example of the "intense" drama of the Holy Sonnets.

Buckley (1965, 29), though finding HSBatter, like many of the Holy Sonnets, "histrionic," also notes that it is "distinctive in its erotic analogies."

Wanninger (1969, 37) states that "a majority of recent criticism" oversimplifies the interpretation of this sonnet by ignoring its "essential duality." She argues that the dual nature of the poem is revealed not only by a paradoxical theme and two kinds of metaphor, but also by elements of structure and concept, such as the differing rhyme schemes of the octave and sestet, and the imagery of war opposed to that of love. To the "obvious oppositions of war and love, holy love and profane love," Wanninger observes, may be added "the counteractions of good and evil, natural and counter-natural forces, illegality and legality, reason and passion, captivity and freedom, active love and passive love, prebaptismal sin and postbaptismal sin, and the opposite boundaries of time."

French (1970, 121–23) claims that the "confusion of thought and feeling" that seems to him characteristic of the Holy Sonnets is most pronounced in HSBatter (121). The main difficulty, he says, is to decide what part or faculty in the writer is attracted to God and what faculty is attracted to the devil. While admitting that he might be guilty of "logic-chopping," French states that the poem "tries to realize a state of anguished doubt about the writer's ability to communicate with and belong to God" and is therefore in one sense "*about* confusion" (122). Donne is not clear whether he is really committed to God, and is trying to decide what part in him is resisting commitment. The poem, French says, is "an attempt to unload the whole mess of feelings onto God and leave Him to sort them out" and is perhaps "a means of getting God's attention" (123).

There is in this sonnet, Halewood states (1970, 80–81), a "rising rhythm," or an "ascent to reconciliation," which is consistent with the "rhythm of meditation." See more under Holy Sonnets: General Commentary.

Stampfer (1970, 258–65) states that the speaker in *HSBatter* suffers depravity, and that only utter violence will penetrate his heart. Therefore, "a rape is called for, not a seduction." The "three person'd God" is not a theological construction, he argues, but an "exasperated summons that all the parts of God slam into his stony heart." The speaker "slams" verb after verb at God, Stampfer writes, "taunting, confronting, demanding a reply." In the middle of the sonnet, at the octave break, Stampfer says, something crumbles inside the speaker: "Where before he would admire, now he suddenly loves God, and dearly." Stampfer finds that the speaker then takes the female role, but Donne's "urgent" language betrays a "strident, awkward, masculine spirit, clumsy with anxiety and articulating too brazenly the call for rape to fit congenially the female role" (258). Stampfer states further that Donne struggled all his life to clarify his ego and arrive at utter intimacy of spirit. The "romantic metaphor" in the closing couplet, he finds, "reads as a gesture of radical self-effacement" and is "simply appalling" in its desperation (264). Stampfer contends that since a strong ego was a male characteristic to the Elizabethans, Donne, by subduing his ego and absorbing the spirit of God, would eliminate his very sexuality (265).

Winny (1970, 141–43) contends that Donne is at first so hopelessly subjugated to sin that gentle inducements cannot persuade him to reform. As a result he cries out to be overwhelmed by the power of God (141). However, by the second line of the poem, Winny states, Donne has passed from "rushing haste" to "something near immobility," first breaking down the natural stops in verse rhythm, and then setting harshly unnatural barriers across it (141–42). Winny observes that Donne "seems to be straining sonnet form to the point of breakdown" and that "the impression that the lines can barely contain all that he crams into them is chiefly responsible for the explosive effect of the poem" (142). The ideas of siege and warfare in the poem "follow naturally" from the context of violent physical effort in the opening lines, Winny says. And, he states, just as Donne eschewed convention in his love poetry, so he avoids custom in his devotional poetry. The prayers of the Holy Sonnets are not respectful and submissive, he argues; rather, they go "straight to the crucial point" (142). *HSBatter* is, he believes, a good example of this kind of approach. With the sestet, Winny notes, the idiom of the poem changes radically: the speaker, "[n]o longer in the thick of a spiritual battle," assumes the stance of a woman "forced into a marriage contract against her will, who looks despairingly towards the man she loves, hoping that he may still claim her" (143). The image of sexual violation in the closing four lines might at first be thought "grotesquely inappropriate," but in fact it "reflects a mode of apprehension natural to Donne, and not a deliberate attempt to be sensational" (143). Winny argues that for Donne to feel secure, God must take him with the "sudden ferocity of possession" that the metaphor implies; the metaphor of rape, he states, ties together the diverse elements of love and violence in a "firmly unified conclusion" (143). By the end of the poem, Winny concludes, Donne has worked out an answer to his distracting spiritual problem.

Kerrigan (1974, 351–56) argues that the rape described in HSBatter should be read as "implicit in the ancient theological conceit of the righteous soul's marriage to God" (351). He writes that given Donne's view of "sacred metaphor," the "accommodated marriage" would "compress all the things that attend earthly marriages" (352). He notes that at the time he wrote HSBatter Donne was "imprisoned by the father of the bride," and thus the poem recalls the "drama of his own marriage" (352). He argues that HSBatter evolves towards a single metaphor, noting that the text's subsidiary conceits have primary reference to the love relationship, itself "an accommodated vehicle for the spiritual life of the soul" (353). Kerrigan argues that though we realize that "sexual rape" is in the poem a "metaphor for the forcible entrance of the deity into an otherwise impenetrable soul," there remains an "extraordinary emphasis" on the "penetration of a tight body," since "insofar as the tropes reach out of local context to describe the climactic invitation, that sexual event acquires the force of a tenor" (354). Kerrigan argues that "the commands of the poem proceed through a series of transformations in assaulter and thing assaulted," with the "vehicles of her wish" flowing together: the "battered heart" changes to the "attacked city" which then becomes the "ravished vagina"; the "tinker's tools" are transformed into the "monarch's engines which become, indeed, the penis of God" (354–55). Kerrigan notes that in the closing paradox "the equation of ravishment and chastity deflects the perilous situation reached through the unraveling of accommodated love," and that, "having painted himself into a corner, Donne proceeds to extricate himself "by switching colors" (355). He writes that faced with the threat of a God who appears to be "irregular" or imperfect, Donne "introduces a 'complete and excellent' anthropomorphism, equating the imputed human vice to the appropriate and opposite human virtue" (356).

Cathcart (1975, 161–63) discusses the casuistry of HSBatter, as in this sonnet Donne deals with a "double truth, arriving in the end at a paradoxical conclusion" (161). For Cathcart, the poem tries to reconcile resistance and attraction and the conflicting claims of reason and body.

Fowler (1975, 105) notes that HSBatter exhibits "a combination of siege and marriage metaphors."

Stringer (1976, 193) remarks that the climax of the Holy Sonnets is HSBatter, where the speaker's prior, apparently ineffectual efforts to assure his election through various meditative gestures are swept away in an anguished call for "forcible rape."

Aers and Kress (1981, 66–68) note that, given Donne's emphasis in the sonnets on the instability of the self, his desire, as expressed in HSLittle and HSBatter, "is an idiosyncratic and violently assertive demand to be raped, overwhelmed and drowned," to be denied "all vestiges of the responsibility that might be part of a version of a self which attributed some powers of conscious agency to the individual, however 'fallen'" (66). According to Aers and Kress, God is seen as a "terrorising and brutal force uninterested in personhood or individual nuances and developments of awareness and love in his creatures" (67). Thus, Aers and Kress argue, Donne "begs this power to fix his identity in the most absolute way," even to "imprison" him, thus "virtually renouncing the fundamental idea of Christian Liberty so important to the history of Protestant thought" (67). The sexual imagery that Donne employs, they say, is linked to his "prophane Love" and gives rise to "desperate, contradictory [experiences] fusing massive self-assertiveness with self-annihilation" (67). Aers and Kress call attention to a significant problem in Donne's desire for this "coveted state," namely, the absence of an "identity to whom the achieved stability could be attributed," as well as the lack of "any specifiable moral commitment or framework" to this state (68).

Carey (1981, 53, 57) claims that in HSBatter Donne expresses his love for God, but "it does no good," for "he feels no reciprocal love from God" since "the devil has him" (53). The sonnet affirms that "assurance must come from outside," but, says Carey, "as a Protestant," Donne has "cut himself off from that outside assurance which, for the Catholic, the Church and the sacraments supplied" (57).

Miller (1982, 836) cites Clements (1961) and others (see HSBatter: Themes) who have viewed the sonnet "as hieroglyphically illustrating the Trinity in its three-part structure." The persona's soul is described by Miller as "the beloved of God though betrothed to his enemy and longing for divorce." Miller finds the resolution of the sonnet in the way that it "turns on a paradoxical sexual image as the persona says that his soul will never be chaste unless God ravishes him." Miller finds a "similar complex of imagery," although "in a less startling fashion, in HSDue."

Yearwood (1982, 210, 217–18) finds that the conversion process in Donne's first twelve Holy Sonnets (following Gardner's 1952 ordering) "begins in pride, proceeds to confession and despair, and culminates in a humble joy and confidence" (210). The tenth sonnet in the sequence, HSBatter, records, in Yearwood's view, "the ultimate expression "of fear and despair as the speaker fails to attain a conversion through his own efforts, but the sonnet does culminate in the speaker's resignation, or "indication of dependence which is necessary for complete acceptance of absolution" (217–18). Yearwood contends that the speaker, because of his "inordinate despair" at this point, "throws the responsibility for his salvation too completely on God" (218).

Hamburger (1985, 17) observes that the speaker's conversation with God in HSBatter is dramatic and pushes towards action, adding that for such exchanges Donne develops his own dramatically-shaped poetry, but poetry that is also conscious of form and genre.

Veith (1985, 119, 121) finds that here as well as in his sermons, Donne "often sounds Calvinist or Lutheran," yet in Donne the "tightly knit structure of Reformation theology, as articulated by Luther and systematized by Calvin, begins to unravel" (119). Although he acknowledges that it may oversimplify Donne's religious position to call him an Arminian, Veith nonetheless argues that with regard to a number of issues, and "especially on the question of whether salvation can be lost," Donne tended to be "in the Arminian camp, with Herbert in the Calvinist" (119). Veith points out that the sonnet "seems a celebration of irresistible grace, of the Calvinist God who breaks strongholds and ravishes," but the sonnet's conception of the human will is "essentially Arminian," in that "the speaker's will is directed to God, but it is hemmed in by sin"; by contrast, according to the Calvinist view, "the will is rebellious, but is hemmed in by God" (121). In Donne's sonnet, Veith observes, the speaker is "frustrated" by his sinfulness, "which he feels excludes him from God's presence" (121). Veith suggests that part of the strength and richness of Donne's religious poetry derives "from his standing at a transition point between Calvinism and Arminianism," positioning himself "between the view that God accomplishes everything for salvation and the view that the burden lies essentially on the self" (121).

Booty (1990, 39) briefly discusses individual sonnets, focusing on *HSBatter*, which for Booty is an expression of the "frustration of the penitent soul" and a "fervent confession of sin, an expression of sincere contrition, an admission that he is totally reliant upon God." Although the speaker "rails at God" in the octave, he finds the answer "is in acceptance of God as God is—God the Father who knocks, God the Spirit who breathes, God the Son who shines—and in adoration, with contrition, to live in the knowledge of God's love day by day."

Coiro (1990, 86) sees Donne as a poet who "draws clear sexual lines and usually talks to his God as one aggressive guy to another." She finds that "the most complete self-abnegation that he can imagine" is, in *HSBatter*, to "place himself before God as a woman, a woman begging to be raped."

Martin (1990, 60) says that *HSBatter* is "antithetical, paradoxical and violent" but that the "basic plan" of the sonnet is "quite simple": the speaker "urgently wants God to possess him and show him grace."

Ray (1990b, 46–48) points to the sonnet's use of the conceit of "the military analogy of the sinner to a fortified city," usurped by Satan, which "pervades the octave" (46). The speaker contends that what is needed, according to Ray, is a total destruction of the "old man" so that "a completely new, regenerated town/man can be constructed from the foundation up," for "destruction of the sinful generates the pure, in Christian terms" (46). Ray finds that the sestet introduces another conceit ("God as a lover") and the speaker's "wish to be reconquered by Him in terms of love, sexuality, and marriage" (47). The feminine soul, Ray states, "feels that she has been forced into a marriage with the conqueror and usurper Satan (i.e., sin)," feels, in other words, "betrothed unto Your enemy" (l. 10) (47). Thus, "spiritual purity comes to an individual soul when God takes it completely," a paradox which Ray regards as "the high point of the love motif in the sestet" (47–48). Ray concludes that the conceits of "military and sexual conquest" express the speaker's "senses of deep entrapment by sin and the necessity for God's power and love to rescue him" (48).

As illustration for her argument that the twelve sonnets from 1633 are formed into two groups of six, with each poem in the first group having a counterpart in the second group, Albrecht (1992, 24–30) focuses on *HSScene* and *HSBatter*. In *HSScene*, she says, we find "the creature seeking purgation from world/flesh/devil," and in *HSBatter*, "the creature seeking purgation and divorce from Satan's bond" (24), adding that in the latter poem the actor/speaker "is desperate for a quick escape, or at least closure" (27). The "theology" of *HSScene* is, she argues, replaced by "military science" in HSBatter (27). Given the failure of the male speaker of HSWhat (which immediately precedes HSBatter in 1633) in his attempt to "woo Christ," the speaker/ actor in HSBatter, Albrecht suggests, "tries to 'play it again,'" but this time by assuming a female voice which is also "a failure, because the actor is unable to strike the right tone" (28). Albrecht finds that the "barrage of b's" in the opening four lines of HSBatter betrays the male voice that "lurks behind the ventriloquized female voice, creating a form of linguistic rape" (29). Albrecht concludes that "this woman cannot control either of the masculine forces pinning (penning?) her down," for as Satan has "enthralled her," so has "the masculine discourse of the transvestite ventriloquist," and thus "God does not answer the speaker's prayer because it is the wrong prayer," that is, "it is a masculine prayer, demanding ravishment" (30).

Low (1993, 69, 79–81) observes that the view of God in HSBatter is that of "a king who has left a deputy to command his city" (69). He also regards HSBatter as "the only divine poem in which Donne assumes the female part unequivocally to the end" (79). Low acknowledges that many studies have argued the sonnet's "three-part development of the imagery": namely, "the prayer for destruction and remaking, the prayer for relief of the besieged town usurped by Satan, and the prayer for a forcible divorce from Satan and a divine ravishment." Once again, Low claims, Donne's poetry indicates that "Donne cannot surrender himself to God," that is, "he must be forced, broken, burned, entirely remade," and, ultimately, "raped" by God. Low observes that the ending of the poem "casts its influence backward," so that with a second reading the sexual implications are present from the beginning. Low does not find adequate the recurring explanation that the speaker cannot submit to God because of "the Calvinist strain in Donne's thinking" (80). Most theological explanations, in Low's view, do not explain why Donne cannot surrender himself to the "terms of the biblical marriage trope." Low offers what he regards a "simpler explanation," that is, "unless forced," Donne "simply cannot submit to the woman's passive role" (81).

The Poet/Persona

Praz (1925, 69–70) observes that in HSBatter Donne makes desperate appeals from the depth of his heart for expiation and purification.

Payne (1926, 142–43) quotes the poem in full as an example of Donne's "burning desire for an assurance of forgiveness."

MacCarthy (1932, 35–36) observes that in the poem Donne does not so much repent as he desires to repent and that he is moved only by "the *effort* to feel deeply."

To Leishman (1934, 88–89), Donne is continually reexamining the premises of his faith in HSBatter and so can never achieve that "complete self-surrender and perfect union with Christ for which he longs."

Potter (1934, 14), emphasizing Donne's persistent search for self-knowledge throughout his poetry, identifies "the painfully fierce self-searchings" found in the Holy Sonnets, as in HSBatter.

Schirmer (1937, 299) finds HSBatter to be an expression of Donne's desire but inability to achieve a spiritual union with God.

Hardy (1942, 179–80) quotes HSBatter in full as "the most magnificently brazen" of the Holy Sonnets. Donne, she observes, resembles a prisoner pleading with an "Inquisitional gaoler," using images that emphasize his mental torment.

Scott (1945, 11) observes that Donne in his early years failed "to integrate his own life" and consequently he was never able to fully believe that "sins committed and repented were in fact forgiven." His consciousness of sin can be heard in the "heart-felt cry" of ll. 1–2 and "his unending agony of spirit" in ll. 5–10.

Policardi (1948, 112–113, 145) observes about the sonnet that Donne's restless intellect prevents him from achieving a sense of repose and perfect abandonment to the union with Christ to which he aspires (112–13). Policardi adds that the poet becomes excited when the theme is remorse and the desire to repent (145).

Leishman (1951, 261) finds that whereas *Father* ends "on a note of peace and security," *HSBatter* has the more usual note of "agonized striving" to be found elsewhere in Donne's religious poetry.

Umbach (1951, 102) finds the poem "an outstanding self-revelation."

Adams (1958, 111) thinks that Donne is often self-consciously theatrical, as in *HSBatter*.

Cruttwell (1966, 28–29) quotes the whole of *HSVex*, *HSBatter*, and *HSRound*, commenting that Donne's "rage and disgust" at the "inadequacy of his own devoutness" in *HSVex* are also evident in the "almost hysterical" *HSBatter*. For "some tastes," Cruttwell acknowledges, these two poems are "too obviously egoistic" for religious verse.

Yepes Boscán (1966, 33–58) writes of Donne's identification with the role of prophet in *HSBatter*, arguing that Donne is not only a metaphysical poet in the strictest sense of the world but also a theological poet whose style responds faithfully to new ideological/spiritual structures, attempting to bring us closer to God not simply through rational processes but particularly through the aesthetic process.

Jackson (1970, 111) notes that *HSBatter* is unique among the Holy Sonnets in having a female persona for the soul and having this "she," or "I," as the speaker of the poem.

Fiore (1972, 6) compares the speaker of *HSBatter* to "the ascetics of old," in their determination to describe "their most contemplative experiences in terms of sex," and he points particularly to the "expressions of rape" in "enthrall mee" (l. 13) and "ravish mee" (l. 14), actions that coincide with the desire to be "ever chast" (l. 14).

Stachniewski (1981, 689–91) sees Donne's religious despair rooted in his "fundamental inability to forfeit, as Augustine wills to do, his independent identity." Consequently, Donne's only hope, in Stachniewski's view, is for "divine rape," for "Calvinist conversion involved God's simultaneous and irresistible seizure of all the faculties," an action Donne invites in *HSBatter* 12–14. Stachniewski cites Lewalski's (1979) remarks (see *HSBatter*: Themes) on "the paradoxical reversal of Christ's customary relationships with the soul—as liberator . . . and as Bridegroom," which evokes a "complexity of feeling" in Donne (689). Stachniewski shows that the sonnet underscores the distrust of reason, which, in Calvinist terms, "bolsters the need for divine intervention" (691).

Garrett (1986, 35) finds that all of the features of *HSBatter* combine in the poem's insistence on "physical intervention by God in the life of this habitual sinner," reflecting that "the carnal consciousness of the younger Donne" is still evident, for the poet "remains unable to grasp a reality that does not manifest itself in flesh, bone and blood."

Nardo (1986, 159) finds the speaker in both HSBatter and Father "equally perverse" in their doubt of "the efficacy of the shining Son."

Rollin (1986, 144) pairs HSBatter with HSLittle in that both sonnets are "fraught with aggression" and with "major depression." But even though the sonnet displays "spiritual impotence," it, like HSLittle, possesses an energy level that is "nothing less than manic." Both sonnets, he concludes, are "dynamic poems about paralysis."

Strier (1989, 374–77) feels that "it is no accident" that critics disagree about whether the sonnet is lodged in a Roman Catholic or Calvinistic frame of mind, given Donne's own "uncertainty about the status of the self vis-à-vis God" (374). Strier finds that the opening and closing of the sonnet "are brilliant formulations of the Reformation perspective," that is, the individual's "total spiritual dependence on God" (375). But, in Strier's view, the poem does not persist in this perspective, and lines 5–10 are "conceptually uncertain" (375). In fact, by the beginning of the sestet, according to Strier, "the self's intentions are pure," and "it becomes even clearer that what hampers the self's relationship to God is merely external, almost technical," as expressed in ll. 9–10 (375). But, says Strier, the speaker soon realizes (l. 11) that "if the self merely needs to be freed from impediments (usurpations, unwilling betrothals), it does not have to be made new" (376). Strier contends that the "deepest conflict" in HSBatter is seen in its "imagination of violence, which is divine in the beginning and ending, and demonic in the middle" (377). Strier views this as a product of Donne's intellectual landscape at that time, arguing that, "through his ordination in 1615," Donne could "imaginatively enter into Reformation theology only by conceiving of grace as violence" (377).

Skulsky (1992, 116–17) finds that HSBatter, as well as HSDue, creates the "impression" that "sin is something that *happens* to the sinner rather than something he *does*," which Skulsky describes as a "diversionary *littera* fostered by the speaker's fear of his ultimate judgment by God" (116–17). Skulsky contends that the speaker's vain attempts to "admit" God point to a metaphor for "inability or reluctance to love, not for loving, much less for loving 'dearly'" (116). Skulsky finds "a second suspicious contradiction," noting that betrothal to somebody "is to be morally 'due' or obliged to marry that person; if the speaker is betrothed to the devil, then how can he also be 'due' to God and be simply *usurped* by the devil?" (116).

Baumgaertner (1994, 4–5, 8) frames her discussion of the sonnet by pointing to the appeal of Donne's poetry, particularly in mid-century, to New Criticism, which had claimed that "paradox and ambiguity were the *sine qua non* of great poetry," and HSBatter provided that for these critics (4). Baumgaertner agrees that the poem is based almost entirely on paradox, but, she adds, anyone seeking a "clear and consistent theological viewpoint" in HSBatter and many of the Holy Sonnets will be disappointed (4). Baumgaertner cites approvingly Strier's reading (1989) of uncertainties and contradictions in HSBatter and claims further that the poem reflects "downright theological confusion" (5). Indeed, according to Baumgaertner, the poem ends with what she regards as a perverse paradox "in which Donne uses rape as a metaphor for God's grace," providing evidence of "the voice of the male imperialist" (5). Baumgaertner emphasizes that "this is not a poem a woman would ever have written" (5). Behind the apparent theological confusion, in Baumgaertner's view, is Donne's "struggle with and against the Roman Catholic Church," which had occurred over a number of years (5), and she concludes that his poetry presents us with the most problematic texts of all the seventeenth-century metaphysical poets, primarily because of his "indeterminate stance," influenced as it is by "the languages of recusant, apostate, Anglican divine, patronage seeker, melancholy lover, and political aspirant" (8).

Coyle (1994, 144–46) finds that the sonnet begins with the speaker's assertiveness toward God, but then begins to articulate the "problem" that the desire for submission reflects the knowledge the speaker has of his own power and separateness from God" (144). Here, according to Coyle, we sense the "rift between subject and God," but also the "continuing desire of the subject to be separate" (145). In Coyle's view, the "desire for submission" is "paralleled by a desire to be other than 'I', to be a different subject," but "through, paradoxically, the desire to be worthy of God" (145). Thus, in HSBatter, "underlying the desire for God is simultaneously a desire to be other, to be free by being at once man and woman," but Coyle adds that God cannot "comply with the speaker's commands and pleas, for to 'enthral' and 'ravish' the speaker is to set him/her free and to allow a new 'me' to take control" (146).

Strier (1994, 235–36) regards HSBatter as the "most brilliant expression" of Donne's view that the Protestant devotional stance "devalued agency and threw itself entirely on grace," a stance that Donne "had trouble fully inhabiting" (235–36). Although the sonnet begins, "Batter my heart," and ends with "an eroticized version of this prayer," the poem, in Strier's view, "does not maintain the stance of the opening and closing prayers" (236). Between the opening and closing visions, according to Strier, Donne offers a "different vision," one in which the self or soul struggles "to admit" God (l. 6), but Donne is "best," Strier contends, when he makes these "instabilities" the subject of his poems, as in HSMin, HSSighs, and HSVex (236). Here, Strier adds, and in his later religious poetry, such as Father, Donne displays his reluctance to submit to "self-abandonment" (236).

Genre and Traditions
Bethell (1948, 61, 67–71) distinguishes between "two great streams of English poetry," "Group A," exemplified by Shakespeare and Donne, and "Group B," by Spenser, Milton, and Tennyson (61). Bethel quotes HSBatter as an example of the former in that the language is colloquial, that is, concrete and immediate, using words that "do what they say." The poem's rough rhythms, he continues, imitate the speech of impassioned thought, and the varied imagery reflects fusion of intellect and emotion in "the multiple worlds of human discourse" (67). Bethell argues that the "physical shocks and strains" of the poem are justified by its "subtle, complex thinking" in the "white heat of emotion," combining various levels of experience in a strong, unified mental act. He concludes that Donne's poems "are not reflections done into verse" but are "truly acts of the mind" and that what dominates in his works is "the

intellect" (71). Bethell undertakes a detailed explication of words and phrases to illustrate his argument (68–69).

Wilson (1958, 51), acknowledging his debt to Martz (1954—see Holy Sonnets: Genre and Traditions), observes that the Ignatian method of meditation "saw the divine in terms of the human," so that in the urgency of works like HSBatter "religion and ordinary life remain in contact" through the medium of its "direct and unliterary" language.

Kermode (1974, 93) cites HSBatter as a sonnet exhibiting Donne's characteristic emphasis on the break between the octave and the sestet as, in this instance, the first eight lines have a "forced, meditative excitement," with the final six concluding with a "humble plea."

Zunder (1991, 1483) attributes the forcefulness of the appeal to God in HSBatter to the profound changes Donne was experiencing personally and culturally, to what Zunder calls this "moment of personal and cultural crisis." Zunder offers a detailed reading of the sonnet in which he calls attention to the violent emotion of the opening quatrain and Donne's containment of it within the sonnet form, along with the "desperate need for some sort of inner renewal." Zunder notes "a shift in tone and a transition of thought" as the "I" of the poem changes to "political imagery" in line 5, but Donne, he says, is "helpless," given "the rapidly and radically altering world of 1609." At the sestet, the sonnet turns to the resolution, and Zunder finds the lines calmer and more rational than the opening quatrain. Yet, Zunder notes, Donne continues to feel "betrothed" to Satan and "to a world that does not want him," all of which produces a renewal of the anxiety that suffuses the opening quatrain, and the command that God "imprison" him. In the third quatrain, according to Zunder, "emotion breaks through the form," with the thought carrying over "into the concluding couplet." Zunder points out that as with all the Holy Sonnets, Donne "combines the Italian with the English sonnet form, in order to attain the possibility of a resolution of sentiment in the English sonnet final rhyme." Zunder concludes that the resolution of the sonnet "is one of absolute submission to an external authority," expressed as paradox and resting on God taking Donne by force.

Language and Style

Drew (1933, 58) cites the sonnet as a work with which the reader can disagree intellectually but fully accept emotionally, one that can be appreciated for its poetic elements alone.

Untermeyer (1938, 16–17) quotes the sonnet in full to illustrate that in Donne's religious poetry the "figures of speech are particularly violent, the similes most torturous, and the wit most agonized."

Bush (1945, 134) cites the poem to illustrate that Donne's "anguished cries are composed of contrition, fear, and hope, of passionately humble entreaty and almost imperious demand."

Daiches and Charvat (1950, 660) comment on the important role played by paradox in the poem.

Louthan (1951, 123–24) draws attention to the "siege-imagery" in which the figure of God as the ram exerts a "binding force" in HSBatter. God, he observes, is to be a battering ram at the gate, that is, the poet's heart, rescuing him from the usurping enemy. Louthan cites the pun in *Cor7* 9–10, where the "strong Ramme" and the "milde Lambe" combine efforts to work the poet's salvation.

Gardner (1952, xxx–xxxi) cites the "violence" of the poem to illustrate "a note of exaggeration" in the Holy Sonnets (xxx). Quoting *HSBatter* 12–14, she remarks on Donne's "plain unadorned speech" that gives "extreme emphasis to the personal pronouns" (xxxi).

Reeves (1952, 101–02) notes that the poem's "nervous, jerky rhythm, intensity of feeling, and almost over-strained language" is highly characteristic of Donne's style.

Martz (1954, 145) finds in the sonnet that "the noise of thoughts is clamorous" and that "the grief pours forth in anguished eruption," contributing to a mood of "violence and tumult."

Kermode (1957, 39–40) quotes the poem in full, observing that some of the Holy Sonnets contain images that, though commonplace in Donne's time, are no longer; hence "their wit is always likely to seem indelicate as well as passionate" to the modern ear.

Coanda (1957, 181) finds the poem to have "a seemingly unsurpassable intensity and concentration."

Hooper and Harvey (1958, 13, 15) find that the principal effect of the imagery and rhythm is to project a sense of urgency (13). They argue that the drama of the sonnet is heightened by the sense that Donne writes as if he is actually experiencing the conflicting feelings, and, overcome with guilt and helplessness, asks God to use force as a last resort (15).

Yepes Boscán (1966, 66), writing at length on *HSBatter*, finds that Donne uses paradox and literary realism as co-natural elements, the first because of its affinity with the paradoxical language of Christianity and the second because its product is a vital religious realism which cannot be revealed in idealized form. Imagery, style and rhythm, he thinks, lead one to conclude that Donne's poetic universe is incomprehensible in mere analytical and rational terms, for Donne is an integral man.

Leech (1969, 143) cites *HSBatter* 13–14 as an example of paradox, noting that Donne's figures here are traditional and should be interpreted in a metaphorical sense. He argues that Donne's use of paradox is effective because it places "emphasis on the violence of God's taking possession of the Soul" (143).

Halle and Keyser (1971, 165–66) note that *HSBatter* has "an initial troche, as well as a verse-medial heavy foot in the phrase 'three person'd God' and a verse-final pyrrhic," while the second line and the fourth line contain spondees. The third line exhibits an "initial pyrrhic foot and an extra slack syllable, 'me, and.'"

Miller (1971, 131–32) remarks that the tenor "heart" is synecdochical for "self" and emblematic of soul, but, he says, "both these metaphoric movements are moribund" (131). He observes that there are two submerged metaphors which unify the first quatrain, advance its argument, and establish "firmness in logical progress" (132).

The language of *HSBatter*, Sanders (1971, 130–31) argues, performs its minimal function—"to convey information and nothing else" (130). The problems that Sanders finds with *HSBatter* are "the fumblings of ineffable banality" (130). Sanders is more comfortable with those Holy Sonnets that do not arouse expectations of a genuinely religious encounter, those that are "decently conventional" and that display an "appropriateness" of subject, such as *HSRound* (131).

Ansari (1974, 144) writes that *HSBatter* possesses violent imagery which points to Donne's "masculinity of temperament."

Kerrigan (1974, 356–62) argues that the startling sexual metaphors in *HSBatter* and *HSShow* result from the use of accommodated speech. While an anthropomorphic understanding of God must necessarily be deficient, Kerrigan states, the only way we can understand God is anthropomorphically. But the words we use to describe God, being accommodated speech, and the metaphors we use to understand him are not only inadequate but, taken to their logical extension, perverse. Kerrigan says that Donne pushes the limits of our anthropomorphic understanding of God by depicting God's actions in sexual terms. Further, he says, "since we know only human perfection, we can indicate our recognition of the failure of accommodation by conflating earthly weakness with earthly virtue: we can reaccommodate the failed accommodation" (356). In this view, the rape in *HSBatter* preserves, rather than destroys, chastity, and the seduction and adultery in *HSShow* is a seduction into purity, or "exemplary fidelity" (358). God is fearful to us because he is incomprehensible, says Kerrigan, but he is fearful to us also because we understand him only in our fallen anthropomorphic terms (362). Donne was, according to Kerrigan, the "one great poet of the English Renaissance" who exploited "the fearful consequences of accommodation in his devotional verse" (360).

Tsur (1974, 414–23) writes that in a grammatical analysis one notices the predominance of the vocative in line 1, the imperative in lines 1–4 and 11–12, and the second person pronoun throughout the poem. He argues that these features suggest a "possible dominance of the conative function." He notes that in lines 5–10 "indicative sentences prevail" (414) and that the impulsive energy carried by the imperatives and the figurative language serves to affect the addresser as much as the addressee. Consequently, in order for the experience to be genuine, a much more intense mental activity is required from the meditating person than from the praying one (415). He argues that when reading *HSBatter*, the reader "contemplates a 'dramatic' situation in which the speaker, a devoted Christian, addresses God" (416). However, he notes that the identity of the speaker is complex in that he could be understood in various ways. He says that a person of any religion may appreciate *HSBatter* because a reader "only must believe that the speaker believes in a three-personed God" (417). He writes that the poem is shaped as "an 'emotive' *crescendo*" whose "imagery presents the experience as highly unified and suggests some type of gradually heightened intensity." Tsur notes that the first three verbs in succession have "no reference to the respective persons of God," but then a second succession of verbs occurs, likewise "with no reference to the respective persons" (418). Thus, Tsur argues, attention is given to the "amplification from gentle to violent action." He notes that "the cumulative impact" of the verbs is foregrounded rhetorically by both asyndeta and alliteration and prosodically "by the tension between the linguistic stress pattern and the alternating weak and strong positions in the iambic pattern" (419).

Gregory (1974, 113–15) comments on several features of language and style, noting for example that *HSBatter* includes patterns of violence and the refurbishing of metals, with the linking of these patterns to the activity of maintaining metals in the seventeenth century. Gregory also notes that lines 1–4 are imperative in mood, 5–10 declarative, and lines 11–14 again imperative (115). Correspondingly, he observes the shifting of grammatical person from a "full range of person" to a return to the first and second person (115).

Low (1978, 68) writes that in *HSBatter* Donne uses vocal prayer instead of Ignatian meditation and notes also the use of strong *b* alliteration in the poem.

Vernon (1979, 73–74, 77, 79–81) reads the sonnet as reflecting the Elizabethan view of language as "engaged in the act of creating the world" around them (73). He finds an "intimacy between words and things," an intimacy grounded in the Elizabethan "tendency to see correspondences between things" (73). Vernon thus reads the sonnet as a linguistic manifestation of its words. For example, the words with which the poem opens contain "tremendous desire" (74), and, in fact, the opening four lines contain a preponderance of verbs, all "seeking an object to couple up with and transform" (74). Because, for Vernon, the sonnet is a form "that has to complete its gesture," the words do not "really become themselves until they call up the ones they've been yearning for" (77). The shift, therefore, from "batter" to "ravish" at the end signifies "a presence, a touch . . . an intrusion of the unknown" without "the harshness of 'batter'" (81). And thus the end of Donne's sonnet, in Vernon's view, both fulfills itself and waits for a reply, for the poem "exists entirely in the mode of waiting" (79).

Sloane (1981, 47–48, 59) calls attention to the pronounced visualization of Donne's poetry, and in particular *HSBatter*, stating that this approach reflects the poet's "attempt to intensify his meditation, to relate it directly to himself as he subjects the composition of place to his understanding and tries to give it qualities that, as St. Ignatius Loyola had suggested, would enable the meditator to feel that the meditation was passing through his own heart," features that Sloane finds in the poetry of both Herbert and Donne (47–48). Sloane sees greater "activity and intimacy" in Donne's appropriation of emblematic practice in his poetry and in particular with *HSBatter* (47). The reader, according to Sloane, is therefore "drawn into the poem" through the "visual presentations" of psychological feelings or states rather than through descriptions of them (48). Sloane points to Höltgen's (1964) study (see *HSBatter*: Themes) as further evidence of the existence of emblematic parallels for Donne's verbs in the poem and of the connection between *HSBatter* and the meditative tradition (59).

Yarrow (1981, 210–11) reads the poem as concerned primarily with realizing a "particular and more than ordinary condition of consciousness" on the part of both the speaker and reader (210). The poem, therefore, in the strong physicality of its language and style, seeks to communicate its subject "not merely as an idea, but by admitting it as direct experience" (210). Yarrow finds that Donne employs three "mechanisms" to accomplish this experience and that these devices enlist writer, poem, and reader: "shock tactics to force the reader to stop in his tracks and abandon a-priori conceptions," the "establishment of a kind of gap or vacuum in consciousness which parallels the moment when all limits are transcended," and the "recognition of this gap as not only the result of abandoning previous categories, but also as . . . the impetus for perceptual and conceptual renewal" (211). Yarrow points to the speaker as expressly desiring a change of consciousness: "make me new" (211).

Kerrigan (1983, 154–55) calls attention to "the orthodox trinity," which "invites diagrams and analogy, as in the triple verbs and three conceits" of the sonnet's "three-personed God."

Romein (1984, 13–14) offers a reading of the sonnet that conceives of God as a glass-blower rather than the more frequent view of God as a metal-blower, "who uses his breath to fill the vessel and give it new form" (13). Romein finds that the two verb series, "knock, breathe, shine" and "break, blow, burn" move toward "more emphatic action," and thus the speaker says, "Please break rather than knock, blow rather than breathe, and burn rather than shine" (13). Romein contends that the word "blow" is "particularly suggestive," indicating that the "new vessel" is in fact "being filled with the Holy Spirit," whereas in the metal-blower metaphor the "breath of spirit is applied to the fire, not to the vessel itself" (14). Moreover, Romein notes, "a flawed metal vessel could possibly be mended, but a misshapen piece of crystal would have to be destroyed before it could be made perfect" (14).

Willmott (1985, 22), noting the dramatic quality of Donne's poetry, observes in the sonnet "not only the shock opening, but a string of heavily accented monosyllabic verbs in succession to suggest the vigorous action needed." Observing that the poem is "carefully structured"—not just an "unrestrained outburst of verbal energy"—Willmott notes the "more forceful" verbs of line 4 as against those in line 2, since God, the "blacksmith of Donne's heart," must not simply "seek to mend" (l. 2) but must "make [him] new" (l. 4). Willmott also finds the "deliberate juxtaposition of 'stand' and 'o'erthrow'" in the paradox of line 3 to be additional evidence of the "care with which Donne organises his verse" (22).

Marotti (1986, 259) contends that "the indecorous sexualization" of the speaker's relationship to God is one example of the "rhetorical sadomasochism" to be found in the Holy Sonnets and of Donne's "conflict of assertion and submission." Marotti finds the sonnet "shocking" in part because the poem "has the shape of a passive homosexual fantasy," a reformulation of Petrarchan love into a homosexual relationship that "suited," according to Marotti, both "male-male patron-client transactions generally" (as in the sonnets of Shakespeare) and "Jacobean courtier-King relationships specifically."

Martinet (1987, 63–64) describes Donne as the poet of negation, referring specifically to Father 5 ("When thou hast done, thou hast not done") and noting the recurring syntactical negations which are supported by the enigmatic imagery, so that the sign does not bring us closer to the meaning, but paradoxically places it at a distance (63–64). The overtaking of all signs is found in HSBatter, a unique text, according to Martinet, where Donne addresses himself to God with the plural "you" in order to emphasize the Trinity (63). Here, in Martinet's view, Donne presents analogies with the writing of Meister Eckhart on the castle of the soul, where even the God of three persons cannot enter, and thereby places value on the impossibility of penetrating the soul, and the inadequacy of so many of the images of the divinity that are intractable to humanity (63). Martinet finds that the negative theme appears explicitly in the "except" at the end of *HSBatter*, but all of the poetic is, in fact, a definition, by way of irony (antiphrasis), of the inaccessibility of the self (63).

G. Smith (1987, 167–69), as part of a larger comparison of the poetry of Gwendolyn Brooks and Donne, analyzes *HSBatter* to illustrate "the difficulties associated with metaphysical poetry" (167). Smith explains that the octave of Donne's sonnet "summarizes the persona's paradoxical religious feelings," and records the speaker's plea to God "to save him from the inner forces that threaten to destroy his religious faith." But, Smith points out, the "volta" in line 9 "begins the turn toward a partial resolution of the persona's ordeal," as the speaker's "less strident" voice "resolves his predicament with a simple declaration of love." Smith notes that Donne alters the usual pattern of Petrarchan rhyme "by adding a Shakespearean couplet to the final quatrain," thus producing two voltas. For Smith, one doubling of the volta "thwarts the reader's expectation for an early resolution of the persona's paradoxical dilemma," while it also "lessens the dramatic distance between the opening conceit" ("Batter my heart, three-personed God") and the final one ("Except you enthrall me, never shall be free") (168). Furthermore, Smith adds, the "vessel-town-woman" metaphor yields many interpretations, "none of which totally answers the sonnet's paradoxical question: How can the persona's fractured religious faith be restored by a three-personed God?" Smith contends that the language surrounding these three metaphors "startle[s] the reader into an awareness of the subliminal relationships between words and ideas" (169). See also The Holy Sonnets and Other Works.

Warnke (1987, 108–09) locates the "unit of tone" in the poem in the qualities of "force and violence" that prevail, namely, in "the violence of physical labor in the first quatrain, the violence of warfare in the second," and the "sexual violence" in the sestet (108). Warnke contends that the "dazzling paradoxes" at the end of the poem "reaffirm the degree to which Donne was an artist of the baroque," that is, "in a world where all is illusion, divine truth inevitably presents itself in terms that seem absurd or self-contradictory to earthly wisdom" (109).

Clements (1990, 69–75) finds *HSBatter* "fairly representative" of "the characteristic spiritual state and stance" of the Holy Sonnets and of the divine poems as a whole (69). Clements's analysis of the poem focuses on Donne's use of paradox as the central animating principle of the poem. The three powers of the Trinity, symbolized by the words "knocke, breathe, shine," which Donne subsequently transforms into "breake, blowe, burn," are, in Clements's view, a unified concept rather than individual descriptive terms for Father, Holy Ghost and Son (69–70). For Clements, it is crucial to our understanding of the paradox at the center of the poem that the Trinitarian paradox be preserved. Each of the other Persons of the Trinity, according to Clements's reading of the poem, is "'involved' in the activity of any one" (70). Clements emphasizes that "all the triple strength of the Three Persons acting as one, with true trinitarian force, is required to raise Donne from his deeply sinful life and hence to effect his salvation" (72). Clements, finding this same kind of religious paradox operative throughout the poem, claims further that the "paradox of dividing in order to unite, destroying in order to revive, throwing down in order to raise, determines the choice of and finds expression in the poem's figurative language" (72).

Clements identifies two principal kinds of figurative language: one is "warlike, military, destructive, dividing," the other "marital, sexual, or uniting," but he points out that the words "divorce," "enthrall," and "ravish" (ll. 11, 13, 14) "partake of both kinds of metaphor: a divorce is a dividing, yet the word is associated with marriage; to enthrall is both to subjugate and to captivate or enamor; ravishing is both sexual and violent" (73). Here, Clements notes, Donne fuses or unites the two kinds of figurative language so as to achieve with the metaphors "what Donne wishes to achieve with God" (74). Thus, in Clements's view, "the paradox of death and rebirth" is both the "organizing principle" of HSBatter and the "central paradox of mysticism and therefore of Christianity," but here "this paradox is prayed for, not realized," so that, typical of contemplative verse, the paradox of the Trinity is not here a mystical paradox (75). See also Clements (1961) under HSBatter: Themes.

Martin (1990, 61–65) acknowledges that the "violently contorted language" and what seems to be a "theatrical kind of masochism" have bothered readers of HSBatter, and he suggests that a change in two "cultural codes" contributes to this uneasiness: a change in the "witty code of paradox" and in the "Biblical code of metaphor and allusions" (61). Martin finds throughout the poem crucial evidence of paradox and metaphor grounded in biblical contexts and concludes that for the ideas of HSBatter "there was no adequate language other than the multi-dimensional metaphorics of the Bible" (65).

Manlove (1992, 97–98) argues that HSBatter preserves the distinction between the operation of imagination in the octave and "sense" in the sestet, adding that the first image of the poem "appears to blame God for the weakness of His assault on the speaker," while the following two images indicate "that the fault is not just God's but also the devil's." Further, Manlove adds, none of the images "blames the speaker himself" (97). Manlove points out that "it is theologically orthodox that only God's grace may rescue us from our mortality and sin," but quite unorthodox "to blame God for failure to penetrate the wicked soul." Yet he thinks that Donne "dances on the edge of the permissible, delighting in it." In Manlove's view, there is no need for three different images of God (as blacksmith, besieger, and lover, since "each simply asks God to do more") other than the pleasure that the speaker derives from "the ingenuity involved in thinking up three different pictures which convey the same meaning," as well as enjoying "the potential for paradox that they carry." What we have, according to Manlove, is the "daring" of a poet "on a theological high wire, attempting a triple somersault," with "the fantastic imagery loosely tethered to the sense." Manlove concludes that God's enemy in the poem is not reason but imagination, an imagination "which has so delighted in various images for the speaker's plight that the gravity of that plight has been lost" (98).

Rogers (1992, 163) finds that the Holy Sonnets share qualities with the love poems, such as the "insistent imperatives" throughout HSBatter and the "development of an idea to its absolute," as in HSBatter 12–14. Rogers contends that the "startling paradox" of "chastity co-existing with rape," which brings together "strong metaphors for the union of the individual soul with God," is "exceptional" in the Holy Sonnets, which he judges "usually less witty." Rogers thinks that in this regard the "regularity of the form" of the sonnet and its "brevity" perhaps offered Donne less "scope and variety or that he might have seen these "Divine meditations" as something closer to "serious theological essays."

Singh (1992, 100) attributes the "vigour" of the sonnet to its "direct colloquialisms, force of expression, and the startling use of sexual imagery," further noting that the poet "demands extreme measures from God as being the only way his soul can be won over."

Spurr (1992, 21–22) contends that *HSBatter* is Donne's "noisiest poem, containing a series of alliterated, onomatopoeic and violent verbs proclaiming the rigorous purgation he requires and, thereby, indicating the deep-seated sinfulness which demands such a purifying process" (21). The "startling incongruity" between the request for a "battering" from "the transcendentally spiritual Trinity" indicates, according to Spurr, "the absolute separation of Donne from God even as it conveys his earnest desire to bridge it" (21). As an Anglican, Spurr notes, Donne "believed that reason, with grace, should assist the believer's progress to truth," but "his mind has the habit of thwarting, rather than aiding, his faith" (22). And, thus, according to Spurr, *HSBatter* "closes, as it opened, in paradox, as intellectual acuteness is vivified by a clamour of powerful verbs" (22).

Prosody

Louthan (1951, 123) finds that metrical stresses reinforce meaning in the poem, since "heavily accented syllables connote violence," producing "a sort of sledgehammer effect."

Esch (1955, 49–50) finds the tone of the poem at variance with most of the other sonnets, where there is a sharp antithesis between octave and sestet. The entire poem is uttered with a kind of "breathlessness" ("Atemlosigkeit"), more in keeping, Esch argues, with Donne's actual experience. See more under Holy Sonnets: Prosody.

Hooper and Harvey (1958, 13) observe that the run-on lines and "laboring rhythm" give the impression of spontaneity and surging emotion.

For Dalglish (1961, 136) *HSBatter* possesses unusual flexibility of meter, sounds of words, and imagistic range.

Graham (1968, 64–65) asserts that *HSBatter* is centered on a personal experience, and that since Donne is trying to comprehend and master his experience, the poem has a tight structure. Graham identifies three separate "units" in the poem (4-4-6) (64), though he also notes that most of Donne's "sense units" in the poem are pairs of lines. Graham argues that there is a complex interplay between the rhyme-scheme and the "sense units," suggesting that Donne's experience is "too urgent and troubling" to be put into smooth, regular verse. The poet, in Graham's view, seems to be trying to control and master his passionate sense of loss in order to make his desperate plea to God (65).

Gregory (1974, 116) discovers a "pattern of threes and twos" in the recursion of verb elements. He writes that *HSBatter* "exhibits high *verbality* in the grammatical sense of the word," noting that of "forty-seven lexical items," "thirty-one are exponents of verbal elements of structure." He argues that the "dynamism" of *HSBatter* is "reinforced phonologically by the frequency with which strong stresses fall on a verb item."

Fuzier (1983, 40–48) examines the relationship of the prosodic elements and the rhetorical form of *HSBatter*, beginning with a detailed scansion of the sonnet (42) and its dominant rhyme scheme (abba abba cdcd ee), noting that the poem follows the pattern of an Italian sonnet in the octave and a Shakespearean sonnet in the sestet. Furthermore, the syntactical division, according to Fuzier, clearly splits the meaning into two quatrains and two tercets, which in fact links the form to the Italian and French traditions. Fuzier's analysis points to two fundamental metaphors: a military metaphor in the octave and a matrimonial one in the sestet, wherein the soul rightfully aspires toward her divine husband. The two metaphors appear distinct, but as Fuzier notes, are intricately linked through a shared erotic motif (43). The erotic orientation of the military metaphor is recognized by the reader retrospectively when, in light of the last lines of the sonnet, the reader realizes that the terms which describe the hoped-for military assault evoke in a way no less precise the gestures of a hoped-for sexual aggression, facing which the victim gives proof of an active good will (43–44n9). It is in this union that the conceit inheres, that is, by the desired violation underlying both metaphors and the battering ram motif in both lines 1 and 14 (43). Fuzier finds that the enjambment produced at the end of the first line effects a disequilibrium by opposing an imperative of eight syllables ("Batter my heart, three-personed God") to a statement consisting of twelve syllables ("for you . . . seek to mend"). This opposition reveals the insufficiency of the weak and dispersed efforts at redemption that God until now had exercised in contrast with this last call of the poet for a unique and violent gesture (44). Fuzier comments on the first line of the second quatrain, which explains the metaphor "Batter my heart" by way of a comparison ("I, like an usurp'd town") as a prosodic structure that unveils a series of rhythmic upheavals, which Fuzier demonstrates, through a detailed analysis, as persisting and intensifying throughout the three following verses, and reflective of the microcosmic disorder that the speaker conveys (45). Fuzier claims that Donne's prosodic changes are not a deliberate effect, but rather an organic necessity, and he identifies such features as prosopopoeia, antithesis, antimetathesis, and especially synaeresis. For Fuzier, synaeresis (the joining of two vowels to create a single syllable) is the clearest sign of Donne's desire to break from the restrictions imposed by the inflexible rules of Elizabethan poetry, which shackle the spontaneity of his expression (48). The sonnet includes nine instances of synaeresis, seven of which are signaled by apostrophes in the 1633 edition, Fuzier contending that in its frequent use of synaeresis, *HSBatter* is the most notable example in all of Donne's writing of his effort to liberate himself from poetic conventions. Fuzier concludes that his analysis of Donne's sonnet testifies to the informing role of prosodic and rhetorical elements, and thus confirms that the poem is indeed the formality of the essence (48).

Linville (1984b, 67–68) finds Donne's "more radical kind of metric disruption" in this sonnet difficult to notate (67). Scansions reveal, in Linville's view, that the disruptions are consistent with the meaning (68). Linville explains this feature of the sonnet by pointing to "the plea for a personal apocalypse or destruction of the old world of the self and the summoning up of souls on Judgment Day," both of which "entail annihilation of present temporal and spatial order, an annihilation which rhythm helps to reflect" (68).

Garrett (1986, 25, 50–53, 55) points out that whereas poetic rhythm may reflect an ordered world, this is not always the case, and particularly not for Donne (25). For example, HSBatter, in Garrett's view, is a poem about disorder, and the rhythm tends to be disordered as well (25). The two opening lines, expressing "the speaker's spiritual crisis," follow, says Garrett, an "underlying pattern of iambic feet but with considerable metrical variation and extra stresses, suggesting "mental 'stress'" he is experiencing because of his "fears about his spiritual shortcomings" (25). Garrett also notes the presence of "verbs of violent action" that suggest the "force" the speaker believes is "necessary for his 'reshaping,'" while, at the same time, the speaker himself "does violence to the iambic pentameter of the verse" (52). Furthermore, Garrett says, "the heavily stressed plosives" of each verb mimics "the rhythm and the compressed and concentrated energy of the blacksmith's hammer as it pounds old metal into new material" (53).

Young (1986, 152, 154), in discussing Thomas Hobbes's view of poetry (in his correspondence with Sir William Davenant in 1650 concerning Davenant's epic Gondibert) and the role of Hobbes in the development of neoclassicism, points out Hobbes's stated preference for verse written in "'measur'd'" lines (152). Young concludes, therefore, that Donne most likely is one of those earlier poets against whom Hobbes is reacting, and he cites the "violently irregular rhythm, the series of strong accents in place of regular iambic feet" in HSBatter (154).

Sacred and Profane

Hamilton (1926, 610–11) observes of Donne that the mixture of "sensuality and religious feeling strangle" meaning to the extent that "some of his physical verse is detestable." Hamilton regrets that the "masculinity" of the opening lines of HSBatter is spoiled by "a jarring sexual metaphor" at the end.

Fausset (1931b, 342), analyzing Donne's appeal, argues that his "cry to God" and the sensuous image of the final lines "finds a responsive echo" among those "whose imaginative life has been impoverished by intellectual sophistication and the mechanical triumphs of the practical consciousness."

Untermeyer (1938, 16–17) finds in the poem "the Elizabethan theme of the impatient lover and his reticent beloved," but it is the poet who is the "half-willing, half-resisting woman." It is "the town, the virgin body, the eager spirit" that is subject to rape as the reader "looks on with a kind of terror as the word is made flesh." Untermeyer asks whether it "is anguish or ingenuity that can turn an appeal to God into a game, a verbal trick" of oxymoronic contradiction.

Louthan (1951, 124) points out the paradoxes of the poem—overthrow vs. rise and stand, imprison vs. free, ravish vs. chaste, the last of which "strikingly combines secular and sacred love"—to indicate that there is both violence and meekness in Christian doctrine.

Newton (1959, 11) finds in the metaphors of the sonnet "striking echoes" of Donne's earlier love poems.

The last line of HSBatter, Gransden says (1969, 130), presents the idea of God as the lover whose love alone is chastity. With the contemporary language of profane love, Grandsen states, Donne realizes the "traditional idea of divine love as a concrete and important experience."

Gregory (1974, 114) observes that the final six lines are "dominated by the lexis of a Love/Sexual relationship."

Roston (1974, 172–75) argues that HSBatter illustrates the "mannerist assault upon the normal patterns of logic or belief" (172). He writes that Donne brushes aside conventional notions of prayer, and that he reflects the mannerist theme in which "the *sprecher* or saint is flung head over heels by the force of the vision, to see the world afresh from a physically inverted but spiritually more valid view point" (173). Roston traces the use of the sexual imagery of HSBatter to Counter Reformation practices in which "nothing was secular, nothing profane if it could be made to serve the purpose of the spiritual life" (175).

Mano (1979, 5–6,10) contends that "for any Christian writer the obscene, the grotesque, the violent seem almost prerequisite," for such writers are "trafficking with an ineffable theme: the transcendent God," and writers "don't much care for ineffabilities" (5). Thus, images are required that are "vivid enough to move an atheist or a fallen-away Christian to some crepuscular feeling for the benevolent savagery of grace" (6). Mano expresses admiration for Donne's language in HSBatter, for "only the sexual act can approach—in its wild animal consummation—the working of God's love in the human soul" (10).

Willy (1979, 311) claims that the death of Donne's wife "strengthened the wholeness of his own surrender to religion." Yet, HSBatter entreats God to "penetrate the citadel of his spirit with an ardour as personal and passionate as for any of his human loves," according to Willy, who notes also the "audacity of the culminating erotic metaphor ('Nor ever chast, except you ravish mee')."

Sherwood (1984, 151–52) sees in HSBatter the recurring "conflict between loves" along with "the notion so basic to Donne's religious thought that only the power of God's affliction can break that conflict" (151). The poem centers, says Sherwood, on the "pivotal spiritual problem" of the Holy Sonnets, namely, the "stubbornness of profane love" and divine love, which "alone can redirect the will's stubborn inclination" (152). Donne's use of "arresting sexual language," Sherwood adds, emphasizes "the sexual dimension of ravishment and the feminine soul as a besieged fortress" (151).

Singer (1984, 204) comments that HSBatter reflects "a richness that exceeds the limits of conventional mysticism: the ravishment for which the religious soul now yearns takes on heightened significance once we remember how great a value passion had in the sexual love to which Donne previously devoted himself." See also Holy Sonnets: Sacred and Profane.

Schoenfeldt (1990, 290) cites HSBatter and HSShow as examples of Donne's "stunning blend of erotic and religious impulses," an interest that is "easily comprehended precisely because the eroticism is so explicit." See Holy Sonnets: Sacred and Profane.

Handley (1991, 44) finds in this poem evidence that the Holy Sonnets and the love poems "have a shared body of images and that the passion of a sexual nature has here been transmuted, though in like language, to spiritual passion."

Guibbory (1993, 141–42) states that the sonnet serves as an opportunity for Donne to exploit the analogies between religious and sexual love (141). Many of the "unsettling" implications arise, according to Guibbory, when "the biblical notion that Christ is the bridegroom (and the soul the bride) is conjoined to the Christian paradox that one is only free when bound to God" (141).

Davies (1994, 51–52) finds similarities between certain of the Divine Poems and the more overtly erotic secular poems (51). In *HSBatter*, according to Davies, the persona "presents himself as a feminine vessel soliciting a 'holy rape' by the Almighty," with the rhyme scheme of the octave functioning as "an oral mimesis of the enclosed space of the city desirous of being stormed and entered" (51). Davies identifies 14 verbs in the first four lines, "dominated by the command or demand of the initiating word, 'Batter', that open up a "sphere of powerful emotional activity whose throes are contained within the city-walls of a rigorously observed metrical form" (52). The second quatrain, in Davies's view, is "more reflective," though the "exclamatory 'Oh, to no end'" maintains the "passionate momentum," culminating in the "climactic sexuality of the sestet" (52). Davies points out that "the besieged walled town was a familiar emblem of the desired womb or woman," which Donne had employed in *ElWar* (52). Davies adds that "the final couplet, wittily calculated to shock and excite, glamorizes rape by raising it to the status of a spiritual principle" (52). And yet, Davies notes, the voice of the poem has a "potent and imperious sonority" that readers have often identified with Donne's "'masculine, persuasive' language" (52).

Grey (1994, 363, 365–66) argues that one of the important challenges for feminist theology is "to re-image the concepts of transcendence and immanence in such a way as to break free from the sexist interpretations of patriarchal theology," and particularly of the Trinity. Grey's theoretical approach is grounded in "a psychological and philosophical relational perspective, in an effort to re-think transcendence and immanence." Grey cites Mary Daly's critique of Trinitarian theology (*Beyond God the Father*. Boston: Beacon, 1973; The Women's Press, 1986), which focuses on "the relation between divine transcendence as imaged in trinitarian doctrine, and the toleration of rape, genocide and war" (363). Grey contends that in the context of "trinitarian doctrine" there is no greater evidence of the "blatantly violent interpretation of transcendence" than in *HSBatter*, adding that "even the language of love can never be innocent of its social connotations" (365). According to Grey, in *HSBatter* we find "the transcendent God battering from the outside, invited to take the poet by force," and she exclaims, "this is a model of Christian love which uses the language of rape and seduction!" (365). Grey adds that *HSBatter* "inspired Oppenheimer to code-name that atomic bomb 'Trinity'!" (365–66). For Grey, this is "truly apocalyptic destruction, heavily disguised as love," creating, therefore, an "urgent need to re-image transcendence and immanence." Grey's study explores the philosophical and theological foundations for a new image of God that "breaks out of patriarchal space, that is, out of harmful dualistic interpretations of transcendence/immanence" (366).

Coakley (1995, 74–76, 82) contends that *HSBatter* reveals the "intrinsic, if initially puzzling," links between sexuality, spirituality, and the doctrine of the Trinity.

Coakley further notes that Donne's thematizing of his "encounter with God" in terms of "battery and seduction" has been the subject of feminist critiques, citing, for example Grey (1994). Coakley finds that the "erotic connections" that have been assigned to the Trinity were apparent to the Church Fathers, "though sometimes veiledly." Her study seeks "to face this messy entanglement of sexual desires and desire for God, and inquire why the Trinity specifically focuses it," but she adds that her intention is not "to exonerate Donne from the potential of an abusive interpretation" (74). According to Coakley, Donne's "genius" is found in his "perception that within the Christian provenance, trinitarianism both reflects and permeates our most basic preoccupation—with sex, power, pain, death, and political arrangements," but "what the Fathers veiled and the scholastics obscured, Donne openly revealed." Donne's perception that his "ensnarement to sin, his own tragic sense of disjunction between human and divine loves," was "capable of resolution only by divine invasive intervention" can be understood best in the context of his "Western, Augustinian heritage," that is, "in the formative trinitarian period of the fourth and fifth centuries." For Coakley, the work of a "Christian feminist" is to "ferret out" the political, spiritual and sexual implications of the Trinity, and where necessary, "criticize and redirect them" (75). Coakley claims that "at the very least," feminist perspectives and criticism should have "vindicated" Donne—"at least to the extent that he makes these connections explicit" (76). But, Coakley emphasizes, other elements of Donne's poetry "yearn toward a more integrated understanding of sexual and divine loves." Coakley finds that Donne's early love poetry and his Holy Sonnets "invite collocation" for "divine and human loves feature in both," and she notes that on the death of his wife, Donne "explicitly voices his conviction of some alignment of these loves" in HSShe 5 (82).

Labriola (1995, 99) finds that the sonnet "evolves from a central conceit of possession, whereby the competing claims and alternating presence in the human heart by Satan or the Lord are reflected." According to Labriola, "however unnatural or outlandish the conceit of possession may appear, especially when its sexual implications are pursued to the point of ravishment," the speaker is "contemplating the apocalyptic union of his soul with the Lord," who, in the Bible, is likened "to a bridegroom yearning for his beloved on their wedding night."

Osterwalder (1995, 199–200, 206–08) examines the love imagery in both the secular and religious poems of Donne in an attempt to give partial answer to the "vexed question whether Donne, as a 'great visitor of ladies,' accepted the bodily aspect of human love, or whether he was part of the 'anti-body' league spearheaded by Marsilio Ficino" (199). Osterwalder notes that "the vehicles for human love are drawn from Christian Neoplatonism, whereas in some of the Holy Sonnets rape and prostitution are the chief metaphors" (200). While many studies have called attention to the violent images in the "accumulation of verbs" in the first quatrain of HSBatter, Osterwalder stresses the "crescendo effect of these asyndetic pileups," finding an "erotic undercurrent" in line 4, while the metaphor of the besieged town/woman in the second quatrain "heightens the potential sexual overtones and hints at the combination of violence and sexuality which is yet to come." Osterwalder observes further that these "connotative erotic overtones" are made explicit from line 8 forward:

"paired in binary opposition the vocabulary of worldly love is presented with a crescendo effect"—"untrue"/"love," "betrothed"/"divorced," "enthrall"/"free," "chaste"/ "ravish"—but "the obvious culmination is the rape image in the last line" (206). Osterwalder finds "striking" and "daring" the "pervasive use of erotic and overtly sexual imagery to illustrate the love of God to man" but adds that Donne here follows the "tradition of Christian mysticism" and its use of the "symbolism of ravishment," pointing to precedents in John of the Cross's *Cantica Espiritual* and, from a different tradition, Plotinus's *Enneads* (207). Nonetheless, Osterwalder concludes that "the combination of images of violence and sexuality is idiosyncratic on Donne's part," taking the reader away from the "tradition of Petrarchism and Renaissance Neoplatonism still current at his time" (207–08).

Themes

An anonymous editor (1840, 271–72) compiled a number of Donne's works and printed various poems under original headings. *HSBatter* is printed under the heading "Prayer for Grace."

Simpson (1948, 212) detects "a kinship of spirit" between the prayers in *Essays* and those in the Holy Sonnets. She finds that Donne's "plea to God" to provide "an overpowering access of grace" so as to overcome his stubborn will "reaches its finest expression in the intensity" of *HSBatter*.

Spörri-Sigel (1949, 85) notes that the poem clearly defines the tension between God and Satan. Donne, she observes, conceives of himself as married to Satan, preventing his union with God; and only God has the power to divorce him from evil. This he can do, however, only through violence, which is defined in the poem in the language of warfare, the confrontation of two enemy powers, God vs. Satan.

Reeves (1952, 101) finds the paradoxes of the poem "brilliant" as Donne "begs God to take possession of his heart."

Simon (1952, 115) senses that Donne's "ascent to God" is a hard one, "for his reason is never silenced" and he needs help from outside: "he must be battered, overthrown, bent, broken, blown, burnt before he can 'admit' God." See also Holy Sonnets: Themes.

Levenson (1953, item 31) finds that the dramatic "switching of verbs" throughout the poem suggests a central metaphor: "God as a tinker, Donne a pewter vessel in the hands of God the artisan." On the image of God as a tinker, see also Herman (1953), Levenson (1954), Knox (1956), Schwartz (1967), Heist (1968), and Jerome (1968).

Herman (1953, item 18) dismisses Levenson's suggestion (1953) that God as tinker and Donne as pewter vessel is a central metaphor of the poem since at most it could only apply to the first quatrain. Herman proposes rather that the image of the "three-person'd God" unifies the poem, as Donne asks that greater violence be employed to redeem him. God the Father needs to break rather than knock at the heart, God the Holy Ghost to blow rather than breathe, and God the Son to burn rather than shine on the "heart-town-woman." On the image and role of the Trinity in *HSBatter*, see also Clements (1961), Parish (1963b), Cornelius (1965), Ruotolo (1966), Schwartz (1967), Heist (1968), Steele (1971), Moseley (1980), and Lawrence (1985).

Levenson (1954, item 36) rejects Herman's position (1953), which he character-izes as a contention that no good poet "would develop a conceit of a metal-worker in his first quatrain, a military conceit in his second quatrain, and a sexual conceit in his sestet" in such a short work. Levenson argues that this is precisely what Donne does, using "the common denominator of violence" and certain verbal links to cre-ate a unified poem. He finds Herman's notion of a "heart, which is also a town and a woman," to be a "specious simplification," though he acknowledges that Donne had a "habit of shifting metaphors," as in *HSBlack*, *HSMin*, and *HSDeath*. Levenson insists that the image of God as metal-worker is appropriate but acknowledges that "tinker" may have been ill-chosen, since the poem asks God to cease "tinkering" and use more violent means. He argues that Herman's "three-person'd God" theme "rests on untenable theological premises" unless it is determined by the "metal-work-ing metaphor."

Umbach (1954, 19) suggests that the sonnet illustrates Donne's method of prayer.

Denonain (1956, 153) notes that Donne asks for God's "brutal and saving sever-ity" ("sévérité brutale et salvatrice") because of the inability of human reason to save him.

Knox (1956, item 2) finds that the readings of both Levenson (1953, 1954) and Herman (1953) fail to define the unity of the poem, in that the former's "God-the-tinker" idea applies only to the first quatrain and the latter's "woman-town ratio" spoils his argument. Knox argues that the Father represents power, the Holy Ghost "the infusion of love or Grace," and the Son light, all appropriate to "knock, breathe, shine." When applied to the "unregenerate ego," however, these forces must change to "break, blow, burn." Thus, Knox continues, God's Trinitarian powers fail to re-lieve the town because of the speaker's weak reason, so the alternative is a "forceful overpowering and violent reshaping" represented as love: the "fallen one must be ravished before he becomes spiritually chaste." Knox finds Herman's identification of the speaker as a woman strained, since the symbol of ravishment is traditional in Christian mysticism regardless of gender.

Hooper and Harvey (1958, 13–14) call the sonnet "a cry for help," but one para-doxically requesting the use of force against the pleader. The authors find the poem "a well-knit compact unit" with the image of the "usurpt town" in the octave matched by the lover "betroth'd" to the Devil in the sestet. God is asked to lay siege to and to ravish his heart so as to break the Satanic hold. The unifying idea of the poem, they propose, is that of a spirit "desiring God's help, but incapable of achieving it alone."

Newton (1959, 10–12) offers a reading of the poem in the light of Paul Tillich's *Love, Power, and Justice* (London, 1954). Newton finds that though the metaphors depict power, the poem is about love; and justice, he explains, is achieved, accord-ing to Tillich, by compulsion of a kind that reunites things separated. Hence, argues Newton, Donne implores God to use his power to compel his heart, separated from the Deity by sin, to achieve a just reunion in his love. Love is central to the poem, Newton concludes, expressed in explicit metaphors reminiscent of Donne's erotic poetry, but they have meaning only in relation to the divine power and justice that will effect the desired reunion.

Peterson (1959, 512–13) argues that the sonnet is a culmination of the desire and need "to satisfy the requirements of contrition" and the penitent must now find a way to return God's love. The poem concludes, according to Peterson, with the poet's acknowledgment that he has done all he can and now needs divine aid if he is to do so sufficiently (ll. 11–14). Peterson notes that the plea is the same as that in HSDue, the first in the sequence, differing only in the intensity of feeling. See more under Holy Sonnets: Themes.

Clements (1961, 253–55) maintains that Donne is exploiting the traditional distinctions between the Three Persons (Father=Power, Son=Light, Holy Ghost=Breath) and also the traditional biblical values and associations of "knocke," "breathe," and "shine," and thus the poem suggests that the "triple strength of the Three Persons acting as one, with truly trinitarian force," is needed to lift Donne from his "deeply sinful life and hence to effect his salvation" (253). The sonnet's structure, according to Clements, is viewed as the development of three quatrains, each separately assigned to each of the Three Persons. There is thus a paradox of dividing in order to unite, destroying in order to revive, throwing down in order to raise, that determines the choice of and finds expression in the poem's figurative language, which is of two kinds: the one is warlike, military, destructive, dividing; the other is martial, sexual, or uniting. Each kind of figurative language operates throughout the sonnet (254). Clements concludes that even though the poem is "highly emotional and personal," Donne's "characteristic intellectual mode" is "enhanced and compounded" not just by a "juxtaposition" but by a "fusing or uniting of the two kinds of metaphor" such that they are made to achieve as metaphors "what Donne wishes to achieve with God" (255).

Mueller (1961, 312–14) maintains that an appreciation of this sonnet depends on biblical imagery (312), and "heart" equals the whole inner life or character of the human being. The two central images of the sonnet, he notes, are war and marriage, for the victor at war will also be the victor at marriage: at stake is the heart or the speaker himself. Mueller observes that the key to the meaning of the imagery is the Bible; Mars has nothing to do with this battle and Venus nothing to do with this love (313). Donne represents himself in HSBatter to be as "firmly knit to the Adversary as was Israel in her days of defection," and much as the prophets of Israel "called their people to an account of their sins and called upon God for atonement," so Donne reveals "his own lost position" and prays for "the kind of reconciliation that will lead to freedom" (314).

Parish (1963b, 300–02) does not believe that the sonnet is divided into three parts devoted respectively to the Father, the Son, and the Holy Spirit; the sinner's only reason for addressing God as "three-person'd" is to implore him to exert his complete and triple power (300). The sonnet is unified, Parish asserts, by a shifting viewpoint that produces the effect of God's boring from the outside into the very center of the human heart (300). Parish sees the subject of this sonnet as remorse, calling it "a sonnet in which Donne, with his accustomed daring, requires the reader to see God wearing (with a difference) the rue of a Petrarchan lover" (302).

Cornelius (1965, 25) thinks that this sonnet is developed in three images corresponding to the three persons of the Trinity, reflecting power, wisdom, and love, and notes that three metaphors are used: the blacksmith as creator, the heart as a usurped town, and the soul as a woman appealing for a "holy rape." *HSBatter*, says Cornelius, is a microcosm of Christian experience based on the Trinity as if a drama in three acts, all of them implicit in the initial act of creation.

Ruotolo (1966, 446) believes that the poem has a Trinitarian perspective influenced by St. Thomas Aquinas's discussion of the Trinity and the nature of sanctifying grace. Ruotolo argues that Donne's poem reflects the essentially Thomistic notion of God the Father as begetter and generator (and thus the figure of sexual ravisher is entirely apt); God the Son as begotten who breathes forth love; and God the Holy Spirit whose love illuminates man through the affections and the will (446). Ruotolo notes that Donne displays the procession of the members of the Trinity, and he also reveals sanctifying grace in which the "dread" of the eternal faces the temporal. The sexual language of the sestet, observes Ruotolo, reflects the traditional Christian struggle between man and God and the finite self's resistance to grace, and he finds Donne's theology solidly based, for he roots mankind's ultimate salvation and freedom in his capacity to endure this confrontation. The plea at the close of the poem, Ruotolo says, asserts the faith that God's ravishment leads to chastity (446).

Schwartz (1967, 13–16) argues against the belief that the controlling idea of *HSBatter* is either the doctrine of the Trinity or a single figure. He believes that these views are irrelevant, because they ignore the poem's "dramatic immediacy" (13). He sees the poem based on a series of three figures which are functional vehicles that convey progressive spiritual changes in the speaker. The sequence of metaphors figures human progress "from creation, to the Fall, and at last to the love of God and union with Him" (16). Schwartz thinks that there is a rational and a spiritual development in the poem: as the speaker's thought moves toward a true view of his condition, the speaker's soul moves from terror and despair to love and hope. The three metaphors in the poem—the submerged "tinker" in the first quatrain, the besieged town in the second, and the nuptial metaphor in the third—promote our awareness of the dramatic and spiritual progress of the speaker. For Schwartz, the tinker figure conveys two ideas at once: first, the speaker recognizes his "creatureliness" and his dependence on God, and second, he wrongly imputes to God all the responsibility for his condition and his salvation, failing to recognize his own role in his salvation. Schwartz notes further that there is a suggestion that God is not a good workman and may therefore be responsible for the imperfections of his creature. He states that the besieged town metaphor shows the speaker's incipient awareness of his responsibility for his sins and his realization that he is unable to resist sin without God's grace. Schwartz finds that in the nuptial figure the speaker passes to the next stage, that is, true contrition, which is marked by a genuine love for God. The third quatrain expresses the mystery that the speaker now experiences, namely, his longing and love for God and the sense that he must receive grace from God to love him and to be loved by him. By the end of the sonnet, Schwartz says, the speaker's spiritual state has prepared him for this union, even while he continues to pray for it (16).

Shawcross (1967, 408) says that the first quatrain "pleads for the heart to be freed of sin," the second, "for the mind," while the sestet "involves both of the preceding by pleading for the body to be freed." At the same time, Shawcross remarks that because Christ is the Bridegroom (as in *HSShow*), the sonnet provides sexual images that symbolize the author himself as His consort. Moreover, the poet wishes to be "overthrown," or ravished, and line 4, according to Shawcross, thus refers to "passionate and productive intercourse." A kind of phoenix symbol is contained in this same line, Shawcross notes, for there is a wish for death and rebirth, and the final lines depict the "hoped-for ravishment."

Graham (1968, 30) argues that the words "enthrall" and "ravish" are ambiguous: "enthrall" means "put me in your thrall, enslave" and "fill with delight, enrapture," while "ravish" means both "rape, take by force, despoil" and "fill with pleasure, enrapture." Therefore, he says, the words provide one meaning which is paradoxical and another meaning which is not. That is, Graham argues, it is possible to read the lines as saying that the poet will never be free and chaste unless God fills him with delight.

Heist (1968, 311–20) writes especially in response to Parish (1963b) and also to the various critics whose ideas Parish addresses, asserting that there is "little room for doubt" that the initial image in *HSBatter* is that of a "metal-smith working upon the speaker," an image Heist associates more specifically with a tinker (312). Heist argues against the view that the three persons of the trinitarian God perform three different actions in the poem, and he argues as well against Parish's view that the poem works through a "single parable" that is realized through interconnecting images of a town and bride (314). The "internal structure" of *HSBatter*, he thinks, consists of "three parallel images arranged in ascending order of intensity": in the first the speaker is "simply an old pot, to be melted down and recast"; the second is taken from the world of war and politics; and the third involves "one long crescendo concluding with two paradoxes, that freedom can be found only in thralldom and chastity only in ravishment" (317–18). In Heist's view *HSBatter* is "a series of figures expressing in three images—material, social, and personal—the necessity of Divine Grace," and he finds the unity of the poem not in its imagery, "for the figures of the sonnet cannot be harmonized," but in its theme (320).

Calling *HSBatter* "baroque," Jerome (1968, 301–02) states that the poem strains against its containing form. Violence, paradox, and asymmetry, he finds, all erupt in the first line. He paraphrases the first two lines: "My corruption is such that you will not improve me by tinkering, as one patches an old pot. Rather, I must be smelted, reduced to liquid and reconstituted." The second quatrain shifts to military imagery, Jerome says, the usurper being the devil and the rightful ruler being God. Since the besieger is God, he states, "defend" must be taken in a much more general sense of "look out for my true interest." In the sestet, Jerome continues, the imagery is of a bride begging for bondage to God and then for abduction and rape. Jerome argues that the poem "dramatizes for us a mind scattered, desperate, reaching wildly and indiscriminately for the language, the images which will express his anxiety," and he suggests that the experience the speaker desires is "mystical—there is the violence of rebirth, of seizure, of the rape of God." But such an experience is not realized, Jerome says, and at the end "we sense he will never actually be free or chaste on the terms he requires" (301). And yet Donne's wit, Jerome thinks, leaves his emotion intact. For example, the "three person'd God" of the first line does embody the mystery of the Trinity, but at the same time those words "loom a little like a multi-headed monster of mythology" and thus they undercut credibility (302). Similarly, Jerome continues, the thought of God performing the actions of a tinker "seems somehow amusing, condescending, a tonality which works against the passion and violence the quatrain calls for." The second quatrain, Jerome argues, is convoluted with ingenuity, again obstructing the stream of unreflective desire which Donne is laboring to express. Finally, he says, the sexual incongruity of the sestet "obtrudes and qualifies the appeal" (302).

Bell (1969, 16) argues that Donne makes extensive use of the figure of atonement in HSBatter. See more under Holy Sonnets: Themes.

Steele (1971, 74) suggests that Donne uses the form "you" as second person plural. The belief that Donne is singling out the Father in the first quatrain, the Son in the second, and the Spirit in the third, he contends, is untenable. Steele says that it is "almost unthinkable" that Donne would have wanted the sexual meaning of "you ravish"—in the plural—to be primary. Another meaning of "ravish," however, that is, to take away, or to remove spatially, would fit well with the third quatrain. The sexual meaning is inevitably present but secondary next to the request by the persona of the poem "to be taken away from her bondage to the enemy of the three-person'd God."

Willy (1971, 79–80) thinks that the poem derives its imaginative energy from Donne's "powerful" and "central" use of paradox, expressed in line 3, emphasizing that the "ideas of freedom through imprisonment and enslavement, and chastity through spiritual ravishment" are supportive of this paradox (79). Willy identifies a "fierceness of feeling" that is evident in the impact of harsh onomatopoeic words like "batter," "knocke," "breake"; in the "impetuous, flexible rhythms with their subtle variations of emphasis"; and in the "analogies of forcible possession," all of which culminate in the "audacity" of the erotic metaphor of the last line (79). Donne is saying that if divine love is to prove irresistible it must "storm the citadel of the spirit" rather than woo it. This "invasion of the self," Willy argues, is similar to the experience of human love (79).

Beer (1972, 45–48) states that in HSBatter Donne pursues with "extraordinary intensity" the traditional connection between religious and sexual imagery (45). Further, she says that the "violence of the sentiment" is served by Donne's technique in the poem. Calling the poem a "genuine example of onomatopoeia," Beer says that Donne does not state his theme so much as enact it. The battering of which Donne speaks is felt and heard throughout the poem: "it is a very noisy poem," she says (46). The sonnet includes two devices that Donne was fond of using, Beer observes. First, there is the catalogue or list ("knocke, breathe, shine, and seek to mend"), which Donne also employs in HSRound and HSDeath. Second, there is the use of "Oh" and "Ah" (l. 6), a practice which, Beer states, is "fraught with great danger" (47). Finally, Beer notes that HSBatter demonstrates particularly well Donne's handling of meter (48).

White and Rosen (1972, 54–55) argue that in HSBatter God is implored to act as the blacksmith of the soul (54). The soul is a tower besieged from without by God, they state, but within, the soul is subject to the power of sin, which has captured Reason, God's viceroy or lieutenant. Finally, they claim, God, the divine lover, is implored to oust the devil to whom the soul is betrothed, and to free the soul by making it captive and to make it chaste by ravishing it himself (55).

In *HSBatter*, Altizer (1973, 86–87) asserts, "violent and erotic imagery transforms paradoxes of the Trinity into a unified *force* transcending dogma and logic" (86). As the paradoxes are presented in increasingly erotic form, she says, they not only triumph over reason, but also seem almost on the verge of ravishing the poet's whole being (87).

Blanch (1974, 481–82) writes that in *HSBatter* Donne professes "a passionate love of God," suggesting further that the images of "sexual violence" show that Donne has "no doubts . . . no fears" but has realized a "high degree of spiritual intimacy with God" (481). Blanch notes a "dichotomy between the octave and the sestet": the octave shows that the speaker "wishes God to employ all his power to precipitate a spiritual rebirth," but then in the sestet the speaker is "too weak-willed to do little more than co-operate with God" (482).

Gregory (1974, 117) argues that the "unity of vision" in *HSBatter* is evident in the "sustained assertion" that "in the context of man's relation to God, violent intervention is necessary to bring about a change of state, a salvation." He points to the "complexity" of the poem in realizing this vision: its "actualization in terms of metals through their destruction, the forceful relief of siege in an usurped town, the breaking of a triangular love relationship." He writes that Donne expresses the experience of "man's relation to his God" in terms of the known and argues that *HSBatter* exhibits a "unified sensibility . . . in which thought enlightens feeling and feeling energizes thought."

Wall (1976, 200) argues that *HSBatter* exhibits the full pattern of the lament-psalm, writing that it points to the "essential paradox at the heart of Christian redemption, that the speaker is powerless to effect that which he desires." He notes that the imagery of *HSBatter* (and of *HSShe*) reflects this paradox "by inverting the usual conventions of language and action in Elizabethan sonnet cycles." That is, he argues, in contrast to secular sonnets in which the speaker attempts "to overcome his beloved's passive resistance and convert it to passive yielding," in the Holy Sonnets "the one to be overcome is the speaker himself."

Parini (1977, 305) writes that "the forceful colloquy with God" in *HSBatter* "draws its pathos from the sense of ineradicable sin" which has been gathering throughout the whole sequence of the Holy Sonnets.

Lawler (1979, 91–97) examines Donne's approach to "the excruciating historical and theological dilemma of allegiance to richly painted Romanism or to lamenting and mourning Protestantism" in *HSBatter* (91–92). For Lawler, "the absolute-contingent relationship is the ultimate metaphysical issue," not only for Donne's sonnet, but for "the philosophical-religious views of the entire era" (92). Lawler finds that Donne draws a contrast between "a being that merely patches and polishes" and "a being that recasts and utterly transforms." In other words, according to Lawler, there is a contrast between the Lutheran doctrine of "imputation" through which one is not "intrinsically changed" but is "merely cloaked" in the "merits of Jesus," and the

Catholic doctrine "that the soul is modified in its very substance by 'sanctifying grace,'" while also retaining "its own personal identity" (93). The latter position, in Lawler's view, is the one Donne "affirms" in HSBatter. In this way, according to Lawler, Donne supports the view held by the twentieth-century Catholic Martin D'Arcy, who argues the "mutuality" of eros and agape—or, their "enjambment"—rather than their antagonism (94). Donne, like George Herbert, in Lawler's view, seeks "to be transformed into the infinite," while at the same time retaining "his own finitude" (97).

Lewalski (1979, 271–72) states that HSBatter "is explicitly about regeneration, 'making new,'" but Lewalski adds that the progressive process of regeneration is never completely attained, though "the corruptions of sin are purged from [the soul] and the image of God is restored in it" (271). The speaker's regeneration is dramatized, according to Lewalski, "in uncompromising Calvinist terms, as solely the effect of God's grace upon his passive and helpless self," and furthermore, "mere mending will not suffice to his regeneration: he must be made new by violence," given that he is now in "the possession of an enemy" (272). The Calvinist perception of the individual's "total dependence upon God's grace," given original sin, finds, says Lewalski, a "powerful and paradoxical expression" in the speaker's "declaration that Christ can be liberator of the soul only by becoming its jailer; and can be its Bridegroom only by becoming its ravisher" (272).

Moseley (1980, 103–07) reads the sonnet as an "essay on the Triune nature of God and the action of that nature on man" (103–04). He emphasizes two aspects of Donne's sonnet: "the extent of Donne's debt to Biblical (especially Pauline) theology and Christology" and "the movement of ideas through the poem." Moseley feels that the poem should be read as "a celebration of a property of each Person of the Trinity in turn, forming nevertheless a unified poem." He divides the poem into three parts, with the divisions at line 4 and line 8. The first section of the sonnet, in Moseley's view, centers on "the idea of a creating, making God, a Deus Artifex, who is "reforging his material" (104). Moseley finds that the succeeding sections of the poem "do not present a development of any argument so much as an elaboration of the original impulse." Lines 5–8, in Moseley's view, "are dominated by the conceit of the 'usurpt Town,'" with the usurpation effected by sin, namely, the corruption of Reason "by subterfuge from its duty as captain of the little world." Rectification can come about, according to Moseley's reading, through "intervention by the risen Christ," who "broke the gates of Hell, a city likewise held against him." Moseley sees Donne's debt here to Pauline theology, and in particular to Rom. 7.15, 23–25 (105). Although the word "yet" in line 9 signals a change in the course of the argument, Moseley points out that what mostly occurs "is more a change in tone and register," for "the creative violence of the furnace and the potter's wheel, of the military campaign," yields momentarily to the "tender simplicity of 'Yet dearly I love you, and would be loved faine,'" which Moseley characterizes as having a feminine tone. He finds the verse moving from physical and sexual love through captivity and imprisonment to slavery, or being owned by another, but these ideas are immediately followed by "free," which Moseley relates to the paradox of the Prayer Book's "In whose service is perfect freedom" (106). The "mounting passion" of the poem reaches its climax in the juxtaposition of the words "chast" and "ravish," of which, Moseley notes, "ravish" implies a "violent, selfish, overwhelming and *desired* sexual attack," but the result of this ravishment is "chastity." Moseley concludes by pointing out that the sestet is "an appeal for the operation of the Holy Ghost" in the speaker, a "necessary conclusion to the threefold structure of the poem." Each of the Persons of the Trinity, Moseley says, is "involved in the activity of any One," so that "the poem is itself an image of the Person it addresses," that is, "its structure is itself a trinity" (107).

Mallett (1983, 55, 59) notes that the argument of the sonnet, the "plea for God to enter and take over the poet," is achieved through "two images of assault, one military and one sexual." Acknowledging the dramatic effect of the literally drawn images, Mallett also suggests that a modern reader might be "uncomfortable" (59). Finding some of the Holy Sonnets "forced and unnatural," Mallett views *HSBatter* as trying to be both a "lavish and wilful [sic] display of Donne's intellectual virtuosity" and an "assertion of the poet's desire to surrender his individuality by submitting entirely to the will of God" (55).

Young (1984, 140–41) claims that, except for Richard Crashaw, Donne is probably the most obvious instance of "an English baroque poet," evident, for example, in *HSBatter* (140–41). Young finds the sonnet's "passionate and daringly erotic language" to be that of the devotional baroque lyric, though he also sees it as structured according to "the principles of the Ignatian meditation" (141).

Lawrence (1985, 236) discusses the importance of a number of "trinities" in the poem, suggesting their connections to the divine Trinity and also arguing that the specific identifications are "less important than the general pattern in which three coalesce into one—in this case, a single vision of renewal through the paradoxes of spiritual violence and violation."

Patrides (1985a, 443) points out that the relationship between God and humankind has been figured "in terms of marriage or adultery" since the writings of the great Hebrew prophets. Within this context, Patrides, citing Mueller (1961), notes that Donne described adultery as "every departing from that contract you made with God at your Baptisme" (*Sermons* 9:399).

Gilman (1986, 63, 79–80, 88) examines Donne's poetry in the context of the iconoclastic controversy and attacks on sacred imagery (63), finding *HSBatter* imbued with the Reformation desire to resist any form of idolatry (79). According to Gillman, the iconoclasm urged historically in Deut. 12.3 "must be completed morally in the heart still drawn to the lure of 'their images,'" but the strength of the renewed iconoclasm, in Gilman's reading of the sonnet, is "stronger than the power of mere persuasion to keep [it] out" (79). Gilman contends that "to be made new on the Pauline and Augustinian model demands that the old self and its idolatrous artifacts, be marred—broken, blown, burned" (88). Thus, "the sincerity of the divine poems," in Gilman's view, "would seem to depend all the more on their making a clean break from the idolatry of the love poems," which is also at issue in *HSWhat* (88).

Guibbory (1986, 97) finds that Donne "often reveals" (especially in the Holy Sonnets) a "deep sense of man's essential helplessness." She points out, for example, that in HSBatter the speaker, as a "usurpt towne," appears as a "victim," scarcely responsible for "being 'betroth'd' to Satan," and thus his "rescue depends on God's actions rather than his own" (ll. 11–12). Guibbory adds that although in HSDue memory "instills in Donne a sense of his sinfulness and of God's love and mercy and thus leads him to resign himself to God," in HSBatter the "'devill' continues to 'usurpe' on him" (HSDue 9).

Stein (1986, 96–97) finds in Donne's religious poetry "an imagined dying, a turning away from past considerations and toward the last act conceived and felt as immediately present," which, for Stein, produces "a certain violence" in the poetry, both physical and mental (96). But, according to Stein, the violence in the poetry may be a product of the "strain of near-exhaustion," so that "what is spoken will strive toward the naked utterance of simple truth, the last words that will be validated by the last act," which "might represent a death of the personal will," such as Stein observes in HSBatter (96). Here, Stein emphasizes, there are moments when the violence is "prominent," but there are intervening periods "drained of energy," such as the closing lines (11–14), bearing "images that seek valid ends of religious desire while destroying the traditional frames in which valid concepts of free will and chastity are held" (97). Whereas in his love poetry, Donne "establishes himself in the full and varied character of the masculine lover," in the religious verse, according to Stein, "when he makes love to God," "absolute need" is evident, a "helplessness which must be mastered from without" (97). In this state, Stein adds, Donne assumes the nature of the "traditionally feminine," of "utter subordination and dependence and the brutal psychic condition of ravishability" (97). Stein suggests that what Donne "seems to be willing here is a sacrifice represented by a death of the masculine will" (97).

Van Emden (1986, 53–54) finds that HSBatter reflects neither "the despair" of HSDue nor "the certain faith" of HSDeath (53). HSBatter, she concludes, reflects "the self-tormenting vacillation of hope and despair which is the need he brings to God" (54) and reveals, in the paradox of line 3, "the dramatic action which the poet desires" (54).

Young (1987, 30–31) points out that at first glance HSBatter seems to reflect, particularly in its conclusion, "the severities of Calvinism," but he emphasizes that the sonnet is "precisely a prayer to God for grace, which, if the Calvinist notion of the irresistibility of grace be true, is essentially pointless" (30–31). Young adds, however, that the sonnet nonetheless "expresses a sense of profound depravity and fear of damnation," so that it is "questionable" whether the close of the sonnet "yields a clear theological resolution" (31).

Fallon (1991, 225) points out that both George Herbert and Donne draw on the courtly love tradition in their religious poetry and that the language of that tradition "often reflects an analogy with war." Fallon claims that the "martial aspect" of courtly love often is employed to represent the relationship between God and man, but that the combat is usually "one-sided," as when Donne pleads with God at the opening of HSBatter.

Spurr (1991,171–72) comments on the way in which HSDue calls to mind HSBatter, namely, that "the conviction of ravishment by Satan" in HSDue underlies

Donne's request for ravishment by the Trinity in *HSBatter* (171). Spurr finds that the speaker's "sense of the thoroughness of his sinfulness is extended by the violence of the means required to save him from it" (171–72). Spurr further points to the way Donne "quietly undercut[s]" the dramatic evocation of God by the "measured certainty of his impotence for penitence," as in lines 7–8 (172). Spurr notes that even though the sestet is "pregnant with reconciliation" ("Yet dearly I love you, and would be loved faine"), the "design proves abortive" ("But ame betroth'd vnto your enemy") (172). The concluding couplet, according to Spurr, proposes God's action in a way that "so exaggerates orthodox conceptions of the operation and experience of grace as to be a parody of them" (172). But, Spurr contends, "only such a rigorous epiphany would suffice, for Donne, to compensate for the satanic rape he has already endured" (172).

Sabine (1992, 26) points out that in *HSBatter* Donne "expresses what must have been a common Protestant uncertainty as to whether God was a redeemer or a tormentor," for "Protestantism insisted that salvation did not derive from good works or human virtue but solely from Christ's righteousness."

Wiltenburg (1992, 413, 424–25) finds that the Renaissance preoccupation with the "fortunes of the self," that is, "its making and unmaking, its struggle to be known or heard," is framed in the divine poems as a dialectic "between self and soul," and in those poems Donne "envisions a clear program: the overthrow of the self by whatever means necessary" (413, 424). Wiltenburg contends that "the clearest (and most vehement) statement of this inner division" is seen in *HSBatter* (424). Despite "the Augustinian consummation so devoutly wished for," Wiltenburg emphasizes, it is "never quite achieved." According to Wiltenburg, the impact of *HSBatter* "depends precisely on its equivocal presentation of the 'I' (and 'me') who writes and speaks the poem: Is it the soul, crying *de profundis* in its desperate longing to be made 'new,' or is it the self, performing a star turn *as* the soul crying, etc.?" Wiltenburg contends that it is both at once, and the "brilliant, inextricable mixture of motives and voices dramatizes man's inability, without divine help, to make conversion out of the interminable inner conversation." Finally, Wiltenburg notes, "this is as it must be," for "the soul is of necessity in the self's keeping" (425).

Loewenstein (1993, 11) points to the God addressed by Donne as his "Calvinistic God," who is "capable of making and unmaking his sinful, helpless subject," a God who becomes in the course of the three quatrains, "a metal worker, a warrior-king, and a male lover." Loewenstein notes that Donne paradoxically resists and appeals to God to be forceful in regenerating his sinful soul.

Rambuss (1994, 271–73), finding homoerotic features in the poetry of Crashaw and Herbert, claims that even Crashaw's baroque poetry cannot surpass the homoerotic features of *HSBatter* (271). Rambuss calls attention to Donne's desire to be raped, not by Jesus alone, but by the whole "three-personed" Godhead, or what Rambuss describes as "a kind of trinitarian gang-bang" (272). Moreover, Rambuss posits that Donne "calls up the suggestion of anal penetration" in the lines "I . . ./ Labor to admit you, but oh, to no end" (ll. 5–6). According to Rambuss, "it is as though Donne wants to be enthralled and ravished so that he can remain potent and erect" (273).

Creswell (1995, 184, 187–96) reads *HSBatter* as part of his larger contention that Donne's religious verse manifests "an iconoclastic skepticism about the truth of images" (184). Creswell argues that, through "invoking the Word," the speaker "moves from the figures of praise to the figures of address and in doing so redefines the project of the sonnet and the very status of the subject" (187–88). According to Creswell, the "endlessly self-referring rhetoric" found in Renaissance texts is "frequently figured as the seductive, excessive, and particularly female body," and thus, in Creswell's view, the speaker of *HSBatter* "seeks just such a figure and just such a radical union," "invoking the Word as the force that elides differences" (188). The speaker in Donne's sonnet "takes the position not of the sonneteer but of the besieged citadel or mistress," and in this respect, he is reminiscent of God's beloved in Song Sol. 5, who is described as a "garden inclosed" and who "invokes the winds to 'blow' upon her and yet struggles to give entrance to her beloved." Creswell argues that the "chief figure" of *HSBatter* is apostrophe, adding that this "figure of address" giving "voice or face to the absent" is "invoked" in *HSBatter* so that the speaker "may in turn receive life," as in lines 3–4 (189). Therefore, Creswell contends, the power of the Word in *HSBatter* is to "repeatedly 'o'erthrow' the figure it instates," and "rather than enlivening the speaker by breaking him in order to make him new," the God who is apostrophized is "neither life nor death, spirit nor flesh, but the force that folds these categories in upon one another" (193). According to Creswell, the speaker's apostrophe is thus "his attempt to give voice and form to God so that in turn he might be recovered," but "in not seeking an image but a forceful voice, the speaker would mimic the divine decree," and in doing so gives face "to that which lies prior to and exceeds presentation." Creswell proposes that the "open body figures" of *HSBatter* and *HSWhat* "do not merely thwart reference but split the subject," and therefore "imply not merely an attack against the iconic image of 'visual poetics' but a shattering of vision itself" (194). Creswell concludes that "the more one invokes the Word the more one misdirects," is "left bereft of language," and "yet the Word manifests itself only through these doubly veiled figures" (195).

HSBatter and Other Works

Fausset (1924, 244) compares the sonnet to Thompson's "Hound of Heaven" in that both poems propose to take God's heart by force.

Bethell (1948, 61, 67–68) compares *HSBatter* to Tennyson's "Tears, Idle Tears" to illustrate the difference between "the two great streams of English poetry" (61), that is, between works in which words "do what they say" and those in which they are largely sensuous and emotive (67–68). See more under *HSBatter*: Language and Style.

Daiches and Charvat (1950, 659–60) note that the poem shows the "intense inner conflict" of Donne's faith, in contrast to the "more equitable" tone of Herbert's poems. For other comparisons of Donne and Herbert, see Hooper and Harvey (1958), Slights (1981), Sloane (1981), and Sherwood (1989).

Louthan (1951, 123) suggests that the rhythm and alliteration of the poem "point backward to *Beowulf*, and forward to Hopkins and Auden." On *HSBatter* and Hopkins, see also Morris (1953) and Coanda (1957).

Morris (1953, 73–75, 99) finds that Donne and Hopkins share an awe at the power of God and a sense of spiritual struggle as physical, as in *HSBatter* and "Carrion Comfort." He further compares Donne's sexual image of religious concepts to Hopkins's effort to relate the birth of a poem to human fertilization in "To R.B.," both of them linking the material and spiritual worlds (75). Morris observes that Donne's sense of spiritual struggle, as expressed in *HSBatter* (as well as *HSVex*) may also be found in T. S. Eliot, as in "Ash Wednesday" (III, 1–6), where salvation is a flight of stairs to be climbed with difficulty (99).

Coanda (1957, 182, 187) thinks that, while Hopkins came close to a mystical vision, as in the first stanza of "The Wreck of the Deutschland," Donne was never close to God, as is evident when "he *begs* Him to batter his heart" (182). Coanda further argues that *HSBatter* and Hopkins's "Carrion Comfort" are "two sides of a coin" in that their dominant metaphor is a God "ravishing, or wrestling with, a recalcitrant sinner in order to humble and cleanse him." They resemble one another further, he says, in that both are "rich with alliteration, assonance, rhyme, parallel verbs, caesuras, interjections, paradox, terseness, irregular meter"; and, Coanda concludes, both "reach the apex of religious and metaphysical sonneteering" (187).

Hooper and Harvey (1958, 13) suggest a comparison with Herbert's "Love."

Richmond (1958, 534–35) argues that the passionate style and meaning of the sonnet owe something to Ronsard's *Amours* (2.9). See also Richmond (1970), Prescott (1978), and Richmond (1981).

Ellrodt (1960, 2:259n83) suggests that Jacques Grévin's sonnet "Souffle dans moi, Seigneur, souffle dedans mon âme" reminds one of *HSBatter*.

Höltgen (1964, 347–52) describes Donne's *HSBatter* as illustrative of and influenced by the traditional emblem sequence of the uninstructed heart. Both divine love and erotic love are brought together in Donne's poem as they are in many emblematists of the time. Höltgen comments on these pictures or emblems of the heart (evoked by "knocke, breathe, shine, seeke to mend" and "breake, blowe, burn, make me new") by pointing to Christopher Harvey's *Schola Cordis* but also (and especially) to Georgette de Montenay's *Emblèmes* (Lyons, 1571), Antoon Wiericx, *Cor Iesu Amanti Sacrum* (about 1600 or earlier), Daniel Cramer, *Emblemata sacra* (Frankfurt, 1624), Hermannus Hugo, *Pia Desideria* (Antwerp, 1624), and others. No single work, he notes, can be cited as a source for Donne, and in any case many of the emblem books are too late for him to have seen. But there can be no doubt that Donne's imagery in *HSBatter* belongs within the emblematic tradition though one can hardly prove his knowledge of any particular emblem book or writer. One may also see the continuity of this tradition by looking at Donne's influence on Harvey himself, Höltgen observes; the conventional materials could be endlessly varied. But *HSBatter* makes use of these materials in an individual way, he thinks, for Donne possesses "a personal predilection for the methods of the emblematic tradition" ("eine persönliche Vorliebe für die Methoden der Emblematik") (352).

In answer to Ruotolo (1966—see *HSBatter*: Themes), Lloyd (1969, 251–52) contends that Donne received his inspiration for *HSBatter* not from Aquinas but from the second collect (for peace) in the office of morning prayer in the Book of Common Prayer. He comments specifically on Donne's adaptation of certain phrases from the collect, notably "O God . . . in knowledge of whom standeth our eternall life" and "in whose service is perfect freedom" (251).

Richmond (1970, 141–44) argues that HSBatter borrows "ideas, images, or situations from Ronsard, who offers consistently relevant precedents for Donne's idiosyncrasy, subjectivity and verve" (141). He writes that the structure, thought and imagery of this sonnet derive inspiration from Ronsard's "Foudroye moy le corps, ainsi que Capanée" (141). Although Richmond thinks that Donne provides his own "bizarre" heightening in the allusion to the Trinity, he notes that HSBatter takes its military imagery from Ronsard. Donne, moreover, makes use of Ronsard's sense that man desperately needs God's grace on account of the intransigent sinfulness of human nature that reason betrays (144).

Prescott (1978, 115) states that HSBatter shares with Ronsard's sonnet "Foudroye moy le corps" the image of a warring city betrayed by Reason, a violent tone, and a plea for God's overpowering force to do for the speaker and his inner divisions what his own defective will cannot. See also The Holy Sonnet and Other Works.

D'Amico (1979, 24, 26), discussing the importation of Petrarchan features into the English tradition, compares Drayton with Donne. Drayton (as in "Truce, gentle Love") "introduces an original touch, characteristic of his sonnets, by using the technical language of a truce and a witty conclusion in which it is suggested that to be conquered by love is to win," but the paradox is "the conquering woman does not do unto them as they would like to have done unto her" (26). Donne, however, in HSBatter, "can turn this situation around and call upon his God to attack, overcome, and ravish" (26). In Donne's sonnet, according to D'Amico, "defense is now a sign of betrayal, because the heart and soul are only fulfilled when united with God," and "sexual-spiritual consummation—to die—can only take place when the heart is divorced from the 'enemie' and wed to God" (26).

Milward (1979 [1988, 77–79]) observes that even though it is less evident than in other sonnets, HSBatter remains "Ignatian in spirit with its vein of military metaphor and even its imagery of marital love." Milward adds that "the opening petition, 'Batter my heart,' is mindful of "the second prelude of the Meditation on the Kingdom of Christ," with "the address to 'three person'd God'" echoing "the subsequent Contemplation on the Incarnation." The closing three lines of the sonnet call to mind "the concluding Ignatian Contemplation for Obtaining Divine Love, with its act of self-oblation" (77). And, paradoxically, "the only way to make him 'rise, and stand' on his spiritual feet," Milward observes, is "by overthrowing him—as the angel of God overthrew Jacob in their wrestling together" (Gen. 32.24). The metaphor of the besieged town recalls "the siege of Pamplona in which Ignatius was struck in the leg by a cannon-ball and thus converted from a worldly life to the service of God" (78). In the sestet, Milward notes, the speaker longs to be loved by God, but "there is a serious obstacle: he is already betrothed to the devil," and "so he prays God to effect a divorce, a forceful breaking of this conjugal knot"—"that subtle knot" (cf. Ecst)—which "makes him less than a man, a slave to Satan." Milward adds that one may also perceive here an "echo" of Viola's prayer in TN 2.2.41: "O time, thou must untangle this, not I;/It is too hard a knot for me to untie" (79).

Novarr (1980, 128–29, 179–82) notes that Gardner (1952) draws a comparison between *HSShe* and *Christ*, given the sonnet's emphasis on "the idea of God as a jealous lover," which Novarr finds also present in *HSBatter* (128, 128n). Novarr further notes the similarity between *HSBatter* and the last line of *Sickness* ("Therefore that he may raise the Lord throws down"), suggesting their possible common connection to Ps. 146.8, and later 1 Cor. 9.27, and the view that God brings humans to death that He might raise them to life everlasting (179–82).

Klinck (1981, 249–50) finds that a close comparison of *HSBatter* with *Lit* confirms the view that the Trinity is "structurally and thematically important throughout the poem and not merely in the apostrophe of the first line" (249). Klinck points out that in the first three stanzas of *Lit*, the "Persons of the Trinity are associated with specific aspects of regeneration," while in *HSBatter*, "each quatrain introduces a different aspect of the process the speaker wishes to undergo": namely, the Father-Creator, who must "re-create the speaker, that he may be 'new fashioned'"; second, "the speaker is like something belonging to God originally," but now "in need of redemption"; and, finally, "the Holy Ghost is associated with the will or love," which emphasizes "the union of the soul with God" (249–50). Klinck adds that Martz (1954) also has commented on the form of a meditation as analogous to the Trinity in the human soul: "memory, understanding and will" (250).

Richmond (1981, 229–34) makes the claim that much of what has been regarded as distinctive to Donne's poetry can be found in earlier poetry such as that of Ronsard. Richmond finds *HSDeath* "typical" of the Holy Sonnets in that, "under the pressure of his religious anxieties and divided ecclesiastical loyalties," Donne has "transposed what had been an amatory motif to more religious meaning," and he notes "the same ethical evolution" in *HSBatter*, an "infinitely more powerful and moving sonnet" than *HSDeath* (229–30). The "deep ambivalence" evoked by the amatory and the religious (which gives *HSBatter* its "religious desperation"), is also evident in Ronsard's "Je veux brusler pour m'en-voler aux cieux," and Richmond considers Ronsard's sonnet "Foudroye moy le corps, ainsi que Capnée" to best reflect the earlier treatment of certain themes that we find in Donne, and in particular in *HSBatter*. Richmond claims that Ronsard's sonnet is "conclusive evidence" that the "deep emotional ambivalence, powerful language, and compressed imagery" associated with Donne are "quite traditional" (232). Richmond adds that even the "sexual tension" in *HSBatter* "derives from the more emphatically amatory context of Ronsard's sonnets" as does the "kinetic phrasing," or "violent language" (233). Richmond finds that Donne adds "two distinctive heightenings," namely, giving God the "triple identity of the Christian trinity," and providing the "imagery of rape" that yields a "climactic shock value" (233). Richmond adds that while Ronsard is "quite deliberate in his provocative exploitation of sexuality," he does not achieve the "progression of emotion and argument" evident in Donne, who "tightens the structure and heightens the tone of his models" (233). In both *HSBatter* and "Foudroye moy le corps," Richmond argues, "the tension is increased by a Reformation intensity of moral concern and by the ominous overtones of the allusions to military sieges" (233–34).

Slights (1981, 237–38) compares *HSBatter* and Herbert's "The Crosse" to illustrate their key differences on the question of "how to achieve assurance, avoiding both despair and presumption," which Slights, citing Peterson (1967), finds central to the anxiety of the Holy Sonnets (237–38). Herbert's "resolutions that direct to moral action," such as that found in "The Crosse," Slights says, distinguish Herbert's poetry from Donne's (237). Although HSBatter and "The Crosse" "explore the ambivalence of fear and desire," Herbert resolves the tension "in the paradox of the cross, finding evidence of grace in the recognition of guilt and intention to do God's will." Slights views Donne, on the other hand, as using paradox "not to resolve contradictions but to define the problem of simultaneously longing for and resisting grace, of loving and fearing God." Slights acknowledges Cathcart's argument (1975) that the "business of the poem" is the reconciliation of contradictions and she agrees that in the "rape metaphor" Donne seeks recognition "of the powers of both the reason and his physical nature," but for Slights the metaphor "expresses the violent tension between desire and fear, not the peace of reconciliation" (238n41). Slights notes that Donne uses "meditative techniques to evoke the fear and love of true contrition," but "his moral stance" in the Holy Sonnets is "passive." Slights points out that Herbert also wrote poems that exhibit unresolved longing, but in "The Crosse" "doubt yields to love" (238).

Sloane (1981, 55–61, 76) points to Donne's and Herbert's use of emblematic techniques such as the "personification of the soul . . . as an actor in the drama" of the poem, noting also Francis Quarles's personification of the Anima in his Emblemes. Using this device, according to Sloane, "the poet tries to draw the reader into his own meditative world" (55). The heart emblem, Sloane adds, functions much the same way in HSBatter. Sloane notes that Höltgen (1964—see HSBatter: Themes) finds justification for the violence of Donne's images "in the light of the purgation, illumination and unification of the meditative tradition" (59), and concludes that the similarities between "the heart emblems" and those found frequently in the poetry of both Donne and Herbert make it difficult to think that the two poets did not draw from such emblematists as Georgette de Montenay (1571) and Daniel Cramer [Emblemata Sacra (1624)]. Cramer's image of the heart provides, according to Sloane, "an excellent example," showing "a heart being beaten by a hammer held by a hand—a typical image, usually regarded as the hand of God—extending from the clouds" (60). Sloane compares the use of the heart emblem in HSBatter and Crashaw's "To the Noblest & best of Ladyes, the Countesse of Denbigh," and concludes that, unlike Donne's effort, Crashaw's poem does not "draw us into the picture" (76). In Sloane's view, the reader does not "feel" the images in Crashaw's poem as in Donne's, for Crashaw "has not interiorized his thought," or objectified his soul in the way that Donne dramatizes it (76).

Paulissen (1982, 149–52), having claimed that Lady Mary Wroth knew and emulated Donne, draws a comparison between Wroth's Sonnet 27 ("Fie, tedious hope, why do you still rebel?") and HSBatter (149–50). Paulissen finds a close parallel with Donne's sonnet in the tercet following the second quatrain of Wroth's poem: "No towne was won by a more plotted fight/Then I by you, who may my fortune write/ In embers of that fire which ruin'd me" (ll. 9–11). In the tercet, according to Paulissen, Wroth "attacks Hope, who has misrepresented herself," but "this time with a conceit of a besieged city, like a soul bereft of Hope, falling to the enemy and being burned" (151–52). Paulissen finds Wroth's imagery "suggestive of Donne's sonnet," in which he compares himself to a "usurpt towne," adding that Wroth's "fire" may refer either to "the literal fire of a razed city or to a sexual fire." And, again, "like Donne, who ordered God to batter down his hardened heart," Wroth demands with "enthusiastic zeal" that the "virtue of Hope return to her and save her from the spiritual aridity in which she now suffers" (152).

Dollimore (1984, 180) argues that the sonnet presents a speaker who is in "a relationship with sado-masochistic power (and desire)" and who is quite different from the "exploitative rake" of *LovUsury* (180). Dollimore associates the sensibility in *HSBatter* with Donne's "obsession" with the "instability" of the self, and a consciousness of "the complex interrelations between power, violence, and desire, as they traverse and constitute subjectivity" (180).

Young (1984, 141–43) finds a number of similarities between *HSBatter* and poems of Lope de Vega (141). For example, Donne's speaker "beseeches God for the ecstasy, the rapture of surrender," which is the goal of Lope de Vega's *Rimas sacra*, in Young's view (142). But Young points out that, in the instance of Donne, "genuinely voluntary surrender is impossible to the enslaved will of Protestant theology" (142–43). Whereas in Lope de Vega's sonnets, the speaker is a "faithless wife or a slave" who has escaped from a "rightful master," in Donne's sonnet, the speaker is "not merely captured by Satan but is "'betroth'd' to Satan and hence rightfully belongs to God's 'enemie'" (142). Hence, the speaker's "release demands from God an act of lawless violence—a rape, a conceit which implies that the sinner's soul does not yield, does not consent to God'" (142). Young isolates the tension in the poetry of Lope de Vega between " the poet's desire to gratify his own pride and lust and his desire to do the will of God," and in Donne's poetry between "the poet's longing and experience and his Reformation theology" (142). Young concludes that, poetically speaking, Donne's theology is ultimately "anti-poetic" since, in "eliminating all contingency from man's destiny," it thereby "cancels any sense of drama, which is the heart of literature" (142–43).

Gaston (1986, 208–09) observes here, in the second of the nine Holy Sonnets that Benjamin Britten set to music in 1946, Britten's challenge to his audience as "the repetitive, inexorable accompaniment rises and falls by its own logic as the voice interposes the sonnet's hard monosyllables in dissonant bursts" (208). Gaston notes that with this setting, Britten creates the "strongest possible contrast" with the setting of *HSBlack*, which immediately precedes *HSBatter*, and so "defines at once the polarities between which his penitent will move" (208–09).

Guibbory (1986, 97) notes that although in *HSDue* "memory instills in Donne a sense of his sinfulness and of God's love and mercy and thus leads him to resign himself to God," in *HSBatter* the "'devill' continues to 'usurpe' on him (l. 9)."

Frontain (1987, 163–69,172–74) examines *HSBatter* in the context of the Reformation emphasis on the typological model for "the individual to explore one's own spiritual state" and to discover, as Donne says in a sermon, "the repeating againe in us, of that which God had done before to Israel" (*Sermons*, 3:313). Frontain finds that in communicating to a Christian trinitarian God "his readiness and complete desire for salvation," the speaker evokes three images "most often used in tandem by the Hebrew prophets to denounce sinful, apostate Israel: a vessel in need of repair, a usurped town under siege, and a woman trapped in a degrading sexual relationship" (163). Frontain notes that the speaker "must be broken, beaten, and divorced just as Israel was for having been unfaithful to the one true God" (164). Frontain acknowledges the value of those studies, such as Clements (1961), that align the three conceits with the three persons of the Trinity but also finds that such analyses "unfortunately" take attention away from the "likewise deeply Hebraic resonance of the poem's three conceits," which have their "basis in the covenant which Yahweh made with Israel in which the Israelites' undeviating worship of Yahweh as their one true god guaranteed them this protection as his chosen people" (165). Frontain proceeds to associate in considerable detail the images of the potter, the besieged town, and the woman in a problematic sexual relationship with images drawn from Hebrew scripture, concluding that biblical Israel's "historical drama of disobedience and chastisement" significantly "adumbrates the interior drama" evident in the speaker of HSBatter (168). Frontain suggests that the difficulty a reader might have in perceiving the typological dimensions of the sonnet may be attributed to Donne's "conflation of the images." He notes that Clements's (1961) study shows that the individual members of the Trinity are also "conflated theologically into one 'three-person'd God,'" much as the "verb actions" most appropriate to a particular member are also applicable to other members of the Trinity, and he argues that an even larger conflation occurs, as "type and antitype are subsumed into an eternal drama in which the actors are both Israel and Yahweh, the individual Christian and the grace-giving Trinity" (169). HSBatter offers no certain closure or evidence of the speaker's "peace of mind," notes Frontain, and he thus identifies the speaker as a "peculiarly Donnean sort of prophet, one who employs prophetic language to prophesy to God against himself" (173). Thus, Frontain concludes, "rather than attacking the people's complacency and denouncing a sinful nation, the speaker storms God's ear to denounce himself, for unless God recognizes the speaker's contrition and acknowledges his desire to repent by offering him the gift of prevenient grace, the speaker is eternally lost." Hence, he says, "by describing his situation typologically, the speaker attempts to prod God into acting in the necessary way" (174).

Moseley (1989, 19, 167) finds the "Schola Cordis tradition of self examination and personal devotion" evident not only in English emblem books but also in the strategies of poets such as Herbert and Donne, who used "devotional emblems" as "image sources and reference points and as ways of conceptualising their own self-examination" (19). Both HSBatter and Herbert's "Grace," he says, "depend on a memory of emblems of the heart being hammered on an anvil, or refined in an alembic, by God's grace" (19). He further notes the influence of Hermannus Hugo's Pia Desideria (Antwerp, 1624) on poems such as HSBatter and "Grace" (167).

Sherwood (1989, 37), in his comparison of Herbert's conception of love for God with that of Donne, finds that Donne's "calculated shock in inviting a divine rape . . . is merely a flamboyant heterosexual embrace to express union."

Creswell (1995, 184, 189–92, 194–95) finds close parallels between HSBatter and Song Sol. 5 as well as Deut. 12.3, 13.15–16 and 12.30, and in particular with regard to Donne's apparent "skepticism about the truth of images" and his new emphasis on "voice," or sound (184, 189–90). Creswell notes, for example, the poem's "images of breaking and burning" that "echo Deuteronomy's call for the destruction of idols or the carnal icon." *HSBatter*, in Creswell's view, not only invokes the "blazon of God the beloved" in Song Sol. but repeats the "injunction" in Deut. "against any such image-making." Creswell cites Gilman's assertion (1986—see *HSBatter*: Themes) that the iconoclasm in Deut. "must be completed morally in the heart still drawn to the lure of 'their images'" (190), and he suggests that *HSBatter* "does not present a new, truer figure but disavows the figurative speech it instates," asserting and crossing out "the very act of presentation" (190–91). Creswell states that the speaker's apostrophe to God is "his attempt to give voice and form to God so that in turn he might be recovered" (194). And yet, Creswell maintains, "the speaker's apostrophe can only address another trope, not an iconic sign but only a chosen figure," and thus the sought-for "mystical union may not be a consummation that makes whole but a binding that ceaselessly rends apart" (194–95).

Notes and Glosses

1–8 *Batter . . . proves weake and vntrew.* **LEISHMAN** (1951): these lines offer the usual "note of agonized striving" to be found in Donne's religious poetry (261). **BELLETTE** (1975) argues that there is a "strong controlling pattern" in the octave of *HSBatter*, with a temporal and logical sequence that begins to break down in the second quatrain (330).

1–6 *Batter . . . to no end.* **PRAZ** (1931) compares the religious poetry of Donne and Michelangelo, finding that they both struggle against "the aridity of their hearts," feeling that there is a barrier between themselves and God, which only He can break. Cites ll. 1 and 5–6 to illustrate (69–70).

1–4 *Batter . . . and make me new.* **SYMONS** (1899) says that in the Holy Sonnets "thought crowds in upon thought," as in the "too knotted beginning" of this poem, showing Donne to be "too often ingenious rather than felicitous" (743). **FAUSSET** (1938): Donne's consciousness of "the prison of himself" is powerfully expressed in these lines where "he bade God to punish him like a pugilist" while the "hammer blows of the monosyllables" reveal his "hunger after the spiritual" (x–xi). **ANONYMOUS** (1938): Donne's "turbulent mysticism" is often expressed in images of violence and suffering (814). **HAMBURGER** (1944): the rhythm "conveys an impression of agony and violent conflict," which a smoother rhythm would have failed to create (159). **STAUFFER** (1946), arguing that effective poetry depends upon concrete images engaging tactile sensations, cites the lines as images of "straining figures." Points out that the sense of struggle and effort is heightened by "the force and heaviness of the extra accented syllables" (135–36). **LOUTHAN** (1951) finds the fact that the God is "three persond" to enhance the strength of the battering. Observes that the image is pursued in the two groups of single verbs in ll. 2 and 4: God the Father must break instead of knock, God the Holy Spirit blow instead of breathe, and "God the Son (Sun)" burn instead of shine. (Similarly, Martz [1963, 90].) Notes further that the violent verbs alliterate with "batter" (124). So also Fuzier (1983). **MILES** (1951)argues that Donne's words are "abstract, active, and evaluative," appropriate to sentences that are primarily "address and argument." (Revises later [1957, 21–23] to say that Donne's language is "vocative, predicative, abstract.") Observes that poets in the Donne tradition relied heavily on verbs, using one "for every two substantives," unlike others, such as Milton, for whom the ratio might be as high as one for four. Cites *HSBatter* 1–4, a poem of "action and address," to illustrate (38–40). **WHITE** (1951): Donne is to be admired for "the remarkable energy and immediacy" with which he conceived of theological doctrine, as here with the Redemption (366). **MORRIS** (1953) finds a "striking similarity in thought and passionate expression" between Hopkins's "The Wreck of the Deutschland," (*st.* 2) and Donne's lines (21–22). **HUNT** (1954): here and in ll. 11–14 his "dramatic bent can also lead Donne to the forced sensationalism of melodrama, especially when he gets his hands on an erotic conceit" (136). **WILLEY** (1954) notes the "sledge-hammer effect" of Donne's "impassioned pleading with God" (364). **COX** (1956b) quotes the lines to illustrate that, like the love poetry, the "dramatic power" of the religious verse "expresses his mental conflicts" (51). **UL-HASAN** (1958): Donne humanizes Christ, cast here in the "workman-like role" of a chemist (36). **SHAWCROSS** (1967) writes that "the Father, who is power, now only knocks but is asked to 'breake'; the Holy Spirit, who is the infusion of love, now only breathes but is asked to 'blowe'; the Son, who is light and synonymous with the sun, now only shines but is asked to 'burn.'" Observes that the entire Trinity thus both seeks to mend the author's sinfulness "by these only partially destructive forces" and is asked to "make him new by complete destruction." Concludes that the speaker "rises (to heaven) by being overthrown" and "stands upright (firm in Faith) by the bending of God's force" (408). **LEVER** (1974) notes the "overriding of regular metre by impetuous stress effects," finding also that the conceit of the heart "as a besieged fortress" comes from romance and here "suggests contemporary cannons and mines" (181). **MOSELEY** (1980) notes that the "subliminal images" suggest God "as a blacksmith or possibly Jeremiah's potter" and points to Jer. 18.3–4 and Ps. 1.9 (104). Cites Gregory's comment (1974) that Donne's father was an ironmonger but observes that "the image of God as craftsman is common enough" (104). Adds that these lines "could almost be an expansion, after meditation," of Ezek. 18.31: "Cast away from you all your transgressions, whereby ye have transgressed; and make you a new heart and a new spirit; for why will ye die, O house of Israel?" Concludes that the "fundamental unstated ideas" behind Donne's exact "visual paradoxes" is Jesus's remark that "He that would save his life shall lose it; he that shall lose his life, for my sake, shall save it" (105). **BEDFORD** (1982) surveys the varying interpretations of the opening lines and images and believes that the "most useful" suggestion is Levenson's identification (1953) of God as a "tinker" and the speaker as a "pewter vessel" (see *HSBatter*: Themes) (17). Points to images of God as potter in Isa. 30.14 and 64.8 and Jer. 18.4 and notes the increasing activity called for: "knocks, breathes on, shines the defective clay pot" ("taps it to test its strength, breathes on it and shines it up to make it look all right superficially") give way to more extreme redoing ("the pot must be broken, the bellows worked, the kiln fired again") (18). Suggests that interpreting the imagery is difficult because Donne seems to be "thinking of two incompatible ideas at the same time": that the vessel in its original state is marred by original sin, and that God's remaking of the vessel "can only be interpreted as the grace which regenerates marred and fallen men" (18). Asserts, however, that the "basic material is nothing more than clay in God's hands" (18). Cites Jer. 19.10–11 and concludes that the opening conceit is one in a series of three metaphors "assigned to the Father (the potter), the Holy Ghost whose inspiration releases captive reason, and the Son whose Bride Donne prays to become" (19). **FUZIER** (1983): the twelve-syllable element of ll. 3 and 4 ("and bend/Your force, to break, blow, burn, and make me new") in contrast with its homologue of ll. 1 and 2 is a sign of massive and irresistible force, and at the same time underscores the truth of the profound sentiments which gives shape to the prosodic and rhetorical elements expressed in this meditation (44n11). **LINVILLE** (1984b): the "'bending' of one line into the next copies what the speaker demands and desires: a radical 'bending' of God's force to break and utterly transform him," and thus the "shape and rhythm of the lines" in the opening "underscore and act out its central paradox: that renewal and regeneration are only possible through radical disruption and creative destruction" (77). **CRAIK and CRAIK** (1986): "The dominant imagery is of repairing a metal utensil: tinkering is unfavourably contrasted with reforging" (280). **SMITH** (1991) argues that the "sheer force of the petition" points to the "extremity of his struggle with himself and with God's adversary, as well as the majesty of the universal conflict which is waged in him and which God has an interest in his winning" (135). **SMITH** (1992): an example of the Holy Sonnets' opening "the sinner to God, imploring God's forceful intervention by the sinner's willing acknowledgment of the need for a drastic onslaught upon the present hardened state" (88).

1–2 *Batter . . . and seeke to mend;* **HAMER** (1930): "the opening phrases generally march straight across the line limit" (200). **KLINCK** (1981), finding *Lit* to be Donne's most sustained treatment of the Trinity, sees *HSBatter* as a poem that epitomizes "the difficulties inherent in applying a trinitarian analysis to Donne's poetry," particularly since it addresses the "three-person God" (248). Reviews the controversies surrounding the Trinitarian framework of Donne's sonnet and cites Knox (1956), Clements (1961), Ruotolo (1966), Schwartz (1967) (see *HSBatter*: Themes) and Wanninger (1969) (see *HSBatter*: General Commentary). Adds a further problem to be found in "an extensive trinitarian reading of this sonnet," namely, that "the order of the verbs ('knock, breathe, and shine')," suggesting the sequence "Father, Holy Ghost, Son" is "unconventional" but points out that Donne "regularly associates the Third Person with shining" (249). **SINGH** (1992): the speaker represents his heart "as a door that needs to be forcefully battered down," though at present God is "only knocking at it" (l. 2) (101).

1 *Batter my hart, three-persond God, for you* **READ** (1928) cites this as an example of Donne's lines that contain images and expressions of "the same dialectical subtlety and impassioned majesty" as appear in his early works (66). **WELLS** (1940):

Donne wrote in the tradition of the dramatic monologue, often proposing, as here, "an astonishing task" (186). MOLONEY (1944) quotes the line to illustrate "the transmutation of the traditional silken sonnet of the Elizabethans into a lyric of highly dramatic propensities" (132). STAUFFER (1946) remarks about the line that the "abstract and the concrete, the intellectual and the tangible, are not easily separated in Donne's mind; one grows from the other, and neither can be said to come first" (152). BETHELL (1948): the concentrated force of a "desperate petition" is reinforced by the hard open vowels and sharp consonants (68). MORRIS (1953): in Donne spiritual conflict is a physical experience, as it is for Hopkins in "Carrion Comfort" (5–6) (30). WINNY (1970) calls this opening "brutally violent" and says that "the suddenness of the onslaught takes us unawares" (141). LEWALSKI and SABOL (1973) observe that this address to the Trinity "turns upon several series of three—trinities of actions and of petitions" (155). BROADBENT (1974) finds in the word "batter" an allusion to a "blacksmith (as in Hopkins's *Felix Randall*) or an army, as opposed to a mere tinker." Notes that the image "changes to sex and imprisonment" and calls HSBatter a "[s]trongly antithetical poem" (128). GILL (1990), citing the line, notes that "as in many of the love poems an examination of the frequency and impact of the first and second person pronouns is illuminating" (105).

1 *Batter* BETHELL (1948): the meaning of the word is "undecided" until the verbs of l. 4 and the siege imagery of ll. 5–6, where it becomes clear that "God is the ram" (69). HOOPER and HARVEY (1958): an image of a medieval battering ram used to destroy the gates of a besieged town (14). WILLMOTT (1985) calls the "forceful opening" apt for both the "image of the blacksmith hammering on the anvil" and the "siege images which follow" (69).

1 *three-person God,* (Many commentators have identified the "three-person God" with the Christian Trinity. For more extensive discussions see especially the entries under HSBatter: Themes.) UPHAM (1908) suggests that Donne's use of compounds may have been influenced by Du Bartas (179). KERMODE (1957) finds the reference appropriate to a poem about the paradoxes of the Christian faith, since the Trinity is one of the most important of them (40). SULLENS (1964) cites "three-person" as a word combination the OED does not record (206).

2–4 *As . . . and make me new.* KORTEMME (1933): Donne beseeches God passionately for grace, the intensity of his feeling especially evident in the verbs (45). HOOPER and HARVEY (1958): Donne deliberately contrasts the half-measures of l. 2 with the more vigorous methods of l. 4 (14). MOSELEY (1980) suggests that the verbs may point to the Persons of the Trinity: "knock" (l. 2) is used in Rev. 3.20 and elsewhere as Jesus knocks "for admission to the human heart"; "breathe" is "commonly used of the action of the Spirit"; and 2 Cor. 4.6 refers to God "shin[ing] in our hearts" (104n). FUZIER (1983): the initial unstressed foot of l. 3 reduces to four the number of accents, all of which occur in the four verbs in company with the paradoxical antithesis: "That I may rise, and stand, o'erthrow me, and bend." Lines 3 and 4 are remarkable for their perfect prosodic parallelism (rhetorical and semantic) with l. 2, and their identical accentual schema. These same lines furnish an uncommon example of isocolon (a type of symmetry) doubled with "amplificatio" (a type of intensification). The triple alliteration ("break," "blow" and "burn") by way of the intermediary "bend" echoes "batter," a key word of the entire sonnet, and conveys perfectly the convergence of efforts in a radical renovation by the violence that does not exist in "knock, breathe, shine" (44). GILL (1990): the fourth line "answers" the second by providing "stronger verbs," such as "break" in place of "knock." Such juxtapositions may suggest the "desperate state of the poet" but may also "disturb" because of the "almost blasphemous substitution of violent words for ones which are steeped in biblical associations." Christ in Rev. 3.20 is seen as saying: "Behold I stand at the door and knock," whereas in Matt. 6.19 thieves are the ones who "break through and steal" (105). HANDLEY (1991): the images are perfectly balanced, "almost likening God to a blacksmith" (44). LABRIOLA (1995) suggests that the order of verbs may be associated with the Father, Son, and Holy Spirit, respectively (99).

2 *As yet but knock, breathe, shine, and seeke to mend;* MORRIS (1953): both Donne and Hopkins, in his sprung rhythm, overload a line with stressed syllables by including one that demands emphasis in the place of a normally slack syllable, as here, in l. 4, and in Hopkins's "The Soldier" (l. 6) and "To R.B." (l. 6) (47).

2 *knock,* BETHELL (1948): the word "suggests the familiar knocking of the heart and a Gospel reference" (69). HOOPER and HARVEY (1958): an echo of Rev. 3.20, "Behold, I stand at the door, and knock" (14). [So also, Booty (1990, 109) and Martin (1990, 62).] FOWLER (1991): "(1) test by tapping; (2) beat the breast in contrition" (118).

2 *breathe,* HERMAN (1953): the word may also have the OED definition, "to taint, corrupt" (item 18). HOOPER and HARVEY (1958): an echo of Gen. 2.7, "breathed . . . the breath of life" (14). MARTIN (1990) points to Christ's breathing on his disciples in John 20.22 (62–63).

2 *shine,* HOOPER and HARVEY (1958): an echo of Ps. 31.16, "Make thy face to shine upon thy servants" (14). [Similarly, Martin (1990, 63).] MALLETT (1983): "polish" (59).

2 *mend;* SHAABER (1958): "heal, cure" (104).

3–4 *That . . . make me new.* STAUFFER (1946): the poet achieves intensity and momentum "by delaying the completion of the thought while he crowds together" compound verbs (74). BETHELL (1948) notes that the words "do what they say." Observes that the extra syllable, "mee," reflects "the strain of overthrowing" and the line-end gap between verb and object enacts "the difficulty of the operation" (68–69). MORRIS (1953): Donne's physical imagery of spiritual conflict is similar to that of Hopkins in "Patience, hard thing!" (10–11) (74–75). DUNCAN (1959): Donne anticipates Hopkins's notion of a "divine union of love and force and the steady clenched blows of his idiom" (97). **NEWTON** (1959): Donne is a vessel or metal utensil "which needs more than reparation, which needs to be recreated in God's smithy" (12). **SHERWOOD** (1984) notes that Augustine and Bernard "share a psychology of the soul or will 'bent' by Original Sin, needing to 'turn' from the world back to God" (161). Observes that for Augustine, "the 'heart' or the soul, and alternately the will, are bent (*distorta; curva*), unlike God's will, '*Distortus tu es, ille rectus es*'" (*Enarratio in Psalmum*, XLIV, 17 in *PL* XXXVI, 503–4) (218n) and that conversion "conforms man's bent will to God's straight will" (161). Similarly points to Bernard's view that the soul "before returning to God is 'blind, bent' (*curvam*) earthwards" (*Eighty-six Sermons on the Song of Solomon*, in *Life and Works*, IV, tr. S. J. Eales [London, 1896], XXXVI, 5, p. 237; *PL*, CLXXXIII, 970) (218n). Also cites Calvin on God's "bending, forming, and directing, our hearts to righteousness" (*Institutes*, II, iii, 6) (218n) and concludes that the position of "bend" allows it to act on both "mee" (l. 3) and "Your force" (l. 4), "with the meaning shifting in line 4 accordingly" (218n). **MARTIN** (1990) points to images of the hard heart in Exod. 8 and Mark 8.17, and in Renaissance devotional literature, noting the various actions recommended to "break" it and make it "new" (63).

3 *That I may rise, and stand, orethrow me; and bend* **FAERBER** (1950): an incomprehensible paradox gives us reason to deny the equally incomprehensible thought that God has abandoned us (30). [See more under Holy Sonnets: Language and Style.] **WILLEY** (1954) finds here and in ll. 12–14 examples of Donne's paradoxical expression of the redemptive force of God (363). **STEPHENSON** (1959): the line "expresses the continuity between death and resurrection" (320).

3 *orethrow* **BETHELL** (1948): "a touch of Jacob and the angel, but in reverse" (69). **LEVENSON** (1954) sees in the word a verbal linkage in the move from the image of "the artisan's workshop" (ll. 1–4) to that of "the beleaguered town" (ll. 5–8) (item 36). See also *HSBatter*: Themes.

3 *bend* **MALLETT** (1983): "direct, apply" (59).

4 *Your force to breake, blow, burne, and make me new.* **BETHELL** (1948): the "b" of l. 1 is taken up in alliterative verbs of destructive force (68). **MORRIS** (1953): both Donne and Hopkins employ assonance and rhyme to unify lines, as here with "break and "make" and in "The Wreck of the Deutschland" (2:3) with "lash" and "last" (58–59). **WILLEY** (1954) cites the line in arguing that Donne "had to wrestle daily with his God" (359). **WILLMOTT** (1985) finds each verb to be a "stronger counterpart of those in line 2; the poet is like an object which is past repair and must be completely re-made" (69). **LOEWENSTEIN** (1993): "The alliteration and forceful verbs of l. 4 (God's spirit blows rather than breathes, his face burns rather than shines) convey the divine power and violence needed to break Donne's resistance and make him anew, especially when he is 'betrothed'—as he is in the third quatrain—to God's enemy, Satan." Donne thus "urges God's sexual assault and penetration" since he is "betrothed to Satan (though he dearly loves God)" (11).

SHULLENBERGER (1993): "The act of rightful possession by God would be an act of erotic violence, a punitive and purgatorial ravishing that would 'breake, blowe, burn, and make me new" (55). CRESWELL (1995): the images of breaking and burning echo Deut. 12.3, 12.30, and 13.15–16 and its "call for the destruction of idols or the carnal icon." *HSBatter* thus invokes both the "blazon of God the beloved" from Song Sol. and the "injunction against any such image-making" (190). OSTERWALDER (1995) notes the "erotic undercurrent" in l. 4, where "Blow" can also suggest "to bring into discredit" and where "make" may well have (as it does in Shakespeare) "bawdy overtones" (206).

4 *breake,* HOOPER and HARVEY (1958): the word is an echo of Ps. 2.9: "Thou shalt break them with a rod of iron" (14).

4 *blow,* HERMAN (1953): the word may reflect the *OED* definition of "blow upon": "to bring into discredit, defame" (item 18). HOOPER and HARVEY (1958): the word is an echo of Isa. 40.7: "The grass withereth, the flower fadeth: because the spirit of the Lord bloweth upon it" (14).

4 *burne,* HOOPER and HARVEY (1958): the word is an echo of Luke 3.17: "the chaff will he burn with fire unquenchable" (14).

4 *make* HERMAN (1953): the word "had the appropriate popular meaning in Donne's day that it has today" and may be a conscious pun (item 18). SHERWOOD (1984): "The pun on *make* can work several ways: begetting, fashioning, repentance, siege, conversion; *make,* the old synonym for *mate.*" See *OED* and *HSShow* 10: "First travaile we to seek and then make love?" (216n).

5–14 *I like . . . you rauishe mee.* FRIEDERICH (1932) quotes the lines as an example of a Baroque poet's appeal to God to save him from the "self-centeredness" ("Eigensucht") that separates him from divine love and leaves him enthralled to the devil. Observes that these poets, like Donne, call for help but only fall into despair at the thought of original sin (138). HERMAN (1953): the "town-woman" asks God to end her possession by or break her betrothal to God's enemy, and to ravish her, that is, to make her chaste (item 18).

5–8 *I like . . . proves weake or vntrew.* WHITE (1936) notes that the lines are an example of the "tension between faith and reason" (140). RUGOFF (1939) cites the lines as an image where "Love is warlike or violent." Compares them to *LovExch* 24–28, where Donne is also a "beleaguered town," though the conqueror is love, not Satan (158). HOOPER and HARVEY (1958): in the besieged town it is the "enemy within the gates who refuses to allow the would-be loyal citizens to open to the relieving force" (14). UL-HASAN (1958): the passage is a political image in which God appears as a king and the human soul his subject, administered by reason, his viceroy, over the city of the body (50, 54). MOSELEY (1980): "By the Fall, the Will has become divorced from knowledge of the truth. Hence, while Reason in fallen man can still show the truth, this is not enough." See Rom. 7.15, 23–25. The images of "besieging and war" in this section suggest "something of the military triumph of Christ in the Harrowing of Hell," and remind one of poems of the Middle Ages on the theme *"Quis est hic qui pulsat ad ostium?"* (105).

5–6 *I like . . . to no end.* **GRANSDEN** (1954): Donne asks God to take possession of his soul by force (128–29). **EVANS** (1955) notes that the image of the besieged fort was traditional in religious writing but not with the sexual associations of Donne's lines (107, 166). **NEWTON** (1959): Donne is a usurped town that "desires to have the power of God manifested to restore it to His suzerainty" (12). **SHAWCROSS** (1967): "he is usurped by Satan but belongs to God" (344). **LEVER** (1974): the heart "secretly sympathizes with the attacker, God, who is reclaiming his own domain usurped by Satan" (181). **SPURR** (1992): in a typical fashion, Donne "conflates religious and secular emotion in the poem's second analogy." Having been "conquered by sin," he "animates his effort to resist the usurper in the forceful verb, 'labour,' and the cry of desolation, 'oh, to no end'" (21–22). **CRESWELL** (1995): the speaker, as both a "usurped town" and a "beloved's stoney heart," invokes the God of Song Sol. and the "lover-warrior of countless iconographies, emblem books, and secular lyrics." The speaker is especially suggestive of Song Sol. 5, where the beloved is a "garden inclosed," struggling "to give entrance to her beloved" (cf. Song Sol. 4.12, 16 and 5.2) (189).

5 *vsurp'd* **WILLMOTT** (1985): "captured (by the devil); stress on first syllable" (69). **GILL** (1990): "a town in which power has illegally (and probably violently) passed from a legitimate ruler to an invader" (105).

5 *to'another dew* **SMITH** (1971): "owing duty to somebody other than its usurping occupier" (632). [So also, Craik and Craik (1986, 280) and Lloyd-Evans (1989, 299n45).] **WILLY** (1971): "owed to another—i.e. to God" (80). **HOLLANDER and KERMODE** (1973): "owing allegiance to someone other than the usurper, in this case the devil" (1052). **MALLETT** (1983): "owing duty and obedience to another" (59). **WILLMOTT** (1985): "owing allegiance to another (i.e. God)" (69).

5 *another* **GILL** (1990): "it is not clear who or what *another* is; it could be the devil, death, sin, doubt, despair or a human lover" (105).

5 *dew* **GRANSDEN** (1954), reading "dew" as "due," notes that the word appears as well in *HSDue* 1 (129). **FOWLER** (1991): "belonging by right" (118).

6 *Labor* **ESCH** (1955): the word prepares for the sexual metaphor of the sestet (50).

6 *Oh* **BENNETT** (1934): Donne often indicates "a pause or intake of breath by means of an exclamatory monosyllable," such as "Oh" (48).

6 *to no end.* **MALLETT** (1983): "unsuccessfully" (59). **WILLMOTT** (1985): "to no avail" (69). **CAYWARD** (1980): "no explicator, to my knowledge, has called

attention to the anagram in line 6 of the poem." The lines "compare the speaker, the poet (Donne), to a town captured by Satan and powerless (through weakness of will) to admit, or readmit, God to His rightful place as ruler of the town." Furthermore, "if the letters of 'no end' in line 6 are rearranged, they form 'donne' (Donne), reinforcing the simile of the poet as a captured town by spelling out the poet's name" (5).

7–12 *Reason . . . emprison me*, **UL-HASAN** (1958): Donne is consumed by a sense of sin, finding himself unable to escape its grip, and so begs God to break its hold, though he will not be entirely reassured until he is imprisoned (42).

7–8 *Reason . . . weake or vntrew.* **HARDY** (1942): reason is not the key to reconciliation with God (240). **CAREY** (1981): "These lines imply that reason, if only it functioned freely, would bring him close to God, but in other contexts he denounced attempts to make God intelligible to the reason as a 'lamentable perversenesse', and warns his congregation that Scripture will be out of their reach if they believe it only in so far as it concurs with 'Reason' or 'Philosophy' or 'Morality'" (*Sermons* 9:256, 2:308) (241).

7 *Reason your viceroy in me, me should defend*, **MORRIS** (1953): both Donne and Hopkins vary iambic pentameter, on occasion with a reversed foot at the beginning and another in the middle of the line, as here and in Hopkins's "I wake and feel the fell of dark" (l. 7) and "Thou art indeed just" (l. 14) (45–46). **SHAWCROSS** (1967): "[Reason] should maintain me against the force that has usurped me" (344). **MALLETT** (1983): "his reason should rule him in God's name and on God's behalf" (59). **WILLMOTT** (1985): "Reason is God's deputy, planted in man to enable him to distinguish between right and wrong, and so should be available to 'defend' him from 'the crafts and assaults of the devil'" (cf. "The Litany" in the Book of Common Prayer) (69). **SINGH**: (1992): cf. the "role of reason in the individual to that of nature in the world" in *Goodf* 19 (101).

7 *Reason your viceroy* **FAUSSET** (1924) finds Donne complaining that reason, "God's viceroy, has only made him the more calculated and efficient a sinner," having "proved alike" both its power and its impotence. Observes that reason "brings consciousness, but not necessarily virtue or harmony"; it "enslaves, as instinct does; and freedom can only come when the two are related to some higher idea" (244). **BETHELL** (1948): "a typically elaborate Elizabethan-Jacobean analogy" in which "God is the true King of man, reason a mere viceroy" (69). **WILLY** (1971): "Reason, ruling as God's deputy in me" (80). **LEVER** (1974): "Governor of the 'fortress' of the heart" (181).

7 *viceroy* **GROSART** (1872–73): "usually and grossly misprinted 'victory'" (2:291). **SULLENS** (1964) notes that the *OED* does not record a figurative use of the word as Donne has it here (267).

8 *But is captiv'd and proves weake or vntrew.* **MELTON** (1906): in Donne's meter an insignificant word often carries the stress, as "or" does here (69). **MARTIN** (1990)

points to Calvin, who thought that reason, "the prime characteristic of humanity, had been almost hopelessly corrupted by the Fall" (63). **SINGH** (1992): the point of the line is that, while Reason "should preserve Donne's soul for God," it has "either been imprisoned by the usurping enemy Satan in the same way that a town's governor may be imprisoned by an invader," or has "proved too weak in its post as God's viceroy," or else has, "like a traitor," "allied itself to the enemy" (101).

8 *captiv'd* **SMITH** (1971), reading "captived": "the stress falls on the second syllable" (632).

8 *weake or vntrew.* **LEVENSON** (1954): the words provide a transition "from thoughts of siege to thoughts of sex" (item 36). [See more under *HSBatter*: Themes.]

8 *vntrew.* **KNOX** (1956): the word "carries us on from 'heart' [l. 1] and further anticipates the love-courtship theme" (item 2). **SHAWCROSS** (1967): "unfaithful (to God, for whom reason is viceroy)" (344). [Similarly, Booty (1990, 109).]

9–14 *Yet . . . except you rauishe mee.* **RUGOFF** (1939): the speaker approaches God "as a kind of holy mistress" (87). **WEDGWOOD** (1950), citing these lines, notes that the "pulse of passion still throbs" in Donne's religious poetry, with its "rich inlay of worldly knowledge and sensation, and its unusually violent exploitation of sensual metaphors" (68). **ESCH** (1955): the request to God is couched in sexual metaphor, as the most personal of relationships (50). **NEWTON** (1959): Donne is a betrothed woman who would have God forcefully destroy her unwelcome tie so that she can submit herself to his greater power (12). **HOLLANDER and KERMODE** (1973): "For the sestet the figure changes to one of love, marriage and rape" (1052). **BELLETTE** (1975) notes the absence of "prayer and submission" in the sestet, as the "sequential argument" that would typically carry the sonnet "through to a resolution" instead "collapses as syntactic units become smaller and increasingly antithetical." Comments that in spite of the "much-remarked-on energy" of *HSBatter*, the "basic movement is 'to no end,'" with its "final state a paralysis of the will" (331). **GRAY** (1975) says that while Christ frees the soul from the captivity of sin and death, he paradoxically makes human beings his captives. Cites the sestet of *HSBatter* as a literary example of this paradox (3). **MARTIN** (1990) finds behind the sestet and its marital imagery a number of biblical texts, including Exod. 16.30–32, Isa. 55.5, and Isa. 62.5–6, showing both the perils of unfaithfulness and the "moral relationship of loving authority over a dependent" to be "humanised" in marriage (64).

9–12 *Yet dearly . . . emprison me, for I* **FUZIER** (1983) finds richly suggestive the false rhyme occurring between lines 10 and 12, i.e., "enemy" and "I." Notes that though a traditional rhyme, it seems here to indicate the refusal of the subject "I" to belong to the unnamed "enemy," a negation signaled by the rhymes in lines 9 and 11 that frame the word "enemy," of which the phonetics of the time permit a perfect rhyme with "me." Concludes that this subtle phonetic game underscores the opposition between the "enemy" and "I" (48n14).

9–10 *Yet dearly . . . vnto your enemy:* **FAERBER** (1950): Donne's consciousness of sin and of his inability to escape it hinders him from achieving a certitude of faith (21).

9 *Yet dearly I love you, and would be loved faine:* **FUZIER** (1983): this initial line of the sestet marks the turning-point of the sonnet with a double-accented foot, its accentuation now being regular, unlike in the octave (with its two instances of synaeresis), so that this line is read as an alexandrine. The parallelism of the accents brings out the rhetorical parallelism of the "paregménon" "love/loved," which confirms the absolute reciprocity desired by the speaker between the love he experiences for God and the one that he is waiting for in return (46).

9 *and would be loved faine:* **SMITH** (1971): "he eagerly wishes to be loved" (632). [Similarly, Willy (1971, 80), Mallett (1983, 59), Willmott (1985, 70), and Lloyd-Evans (1989, 299n46).]

9 *loved* **GARDNER** (1952) prints the contraction of 1633 ("lov'd"), suggesting that in this "forceful and colloquial sonnet" it is unlikely that Donne would have used the "poetical and archaic form 'lovèd.'" Also keeps one elision from 1633 ("dearely'I") but removes another ("you,'and") (71).

9 *faine:* **SHAWCROSS** (1967): "with joy" (344). **PATRIDES** (1985a): "gladly" (443). [So also, Booty (1990, 109), Gill (1990, 105), and Singh (1992, 101).]

10–11 *But ame betroth'd . . . agayne,* **FUZIER** (1983): l. 10 signifies, by its two inverted feet—although weakly accented, but nevertheless reflecting the confusion of the preceding quatrain—that the soul, now betrothed instead of imprisoned, is no longer in the grip of the enemy. The calmed prosody of line 11, which is perfectly regular, given the artifice of a synaeresis, thus reflects the hope that God will respond to the prayers of those who love Him by bringing into His service whoever is betrothed unto Him (46).

10 *enemy:* **LEVENSON** (1954): the word provides linkage by reaching "back in association" with the military image (5–8), "though the enemy is now singular rather than collective" (item 36). [See more under *HSBatter:* Themes.] **WILLY** (1971): "Satan" (80). [So also Lloyd-Evans (1989, 299n47).]

11–14 *Diuorce me, . . . except you rauishe mee.* **SPÖRRI-SIGEL** (1949): only God can break the bond between Donne and the Devil (85–86).

11 *Diuorce me, . . . that knott agayne,* **KORTEMME** (1933): the intensity of Donne's feeling is especially evident in the verbs as he beseeches God for grace (45). **SMITH** (1971): "dissolve the attachment, annul it, or separate the parties by force" (632). [Similarly, Fowler (1991, 118).] **McCORMICK** (1983): the line "would not have failed to stir in the minds of Donne's contemporaries memories of that most famous plea for divorce in English history, Henry VIII's request of the Pope that he

'untie' the knot which bound him to Catherine of Aragon" (23). Breaking that knot "againe" also calls to mind that it was the Pope who granted the divorce that allowed Henry VIII to marry Catherine (23); thus, the reference to "divorce" may draw a parallel between Donne's situation and that of Henry, namely, that the poet is seeking permission to be released from the Catholic church to enter into "a potentially more fruitful" union with the Anglican church, much in the same way that Henry sought permission from the Pope to divorce a wife who had not born him a male heir (23–24). But an alternative reading of the word "againe" could point to the speaker's release from the "knot" that presently ties him to the Anglican church and for his imprisonment "in his former cell, the Catholic Church" (24). The paradox at the center of the sonnet's closing line reflects Donne's "quite irreconcilable religious impulses" (24). **CRAIK and CRAIK** (1986): the verbs "untie" and "break" ("that knot") are "increasingly vivid synonyms" for "Diuorce" (280).

11 *Diuorce* **MOSELEY** (1980): the language begins to suggest the "virtual impossibility of human agency dissolving marriage" (106). Donne may also have in mind "Hosea's image of Israel as the harlot wife," reinforced by "the idea of unchastity." See also Rom. 7.2–3, which "provides a parallel to the key idea of being bound in marriage by law" (106n). **MAROTTI** (1986): the word may express Donne's "deep misgivings about his marriage" (259). **GILL** (1990): the word is crucial in "an implied story which acts as a parallel to the poet's religious state: a woman has desperately fallen in love (9) but is betrothed, married or has been stolen by another so cannot be *free* (13) or *chaste* (14) (the word was applied to married couples) until her true love divorces her from the one to whom she is bound." But such an idea is "hardly Christian" and therefore the poet may be "indulging a love of paradox at the expense of the word's meaning." In other words, can the word "divorce" ever be "appropriately used of God's relationships with his people?" (105).

11 *that knott agayne,* **SHAWCROSS** (1967): "the first time occurring with Christ's Incarnation and Passion (344). [Similarly, Booty (1990, 109).] **WILLY** (1971): "of betrothal to sin" (80).

11 *knott* **MOSELEY** (1980): the knot to be broken is "the knot of spousal—ironically a lovers' knot," but may remind us of "the subtle knot that makes us man (*Ecst* 64) ("the linking of matter and spirit") and Donne may also be "glancing back" to the idea that opens the poem: "the remaking of human nature." The speaker's nature, "wedded to Satan (Death) as it is, cries out as Augustine did for purity—but, unlike Augustine, for immediate purity" (106). **MALLETT** 1983): "that is, the 'knot' which is said to bind together the partners in marriage" (59).

12–14 *Take . . . except you rauishe mee.* **BENNETT** (1934): Donne "cries out to God in the accents of love," and "expresses his love for God in terms of a lover for his mistress, or, as here, a woman for her lover" (27). **FAUSSET** (1938): Donne struggled to escape from "the prison of himself" to achieve the spiritual life (x–xi). **BROOKS** (1939), arguing that wit and sincerity need not be antithetical in poetry, cites *HSBatter* as a work that transmits "a sense of seriousness." Asserts that while the linking of the sexual figure and spiritual chastity is "audacious," no one doubts Donne's seriousness (25–26). **RAINE** (1945): the imagery of erotic love is elevated to "a symbolic language to speak of God, and to God" (390). **STAUFFER** (1946): "the paradox shocks us into attention" and produces "a deeper realization of religious faith" (85). **FAERBER** (1950) argues that Donne sees the only way out of the paradox of human existence to be through a miracle, though it is but another paradox in which something incomprehensible allows us to enter into God's grace and avoid the equally incomprehensible thought that God has abandoned us (30). Notes that Donne's paradoxes encompass various levels of experience and belief (69). See more under Holy Sonnets: Language and Style. **GARDNER** (1952) quotes the lines as an example of Donne's plain unadorned speech, in that he gives extreme emphasis to the personal pronouns (xxxi). **WILEY** (1954) notes that for Donne verbal ingenuity, as in metaphors depicting spiritual love in sensuous terms, was not incompatible with serious purpose (103). **COANDA** (1957) finds that Donne and Hopkins made liberal use of the personal pronoun, as here and Hopkins's "Thou art indeed just, Lord" (186). **KERMODE** (1957) observes that the lines suggest a number of the paradoxes of the Christian faith: God as "a monster of mercy," an infant, and a malefactor; "Justice as Mercy"; and "Death as Life" (40). **NEWTON** (1959): the sexual metaphor is entirely appropriate in terms of Paul Tillich's definition of *agapē* (12). [See also *HSBatter*: Themes.] **SICHERMAN** (1970), citing these lines as an example, says that in some of the "most successful" of the divine poems— "successful both as art and as attainments of decision—paradox alone can provide a conclusion" (128). **SMITH** (1970) observes the "outrageousness of the sexual figure in a pious context" (166). **MOSELEY** (1980) points to the "climactic paradoxes" of the final three lines (with "emprison," "enthrall," and "rauishe" set against "free" and "chast") and suggests that the notion of captivity in "emprison" and "enthrall" develops "interestingly" from the claim that "Reason" is "captiv'd" (ll. 7–8), which "exactly parallels" Paul's idea in Rom. 7.23: "But I see another law in my members, warring against the law of my mind, and bringing me into captivity to the law of sin which is in my members" (106). Believes that it is "more than possible" that *HSBatter* is the "fruit of meditation" on Rom. 7 (108). **FUZIER** (1983): the speaker implores God to consummate the marriage of his soul to God ("Take me to you"), which has the precise meaning of "Take me for your spouse." The words "rauishe mee," though referring unambiguously to a nuptial violation or rape, are finally justified by the two last lines in which the serene accentuation (especially of l. 14) translates into the hoped-for-happiness. The justification is effected by means of a double paradox, which recovers and explains "take" and "emprison" under the form of a semantic antimetathesis, with line 13 referring back to the second of these terms ("emprison") whereas l. 14 refers back to the first ("take") (46). **ROSTON** (1987): in the art of the High Renaissance, we see "the forcible snatching up of the soul from its bodily setting," the "enthralling and ravishing" that is quite different from the "traditional Renaissance form of serene classical allegory." It is witnessed "both more intensely and more passionately as the worshipper, often with the shock of overt paradox, pleads for divine aid in releasing himself from the bonds of intellect and of the actual in order to enter the luminous world of religious paradox" (313). **A. SMITH** (1987): the "outrageousness of the sexual figure in a pious context parallels the effrontery with which [the speaker] blatantly applies to Christ the casuistry he had once used to seduce women" (cf. *HSWhat* 9–12) (166). **ELLRODT** (1993) finds that here Donne turns to violence and calls the violence divine: "Take me to you" has an erotic sense, and "rauishe" signifies at the same time to ravish in ecstasy and to violate (rape) (456).

12 *emprison* **MOSELEY** (1980): "suggests something violent, something that actually changes a captive's nature so that he becomes a menial—that 'enthralls' him. The captivity intensifies from external captivity, like being a prisoner of war, with its conventions of honourable treatment, to imprisonment—a suppression of liberty—and finally to thralldom and slavery, where one being is *owned* by another" (106).

13–14 *Except you enthrall me . . . rauishe mee.* **MILWARD** (1979 [1988]) observes the strength of the concluding paradox: "It is only by being enthralled to God that he can be freed from the slavery of Satan; and it is only by being ravished by God that he can be chaste, purified from the embrace of passion." Claims that "in this conclusion, more than in any of his other sonnets, and perhaps more than in any other poem of his age, Donne gives powerful expression to the tormented spirit of Italian Baroque art in English poetry" (79). **WILLMOTT** (1985): the paradoxes "reinforce" the point of l. 3, with the "lover image" in particular stressing the poet's "sense of helplessness unless God will take the initiative" (70). **LOEWENSTEIN** (1993): For Donne, "God's enthralment paradoxically enables Donne's freedom, just as God's ravishment paradoxically enables Donne's chastity" (11). **LABRIOLA** (1995) says that the paradoxes "highlight the intensity required for his disunion from Satan and repossession by the Lord" (99).

13 *Except you enthrall me* **WILLY** (1971): "Unless you enslave me. [So also, Campbell (1989, 232).] T. S. Eliot calls the last two lines 'in the best sense, *wit*'" (80).

13 *Except* **PATRIDES** (1985a): "unless" (443). [So also, Booty (1990, 109).]

13 *enthrall* **KNOX** (1956): "bent and mended in accordance with God's will, which is complete love" (item 2). **SMITH** (1971): "make a slave or prisoner of" (632). **HOLLANDER and KERMODE** (1973): "take prisoner" (1052). **MALLETT** 1983): "make a slave of me" (59). **WILLMOTT** (1985): "enslave" (70). [So also, Booty (1990, 109) and Fowler (1991, 118).] **PATRIDES** (1985a): "reduce to slavery; also, enchant" (443).

14 *Nor euer chast except you rauishe mee.* **BETHELL** (1948): Donne's imagery of sex and marriage, common to mystical and Baroque writing, is not in bad taste; it is "so purely of the intellect" that "we are left marvelling" at it (69). **UL-HASAN** (1958): Donne describes the height of spiritual love in terms of the sex act (11) and

casts Christ in the role of husband, humanizing him (36). **MAROTTI** (1986) reads in this an allusion to King James's homosexuality, along with an "allocation of power to male favourites," which "created a cultural matrix in which the poem's homo-erotic submission could be equated with the gaining of royal (and hence divine) favour" (259–60). **CAREY** (1990a) questions Marotti's view, finding it "strange" that, if Marotti is right, Donne should "be able to count on the poem's male coterie readership responding to sodomy as kingly and divine," and noting that Donne in *Pseudo-Martyr*, a work addressed to James, treats sodomy "with unsparing derision" (279). **MARTIN** (1990) calls attention to the fact that both "chast" and "rauishe" had meanings not limited to the sexual, "chast" suggesting "morally pure, innocent" and "rauishe" meaning "to carry away (especially to heaven) in a mystical sense," both meanings important to the intent of the sonnet overall (61–62). **ROSTON** (1990) draws an analogy between "scenes of ravishment," such as the painting "Rape of Europa" by Guido Reni and "the anguished conclusion" to *HSBatter* (209). **HANDLEY** (1991) calls the image "audacious" (44).

14 *rauishe* **GRANSDEN** (1954): the word appears here, and in *HSDue* (10), as a cry to God to take an active role in his life and release him from his "regretted thraldom to Satan" (129). **SULLENS** (1964): the word is used here in a figurative sense earlier than the first recorded entry in the *OED* from 1664 (229). **CHING** (1978): a pun here "is crucial in producing both the dissonance and consonance in the poem" (1). **MALLETT** (1983): "unless you rape me" (59). **PATRIDES** (1985a) glosses as "violate"; or alternatively, citing Steele (1971—see *HSBatter*: Themes), "take away or remove spatially," as well as "overwhelm with astonishment" (443). **CRAIK and CRAIK** (1986): "in two senses: (1) carry off; (2) violate (this second sense making a strong paradox with *chaste*; compare *enthral* and *free*, l. 13)" (280).

 *HSBlack*

COMMENTARY

General Commentary

An anonymous author writing in *QR* (1862–63, 85) prints *HSBlack* with the comment that it is "one of the sonnets written in the agony of . . . [Donne's] soul, apparently in the last struggle, between doubt and conquering faith."

Gransden (1954, 128, 136) describes *HSBlack*, *HSMade*, and *HSScene* as "rather sombre" sonnets that present a poet "seeking strength, grace, and forgiveness from Christ." In the poems, Gransden argues, Donne is "not speaking professionally or doctrinally but is meditating privately" on the human soul (136).

Cohen (1963, 168–69) observes that this sonnet possesses "agonized but sure-footed reasoning, expressed in the simple imagery of treason, prison, and execution." Donne's move from the "pilgrim" to the thief who awaits sentence before receiving his punishment "heightens the tension and strengthens the analogy between the poet's state and the prison in which both captives languish." He adds that the images are "of the simplest, yet they are marked with Donne's personal imprint."

Donne's color imagery, remarks Herbold (1965, 284) was susceptible to "balance." In *HSBlack*, he adds, Donne "found a structure in the opposition of a black soul . . . to the red face of a blushing sinner and to Christ's blood."

Halewood (1970, 80) remarks that Donne expresses reconciliation in the Holy Sonnets, with *HSBlack*, for example, moving "surely from the soul's sin to Christ's redemptive power."

According to Sanders (1971, 128), *HSBlack* presents the cliché of washing in Christ's blood, and "the verbal games with colour-symbolism turn the drama of redemption into the antics of a moral chameleon."

Altizer (1973, 84) thinks that in *HSBlack* Donne attempts to find the "grace to begin" (l. 10) by creating a symbolism of color linking the poet's "sick soul" and Christ's redeeming blood. The paradoxical conceits in the poem may lead to a deeper understanding of Christian symbolism, Altizer states, but not necessarily to grace or repentance.

Blanch (1974, 480) also believes that the use of color symbolism is significant in *HSBlack*, writing that "the blackness of sin must be transformed into the black garb of mourning—the initial step towards spiritual rebirth, whereas the redness of sin (sins of passion) must turn into the blush of shame." He adds that "through Christ's redeeming blood . . . the poet may put on the white robe of supernatural life."

Sloane (1974, 77) writes that Donne, "like the emblematist," works with "similitudes" in this sonnet. See also HSDeath: Themes.

Evans (1978, 117) remarks that in HSBlack Donne compares the progress of an illness with the movement from life to death.

Mackenzie (1990, 76) identifies HSBlack as one of the Holy Sonnets that falls short of their potential, in that the "dramatising of terror outweighs the salvation that should swallow it up." HSBlack, according to Mackenzie, "makes the dramatising of sin and terror in the octave suspect," for sweeping away the sin and terror later in the poem appears too easy and "contrived."

Low (1993, 69) states that the view of God in the sonnet is that of "a great king against whom the soul has committed treason."

Date and Circumstances

Martz (1954, 140) suggests that the occasion of the poem "may be one of actual sickness."

According to Gransden (1954, 127–28), HSBlack, HSMade, and HSScene probably refer to Donne's illness in 1608, not that in 1623.

The Poet/Persona

Payne (1926, 139–40) quotes the poem in full as an example of Donne's sense of unworthiness when he turns to God for comfort.

Stachniewski (1981, 699) analyzes the sonnet against the background of Calvinist theology, stating at the outset that "the rationale for Calvinist theology was that it boosted God's sovereignty at the expense of human autonomy: man was made quite powerless, powerless to contribute to his salvation in any way," and Donne's "extreme passivity is a strikingly consistent feature of the sonnets." Stachniewski finds HSBlack's development "interrupted" by the "But" of line 10, and thus the structure of the poem "enforces the [Calvinist] implication that the necessary grace may be withheld." Stachniewski adds, however, that Roman Catholics "insisted that God readily offered the grace to repent."

The sonnet's speaker, in Radzinowicz's view (1987, 47), "separates himself from his black soul to admonish it." The speaker tells the soul that there are two means to grace, namely, contrition and belief, but, Radzinowicz says, "the speaker is compassionate but impotent, the soul responsive but helpless; grace affords active compassion and enables response." The "hero" of the poem, Radzinowicz concludes, is "neither the speaker nor the soul, but the suffering Saviour."

Strier (1989, 370–72) finds that HSBlack, unlike some other Holy Sonnets, "brings the issue of agency to consciousness," for after an octave that "powerfully" evokes ("perhaps in recusant terms"—e.g., "a pilgrim, which abroad hath done/Treason [ll. 3–4]") a condition of "spiritual confusion in the face of imminent death," the sestet appears to "offer a solution: 'Yet grace, if thou repent, thou canst not lacke'" (370). But Strier claims that the final couplet raises other problems with respect to either a Catholic or Protestant reading of the poem. Although for Strier the last lines present a "poetic solution," he finds "the logical and syntactical stress of the couplet" to be on "the physical redness of the blood," and therefore "the lines establish no logical or conceptual relation between the physical process they envision and the moral, psychological, and theological terms of the poem" (372). For Strier, the relation of the lines to the poem as a whole "is entirely imagistic" (372).

Hester (1991a, 175–77) reads HSBlack in the context of his larger reading of the Holy Sonnets as "vigorous explorations" of the speaker's effort to "re-sign his self *in imagines dei* and of the poems' efforts, primarily "ineffectual," to "affirm any enduring sense of assurance" (175). HSBlack, for example, issues, according to Hester, in a "playful gesture" that "privileges the prestidigital words of the clever speaker over the ontological transfigurations of The Word" (176), especially as seen in the way Donne plays "gratuitously" on the literal and metaphorical meanings of "red" in the final lines of the poem (176–77). Hester thus concludes that "on its own, absent of the Sign of divine erasure, the text of the self can only be read as an insignificant trace fondly inscribed by fallen man" (177). See more under Notes and Glosses to HSBlack, lines 11–14.

Spurr (1992, 19–21) finds that Donne's religious poetry is marked by "extremity," given his preoccupation with his sinfulness and the challenge for him to live a life that will make him "worthy to receive God's grace and be acceptable in the hour of death and on the day of judgement" (18). For Spurr, this anxiety in Donne, which gives his religious poetry "a dramatic immediacy and vitality," is "perfectly" captured in HSBlack (19). Spurr points to the opening of the sonnet, which declares "the sin-laden state of his being," and where "urgency" is added to his anxiety since his present illness could be fatal, and judgment, therefore, could be imminent (19). Donne then, according to Spurr, "embellishes his meditation with two similes from secular life" (the "foreign traveller who has betrayed his country abroad and is terrified to return home" and the "convicted thief who wants to be released from prison, but when release is offered in the form of execution prefers to remain in gaol" (19)), but in the sestet, Spurr notes, Donne "proffers the Christian solution to the problem posed in the octave," namely, that "God's grace will absolve even the blackness of his soul" (20). Spurr calls attention to the progression of the sonnet from "black" to "white," but cautions readers that "at the heart of the sonnet is that contingency, 'if thou repent,'" for "this is what Donne would desire, not what he has actually achieved" (21).

Genre and Traditions

Kermode (1957, 38) observes that the poem owes much to the Ignatian method of meditation, which directs one "to achieve a vivid image, enforce it with appropriate similitudes, and then to pray accordingly." Donne here imagines his deathbed, he notes, pictures the soul as an exile afraid to return home and a prisoner fearful of freedom, and then prays for grace to repent.

Sloane (1981, 53) observes that the readers of the sonnet "are expected to identify with the action and thus participate in it," which reflects a different kind of emblematic poem from that in which the emblem functions as a symbol and the dramatic action itself is not significant, such as the emblems in various editions of Andreas Alciati (*Emblematum Liber*, 1531).

Heffernan (1991, 60) labels HSBlack "an emblem poem" (a "verbal picture of an invisible reality spoken of as visible") and a "hieroglyph, a shadowy sign, that points to a higher and better meaning hidden within the Soul's sinful condition." Heffernan suggests that "in this hieroglyph the visualized Soul conceals and gradually reveals the truth and beauty hidden in the Soul's capacity to be re-formed."

Language and Style

Morris (1953, 74) finds the dark tone of the sonnet to resemble that of Hopkins in "I wake and feel."

Levenson (1954, item 36) observes that the sonnet illustrates Donne's use of "shifting," or varied, metaphors in a short poem, as here where the soul is "successively pilgrim, prisoner, and penitent, and even changes from black to red." See also HSBatter: Themes.

Linville (1984a, 142–43, 148), in her study of closure in devotional poetry, suggests that the force of closure often depends upon an extra-poetic truth that cannot be proven in the poem itself (142). But in some instances, according to Linville, the "extra-poetic model" may work against closure (148). Linville cites studies of HSBlack providing different readings: Halewood (1970—see HSBlack: General Commentary), for example, sees the poem as providing "emphatic reconciliations," while Ellrodt (1960, 1:222) claims that the final paradox is false, a figurative expression. For Linville, HSBlack "leaves some lingering sense of unbridged gaps: between words and things, between a verbally actualized potential and practicable action, and between the desired contrite sorrow and the workings of Christ's redemptive activity" (148). Linville concludes that the role of the extra-poetic model is actually twofold: first, "it lends authenticity to the closing images," and secondly, it brings the reader to realize that "the two alternatives proposed at the sonnet's conclusion should not ultimately be seen as alternatives," for "true contrition and faith in Christ's redemptive power must work as one" (148).

McNees (1987, 110–11) studies the impact of the Anglican Eucharist on the Divine Poems, underscoring the necessity that an individual first experience "internal crucifixion through penitence" in order to realize Christ's presence. HSBlack, according to McNees, adopts the language of Goodf, as in HSBlack 4, "to argue toward final repentance," but in the sonnet the speaker "addresses his own soul, not Christ," and "grants his soul two alternatives": the first (ll. 11–12) "concerns penitence and mortification," but the second (ll. 13–14) "offers a more tangible and reciprocal alternative" (110). McNees thus claims that "through true identification—both physical and spiritual—with Christ's blood in the Eucharist, the speaker may find himself replenished and purified" (110–11).

Warnke (1987, 106–07) finds Donne's use of paradox and conceit in the Holy Sonnets "unmatched even in the amorous lyrics" (106). For example, Warnke states, the "elaborate metaphors" in HSBlack that identify "the sinful soul with an exiled traitor and then with a condemned thief" lead to "a blaze of self-contradictory imagery, in which the color red assumes three different symbolic valences and then operates in a manner that contradicts normal experience" (106–07).

Osmond (1990, 128–29) points to the movement in the seventeenth century away from "sustained allegory" to "more direct and dramatic modes of presentation," observing that "the needs of dramatic presentation fostered not only the concrete representation of the soul but the portrayal of it in situations of conflict," as in *HSBlack*. Osmond emphasizes that Donne's poetry "typically casts the soul in conflict" (128). In this poem, she says, the soul is summoned "by sicknesse, deaths herald" (l. 2), calling it to "the bar of judgment," the whole of the experience "made more vivid by a series of comparisons in which the soul becomes a pilgrim that has committed treason or a prisoner hauled to execution" (128–29). Discrepancies between Donne's views of "the body's role in the transmission of original sin," as seen in his sermons and in his poetry, may, she thinks, be attributed to "just such perceived literary demands" (129).

Stephens and Waterhouse (1990, 13, 59–63) examine *HSBlack* in relation to its "syntagmatic and paradigmatic patterning," rather than as a more conventional octet/sestet or rhyming pattern (59). The "syntagmatic axis," according to Stephens and Waterhouse, relates to the "horizontal, linear progression of the text (the process of thinking)," whereas the "paradigmatic axis" points to "what happens at each of the links, that is, the process of selection which occurs at each place or slot along the syntagmatic axis" (13). They print the poem in a form that schematizes it according to its syntagmatic and paradigmatic patterning, offering several specific illustrations to support their reading (59–60). Stephens and Waterhouse emphasize that Donne plays with and against "the norms of language" by using "fairly ordinary and easily apprehended syntax to transfer the signifiers from their most common signifieds to less common, even if sometimes quite conventional signifieds" (61). They note further that within the octave of the sonnet, the "analogies for the soul's state" grow out of "seventeenth-century cultural and societal hierarchies," with the "descending social status and diminishing freedom of the soul" exhibited in the "free man challenged to trial by combat," the "exiled pilgrim," and finally the "disreputable thief" (62). They emphasize and illustrate what they deem to be "a key aspect" of the sestet, which is a "play with signifiers, with more than one signified denoted by the same signifier" (62–63). In sum, in the view of Stephens and Waterhouse, an analysis of the sonnet concentrating on the "interrelationship of syntagm and paradigm" demonstrates how the poet "both generates meanings within and controls a rather complex discourse" (63).

In a detailed reading of the sonnet that includes a comparison of *HSBlack* to *Everyman*, Hester (1991b, 17–25) reveals the "troubled wit" of the sonnet, the way in which the rhetorical figures "enact their own 'might' as fictions of transfigurative desire and signs of moral limitation" (18). Hester comments that the octave "figures forth the mortality of man," as the "black marks that trace the self . . . create only a parodic mirror of divine creativity," revealing man's "inability to 'turn' himself into an object worthy of liberation without God's grace," and therefore the "emblematic figure" at the beginning ("Oh") "aptly expresses man's desperation," "succinctly" capturing the "circular, self-cancelling shape of his argument and his language" (19). Hester notes that Everyman's search for meaning is similar but that, unlike Donne's speaker, Everyman is "suddenly (and miraculously) aided by the Grace of Knowledge," who leads him "to Confession and the 'jewel of penance'" (20). The project of the sestet, then, according to Hester, is "to re-write, to transfigure, or, literally, to change the rhetorical colors of the text (of the self) so that it 'might' be 'read' mercifully by God—thus moving from the emphasis of the morality play on the scheme of Penance in order to focus attention more fully on the paradox of fallen man denied the 'might' of that sacrament" (18). Hester believes that "on its own, as the shape and language of this meditative sonnet illustrate, the text of the self can only be read as an insignificant trace of fallen man's nugacity," and though Donne "may have framed the moral meter of his meditative voice in the syllables of the Reformation debate about how to read the hermeneutics of God's Word in the operation of Grace," HSBlack appears "poised more to test or try the Reformed doctrine than to affirm it" (23). Hester finds no such "unresolved reading" at the end of Everyman, but neither does the play end with assurance, for the "provisionals of the Doctor's final words remind the reader that man will be damned or saved only by God's 'saying': 'None excuse may be there for every man.'" Nonetheless, Hester proposes that "such a view of man's salvation history still seems closer to the texture of Donne's fearful meditation than does the Protestant doctrine of election and assurance" (24). Hester notes on this point that "the issue of Donne's residual and abiding Catholicism continues to be central to readings of his poetry," so that the sonnets, on one level, render "how Donne could not accommodate his moral conscience to the current doctrines" (25n2). It therefore seems, in Hester's view, that HSBlack "offers an analogy for Donne's own situation," conveying "dramatically" as it does the "desire for and the insufficiency of man's attempts to trans-figure the 'selfe'" (24). For Hester, "this ability to dramatize the dynamics of human paradox remains the major achievement of Donne's poetry of wit" (24).

McNees (1992, 62–63) states that the sonnet "initiates the soul's quest for purity through Christ's blood." Noting that the octave, which is "addressed to the sinful soul," illustrates the "death-in-life fate of an unrepentant soul," McNees finds that the sestet "turns on the word 'grace,'" suggesting a "course of action the static predicament of the octet lacked." In the course of HSBlack, according to McNees, Donne "plays on the secular and sacred connotations of black and red," allowing secular meanings to be "consecrated" (e.g., "sinful black becomes the black of holy mourning; red shame washed in Christ's blood is transformed to pure white"). Furthermore, McNees adds, the similes of the octave ("like a pilgrim," "like a thief") are "transmuted to active metaphors in the sestet" (62). McNees explains this "metaphorical action" as derived from "the speaker's own penitential ability to 'make' himself black with mourning and red with blushing in preparation for Christ's eucharistic offering 'dying red soules to white'" (l. 14) and further concludes that the act of "washing oneself in Christ's blood derives specifically from the Anglican liturgy of Holy Communion" (62). McNees adds, however, that as with Goodf, HSBlack and other Holy Sonnets "fall short of realizing actual communion with God" (63).

Labriola (1995, 95–99) finds that Donne's Holy Sonnets and other religious poetry bear the same "hallmarks" as the "amatory poetry," with the exception that "the loving interaction is between God and humankind, not man and woman" (95). In the Holy Sonnets, according to Labriola, "the conceit is the central device whereby thought and feeling are fused" (98). In HSBlack, in Labriola's view, the dominant conceit is blackness, "which alternately signifies sinfulness and penitence, both the malady and the remedy" (99). Labriola observes that "black is the typical color worn by the prisoner, pilgrim, and penitent, all three of whom provide a framework of comparison for the speaker" (99).

Yen (1995, 226–27) finds that the speaker "recognizes that previous sins have led to his spiritual decay," and that the word "treason" (l. 4) (expressing "religious betrayal") encourages the reader to understand the poem "in political terms" (226). According to Yen, line 9 is "pivotal" in "signifying the turn in the argument towards hope" and appears "to hold the promise of satisfaction, both the divine grace of mercy as well as the political favor of an appointment" (226). But she finds that the argument "immediately takes another turn" in line 10 and thus the balance of the sonnet provides "no answers, only an exhortation and an overworked paradox," namely, that "baptism in the Savior's blood will transform the sinfulness of scarlet souls to white innocence," a "facile paradox" that "fails to carry the force of conviction" (227).

Prosody

Linville (1984b, 72) calls attention to Donne's use of enjambment to reinforce the subject matter of the sonnet; that is, the "'turning' or 'doubling' back" of enjambed lines (e.g., ll. 2–3) as well as their doubling of rhyme "become formal extensions of the concept of doubleness (double-dealing, etc.)" that "permeates" HSBlack. Beyond this, according to Linville, Donne's end-stopped lines (e.g. ll. 3–8) "complement the idea of construction and enclosure," so that the word "'prison' is literally 'imprisoned' in the enveloping rhyme" as the sonnet reflects further correspondences between the thematic "double-binds" and its formal features.

Themes

An anonymous editor (1840, 264) compiles a number of Donne's works and prints several poems under original headings. HSBlack is printed under the heading "Repentance and Faith."

Addleshaw (1931, 52) quotes the poem in full to illustrate that Donne was a teacher of the Cross rather than the life of Jesus, and that he saw no hope for sinners, torn by the convulsions of their nature as they came nearer to death, except in the blood shed by Jesus upon the Cross.

Spörri-Sigel (1949, 86) finds that the tension between God and Satan is conveyed in the opposition between sin, death, and damnation, and God's grace. She observes that while it appears there is still a question as to whether grace is bestowed, sin does not have the same power to lead astray as portrayed in HSMade. The tension remains, she says, but it is not as intense.

Reeves (1952, 100) paraphrases the poem: "An agonized cry for the grace without which he cannot begin to be truly repentant and so save his soul from damnation."

Denonain (1956, 152) notes Donne's belief that the sinner's soul needs simply repentance, which only God can provide.

Peterson (1959, 509) finds the poem to reflect the Ignatian method of contemplating the Last Judgment so as to arouse fear of God in the penitent: the octave meditates on "the endless misery" confronting the sinner and the sestet the means, through Christ, of averting punishment. See also Holy Sonnets: Themes.

Lewalski (1979, 267) observes that in HSBlack, the speaker finds his "black Soule" "summoned by sickness, death's herald, and, like an exiled traitor or an imprisoned thief, he fears execution far more than present miseries." The speaker comes to recognize, according to Lewalski, that it is God who must give "the prevenient grace and the repentance itself."

Yearwood (1982, 210–13) finds that the conversion process in Donne's twelve Holy Sonnets, following 1633 and Gardner's (1952) ordering, "begins in pride, proceeds to confession and despair, and culminates in a humble joy and confidence" (210). The second sonnet in the sequence (HSBlack), according to Yearwood, "corrects" the speaker's misconception in the first sonnet (HSDue) that he can effect his own salvation and that "he will be judged on his own merits" (212–13). Yearwood identifies the second voice in HSBlack as "the voice of grace," who "leads from within," and "diagnoses the speaker's spiritual evasion in corrective comparisons," leading him to "recognize and accept his sins" (213).

Mallett (1983, 56) says, in summary of HSBlack, that it is "a prayer for the grace without which the poet cannot be truly repentant of his sins."

Martz (1985, 14–15) finds that HSSighs and HSBlack (the third and fourth sonnets in 1635) continue the emphasis on "utter sinfulness," but in the sestet of HSBlack "a problem in controverted divinity emerges, the protestant problem of the action of grace" (14–15). According to the "old religion," Martz points out, one must only confess to the priest, "penance will be awarded, and forgiveness will follow" (cf. l. 9) (15). But now, Martz adds, one has to ask: "But who shall give thee that grace to beginne?" (l. 10) (15). Donne's sonnet offers several possible answers in the closing lines, according to Martz: "the words 'make thy selfe' seem to imply some power of free will in the speaker," but "the action of the blood of Christ" is also required (15). And this is to be obtained, Martz points out, "by faith alone," according to "the strict reformed theology," "by the Eucharist, devoutly taken, the old religion would say," but "by both working together, many, perhaps most, in the Church of England would say" (15). Martz concludes that "with this double strand of hope the sonnets make their uncertain way toward greater confidence" (15).

Heffernan (1991, 58–59) believes that Donne, like St. Augustine, saw the interconnection of the psychological life of the individual with history, given that all of human life is a protracted process of conversion [Confessions XI.26–28; De Genesi ad litteram libri duodecim 1.8.14]. Heffernan finds that HSBlack manifests this "interrelated pattern." The Soul, in Heffernan's view, is "like a pilgrim, which abroad hath done/Treason, and durst not turne to whence hee'is fled" (ll. 3–4); that is, "the soul has sinned against her Maker" (58). Consequently, Heffernan finds, the Soul is now "like a prisoner whose own unaided will is ineffective, yet the Soul's re-creation or re-formation is possible" ("Yet grace, if thou repent, thou canst not lacke:/But who shall give thee that grace to beginne? [ll. 9–10]") (59). Heffernan contends that "a prelude to the Soul's re-creation is contrition—repentance after sorrow and grief for sin," an allusion to 2 Cor. 2.7: "godly sorrow worketh repentance" (59).

Klawitter (1991, 144–49) finds that HSBlack "raises a nuance about 'the grace to begin grace'" that is not raised elsewhere in Donne's poetry. The sonnet, in Klawitter's view, begins as a vision in which the speaker, who is facing death, wishes to be returned to his sickness rather than "face the uncertainties of the after-life." The underlying concern, Klawitter emphasizes, is not so much the separation of the body and the soul "as it is separation of the soul from God" (144). In Donne's view, according to Klawitter's reading of the sonnet, grace is "dependent upon our repentance," but "how we can be moved to repent in the first place if we are not given the grace to be so moved: 'Who shall give thee that grace to begin?'" (l. 10) (144–45). Klawitter sees the sonnet as providing two "avenues of action" for the sinner: first, creating "an inner environment through 'mourning' and 'blushing'" to show that one is aware of one's sinfulness and "estrangement from God" (145), and second, receiving grace "through reception of the sacraments," specifically Baptism (cf. l. 13) and the Eucharist, "since the poem is addressed to adults already baptized" (cf. *Sermons*, 2:258, 10:76) (146–47). Klawitter contends that it is evident that the "initiator of the 'automatic' grace" must be the "sinner himself" (149), and he notes that the "closing couplet simply evokes supernatural aid quite mechanically without the torture involved in a personal struggle against all forces." In contrast, *HSMade*, according to Klawitter, gives us a speaker who "gives in to divine power rather than cooperates with its infusion." Donne's "independent" speaker in *HSBlack*, however, reflects Donne's private, litigious soul, his vaulting ambition, his worldly and ecclesiastical pursuits," all of which "corroborate the counsel he gives in verse and prose: act, do not wait to be acted upon." Klawitter concludes: "how far from *solum fide* could a man be?" (149).

Ellrodt (1993, 455) notes the sonnet's emphasis on the impotency of the soul, in that the soul came from heaven and, having betrayed God on earth, does not dare to rejoin its native country.

HSBlack and Other Works

Milward (1979 [1988, 46–48]) finds this sonnet deriving most closely, not from one of the meditations in the *Spiritual Exercises* of St. Ignatius, but from the "Second Addition of the *First Week*," in which the exercitant imagines himself in "various situations" (46). Milward compares some of the situations to those found in *Everyman* and *Hamlet*, and to situations reflecting contemporary religious issues, particularly those of the treatment of Catholics. In the sestet, following these comparisons, the speaker, in Milward's view, "exhorts himself to repentance" (48). But he comes to recognize by the end of the sonnet, Milward says, that he will require God's grace to even begin to repent.

Gaston (1986, 206–07), discussing *HSBlack* as the first in the cycle of nine Holy Sonnets that Benjamin Britten set to music in 1946, says that Britten establishes a "persistent analogy for the physical and spiritual dis-ease that informs the poem," and "by sharply limiting melodic material in the setting," the composer "conveys the narrow compass of the invalid's desperate ingenuity" (206–07). But, Gaston points out, Britten places emphasis on the assertion of faith with which the poem concludes: "the voice rises to its affirmation as the uneasy tritone beneath relaxes and supports it" (207).

Radzinowicz (1987, 45) draws a comparison between the sonnet and Ps. 142 and 143, all of which employ the poetical device of *anima mea*, the dialogue of a man with his soul.

A. Smith (1987, 164) observes that poems by George Herbert often "evoke an external object, a posy of flowers or the monuments of a church, only to move inward by a sharply perceived likeness towards an intimate self-perception," as in his poem "Life." But a poem such as *HSBlack*, according to Smith, "moves wittily out to occupy one's mind with a diversity of vivid actions going on in the world at large," such as "a challenge to a tournament, a self-exiled traitor, and the dilemma of a condemned thief."

Hester (1991b, 16–25) offers a detailed reading of *HSBlack* and a comparison of the poem's "central paradox" with the "dramatic exposition" of the issues of assurance and "election" in *Everyman* (16). For Hester, the Holy Sonnets generally are ineffective, "at least in their nervous attempts to affirm any enduring sense of assurance or 'election,'" and he locates the site of the conflict in the "space" (cf. *HSRound* 9) between "Grace and reason in which *moral consciousness* discovers and expresses itself." Hester claims that "both the promptings of moral desire and the inability of current Protestant soteriology to satisfy that desire" are especially apparent in *HSBlack*. Hester believes that both *Everyman* and *HSBlack* offer a "dramatic self-examination initiated by the prevenience of Death." In the morality play, Hester observes, when Death summons Everyman, because he has been a "thief" and a "traitor deject," to a pilgrimage from which he will not "turne again," Everyman's reaction to this summons ("this blind [obscure] matter troubleth my wit . . . my writing is full unready") is apt for the "moment and texture of Donne's poetic meditation." Donne's speaker, Hester observes, "similarly provoked to repentance," also characterizes himself as a "pilgrim," a traitor, and a "thiefe" (17). Hester also finds that both speakers "describe their unreadiness similarly" and that both works "focus attention on this pivotal moment in salvation history" (18). See more under *HSBlack*: Language and Style.

NOTES AND GLOSSES

1–8 *Oh . . . he might be'imprisoned.* **FRIEDERICH** (1932): Donne attempts to distance himself from his youthful follies, using them in later life as a basis for prayers and sermons. He often implies that he is "dying an eternal life and living an eternal death" ("als ob er ein ewiges Leben sterbe und einen ewigen Tod lebe") (158). **MARTZ** (1954): the lines reflect the "composition" stage of the Ignatian meditation (31). [See more under Holy Sonnets: Genre and Traditions.] **MAROTTI** (1986) finds in the octave "an aura of self-consciously witty melodrama" (256). **SMITH** (1991) notes that rather than "dwelling on his own suffering," the speaker "wittily reviews a series of situations in the world which bring home the peril to his soul such as a challenge to a combat, the quandary of a treasonous defector, the dilemma of a condemned thief." Adds that the "system" suggests a "correspondence between the spiritual and the temporal states which annuls the supposed barriers between them" (136).

1–5 *Oh . . . as a thiefe* **BUCKLEY** (1965) quotes the opening lines to illustrate that something is "subtly wrong with the pitch" of some Holy Sonnets (29). SMITH (1970) notes that though opening with an "occasional event" such as sickness, HSBlack immediately "moves wittily out to occupy one's mind with a diversity of vivid actions going on in the world at large" (164).

1–2 *Oh . . . Deaths Harold and Champion;* TROST (1904): an example of alliteration extended over two lines (56). GRANSDEN (1954): the lines allude not only to spiritual, but to physical illness, such as Donne's afflictions in 1608 (128–29). MARTZ (1954): Donne's focus is on the fearful voyage of the soul to judgment at the hour of death (139). [See also Holy Sonnets: Genre and Traditions.] MARTZ (1963): "The image is that of being *summoned* in the legal sense to undergo a trial by combat, in which sickness is the *champion* or official representative of death" (85). MILWARD and ISHII (1976): the opening words remind one of *Everyman*, where Death as God's messenger issues a summons to Everyman to appear before the divine judgment seat. But here the summons is issued not directly by Death but indirectly by Sickness, as "Harold and Champion" of Death. The terms of the metaphor are thus changed "from legal to chivalric," with Sickness assuming the offices of Harold "announcing the combat" and Champion "actively engaging in the combat on Death's behalf" (139–40). MALLETT (1983): "the reference is to a joust or tournament, where the herald summoned two rivals to combat; a champion was one who fought for or on behalf of someone else" (56).

1–2 *summoned / By Sicknes,* WILLMOTT (1985): "Sickness is a summoner to God's court because it leads to death which is followed by judgement" (66).

1 *black* WILLMOTT (1985): "with sin" (66).

1 *summoned* SMITH (1971): "Pronounced as three syllables" (626).

3–8 *Thou'art . . . might be'imprisoned.* HARDY (1942) quotes the lines as an example of the chasm that separated Donne from his God, finding in the images of "his exiled forbears" and the condemned man being led to execution evidence of Donne's deep remorse at his inadequacy, his indulging in an endless cycle of sin and repentance (179). MILWARD and ISHII (1976) point out that the two comparisons here may have been suggested by Ignatius's *Spiritual Exercises* and specifically by one of the "additions" to the first week, where exercitants are advised to imagine themselves in various difficult situations, including being imprisoned as criminals and bound in chains before a judge. Note that both images may grow out of contemporary religious controversy, where Catholic "pilgrims" were regarded as treasonous and faced punishment that was worse than that accorded thieves (140). ARCHER (1977) writes that "comparison of the soul to a pilgrim holds rich possibilities for development, but Donne ignores them, limiting the association to feelings of dread that accompany the necessity to return home." Finds the "confrontation" in the second simile to be "much more dreadful, brief, and dramatic, as the criminal faces his final brief journey" (176–77).

3–4 *Thou'art . . . to whence he'is fled,* **RUGOFF** (1939): "the soul summoned by death is described as a traitor who dares not return home" (154). **LEVER** (1974) says that Donne adds a "contemporary note" to the traditional pilgrim image by including "an act of treason [that] prevents the 'pilgrim' from returning to his own country" (179). **CRAIK and CRAIK** (1986) point out that human life was "traditionally called a pilgrimage" and cite *HSScene* 2. Add that here the analogy is with "a pilgrim who, while abroad, has committed treason against his own king" (277).

4 *darst not turne* **MALLETT** (1983): "does not dare to return" (56). [Similarly, Handley (1991, 42).] **HESTER** (1991b): "denotes both the speaker's lack of trust in the mercy of the Word" (cf. Zech 1.3 and Ps. 121) and "his inability to 'turne' to himself for a cure." As with the other comparisons in the octave, the pilgrim/traitor similes are forms of "mis-namings" (as found in Renaissance handbooks), "reductive substitutions of alibis and self-protective excuses for the surrender of the self in which he should engage." The "durst not" [sic] of the speaker's "fearful misreading of the relationship to Christ" is "mirrored" by the "unfolding presentation of the pilgrim conceit in which the initial premise of the comparison is negated by the subsequent 'traitorous' amplification." This rhetorical strategy "reinforces that each choice negated by the speaker's fearful desire here is a rejection, a repeated and reiterated rejection, of a biblical counsel" (18–19).

4 *turne* **SMITH** (1971): "return" (626). [So also, Hollander and Kermode (1973, 1050) and Patrides (1985a, 436).]

5–8 *Or . . . might be'imprisoned.* **RUGOFF** (1939): "the soul at the final summons" is described in terms of "the ways of thieves." Cf. *Sappho* 39–40 (81). **WILSON** (1958): Donne "saw the divine in terms of the human" as in the "image of his soul as a condemned prisoner" (51). **LEVER** (1974) thinks that Donne's conceit here may derive from "the figure of life as a prison from which all are taken to execution" in Thomas More's *Four Last Things* (179).

5 *death's doome* **SHAWCROSS** (1967): "Judgment Day" (339). [Similarly, Booty (1990, 107).] **SMITH** (1971): "sentence of death" (626). [Similarly, Mallett (1983, 56), Patrides (1985a, 436), Willmott (1985, 66), and Craik and Craik (1986, 277).]

5 *red* **PATRIDES** (1985a) (reading "read"): "cf. 'red', lines 12 and 14" (436). **HESTER** (1991b) calls attention to the play on the word "red" ("read") here and in the final lines (22–23). See more under notes to ll. 11–14.

6 *deliuered* **LEVER** (1974): "Released" (179).

6–7 *prison . . . execution* **STEIN** (1942): an example of rhyming of masculine and feminine endings (679).

7 *damn'd* **MARTZ** (1963): "condemned" (85). [So also, Warnke (1967, 267),

Smith (1971, 626), Mallett (1983, 56), Patrides (1985a, 436), and Craik and Craik (1986, 277).]

7 *haled* GROSART (1872–73), reading "hal'd," says, "'hal'd' [or 'haul'd'], not 'halèd,' because, as frequently in Donne and in Marlowe, &c. '-tion' at the end of the line is a full dissyllabic foot. Cf. 'cham-pion,' 1.2" (2:290). MILWARD and ISHII (1976): the word has the grim connotation of being bound to a hurdle and dragged by horses through the streets to the public place of execution at Tyburn (140). MALLETT (1983): "dragged" (56). [So also, Willmott (1985, 66).]

7 *execution* SMITH (1971): "Pronounced as five syllables" (626).

8 *be'imprisoned.* LEVER (1974): "'be' elides with the first syllable of 'imprisoned'" (179).

9–14 *Yet grace, . . . Soules to whight.* STEIN (1962): "With Donne the anger, punishment, and burning are less metaphysical than actual; and the violence of the necessary means, whether the same ultimate 'image' be 'restored' or not, must proceed by unfamiliar paths to an uncertain destination" (193).

9–12 *Yet grace, . . . art with Sin.* SMITH (1991): the "struggle for grace to redeem sin may be resolved only in a drastic reformation of our entire nature such as transforms vice into penitence and guilt into shame," for "we must merit death even though our redemption is at hand, yet we cannot even begin to repent without grace" (133–34). SMITH (1992) thinks that these lines point to Donne's sense of "his own unworthiness, his sense that he could not possibly merit God's grace," but they do not suggest that his "reluctance to become a priest" came from "a lack of faith" (88).

9–10 *Yet grace, . . . to begin?* STEIN (1962): "So long as that question [of l. 10] can be raised it is unanswerable" (193). LEVER (1974): "Repentance will win grace; but grace is first needed for the soul to repent" (179). MILWARD and ISHII (1976), observing that the poet addresses his colloquy not to God or Christ but to his own soul, point out that, like Shakespeare's Claudius, he reflects on God's readiness to forgive if he will only repent but that, also like Claudius, the "if" is his problem. Cite *Ham.* 3.3.65–66 (140). MALLETT (1983): "in line 9 'grace' is the mercy of God, which would not be denied to those who truly repented; in line 10 it refers to the state of mind in which the need for repentance is admitted, and which could only come about as the result of God's prompting" (56). SINFIELD (1983): the speaker "would repent [for his unworthiness]," but that is in "God's gifts" (11). VEITH (1985) points out that Donne believes that "one is saved by grace," but the "conditional clause" is "significant." Notes that a Calvinist "would not make grace contingent upon repentance, but would make repentance contingent upon grace," yet Donne "does not permit grace to do everything." Argues that Donne "sometimes questions his own Arminianism" and that here the conditional clause ("if thou repent") "intrudes itself between grace, offered as an alternative to damnation" ("yet grace") and its "abundance" ("Thou canst not lacke"). Finds that in l. 10 the conditional clause is itself "scrutinized" (124). **WILLMOTT** (1985): "God's grace (the unearned gift of God's favour) is freely available as long as the sinner chooses to repent and to accept it, but the poet needs grace in order to repent in the first place" (66).

10–14 *But . . . red Soules to whight.* **SIMPSON** (1924): Donne was "sufficiently convinced of the truth of the Christian doctrine of Atonement to believe that his repentance for these sins had been accepted in virtue of his faith in the blood of Christ" (117). **PRAZ** (1931) cites these lines to compare the Holy Sonnets favorably with the poetry of Michelangelo, especially for their "earnestness and intensity of religious thought." Conjectures that faith proved so difficult for them both that "they are continually afraid of slackening in zeal" (69–71). See more under The Holy Sonnets and Other Works.

10 *But who shall give thee that grace to begin?* **HANDLEY** (1991): a "rhetorical question" (42).

10 *grace to begin?* **HOLLANDER and KERMODE** (1973): prevenient grace, without which the repentance which gains further grace is impossible (1051).

11–14 *Oh . . . red Soules to whight.* **TURNELL** (1950) finds that "the poetic achievement is uncertain" in the poem, since though it has an impressive opening (ll. 1–2) and one lovely line (11), the three that follow (12–14) are among his "most affected" (273). **CRAWSHAW** (1972) says that Donne uses a "straightforward liturgical symbolism," for an "alchemical reading makes nonsense of it." Asserts that the alchemical progression is "unequivocally black, white and red" (348). **VEITH** (1985) notes that *HSBlack* ends "by positing two alternatives" and that a "more assured religious poet" might have used "and" rather than "or" i.e., "repent *and* Christ will cleanse you." Sees Donne as presenting "the two terms as alternatives": salvation is seen as "a function of the self or Christ, of repentance or atonement," and thus Donne "denies himself any confidence" (124–25). **HANDLEY** (1991) cites the "vivid physical effects of the spiritual experience" (42). **HESTER** (1991b): the "most remarkable feature" of the final lines is "the way in which they call attention to their own wit, to the speaker's creation of a rhetorical 'color' in imitation of the recreative power of Christ's sacrifice." From this view, the "playful gesture" (cf. "dyes") "privileges the prestidigital words of the clever speaker over the ontological transfigurations of The Word," and the play on "red"/"read" suggests that the speaker's "true hope lies in that faith 'read' in the death of Christ which alone, 'being re[a]d' by God, can sanctify man's 'blacke Soule.'" Thus "only if the text of the self is *misread* or *not read* at all by God, only if it is repenned/'repent' [l. 9] by Grace (and perhaps by man's cooperation with Grace), can it hope to be 'White'" (22–23). **SINFIELD** (1992): Christ's blood may well have "this might," but the question remains as to whether its power will extend to Donne. As expressed, the "mourning and blushing" are not "achieved states" but are "imperatives" Donne addresses to himself, and while he urges himself to "make thyself" he has already confirmed that "grace is necessary first." The ending is thus both "provisional" and even "rather conventional" (e.g., cf. William Perkins, "Dialogue of the State of a Christian Man" (1588) (161). SPURR (1992) calls attention to the "evolution of the colour conceit," as the "blackness of sin becomes that of mourning (sorrow for sin); the scarlet of evil becomes a red blush of regret; and the miracle of Christ's blood is that it changes the redness of sinful souls to a white purity." Notes that Donne puns on "dyes" and "dies" and that, through Christ's death, "souls die to sin and are reborn to sinlessness." Stresses the importance of the sonnet's progression from "black" to "white" (20–21). BORKOWSKA (1994) cites approvingly Hester's comments (1991b) on the association between writing and "re-pen(t)ing of the self" and suggests that the pun on "red"/"read" indicates that "man's way to salvation and his true hope lies in Christ's blood, that is faith as read (red) from this sacrifice." Further observes that the "interplay of colours" is important because it implies that "the Christian message only when correctly and passionately read (red), that is justly interpreted" or "re-pen(t)ed by Grace" can make a "new self, make it sin-less, 'white' (also the white, unwritten page of the text)." Adds that in his sermons Donne "condemns ignorance and neglected learning," comparing it to "blindness obstructing constructive hermeneutics" (34).

11–12 *Oh . . . as thou art with Sin.* PATMORE[?] (1846) cites these lines as an example of "splendid thoughts and splendid words" in the Divine Poems (236). MORRIS (1953): the sense of sin, as expressed by Eliot in "Ash Wednesday" (32–33, 40–41), is the same as Donne's (98–99). PETERSON (1959): the lines imply "sorrow for sin itself rather than sorrow occasioned by fear of punishment" (509). SHAWCROSS (1967) says that red was "the color of sin and remorse; black indicated its foulness" and that in alchemy black "signified penitential purification; red, the resurrection or immortality." Notes that the pilgrim, the prisoner, and the penitent "would all be pictured in black" and, finally, points to the pun on "red/read" (l. 5) (339). HEFFERNAN (1991) finds multiple allusions in these lines—e.g., the speaker alludes to Ezek. 18.4 and to Rom. 5 and 6, "where St. Paul teaches that by Christ's grace 'we . . . are dead to sin'" (Rom. 6.2), as well as to "colors mentioned in Scripture that present related meanings by stated or implied antithesis," such as Jude 13, where "the picture of grace refused is 'the blackness of darkness for ever,'" and Isa. 1.18, where the "antithesis is red and white: 'Though your sins be as scarlet, they shall be as white as snow; and, though they be red like crimson, they shall be as wool'" (59). Notes also that John "uses white for the garment of salvation" in Rev. 3.5 and concludes that these allusions "invest the meaning" of the final lines (59–60).

11 *blacke* WILLMOTT (1985): "no longer with sin (line 1), but in mourning repentance for sin" (66). BOOTY (1990): "indicating foulness" (107). HESTER (1991b): "blacke" has an "ameliorative connotation" in the "amplification of 'holy mourning'" and the line suggests a "desire to 'turne' to the octave's pilgrim simile," not this time to be "like" a pilgrim but to "*be* a pilgrim internally and spiritually" since it is for "being" that the speaker "yearns." But there remains the problem that this line may be "yet another act of 'treason,'" for in view of the "self-conscious

myopia" of l. 10, the "admonition to 'make thy self'" may promote "another refusal to 'turne' to God for the gift of mercy" (20–21).

12 *red with blushinge* **WILLMOTT** (1985) reads as "blushing with shame for his sins which are also 'red' (most wicked)" and cites Isa. 1.18 ("though your sins be as scarlet, they shall be as white as snow; though they be red like crimson, they shall be as wool" [so also, Craik and Craik (1986, 177)] (66). **BOOTY** (1990): "color of sin and contrition" (107). **LABRIOLA** (1995): "the flushed appearance, symptomatic of ill health, is a metaphor of the spiritual malady of the soul," but "health is restored . . . with 'Christ's blood,' which 'being red' then 'dyes red soules to white.'" The biblical texts that underlie this conceit are Isa. 1.16–18, 1 John 1.7, and Rev. 7.14 (99).

13–14 *Or . . . red Soules to whight.* **THOMPSON** (1935) finds that the lines reflect Donne's belief that both sin and death can be conquered through Christ's blood (14). Notes also that they are an example of his use of paradox until it becomes a "labyrinth of logic" ("Irregarten von Logik") in which he requires his soul to repent (77). **SIMPSON** (1948) observes that the Holy Sonnets and *Essays* have a common source in the Book of Revelation, here in "the dyeing of the souls in Christ's blood which makes them white," a reference to Rev. 7.14 (211). **FAERBER** (1950) explains that Donne's paradoxes of Christ often involve a play on words, as here the traditional image of Christ's blood is ripped out of the conventional context and intensified by means of the demonstrative additive, "being red" (26). Finds that Donne's paradoxes are far stronger than those of the other metaphysical poets, most of whose lie outside the contradictions rather than within them (32). See also Holy Sonnets: Language and Style. **A. SMITH** (1987): "the witty order of the Christian truth" celebrated confirms the "inherently paradoxical nature of truth itself, as we must see it," and, furthermore, "points the paradox at the heart of our reality" (166). **LABRIOLA** (1990) identifies here "the paradoxical adaptation of the Deity's omnipotence to the self-sacrifice of the Son" in Donne's use of the word "might" (64–65) and explains that in the paradox Christ's blood is "likened to a tincture that has the 'might' to transform the soul's red condition of sinfulness to whiteness or purity," a "transformation" revealed in Isa. 1.16–18 and Rev. 7.14 (65). Adds that "in illustrated Bibles, books of hours, paintings, frescoes, and stained glass, the blood of the crucified Christ drops onto the earth, where the skull and bones of Adam were exhumed, as the legends of the Cross recount," and "in sequential iconographic depictions Adam, at times, acquires flesh; he rises; and he collects in a vessel the effusion of water and blood from Christ's side, an elixir of life that he imbibes" (65). Emphasizes that through the juxtaposition of iconography of "the creation of Adam and the Crucifixion," readers may "perceive the reconciliation of Old and New Testament conceptions of the Deity" (65). Points to illustrated Bibles, for example, in which "God the Father breathes life into Adam, whose name (from the Hebrew word *adamah*) signifies red earth," and "at the redemption, analogously, Christ's blood reddens the earth; like a tincture on the bones of Adam, it has the 'might' to recreate humanity" (65).

13 *Christs blood,* **SHAWCROSS** (1967) notes that, "alchemically, blood was thought to act as a tincture" and cites 1 John 1.7: "But if we walk in the light, as he is in the light, we have fellowship one with another, and the blood of Jesus Christ his Son cleanseth us from all sin" (so also, Booty [1990, 107]) (339).

13 *might* **MALLETT** (1983): "power, property" (56). **WILLMOTT** (1985): "power" (67).

14 *dyes* **WILLMOTT** (1985) says that sin "*dies* and the soul is *dyed* a new colour being washed free of sin" and cites Rev. 7.14 (67).

14 *red Soules to whight.* **LEVER** (1974): see Isa. 1.18—"though your sins be as scarlet, they shall be as white as snow" (179).

14 *red* **SULLENS** (1964) notes that no figurative use of the word recorded by the *OED* is as early as Donne's here (229).

14 *whight.* **MALLETT** (1983): "white was the colour of innocence" (56).

HSDeath

COMMENTARY

General Commentary

De Quincey (1818 [1890, 70–71]), explaining some of the reasons Donne "is now almost forgotten," nonetheless says that fuller attention to his verse is warranted and quotes in full *HSDeath*, to which, he says, "high place is due."

Dyce (1833, 214) observes that *HSDeath* is "[d]eep-thoughted; and forcible."

Wordsworth (1833 [1979, 5:604]) responds to Alexander Dyce's request for advice about selections for his *Specimens of English Sonnets* (1833), commenting that *HSDeath* should be included because it is "so eminently characteristic" of Donne's "manner," as well as "so weighty in thought, and vigorous in expression." Wordsworth also admits that "to modern taste it may be repulsive, quaint, and labored."

The unnamed editor ("H.E.M.") of *Dies Consecrati: or, A New Christian Year with the Old Poets* (1855, 294) prints *HSDeath* as a poem appropriate for the Burial of the Dead.

An anonymous author writing in *QR* (1862–63, 43–90) prints *HSBlack* as a poem illustrating the struggle between doubt and faith, and then *HSDeath*, remarking that the second poem "was composed when the victory had been achieved, and, in imagination, the last enemy was already trodden under foot" (86).

Hunt (1867, 78), though expressing general disappointment about Donne's "sincere" but "not healthy" piety, acknowledges *HSDeath* to be "the best sonnet he wrote." Written on a subject with which, Hunt thinks, Donne "was in more than one sense of the word least happy," the poem is in his judgment "equally unexceptionable and noble."

MacDonald (1868, 121–23), both praising and criticizing the Holy Sonnets, quotes in full *HSMade*, *HSSouls*, and *HSDeath*, describing them as "very fine" (121).

Deshler (1879, 125–26) writes about Donne in the form of a dialogue between a professor and a student. The "professor" comments negatively about Donne's poetry and cites as characteristic of Donne's verse *HSRound* and *HSDeath*. The "student" is initially more positive, observing that "[t]here is something delightfully impudent in Donne's contemptuous banter of Death" in *HSDeath* and also commenting that the final couplet "in a measure redeems the extravagant braggadocio that precedes it" (126). Nonetheless, the student acknowledges that Donne's response is "inferior in true grandeur" to St. Paul's words in 1 Cor. 15.55 ("O death, where is thy sting? O grave, where is thy victory?") and to Raleigh's apostrophe to Death at the close of *History of the World*.

Noble (1880, 456–57), though hinting that most of Donne's sonnets are "chaff," says that one of the "wheat-grains" is HSDeath. Noting that, other than the topic of love, death "has been the most favoured motive of lyrical poets," Noble doubts that there is in English "any invocation to Death which, for manliness, weight, and dignity, deserves a place beside this high utterance of the first of our miscalled 'metaphysical poets'" (456). After printing the poem, Noble affirms that there is "nothing of the same kind in English poetry more impressive than this solemnly triumphant close" (457).

Caine (1882, 276) calls HSDeath "magnificent" and a "masterpiece" and observes that "there can hardly be a doubt that it is the weightiest, most forceful and ful-thoughted of all the many English sonnets written on the subject."

Pollitt (1890, 70–71) explains generally why Donne, though with a "splendid reputation" in his own time, is now largely neglected because of such qualities as "the extreme harshness of his metre, and the obscurity of much that he wrote" (70). He says, furthermore, that a "just expression of respect for the memory of this distinguished man" would be to print a representative selection of his verse, and he chooses HSDeath with the belief that readers will think "that a high place is due" to that sonnet.

An anonymous author in Ac (1900, 609) quotes the poem in full to illustrate that Donne's Divine Poems "have the same intensity of imagination, the same fine exordia" as his secular verse.

Grierson (1909, 248) notes that in a manuscript collection made between 1619 and 1623 BoulRec and an "Elegie" beginning "Death be not proud" (not HSDeath—ed.) appear together, the latter seemingly in answer to the former. Despite this coincidence, he suggests that "Elegie" was not composed by Donne but possibly by the Countess of Bedford. Grierson later (1912, 2:cxliii–cxlv) identifies two manuscripts, H6 and O21, in which the "Elegie" appears as a continuation of BoulRec, but again argues, on the basis of style and content, that the former is not Donne's, adding that the poem may or may not be by the Countess of Bedford.

Schelling (1910, 133), discussing the composers of religious sonnets in Shakespeare's time, cites Corona and the Holy Sonnets, "both of questionable date," as collections that contain poems "worthy of Donne's great repute." He quotes HSDeath in full as an example.

Hillyer (1941, xxxiv) praises HSDeath as "one of the triumphs of the sonnet form in English."

Garrod (1946, x) singles out HSDeath and HSWilt from among the Divine Poems as works "men will not willingly let die."

Brooke (1948, 635–36) is of the opinion that among the Holy Sonnets HSDeath ranks second only to HSRound.

Buckley (1965, 29), though identifying HSDeath as "histrionic," also finds that it has "magnificent moments."

Bush (1965, 75) refers to HSDeath as a poem "in which the poet challenges the great enemy in the strength of Christian faith."

Sanders (1967, 353) writes that, in HSDeath, Donne "apostrophizes from an imperative opening into a series of arguments and refutations, developing his statement much as an accomplished debater might." He argues that Donne minimizes death by quickly taking the reader past "fearful spots."

Dickinson (1967, 6) notes that this poem is concerned with "immortality of the soul, a concept made immediate and real by means of the argument the poet advances in an implied debate with personified Death."

Mulder (1969, 63–64) believes that while HSDeath is sometimes cited as an example of confident hope in eternal life, it would have been read by Donne's contemporaries as a cry of anguish. He says that its logic is a series of false syllogisms, a "hopeless argument from a helpless voice" (63). "Sheer animal fear" of losing his body in death causes the speaker to cast about for arguments against death, Mulder says. Contending that the speaker's "specious reasoning" shows his anxiety, Mulder finds the speaker's one-sided debate as he attempts to silence death to be a desperate effort to silence his own anguish. This sophistry, he argues, proves the impotence of human reason in the face of death and points to the Christian's only recourse: the hope of heaven founded on faith (64).

Had he feared death, Roy and Kapoor (1969, 121) write, Donne would not have been able to defy death as he does in HSDeath. Further, they argue, Donne focuses on death because "it brings to the fore his consciousness of his sins."

French (1970, 113–14) claims that this sonnet reveals a fear of death despite the assurances in the poem. Furthermore, he states, Donne's analogies are "so desperately evasive that we can only conclude he must have had something considerable to evade." French calls the poem a "sustained piece of bluff."

Smith (1970, 161) declares that the "hammering grandeur" of such poems as HSDeath reveals the "momentousness" of the subject matter. Donne's writing, Smith contends, "invests our human affairs with a dignity that befits man's standing, at the centre of a cosmic drama." There is, he says, no inward conflict or personal anguish.

According to Sanders (1971, 114–15), this sonnet displays a "bland superficiality" and a "triumphal brassiness." See more from Sanders in the General Commentary on the Holy Sonnets above.

Willy (1971, 80) thinks that Donne is proclaiming the "ultimate invincibility of man's immortal soul" by "defiantly" challenging what in a 1621 sermon he calls "the last and in that respect the worst enemy" (Sermons, 4:55).

Granqvist (1975, 126–28) notes that HSDeath is "[b]y far the most popular" of the Holy Sonnets in the anthologies he surveyed from the 1830s to 1860s, followed by HSDue and HSRound (128).

Jones (1978, 38–40) writes that Donne "could not conceivably have been aware of how bad his arguments are" in HSDeath, suggesting that the "badness" of these arguments "must be taken as part of the meaning of the poem" (38). He observes that what is admired in Donne's poems of faith "is his refusal to be intimidated by reasons" (39) and that in HSDeath there is enacted "an encounter between man and more-than-man" (40).

Low (1978, 66) argues that this sonnet, the best known of all Donne's devotional poems, is not a traditional devotion because "it balances indirect meditation on death with vocal thanksgiving for salvation."

Manlove (1978, 11–12) describes HSDeath as a "striking demonstration of Donne's commitment to mind in opposition to external phenomena," as in this poem "wit takes on death itself." He notes that, until the final couplet, Donne "proposes to devalue death by purely human intelligence and argument," but in that effort Manlove finds Donne largely unsuccessful. The arguments, he says, "do not convince" (11). The final two lines, he thinks, make a point that might have formed the basis for the argument of the poem as a whole and thus have "saved" it, but, "thrown in" at the end, it "seems one more in a list of self-delusions," for, indeed, it "glosses over the possibility that eternal waking might be in fields not Elysian." Finally, Manlove asserts, "to say that death will die is to give back to the notion of dying all the weight and meaning that the poem has tried to remove from it" (12).

Carey (1981, 199) finds that "part of the strength of this poem is that its argument is so weak." As Carey explains, even though the speaker claims that death is nothing to fear, "the speaker can hardly, at the end, use death as a threat . . . without ludicrously betraying himself." Donne's "ill-assorted reasons tumble out in no recognizable order, reflecting inner disarray," in Carey's view, presenting us with a speaker who is "plainly trying to convince himself, and failing so badly that he cannot even decide whether he wants to say sleep is better than death or vice versa."

Hyman (1982, 49–50) considers HSDeath in the context of the larger question of how "humanists and other non-believers" can appreciate religious works and focuses on the poem as "experience" rather than a series of statements providing simple answers. Hyman finds the claims of the sonnet "unambiguous" and set out in three arguments: "we should not fear death because the image of death ('sleepe') gives pleasure, because death is itself subject to 'Fate,' and, finally, because we are promised eternal life." Since the first two arguments are "specious," according to Hyman, but "are presented with so much more vigor and wit than the third," one finds it difficult "to decide which reason is more effective within the poem." And Hyman adds that "there is nothing in the poem to indicate that the third reason, the belief in the immortality of the soul, is of a different order of seriousness than the obviously specious reasons that precede it" (49). Hyman indicates that he is not "suggesting that the poem does not mean what it says," but rather that, at the end, "we should respond to the entire poem and not just to the conclusion." Doing so, he believes, will allow us to read the poem not as a "statement" but as an "experience," that is, the experience of "the extreme difficulty, logically and emotionally, of the speaker's overcoming his fear of death as well as the courageous resolution to do so" (50).

Gill (1990, 103) finds the repeated change of moods in the sonnet a product of "a kind of poetic duel with death." Gill sees the falsity of the argument itself as posing an interpretive problem, but he offers two defenses of this approach: 1) because the poem is about "the *language* we use to speak of death," then "what the poet does is playfully exploit some of the ways in which people speak of death in order to belittle the kind of talk that calls it *mighty* and *dreadful*"; and 2) "what matters is not the argument itself but the creation of an anxious mind that seeks to control the terrible threat of death by bracing itself with as many images as it can." Gill also observes that God is not mentioned in the poem, and he wonders if the speaker "feels death to be more immediate than God" or if there is a "quiet confidence in the restraint of the language" that makes it "more appealing and religiously profound" than the more direct language of a poem like HSBatter.

Ray (1990b, 86–87) points to the speaker's "absolute confidence in his eternal salvation and triumph over physical death" (86), finding as well a "grimly humorous pun" in the image of Death as a "corpse that is swollen: the speaker sees the effect of physical death on a dead body as exemplifying the pride in Death personified," and yet, "it is pride without justification," as he shows (87).

To González and de Sevilla (1991, 552–53) HSDeath offers a blunt demystification of death. The poem begins, they observe, by recognizing that to some, death is great and powerful but proceeds to show that its influence and action are limited and very much earthbound.

Handley (1991, 43) calls HSDeath a "finely economical" poem that is "rich in single word effects" and that features a "sustained personification of 'Death' throughout giving it a curiously triumphant tone."

Singh (1992, 99) states that the sonnet "affirms the Christian belief that the death of Christ on the cross has freed mankind from the fear of death."

Date and Circumstances

Chambers (1896, 1:246) says that HSDeath must have preceded BoulRec, written in 1609, because the latter alludes to the former.

Carpenter (1897, 113) says that HSDeath was written "before 1607."

Martz (1954, 217–18), like Chambers (1896), argues that the opening lines of BoulRec (1–4) represent "a recantation" of the opening lines of HSDeath (1–4), that lines 9–10 of BoulRec "appear to reinterpret lines 7–8 of the sonnet," and that "all the first half of the elegy (1–34) amounts to a denial of the sonnet's ending." He concludes, therefore, that since Mrs. Bulstrode died on 4 August 1609, HSDeath must have been composed before that date.

Milward (1979 [1988, 66]) also notes a relationship between the two poems, finding BoulRec a "strange recantation" of HSDeath. Milward points out that in some manuscripts BoulRec "is immediately followed by another poem, beginning with Donne's own words, 'Death be not proud,'" but the poem is not by Donne himself. Milward notes Grierson's suggestion (1909 and 1912—see HSDeath: General Commentary) that the poem may have been written by Donne's patroness, the Countess of Bedford. If this is true, then, Milward argues, "together the two elegies serve to fix the date" of HSDue, HSBlack, HSScene, HSRound, HSMin, and HSDeath "within the first half of 1609 which was also the year Richard Sackville succeeded to the title of Earl of Dorset and received this poetic offering from Donne."

Singh (1992, 99) points out that the view that "after death our souls will sleep till they awake on the Day of Judgement" is helpful in dating HSDeath and related Holy Sonnets. Singh cites Gardner's suggestion (1952) that not until the writing of Pseudo-Martyr (1609) did Donne determine "that the souls of the righteous are admitted to God's presence at the moment of death rather than having to wait till the Day of Judgement." Thus, Singh observes, the perspective in HSDeath that death is "followed by a short sleep," indicates that it must predate August 1609.

The Poet/Persona

Praz (1925, 68–69) finds that, in trying to calm his fears of being weak and sinful, Donne considers death to be a passage to a beatific life.

Leishman (1934, 90), echoing Walton (1640), observes that Donne never feared death and that in this "the finest of his sonnets he faces the great enemy."

Mims (1948, 55–57) quotes HSDeath in full to show that although death "fascinated and terrified" Donne, in the end he was "perfectly sure in his faith," confident that Christ by his death and resurrection had "opened up to man a vision of triumph over death" (57).

Spörri-Sigel (1949, 78) finds in the poem Donne's most powerful and passionate exposition of death, one in which he compiles proof after proof of its weakness and its "nothingness" ("Nichtigkeit") in the face of the promise of eternal life. But she argues that in asking the question "why swell'st thou then?" Donne implies a continuing struggle, though he does not want to admit to himself the power he ascribes to death. In personifying death he makes it his personal opponent, one which he can overcome only after violent struggle.

Faerber (1950, 31) claims that the paradox of death's defeat has the effect of calming the irritation caused by the contradictions of Christian doctrine, thereby arousing a sense of piety. He argues that in reality Donne has a great fear of death; hence the sonnet is not the serene testimony of one who has overcome that fear, but a powerful teaching of the dogma which is supposed to magically banish it.

Gransden (1954, 136) contends that in the ultimate defeat of death Donne places "all his faith in the New Testament" and its promise that those who learn to repent will achieve salvation.

Frankenberg (1956, 372) observes that the confidence Donne expresses in the poem was not easily won, but is a consequence of "an active and continuous conquest of doubts and of his recurrent state of ill-health."

In Sicherman's reading (1971, 85), the speaker claims to have transcended fear of death, but his words "smack more of cliché than reflection" and the conclusion "is of scant comfort" to persons not yet resurrected.

Stachniewski (1981, 691–92) finds that the tone of the sonnet "is one of bravado rather than assurance," and "by pretending that death is a person Donne can believe, or appear to believe, that he dominates it" (691). He reads the closing line as "a theatrical gesture," for if death had been "diminished, the verb 'die' would not have seemed a strong one with which to conclude." The ending, then, in Stachniewski's view, "confirms the fear which is the basis of the poem" (692).

Marotti (1986, 257) explains that the sonnet may rest "on the conventional devotional sharing in Christ's victory over death through the redemption," but he also finds the speaker to be engaged in a particularly self-aggrandizing act. The two attitudes, in Marotti's view, "are hard to disentangle."

Wolny (1991, 188) calls attention to Donne's distancing of himself from this sonnet and its ideas. For Wolny, Donne is "absent from the poem (no subjective 'I', so frequent in other pieces)." Wolny finds here that Donne "describes death such as it is <u>not</u> for him."

Structure

Ward (1949, 2) notes that the sonnet is in the Shakespearean tradition of three quatrains and a couplet but has the Petrarchan octave and sestet.

Esch (1955, 52) finds the sonnet, though Italian in structure, at variance with the traditional form in that the concluding couplet rounds off the question raised in the first twelve lines, "why swell'st thou then?" See more under Holy Sonnets: Genre and Traditions.

Stampfer (1970, 247–50), looking at the development of the poem as a whole, says that the octave comprises the thesis, which is "vehement, illusory action" (247): the speaker would by a force of spirit evoke Judgment Day. Stampfer then identifies lines 9 to 12 as the antithesis of "befuddled helplessness" (247), where the speaker falls back on his fallen condition for possible penance. The synthesis Stampfer finds in the last two-and-a-half lines, which have a muted sincerity as the speaker asks for a lesson in repentance: "Standing now on a glum, flat truth, sensing he requires a fresh stirring of soul, he begins at last to pray in earnest" (247). Stampfer asserts that *HSDeath* is structurally "odd," for Donne's equilibria keep shifting ground "between shadow and substance, antagonist and self, confrontation and utter isolation" (249). For example, he notes, the opening octave confronts death, the speaker then denies death the ferocity to possess the world, and by the end of the octave death has been internalized "from a confrontation to a biological process" (249). In the sestet death looms again, observes Stampfer, but it is ineffectual: "The speaker has blocked death off, annulled it, cancelled its existence" (250). The final couplet marks for Stampfer the arrival of the metaphysical poet who stands confronting death, as the strenuous existential believer. No final resolution is possible, Stampfer concludes; there remains only the towering defiance of the speaker.

Fuller (1972, 22–23) remarks that the history of the English sonnet in late Elizabethan times is largely one of assimilation with the Italian sonnet. He argues that Donne, like Milton, presided over the general blurring of the sonnet's musical form. In *HSDeath*, for example, there occurs an Italian octave followed by an enclosed quatrain and couplet. Fuller observes that the rhyme scheme in *HSDeath* is identical to Milton's sonnet on Cromwell. However, the two poems differ, he notes, in that Donne "feels no obligation to turn at line 9 or anywhere near it, whereas he clearly feels the quatrains as developing units" (23). In the first quatrain, Fuller states, death's power is a pretence; in the second, death is a welcome release; and in the third death is shown as essentially weak.

Dasgupta (1981, 84–92) identifies four sections in the sonnet, "constituting a point-by-point refutation of death's claim as the destroyer": lines 1–4 reject "the grounds for death's pride"; 5–8 are "a recognition of death as soul's liberation"; 9–12 reveal "death's subordination to other agencies and modes of destruction"; 13–14 are "a triumphant assertion of the death of Death" (87–88). Dasgupta's reading distinguishes the "more vigorous and positive" focus of the sestet from "the more subdued tone of negation and qualification in the octet" (89), arguing that the "ultimate conviction" of the poem is "fully convincing because it is *believed* in, not rhetorically *imposed*, by Donne" (91–92).

Language and Style

Schirmer (1937, 299) notes that in contrast with the "rousing" ("rauschenden") tone of HSRound, HSDeath achieves a certain "joyous piety" ("heitere Frömmigkeit").

Ward (1949, 2–3) observes that the poem opens in a "colloquial, almost conversational" tone and builds to a triumphal ending (2). The notes of scorn in the first quatrain, she explains, and of contempt in the second, produce the humiliation in the third, setting the stage for the "final blow" of the couplet (3).

Daiches and Charvat (1950, 659) note the difference in tone between the religious and secular poetry, HSDeath, for example, having a "massive quality" not found in the Songs and Sonets.

Martz (1954, 144) finds that, though the sonnet's approach to death is relatively calm, still "there is a note of stridency, almost of truculence—a sense of daring to stand up to the terror."

Frankenberg (1956, 372) detects a calm tone unlike that of the other sonnets, such as HSBatter and HSMade, where Donne spars "with his God, as with a beloved adversary."

Sanders (1967, 353) notes the use of irony throughout the text, as well as its "rugged" metrical movement, and finds the tone of the sestet "embarrassingly personal (or magnificently sure)."

Patterson (1970, 105–08), tracing Renaissance satire to the Neoplatonic Ideas of Hermogenes, and in particular the three Ideas of Reproof (Asperity, Vehemence, and Vigor), argues that HSDeath is in the Vigorous style.

White and Rosen (1972, 53) call this the best-known of the Holy Sonnets, remarkable for the "rallying mockery of its tone." This mockery is effective and wittily delivered in a series of arguments, they point out—arguments by analogy, by syllogistic logic, and by example.

Bartine (1979, 1, 4–5) is concerned with features of a "primary performative utterance," as distinguished from a "performative" utterance, explaining that in both the speaker is "doing something rather than merely *saying* something," but with the latter, "the performative (e.g. I urge you, I order you) is not explicitly stated" (1). Bartine notes the relationship between "primary performatives" and personification, observing that "the speaker in directing a primary performative at an abstraction (death, time, etc.) chooses to rely heavily on personification for the necessary constitution of the audience to whom the primary performative is directed" (1). Bartine draws upon HSDeath as illustrative of this device, noting that with this sonnet "we quickly recognize the impoverishment of paraphrases such as *the speaker is commanding death* or *urging death*" (4–5). Bartine claims that "much of the complexity of this poem is a result of the three simultaneous functions of personification: it acts as the device supplementary to the primary performative and carries clues to the speaker's state of mind; it serves to constitute the audience of the utterance; and it functions as a central principle of structure for the entire utterance," the whole becoming "an increasingly-complex accumulation of clues about the speaker's state of mind." Bartine finds that personification enables "that which is addressed" to become available by "filling out dimensions which are incomplete for the speaker" and that in the case of HSDeath, death is "almost wholly unavailable" prior to personification (5).

Handscombe (1980, 98–108) suggests that whereas one might think that a poem in "plain" style (e.g., *HSDeath*) would pose less difficulty in interpretation than one that is "embellished" (such as *HSBatter*), in many instances "the contrary is true" (98). Handscombe notes that *HSDeath* offers a "clearly accessible primary meaning," and the "few supporting images" may lead us to think "that that is all there is," but, he argues, this sonnet demands that we look at "the range of semantic options open to the author, the reader, *and the language as a whole*" (99). Handscombe then suggests a range of issues and questions, including: the use of the word "death" "as a concrete or abstract noun" (100); the poem as (possibly) "a personal obsequy, at once anguished and consoling, written for the real death of a real person" (101); the speaker's sincerity, age, and gender or, even, the speaker as Christ; the poem as "a picture representing, say, a Dance of Death," reflecting "the thoughts of the most indignant-looking participant" (105). Handscombe also suggests a possible allusion to the Book of Revelation in the final line, for in this biblical text, death does in fact die. Thus the multiplicity of possible readings can, in fact, have a "common ground" because for Donne, in Handscombe's view, "any human experience is a potential means of making contact with God through the sacrifice of Christ," and the poet's purpose is "to show that it is not just for 'mee' that Death will die, but for all mankind" (107–08).

Sloane (1985, 149, 233–38, 246–48), in a comparison of Milton's "On Time" and *HSDeath*, observes that in Donne's sonnet, Death is "personified, but, paradoxically, in less than human terms," which Sloane regards as "the entire point" of *HSDeath*: "sealed by the final reversal, it is death who is truly mortal, not we" (237). Sloane finds the speaker in control throughout, evident in "the confident manner in which he confronts his adversary, in the evenness of his tone, and in such local effects as the denigrating address to 'poore death' and the *zeugma* of lines 5 and 6" (237). In Donne, Sloane finds both rhetorical (in the sense of argumentation) and nonrhetorical styles, and he believes that Donne "never escaped sounding like a lawyer" or, more specifically, "thinking like one" (149). According to Sloane, "the conditions of rhetoric, the constant and functional oppositions," are "more evident in Donne than in Milton" (248), and he proposes that while Donne "thought controversially," Milton "apparently, did not" and thus "in that negative observation humanist rhetoric as an approach to Milton ends" (248).

Stein (1986, 161–62) notes that in several of Donne's poems, including in particular *HSDeath*, the power of death is diminished in the course of the poem. At the outset of the sonnet, Donne "rehearsed some familiar images of death," then "shrewdly observed a few apparent limitations of death's power, and ended with a restatement of the promise which alone could validate his argument" (161). Stein states that the "bravura" of Donne's rhetoric "is paired with a kind of cunning intimacy that reduces the size and remoteness of the foe," and the "status of death" is apparent from the "wretched company it keeps" ("poyson, warre, and sicknesse") and by the fact that it is dependent on the "whims of 'Fate, chance, kings, and desperate men'" (162).

Mazzaro (1987, 250), in the context of a comparison of Donne and Herbert, says that *HSDeath* "gains immediacy" through "apostrophe, enjambment, imbalance, rhythmic irregularity, and paradox." Various poetic devices, he asserts, coalesce to "delineate a particular vantagepoint." By mediating the event "through the contingencies of this vantagepoint," he argues, Donne creates a context "against which opacity emerges and language can rebound."

A. Smith (1987, 161) contends that "the odd notion of a witty piety," though "basic" in Donne's religious poetry, "may strike one less at first than the sonorous address and sheer dramatic impact of some of the poems." In *HSDeath*, for example, "there is no question" of "an inward conflict or a personal anguish," for "the rhetoric itself is an affirmation," proclaiming the "possibility of a heroic triumph snatched from likely defeat."

Nash (1989, 34–37) points out that although Donne's sonnet may have "the air of unconstrained emotional utterance," it is "a well-known demonstration of affective rhetoric," clearly in debt to St. Paul's epistle, "and like those of the Pauline rhetoric, its passions are discernibly *argued*" (34). Affective rhetoric, according to Nash, has as its objective "the entrapment of the audience, the enforced complicity in a ritual act" (37). Nash states that "the form of the argument is quite close to that of classical forensic oratory, except that the process of *confutatio* is absent," but "in any case, the whole poem is a confutation of Death's alleged might; *confirmatio*, the arguments of faith, and *confutatio*, the case against despair, here run together" (34). The sonnet appears to follow the Petrarchan model, that is, with an octave and sestet, but Nash observes that the sonnet's argument "is not constructed on the octave-sestet division" (34). Instead, Nash demonstrates, "the prosodic basis of Donne's argument in this poem is the distich; he proceeds two lines at a time" (35). Nash further notes that the shape of the poem is "a rounded utterance," by virtue of "the apostrophe to Death at the beginning and end" (36). Although there is a sense of distance between the speaker and reader at the beginning of the poem, the change in pronouns in the sixth line prepares for the engagement of the reader by the end "when the *rhetor* is thus able to say to us 'this touches you personally'" (37).

Müller (1992, 367) finds that in *HSDeath* Donne constructs paradox through wordplay. Death was perceived in the Baroque era, according to Müller, "as omnipresent and almighty," but the speaker confronts death in a "bold way and disputes in a stubbornly insistent, passionate argument its horror and power." The last two lines of the sonnet, in Müller's view, deal Death a "rhetorical deathblow." Müller suggests that Donne employs, in a rhetorical sense, a *figura etymologica*. "Expressed in a grammatical way," Müller adds, "the predicate ('die') is assigned to a subject ('death') with which it does not logically fit."

Prosody

Schelling (1895, xlviii) cites *HSDeath* as an example in which Donne, like some other poets, shows "much freedom and art in phrasing and in the employment of the overflow [enjambment—ed.]."

Brooks and Warren (1938, 524) offer the poem for analysis, using the method they applied to the study of *HSMin* (520–24). See more under *HSMin: Prosody*.

Daniels (1941, 275–78) analyzes the prosody of *HSDeath* to explain how Donne makes an effective poem of an analytical argument, citing caesuras of varying strengths, irregular stresses, paradoxes, concrete imagery, and the "sudden flash of the final statement" (278).

Levenson (1954, item 36) observes that in a short poem Donne can shift swiftly between metaphors, as here where death, once "mighty and dreadful," is reduced to a "slave, criminal, and soporific" in the sestet.

Wolfe and Daniels (1967, 116–17) point to the rhymes of *HSDeath* to illustrate the poem's attention both to the death of Death and to eternal life. By placing "eternally" first in the final couplet, they note, Donne "produces a momentary ambiguity of rime," which yields a striking conclusion to both lines while giving the death of Death the "greater prominence"; "eternally" appears to be the culminating rhyme word to the rhymes introduced in lines 1, 4, 5, and 8 ("thee," "mee," "bee," and "deliverie") and thus concludes the development of the subordinate theme of the sonnet. But they observe that the presence of "die" (l. 14) has the effect of giving even greater emphasis to the final line, combining, paradoxically, the appearance of being exactly rhymed with the distinctiveness of being unrhymed. If line 13 echoes as well as completes the idea of the beginning, they conclude, then we may see the structure of the poem faintly reflecting Donne's idea, which is to show that "in our end is our beginning" (117).

Themes

An anonymous editor (1840, 271) collects and prints a number of Donne poems under various original headings. *HSDeath* is printed under the heading "Death and Resurrection."

Aronstein (1920, 82–83) finds the poem a song of triumph of belief and victory over death.

Friederich (1932, 175) observes that the thought of the death of Christ joyfully released "oppressed, conscience-stricken Baroque mankind" ("den neider gedrückten, gewissensgequälten barocken Menschen") from the great burden of fear of death which they bore.

Daniels (1941, 275–78), in explicating the sonnet, acknowledges that the thought is commonplace but says that Donne has written "one of the best English poems on the subject." The poet's approach, he asserts, is original, a denial that death is "proud and powerful"; and he addresses the subject colloquially, as if engaging death in conversation. Daniels finds that this tone does not last, however, for after the first lines it is apparent that the poet is in "dead earnest." The poem is not emotional, as one might expect of the subject, but takes the form of a reasoned argument, a dramatized debate in which only one side is heard (275–76). Daniels analyzes the elements of the argument: the analogy with rest and sleep; the fact that "our best men" go, and "the best can't be wrong"; death as a slave; and drugs as equally effective in producing sleep. For Daniels, the effectiveness of the poem arises from its refusal, though it dramatizes a feeling, to allow emotion to take control. Daniels summarizes the poem (e.g., the dramatic opening, the personification of Death, the list of reasons Death has no justification for pride, the closing question, "Why swell'st thou?," and the final paradox) and concludes that *HSDeath* is one of the "first class" of its kind (278).

Roth (1947, 16–17) finds that by personifying death Donne reduces it to a human level, thus lessening its impact and inducing a feeling of content.

Ward (1949, 1–4) asserts that the sonnet is built upon an extended conceit, "the confutation of Death" (1). Acknowledging that the argument is absurd literally, Ward nonetheless finds a forceful expression of the emotion aroused by the conviction that Christian faith will triumph over death, and as such it can only be appreciated as a union of thought and feeling. Ward argues that the key to the poem is in the opening four words—the attack on death's pride—and that each quatrain continues the assault, the first refuting death as "mighty," the second as "dreadfull," and the third humbling it to the level of a slave (2–3). In the final couplet, Ward concludes, the once "swelling" death is defeated by the thought of immortality (3–4).

Reeves (1952, 101) summarizes the poem: "Death is not the all-powerful tyrant it is sometimes called," but only a servant, "and will in the end give way to eternal life."

Wiley (1954, 99) observes that although Donne, like his contemporaries, was obsessed with death, their "Christian faith stood firm"; thus the sonnet expresses a "great final affirmation" of victory over it.

Sypher (1955, 138), discussing Jesuit casuistry (e.g., the application of a "pliable and provisional law of pro and contra" to reconcile opposites), observes that HSDeath, with its "legalistic wit," succeeds "surprisingly" in accommodating contradictions.

Denonain (1956, 154, 290) notes that the poem is a sarcastic address to impotent death (154), adding that Donne "consecrates" ("consacrer") the defeat of death by divine grace (290).

Frankenberg (1956, 372) finds that the triumph of the poem is over sorrow, unlike the love poems, which defeat disappointment and cynicism.

ul-Hasan (1958, 58) observes that Donne sublimated his fear of death by turning it into a longing, as a means of attaining eternal life.

For Peterson (1959, 510) the poem "dismisses death as a valid motive for fear."

Wolfe and Daniels (1967, 116–17) observe that Donne presents death in the image of a being who will die and that, while eternal life is a secondary theme, it is "remarkable" that it emerges "so strongly without seeming to compete for attention with the ostensible major theme." The delicate balance between major and minor themes is, they assert, maintained "not only by unified imagery but also by the rime scheme" that almost creates the effect of a double ending (116). See more under HSDeath: Prosody.

Roston (1974, 189–90), identifying the Pauline "contempt for physical death" as the "central theme" of HSDeath (189), finds that Donne deflates Death's pride by using techniques similar to those found in his secular poetry. Roston argues that in HSDeath the personification of Death, familiar to allegory, "is turned inward upon itself" because Donne treats it with "a sly literalism which transforms it into near absurdity" (190).

Sloane (1974, 77) notes that "not only has sickness been given the dramatic role of herald and champion of death, but, as in Quarles's emblems, other similitudes also are capable of actions that represent the soul's guilt."

Lewalski (1979, 270) proposes that the placement of HSDeath after HSMin in the 1635 edition is a consequence of "a kind of victory over [the speaker's] sins" at the end of *HSMin*, in light of the speaker's "true repentance and faith." *HSDeath*, in Lewalski's view, thus next takes up the speaker's "conquest over death," for the speaker no longer fears the power of death over him.

Dasgupta (1981, 84–92) acknowledges the importance of studies of the Ignatian meditative tradition for understanding Donne's religious poetry, but finds that "the tradition alone does not fully explain Donne's preoccupation with death in his secular and divine poetry" (84). Dasgupta believes that Donne's protracted interest in death and decay is "as much the product of the Jacobean Zeitgeist as of the privation and insecurity he suffered after marriage" (85), citing evidence from the Songs and Sonets, the two Anniversary poems, and the prose works, with Donne's "obsessive concern" with death reaching its "climax" in the Sermons (85–86). Whereas, according to Dasgupta, the first five sonnets [following Gardner's (1952) grouping—ed.], *HSDue, HSBlack, HSScene, HSRound,* and *HSMin,* evoke "a sense of fear and horror of judgement," the sixth sonnet, *HSDeath,* "dismisses the last enemy with an unruffled, solemn majesty" (87). Here, in Dasgupta's view, Donne regards death as "a gateway to a greater life beyond the grave" (87). The poem, for Dasgupta, is an expression of "private experience with public appeal where Donne's personal musings re-create for us a situation which provides a momentary but vivid glimpse of the momentous drama awaiting enactment in Eternity" (92).

Shaw (1981, 26–28) finds the speaker "protesting overmuch" in the sonnet, thus calling into question the speaker's efforts "to diminish the awesomeness of Death" (26). In the beginning, according to Shaw, the speaker "seeks to establish superiority over his enemy by gainsaying Death's reputation ('thou art not soe'), condescending to him ('poore death'), and boasting exemption from his power ('nor yet canst thou kill mee')" (26). Shaw notes that the speaker then shifts his line of reasoning and attempts "to invest [Death] with some reassuring qualities," that is, "Death as a bringer of rest," a strategy Shaw does not find "compelling enough to obviate the previous vision of Death" (27). Shaw concludes that the speaker makes his point in the concluding couplet, "by dint of dogmatic prophecy," but not quite assuredly (28).

Yearwood (1982, 210, 215–16) finds that the conversion process in Donne's first twelve *Holy Sonnets* [following Gardner's (1952) ordering—ed.], *HSDue, HSBlack, HSScene, HSRound, HSMin, HSDeath, HSSpit, HSWhy, HSWhat, HSBatter, HSWilt, and HSPart,* "begins in pride, proceeds to confession and despair, and culminates in a humble joy and confidence" (216). But the sixth sonnet, *HSDeath,* reflects a "static" state, according to Yearwood, like the twelfth, *HSPart*; that is, "it records a plateau, a resting place marked by persisting misconceptions as well as exultation in repentance" (215). One sign that the speaker's conversion process is incomplete is "his persistent delusion that death is like sleep, that it brings merely rest and delivery," and seems, in Yearwood's view, to reflect a speaker who "has not yet come to terms with Judgment Day" (216).

Mallett (1983, 58) summarizes the argument of the sonnet: "Death is not all-powerful, since it must eventually give way to eternal life."

Van Emden (1986, 53) observes that whereas other sonnets arise out of the fear of despair, this sonnet is "a clarion call of hope, indeed of certainty, that death is always followed by resurrection," and further that the poem ends with "the bold assertion that death can bring only pleasure."

Nash (1989, 36) finds in *HSDeath* "a deliberate process of hypostasis, a confusion of death (small d) as natural event, and Death (capital D) as personification." Thus, according to Nash, Donne's "theme" is primarily the "fear of death as a natural event," the speaker arguing "in part" from the perspective that "death (small d) is natural, like falling asleep, or easy, like taking a sleeping draught," while also raising a "moral case against Death (capital D) as a bad character." Thus, Donne's argument, in Nash's view, is that "death (small d) is natural, and therefore not to be feared, and that Death (capital D) is a reprobate and therefore to be despised." The argument, however, is not rendered "in the form of close reasoning," Nash emphasizes, but "as a sequence of commonplaces (*loci communes, koinoi topoi*)," the most common of which is "the comparison of death with sleep."

Wolny (1991, 179–80, 182–83, 186–88) finds in Donne's religious poetry a prevailing interest in death. Wolny explains this preoccupation with death by linking it to Donne's belief that "his God lives not in Heaven's but in Death's kingdom." Donne's attitude toward death, Wolny explains, is not a "typically religious" attitude (179). It derives in part, according to Wolny, from Donne's "unhappy" conversion: "as a Catholic, he was given an alternative: a professional career or his faith, the latter meaning definitely death in Protestant England" (180). Wolny compares, for example, Ben Jonson, who regarded death "as sorrowful and disastrous" (182), with Donne, who, especially in his Holy Sonnets, finds death "destructive for everyone but him," due in part, perhaps, to Donne's conversion, "which places him beyond society and standards assigned to it" (183). Wolny points out that *HSDeath* reinforces this view in that Donne "very clearly distances himself" from the sonnet and its ideas (188). Donne, Wolny notes, is "absent from the poem (no subjective 'I', so frequent in other pieces)" (188), and therefore, in Wolny's opinion, the image of death Donne describes in *HSDeath* "had little, if any, appeal to him" (186). Wolny concludes, based primarily on his reading of *HSDeath*, that what Donne "strongly believes in is the resurrection of the body and its final integration with the soul" (187). See also Wolny under *HSDeath*: The Poet/Persona.

HSDeath and Other Works

Gosse (1899, 2:108–09) says that the invocation to Death was "peculiarly in the spirit of the age" (108) and argues that there is "more than an accidental resemblance" to Raleigh's "famous appeal" to Death published in 1614. Gosse finds this "an almost solitary example in which the work of an English contemporary is found exercising an influence on the style of Donne" (109).

Brooke (1948, 636) observes that the poem "invites comparison" to Shakespeare's sonnet 146.

Daiches and Charvat (1950, 659) note that Donne used the same modification of the Petrarchan sonnet as did Wyatt.

Stevenson (1954, 7) finds an affinity between Donne and Shakespeare, suggesting that *HSDeath* is a "conscious or unconscious reply" to *Jn.* 4.3.35, *Ham.* 5.2.378, and *Ant.* 4.15.87.

Coanda (1957, 187) argues that *HSDeath* and Hopkins's "No word, there is none" contrast and resemble one another "as pessimism contrasts and resembles desperate optimism."

Lever (1974, 180), pointing to the opening lines of *BoulRec*, says that Donne "later regretted the overconfidence" evident in *HSDeath*.

Milward (1979 [1988, 63, 65]) finds that, unlike the first five of the Holy Sonnets (following Gardner's [1952] dating—ed.)—*HSDue*, *HSBlack*, *HSScene*, *HSRound*, and *HSMin*—this sonnet, in its meditation on Death, reveals "very little relation" to St. Ignatius's *Spiritual Exercises* (63). The entire sonnet, Milward emphasizes, "stands from beginning to end not as a colloquy, but as a defiant challenge to Death, personifying him and depreciating him with a series of ingenious arguments" (63). This is true, according to Milward, for both the octave and the sestet. He notes that the concluding couplet ends as if "it were putting the last nail into Death's coffin" (65).

Shawcross (1980, 58–59) finds that Donne employed Plutarch's *Moralia* for "ideas, narrative, and images" and points to a 1544 Paris edition of Plutarch that included a thorough index that Donne might have used (58). Shawcross comments on the similar treatment of sleep in *HSDeath* and Plutarch's "letter of condolence to Apollonius," which quotes Pindar on the "sleep of death." Shawcross adds that the "sleep of death is also specifically discussed in this same essay, cited from Socrates (Plato's *Apologia*, 40C)" and that Plutarch says that "sleep is really a preparatory rite for death" (59).

Dasgupta (1981, 87) says that *HSDeath* recalls Herbert's poem "Death," "where, from being 'once an uncouth hideous thing,'" (l. 1), Death becomes "fair and full of grace" as a result of "Christ's sacrifice in expiation for the sins of mankind." Like Herbert, Dasgupta suggests, Donne "looks upon death as the gateway to a greater life beyond the grave." See also Sloane (1981), Kawada (1985), Strier (1990), and Allen (1995).

Richmond (1981, 223–24, 229–30) elaborates his view that many of what were once regarded as distinguishing features of Donne's poetry are now recognized as evident in earlier poets such as Ronsard (223–24). Richmond points to similarities between Ronsard's sonnet "Douce est la mort d'autant plus qu'elle est brève" and Donne's *HSDeath* (229). Donne's sonnet, according to Richmond, is representative of the Holy Sonnets in that, "under the pressure of his religious anxieties and divided ecclesiastical loyalties," Donne has "transposed what had been an amatory motif to more religious meaning" (229–30).

Sloane (1981, 55–56) contrasts the figures of Death in *HSDeath* and Herbert's "Death," observing that Donne proceeds from his image "to draw intellectual conclusions," whereas Herbert "gives Death decidedly sensual human characteristics" (56). Sloane also points to Donne's and Herbert's use of emblematic techniques such as the "personification of the soul . . . as an actor in the drama" of the poem (55). Sloane compares the personification to that of *Anima* in Francis Quarles' *Emblemes*, in which the personification of the soul appears (55). By doing this, according to Sloane, "the poet tries to draw the reader into his own meditative world" (55).

Den Boer (1982, 76) discusses Victor E. Vriesland's translation of *HSDeath*, noting the sonnet's mocking tone.

Riemer (1982, 85–86) emphasizes T. S. Eliot's indebtedness to poetic models provided by Donne and Herbert, citing "The Journey of the Magi" as an example. In particular, "the juxtaposition and the confounding of birth and death" in the poem ("All this was a long time ago, I remember....this Birth was/Hard and bitter agony for us, like Death, our death") recalls, in Riemer's view, the sestet of Donne's *HSDeath*, and its "flamboyantly paradoxical spirit," which "Eliot may be seen to be attempting to habituate to the modes of modern poetry" (85–86).

Briggs (1983, 14) suggests that the sonnet, "though probably written earlier," could be read as an answer to Raleigh's claim in *History of the World* (1614): "O eloquent, just and mighty death! . . . thou hast drawn together all the far-stretched greatness, all the pride, cruelty and ambition of man, and covered all over with these two narrow words, *Hic iacet*" (bk. 5, ch. 6, sect. 12).

Ferry (1983, 220) notes the resemblance between *HSDeath* and Shakespeare's Sonnet 19 in that both employ "the rhetorical strategy of boastfully challenging a personified abstraction."

Raspa (1983, 16) claims that the sonnet celebrates "the imminence of death with a daunting equanimity and longing that would have confused the [Anglo-Saxon and Medieval] authors of 'Dream of the Rood' and 'Pearl.'" For Raspa, there is a crucial distinction between the "baroque writer" and Anglo-Saxon and Medieval views: "the sense of abandonment of the faithful Christian" found in the "Dream of the Rood" and "Pearl" is denied by the "baroque man." Raspa adds that "Christ's Agony in the Garden was not for this time a popular or intelligible theme," given the baroque writer's inability "to believe in the eternal love of God without enjoying the belief of its immanence in primary graded forms of creation." "The gradation of the affections," which includes divine love, was, in Raspa's view, "of necessity matched by a gradation of things."

Tromly (1983, 390–93) acknowledges the absence of any reference by Milton to Donne or any borrowings by the later poet. He maintains, however, that a link exists between the two poets in Milton's poem "On Time" and Donne's *HSDeath*, and that when we read the two poems together, "we can understand why Milton found so little use for Donne's poetry" (390). He further points out that in a Bodleian Library version of "On Time" (which Tromley believes to be an early draft that was subsequently revised) the last line clearly echoes *HSDeath*: "Where death and Chance, and thou O tyme shall be noe more" (390). Tromly notes that both poems are "highly rhetorical, declamatory credos which invoke and then proceed to confute a personified metaphysical antagonist" (391). Each poem, he suggests, is organized around three parallel sections, with the two poems "closest together" in their conclusions and their penultimate lines "virtually isomorphic" (391). But Tromly draws a sharper distinction between the two poems with respect to their "tone and movement" (392). *HSDeath*, according to Tromly, has a "brittle, shifting tone," and to that Milton's poem is "diametrically opposed," suggesting that Milton wrote his poem as a direct "counterstatement" (392). Unlike Donne's poem, Tromly claims, Milton's "persona sustains the sublime equipoise with which he begins," and "allows no personal anxieties to disrupt his declaration" (392). And, furthermore, according to Tromly, whereas Donne's sonnet "has a circular movement," Milton's poem "advances through a steady, linear progression of ascent and purification" (392). Finally, Tromly proposes that Milton read Donne's sonnet soon after its publication, "found its choplogic and ambivalences disconcerting, and responded with a poem which attempts to make good its dubious triumph over mortality" (393). See also Sloane (1985).

Schlüter (1984, 323–25, 336–41) questions limiting the generic classification of sonnets to their metric form alone so that sonnets exist in a category separate from ballads, odes, elegies, hymns and songs (323), and he proposes a study of the prayer hymn (its origins in Greek religion), with its combination of praise and prayer, the speaker's address to "a specific power, praising and describing it, and calling upon it for assistance in his need," and a beginning invocation of the god addressed (325). The prayer hymn, according to Schlüter, specifically provides for a rich comparison with HSDeath, which Schlüter later describes as an "anti-hymn" (338). Donne, he thinks, strives to demythologize and disempower death by such strategies as overturning the hymnic-like epithet "Mighty and dreadful" and replacing it with his own epithet "poore" in order "to show up Death's inferiority" (337). Schlüter identifies other hymnic inversions—e.g., turning praise into dispraise—noting specifically the speaker's deflation of Death by the question "why swell'st thou then?" (339). It appears, then, says Schlüter, that the mortal speaker emerges in the end as the triumphant one, who, paradoxically, succeeds "in the surety of his own immortality" (341).

Kawada (1985, 129–48) elaborates on the similarities and differences between Donne's and Herbert's treatment of death, citing particularly HSDeath and Herbert's "Death" and "Time."

Sloane (1985, 235, 238, 248) illustrates Milton's "nonrhetorical thinking" by contrasting his poem "On Time" with HSDeath, finding HSDeath more confrontational and adversarial (235). In HSDeath, Sloane argues, Donne "poses the problem adversarially" and though the speaker "wins out by posing . . . a largely verbal form," it is only after a "hard-fought and narrowly victorious battle, and we see and hear the entire process" (238). For Sloane, the "conditions of rhetoric, the constant and functional oppositions," are thus more apparent in Donne than in Milton (248).

Gaston (1986, 211–13) finds that Benjamin Britten's musical setting for HSDeath, the final sonnet in his cycle, "develops in three broad sections: the first and third represent proud assertion of the confident redeemed man against death, the second, a somewhat less forceful exposition of the means and universality of death." Furthermore, he says, "in the assertive sections, the vocal line assumes full authority; the bass line in the accompaniment gently supports, and in places follows, the voice" (211–12). Gaston observes that "at no point does the calm passacaglia compete with or provide a critical commentary on the vocal line" (212). "Assurance of victory remains firm," in Gaston's view, and thus "the singer addresses death on a strong F-sharp for two measures, then drops an octave 'thou shalt'—and concludes triumphantly on the tonic B, 'die'" (213).

Lewalski (1987, 75) notes that the Countess of Bedford's single extant poem, an elegy occasioned by the death of Cecilia Bulstrode, "is from a poetic exchange with Donne in 1609," a poem "good enough to be ascribed to Donne himself in the 1635 edition and often thereafter." The opening line of her poem ("Death be not proud, thy hand gave not this blow") begins by quoting the first line of HSDeath, notes

Lewalski, and the Countess's poem provides a "deft response and correction" to Donne's first elegy for Bulstrode (*BoulRec*), which begins by alluding to *HSDeath*, but which recants its argument by describing the "whole world as a universe of death." Lewalski adds, however, that in keeping with "the spirit of Donne's sonnet," the Countess "affirms that Death cannot harm the just, that it has power only over the reprobate—defined in Calvinist terms as 'people curst before they were.'"

Manlove (1989, 93–98) draws a detailed comparison of *HSDeath* and Dylan Thomas's "And Death Shall Have No Dominion," beginning with the most obvious difference: whereas Donne's sonnet is 14 lines, Thomas's poem is three stanzas of nine lines each (94). Manlove accounts for this difference by noting that Thomas's poem is "founded much more on feeling, and the emotional certainty perhaps takes time to realise itself," whereas Donne's sonnet "seems much more of an argument, moving from point to point." Manlove next considers how "each poem denies death's power," finding that while most readers assume that Donne's stance rests on his "Christian faith and his assurance of resurrection," in fact most of the poem is a "series of arguments operating from quite secular or empirical premises" (95). Donne's poetic devices underscore his "mental attack on death," whereas "Thomas seems much more concerned with the nature of life itself as an answer to death" (96). The "principle" in Thomas's poem that seems to defeat death, according to Manlove, is the act of taking away "all that the self has," and thus we "become part of the larger universe from which the self and its feelings and principles spring." Manlove concludes that "the whole victory" of Thomas's poem "depends on the loss of the self's apartness," and that experience "depends on the removal of the kind of mental organising of experience that we see in Donne's poem" (97).

Strier (1990, 129), in discussing approaches to teaching George Herbert, finds it valuable to compare Herbert's "Death" with Donne's *HSDeath*. Strier finds that whereas *HSDeath* is "forced in its tone and argumentation and more convincing in its Socratic mode than in its Pauline mode," Herbert's "Death" is "unequivocal in its gaiety and imaginative freedom."

Badenhausen (1992, 181–91) theorizes that the poetry of Donne may have influenced the poetry of Wilfred Owen, and specifically his poem "The Next War" (181–82). Owen, writing during World War I, may have known Donne through Grierson's edition (1912) or the 1912 edition of *The Oxford Book of English Verse* (182). Badenhausen notes Paul Fussell's observation in *The Great War and Modern Memory* [New York: Oxford University (1975)] that the *Oxford Book of English Verse* "presides over the Great War in a way that has never been sufficiently appreciated," (182), and he points out that the Oxford editor entitled Donne's sonnet "Death," which, Badenhausen suggests, "would have captured the attention and the imagination of a young man in the trenches leafing through his volume of poetry in a vain attempt to relieve the wartime tedium" (182). Badenhausen identifies a number of similarities between Owen's poem "The Next War" and Donne's *HSDeath*, suggesting that the "most provocative bond" is the way each poet "uses the last two lines to resolve the dilemma in his sonnet" (188). Whereas Donne's couplet rests on belief in "the existence of a Christian afterlife" rendering Death "insignificant," Owen's couplet is, according to Badenhausen, a "secular version of Donne's ending," in that modern warfare, or "The Next War," will overthrow Death, because "men will fight for social causes at home instead of political rights abroad" (189). Badenhausen concludes that while Donne "adapted a form previously associated with love poetry so that it accommodated religious meditation" (the sonnet "could not be 'Holy' before Donne"), Owen includes in the sonnet a "graphic description of wartime conditions," and, indeed, until the Great War, few English sonnets "are as violent as Donne's" (191).

Skulsky (1992, 124) states that, like *HSDeath*, Herbert's "Church-monuments" is the story of a speaker attempting to "stare down" his fear of death, adding that it is also about "linguistic perversion: an attempt to own up to the fear—in language that sidesteps the admission if taken literally."

Allen (1995, 122) notes that the opening of George Herbert's "Death" ("Death, thou wast once an uncouth hideous thing,/Nothing but bones") is mindful of *HSDeath*. Allen finds Herbert's conceit "more grotesque" and "intellectual" than Donne's, but also identifies Herbert's "ingenuity" as "pastoral." And, Allen adds, rather than Donne's "catalog of abstractions and final broadside of spondees," Herbert offers a "comforting story and melodious conclusion: the pastor can befriend even Death and make him sing, can help once-frightful Death to be 'full of grace.'"

NOTES AND GLOSSES

1–8 *Death . . . Soules deliueree.* **MAZZARO** (1987), noting that the biblical origins of death (ll. 1–4) and the classical origins (ll. 5–8) are "inconsistent," cites Johnson's comment in *Rasselas* that inconsistencies may nonetheless be "true." Argues that Death's "pride, which is based on power, is challenged by his eventual defeat" and cites 1 Cor. 15.54 and 1 Tim. 1.10 (250).

1–4 *Death . . . canst thou kill mee.* **THOMPSON** (1935) finds that in early life Donne's "solution to the problem of death" ("Lösung des Todesproblems") was colored by Christian teaching about the horror of death, but later, as here, death appeared no longer to frighten him (46). **WHITE** (1936) quotes the lines as an example of a "freshness and trenchancy" in the music of Donne's poetry, arising from his experimentation "with variety of form in line and stanza pattern." Finds their musical quality "typical of the usual Donne effect" and notes further that "here is the perfect musical counterpart of the emotional effect found so often in Donne where the imagination seems to fly out into infinity only to be caught swiftly and noiselessly back" (92–93). **WARD** (1949) observes that the quatrain is a refutation of the word "Mighty" (l. 2), in that death is depicted as impoverished, impotent, and possessed of only false strength (2). **SLOANE** (1981) finds here "a picture of Death consistent with the personifications of death in the emblem prints, adding that "it is almost as if he were addressing one of the many figures of Death as a powerful skeleton who, in the emblem books, stands ready to part man from his worldly possessions" (56). **MARANDON** (1984): the French research group *Groupe d'Etudes et de Recherche Britanniques* offers a translation of *HSDeath* at variance with a previously existing translation. An example is seen in translations of the second part of l. 3 ("tu prétends avoir anéantis" and "tu prétends avoir jetés à bas"). As a concrete image "jeté à bas" corresponds better than "anéantis" to the language of overthrow (155–56). WOLNY (1991): the invocation is "almost blasphemous in negating death's might," providing further evidence that Donne holds an atypical religious view of death, namely, that "death remains destructive for everyone but him," a view perhaps resulting from his conversion (183).

1–2 *Death . . . thou art not so.* WORDSWORTH (1799? [1992]) copied this section of *HSDeath* into her notebook, presumably at her brother William's request, during their stay in Berlin during 1798–99 (729). HAMER (1930): "the opening phrases generally march straight across the line limit" (200). WHITE (1936) comments on elements of both Elizabethan and Augustan tendencies in Donne, the former "in the audacity of his assault upon a theme and the richness of the associations he brings to its unfolding," the latter "in the precision with which he seeks to gather all the strands of his thought into his hands." Cites *HSDeath* as an example of the Elizabethan influence, quoting the first two lines as "the rich opening out of implication in the adjectives" (146–47). HANDLEY (1991) calls this a "magnificent rhetorical opening" that "sounds the note of Donne's late sermons" (43). SMITH (1992): "Christ's double nature, as God and man at once, assures his power to transform events in time; and it also confirms our power to outbrave our last enemy" (88).

1 *Death be not proud, though some haue called thee* ROTH (1947): the line has a tone of "majesty, of pomp and circumstance" (17).

1 *Death be not proud,* WARD (1949): the key to the poem is "a direct assault on Death's pride" (1). GARDNER (1952): "These words also open an Elegy to Mrs. Bulstrode, which is almost certainly not by Donne." Cf. Grierson (1912) (69).

1 *proud,* GILL (1990): "the word has the sense of being impressive and awe-inspiring as well as the standard meaning of boastful self-confidence. Both senses are also present in *swell'st* (12)" (103).

3 *overthrow* DANIELS (1941): a detail developing the figure of battle concretely (278).

4 *Dy not poore death, nor yet canst thou kill mee.* WILLMOTT (1985): "To the Christian, death is merely the gateway to eternal life" (68).

4 *nor yet canst thou kill mee.* GILL (1990): "the quickened pace of these heavily stressed monosyllables might suggest a lively confidence that the poet has the measure of his opponent, or they could be a defensive thrust at a strong adversary whom he fears" (103).

4 *yet* LEVER (1974): "Moreover" (180).

4 *mee.* LEVER (1974): "My soul" (180).

5–8 *From rest . . . and Soules deliueree.* **WARD** (1949): the lines refute the word "dreadfull" (l. 2) by comparing death to rest and sleep (2). **MARANDON** (1984): the French research group *Groupe d'Etudes et de Recherche Britanniques* (G.E.R.B.) offers a translation of *HSDeath* at variance with another translation. The G.E.R.B translation of the end of l. 7, for example, with the cliché "se courbent sous ta loi," fails to match the simplicity of Donne's "with thee do go" (156–57). **CAMPBELL** (1989): "death is a rest for the body and a liberation (delivery) for the soul" (232).

5–6 *From rest . . . much more must flow,* **MAIN** (1880) points to the last line of a poem by William Drummond ("I long to kiss the image of my death"). Adds that Donne is "thinking of Cicero's argument (*Tuscul. Disput.* i, 38): 'Habes sumnum imaginem mortis,'" and also cites *MM* 3.1.17–19: "Thy best of rest is sleep, / And that thou oft provok'st; yet grossly fear'st / Thy death, which is no more" (308). **DANIELS** (1941): Donne asserts that there is nothing to dread in Death, since its images, rest and sleep, give pleasure (276). **WIGGINS** (1945): an example of Donne's use of elements of formal logic, in this case "the argument of *more or less* by *comparison*," an aspect of "the *predicament relation* and its *post-predicament opposition*" (54–55). **ELLRODT** (1960): Donne presents the resurrection of the flesh as the resurrection of the entire person; death was, for Donne, a violent uprooting, a tearing apart of the human person (1:381). **DALGLISH** (1961) paraphrases these lines: "Since we get much pleasure from rest and sleep, which are only imitations of death, we shall get even more from death itself" (136). Similarly, Smith (1971, 629), Willy (1971, 81), Hollander and Kermode (1973, 1052), Mallett (1983, 58), Willmott (1985, 68), and Singh (1992, 100). **JONES** (1978) says that we don't take these lines seriously because "we do not accept the premise that the relation between sleep and death is in all relevant respects the same as the relation between a picture and the thing depicted . . . we cannot for a moment believe that if a picture gives us pleasure the thing it depicts must necessarily give us more pleasure" (38–39). **JONES** (1986) repeats some of his observations from 1978, suggesting that Donne could not have found the argument of this analogy "convincing," but noting that we are not therefore forced to conclude that Donne was being "insincere" in writing *HSDeath* (52–53). Thinks that if there is too simple an insistence on "sincerity," the reader might miss the contrast between the "calm assurance" of the final couplet of the poem and the "desperate bravado of the other arguments" (53–54).

5 *pictures* **LEVER** (1974): "Symbols, figures" (180). **HANDLEY** (1991): "Images" (43).

7–8 *And soonest . . . and Soules deliueree.* **DANIELS** (1941): Donne's theme is that there is nothing terrible about Death, since our best men go to it and "our best men can't be wrong" (276). **MORRIS** (1953) observes that both Donne and Hopkins were "fascinated by the relationships between diverse objects and ideas, by the sameness lying behind the diversity of things," and they both linked words diverse in meaning by assonance and alliteration, as here and in "God's Grandeur" (l. 6), "Starlight Night" (l. 4), and "The Wreck of the Deutschland" (12:5–6) (60–

61). **MANLOVE** (1978), finding Donne's arguments overall unconvincing, reads these lines to mean either "the good die young" or "the good are readiest to die," but the first is false in claiming (1) "that they all do" and (2) "that of those of them who do, all go willingly." Further argues that the second meaning is "highly debatable" and its sense "could be reversed and reduced to its arbitrary foundation, namely, the presupposition that those most willing to die are good" (11). **WOLNY** (1991) refers to Smith's (1971) reading (see notes to l. 7 below) that these lines should be given "a two-fold interpretation: either: the best men die young, or: good men make least fuss in dying" (185). But says that "none of these seems satisfactory" (185). Considers Donne's references to death in other of his writings and concludes that the image of death Donne presents in *HSDeath* "had little, if any, appeal to him" (186). Thinks that Donne "considered himself a special case, partly from his "strong feeling of not belonging to the society, and partly from his unquestionable egocentrism" (186). Points to words from *ValName* to reinforce this view: "In it offend'st my Genius" (l. 48) (186). Cites Carey (1981, 226) as further evidence in support of his own view: "'Even if death meant only the separation of soul and body, it was still repugnant'" (186). See also Wolny's glosses on ll. 9–10, 11–12, and 13–14.

7 *And soonest our best men with thee do go,* **GARDNER** (1952): "The reference may be to the proverbial saying that the good die young [so also, Shaaber (1958, 103) and Craik and Craik (1986, 279)], or to the death-bed of a righteous man," as in *ValMourn* 1–2 (69). [Similarly, Smith (1971, 629), Willy (1971, 81), and Singh (1992, 100).] **HOLLANDER and KERMODE** (1973): "the good die without fuss" (1052). **WILLMOTT** (1985): "'The virtuous die young', or more probably, 'the virtuous are happy to die'" (68).

7 *soonest* **MAIN** (1880): "=most willingly [so also, Dickinson (1967, 6)] (*rathest*, as he might have said, had not the form already been allowed to drop). Or did he mean (literally) earliest, in allusion to the proverbial 'Whom the gods love die young?'" (308).

8 *Rest of ther bones, and Soules deliueree.* **SCHELLING** (1895): "These words are in apposition with thee in the verse above" (272). **ADAMS** (1962): "our best men go with you to find rest for their bones and freedom ('delivery') for their souls" (785). [Similarly, Smith (1971, 629.] **WILLY** (1971): "i.e. Their bodies find rest, their souls 'delivery'—rebirth into immortality—from the body" (81). **WILLMOTT** (1985): "Death gives rest to their bodies and sets free their souls; there is a suggestion of re-birth in 'delivery'" (68). **CRAIK and CRAIK** (1986): "Death gives rest to their bodies (*bones*) and is a freeing (*delivery*) of their souls from the prison of the body" (279).

8 *bones,* **DANIELS** (1941): a detail developing the figure of rest concretely (278).

8 *Soules deliueree.* **GARDNER** (1952): "Death is both the soul's birth, and its 'gaol-delivery'" (69). **GILL** (1990): "the soul is delivered in the sense that at death

it is born into eternity and also in the sense that it is delivered from the prison of life" (103). **HANDLEY** (1991): "i.e. the freedom of the soul when the body dies" (43).

8 *Soules* **DANIELS** (1941): a detail developing the figure of delivery concretely (278).

8 *deliueree.* **SHAABER** (1958): "deliverance, release" (103). [Similarly, Lever (1974, 181).] **MARTZ** (1963): "release, liberation" (88). **WARNKE** (1967b, 269): "liberation." [So also, Booty (1990, 108).] **PATRIDES** (1985a): "deliverance, liberation" (440). **FOWLER** (1995): "(1) birth; (2) emancipation" (261).

9–12 *Thou art . . . why swellst thou then?* **WARD** (1949): building on the scorn and contempt of the octave, the sestet humbles death to the status of a slave (3). **WILLMOTT** (1985): "Death is asked contemptuously why it swells with pride since it is a 'slave', keeps bad company, and is no more effective than a sleeping drug ('poppy') or spell" (68).

9–10 *Thou art . . . and sicknesse dwell;* **DANIELS** (1941): death has nothing to be proud of, since it is a slave to other forces and is "associated with unpleasant things" (276). **CRAIK and CRAIK** (1986): cf. *HSRound* 6–7 (279). **WOLNY** (1991): these lines provide further evidence that Donne considered himself "a special case" in matters of death since "he calls the death he ascribes to other people inferior" (186). **DUNDAS** (1994): unlike the personification of Death in *HSMade*, here Donne "reverses the strength of death relative to the speaker," as he "addresses death using *meiosis*, or the figure of belittlement," what Puttenham calls "the disabler" in *The Arte of English Poesie*. The "bad company death keeps reveals its weakness," and its "resemblance to sleep further diminishes its power" (ll. 11–12). In a sermon (*Sermons*, 8:189–90) Donne "notes that this analogy between sleep and death only begins to flourish in the Christian era when the conviction of resurrection gives significance to the parallel" (127).

9 *Thou art Slaue to Fate, Chance, kings, and desperat men,* **MOLONEY** (1950): the "centroidal grouping" of words in the line produces emphasis, an effect found frequently in Milton (238). **WILLY** (1971): "i.e. Far from being a 'mighty and dreadfull' despot, death is the mere slave of its own agents, circumstance and accident, kings who condemn men to die and the murderers or suicides ('desperate men') who inflict death" (81).

9 *Slaue to* **SINGH** (1992): "you are used or exploited by" (100).

9 *kings,* **MAROTTI** (1994a): Donne's use of the term even in a negative sense nonetheless signals his "insistent awareness of the political order" (79).

10 *And dost . . . sicknesse dwell;* **MANLOVE** (1978): the line "says no more than that death keeps bad company, which is hardly a way to belittle" (12).

11–12 *And Poppy . . . why swellst thou then?* DANIELS (1941): there is "nothing peculiar" in death's power, since drugs can produce sleep as well (276). RASPA (1983) cites these lines to illustrate the poet's move from the personal to the universal, noting that the "nature of imitation [and poetic meditation] encouraged the discussion of psychological and moral states as impersonal and general." Comments that "sensory images were constantly impressing their universal character" on Donne's imagination" and that even "the most personally felt state of alienation, like that due to mortality" in *HSDeath*, "ended quickly in the consideration of the universality of the demise of death not in the self but in the world" (87). WOLNY (1991) reads these lines, in which Donne compares death to sleep, as implying "that if death is to be understood as a mere sleep-maker and to this its role should be limited, therefore, death has no right to puff itself in pride, since some other things, narcotics or charms, make that [i.e., sleep] better" (187).

11 *Poppy or Charmes* CRAIK and CRAIK (1986): "opium or hypnosis" (279). BARAŃCZAK (1984) notes that opium can be made of poppies and points to *Oth.* 3.3.330–33 (161). SINGH (1992): "Poppy or opium is a soporific. Charms may refer to other sleep-inducing drugs" [similarly, Handley (1991, 43)] (100).

11 *Poppy* DANIELS (1941): a detail developing the figure of drugs concretely (278). SMITH (1971): "the juice of the poppy is a narcotic" [so also, Mallett (1983, 58)]. See *Oth.* 3.3.330–33 (629). ADAMS (1979): "Opium" (1101). FARMER (1984) notes that the poppy is "commonly a symbol of sleep, ignorance, extravagance, and indifference" and that in this vein Donne "associates it with death" (101). HAMBURGER (1985): the poppy plant is used for the production of sleeping and relaxation potions (181). [Similarly, Campbell (1989, 232).] HANDLEY (1991): producing sleep "because it contains opium" (43).

11 *Charmes* LEVER (1974): "Perhaps 'soothing songs' rather than incantations" (181). CAMPBELL (1989): "magic spells" (232).

12–14 *And easier . . . Death thou shalt dy.* FAUSSET (1938): Donne "turns the tables" on death (xiii).

12 *And easier . . . then?* ELLRODT (1960): Donne reveals the terror of a man confronting his fate who is suspended in the judgment of an angry God (1:419).

12 *And easier then thy stroke,* GARDNER (1952) (reading "better then") says that "better" offers a hyperbole, while "easier" "merely means more pleasantly" (69). MALLETT (1983) (reading "better than"): "the sleep brought on by drugs is heavier and more refreshing than that of death. The idea evidently conflicts with ll. 5–6 above" (58).

12 *stroke,* DANIELS (1941): a detail developing the figure of battle in l. 3 concretely (278).

12 *why swellst thou* DANIELS (1941): a detail developing the figure of Death

concretely as a person who is proud (277). **WARD** (1949): the phrase recalls the image of "the martial puffing and strutting figure" implied earlier (3). **ADAMS** (1962): "Puff up with pride" (785). [So also, Smith (1971, 629), Lever (1974, 181), Craik and Craik (1986, 279), Campbell (1989, 232), and Booty (1990, 108).] **MANLOVE** (1978): a question that seems "not so much a triumphant sneer" as a subject "fearfully to be asked" (12).

12 *swellst* **MAIN** (1880) glosses as "boastest" or "brag" and cites Shakespeare's sonnet "Shall I compare thee to a summer's day?" ("Nor shall Death brag thou wander'st in his shade"). Notes that an "instance of the adjectival form, as in Scripture and in Shakspeare [sic] frequently, may be cited from the posthumous version of Drummond's sonnet, CXXIV (*Poems*, ed. 1656, p. 103): 'A *swelling* Thought of holding Sea and Land)'" (308). **SCHELLING** (1895): "*I.e.*, with pride" (272). **SHAABER** (1958): "exult, puff up" (103). **DICKINSON** (1967, 6): "swell with pride." [Similarly, Mallett (1983, 59) and Singh (1992, 100).] **HIEATT** (1987): "vauntest" (239). **FOWLER** (1991): "be arrogant" (117).

13–14 *One short . . . Death thou shallt dy.* **FAUSSET** (1923): Donne had a "physical horror" of death, and yet penned these lines (98). **THOMPSON** (1935) observes that although the concept of death changes over the centuries, the Anglican attitude has always been more or less that which we hear today (87). **DANIELS** (1941) observes that the caesura of l. 13 calls for only a slight pause, whereas that of l. 14 "cuts the line clearly into two distinct halves." Notes further that the stress is piled on at the beginning of l. 13 and the end of l. 14, slowing the movement to emphasize the weakness of Death (277). **WARD** (1949): death is finally defeated by the idea of immortality (3–4). **WILLY** (1971): the concluding couplet is a "decisive statement" that "strikes home with monosyllabic force and finality" (80). **MARANDON** (1984): the translation of *HSDeath* offered by the French research group *Groupe d'Etudes et de Recherche Britanniques* (G.E.R.B.) is at variance with another translation, as in these lines. The translation of the G.E.R.B. is more stylistically far-fetched (157). **WOLNY** (1991) reads the conclusion of Donne's sonnet as claiming that death serves "a greater and far more important task." Argues, in other words, that "by negating death, Donne gives a hint that there is something beyond and, in a sense, superior to the image of it presented in the poem." Asserts that the superior state beyond death is to "wake free from such sleep to eternal life," for "death appears to be the last enemy to be overcome and destroyed" (187).

13 *One short sleepe past, we live eternally* **DANIELS** (1941) (reading "live" as "wake") notes "the careful placing of *sleep* against *wake*, *short* against *eternity*" (277). **GARDNER** (1952) (reading "live" as "wake") says that "wake" provides a "better antithesis to 'sleepe' than 'live' does" (69). **SIMON** (1952): "the firm belief on which he relies" (131). **WILLMOTT** (1985) (reading "live" as "wake"): "we wake from death to eternal life" (69).

14 *And Death shalbe no more, Death thou shallt dy.* **SMITH** (1971) points to 1 Cor.

15.26, 54: "The last enemy that shall be destroyed is death . . . . Death is swallowed up in victory" (629). Similarly, Lever (1974, 181), Mallett (1983, 59), Barańczak (1984, 161), Hamburger (1985, 181), Patrides (1985a, 441), Willmott (1985, 69), Craik and Craik (1986, 279), Lloyd-Evans (1989, 299n43), Booty (1990, 108), Carey (1990b, 454), Singh (1992, 100), Di Nola (1993, 118–19), Ellrodt (1993, 456), and Fowler (1995, 261). **HANDSCOMBE** (1980): there is a possible allusion in the closing line of the sonnet to the Book of Revelation, for here, Death does die (106). "The sonnet's speaker could now be the Second Death. But it is more likely to be the righteous warrior, The Word of God, Christ himself" (107). **HOLDSWORTH** (1990) cites, in addition to 1 Cor. 15.26 and 54, Hos. 13.14: "I will redeem them from the power of the grave: I will deliver them from death: O death, I will be thy death: O grave, I will be thy destruction." Suggests that Donne must have been remembering the version of either the Geneva Bible or the Bishops' Bible (183).

14 *Death thou shallt dy.* **MAIN** (1880) cites Rev. 21.4 and its metrical paraphrase, along with Shakespeare's Sonnet 146, l. 14 ("And death once dead, there's no more dying then"). Refers to *BoulRec* and notes Dyce's comment (in the flyleaf of Dyce's first edition of Donne's *Poems*) that Wordsworth had recommended *HSDeath* for inclusion in *Specimens of English Sonnets* (1833) (308–09). (Cf. Wordsworth's letter [1833] to Dyce under General Commentary on *HSDeath*.) **KORTEMME** (1933): the phrase is an example of an antithesis in the form of contrary or contradictory opposites, a type that Donne employs at times with great brevity (47). **DANIELS** (1941) notes the comparative strength of the second half of the line "following the quieter, vaguer" first half (277). **WARD** (1949): the paradox is "a command, a prediction, and a summary" of the poem (4). **CRUTTWELL** (1954): the final couplet of Shakespeare's 146th sonnet is "very close" to Donne's ending (12). [Similarly, Carey (1990b, 454).] **MURAOKA** (1970) suggests that this line is influenced, in both its substance and its language, by the concluding line of Shakespeare's Sonnet 146 ("And Death once dead, there's no more dying then."), acknowledging a difference between the two: Donne directly addresses Death and points out its nature, while Shakespeare describes Death's nature objectively. Supposes that when he read Shakespeare's sonnet, Donne, fascinated with paradoxes, anticipated composing a sonnet in which the paradox was repeated, though in a different manner (246–48). **GILL** (1990): one might question dismissing the fear of death throughout the sonnet, and then serving "it up as a threat to Death itself at the climax," but that reading of the sonnet "might miss the point that Death is only terrible within the world, for, paradoxically, when people die they leave Death's realm and so to them Death is dead" (103–04). **RAY** (1990b): the last four words of the sonnet "create a parallel and contrast to the opening four words of the sonnet," providing the "definitive answer" as to "why Death should not be proud." This "paradox and contrast" bring the reader "full circle in the poem, just as the circle symbolizes (for the Christian speaker) the infinity that ends death" (88).

 *HSDue*

COMMENTARY

General Commentary

In an eighteenth-century Moravian Brethren's hymn-book (*A Collection of Hymns*) (1754 [1966, 19–20]), four Holy Sonnets—*HSMade, HSDue, HSSpit,* and *HSWhat*—are used, slightly altered, and combined to make up hymn number 383.

Trench (1868, 403–04) prints *HSDeath* and *HSDue* in his *A Household Book of English Poetry*, noting of the latter that it is a "rough rugged piece of verse" and, like almost all of Donne's poetry, "imperfect in form and workmanship." But he adds that it is "the genuine cry of one engaged in that most terrible of all struggles, wherein, as we are winners or losers, we have won or lost all." In that, Trench observes, Donne reminds us of St. Augustine.

Lightfoot (1877, 9) cites Trench's comment (1868) on *HSDue* and says that Donne was no doubt "sensual."

Furst (1896, 230) refers to *HSDue* and cites approvingly Trench's comments (1868) about it.

Gardner (1952, xl) notes that the poem is "a preparatory prayer before making a meditation."

Wagner (1965, 19) sees this sonnet as an expression of Donne's often paradoxical attitudes towards religion, "here expressed through structure as well as content." The octave is optimistic, presenting humankind's submission to God, the sestet pessimistic, describing humanity's ties with the devil.

Grant (1974, 74–75) notes that *HSDue* "becomes fraught with strain and anxiety" (74), that it "must discover in anguish that the desire for self-resignation is a self-willed desire," and that it thus "ends by denying what it set out to affirm" (75).

Sellin (1974, 191–92) argues that *HSDue* portrays a man who believes that he has a right to share in God's promises but who finds himself still in the power of Satan and therefore fears that he might be reprobate. The poem, he says, "captures a man in an instant of passion" and, moreover, the speaker of the poem is clearly one who, though longing to be among the elect, knows that he is not yet there, "knows that grace cannot be commanded or acquired, and that the strange ways of God carry the real possibility that from him individually grace may be deliberately withheld" (192).

Brink (1977, 101) says that Donne appeals to "the procreating father as well as the Father in heaven to lift the guilt of a misspent erotic life."

Low (1978, 60) echoes Gardner (1952) in asserting that *HSDue* is a preparatory prayer to the main cycle of twelve sonnets. He writes that the sestet addresses the soul "and so is neither a petition or colloquy," but an attempt to make a resolution based on the foregoing meditation.

Linguanti (1979–80, 25–47) offers a detailed overview and analysis of *HSDue*, with attention to its theme, language, form, rhetorical structure, and various stylistic features.

The Poet/Persona

Jackson (1970, 105–07) suggests that the speaker of *HSDue* discovers to some extent "the unconscious in the persona of the devil" (105), which is a "sign that he is still in an improper relationship to himself" (105–06). What is anticipated, says Jackson, is the "psychic marriage" with God (107).

Wall (1976, 192–94), analyzing the speaker's role in the context of the development of the poem, notes that he "moves from passive acceptance and praise of God's actions for all mankind to active, desperate appeal for God to act again in his own, individual behalf" (192). He argues that in the octave "the first four lines represent an *anaphora* in the strict liturgical sense," a "remembering of the salvation history," and that the second four lines "shift to the present tense to describe in Biblical terms the speaker's understanding of his relationship with God," the whole of the octave thus presenting the speaker "in a reconciled relationship with God through confession, the action of the memory and the understanding." Reading *HSDue* as an "address to God," Wall notes that the octave "speaks not just for the individual *persona*, but also generally and symbolically for all mankind" (193), adding that the speaker of the sestet is "more personal and particularized, a concrete, specific individual at a definite time and place who realizes that God's reconciliation with mankind may not include him" (193–94).

Stachniewski (1981, 700–01) finds that the sonnet "registers Calvinist influence in its reversal of the usually attempted move from fear to hope" (700). According to Stachniewski, the sonnet begins by setting forth all that God has done for the speaker, but it ends "by entertaining the doubt that God will not trouble Himself over his individual soul, despite His love for mankind," as expressed in line 13 (700–01). Stachniewski concludes that the sonnet "is decidedly Lutheran and Calvinist," in that the speaker is "haunted by the fear" that "God could exert Himself to beat off the devil, but whether He does so will depend on His free, unobligated choice" (701).

Docherty (1986, 138–39) finds that *HSDue* explicitly identifies the speaker as "Image" or representation of God (139), adding that "the tenor" of the argument of the sonnet is that "repetition and a re-signature" are required: "As due by many titles I resigne/My selfe to thee, O God," that is, a re-signing in the name of God (139). And in so far as Donne is conceived of as "a repository of the breath/spirit," in Docherty's view, he becomes the "medium through which the spirit articulates itself in history" (139).

Rollin (1986, 139–40) sees the sonnet as an example of the "marked alternations of mood between as well as within individual poems." "On the surface," according to Rollin, the poem's octave "suggests not only the speaker's understanding and acceptance of his relationship with God but also an easy compatibility between his ego and his superego" (139). But following "the legalistic and mercantile metaphors," which "may reveal a latent tension," the "concluding mood" of *HSDue*, in Rollin's view, is "one of depression so profound as to verge on hysteria: 'Oh I shall soone despaire'" (l. 12) (140). Rollin cites Stachniewski's (1981) study of the prevailing despair in the Holy Sonnets and the Calvinist influence on *HSDue* and other poems. But Rollin finds a difficulty in Stachniewski's argument, namely, his assertion that the speaker of the Holy Sonnets is "no less and no more than John Donne himself," and that consequently we are asked to believe that Donne was a "closet Calvinist" (140n20). Rollin then cites Carey (1981), who believes that Donne was "deeply influenced by Calvinism" but that he was also an admirer of Aquinas, and ultimately "adhered to the more 'moderate' (Aquinian) view" (140n20). But Rollin argues "a yet more conservative view," namely, that Donne "creates a speaker who often errs" and who, much like the "erring characters of the drama, takes on interest and serves as something of an object lesson" (140n20).

Strier (1989, 361, 368, 370) finds in *HSDue* the same tension evident in other Holy Sonnets, namely, whether the speaker is "claiming salvation on the basis of an achieved condition or throwing himself on God's mercy" (368). In the first quatrain, according to Strier, the speaker seems to be listing titles "by which he is obliged to resign—titles of honor rather than debts," but in the second quatrain the speaker appears to list "'titles' by which he has a positive claim on God" (368). In the last four lines of the sestet, however, Strier says, Donne "turns to God, but instead of a prayer for unmerited mercy, he produces something like a threat" (370). For Strier, the ending is troubling, because it includes "petulance" but "without humor or self-directed irony" (370). As in other of the Holy Sonnets, in Strier's view, the speaker fails "to acknowledge fundamental theological confusions" (361).

Fish (1990, 242), citing Hester (1987—see *HSDue*: Language and Style), asserts that "the gesture of resignation is at the same time a reaffirmation of the resigner's independence," concluding that the sonnet appears to be a plea to be possessed fully by God, but "in fact," is rather a "desperate attempt to leave something that will say, like Kilroy, 'Donne was here.'" The same desperation, according to Fish, informs *HSSouls*.

Skulsky (1992, 116–17) finds that *HSBatter*, as well as *HSDue*, creates the "impression" that "sin is something that *happens* to the sinner rather than something he *does*," which Skulsky describes as a "diversionary *littera* fostered by the speaker's fear of his ultimate judgment by God." See more under *HSBatter*: The Poet/Persona.

Genre and Traditions

Martz (1954, 47–49) quotes *HSDue* in full to illustrate a sonnet that corresponds to but one of the three steps of an Ignatian meditation, the "colloquy," and he compares the poem to a passage from Luis de la Puente's *Meditations*. See more under Holy Sonnets: Genre and Traditions.

Structure

Simon (1952, 123–25) stresses "the organic structure" of the sonnet in which "every part depends on, and reacts on the other parts." She detects in the coldly legal tone of the first quatrain a speaker who accepts his surrender rationally but without "the natural overflow of his *feelings* toward God" (123–24). In the second quatrain, Simon continues, the tone is softened by the thought of Christ's sacrifice (l. 4) so that the "relation is no longer that of owned to owner, but of son to father" or "of kind master to servant, of shepherd to sheep"; but the speaker confesses that he has betrayed this trust (ll. 9–10), which leaves him open to the devil. That is, "because he himself has destroyed God's titles of possession, he cannot expect to be restored by his own efforts; God alone can restore him." In the end, Simon concludes, the pent up emotions "are released by his surrender to God" in an appeal for Grace as the only hope for salvation. She observes that the expression of a desire to be "enthralled by God" derives from Matt. 7.7 (124–25).

Esch (1955, 49) thinks that in contrast to other sonnets the octave is less dramatic than the sestet, but appropriately so for the first poem of a meditative sequence that begins traditionally with an opening prayer. See also Holy Sonnets: Genre and Traditions.

Bellette (1975, 328–30) observes that the first two quatrains of *HSDue* are "compact units built up through a series of parallel phrases governed by strongly placed subordinating elements," which produce the effect of "order and proper relationship" (329). He argues that the sense of logical progression of the poem is destroyed by the "Why," "Except," and "yet" sequence (ll. 9, 10, 11, 13, 14) (329–30). Furthermore, he notes that the octave's logical purpose is destroyed by the "unsatisfying paradoxes" of the closing couplet (330).

Language and Style

Linville (1984a, 149–152), in her study of closure in devotional poetry, suggests that *HSDue* reflects Donne's ability to make "unresolvedness much more explicit in the substance and structure of his devotional poetry," given the way the "form mediates the uneasy relations of self and doctrine." Linville underscores the sonnet as "one of surprises and reversals" (149). For example, according to Linville, instead of developing in the octave "the problems of fallenness and estrangement," allowing the sestet to resolve them, *HSDue* "reverses this process and concludes by refuting what it initially seeks to affirm" (150). Linville also calls attention to Donne's deliberate creation of disjunctive rhyme to underscore the speaker's spiritual dilemma: his "oneness with God" that is "harmoniously figured by rhyme and by biblical metaphor in the octave" is disrupted by the "initiation of the 'Why's,' which in turn initiate his description of his own alienation, internal division and disorder" (151). Linville concludes that "the strain in this sonnet stems from something characteristic of Donne: his presentation of himself as he is rather than as he should be—that is, divided, complex." Moreover, this "doubleness of form," in Linville's view, "marks his entire 1633 sequence" (152).

Hester (1987, 60–65) finds the "central concern" of the sonnet to be that of the religious lyric, namely, "the power of words to signify the self as an image of The Word," or in the language of the poem itself, "the capacity of 'titles' to 're-sign' the self in humble resignation to the handwriting of God" (60). *HSDue*, in Hester's view, "applies that central topos of Renaissance homiletics and poetics—man as a word striving to communicate with The Word—in order to explicate the limitations and powers of man to re-create himself in *imagine dei*" (60). Hester points to "the central motif of God as an artist," which "establishes a paradoxical analogical pattern of divine re-creation which the speaker meditatively strives to imitate" (61). Because the speaker cannot accomplish this re-creation, the sestet, in Hester's view, challenges the argument of the octave. Hester also notes the increasing ambiguity of the poem as well as the growing stasis of the rhyme scheme, mirroring the gradual "fall" of the speaker along with "the progressive separation of man from The Word" (63). Hester concludes that "the changing shape of his language in the octave subtly traces man's fall from union with the signifying divine Word into the isolated limitations of human signs," that is, "into the enigmatic text" of the self (65).

Warnke (1987, 105) claims that this sonnet has the "rigorously argumentative structure that practically defines not only Donne's lyric poetry but, indeed, Metaphysical poetry as a whole."

Ray (1990b, 38–39) notes that the "dominant imagery" in the sonnet is "legal (contracts, property, things bought and sold)" (38) and explains that following the "relatively moderate, logical tone and feeling" found in the octave, the sestet presents a "more emotional" speaker who is "indignant at Satan but also at God," for "Satan has had the audacity to 'usurp' (seize or overthrow) the speaker who belongs to God." The speaker ends, Ray argues, on a "resentful, sarcastic, and paradoxical note," and Ray finds the "accusatory, argumentative, challenging, and questioning" qualities of *HSDue* representative of several other Holy Sonnets (39).

Frontain (1992, 85, 92–93) finds in Donne's Holy Sonnets heightened anxiety instigated by the Protestant Reformation's emphasis on the absolute dependency on God for one's salvation (85). Frontain notes in *HSDue*, for example, that "the initial tone of humble resignation and of calm, logical, dispassionate thought" gives way ("subtly") in the second quatrain to the speaker's "iteration of the reasons for his resignation," also suggesting the "reason why such resignation is so necessary at this particular moment" (92). Having "'betray'd' the divine Spirit inherent in him as a son of God," the speaker is "consequently in desperate need of God's further action on his behalf if he is not to be lost eternally to sin and Satan" (ll. 5–8) (92). Thus, Frontain states, "gratitude for past acts," as in lines 3–4, yields to "anxiety over present necessity" and the "impassioned questioning" of lines 9–10 (92). The closing lines, according to Frontain, "emphatically state the conditions of the speaker's salvation, succinctly summarizing the drama of his election," and he points to the inherent ambivalence in the speaker's contractual relationship to God, "for as the speaker reiterates his many obligations to his Creator, he implicitly reminds God of His reciprocal obligation to His creature" (92–93). Thus, Frontain argues, even as he admits his sinfulness, the speaker "entreats or tries to provoke God to act on his behalf" (93).

Pallotti (1993, 173–75) finds that the speaker "does not simply state the obvious," that is, that God is supreme, but instead he wishes to underscore that there "*is* a relationship and that *that* relationship constitutes a permanent and inevitable bond." The speaker accomplishes this by "the processes the verbs express, the insistent repetition of pronouns of the first and second person, especially possessives, the tense itself, constantly shifting from present to past, from past to present, in order to cover the whole of human history from creation to fall to redemption," all the elements serving "to highlight the existence of an 'essential' tie, a 'natural' bond holding between God and the individual." Pallotti notes that "all the linguistic forms employed in order to define the *I* are loaded with religious significance" and "more or less explicitly refer to or are related to Christ with whom, thus, the speaker appears to equate himself," and which appear to "justify his audacity in calling Him into question" (173). Moreover, "rhetorically," Pallotti claims, "the passage from the declarative to the interrogative appears to carry a pattern of assertion and challenge," with the sonnet closing "with the speaker's doubt, and uncertainty, about God's intervention, the performing of an action that will assure him of salvation" (174). And, "grammatically," according to Pallotti, the poem "registers the passage from the *I*, weak but still tentatively active" at the beginning, to a "*mee*, a passive and abandoned object completely at the mercy of the 'subtle foe' [HSMade 11]" (175). Pallotti concludes that "the assertion and simultaneous challenge of divine power and authority implicitly open up for consideration the question of God's dealings with man and eventually the question of heavenly Justice" (175).

Yen (1995, 214–15, 226) finds that the sonnet can be read through the lens of the metaphor of the *pharmakon*, which simultaneously is "both a poison and a cure," a strategy that Donne employs in the Holy Sonnets "to praise and court God in 'prayers, and flattering speaches' [HSVex 10]" (214–15). For example, according to Yen, line six could be understood to have Donne's "political as well as religious imperatives in mind," and therefore would "take on ironic meaning: not praise of God expressing faithful obedience, but veiled criticism of a King who has *not* rewarded faithful service" (226). And lines 12–13 of the sonnet could be "giving voice to his political disappointment as well as his religious torment" (226).

Prosody

Winters (1967, 75) notes that in HSDue the accentuation violates poetic principles, suggesting that in line 6 the language must be deformed in order to fit the line into a pentameter pattern. He believes that Donne often violates poetic form and concludes that the high incidence of these violations shows "a relative unawareness of the nature and importance of sound."

Sacred and Profane

Low (1993, 77–78) points out that the marriage trope can be found in a number of Holy Sonnets, including HSDue, where it is suggested in the "rivalry between God and the devil, who has usurped, stolen, 'nay ravish[ed]' what belongs to God" (78).

Themes

Dennis (1873, 56) prints HSDue under the heading "Self-Dedication."

Reeves (1952, 100) paraphrases the poem: "He belongs to God by right, yet he feels that God has abandoned him and only the Devil seeks him."

Simon (1952, 123), in an extended explication, demonstrates that the sonnet has the "note of true grief and sincere appeal for mercy" characteristic of most of the

Holy Sonnets. The poem, she contends, develops from a "hard and cold," almost grudging, acknowledgment of the speaker's surrender to God in the octave to the "sharp cries" of lines 9–10 and the "passionate appeal to be taken by force" of lines 11–14. He "confesses his despair and beseeches God to help him," Simon says, since he is too weak to sustain the struggle. See also Holy Sonnets: Themes.

Denonain (1956, 151) notes that the theme of abandonment by God is scarcely expressed in the Holy Sonnets, and never as a central theme, except in HSDue.

Peterson (1959, 508) finds that, as the first sonnet in the sequence, the poem represents the first steps in the Anglican experience of contrition, the acknowledgment of sin (1–10) and the prayer for grace (11–14). See also Holy Sonnets: Themes.

Stampfer (1970, 243–44) observes that the poem has a highly formal relationship between the speaker, God, and the devil, under a dominant legal metaphor, employing the ideas of landed property and usurpation. The "I" and the "self" in the opening two lines are not the same, he says: "the 'I' keeps itself carefully defined; the 'selfe' is a piece of unknown property, at most registered in an attorney's office." And throughout the metaphor of property, Stampfer states, echoes the doctrine of original sin: "sin, like property, can be passed from generation to generation automatically." However, Stampfer continues, behind the legal metaphor stand relationships to God of greater intimacy—specifically, a family metaphor (243). For example, he says, the final prayer in the poem, that God "rise and for thine owne worke fight," refers to property; but then the uneasiness that God may not choose the speaker, though he loves him, is a family metaphor, the fear of being rejected for another love. The poem is thus "forced, muffled, and formalized," Stampfer contends; the helpless speaker addresses God yet feels Satan inside him. The divine presence, he says, is distant and unfelt (244).

Sicherman (1971, 85) remarks that this sonnet displays a "conventional submission" to God by giving a "facile and general" catalogue of sins and debts. To improve his knowledge of God's love, she says, the speaker undertakes the discipline of fear.

Blanch (1974, 479) writes that in HSDue Donne acknowledges a "legal contract between the poet and God" and thus "attempts to establish himself as God's property" in the octave of the poem. Arguing that the sestet of the poem "implies a state of warfare between God and Satan," Blanch describes the poet as tortured by the fear that his fate is contingent upon God's whims and that he may have no place in the divinely ordered scheme.

Lewalski (1979, 266) defines the concern of the sonnet as "the problem of election." At the beginning, she suggests, the speaker sets forth a series of titles which might demonstrate his "election," but by the sestet the speaker recognizes that Satan has gained control, and he fears that he may not be one of the elect.

Milward (1979 [1988, 43–44]) identifies the subject-matter of the sonnet as a "free development" of the initial consideration of the Ignatian Exercises entitled Principle and Foundation: "Man is created to praise, reverence, and serve God our Lord, and by this means to save his soul" (43). The speaker thus begins, according to Milward, by considering "the 'many titles', or legal grounds, of his dependence on God" (43), all of which "prompts him to 'resigne' or make himself over to God in return" (44). Milward concludes that "by recalling these titles, the poet seeks in the octet to raise his mind to God on high; then in the sestet, he cannot help reflecting on himself and contrasting God's holiness with his own sinfulness" (44).

Shaw (1981, 43–45, 51) states that "the creature" in the sonnet "seeks to clarify his relationship to the Creator by harking back to its original terms" (43). Shaw posits that Donne's use of the word "titles" in the first line invites the reader "to expect an argument couched in legal terms," but the speaker has "little room to maneuver, for the titles by which he is reckoned God's property are not disputable" (43–44). Shaw contends that the titles signify both God's "lawful" possession of the creature and the status of the creature: "sonne," "servant," "sheepe," "Image," "temple." Shaw adds that "the sonnet betrays a mounting impatience with the legalistic image it first invoked," and in turn uses "the charged word 'ravish,'" which "could be read as a glancing attempt to appeal not merely to God's rights as a proprietor but to his honor as a lover, arousing his jealousy of a rival suitor" (44). In the penultimate line, Shaw concludes, the speaker, "the unchosen one, stands at a forlorn distance from the object of God's love, 'mankind'" (44–45). Shaw claims that although the "possibility" of Grace is expressed in the Holy Sonnets, there is no clear indication that Donne "has experienced it as a reality—has received justification, as theology would say" (51).

Yearwood (1982, 210–12) finds that the conversion process in Donne's first twelve Holy Sonnets, following the 1633 and Gardner's (1952) ordering, "begins in pride, proceeds to confession and despair, and culminates in a humble joy and confidence" (210). HSDue (the first of the twelve) begins with the speaker's "misconception" that "he must accomplish his own salvation by a sinless life," but discovers by the end, according to Yearwood, "that he cannot *not* sin" (212). Yearwood adds that in the closing lines the speaker despairs and blames God (212).

Mallett (1983, 55) summarizes the argument of the sonnet: "Donne belongs to God by right; but in his despair he feels that God has abandoned him, and only the Devil seeks him."

Martz (1985, 14) notes that although "traditional comforts" are of no avail in Donne's "sense of utter sinfulness and the utter necessity of relying wholly upon the will of God for salvation," he does summarize them in the octave of the sonnet. Hope, however, "is corroded by the fear that he is not one of the chosen," says Martz, as expressed in lines 11–14.

Guibbory (1986, 94) observes that "it is not just memory of his sinfulness that helps restore the connection between man and God" and that, indeed, "memory of God's many mercies work a similar effect." For Guibbory, Donne's "recollection that God originally created him as a 'temple of thy Spirit divine' [l. 8] and redeemed him 'when I was decay'd'" [l. 3] "compels" him to "'resigne' himself to God."

Marotti (1986, 255) finds the "conflict between assertion and submission" played out in the Holy Sonnets in the "thematic and rhetorical interplay of spiritual pride and humility." HSDue, for example, in Marotti's analysis, "seems more concerned with blaming God than with loving Him," a "spiritual attitude" that the succeeding sonnets must change. According to Marotti, "the speaker arrogantly puts all the responsibility on God."

Spurr (1991, 170–71) finds that *HSDue* appears to reverse the usual despairing tone of the octave of many of Donne's Holy Sonnets, as it begins with a "quasi-catechetical catalogue" of his "theoretical godlikeness," but it continues with his fall and redemption, a "summary" which Spurr claims is "preparatory to meditation" (170). The sestet, then, according to Spurr, displays "the extremity of the persona's dismay at the loss of his purity and innocence," which "brings the poetry to life" (170–71). Given such "utter corruption," Spurr contends, "extraordinary redemption" is necessary, so the speaker stresses again "the exceptional operation of God's saving power" in line 11 (171). Spurr finds lines 12–13 theologically controversial when Donne "threatens God with his indifference to him," and the poem ends, Spurr emphasizes, "not on a note of confidence even in the possibility of God's gift of grace, but in sure knowledge of the perverse possessiveness of the Devil" (171).

HSDue and Other Works

Young (1987, 27, 29) draws a comparison between *HSDue* and the penitential lyrics in the *Heráclito cristiano (Christian Heraclitus)* (1613) by Francisco de Quevedo (1580–1645), noting that both collections "focus on the spiritual condition of the poetic persona." The first octave of Donne's sonnet "establishes the misery of man's natural condition," but Young observes that "the proliferation of metaphors, suggesting various relationships with God, is an indication of the speaker's uncertainty and the feebleness of his position." With the sestet, therefore, the speaker "dwells queasily on the prospect that the proffered self may not be worth the cost of refurbishing, that only the devil is still interested: 'Why doth the devill then usurpe in mee!'" (27). Young cites another poet who writes in this vein: the Frenchman Jean de la Ceppède (1550–1622), whose collection of religious poems is entitled *Théorèmes Spirituels* (1613–21) (29).

Spurr (1991, 171) comments on the way in which *HSDue* brings to mind *HSBatter*, in that "the conviction of ravishment by Satan" in *HSDue* underlies Donne's request for ravishment by the Trinity in *HSBatter*. See more under *HSBatter*: Themes.

Notes and Glosses

1–8 *As due . . . Temple of thy Spirit divine.* **SIMON** (1952) argues that the speaker's consideration of "God's titles of possession" strikes the reader "as hard and cold, as though he was bartering and loth to admit the many titles by which he is 'due' to God" (123). See also *HSDue*: Themes.

1–4 *As due . . . the which before was thyne.* **GARDNER** (1952), calling *HSDue* a "preparatory prayer," quotes these lines to show that it begins "with an act of recollection" (xl). **SIMON** (1952) finds the first three lines a "hard turn," in which the speaker implies that "his surrender is imposed upon him by his *reason*, and not the natural overflow of his *feelings* toward God." Observes that this "hard legal tone" is relinquished in l. 4, showing that this attitude is wrong (124). See also *HSDue*: Themes.

1–2 *As due . . . first I was made* **FAERBER** (1950) observes that Donne employs hypotaxis, that is, the use of coordinating conjunctions, in his language, rather than omit them, or parataxis, because the latter is inadequate to express his meaning. Notes that in this regard he differs from Herbert and the other metaphysical poets (18). Contends that the two sides of Donne's paradoxes are not always balanced; rather, they juxtapose experience and a constructed image of his being, here starting out with a personal experience followed by a statement of belief (69).

1 *titles* **MARTZ** (1963): "in legal usage, the proofs of ownership" (83). **SMITH** (1971): "legal rights or entitlements" (625). [Similarly, Mallett (1983, 55), Patrides (1985a, 435), and Booty (1990, 107).] **LEVER** (1974): "Donne refers to God's 'titles' (i.e. claims), not man's" (179). **CRAIK and CRAIK** (1986): "legal entitlements (as listed in ll. 2–8)" (276). **HANDLEY** (1991): "i.e. dues (to God)" (42).

1 *resigne* **MARTZ** (1963): "give up, hand over" (83). **MALLETT** (1983): "surrender" (55). **PALLOTTI** (1993): beyond "resignation" or "surrender," "resign" suggests "re-sign" or "sign again, or writing one's name with the implication, here, that the speaker re-signs not in his own name, but in the name of God" (cf. Docherty (1986, 138–39). Since name indicates "identity, a re-signation implies a change in, a renewal of, identity," and further, "sign" also has the "specific Christian meaning connected with the sign of the cross. Thus re-signing oneself is an act that implies also a renewed profession of faith" (182n15).

2–10 *(O God) . . . nay ravish that's thy right?* **FAERBER** (1950): the situation of mankind is a shrill contradiction of the redemptive power of Christ's death, which loses itself in "tragic unavoidability" ("tragische Unausweichlichkeit") (29). See also *Holy Sonnets: Language and Style.*

2–4 *(O God) . . . before was thyne.* **FAERBER** (1950): Donne revolts against the ancient contradiction that God's creatures have been left to corruption, sensing that the concept that we are thrown without meaning or purpose into the world ("Geworfenheit") conflicts with the belief that we are all children of God (29). See also *Holy Sonnets: Language and Style.* **KLINCK** (1981): the first three "titles" which "lead the speaker to resign himself to God" are "directly correspondent to the Persons of the Trinity as creator, redeemer, and sanctifier" (251).

3 *By thee, and for thee, and when I was decayde* **MORRIS** (1953): both Donne and Hopkins employ the "outride" or "hanger," an extra half-foot, in the iambic pentameter line, as here and in "The Caged Skylark" (l. 4) (46).

3 *and for thee,* **STEIN** (1944) thinks the eye "may accept" but the ear will refuse the elision of "for" (392).

3 *decayde* **SMITH** (1971): "corrupted by sin" (625). [Similarly, Mallett (1983, 55) and Handley (1991, 42).] **LEVER** (1974): "by man's first sin" (179). **PATRIDES**

(1985a): "fell in the Fall of Adam" (435). [Similarly, Craik and Craik (1986, 276) and Booty (1990, 107).]

4 *Thy blood bought that, the which before was thyne.* **FAERBER** (1950): a paradox in that Christ's sacrificial death should not have been necessary (27). See Holy Sonnets: Language and Style. **GASTER** (1986) says that Donne, like the later Bunyan, felt the "full weight of his own unworthiness in the face of a God who was paradoxically redeeming what was already His" (5).

4 *bought* **SHAWCROSS** (1967): "redeemed" (338). [So also, Patrides (1985a, 435) and Booty (1990, 107).]

5–8 *I ame . . . Temple of thy Spirit divine.* **SIMON** (1952) finds that the thought of Christ's sacrifice in l. 4 softens the "hard legal tone" of ll. 1–3, hence that the relation between man and God "is no longer that of owned to owner, but of son to father," of servant to kind master, or sheep to shepherd. Observes that the speaker confesses his misery at having betrayed the trust of those relationships, a weakness which opens him up to the enemy (124). See also *HSDue*: Structure and *HSDue*: Themes.

5 *I ame thy Sonne made with thy selfe to shyne,* **KORTEMME** (1933) notes here that "wordplay" ("Wortspiel") often intensifies the paradoxical effect (48). **GARD-NER** (1952): cf. Matt. 13.43: "Then shall the righteous shine forth as the sun in the kingdom of their Father" (65). [So also, Lewalski and Sabol (1973, 151), Lever (1974, 179), Craik and Craik (1986, 276), and Carey (1990b, 454).] **MALLETT** (1983) points to the wordplay on "son" and "sun" (similarly, Smith [1971, 625], Patrides [1985a, 435], Craik and Craik [1986, 276], and Handley [1991, 42]), comments that the "believing Christian is 'the child of God,'" and refers to the "biblical promise" of Matt. 13.43 (55).

6 *Thy Servant, . . . hast still repayde,* **LEVER** (1974): the line alludes to Matt. 20.1–16 and the parable of the laborers in the vineyard (179).

6 *whose paines thou hast still repayde,* **MALLETT** (1983): "Christ's sufferings on the Cross were seen as the payment of a ransom, freeing those who held to the Christian faith from the pains they would otherwise have had to endure in hell" (55).

6 *paines* **CRAIK and CRAIK** (1986): "labours" (276).

6 *still* **SHAWCROSS** (1967): "always" (339). [So also, Patrides (1985a, 435) and Booty (1990, 107).]

7 *Thy Sheepe, . . . Spirit divine.* **LEVER** (1974) notes that the biblical images of sheep (Matt, 18.12–14), image (Gen. 1.27), and temple (1 Cor. 6.19) "become increasingly impersonal and remote" (179).

7 *Thy Sheepe*, **MALLETT** (1983) notes that God's love for humankind in the Bible is frequently compared "to that of the shepherd for his sheep" (56).

7 *thyne Image;* **MALLETT** (1983) cites the biblical account in Gen. 1.27 that "God created man in his own image" (56).

7 *betrayde* **HANDLEY** (1991): "Succumbed to temptation (of the devil)" (42).

8 *My selfe) a Temple of thy Spirit divine.* **MALLETT** (1983): "according to Christian teaching, the Holy Spirit dwells in all Christian believers, who may thus be said to resemble temples" (56). **MÜLLER** (1986): the metaphor is of biblical origin: "Know ye not that ye are the temple of God, and that the Spirit of God dwelleth in you? If any man defile the temple of God, him shall God destroy; for the temple of God is holy, which *temple* ye are" (1 Cor. 3. 16–17) (74). The same metaphor appears in the third stanza of *Lit* (74).

9–10 *Why . . . ravish that's thy right?* **SIMON** (1952) finds the two questions to "cut like sharp cries," revealing the speaker's "fear of the enemy that is seeking to steal what is God's by right" (123). See also *HSDue*: Themes. **PALLOTTI** (1993) sees "behind" these questions a "powerful echo" of the "distressing complaint from Jesus on the cross" in Matt. 27.46 ("My God, my God, why hast thou forsaken me?") (182n19). **MAROTTI** (1986): Donne asks these questions "petulantly" and "accusingly," as if it is "God's fault that he is plunged in sin" (255).

9 *Why dothe the deuill then vsurpe in mee?* **FAERBER** (1950) notes that the same imagery is to be found in some of Donne's love poems (69).

9 *vsurpe in mee?* **GARDNER** (1952), printing the phrase as here, notes that "vsurpe on" is the "more common phrase" but that it is usually used "with the person whose rights are 'usurped on'" (66). **SHAABER** (1958): "wrongfully appropriate" (100). **SHAWCROSS** (1967): "practice his power of seizure" (339). **LEVER** (1974) notes the alternate reading in 1633 ("on" rather than "in") but says that "the devil's usurpation is not *on* man, but on the divine 'titles' *in* man" (179). **MALLETT** (1983): "unjustly claim possession of me (compare the first line of the poem" (56).

10 *ravish* **GRANSDEN** (1954): both here and in *HSBatter* 14 Donne begs God to be more active in his life and rescue him from his "thralldom to Satan" (129). **UL-HASAN** (1958): the height of spiritual love is compared to the sex act (11).

10 *that's* **MARTZ** (1963): "that which is" (84).

10 *that's thy right?* **MALLETT** (1983): "that which rightly belongs to God" (56).

11–14 *Except . . . is loth to loose mee.* **HARDY** (1942): the lines define the bridgeless chasm that Donne sees lying between his soul and God (179). **SIMON** (1952) finds the speaker helpless against the devil, against whom only God can prevail, but God "must fight for His Possession" (123). Observes that the speaker, after the rational and legalistic tone of the octave, finally releases his "pent up emotions" in his surrender to God. Notes that the repetition of "mee" in ll. 13–14 is a sign of his feeling of "dereliction" and "belief that the power of Grace is the only hope of salvation" (124–25). See also *HSDue*: Structure. **FAERBER** (1950): Donne does not surrender his titles unconditionally or stereotypically, but requires certain guaranties from God in return (18). **HEBAISHA** (1971) finds the "colloquy" at the end of *HSDue* not a "prayer in the usual sense" but a "desparate [sic] cry for Christ's help in this difficult situation" (60).

11–12 *Except . . . when I do see* **PRAZ** (1931) compares the religious poetry of Donne and Michelangelo, here in their appeal to God to break the barrier between him and their hearts (69–71). See also The Holy Sonnets and Other Works. **MAROTTI** (1986): the speaker is here delivering to God a kind of "moral ultimatum" (255).

11 *Except* **MALLETT** (1983): "unless" (56).

11 *worke* **HANDLEY** (1991): "i.e. because you have made me, I am your 'worke'" (42).

12–14 *O I . . . is loth to loose mee.* **MORRIS** (1953): Donne is "almost in despair over his weakness in the face of evil," approaching the mood of Hopkins in "I wake and feel" (74). **GRANSDEN** (1954): in the last years of his secular life Donne senses that though the world has rejected him, he still cannot surrender himself wholly to God, and so asks Him to "take back his creature by force" (128–29). **CAREY** (1981) says that the final three lines are a "warning to God: he may go too far, may look away too long. Implicit in them is that frantic attempt to blackmail God with promises or threats which we are all tempted to resort to, in moments of unbearable stress, whether we believe in him or not" (53–54). **SINFIELD** (1983): the lines disclose Donne's response when he finds that he is "not among the few to whom [divine mercy] is extended" (11).

13–14 *That . . . is loth to loose mee.* **KORTEMME** (1933) finds in the lines a paradox in which opposites, here love and hate, are bound together in an inharmonious fashion (50). **FAERBER** (1950) argues that Donne does not see a reasonable solution to the dilemma of the conflicting concepts that we are thrown into the world without meaning or purpose and the belief in God's patrimony (29). Notes that the paradox need not determine and control the religious vision (32). See also Holy Sonnets: Language and Style. **VEITH** (1985) argues that while the lines appear to stress the "exclusivity of God's election associated with Calvinism," they in fact express "Arminian Universalism, which stresses God's love for all mankind, so that God does not choose individuals whom He will save" (120). **HANDLEY** (1991) notes the "careful antithetical balance" of "lovst," "chuse," "hates," and "lose," an "equivalent to the balance between good and evil" (42).

13 *yet wilt not choose mee,* **LEVER** (1974): "By refusing to 'choose' (i.e. elect to eternal life) God lets his 'titles' go by default" (179).

13 *wilt not* **STEIN** (1944): the apostrophe after "wilt" [as, for example, in the editions of Grierson (1912) and Gardner (1952)—ed.] was probably added by a later transcriber who noticed the eleven syllable line and thought "mee" should be stressed, but failed to notice the feminine rhyme of the two lines (391). **GARDNER** (1952), reading "wilt'not," argues that the contraction is correct though it has "no manuscript support." Says that the line is decasyllabic, with the stress falling on "mankind" and "me," but that l. 14 is properly read with eleven syllables. Adds that "the most sensitive metrists" either never or seldom took advantage of the "license" to rhyme a tenth syllable with an eleventh syllable and that there is "a particular lack of tack" in this example, "for the ear and eye are haunted by the true feminine rhyme "chose me" and "loose me" (66). (Later, Gardner [1978, 66, 152] rejects the contraction.) **LEVER** (1974) argues against Gardner's (1952) contraction, saying that Donne "speaks as a representative man, not an individual sinner" (179). **MILWARD** (1979 [1988]) addresses Gardner's (1952) criticism of Donne in the final couplet and explains Gardner's "difficulty" as deriving from her insertion of a contraction mark in "wilt'not" and then "treating the contraction as one syllable" (45). Prefers to leave the words as two syllables, without the contraction so that "the whole line is naturally extended to eleven with the feminine ending 'choose me'" (45).

HSLittle

COMMENTARY

General Commentary

Gosse (1899, 2:107–08) finds that, as Donne "reflects upon his frailty" in *HSLittle*, his "old intellectual ingenuity" returns, and he "calls on the discoverers of America to lend him their new seas to add to the old," wishes to make a "flood deep enough to quench the fires of lust and envy before they have consumed his soul away," and hopes "to save as much of that soul as possible to be the prey of a very different conflagration, the zeal of the Lord and of His house burning him up" (108).

HSBatter and *HSLittle* are, Altizer (1973, 86–87) says, "the only two examples of Donne's plea for personal apocalypse" (86). There is violent imagery in both, but it is more subdued in *HSLittle*, Altizer argues, residing neither in accumulation of paradox nor in erotic imagery, but in the symbolic force of the reiterated verbs "drowne" and "burne." Altizer contends that both *HSLittle* and *HSBatter*, as "semi-apocalyptic" poems, tend to be self-conscious and logical, their plea for the overthrow of reason and selfhood answered in part by the very image of the Holy Spirit that the poems create. Altizer states, however, that there is little reason to suppose that when these two poems were written Donne was on the verge of discovering the Adam and the Christ within himself (87). See also *HSBatter*: Themes.

Blanch (1974, 480) writes that *HSLittle* contains "an interesting *mélange* of astronomical and religious imagery to underscore the internal conflict in the poet's 'little world.'"

Carleton (1977, 64) supposes that in *HSLittle* Donne "speaks of body and soul united in human love, or gives voice to his spiritual struggles and yearnings."

Partridge (1978, 134–35) thinks that *HSLittle* is unusually structured "because the plaint about sin overflows the limits of the octave by a line" (134). He notes that the first quatrain presents man as a microcosm and that there are two biblical references in the poem: one to 2 Pet. 3.7 and another to Ps. 69.9–10. Partridge rejects Empson's reading (1935—see *HSLittle*: Themes) for not being "based on a close reading of the text" (135).

Aers and Kress (1981, 66–68) note that, given Donne's emphasis in the sonnets on the instability of the self, his desire, as expressed in *HSLittle* and *HSBatter*, "is an idiosyncratic and violently assertive demand to be raped, overwhelmed and drowned" (66). See more under General Commentary on *HSBatter*.

Ray (1990b, 174–75) points to the "central analogy" of the microcosm at the opening of the sonnet, observing that the speaker "is made of the elements (i.e. his body) and a spirit (i.e. his soul)," but because of sin, the body and soul will die and be condemned to everlasting damnation unless the speaker can find a remedy that will redeem him. The speaker turns to the astronomers and discoverers who are finding "new facets of creation that before seemed nonexistent," Ray notes, with the speaker hoping for a similar experience in the "parallel universe/earth of himself" (174). According to Ray, the speaker considers "seas" of tears to wash him clean as well as God's purifying "fires," recalling Ps. 69.9, the fire that "will burn up the old charred world of his sinful self: paradoxically, it is an 'eating' up that will 'heal' him spiritually by making him a 'new earth,' a new world" (174–75).

Low (1993, 69) states that the view of God in the sonnet is that of "lord of a 'house,' which the poet wants to join, that is, he is head of a family, tribe, or nation."

Date and Circumstances

Coffin (1937, 185–86) proposes that the reference to "new Sphears" and "new Lands" in the poem (l. 6) was inspired by Galileo's discoveries as reported in his *Sidereus Nuncius*, and that since that work was published in 1610, the sonnet must have been composed after that date.

Gardner (1952, 75–76) questions Coffin's dating of the poem (1937) on the basis of the publication of *Sidereus Nuncius* in 1610. She doubts that the reference is to any specific "astronomers of the old and new schools" but is more likely Donne referring to discoverers more generally: "astronomers who find new spheres and explorers who find new lands."

Adams (1962, 758) notes that *HSLittle* first appeared in 1635 but that determining its date of composition, like the dates of most of the Holy Sonnets, is based on the "scanty marks of internal evidence" (758). See more under Holy Sonnets: Dating and Order.

The Poet/Persona

Bush (1945, 133–34) finds that the contrast between "divine goodness and human weakness" was Donne's "chief torment" and that the "stage, or rather the battleground, is not the macrocosm but that 'little world made cunningly,'" the Donne who is but a "man facing his Maker."

Docherty (1986, 138) finds that *HSLittle*, like *HSMade*, seeks "a re-incarnation of Donne, in the figure of Christ," but here the equation of Donne with Christ is less explicit. Donne seeks "new elements" for the re-incarnation, says Docherty, such as "new writings" and "new maps" that "constitute new geographies and new configurations," as well as "new people." The "fire" that Donne seeks is one that consumes him, which Docherty reads as a "digestive metaphor," recalling "the eucharistic idea of rebirth, purification and incarnation which has been submerged through the poem," and which "makes of Donne a 'new I,' as it were, a 'crossed I' (self-differential) in the configuration, metaphorically attained, of Christ."

Strier (1989, 377–78) also finds *HSLittle* similar to *HSMade* in that both approach but do not parallel the "sophistry" of *HSScene* with respect to the relationship between the self and God (377). The poem's "ethical world," Strier points out, is clear: "black sin hath betraid to endless night/My worlds both parts, and (oh) both parts must die" (ll. 3–4). What Strier finds "striking" about the "cognate final prayers" of *HSLittle*, *HSMade* and *HSBatter* is "first, their thoroughly Protestant theology of grace, and second, their imaginative apprehension of this theology in images of violent and essentially impersonal phenomena," that is, "God is a force and the soul is an object" (378). See also *HSMade*: The Poet/Persona and *HSScene*: The Poet/Persona.

Genre and Traditions

Martz (1954, 52–53) analyzes the sonnet to demonstrate its inclusion of all three stages of Ignatian meditation, though it oversteps the traditional Petrarchan structure in line 9: The first quatrain is a "composition by similitude," defining the problem; in the next five lines the intellect in "a mode of violent hyperbole" examines the issue; the last five lines, ending in a "petition in colloquy with God," express the passionate affection aroused by the problem posed. See more under Holy Sonnets: Genre and Traditions.

Structure

Esch (1955, 51) finds the poem a variant from the Italian structure in that the "concluding part" ("der Abgesang") is reduced to five lines. See more under Holy Sonnets: Prosody.

Stampfer (1970, 269–70), viewing the development of the poem overall, says that while the opening couplet suggests a unified being of the ideal self before the fall, sin has split the speaker into two parts, both of which are consigned to death (269). Stampfer finds that the effect of the second quatrain is slack torpor: Donne cannot move by human means. The image of fire repeated several times in the sestet, Stampfer says, "establishes the feeling tone of an extreme fanatic, one who would altogether excoriate the old man" (270).

Conrad (1985, 234–37) focuses on Donne's preoccupation with "the encroachments of nothingness," and specifically in *HSLittle*, where Donne sees himself and the poem as "a little world made cunningly" (234–35). According to Conrad, Donne's "analytic mind delights in controlled destruction or disintegration," and so in *HSLittle* his "physical carcass and his 'Angelicke spright'" are "at mortal war in him, and at odds structurally in the poem." Conrad finds that "Donne exacerbates the self-division of the sonnet, making octave and sestet schizophrenically clash." Donne "consigns his sinful parts to their various perditions of water and zealous fire," and simultaneously as Donne is "undoing the sonnet," we find, according to Conrad, "the octave is about the self's hydroptic swelling to extend into new lands and spheres, the sestet about its vengeful destruction." Conrad contends that "the structural virtue of the sonnet is the cleanliness of the incision it makes between soul and body" (235). Conrad locates a similar state of mind in Donne's use of "the fatal monosyllable of exclamation" ("O" or "oh"), which is "language's and life's surrender of breath" (cf. l. 4) (236). Here, according to Conrad, the monosyllable "warns of severance, the poisoned body's sundering from soul" (237).

Language and Style

Battenhouse (1942, 245) notes the prominence of the macrocosm-microcosm analogy in the poem.

Sloane (1981, 66, 69) notes that Donne's equation of the physical world and the human body "had its roots in the concept of a correspondence between the macrocosm and the microcosm and, thus, was one of the ubiquitous metaphors of the Renaissance" (66). Sloane notes further that Donne, through his emblematic use of eyes and globe in the sonnet, objectifies the subject of the poem, and then places the original images "in new relationships to each other" (69).

Clark (1982, 77) says that "neotypological lyrics," such as *HSLittle*, present "personally dramatic, exemplary self-portrayals through a persona so closely identified with a type that he becomes a neotype of Christ in some common seventeenth-century predicament." In the beginning, Clark points out, "the persona declares that his penance is necessary, yet wonders if it is necessary to drown his little world in tears." Later, he "recalls that the world is to be destroyed by fire" (cf. 2 Pet. 3.10) and "prays for the zeal of God's house to devour and heal him" (ll. 13–14). See also notes to l. 14.

Raspa (1983, 125–26) finds that the function of the enthymeme in the Holy Sonnets is the same as in *Corona* (125). That is, "in both sets of poems," according to Raspa, "every image and hence every enthymeme aspired after an antithetical effect proper to itself, different from that of the extended paradox of ancient epigram" (125–26). For example, *HSLittle*, in Raspa's analysis, combines "images of the cleverness of divine creation and of darkness" for the purpose of "organizing a series of compressed images into a provocative general picture of Christian truth emotionally significant to all men" (126).

Dickson (1987, 259), discussing the forms and uses of biblical typology, sees *HSLittle* as a poem that "links persona and sacred history together, revealing how one essential salvation drama is being played through the archetypal patterns of the Christian *mythos*."

Warnke (1987, 107) finds this sonnet "rather more hopeful" than most of the Holy Sonnets, and in that regard it bears a "certain affinity" with *HSDeath*.

Osmond (1990, 128) points to the movement in the seventeenth century away from earlier "elaborate systems of correspondence" which had fostered the literary use of "sustained allegory" to the freedom for "more direct and dramatic modes of presentation" as seen in the "startling effects" of much metaphysical poetry. Osmond thus finds that *HSLittle*, though beginning with "the conventional image of man as a little world," proceeds in a "most unconventional manner," with the allusions to "new sphears" and "new lands" and the desire that "new seas" might be "poured into his eyes so that they can then 'drowne' this world with weeping."

Sacred and Profane

Williamson (1931, 159, 162–63) quotes the poem in full to illustrate "why the ardor of the lover and the experience of the mystic pass so easily from one region to the other, and why one expression and even the same image serve for both." He concludes that in such works the "world of metaphysical concept and the world of sensuous fact meet and exchange significance; the metaphysical word is made flesh" (159). Williamson compares the "deluge" image in HSLittle 7–9 to similar figures in ValWeep, Noct, and SecAn to argue that Donne "achieved a definite extension of the sensibility of poetry in his time," making possible both "the fine religious poetry of this century" and "the love-poetry able to raise the dark and paradoxical aspects of passion to the level of vision" (162–63).

Themes

Fausset (1924, 243) quotes the poem in full, observing that Donne believed "one moment's slackening" of his faith would "change victory into defeat," hence rejecting sin "with the same violent subtlety with which he had embraced it."

Empson (1935, 73–76) argues that HSLittle reflects Donne's attraction to the "Renaissance desire to make the individual more independent than Christianity allowed" (73). Empson observes that the poem imagines the soul as isolated and complete in itself, as in the world of the new astronomy, and thus if there are other worlds (ll. 5–6) whose inhabitants can live as they like, then the uniqueness of Christ and divine justice itself are called into doubt: a heaven "most high" (l. 5) is safely distant and difficult to reach (75). Empson argues that the reference to "spright" and "elements" (l. 2), that is, spirit and body, reflects the day and night of the world (here the globe) and the fusion of body and soul, a frequent theme in Donne. Both, then, are to be drowned and the soul is safe from punishment, since it will die as well. But the flood and the fire pull the reader back from the thought, as does the image of healing by eating (l. 14), and the reader, Empson concludes, "is now safely recalled from the interplanetary spaces, baffled among the cramped, inverted, cannibal, appallingly tangled impulses that are his home upon the world" (76).

Empson (1949, 580), citing his earlier work (1935), finds in the poem a tension between "a remorseful hope for atonement with God" and a "hunger for annihilation and escape from God."

Reeves (1952, 100) observes that the subject of the poem is the same as that of HSBlack and paraphrases it: "He prays for Christian zeal to burn up his soul, as it had formerly been burnt by the lusts of youth."

Denonain (1956, 152) notes that Donne asks if tears are necessary to cleanse or drown this little world that sin has seduced and dragged to death, and concludes that the body must burn with zeal toward God as it did with lust and greed in youth.

Peterson (1959, 514) finds the poem "a lamentation for sin," expressing the penitent's desire that he had not transgressed. See also Holy Sonnets: Themes.

Lewalski (1979, 267) suggests that HSLittle may be the fifth sonnet in the 1635 edition "not only because of the continuation of the motif of grief and repentance" found in the fourth—HSBlack—"but also from the conception of the 'blacke Soule' now threatened with imminent death." Lewalski observes that "the inevitability of this result for his little world" is suggested as the lines "play off against" such texts as Rom. 5.12 and 6.23.

Milward (1979 [1988, 89–92]) finds HSLittle less directly related to the Ignatian

Exercises than some of the other Holy Sonnets, instead suggesting that it looks back to the Songs and Sonets and forward to *Devotions*. Milward points out that the idea of man as "a little world," or microcosm, is shared with many writers and thinkers—including Hooker, Bacon, Browne, Shakespeare, and Sir John Davies, and he notes specifically the description of King Lear as one who "strives in his little world of man" (3.1.10). Citing God's warning to Adam in Paradise (Gen. 2.17), Milward says that Donne's speaker "laments" as well "the strife that sin has brought into his little world, incurring the penalty of death" (89). The macrocosm/microcosm comparison, according to Milward, "aptly summarizes the mediaeval metaphysic to which Donne was so attached from the time of his university studies" (90). The cosmological comparison leads the speaker "to a further astronomical and geographical one in the second quatrain," which, Milward indicates, is so often the case in the Songs and Sonets, where Donne's speakers delight "to contemplate the new discoveries of his age," and in particular those who have, like Galileo, "found new sphears" (90). All of this, according to Milward, brings the speaker to meditate on the inevitable fire that will consume the world at the end of time. The sonnet ends, however, with a colloquy with Christ, in which the speaker, Milward notes, "prays that he may be burnt, no longer with 'the fire of lust and envie' nor yet with eschatological fire, but 'with a fiery zeale of thee and thy house'" (92).

Raspa (1983, 73–74) notes that the faculty of understanding in the "apparently conventional" sonnets of Donne "performed the functions allotted to it in meditative thought," and he cites *HSLittle* as a good example. Donne offers in the sonnet, according to Raspa, "the classical Christian duality of human body and soul," but Donne "marvelled at the union of these contrary forces in himself" (73). Moreover, Raspa observes, the "spirit of the poet at work in the poem" was able to draw "analogies between temporal experience and eternal emotive realities," which "was not the logical faculty described in the *curricula* of Renaissance books of education marvelling at man's place in the Great Chain of Being" (73–74). Raspa argues that in Donne's sacred verse "psychology and the senses became the predominant human traits," and he concludes that the "references to man, reason, and poetry" in Donne's verse are "stronger indicators of his place in the history of Ignatian aesthetics than his factual connections with Jesuit verse" (74).

Guibbory (1986, 90–91) points to this sonnet as illustrating Donne's recognition that he "must personally reenact biblical history in order to expiate his sin," for "just as in Noah's time the sinful world had to be punished with the Flood, so now Donne longs to 'Drowne my world with my weeping earnestly' (l. 8)." But Guibbory adds that Donne recognizes that "the postdeluvian [sic] world continued to sin," and that he, too, "will need a more devastating punishment" (90). Consequently, he "prays for an apocalyptic fire that will at once destroy and recreate him anew, much as God will do to the world at the end of time" (cf. ll. 13–14) (90–91).

Dickson (1987, 254, 268–69) discusses the importance of biblical typology and stresses the recognition of three typological modes: the Christological (stressing type and antitype), sacramental ("through which the individual's salvation history is told in imitation of Christ"), and eschatological ("through which the ultimate glorification of Christ, man, and the universe is foreshadowed and fulfilled") (254). Dickson comments on Donne's indebtedness to these typologies, noting in particular Donne's treatment of history in *HSLittle*, which "features the eschatological relationship between the flood and the apocalypse" and which "links personal and sacred history together, revealing how one essential salvation drama is being played through the archetypal patterns of the Christian *mythos*" (268–69).

McNees (1992, 64–66) claims that both *HSMin* and *HSLittle* "allude to the hope that the Eucharist will drown or wash away black sin" (64), and she finds that, like the love poems, *HSLittle* "plays on the microcosm-macrocosm connection between the seas and tears" (ll. 7–9) as the speaker "demands the motivation to repent through alternative actions separated by the conjunction 'or,'" but "these alternatives, uncoupled with Christ's blood, fail" (65). When he finally addresses God in the final couplet, the speaker, according to McNees, "transfigures the word 'burne' from its secular to sacred use by imploring God's intervention as opposed to that of the secular explorers" (65–66), thus surrendering his "temporal control over language to God's sacred control." Acknowledging as one source Ps. 69, McNees also thinks that Donne converts David's lines ("For the zeal of thine house hath eaten me up and the reproaches of them that reproached thee are fallen upon me") to "a request for fulfillment through participation in the eucharistic meal," for David can only "pray for salvation and deliverance from his enemies" while the speaker of *HSLittle* can "participate in sacramental salvation" (66).

Haffenden (1993, 18–19) cites *HSLittle* to show that Donne laments that he has "betrayed his body and soul into 'black sinne' and proceeds to an invocation" that is, as Carey (1981—see notes to ll. 5–9) says, "a vast gesture of despair" (18–19). Haffenden also finds through images of "new sphears" and "new lands" evidence that Donne understood the "breathtaking implications of an infinite universe" (19), and he questions Gardner's suggestion (1952—see *HSLittle*: Date and Circumstances) that Donne may have been thinking of "discoverers generally" (19).

DiPasquale (1994, 403–07, 411–12) contends that the sonnet's movement from flood to fire is insufficiently explained by its debt to Gen. 9.11 and 2 Pet. 3.12 (403). In DiPasquale's view, one must understand the "typological relation" between the "water of the Deluge" and the "'figure' of baptism" (cf. 1 Pet. 3.20–21) (403–04). In order to solve the problem that he has created, DiPasquale notes, Donne first tries to circumvent the need to drown his world by "suggesting that his world may be 'washed' in tears even if it can no longer be drowned." DiPasquale observes that this kind of cleansing should be the "perfect completion" of Donne's typological comparison, but, according to DiPasquale, "the speaker's state is one of near, if not complete, despair" (404). By line 10, DiPasquale notes, the poem's water imagery has turned to fire, so that the poem's "desperate logic" is evident: since "the macrocosm 'must be drown'd no more' after Noah's flood, it will instead be destroyed by fire" (cf. 2 Pet. 3.7) (405). In DiPasquale's view, the speaker is "trapped by the parallels that his own wit has generated," that is, "according to the artful parallel he has established, both parts of his 'little world' are 'reserved unto fire,'" as are "the earth and sky of the macrocosm" (405). DiPasquale finds that the "near-despairing" tone of the sonnet arises from the speaker's "sense that he has been *un*faithful to the commitment he made in baptism," but she does not find the poem ending in despair; instead, the speaker turns from his meditation on one sacrament, baptism, "to find hope in the thought of another—the Lord's Supper," as suggested by lines 12–14 (407). What Donne achieves by the end of the sonnet, according to DiPasquale, is to "rework the image of burning, relying on the fact that flames—like the bread and wine of the Lord's Supper—have more than one use," that is, "fire may destroy, or it may be an agent of purgation and digestion" (411). DiPasquale thus claims that through "the eucharistic flexibility of poetic language," the poet "redefines and transforms the sonnet itself," so that "poetic utterance remedies the despair that was spoken into being through poetry" (411–12).

HSLittle and Other Works

Holmes (1929, 100–01), in describing Donne's influence on Chapman, finds similar images in *Hymnus in Noctem* and *HSLittle*, "where the starting-point is the favorite idea of the other 'world,' the 'microcosm' of man, and the further allusion seems to be to the fabrications of the 'Crystalline' heaven." Holmes concludes that a "full comparison" illustrates the "enrichment, both intellectual and emotional," that Donne "effected in this kind."

Coanda (1957, 187) observes that both Donne and Hopkins strained the sonnet structure, as in *HSLittle* where the poet "mirrors the cosmos in microscopic man," and in "Spilt from Sibyl's Leaves" where night is the "womb-of-all, home-of-all, hearse-of-all."

Ferry (1983, 220) finds that both Shakespeare, in Sonnet 146, and Donne, in *HSLittle*, "expand in comparable ways a traditional metaphor of man's body and soul as a world."

O'Connell (1985, 13) draws a comparison between *HSLittle* and *Goodf*, given their "structural, verbal and thematic parallels": both poems begin with "a microcosm-macrocosm analogy, proceed to the speaker's recognition of his own sinfulness, and conclude by addressing the Lord directly, in each case to ask for the purifying action of fire." O'Connell notes the "reference to the redemptive death of Christ" in both poems—in the final couplet of *HSLittle* and in the central section of *Goodf*—but also highlights some of the ways that Donne has "refashioned" traditional images in *Goodf*.

Schoenfeldt (1990, 297) notes in his comparison of *HSLittle* with the second sonnet entitled "Love" in Herbert's *The Temple*, in which the "'greater flame' of God will 'kindle in our hearts such true desires,/As may consume our lusts,'" that Donne "provides a similar contrast between carnal and purifying flames, comparing 'the fire/ Of lust and envie' to the 'fiery zeal' of God, 'which doth in eating heale'" (297n11).

DiPasquale (1994, 406) believes that Heb. 6.4–6 "sheds significant light on the emotional logic" of *HSLittle*, noting that this particular passage "invokes the image of earth which takes no benefit from having been watered," and thus "those who bear no fruit when they are blessed by God's rain of grace will meet a fiery doom."

Shawcross (1994, 191) draws a brief comparison between Vaughan's poem "The Retreate" and *HSLittle*, focusing on Donne's image of "Angelike spright" and Vaughan's "Angell-infancy." In both poems, according to Shawcross, the speakers look to that "state in which [they] came into life" as a sought-after "retreat."

1–8 *I ame . . . with my weeping ernestly.* **ROGERS** (1862) prints these lines opposite one of his emblems exemplifying "The Present" (26). **HOLMES** (1929) quotes the lines to illustrate Donne's influence on Chapman (100–01). **MILWARD and ISHII** (1976) note that the idea of humankind as a "little world" is one Donne shared with learned contemporaries and point to *Devotions*, Meditation 6 for further evidence of Donne's interest in the metaphor (414).

1–4 *I ame . . . both parts must dy.* **FAUSSET** (1923) observes that Donne had difficulty "reconciling the fact and the idea," and that for him "the soul and body in human love were constantly in conflict," rarely coinciding, as they do in these lines (98). **SPÖRRI-SIGEL** (1949) argues that in the Holy Sonnets Donne comes to terms with God personally and directly. Observes that here he deals anxiously with the conflict between sin and grace, in which death is an existential question for the poet (70). **ANSARI** (1974) points out that the opening four lines develop from the familiar Renaissance notion of the microcosm—"a microcosm in which the body is composed of the four elements and the soul is invested with an immortal substance." Argues that the body and soul are "held together by some sort of inner nexus and it is there in the background of his mind" but that both body and soul are "submerged in the sea of sin encompassing us on all sides." Finds that the "body-soul complex" risks "becoming extinct" but can be saved "by an act of repentance and the application of sacraments." Concludes that the "storm of tears" arises from someone to whom "the immensities of the universe stand revealed by new scientific advances made possible by Galileo's telescope" (145–46). **CARLETON** (1977) finds the microcosm metaphor to be "dramatically located by the fervent acknowledgment of a sense of sin" (64–65). **RASPA** (1983): the sonnet "suppressed the first premise of the syllogism underlying its opening four lines," a premise that would "state generally that the fall of creation sharpened Donne's consciousness of his own weak condition," so that the end of the quatrain "leads us on little reflection to grasp the absence of that first premise." Thus the opening enthymeme of *HSLittle* "fulfilled its end of provoking a picture of Donne's condition as racially common without his ever having stated its presuppositions" (126). See also *HSLittle*: Language and Style.

1–2 *I ame . . . an Angelique Spright,* **LEWES** (1838) confirms the legitimacy of the microcosm-macrocosm metaphor and exclaims: "Thus tersely and finely does Donne express it" (376). **WHITE** (1936) quotes these lines as an example of Donne's "extraordinary capacity for self-observation" (127). See also Holy Sonnets: The Poet/ Persona. **LOUTHAN** (1951) observes that Donne "never fails to utilize a potential relationship between the microcosm and the macrocosm" (174). **MATSUURA** (1953): the soul, which during life is only an "angelic spirit," upon death becomes equal to celestial beings (11). **BOTTRALL** (1958): despite advances in science and medicine the medieval view of "the relation of the soul to the body and of man to the cosmos" persisted into the seventeenth century (17). **SLOANE** (1981) notes that equating the physical world with the human body "had its roots in the concept of a correspondence between the macrocosm and the microcosm" and points to Nicolson's observation (1950) that "when Harvey first described the human circulatory system he did so by comparing it to evaporation and rain" (66).

1 *I ame a litle World, made cunningly* RAMSAY (1917): the line reflects Donne's adherence to the Paracelsian concept of the microcosm and the macrocosm (275). WAGNER (1947): the divine message of Donne's poetry is that there is "a world, a home, inside each of us" and that we must "descend into ourselves to save ourselves" (256). NICOLSON (1950) quotes the line to introduce her argument that to seventeenth-century writers man *was* a little world," a microcosm of the larger one, made up like it of four elements (1). SMITH (1971) notes that the metaphor is a "Renaissance commonplace" (626). Similarly, Crennan (1979, 20) and Booty (1990, 109). BARAŃCZAK (1984): the conviction that man is a microcosm belonged to the Renaissance *loci communes* (161). PATRIDES (1985a) joins others in noting that "man was habitually said to be the microcosm or 'abridgment' of the universe" and points to *Har* 110 (437).

1 *cunningly* MARTZ (1963): "skillfully" (85). RUOFF (1972): "skillfully and with purpose" (913). [Similarly, Lever (1974, 182).] DIPASQUALE (1994): the word "evokes a connection between the poetic activity of the poet's 'Angelike' spirit and the divinely-inspired and commissioned work of the craftsmen chosen to make the cloth of the tabernacle, which is to be adorned with 'broidred' cherubim" (Exod. 26.1). Cf. the Geneva Bible's marginal gloss ("of moste conning of fine worke") and the King James translation ("with cherubim of cunning work shalt thou make them") (414n22).

2 *Of Elements and an Angelique Spright,* MELTON (1906): Donne often repeats the same sound in successive stressed and unstressed syllables (156). EMPSON (1935): the two words "Elements" and "Spright," reflecting "spirit and body, correspond to the day and night of the imagined globe, a fine case of the fusion of body and soul which Donne often attempts" (76). ADAMS (1962): "Both body and soul— the former made of 'elements,' the latter 'angelic sprite' (spirit)" (784). SMITH (1971): "matter and spirit. The four elements of material substance are coupled with an angel-like intelligence or soul" (626). [Similarly, Craik and Craik (1986, 277).]

2 *Elements* WARNKE (1967): "the four humours, of which man was believed to be composed" (272). PATRIDES (1985a): "the traditional four (earth, water, air, fire)" (437). [So also, Booty (1990, 109).]

2 *Angelique Spright,* COFFIN and WITHERSPOON (1946): "Spirit" (33). [So also, Martz (1963, 85), Patrides (1985a, 437), and Booty (1990, 109).] MATSURRA (1949) cites the phrase to identify the soul which in *SecAn* enters the final stage of its journey through the Ptolemaic universe to Heaven (138–39). LEVER (1974): the "indwelling spirit," corresponding in the speaker's "little world" to the angels "in the empyrean or highest sphere of the macrocosm" (182).

3–4 *But blacke sinne . . . must dy.* **LINVILLE** (1984b): "the absence of an end-stop becomes a figure of the endless, the eternal, of unbounded time" (76).

4 *My Worlds . . . must dy.* **ANSARI** (1974): this line ends "with the conviction that man's body and soul are in a state of perdition"; "must" implies a "certain degree of inevitability about extinction," but the last line of the sonnet changes this despair to hope (147).

4 *Oh* **SHAW** (1981): the sigh "seems to comprise both wonder at the noble intricacy of man, the crown of creation, and horror at his imminent dissolution." Donne has succeeded in "reversing" the "rhetoric of humanism, the figure of man as microcosm," which "can lend itself to statements of extraordinary optimism about man's innate powers and apparent potentiality" (47).

4 *both parts* **SHAABER** (1958): "body and spirit" (101). [Similarly, Patrides (1985a, 437).] **SHAWCROSS** (1967): "his soul and his body, which contains his 'Angelike spright'"; cf. 1 Cor. 6.19: "know ye not that your body is the temple of the Holy Ghost which is in you" (347). [Similarly, Booty (1990, 109).]

4 *must dy.* **PATRIDES** (1985a): "a potentially dangerous notion, since the soul is immortal" (437).

5–9 *You, . . . be drown'd no more:* **COFFIN** (1937), quoting these lines, suggests that speculation about the nature of space among intellectuals and astronomers of the time—Copernicus, Digges, Bruno, Galileo, and Kepler—influenced Donne's thought and poetry (185–86). **GRANSDEN** (1954): Donne "puts secular passions to divine use," here recalling "the world of tears" of his love poems (130–31). **NICOLSON** (1956): "Donne does not hesitate to suggest the existence of other worlds, though without theological implications" (55). **ADAMS** (1962): "Donne asks the astronomers and explorers to find new oceans for tears to weep or waters to wash away his sins" (784). **ANSARI** (1974): these lines suggest "the effect of widening the limits of exploration," with l. 5 pointing to "the state of knowledge that was possessed till then." The "mighty tides of acquisition made possible now are employed in order to highlight his own predicament at the moment" (146). **CAREY** (1981) finds that though the Holy Sonnets are indebted to St. Ignatius Loyola's *Spiritual Exercises*, Donne is also capable of modifying them. Notes that Ignatius recommends that the contemplation of Christ's passion include a request for "grief, tears, and pain in union with Christ in torment," but here Donne's petition is not so much "self-abasing or lachrymose" but a "vast gesture of despair at his own aridity and unresponsiveness" (50). **DIPASQUALE** (1994): the lines address "the saints, the heroes of the Church Triumphant," as well as "heroic Renaissance scientists and explorers." However, the speaker follows a "false lead" by asking "those who have traveled beyond the old world to supply him with water drawn from the oceans they have discovered; for the saints have not yet seen the 'new heavens and new earth' which will be fired into being at the end of time." Indeed, "only the words of the divine author Himself can provide an escape from the typological cul-de-sac that the human sonneteer has constructed for himself" (409).

5–7 *You, . . . in myne eyes,* **HIEATT** (1987): "Those who have invented new heavenly spheres beyond the supposed outermost one of the universe (the macrocosm) or have discovered new earthly regions are invited to pour new seas into the microcosm, or little world, of the speaker" (241).

5–6 *You, . . . new Lands can wright* **GROSART** (1872–73): "It is not clear whether the Poet means astronomers, or, as is more probable, those discoverers who have found new lands beyond the equator" (2.290). **GARDNER** (1952) questions Coffin's suggestion (1937—see *HSLittle*: Date and Circumstances) that the reference to "new Sphears" and "new Lands" in l. 6 was influenced by Galileo's *Sidereus Nuncius*, published in 1610. She doubts that "a precise meaning can be given to these words," citing earlier astronomers, Ptolemy, Alphonsus of Castile, and Copernicus, who had postulated new spheres. She thinks "it is more likely he is calling on discoverers generally; astronomers who find new spheres and explorers who find new lands" (75–76). **MARTZ** (1963): referring to the "astronomical controversies of Donne's time, when the theory of the Ptolemaic universe, with its concentric spheres, was being questioned, altered, and rejected" (85). **WARNKE** (1967): "a reference to the new astronomers" (273). **KERMODE** (1968): new spears "added to the original eight in an attempt to explain the heavenly motions otherwise unaccounted for" (182). **LEWALSKI and SABOL** (1973): "a reference either to the newly discovered immensity of the universe or to the efforts of the Ptolemaic astronomers to save the appearances by adding new spheres and new motions" (158). **LEVER** (1974): "Those who, rejecting the Copernican system, posit spheres beyond the traditional nine" as, for example, the Jesuit mathematician Clavius (182). **CRENNAN** (1979): the lines point to Donne's awareness "of the great changes around him—the discovery and exploration of the New World, the changing models of the universe, the daily facts of life," which "are all eagerly seized upon in the poetry" (5). **PATRIDES** (1985a) says that the lines refer to "the celestial regions observed telescopically by Galileo, but perhaps the suspected plurality of worlds too" and cites Coffin (1937) (437). **ELLRODT** (1993), noting that *HSLittle* was written after the discoveries of Galileo, observes that the plurality of worlds was a hypothesis circulated even before Galileo (455).

5 *You,* **SHAWCROSS** (1967): "Christ" (347). [So also, Booty (1990, 109).] **SMITH** (1971): "(a) recent astronomers; (b) the blessed, who have ascended to a heaven beyond our apprehension" (626). **CRAIK and CRAIK** (1986): "astronomers and geographical discoverers" (277).

5 *that heauen, which was most high* **SMITH** (1971): "what men formerly took to be the extent of heaven" (626).

6 *new Sphears,* **EMPSON** (1957) finds "sphere" to be an "ambiguity" in this poem, adding that the "converted" Donne initially "reflected on his old idea of the sepa-

rate planet, as an escape from the Christian Hell," and then wrote *HSLittle* "specifically to renounce this heresy" (374). Also finds that in the image of ll. 5–6 "Copernicanism puts Heaven further off" (380). **SHAABER** (1958): "those added to the Ptolemaic system by later astronomers" (101). **SMITH** (1971) glosses "new Sphears" and "new lands" as "(a) the discoveries of recent astronomy; (b) the true domains of heaven, unimagined by us here below" (626). **PATRIDES** (1985a) cites the reference to "spheres" in *LovGrow* 23, noting that these are the "transparent, 'pure' spheres in which the planets were thought to be embedded" and that they were "concentrique" (*LovGrow* 24) to the earth (437). **CAREY** (1990b): "Ptolemy had added a ninth sphere, the Primum Mobile, beyond the fixed stars; later astronomers posited tenth and eleventh spheres" (455).

6 *new Lands* **LEWALSKI and SABOL** (1973): "a reference either to the new lands of the moon seen through Galileo's telescope, or to the various new lands terrestrial explorers found" (158). **LEVER** (1974): "Notably in the Americas and Indies" (182).

7–14 *Powre . . . in eating heale.* **SLOANE** (1981) observes that after Donne describes himself as "'a little world made cunningly,' divided that world into flesh and spirit, and indicated that both parts must die because sin has betrayed them, he expands on and complicates the globe image" in the closing eight lines (68). Notes that although tears and globes were recurring images in the emblematic tradition, Donne, subjecting them "to the meditating mind of the metaphysical poet," places the tears and globes "in new relationships," so that "the eyes become so large that they can contain seas which can either wash or drown his world," and even confers on them the "possibility that an emblematic globe could be subjected to—burning" (68–69).

7–9 *Powre . . . be drown'd no more:* **WILLIAMSON** (1931) compares the "deluge" image to similar figures in *ValWeep, Noct,* and *SecAn* to argue that Donne extended "the sensibility of poetry in his time," making it possible to raise "passion to the level of vision" (162–63). See also *HSLittle*: Sacred and Profane.

7–8 *Powre . . . my weeping ernestly.* **RICHTER** (1902): the lines are an example of "irregular meter" ("doppelte Taktumstellung") (395). **UL-HASAN** (1958): the comparison of tears to the sea implies a kinship between the turmoil of "the human soul and a stormy sea" (31). **LEVER** (1974): "In the microcosm tears become *new seas,* and weeping earnestly suggests a new Flood to *Drown my world*" (182). **DIPASQUALE** (1994): the speaker of *HSLittle* "may feel the need for 'new seas' to be poured into his eyes" because he feels, as does the speaker of *HSSighs,* that he had previously "spent" (*HSSighs* 2) all of his tears when he "mourn'd in vaine" (*HSSighs* 4) as "an idolatrous lover" (412n5).

7 *Powre* **BOOTY** (1990): "pour'" (109).

7 *new Seas* **SMITH** (1971) says that these are "heavenly seas yielding penitential tears, instead of the terrestrial seas which supplied his amorous grief," and notes

that Renaissance cosmographers "conjectured that there is a region of seas in the heavens beyond the fixed stars, the 'waters above the firmament'" as stated in Gen. 1.7 (626).

8–9 *Drowne . . . washe* EMPSON (1935): the distinction between the two words raises the question whether the soul is to be drowned as well (76).

9–14 *Or . . . in eating heale.* MILWARD and ISHII (1976): Donne recalls God's promise to Noah (Gen. 9.11) not to destroy the earth again by flood and also thinks of the use of water for washing or baptism (cf. also *Devotions*, Meditation 19). Thinking about the flood whose destruction he escapes leads him to consider the fire that will consume the world in the end. Cf. 2 Pet. 3.7–12, 1 Cor. 3.13–15, and *Devotions*, Meditation 10 (414).

9–10 *Or . . . alas the fyer* GARDNER (1952): cf. the promise to Noah (Gen. 9.9–17), and the belief derived from 2 Pet. 3 "that the world would end in fire" (76). [Similarly, Martz (1969a, 81), Ansari (1974, 146), and Hieatt (1987, 241).] SMITH (1971) notes the "widely held" belief that "the world would end either in a new flood or by fire" (627).

9 *Or . . . drown'd no more:* COFFIN and WITHERSPOON (1946) point to Gen. 9.11 and the "Divine promise" that the earth "will not again be destroyed by a flood" (33). Similarly, Spencer (1952, 430), Adams (1962, 784), Lewalski and Sabol (1973, 158), who add that the promise to Noah "supported the belief in the final destruction of the world by fire," Bergman and Epstein (1983, 353), Patrides (1985a, 437), Craik and Craik (1986, 277), and Booty (1990, 109).

10–14 *But . . . which doth in eating heale.* GARDNER (1952): "As often, Donne abandons an extended parallel for a contrast. The fires of lust and envy, unlike earthly fires, have not purged, but made him 'fouler.' The fire he prays for, unlike the fire which will destroy the world, will 'in eating heale'" (76). ANSARI (1974): these lines express an alchemical metaphor: the "body-soul complex, instead of being washed, stands in need of purification by burning," not the fire of lust and envy which is destructive but the fire of zeal or piety which is truly purgative (146). DICKSON (1987) finds these lines connecting "the promise to regenerate the macrocosm by fire with the speaker's sacramental participation in the double baptism of fire and water" (269).

10–11 *But . . . burnt it hertofore* HARDING (1951) finds this to be Donne's "rather conventional" expression of his sense of inadequacy (429).

10 *But oh . . . burn'd;* COFFIN and WITHERSPOON (1946): "That is, at the Day of Judgment." Cf. 2 Peter 3.5–7 [so also, Booty (1990, 109) and Carey (1990b, 455)] (33). SHAABER (1958): "by the fire expected in the end to destroy the world"; cf. *HSRound* 5 (101). [Similarly, Craik and Craik (1986, 277).] LEVER (1974): "Individual punishment in hell flames was a 'correspondence' to the future destruction of the world by fire" (182).

11 *hertofore* **GRIERSON** (1912): "hitherto" (2:232).

11 *Lust and Envy* **GRIERSON** (1912): in the reference to "Lust" Donne "thinks mainly of his youth," in the reference to "Envy," "his years of suitorship at Court" (2:232).

12 *fouler;* **CRAIK and CRAIK** (1986): "uglier (because the *fire*—here twofold, hence the plural verb *have*—of lust and envy has blackened it)" (277).

13–14 *And . . . which doth in eating heale.* **EMPSON** (1935) paraphrases the lines: "You, by our eating of you, heal me, and heal your house; your house, in eating you, heals itself; you, by eating with the fires of hell lust and envy, your house, by eating with the fires of Smithfield such heresies as are at the back of my mind, heal me" (76). **COFFIN and WITHERSPOON** (1946) point to Ps. 69.9: "For the zeal of thine house hath eaten me up" (76). So also, Gardner (1952, 76), Spencer (1952, 430), Shaaber (1958, 101), Adams (1962, 784), who notes that the passage "involves three sorts of flame—those of the Last Judgment; those of lust and envy; and those of zeal, which alone heal," Martz (1963, 86), Shawcross (1967, 347), Warnke (1967, 273), Patrides (1985a, 437), Craik and Craik (1986, 278), Hieatt (1987, 241), and Booty (1990, 110). **MROCZKOWSKI** (1981) reads these final two lines as an example of Donne's capacity to be reasonably simple and straightforward (219).

13 *And . . . a fiery Zeale* **MELTON** (1906): an insignificant word, here "with," often carries the stress in Donne's meter (79). **MORRIS** (1953): the image of God burning his will into Man's soul is to be found also in Hopkins's "The Wreck of the Deutschland" (1:5–8) (76–77).

14 *Of thee,'and . . . heale.* **SHAWCROSS** (1967): "which by consuming me restores me; which by my partaking of the Eucharist (the body and blood of Christ, constituting His house) nullifies my black sins. In the background may be a phoenix-like resurrection" (347). **DELANY** (1970): in addition to Psalm 69.9 see James 5.3 ("Your gold and silver is cankred, and the rust of them shal be a witnesse against you, and shall eate your flesh, as it were fire" [Geneva version]). Also, the angel in Revelation warns of the "eating fires" to come. The resolution of the poem comes from the union of "fire" and "zeal" since one kind of fire will consume those guilty of greed and lust by eating their flesh, while another kind, the fire of zeal, will heal the sinner and prepare him for resurrection (7). **CLARK** (1982) notes with approval the "meaningful ambiguity" identified by Shawcross (1967)—that "eating" can be read as either passive ("being eaten") or active (as a reference to partaking of the Eucharist, "Christ's house or tabernacle") and points to the kenosis of Phil. 2.6–8 and the opening of John. Concludes that "through this ambiguous syntax Donne is reinforcing the affirmation that faith leads to salvation by accenting a Christian paradox inherent in the neotypological structure of the poem" (77–78).

14 *thy house,* **LEVER** (1974): "God's temple, located in man's body" (182).

14 *eating* **LEVER** (1974): "Consuming with fire" (182).

 *HSMade*

General Commentary

In an eighteenth-century Moravian Brethren's hymn-book (*A Collection of Hymns*) (1754 [1966, 19–20]), four Holy Sonnets—*HSMade, HSDue, HSSpit,* and *HSWhat*—are used, slightly altered, and combined to make up hymn number 383.

Lofft (1813, n.p.) includes Donne in a group of poets who have, with respect to the sonnet, "eminently contributed to its Dignity and Beauty, or that of the *Quatuorzain,*" and prints *HSMade, ED,* and *SB.*

The anonymous author of an article on Donne in *The Leisure Hour* (1864, 557) comments briefly on the poetry and prints *HSMade,* observing that in it Donne "expresses the conflicts of his soul."

MacDonald (1868, 121–23), both praising and criticizing the Holy Sonnets, quotes in full *HSMade, HSSouls,* and *HSDeath,* describing them as "very fine" (121).

Gosse (1899, 2:107) says of *HSMade* that "[r]arely was the natural language of the heart sustained so long by Donne in his verse as in this noble sonnet."

Sinclair (1909, 197) praises the poem as one of a number of sonnets "of remarkable beauty from Donne in a later life and graver mood."

Gransden (1954, 128) describes *HSBlack, HSMade,* and *HSScene* as "rather sombre" sonnets that present a poet seeking "strength, grace, and forgiveness from Christ."

Rawlinson (1968, 105–13) states that in *HSMade* Donne, "obviously in middle or advancing age, and no longer with the optimism of youth, feels acutely aware of his own weakness, his inability to lead the good life without God's help" (105). The sonnet, he says, could only have been written by a man at a particular time of life: Donne feels the onset of physical decay, Rawlinson contends, and he fears approaching death and possible extinction. He writes that Donne is trapped between his despair, that is, his sense of guilt for past pleasures, and his fear of death, and both are too terrible to contemplate (112). Further, Rawlinson notes, the language of *HSMade* enacts its meaning in us: "we recreate for ourselves his moment of paralysed panic" (112). Rawlinson argues that there is a downward movement in the octave, which is replaced by an upward movement in the sestet, as the "inrush of life and hope into a feeble ageing man" becomes evident. The sonnet is "incomparably vehement," he concludes, Donne's prayer "desperately urgent" (112–13).

Schwartz (1968, 351–54) argues that once we have grasped the literal meaning of HSMade we may then understand the poem as a dynamic image, that of a terri-fied man engaged in fervent prayer (351). He observes that as the fictive prayer unfolds, we discern the spiritual "movement" of the speaker's soul, the action which the poem imitates (354). The speaker, he says, "moves" from the desperation of the opening lines to a recognition of his sinfulness and helplessness without grace, to an awareness of God's saving power, to chastened humility. The poem, he contends, is thus "a fictive prayer which 'actually' works" (354).

Stampfer (1970, 267–69) believes that the opening couplet of HSMade makes the entire passage not a sudden, shocking experience but a vivid set-piece (267–68). Stampfer contends that Donne's despair is rhetorical: the changes in direction in the poem, he says, are "the strokes of an orator, not the shifts of a wayward spirit" (268). Donne's earlier confessional sonnets, Stampfer remarks, read as poignant dra-matic monologues; here, however, they are altogether static, carefully shaped offer-ings of prayer. Stampfer notes that the poem suggests the resurrection of the body. The dualistic Donne could, he says, "consign the body to the grave, and remain with his soul." But the resurrection of the body, Stampfer argues, gives the flesh a gravity toward heaven, counteracted by sin weighing it toward hell (269).

White and Rosen (1972, 51) say that the dominant image in HSMade is taken from science: the "iron heart" combines the literal and metaphorical force of "iron." The iron heart is by its own sin drawn down toward hell, they note, and the poet implores God's grace to act as a more powerful magnet by drawing it toward heaven instead.

Pollock (1973, 524) argues that the essence of Donne's HSMade is that "God has *not* seized possession of the self and will." But Pollock sees Donne as wishing that God might do so.

Bellette (1975, 334–41) writes that the idea of Christ on the cross affects the form of HSMade, HSScene and HSRound, and notes that these three sonnets may be read as forming a sequence "depicting . . . the transition from this world to the next" (334). In these texts, Bellette says, the conventional form is not subverted and the final couplet "assumes its true and traditional weight" (335). He writes that these three Holy Sonnets all begin "in conflict and disjointed time, reflected in unsubor-dinated and antithetical grammatical structures" and that "all three at the end find a new orderliness of grace" (337). Bellette believes that the "general structure of the Christ-centered sonnets" is best understood in the "movement from a specific ques-tion or object of contemplation to a final statement of a general and enclosing truth" (341). He notes that this truth is implicit at the beginning of the poem and only awaits full development. In these poems, when fragmentation does occur, he says, it is "contained within a strong subordinating grammatical order which corresponds naturally to the lines of the quatrain" (341).

Granqvist (1975, 51) says that Lofft (1813) "reluctantly inserted" HSMade into his *Laura; or, An Anthology of Sonnets.*

Brink (1977, 101) says that in HSMade and HSDue Donne appeals to "the pro-creating father as well as the Father in heaven to lift the guilt of a misspent erotic life."

Bond (1981, 26–33) thinks that in the Holy Sonnets Donne frequently "crammed so many implications into a sonnet that an explicator must resort to very expansive critical reading in order fully to understand them" (26). For example, Bond believes that Martz's analysis (1954) of HSMade and its indebtedness to Fray Luis de Granada's *Of Prayer and Meditation* (1612) (see Genre and Traditions and notes to ll. 1–9) "does not sufficiently recognize that the poem is more than a meditation on the imminence of death and the subsequent effects of that fact on the speaker" or that it is "a statement of how God's power overcomes death and of how that assurance affects the speaker" (26–27). According to Bond, Martz "attributes too much importance" to "fear and terror" by "failing to distinguish between contrition and attrition" (33n5). Bond shows also that although the pattern of the sonnet seems close to 2 Cor. 4, it "adumbrates a variety of doctrinal commonplaces within the sonnet's little rooms" (28). Bond finds that despite "the poem's sense of urgency and immediacy" HSMade responds to what Donne in a sermon calls "the whole compasse of Time, Past, Present and Future" (*Sermons*, VII: 53), for the speaker begins "with Creation, moves to a point where an eschatological 'end' is imminent, and then rises above the moment of final judgment in the sestet" (28). Bond sees this "conjunction of the personal crisis with the 'grand design of God'" as suggesting a "typological organization for the poem," pointing to Donne's use of the "notion of three 'births' that he was fond of engaging as a doctrinal framework," namely, *per generationem, per regenerationem* and *per resurrectionem*" (28). The movement of the sonnet thus traces the speaker's inability to look up and contemplate heaven in the octave, reflecting his "sorry sense of defeat" and an "'irreligious dejection of spirit' [*Sermons*, 7:243–44] that deepens the depths into which he has fallen" to a point in the sestet where the persona is "rising again" (30–31). Bond emphasizes that the important point is that "God's generosity is exclusively responsible for man's ability to become a regenerated, re-created man," for the word "onely" at the beginning of the sestet "limits, and thus defines, the mercy made manifest in the resolution of the poem" (31). Thus, according to Bond, the sonnet "achieves more than an articulation of the doctrine of grace: it dramatizes the speaker's misguided use of the doctrine in order to trace reflexively, within the poem itself, the regenerative workings of grace within the human soul" (33).

Mackenzie (1990, 77) finds HSMade to be the "finest" of the Holy Sonnets, as it "moulds the experience of instability towards the beautiful interplay of its close," where, according to Mackenzie, the "flutter of hope" in line 13 is "overborne by the assurance" of the final line.

Ray (1990b, 322–24) finds that the speaker questions God concerning his apparent neglect and does so with words of urgency "because he feels that his death ('mine end') is rapidly coming" (322–23). The sestet, Ray suggests, "poses the solution for God's urgent consideration," while also shifting the imagery from a dismal downward-looking motif to one involving looking up toward God and heaven." In his ability to turn toward God, Ray emphasizes, "the speaker becomes optimistic" (323). The speaker recognizes that he "cannot save himself after succumbing so entirely to sin" and must "depend on God's grace to rescue him" (323). In the final line of the sonnet, Ray notes, "God becomes like a magnet ('adamant') that attracts the heavy iron (the sin) that is weighing the sinner down toward hell" (323–24).

Date and Order

According to Gransden (1954, 127–28), HSBlack, HSMade, and HSScene probably refer to Donne's illness in 1608, not that in 1623.

Grove (1984, 67) proposes that, in considering the order of the Holy Sonnets, HSMade is "surely placed first in its group because the undeclared image around which it forms is that of the hour-glass," similar to what is found on the writing desks of "saint or penitent or holy man" in various contemporary portraits, and thus there is at the beginning of these poems a "*memento mori*" on "sin, death, and the Last Things to be ever remembered."

The Poet/Persona

Fausset (1924, 241) reads the poem as an example of Donne's "personal veracity," his admission of the "flaws and fluctuations of his nature." Terrified of "Despair behind" and "Death before," Fausset continues, he considers his youth as "God's picture marred," and even finds remorse a sin "because it perpetuates the discord which he would resolve."

Praz (1925, 66–67) observes that Donne is afraid of death because he believes himself not yet worthy of salvation.

Leishman (1934, 88) notes that Donne rarely achieves a "mood of perfect joy and security" and that HSMade, like almost all his sonnets, is a record of his struggle with the sin of fear.

Schirmer (1937, 299) finds the poem an expression of passionately troubled self-examination.

Grierson (1948, 313) quotes the poem in full to illustrate Donne's desire to be penitent for his sensuous, ambitious nature, a desire countered "by something stubborn in his own heart that only the spirit of God can relax."

Spörri-Sigel (1949, 72) finds in the first line an expression of the bitterness of dying and the terror of death. For Donne, she continues, death comes as a consequence of sin; for him all happiness is in the past and the future holds only the terror of death.

Blanch (1974, 479) writes that Donne is a "victim of spiritual paralysis" when a movement towards God and light is "demanded," and "only through the grace of God may the poet aspire to the *visio pacis*."

Schmidt (1980, 144) states that HSMade gives us "a vision of a man hemmed in before and behind, and like Faust weighed downward by his own sin," with God functioning as "a magnet drawing him to heaven." Schmidt compares the sonnet to the love poems, wherein "emotion—in this case fear born of a sense of unworthiness—is a stimulant to thought," the effect of which is to accentuate the speaker's egotism. The extremity of the emotion "transcends," in Schmidt's view, "its poetic bounds."

Carey (1981, 52–53) questions Martz's (1954) reading of the sonnet (see Genre and Traditions), namely, that the octave deliberately arouses feelings of despair, which the sestet repels "by confidence in God's grace" (52). Carey instead finds that the "relief" Donne expresses in the opening ten lines is undercut by Satan, the "subtle foe" of humankind, who "ensure[s] that this relief is temporary" (52–53). It is true, according to Carey, that for Donne "Grace may wing me to prevent his art" (l. 13), but Donne remains unsure that God ultimately will redeem him (53).

Stachniewski (1981, 699–700) contends that the question posed in the first line is not "an idle one assuming a negative reply." The sonnet continues in a despairing voice, according to Stachniewski, expressing Donne's "feeling that sin is weighing him down towards hell" (699). Stachniewski cites Martz's reading of the sonnet (1954) (see Genre and Traditions) in which he contends that in the sestet Donne "repels" the thoughts of sin and hell expressed in the octave, "by confidence in God's grace." Stachniewski, however, finds that Donne is "so strongly tempted by the devil to despair" that he "cannot sustain himself for one hour," and moreover, he argues that the verb "may" (l. 13) is "consistent with the other examples of Donne's sense of being at God's mercy" (700).

Harman (1982, 42–43, 217–19) finds that the speakers in Donne's religious poetry regard "privacy" as both "isolating and threatening," and thus turn to speech as "a way of insisting upon one's presence in a world that seems far more hospitable to death and disappearance" (42). Harman cites HSMade as an example of a sonnet in which a speaker, who, as long as he can continue to speak, "can 'sustaine' himself another hour (l. 12)—or perhaps long enough to clarify the terms for escape from an annihilating present" (43). Here, and in HSBatter, according to Harman, we have a speaker "as he appears prior to and in the absence of relationship, where relationship would at once save, and annihilate, the self as we know it" (218–19n). In neither poem, in Harman's view, does the speaker "portray the self *in relationship* to God" (219n).

Van Emden (1986, 53) sees the poet "weighed down" by the imminence of death and despair, as "the forcing of words into the confined space of a five-stress line (as at l. 8) suggests a rising panic." With the turn at the ninth line, however, Van Emden identifies the return of hope, with the "double significance" of "only": "God alone is above" and "only God Who is above." And yet, she concludes that the recognition that hope comes from the grace of God rather than from his own doing appears insufficient for the poet on at least an emotional level.

Rollin (1986, 143–44) describes the speaker here as "all but catatonic": "I dare not move my dimme eyes any way" (l. 5); "not one houre I can my self sustaine" (l. 12) (143–44). Moreover, in Rollin's view, the speaker "reduces himself to an artifact": "Thou hast made me" (l. 1); "thy worke" (l. 1); "Repaire me" (l. 2). Rollin adds that "if he is man, he is a hollow man, 'feebled flesh,' or he is but a sack of sin, wholly dependent on outside forces to prevent his plummet into hell" (144). In Rollin's view, HSBatter presents an analogous situation.

Strier (1989, 377) finds that HSMade, like HSLittle, "build[s] to images of redemptive violence," while avoiding the "incoherence and sophistry" evident in other Holy Sonnets with respect to the question of salvation. Furthermore, according to Strier, the sestet "makes it clear that the conception of sin in this poem concerns the whole person," rather than simply the physical self, and that "God is truly a solution here." For Strier, "the Reformation position leads to precision and humility, not to incoherence or unacknowledged puzzlement."

Fish (1990, 241–42) examines HSMade in relation to the exercise of power that he finds elsewhere in Donne's poetry (241), arguing that the poem is, in a significant way, "simply a rewriting" of *ElNat*, a poem that might itself be titled "I have made you, and shall *my* work decay?" (241–42). Fish contends that both poems have a structure in which "masochism (and now sado-masochism) is elevated to a principle and glorified," in *ElNat* "in the name of a frankly secular power," in *HSMade* "in the name of a power that is (supposedly) divine." For Fish, the fact that Donne "now assumes the posture of a woman" and (like the church of *HSShow*) "spreads his legs (or cheeks)" is important, but there is no significant change "in his attitude toward women and power," but rather an indication of "how strongly that attitude informs a poetry whose center is supposedly elsewhere." Fish adds that "even as Donne casts himself in the female role, he betrays an inability to maintain that role in the face of a fierce and familiar desire to be master of his self, even of a self whose creaturely nature he is in the process of acknowledging" (242).

Genre and Traditions

Martz (1954, 132) argues that the poem reflects the meditative practices of Scupoli's *Spiritual Combat*. In the octave, he observes, Donne arouses a sense of terror and despair at the thought of sin, death, and hell, and then in the sestet repels such sentiments through confidence in God's Grace. See more under Holy Sonnets: Genre and Traditions.

Raspa (1983, 154) regards the sonnet as "an example of the transformation of a genre by paradox." The opening three lines of the sonnet, Raspa emphasizes, are a sequence of three paradoxes, and "all three of their propositions were theologically impossible to Donne as well as to his first readers." Raspa claims that "from such theological impossibilities there sprang all the force of Donne's paradoxes reflecting the exigencies of the Christian mythological universe for which his theology spoke."

Structure, Language, and Style

De la Mare (1913, 376) quotes the poem in full to illustrate that throughout Donne's life "the same bare, emotional directness is apparent," from *Canon* to the Holy Sonnets. "Reading him," de la Mare continues, "we do not throw off the world; we are not, as by a miracle, made innocent and happy."

Simon (1952, 120–22) observes that the structure of the sonnet is based on "the organic development of the theme." Verbal relationships are important in the juxtaposition of death and Grace, and the way in which decay, death, and despair are "gathered in *sin* and *weigh*." She also finds important the implied physical forces, driving the speaker onward, imprisoning him, and weighing him down, all of which are defeated by the power of Grace over nature so that the spirit rises, wings, and is drawn (ll. 10, 13, 14). Further, Simon argues that the contrasts between different parts of the poem suggest the spiritual struggle under way, the forces rushing toward death, the paralysis of fear, and wasting flesh countered by the spirit rising and being drawn by Grace (120–21). She concludes that the dramatic impact of the poem arises from the image in the octave of "the poet struggling, which creates an impression of breathless expectancy" (122). See also *HSMade*: Themes and Holy Sonnets: Themes.

Esch (1955, 47) finds that the Italian structure suits well the theme, where expressions of despair, death, and sin in the octave contrast with the image of a gracious and forgiving God in the sestet. See also Holy Sonnets: Genre and Traditions.

Stull (1982a, 87–90) finds that HSMade is an example of the new "plain style" of the sonnet—that is, "intellectual, dynamic, and often self-consciously difficult . . . meditative, aimed at self-persuasion" and distinguished by "freedom—in subject matter and form"—that succeeded "the decline of Petrarchism at the end of the sixteenth century" (87–88). HSMade, according to Stull, resembles "Attic" usage in that the "language is colloquial," the words "mostly monosyllables of native origin," and with the "personal intimacy of a versed letter" (89). Donne also keeps "the caesura in his lines free-moving," subordinating "meter to meaning," and using metaphor sparingly (89). Stull adds that even though Donne's references to Biblical passages are perhaps less obvious than in earlier moral and religious sonnets by Gascoigne, Barnes, Breton and Lok, they nevertheless are "pervasive" (89). In HSMade, for example, "the image of the frightened sinner pursued by Satan but afraid of God [ll. 5–7]" points us to two biblical archetypes: the first is "Jonah's flight from God," the second "the parable of the Prodigal Son," which is "an allegory of forgiveness and redemption" (89). According to Stull, unlike earlier sonneteers such as Lok or Drummond, only Donne realizes "the full meaning" of the biblical archetypes, which, for Donne, are "parables of regeneration and grace" (90).

Skulsky (1992, 112–14, 264–65) focuses on the "diversionary littera" in the Holy Sonnets, where the speaker undertakes "a hysterical effort to deceive the Undeceivable" (112); in other words, it is as if Donne is "trying to put off the pronouncement of sentence with a nonstop filibuster, knowing that at any moment a rap of the gavel will silence him for good," and so "his only hope is to divert the judge in both senses of the word" (112). In HSMade, for example, the speaker's "religious panic takes the form of a nightmare chase in which the fugitive's escape is blocked at both ends of a corridor" (112). Donne's speaker, according to Skulsky, "tries to have it both ways," that is, "to tell the truth in language that will carry a falsehood to a superficial reader," but "the God he believes in is no such reader" (113). Skulsky notes that "unlike Donne, the speaker is no Calvinist," for "Calvin doesn't reduce justice to supremacy" (264n43). Thus, in Skulsky's view, "the speaker tries to equivocate to heaven, even though in the back of his mind he knows as well as Macbeth's Porter that the ploy is doomed" (114). Skulsky notes the Calvinistic tenor of Donne's view that "after receiving grace the sinner spontaneously 'cooperates' with God," and he adds that the "catch is that grace does all the work" (265n45).

Themes

Spörri-Sigel (1949, 86) observes that the tension in the poem is depicted in terms of "the medieval space conception of the below and above" ("der mittelalterlich-räumlichen Vorstellung eines Unten und Oben"). Donne, she argues, finds himself sinking toward Satan under the weight of his sins, realizing that only in looking up to God can he be released from Satan's power. Donne, she concludes, finds himself powerfully attracted to sin, like the moth to the flame, so much so that there is a question as to whether grace can ever destroy his connection to Satan.

Reeves (1952, 100) paraphrases the poem: "A grave and despairing appeal to God to sustain him as he feels death approaching."

Simon (1952, 117–20), in an extended explication of the poem, finds that like many of the Holy Sonnets it opens with an expostulation to God in which Donne "seems to be reproaching his Maker," builds to a climax with thoughts of fear and imprisonment, and then reverses as he "relinquishes the way of reason" (117). The poem opens, Simon argues, by raising "the question of God's purpose in creating man" and praying for help "now" since death impends. The implication is that there is some doubt as to who is responsible for his misery, God or himself. The second quatrain, Simon notes, emphasizes a "sense of vanity and helplessness," as the speaker "is reduced to complete inaction" by the "terror" of hell to which his sins are forcing him (118). In the third quatrain the thought of God causes him to look up "to the only light that breaks through the prison walls," but he is still enthralled to sin and cannot "sustaine" himself. Simon finds this "the real theme of the poem": a realiza-tion of "man's incapacity to help himself" and the need for Grace to defeat the "subtle foe." The final lines present the power of Grace to lift and draw the soul, defeating the forces of nature which weigh down the flesh in sin. The poem, Simon says, be-gins on a note of despair but "ends in Donne's confession of his utter reliance on God" (120).

Denonain (1956, 151–52) observes that the poet develops an argument by estab-lishing man's debt to God, and then in "a touch of blackmail" ("d'un leger chanter") Donne cries out indignantly that God has abandoned him to Satan.

Peterson (1959, 513) finds the poem both a "supplication" and a "confession," expressing the penitent's desire that he had not sinned. See also Holy Sonnets: Themes.

McGuire (1974, 67–68) says that HSMade is a "clear example of a poem com-posed in accordance with specific rules for a certain kind of prayer, the prayer of petition" (67). He notes that the order of the poem aligns "almost exactly" with the "foure things" advised by Elnathan Parr in Abba Father (3rd ed. 1611)—that is, a "description of God," "confession of faultinesse," an "acknowledgement of impotency," and a "craving thou desirest" (67–68).

Lewalski (1979, 266) links the first sonnet in the 1635 edition, HSMade, to the second sonnet, HSDue, which is the first sonnet in the 1633 edition. HSMade, ac-cording to Lewalski, "sounds the leitmotifs of the entire series—creation, decay, death, sin, reparation"—"graphically" presenting the "condition of anguish, terror, help-lessness and despair accompanying the conviction of sin and guilt which is the first effect of God's calling" and echoing Ps. 6.6–7.

Klinck (1981, 251) finds in several of the Holy Sonnets evidence of Donne's "trinitarianism," pointing out that the first line of HSMade "raises the issue of cre-ation" ("Thou hast made me") and the "need for re-creation" in the face of his impotence due to profound sinfulness. Here, in Klinck's view, Donne views "regen-eration as a threefold process, involving a re-making, a clarifying of 'vision,' and an infusion of love."

Shaw (1981, 49–50) argues that the speaker is "overwhelmingly conscious of the perils of his position," for "although the grace of God may draw his gaze upward, the temptations of the devil are always present to weigh him down" (49–50). In Shaw's words, God and the devil "inconclusively contend" for his heart (50).

Kamholtz (1982, 483–84), studying "how Donne's poems respond to and are subject to time," states that "time is one of the factors that imposes limits upon the working of Donne's mind" (483–84) and that HSMade illustrates Donne's view of time most clearly. Time, he notes, is a "hierarchical scale of value," and Donne thus must "ascend from his collapsing, mortal, horizontal experience where decaying things are subject to postlapsarian time and journey upwards toward God's eternal, intangible time" (484).

Low (1982, 72–73) observes that the conception of motion as understood in the old science, which the Renaissance inherited from Aristotle, typically has "moral and teleological implications" which are absent in the seventeenth century's shift to "a mechanical model of the universe" (72–73). The older model, according to Low, underlies the conception of motion in HSMade, wherein the speaker "admits to a deadly motion caused by sin and the fall: 'I runne to death, and death meets me as fast,'" but, "fortunately," Low adds, "grace initiates a counter-motion: 'Onely thou art above, and when towards thee/By thy leave I can looke, I rise againe'" (73).

Rissanen (1983, 44) finds HSMade reflective of Donne's "heavy existential anguish," noting the prominence of the "theme of death, decay and destruction" and arguing that this theme is "obviously the real cause of his anguish." Rissanen adds that in Donne's description of his state there is "only a very slight veneer of religious frame of reference," for he no longer tries to portray "the religious soul" so fully as he did in Lit.

Docherty (1986, 132–34) finds a recurring theme in Donne's Holy Sonnets, namely, "the turning of the face away from [the] 'reality' of a holy or spiritual ghost," a turning which is a "revolution." In HSMade, according to Docherty, the "turn" focuses on whether the speaker can "turn the face to the God who has 'gone,'" a God who exists now as a ghost. Docherty further suggests that throughout Donne's poetry human love of another person or love of God is "always the love of a 'ghost'" for the "object of desire has always 'gone'" (132). Thus, it is only through "the infidelities of inconstancy," in Docherty's view, that the speaker can "re-new, re-begin or re-present the contractual commitment to love" (132–33). Docherty finds that HSMade, among other subjects, is about "the construction of a cross," organized around "a 'crossing' or trafficking-point," and as such it focuses on "the relations between horizontality and verticality" (133). According to Docherty, the poem presents "an entropic decay of the speaker's horizons," but as in other of Donne's sonnets, there is a "turn," which "converts the horizontal into the vertical, thus generating the cross which informs both the poem and the 'identity' of its speaker." Docherty locates a similar organization—grounded in the resurrection—in Donne's Cross (134).

Stein (1986, 97–98) states that only the opening of HSMade has a "direct appeal" to God, for the remainder of the sonnet acts out "an indirect appeal." For Stein, "the prospect of death is but the emergent occasion and not the subject," for "'decay' does not refer to the physical condition, and 'Repaire'" (possibly calling up the "etymological sense of 'return home' (*repatriare*)") is a "near-equivalent to the 'Restore thine Image'" of *Goodf*. According to Stein's reading of the poem, "the prospect of death is the moment of time and action and is the essential element that releases the attributes that are acted out to demonstrate and support the appeal" (97), and he adds that the movements of death and the speaker toward each other "create so intense a pressure that the will is paralyzed," with the "stage of paralysis followed by despair" and leading to the "downward movement, the nadir of hell." Now, according to Stein, "only the rising, which he looks for and which, when had, is easily available, lies wholly outside his will as he brings his personal history up to date" (98).

Malpezzi (1987, 71–76) examines *HSMade* within the context of the "tropological level of allegory," a "pilgrimage through sacred time" that is a "journey not only to the spiritual past of humanity, but to the future as well" (71). *HSMade*, according to Malpezzi, "is just such a hierophantic progress, the memory's movement toward the apocalyptic revelation," in "the speaker's imaginative rush toward death and judgment." Donne thus "translates his reader from the profane to the sacred, providing in his speaker a model for the internalization of the Christian Psychostasis, the weighing of the souls of the dead" (72). Donne's speaker, according to Malpezzi, "flanked by death and despair," thus "complains of his 'dimme eyes' (l. 5) and his 'feebled flesh,' flesh wasted by sin that also weighs it toward hell (ll. 7–8)." The speaker, Malpezzi notes, "finds himself running toward death," but there is also "stasis," as the speaker feels "frozen, paralyzed" (cf. ll. 5–7) (73). Malpezzi summarizes the "paradigmatic journey": in the first section of the poem, as "the decaying speaker envisions his death," he moves toward the "sacred time of judgment," yet as he is "plummeted toward hell," God answers his "prayer for renewal, for recreation," and grants him "reparation of his vision." Thus, Malpezzi concludes, "despair, a type of spiritual blindness, is, for the time, remedied, and he now looks with hope to the Lord" (74). Nonetheless, she says, Donne's speaker "realizes that his eternal destiny hangs in the balance throughout his temporal existence," and, as the closing lines of the sonnet make clear, he has come to "a greater knowledge," namely, that "it is only through the power and goodness of God that he is made and remade," therefore "preparing him for the ultimate revelation of Judgment Day" (75–76).

Spurr (1991, 165–66, 168–70) finds that the sonnet offers an instance of the "extremity" of Donne's religious poetry (165) between "a preoccupation with grace and the conviction of sinfulness" (168). The opening sestet, according to Spurr, bespeaks "a harrowing concentration upon a unique experience," in its repetition of "now" and "death" (ll. 2–3) (166). Spurr notes that Donne's sestets "often proffer the saving antidote for his poisoned octaves," but Spurr cautions against too easily interpreting them as "'comfortable words'" (168). The sestet in *HSMade*, Spurr observes, promotes, not "burgeoning confidence, but the precariousness of 'By thy leave' and 'Thy Grace may wing me,'" while at the same time "embedded at the heart of this putative panacea and uninhibited by the ambiguity which encloses him is the Devil, distressingly personalized," as in lines 11–12. In the end, according to Spurr, the sonnet dwells upon the "Despair" of the octave, and ultimately, in Spurr's reading, the sonnet "is animated by the realization of an inability to 'turn', in the brief space of the spiritual exercise, 'from his wickedness and live'" (169). Spurr finds that "Donne's inspiration for persistence in meditation derives as much from the experience of failure in it, as from his knowledge of his sins" (170).

Davies (1994, 63–64) calls attention to the sense of urgency in the sonnet despite its "restrained" manner. For example, Davies notes, the opening words articulate an "unquestioning faith from which rushes a question which breaks faith with it" ("And shall thy works decay?"), suggesting that there is "no time to address his Maker with the respectful devotion for which he might have leisure" if he had more than 14 lines "in which to wrestle his soul from Hell to Heaven" (63). Davies finds that the speaker "sheers headlong against his will toward his enemy, who rushes to meet him as if charging backwards along the same line" (l. 3). The sonnet's "alliteration" and "paratactic structure," in Davies's view, "builds to a crisis which suddenly and beautifully modulates in the sestet," with a "statement of wistful faith" ("Onely thou art above") and a "profound and virtuoso paradox" in a new rhyme in the final couplet. Thus, Davies concludes, "out of the impasse between God's 'can' and man's 'can't' proceeds the mediating 'may'" (64).

HSMade and Other Works

Furst (1896, 230–37) says of HSMade that it "strongly recalls," in both "matter" and "expression," Michelangelo's "Prayer for Purification" (230).

Winters (1948, 457–66) compares the poem to Robert Bridges's "Low Barometer" and Gerard Manley Hopkins's "No worst, there is none." HSMade, Winters contends, expresses "an orthodox theological definition of a predicament" shared by all of humankind, that is, their helplessness and need of God's grace to escape sin. Bridges's poem has a similar theme, expressed, however, without theological language (457–58). Winters finds Hopkins's sonnet on the theme less effective because of the meter, which produces "emotional overemphasis" (466). For more comments on Hopkins and HSMade, see also Coanda (1957), Stephenson (1959), and the notes to lines 1, 5–8, 9, and 14.

Coanda (1957, 187) notes that the poem resembles Hopkins's "Thou art indeed just, Lord" (ll. 5–14).

Stephenson (1959, 303) discovers affinities between HSMade and the first three stanzas of Hopkins's "The Wreck of the Deutschland." Both speakers, he observes, panic before God's majesty, fall, and are raised again on "wings of grace"; and both describe the "precarious stability" set up by "opposing pulls and contrary tides of nature and grace."

Hemmerich (1965, 18–23) compares Gryphius and Donne, both of whom wrote over a number of years, with developing interests. Hemmerich quotes briefly from HSMade and HSVex to support his claim that fear and love are the object of both poets, and he notes that in Donne contrition always provokes passion.

Cameron (1979, 45–46) compares Donne with Emily Dickinson and their common interest in the experience of "being apprehended by—caught at the center of—the various aspects of one's experience that refuse one the singleness of interpretation, for interpretations depend upon the hierarchy or ordering of phenomena, which in turn depends upon one's ability to achieve momentary distance from them" (45).

Cameron finds this experience "palpable" in *HSMade* and further claims that the sentiments in Donne's sonnet are those about which Dickinson "spent her life writing," epitomized in Donne's line "I dare not move my dimme eyes any way" (l. 6) (46). Cameron elaborates on the experience, noting that, "bound to the moment (without memory or imagination, that is, without concept of time), the spatial dimensions of the world overwhelm, for they alone determine and delimit one's place in it" (45), and thus the effect is a "heightened awareness of one's body" (45–46). What is needed, according to Cameron, is "outside presence," which Donne called "Grace," for "the self is at one with its insufficiency," and consequently "connection is redemptive" for both Donne and Dickinson (46).

In Lewalski's view (1979, 266), the only hope offered by *HSMade* is in the final couplet, "evoking a striking emblem from Georgette de Montenay [*Emblemes, ou Devises Chrestiennes* (Lyons, 1571), p. 5] of an iron heart drawn irresistibly by an adamant stone held out from heaven."

Milward (1979 [1988, 86–88]) finds *HSMade* to be penitential in nature, following in its main line of development in the octave—"from his creation by God, through his decay in sin, with his consequent fear of death and hell"—the *First Week* of the *Exercises* of St. Ignatius (86). In the second quatrain, in Milward's reading, the speaker is filled with such profound fear as he recalls his past that his despair ultimately brings him to feel that "he can 'rise again,'" in that he can look towards God by God's gracious leave" (87). Milward draws a comparison with Claudius in *Ham.*, who "rises from prayer while his 'thoughts remain below'"; Donne's speaker, however, now feels he can petition God "for divine grace to 'prevent,' that is, to anticipate or forestall, the 'art' of the tempter" (88).

Gaston (1986, 211) finds "the exuberant *moto perpetua*" of the penultimate setting for the eighth sonnet in Britten's sequence "to be a release in several senses." He says that both piano and voice are able "to compete in exhibitions of athletic prowess"; moreover, Gaston adds, "the sonnet is itself witty" and he points to lines 11–14 as examples. Moreover, the "lightening" found in this setting "enables us to respond more directly," Gaston claims, to the "grand seriousness" of Britten's "conclusive interpretation" in *HSDeath*.

Rollin (1994, 55) finds that the diction of Devotion 6 in the *Devotions* is mindful of *HSMade*, observing about the former that the "anxiety expressed by the doctor communicates itself to his patient, who wryly notes: 'I observe the physician with the same diligence as he the disease; I see he fears, and I fear with him, I overtake him, I overrun him in his fear.'" In *HSMade*, Rollin says, the speaker "wails 'I runne to death, and death meets me as fast,'" but in the Expostulation of Devotion 6 the fear of death is "displaced by the fear of God . . . which is revivifying: 'O my God, thou givest us fear for ballast to carry us steadfastly in all weathers.'"

Schoenfeldt (1994, 83–85) claims that in both *HSMade* and *HSDue* Donne "approaches his God through strategies that are strikingly similar to those he employed toward his mortal patrons" (83). Schoenfeldt cites letters to James Hay, Robert Carr, and Sir Henry Goodyer that reinforce the similarities, but with the crucial difference that in the Holy Sonnets Donne is invoking "divine aid" (84–85). Schoenfeldt cites Stachniewski (1981, 702–03), who says that Donne "felt his dependence on

God to resemble his dependence on secular patronage with its attendant frustration, humiliation and despair (85).

Notes and Glosses

1–8 *Thou . . . towards hell doth weigh.* **ANONYMOUS** (1938): Donne writes in fear of death, the unknown, and God and is here "as lost and helpless" as he once was "in the clutches of physical love" (814). **MILES** (1951) quotes the lines, concerning "the work of making and unmaking," to illustrate Donne's use of "abstract, active, and evaluative" words in poems of "argument and logic" (38–40). **GRANSDEN** (1954): Donne may have written some of his most personal sonnets in the years 1607–09, at the lowest point in his temporal and spiritual fortunes, those that record, as in these lines, "a ruined life wasting away, to imminent death, to sickness, to failure and to despair" (27). **MARTZ** (1954) finds the passage close to the wording of Fray Luis de Granada's *Of Prayer, and Meditation* in its evocation of "the primal horror, the grimmest terror" of the soul on its voyage to judgment (139). See also Holy Sonnets: Genre and Traditions. **DEN BOER** (1982) hears a dominant note of despair in the opening lines (31).

1 *Thou hast made me, and shall thy worke decay?* **THOMPSON** (1935) sees here a fear of dying rather than of death itself (45). **SPÖRRI–SIGEL** (1949) notes that Donne had an overwhelming fear of death as a force ending life (54). **FAERBER** (1950) says that Donne's paradoxes of human existence are not always expressed explicitly (29). Argues that the two parts of Donne's paradoxes result not in a balanced connection but in the juxtaposition of experience and the constructed image of his being, comparing a personal experience to something else, a supposition, an expectation, or a statement of belief (69). **SIMON** (1952): the line "raises the question of God's purpose in creating man, a being lost in darkness, unable to help himself to reach his true end" (118). **UNGER and O'CONNOR** (1953): an example of a "condensed conceit," which unlike the "expanded" is a single, simple statement in which the basis for comparison is implied rather than explained (109). **MORRIS** (1953) argues that Donne is too much tortured by doubt, constantly questioning God, to be possessed of the kind of humility Eliot expresses in "Ash Wednesday" (III, 23–26, V, 13–14) (99–100). Notes that the same theme is to be found in Hopkins's "The Wreck of the Deutschland" (1:5–8) (77). **MROCZKOWSKI** (1981) finds the beginning of HSMade an example of Donne's capacity to be direct and unfanciful (219). **TEAGUE** (1987): the lines support the view that Donne's "trust in God seems often to take the form of a profession of complete human helplessness," often expressed in "an aggressive putting off of responsibility onto God" (32). **DI NOLA** (1993) argues that the line is rhetorical since Donne knows that, as a creature of God, humankind cannot completely perish or die (118).

1 *Thou hast made me,* **STEPHENSON** (1959) finds the phrase similar to the

opening lines of Hopkins's "The Wreck of the Deutschland" (1.1–5). Notes that both poets go on immediately to express a "sense of dissolution" (303).

1 *decay?* **LEVER** (1974): "Fall into destruction" (182).

2–8 *Repaire me . . . towards hell doth weigh.* **FAERBER** (1950) finds that for Donne death was a demonic force that cast its shadow over his entire life. Observes that he speaks of death in each of his illnesses and views everyday events with death as a precondition (14).

2–4 *Repaire . . . are like yesterday.* **GRANSDEN** (1954): an allusion, not only to spiritual, but to physical illness, such as that Donne suffered in 1608 (128–29).

2 *Repaire me now, for now myne end do'th hast.* **SIMON** (1952): the speaker "needs help at once, for his end 'doth *haste*'" (118).

3–7 *I run . . . fleshe doth wast* **GRIERSON** (1921): cf. Ps. 6.6: "I am weary of my groaning; every night wash I my bed; and water my couch with tears" (228). **SMITH** (1991) quotes the lines, first observing that the "present moment may define us forever. To imagine ourselves in mortal sickness or at the point of final judgment is a way of making our predicament immediate, bringing us up sharp against a reality which our daily lives obscure from us" (134). **DUNDAS** (1994), arguing that initially the word "death" does not appear to be a personification, observes that when "death" and "despair" are "given an action to perform" (ll. 6–7), a "fiction develops." Comments further that "the traveler beset by these enemies, which are only phantoms, is a familiar theme in both literature and the visual arts" and cites Dürer's *The Knight, Death, and the Devil.* Suggests that Donne, more directly than Dürer, "emphasizes the weakness and helplessness of the central figure—himself—so that he must turn to God for support" (127).

3 *I run to death, and death meets me as fast,* **KORTEMME** (1933): the line is an example of a paradoxical antithesis in which two relationships are reversed (47). **SIMON** (1952): the line suggests "physical forces driving man forward like a ball rolling" or "the inevitable crash of trains rushing toward each other" (121).

3 *I run to death,* **SIMON** (1952) observes that the phrase implies that the speaker is the cause of his own death, "which qualifies the question of the first line." Suggests that the shift from "Thou" (l. 1) to "I" implies that he considers himself responsible for his own fate (118). **WOODHOUSE** (1965) finds the phrase "significant of Donne's recurrent preoccupation" with Death (61).

3 *fast,* **SHAWCROSS** (1967): "both 'as rapidly' and 'as tenaciously'" (346).

4 *And all my pleasures are like yesterday.* **SIMON** (1952): the line "conveys vanity," as if "his pursuits have been nothing but vexation of spirit" and have "grown stale" (118).

4 *like yesterday.* **LEVER** (1974): "Passed into memory" (182).

5–14 *I dare . . . myne Iron hart.* **SIMPSON** (1948): the lines express a strong sense of guilt but also a belief that "conversion is the first stage of the soul's pilgrimage towards God," a "turning away from our sin and a returning to God" (81–82).

5–8 *I dare . . . towards hell doth weigh.* **MORRIS** (1953): Donne's image of the poet seeking escape from the terrors of Judgment Day is matched by Hopkins in "The Wreck of the Deutschland" (3:1–3 and 10:1–2) [similarly, Stephenson (1959, 303)] (76). **EVANS** (1955) cites the lines as an example of Donne's "greatest achievement," that of developing "the dramatic impulse in non-dramatic poetry," here realizing the dramatic potentialities of the conflict he felt within him between God and the Devil (168). **COX** (1956b): the lines have a note of "torment and struggle, and the style expresses this passionate conflict with dramatic vividness" (55).

5 *I dare not moue my dimme eyes any way,* **SIMON** (1952): we see Donne "staring in the dark, not moving one limb lest he disclose his position to the enemy" (118).

5 *dimme eyes* **POLLOCK** (1978) says that "dimme eyes" may be a pun on "demise," implying that Donne is "afraid both of prolonging his life and hurrying his death." Notes that in Donne's time "demise" could be used as a legal term meaning "conveyance or transfer of an estate by will or lease." (Similarly, Patrides [1985a, 434].) Finds the pun artistically effective because it "equates Donne's failing eyesight directly with his approaching death," thus emphasizing "his spiritual dilemma" as he both "runne[s] to death" (l. 3) and "dreads it" (83).

6–8 *Dispaire . . . towards hell doth weigh.* **GRIERSON** (1921) quotes the lines as an example of "the deeper scars, the profound remorse which gives such a passionate, anguished timbre to the harsh but resonant harmonies" of the Divine Poems (xli). **BLANCH** (1974): Donne mixes his metaphors in ll. 6 and 7; images of spatial mobility juxtaposed with images of light and darkness clearly indicate that the poet cannot save himself (478).

6 *Dispaire behind, and death before* **MIMS** (1948): the sentiment may reflect Donne's response to the death of his wife, who "led him to faith hard won" (186).

6 *doth cast* **CRAIK and CRAIK** (1986) say that the singular verb "doth" is "governed" by both "despair" and "death" and that in l. 7, "doth waste" is "governed" by "flesh" (276).

7–8 *Such . . . towards hell doth weigh.* **GRIERSON** (1921) compares "my feeble flesh doth waste by sinne in it" to Ps. 38.3: "There is no health in my flesh, because of thy displeasure: neither is there any rest in my bones, by reason of my sin" (228). Similarly, Fowler (1995, 260).

7 *Such terror,* **SIMON** (1952): "a cry of anguish" (118).

8–14 *By Sin in it, . . . draw myne Iron hart.* **GROVE** (1984): since the "unde-clared image" around which the poem forms is "that of the hour-glass, such as we find on the writing-desk of saint or penitent or holy man in the appropriate con-temporary portraits," with the eighth line, "we are at the waist or turning-point," in which "the poem is turned—not by reversing the glass (which would not stop time's running out), but by finding resurrection in the mounting-up of mortality itself." Thus, "to realize that, unaided, one's life is lost, restores it, for at last the gaze turns upward, other way, to God." But "life, if it is only dust, mounts upward self-undoingly, since 'our old subtle foe so tempteth me.'" In its close, then, "the sonnet must tran-scend itself," for "the unyielding heart, which is what has most resisted God, is proved to be the very thing His adamantine power draws irresistibly to itself" (67).

8 *By Sin . . . weigh.* **SHAWCROSS** (1967): cf. Isa. 26.7: "The way of the just is uprightness: thou, most upright, dost weigh the path of the just" (346). [So also, Booty (1990, 109).] **LEVER** (1974): the "weight of sin pulls the feeble flesh (l. 7) down to hell" (i.e., the "centre of the earth") (182).

8 *weigh.* **PATRIDES** (1985a): "carry; also, incline" (434).

9–14 *Only . . . myne Iron hart.* **COX** (1956a) remarks of the Holy Sonnets that the "best" reveal the "characteristic wit reinforcing the emotional intensity" and quotes these lines as an example (113).

9 *Only thou art above; and when towards thee* **SIMON** (1952) suggests that the line can be read in two ways, depending on whether the stress comes on "thou" or "art": if on "thou" it means that God will not let his creatures decay, if on "art" that the very existence of God will save them. Prefers the latter, believing that Donne "first expresses his confidence in God's *existence*, then considers His *nature*, and fi-nally realises that the hard God whose dark purpose cannot be fathomed [l. 1] is also the loving God" (119). **MORRIS** (1953): both Donne and Hopkins vary the iam-bic pentameter line, on occasion with two reversed feet running, as here and in "The Handsome Heart" (l. 10) (45).

9 *Only thou art above;* **STEPHENSON** (1959) finds the phrase echoed in Hopkins's "The Wreck of the Deutschland" (21.5) (303).

9 *Only thou* **LEVER** (1974): "Thou alone" (182).

9 *Only* **CRAIK and CRAIK** (1986): "but" (276).

10 *By thy leaue* **SHAWCROSS** (1967): "both 'by thy permission' and 'by thy releasing me from life'" (346).

10 *I can looke,* **SIMON** (1952) says that the speaker thus far "has kept his eyes riveted to the ground" but once realizing there is no hope there, he can look up to God "as to the only light that breaks through the prison walls" (119).

10 *agayne.* SIMON (1952): the word "suggests that the fall and rise has occurred more than once, and hence is likely to occur again, that this is not final" (119).

11–14 *But . . . myne Iron hart.* WILLIAMSON (1930) quotes the lines as an example of the combination of "imaginative distance," "fundamental brain work," and "emotional intensity" of Donne (85–86).

11–12 *But . . . my selfe sustayne.* SPÖRRI-SIGEL (1949): in the conflict between God and Satan, Heaven and Hell, grace is "a possibility but not a reality" ("eine Möglichkeit, aber keine Wirklichkeit") (86).

11 *But our old subtile foe so tempteth mee* SMITH (1971): "Satan tempts him to despair, in this extremity" (625). CRAIK and CRAIK (1986): "But Satan so strongly tempts me to despair" (276).

11 *foe* SHAWCROSS (1967): Satan, as serpent (346). [Similarly, Lever (1974, 182), Patrides (1985a, 434) and Booty (1990, 109).]

12 *That not one hower I can my selfe sustayne.* SIMON (1952) concludes that this is the "real theme" of *HSMade,* the fact of "man's incapacity to help himself, and the necessity to look for help outside himself" in the form of God's Grace (120).

12 *hower* SPURR (1991): the word "refers both to the penitent's general state, with its less momentous, pleasurable misdemeanors, and his experience in meditation itself," the "hour" being typically associated "with the daily period of prayer" (169).

13–14 *Thy . . . myne Iron hart.* WHITE (1936): "For if man seeks God, no less does God seek man, like adamant drawing his iron heart" (137). MOLONEY (1944) quotes the couplet as an example of Donne's "high poetic accomplishment" and then explicates the lines: "The likening of the attraction of Divinity for the erring human heart to the action of the magnet upon iron is highly felicitous, while the labored movement of the predominantly monosyllabic line suggests the agony involved in the tearing of that heart from its baser affections" (132). MCGUIRE (1974) notes that the final couplet is not only a recognition of God's power but also a "statement of praise and is tantamount to another 'ground' for the petition 'Repaire me now,' because in this context praise of God's power is also an implicit invitation to exercise it on the speaker" (68). Writes that "iron heart" is a "confession of the speaker's sinfulness, and the complete figure, which suggests the helplessness voiced in ll. 9–12, emphasizes the possibility of Christ's omnipotently drawing the speaker to him" (68). CRAIK and CRAIK (1986): "May thy grace give me wings to frustrate his craft, and mayst thou, like a magnetic lodestone (*adamant*), draw mine iron heart to thee." Cf. *MND* 2.1.195–98 (276).

13 *Thy grace may winge me, to preuent his art* FAERBER (1950) contends that a denial of self is alien to Donne. Finds that in the poem, as in these lines, he is un-

able to resign himself to that denial, but depends on God to free him from sinfulness (22).

13 *winge me,* **SHAABER** (1958): "give me wings" (100). **ADAMS** (1962): "strengthen" (784). **SHAWCROSS** (1967): transport, give me wings (to fly away) (346). **LEVER** (1974): "Add wings, as in falconry feathers were 'imped' to a hawk's wing" (182).

13 *preuent his art* **GARDNER** (1952): "Satan's art is to make men fall into despair" (75).

13 *preuent* **GARDNER** (1952): "frustrate" (75). [So also Shaaber (1958, 100), Kermode (1968, 182) and Booty (1990, 109).] **MARTZ** (1963): "anticipate, forestall, balk" (83). **ADAMS** (1962): "counteract" (784). **SMITH** (1971): "forestall, frustrate" (625). [Similarly, Lever (1974, 182), Patrides (1985a, 434) and Fowler (1991, 116).] **FOWLER** (1995): "anticipate, forestall" (260).

14 *And thou like Adamant, draw myne Iron hart.* **WILLIAMSON** (1930) argues that this is "one of the finest lines in Donne" and is a "complete vindication of the conceit as a means of expressing a particular way of thinking and feeling" (86). Finds that in it meet "Donne and his shroud, Donne and his age" (98). **WINTERS** (1948): "a pun which makes one of the greatest lines in English poetry" (458). **SIMON** (1952) sees the speaker's "Iron hart" as the weakness he complains weighs him down (l. 8), and Grace's adamant, "one of the most mysterious forces of nature" at the time, as the only force powerful enough to "draw" it (120). Argues that the "iron" emphasizes the conflict within man, since paradoxically it is heavy and cannot rise by itself but at the same time because it is iron it can be attracted by God's "Adamant" love. Concludes that Grace achieves a victory over the laws of nature "by a power that is in nature (adamant) but can transcend" nature's laws (121–22). **MORRIS** (1953): Donne merges the physical and the spiritual, as does Hopkins in "Carrion Comfort" (ll. 13–14) (36). **SMITH** (1971): "God may if he chooses draw the poet's heart to him" (625). **LEVER** (1974): the paradox rests "in the *iron* hardness of the heart, which enables God to draw it up as if with a magnet (*adamant*)" (182).

14 *And* **GARDNER** (1952) notes that "'And,' used as a conditional conjunction, takes the subjunctive" (75). **SHAABER** (1958): "if" (100). [So also, Fowler (1995, 260).]

14 *Adamant,* **PALGRAVE** (1889): "magnet" (19). [Similarly, Coffin and Witherspoon (1946, 33), Willey (1954, 386), ul-Hasan (1958, 19), Shaaber (1958, 100), Adams (1962, 784), Patrides (1985a, 434), Booty (1990, 109), and Carey (1990b, 455), some of whom also identify the magnet with the loadstone.] **JUDSON** (1927): "Adamant was at this time confused with the loadstone or magnet" (250). **GARDNER** (1952) observes that "'Adamant' implies both steadfastness and an attractive force which is irresistible." Adds that Donne "comments on the dangers of the doctrine of the 'irresistibility of grace'" in *Sermons* 7:156 (75). **STEPHENSON**

(1959): the word corresponds to "dovewinged" and "carrier-witted" in Hopkins's "The Wreck of the Deutschland" (3.6–7) (303). **MARTZ** (1963): "a stone of extreme hardness; also, of magnetic power" (83). **SHAWCROSS** (1967): "ironically [the loadstone] is supposed to be of impenetrable hardness" (346). **SMITH** (1971): "(a) lodestone, a magnetic stone; (b) adamantine rock, a proverbially hard stone which here figures the unyielding determination God might show in drawing the poet's heart to him" (625). **FOWLER** (1991): "(1) lodestone, magnet; (2) diamond (emblem of faith)" (116). Similarly, Fowler (1995, 260).

14 *draw* **PATRIDES** (1985a) points to the "commonplace notion that love has 'an Adamantine power that is able to draw the hardest heart'" (434).

14 *Iron* **SHAWCROSS** (1967): "sinful [so also, Booty (1990, 109)] and obdurate" (346). **SKULSKY** (1992): in "iron" there is, as with "adamant," a "metalepsis": "things made of iron are *hard*; hard things are *unyielding*," and therefore "there is nothing promising in the hardness of a 'hard heart,' not in the biblically charged dialect of Donne's language community. To be hardhearted is to be naturally resistant to the love of God" (114). Adds that "if the speaker's heart is supposed to be seeking God the way iron seeks adamant, then 'iron' doesn't mean *stubbornness toward God* here" (265n44).

 *HSMin*

COMMENTARY

General Commentary

Potter (1934, 18–19) writes about Donne's "search for himself" that pointed him eventually towards religion. Noting that Donne's religious writings reveal his continuing quest and show that "he was not always satisfied to wait patiently till death should open wide the gates and let him in" (18), Potter cites *HSMin* as a poem that results from "such impatience," adding that few churchmen went as far as Donne does in this poem "in questioning the justice of God's ways to man" (18–19).

Ansari (1974, 143) writes that there is "a sharp and strong protest against the inscrutable cosmic order" in *HSMin*.

Roston (1974, 58–59) argues that in *HSMin* Donne achieves an "inversion of the familiar" by placing the "hyperbolic vocabulary of the Counter Reformation" in a "new setting."

Sellin (1974, 192–96), noting that with the Reformation, God became less a benevolent deity and more a God who lay beyond the scope of human reason, thinks that *HSMin* dramatizes the position of Luther and Calvin on man's relation to God and God's will (192). Sellin states that Protestants lost the psychological comfort of being able to discern with certainty the Lord's intentions and that with the emphasis on predestination one was unable to know for certain whether one was elect because God's ways were unsearchable. This perception of God, Sellin says, is discernible in the drama and the lyric poetry of the Renaissance, and it is evident in the Holy Sonnets, specifically *HSDue* and *HSMin*. In *HSMin*, says Sellin, the octave raises Luther's question, namely, "why does God lay our destruction to the charge of human will, when man cannot avoid it?" (193). Sellin states that in the sestet Donne answers the question the way that Luther answered it: "though you should ask much, you never find out" (193). See also Sellin under Holy Sonnets: General Commentary.

Miller (1982, 836) finds that the sonnet opens "audaciously by accusing God of unfairness in the consequences He has decreed for original sin," but in the sestet the persona recognizes his unworthiness to dispute with God, begging that his "tears of guilt" might bring God "to overlook his sins rather than actually forgiving them." Although this sonnet, unlike *HSBatter*, "does not turn on a sexual image," Miller notes, it nonetheless contrasts "the lot of fallen man unfavorably with that of lecherous goats, who have no decree of damnation over them."

Sherwood (1984, 154) contends that the Holy Sonnets do not affirm rational skepticism, but instead "portray reason's share in the debility from sin while granting its essential contribution in erecting the soul through repentance," for "it is sin that makes reason 'untrue.'" For example, in HSMin, according to Sherwood, the argument of the octave "ignores the difference between man and lower creatures until reason itself in the sestet, by ensuring such misguided 'dispute' and demolishing its own untrue constructs, ironically dramatizes that difference."

Schoenfeldt (1994, 82) observes that although the sonnet "begins with a brazen interrogation of divine justice," it turns to "an interrogation of the speaker's own identity and status in discourse with God," as in line 9. The ending, Schoenfeldt notes, "equivocally prais[es] God's mercy."

The Poet/Persona

Payne (1926, 141–42) quotes the poem in full to illustrate the conflict between Donne's "self-abasement" and his "doubting intellect."

Mahood (1950, 124–25), assuming a later date for the Holy Sonnets, argues that they reflect a "new humanism" to be found in Donne's work, one theocentric rather than Renaissance in spirit. Mahood contrasts Metem 101–20, which he accepts as earlier, with HSMin, finding in the former a "protest of free reason against the apparently irrational scheme of the world," a sentiment repeated in lines 1–4 of the sonnet. The sestet, however, reveals an acceptance based on self-discovery, observes Mahood, and a new understanding of "the reason of the heart" which goes deeper than that of the mind.

Martz (1970, 105–06) cautions against overestimating the influence of Donne upon the course of devotional poetry in the seventeenth century, arguing that Donne's religious consciousness is peculiar to Donne. Illustrating this point with the examples of HSMin and HSShe, Martz comments that HSMin "develops a remarkably intricate series of dramatic postures" (105) and notes that the most striking feature of the poem is the continuously shifting nature of the argument, "the way in which the speaker's mind seems to be racing ahead of itself, answering questions implicitly even while they are being asked." Martz argues that this constantly shifting nature of the speaker's stance within a given poem is what makes Donne's poems basically inimitable. HSMin begins, he says, with blasphemous thoughts and continues with "evasions and curious questions." In the sestet, however, reason "emerges triumphant" with an exact command of the theology of redemption (106).

Altizer (1973, 84–85) argues that the octave of HSMin is full of reason and indignation, but this gives way to pleas for forgetfulness and mercy in the sestet. The sestet implies that if God would forget the poet's sin, then the poet could also forget it. Thus, she says, the idea that repentance requires self-forgetfulness is alluded to obliquely, but not within a "coherent framework" (85).

Pop-Cornis (1975, 20–21) declares that in HSMin, rather than writing a "poem of statements," Donne resorts to questions, "many unanswered, that are more provocative and dramatic." He notes that the octave poses questions that "all center around one unfair contrast," and he sees in them an "implicit criticism of God's ways." He writes that, in the sestet, instead of answering the question, Donne poses another question which constitutes "an abrupt turn of logic" (20), with the last two lines expressing a paradox. He argues that the argumentative "device" of *HSMin* aims "to make a new and striking point by a syllogism concealing a logical error." He writes that the error Donne describes in *HSMin* "is in accepting the fact that reason, which initially was given to man to save him from inferior nature, is also the source of damnation." He further says that Donne "also tries to persuade himself that he has to ask for forgetfulness and not forgiveness or remembrance which God cannot give" (21).

Low (1978, 64) writes that *HSMin* arouses "impious emotions in order to purge them," noting that Donne places himself among the poisonous minerals and arguing that he "strikes a pose that the poem as a whole deliberately undercuts."

Stachniewski (1981, 694–96) focuses on the unreconciled disparity between the octave and the sestet. In the octave, he says, Donne despairs of his sinfulness and of "his innate capacity for damnation, unshared by the non-human created world." In Stachniewski's view, "the burden of being human under a God of Calvinist character seems to Donne too heavy" (694). The sestet, however, focuses on Donne's repentance for his sinfulness, but Stachniewski points out that "there is no attempt to reply to the question of lines 7–8 ("And mercy being easie, and glorious / To God, in his sterne wrath, why threatens hee?") (695). For Stachniewski, it appears that Donne was "reluctant to deny his perception of God's predilection for sternness while presenting an elaborate show of submission" (696).

Rollin (1986, 139) finds a "fantasy" embodied in this sonnet, as in *HSRound*. But whereas the fantasy in *HSRound*, in Rollin's view, is "an untenable power fantasy," here there is a fantasy of "intellectual dominance." For Rollins, this second fantasy also "collapses under the onslaught of the speaker's superego." Rollin attributes the shift in mood in the sestet to "an attack of anxiety arising out of his recollection that God is capable of 'sterne wrath' as well as mercy," such that the speaker's reaction to this fear is "submission and a plea that God forget him." Rollin notes that the speaker's belief that God will forget is "yet another indication of the speaker's theological ineptitude." But Rollin finds even more important "the speaker's impulse toward oblivion," which, in his psychological reading of the sonnet, he sees as a sign that "he is sinking into depression." See also *HSRound*: The Poet/Persona.

To Strier (1989, 382–84), *HSMin* is clearly an instance of "deliberate sophistry" and thus can enable us "to determine when we are confronting such a case, and when not," for here Donne "explicitly calls attention to assumptions or arguments he has pretended to make" with respect to his relationship to God. For example, Donne presents the argument of the octave of *HSMin* so as "to call attention to its own lack of seriousness." For Strier, the words "threw death" (l. 2) and the "insistently moral epithets applied to animals give the game away" (382). The sophistry of the octave, according to Strier, may manifest a "Reformation distrust of reason and disgust with the incessantly disputatious self," for in the octave Donne "dramatizes" what Carey (1981, 47), speaking of *HSWhat*, calls "a mind humiliatingly aware of its limits, when faced with the divine." (See *HSWhat*, notes to ll. 13–14). The plea following the "turn" of the sestet, in Strier's view, is "consciously Protestant" when it ascribes merit only to Christ ("thine onely worthy blood" [l. 10]) and when it asks God "to take decisive action," but the "paradox" of line 11 ("a heavenly

Lethean flood") fails to "lead Donne to a vision of divine forgiveness in normal Protestant or biblical terms" (383). According to Strier, "there is no positive version of divine remembrance in the poem." The "entire prayer," Strier contends, is that God "will not see the sinner himself," and consequently a "Calvinist sense of sin has banished merit as the way to salvation, but nothing—or rather, nothingness—has replaced it." Strier concludes that it is difficult for Donne "to accept being saved as a sinner," but neither can he "convincingly imagine being free from sin," and thus absent either of these alternatives, Donne's "deepest prayer" is "either to be ravished into chastity, or, like Faustus, to escape from God's attention" (384).

Skulsky (1992, 112, 114–15) examines the diversionary tactics of Donne's fearful speakers in their efforts to circumvent the inevitable, the "pronouncement of sentence" by God, efforts Skulsky finds utterly futile (112). In HSMin, according to Skulsky, the speaker "puts himself forward as an attorney for people in general and himself in particular," given that "a mass verdict of guilty has been handed down, along with a sentence of capital punishment," although both judgments are "tainted by species favoritism" (114). Skulsky notes that the "only visible difference is that the sins of the exempted are committed without intent or reason" (114). Skulsky believes that "the argument is designed to shift the burden of proof on to God," so long as God "falls for the semantic illusion of the 'sins' of minerals, vegetables, and dumb animals" (114–15). Skulsky concludes that "we're given no reason to doubt that the speaker is sincere when he ends with a powerful outburst of loathing for his sins," and he adds that Donne could have introduced his "unfairness argument" by substituting the "arbitrary predestination of the elect" for the "arbitrary exemption of nonhuman 'sinners'"—that is, "replacing a bogus difficulty with a genuine and notorious one"—but "bogus difficulties" are part of what HSMin is about, the "unholy alliance of wit and terror." For Skulsky, "the heart of [the sophism] is a diversionary littera" (115).

Genre and Traditions

Martz (1954, 52, 132–33) quotes the poem to illustrate how some of Donne's sonnets include all three steps in the traditional Ignatian meditation: the first quatrain proposes Donne's "besetting sin of intellectual pride"; the second analyzes the proposal by giving "the proper theological answer" to the matter and questioning God's justice; and in the sestet the blasphemous argument collapses into "one of Donne's most vehement colloquies" with God, ending in the real answer to the questions posed (52). Martz also contends that Donne is engaging in the "exercise" of self-analysis proposed in Scupoli's Spiritual Combat when he deliberately cultivates blasphemous thoughts by disputing with God and then rejects them in the sestet by appealing to God's mercy (132–33). See more under Holy Sonnets: Genre and Traditions.

Structure

Roth (1947, 17) finds the speaker's mind to be "tortured and mangled with doubt," observing that in the octave the poet disputes with God but that the tone shifts sharply to intense humility in the sestet, where he is "chagrined at his subversive calculations." For Roth, the sestet is anticlimactic, and she judges the octave, "with its intense brooding over man's precarious situation," as "the strength of the sonnet."

Esch (1955, 53) finds the sonnet artistically less satisfactory than others which, like it, achieve a synthesis of the Italian and the English sonnet form. The Italian division is present, with the speaker reasoning with God in the octave and in the sestet asking Him to drown his sins in a flood of forgetting, but the couplet, Esch concludes, fails to reach a fitting climax, ending the poem in "a pale cliché" ("eine blasse Wiederholung").

The speaker's initial "huff of disquiet" at divine judgment in *HSMin* is resolved in the sestet of the poem, Stampfer (1970, 248) observes. He says that the octave is the thesis of the sonnet, and that it presents a speaker who is "chafing," demanding to know why his guilt should be greater than that of evil and depraved creatures. Identifying the antithesis of line 9 as an answer to the speaker's "aggressive disquiet," Stampfer views the last five lines as a synthesis in which the speaker's spirit enters a "taut movement of rapport with his environment, engaging God in a direct confrontation."

Language and Style

Brooks and Warren (1938, 520–24) find the poem dramatic in that it is a prayer couched in the form of an argument. They offer a prose summary of the argument and then examine the sonnet to determine how Donne invests it "with the emotive force necessary for poetic effect" (521). In discussing the organization and structure of the sonnet the authors emphasize three poetic devices: (1) the sequence of three questions in the octave that heightens the dramatic effect, since questions are "more provocative" than statements; (2) the exclamations (ll. 4 and 10) that achieve the same dramatic effect and that are not placed at the beginning of the poem, where they might create the effect artificially, but at points which signal a turn in the thought of the work (522–23); and (3) the series of contrasts that develop the ideas of the poem in the octave: lower creation and humankind (ll. 1–4), the paradoxical possession of reason (ll. 5–6), God's mercy and justice (ll. 7–8), and human reason and divine justice (l. 9) (523). Brooks and Warren then contrast these effects with those in the sestet, where the speaker abandons the argument and resorts to an appeal to the promise of redemption, concluding with a final contrast between those who pray to be remembered and those like himself who hope "for salvation by divine forgetfulness." The authors observe that the poem is spare of simile and metaphor, which makes the image of Christ's blood and the penitent's tears in the sestet "especially bold" in contrast to the more direct method of the octave (523–24).

Pallotti (1993, 175–78), in his study of the interrogative mode as the prevailing discourse pattern between the speaker and hearer of the Holy Sonnets, claims that "personal salvation and the role God has in it is a pervasive theme in the Holy Sonnets, if not the theme *par excellence*" (175–76). Pallotti points to the "disturbing sensation" provoked by the opening question of *HSMin*, but he notes also the "formal syntactic patterning of the structure of the four lines (*if . . . and if . . . If . . . if . . . why*)," as if the "emotional intensity of the speaker's underlying feelings were curbed by the logical consistency of his reasoning" (176). In the second question (ll. 5–6), according to Pallotti, the speaker's "reasoning becomes more subtle," for "since what distinguishes man from other creatures, 'intent' and 'reason', are innate faculties, independent from human will, it cannot be man's fault if he possesses them" (176). The speaker's "protest" reaches a "climax" and is "almost subversive" in lines 7–8, Pallotti thinks, and leads to the opening of the sestet, with its "direct address," a "shift in thought and emotion," as well as the speaker's new "posture of humility and self-distrust" (177). Pallotti concludes that "in the discursive situation of the poem, the subject appears to be split into two roles," for he is "both the object of the dispute and, simultaneously, the disputer," and, Pallotti adds, God "is also described as performing two different roles," appearing as the "judge" as well as the "defendant in the case," implying that God is "the individual's adversary." Thus, "inevitably," Pallotti emphasizes, "discourse refuses a single, monological point of view and becomes an arena where different, conflicting voices can be heard" (178).

Kullmann (1994, 121, 128–29) identifies drama as the characteristic that distinguishes Donne's Songs and Sonets and religious poems from both earlier and contemporary Elizabethan poetry (121). The religious poetry, according to Kullmann, is often an intense and complicated dialogue with God, combined with vivid and insistent self-questioning, qualities HSMin illustrates (128). Kullmann notes that the change in the form of address—from "He" to direct address—is more dramatic and the imagery more concrete and dramatically vivid (129). Kullmann states that the chosen image, God's blood, in combination with the speaker's tears, will become a mythological river in which the memory of the speaker's sins are drowned, thus creating a dramatic replication not only of the ritual of communion, but also the divine events of salvation (129).

Prosody

Chatman (1965, 9–11, 148), demonstrating the "utility of structural linguistics in developing a theory of English meter" (9), cites HSMin 3–4 to illustrate the "accentual" pressure that operates "to reverse a metrical set"—that is, the iambic foot, which is expected, is reversed to become a trochee (148).

HSMin reminds Nelly (1969, 140–41) of Gerard Manley Hopkins's works in its conveyance of emotion by broken rhythm and irregularly occurring caesurae (140–41). But, she maintains, "the dialectic links are weak, and the passion is dissipated, as Donne seems to jump from one ground of appeal to another." While there is a "moving pathos" in the final couplet, Nelly says, "we miss the tension, the ambiguity, 'the anguish of the marrow,' which give an almost elemental force to his great love lyrics" (141).

Themes

Empson (1935, 73–74) detects in HSMin the "Renaissance desire to make the individual more independent than Christianity allowed" (73). The poem, he argues, strikes a balance between the idea of rebirth of the soul and metempsychosis—a form of pantheism—with the animal imagery of lines 3–4 hinting at the latter. Empson finds in the contrast of the final couplet some doubt as to which destiny

Donne is referring to, since Lethe was "where the souls forgot everything before rebirth" (74).

Brooks and Warren (1938, 520) interpret the theme of the sonnet posed as a question: "what should be the attitude of sinful man toward God's justice?"

Gardner (1952, 68) observes that the "sonnet has no *compositio loci*," and that the "torments of the damned are usually handled at length" in the Ignatian method of meditation, "which Donne is drawing on."

Reeves (1952, 101) paraphrases the poem: "If plants, stones and animals are not damned for their wickedness, since they lack reason and intention, why should I be? Yet I must accept the will of God and pray for his mercy."

Peterson (1959, 510) observes that Donne questions God's justice (ll. 1–6) but then, fearful at having done so, acknowledges that he must accept it on faith and "throw himself on His Mercy." The ending (ll. 9–14), he says, transforms "sorrow incited by fear to sorrow incited by love," a necessary condition for true repentance.

French (1970, 112) argues that the tone of HSMin is one of defeat—either the defeat involved in a feeling of deep unworthiness or the defeat involved in giving up the struggle to reconcile mercy and "sterne wrath." And while French cites Martz (1954, 132–33—see HSMin: Genre and Traditions) as saying that the tone of the sestet provides a satisfactory answer to the agonizing questions raised in the octave, he is doubtful, owing to the "defeated tone" of the sestet, whether Donne was ever convinced by his own argument.

Lewalski (1979, 269–70) finds that HSMin "enacts the speaker's true repentance and faith," so that by the end of the octave, the speaker "throw[s] himself without reservation upon Christ's mercy in the earnest hope of justification." Lewalski adds that the sonnet is devoted to the speaker's defining of himself against the backdrop of Job, who, unlike Donne's speaker, "maintained his integrity and righteousness before God, implying that God has unjustly dealt with him" (269). The speaker in HSMin, according to Lewalski, "finds his best hope in God's total forgetting," which reflects the Calvinistic view of justification (269–70).

Klinck (1981, 251) locates Donne's trinitarianism in the sonnet's attention to the three kinds of sin corresponding to the three Persons of the Trinity: the "lower orders of creation can 'sin' only from weakness, only, perhaps, against the Father," but humankind is "capable of the more damnable sins associated with reason and intent: sins against the Son and the Holy Ghost."

Yearwood (1982, 210, 214–15) finds that the conversion process in Donne's first twelve Holy Sonnets (following 1633 and Gardner's [1952] ordering) "begins in pride, proceeds to confession and despair, and culminates in a humble joy and confidence" (210). The octave of HSMin, the fifth sonnet in this sequence, Yearwood says, "demonstrates nearly every presumptuous misconception possible" (214). But having "tried out blasphemy," he adds, the speaker is "prepared for true humbling of himself," and the sestet thus ends with the first part of his conversion: "a complete confession" (215).

Mallett (1983, 58) summarizes the argument of the sonnet: "the poem is a prayer that God will forget the poet's sins, and so allow him to escape the damnation he has deserved."

Klause (1986, 421) concedes that on occasion Donne "must have meditated on the words of Saint Paul (Rom. 7:7–8) concerning the deadliness of law." But Klause finds in *Biathanatos* Donne's acknowledgment of God's freedom to "retract his precepts as he wills": "nothing is so evil," writes Donne, "but that it becomes good, if God command it." Knowing that the "moral law and its application are flexible," Donne sometimes wonders about the "absolute necessity of a sentence unto damnation," as we find in *HSMin*.

Guibbory (1986, 93–94) points to this sonnet as "one of the most striking examples" demonstrating that Donne's "holy meditations" are "affected by his sense that it is memory rather than understanding or will that best leads a person to God" (93). For example, Guibbory explains, the sonnet begins with a series of questions that "suggest the speaker's separation from God," but "the poem (and the speaker's spiritual state) turns abruptly at line 9 as he remembers his unworthiness," an "act of memory" that, significantly, "marks the speaker's direct address to God for the first time in the poem" (93–94). Thus, "his remembrance of his sin," according to Guibbory, "leads him to long for the restoration of his original harmony with God, which can only take place if God blots out or forgets Donne's sinfulness" (94).

McNees (1992, 64–65) claims that both *HSMin* and *HSLittle* "allude to the hope that the Eucharist will drown or wash away black sin." The former sonnet, according to McNees (citing Paul Ricoeur ["The Logic of Jesus, the Logic of God," *Anglican Theological Review*, 62.1 (1980): 37–41], opens with the "harsh Old Testament logic of God." Ricoeur distinguishes between Old Testament "logic of punishment" and New Testament "logic of superabundance," with the former associated with "sin, law and death" and the latter "justification, grace, and life" (64). McNees finds that the sonnet "pits these two logics against each other and acknowledges the need for punishment as a prerequisite for redemption," explaining that the octave "describes an Old Testament world—the Garden of Eden—with its nonhuman elements," while the sestet "charts the New Testament logic of superabundance based on Christ's passion," with the speaker understanding the "need for mutual sacrifice." McNees believes that Donne "stops short of Christian absolution," mixing as he does "mythological and biblical references (Heaven and Lethean Hades' river of forgetfulness) into an oxymoronic conceit" and questing for "blind forgetfulness over remorse and contrition" (65).

Loewenstein (1993, 11) places *HSMin* among those Holy Sonnets that reflect Donne's "Calvinistic terror of damnation and sense of sinfulness as he confronts his personal and awesome God." Loewenstein finds that whereas in the opening lines of the sonnet Donne becomes "contentious with God as he envies the rest of creation," later, having recognized "the all-powerful nature of his Protestant God who can forget Donne's human sins," Donne withdraws from his contentious attitude.

HSMin and Other Works

Brooks and Warren (1938, 535) propose that the reader compare Sidney's control of tone in "A Farewell" to Donne's in *HSMin*.

Milward (1979 [1988, 60–62]) describes this sonnet as the only one of the first six Holy Sonnets in 1633 that corresponds to "a particular exercise" of the *First Week* of the *Spiritual Exercises* of St. Ignatius, namely the *Meditation on Hell*, which applies the senses to experiencing "an interior sense of the pain which the damned suffer." Although the speaker recognizes that he deserves being damned for his past sins, Milward notes, he "still protests against the just judgment of God," much as did Job (ch. 23) and Jeremiah (ch. 12) (60). The "thought of mercy" in the sestet brings the speaker "to change his tone and to turn his thoughts from himself to God," and to his appeal, according to Milward, to God to show him mercy by forgetting his sins, according to the promise of God in Jer. 32.34: "I will forgive their iniquity, and I will remember their sin no more" (62).

Sherwood (1989, 27) finds that whereas Donne speaks in his own voice in the *Devotions*, in the Holy Sonnets, and in *HSMin* in particular, he is "distanced self-consciously from the speaking voice by irony." According to Sherwood, "the speaker's sinful logic" in *HSMin*, "delimited by assuming that non-rational goats and human beings should be categorized together, reflects this sinful self-concern." Consequently, he thinks, "the irony separates the speaker from Donne himself, who thus gives an accurate fictional image of his own impulse to self-delusion while praying."

Kullmann (1994, 132) contends that the meditative elements in Donne's poetry are obvious, and that Donne, raised as a Roman Catholic, knew Ignatius of Loyola's spiritual exercises firsthand, and that although he was later an enemy of the Jesuits, this did not prevent him from making use of what he learned from his Catholic education and specifically about meditative practices. He cites *HSMin* as a sonnet that does not begin with an explicit "compositio loci" found in many poems informed by Ignatian meditation, but begins, as Gardner (1952) observes, with a "point" from a meditation on hell. The poem ends, in Kullmann's reading, with an Ignatian colloquy, or personal address to God.

NOTES AND GLOSSES

1–8 *If . . . why threatens hee?* **FAERBER** (1950) observes that Donne utters a simple plea for God to take the gentle path, wishing to be spared divine wrath and arguing that indeed he is entitled to such leniency, but acknowledging in the end his unworthiness. Concludes that the important point is that the first thought was even considered (19). **MARTZ** (1959): Donne's poems begin typically with a vision of "the follies and foibles and infidelities of the world," as in "the fierce and bitter opening" of *HSMin* (272–73). **YEN** (1995) finds in these lines, as in *HSSighs*, evidence of "Donne the courtier complaining about the injustice of the political system that had consistently refused to reward him." Adds that since the King "handed out favors with apparent ease," Donne wanted "his rightful share." But notes the sudden change in argument in l. 9, "as the speaker realizes his presumption in arguing with his Maker," the question posed there signaling the "recognition of a supplicant that he can only rely on divine grace for any hope of gaining success" and thus the poem will end with the speaker "praying for God's mercy" (225).

1–4 *If . . . why should I bee?* **FAERBER** (1950) sees here a rejection of the Christian paradox of human existence (29). See also Holy Sonnets: Language and Style. **LEVENSON** (1954) notes that Donne swiftly shifts metaphors, as here "where the mineral, vegetable, and animal kingdoms are traversed in just three lines" (item 36). **MARTZ** (1954): the opening is "an audacious, blasphemous evasion of responsibility" (52). **MARTZ** (1970): there is "wilful misunderstanding" here, as if the tree were at fault, and of course the one serpent has been damned; the crying question will be implicitly answered in line 5 (105–06). **SMITH** (1991): "At the personal level Donne's religious wit follows out the prospect which Christ's double nature opened to us, rehearsing the paradox and the dilemma of our ambiguous state. An animal being nonetheless bears moral responsibility" (133).

1–2 *If . . . els immortall vs,* **GROSART** (1872–73) says that the line, recalling even the rhythm of the opening of *Paradise Lost,* "tells us that Milton read Donne" (2:44). **GOSSE** (1899) finds it "difficult" to believe that Milton "did not read and recollect" these lines (2:108). **MOLONEY** (1944), comparing the lines to the opening of *Paradise Lost,* remarks that Milton "must have known and treasured" them (132). **MOLONEY** (1950) suggests that the similarity between these lines and *Paradise Lost* 1:1–2 represents the only "direct echo of Donne in Milton" (238). **COANDA** (1957): the passage is an example of Donne's "morbidity" (181). **MALLETT** (1983) notes that "death came into the world when Adam and Eve ate the fruit of the tree of the knowledge of good and evil, which God had forbidden" and points to Gen. 3 (58). **PATRIDES** (1985a) alludes to the opening lines of *Paradise Lost* but says, *contra* Moloney (1944), that "there is no evidence that Milton 'must have known'" *HSMin* (440).

1 *If poysonous Minerals, and if that tree* **MELTON** (1906): an insignificant word is frequently stressed in Donne's meter, here "if" (72).

1 *poysonous* **RICHTER** (1902): Donne frequently slurs an unaccented syllable, as here (403–04).

1 *tree* **SHAWCROSS** (1967): "the Tree of Knowledge of Good and Evil of whose fruit Adam and Eve ate, breaking their covenant with God" (341). [Similarly, Lever (1974, 180), Adams (1979, 1101) and Booty (1990, 108).]

2 *threw* **SHAW** (1981) notes the "startling use of the aggressive verb 'threw,'" allowing the speaker to suggest that the fruit, not "the human hand that plucked it," caused the Fall. Further observes that the speaker "then pulls himself up short with the great question" of ll. 9–10 and retreats "from an advocate's to a supplicant's posture" (46).

2 *els* **SULLENS** (1964) points out that Donne's use of the word in this sense is earlier than the first such use noted in the *OED* (adv.4.d.) (213).

3–4 *If . . . why should I bee?* **LOUTHAN** (1951) compares the "Cocks and Lyons" of *Fare* 22 to these lines, both poems reflecting "the nostalgic thought that animals, like infants, are exempt from ethical responsibility" (156). **SMITH** (1971): "only creatures having the power of reasoned choice can incur damnation" (628). [Similarly, Hollander and Kermode (1973, 1051), who cite *Dr. Faustus* XVIII.171ff., and Mallett (1983, 58).] **CAREY** (1981) thinks that the lines signal "symptoms of religious despair," for Donne "envies the animals, because they cannot be damned, as he can" (55). Adds that Donne, suspecting that "his wickedness outweighs that of all the rest of creation" (55), concludes that "we should simply be extremely grateful if we are among the elect" (242).

3 *Lecherous* **RICHTER** (1902): Donne here slurs an unaccented syllable (403–04).

3 *gotes, . . . Serpents envious* **SHAWCROSS** (1967) notes that the goat was associated with Pan "and thus with Satan," while the serpent "was, of course, also identified with Satan" (341). Similarly, Booty (1990, 108). **LEVER** (1974) notes that goats were traditionally regarded as the "most lecherous" creatures. Points to Gen. 3.14–15 regarding the serpent and adds that "envious" means "malicious" and that Donne refers, not to the "archetypal 'serpent' Satan" but to "natural serpents after the Fall," since Satan was "indeed damned" (180).

4 *why should I bee?* **SHAWCROSS** (1967): the speaker "has covered the mineral, vegetable, and animal kingdoms in lines 1–3" (341).

5–6 *Why . . . more heinous?* **MARTZ** (1970): the traditional answer is obvious, for "the power of reason . . . makes man damnable when 'minerals' or trees cannot be damned" (106). **LEVER** (1974) claims that Donne's "protest is based on the Augustinian doctrine that man alone is damned since the Fall by his reason, yet cannot save himself by reason" (180). **PATRIDES** (1985b) finds that Grierson's editorial decisions with respect to the punctuation of Donne's poems were governed by "the general tendency among editors to 'methodize' Donne's poetry" in order to "lessen the turbulence of Donne's more aggressive rhythms," citing as an example these lines from *HSMin*. Notes that the 1633 edition reads: "Why should intent or reason, borne in mee,/Make sinnes, else equall, in mee more heinous?" But finds Grierson (1912) altering the rhythm and tone of the second of these lines "by the unwarranted addition of yet another comma: 'Make sinnes, else equall, in mee, more heinous?'" (371–72).

5 *intent, or reason,* **HANDLEY** (1991): "Will, and the ability to think and judge" (43).

5 *intent,* **GROSART** (1872–73): "thought, or purposing thought" (2:291).

6 *els equall,* **SHAWCROSS** (1967): "otherwise (except for intent of reason) the same as the sins of goats (lust) and serpents (envy)" (341).

7–8 *And . . . why threatens hee?* **KORTEMME** (1933): the paradox is a form of antithesis in which seemingly contradictory characteristics of God are contrasted

(50). **MORRIS** (1953): one way in which Donne rebelled against Petrarchan smoothness was by indicating a pause after the first foot of a line, as in line 8, a device employed by Hopkins in his sprung rhythm, as in "I wake and feel the fell of dark" (l. 3), even on occasion pausing after the first syllable, as in "Carrion Comfort" (l. 13) (53). Donne and Hopkins share a sense of the terror of God, as here and in "Carrion Comfort" (ll. 5–6) (73). **MARTZ** (1970): it is as if the "mention of God reminds the speaker that he is . . . speaking in the presence of his God" (106). **SMITH** (1971): "why does God threaten in anger when it is easy for him to show mercy and his doing so redounds to his glory?" (628). [Similarly, Mallett (1983, 58).] **LINVILLE** (1984b): Donne's use of synaphie underscores his argument for a "ready, compliant outpouring of mercy from God, which he errantly asserts is his due" (72). Donne therefore strives for "an especially smooth, effortless overflow" of line 7, along with the polysyllabic end-word, to create the effect of expansion, making the "carry-over" "easy" and "inevitable," hinting at "that same lenience and flexibility the speaker wishes from his maker" (72–73).

9–14 *But . . . if thou wilt forgett.* **GARDNER** (1952) quotes the lines to illustrate "a note of exaggeration" and "a strained note" in the Holy Sonnets. Compares the feeling in the final couplet to that expressed in Donne's other works and finds that "the close of the sonnet seem[s] facile" (xxx). **COANDA** (1957): the lines parallel Hopkins's "Thou art indeed just, Lord" (ll. 1–4) (187). **MARTZ** (1970): at the beginning of the sestet, the speaker's resistance "breaks down in anguish and fear" (106). **HOLLANDER and KERMODE** (1973) note the change of tone in the sestet, with the speaker reproving himself "for arguing with God's dispensations" (1051). **LEVER** (1974) says that the sestet appears to be "a desperate plea for oblivion" (180).

9–12 *But . . . Sins blacke memoree.* **ROSTON** (1990), calling Donne the "leading English exponent of [meditation]," points to these lines as "marked by a confessional privacy so intense as to bestow upon the speaker a sense almost of eavesdropping"—in contrast to "Late-Baroque versions" where a kind of "theatricalism" prevails, where there is more concern with a "dramatic effect" of scenes upon spectators than with the "intimacy of the personal experience" (63).

9–10 *But . . . only worthy blood* **FAUSSET** (1938): to struggle with God "was the only way in which Donne could come near to the reality he sought and ease the frenzy of his mental solitude" (xiii–xiv). **GARDNER** (1952) (reading the lines as "But who am I, that dare dispute with thee? / O God, Oh! of thine onely worthy blood") keeps the punctuation of 1633, suggesting that it offers a "finer rhythm" and puts the stress "firmly" on "I" and "thee" (68–69). **STEPHENSON** (1959): the lines recall, in their "accent and plainness of diction," Hopkins's "Thou are indeed just, Lord" (304). **LEVER** (1974) cites Job 40.2: "Shall he that contendeth with the Almighty instruct him?" (180). **SINFIELD** (1983): the speaker has exhibited a "trace of resentment" in preceding lines but the complaint is a "gross sin" that is withdrawn with the "Pauline cut-off" (cf. Rom. 9.20) (11). **SINFIELD** (1992):

"'Thine only worthy blood' suggests Christ's generous sacrifice, but 'dare dispute' suggests power rather than goodness: threat and beneficence are inseparable," and thus "the argument is not resolved" (161–62). PALLOTTI (1993) finds in the lines an "echo" of St. Paul's "intense question" of Rom. 9.20 ("O man, who art thou that replies against God?"), a "well-known passage about predestination" (182n23).

9 *with thee* PALLOTTI (1993): "By specifying that the disputation is directed to God ('with thee'), the speaker makes us modify our perspective on the kind of discourse contained in the octave and we are made aware that God has (over)heard the entire discourse" (178).

10–11 *O God? . . . a heauenly Lethean flood* GRANSDEN (1954): Donne's sonnets deal with theological issues but they always have a "personal point of return," here his "tearful expostulation" (131).

10 *O God? O* GRIERSON (1912) insists that the "O" must stand alone, not as one of a "hurried series of exclamations" as in the "O God, Oh!" of recent editions. If the "O God?" completes the previous sentence, the "O" may be heard as "a sigh drawn from the very depths of the heart" (2:233). PALLOTTI (1993): the "vocative 'O God'" not only "identifies explicitly the internal addressee but also brings into prominence God's role in the state of affairs described" (182n24).

10 *thyne only worthy blood* SHAWCROSS (1967): "only God's blood has merit, moral excellence" (341). SMITH (1971): "Christ's blood which alone is worthy to drown the memory of our sins" (628). [Similarly, Hollander and Kermode (1973, 1051), Mallett (1983, 58), and Handley (1991, 43).]

10 *only worthy* CRAIK and CRAIK (1986): "alone having value" (278).

10 *only* PATRIDES (1985a): "alone" (440). [So also, Booty (1990, 108).]

11 *heauenly Lethean* HANDLEY (1991) notes the combination of the pagan and the Christian in the image (43).

11 *Lethean* SHAABER (1958): "causing forgetfulness" (102). SHAWCROSS (1967): "referring to the river of forgetfulness. By 'heavenly' he asks heaven to forget and calls such lack of memory comforting and blissful" (341). SMITH (1971): "Lethe in ancient myth is a river of Hades, out of which the souls of the departed drink oblivion of all their early existence" (629). [Similarly, Lever (1974, 180), Adams (1979, 1101), Mallett (1983, 58), Patrides (1985a, 440), Craik and Craik (1986, 278), and Booty (1990, 108).]

13–14 *That thou . . . if thou wilt forgett.* FAERBER (1950): an example of "reaching back" ("ausholen") by contrast, in which the remembering of the first line adds intensity to the forgetting of the second (11). [See also Holy Sonnets: Language and Style.] GARDNER (1952) thinks that the reading in some mss. ("remember them no more") results from the copyist substituting this familiar phrase for the correct one. Notes that there is much "Scriptural warrant" for the idea of God forgetting sins (69). SHAWCROSS (1967) reads l. 13 to mean "Some people require as a debt owed to them that you remember their sins and them" (341). Cites Ps. 25.7: "Remember not the sins of my youth, nor my transgressions: according to thy mercy remember thou me for thy goodness' sake, O Lord" (408). MARTZ (1970): HSMin "stands on the edge of despair, but never quite falls into the pit." Donne shows at last "an exact command of the theology of redemption" (106). ARCHER (1971) supports Shawcross's reading of l. 13, saying that it emphasizes the antithesis between "some people" and "I," the persona of the poem. Suggests that behind the passage lies a biblical reference to St. Paul, especially Rom. 4.4–5: "Now to him that worketh is the reward not reckoned of grace but of debt. But to him that worketh not, but believeth on him that justified the ungodly, his faith is counted for righteousness." Contends that this antithesis appears in the poem and paraphrases the concluding couplet as follows: "That thou remember them for the merit of their works some claim as debt, salvation being their due; I think it merciful if thou wilt forget my works, good and evil." Remarks that Donne's further purpose in the couplet may have been to discredit a view of salvation based upon works (item 4). SMITH (1971): "some people entreat God to remember their sins and so forgive them as part of the general debt to Christ discharged" (629). [Similarly, Hollander and Kermode (1973, 1051) and Mallett (1983, 58), who adds that the poet "prefers to hope that God will simply forget his sins" and cites Jer. 31.34, as do Barańczak (1984, 161) and Booty (1990, 108)]. LINVILLE (1978) disagrees with Archer's reading (1971) of the concluding couplet, saying that Archer introduces concepts which he supports with scripture, but not with what the poem actually says. Argues that the difficulties in understanding the couplet have stemmed from the tendency of critics to identify the referent of "them" as either "some people" or "their sins" or both, while the context of the poem suggests a more specific antecedent for "them," and a separate identity for "some." States that immediately before the couplet the speaker asks that his sins be erased from his memory and from God's: that the speaker is able to forget is "dependent upon God's prior act of mercy in the forgiveness and forgetting of these sins." Further observes that the speaker "also recognizes the 'claim' that God should be mindful of his sins—the speaker's own sins—just as He is mindful of the sinful state of fallen man, of original sin." Thinks therefore that "some" (l. 13) is "not specific, but refers generally to all who maintain this theological position" (21). Believes that the sonnet "concludes with a plea for mercy greater than justice, greater than fallen man could ever 'claim as debt,'" namely, a reiteration of the plea that God should forget the speaker's sins, noting that the sonnet "moves from prideful disputation, in which reason attempts to exempt itself and man from [this] special position . . . to a humility which recognizes both the rational claim that man's culpability should not be forgotten, and the supra-rational process through which Christ's sacrifice and the speaker's contrition can cancel out that debt." Says that this reading "restores the poem's moral and thematic integrity by showing how its conclusion is related to all its parts" without needing emendation or departing far from the text (22). CRAIK and CRAIK (1986) paraphrase as: "Some people ask thee to remember them (that is, be good to them) as recompense for their faithful service (*as debt*); I think it mercy in thee if thou wilt forget me (that is, forget what a sinner I am)." Notes that the "point" is found in the paradox of l. 14, "since to forget the sinner absolutely would be not mercy but the severest justice" (278–79). **ELLRODT** (1993): sins make up part of the debt paid by Christ, and therefore can be erased only if God remembers them (455). **SCHOENFELDT** (1994): "Although the object of *them* is ostensibly the 'sinnes' of the previous line, it also may include the subsequent 'some.' If so, it curiously praises as an act of divine mercy what George Herbert, in the conclusion of 'Affliction (I),' depicts as the ultimate psychological terror: being forgotten by God" (82).

13 *them,* **LEVER** (1974): the reference is "ambiguous," the pronoun appearing to "refer back to *sins*," but it may more likely refer to the "some" that follows (180). **CAIN** (1981): "referring to sins, not 'some'" (312). **PATRIDES** (1985a): "the speaker's own sins" (440).

13 *Some* **EMPSON** (1935): "some people," not "some sins" (74). **PATRIDES** (1985a) identifies "Some" as "those who maintain this view" and cites Linville (1978) (see notes to ll. 13–14) (440).

13 *Some clayme as dett,* **SHAABER** (1958): "since God can pardon only those sins he remembers" (102).

13 *dett,* **PATRIDES** (1985a): "the debt generally discharged by Christ" (440).

14 *I thinke it Mercy if thou wilt forgett.* **MELTON** (1906): in Donne's meter an insignificant word often carries the stress, here "if" (72). **HARDY** (1942): the line reflects Donne's remorse at his inability to break out of an endless cycle of sin and repentance (179). **SMITH** (1971): "for I will forgive their iniquity, and their sin will I remember no more" (Jer. 31.34) (629). [So also, Lewalski and Sabol (1973, 153) and Patrides (1985a, 440).] **HANDLEY** (1991): i.e., forget "my sins" (43).

 *HSPart*

COMMENTARY

Poet/Persona

Ricks (1966, 190) describes *HSPart* as "a prayer affirming the poet's new-found religious confidence."

Stampfer (1970, 265–66) remarks that there is in *HSPart* a "stately procession of couplings," which are emblematic of the coupling of God's will with the speaker: the father and son share one kingdom, the son having a double interest; the twice-slain lamb has two wills, invested with the legacy of a joint kingdom; grace and the Holy Spirit revive the victims of law and letter; and the speaker is a "disrupted two" that must come to a coupling—the two of body and spirit, torn apart, must arrive at a jointure of body and earth, spirit and God. Stampfer says that the prayer in the last line of the poem represents a culmination of the twelve sonnets in 1633, the "entire bent" of the twelve-sonnet sequence blending "the speaker's will to the will of God." In the closing prayer, he concludes, there is no qualification or confrontation between man and God, but a single will, belonging to them both.

Sicherman (1971, 86–87) points out that the speaker knows in *HSPart* that God's last command "Is all but love" (l. 14), and thus he emerges with the faith that Christ conquers death and the knowledge that God's grace compensates for human insufficiency.

Young (1987, 38) observes that even though Donne's persona in many of the Holy Sonnets is "hag-ridden by doubts of his own sincerity, and hence by doubts of the validity of his sense of grace," the "Calvinist dynamic" does not ultimately "dominate" the Holy Sonnets. Young points out that *HSPart*, Donne's last sonnet in 1633 and 1635, ends with "the law of love—not faith—as the ultimate Christian obligation." According to Young, Donne here is not "taking a position on the theology of justification and grace; he is praying for grace and exhorting himself to love." Young finds Donne "typical" of devotional poets in England in the seventeenth century, "who, though generally Protestant, are not, *in their poetry*, so much militant proponents of the Reformation as Christians confronting God."

Strier (1989, 379) finds *HSPart* to be "carefully and explicitly Protestant—denying that man can fulfill the moral law, a position that it characterizes as being 'argue[d] yet' [l. 9]—but it never generates any emotional intensity," with the final prayer "ambiguous, either a personal plea for grace or a generalized plea for human solidarity."

382

Language and Style

Williamson (1940, 62–64) considers the change effected in *HSPart* by alterations to the pronouns. Line 9 of the 1633 text reads "these laws," he notes, which Grierson (1912) changes to "thy laws"; and line 11 reads "thy all-healing grace" which Grierson alters by omitting the pronoun "thy" (63). Williamson observes that "[h]aving distinguished Father and Son, and having made the Son the author of both Wills," the poet cannot say 'thy laws' without having them refer back to the Father, since Christ's pronoun in the poem is "his." He thinks that "since this is the impossible Will, it is best spoken of without a possessive" (i.e., as "these laws"), indicating the "multiplicity which makes them impossible of fulfillment" (63). Donne is orthodox in referring to Christ as the agent of God's actions, he argues, and he appropriately enough separates the Father from the fatal laws: the "lawes abridgement" is "sufficient to make quite certain the proper context for the two Wills or 'testaments'" (64).

Clark (1982, 76) describes *HSPart* as a homiletic poem, explaining that "the first compact is the legal obligation no man can live up to," but the second, as expressed in lines 13–14, is "merciful redemption."

Linville (1984a, 152–53) finds Donne's awareness of his "divided, complex" self throughout the 1633 sequence, that is, his consciousness of his "changeableness" (152). According to Linville, *HSPart* captures the "doubleness of feeling," in that it does not reflect "a composed, complete, integrating vision" but "provides a final dramatization of the antithetical impulses that have characterized the sonnets throughout the sequence" (152). More specifically, in Linville's view, "the complicated, convoluted, juridical argument" of *HSPart* and its "correspondingly convoluted syntax" have a tendency to "belie or negate the simplicity of soul and faith implied in the concluding request" (152). The inherent tensions in the poetry, for Linville, can serve to "revivif[y] faith by presenting it, not as static ideal, but as process" (153).

A. Smith (1987, 163) contends that it is not clear what the "egregious quibbles and paradoxes" of *HSPart* "have to do with sincere faith." For Smith, "the question is how far the wit becomes its own end." Smith notes that Donne "envisaged a right functioning of religious wit, or rather, a religion that is witty in itself," as in *BedfHon* 44–45.

Themes

Gardner (1952, 72–73) notes that Donne elaborates on the theme of *HSPart* in a sermon on John 14.20, and she quotes from *Sermons*, 9:232.

Reeves (1952, 102) finds Donne's device of combining legal and theological themes "obscure and involved." According to Reeves, the poem concludes that "in order to be a partaker in God's kingdom, man must obey his laws; but since no man can do this wholly, God's love and mercy must make allowance for man's shortcomings."

Peterson (1959, 513) argues that the poem concludes the sequence of the 1633 sonnets by affirming that God's love transcends his justice and that in his command to love lies the penitent's only hope. See more under Holy Sonnets: Themes.

Stein (1962, 41) notes that *HSPart* refers to the Old Law in terms of human love.

Galdon (1975, 122–23) observes that "lamb typology" (i.e., the Lamb of God), with its "mystical applications," is used in HSPart and HSBlack.

Low (1978, 70–71) writes that the poem's style "appropriately" reveals the "difficult questions of law, justice and love" that Donne considers here (70), but he also notes that the mood is "impersonal" (71).

Lewalski (1979, 273) states that HSPart, the last sonnet in both 1633 and 1635, confronts the issue of "how the regenerate Christian should serve God, how he should exhibit that 'new obedience' to God's will that was understood to be the effect of regeneration and adoption." According to Lewalski, the resolution resides in the speaker's recognition that the "New Covenant Law, the summary and epitome of the Old Law, is simply love of God and neighbor."

Yearwood (1982, 210, 219) finds that the conversion process in Donne's twelve Holy Sonnets (in 1633 and following Gardner's 1952 order), "begins in pride, proceeds to confession and despair, and culminates in a humble joy and confidence" (210), and she interprets HSPart as the attainment of full conversion (219). She notes that in this poem (and "for the first time") the speaker addresses God as "Father" (l. 1) and that he assumes and accepts "his sonship as a gift he has been given because God was 'made like man'" (HSWilt 14) not, as he mistakenly asserts in HSMade, because "he was made by God." Yearwood calls attention to the quiet and assured tone, and the form of the poem as a prayer (219).

HSPart and Other Works

Milward (1979 [1988, 83]) regards HSPart in the group of twelve (in 1633 and following Gardner's order [1952]) as a continuation of the Ignatian meditative exercise on the Contemplation for Obtaining Divine Love found in HSWilt. In this sonnet, in Milward's analysis, the speaker "concentrates on the sacrificial love of the Son, as Lamb of God."

Notes and Glosses

1–8 *Father, . . . thy Sonnes invest.* SMITH (1970) says that it is not immediately clear how the "egregious quibbles and paradoxes" in these lines pertain to "sincere faith" but goes on to assert Donne's belief in a "right functioning of religious wit" (163). SMITH (1991) acknowledges that Donne's "pious wit can seem unaccommodatingly knotty," but asserts that the "legal quibbling is not wanton ingenuity." Suggests that it develops the "intricate interrelation of divine being with human nature, timeless events with history" (135).

1–4 *Father, . . . his deaths Conquest.* RUGOFF (1939) comments that Donne's use of images of commerce, as in these lines, is an aspect of his "rejection of Petrarchan and Spenserian conventions" (144).

1–2 *Father, . . . thy Sonne giues to mee;* LOW (1993) notes that in this poem God is "king, father, and property owner, as well as creator" (69).

1 *Father, part of his double interest* **MOLONEY** (1950): the line is an instance of "centroidal grouping" of words to produce emphasis, similar to lines in Milton (238). See also The Holy Sonnets and Other Works.

1 *his double interest* **GARDNER** (1952): "his two-fold claim" (73). [So also Kermode (1968, 181), Smith (1971, 633), and Patrides (1985a, 444).] **MARTZ** (1963): "legal claim to or participation in ownership" (91). **SHAWCROSS** (1967): "as part of the Trinity and as blessed man" (345). [Similarly, Booty (1990, 109).]

3–4 *His . . . his deaths Conquest.* **UL-HASAN** (1958) notes that the powers of God are often expressed in legal terms (47).

3 *ioynture* **GARDNER** (1952): "'the holding of an estate by two or more persons in joint-tenancy' [similarly, Martz (1963, 91), Shawcross (1967, 345), Kermode (1968, 181), Smith (1971, 633), and Booty (1990, 109)] (O.E.D., now obsolete)" (73). **SULLENS** (1964) says that the OED does not record a figurative use of the word as Donne has it here (262). **PATRIDES** (1985a): "joint possession" (444).

3 *knotty trinitee* **KLINCK** (1981): "here the Father, as power or sovereignty, is spoken of as having a 'kingdome' [l. 2]; the Son, as redeemer, has invested mankind with an interest in this 'kingdome'; man, however, cannot fulfill the laws of this kingdom without 'all-healing grace and spirit' [l. 11]" (251).

3 *knotty* **GARDNER** (1952): "entangled, or inextricably tied together; and 'full of intellectual difficulties, hard to explain' (O.E.D.)" (73). [Similarly, Smith (1971, 633) and Patrides (1985a, 444).] **SHAWCROSS** (1967): "difficult to comprehend or unravel, alluding to the problem of explaining three persons indivisible" (345).

4 *He keepes, and giues me his deaths Conquest.* **GARDNER** (1952) believes that the irregular meter derives from the poet's "intention," noting that a "marked pause" in the line provides "rythmic compensation for metrical deficiency" (62).

4–5 *Conquest. . . . blest* **STEIN** (1942): Donne at times shifts the stress in the fifth foot of his couplets, producing "a feminine rime which is invariably matched with a masculine" (681).

4 *deaths Conquest.* **SMITH** (1971): "what he won by his death" (633). **PA-TRIDES** (1985a): "conquest of death" (444). [So also, Booty (1990, 109).]

5–6 *This . . . Worlds beginning slayne, and hee* **SIMPSON** (1948) detects a linkage between the Holy Sonnets and the *Essays*, for example in their reliance on imagery from the Book of Revelation, here "the description of Christ as 'the lamb slain from the foundation of the world'" in Rev. 13.8 (211–12). **FAERBER** (1950): the lines describe one of the paradoxes of God, similar to a paradox of Christ. [See more under Holy Sonnets: Language and Style.]

6 *Was from the Worlds beginning slayne, and hee* **GARDNER** (1952) cites Rev.

13.8: "the Lamb slain from the foundation of the world." (So also, Shawcross [1967, 345], Martz (1969a, 86), Smith [1971, 633], Lewalski and Sabol [1973, 156], Patrides [1985a, 444], Booty [1990, 109], Carey [1990b, 455], and Ellrodt [1993, 456].) Notes that all "English versions before A.V. have 'from the beginning'" (similarly, Lewalski and Sabol [1973, 156]) (73).

7 *two Wills,* GARDNER (1952): "The two Wills are the two Testaments. [So also Martz (1963, 91), Shawcross (1967, 346), Smith (1971, 633), Lewalski and Sabol (1973, 157), Cain (1981, 312), Patrides (1985a, 445), Booty (1990, 109), and Carey (1990b, 455).] Both are of force by the death of the Testator"; cf. Heb. 9.15–17 (73).

8 *doth thy Sonnes invest.* SHAWCROSS (1967): "do envelop men; do commit men to a course of action (in order to gain the legacy); do offer men opportunity for moral profit" (346).

8 *invest.* MARTZ (1963): "place in possession of" (91). PATRIDES (1985a): "grant the rights to" (445).

9–11 *Yet . . . all-healing Grace and Spiritt* STEIN (1942): the passage is an example of Donne's frequent rhyming of masculine and feminine endings ["yett" and "Spirit"] (680). MORRIS (1953): both Donne and Hopkins elide whole phrases to avoid repetition, as here (the absence of "fulfill those statues" after "None doth") and in "To seem the stranger" (ll. 13–14) (66–67).

9 *Yet such are thy Laws, that Men argue yett* MELTON (1906): Donne frequently begins and ends a line with the same word (150).

9 *thy* PATRIDES (1985) (reading "these") notes that various mss. read "those" or "thy" and cites Williamson (1960 [rpt. from 1940—ed.]—see *HSPart:* Language and Style) (445).

10 *those Statutes* SMITH (1971): "God's laws, such as the Ten Commandments, that set down the conditions on which men can inherit Christ's bequest to them in the Testaments" (633).

11–14 *None . . . last Will stand.* RASPA (1983) comments that here Donne exalts "all-healing grace" but limits its "power by declaring 'love' the divine 'last Will' to stand" (64–65). Suggests that the poet's "inability to win grace except as a gift" hints at "strong Puritan and Lutheran origins," but as a gift "undeserved by men, grace did not eliminate the will as the link between the poet, the baroque world, and meditative verse" (64).

11–12 *None . . . what Law and Letter kill.* GARDNER (1952) cites John 1.17, "The law was given by Moses, but grace and truth came by Jesus Christ" (so also, Lewalski and Sabol [1973, 157]) and 2 Cor. 3.6: "The letter killeth, but the spirit giveth life" (so also, Cain [1981, 312], Patrides [1985a, 445], Booty [1990, 109], and Carey [1990b, 455], who cites both biblical texts). Argues that "the capital of 'Spirit' is right, and that Donne intends a reference to the Holy Spirit, the bequest of Christ in his 'last Will,'" adding that "Spirit" and "Holy Spirit" are frequently found "without an article in the Greek New Testament" and pointing to Donne's discussion in *Sermons*, 5:60–61 (74). **SMITH** (1971): "by the law and letter of the Old Testament we merit death, but the grace of Christ and the operation of the Holy Spirit (Christ's bequest to us) offer us life" (633). **LEWALSKI** (1979): "these lines echo a medley of Pauline texts" such as Gal. 5.1 and 2 Cor. 3.5–6 (273).

11 *None doth; but all-healing Grace and Spiritt* **GARDNER** (1952) suggests that the "metrical irregularity" of the line is intended by the poet (73–74).

11 *but all-healing Grace* **PATRIDES** (1985a) (reading "thy all-healing grace") notes that "thy" is omitted in some mss. and by some modern editors (e.g., Grierson [1912] and Gardner [1952]) but points to Williamson's discussion (1960) (445).

13–14 *Thy Lawes abridgment, . . . Oh let that last Will stand.* **BARAŃCZAK** (1984): *HSPart* emphasizes the "difference between the Old Testament's severe law of the Decalogue, and the New Testament, based on love." Cf. John 13.34: "I give you a new commandment, that you love one another. Just as I have loved you, you also should love one another" (162).

13 *Lawes abridgment,* **GARDNER** (1952) cites *Sermons*, 9:150: "Where the Jews had all abridged in *decem verba* . . . the Christian hath all abridged in *duo verba*, into two words, love God, love thy neighbour" (74). **KERMODE** (1968): "To love God and one's neighbor" (182). **SMITH** (1971): "the Ten Commandments, which epitomize God's law" (633). **CAREY** (1990b) cites Mark 12.29–31 (455).

13 *thy last Command* **GARDNER** (1952): Cf. John 13.34: "A new commandment I give unto you, That ye love one another" (74). [Similarly, Lewalski and Sabol (1973, 157) and Carey (1990, 455).]

14 *all but Love;* **GROSART** (1872–73): "curious English for 'is all love *only*,' i.e. is all love and love only" (2:291). **MARTZ** (1963): "*but* in the sense of *only*: 'nothing but love'; see John 13:34" (92). **SMITH** (1971) points out that the Ten Commandments "rest upon the notion of a just reward for obedience rather than upon love and notes that Christ "added a commandment when he enjoined us to love one another" in John 13.34. Observes that "it is upon Christ's mercy and love for us that our salvation depends, since in strict justice we stand condemned" (633). **PATRIDES** (1985a): "nothing but" (445).

14 *Oh let that last Will stand.* **SMITH** (1971): "uphold the New Testament and put aside the Old Testament; let our salvation stand upon love and mercy, not upon justice" (633). **GARDNER** (1952) prefers "that last Will" over "thy last Will" (as found in some mss.), suggesting that "that" is stronger in emphasis (74).

14 *last Will* **SHAWCROSS** (1967): "Jesus's last command" (John 13.34) (346). [So also, Booty (1990, 109).]

 HSRound

General Commentary

Richards (1929, 4, 42–50, 365) includes the responses to *HSRound* of a number of readers who commented upon it without knowing its title or author. Richards identifies the majority of them as "undergraduates reading English with a view to an Honours Degree," though some were reading in other subjects and there was a "sprinkling" of non-academics (4). Richards, in classifying responses, characterizes them as the consequence of "doctrinal grudge" (44), "anti-religious prejudice" (45), "moral objection to the poet's attitude" (45), "ignorance of Christian cosmology" (47), "inexperience" or "lack of familiarity" with even "simple verse movements" (49), and "frustrated visualization" (49). In reporting the relative popularity of the thirteen anonymous poems examined, Richards lists the responses to *HSRound* as 30 "favourable" (11th of 13), 42 "unfavourable" (tie for 5th of 13), and 28 "non-committed" (13th of 13) (365).

Eliot (1930, 552–53) distinguishes between religious and devotional poetry, the former arising from a religious feeling, the latter from something connected with revealed religion; and he quotes *HSRound* in full as an example of Donne's best "religious poetry."

Bush (1945, 134) cites the poem as an example of Donne's "medieval learning."

Brooke (1948, 635) says of *HSRound* that it "rises easily above all the rest" of the Holy Sonnets.

Turnell (1950, 273) identifies *HSRound* as one of Donne's "greatest poems and one of the greatest sonnets in the language."

Gransden (1954, 135) cites *HSRound* as a "fine example" of Donne's use of "traditional medieval material."

Sanders (1971, 132) says that *HSRound* does not offer much for our understanding of what it means to "behold God."

Bellette (1975, 334–41) writes that the idea of Christ on the cross affects the form of *HSMade, HSScene* and *HSRound*, and notes that these three sonnets may be read as forming a sequence "depicting . . . the transition from this world to the next" (334). See fuller commentary under *HSMade*: General Commentary.

Skelton (1978, 67–68), writing about the relationship between a poet's beliefs and those of his readers, observes that in a poem like *HSRound* it is important for a reader to know about the intense feelings involved in the Last Judgment, not necessarily to endorse those beliefs but to appreciate the anguish of the speaker. *HSRound*, he suggests, like the other Holy Sonnets, "relies upon expressed beliefs only to the extent that these are symptomatic of all beliefs of a certain kind" (68).

Wellek (1986, 227) cites Richards's critical study (1929), noting that Richards views *HSRound* as a poem that may evoke the "fullest emotional belief while withholding intellectual belief," but Wellek understands this to be an "inferior" response, since Richards goes on to contend that *HSRound* "requires *actual belief* in the doctrine for its full and perfect imaginative realization."

Zemplényi (1986, 157–58), noting that both Gardner (1952—see Holy Sonnets: Dating and Order) and Martz (1954—see *HSRound*: Genre and Traditions and Holy Sonnets: Genre and Traditions) analyze *HSRound* as "a poetic meditation," finds another interpretation of the poem possible: "while the theology represented in the sonnet is absolutely orthodox, both from Catholic and Anglican sides, the poem's whole structure is ironic," with the greatest irony in the beginning and the ending, giving "an ironic frame to the work," which is directed in part "against poetic tradition" (158). See also Notes and Glosses to lines 1–2.

Ray (1990b, 39–40) identifies the speaker of *HSRound* as "a Christian ready for the end of the world and the Last Judgment," waiting "to see the four angels standing on the four corners of the earth blowing their trumpets" (Rev. 7.1) and the resurrection and reunion of souls to bodies in anticipation of Final Judgment (39–40). Ray notes that Donne "conveys the drama and grandeur of the unfathomable massiveness in such an assembly by the inclusive listings and by repetition and heavy stresses on 'all.'" But the sestet, according to Ray, presents the speaker as "suddenly fearful and having misgivings," a change "evident in the word 'But' that begins the sestet." Perceiving the need for more time to pray and repent, the speaker, Ray argues, "reverses himself by asking God to, after all, wait a bit longer before he causes the end of the world and the resurrection of the dead ('let them sleep')." The speaker wants God to teach him how to repent in the "'here' and now," which, for Ray, is an "important" initial step "to assure his salvation" (40).

Levi (1991, 93–94) finds "visionary passages" in Donne's poetry, much as there are "visionary sentences" in his sermons, and yet, he thinks, Donne "never maintains visionary intensity throughout an entire secular poem." But Levi finds Donne "capable of unearthly visions," such as those present in *HSRound* (93). Levi maintains that Donne's "constant urge is to outsoar his own mind's boundaries, to race towards a receding horizon, to come close to saying what cannot be said," but he also finds Donne "too passionate for innocent visions, and too thoughtful for simple ones" and thus "his greatness lies elsewhere." In Levi's view, *HSRound* "droops away into religious melancholy about sin, as so many of Donne's religious poems do" (94).

Ellrodt (1995, 21–22) notes that Donne wrote in one of his letters (*Letters* 70–72) that "since men have various affections, therefore various minds," and therefore, "out of this variety of minds it proceeds, that though our souls would go to one end, heaven, and all our bodies must go to one end, the earth; yet our third part, the mind, which is our natural guide here, chooses to every man a several way" (21–22). Ellrodt comments that an "unorthodox theologian" might think that the soul "only survives as an impersonal spiritual principle in the period between death and the resurrection," but he adds that Donne does not explicitly state this view, though it would be "consonant with his dallying with the mortalist heresy" in *HSRound* (22).

Date and Circumstances

Rosenthal, Hummel, and Leichty (1944, 407) observe that the sonnet was written "after the young-man-about-London had found his career in the Church."

The Poet/Persona

Praz (1925, 68) notes that in the poem Donne implores God to delay judgment so he will have time to repent.

Payne (1926, 141) quotes the poem in full to illustrate Donne's conviction that repentance must precede the remission of sins.

Leishman (1934, 87) observes that Donne, so concerned with his own spiritual inadequacies, often dwells on "the awfulness of God," but calms his fears by contemplating eternal glory, as in *HSRound* where the terrible vision of the Last Judgment is followed by the thought that no terrors need shake the sincerely repentant.

Leishman (1951, 259–60) quotes *HSRound* in full to illustrate Donne's need "to exaggerate the sins of his youth in order to bring home to himself the need for repentance" and to do so by "dwelling on the terrors of death and the possibility of perishing, as he expresses it, on the shore" (259). It is, Leishman continues, as if in order to persuade himself "of the need for repentance here and now, Donne had first to fill his imagination with the sound and spectacle of the Last Judgment, when repentance would be too late" (260).

Hunt (1954, 187–88) questions Bennett's contention (1934) that the poem is not philosophical in content (see notes to ll. 1–4). Hunt argues that Donne is a "practitioner of Eliot's 'objective correlative,'" using "abstract ideas" in his verse because he is inquiring after, in Eliot's words, "the intellectual equivalents of emotion." Hunt finds "unhistorical" Bennett's theory that Donne uses metaphysical images such as those from alchemy and astrology "because they are the mode by which his mind articulates states of feeling." Modern thinkers, he argues, have methods unknown to the Renaissance by which "to draw a sharp division between fact and fantasy in the realm of theoretical speculation about the natural world." Donne, on the other hand, Hunt concludes, like others of his era, "could not make up his mind about whether these ideas are true or false"; hence "in his poems he is presenting those conceits fundamentally as philosophical statements which are, or may well be, factually true."

Ricks (1966, 190) regards *HSRound* as one of those sonnets that forms "a meditation by means of which the poet arrives at a realization of the relevance of redemption to him personally."

French (1970, 115–16) contends that Donne is bluffing in *HSRound*, in the sense that he is "simultaneously trying to represent himself as very sinful and not very sinful" (115). The whole progress of the sonnet is confused, French asserts, because Donne is suggesting at the same time that he is no more culpable than a man who dies of an ague and that he is yet very culpable, indeed. Donne might be suggesting the latter, French says, because he wants God to take notice of him. Feeling "lonely, and small, and rather deserted," the speaker "can feel himself to be someone important," French claims, if he can say, "above all these, my sinnes abound" (115–16).

Sicherman (1971, 85) writes that Donne wishes to improve his knowledge of God's love; therefore, the speaker undertakes the discipline of fear of judgment in HSRound, evoking intense terror in the octave and penitence in the sestet.

Kremen (1972, 113–14) notes that Donne's imagination is characteristically attracted to last things, and she states that HSRound dramatizes not only his "eschatological imagination but also his personal, urgent *agon* of proper penance." The theology of HSRound, Kremen argues, is traditional, except that it delays the saved soul's resurrection to God's presence from the hours of death until after the general last judgment. Donne's deviation is dramatically and theologically justified, she contends, since Donne desires to delay God's last judgment on him until he has had a chance to repent of his sins.

Roston (1974, 62–63, 101) argues that HSRound is the "reverse" (62) of Milton's sonnet on his blindness, noting that HSRound begins with "the magniloquence of the baroque" and closes with "the quiet voice of the speaker's own soul" (63). Roston argues that the opening lines of HSRound show Donne transcending "the mechanistic universe" posited by Copernicus, Galileo, and Kepler as "irrelevant to man's spiritual concerns" (101). Roston argues that, in HSRound, Donne prefers the imagined world over the physical world.

Parker (1975, 55) writes that though HSRound is in part an expression of "affirmation and joy," it also has a "dying fall," the sestet confirming the speaker's realization of his own "need for grace."

Berry (1976, 15–16) argues that HSRound is expressive of a conservative political outlook, observing that in this sonnet "'Puritanic' eschatological preoccupation and personal sense of sin both emerge clearly" (15). He believes that Donne's use of "as if" in the final line of the poem is indicative of a "tentativeness" that reinforces and echoes the poet's willingness to live in the uncertainties of this life "here" because only in due course of time will he arrive "there" (16). Present and future are run together in the first line, he says, and are separated as the poem progresses.

Wall (1976, 195–96) writes that, though the sestet of HSRound begins on a note of reconciliation, the speaker loses confidence and prays for more time in which God can help him achieve true assent to God's Love. He argues that HSRound "establishes a context" in which a dramatic movement of achieving reconciliation takes place.

Carey (1981, 202–03, 229) argues that "death preponderates in Donne's religious poems even more markedly than in his love poems." According to Carey, Donne craves death in his religious poems, such as HSRound, because, for one reason, "dead he will at last know whether or not he is saved" (202). Carey explains Donne's request at the beginning of the poem for the Last Judgment to take place immediately as relieving Donne "of the necessity of dying and rotting, as everyone else in history has had to do." Hence, in Carey's view, the speaker initially asks "impatiently" that the Last Judgment occur "without more ado," but what finally deters the speaker in the second part of the poem is not the thought of other lives that would be cut short but the recognition that an "immediate apocalypse" might not "ensure his salvation." Carey contends, finally, that the poem is a "characteristic display of egotism" (229).

Marotti (1986, 255–56) sees "the conflict between assertion and submission," which is enacted in the Holy Sonnets, taking a turn after *HSDue*, the first Holy Sonnet in 1633, and thus the speaker adopts an attitude evident in a number of the other sonnets, namely, an "affectionate humility that is a precondition to receiving divine grace" (255). *HSRound*, for example, shifts from "prideful assertion" in the octave to "humble submission" in the sestet (256), but Marotti finds here and in several other Holy Sonnets an element of boastfulness and an over-dramatization of the self, despite "the gestures of self-effacement" (256).

Rollin (1986, 138–39) interprets the speaker's perception of repentance as a skill that one needs to be taught as "yet another instance of the confusion of Donne's persona." Rollin finds that "what most marks the confusion of Donne's speaker" is "his claim that learning how to repent will be 'as good/As if thou'hadst seal'd my pardon, with thy blood'" [ll. 13–14], noting that "the conditional mood used here is shocking if not heretical" (138). Even if the speaker "*mis*interprets," the guiding question for the speaker, according to Rollin, is whether the employment of a concept enables him to engage in "the doctrinal interpretation of life situations." "Implicit in the speaker's rhetoric," says Rollin, is "the replacement of an untenable power fantasy, in which he presides over the world's destruction, by a more appropriate fantasy of submission, in which he represents himself as suppliant, student, and criminal" (139).

Nash (1989, 143–45) claims that an analysis of the "figurative rhetoric" of *HSRound* would be "meaningless without the statement of a crucial distinction between octave and sestet, a distinction between roles adopted by the poet-speaker." For Nash, the poet assumes the role of "an immortal or a divine being" in the octave, as he calls to the dead to "rise from their graves," and he "commands the trumpeter angels to sound the call that will begin the Resurrection" (143). But in the sestet, according to Nash, the role of the poet-speaker is "abandoned and reversed; the speaker is now the miserable sinner, confessing to God his need for repentance and atonement." The contrast between the octave and sestet is, for Nash, more than simply a "change of tone"; rather, it is "a change of authorial role, of stance," that is, "the power-posture of the octave yields to the stance of humility in the sestet." Nash also notes the reduction in figurative elements in the sestet as the poet-speaker assumes "a healthier sense of reality" (144). Nash thus emphasizes that *HSRound* is an example of how "figures of speech" can nonetheless have "organic significance in works of literature" (144–45).

Genre and Traditions

Hamer (1930, 201) quotes the poem in full as an example of Donne's departure from conventions to make the sonnet a "less formal and a more impressive instrument." Hamer scans the poem to illustrate Donne's use of substitution, especially spondees, his shifting caesura, and the frequency with which he employs "overflow," a run-on line that disregards the customary divisions into quatrains and couplets.

Martz (1954, 50–51) finds that the sonnet includes all three steps of the traditional Ignatian meditation: in the first quatrain the speaker calls on the memory of Doomsday in the Book of Revelation; in the second he analyzes the causes of death; in the sestet, a "colloquy with God," the will expresses its "affections" in a petition. See more under Holy Sonnets: Genre and Traditions.

Hussey (1981, 97) describes HSRound as "a concise example of a controlled poetic meditation along Ignatian lines."

Structure

Gransden (1954, 135) asserts that the octet "transports our imagination to the traditional scene of the Last Day," but the poet himself, Gransden maintains, "is not part of this scene." The sestet, by contrast, is "a prayer that what has just been depicted shall not take place until he has learned how to repent."

Stampfer (1970, 247) asserts that in HSRound, HSMin, and HSDeath, Donne prays "in attunement to the universal human condition." The octave of HSRound comprises the thesis, Stampfer states, which is "vehement, illusory action": the speaker would by a force of spirit evoke Judgment Day. Lines 9 to 12 contain the antithesis of "befuddled helplessness," he says, where the speaker falls back on his fallen condition for possible penance. The synthesis, which is in the last two-and-a-half lines, Stampfer notes, has a muted sincerity as the speaker asks for a lesson in repentance. "Standing now on a glum, flat truth," Stampfer concludes, "sensing he requires a fresh stirring of soul, he begins at last to pray in earnest."

Power (1972, 26–27) finds in HSRound an "abrupt change in attitude between octet and sestet," a change not so much because of the evident "evolution" of the speaker's "thoughts or feelings" but because of the progress implicit in the form of Ignatian meditation. In the octet, she says, we have the "assured, egocentric voice of the love poems" that commands, but in the sestet the speaker "implores," changing from "confidence to doubt," from "addressing men and angels to addressing God," from "projecting himself imaginatively in the Day of Judgment to returning to the present," and thus from "invoking an imagined end of the world to asking for its postponement." The speaker's change, she suggests, apparently comes from his "awareness of his own sins," but the "thoughts which prompt the shift," she argues, remain absent from the poem (27).

Kermode (1974, 91–92) is especially interested in the break between the opening octave and the sestet of HSRound. The octave, he says, has "a picture of the end of everything," and, characteristically, Donne "wants to get everybody in." But in the sestet, he notes, "the tone is deliberately lowered," becoming more focused on the speaker and his need for "grace abounding" (92).

Ellrodt (1980, 172n45) identifies three steps in the progression of the argument of the poem: (1) (ll. 1–4) "a supposition based on the assumption that angels and blessed souls alike can know the minds of men intuitively, i.e. what Donne, following St. Thomas, habitually denied" (cf. Sermons, 4: 316, 10: 58); (2) (ll. 5–8) "another supposition obviously derived from St. Thomas, who granted angels some knowledge of men's thoughts when manifested through outward signs in the body (Summa, Ia, q. 57, art. 4), hence the fear of misinterpretation" (ll. 9–12); and (3) (ll. 12–14) "the problem is dismissed by the poet since the essential thing is that God should know his thoughts."

Conrad (1985, 235), discussing several Holy Sonnets in terms of the relationship between the octave and the sestet, observes that HSRound "makes a portentous noise in its octave to orchestrate the last judgement," and then proceeds, "having summoned to resurrection these 'numberlesse infinities,'" to decide in the sestet "on their quietening and its own more studious quieting," as in line 9.

Gill (1990, 101–02, 141–42) finds "striking contrasts between the octave and the sestet" (101), asking "what is to be made of the way the colourful, highly peopled and even theatrical opening is followed by a visually spare and highly individualistic close?" He finds "the overall stance" of the poet "puzzling," for in the octave he "speaks in bold imperatives, while in the sestet he is fittingly humble" (102). Gill proposes that one explanation may reside in the tension between Catholicism and Protestantism in Donne's verse. In HSRound, Gill states, the octave is "highly visual and essentially Catholic in its communal imagery, thought and feeling," whereas the sestet "seems quite Protestant in its emphasis upon the individual's relationship with God and the way it is visually restrained" (141–42).

Language and Style

Garnett and Gosse (1903, 294) quote the poem in full as one "in which the majesty of his sombre imagination is finely exemplified."

Symons (1916, 103), citing HSRound specifically, finds the Holy Sonnets "a kind of argument with God" in which "they tell over, and discuss, and resolve" matters of faith and reason.

Aronstein (1920, 83) remarks on the sonnet's powerful "stream of poetry" ("Strom der Poesie").

Bennett (1934, 16) argues that Donne was able to pass abruptly "from the trivial to the sublime." She contrasts the "magnificence" of lines 1–4 with the catalogue of "a motley assortment of human ills" in lines 6–7, and concludes that it "is an essential character of his mind that he recognizes trivial mundane affairs as part of the same experience as death and the dread of eternity."

Schirmer (1937, 299) finds that in contrast to the peaceful tone of HSDeath, the poem is "rousing" ("raushenden"), revealing Donne's spiritual insecurity.

Rosenthal, Hummel, and Leichty (1944, 412), in comparing HSRound and SGo, find the sonnet superior in its employment of the imperative mode: (1) it is used "in a grave appeal" rather than "half-sarcastically"; (2) the sonnet opens with "a mighty phrase" rather than a command; and (3) the imperatives following add dignity to the opening "with their own compelling sonorousness."

Daniells (1945, 401–02) cites the poem to illustrate baroque elements in Donne's verse, the "sequence of outbreak, compound fracture of smooth convention and smooth line, and then the masterly moulding of language to carry out the dramatic pattern."

Mims (1948, 56) finds in HSRound "a vigor of imagination that has rarely been surpassed."

Brower (1951, 67–70), in a detailed examination of sound in the poem, finds the sonnet "conceived in two sharply contrasting situations and tones: the imagined judgment day in which the poet all but assumes the voice of God, and the meditation in which he speaks to his Lord in humble intimacy," a contrast brought into focus by the "there" and "here" of line 12 (67). Brower argues, however, that there is a continuity between the two parts of the poem, one achieved by a variety of effects: first, the reader's memory of the "grand and awful scene in the opening lines" underlies the sestet; second, Donne duplicates the "continuous stresses and sharp pauses" of the octave, as in lines 6–7, in the "freely distributed pauses of reflective conversation" in the sestet (68–69); and third, there is the "adjustment of particular sound patterns to meaning." Brower adds that the repetition of the long "o" in the opening lines, appropriate to the "Tuba mirum spargens sonum" of the Requiem, achieves an "immediacy" that carries over into the second half, as in lines 13–14 where Donne contracts, elides, and "brings together consonants of very similar sound" to "relax our utterance" into the tone of casual speech. Finally, according to Brower, continuity is achieved by the variety of rhythms throughout, as in the shift in meter of "All whom" (ll. 5–6) and the reversal of accent of "there; here" in line 12 (70).

Hunt (1954, 158–59) detects in the use of "imagind" in l. 1 evidence of Donne's inclination to "submit his mind to things" in the Baconian sense; he has a need "to run a quick laboratory check" on medieval thought "before he would cut his mind loose on a traditional religious concept" (158). Hunt finds that in a poem depicting "the dreadful reality of the Day of Doom," Donne pauses to point out that "Revelation is a little off on its facts," that "four angels cannot possibly stand at the four corners" of a "round earth." Hunt argues that the use of "imagind" throws a "skeptical, empirical qualification into a poetic picture of the Day of Judgment," in effect testing "religious doctrine against scientific fact," running a "scientific check on the myth of Judgment Day" (159).

Cox (1956a, 113) finds "no essential change of style" within the Holy Sonnets, noting that they can express "conflict and doubt or fear" and with "unparalleled force." He points out, for example, that Donne "can stop to remember that the round world's corners are 'imagin'd'" without destroying the power of his vision of Judgement Day."

Buckley (1965, 29–30) declares HSRound a "splendid exception" to his general claim that the Holy Sonnets are overly "histrionic," and he notes that this is a poem "of resurrection rather than self-accusation or self-reproach," tempting the poet perhaps to "violent affirmation," but not, Buckley argues, to "histrionics" (29–30). In the poem, Buckley notes, we see the "unique quality of Donne's passion" and witness an example of the "finest paradox" of religious poetry. He further points to the "rhetorical magnificence" of HSRound, concluding that there is not in the poem "a single note of cheapness" and that its "final effect" is not "of persuasion but of revelation" (30).

Citing HSRound, Smith (1970, 161–62) calls Donne's rhetoric an "affirmation"; that is, "it proclaims the possibility of a heroic triumph snatched from likely defeat" (161). He believes that the "slackened tension" in the poem "takes with it the whole force of an assured resurrection which is the sense of the poem" (162).

In his analysis of the rhythmic structure of English verse, Kiparsky (1977, 202) contrasts the poetry of Donne and Milton. Citing lines from HSRound and HSSouls, he states that the "simultaneous bracketing and labeling mismatches, occasionally encountered in Donne, simply do not occur in Milton."

Asals (1979, 128–29, 134) contends that "the practice of the grammar of redemption" gives *HSRound* its meaning, in the "dynamic by which word becomes effect and by which the poet's own words (in imitation of his God's) may effect his own redemption" (128–29). In a detailed reading of the sonnet in the context of the "grammar of redemption," Asals argues that "considering the significance Donne finds in the difference between God's primary idiom, imperative command, and his secondary idiom, the hortatory 'let,'" we must be especially attentive to the change from imperative (ll. 1–2) to hortatory (l. 9). According to Asals, "let" signals that "now is the time for concurrence, now is the time for the speaker's participation in God's idiom of dialogue and consultation." Asals adds that the "lowly ground" (l. 12) "on which Donne asks to be taught repentance" is poetry, and the "lowly ground of poetry is the logical ground for salvation" (134).

Carey (1981, 202–03) maintains that the subject of death "attracts because it is a crisis," and "its insertion into poems, secular or divine, can help to make them urgent and momentous as the self-dramatizing Donne needs them to be."

Sloane (1981, 83) calls attention to Donne's emblematic practice, in which it is expected that the picture he creates "of the corners of the earth, the trumpets, and the angels," will "call forth everything that the reader has learned about the last judgment from the Book of Revelation."

Sloane (1985, 159–60, 178–81) examines the sonnet in order to call attention to "the effects of controversial thinking on conventions." Sloane points to the opening of *HSRound* in which the earth's "roundness is a given" and its corners "imputed," and "yet the angels are asked to sound the Day of Judgment." Sloane contends that the Day of Judgment "*emotionally* overwhelms both the given reality and the imputed construction" to the extent that it "seems to belong to another order of things altogether beyond the reality of the earth's roundness or the imputation of the corners" (159). Sloane describes this change as similar to "typical [rhetorical *controversia*] built on prolepsis and reconciliation: when two matters are in controversy, one gives way to another or they both give way to a third—either in the poem or in the mind of the audience" (159, 181). Sloane claims that even to the "slight" extent that "as if" (l. 14) "leaves the door open for the reader who is no literalist," even such a reader "must nonetheless reconcile the controversy on the level of personal belief, or fail to reconcile it" (159–60). And therefore, according to Sloane, "the controversy is between personalism and convention," which are "joined at the conclusion" by a "conditional" (160). Sloane considers the value of the rhetorical approach to our understanding of the sonnet, and he concludes that it "is able to offer little more than a view of the poem as the working out of a stance toward eternal religious verities" (178). But, according to Sloane, Donne's speaker "would seem to be skeptical of all truths but those he can immediately experience" (178). What Sloane finds in Donne's poetry is that "external events, like an external audience, are interiorized, questioned, and transformed into truth" (178), and he concludes that in *HSRound* (or "any of Donne's poems"), we must grasp an "interiority that is Donne's highest artistic achievement, self-fashioned but ultimately in imitation of Christ who, as Erasmus stated, drew all things unto himself" (179).

Flanigan (1986, 50–53, 55) accounts for some of the difficulty in interpreting the sonnet, and literature in general, "in terms of a general failure to read the poem as the words of a pretended speaker who is following the accepted conventions for speech in a particular context of action." She finds that the application of speech-act theory to literary criticism overcomes some of the "problematic features" of the sonnet. The theory focuses on three aspects of the speech-act: "locutions (the physical words or utterances themselves), illocutions (the words viewed in terms of their meaning or 'point' in a particular context), and perlocutions (the effects or consequences of the words in the 'real' world)." Flanigan adds that "the literary speech act is *mimetic* of real speech acts; it is fictive, or imaginary, 'make-believe' or pretended discourse, with the usual rules of social speech suspended" (50).

In looking at Donne's sonnet as a mimetic speech act, then, Flanigan notes that it "becomes apparent that an imagined speaker (not the poet) is performing various illocutionary acts; whether they are felicitous [appropriate] depends on their 'fit' not with our world, historical or modern, but with the pretended world the poem presents" (51). Flanigan's analysis of *HSRound* identifies two principal kinds of illocutions: "directives and representatives." Thus, for example, "the speaker commands the angels to blow their trumpets at the four corners of the earth, and he also directs the 'numberless infinities' of the dead to arise from the grave and rejoin their bodies." Donne's speaker makes it clear that this is a world "with *imagined* corners, thereby placing the world of this little frame into the established fictive frame of earlier Christian cosmology," so that "within this now legitimized, if fictive, social structure, the speaker can not only address angels with felicity, he can also talk to disembodied souls" (52). Flanigan finds the "sanction" for such an address not only in scripture ("when Abraham wrestles with an angel and Job argues with God") but also "from the Christian meditative tradition," in which one "imagines" a scene drawing upon divine events, followed by "colloquy" with God, that is, in the words of Loyola, to "'enter into conversation' with Christ or the Father" (52–53). Thus the problematic "as if" clause of the last line of the sonnet is, in Flanigan's view, "clearly ironic, a pseudo-subjunctive: repentance, the speaker says, would be as 'good' (or valid) *as if* a divine pardon had been sealed in blood, and in fact it has" (55). In this way, Flanigan claims, "the entire sonnet becomes a series of mimetic speech acts asserting or attesting to the faith of the speaker in a system of accepted certainties" (55).

Rollin (1986, 138), in keeping with his psychological reading of the Holy Sonnets, notes that the sonnet preceding *HSRound* (in 1633 and 1635) is *HSScene*, so that a poem addressing the speaker's "imminent death is followed by one in which he calls for the death of the world itself." Rollin, noting the sudden alterations in mood in Donne's Holy Sonnets, finds that *HSRound* "opens busily and stridently, with the issuance of rapid-fire imperatives" ("blow," "arise," "goe"), and in doing so intensifies "the manic quality of the octet," but "the sudden shift of mood with line 9 is almost histrionic: 'But let them sleepe, Lord, and mee mourne a space.'" Rollin claims that "grandiosity gives way to guilt."

McNees (1987, 111), in her study of the impact of the Anglican Eucharist on Donne's divine poems, argues that *HSRound*, like *HSBlack*, "ends with an allusion to eucharistic Real Presence," although the final couplet of *HSRound* "commands" God in a tone that is reminiscent of *Goodf*. According to McNees, "repentance here appears to take the place of participation in the Sacrament, not to be a prerequisite for it," and "the conditional note, like that of the ending of *Goodf*, appears to hover between two poles—that of inward repentance spurred on by God's corrective affliction and that of true identification with Christ in the Eucharist." Thus, "fearful of his own unworthiness," Donne "often falls short of wholehearted belief in Real Presence," in McNees's view, "and instead dwells on the problem of contrition."

Manlove (1992, 94–96) sees *HSRound* as "dialectical" in the way that it plays the imagination in the octave against the "sense" of the sestet (94–95). On another level, according to Manlove, the octave "describes a longing for the great consummation of apocalypse," but the tone abruptly shifts in the sestet as the poet realizes "that he would be included in the numbers he has raised, and the Last Judgment is not just a wonder, but a terror to those whose sins are still black, and that he is such a one." Manlove finds that the poem seems to stress "the delusional flights of an imaginative picture that becomes caught up with itself." The sonnet also may be read within a related context, namely, meditative practices "in which the sinner deliberately calls up a picture of the Last Things or of Christ, in order to heighten for him now the terrifying reality of his own sin and the immediacy of his need for repentance and absolution," but, for Manlove, the poem seems "much less deliberate" in its development. Rather, says Manlove, the sonnet portrays "an ignorant sinner caught out in the indulgence . . . of the imagination," the speaker's ignorance "underlined" in the conclusion of line 14 (95). But read another way, according to Manlove, the poem allows a way for the speaker to abdicate himself "from personal responsibility by imagining the end of time," a circumstance "in which he need do no more, for God will be doing it all" (96).

McNees (1992, 63) contends that *HSRound* is the "most explicitly eschatological" of the Holy Sonnets, noting that the octave "begins with a discursive description of the Last Judgment," while the sestet "shifts inward" like that of *HSBlack*, "begging for the grace to begin repenting [ll. 13–14]." The closing couplet, according to McNees, "echoes Donne's belief in the sacrament as a 'seal of grace': if the persona learns to repent, he will be able to participate worthily in Holy Communion and have his pardon 'sealed.'" And yet, McNees emphasizes, "the conditional 'as if' alerts the reader to the actual absence of pardon," for "repentance does not constitute pardon." Thus, "God is present only as a passive listener," with "the entire drama occur[ring] within the speaker."

Spiller (1992, 20, 32–33, 178–80) compares Donne's poetic style with that of the *stilnovisti*, who "adopt a straightforward syntax, and a vocabulary that is not particularly extended" (33). Spiller defines "straightforwardness" as that which "allows its clausal and phrasal units, when these are in the order of normal speech, to align with the poetic units" (33). Spiller points to the first quatrain of *HSRound* as illustrative of normal speech, but the words are not aligned with the poetic units: "the entire sentence coincides with the quatrain, but at the end of each line a normally unified phrasal group is broken by being separated across the lines (enjambed)" (33). Italian perhaps tolerates inversions more than English, according to Spiller, but the *stilnovisti* "avoid the more elaborate reversals of syntax, and take care that such inversions as do occur coincide with poetic units" (33). Spiller associates Donne's style with "the extremely complicated wordplay" of Guittone d'Arezzo (20), and calls Guittone "the John Donne of early Italian poetry" (32).

Labriola (1995, 100) finds that, having "visualized Christ in session at the Final Judgment and then being confronted with the prospect of damnation," the speaker "changes his tone from initial presumptuousness to earnest plaintiveness," particularly when he "recognizes the depth of his sinfulness."

Prosody

Payne (1926, 149) calls *HSRound* the best of the sonnets, observing that its idea is "perfectly modulated" and the octave "so dignified as to be almost Miltonic." The poem avoids the "normal effect" of the final couplet, Payne continues, by beginning its thought in the middle of the twelfth line.

Brower (1951, 70) observes that the "movement of drama in *HSRound*, from "cosmic vision to private confession," is aligned with a "movement of sound that is exquisitely adjusted to the moments of most significant change."

Esch (1955, 46–47) finds the Italianate structure of the poem "taut and at the same time balanced" ("gespannt und doch ausgewogen"), observing that the first quatrain flows dramatically with enjambment, the second by contrast is abrupt in its systematic enumeration of the causes of death, and, in countermovement, the sestet is more peaceful and assuring of forgiveness. Esch concludes that the feeling of tension in the sonnet is achieved by the pauses, by the mixing of monosyllabic and multisyllabic "Romantic" words, by the fusing of images of the Apocalypse with those of science and the everyday, and chiefly by the union of "rhythmic passages" ("rhythmischer Bögen") with strong asyndetic sequences. See also Holy Sonnets: Genre and Traditions.

Masson (1967, 60–61) discusses "sound-linkages" in *HSRound*, suggesting, for example, that the "glory of the image" of lines 1–3 is in part enhanced "by the repetition of sounds" and concluding more generally that the poem exhibits "short-lived themes" that reveal "a mind jumping from one idea to another, living always at fever-pitch of thought and perhaps of feeling."

Winters (1967, 78), suggesting that Donne's "greatest poetry and some of his worst meter can be found in the Holy Sonnets," finds *HSRound* to be one of the best Holy Sonnets because it is largely free of metrical problems.

Lemon (1969, 97–98) analyzes the first quatrain of *HSRound* and finds that in it Donne fully exploits the potentialities of the meter (98). Donne's problem in the poem, Lemon says, is to use the form "so that it convinces the reader of the speaker's boldness and of the grandeur of what he is commanding be done" (97). Donne deliberately makes the meter jar, he notes, "to help capture a sense of the catastrophic power of the end of the world" (97). Further, he says, in the first line Donne places the caesura late, just before "blow," with the result that "it is all but impossible to avoid pronouncing it forcefully" (98). The result, Lemon argues, is a kind of dynamic, explosive quality about the passage that perfectly matches the meaning of the lines.

Patterson (1970, 170–71) shows that in *HSRound*, and specifically in the first four enjambed lines, there is the use of the "Hermogenic Idea of Speed," that is, the technique of enjambment or the run-on line.

White and Rosen (1972, 52) observe that *HSRound* is memorable, equally with *HSMade*, for its "breathtaking sweep of vision from alpha to omega, from Creation to the Day of Judgment," and for its "splendors of sound." They state that the sestet exhibits the "characteristic turn of mood" of the Italian sonnet "as the poet's vision shifts from past and future to his own present, the reality of sin." The poem concludes, they note, with an "extraordinarily effective" paradox.

Linville (1984b, 79–80) finds, through analysis of the sonnet's mimetic line forms, that Donne's "aim is to dramatize an expansion into the infinite, rather than compression," such as Linville finds in *HSScene*. Here, Donne seeks "to convey the awesome tumult of Judgment Day" (79). For example, Linville shows that whereas in *HSScene* Donne "created increasing line and syntactic constriction to suggest the pressures of diminishing time and space," the effect in *HSRound* is "reversed," as he "moves from a line as short as 'From death, you numberlesse infinities,' to the expansive list that constitutes lines six and seven" (79–80).

Willmott (1985, 22) finds in the opening lines of the sonnet that "the relentless forward motion of a breathless account of Judgement Day is maintained by running the sense on from the end of each line."

Russo (1989, 228), in discussing Richards's scorn for a strict adherence to an analysis of rhythm and meter, cites his reaction (1929) to an unnamed reader who indicted *HSRound* as a "rotten sonnet" because the reader could not "even by cruel forcing and beating the table with my fingers" manage to identify the "customary five iambic feet to the verse." To Richards, Russo notes, this "mechanical" view of rhythm was a particular threat to "good reading." Russo adds that, in Richards's view, this kind of analysis "flattened nuance and created false expectations in readers who counted missed beats against the author." See Richards (1929) under *HSRound*: General Commentary and *HSRound*: Themes.

Sacred and Profane

Cox (1956a, 113) observes that Donne "treats God as a conqueror or a ravisher, or employs the kind of wooing used to his 'profane mistress.'"

Themes

An anonymous editor (1840, 270–71) prints a number of Donne poems under original headings, including *HSRound* under the heading "Repentance."

Richards (1929, 272–73, 278), in discussing readers' responses to the poem, addresses the doctrine defined in it. He acknowledges it "very difficult not to think that *actual belief* in the doctrine that appears in the poem is required for its full and perfect imaginative realisation," adding that the "mere assumption of Donne's theology, as a poetic fiction" may seem to some readers "insufficient in view of the intensity of feeling which is supported and conveyed to us by its means" (272–73).

Later, however, Richards make a distinction between intellectual and emotional belief in the ideas of the poem. He argues that Donne "probably gave both forms of belief to these ideas," a fact which need not "prevent a good reader from giving the fullest emotional belief while withholding intellectual belief, or rather while not allowing the question of intellectual belief to arise." Richards points out that in such doctrinal poems the "absence of intellectual belief need not cripple emotional belief." When it does, he concludes, "Good-bye to poetry" (278).

Bennett (1934, 1–2) argues that Donne cannot be called a philosophical poet simply "because he makes use of ideas." He does not, she observes, speculate "about the nature of things" (1). Bennett quotes HSRound 1–4 as an example, observing of the lines that Donne "is not defining the doctrine of the church about mortality or describing the new cosmology," but is, rather, "expressing a state of mind by referring to a background of ideas" (2).

Spörri-Sigel (1949, 86) finds tension in the poem described in terms of the opposition between sin, death, and damnation, and the grace of God. The tension, she contends, is not as intense as in HSMade, for while there is still some question as to whether grace will be bestowed, sin does not here have the same power to lead astray as in the other poem.

Baker (1952, 61) argues that Donne was "painfully aware" of evil in man and constantly prayed for zeal in purging his own sins, confident in his capacity for regeneration.

Reeves (1952, 100–01) paraphrases the poem: from a contemplation of Judgment Day Donne "sinks to the humble contemplation of his own miserable lot" and begs that since his "sins exceed all other men's," he be "given grace to repent before it is too late."

Peterson (1959, 509–10) observes that Donne rejects the argument that since the sinful body will be separated from the pure soul at death, the soul will be purged of sin (ll. 1–4), stating rather that pardon for sin will only be won through repentance "on this lowly ground" (ll. 11–14). See also Holy Sonnets: Themes.

Herbold (1965, 277–94), writing of dialectics in Donne, says that the "keynote" in Donne's dialectics is his "search for an equilibrium between balanced polarities" (280) and that in the Holy Sonnets this position occurs chiefly between Faith and Doubt. HSRound, he says, "with its splittings into soules-bodies, flood-fire, law-chance, behold-taste, them-mee, there-here is representative of the divine poems that split down the middle" (284).

For Crennan (1979, 13–14) HSRound is one of the Holy Sonnets that treat "the eschatological themes of Death and Judgement." Crennan observes that the sonnet specifically addresses the "general resurrection of the Dead, which is to precede the last Judgement in which souls will be finally allotted Paradise or Hell." The octave, according to Crennan, "summons all the souls of the dead to return to their bodies and thus rise from death," while in the sestet the speaker "recollects himself and asks God to delay this general resurrection." The request for a delay is needed, Crennan explains, because the speaker "has many sins."

Zitner (1979, 66, 69, 75) approaches the sonnet against an interpretive framework that combines both the rhetorical and doctrinal issues in the poem. In doing so, Zitner finds an uneasy relationship between the two, which is clearest in lines 1, 8, and 14. The tension Zitner finds in the first line of the sonnet—"between a round-ness that is self-evident, or at least requires no qualification, and corners that need the qualifying word 'imagin'd'"—underscores the nature of the tensions elsewhere in the sonnet, that is, the tension between the "immediate" and the "apocalyptic" (69). Zitner extends the reading by suggesting that the last lines of the octave "seem to join the apocalyptic with the immediate," by addressing "those who will be alive at the Second Coming, those for whom Judgement is a possibility that may overtake them in the midst of literal existence" (69). The last two lines of the sonnet—which have prompted considerable critical study because of Donne's use of "if" in the final line—conclude the sonnet, in Zitner's view, "as it began"—that is, "with something accessible to experience (albeit with the guidance of doctrine), being weighed against something more remote because it depends on a problematic use of doctrine and belief," but without seeming "to denigrate it" (75). For Zitner, HSRound "provides a picture of hesitation, not on the brink of belief, but within it" (75).

Ellrodt (1980, 165, 171–72) finds that Donne had a long-standing interest in angels "as objects of intellectual speculation," and "in an age when man was defined as 'a little world made cunningly / of Elements, and an Angelike spright' [HSLittle 1–2] no one denied the angels a place in the great Chain of Being." Ellrodt therefore regards Donne's understanding of angels as expected, and he cites Sermons, 8: 106: "They are super-elementary meteors, they hang between the nature of God, and the nature of man, and are of middle Condition" (165). Donne's interest in what angels and man share with respect to the faculties of understanding is addressed in HSRound, but here, according to Ellrodt, "the poet does not choose between two hypotheses: our hearts may be known to angels (hence to blessed souls) either intuitively or only through appearances" (171–72). Ellrodt finds the "practical conclusion" to be "that God 'knowes best', that is, knows better than angels the sincerity of the poet's repentance, not that it is known to Him alone." Ellrodt concludes that "what characterizes Donne's attitude is this very tension: on the one hand a Christian readiness to admit that speculative knowledge is unattainable and anyway superfluous for salvation; on the other hand a persistent intellectual curiosity, an irritability of the mind" (172).

Yearwood (1982, 210, 214) finds that the conversion process in Donne's twelve Holy Sonnets (following 1633 and Gardner's [1952] ordering) "begins in pride, proceeds to confession and despair, and culminates in a humble joy and confidence" (210). In the fourth sonnet, HSRound, the speaker, having recognized that he has not fully repented, "achieves," according to Yearwood, the "necessary spiritual posture," and "seeks repentance," but through the wrong means, namely, "doctrinal misconception and systematic illogic" (214).

Mallett (1983, 57) summarizes the argument of the sonnet: "in this poem Donne imagines the Day of Judgement, and begs for time to be allowed for him to repent his sins."

Fleck (1994, 66–67) discusses the way in which HSRound "focuses on spiritual fulfillment of eschatological prophecy without abandoning final, literal fulfillments," calling attention to the sonnet's "tense substitutions and shifts" that "depict repentance in an eschatological light" (66). The octave, Fleck notes, is based upon Rev.

7.1, and "commands the resurrection of the body," while in the sestet, "the speaker retreats in fear from the prospect of God in judgment" (66–67). Fleck argues that "the shift from future to present tense corresponds with a shift in emphasis from the eschaton to realized eschatology," that is, "the speaker's imaginative projection into the future and meditation upon the last judgment result in a retreat to the present for sober examination of his spiritual condition" (67).

HSRound and Other Works

Chadwick (1900, 46), quoting the sonnet in full, finds in it "a stately music as if Milton were being heralded." See also Eliot (1930).

Eliot (1930, 553) finds the poem to anticipate "the magnificent style of Milton's religious sonnets."

Rosenthal, Hummel, and Leichty (1944, 406–12) compare HSRound and SGo, finding the former superior since in it Donne addresses "an important and original idea, one worthy of his mind and spirit" (407). Pursuing the comparison, the authors find the first line of the sonnet "long and grave, instead of brief and tripping" (407). Donne addresses the angels and souls in the octave, they note, calling for the Day of Judgment, and God in the sestet, appealing for delay, a contradiction showing "signs of fervent piety," with the implication of the poet's "consciousness of the tragedy of human death" and the "tremendous urgency" of life (410).

Coanda (1957, 186–87) compares HSRound with Hopkins's "That Nature is a Heraclitean Fire," finding both to be resurrection poems that begin "with movement on a grand scale" and end "with diminutive motion." Coanda further observes that both Donne and Hopkins put a strain on the sonnet form, as in HSRound where all creation is represented in fourteen lines, and in "No worse, there is none" where Hopkins explores "the vaulting geography of man's mind."

Sloane (1974, 74–79) compares HSRound to an emblem of Georgette de Montenay (1571) that depicts the four winds at the corners of the print and a trumpet-blowing angel in the center.

Wennerstorm (1978, 59–60) discusses the results of a workshop that looked at Benjamin Britten's settings of poems by Shakespeare, Donne, and Keats, giving specific attention to the setting of HSRound. There are some close correlations between the poem and the music, according to Wennerstorm, including the larger structural divisions (4-4-6) and smaller details, such as the representation of HSRound 6–7 "with a compressed musical sequence," though overall, "meaning in language cannot be transposed directly into music" (60). See also Gaston (1986).

Crennan (1979, 14) contrasts Donne's summoning of the dead in the sonnet, which is "hortatory" and urges "the souls to hurry to judgement," with the older epic convention of summoning the dead, which we find in Vergil, a summoning marked by melancholy and a sense of loss. Vergil alludes to "the variety of life left behind," whereas Donne's summoning "emphasizes not the loss and sadness of death, but its multiform and unpredictable variety and its suddenness, together with the fact that it is to be followed by judgement." In Donne, says Crennan, the souls, "being dead, have much to do, and face."

Lewalski (1979, 268–69) finds a possible connection between *HSRound* and *HSScene*, the poem that precedes it in 1635, in that "the consideration of the moment of death leads logically to meditation upon the Day of Judgment" (268). Lewalski adds that *HSRound* is "one of the two or three which exhibit the full Ignatian meditative structure," beginning with a clear *compositio loci* resembling the scene in Revelation 7.1, culminating with a plea to God "for more time to mourn his sins," and asking "for the divine gift of true repentance" (268–69).

Milward (1979 [1988, 55–58]) assigns the source of the sonnet's meditation on the "General Judgment" to the scene suggested in Rev. 7.1 (55). Milward also sees close parallels between Donne's dramatic language and mood and that of Shakespeare's *Macbeth* when Macduff discovers Duncan's murder (2.3) (56). Following a consideration of individuals who die in various ways, Milward says, the speaker, "in an abrupt contrast" with the "noise and throng of the last judgment," next turns to the sestet and to "a silent colloquy with God," seeking divine grace here on earth through his repentance (58).

Den Boer (1982, 76) cites and discusses alternative Dutch translations by G. H. M. van Huet and Victor E. Vriesland.

Burgon (1984) composed music for *HSRound* for soprano (or tenor), trumpet in C, and organ.

Sloane (1985, 159) finds that the opening of the sonnet is similar to *Sidney*, a poem Donne wrote perhaps ten years later. Sloane notes that "both poems begin with the impossibility of either squaring a circle or circling a square," an assertion that is like a "rhetorical *correctio*: possibility is denied, only to remain as another kind of possibility, one that is beyond our reach, including the reach of our linguistic conventions," and "in this way, the conventions themselves are not exactly rejected but are used, for all they're worth."

Gaston (1986, 211) observes that Britten's musical setting for *HSShe* prepares for the opening of the next setting for *HSRound*, namely, *largamente*. Affirming the view of Rembert Bryce Herbert ["An Analysis of Nine Holy Sonnets of John Donne to Music by Benjamin Britten," Ph.D. diss., American University, 1974, p. 31], Gaston emphasizes that from this point forward in Britten's cycle, "the relationship between God and the supplicant grows more and more straightforward, and the voice we hear in Britten's settings grows more and more confident."

Hester (1993, 346–50) finds that "the crucial turn of the sonnet which initiates the surprising sestet" calls to mind the biblical passage describing St. John's vision (Rev. 6.9–11), an allusion not mentioned in previous studies (346). Hester finds that the implications of this biblical allusion help "to explain the chord of frustration with which this poetic meditation concludes" (346). The "turn," in Hester's view, might call to mind the "damned Dr. Faustus's eleventh-hour plea that time, motion, and Justice cease," and thus "begs for a 'space' outside the scheme of Justice" (347). In light of the biblical allusion to the vision of St. John, it becomes clearer, according to Hester, "why Donne might well have feared himself to be outside the 'seal' of selection which the poem contemplates," that is, the speaker's "vision of his own place in the divine scheme derives from the juxtaposition of those who 'sleepe' [in Revelation] to his own desire for the additional 'space' to 'mourne'" (348). *HSRound*, in Hester's view, serves "as the site for Donne's meditative attempts to appraise the moral virtues of the rivals in the Counter-Reformation debate," so that the Holy Sonnets may be seen as the "fullest" statement of the "space" in which we find, according to Young (1987), Donne "trying out different versions of grace" but "without betraying his family tradition" (349–50).

Fleck (1994, 67–72) compares *HSRound* and Milton's Nativity Ode, noting that in both poems "proper responses to meditation upon the last judgment are watchfulness and repentance" (68). Donne's sonnet and Milton's Ode, according to Fleck, employ the grammar of eschatology, which includes tense shifts and substitutions which give the prophetic verse the sense that the eschatological prophecies have already occurred or at the least the "certainty of eschatological fulfillment is indicated by the futuristic present tense" (69–71). Fleck concludes that in *HSRound*, more than in Milton's poem, "eschatological grammar pushes beginnings back in time and demonstrates that the end is implicit in the beginning of an action, itself a prophetic fulfillment," thereby "celebrating the ever-present reality of eschatological redemption" (72).

Notes and Glosses

1–8 *At the round . . . deaths wo.* **GOSSE** (1899), quoting these lines, says that Donne "conceives that death is absolutely upon him, and he breaks forth into a burst of almost Miltonic magnificence" (2:108). **RICHARDS** (1929) observes that Donne is "perhaps the slowest mover in English literature and here the trumpets are still blowing right down to 'taste death's woe'" (47). **WHITE** (1936) thinks that Donne, although he "cannot be considered a mystic" himself, inspired poets like Herbert and Crashaw, who were. Quotes the lines, calling the poem "a trumpet call to the mystical poets of his tradition" (148–49). **RAINE** (1945): the poet summons up the angels "in Baroque imagery of unsurpassed grandeur" (390). **SIMPSON** (1948) finds in these lines a linkage between the Holy Sonnets and the *Essays* in their common reliance on the Book of Revelation, referring specifically to Rev. 7.1, 8.2 and 6–12, and 20.13–14 and citing references to the Last Judgment in *Essays*, pp. 61, 63, 113, and 168 (211–12). **WILLEY** (1954): Donne's poetry can soar (ll. 1–4) but the emotion is often checked, as in this case by "thudding monosyllables" that follow (ll. 5–8) (364).

1–6 *At the . . . age, agues, tyrannyes,* **BENNETT** (1934) cites these lines as an example of Donne's ability to pass abruptly from the sublime to the trivial (16).

1–4 *At the . . . to your scattered bodyes go,* **BRADFORD** (1892): though Donne's poetry reflects a "wanton disregard of the laws of English versification," it does occasionally have "lines of extraordinary rhythmic power" such as these (359). **SYMONS** (1899), while finding that often in the Holy Sonnets "thought crowds in upon thought," points out the "splendour" of these lines (743). **GRIERSON** (1912): the lines are equal to the "magnificent openings" of Donne's love poems (2:lii–liii). **READ** (1928) finds the lines to contain images and expressions of "the same dialectical subtlety and impassioned majesty" as those in Donne's early works (66). **WILLIAMSON** (1930) detects echoes of these lines, "though with a Neo-classical accent," in Dryden's "Ode to Mrs. Killigrew" (219). **BENNETT** (1934) argues that Donne is not philosophical here; he is simply "expressing a state of mind by refer-ring to a background of ideas" (2). **COFFIN** (1937): the "concepts of space and of the world's immensity are always emerging as intimate parts of Donne's imagina-tion" (192). **WELLS** (1940): Donne's poems are often dramatic monologues, here addressed to the angels (186). **DANIELLS** (1945): the lines illustrate baroque ele-ments in Donne, here "the effect of superimposing continuous movement over the set frame" of the sonnet form (401–02). **STAUFFER** (1946), in his discussion of concreteness, argues that not all images are visual, and those that are do not con-jure up the same visual impression for all readers. Observes that the second sen-tence (ll. 2–4) evokes an image that has become somewhat conventional, since it has been depicted frequently in religious art, but that the first sentence (ll. 1–2) lends itself to a variety of visual impressions: Is it a globe or a flat map? How does one visualize angels? Are we standing on earth looking up or in space looking down? Suggests finally that it is possible to enjoy the sound of the lines without calling up a visual image at all (139–40). **TUVE** (1947), discussing decorum in imagery, quotes lines 1–2 as intended to depict the unimaginable scope of the world and lines 3–4 to amplify the numbers of the human race. Finds the "same crowd" similarly en-gaged on that "last busie day" in *Relic*, though there the intent is to diminish the importance of their activity when compared to the lovers' last meeting (199–200). **SPÖRRI-SIGEL** (1949): in the opening figure of a round earth's corners, Donne appeals to the reader's imagination to conjure up thought of the resurrection of the body, which will finally conquer death (77). **NICOLSON** (1950) quotes the lines to illustrate her argument that in the seventeenth century the circle reflected both God's nature in the heavens and the cycle of time that will end where it began with the Last Judgment (67). **HUNT** (1954) acknowledges that on occasion the open-ing lines of Donne's poems have "superb dramatic power" (135). **GRANSDEN** (1954): the lines reflect the individual's sense of inadequacy at the traditional scene of Judgment Day; but Donne is not a part of the scene, rather asking that it be de-layed so that he can repent (ll. 9–12) (135). **UL-HASAN** (1958) observes that Donne did not often "produce sound-sensations" through his imagery, preferring to employ "rhetorical tricks" by imposing sound patterns on his lines, here the word "round" and the repetition of "arise," which add a "sensuous quality" to the passage (80–81). **SMITH** (1970) finds the lines an example of rhetoric that is itself an "af-firmation": to rephrase these lines "by syntax alone" would diminish both their "vivid articulation" and their "point" (161–62). **SLOANE** (1981) finds that, with "the economy of the emblematist," Donne sets up his images, as here. Compares the lines to an image of Georgette de Montenay (1571) and notes that Donne's image "is expected to call forth everything that the reader has learned about the last judg-ment from the Book of Revelation" (83). **A. SMITH** (1987): the "vivid articula-tion Donne gains by running the sense across the lyric pattern," as in ll. 2–4, and "the slackened tension, like a paean on a damp string, takes with it the whole force of an assured resurrection which is the sense of the poem" (162). **SMITH** (1991) says that the "real apprehension that final issues are imminent in our everyday lives gives the *Divine Meditations* their dramatic urgency, setting the trumpets blowing here and now to proclaim the sudden irruption of the Day of Judgment" (134). **SMITH** (1992): the "ringing rhetoric sustains a mighty shout of defiance" and proclaims the "possibility of a heroic triumph snatched from likely defeat." This "magnificent declamation gives our moral life the grandeur of a universal drama that is perpetually reenacted" (88).

1–2 *At the . . . Arise Arise* **JUDSON** (1927) cites Rev. 7.1: "I saw four angels standing on the four corners of the earth" (250). [So also, Coffin and Witherspoon (1946, 33), Gardner (1952, 67), Spencer (1952, 430), Martz (1963, 86), Smith (1971, 627), who notes that maps depicting earth as a round body appeared as early as the sixth century BC, Lever (1974, 180), Cain (1981, 312), Mallett (1983, 57), Barańczak (1984, 161), Patrides (1985a, 438), who adds that, "[c]oncerned as the poem is with the Last Judgement, echoes from the Book of Revelation are necessarily numerous," Willmott (1985, 67), Craik and Craik (1986, 278), who note that the angels of Rev. 7.1 have no trumpets and that these instruments "enter the poem" from 1 Cor. 15.52, Pritchard (1986, 348), Hieatt (1987, 239), Booty (1990, 108), Carey (1990b, 454), Handley (1991, 43), and Fowler (1995, 261), who adds that in Donne's time, "maps of the world often had wind gods, putti, or angels in the four corners, as in Cornelis de Jode, *Speculum Orbis Terrarum* (1593)."] **MOLONEY** (1944) quotes these lines to refute the "common imputation to Donne and the metaphysicals of an unending search for fanciful subtleties to the detriment of the true powers of the imagination" (132). **TUVE** (1947): "the bold spondee and triumphant upspringing rhythm underline the extension of the earth's limits rapidly denoted through the remaking of the doubly familiar image (*round, corners*)" (199). **FAERBER** (1950): the contradiction in the lines involves a shift from one level to another in which the traditional imagery and the knowledge of the new philosophy collide, forming an absolute paradox (73). **MARTZ** (1954): the opening lines reflect the "composition" or "proposing" stage in the traditional Ignatian meditation (31). [See also Holy Sonnets: Genre and Traditions.] **CRENNAN** (1979): the image of the round earth with its imagined corners suggests that Donne "is seeing with a double vision." One perspective "focuses on the iconographic tradition of the earth as a flat map, with the four corners corresponding to the points of the compass on each end of which there is an Angelic being." The second perspective "focuses on the physical fact that the world is a sphere." The effect of this double vision is "to affirm that there are two orders of being: the physical world and the spiritual world," the latter "registered by symbols and convenient, agreed-upon fiction." But "both exist; one follows the other" (14–15). **WILLMOTT** (1985) notes that in Rev. 7.1 St. John "gives a visionary account of the end of the world in which each new disaster is heralded by an angel blowing a trumpet," an account that is preceded by a description of the saved. Suggests that the "corners" are not simply "imagined" in the sense of "being unreal, but as part of a spiritual exercise (imagining the end of the world) which leads to the repentance expressed in the contrastingly subdued sestet" (67). **PRITCHARD** (1986), noting that the angels "derive" from Rev. 7.1, adds that "in Jewish and cabbalistic tradition, these were the archangels Michael, Gabriel, Raphael, and Uriel" (348). Points out that "this tradition was followed by Renaissance magicians," as, for example, in John Freake's translation (1561) of Heinrich Cornelius Agrippa of Nettesheim's *De occulta philosophia* (1533) ("whose work Donne certainly knew"), where there is a table [cited in S. K. Heninger Jr., *Touches of Sweet Harmony, Pythagorean Cosmology and Renaissance Poetics* (San Marino, California, 1974), fig. 25] "showing how the cosmos is organized on the principle of the tetrad" and identifying the Tetragrammaton ("God's name in four Hebrew letters") with a list of the four elements, four humours, four seasons, etc., as well as the "Four corners of the world" (East, West, North, and South) and the "Four Angels ruling over the corners of the world" (Michael, Raphael, Gabriel, and Uriel) (348). Finds that Robert Anton's "diagram of the tetrad (in *The philosophers satyrs*, London, 1616) [also cited in Heninger, fig. 34] is particularly clear" and that from such a diagram we associate Michael with Mars, "the choleric humour, 'warre,' and 'dea(r)th,'" Raphael with Jupiter, "the sanguine or blood humour, 'age,' and 'agues,'" Uriel with Saturn, "melancholy, 'tyrannies,' and 'Despaire,'" and Gabriel with Luna, "phlegm, 'law,' and 'chance'" (349). **ZEMPLÉNYI** (1986) interprets the lines as grounded in paradox and "strong irony." Points out that studies of the poem already have noted the paradox of l. 1, namely, its "juxtaposition of the 'new philosophy,' of Copernican cosmology . . . and Biblical faith," with its allusion to Rev. 7.1. Adds, however, that what has not been observed by critics is Donne's amalgamation of Rev. 7.1 and Rev. 8.2–6 ("and I saw the seven angels which stood before God; and to them were given seven trumpets...And the seven angels which had the seven trumpets prepared themselves to sound"). Regards the handling of the biblical material as important primarily because of two effects: (1) it reveals Donne's sense of a "contradiction between modern science and Biblical revelation," and (2) it shows him making "the less important four angels sound the trumpets of Doom, focusing attention on them, giving them greater relief, because it is in this way that he can place them on the . . . four corners of the earth, making the contrast stand out sharply." Concludes that here Donne makes clear that, "in matters of the spirit, the factual and the rational are nugatory beside the transcendent paradox" (159).

    1 *At the round Earths imagind corners blow* **G[ILES] O[LDISWORTH]** (c. 1650), making notes in a copy of the 1639 *Poems* (C), has written "Resurrection" in the right margin next to this line (335). **TROST** (1904): an example of Donne's use of oxymoron (51). **WILLIAMSON** (1930): an example of the "mystical expression" of the "nature of the unseen world of life, love, death, and eternity" (236–37). **RAIZISS** (1952) finds an echo of the line in Allen Tate's "Sonnet at Christmas: II," l. 7 (191). **ADAMS** (1962) says that Donne "may have been thinking of the angels on old maps, who blow their trumpets to the four points of the compass," and cites Rev. 7.1 (784–85). **SHAWCROSS** (1967): "Roundness was considered perfection; angular things, imperfection" (340). **BROADBENT** (1974) says that "[t]his kind of imagination" was a recognized feature of the systematic devotional meditation urged by St. Ignatius Loyola and that a poem written in such a mode might follow the progress of meditation found in Ignatian meditation (131). See also Martz

(1954) under Holy Sonnets: Genre and Traditions. **J. THOMAS** (1976) identifies Donne's use of the square as a symbol of "man's poor wit" and adds that Donne "resists the corners of the square so consistently" that it should come as no surprise that he "locates the angels who blow their trumpets to announce the resurrection not at the corners of the earth but at 'imagined' corners" (93). **GILL** (1990) notes that "the effect of coupling *round* and *corners*" and adding the word *imagined* seems intentionally ambiguous in order to draw attention to "an event so unparalleled that words have to be stretched and extended beyond their ordinary meanings in order to imagine it" (102).

1 *imagind* **HUNT** (1954) charges that in using the word Donne is testing "religious doctrine against scientific fact" or running a "scientific check on the myth of Judgment Day" (159). See also *HSRound*: Language and Style. **A. SMITH** (1987) says that the word "pulls one up sharp," calling to mind the final judgment and inviting thought about the "discrepancy between what we once took for knowledge and what we think we know now" and encouraging an understanding of the "relativity of the mind's grasp" (165). **FOWLER** (1991): that is, "in maps" and in Rev. 7.1 (117). **ELLRODT** (1993) states that referring to these corners as imaginary is characteristic of the care for truth that Donne manifests in the use of figurative language. Adds that the power attributed to repentance in the poem seems contrary to Augustinian theology, but the very fact of being able to repent gives the sinner the assurance of being one of the chosen (455).

2–4 *Arise Arise . . . bodyes go,* **GARDNER** (1952) finds the idea here, with the notion of souls arising from death, "quite inconsistent" with the point of view in Donne's sermons (xliv–xlv). **SHAABER** (1958) notes that this idea of the death of the soul is exceptional in Donne. Observes that in *HSScene* 7–8 "the soul parts from the body at death and immediately sees God face to face" (102). **LEWALSKI and SABOL** (1973) point out that here Donne suggests "the death or sleep of the soul until the Last Judgment" but that in the Anniversaries and his Sermons he "supposes the soul's immediate transmission to heaven" (152). **CAREY** (1990b) says that the belief expressed here ("seemingly Donne's") "that the soul dies, and later rises from the grave, was a version of the heresy known as Mortalism" and points to *HSScene* 7 (454). **FISCHLER** (1994): "Human beings return briefly to the natural world in the moments before the Last Judgment" (181).

2 *Arise Arise* **TROST** (1904): an example of repetition to achieve emphasis (51).

3–9 *From Death . . . mourne a space,* **KLAUSE** (1987) observes that "[w]hen Donne religiously longs for a heaven that will level many distinctions, he must try to achieve a sense of his soul's uniqueness" (61). Notes that Donne "believed that the human mind loses its sense of the miraculous when miracles become common," and therefore one "can recover a sense of the admirable" through "an imaginative awareness of what is unique to a privileged initiation" (61).

3–4 *From . . . scattered bodyes go,* **BROWER** (1951): "the controlling metaphor" of the octave is "the numberlessness of the dead" (67). **CRENNAN** (1979) finds "numberless infinities" to be "abstract and mathematical," but also capable of being addressed: "you numberless infinities." Notes further that "the bodies to which the numberless infinities are to go are 'scattered'—which suggests beautifully the random disarray of the remains." Concludes that this strategy of "tying an abstract or general phrase to a personal address and a specific physical ingredient" is "very effective" here (15).

3 *From Death you numberles infinities* **GARDNER** (1952), in arguing for Donne's "plain unadorned speech," quotes the line as an example of one "lengthened by heavy secondary stresses, which demand the same emphasis as the main stress takes" (xxxii).

4 *scattered bodyes* **SMITH** (1971) says that this refers to "bodies dispersed about the earth as dust and bones" and cites *Relic* 10–11 (627). **WILLMOTT** (1985): "Souls return to their bodies for the resurrection of the dead" (67). **PATRIDES** (1985a): "at the Last Judgement the souls are to rejoin their resurrected bodies wherever these may have been previously scattered" (438). [Similarly, Gill (1990, 102).]

5–7 *All . . . hath slayne,* **SPÖRRI-SIGEL** (1949) observes that Donne lists various causes of death, a list that could be extended indefinitely. Finds that in his rhetorical compilation he emphasizes the power of death, in contrast with *HSDeath*, where its power is contingent on other forces (54). **MORRIS** (1953): both Donne and Hopkins achieve greater power and dignity by occasionally overloading lines with stressed syllables, as here and in "I wake and feel the fell of dark" (l. 11) (47–48). **STAUFFER** (1946) cites the lines as an example of the poet achieving intensity through grammatical ellipse (73) and by crowding compound subjects together to create momentum, delaying completion of the thought until the final words (74). **PATRIDES** (1985a) says that in Donne's verse, Death is "present where he appears to have been virtually stilled into extinction" and that the "departure from the basic iambic beat in the octave induces a counter-movement, affirming through the disturbed rhythm what the sweeping movement endeavours to bypass" (32–33).

5 *All whom the Flood did and fyre shall overthrow* **DALGLISH** (1961): "All who were drowned in the Flood (Noah's) and who shall die by the fire that will consume the world on the last day" (136). [Similarly, Lever (1974, 180), Mallett (1983, 57), who cites Gen. 6–9 and Rev. 6, Gill (1990, 102), who cites Gen. 6–8 and Rev. 8, and Handley (1991, 43).] **SHAWCROSS** (1967): fire signifies "the great conflagration in which the world will be consumed" (cf. 2 Pet. 3.10) (340). [So also, Patrides (1985a, 438) and Booty (1990, 108).] **SMITH** (1971) cites *HSLittle* 8–10, *Fever* 13–16, and Rev. 6–12. **WILLMOTT** (1985): "all who have been and will be killed in the course of history from Noah's flood to the fires that will end the world" (cf. Rev. 8 and 9) (67). **LLOYD-EVANS** (1989) cites Rev. 6–12 (299n41).

6–7 *All . . . and you whose eyes* **MOLONEY** (1950): the passage is an example of "centroidal grouping" of words to produce emphasis, similar to lines in Milton (238). **BROWER** (1951): "the meter disintegrates in a series of continuous stresses and sharp pauses" which fit "exactly the helter-skelter gathering" Donne describes (68–69).

6 *All whom Warr, dearth, age, agues, tyrannyes,* **GROSART** (1872–73), reading "All whom death, war, age . . .," says that "death" was probably supposed to "present the wide thing and word, and the after 'warr, age,' &c the various forms or modes" and that therefore he has "ventured to place 'death' before 'warr'" (2:290–91). **GARDNER** (1952), in describing Donne's "plain unadorned speech," quotes the line as an example of one "weighted with heavy monosyllables" (xxxii). **LEVER** (1974): the list reveals a "critical awareness" of "avoidable social ills" (180).

6 *dearth,* **GRIERSON** (1912) prefers "dearth" to the "death" in several mss. and editions, since Donne "is enumerating various modes in which death comes" and "death itself cannot be one of them." Points to "death" in l. 8, which "makes the error even more obvious" (2:232). **HAYWARD** (1929), citing Grierson (1912), finds "death" "obviously incorrect." Compares the line to a sermon (*Sermons*, 9:184) to support the Westmoreland version (NY3) (778). **GARDNER** (1952), though arguing that choosing "dearth" over "death" is not as simple as Grierson (1912) suggests, nonetheless finds "dearth" less awkward and more likely Donne's intended word (67–68). **LEWALSKI and SABOL** (1973) echo Grierson (1912), noting the "manuscript authority" for "death" but arguing that "dearth" ("famine") is the "better reading in this list of specific causes of death—which appears as a general term in ll. 3 and 8" (152). Similarly, Lever (1974, 180).

6 *agues,* **PATRIDES** (1985a): "malarial fevers" (438). **GILL** (1990): "diseases" (102).

6 *tyrannyes,* **MAROTTI** (1994a): Donne's use of such a term as "evil and destructive" nonetheless signals "his insistent awareness of the political order" (79).

7 *Dispayre, Law, Chance, hath slayne,* **CRAIK and CRAIK** (1986): "Those slain by *despair* are suicides, those slain by *law* have been executed, and those slain by *chance* have died in accidents" (278).

7–8 *you . . . never tast deaths wo.* **COFFIN and WITHERSPOON** (1946) cite Luke 9.27: "I tell you of a truth, there be some standing here which shall not taste of death till they see the kingdom of God" (33). Similarly, Adams (1962, 785), Martz (1969a, 82), Cain (1981, 312), Mallett (1983, 57), Patrides (1985a, 439), and Booty (1990, 108). **WILLEY** (1954): "you who will be alive at the time of the Last Judgment" (386). [Similarly, Ruoff (1972, 915), Lever (1974, 180), and Craik and Craik (1986, 278).] **SMITH** (1971) quotes 1 Cor. 15.51–52: "We shall not all sleep, but we shall all be changed, in a moment, in the twinkling of an eye, at the last trump" (627). Similarly, Ruoff (1972, 915), Willmott (1985, 67–68), who refers to "those still living at the end of the world who will therefore find themselves face to face with God without experiencing death," Hieatt (1987, 239), Lloyd-Evans (1989, 299n42), Booty (1990, 108), Carey (1990b, 454), and Fowler (1995, 261).

7 *you* SHAABER (1958): "the righteous, who are exempt from the penalties of death" (102).

8–14 *Shall behold . . . with thy blood.* G[ILES O[LDISWORTH] (c. 1650), making notes in a copy of the 1639 *Poems* (C), writes at the bottom of a page containing these lines and the beginning of *HSSouls*: "To my lord & from/ my lord" (336).

8 *deaths wo.* GARDNER (1952): "the return of the body to dust." Cf. 1 Cor. 16.51 (68).

9–14 *But let them . . . with thy blood.* BROWER (1951): the poet "speaks to his Lord (now Christ) in a tone that is everyday and even a little offhand, touched by the irreverence that is the sign of assured faith," with the breaks and pauses of "re-flective conversation" appropriate to the "intimacy of Donne's prayer" (68–69). SMITH (1991) says that the sonnets—including specifically *HSRound*—open a "time-less prospect to us" but also allow a "space in which to prepare ourselves for a final reckoning with the transgressions which might endlessly alienate us from God" (134). SMITH (1992): "The poet is always fearfully aware that we cannot command such triumphs for ourselves, and that we may have part in them at all only by submitting ourselves to a course of repentance that will open us to God's grace at last" (88).

9 *But let them sleepe, Lord, and me mourne a space,* EVANS (1955): Donne "ex-ploits the sudden change of mind as an occasion for drama or for humour" (171). HOLLANDER and KERMODE (1973): "But" signals "the characteristic change of tone for the sestet" (1051). MALLETT (1983): "that is, delay the Day of Judge-ment" (57). TEAGUE (1987) finds the line to be evidence of Donne's "aggressive-ness" in his relationship with God, interpreting it as "a form of Christian confidence even in the astonishing conceit of asking God to delay the General Resurrection" (32). GILL (1990): these words "could be the impudently blasphemous request (de-mand?) of a grossly egocentric man, or there could be an uncertain humour about the words that draws attention to the gulf between the poet and Christ" (102).

9 *a space,* LEVER (1974): "For a while" (180). CRAIK and CRAIK (1986): "for a time (relating to both *sleep* and *mourn*)" (278).

10 *above* SHAABER (1958): "more than" (102).

10–11 *my Sins abound . . . thy grace.* HOLLANDER and KERMODE (1973): see Rom. 6.1 (1051). GILL (1990) points to Rom. 5.20: "where sin abounded, there grace abounded much more" (102).

10 *abound* HANDLEY (1991): "i.e. are measured more than" (43).

11 *Tis late* **MALLETT** (1983): "it will be too late" (57).

11 *grace* **WILLMOTT** (1985): "forgiving favour" (68).

12 *When we are there: Here on this lowly ground* **BROWER** (1951): "The reversal of accent increases the stress and makes us put in a pause for the unaccented syllable we have lost; while 'here' gets a further stress due to the chiasmus and the lack of a connective corresponding to 'when'" (70). **MORRIS** (1953): both Donne and Hopkins often substitute a simple word for a phrase, as with "there" in this line and "as" in "The Handsome Heart" (l. 8) (66–67). **MARTZ** (1954) comments that the line resembles "a part of the traditional colloquy with God" on the Last Judgment, with "we" representing all sinners as well as the individual soul, and "there" the throne of Judgment, in contrast with "the lowly ground" where the speaker prays. Notes that "we are there" puzzled the students of I. A. Richards (1929—see *HSRound*: General Commentary) and cites Gardner's contention (1952—see Holy Sonnets: Dating and Order) that the poem can be interpreted in accordance with the Ignatian method of worship (51–52). See also Holy Sonnets: Genre and Traditions.

12 *there:* **LEVER** (1974): "In heaven, before the throne of judgment" (180). [Similarly, Willmott (1985, 68).] **CRAIK and CRAIK** (1986): "in God's presence" (278).

12 *this lowly ground* **WILLMOTT** (1985): "earth" (68). **HANDLEY** (1991): "i.e. earth, in life" (43).

13–14 *Teach . . . Seald my pardon with thy blood.* **WYLD** (1923) argues that the lines rhyme according to the pronunciation of the time, noting that the "agreement in sound was perfect," approximating the vowel sound of modern "food" (76–81). **RICHARDS** (1929) finds these lines a test of "the distinction between words whose feeling tends to dominate their content and words of a more malleable nature" (212). **BROWER** (1951): Donne offers here "one of his pieces of coalescing sound" (70). **GARDNER** (1952): "True repentance is a guarantee that the general pardon purchased by Christ's blood is sealed to a man individually" (68). **KREMEN** (1972) states that the model of salvation implicit in these lines typifies Donne's interpretation of traditional theology, suggesting that while Donne recognizes God's grace as the necessary and sufficient cause of redemption, he also believes that salvation arises from the simultaneous cooperation of divine and human wills. Claims that, in effect, to the gospel of divine forgiveness of sins, Donne adds human penitence (114). **CRENNAN** (1979): the lines are marked by "a tone vibrant with certainty," given that "this, in the sacramental scheme of things envisaged by Donne and repeated in Christian liturgy, is precisely what God *has* done" (15–16). **CRAIK and CRAIK** (1986): "True repentance will assure the sinner that God has confirmed his pardon with his (Christ's) blood. The image is of a royal pardon with the king's seal upon it" (278). **STRIER** (1989): the ending "duplicates the problem of seeing individual repentance and Christ's sacrifice as alternative ways to salvation," for rather than being "coordinated" they are "equated in value and efficacy." And thus "again, the problem is evaded not acknowledged by the poem" (372). GILL (1990) questions if the tone of the ending is "assured" or "anxious," noting that the "almost colloquial" "for that's as good" could suggest "confidence or nervous bluster." Comments that Christian doctrine "asserts that Christ has sealed everybody's pardon with the blood of the cross" but that the effect of "As if" could "make the final line sound more tentative" (102). FOWLER (1995): "True repentance, ensuring a share in mankind's general redemption, is as effective as an individual pardon" (261). LABRIOLA (1995) says that the conceit of the final couplet "echoes the terminal true rhyme of 'good' and 'blood,'" arguing that for Donne, "good" was "nearly homophonous" with "God" and that thus "the conceit of God's blood, both visually and aurally, ends the poem," becoming a compression of the speaker's "thoughtful process" (100).

13 *Teach me how to repent, for that's as good* RICHTER (1902): the line is an example of "irregular meter" ("doppelte Taktumstellung") (395). HARDY (1942): the line suggests Donne's remorse at his spiritual weakness, his indulgence in an endless cycle of sin and repentance (179). LEWALSKI and SABOL (1973, 153): "*Repentance* is the sign, the evidence of election and pardon."

13 *Teach me how to repent,* TOMKINSON (1931): the words reflect Donne's humility and dependence on the Grace of God (345). THOMPSON (1935) observes that this must be everyone's prayer, since sin can damn the eternal soul (13). LEVER (1974) points to HSBlack 9–10 (180).

13 *that's as good* DREW (1933) draws attention to the "verbal boldness" of the words, asking whether the colloquial tone of the phrase adds to the poetic effect or undermines it, whether it sharpens the emotional impact or damages it (178–79).

14 *As if thou hadst Seald my pardon with thy blood.* ZEMPLÉNYI (1986) calls attention to the ironic nature of the line, namely, that "in spite of all theological orthodoxy, the ending questions the fact of salvation for the speaker himself, and is, by this fact, bitter, even tragic; it contains a strong sense of doubt." Extends his reading of the line by noting that the tense of the last line is "the third type conditional," which suggests the meaning "that thou hadst not really." Believes that the speaker is "not yet saved by the act of Redemption—for that he needs the special grace of God, which is the don of repentance, of penitence, contritio." Adds that "[a]ll this is naturally perfectly in accordance with both Catholic and Anglican theology, while in the modality of its poetic handling still carrying some disquieting element" (162).

14 *Seald my pardon* SHAWCROSS (1967): "both my remission of penalty and my indulgence" (341). SMITH (1971): "true repentance can earn for the poet the general pardon that Christ's sacrifice offered to mankind" (628). MALLETT (1983): "Christ's death on the Cross purchased an offer of pardon for all men; if Donne learns how to repent his sins, his particular pardon will be confirmed or authorised" (57).

14 *Seald* SMITH (1971): "(a) authorized with the necessary imprint; (b) pledged,

confirmed" (627). **HOLLANDER and KERMODE** (1973): "confirmed" (1051). [So also, Willmott (1985, 68), who adds, "Christ's death saves man from sin and his blood is like the wax stamped with an official seal to authorise a pardon," citing Rev. 7.3 "in which the 'servants of God' are 'sealed . . . in their foreheads.'"] **PA-TRIDES** (1985a) notes that this is "the precise theological term attesting confirmation, witness the usual definition of a sacrament as 'a seale of saving graces,'" and cites C. A. Patrides, *Premises and Motifs in Renaissance Thought and Literature* (Princeton: Princeton UP, 1982) (439).

14 *thy blood.* **GROSART** (1872–73), reading "my blood," says that "my" is "usually, but erroneously, 'thy,' which is perhaps a later form of theologic speech." But also points to *HSBlack* 13–14 (2:291). **SHAWCROSS** (1967): cf. *HSBlack* 13–14 (341).

 *HSScene*

COMMENTARY

General Commentary

Gransden (1954, 128) describes *HSBlack*, *HSMade*, and *HSScene* as "rather som-bre" sonnets that present a poet seeking "strength, grace, and forgiveness from Christ."

Bellette (1975, 334–41) writes that the idea of Christ on the cross affects the form of *HSMade*, *HSScene* and *HSRound*, and notes that these three sonnets may be read as forming a sequence "depicting . . . the transition from this world to the next" (334). See fuller commentary under *HSMade*: General Commentary.

Partridge (1978, 132) writes that *HSScene* has a "less explosive opening" than most of Donne's poetry, arguing further that because Donne finds at the end of *HSScene* and *HSRound* that "consolation is in vain," one may appropriately read the two poems together.

HSScene, Rollin (1986, 141) says, is an example of "Christian 'comedy'" as iden-tified by Robert Burton in *The Anatomy of Melancholy*, that is, "a miniature religious drama with a happy ending."

Shawcross (1988, 301–10) analyzes the text and textual variants of *HSScene*, cit-ing it as a poem that, though "seemingly simple textually" (306), confirms in fact that for Donne there appear to be "no uncomplicated texts, only deceptive pitfalls" (310).

Ray (1990b, 321–22) notes the speaker's emphasis on the "very end of several things" and describes the speaker's state of mind as "a complex combination of an-ticipation and fear," including the "Christian fear of the Last Judgment" (321). But the sestet, according to Ray, resolves the issue for the speaker as he "imagines his soul ascending to heaven," thereby assuring himself that "his sins that came of the body will fall with the body and leave his repentant soul ['imputed righteous by Christ himself'] free" (322).

Albrecht (1992, 24–30) offers an extended comparison of *HSScene* and *HSBatter* as part of her argument that the twelve sonnets from 1633 are formed into two groups of six, with each poem in the first group having a counterpart in the second group. See more under *HSBatter*: General Commentary.

Oliveros (1992, 143–65) includes *HSScene* among four English Baroque poems he translates and comments on, analyzing the meditative and Ignatian elements in the sonnet and citing it as a prime example of the Baroque in English.

Shullenberger (1993, 55) notes that the "ocular motif," which dominates the religious poems, is present in *HSScene*, where "the gaze of God" "whose feare al-ready shakes my every joynt" (l. 8) is "omniscient and threatening."

Date and Circumstances

Mims (1948, 56) says that the poem was written in 1618.

Gransden (1954, 127–28) believes that *HSBlack*, *HSMade*, and *HSScene* probably refer to Donne's illness in 1608, not that in 1623.

The Poet/Persona

Payne (1926, 140) quotes the poem in full as an example of Donne's awareness of how short a time is left him.

Leishman (1934, 88) notes that *HSScene*, like almost all of Donne's sonnets, is a record of his struggle with the sin of fear, one that finds him only rarely achieving a "mood of perfect joy and security."

Miner (1969, 173) observes that Donne reduces the reality of the world almost to nothing in *HSScene* and that, outside of himself, the speaker is most conscious of God.

Stampfer (1970, 242) states that the speaker, "wallowing in a purposeless chaos, struggles to define some future he is helpless to control." The speaker is helpless in his sinful condition, Stampfer says; hence, he prays "without a will for grace" and "projects visions not knowing who listens to his prayers."

Sicherman (1971, 85) asserts that, to improve his knowledge of God's love, the speaker undertakes the discipline of fear of death.

Sanders (1971, 128) contends that there is "frightening inadequacy" in the dogma invoked in *HSScene*, a "blatant theological sophistry" that does no more than dramatize Donne's "logical bankruptcy."

Parfitt (1972, 381–82) regards *HSScene* as a striking illustration of Donne's use of the first person (381), remarking that Donne's poetry generally "tends to exclude considerations outside the individual self and the figure of God," giving the impression that God is "a concept to which Donne can respond only in closely personal terms" (382).

Young (1987, 31–34) finds the equivocal nature of Donne's views on imputed righteousness present in *HSScene*, which makes "explicit reference to imputed righteousness" in the closing couplet (31). The octave, according to Young, presents a traditional Ignatian meditative setting, the deathbed and judgment, two of the "Four Last Things," and the sestet focuses on the remaining two, heaven and hell (31–32). Young agrees with Sanders (1971) regarding the sophistry of the lines, finding as well an "air of nervousness" in the sonnet regarding the effectiveness of "imputed righteousness" (34).

For Strier (1989, 374), both *HSScene* and *HSBlack* show us Donne's "deep inability to accept the paradoxical conception of a regenerate Christian" as at once "righteous and a sinner." According to Strier, Donne's imagination "hungered for actual purity, for imparted or attained not imputed righteousness," and "this desire was one of those deep 'impressions of the Romane religion' very difficult to 'blot out.'"

Hester (1991a, 177–90) reads *HSScene* in the context of his belief that the Holy Sonnets "affirm man's limited powers of recreation" while they reveal the "tensions inherent to, and the psychic questions raised by, the Protestant doctrine of imputation to the human condition." *HSScene*, Hester believes, offers a "more direct consideration of the issue of imputation" and "enacts man's attempts to *write*/'right' a text of the self that God might read as 'righteous'" (177). In a detailed reading of the sonnet, Hester contends that it "stages a three-step 'purg[ing]' of the self's corporeality in order to attain psychic (or moral) assurance," but, in Hester's view, "the positing of a (Gnostic) dualism of body and soul to overcome the self's death achieves only an ill-founded 'confidence' that is contradicted by its strained verbal gestures and the absence of Grace which it ironically calls into presence" (179). Whereas the first quatrain of the sonnet, Hester observes, is "dominated by reference to and the perspective of the 'world,' and the second by the 'flesh,' so the third enacts a commitment to the temptation of the 'devill'" (185). By "positing the most radical extension of his dualism," Hester says, the speaker "strives to 'take flight,' but concludes the section by focusing on the fear of physical pain—'presse'" (185). Hester concludes that the "final import" of *HSScene* underscores the "'idle talke' of a dying man, foolish in its rationalized literalizations and in its sensual and hyperbolic application of conventions," in its "idolizing of the self" (189). But, Hester emphasizes, "emotionally it is valid and true—as an evocation of the meaninglessness of life without love/Love, the nothingness of words without the gracious response of the Beloved," and as such, the sonnet "dramatizes the fond rational foundations of any mechanical doctrine of justification that evades the problematics of human virtue and the mystery of imputation at the same time that it explores the desperate foundation of such doctrine in the human desire for signification" (189–90).

Nardo (1991, 56, 71) states that Donne prefers themes that "capture the experience of being in between," with the "peak-moments of in-betweenness" occurring "during sex, sickness, and suffering." According to Nardo, Donne "always felt himself to be a body, to be in the flesh," and thus "to reach beyond the self to another (whether to a lady or God), he had to experience the other with his flesh" (56). Nardo emphasizes that "beds provide settings for these moments" in many of Donne's poems, and, in particular, in *HSScene*. Nardo adds that beds are like "playgrounds," or "the threshold between multiple realities," in which "Donne indulges his 'antic disposition'" (56). Nardo concludes that Donne was "a liminal man in a liminal age" (71).

Structure

Esch (1955, 52–53) contends that the poem achieves a synthesis of the Italian and "the English sonnet structure" ("der national-englischen Struktur"). He detects "a dark tension" ("eine dumpfe Spannung") weighing down the octave through the condensation of time and the repetition of the word "last," a tension that climaxes in line 8. It is released, Esch senses, in the sestet, but the emotion is packed into the final couplet, as it is in the Surrey-Shakespeare structure. See also Holy Sonnets: Genre and Traditions.

French (1970, 116–18) says that a sense of sinfulness is supremely important and dominant in *HSScene* (116). French finds a note of "uncontrollable terror" in the octave and observes that the idea in the sestet of sins falling away to hell is "rather queer" (116). The change in tone between the octave and sestet, French says, suggests a sudden burgeoning of faith as the result of an act of grace on God's part.

There is according to French no contrition in the poem and "very little suggestion of any moral activity on the writer's part," adding that the phrasing of the first quatrain is "curiously mechanical" (117), a reflection of the "abject impotence of man, his total lack of control over his destiny." The "dislocation of tone between the octave and sestet" may be due, he says, to "the attempt to render in verse God's gift or faith (or grace) which, being arbitrary, *cannot* appear to arise naturally from the postulates of the poem" (118).

Roston (1974, 182–83) writes that in the octave of *HSScene* "the reader is drawn into a personal confrontation with death" through Donne's "elongation and compression of time and space." He notes that in "asserting paradoxical truth" in the sestet of the sonnet, Donne shows off a wit that is more evident in his secular verse.

Rollin (1986, 141) identifies one "difficult moment" in *HSScene* at lines 7–8 but says that overall the "mood" of the poem is "composed," arguing that the "near-clichés" associated with death in the octave and the "conviction of salvation" in the sestet keep the mood of the poem generally "elevated" and "expansive."

Strier (1989, 373–74) shows that the octave, in its move to the presence of "that face" in line 7, prompts a "reaction of terror on the part of the speaker"—"Whose feare already shakes my every joynt" (l. 8). But instead of focusing on the fear and guilt inspired by "that face," the sestet moves to what Strier calls "a fantasy of material purification." Strier concurs with French (1970) that it is difficult to grasp the movement from "the face that is terrifying" to the soul's rising to heaven, and he endorses French's notion that the vision of the poem is "rather queer." Strier suggests that Donne may have sensed that *HSScene* "has slipped its theological moorings," and thus attempts to correct it in the closing couplet. But Strier finds the effort unsuccessful in that while it begins with a "self-consciously Protestant prayer," the "Reformation vocabulary" of the couplet fails to support the "vision" of the final lines (373). The "self-congratulatory tone" of "thus I leave" (l. 14), Strier says, "strongly supports the materialist, anti-Reformation reading of 'thus purged'" (374).

Gill (1990, 100) finds that in the opening octave of *HSScene* the poet "creates in detail the intense musings of a man anticipating his own death," but in the "cooler and more theological sestet" that follows he "attempts to calm the fears aroused by the opening through the consoling hope of imputed righteousness."

Language and Style

Cruttwell (1954, 42) argues that Donne's youthful experience attending the theater made the play a "natural" metaphor, as with Shakespeare, for the expression of his deepest emotions. Cruttwell cites *HSScene*, where Donne "contemplates his own dissolution," as an example.

Sypher (1955, 129–30) argues that Donne is able "to assimilate opposite and diverse appetites and experiences" in his poetry, but that he "reflects the mannerist instability and tension" in his reaction to the gulf between Renaissance optimism and Medieval faith. Sypher quotes *HSScene* in full as an example of "the mannerist tension, dissonance, and perversion," in that while Donne claims not to fear death he only barely conceals his horror of the grave.

Asals (1979, 128–29, 132) finds the meaning of *HSScene* in "the practice of the grammar of redemption," in "the dynamic by which word becomes effect and by which the poet's own words (in imitation of his God's) may effect his own redemption" (128–29). Asals reads in the sonnet an emphasis on time and the "end of man's own time." The poem introduces us, says Asals, to the "method of God's language (its indifference to the consistency of temporal point of view) which is dramatized in the speaker's flagrant lack of commitment to any single verb tense." Furthermore, she says, HSScene concludes with an imperative ending ("Impute me righteous"), "demonstrating the power of the Word to . . . effect and fabricate from the present and the future a participle of the past tense." Thus, Asals points to the structure of the poem as involving a "present-future-release into past effect with the imperative operation of the Word" and a movement "towards the idiom of the divine Word" (132).

Sloane (1981, 52–54) finds Donne's use of the "active emblem" to be consistent with an observation made by Martz (1954) in his study of meditative poetry, namely, that the techniques employed by various Renaissance religious writers, including Ignatius Loyola, "resulted in an interior drama in which the poet sees his soul as an actor on a stage in the presence of God" (52–53). For Sloane, HSScene epitomizes the technique.

Raspa (1983, 125–26) discusses the function of the enthymeme in the Holy Sonnets, noting that "every image and hence every enthymeme aspired after an antithetical effect proper to itself, different from that of the extended paradox of ancient epigram" (125–26). He says that HSScene includes "confused images of drama, race, pilgrimages, and span," designed "to create an enthymemic effect" by "organizing a series of compressed images into a provocative general picture of Christian truth emotionally significant to all men." Raspa observes also that "the profusion of time and space images" seen in the octave depicts "the terrifying proposition that the 'last mile' of life is heaven-appointed," although it masks "the more pleasing prospect that human life was created at all only in order to end, and then to enter into a better state" (126).

Conrad (1985, 234–35) focuses on Donne's preoccupation with "the encroachments of nothingness" here and in HSLittle, the two poems functioning together, according to Conrad, to "exploit the sonnet's lacerating courage of self-contradiction" (234–35). Since the two sonnets "are about man as a walking paradox, made of both mire and grace, they couple two incompatible and separable poems in a single unit, and the argumentative pivot or turn in the ninth line is always a point of unhinging, which reveals how the deathly, salutary dis- or (as Donne calls it) unjointing might mercifully be achieved." In HSScene, Conrad asserts, "the octave considers the body's profane earthly incarnation; the sestet consigns it to burial and frees the spirit for flight" (235).

Warnke (1987, 106) finds HSScene emblematic of the Holy Sonnets in its "relentlessly dramatic, immediate, and colloquial quality." And, in Warnke's view, "the irregular, yet inescapable recurrence of the word *last*, with its variant *latest*, anticipates the technique Donne was to employ later as preacher," the "ubiquitous baroque topos of the theater" serving to "intensify the macabre effect."

Skulsky (1992, 116–17) states that HSScene, like other of the Holy Sonnets, employs the "diversionary *littera*" in order to "conjure up a convenient double," which in this instance is "his own soul," whereas in *HSBatter*, Skulsky shows that the double is "a whipping boy" (116–17). The soul, in *HSScene*, says Skulsky, "is packed off to face the ultimate terror while the speaker is safely unconscious [ll. 5–8]." "Unfortunately," Skulsky notes, "if his soul sees that face, he will, too." According to Skulsky, "what [the speaker] really anticipates after death, for his waking self, not his joints, is that his new fear will just keep on mounting until it confronts its terrible object." But all that the diversionary *littera* can actually do to relieve the speaker, Skulsky adds, "is let him imagine he is denying [the terrifying belief] or defying it," as in *HSDeath* (117).

Prosody

Sypher (1955, 130) argues that "the wavering caesura, the sliding meter, the wrenched accents" of the poem reveal the tension between its psychological and rhetorical dimensions, suggesting "the curious torment in mannerist faith—and mannerist doubt."

Linville (1984b, 77) finds, through a detailed analysis of the sonnet's mimetic line forms, that Donne's "initial aim" is to "dramatize a progressive diminishment or compression of his life's time and space on earth, until, at octave's end, temporal perspective is obliterated, and the speaker stands trembling on the brink of judgment and eternity."

Themes

An anonymous editor (1840, 270) prints a number of Donne poems under original headings, including *HSScene* under the heading "Thought on Death."

Fausset (1924, 242), quoting the poem in full, finds that it characterizes "Death as the liberator" and that Donne imagines himself "as about to endure the terror and triumph of dissolution."

Mims (1948, 56) cites the poem as an example of Donne's terror of death. In *HSScene*, Mims says, Donne "pictures death as unjointing his body and soul" and calls upon God to save him from hell by purging him of evil.

Reeves (1952, 100) paraphrases the poem: "Convinced that he is about to die, he imagines his body returning to the earth, his sins to hell, and his soul to Heaven."

ul-Hasan (1958, 68) observes that the poem presents life as a stage, implying that it is "a mere imitation of something else and is an empty show."

Peterson (1959, 509) contends that Donne, in fear of punishment, argues fallaciously that since the body has sinned and the soul has remained pure, at death he will be purged of evil and God will impute him righteous. Peterson notes that in *HSRound* 1–4, the next sonnet in the 1633 sequence, Donne rejects the argument. See also Holy Sonnets: Themes.

Collmer (1961, 327–29) says of the Holy Sonnets generally that "though they are in the *meditatio mortis* tradition, they do not offer any example of a mystical ecstasy produced by thinking of death" (327), but he goes on to add that in *HSScene*, the speaker does suggest that "one should think about his own near death so that he won't want to sin." In this theme, Collmer says, lies the meaning of *HSScene* (329).

Roy and Kapoor (1969, 120) state that in such poems as *HSScene* Donne refers to the point of death in order to reveal the significance of the moment when the soul leaves the body.

Wall (1976, 195) notes that there is a "slight note of apprehension" in *HSScene*, but argues that "it is caught up in the calm joy which comes with the confidence that with death sin and the chance of new sin are left behind."

Low (1978, 61–62) writes that in *HSScene* "Donne combines three traditional metaphors: life as a play, life as a pilgrimage or exile from heaven, and life as St. Paul's footrace." Low argues that death is made more disturbing "for being left pictorially vague," and that "its force is felt not by the eyes but by the deeper kinesthetic sense of bodily integrity" (61), concluding that the sestet uses the emotion of the octave to "motivate a resolution" (62).

Lewalski (1979, 268) regards *HSScene*, the sixth sonnet in the 1635 volume, as "something of a turning point" in that the speaker "imagines himself at the moment of death, but not by evoking a deathbed scene in the manner of an Ignatian *compositio loci*." Rather, she says, the speaker "calls upon the very familiar biblical metaphors of life as pilgrimage and as athletic race." When, in the final couplet, the speaker cries out to God to "impute me righteous," Lewalski claims, the cry "indicates that he clearly understands his need and that his faith is now strong enough to formulate it," in terms reminiscent of Rom. 4.6–24.

Yearwood (1982, 210–13) finds that the conversion process in Donne's twelve Holy Sonnets of 1633 (and following Gardner's 1952 ordering) "begins in pride, proceeds to confession and despair, and culminates in a humble joy and confidence" (210). In *HSScene*, the third sonnet in that sequence, the speaker begins what he was told to do in the second sonnet, *HSBlack*, by "the voice of grace," according to Yearwood, namely, "recognize and accept his sins" (213). But Yearwood points out that the speaker's admission of sin "moves him only to fear" (213).

Mallett (1983, 56) notes that in this poem Donne "imagines that he is on his death-bed preparing to meet God's judgement," and he suggests the value of comparing *HSScene* with Donne's actual preparations for death undertaken in 1631.

Sabine (1992, 105) contends that Donne shifted his iconographic focus from Mary, Mother of Jesus, to Jesus himself. Whereas in the Anniversaries, according to Sabine, Donne had believed that the face of Mary "most closely reflected Christ's," conceiving of the work "as a divine mirror formed of feminine prisms," in *HSScene* the face he "felt authorised to contemplate" was Christ's, not Mary's, a "face / Whose feare already shakes my every joynt" (ll. 7–8). In Sabine's view, Donne "showed his determination to restamp the versical papers which were his spiritual passport back to Protestant England."

HSScene and Other Works

Friederich (1932, 165–66), in discussing poetry about death, contrasts *HSScene* with Herrick's "A Good Death," arguing that Herrick had no fear of death, but for Donne and others in the period it was "terrifying" ("Fütchterliches"), conjuring up images of the Last Judgment and of Hell.

Bennett (1934, 7–8) quotes the poem in full, contrasting it with lines from Thomas Nashe's *Summer's Last Will and Testament*, to argue that while the pattern of

Nashe's work is "a symmetrical design without development," Donne's is the pattern of thought "of a mind moving from the contemplation of a fact to deduction from a fact and thence to a conclusion" (7). Bennett concludes that while Nashe "excites emotion," Donne "appeals through the ear to the intellect" (8).

Milward (1979 [1988, 50–54]) connects the subject of the sonnet, in its focus on death, to the Ignatian *Spiritual Exercises*, and in particular to the Sixth Addition to the *First Week* (50). Milward also connects the sonnet's emphasis on death to the writings of both the Jesuit Robert Persons, in his well-known *Christian Directory* (1585), and the Spanish Jesuit Luis de la Puente, in his equally popular *Meditations* (1605) (50–51). Donne's images in the sonnet, according to Milward, also follow closely images in the Bible and in the plays of Shakespeare, such as the image of Death in *Rom.* 5.3.45 and the reference to "pilgrimages" in *AYL* 3.2.138–41(51–52). But in the sestet, the speaker "immediately moves from fear to hope, or rather to prayer" (54). Here, Milward asserts, the speaker echoes "the Aristotelian idea of everything moving to its proper place," so that the soul, whose destination is heaven, "must take her flight upwards on being released from the body," whereas the body, "born as it is of the slime of the earth, must dwell 'in the earth,'" which Milward notes is a view reminiscent of the words of the dying Richard II in Shakespeare's play (5.5.112–13) (54).

Nelson (1979, 272–81) compares sonnet 52 of Sidney's *Astrophel and Stella*, Sir John Harington's epigram "A Dish of Dainties for the Divell" (published in *The Metamorphosis of Ajax*), and *HSScene* to highlight their unexpected similarities, given the "frivolous" nature of the Sidney and Harington poems. Nelson finds such similarities as their "attempt to justify a dissociation of earthly things from spiritual ones"; "the conscious use of sophistry" (274); and the image of "the reverend man sitting on the privy" in the Harington epigram and, possibly, in the Donne sonnet (276). Nelson asserts that both Sidney and Donne (in some other Holy Sonnets) show that they are aware that "soul, body, and sin are implicated in one another" and thus "cannot be neatly separated," as envisaged in *HSScene* (274). Nelson cites approvingly Peterson's comments (1959) on *HSScene* and also suggests a possible connection between the poems of Harington and Donne in relation to Harington's epigram about "the reverend man sitting on the privy," citing lines from each: from Harington's epigram: "Ech take his due, and me thou canst not hurt,/To God my pray'r I meant, to thee the durt..."; and from Donne's sonnet: "So, fall my sinnes, that all may have their right,/To where they'are bred, and would presse me, to hell" (ll. 11–12). Nelson cites a sermon by Donne (*Sermons*, 1:190) that takes up a similar issue, as Donne describes God taking away the uncontrite man "*as a man takes away dung, till it be all gone*" (276). Nelson also cites Rabelais, who suggests, in *Gargantua* (ch. 23), that "time spent on the privy should be used for the exposition of Biblical texts" (280). The possible conceit, for Nelson, associates sin with dung, though he acknowledges that it is "submerged" in Donne (281). Nelson's primary interest here is in the "process of thought" that could lead early modern writers "to use scatological imagery in an eschatological context" (277).

Veith (1985, 126) finds that whereas Herbert's poem "The Glance" (ll. 19–24) "anticipates with the greatest yearning beholding God face to face," Donne's sonnet stands "in marked contrast," in that the anticipation of God "remains terrifying" (cf. ll. 6–8).

Sullivan (1995, 345–46) believes that the conceit in which "gluttonous death sieves the soul" may have been suggested by Robert Southwell's "Sinnes heavie loade," suggesting that Donne had connections to "Southwell's circle." Noting Gardner's (1952) suggested date of 1609 for this poem, Sullivan points out that Southwell's poems were frequently issued from 1597 onward and that *HSScene* and the 1620 edition of Southwell's works "shared the same dedicatee, the third Earl of Dorset" (346).

Notes and Glosses

1–6 *This is . . . sleepe a space,* **PARFITT** (1972) cites these lines in particular to illustrate Donne's emphasis on the self, noting that the "stress upon the first person" is evident throughout the poem (381). **ANSARI** (1974): there is an expression of "insecurity and "sheer hopelessness" in these first six lines (144).

1–4 *This . . . my Minutes last pointe.* **GRIERSON** (1912): the passage is comparable to the "magnificent openings" of Donne's love poems (2:lii–liii). **SPÖRRI-SIGEL** (1949): Donne's fear of death appears most strongly in these lines (54–55). **MARTZ** (1954): the lines are an instance of the "composition" or "proposing" stage of the Ignatian meditation (31). [See also Holy Sonnets: Genre and Traditions.] **ESCH** (1955) finds that the lines achieve "a dark tension" ("eine dumpfe Spannung") through the condensation of time, "scene-mile-pace-inch-point," and the heavy echo of the repeated "last" in each of the lines. Observes that the tension arises from linking the heavy vowel of "last" with the lighter ones of the nouns, and from the metric structure, where the word, though it appears as an unstressed syllable, requires the stress, thus creating a series of spondees leading up to the entrance of death in line 5 (53). **LEVER** (1974): the images point to a "gradual constriction of space and time to the instant of death" (179). **MAROTTI** (1986) sees the "chain of epithets" in the opening quatrain as "less functional than wittily overdramatic" (256).

1–2 *This . . . Pilgrimages last Mile,* **MARTZ** (1966) finds the first two lines "almost too good to be true" (5).

1 *This is my Playes last Scene,* **GRIERSON** (1921) recalls the characterization of Donne as "a great Frequenter of Plays" (228). Similarly, Handley (1991, 42). **LEVER** (1974) says that "More's figure of life as a stage-play is close to one of life as a prison" and also points to the end of Marlowe's *Doctor Faustus* (179). **FOWLER** (1995) notes that the "commonplace of life as a comedy" was said to go back to the ancient world in such as Lucian and Pythagoras. Cites, among others, *AYLI* 2.7.139–43 (260).

2 *Pilgrimages . . . race,* **ARCHER** (1977): "the metaphor *pilgrimage* places emphasis on the journey's end—an end well known and, in a pilgrimage, preplanned.

Race is also metaphorically limited: the journey is quick and it follows a prescribed course" (177).

3 *Idely,* **SHAABER** (1958): "indolently" (101). **PATRIDES** (1985a) glosses as "both lazily and foolishly" and cites French (1970) (see *HSScene*: Structure) (437).

4 *My Spanns last inche; my Minutes last pointe.* **COFFIN** (1937) quotes the line, which conceptualizes "the approach of death," to illustrate that "figures of space from geometry" appear in and "increasingly enrich the verse and prose of Donne's maturer years" (184). **MORRIS** (1953): Donne and Eliot are similar in their syntax, e.g., "the piling of parallel epithets" here and in "Whispers of Immortality" (ll. 13–14) (130).

4 *My Spanns last inche;* **MALLETT** (1983): "a span is a small distance, or brief length of time" (56).

4 *Spanns* **SHAWCROSS** (1967): "life-span's." (340). [So also, Booty (1990, 107).] **LEVER** (1974): "The length of the extended hand from thumb to little finger, reckoned at nine inches." Cf. Ps. 39.5 (179–80).

4 *last pointe.* **GARDNER** (1952) adopts this reading but acknowledges that it "gives a defective line." Thinks it likely that the reading "latest point" in some manuscripts and in 1633 was an attempt to correct the defective line but that the textual authority for "last" is very strong. Believes that the "crescendo" of the repeated word "last" is "so powerful that it is impossible for the sake of metrical regularity to prefer the less authoritative and tamer 'latest'" (67). **LEVER** (1974), reading "latest" and finding that Gardner's (1952) emendation "upsets the metre," glosses as the "last minute mark on a clock face" (180).

5–8 *And . . . shakes my euery ioynt.* **FAERBER** (1950): a paradoxical expression of Donne's fear of death (14). **MARTZ** (1954): the lines reflect the Jesuit practice of meditation on the hour of death, especially Fray Luis de Granada's emphasis on the fearful voyage of the soul to judgment (139). [See more under Holy Sonnets: Genre and Traditions.]

5–6 *And . . . I shall sleepe a space,* **THOMPSON** (1935) observes that poets were uncertain when the soul would be separated from the body. Notes that Donne suggests here it will be at the hour of death, but says elsewhere at the Last Judgment (40). **GRANSDEN** (1954): the passage is a reference to the actual illness Donne suffered in 1608 (127–28).

5 *gluttonous* **OED** (1897–1900) cites this use as the first instance to mean, in a figurative sense, "Given to excess in eating; characterized by, or of the nature of, a glutton" (1.*fig.*). **RICHTER** (1902): Donne frequently slurs an unaccented syllable, as here (403–04). **UL-HASAN** (1958): death is pictured as "devouring and swallowing" in "undignified haste, greediness, and unhealthy hunger" (58).

5 *vnioynt* ANSARI (1974): expresses a "sense of strain" and suggests "the awareness of life coming to a close" (144). LEVER (1974): "Disjoin, with a suggestion of breaking joints" (180). MALLETT (1983): "separate" (56). CRAIK and CRAIK (1986): "divide from each other" (278). HANDLEY (1991): "Divorce, separate" (42).

6–7 *I shall sleepe . . . see that face* MALLETT (1983) (reading l. 7 as "But my ever-waking part shall see that face") says that here "'I' is the body, the 'ever-waking part' the soul," noting that Donne believed "that the soul was judged at the very instant of death, while the resurrection of the body had to wait until the final Day of Judgement" and points to the "general thought" of *Relic* 8–11 (57).

6 *and Soule,* PATRIDES (1985a) notes that the printings in 1635–69 and most mss. omit the "and" though it is included in 1633 (438).

7 *Or presently, I know not, see that face* GRIERSON (1912), reading the line as here, argues that Donne revised the line to read "But my ever-waking part shall see that face" because the "I know not" implied the unorthodox, "even heretical," doctrine that departed souls will not see the face of God until Judgment Day, a belief that he rejected more than once in his preaching (cf. *Sermons*, 7:134). Draws attention to the fact that Donne did accept two related doctrines, "not strictly orthodox": (1) a period of preparation, as in Purgatory, and (2) "Conditional Immortality," the belief that the soul is not immortal by nature, but only because God preserves it, as in *BedfWrit* 58 (2:232). FAUSSET (1924) observes that "conventional piety" required that the line be altered to omit the phrase "I know not" in some versions, but that it accurately reflects Donne's "agnosticism." Argues that his "naturalism and scepticism were not submerged in mystical faith," which accounts for the "terrible and sublime" reality of his religious verse (242–43). GARDNER (1952) adopts the reading "But my'ever-waking part shall see that face" but believes that the line as given here was Donne's original. Says that the "deliberate expression of doubt" suggested by "I know not" is "the more impressive" in view of the fact that the sestet "assumes that the second alternative" ("presently") is true. Argues that Donne emended the line "some time after he had made up his mind on the point" (xlv). LEVER (1974) says that the line was changed "for doctrinal reasons," thus "eliminating the doubt expressed" (180). PATRIDES (1985a) (reading the line as "But my ever-waking part shall see that face") cites the alternative (as here) given in several mss. (438). PATRIDES (1985b) finds that the elimination of "'defective' or 'clumsy' readings from Donne's poetry is often based on principles that tend to shift as the occasion may happen to demand." Notes that in "all early editions" *HSScene* 7 reads as "But my ever-waking part shall see that face," though a "battalion of manuscripts" (including NY3 the "most authoritative" ms. for the Holy Sonnets) read the line as given here. Suggests that one might have assumed that editors would have endorsed "the latter reading from the reported manuscripts," but instead they "endorsed the former one from the printed sources" (370). Points out that Shawcross (1967), with respect to this sonnet, both rejected NY3 in line 7 and ac-

cepted it in line 14 ("and devill" rather than "the devill") "in spite of the congregated witness of all early editions to the contrary" (371). **CAREY** (1990b): the version of several mss. (as here) suggests that Donne, "like other 'advanced' thinkers, suspected the soul might not go to heaven (or hell) at death, but sleep in the grave till the Last Judgement" (454). **HESTER** (1991a) points out the reading of this line as given here and notes that several editors have seen it as an earlier, less "orthodox" position. Argues, however, that orthodoxy is "slender grounding for textual decisions about the Holy Sonnets, since they seem more concerned with expressing the problematic nature of 'accepted doctrines.'" Finds the reading (as here) in NY3 and other mss. "preferable" not "in spite of but perhaps even because of its unorthodox position." Notes that Gardner (1952) commented on the "more impressive" reading of this line, even though she rejected it, and concludes that "I knowe not" effectively evokes the "limitations of the speaker's view of the afterlife" and points to the "essential limitations of fallen man who, as sinner, actually 'knowes' only 'not'—whose vision in this case is capable of 'seeing' the eternal only as the absence of the physical" (178n5). **ELLRODT** (1993) comments that in his edition he has retained the earlier version of the line (as given here) where Donne "hesitates" ("hésite") between the orthodox view of the immortality of the soul and the mortalist heresy. Acknowledges that the doubt disappears in the final version of this line but says that Donne "forgot" ("oublié") to correct it in poems such as HSRound 2–3 and HSDeath 13, where the lines seem to represent the resurrection of the body as the resurrection of the entire person (27). **SULLIVAN** (1995) suggests a connection between HSScene and Robert Southwell's "Sinnes heavie loade" (see HSScene and Other Works) and proposes that the latter's endorsement of "an orthodox Catholic view of purgatory" might provide added justification for retaining the reading "Or presently, I know not, see that Face" as "expressing Donne's earlier recusant sympathies" (346).

7 *presently, I know not,* **SHAABER** (1958) (reading "my ever-waking part"): "the soul" (101). [So also, Shawcross (1967, 340), Patrides (1985a, 438), and Booty (1990, 107).]

7 *that face* **SHAWCROSS** (1967): "the face of God at Judgment Day" (340). [Similarly, Craik and Craik (1986, 278), Booty (1990, 107), and Handley (1991, 42).] **PITTS** (1971): the face of Satan. If the face is the devil's, the notion is not heretical but an expression of popular belief consistent with Donne's sermons. Interpreting the face as God's or death's "weakens the otherwise tight parallel structure and unity" of the poem. **DANIELS** (1972) disagrees with Pitts, citing as the "crucial obstacle" to Pitts's reading the form of l. 7 (as given here), thought by Grierson to be Donne's first version of the line: "Or presently, I know not, see that Face." Argues that while Pitts suggests that the speaker in ll. 6 and 7 "seems uncertain when the face will be seen, either just before or at the moment of death," Donne refers to time *after* the instant of death." States that the poem points to three moments of time: (1) "in lines 5–6 death comes"; (2) consequently, in l. 6 the "first possibility is that the speaker may 'sleepe a space,' which hardly would allow him to

see the face at the moment of death"; and (3) the "alternative possibility" based on the variant l. 7 is "an immediate meeting of the face ('presently,' i.e., right after death)." Concludes that Donne is "hesitating between the Mortalist heresy, which holds that the soul will sleep until the Judgment Day, and the orthodoxy that the soul will see God immediately after death" (item 12). PATRICK (1972) also opposes the interpretation of Pitts. States that the speaker is in the last moment of his life, just before the instant in which death will unjoint his body and soul and argues that the speaker is fearful "because after death, when his soul reaches heaven and sees God's face, he will be judged for his sins." Emphasizes the "persistent ideas of unjointing and of the world, flesh, and devil (or sins)" to counteract Pitts's claim that understanding the face as God's weakens the structure and unity of the poem (item 12). PATRIDES (1985a) glosses as "God's—or, on the contrary, Satan's" and cites Pitts (1971) (438). GILL (1990): it is uncertain whether the identity of "that face," and whether "the fact that there are a number of answers—God, death, the devil"—adds richness to the poem "by highlighting the poet's fear and uncertainty," or diminishes it "by making the fear vague" (101).

8 *Whose feare* SHAABER (1958): "fear of whom" (101). [So also, Patrides (1985a, 438) and Booty (1990, 107).]

8 *shakes my euery ioynt.* MORRIS (1953): Donne and Eliot often use a vocabulary that is more realistic than poetic, as here with "shakes my euery ioynt" and in *Relic* (120).

9–14 *Then as . . . the world, the fleshe, and deuill.* FAERBER (1950): Donne's concretization of the relationship between God and Satan runs into certain contradictions, which would end in despair if God did not rise up to wrench his creature from that state of mind (18). [See also Holy Sonnets: Language and Style.]

9 *Then as my Soule, to'heauen her first Seate takes flight,* MORRIS (1953): both Donne and Hopkins "mould syntax to suit the rhythm," stressing successive words to add emphasis, as here and in "The Wreck of the Deutschland" (l. 5) (68). PARTRIDGE (1964) says that "to'heauen her" is an example of the kind of elision, common in the Holy Sonnets, that is really a "metrical fiction, designed to indicate the desirability of retaining the full forms in reading." Adds that here the four syllables require metrically to be reduced to two (91–93).

9 *to'heauen* RICHTER (1902): Donne frequently slurs an unaccented syllable of the form vowel + v + e + consonant (403–4).

9 *her first Seate* CRAIK and CRAIK (1986) cite *HSBlack* 4 (278).

9 *Seate* MARTZ (1963): "place of residence" (86). [Similarly, Shawcross (1967, 340) and Booty (1990, 107).]

10 *earthborne* PATRICK (1972) (emphasizing "borne"): meaning both "generated" and "carried" (item 12).

11–12 *So fall my Sins, . . . to hell;* **SHAWCROSS** (1967): "The sense is: So let my sins fall in order that all of them may have their just claim upon the place where they are bred, the same place to which they would force me by their weight (that is, hell)" (340).

11 *So fall* **LEVER** (1974): "So let (them) fall" (180).

11 *that all may haue their right,* **LEVER** (1974): "The sins are sardonically granted repatriation in hell; but they are trying to jostle the poet with them. The conceit resembles the finale of *Doctor Faustus* (180). **MALLETT** (1983): since "his soul will go to its proper home in heaven, and his body will return to the earth," it is "only fitting that his sins should go to their natural home in hell" (57).

12 *and would presse me,* **MALLETT** (1983): "his sins want to thrust him into hell" (57).

12 *presse* **PATRICK** (1972): meaning both "bearing down" and "impressing into conscription" (item 12).

13–14 *Impute . . . the world, the fleshe, and deuill.* **STEPHENSON** (1959): Donne's "one-sided theory of justification rather too easily disarms the wrath of God" by dictating "an oversimplified theology [where] even God must walk by predetermined paths" (310). **LEWALSKI and SABOL** (1973): "The soul which bears the imputed guilt of Adam can only be saved by being imputed righteous through Christ's merits" (152).

13 *Impute me righteous* **GRIERSON** (1921) cites Rom. 4.6, both the "obsolete" usage in Tyndale, "God promiseth to forgive us our sins and to impute us for full righteous," and the "regular use" in the Great Bible, "David describeth the blessed fulness of that man unto whom God imputeth righteousness without deeds" (228). Similarly, Sinfield (1992, 147). **GARDNER** (1952) notes that though "purged of its actual sins by penitence, the soul is not righteous—it bears the 'imputed guilt' of Adam; it can only be 'imputed righteous' by the merit of Christ." (Similarly, Smith [1971, 627].) Cites Article XI of the 39 Articles (so also, Shaaber [1958, 101]) and *Paradise Lost* 3:9 (so also, Patrides [1985a, 438]), "where Milton sets out this distinctly Protestant doctrine" (67). Similarly, Fowler (1995, 260). **MALLETT** (1983) says that here Donne borrows an idea from Calvin, who argues "that men were unable to win salvation through any merit of their own, but a few were chosen by God to be saved because the righteousness or 'grace' of Jesus Christ was 'imputed' or credited to them: that is, they were saved for merits which were not strictly their own" (28). **CRAIK and CRAIK** (1986): "still bears the hereditary sin of Adam and must therefore be *imputed righteous* (have righteousness attributed to it) by the merit of Christ" (278). [Similarly, Lever (1974, 180).] **GILL** (1990) identifies this "essentially Anglican rather than Roman Catholic cry for help" as deriving "its force from the doctrine that since Adam's sin, due to the fall, is attributed, or imputed, to all, salvation is only possible if people are correspondingly imputed righteous by the merits

of Christ's suffering and death upon the cross." Notes further that the sermon in the second *Book of Homilies* (1563) explaining Article XI (on justification) contains this remark: "we cannot be accounted righteous, but by Christ's merits imputed to us" (101). **BOOTY** (1990): "See the doctrine of justification wherein the Christian is made righteous by imputation of Christ's merits" (108). **CAREY** (1990b): "According to Protestant doctrine, no soul can be saved through its own righteousness, only through Christ's 'imputed' to it" (454). **HANDLEY** (1991): "allow me to be accepted as righteous now that I have purged myself of my sins" (42). **ELLRODT** (1993) notes that the "mérite imputé" is from Christ and that the language, if not the doctrine, is here Calvinist (455).

13 *righteous* **SMITH** (1971): "Pronounced as three syllables" (627).

14 *For thus I leaue the world, the fleshe, and deuill.* **GOSSE** (1899), though not identifying this line explicitly, says that with "strenuous abhorrence" Donne "repudiates the World, the Flesh, and the Devil, and for the future his life shall be dedicated wholly to God" (2:108). **GARDNER** (1952) compares the line with *SecAn* 214–15, where Donne calls death the soul's "third birth" since "Creation gave her one, a second, grace." Notes that the line "recalls the renunciations which precede the administration of baptism in the Book of Common Prayer" (67). Similarly, Lever (1974, 180), Wall (1976, 195) and Fowler (1995, 261). **GILL** (1990): the ambiguity surrounding the "state" in which the speaker leaves the world is not "resolved" by the words "the world, the flesh and devil": "they are a reference to the Baptism Service in *The Book of Common Prayer* but they could equally mean that, as at baptism, the poet has renounced them or that, since he is still polluted, he draws attention to this in order to strengthen his plea for mercy uttered in the previous line" (101).

 *HSShe*

COMMENTARY

General Commentary

Gosse (1893, 429–36) comments on the "pathetic sonnet" from the Westmoreland ms. (NY3) (as yet unpublished) that shows the effect of Donne's "bereavement" over the death of his wife and prints *HSShe* for the first time (433).

Kermode (1974, 93), acknowledging that *HSShe* is "rather famous," suggests that it is "not . . . a very good poem," being rather "extremely flat and laboriously worked out."

Marotti (1986, 138–39, 177, 278–79) finds that the further Donne was from the date of his marriage, the "stronger" his "ambivalent feelings about his spouse seem to have grown" (138). For example, he argues, Donne's puns in his sermons and in such poems as *Father* and *Christ*, as well as *HSShe*, reveal "deeply disturbing fear and guilt" (138). Marotti locates the source of the tension in the conflict between Donne's "spiritual motives and secular attachments" (278), and he emphasizes that in *HSShe* Donne claims that the death of his wife "moved him to orient his desires toward heavenly, rather than worldly, ends" (278). Marotti adds that it is as if Donne's love for his wife stood in the way of his full commitment to God (279). Marotti also finds that, while love poetry written before their marriage professes "strong amorous feeling" (139), poems such as *ValMourn* and *HSShe* demonstrate that it is "inevitable" that "the human relationship of the lovers be diminished in importance even as it is philosophically and religiously expanded" (177).

To Warnke (1987, 110), this is a "deeply moving" sonnet in which Donne complains that "despite the consolations of Christian Platonism, he cannot satisfy himself with the love of God alone."

Ray (1990b, 302–03) points out that death was "commonly referred to as the last debt that any individual owes to nature (i.e., to one's physical, moral nature)" (302). Donne, according to Ray, responds to his wife's death as having taken "all 'good' from the earth," and, therefore, he "turns his mind entirely to things of heaven." But, Ray adds, Donne still wishes for more, suggestive of "his desire for some absolute assurance of God's love and grace," which is the state of mind on which the octave closes. Ray finds that "the problem is resolved" in the sestet when Donne "realizes that he does not really need to beg for more love from God, because he recognizes that God actively, masculinely courts Donne's soul" (303).

Porter (1991, 10) identifies *HSShe* as the "most personal" of the Holy Sonnets.

Smith (1992, 90) finds the poem "movingly restrained and dignified," as Donne transforms "his worldly loss to an occasion of final good in that he now finds only one sure way to be reunited with her," for she "becomes the means by which Christ woos his soul toward a remarriage in heaven."

Spurr (1992, 23–24) accepts Gardner's (1952) dating of HSShe in 1619 and thus interprets the poem as Donne's meditation on both the memory of his wife's death in 1617 and "his spiritual journey in the intervening years." As always, according to Spurr, the spiritual journey is "incomplete," for even though Anne leads to the "source of the divine," Donne remains "possessed of sin (here represented as a fever, with its unquenchable thirst)" (23). But in the sestet, Spurr says, Donne's "humility restrains his complaint" (23–24), and HSShe, marking Donne's advancement to the love of saints and angels, is "more optimistic than most and touchingly personal in its tribute to his wife's example" (24).

Yen (1995, 223–24), drawing on "the metaphor of the *pharmakon*, or 'physicke,'" employed by Plato in the *Phaedrus*, with its simultaneous meanings of a poison and a cure, finds that HSShe figures Donne's "spiritual struggles as a continuing disease of discontent," as in lines 7–8. Yen cites Aers and Kress (1981), who find Donne "at peace with himself," and Marotti (1986), who finds the speaker unable to reconcile "his spiritual and worldly desires" since Anne remains "an obstacle in the way of a wholehearted religious commitment" and concludes that neither view seems compelling (223–24). Yen contends that the assertion of line 4 ("Wholy on heavenly things my mind is sett") is "undercut" by the last half of the poem. The speaker, according to Yen, "unable to reconcile the contrary images of the Old Testament God of wrath with the New Testament God of mercy," views God in terms of "his own emotions of fear, doubt, and jealousy." As an example, the speaker refers to God's "tender jealousy" rather than the more familiar "tender mercies," thus revealing, Yen says, a "troubled state of mind." Yen argues that the various "instabilities" and unresolved questions in the text "reveal the potential poisonous nature of the *pharmakon* metaphor," for, while "seeking a cure for the spiritual disease of despair, the speaker vows that his mind is completely set on God," but the end of HSVex confirms the "continued presence of 'the World, fleshe, yea Devill'" in the speaker's life (224).

Date and Circumstances

Simpson (1924, 103) comments that the poem was written "soon after" Anne Donne's death. Many critics have commented similarly, including Adams (1962, 783–84), Warnke (1967, 274), Martz (1970, 106–07), Sanders (1971, 136), Hollander and Kermode (1973, 1050), and Lewalski (1979, 273).

Umbach (1951, 102) calls the death of Donne's wife the "central influence"—other than "love of his Savior"—in what he terms Donne's "later saintliness."

Gardner (1952, 78) believes that, although Donne's wife died on August 15, 1617, the "tone of resignation" in the poem suggests that it was not written immediately thereafter, suggesting that, since HSShe "reads like a first working-out of an idea" expressed "more powerfully" in Christ, a more probable date is shortly before Donne's journey of May 1619.

Bald (1970b, 328), while not commenting explicitly on HSShe, emphasizes that the death of Donne's wife "marked a turning-point" in his career and "deepened his sense of religious vocation." After 1617, he says, Donne displays "increased intensity of religious feeling" in all his life and work.

Smith (1971, 634) notes that Anne Donne was 33 when she died "after giving birth to their twelfth child."

Milward (1979 [1988, 99–102]) identifies HSShe as the only poem Donne "explicitly dedicated" to Anne, who had "exercised so deep an influence on him in his previous life and poetic work" (100). The sonnet records, in Milward's view, Donne's "deep sorrow" and his present resolve to set his mind "wholy in heavenly things" (l. 4) (100). Milward cites approvingly Bald's comments (1970) on Donne's devotion to his wife and the impact of her death on his "religious vocation" (101). In the sestet, according to Milward, the poem takes "a characteristic sharp turn," for while he had before "been seeking God by way of his wife," since her death God leads him "by the higher, purer way of divine love—'for hers offring all thine' [l. 10]" (102).

Novarr (1980, 122–27) finds parallels between HSShe and HSVex in that both are concerned with "the discreteness of the secular and the holy" and seem to be written by a man who engages in intense self-scrutiny because new circumstances have not changed him as he had expected (122–23). HSShe, he observes, focuses on the poet's "response to the death of the woman he loved," and since her death, "his mind is wholly set 'in heavenly things'" (l. 4). But Novarr points out that despite a "surface of calmness and acceptance," there is a "discordant rub" in the phrase "and to hers, and my good is dead" (l. 2) (123). Novarr explains that the first two lines of the sestet express the conclusion more fully than the final couplet, a conclusion that signifies, in Novarr's view, that the speaker "needs more love than God has thus far showered on him because God's love has thus far been an insufficient substitute for his earthly love and for the love he still has for a woman who has become a saint and an angel" (124). The implication here, according to Novarr, is that Donne has "already found God, and God has, indeed, fed his thirst, but he still remains subject to temptation, and God must work still harder." This reading, in Novarr's view, may lead us to think of this sonnet as a late one (125), as do two other features of the sonnet: that Donne here "dichotomizes earthly love and heavenly" and that HSShe is "extraordinarily passionate" in its expression of the effect on the speaker of a woman's death (125–26). Novarr speculates, therefore, that the attention the sonnet gives to the inferior nature of earthly love may reflect "the perspective of a man in holy orders," and the passionate expression of loss is, for Novarr, "elegiac," suggesting that only the death of his wife could have caused such emotion (126). But Novarr points out that the conjunction of such emotion and death also occurs in Noct, and we are reminded that Donne "had expressed such emotion earlier" (127).

Gill (1990, 106–07) finds that "an autobiographical approach" to HSShe is called for, given the sonnet's connection to the death of Anne (107). Gill adds, however, that HSShe "might not have been written immediately afterwards," noting that Gardner (1952) suggests 1619 as a possible date (106).

The Poet/Persona

Simpson (1924, 37–38, 64) quotes the poem in full as a description of Donne's state of mind after his wife's death and of "his increased longing for holiness" (37–38). She finds in the poem an indication that Anne More was "a woman of tender piety" whose death "left a gap in Donne's life which he never turned to earthly love to fill" (64).

Fausset (1924, 239) observes that Donne's religious faith was "the climax of his domestic" life and that in approaching God "he showed the same remorse for past infidelity as he had to his wife."

Fausset (1938, ix–x) observes that in dying Anne More carried upward Donne's "love from earthly to heavenly things," but that his desire for heavenly good was insatiable, a "holy thirsty dropsy" (l. 8). It was never fully realized, Fausset concludes, because Donne was so conscious of "the prison of himself."

Mahood (1950, 87–88) argues that Donne did not change over time but in his later years retained the emotional and intellectual qualities of his youth. The "holy thirsty dropsy" (l. 8) of the sonnet, he observes, was a thirst for God, replacing with equal intensity the thirst of his early years for learning, transforming into a theocentric humanism the Renaissance spirit of Jack Donne.

Leishman (1951, 188–90) argues that in comparing Donne's "deliberately outrageous poems" with those more serious in tone and attitude, the reader detects, not so much "the reformation of a rake," as Bennett contends (1934, 22), but the "more continuous actualization" in him "of potentialities which he had hitherto only occasionally experienced and expressed" (188), and he cites Walton's sentiment (1640) that after his wife's death Donne became "crucified to the world and had left trifles and trifling behind him" (189).

Coffin (1952, xxxiv) cites the sonnet as evidence that upon Anne More's death, Donne began the final phase of his career with a mind set "wholly on heavenly things."

Grenander (1960, 95–105) asserts that *HSSouls* and *HSShe* provide contrasting examples of Donne's wit, the former plain, straightforward, and non-symbolic, the latter a "brilliant instance of the peculiarly daring and subtle symbolism" found often in Donne's poetry (100). *HSShe*, Grenander says, is "a symbolic poem involving a change in thought and an accompanying change in emotion" (101), a change expressed "imagistically, with the image changing at intervals corresponding to the changes in thought and emotion" (105). See more under *HSShe*: Sacred and Profane.

Martz (1970, 105–08) says that in this sonnet, as in *HSMin*, one is deceived by the opening posture of serenity, which is quite illusory, for the speaker is, as always, dissatisfied.

Sanders (1971, 137–38) states that while *HSShe* is suffused with a great warmth of feeling for Donne's wife and for God, there is also an incompleteness about the poem. A "great and courageous candour" calmly lays itself bare in the sonnet (137), Sanders says, and he remarks that the "equanimity" evident at the end of the poem "recognises the very personal route by which Donne has reached faith, and the painful incompleteness of that faith." Divinity, love, and wonder, Sanders concludes, are momentarily one (138).

Thomas (1972, 348) remarks that Donne appears to have turned to religion after the death of his wife, and that "there is no reason to doubt the sincerity with which, on losing his wife, he made a fresh covenant with God" as expressed in the first quatrain of HSShe. Thomas argues that for all Donne's inability to make profession and practice one, he had, "in rare degree," the virtue of honesty.

Porter and Thwaite (1974, 102, 107) claim that the one consistent attitude throughout all of Donne's writings is his casting himself in the role of a wooer, either of women or of God (102), and they cite HSShe as an example of how Donne felt love to be "the mainspring of human life and of poetical creation" (107).

Wall (1976, 200) notes that the imagery of HSShe, like that of HSBatter, reflects the paradox of Christian redemption "by inverting the usual conventions of language and action in Elizabethan sonnet cycles"—the powerlessness of the speaker to effect what he desires. In contrast with secular sonnets, Wall notes, in which the speaker attempts "to overcome his beloved's passive resistance and convert it to passive yielding," in HSShe (and throughout the Holy Sonnets) the speaker himself is the one to be overcome.

Aers and Kress (1981, 69–70) view this sonnet as one that "evokes a version of self and a stance towards God which are not at all characteristic of Donne's religious poetry" (69). It is, in fact, according to Aers and Kress, Donne's "most impressive and self-aware of poems," moving to the "stunningly candid confession of God's inadequacy" and "acknowledging that he has 'found God' and God has now offered all his love—an "extremely rare feeling about God" in Donne's religious verse. Aers and Kress observe that "perhaps it is reasonable to speculate that the calm assurance and frankness" of HSShe are associated with the fact that by the time of its composition, Donne was "well on the path to incorporation in the social world of the establishment." Here, they say, the self "moves in time as a choosing agent and is the subject of transactive verbs deploying a range of tenses" and revealing a "continuity in change" that contrasts with "the unpredictable bursts of emotion and the wish for total self-annihilation" seen in other poems (70).

Carey (1981, 58–59, 73) considers the subject of the poem to be Donne's "unassaugeable desire for love" and his inability "to believe that he was loved enough, even by God" (58–59). Carey calls attention to the "absence of grief" in the sonnet, which he interprets as Donne's view of his wife's death as "a good thing," in that it is "good for her, and good for him, because she has gained heaven and he is freed from earthly lusts" (58). Carey finds Donne's feelings "outstandingly honest, and poignant in its honesty" (59). But Carey emphasizes that "Donne's fidelity to Ann was absolute; when he had her, he wanted no other woman" (73).

Stachniewski (1981, 686–87) finds that this sonnet, along with HSBatter, reflects Donne's attempt to frame his feelings within the discipline of the sonnet form, but in both instances "the thoughts and feelings escape." Whereas in the octave of HSShe Donne writes of "the gentle love of God to which his wife introduced him," the sestet, Stachniewski observes, presents "a stiffly Protestant conception of God as jealously intrusive in Donne's life" (686). The second God, in Stachniewski's view, is "the anthropomorphized Protestant God who will not tolerate sharing human devotion with saints and angels, let alone women" (687).

Egan (1985, 29–30) focuses his study on Donne's preoccupation with death and on his mastery of wit, finding HSShe characteristic of what he describes as Donne's "wit of death," a sonnet in which Donne "meditates on both a literal and a metaphoric death": that of his wife and the effects of "'dying' to the things of this world in order to enrich his spirituality" (29). In Egan's view, the speaker's reference to Anne's soul having been "ravished" into heaven (l. 3) has "bitter connotations," implying that he is "the cheated lover who has lost more than he could have imagined." The poem, according to Egan, portrays God as "an indecorous, heavy-handed wooer" refusing to permit "a proper time for grief before resuming his eager courtship of the narrator's soul." Egan concludes that in the secular poems Donne was "love's fool," and in his religious poems a "holy fool," but in HSShe "he is both" (30).

Rollin (1986, 144–45) finds this sonnet ambivalent about the source of its melancholy—whether love or religion: on the one hand, the speaker indicates that only since his "good" (l. 2) has died has his "commitment to 'heavenly things' been "total," but he also professes that his earthly love "'did whett' his mind to seek God" (l. 5). But, in Rollin's view, the sonnet is about religious melancholy, and furthermore, Donne's speaker "seems reconciled to his loss" (144). In the last four lines, according to Rollin, "the speaker's ego unconsciously attempts to defend against anxiety by projecting that anxiety onto God, attributing to the Omniscient some uncertainty as to whether he (the speaker) will ultimately attain salvation" (145).

Larson (1989, 89, 138) cites HSShe to illustrate the varied and uncertain picture we are given of Donne by way of his writings. When confronting the question of how Donne felt about the death of his wife, one finds the sonnet to be "a record of his feelings," says Larson, but at the same time some find that the poem "says more of the poet's feelings about himself than of his feelings for his wife" (89). Larson cautions, however, against making "little or no distinction" between persona and poet on this issue and emphasizing "only one side of Donne's mind" (138).

Gill (1990, 106) suggests that the sonnet "seems unfinished" and notes that in view of God's attitude toward the poet (ll. 9–14), the reader "looks for the poet's response but finds none." Gill proposes that "what is fascinating (and moving?)" about HSShe is the poet's "uncertainty about the nature and the rightness of his desires and his less than successful attempt to accept the situation in which he has found himself."

Gorbunov (1993, 124–25) finds the three late Holy Sonnets—HSShe, HSShow, and HSVex—detached from Ignatian meditative exercises (124), identifying in HSShe, for example, a deceitful calmness on the surface, beneath which there is both the indescribable bitterness of a loss and an unfulfilled desire for love. Gorbunov, describing the speaker as a hero, finds that his appreciation for God cannot be separated from pain, for God deprived him of earthly joy due to his "tender jealousy" (l. 13) so that he could be drawn to Him fully (125).

Langley (1993, 191–93, 210) takes issue with Carey's analysis (1981) of HSShe and his emphasis on Donne's emotional outpouring in the sonnet, finding, on the contrary, that Donne's feelings "are subject to a pervasive and controlling, if agonised, irony" (191). Langley wonders if Donne's "thirst for 'heavenly things' and the love of a 'jelous God' who in Exodus 22.5 declares Himself resentful of all rivalry (and has, perhaps, lately ravished away one threat for her and her husband's good)" is "quite as unadulterated as he pretends" (192). Langley sees Donne as having "a persistent appetite for his wife's body which had brought her to a twelfth and fatal childbed," and now, with the final "installment of her marital debt" having been paid—"with his wife out of the way which he claims she had cleared"—Donne is "free to concentrate on God exclusively." Noting that, unlike George Herbert, who "avoids sexual complications" in describing his relationship with God, Langley finds Donne's "masculine wit" rising "vigorously to the challenge of being a 'bride of Christ,'" and thus one reading, Langley suggests, is that God "offers all His love in exchange for that of Donne's (feminine) soul" (193).

Davies (1994, 53) states that the sonnet "begins as a moving valediction and tribute to his wife," but as the sonnet develops, Anne is "eclipsed behind the lonely, artful play her husband makes for the attentions of the amorous Deity, whose provocative 'tender jealousy' has 'ravished' her in order to ensure the exclusive affection of Donne himself."

Language and Style

Moloney (1944, 144–45), discussing Medieval and Renaissance influences on Donne, quotes the poem in full and suggests that it reflects his "deeper recollection of the older age" in its "Dantesque reverence for womanhood."

Partridge (1978, 137) writes that the language of HSShe is meant "to enhance the conceit that a jealous God had not only replaced Donne's deceased wife, but possessively guarded him against the secular world, the flesh and the devil."

Stein (1986, 139–41) thinks that though Donne "yearns for 'more love' from God," the poem does not show him begging, for that "lies among other silences in the poem" (139–40). Stein finds the speech of the poem "unique and mysterious" in "expressing the self to the self and to God" through "firm, brief affirmations" and "almost inaudible undertones." Moreover, Stein observes, Donne's wife is "only spoken of, kept in a careful third person," and "no human audience is intimated" (140). Whereas "in the world of nature," according to Stein, "the otherness of his dead 'good,' of 'she whome I lovd,' cannot be translated in any way" but is "fixed and denies relationship," in the world Donne identifies here "her soul is not dead and not other, it does not deny relationship" (140–41). Stein concludes that in admiring Anne, Donne's mind "turned toward the origin of her soul in God, and that action is further advanced when God translates her soul into a new relationship—a present courtship in which God fully participates, as He did not in her death, presided over by 'Nature'" (141).

Novarr (1987, 286, 289–91), citing Morris (1973) and David Leigh ["Donne's 'A Hymne to God the Father': New Dimensions." SP 75 (1978): 84–92], discusses the strong temptation to read a pun on "more" in HSShe because the poem appears to be a private poem in light of its initial appearance in NY3 (289). For Novarr, Donne most likely would include such "idiosyncratically private references" only in private verse, such as HSShe, written after his wife's death (290). By contrast, Novarr regards Donne's three Hymns as public verse, and in them he does not find convincing evidence that Donne is punning on "more" (290–91).

Prosody

Tillyard (1956, 6–7) admires the division of the sonnet, in that the verse of the octave is appropriately "clotted" while in the sestet "it becomes thin, clear, exalted, betokening a cleansed state of the spirit."

Themes

Williamson (1961, 40) says that HSShe illustrates "the wit of discordant feeling," i.e., the "contrariety of his feelings is disclosed by means of discordant objects or claims of feeling"—here the fact that the death of his loved one "has set his mind wholly on heaven." The poem reveals, Williamson asserts, the "ambiguities of feeling involved in saying 'my good is dead.'"

Lewalski (1979, 273) observes that the first of the three sonnets from the Westmoreland ms. (NY3) is, like the remaining two sonnets, an occasional piece, in that all three are "concerned with one or another of the exigencies of the regenerate Christian life," adding that in HSShe the speaker "adopts a Platonic doctrine, viewing his love for his wife as the means which led him to seek God." The speaker, in Lewalski's view, remains unsatisfied, however, but in the sestet he acknowledges that he has "no grounds for complaint: God has offered all his own love in exchange for his wife's, and has every reason to be jealous of the speaker's propensity to give his love to others." Lewalski concludes that the sonnet "seems less unified and effective than is usual with Donne."

Mallett (1983, 59) says that Donne's principal aims in HSShe are "to persuade himself that her death was in accordance with divine justice and mercy, and to calm his sense of anger and bitterness" (59).

Zunder (1988, 88–90) finds in Donne's poetry the expression of doubt about the "sufficiency" of an individual love relationship, expressed in the Holy Sonnets primarily between 1609 and 1611 when Donne had moved to Mitcham and began to reapply for a government position following his marriage to Anne More (88–89). He contends that Donne's poetry shows that the "commitment is transferred from the individual human relationship to an individual religious relationship," a "transference in a virtually Freudian sense" (89). In HSShe, according to Zunder, the transference occurs following the death of Donne's wife, but still, in Zunder's view, "the new love is not settled," for "it is like a troubled marriage or affair," whereby "Donne wants more love, greater assurance." But, Zunder notes, "the irrationality of this is acknowledged, since God himself is an anxious lover, chasing Donne's soul rather than Ann's, and jealous not only, tacitly, of Ann and other beautiful rivals — saints and angels — but also of ugly competitors for Donne's love, the world, the flesh, and the devil" (90).

Sabine (1992, 28–29) states that "an ungovernable Catholic bias programmed" Donne to "behold the woman landing him in trouble as the 'lady' leading him by the hand out of the darkness" (28). Sabine adds that as late as HSShe Donne was not able to decide whether Anne "had been divine retribution or recompense for the feminine-featured faith he had sacrificed in the pride of life" (28–29).

Sacred and Profane

Bennett (1934, 16), emphasizing Donne's recognition of "the unity of experience," secular and spiritual, compares GoodM 6–7 and HSShe 5–6.

Louthan (1951, 125) explicates the sonnet, emphasizing the secular-sacred imagery, which shows that love for his wife has "whetted Donne's love for God," and concluding that in the poem a jealous God is depicted as a jealous lover, with the "Platonic ladder" leading "upward from love of woman to love of God."

Gardner (1952, 78) observes that within the poem Donne "tries to find in the infelicities of his life a proof of God's love, by seeing them as a lover's stratagems," a theme to be found in Christ as well.

Reeves (1952, 102) summarizes the poem: since the death of his wife Donne "has sought only the love of God, the source of his love for his wife. Although he is thirsty for God's love, God woos his soul on behalf of her who is in heaven, and is jealous lest Donne's love should revert to the world, the flesh, and the devil."

Smith (1956, 406–07) paraphrases the octave of HSShe as an expression of Donne's anxiety that he does not have enough of God's love for salvation, and the sestet as allaying that concern, since God is already wooing his soul "for" his wife. God's love, Smith explains, is "a dowry" for her to obtain his soul.

Peterson (1959, 515) argues that the poem rounds out the Holy Sonnets sequence "dedicated to the experience of contrition." It is a warning against "excessive scrupulosity," he says, in this case the "spiritual sickness" expressed in the octave of an inordinate desire for signs of God's love. The sestet corrects the "sickness," he suggests, asserting that it is sufficient that the penitent feel in his heart God's love for him, and his desire that he remain sinless. See more under Holy Sonnets: Themes.

Grenander (1960, 100–05), stressing the change in thought and emotion in HSShe, says that "in order to understand how this change is brought about, one must inquire into the relationships involved in the poem" (100). He points to the relationship between "the woman, the protagonist, and God," and notes that for "a reunion" between the protagonist and the woman to take place "his attitude must change so that he desires it; and the divine ravisher must either be overcome (obviously impossible), or cease to be a rival" (102). Grenander remarks that line four is "equivocal in meaning" but "suggests a possible solution: that the lovers will be reunited in heaven." Grenander argues that in the following lines Donne analogically equates the woman with God, thus overcoming the barrier of God "acting as a rival for her possession" (102), noting further that in the last two lines of the octave the protagonist's love of God changes from a Platonic love to a physical desire, a change that, in turn, allows for the reunion of the protagonist and the woman. Grenander writes that thus "both barriers" inhibiting "the reunion of the speaker and the woman" have been removed: the "speaker is in a frame of mind to desire the reunion, and God is no longer a rival." Grenander also argues that in the sestet "a divine intercession occurs" in which God "woos the speaker's soul in order to unite it with the woman's" (103). Moreover, he notes that a "change in relationship" in HSShe accompanies "each section or subsection of the sonnet" and that Donne expresses change "imagistically" (104–05). He observes, finally, that the imagery of HSShe is built around the symbol of profane love.

Cohen (1963, 167), citing the opening lines of HSShe, says that Donne "very plainly" tells us "how the main strands of his thoughts and emotion combined, so that love of woman led to love of God."

Broadbent (1964, 66, 85) comments that "when the state took over authority from the Church," it ended the "medieval duality of sacred and profane," but that duality reopened as an "internecine duality of soul and body" (66), a duality he identifies as the "plot" of the Holy Sonnets and as best revealed in HSShe. Broadbent further argues that the love Spenser describes in his Four Hymns (poems based on "the weakest element in courtly Platonism, its impotence") is "precisely" what Donne "rejects as spurious, adulterous and hypocritical" (85). See also Holy Sonnets: Sacred and Profane.

Raspa (1983, 65) holds that in HSShe "grace helped Donne achieve salvation," although "salvation was impossible without love," adding that, for Donne, "human love was a gateway not to grace but to a greater love called divine." As such, in Raspa's view, "grace was a gift while divine love was a form of deliberate cooperation."

Singer (1984, 204) identifies HSShe as a sonnet that captures Donne's belief in the union of human and divine love, asserting that it "reveals the harmony between the two great loves in his life and that Donne's "faith in the merging of human and divine, due to the presence of God's love mysteriously working its way among his creatures, will not brook further analysis." But, Singer adds, Donne also is "writing about the woman he married and lived with until she died," and in that regard she is "not the symbol of theology or even of aspiring spirituality." Instead, Singer emphasizes, "she is a woman, like any other—except that she is the one he loved passionately, the one whose father had him imprisoned for daring to marry her as the outcome of their sexual love." See also Holy Sonnets: Sacred and Profane.

HSShe, according to Mann (1985–86, 546–48) "portrays the positive relation between human love and the love of God," and, moreover, "contains a remarkably precise statement of Donne's ideal of human love in relation to God" in lines 4–5 (546). Citing a sermon in which Donne discusses the faculties of the soul (Sermons, 8:326), Mann suggests that in both HSShe and the sermon Donne "describes a proper participation and hierarchy of love, not a disjunction between the divine and human" (547). Mann concludes that Donne's "portrayals of human and divine love do not support the general perception of a dualism of early profanity and later asceticism in his works," but show him, rather, concerned "with the process which draws natural and spiritual, human and divine into relation, despite difficulty and failure" (548).

DiPasquale (1991, 45–49, 54–55) reads the sonnet as an expression "of the two worst sadnesses" Donne confronted: "to be still a husband—not yet truly widowed—and his wife dead." For DiPasquale, HSShe is "an attempt to cope with those sadnesses, to define who and what he has lost and, in so doing, to redefine himself," since for him Anne "remains, even beyond this life, bone of his bone and flesh of his flesh." Thus, DiPasquale says, Anne "bears a wealth of symbolic meanings," both in death and in the poem, for death has taken away not only the woman he loves but a "human sacrament, a tangible sign that both reveals and conceals divinity." DiPasquale finds that the sonnet reflects an ambivalence in its attitude toward Anne, related in part to "the unresolved conflicts in Donne's sense of the sacramental," and that his response to Anne's "absent presence" mirrors his "response to the Eucharist, the most hotly-debated absent presence of the period" (45). DiPasquale suggests that Donne's "profound ambivalence toward sacramental signs" (including Anne herself) "springs from the difference between sacramental experience and anagogical orientation" (45). DiPasquale locates evidence for Anne's "spiritually salutary role" in Donne's life in HSShe 5–6 (46), and she argues that, for Donne, Anne was not only a "model of virtue" but also a "sacramental sign, a stream which showed the Head" (46). And so his "thoughts," DiPasquale observes, are "fixed upon things celestial" (l. 4) because Anne's death was "the end of his earthly 'good,' the good of marriage itself" (47). DiPasquale notes that Donne's continuing desire for Anne is "ridden with guilt" and that there is "too direct a relation between his conjugal activities and their lethally fruitful consequences," for the end of the sonnet implies, she argues, that had God not intervened she might—"on a more spiritual level—have been the death of him" (48). The ambivalence in his attitude, according to DiPasquale, resides in the fact that God "has taken away his abundance—his More—but he still thirsts for that fleshly abundance, and thus finds himself still wedded to carnal desire" when in fact he should be seeking to become a bride of Christ. For "the God who has 'into heaven ravished'" his wife's soul (l. 3) "is also pursuing Donne's." Thus, she asserts, for Donne "to respond to the divine suitor," he has to "abandon his masculine role and prepare to live in a mansion where Christ, not he, is the head of the household" (49). DiPasquale concludes that "the dilemma of his all-too-husbandly soul is that it cannot gaze upon the example of her femininity without responding to it as a man" (54).

Guibbory (1993, 142–43) finds that HSShe "most painfully presents Donne's sense of anxiety and conflict about the value of human love" (142). For example, according to Guibbory, Donne "has 'found' God [l. 7], yet still 'begg[s]' for 'more Love' [l. 9]"—the last possibly including a pun on Anne "More" and suggesting that he "still longs for her." Guibbory believes that such "contrary impulses" in Donne's poetry may stem from his desire "to possess the full range of love," that is, "both human love and God's love" (143).

According to Low (1993, 74–76), HSShe "directly confronts the difficulties of moving from human to divine love," for even though Donne attempts an "easy transference," the "inward tensions" soon become clear. Low points to the first quatrain, which he finds "ambiguous about Donne's love for God," an ambiguity "strongly confirmed" in lines 5–8, where the speaker argues that "human love has 'whett' his love for God" and that Anne "belongs to the same stream of love that leads back to its source in the Godhead." But Low observes that such "positive affirmations" are rather "blunted" by the acknowledgment that he "still thirsts, under a kind of love that increases his desire rather than satisfies it" (74). And the sestet, Low thinks, "formally introduces the traditional marriage trope, with God a suitor and lover, only to proceed immediately to qualify and confuse it," with the sexual roles becoming increasingly unclear (75). In the end, according to Low, Donne is "consumed with unsatisfied desire" (76), and the "biblical marriage trope" fails to bridge the secular and divine poems, for as in *Christ*, Donne has "severe difficulty accepting the indicated passive female role" (75).

Linsley (1995, 202–210) regards HSShe to be of "central importance in the transition from the poetry of earthly love to that of heavenly love," pointing out that many studies conclude that this transition was realized upon the death of Anne (202). Linsley's detailed reading of the poem seeks to explain Donne's "subtle analysis of his spiritual problems," clarifies the "theological, emotional, and gender conflicts" in HSShe, and "suggests a possible artistic motive for Donne's producing such an intriguing and puzzling text" (202). Linsley "argues that the poem is meaningfully obscure," for "it is a holy puzzle that partly conceals the poet's deep grief and his methods of coping with it" (203). Linsley calls attention to lines 5–8, which confirm the "central paradox" of the poem that, while here, Anne "inspired him to seek God," but with her death he "thinks only of 'heavenly things,' such as the now heavenly Ann" (205). And in the sestet, according to Linsley, the speaker "questions himself and offers some rather suspect sympathy to God for the problems God faces in wooing Donne, 'suspect' because any sympathy a weak mortal offers an omnipotent God suggests a Romantic irony" (206). With respect to possible gender conflicts in the sonnet, Linsley finds there to be a kind of "fantasy scene," a "divine *ménage à trois* with the soul of the live Donne haunting the heavenly scene of God and Ann, waiting for God to woo and win him" (208). Linsley notes that the speakers of Donne's poems "often adopt the feminine role when addressing God" and that "such transsexual artistic switches are common in mystical poetry," but Linsley speculates further about the gender-switching in the sonnet, suggesting that Donne "perhaps emulates the feminine in hopes of inviting seduction, if not ravishment" of the sort Anne experienced, thus indicating "God's power over him" (209). Linsley concludes that "the poem thus exalts the masculine God, who, for the conventional Christian, will always defeat the forces of Nature," and therefore "in a gesture of tribute and humility, he deserts his gender, willing to be 'ravished' or 'wooed' as God chooses" (209). One explanation Linsley offers for Donne's creation of a text "that is meaningfully and calculatedly difficult" is that "he did so as an artistic assertion of his control over Nature," writing a poem "for the few who understand the nature of his loss and who accept this grief for what it is, a grief too deep to express except to those who break through the puzzles of this work" (209–10).

HSShe and Other Works

Tillyard (1956, 4–7, 12, 29), comparing HSShe with Milton's "Methought I saw my late espoused saint," finds the former inferior. Tillyard argues, first, that HSShe is "self-centered," with Donne concerned only with himself, not his dead wife, and, furthermore, the poet "shows no social sense" (4–5), no "public or social obligation" (12). Second, he finds that in logical structure it contradicts itself, revealing a mind that relishes the process of thought rather than arriving at conclusions (5); hence, the poem turns on itself (29). Third, he contends that, though the poem imitates the rhythm of ordinary speech, it is in fact carefully studied rather than spontaneous or natural in its rhetorical effects (5–7).

Morris (1972, 246–48) writes that Benjamin Britten's lyrical setting of *HSShe*, which he judges one of his finest compositions, occurs at the center of his cycle of the Holy Sonnets. He says that "[o]ddly, and probably accidentally," Britten's musical direction ("Adagio multo robato") establishes "the tone for Donne's celebration of the effects of God's 'robbery' of Anne Donne" (246), while the "steady $\frac{3}{4}$ movement of the vocal line against the triplets of the accompaniment encourages the singer to make his own emphases and climaxes" (246, 248). See also Gaston (1986).

Novarr (1980, 128–29) notes that Gardner (1952) draws a comparison between *HSShe* and *Christ*, given the sonnet's emphasis on "the idea of God as a jealous lover," which Novarr finds also present in *HSBatter* (128, 128n). And yet, Novarr outlines important differences that exist between *Christ* and *HSShe* (128), including the sonnet's focus on "opposition" and the hymn's request for "intervention"; the sonnet is more private "in its almost heretical obstinacy" and the hymn is more public "in that its situation is common to all men traversing the sea of life" (129). Novarr states that "the sonnet gets its force from its emphasis on what God must overcome since Donne's earthly love is so great," whereas in the hymn "Donne is more willing to welcome God's love" (129).

Aers and Kress (1981, 71–72), noting that *Christ* and *HSShe* begin with Donne expressing "his confidence in God and his knowledge of God" (71), stress the differences between the two poems. Although there is no more anxiety in *Christ* than in *HSShe*, Aers and Kress observe, "something else has been lost," for there is in *Christ* "no sense of the subtle continuity in the self" so evident in the sonnet, nor "any sense that in such continuity the self may have to discriminate between kinds of love which are finally different but have very much in common." In *Christ*, Donne "still wishes to eliminate process, change and development from the self," they argue, and we are reminded just how "exceptional" *HSShe* is, suggesting that the "self-image and overall movement of that sonnet proved too open-ended, too risky for even an established Donne to live with" (72).

Ferry (1983, 220, 278) finds in *HSShe* echoes of Shakespeare's Sonnet 144 ("Two loves I have, of comfort and despair"). Ferry contends that both sonnets "describe an amorous triangle involving the speaker's soul, a woman whom he calls an angel, and a male figure rivaling the woman in the speaker's love"—God in *HSShe* and a male friend called "my saint" in Shakespeare. Ferry believes that the two sonnets are "close enough, and bizarre enough, to suggest imitation by Donne" (220), adding that if *HSShe* "has been assumed correctly" to be in response to Anne's death in 1617, Donne "could certainly by that date have known the 1609 edition of Shakespeare's sonnets" (278n25).

Gaston (1986, 210–11) finds the musical setting for the sixth sonnet in Benjamin Britten's sequence to be "the most melodic and accessible" while at the same time it "discourages analysis" (210). Gaston cites Morris's comments (1972) on the setting and adds that the music does not encourage "any lapse into the sentimental" (210–11).

Radzinowicz (1987, 52, 56–58) includes *HSShe* among the Holy Sonnets that reflect Donne's debt to the use of *anima mea* in the Psalms, or a dialogic relationship between speaker and soul (52). Radzinowicz identifies Ps. 116 as bearing certain affinities with *HSShe*, particularly in the psalmist's emphasis on his dependency on God (56–57). By the end of the octave, according to Radzinowicz, Donne's desire for God has been unassuaged, for God has taken his Ann into heaven, where Donne may ultimately join her (57). Radzinowicz points out that the octave has "always been read as a conversion of life into art" (57) and that, though the sestet could rest on the "eschatological security" hinted at in Ps. 116, it instead turns, in the closing two lines, on a lack of firm confidence (58). Radzinowicz attributes this slight doubt to Donne's attribution of "so anthropomorphic a love" to God that he "darkens the close of the poem" (58).

Dubrow (1995, 227–28), in her study of Donne's "counterdiscourse" against Petrarchism in his religious poetry, finds the "footprints of Petrarchism" "unsettling" in *HSShe* (227). The sonnet, Dubrow states, "clearly recalls Petrarch's own lyrics on the death of Laura and specifically her position as intercessor, a role often associated with the *donna angelicata*," but Dubrow finds Donne's evocation "ambiguous." For example, according to Dubrow, although lines five and six "explicitly state that earthly love has inspired its spiritual counterpart," the four lines preceding seem to "hint at the opposite," thus perhaps representing an "ongoing struggle as an achieved victory." According to Dubrow, Donne "confounds these integrative problems" when at the end of the poem he "acknowledges God's jealousy" (227). Dubrow offers three possible readings of the closing quatrain, which she claims are not mutually exclusive, but which include both Petrarchan and divine implications, "suggesting that Donne is enacting the very confusion between the spiritual and the secular which he claims to have renounced" (227–28).

Notes and Glosses

1–8 *Since . . . melts mee yett.* **HARDY** (1942): in composing the Holy Sonnets, Donne "sublimated his love and epitomized his sorrow" after the death of his wife (175). [See also Holy Sonnets: The Poet/Persona.] **MARTZ** (1970): the apparent composure of the opening gives way to dissatisfaction, to longing for "the satisfaction of his love for God" (107).

1–6 *Since . . . streames do shew the head,* **LEISHMAN** (1951), quoting these lines, reminds us that Donne's love for his wife was "one of the most important events of his life" (189) and suggests that in the "admiring her" (l. 5), which "whetted his mind to seek God," there was "a progress, a development, a process, in the course of which he discovered much about love, much about life, much about himself which he had not known before" (190).

1–4 *Since . . . my Mind is sett.* **FAUSSET** (1924): the poem records Donne's "new conviction of 'grace'" while it also mourns "its cause and occasion," the death of his wife (238–39). **FRIEDERICH** (1932) quotes the lines as testimony of the "intensity" ("Innigkeit") of Donne's love for his wife (82). **MATSUURA** (1953): Donne was converted to the true religious life after the death of his wife (77).

MARTZ (1954) suggests that *Noct*, like *HSShe*, "deals with Donne's love for his wife," and that its conclusion "seems to point the way" to the opening of the sonnet (214). **GRANSDEN** (1954) cites Walton's report (1640) that, at the death of Donne's wife, he became "crucified to the world" (44). **TILLYARD** (1956) finds the "slow and halting gait" of the first three lines "wonderfully" evocative of "the stupefaction of intense grief," and l. 4 reflective of one who gains control of that grief, emerging "into unstupefied thought and clear rhythm" (6). **UL-HASAN** (1958) observes that the relationship between God and Man is like that between man and wife, in that God like an earthly husband should watch over the soul jealously so that it does not go astray. Argues that the death of Donne's wife left a moral and psychological vacuum which he tried to fill through his love of God (14–15). **ROSSI** (1987): the death of profane love is at the same time a prefiguration of the death of the body, and the heart is consequently inclined toward the imperishable pleasure of Divine Love (75). **GILL** (1990) notes that some critics contend that the poem concerns the poet's grief, basing their interpretation on the sonnet's rhythms—e.g., "heavy stresses at the end of the first line," the rhythm singling out the "painful word early," and the way the sentence leads up to "Wholy"—all indicating "that the words issue from a deeply-felt grief." Questions this reading, pointing out that the "logical" use of the word "Since," the "conventional" portrayal of death "as paying a 'debt / To nature,'" and the "possible reading of the second line to mean that her death is for her and his good," all may suggest that Donne "accepts his loss with little or no anguish" (106).

1–2 *Since . . . and my good is dead* **PAYNE** (1926) believes that this couplet dates the entire series of Holy Sonnets after the death of Donne's wife (143). **GARD-NER** (1952): "The words 'to hers, and my good is dead' may amplify the preceding clause: Death ends the possibility of doing good to oneself or to another. Or they may point forward: her death is for her good and his, since by it she has entered heaven early, and his affections are now all in heaven. The first interpretation seems strained; the second almost intolerably harsh" (79). **FAULKNER and DANIELS** (1976): the first "and" in l. 2 joins the two prepositional phrases "To Nature" and "to hers." The meaning is simply that Anne "has paid her debt to Nature as a human being (all must die) and to her own nature as a woman (the danger peculiar to all women of dying in childbirth)." The phrase "and my good is dead" means: "All that has been good in my life is dead" (11). **HANDLEY** (1991): "i.e. paid her debt to mortality, and to her family" (44).

1 *Since she whom I lovd, hath payd her last debt* **LINVILLE** (1984b) observes that when employing the German prosodic system that focuses on both speech and metrical stress in Donne's poetry, rather than simply focusing on one or the other, the "rhythm that emerges from tension between two kinds of stress" accounts for the effect that Stein (1944) identified, that of "deep pain covered by forced resignation" (67).

1 *She* **GRIERSON** (1912): a reference to Anne More, who died on 15 August 1617 (2:235). [So also, Barańczak (1984, 162), who adds that Anne died after giv-

ing birth to their twelfth child; Willmott (1985, 70) and Patrides (1985a, 445), who both add that she died at the age of 33; Craik and Craik (1986, 280); and Booty (1990, 110).] SHAWCROSS (1967): "apparently" Donne's wife (349).

1–2 *her last debt / To Nature,* SMITH (1971): "'to pay one's debt to nature' was a common way of referring to events that brought home one's human frailty or mortality" (634). LEVER (1974): a "traditional figure" for the "return of her body to earth" (182). MALLETT (1983): "the idea that we all 'owe' Nature a death was more or less proverbial" (59). WILLMOTT (1985): Donne's wife "surrendered her life" (70).

2 *To Nature, and to hers, and my good is dead* TILLYARD (1956) notes that the "hers" is compounded with "Nature" not "my good," a possibility Gardner suggests (1952, 79). Observes that Anne in dying has "rendered her last service to her kin" (77). GRENANDER (1960): the comma at the end of the line should be omitted, thus following the Westmoreland ms. (NY3); "and to hers" is parallel with "to Nature," and "my good" then becomes the subject of "is dead." "In other words, the woman, by dying, has paid her debt to Nature, since all natural things must die; and she has also paid her debt to her (human) nature which is mortal" (100). SHAW-CROSS (1967): "her nature as a human being who is subject to death" (349). SMITH (1971): "the syntax is ambiguous here in that one can take this phrase either with the preceding words or with what follows. If one reads 'To nature, and to hers' the phrase means (a) and to her nature specifically; (b) and to her family and kindred, to whom she can now owe nothing. If one reads 'to hers, and my good is dead' then the sense is that she is dead to the poet's good and her own, beyond worldly concerns in that (a) she can now no longer do good to herself and her husband; (b) she has died — gone to heaven so early — for her own good and for his. The following lines show how her death has worked for his good" (634). LEVER (1974): "Since both are freed from earthly desire" (182). MALLETT (1983): "the syntax of this line is uncertain. Either (a) his wife's death means that she can no longer do anything for her own or for her husband's good, or (b) her death has been for her good (she is now in heaven) and for his (since her death he thinks only of heaven). The first reading offers only the bleak facts, and provides no comfort; the second offers comfort only to a man whose faith is still more powerful than his grief. Possibly both meanings are designedly present in the poem" (59–60). PATRIDES (1985a): "her own nature as mortal" (445). [So also, Booty (1990, 110).] WILLMOTT (1985): "a double ambiguity: 'she has paid her debts **to her family** and my virtuous wife is dead'; or, 'she is dead **to her own good** and to mine'. If the latter, then either: 'she cannot help herself or Donne (in this world)'; or 'her death is to the advantage of them both'" (70). CRAIK and CRAIK (1986): "and is dead to her good and to mine (is incapable of doing good to herself or me)" (280). STEIN (1986): "The good that is dead is the soul of everything in the natural world," the line conveying the meaning "She has paid her debt to nature and to her own nature, and (all) my good is dead" (290–91n4). FOWLER (1991): "dead to her own good, since she can do no more" (119). CAREY (1990b): "Her death is for her good, since she is in heaven, and for Donne's since it fixes his mind on 'heavenly things'" (472). SINGH (1992):

"The line is ambiguous: (1) she has paid her debt to nature, and to her human or moral nature; she, who was my good, is dead. (2) she has paid her debt to nature and is dead, for her good and for mine, since by dying she has gone to heaven and set my thoughts in that direction also. Neither sense is satisfactory" (105). ELLRODT (1993) finds this line and l. 10 ambiguous, suggesting here that death is a "blessing" ("bien") for the wife, which precociously leads her to heaven, and also for the husband, who now is attached more closely to God (456). LANGLEY (1993), responding to Carey's analyses of 1981 and 1990b, says that while Carey's later reading admits some ambiguity in this line, it "remains resolutely monocular." Offers an alternative reading: if "she has 'paid her last debt/To nature, and to hers', in the sense of 'those pertaining to her', family and friends, then Donne's 'good is dead'; and 'good' runs 'God'—witness Matthew 19.17, 'there is none good but one, even God'—disconcertingly close, especially as the poet goes on to reveal that his mind has become set 'Wholly in heavenly things' only since (because?) she has become one of them" (192).

3–4 *And her Soule . . . is sett.* YOUNG (1984) finds here a suggestion that Anne's early death "represents a sacrifice for his spiritual benefit" and that Anne, "taken up into heaven," will be, like Beatrice, a "stream revealing the fountainhead of love in God" (173–74). SPURR (1992) finds startling Donne's word ("ravished") for Anne's soul's entrance into heaven but adds that its "sensuality perfectly conveys the absolute embrace of her by God," which, in turn, has been effected in Donne, suggested by the pun on "wholly"/"holy," that is, "completely and sacredly" (23).

3 *And her Soule early into heauen rauished,* SMITH (1971): the "line is perhaps best scanned with heavy slurring on 'early into heaven'" (634).

3 *early* MALLETT (1983): since Anne was only thirty-three at her death, the line implies that she died "*too* early" (60).

3 *rauished* SHAWCROSS (1967): "transported joyfully" (349). SMITH (1971): "Pronounced as three syllables" (634). MALLETT (1983): "caught up, removed from the earth" (60). GILL (1990): "this can mean being sexually possessed as well as carried away" (106).

4 *Wholy in heauenly things my Mind is sett.* WOOLF (1932) questions whether one of Donne's temperament could ever "be wholly set on any one thing" (35).

4 *Wholy* SHAWCROSS (1967): "with a pun on 'holy'" (349). [Similarly, Gill (1990, 106), who puts it in the form of a question.]

4 *in* MALLETT (1983): "on" (60).

5–14 *Here . . . yea Deuill putt thee out.* SIMPSON (1924): "his love for her had been a step upward in the ladder by which men rise from the love of earthly to that of heavenly things" (103).

5–6 *Here . . . streames do shew the head,* BENNETT (1934) compares the lines to *GoodM* 6–7 to emphasize Donne's sense of the unity of spiritual and secular experience (16). Finds that Donne, though not a "seer or mystic" who yearned for the "immediate sense of God," nonetheless "shared their desire," aware that "human love was not enough" (117).

5–6 *Here the admyring her my Mind did whett / To seeke thee God;* **GRANSDEN** (1954): Donne attributes the dawning of his religious feelings to his meeting with Anne More, suggesting that some of the more doctrinal and less intense sonnets could have been written before *Corona* (1609) (131). **CAREY** (1981) says about Anne that with "hints" such as this, we are able to "construct our images of womanly patience, fortitude, devotion, gentleness," but all we really know about her is that she was "generally pregnant, and that no one recorded for posterity any clear impression of her character" (74). **WILLMOTT** (1985): "My love for her on earth made me eager" (70). **SINGH** (1992): "My admiration for her sharpened ('did whet') my quest for God" (106).

5 *Here* **MALLETT** (1983): "here on earth" (60). **SINGH** (1992): "While she was alive" (106).

5 *the admyring her* **LEVER** (1974): "Wonder at her virtues" (182).

5 *Mind* **SHAWCROSS** (1967): "object of 'whett'" (349).

5 *whett* **MALLETT** (1983): "encourage" (60). **GILL** (1990): "sharpen and make ready" (106).

6 *seeke thee God;* **GILL** (1990) asks "to what extent is this a poem of human or divine love?" Notes that the "cadence leading up to God makes it one of the strongest climaxes in the poem" but urges attention to the "change the sentence undergoes with the introduction of *But*" (l. 7) (106–07).

6 *so streames do shew the head,* **MALLETT** (1983): "just as a stream can be traced back to *its* source, so all human loves can be traced back to *their* source, which is to be found in the love of God" (60). Similarly, Lever (1974, 182) and Singh (1992, 106).

6 *shew the head,* **SMITH** (1971): "reveal the source" (634). **WILLMOTT** (1985): "lead back to their source" (70). [Similarly, Patrides (1985a, 445), Craik and Craik (1986, 280) and Booty (1990, 110).] **FOWLER** (1991): "source (Christ, the fountain of grace)" (119). **HANDLEY** (1991): "reveal where they spring from" (44).

7–8 *But . . . melts mee yett.* **PAYNE** (1926) suggests that these lines and the concluding sonnets in the series (*HSShow* and *HSVex*) demonstrate that he had not yet achieved "permanent satisfaction" from his faith (143). **BENNETT** (1934) observes that Donne often employs images of disease, as here, where his "desire for God is a dropsy" (36). **FAUSSET** (1938): Donne's "appetite for heavenly good" was "insatiable" and never completely satisfied (ix–x). **HAYDN** (1950) insists that in Donne's "wrestling with the problem of reason and faith" the latter won out, though at times he remained "the passionate seeker and doubter" (112–14). Adds that the idea of infinite and insatiable longing for spiritual certainty "never wholly disappears in the Dean of St. Paul's," in "direct contradiction of the traditional Christian-humanist view" (366). **LEVER** (1974) notes that these closing lines of the octave produce a "note of restlessness" rather than "calm devotion" (182). **LINSLEY** (1995): his "thirst for her heavenly love" brings the risk of "distracting him from experiencing God's love directly," much as Jesus told the Samaritan woman at the well: "Everyone who drinks this [earthly] water will be thirsty again. But whoever drinks the water I give him will never be thirsty" (John 4.13–14). Donne is in this "'thirsty' condition, having drunk from the stream (Ann) rather than directly from the source (God)" (206).

7 *But though I have found thee,'and thou my thirst hast fed,* **WILLMOTT** (1985): the "image of the stream" relates to Christ's words in John 4.14: "the water that I shall give him shall be in him a well of water springing up into everlasting life" (70).

7 *fed,* **SHAWCROSS** (1967, 349): "both 'relieved' and 'increased.'"

8 *A holy thirsty dropsy melts mee yett.* **TILLYARD** (1956): Donne continues to thirst for the love of his wife and is "confessing to the difficulty and delay" of realizing the love of God (4, 78). **GILL** (1990): the line raises the question: "is his desire religious, sexual or a fusion of both? The first adjective is *holy*, and *thirsty* can apply to both divine and human love, but *melts* (emotionally affects) is more appropriate to love poetry" (107).

8 *holy thirsty dropsy* **MAHOOD** (1950): Donne's "immoderate desire" was a constant factor in his life, changing only from a thirst for learning to a thirst for God (88). **TILLYARD** (1956) finds the phrase "silly in sound," though acknowledging that some say it mimics "the monotony of dropping water" (5–6). **SHAWCROSS** (1967): "dropsy" is "a disease characterized by an accumulation of fluid and unquenchable thirst" (349). [Similarly, Booty (1990, 110), Handley (1991, 44), and Singh (1992, 106), who also cites *ElFatal* 42.] **SMITH** (1971): "immoderate desire for more" (634). **LEVER** (1974): "An unquenchable, as it were morbid, thirst of the spirit" (182). **MILWARD** (1979 [1988]): "dropsy," used in conjunction with the adjective "holy," may—"in its etymological reference to excess of water"—be contrasted to the "disease" of "th'hydroptique drunkard" in *HSSighs* 9 or of "th'hydroptique earth" in *Noct* 6 (102). **MALLETT** (1983): "a reverent but immoderate desire. The sense is that Donne's thirst for God's love has been fed, but he can never feel that it has been fed enough; the thirst is 'holy' because it is not a sin to desire God's love, but it is also diseased (a 'dropsy') because he remains endlessly unsatisfied" (60). **WILLMOTT** (1985): "an insatiable craving" (70). [Similarly, Norbrook and Woudhuysen (1992, 544).] **PATRIDES** (1985a): "immoderate thirst" (445). **CRAIK and CRAIK** (1986): "here an immoderate thirst for love" (cf. ll. 7 and 9), which "'melts'" (emotionally affects) the poet" (280).

8 *melts mee* **FOWLER** (1991): "touches my feelings" (119).

9–14 *But why . . . Deuill putt thee out.* SMITH (1991): "Even such a personal calamity as the death of his much-loved wife plays its providential part in the drama of God's offer for his soul against the rival enticements of his love" (137).

9–10 *But . . . offring all thine:* WHITE (1936): "For if man seeks God, no less does God seek man," tenderly "wooing him" (137). SMITH (1971): "God woos the poet's soul on behalf of the soul now in heaven, to reunite and marry them there, as a father might plead his daughter's case with a desirable young man; and the offered dowry or ransom is Christ himself, God's only son" (634). MALLETT (1983): "God now offers Donne his divine love in exchange for the human love of which he was deprived with the death of his wife" (60). GILL (1990): the lines offer ambivalent readings: "Is God offering his love to the poet *instead* of that of the dead beloved, or is God cast in the role of a father who supplies a handsome dowry (*offering all thine*) in exchange for the heavenly marriage of the poet and his dead beloved?" (107). SINGH (1992): "There is no need for me to ask for more of your love since you already love me. Indeed, you are wooing my soul in order to unite it with my wife's in heaven, just as a father may woo an eligible young man to marry his daughter here on earth. And just as the father may offer the young man a dowry, so also you have offered me a dowry of all that you possess: your only Son ('all thine' in l. 10)" (106).

10 *Dost woe my Soule, for hers offring all thine:* GARDNER (1952) says that the line as found in NY3, with a semicolon after "hers" (i.e., before any emendation—eds.), does not make sense. Repunctuates the line with a comma before "for" and no punctuation after "hers," offering a "proper antithesis between 'hers' and 'thine.'" Notes that there is a consistent stress on personal pronouns throughout the poem (79). SMITH (1956) questions Gardner's punctuation of l. 10 (1952), agreeing with Grierson (1912) that the mark should come after "hers" rather than before "for" (406–07). GARDNER (1957b) rejects Smith's justification of Grierson's punctuation of l. 10 (1956), arguing that Smith's proposal (see *HSShe*: Sacred and Profane and also Smith [1971] under notes to ll. 9–10) that "God as a father is wooing Donne's soul on behalf of his dead wife, and offering as a dowry all his love" is inconsistent with both the "tender jealousy" (l. 13) at the ending and the Christian idea of Heaven. Insists that the central contrast of the poem is between the highest love on earth and the love of God in Heaven, a theme incompatible with the analogy of an earthly father offering a dowry to his daughter's lover (564–65). WARNKE (1967) believes Gardner (1952) to be "almost certainly" correct in suggesting an emendation of the punctuation of this line by placing a comma after "soul" and removing the semicolon after "hers." Says that the intent of the passage is that God "offers His love in place of that of the beloved" (274). MARTZ (1970) finds Gardner's emendation (1952) "attractive," providing a meaning that leads well into the next two lines (107). STEIN (1986) follows Grierson (1912) in placing the punctuation mark after "hers," reading "for" to mean "for the sake of": "God's offer of love quietly includes Anne and is a gracious act of divine love, not a form of compensation" (290n6). FOWLER (1991): "Offer Christ as dowry, to secure Donne as son-in-law" (119). NORBROOK

and WOUDHUYSEN (1992): "Christ as a dowry in the marriage between the poet's soul and that of his dead wife" (544). ELLRODT (1993) acknowledges the ambiguity of the line, noting that in his edition and translation he has placed the comma after "soul," not "hers" (456).

10 *for hers offring all thine:* **CRAIK and CRAIK** (1986): "offering all thy love to replace hers" (280). **RAY** (1990b) reads the line to mean "in exchange for my soul's love," noting that the soul is frequently referred to as feminine, including *HSScene* 9 and *ElServe* 11. Believes that it is a "one-for-one exchange of love with Donne's soul as the female being courted [by God]" (303). **LINSLEY** (1995) holds that ll. 9–10 are crucial to understanding the sestet (206). Acknowledges there are "at least four plausible readings" of the lines but prefers one, based on NY3: "For the sake of, and in place of, *her* soul God actively woos the poet's soul, offering all His love" (206–07), adding that God "woos Donne" both for His sake and for Anne's, implying that Anne's soul has "continued spiritual influence" on "the soul of Donne" (207). Concludes that since this influence is a "kind of heavenly interference that deflects him from union with God," it might be deemed not "good," but the example of Beatrice, who "actively concerns herself with Dante's salvation," may suggest that similarly Anne "works for the poet's salvation" (207–08).

10 *for hers* **WILLMOTT** (1985): "on her behalf" (70).

10 *offring all thine:* **WILLMOTT** (1985): "God offers all his love in dying on the cross to redeem man, enabling Donne to join his wife in heaven" (70).

11–14 *And dost not . . . putt thee out.* **MARTZ** (1970) finds the lines flowing together "to produce a curious sense of latent threat to the opening security," leading to an ending that is "a most precarious resolution." Suggests that Donne appears to say that God may fear the speaker's love for saints and angels, but it would be "an excess of tender jealousy" if God were to fear that "the world, the flesh, or the devil could ever put God out of the speaker's heart" (108). **LEVER** (1974) identifies the lines as "in effect a quatrain, hinging on a repressed conflict," as God is "gently reproached" for fearing that Donne "might deviate into the Catholic 'error' of loving *saints and angels* (i.e. his wife)," or, more importantly, for His "*tender jealousy* regarding a grosser desertion to *the world, flesh, yea, devil*" (182).

11–12 *And dost not . . . things diuine,* **MARTZ** (1970): a possible allusion in traditional Petrarchan terms but more likely a reference to "the theological problems raised by Catholic devotion to saints and angels" (107–08).

12 *Saints and Angels,* **CRAIK and CRAIK** (1986): "the poet's deceased wife in heaven" (280).

13–14 *But . . . Deuill putt thee out.* **GARDNER** (1952) believes that Donne is thinking about the "general misfortunes of his life," for God both removes his "saint and Angel," lest he "love her too much," and guards him "against temptation by continual disappointments and mortifications" (79). **MALLETT** (1983): Donne "interprets God's treatment of him as that of a jealous and possessive lover," first by removing Anne from him, "fearing that Donne might love her too much," and second by ensuring that "none of Donne's love would be wasted on the pleasures of this world, by providing for him a life of pain and disappointment" (60). **CRAIK and CRAIK** (1986): in these lines God is said "to fear" ("doubt") that "the three foes of mankind" (cf. *Sat3* 33–42)—"even the ugliest of them, the Devil"—may replace Him (i.e., "put thee out") in the "poet's affections" (280). **SINGH** (1992): the point is that "man need not doubt God's love, though God may, with good reason, doubt man's love for Him," yielding the paraphrase: "You are afraid not only that I might give my love to divine beings like saints and angels instead of to you, but also that I might allow the world, the flesh and the devil to usurp the affection that should rightly belong only to you. Therefore you have taken away my wife, the best of saints and angels. You have also sent me worldly disappointments as a way of guarding me against the temptations of life" (106).

13 *tender* **GILL** (1990): "how does the adjective function? Does it show that the poet recognizes that, in spite of his pain, God is compassionate, or does it so clash with *jealousy* as to show the poet's ambivalent feelings about what God has done to him—that is, taken away his beloved?" (107).

13 *iealosy* **SHAWCROSS** (1967): "requirement of exclusive devotion; zealousness" [so also, Patrides (1985a, 446) and Booty (1990, 110)] (349). **WILLMOTT** (1985): "God is seen as a lover" (70).

13 *doubt* **PATRIDES** (1985a): "fear" (446). [So also, Willmott (1985, 70).] **GILL** (1990): "fear and suspect" (107).

14 *the World, fleshe, . . . Deuill* **SHAWCROSS** (1967): "the triple temptation to avarice, gluttony, and vainglory" (349). [So also, Booty (1990, 110).]

14 *putt thee out.* **SMITH** (1971) glosses as "exclude God by claiming the poet's allegiance" and offers a "secondary sense": "that God has deliberately thwarted the poet in this world so as to preserve his allegiance, not only removing loved ones whose origin was divine (saints and angels) but frustrating worldly ambitions or well-being" (634). **WILLMOTT** (1985): "replace you in my affections" (70). **FOWLER** (1991): "outdo God in securing Donne" (119). **HANDLEY** (1991): "i.e. overcome God's influence" (44). **NORBROOK and WOUDHUYSEN** (1992): "exclude, displace, usurp God" (544).

 *HSShow*

COMMENTARY

General Commentary

Gardner (1952, 127) offers a full paraphrase of the sonnet: "Make visible, dear Lord, the Church as she is described in Scripture. Can she be either the insolent, proud Church of Rome, or the mourning and desolate Protestant Church in Germany and here? Am I to believe that for a thousand years or more there was no true Church on earth? Or, that a Church claiming to be truth itself, yet constantly erring—both innovating and deserting what she formerly held—can be she? Am I to believe that now, as of old, and in future, as long as the world lasts, she is to be found in one place only—here, or there, or elsewhere? Am I to believe that she is to be found here on earth, or am I to hold that only in heaven, after our pilgrimage, can we see her as she is? Lord, do not hide thy bride from our sight, but let me woo the gentle spouse of thy marriage song, who is most faithful to thy will and most pleasing to thee, when the greatest number of men seek and receive her embraces."

ul-Hasan (1958, 44) observes, with reference to *HSShow*, that "Donne's approach to religion was that of an explorer and investigator."

Adams (1962, 786), noting that the question of "the marks of a true church" was widely debated in the seventeenth century, observes that few Anglican clergymen "would have expressed an indecision as universal as Donne's" in *HSShow*. He argues that the sonnet was kept out of all seventeenth-century editions because of its skepticism and because of a sense that versifying was unseemly for a clergyman.

Woodhouse (1965, 57), arguing that it is unnecessary "to read doubt or dissatisfaction" into *HSShow*, says that the intent of the poem is "ecumenical": the "spouse is the true Church Universal, which must still be sought in and through Christ."

Stewart (1966, 19–21) points to the "ambiguous meaning" of "Spouse" in *HSShow*, the term that is "the crux of a paradox in which the form and statement of the poem are mutually exclusive" (19). Yet, says Stewart, the speaker of the poem is himself the Bride of Christ, and his "amorous soule" is courting the true Church, "as if seeking some visible sign of the body of which he is already an invisible member" (21).

Kermode (1968, 184), associating the poem with a Protestant defeat in 1620, says that *HSShow* "asks whether the Bride of Christ can possibly be the Roman Church, or the defeated Protestant, or whether we shall not know her before we conclude our earthly quest."

Jackson (1970, 172–74) describes the traditional imagery of the Church as the

Spouse of Christ, but sees Donne himself as the "true bride, the spiritual Israel" (172). The "poet's own spirit is now Christ the husband," Jackson observes, and "the bride of Christ is his body" and thus the "inner self once felt as female" is viewed as male (173). *HSShow* appears to be Donne's "final resolution of the problem of national sectarianism," for the English Church and all churches may be one and the same church: "in having joined the fallen bride of Christ, John Donne also joined the true" (174).

Stampfer (1970, 276–77) claims that *HSShow* "baldly and systematically over-turns the entire courtly love tradition" that "overshadowed" Donne's love poetry (276), suggesting that in this sonnet the church puts on various costumes to in-trigue her worshipers in many faiths, and that her purpose is "beatific promiscuity." This purpose, Stampfer says, echoes an antinomianism Donne expressed through-out his career from his early wavering between faiths to the sentiment in the closing couplet (277).

Henricksen (1972, 9) offers two interpretations of *HSShow*: first, that Christ is married to the church rather than to the individual soul directly; second, that Christ is married to the true church, but he is also the husband of the individual soul in a direct, mystical sense. To Henricksen, the evidence from the sermons shows that Donne would have considered these two interpretations to be irreconcilable and that he would have rejected the mystical one.

Sobosan (1977, 397–98) believes that throughout most of his religious poetry Donne is little concerned with Jesus's humanity, but one exception occurs in *HSShow*, where Jesus appears "as a 'kind husband' to the church." Nevertheless, he argues that this reference to Christ is "metaphorical" and not so much an "actual aware-ness" of the "kindly presence" of Jesus, and that, moreover, in many of the Holy Sonnets and other Divine Poems, Donne refers to Christ in the third person (398).

Carey (1981, 30) regards the most important feature of *HSShow* to be Donne's request to be "granted a vision of the true church," in that it confirms the "lasting disorientation his apostasy entailed." In Carey's view, "a Catholic would not have needed to ask; he would have known."

Fraser (1981, 120) finds that the sonnet "inclines towards the Church of Rome" as the "true Church," adding that "the true Church is traditionally the Spouse of Christ, but can also be thought of as the lady sought by a wandering knight; she is most true to Christ when she is most welcoming, like a harlot, to new lovers."

J. King (1982, 159) finds that the sonnet "resolves the Reformation dilemma by fideistic paradox."

Miller (1982, 836) sees in this sonnet "some of the most shocking sexual imagery in all of religious literature." Miller acknowledges that the use of erotic imagery in describing the soul's relationship with God is a familiar one, but he finds Donne's use of such imagery "of a different order." Like *Sat3*, he thinks, *HSShow* discusses the "competing claims of the various Christian Churches" but moves substantially beyond the "courtship imagery" of *Sat3* "when it praises the Anglican Church be-cause, like a promiscuous woman, it makes itself available to all men."

Gilman (1986, 84–85) finds that *HSShow* centers on two choices, both "unsat-isfactory," that is, "between two spouses chaste in neither case, the one flaunting herself, all too eager to be shown, the other no less exposed, as if the iconoclasm of the Reformation were itself a kind of sexual tampering." The "unhappy choice," Gilman observes, "only spurs the need to see a clearer spouse [l. 1], until the increasingly explicit 'amorous' longing at the end of the poem seems to cast doubt on the very motives of the search underway" (84). But, in Gilman's view, "the lusty snicker in the word 'open' [l. 14] marks the difference between Christ's true church—universal, welcoming, open to the embrace of faith—and the speaker's demand for a vision of that church pleasing to him" (84–85). Gilman concludes that "the poem thus evokes the urgency of the speaker's desire [for an image to embrace] while it reveals the idolatrous, and adulterous, contamination of that desire to 'make love' to the image it seeks" (85).

Marotti (1986, 282–83) explains that although the sonnet alludes to the defeats of German Protestants, as well as "the sympathetic response of their English coreligionists," who were variously unhappy with the policies of James, Donne seems more concerned with an issue that he also raises elsewhere, namely, that of Church unity. Marotti suggests that Donne's support of a Universal Church may reflect his approval of the king's approach to religious conflict in Europe (282). And the wit and sexual-religious metaphors, according to Marotti, indicate that the poem was intended for a select readership, which may explain why Donne possibly withheld it from publication (283).

For Ray (1990b, 299–301), the speaker's opening request, conveyed with a "sense of urgency," arises from the "heavy stress" on the opening line's first syllable, a reversal of the usual iambic foot (299). With the dominating conceit of the "church as various types of women" (300), the poem contends, according to Ray, that "many churches at many locations . . . have made, still are making, and shall make claims to be the true Church." Ray finds that the "shocking paradox" of the final four lines "deliberately echo" Song Sol. 5.2 and that in their erotic connotations, they reflect "amazingly and successfully" Donne's ability to use an "image of an action that would be sin in traditional Christian precepts to convey in symbolic terms what indeed offers spiritual salvation to humanity (i.e., the church's taking in of men)" (301).

Sabine (1992, 11, 38, 64) notes correlations between the sonnet and the travels of Donne's mother, Elizabeth, who "sought religious refuge abroad in 1595" as well as with his younger brother Henry (11, 64). According to Sabine, even though Donne's mother had returned to England by 1606, she was "hounded by the authorities and would regularly be on the move" (38). Thus, "her life-style authenticated the son's depiction of the fugitive female Church" in HSShow (38). And Henry, according to Sabine, "died as a consequence of harbouring a priest and in so doing acquitted himself like Abel, as a keeper of the very shepherd who watched over the sheep" (64). Sabine notes further that "the insinuation that [Abel] is a Cain [as a "family traitor"]" and, like Cain, "a fugitive and vagabond in the earth" (Gen. 4.14) adds resonance to Donne's subsequent description of "the hunted figure of the Church" in HSShow (64).

Baumgaertner (1994, 8) regards the speaker in this poem, as in HSBatter, to be confused and uncertain about the true Church, finding, furthermore, that the initial focus on identifying the true Church is "completely displaced" by what she regards as a "perversion of the spiritual eroticism" of Song Sol., that is, the actions of the woman/church are "rather more akin to those of Hosea's Gomer before her return and repentance." Baumgaertner also believes that the speaker seems unaware of "his conclusion that the church is most pleasing to Christ when she is acting like a whore," and she is, more generally, critical of established interpretive traditions that have ignored some "major flaws" in Donne's poetry.

Summers (1994, 47) finds that the sonnet gives us a vision of the "competing religious sects" of Donne's day that is both skeptical and also tolerant, "juxtaposing their questionable historical records against a transcendent image of unity and love." Donne "finds true religion," in Summers's analysis, "in the love song between his 'amorous soule' and Christ's 'mild Dove,' a union that may be consummated only in a realm beyond the visible world."

Burke (1995, 32) reads the sonnet as one that "steps back and considers the larger question of why the Church described in the Bible contrasts so much with the Church in the world," noting that Donne offers no answers to questions he asks about the Church but, instead, the sonnet ends with an appeal to Christ to reveal to him the universal Church.

Date and Circumstances

Grierson (1909, 233) says that the poem was composed in 1617.

Grierson (1912, 2:235) asserts that Donne composed the sonnet when he was "already three years in orders." Friederich (1932, 188) makes a similar point.

Aronstein (1920, 12) says that HSShow was written in 1618.

Battenhouse (1942, 220) says simply that HSShow was written "sometime after 1617."

Gardner (1952, 124–25) finds the sonnet influenced by the outbreak of the Thirty Years War, specifically the defeat of the Elector Palatine (James I's son-in-law) at White Mountain on October 29, 1620. Leishman (1954, 82), Kermode (1968, 184), Hollander and Kermode (1973, 1050), and Den Boer (1982, 113–15) remark similarly.

Bewley (1952, 646) comments that Donne wrote the sonnet after he had been ordained.

Adams (1962, 758, 784) notes that HSShow did not surface until its appearance in Gosse (1899). Acknowledging that setting the dates of composition of most of the Holy Sonnets is guided by the "scanty marks of internal evidence" (758), he nonetheless suggests that HSShow may be dated more precisely since it appears to be "inspired by the Elector Palatine's defeat" on October 29, 1620 (784). See more under Holy Sonnets: Dating and Order.

Smith (1971, 634–35) notes that some critics have grouped HSShow with Sat3 and dated it prior to Donne's ordination in 1615, "on the ground that it shows him still seeking for the true Church among the several contenders," but he points out Grierson's (1912) dating of the poem alongside HSShe and his further suggestion that HSShow reveals Donne as a priest of "some three years' standing still uncertain whether or not he is in the right communion." But Smith concurs with Simpson (1924) and Gardner (1952) that HSShow is not so much an expression of doubt as an observation "on the distance between the actuality and the ideal, the present state of Christendom and the condition of the true Church as it must be" (635). See also Grierson, Simpson and Gardner under *HSShow*: The Poet/Persona.

Chanoff (1981, 378–79, 383–85) links the debate surrounding the meaning of the sonnet to the biographical context of the poem (378), pointing to the readings of Simpson (1924, 1948) and Gardner (1952) as grounded in the belief that Donne "had resolved his doubts about which Church was the most orthodox years prior to the poem's composition" (378–79). Chanoff notes that Jackson (1970) treats the sonnet "as a coalescence of contradictory views of the Church, man and Christ," but Grierson (1912) held that prior to becoming Dean of St. Paul's, Donne was "still unresolved in his theology." Chanoff offers yet another view, namely, that there is evidence that the sonnet was "the product of a transitional phase in Donne's religious development" (379). According to Chanoff, the Donne who authored the *Essays* was not the Donne who wrote the Holy Sonnets, for after 1610 the "sense of spiritual paralysis and pessimism" evident throughout the sonnets disappears (383). "Clues" to the steps in Donne's conversion in the years 1609–1613 are present, Chanoff argues, in the *Essays*, sermons, and *Devotions*, and include "several axioms of Donne's faith," namely, "the universality of grace," and "the total openness and availability of Christ's mercy." Chanoff contends that the despairing voice so evident in such sonnets as *HSBatter* "gave way to a conviction that no man is under the necessity of damnation" (383). Thus, for Chanoff, *HSShow* reflects Donne's attitude toward the English Church "not long after his ordination," given that his approach is "tentative and questioning" (385). Chanoff claims that Donne "pleads with Christ to reveal the one true Church," but "no authoritative response is forthcoming," and Donne is left "to cope with the problem" in the best way that he can (385).

Rissanen (1983, 75–76) says that *HSShow* was written "probably some time in 1618–20."

Larson (1989, 151–56, 159) examines the history of scholarship surrounding the question of Donne's religious toleration following his ordination. For Larson, *HSShow* provides the greatest support for Donne's religious toleration, but Larson observes that the scholarship on the sonnet indicates that *HSShow* "has caused more problems than it has solved," much of the difficulty arising from uncertain dating. If, Larson claims, the sonnet was written before Donne's ordination, then Novarr (1980) rightly suggests that *HSShow* "reveals one possible reason for Donne's refusing holy orders as long as he did" (151). But if Gardner (1952) and others are correct in dating the poem after 1620, Donne was, according to some, "still questioning the Anglican church after his ordination in 1615" (152). Larson surveys the scholarly debate about the poem's stance toward the true religion with an emphasis on Donne's "supposed religious skepticism and sexual decadence" as evidenced in the sonnet's sexual imagery, and she acknowledges the varied and contradictory views (153).

Daley (1992, 43) interprets *HSShow* —"probably written around 1617—two years after he was ordained"—as an expression of Donne's "anguished preoccupation" with his uncertainties about his personal salvation following his "change of faith."

Norbrook and Woudhuysen (1992, 822–23) note that the poem has been identified with several different periods, from the time of *Sat3*, to a time before Donne's ordination in 1615, to his wife's death in 1617, to the political events of 1620, especially the "collapse of the Protestant cause in Bohemia after the defeat of the Elector Palatine outside Prague."

Fowler (1995, 261) points to line 4 of the sonnet as indicating that *HSShow* "probably" refers to events of 1620.

Gabrieli (1995, 246), assuming that *HSShow* was written three years after Donne's ordination, states that the sonnet reflects Donne's continuing questions about the claims of Rome, Geneva, and Canterbury concerning the True Church.

The Poet/Persona

Grierson (1912, 2:235–36) finds it "clear enough why this sonnet was not published," namely that it reveals that Donne, "already three years in orders," was still experiencing difficulty in choosing among "the three divisions of Christianity—Rome, Geneva (made to include Germany), and England." Donne resolved the difficulty, Grierson believes, in the conviction that "there is salvation in each," hence that since the Church of England had a special claim on him as his country's church, he could devote himself to it as a *via media* between the other two. Grierson concludes, however, that the English Church never appealed to Donne's heart and imagination as deeply as it did to George Herbert.

Ramsay (1917, 72–73) cites the sonnet to illustrate Donne's tolerance toward the various divisions of Christianity.

Aronstein (1920, 13, 82–83) finds the poem to be an expression of the desire for unity of the churches (13), and he detects in Donne's vacilation between faiths a reflection of his loving soul, his magnanimity, and his tolerance (82–83).

Grierson (1921, xxvi) identifies in the poem Donne's "laceration of mind" over "the conflict between the old and the reformed faiths."

Fausset (1924, 239) asserts that the poem is "addressed to the Virgin" but that it does not reflect "a lingering fondness" for Catholicism, but rather a devotion to thoughts of his dead wife.

Simpson (1924, 7, 76–77) argues for "a psychological unity to Donne's career," contending that there is "a thread of purpose which binds together his youth, manhood, and later years." She asserts that he was "always the seeker, who pursued Truth from the early days" through his middle years and beyond, a quest reflected in *HSShow* (7). Simpson quotes the poem in full (76–77), finding in it Donne's conviction "that so long as the Church of Christ is rent into so many portions, men will have difficulty in recognizing her, and will be bewildered by the claims of different factions." She argues that the poet "longed passionately for the re-union of Christendom," and that while acknowledging "that Rome and Geneva, as well as Canterbury, were branches of the One Church," he was troubled throughout his life by Christendom's divisions, a position, Simpson adds, "perfectly compatible with loyalty to the Church of England."

Bredvold (1925, 213) argues that the poem reflects Donne's search "for a church to which he could give undivided, uncritical allegiance." Donne was, Bredvold continues, a "man of unusual intellectual passion and power, whose desire for truth was deep and imperative" though it "always eluded his grasp." Further, he says, Donne was always a "seeker of truth, but pursuing it in vain, he suffered painful dejection and disillusionment," and as a consequence he "lived always intellectually tormented."

Sencourt (1925, 69) remarks that the poem reveals a Donne who was "never entirely happy in his confession" and who "seems to have inclined more to a general tolerance" in his attitude toward contending churches.

Payne (1926, 144–45) quotes the poem in full in arguing that Donne was unconvinced that any of the three religions could lay claim to "absolute truth." Payne concludes that this uncertainty was the source of his "notable tolerance."

Grierson (1929, xiv–xv) finds in the poem evidence that Donne's conversion to the Church of England did not induce the "peace and happiness" that Crashaw and Vondel found in the Catholic Church. Grierson argues that though it would be a mistake to conclude that Donne was "dominated by the conflict between his early Catholicism and his later Anglicanism," a man of his "poetic temperament, susceptible, impulsive, served by an acute and subtle intellect," could not easily escape the influence of his early religious training. The tension between the two faiths produced in him, Grierson says, a degree of "intellectual scepticism" and "spiritual unrest" reflected in the sonnet.

Foster (1931, 409) argues that though Donne "did not die a Catholic," he certainly "did not die a Protestant" either, since no "orthodox Anglican" could have composed a poem like HSShow.

Friederich (1932, 188) argues that Donne believed salvation could be found in any Christian church, hence his Anglicanism was never quite pure, but always included a strain of mysticism and Catholic philosophy. Friederich finds that HSShow reflects Donne's doubts about the correct faith, revealing a "tormented soul" ("gequälte Seele") who could not discover a satisfying balance among the teachings of Rome, Geneva, and Wittenberg. Friederich believes that he achieved this balance later in life when he criticized Catholicism for its intolerance.

White (1936, 95, 380) cites the poem as indicating that even after his formal allegiance to Protestantism, Donne still "found himself at times uncertain and uneasy in that allegiance" (95).

Schirmer (1937, 299) finds Donne here undecided about the choice of faiths, and returning to the theme of Sat3.

Turnell (1938, 25–26) observes that Donne was one of the first great poets forced to choose between conflicting faiths, because he was raised a Catholic and did not find it easy to cast aside that training. Turnell quotes the poem in full as one that reflects a mind experiencing the conflict between the unity of the medieval world and the "spiritual multiplicity of the Reformation."

Battenhouse (1942, 220–21) argues that Donne preferred the church invisible to the visible and the church universal to the national; hence it is doubtful that he "ever found on earth the one true church for which he yearned."

Moloney (1944, 43, 141) quotes the poem in full as "evidence of the division in Donne's mind." He was, Moloney contends, "irrevocably committed to Anglicanism" but "pondered within himself the problem of ecclesiastical allegiance" (43). Moloney suggests that at the same time the poem exhibits "a lingering attachment" to "Catholic devotion to the Virgin Mary, to the Confessions, and to the Virgins" (141).

Bush (1945, 133) argues that Donne's ordination "did not altogether heal some fundamental discords and conflicts in his intense and restless nature." He cites HSShow as an example of his troubled mind, observing that "if the philosophical doctrine of the relativity of truth helped to open the doors of the Church, it also left them ajar."

Grierson (1948, 312–13) quotes the poem in full as evidence that Donne had not "entirely convinced himself of the validity of the Anglican position." Grierson argues that Donne considered the English Church midway between the corrupt Church of Rome and an ideal yet to be achieved.

Turnell (1950, 271–72) argues that Donne is uncertain about which is the true Church and that he "is tragically conscious of being further from his goal" than in his youth. The poem, Turnell continues, reflects Donne's conclusion that one of the Churches may be the Spouse of Christ and reveals his resignation to the necessity of choosing the one he thought least corrupt.

Leishman (1951, 262–63) finds the "continuity between Jack Donne and Dr. Donne" overstated, arguing that the Donne who "in his climbing days" spoke of "corrupt religion" and "pseudo-martyrs" was not the same man who "already three years in orders," according to Grierson (1912), was so conscious of "the difficulties involved in a choice between the three divisions of Christianity," a tension reflected in HSShow, which Leishman quotes in full. In revision, Leishman (1954, 263–64, 272) continues to insist on the differences between "Jack Donne and Dr. Donne," arguing that during the years between his dismissal from Egerton's service and his ordination he exhibited "a continuous deepening, a continuous progress in seriousness, and even in devotional religiousness." Leishman dismisses Grierson's interpretation of the poem (1912) and adopts Gardner's position (1952) that Donne is insisting on the "vast and painful difference" between, on the one hand, "these Churches on earth, whether mourning or rejoicing," and, on the other, the "Spouse of Christ, the promised Bride of the Apocalypse" (264).

Louthan (1951, 126) contends that of the three Holy Sonnets from the Westmoreland ms. (NY3), HSShe and HSVex seem theologically inoffensive, but HSShow "appears too controversial for publication." It is so, Louthan argues, because it reveals, not a priest worrying about his vocation, but a Donne of an independent mind, one who "denied a monopoly on Christianity to any one of its major divisions" and objected to the "cramping narrowness" of each. Christ's spouse, Louthan concludes, is not one of these divisions, but "a truly catholic church."

Gardner (1952, 121–27) discusses HSShow at length, since "it has a bearing on our judgement on Donne's later life" (121). She juxtaposes two interpretations, that of Grierson (1912), who stresses the poet's uncertainties regarding the three principal divisions of Christianity, and that of Simpson (1924, 1948), who concludes rather that he was entirely loyal to the Anglican faith but regretted that there were divisions at all, and "longed passionately for the reunion of Christendom." Gardner agrees with Simpson, arguing that the subject of HSShow is not "Which is the best of existing Churches?" but rather the difference between "the Church promised in Scripture and the Church as it appears in the world and throughout history" (121). In developing her position, Gardner explicates elements of the poem to demonstrate that Donne was more concerned with the general state of religion than he was with doctrinal differences between the faiths. See specific explications under notes to lines 1–10, 1–4, 5–8, and 11–14.

Willey (1954, 357) cites the poem as an indication of the "agonies of study and inward conflict" Donne suffered in deciding "which Church was Christ's true 'spouse.'"

Cruttwell (1954, 89) finds that in the sonnet the older Donne was "still agonizing" over the "conflicting sects of the Church," as he had in Sat3. He contrasts the seriousness of the sonnet's tone with the "easy indifference" of Donne's attitude toward scientific and philosophical issues in the earlier SecAn.

Gransden (1954, 137–38) argues that Donne found the "ideal, universal Church" more meaningful than any individual Church. Gransden compares Sat3 43–46, where Donne is not emotionally involved in the issues, to this sonnet with its "surging stresses of a passionate plea to Christ" for wholeness. HSShow, he suggests, speaks of "something which, like a vision, cannot be argued about, but only prayed for" (137). Gransden comments that the sonnet reveals the larger truth that "the bride of Christ is the mistress of the whole world" (138).

Leishman (1954, 82), in a review essay of Gardner's edition (1952), agrees with her that Donne is not asking which is the true church, but lamenting the divisions among Christians. No one who reads Gardner's argument, he concludes, will ever again "suggest that Donne was less than wholehearted in his allegiance to the Church of England, or that he had any regretful hankering after the Church of Rome."

Sypher (1955, 129) comments that Donne feared eternal damnation and attempted to "jest his God out of His righteous anger."

Empson (1957, 378) mentions Grierson's suggestion (1912) that editors before Gosse suppressed the printing of HSShow because it demonstrates Donne's uncertainty about true religion, but for Empson Donne "is merely expressing a logical readiness to reconsider the question," and he gives evidence of "the habitual direction of his enthusiasm" when he poses questions such as those in lines 9–10.

Cohen (1963, 167–68) notes that Donne does not find it "easy to choose" among religious alternatives (167), pointing out that though he advanced to become Dean of St. Paul's he still asks in HSShow "which is the true Spouse of Christ" (168).

Stewart (1966, 19–21) argues that HSShow exemplifies his claim that "ambiguity is an ever present factor in interpreting many sacred poems," noting that the ambiguous meaning of "spouse" is the "crux of a paradox in which the form and the statement of the poem are mutually exclusive" (19). Stewart also finds that the text deals, to some extent, with the conditions of the English Church. He sees ambiguity in "the figure of the church" and argues that it cannot "be limited to a single level of meaning." Stewart says that in HSShow the condition of the speaker's soul takes precedence over the question of the church. Moreover, he argues that the figure of the spouse contains the "crucial paradox in the poem" (20), noting that the spouse is simultaneously both visible and invisible and that the meditative tradition offers a solution to the dilemma imposed by this paradox. Stewart thinks that the speaker courts the "true Church" because of "the perfect love of God" and that, accordingly, the speaker engages in a search for "some type of visual sign of the body of which he is already an invisible member" (21).

Bagg (1969, 419–21) says that in *HSShow*, Donne turns the question of his relation to God from a rational into a sexual adventure. Donne takes his metaphor "from his knowledge of sex," Bagg states, "where his feelings are alive and directed, to support a realm where his feelings, if no less intense, have not shown him a certain path." In Donne's effort to translate "religious doubt into a sexual context" that is also "bound up with deep-rooted anxieties" (but anxieties that "may be removed by a human and unmistakable gesture"), Donne hopes, says Bagg, that "the anxieties of denominational choice may also be solved" (419). Bagg argues that the poem was meant to be read to other men and that Donne appeals to this audience, "through the daring dramatic situation he has set up," to see if his audience shares the emotions evoked by the situation, specifically "his wish that the pursuit of the true variety of Christianity would be as easy and exciting as chasing a complacent man's wife."

Bagg remarks further that *HSShow* "enacts Freud's thesis that religious 'ideology' is a form of sexual sublimation," noting that Freud's notion "suggests one possible solution as to why Donne instinctively translated his religious anxiety into an Oedipal triangle." Still advancing a Freudian context, Bagg says that men who are "compulsively attracted to other men's wives, or to women possessed by others, usually are governed by an Oedipus complex which triumphantly turns the betrayed husband into the lover's father, who is finally defeated in the battle for the 'mother's' sexual favor" (420). Donne and his readers feel the "favor" of the yielding of one's wife, says Bagg, to be "a sacrifice that only someone beyond the touch of mortal jealousy and sexual anxiety could make." Bagg therefore believes that Donne's "exhilaration" distances him from the "Oedipal crisis" as he "places himself in the hands of a father who does not bar his access to his mother." The "sexual anxiety" that both troubles and finally comforts Donne in *HSShow* "sends its tremors everywhere," Bagg concludes, "sometimes becoming the sympathetic partner of his religious doubts" (as in *HSVex*) and "sometimes itself the guest of honor" (421).

Roy and Kapoor (1969, 114–15) cite *HSShow* as evidence that Donne "was not in any way a confirmed Anglican" and contend that Donne's religious verse "was not propaganda for or an expression of isolated Anglican faith." On the contrary, they state, Donne "speaks to his God, not for or against any religious order," and they argue further that "honest doubt" was rarely absent from Donne's mind for he constantly doubted his integration with religion.

De Silva (1971, 6) claims that in Donne's poetry the "details of ugliness" pile up so often that they bring the poet under the suspicion of perversity. In *HSShow*, De Silva identifies a "licentious conceit" that turns Christian faith into a "more than usually repulsive species of adultery" featuring the Church as a "profligate wife" and Christ as "decadent wittol." For De Silva, the conceit "adds neither intensity nor complexity to the emotion" of *HSShow*, but, rather, "stands outside it and insults it." While this may or may not be "evidence of a radical depravity in the 'sacred' poet," De Silva believes that it clearly reveals a "very grave defect in poetic sensibility" and a "frequent, lamentable lack in Donne of that fine and wise discrimination which need not be identified with fastidiousness."

Kawamura (1972, 49–66), remarking that this poem represents a face-to-face talk between Donne and God, grows out of Donne's personal faith, and confirms Donne's direct relationship to God, concludes that HSShow reveals Donne's tense appeal to God to accept him and his belief that God is most faithful when He accepts as many people as possible.

Pollard (1973, 19) relates HSShow to a history of religious persecution in England and to Donne's own questioning search for the true church, commenting that it cannot be known with certainty why HSShow was not published in Donne's lifetime. He suggests, however, that "Donne the churchman" may have been "outraged by this most daring exploit of Donne the poet" and thus felt it better to confine HSShow to "a small audience with strong literary stomachs."

Blanch (1974, 482) argues that HSShow "reveals the poet's anguished doubt that his adopted religion (Anglicanism) is the way to Truth."

Kerrigan (1974, 356–59) writes that in HSShow "the passionate speaker desires to enjoy the true church promised in the Bible" but that in the accommodated terms of the poem, this desire becomes the eager sexuality of the "amorous soule" (356). He argues that until the final three lines, the revelation is only "distantly sexual" (357) but then the poem moves from "subdued implication to overt proposition." Writing that Donne makes the marriage of the church a "triangular affair by insisting on his actual, rather than symbolic, sexuality" (357–58), Kerrigan notes that HSShow is reminiscent of many of the Songs and Sonets because "the wit of the concluding passage" depends upon our deducing the "fallacious argument" that "preceded the statement before us," as the speaker "offers a proposition admirable as religious desire but startling as sexual desire" ("twisted adultery" is "in accord with the principles of accommodated speech" equivalent to "exemplary fidelity") (358). Kerrigan thus argues that at the end of the poem Donne "almost loses control of his reader's imagination and therefore of his intentional meaning" (359).

Walter (1975, 4–5) writes that the questions that follow the prayerful supplication that begins HSShow express Donne's "indirect criticism of certain recurrent religious attitudes," particularly the attitude that "demands rationalistic purity in all matters of worship and doctrine" (4). He suggests that Donne shows a bias towards the image of the Catholic Church and argues that in HSShow "she at least is open to a kind of love whereas the other woman seems more plunder's victim than love's" (4–5).

Empson (1981, 50), writing in response to Carey (1981) and recalling that HSShow was not published until 1894, points to the sonnet as one in which Donne acknowledges that he has remained "uncertain" regarding "which sect was in the right." Empson regards the poem as a "gratuitous confession made secretly to [his friend] [Rowland] Woodward, impossible for a secret adherent of the pope." Empson adds that "the evidence is bound to be scrappy, but it is consistent."

Rollin (1986, 145) finds anxiety present in this sonnet, but he feels it is "less obvious" than elsewhere in Donne's writing. Whereas in Sat3 43, Rollin notes, "the admonition to 'Seeke true religion'" is "directed toward a silent auditor," in HSShow "Donne's persona is himself the seeker" (145). And, Rollin adds, the anxiety continues to the end, with the concluding metaphor of "Christ as Pandarus to the pious and the True Church as his Holy Whore" (145).

Language and Style

Stauffer (1946, 271) observes that Donne achieves intensity in the sonnet by multiplying uncertainties. In it, Stauffer notes, the poet develops seven possibilities, some with internal divisions, and ends with a paradox.

Brower (1951, 24–25), in a detailed explication of the sonnet's tone, finds the speaker expressing at once "worldly politeness" and "downright insolence," the former in the use of "thy" (l. 12), the "chivalrous sophistication" of lines 9–10, and the "knightly decorum" of line 12, the latter in the imperatives "Show" (l. 1) and "What" (l. 2), the "unflattering adjectives" throughout, and the intimate freedom of "peepes" (l. 5). Donne, he continues, addresses God as would "a man of the world in pursuit of a beautiful woman," characterizing Christ as a "kind husband" and employing the erotic pun of line 14. However, Brower concludes, Donne manages to maintain an equilibrium between the two postures throughout the poem.

Bewley (1952, 645–46) argues that Donne uses cynicism as a means of breaking away from the Catholic Church, but that in the end he remains troubled by the same questions he raised in Sat3. The difference, Bewley senses, is that he is "tired and conventional" in the sonnet, which lacks the energy of the earlier poem.

Morris (1953, 54–55) feels that the irregular pauses in works by Donne and Hopkins are evidence of the "passionate thinking and conflict" they share, especially in poems that pose a series of questions, and he cites six such occasions in HSShow and ten in "Carrion Comfort."

Kerrigan (1974, 356–62) comments on the startling sexual metaphors in both HSShow and HSBatter, observing that both result from the use of accommodated speech and suggesting that HSShow is a seduction into purity, or "exemplary fidelity" (358). See more under HSBatter: Language and Style.

Den Boer (1982, 113–15) notes the high incidence of questions in the sonnet and points to the ecclesiological ambivalence they suggest.

Ferry (1983, 232–33) regards HSShow, as well as HSWhat (see HSWhat: Sacred and Profane), as a sonnet that assaults "the expectations raised by the speaker's language." According to Ferry, the sonnet opens by "evoking the Canticles in a prayer to Christ as the bridegroom of the Church," but this "reverence becomes teasingly intimate in the context of what follows." Donne's speaker, in Ferry's view, "speaks with humorously exaggerated literalness, parodies liturgical formulas, makes a literary joke about chivalric romances, and puns on the word 'travaile' all with an off-handedness that implies Christ will catch and appreciate the verbal play." On the other hand, Ferry claims, Donne's speaker is aware that some readers, other than Christ, will misunderstand his "violation of decorum," but, for the speaker, "the truth in the heart is widely distanced from outward appearance, and not to be known by it" (233).

Spiller (1992, 178) associates Donne with the poetic style of the *stilnovisti*, pointing to such stylistic features as "the agitated questions, running across the boundaries and creating sense pauses in the middle of lines instead," as seen in the "mature manner" of a work such as *HSShow*.

Prosody
Esch (1955, 51) observes that the poem is a variant from the Italian form in that the final part ("Abgesang") is reduced to four lines. See more under Holy Sonnets: Genre and Traditions.

Sacred and Profane
Bennett (1934, 15) writes that it is important that Donne's reader share in the poet's capacity to associate "widely diverse themes and feelings" and to carry with him with each new experience a "vivid memory of what the old had felt like." She quotes *HSShow* 11–14 to illustrate that when, after the death of Donne's wife, he "sought a church as the object of his devotion," his mind fused the "traditional image of the Bride of Christ" with "memories of secular love." See also notes to lines 11–14.

Louthan (1951, 126–28) argues that "the imagery of secular love binds the poem together." The questions of the octave, he contends, concern the church, but in the sestet the "spouse becomes a woman again," one whose "fidelity is paradoxically dependent on her promiscuity." She is, Louthan concludes, "the catholic church" (127). The imagery, he proposes, shows that "Donne the voluptuous hedonist" has become "Donne the voluptuous saint" (128).

Gardner (1952, 80), citing lines 9–10, finds Donne referring to the Church "in terms of two conceptions of love—the domestic and the romantic."

Mollenkott (1981, 23, 30–34) says that Donne's images of androgyny have their source primarily in the Bible, Petrarchan love poetry, Neoplatonism and alchemical discourse, such imagery being "frequently that of the balanced/dialectical type" (23). The biblical imagery in *HSShow*, according to Mollenkott, draws on the belief that "all believers form one mystical body of Christ which is the invisible church," and thus "the visible, organized church is inevitably androgynous as well." Mollenkott notes that Donne refers to the Anglican church as "the Daughter of God, and Spouse of Christ" (*Sermons*, VII: 325), and therefore "just as Christ individually marries each individual Christian, He also becomes the husband of the corporate, visible body as a unit" (30). Mollenkott endorses the view of Jackson (1970) that the "inner dramatic urgency" of *HSShow* arises in part from the fact that the speaker, who is both searching for the bride of Christ and is himself, as a Christian, the bride of Christ, is "looking everywhere except inward for that identification." Mollenkott further shares Jackson's view that in courting the "mild Dove" the speaker is also seeking "an inner union, a sense of reconciliation of the male and female aspects of the speaker's own self" (31). For Mollenkott, the sonnet turns on a speaker who "asks Christ to reveal and share the embraces of his spouse, the church, so that the speaker is both the male seeker and the female object of the search" (32). According to Mollenkott, then, Donne's conception of androgyny here and elsewhere attests to his view that God possesses both a masculine and feminine nature, and Donne presents them "as if they were equals-in-balance" (34).

Schoenfeldt (1990, 290) cites *HSBatter* and *HSShow* as examples of Donne's "stunning blend of erotic and religious impulses," an interest that is "easily comprehended precisely because the eroticism is so explicit." See Holy Sonnets: Sacred and Profane.

Daley (1992, 43) finds that Donne's secular and religious poetry reflect the "anxieties" brought about by his "change of faith." In his secular verse, Daley emphasizes, "Donne's *personae* again and again question the fidelity and constancy of their mistresses," and, similarly, in Donne's religious poetry, and especially in his Holy Sonnets, he "transferred these anxieties and fears to his relationship with God, doubting his own election, fearing his own damnation, and questioning God's seeming indifference."

Low (1993, 76–77, 85) sees a "fundamental difficulty and source of unease" in HSShow in that Donne "has crossed the wires between the two traditional versions of the biblical marriage trope: the marriage between Christ and his Church, and the marriage between God and the soul" (76–77). From the opening, in Low's view, the sonnet appears focused only on the marriage of Christ and his Church, but with the sestet, Donne "unexpectedly introduces a version of the individual marriage trope" (ll. 9–10). The soul, according to Low's analysis, is "a questioning, masculine knight; the object of its love is a maiden, who must first be actively sought and courted before she can be loved." With the introduction of this variant, Low adds, we have "a ménage-à-trois, if not worse," that is, "Christ and the speaker have essentially been transformed into rivals for the lady's affections." The result is that "love between the speaker and Christ finds no logical place in the poem," Low asserts, for "the Church is their common wife." Low concludes that "great difficulties arise because Donne simply cannot allow himself to relinquish his habitually masculine role" (l. 10) (77). Still, in Low's opinion, "the issue of his struggle is strong, admirable poetry" (85).

Osterwalder (1995, 208–09) finds that apart from his use of "ravish" in HSBatter and HSDue, Donne's "most conspicuous use of erotic imagery for the love of God to man" appears in HSShow: "after the conventional Biblical metaphor of the church as Christ's pure bride, the figure of a harlot appears already in the second and third lines . . . followed by a woman 'robbed and tore.'" Osterwalder agrees with Gardner (1952) that the image connotes "not merely lack of comeliness, but of spoliation, even loss of virginity," and he finds "striking" the fact that Donne introduces erotic imagery so early in the sonnet. Osterwalder notes the biblical precedent of the figure of the whore of Babylon from Rev. 17.4, commenting that "attributing sluttish promiscuity to Christ's false bride is nothing out of the ordinary," but it is noteworthy that "Christ's true bride is presented in the same light," that is, in "the paradox that the mild dove is truest when she offers herself to as many lovers as possible" (208). Osterwalder concludes that this otherwise "bewildering reversal of imagery" confirms Mann's view (1985–86) that Donne's "consistent orientation in the treatment of human and divine love is to reestablish and strengthen an ideal continuity and relation between human and divine, natural and spiritual." Thus, for Osterwalder, "the achieved physical union of the lovers in the secular love poems is spiritualized by the Neoplatonic and Christian imagery," whereas "the intensity of God's love for man is rendered by images derived from physical love in order to give it a palpability which religious, spiritual images cannot convey" (209).

Themes

Leishman (1934, 90) finds Donne "unique in his age" in his conviction that Christianity "should transcend particular forms of worship."

Lyon (1937, 13–14, 144, 204) observes that the sonnet reflects the pervasive "intellectual confusion and uncertainty" of the period and a disappointment that the humanistic dreams of the Renaissance had not been realized.

Reeves (1952, 102) notes that Donne's loyalty was divided between the Church of England and the Roman church of his parents and that his doubts are reflected in the sonnet. Reeves paraphrases the poem: "The church is the bride of Christ. Is it to be found, he asks, across the Channel in France and Italy or in Germany and England? He asks Christ to reveal his true bride, since he is happiest when all men court her."

Peterson (1959, 514) finds the poem an expression of the penitent's contrite sorrow in fulfilling God's command to love both him and his "spiritual church," even while mourning the state of the temporal church.

Kremen (1972, 110–11) argues that HSShow expands the marriage metaphor of HSBatter from "the individual to the communal configuration" (110). In his sermons, Kremen states, Donne argues that the earthly church should be a type and figure of the heavenly church. More broadly stated, chronos, or earthly time, is preserved and fulfilled by kairos, or eternal time, and this principle structures Donne's invocation in HSShow. Further, Kremen states, the Christian image of the marriage of Christ with the collective body of Christians informs the metaphor that underlies the last quatrain of the sonnet (111).

Walter (1975, 7) says that Donne is arguing on behalf of the true Church which ignores sectarian disagreements and remains constantly open to all Christians.

Archer (1977, 186) writes that HSShow "makes use of a journey motif as a reference to the church or to a religious vocation," arguing that the imagery suggests "uncertainty and change," while the poet desires "stability and security." He remarks that HSShow shifts from "unfavorable images of the church, which moves and is unstable, to images of men who have to journey in quest of her." But he sees at the end a turn to "stability and domesticity," as the speaker "renews the emphasis upon the church as the spouse of Christ."

Lewalski (1979, 273–74) proposes that HSShow may have been written as a sequel to HSShe, since HSShow moves from "the speaker's love of his own spouse, to his love of Christ's Spouse, the Church" (273–74). The octave, in Lewalski's view, focuses upon "the problem of identifying that Spouse," whether Rome or the Reformed Church. Lewalski notes that the resolution lies in one of Donne's most "outrageous" paradoxes, namely, that "Christ must from Bridegroom turn pander, and so 'Betray' his Spouse to the loves of others," and thus the Spouse "must in the necessary promiscuity of her love to many, turn harlot" (ll. 11–14) (274).

Milward (1979 [1988, 99, 104–05, 108]) sees in HSShow a shift from Donne's thoughts of his deceased spouse to "Scriptural imagery of the 'spouse of Christ,'" the principal source being the concluding chapters of Revelation, "where the Church is presented as the New Jerusalem and the Bride of the Lamb" (104–05). Milward finds that "the sonnet as a whole is framed in the form of a petition to Christ," in which the speaker "expresses his longing desire to see the spouse of Christ, not only as she will be revealed at the end of time as the New Jerusalem of St. John's apocalyptic vision, but also as she is already present in the world" (105). Milward interprets the speaker's inquiry into how the Church is to be identified, whether Roman or Protestant, as revealing his commitment to the Anglican Church, "while glancing with some bewilderment, now at the Roman, now at the Protestant claims" (104). Milward finds it "no wonder" that Donne deemed it "prudent" not to have the poem published while nonetheless "ensuring its preservation" in ms. (108).

Novarr (1980, 135, 139–40] describes the sonnet as "a petition that God reveal to Donne His true Church and allow him to participate in it," in the course of which he "exposes with wit and with scorn the claims of contending theological and ecclesiastical factions" that have "rent the fabric of the Church," which for the speaker is the "Church Universal" (135). Novarr notes, however, that Donne also supported "the lawful civil authority which customarily fettered and imprisoned the word *religion* and immured it 'in a *Rome*, or a *Wittenberg*, or a *Geneva*,'" and he quotes from Donne's letter to Sir Henry Goodyer (*Letters*, p. 245) (139). Novarr cites other of Donne's writings, such as his *Essays*, sermons, and letters, that demonstrate that "his yearning for a Universal Church was customarily tempered by his political pragmatism and by his sensitivity to the opinion of those who were easily scandalized" (140).

To Rissanen (1983, 75–76), HSShow offers the "best starting point" in deciphering Donne's "views on the problem of the division of Churches," which occurred with the Reformation (75–76). Rissanen claims that for Donne the question is "not academic but intensely personal," for he approaches it, not as a "systematic theologian," but as a "soul in uncertainty, yearning to embrace the bride of Christ, but not knowing who, where and in what appearance she is" (76).

Craik and Craik (1986, 281) define the sonnet's theme (implicit in the whole poem) as the wish for unity in the church.

Warnke (1987, 110) points to the paradox that ends the sonnet, namely, that "Christ, the bridegroom of the Church, is pleased when His bride is sexually possessed by as many men as possible." Christ "thus becomes a *cuckold*, or cooperative cuckold—to the Renaissance mind (or to *earthly* conceptions) the most contemptible of beings."

Wall (1988, 174) indicates that the "persistence" of Catholics and Puritans led to "heightened awareness" among Anglicans that their church was one among many and not the "sole expression of Christianity in England," and Wall thus reads Donne's request in HSShow to "Show me deare Christ thy spouse" (l. 1) as "no idle question, as it would have been had Anglicanism's aspirations been realized."

Zunder (1988, 91–94), recalling that in 1621 Donne was to be appointed Dean of St. Paul's and that by 1630 he "was being considered for a bishopric" (94), observes that HSShow nonetheless "reveals no allegiance to any particular church," but instead "each alternative is viewed in turn: the Catholic Church, and the Protestant churches on the continent and at home" (94). Zunder finds in the sonnet "an otherworldly longing of a kind later developed by Vaughan and here expressed in the paradoxical, sexual terms of Donne's inner individualism," an individualism that Zunder defines as Anglican, and, at the time of the Civil War, "Royalist" (91,

94). What Zunder does not find in the sonnet is "any connection between the inner self and the institutional form" (94), and thus the poem, in Zunder's words, reflects "the final position" of Donne, that is, a "dissociation between the inner commitment and the outer life" (93).

Holmes (1992, 25–26, 29–30) examines Donne's handling of "apocalyptic transformation" to reveal its "centrality to his understanding of the re-creation of the body and soul in this life and the next" (25). Holmes finds that Donne's apocalyptic vision conforms to the Reformation emphasis on a "personal relationship to God," thereby locating "the drama of apocalyptic transformation in the individual soul" (29). Holmes reads *HSShow* as reflective of Donne's "prioritization of personal experience" (29). The opening nine lines, according to Holmes, are a "fruitless speculation on the identity of the Bride," and are followed by a quatrain (ll. 11–14) that "begs an immediate unveiling." Holmes cites Summers's claim (1987) that the quatrain expresses an apocalyptic "heavenly ideal," but Holmes finds this view of the intent of Donne's spirituality mistaken, arguing that Donne focuses on a desire to "know in the present the inchoation of personal transformation" (30).

Sabine (1992, xiii, 27–28, 106–08, 110) states that in *HSShow* Donne "attempted, even after ordination, to rearrange the 'peeces' into a feminine figment of the true Church," but "wary of resurrecting Mary's union as Mother with the body of Christ, Donne overworked the metaphors of a spousal relationship" (xiii). Sabine adds that "the bride who is sexually exploited in the infamous couplet of the sonnet brings into shocking focus systematic violations of the Virgin's honour" (xiii). And thus, says Sabine, by virtue of a feminine figure we are alerted to "the cracks in that mask of social and religious unity which Protestant England presented to the world," for what Donne "audaciously brought together in his sonnet was the animal fear of the men who were being systematically hunted down for holding fast to such increasingly outmoded beliefs as Marian devotion" (106–07). Thus, Sabine argues, though *HSShow* was composed some ten years after the Anniversaries, Donne was "still at work on the deconstruction of the madonna figure that he had begun in earnest" in *SecAn*. According to Sabine, the "grotesque contrariety" in lines 13–14 is "consistent with pornography's contrivance to express the female body to the public traffic of the world" (107). Sabine finds that the speaker's "unwillingness" here and in *HSBatter* "to depict his own soul or those of his Christian brethren in feminine and bridelike terms 'betrays' the sexual orientation of the poet's adopted Church," and she notes that the only time this "phallocentric stance falters" is when the speaker "tremulously" begs Christ to "let myne amorous soule court thy mild Dove" (l. 12) (108). Sabine acknowledges that Donne "has our sympathies in his sane desire for normality and defiance of the religious mania for persecution and martyrdom," yet "it was his historical misfortune to be born into a polarised culture that made his choice of life dependent upon the religious rejection of a formative Mother figure" (110).

Singh (1992, 106–07) considers the sonnet in the context of the views of Grierson (1912) and Gardner (1952) about Donne's position on the nature of the true Church, noting that for Grierson the poem suggests the "embarrassing fact that, even after being ordained an Anglican priest, Donne continued to doubt the truth of his Church" (106), but for Gardner Donne is more interested in the possibility of an "as yet hidden figure of the Church Universal, whom he describes as the bride who will be hospitable to all comers" (107). In Gardner's reading, Singh suggests, *HSShow* "becomes an Anglican lament at the rifts which have historically characterized Christianity rather than an anguished utterance of a man who continues to have doubts about the church he has chosen to serve" (107).

Gorbunov (1993, 125) associates *HSShow* with *Sat3*, both of which play with the contrast between the invisible, heavenly Church and its distant, far from being ideal, earthly embodiment. In Gorbunov's view, the erotic paradox that closes the sonnet draws on imagery from the Hebrew Bible, and again one finds that for Donne it is Christian unity that constitutes the true Church, not divisions created by people.

HSShow and Other Works

Praz (1925, 70) hears in the sonnet echoes of the accents of *Sat3*.

Morris (1953, 78) comments that Donne's doubt and uncertainty are echoed in Hopkins's "Nondum" (31–32).

Duncan (1959, 53) finds the conflicting religious attitudes in Browning's *Christmas Eve and Easter Morn* "reminiscent of" *Sat3* and *HSShow*.

Stull (1982b, 133) observes that in 1579, Henry Bynneman printed *A Newyeares Gifte, dedicated to the Popes Holiness, and all Catholikes addicted to the Sea of Rome,* containing a "sequence of six interlaced sonnets subtitled 'The manner and meanes of the Popes beginning'" (133). Stull notes that "these satirical sonnets are in effect the first sonnets on ecclesiastical policy in English," anticipating *HSShow* and Milton's "several sonnets on Republican church politics" (133n14).

Patrides (1985a, 446) cross-references the sonnet with "the search for the 'true religion'" in *Sat3* 43 ff. Many other critics have noted the relationship between these two poems in commentary located in various sections.

Gilman (1986, 83) locates some of the language of the sonnet in an earlier homily by Donne [*The Second Tome of Homilies* in *Certaine Sermons or Homilies* (London, 1623, p. 69)]. But in contrast to the complacency of the Homily, Gilman notes, *HSShow*, in its search for the true image of the Church in the midst of iconoclastic controversies, "travails through a complicated swerve of feeling on its way to the abrupt paradox of the closing couplet."

Summers (1987, 72–3, 76–9, 82) begins by stating that *HSShow* and George Herbert's "The British Church" are both "prompted by schism in the Church," and thus "explore the question of how to recognize true religion" (72). Donne, according to Summers, "contrasts the image of the Bride of the Apocalypse with distinctly unbridelike women who represent various manifestations of the visible Church" (72). Summers finds that the first book of Spenser's *The Faerie Queene* most likely influenced both Donne's and Herbert's poems, with the conflict between Protestantism and Roman Catholicism represented in Spenser's text as Una and Duessa respectively (73). Strikingly close parallels exist between the representation of the Bride of the Apocalypse in both Donne and Spenser, according to Summers, that is, in imagery of brightness and light (73). But Donne, unlike Spenser, "implies considerable skepticism as to the validity of the epic poet's claim to have discovered true religion in Elizabethan England" (76). Summers interprets the opening series of questions in Donne's sonnet as a sign of his "doubt as to whether either Roman Catholicism or Protestantism can genuinely claim to be Christ's Spouse," given their "historical and transient" nature (77–78). The concluding plea to Christ to "Betray thy spouse to our sights" as one who is "open to most men" (ll. 11–14) is, in Summers's view, an expression of Donne's "passionate longing for a truly catholic Church free of division" (79). Donne's "refusal to identify the Church Triumphant with a temporal institution," according to Summers, appears elsewhere in a christening sermon (*Sermons*, 5:126), where he describes the earthly Church as one that "is in a pilgrimage, and therefore here is no setling" (82). But Summers concludes that Donne "does not deny that [the competing Churches] are legitimate" (82).

Schoenfeldt (1990, 285–86), in a comparison of Herbert and Donne, finds that in his poem "The British Church," Herbert "segregates sexual and maternal imagery in order to discover in his mother church a nonsexual, matriarchal edifice which transcends the erotic attraction of both Catholicism and Puritanism" (285). According to Schoenfeldt, for Herbert Rome is a "painted prostitute, seducing her followers with false promises and dazzling cosmetics," while Geneva "affects a plainness which is nearly as salacious as Roman makeup—nudity" (285). Schoenfeldt states that like Donne in Sat3 and HSShow, Herbert "converts religious choice into a question of sexual preference," but that for Herbert, unlike Donne, "the choice is clear: the British Church is one in whom 'Beautie . . . takes up her place,/And dates her letters from thy face,/When she doth write'" (285–86).

Masselink (1992, 95–97), in comparing the sonnet with Sat3, finds that in both poems, Donne "rejects extremes," but "in neither does he identify any earthly church as housing true religion" (95–96). For example, according to Masselink, Donne's admonition in Sat3 to "seeke" truth (l. 74) finds its parallel in HSShow in the "adventuring knights" who "travaille . . . to seeke and then make love" (ll. 9–10) (96). And, Masselink adds, Donne's advice in Sat3 to "doubt wisely" (l. 77) and his series of questions in HSShow express similar doubt "as to where the true church is to be found" (96). Masselink finds a similar view in Donne's sermons, and concludes that the sermons and religious poetry—his public and private voices—resist extremes, and seek instead "to defend the bride of Christ without explicitly identifying her with any particular earthly church" (96). In so doing, Masselink contends, Donne preserves his independence, "the character trait we find so attractive in Donne the poet" (97).

Notes and Glosses

1–10 *Show me . . . and then make Love?* **GARDNER** (1952), pointing to these lines, suggests that the sonnet reflects "the debate as to whether the true Church of Christ is the Visible or the Invisible Church." Finds that by posing the two sides of the argument in a series of questions, "as if neither were tenable," Donne reveals "his sympathy with the Anglican refusal to choose" between them (126).

1–6 *Show me . . . now'outwore?* **CRENNAN** (1979): the lines reveal Donne's desire "to know which is the true Church," as well as his "contact with one of the great issues of the age—the Reformation and the conflicts and personal tragedies it entailed," including his brother's death (10).

1–4 *Show . . . in Germany and here?* GRIERSON (1909), citing these lines, agrees with Gosse (1893 and 1899—see Holy Sonnets: Dating and Order) that Donne was not a "convinced Anglican" in 1607–1610, and had doubts as late as 1617, when he composed HSShow (233). SIMPSON (1924) quotes the lines to illustrate Donne's lifelong search for truth (7). GARDNER (1952) argues that the "Spouse" is not one of the divisions of Christianity but the "Church Universal." Believes that Donne was a loyal Anglican, supporting the church position that membership did not compel him to "'unchurch' other Christians" or to "assert exclusive validity for an episcopal ministry," nor did he believe "the Church of Rome no Church." Adds that HSShow asks Christ "to reveal his bride to men's sight," but Donne finds the claimants to that title "unbridelike," both the "richly painted" church of Rome and that of Germany, "rob'd and tore" by the outbreak of the Thirty Years War (123–25). SABINE (1992): Donne's "gradual dissociation from Catholicism and from the Virgin who gave this religion corporate heart" created "deep psychological scars" that are sometimes evident in the "fabric of his poetry," imagining his soul as "garbed in a piece of the divided raiment of Christ" or picturing the Church as "robed in the torn bridal gown of Christ" (76).

1 *Show me deare Christ, thy Spouse, so bright and cleare.* BATTENHOUSE (1942): "a poignant cry," evidence that it is doubtful Donne "ever found on earth the one true church for which he yearned" (220–21). GARDNER (1952): cf. Rev. 19.7–8: "'The marriage of the Lamb is come, and his wife hath made herself ready. And to her was granted that she should be arrayed in fine linen, clean and white' ('splendenti et candido,' Vulgate; 'pure fyne lynen cloth and shining,' Geneva)" (79). [Similarly, Smith (1971, 635), Lewalski and Sabol (1973, 160), and Fowler (1995, 262).]

1 *Show me* CRAIK and CRAIK (1986): "Compare l. 12, but contrast the plurals in ll. 9–11, 14" (281).

1 *Show* LOUTHAN (1951): the word has two meanings, first, reveal the identity, second, that failing, reveal the person of the spouse herself (127).

1 *Spouse,* WILLEY (1954): "the Church" (387). [So also, Fowler (1991, 119).] SHAWCROSS (1967): "the true Church, with reference to Christ as the Bridegroom" (cf. Matt. 25.1–13) (349). [Similarly, Warnke (1967, 275), Kawamura (1972, 49–66), Barańczak (1984, 162), Patrides (1985a, 446), and Booty (1990, 110).] BROADBENT (1974): "The Christian church is the bride of Christ in Revelation 21–22 and Song of Solomon as allegorized. [Similarly, Craik and Craik (1986, 281), who cite Rev. 19.7–8 and Song Sol. 2.] The first two are not dressed as brides but like a whore (Roman Catholic) and a drab (Lutheran)" (107).

1 *so bright and cleare.* SMITH (1971): "pure and free from error or guilt" (635).

BURKE (1995): the words recall the description of the bride of Christ in Rev. 19.7–8, who is "arrayed in fine linen, clean and white," and also point to the "ideal scenario, in which the true Church is easily discerned among the many options available" (33).

1 *cleare.* FOWLER (1991): "(1) free from confusion; (2) pure" (119).

2–4 *What . . . in Germany and here?* LOUTHAN (1951): the contrast is between "the respective lushness and severity of the Catholic and Protestant ritual," between "a gaudy whore and a disheveled widow" (127). GARDNER (1952) identifies the two images with the Church of Rome and the Protestant church of Geneva and Germany, the first associated with the Whore of Babylon in Rev., the other with the "desolate Virgin of Zion" in Lam. (124–25). ADAMS (1962): the "Church of Rome is 'she which goes richly painted on the other shore,'" in contrast to the "reformed churches 'in Germany and here'" (786). LEWALSKI and SABOL (1973) point to Gardner (1952) and add that the lines following "measure the foolish counterclaims of the churches against that archetypal image of the Bride" (160). HIEATT (1987) notes that "richly painted" suggests the "whorish woman of Revelation," which Protestants would have associated with the "ceremony of the Catholic church." Notes that in lines following the "Protestant church seems just as unlikely a spouse." Points out that "Calvin's doctrine that the Church 'slept' from the time of its primitive purity until the Reformation makes the Visible Church an unlikely bride," as does the "Catholic doctrine that the church is truth, when successive popes change that 'truth'" (241). NORBROOK and WOODHUYSEN (1992): the poem offers "contending images of the Church as a female figure." In Catholic symbolism, the "Church visible was often represented as female," while for many Protestants, "the true Church was the Church invisible of the faithful, whom they identified with the woman wandering in the wilderness" (cf. Rev. 12.6 and Rev. 19.7–8, which "prophesies her marriage with Christ") (822–23). ELLRODT (1993) believes that Donne no longer searches for the true church, as he did in *Sat3*, for the contrast is, rather, between the promised church in Scripture and the diverse Christian churches throughout history and in the present world. Argues, however, that this call for a revealed and "catholique" church open to all Christians is not any less the sign of an ecumenical passion (456).

2–3 *She, which on the other Shore / Goes richly painted?* WILLEY (1954): "the Roman Catholic Church" (387). [Similarly, Shawcross (1967, 349), Warnke (1967, 275), Smith (1971, 635), Barańczak (1984, 162), Patrides (1985a, 446), Craik and Craik (1986, 281), Booty (1990, 110), Fowler (1991, 119), Singh (1992, 107–08), who notes that the "richly painted" woman, like the whore of Babylon, is "very unlike the true Bride" in l. 1, and Burke (1995, 33), who points out that the image was commonly used during the Reformation and who cites Martin Luther's Tract *On the Babylonish Captivity of the Church* to indicate "how loaded this imagery was during the period."] LEVER (1974): in "Catholic France" (183).

2 *What is it She,* GARDNER (1952) inserts a comma after "What" (rather than

Grierson's exclamation mark [1912]) and objects to capitalizing "she." Says that "What" is an exclamation of astonishment, introducing a series of rhetorical questions, expecting a negative answer" (79).

3–4 *Or . . . in Germany and here?* **WILLEY** (1954): "the reformed Church in Germany and England" (387). **SHAWCROSS** (1967): "the Protestant church—such as the Lutheran in Germany and the Calvinist in England" (349). [Similarly, Booty (1990, 110).] **WARNKE** (1967): "the Protestant churches" (275). **SMITH** (1971) cites Grierson's (1912) more limited interpretation and Gardner's (1952) more expansive one (see under *HSShow*: The Poet/Persona and notes to ll. 2–4). Adds that English interests were "deeply involved" in the Protestant cause and that there was "general dismay" when the Elector was defeated (635). **LEVER** (1974): "In England Donne probably had in mind the Puritan sects" (183). **BARAŃCZAK** (1984) also refers both to the traditional identification of the lines with Calvinism and the more recent assertions that Donne had in mind the "collapse of Protestantism in Bohemia" after the battle of Prague (1620) (162). **PATRIDES** (1985a): "Alluding to the Protestant Church inclusive of Lutheranism and Anglicanism" (446). **CRAIK and CRAIK** (1986): "either (1) extreme Protestantism (including English Puritanism), characterized by a contempt for ceremonial; or (2) moderate Protestantism (including English Anglicanism), which suffered a heavy reverse with the Elector Palatine's defeat in Bohemia in October 1620" (281). **SINGH** (1992): "The hopes of the Anglicans were tied up with those of the German Protestants, and so when the Elector lost, the mourning was heard not only among German Protestants but also in England ('here,' l. 4). Donne compares the loss of hope in Germany to the desolation of Jerusalem. In Lamentations the captive Jerusalem is mourned as though it were a raped and robbed daughter, and this imagery may explain why Donne uses the image of a ravaged woman in talking of Protestant Germany's defeat in l. 4" (108).

3 *richly* **WALTER** (1975): "there may be substantial good beneath her external appearance" (5).

3 *rob'd and tore* **BURKE** (1995): the second image of the bride of Christ is "a woman who has been stolen from and whose clothes are torn." This second woman "is the Protestant Church broadly speaking, but in this case centred in Germany, and the fact that "this figure mourns 'in Germany and here' (meaning England) demonstrates the solidarity typically felt among all Protestants" (33).

3 *rob'd* **REEVES** (1952): "robbed" (102).

3 *tore* **RUOFF** (1972): "torn." [So also, Fowler (1991, 119).]

5–8 *Sleepes . . . or on no hill appeare?* **GARDNER** (1952) observes that the wit of these lines is directed not against "Calvinist or Roman" but against those "who would confine the meaning of the word Church" (123).

5 *Sleeps She a thousand, then peepes vp one yeare?* **SMITH** (1971): some Protes-

tant sects claimed that "the true Church had disappeared from the earth for a thousand years, but has now emerged afresh" (635). **LEVER** (1974): cf. *GoodM* 4 (183). **RASPA** (1983): the line takes us back "roughly to 664, when the Council of Whitby according to the seventeenth-century Anglican position integrated the already existing independent English Church into the Roman organization" (113). **BARAŃCZAK** (1984): "some Protestant sects believed that the true Church disappeared from the face of the Earth for the period of one thousand years and was reborn only with their teachings" (162). **CRAIK and CRAIK** (1986): "alluding satirically to the claims of some Protestant sects (with a short expectation of life: *one year*) to have rediscovered long-lost primitive Christianity" (281). **SINGH** (1992): "The Calvinists claimed that the truths of the primitive Church remained forgotten till the time of the Reformation. In this line Donne is making fun of this assertion by asking whether the true Church slept for a thousand years" (108). **BURKE** (1995): a reference to "the reformers' belief that they were recovering the true religion of the Church, which had been hidden by centuries of Roman Catholic domination and misinterpretation." Cf., among other sources, Richard Hooker's *Of the Laws of Ecclesiastical Polity*, the "great defense of the Anglican faith, the first four books of which were published in 1593" (34).

5 *peepes vp* **FOWLER** (1991): "re-emerges reformed (as certain Protestants claimed)" (119).

6–8 *Is She . . . or on no hill appeare?* **KORTEMME** (1933): the paradoxical effect achieved by piling up opposites sometimes appears in a sequence of questions, here using time and number relationships (48).

6 *Is She selfe truth and errs?* **SMITH** (1971): "can the true Church be an institution which claims to be truth itself and yet is in continual error?" (635). **SINGH** (1992): "Donne mocks the Roman Catholic claim to infallibility by asking why, if the Church is the true one, it has been guilty of so many errors" (108). **BURKE** (1995): "Protestants placed authority in the individual and in the Bible, while Roman Catholics believed in the necessity of priestly intervention for salvation" (34).

6 *selfe truth* **WARNKE** (1967, 275): "truth itself." [So also, Patrides (1985a, 446), Craik and Craik (1986, 281), and Booty (1990, 110).]

6 *selfe* **GROOM** (1955): Donne uses words like "selfe" "according to the logic of his memory, not for metaphor, but for impassioned emphasis" (65). **LEVER** (1974): "Pristine, original" (183).

6 *now new, now'outwore?* **SMITH** (1971): "can truth, or the true Church, be a matter of fashion, to be accepted while it is new and discarded when it is not?" (635). **LEVER** (1974): "Can the true church be either 'new' or 'obsolete'?" (183). **BURKE** (1995): the words suggest a "dichotomy between seeing the Church as moving in a new direction and breaking from conventions which many Protestants felt had no basis in scripture, or as building on to tradition" (34).

6 *outwore?* FOWLER (1991): "outworn, discarded like an outmoded fashion" (119).

7–8 *Doth She, . . . hill appeare?* WALTER (1975): the alliteration of "sh" in the seventh line parodies "the animosity and harshness of much religious debate" and "reveals the speaker's irritation with his own question," while the "sing-song repetition of phrases in the eighth line suggests the speaker's increasing boredom with the never-ceasing wranglings of religious fanatics of all sorts" (5). HUNTER (1983) points out that "all commentators" agree that the hill is Mount Moriah, "the location of Solomon's temple," and yet he suggests that, "in the context of the other main contemporary religions" (Roman Catholicism "on seven [hills]" and the "Calvinism of Geneva by a lake" ["on no hill"]), it may be preferable "to identify the 'one' hill as Wartburg, where Luther translated the Bible, a castle atop a precipitous one" (109). LINVILLE (1984b): "the absence of an end-stop becomes a figure of the endless, the eternal, of unbounded time" (76).

7 *Doth She,'and did She, and shall She evermore* BURKE (1995): the three tenses "may suggest Donne's affinities with the Protestant faith since there are three tenses of 'do' in one line and three options for the true Church on the line below it. The present tense corresponds with the Temple of Solomon, the eternal, Biblical depiction of the Church which will always live in Scripture. The next words, 'did she,' correspond to Rome, and the final 'and shall she evermore' relate to Geneva (or Canterbury). This placement suggests that Donne believes that the Protestant cause will endure over the Catholic one, not a surprising opinion considering his livelihood was bound up with the Anglican faith" (34).

8 *On one, on Seauen, or on no hill appeare?* GARDNER (1952): the "one hill" is Mount Moriah, "where Solomon built the Temple"; the "Church on seven hills is the Roman Church, and the Church 'on no hill' is the Genevan" (80). [Similarly, Warnke (1967, 275), Patrides (1985a, 446), Craik and Craik (1986, 281), Hieatt (1987, 241), Booty (1990, 110), Norbrook and Woudhuysen (1992, 545), and Singh (1992, 108).] WILLEY (1954): "Wittenberg, Rome, and Geneva" (387). ADAMS (1962): "The Mount of Olives, the seven hills of Rome, and (perhaps) by Lake Geneva or in the town of Canterbury" (786). BARAŃCZAK (1984): "respectively: Ludgate Hill, on which stood the Anglican St. Paul's Cathedral; seven hills of Rome; Geneva, the center of Calvinism" (162).

8 *one,* SHAABER (1958): "Mt. Moriah, where Solomon's temple stood" (105). [So also, Smith (1971, 635), who adds, "[a]lternatively perhaps, Ludgate Hill on which St Paul's stood," Lever (1974, 183), and Fowler (1991, 119).]

8 *Seauen,* SHAABER (1958): "the seven hills of Rome" (105). [So also, Smith (1971, 635), Lever (1974, 183), and Fowler (1991, 119).]

8 *no hill* LEVER (1974): the "unlocalized seat of Reformed churches" (183).

[Similarly, Fowler (1991, 119).] BURKE (1995): "no hill is likely to be Geneva, the centre of Calvinism, or possibly Canterbury, the seat of the English Church" (34).

9–14 *Dwells . . . and open to most Men.* FAERBER (1950) observes that the paradox reverses the metaphor of the bride of Christ by asking about the true church in the language of worldly love. Notes that the image is in the tradition of ambiguous emblem poetry that sought to represent the strange and baffling in religion (25). TURNELL (1950) finds that the sestet recalls the tone of some of the Songs and Sonets in that "the Spouse replaces the Mistress" and Donne thinks the union with her will bring about the unity he had sought with his mistresses. Concludes that the divided churches trouble him as much as inconstant women once had (272).

9–10 *Dwells . . . and then make Love?* GARDNER (1952) identifies here two "conceptions of the Church" through two "conceptions of love—the domestic and the romantic." Adds that Donne had little "sympathy" with the second and that "allusions to medieval romance are very rare in his poetry" (80). SINGH (1992): "There are so few references to the world of medieval chivalry in Donne that the present one has to be suspected of sarcasm. The implication would be that it is not necessary to quest abroad for the true Church" (108). BURKE (1995): Donne "asks whether the Church lives inside or whether we must search for it. Some critics have seen these lines as Donne asking whether the true Church is invisible or visible, a question the theologians of the day answered in various ways" (34).

9 *with vs,* KAWAMURA (1972): in England, i.e., the Anglican Church (57–58).

9 *adventuring knights* BROADBENT (1974): "knight-errantry of the romances, as opposed to serious love." (107). [So also, Lever (1974, 183), who notes that the conceit points to "an undirected chivalric quest for 'romance,'" rather than "marriage to the 'spouse' at a set place."] BURKE (1995): the "image of the knight errant, a standard one in late medieval and early modern literature, anticipates the eroticism of the final lines" and is "particularly relevant" for *HSShow*, since the "questing knight was not just a figure of romance but also often a Christian warrior searching for the true Church" (34).

10 *trauaile* ADAMS (1962): "The seventeenth-century spelling, *travaile*, includes the idea of labor" (786). [Similarly, Patrides (1985a, 446) and Singh (1992, 108).]

11–14 *Betray . . . and open to most Men.* BENNETT (1934) finds that when Donne "sought a church as the object of his devotion," he conceived of his search in terms of "secular love." Quotes the lines to illustrate, comparing God, a "kind husband" open to an appeal to "betray" his spouse "to our sights," to those who would be "flam'd with the oylie sweat of jealousie" (*ELPart* 43) at the thought (15). GARDNER (1952): the closing prayer "rests on the assumption that, for all her apparent disunity, the Church is still one" (126–27). MORRIS (1953) claims that Donne carries the analogy between the physical and spiritual worlds to a point that shocks his most ardent admirers. Observes that a fusion of spirit and matter marks the poems of both Donne and Hopkins (76). **WILEY** (1954): Donne's verbal ingenuity was not incompatible with serious purpose, as when he describes the soul's yielding in physical terms (103). **SYPHER** (1955): Donne "writes of the Church in terms one usually applies to an adulteress or whore" (129). **KERMODE** (1957) observes that the wit of the poem "ventures where we are reluctant to follow." Suggests that if the modern reader is "uneasy about its taste," it may be because the metaphor, here "The Bride of Christ," is no longer commonplace (39). **LEWALSKI** (1979) suggests that no one but Donne "would so wittily seem to confuse the Bride with her antithesis in Revelation, the Great Whore of Babylon" (see Rev. 17.4–18), "playing upon the contemporary Protestant term of opprobrium for Rome to point up the essential spiritual qualities God's church must display" (274). **CRAIK and CRAIK** (1986) find the lines "paradoxical and daring" and point to Song Sol. 5.2 ("Open to me, my sister, my love, my dove, my undefiled") but note that there is also "a suggestion of a complaisant (*kind*) husband who will prostitute (*betray*) his wife to other men, by whom she will be *embraced* and to whom she will be *open*" (281). **YOUNG** (1994) observes that the poet "who offers to seduce Jesus" in HSWhat "here offers to cuckold him" (171). Notes Ferry's (1983) argument (see HSShow: Language and Style) that Donne stretches the convention of Christ as bridegroom and the Church as bride "to its most shocking limits" (171) but contends that Donne "is not being literal so much as reminding us of the radical nature of the figure: sexual 'grace' is itself a metaphor for *grace*—the ineffable, inconceivable gift by which God grants eternal life, an ongoing existence and identity to the soul or self," so that "the 'shocking' metaphor is intended to startle us into recognition of how very *different* God's love is from ours" (172). **BURKE** (1995): the end of the poem has a "slightly licentious air," recalling the sexual imagery of Song Sol. 5.2. Such imagery is not in the Bible only, for Donne, living his youth in a Catholic household, would have known that "in Counter-Reformation religious poetry physical love was often employed to represent spiritual love." The final image nonetheless comes as a "shock" and confirms that "divine love and human love cannot be thought about in the same terms." In the final lines Donne "offers an insight into the nature of Christ's spouse" but at the close of the poem the "true Church has not been revealed to Donne, nor to his contemporary readers" (35).

11 *Betray kind husband thy Spouse to our Sights,* **TURNELL** (1950) wonders if Donne was "altogether sincere" in the line (272). **UL-HASAN** (1958): Donne humanizes Christ, cast here in the role of husband (36). **LEVER** (1974): an example of Donne's "unregenerate wit" in making Christ a "complaisant husband" (183). **WALTER** (1975), observing the paradox here, says that the "form of the address assumes that a closer affinity exists between Christ's spouse and the woman 'rob'd and tore,'" yet "any simple identification is denied by the speaker's respectful tone" (6).

11 *Betray* **SHAWCROSS** (1967): "reveal" (350). [So also, Booty (1990, 110)

and Singh (1992, 108), who also finds a suggestion of "Christ acting as a pandar or pimp."] **PATRIDES** (1985a): "disclose" (446). **CRAIK and CRAIK** (1986): "word-play: (1) betray; (2) reveal" (281). **NORBROOK and WOUDHUYSEN** (1992): "reveal a secret, or a hidden person, against your will" (545).

12–14 *And . . . and open to most Men.* **RUGOFF** (1939): Donne speaks of the "Church of God" in terms of a "sexual relationship" (86–87). **STAUFFER** (1946): a "deeper realization of religious faith comes from trying to understand" the para-doxes of such lines (85). **BROWER** (1951): the lines reflect "knightly decorum" (25), a combination of the imagery of "courtship" and "curiously passionate rever-ence" (31), and of "insolent and paradoxical wooing" (57). **LEGOUIS** (1958) finds an echo of the conceit in Cowper's *The Task*, where the poem calls nature "free to all men" (Bk. 3, l. 724) (537). **SMITH** (1992) suggests that Donne "resolves his search for the true Church" through an audacious "sexual paradox, petitioning Christ as a 'kind husband' to betray his spouse to our view so that the poet's amorous soul may 'court his mild dove.'" Finds that the evident "indecorum of making the true Church a whore and Christ her complaisant husband at least startles us into recog-nizing Christ's own catholicity" and concludes that the paradox "brings out a truth about Christ's Church that may well be shocking to those who uphold a sectarian exclusiveness" (90).

12 *thy mild Dove,* **GARDNER** (1952): cf. Song Sol. 5.2: "Open to me, my sis-ter, my love, my dove, my undefiled" (80). [So also, Smith (1971, 636), who notes the gloss of the Authorized Version ("Christ awaketh the church with his calling") and the reading of the "whole erotic dialogue in the traditional way as expressing 'the mutual love of Christ and his Church,'" Lewalski and Sabol (1973, 160), Lever (1974, 183), Norbrook and Woudhuysen (1992, 545), Singh (1992, 108–09), who notes that the sexual image is "startling and strong" but has biblical sanction, and Fowler (1995, 262).] **SHAWCROSS** (1967): "symbol of God's mercy and bearer of the olive leaf of peace (as it descended to Noah in Gen. 8:11)" (350). **BROADBENT** (1974): "the bride in Song of Solomon but also Holy Spirit" (107). [So also, Hieatt (1987, 241).] **ARCHER** (1977): the metaphor "mild Dove" "effects a change of tone, identifies the nature of the true spouse in contrast to the unstable ones, and resolves the speaker's dilemma" (186). **MOLLENKOTT** (1981) points out that the dove is male in Song Sol. 1.15, 2.14, and 5.12, and female in Song Sol. 5.2 and 6.9 (31n29).

12 *myne amorous Soule* **GRANSDEN** (1954): the lines reflect Donne's practice of using secular passions in divine poems (130–31).

13–14 *Who . . . and open to most Men.* **LOUTHAN** (1951): "Christ is the only delighted cuckold" (167). **SMITH** (1970) calls the closing sexual paradox "flagrantly shocking," causing one to wonder why comments about "institutionalized Christian-ity" are "cast in a figure which seems calculated to give offence," where, understood literally, the "true Church is a whore and Christ a wittol" (166). **LEVER** (1974): the "true church is the least exclusive," but Donne's "courtly wit creates an erotic paradox" (183). **PARKER** (1984): "The space of deferral which Augustine termed an 'interim age' (*City of God* XI.i) is figured by a female body—Rahab [by patristic writers], the redeemed harlot of Jericho (traditionally the city of 'Error'), whose name (Hebrew for 'broad, wide') is in Latin precisely *dilatio* and who is the type of that other redeemed harlot, the church, a symbolically female figure dilating in order to take in more members, so to speak, before the apocalyptic 'doom.' It is this dilation or opening which informs the culminating sexual pun" of *HSShow* (524). **A. SMITH** (1987) repeats his comments of 1970, adding that the "provocative witty life of the verse . . . breaks down the remoteness of the metaphysical order to show the issues working tangibly in the texture of our daily lives," an approach that admits "no barrier between one order of experience and another." Believes that Donne "sought for what little assurance he deemed possible to us by a coolly persistent determination to see things as they are, stripped of the imposture that our common use maintains" and that the "steady concern to get at the actuality of our human circumstances, and the search for ways of coming to terms with it, are the qualities that bring all his poetry together "in a coherent vision" (166–69). **SMITH** (1991) says that Christ is petitioned "as a 'kind husband' to betray his spouse to our view so that the poet's amorous soul may 'court thy mild dove.'" Acknowledges that the lines may seem "wantonly indecorous," but suggests that they "startle us into a realisation, reminding us how far our presumption of exclusiveness takes us from Christ's own ministry, and how arrogantly it denies Christ's Church" (138).

13 *trew,* **BROADBENT** (1974): "faithful" (107).

14 *embrac'd* **BROADBENT** (1974): "embraced by; you embrace a faith" (107).

14 *open to most Men.* **SMITH** (1971): "open to the generality of mankind (with a glance at the paradoxical sense 'available to the largest number of males'). Universality, not division or exclusiveness, is a note of the true Church" (636). **PATRIDES** (1985a): "possibly the boldest erotic image in Donne's sacred poetry" (446).

14 *open* **SHAWCROSS** (1967): "free, accessible" (350). [Similarly, Booty (1990, 110).] **FOWLER** (1991): "(1) universal; (2) easily available" (119).

14 *most Men.* **KAWAMURA** (1972): refers literally to the majority of people, including Donne, and psychologically Donne alone (65–66).

 *HSSighs*

COMMENTARY

General Commentary

Gosse (1899, 2:107) says of *HSSighs* that Donne worries that his "natural affection may have taken an excessive fleshly form, may have been 'idolatry,'" but that this "temporal sorrow" has brought to him a "holy discontent" [l. 3] that is "obviously salutary." Gosse further observes that, "[t]hrown out of the comfortable security of domestic life," Donne "falls" and is "bruised" but is eventually "lifted tenderly by the Divine hands." He adds that "vehement grief" [l. 13] is not the only cause of the "helpless physical condition in which he finds himself."

The Poet/Persona

Grierson (1921, xxvii–xxviii) finds in the "echoing vowel sounds" of ll. 1–8 of *HSSighs*—the frequent "I," the "sighs," "eyes," "Idol'try," "mine," and "my"— evidence of an "intensely personal religious poet."

Praz (1925, 67) detects in the sonnet a Donne tormented by the memory of his early years of idolatry. Praz interprets the poem as a complaint that since in his youth he gave himself over to every vanity, he should pay the penalty for past illicit joys, but his punishment will be for a troubled rather than a blissful past.

Cruttwell (1954, 92) argues that Donne's self-reproach that he cannot feel as intensely for God as he had for his mistresses is "slightly, though most humanly, comic" in that the author of the Holy Sonnets was simply "not as young as he had been," hence his yearning for a sensuous experience of God came "too late."

Stampfer (1970, 271) maintains that in *HSSighs* the sensualist Donne remembers only "sighs," "tears," and "vehement grief." However, Stampfer claims, Donne was too concerned with establishing his career to risk engaging in public license. Therefore, he says, there is no evidence in the poem that the "sighs and tears" of the octave refer to romance and courtship. Stampfer contends that the sonnet finishes with a bitter awareness of Donne's frustrated ambitions.

Brink (1977, 102) states that in *HSSighs* Donne penitentially reconsiders his idolatrous worship of woman, renouncing his suicidal thoughts in order to place trust in God.

Santisteban Olmedo (1977, 112) states that with his ordination Donne finally found in God the imperishable and unlimited love for which he had been searching all his life. Only when he had found that love, Santisteban Olmedo says, could Donne write *HSSighs*, verses that burn with the "inexhaustible flame of his soul."

Hamburger (1985, 8) calls attention to Donne's melancholy, which weighs even more on him because it is perceived as a sin, and finds that *HSSighs* focuses on this state of mind.

Rollin (1986, 140–41, 144) views Donne's speaker in *HSSighs*, though "in the grip of strong emotions," nonetheless "able to make spiritually productive use of his 'holy discontent.'" According to Rollin, "contrition," not "near hysteria," is the prevailing mood, for Donne's speaker "feels guilt more than abandonment, associating himself with traitors and thieves." Drawing on contemporary psychiatric theory, Rollin notes that such guilt "normally elicits the desire to conciliate the superego and whatever parental or community authority may share the influence of the superego at the moment," and "thus the shift of mood in the sestet—'Yet grace, if thou repent, thou canst not lacke' [l. 9]—is clinically as well as poetically predictable" (140). And yet again, according to Rollin, the speaker "performs a psychological adaptation, consciously bringing doctrine (in this case, correct doctrine, that of the Atonement) to bear on his spiritual state" (140–41). Rollin further classifies this as another sonnet displaying "unrelieved depression" (143), for although the speaker is repentant, he "has fallen prey to religious melancholy" (144).

Sacred and Profane

Leishman (1934, 89) finds Donne's religious poetry "intensely personal," especially in his recognition of the continuity between his early and later years, declaring in *HSSighs* that "because he once suffered the pains of love he must now suffer those of remorse."

Swardson (1962, 167) cites *HSSighs* to indicate that Donne conventionally wrote poetry that shifts from secular love to religious adoration.

Ferry (1983, 239–40) finds that Donne uses associations with the lover's complaint in very different ways in the sonnets. Ferry notes that here the speaker "wants literally to take back his earlier complaints," which he fears have "impoverished himself 'in vaine' [l. 4]" (239). Ferry points to the octave, which "builds a pattern of contrasts between such previous 'waste' and the hope of 'fruit,' between earlier sin and [the speaker's] penitence now." Ferry sees a similar effort on the part of the poet-lover to reject earlier profane expressions of grief in *HSLittle* and in *HSMin*. And yet Ferry claims that in the octave of the "sonnet of complaint," *HSSighs*, Donne's speaker ultimately seems not to reject "his former sighs and tears," but rather "accepts them anew," that is, "rather than asking for purification, he longs only for their return" (239). According to Ferry, Donne "pointedly and repeatedly uses identical terms for inward experiences which seem to be mutually exclusive, here those of complaining lover and penitent sinner, until the closing lines declare them to be indistinguishable" (239–40).

Warnke (1987, 108) finds sexual imagery to be "obsessive" in the Holy Sonnets, much as religious imagery is in the love poems, and such imagery "concentrates with formidable power the dramatic, passionate, and paradoxical elements that virtually define Donne's achievement in the genre of the devotional lyric." In Warnke's view, the "relationship between the amorous poems and the Holy Sonnets is sometimes overt," as it is in *HSSighs*.

Low (1993, 78–79) finds "intertwined sacred and secular love imagery" permeating the entire sonnet. The two loves, according to Low, are "in one sense treated as opposites, for one is idolatrous, the other true," but they are also "treated as precisely alike" in that the two loves are "essentially Petrarchan, and, at least until the present time, as equally unrequited" (78). Low notes that, "surprisingly," Donne "does not accuse himself of lust for mistresses or the world." The speaker mourns like a Petrarchan lover, in Low's view, but with the hope that his mourning will bear "some fruit" (l. 4), but no such fruit yet relieves the speaker from his "holy discontent" (l. 3). Low concludes that God "seems as distant and unobtainable as any Petrarchan mistress" (79).

Prosody

Esch (1955, 47) observes that the sonnet assumes the Italian structure but that it is aesthetically less complete than others in the group. He finds that the dark atmosphere of repentance in the octave contrasts with the sharply drawn figures of the sestet. See also Holy Sonnets: Genre and Traditions.

Stein (1962, 41) believes that HSSighs illustrates Donne's favorite device of making sound accompany meaning for rhetorical emphasis, noting that the final three lines of this sonnet reveal a roughness that refers to immediate objects rather than any kind of personal or satiric attitude that has been awakened, a characteristic feature of Donne's verse.

Winters (1967, 75) sees problems of accentuation in line 11 of HSSighs, which he finds typical of Donne's frequent violation of poetic form, concluding that the high incidence of these violations shows "a relative unawareness of the nature and importance of sound."

Themes

Reeves (1952, 100) says that in the poem the "remembrance of past pleasures comforts the ordinary sinner at the approach of misfortune," for in his "idolatry (i.e., his sinful youth) his sighs and tears were wasted, because he was not, as now, truly repentant." Reeves goes on to observe that since he is "sincerely converted to religion, he feels the need for those sighs and tears he wasted before."

Peterson (1959, 514) finds the poem a penitent's "lamentation" that he had sinned, and a wish that he had not. See also Holy Sonnets: Themes.

Yen (1995, 224–25) finds that this sonnet, like HSShe, "describes religious life as a state of 'holy discontent.'" According to Yen, in the speaker's claim that he has "mourn'd in vaine" (l. 4) and in "his hope that though his current condition is still unsatisfactory, he may now 'Mourne with some fruit'" (l. 4), we perceive Donne's "ambivalence about his family religion which had cost him the career opportunities that were readily available to other young men like him" (224). Moreover, Yen adds, "although he has repented his earlier sins of idolatry, his conversion gives him no peace" (224–25). The speaker laments that "other sinners may have to face 'coming ills,'" but, Yen notes, they "have enjoyed their pleasures and will have the memory of those 'past joyes'" (l. 11) to offer "comfort," but the speaker's situation permits "No ease" (l. 13) (225).

HSSighs and Other Works

Milward (1979 [1988, 93–95]) finds the most likely source of this sonnet, "in which the poet prays for the grace of heartfelt repentance," to be the second prelude to the second exercise of the *First Week* of the *Exercises* of St. Ignatius (93). Milward notes the similarity between the "sighes and teares" here and those described in *Twick*, *ValWeep*, *ValMourn*, and *LovInf* (93–94). Milward calls attention to the absence of the traditional turning-point in the sestet, for here the speaker "allows himself 'No ease,'" and in fact intensifies his suffering by drawing a contrast between his own suffering and that of "the drunkard, the thief, the lecher and the proud man"—four of the seven deadly sins—with an allusion to the drunkard in *Noct* and a further allusion to the lecher in *Oth.* 1.3.336, who is forever seeking "the fulfillment of his 'unbitted lusts'" (94). In the end, according to Milward, the speaker's recurring "grief is at once 'Th'effect and the cause, the punishment and sinne'" (95).

In his comments on this, the third song in Benjamin Britten's sequence, Gaston (1986, 209) finds Britten striving for "a mean between the extremes represented by the first two settings" [HSBlack and HSBatter] for Donne's Holy Sonnets. But Gaston finds that Britten "allows a respite from the energy of HSBatter without relaxing its sense of constraint," for "the single intimation of high feeling in the song at its *poco animato* expresses well the penitent's vexation that he cannot share the sensualist's consolation in remembered pleasures [ll. 9–12]." Gaston adds, however, that after this "moment of resentment," the "setting slows again (*rilassando*) as the penitent recovers his hard discipline of self-knowledge."

Radzinowicz (1987, 45–47) draws a comparison between the sonnet and Ps. 42 and 43, all of which employ the poetical device of *anima mea*, the dialogue of a man with his soul. Radzinowicz finds that though the sonnet "opens with its strongest point," it "does not close with it" (45). Thus, Donne's soul "must be rebuked for having indulged its grief in the past on objects so idolatrous that it can have no 'remembrance of past joyes, for relief/Of comming ills'" [ll. 11–12] (47). The soul, in Radzinowicz's view, must also be rebuked for wasting grief "that could have been used to 'Mourne with some fruit'" (47).

Martz (1988, 21–22) explores what he sees as "essential differences" between the poetry of Donne and Herbert by focusing on "their common theme of sighs and tears" (21). HSSighs, for example, includes "a whole range of human experience that Herbert does not touch," and also confirms Donne's "deep sense of sinfulness," derived from "a vehement, passionate love that he calls 'idolatry.'" For Donne, according to Martz, it is a love that even "led to his marriage" (22).

Stanwood (1992, 181–84) compares Gerard Manley Hopkins's poem "Thou art indeed just, Lord" with Donne's sonnet and also with Herbert's "The Sinner" in terms, first, of the "particular theological outlook common to them all," and, second, "in their poetic imagery and technique" (181). Stanwood finds HSSighs engaged with the poet's repentance of his past, while at the same time "he still suffers, ever grieving, ever thirsting" (182). Stanwood notes that Hopkins's "sots and thralls of lust" remind us of Herbert's "pil'd vanities" and his "shreds of holiness" and that both sonnets "point to Donne's 'holy discontent,' his 'hydroptique drunkard, and night-scouting thiefe'" [ll. 3, 9]. Stanwood adds that the three sonnets locate "an attitude of suffering, disappointment, [and] wretchedness" and ask "why one's best hopes end in disorder" (183). In Donne's sonnet, "the 'sighes and teares' that return once more into the griever's eyes, rending him with deep sorrow and discontent, rain uselessly," but "even so," Stanwood observes, Donne "hints at completeness in the conjunction of redemption and sin, an implicit source of true pleasure" (184).

Notes and Glosses

1–8 *O might . . . I must suffer paine.* **GRIERSON** (1921): the "echoing vowel sounds" of the lines "cannot be quite casual," but represent the "technique" of an "intensely personal religious poet" (xxvii–xxviii).

1–6 *O might . . . my hart did rent?* **CRUTTWELL** (1954): Donne bitterly reproaches himself because he cannot feel the same emotional intensity for God that he had felt for less worthy objects, his "profane mistresses" (92).

1–4 *O might . . . as I haue mournd in vaine.* **GRIERSON** (1921), quoting these lines, acknowledges that Donne was troubled by "the errors of his youth" but that he was even more torn because his "temperament" might have led him to be "an active and useful, if ambitious, civil servant," an inclination "at war with the claims of a religious life which his upbringing had taught him was incompatible with worldly ambition" (xxvii). **RICHARDS** (1929) quotes the lines, citing them as evidence of Donne's regret over "the errors of his youth" (xxvii). **MORRIS** (1953): Donne's sense of sin is the same as that expressed by Eliot in "Ash Wednesday" (ll. 32–33, 40–41) (98–99). **GRANSDEN** (1954) says that tears stand for "regret and for regretted melancholy." Paraphrases the lines as, "In mine idolatry I have lavished tears in idle regret and melancholy—a false grief for unworthy objects. Now this recollection grieves me and I see that tears wasted on sinful things were themselves a sin" (131–32). **VEITH** (1985): "Such 'holy discontent' is essential if grace depends not solely upon the sovereign will of God, as in Calvinism, but in the human act and emotion of repentance" (124).

1–2 *O might . . . I have spent;* **SMITH** (1971) suggests that the speaker "presents himself as a former Petrarchan lover" (625).

2 *spent;* **SHAWCROSS** (1967): "both 'sent forth' and 'exhausted'" (347). **CRAIK and CRAIK** (1986): "i.e. on women, as a lover, in *idolatry* (l. 5)" (277).

3 *holy discontent* **SMITH** (1971) notes that the speaker "contrasts his pious grief now with the profane discontents and vain mourning of his earlier love of women" (625).

4 *in vaine.* **SHAWCROSS** (1967): "in emptiness of result and of true feeling; in self-pity" (347).

5–14 *In my . . . the punishment and Sinne.* **HARDING** (1951) finds that here Donne repents his early sins of grief and despair (429).

5–8 *In my . . . I must suffer paine.* **SIMPSON** (1924) quotes the lines to illustrate Donne's deep sense of repentance for the "sins of the flesh committed in his youth" (116). **ANSARI** (1974) calls this "an expression of repentance which is unalloyed with any virtuosity of argumentative skill or any subtlety of wit" (145).

5–7 *In my . . . now I repent;* **MORRIS** (1953) says that the works of both Donne and Hopkins are "full of question and answer, of argument and conflict," and "the language of passion" is reflected in their irregular rhythm. Compares HS*Sighs* 5–7 and 10–13, Hopkins's "Carrion Comfort" in its entirety, especially ll. 9–10, and Hopkins's "My own heart," ll. 9–14 (58–59).

5–6 *In my . . . my hart did rent?* **MORRIS** (1953): both Donne and Hopkins use syntactical inversion to add emphasis, as here and in "Peace," ll. 3–4 (68).

5 *In my Idolatry* **GRANSDEN** (1954): the phrase, referring to Donne's profane days, is repeated in HS*What* 9 (132). **SMITH** (1971): "worship of women [so also, Carey (1990b, 455)] or of erotic love itself" (626). **PATRIDES** (1985a): "profane love" (435). **HAMBURGER** (1985): in service to women and worldly success (181).

6 *what griefes my hart did rent?* **SHAWCROSS** (1967): "both 'what griefs did burst from my heart, splitting it asunder' and 'what griefs did lease space in my heart'" (348).

6 *rent?* **GARDNER** (1952): "past participle, now obsolete, of 'rend'" [slightly amended in 1978 ed.] (76). **MARTZ** (1963): "rend, tear" (84). **SMITH** (1971): "rend" (626). [So also, Craik and Craik (1986, 277).] **BOOTY** (1990): "tear apart" (110).

7–8 *That . . . I must suffer paine.* **KORTEMME** (1933): the paradox is "a synthetic unity of contradictory opposites" ("eine synthetische Einheit kontradiktorischer Gegensätze") in which the equation, cause and effect, appears paradoxical (50).

7 *That sufferance was my Sin, now I repent;* **GRIERSON** (1912): l. 7 consists of two co-ordinate clauses, with "That" a demonstrative pronoun referring to the sins in the opening sestet; hence ll. 7–8 may be read: "Now I repent. Because I did suffer the pains of love, I must now suffer those of remorse" (2:231–32). **WILLIAMSON** (1940): "sufferance" signifies both "suffering" and "indulgence"; likewise, "suffer" means both "tolerate" and "endure." [Similarly, Patrides (1985a, 436) and Booty (1990, 110).] Thus the poet "repents that indulgence in suffering was his sin; because he tolerated pain he must endure pain. The punishment is like the sin; hence the advantage which the drunkard, thief, and lecher have over him." Grierson puts a semicolon after "sinne" which alters or disguises or even destroys the subtle relationship "between the effect and the cause" (61). **GARDNER** (1952), reviewing the various sources, places a comma after "Sin," preferring Grierson's reading of the line (1912)

to Williamson's (1940), though Grierson has a semicolon, and she identifies the contrast in the line as that "between past and present, his 'unholy' and his 'holy' discontent; '*That* suffering in the past was sin: *now* I am engaged in good work, repentance—but I still suffer'" (76). **LEWALSKI and SABOL** (1973), reading "my sinne I now repent," note that Grierson and Gardner adopt the version of some manuscripts (as here), which "contrasts the tears of the speaker's lovesick days with those of his true repentance." Explain that they adopt the 1635 reading, "which suggests that he mourns specifically for the sin of false suffering for love," an interpretation that seems reinforced by ll. 8 and 13–14 (158). **CRAIK and CRAIK** (1986), reading "my sin I now repent," gloss the line as: "My past suffering was a sinful one which I now repent" and note that in some texts the line reads as here, with the meaning, "My past suffering was a sinful one, but now I repent" (277).

7 *sufferance* **MARTZ** (1963): "suffering pain; also, permission, consent (to engage in such follies)" (84).

7 *Sin, now I repent;* **PATRIDES** (1985a) (reading "sinne I now repent") identifies the alternative "sinne, now I repent" found in some mss. and "all modern editors" and cites Williamson (1940) (436).

8 *Because I did suffer, I must suffer paine.* **GARDNER** (1952) accepts "Because" (rather than "Cause" in some sources) but elides the final syllable of "suffer" ("suffer'l") so as to create no metrical irregularity (76–77). **CRAIK and CRAIK** (1986) note that the "metre has been read in two ways: (1) by discounting the first syllable (some texts have 'Cause'); (2) by stressing *did* and *must*" (277).

8 *suffer* **MARTZ** (1963): "suffer grief (in love); also, allow, permit" (84).

9–14 *Th'Hydroptique . . . the punishment and Sinne.* **FAERBER** (1950): an example of "reaching back" ("Ausholen") by contrast, in which the ability of sinners to remember past joys adds intensity to the speaker's inability to recall anything but grief (12). [See also Holy Sonnets: Language and Style.] **MORRIS** (1953): in the sestet of "I wake and feel the fell of dark," Hopkins describes despair with the same "fusion of passion and intellect" to be found in Donne's lines (22–23).

9–12 *Th'Hydroptique . . . to poore me is allowd* **MORRIS** (1953): Donne's theme of the wicked thriving, rather than the devout poet, is repeated in Hopkins's "Thou art indeed just" (ll. 7–9) (75).

9–10 *Th'Hydroptique . . . and selfe-tickling proud,* **MORRIS** (1953): Donne's realistic vocabulary often includes words with "anti-poetic" associations (120). **GROOM** (1955): Donne duplicates the word-pattern of *The Faerie Queene* II.v.16, though the effect here is more "masculine" and rough (65).

9 *Th'Hydroptique* **RUGOFF** (1939): "an extreme degree of absorptiveness, is used

to epitomize avarice, a drunkard's thirst, or, most interesting of all, the 'immoderate desire of humane learning and languages' that characterized Donne himself" (55). **GARDNER** (1952): "The more the dropsical man drinks the more he thirsts" (77). **SHAWCROSS** (1967): "insatiably thirsty" (348). [Similarly, Smith (1971, 626) and Booty (1990, 110).] **LEWALSKI and SABOL** (1973): "The insatiable thirst of the dropsical" (158). [Similarly, Patrides (1985a, 436) and Carey (1990b, 455).] **CRAIK and CRAIK** (1986): "swollen with drink (as in dropsy)" (277).

9 *night-scowting* OED (1906–07): an early example of the adverbial use of "night" with the present participle, in the sense of "by night" or "during the night" [the only example of "night-scowting" cited by the *OED*—ed.] (sb.IV.12.a.). **GARDNER** (1952): "skulking by night" (77). [Similarly, Martz (1963, 84).] **SMITH** (1971): "(a) spying at night [so also, Craik and Craik (1986, 277)]; (b) flouting the night by working then as other people do in the day" (626). **PATRIDES** (1985a): "night-prowling" (436). [So also, Booty (1990, 110).]

10 *itchy* **GARDNER** (1952): "having an uneasy desire or hankering: the 'lecher' is forever unsatisfied" (77). **CRAIK and CRAIK** (1986): "itching to satisfy his lust" (277).

10 *selfe-tickling proud,* **GARDNER** (1952): "the proud man will owe his pleasure to nobody but himself" (77). **MARTZ** (1963): "the proud man who finds pleasure in admiring himself" (84).

10 *self-tickling* **SULLENS** (1964) cites the phrase as a word combination the *OED* does not record (206). **CRAIK and CRAIK** (1986): "self-caressing" (277).

10 *proud,* **PATRIDES** (1985a): "proud man" (436).

11 *Haue the remembrance of past ioyes for reliefe* **MELTON** (1906): in Donne's meter an insignificant word often carries the stress, here "for" (69).

12–14 *Of comming . . . the punishment and Sinne.* **MORRIS** (1953): the despair is like that in Hopkins's in "I wake and feel" (9–14) (74). **STEPHENSON** (1959) says simply that the lines remind one of Hopkins (304). **TEAGUE** (1987) finds the lines reflecting Donne's modernity, "in being a man of feeling, not of action," and he adds that "[w]here the prophetic tradition pinpoints sufferings in order to overcome them, Donne always shows an inner state about which he feels that he can do nothing" (33).

12 *to poore me* **MARTZ** (1988) comments that he likes the parenthesis around "poor" as printed in 1635, for it "gives just the right touch of conscious self-pity or stagy self-depreciation; this sinner is trying hard to repent!" (23).

13–14 *No ease; . . . the punishment and Sinne.* **KORTEMME** (1933): the lines represent "a synthetic unity of contradictory opposites" ("eine synthetische Einheit kontradiktorisher Gegensätze"), in this case one in which the equation, cause and effect, appears paradoxical (50). **GRANSDEN** (1954) paraphrases the lines as, "for a long time now, I have regretted—and still regret—my past which was itself full of false regret" (131–32).

14 *The Effect . . . punishment and Sinne.* **GROSART** (1872–73) quotes William Drummond of Hawthornden: "J. Done gave my Lord Ancrum [Sir Robert Carr] his picture, in a melancholie posture, with this word about it, *De tristitia ista libera me, Domine*" (2:290).

 *HSSouls*

COMMENTARY

General Commentary

MacDonald (1868, 121–23), both praising and criticizing the Holy Sonnets, quotes in full *HSMade*, *HSSouls*, and *HSDeath*, describing them as "very fine" (121).

The Poet/Persona

Grenander (1960, 95–100) argues that *HSSouls* is a "non-symbolical poem portraying the protagonist in a mood of troubled searching, pondering a question of vital import to himself" (97). Grenander considers the importance of the beginning of the poem to its development and draws attention to the relationship between the speaker, his father's soul, and its spirituality. He notes that the "final object" of the speaker's attention includes "both these aspects, though in a glorified form" (98). Grenander observes that "the relative lengths of the two divisions of the poem are appropriate to the exigencies of each," and that "the proportionate lengths of each of the subsections of the first division are equally appropriate" (99).

Stampfer (1970, 272–73) asserts that *HSSouls* follows *HSSighs* as a poem of solitary but secure faith. Donne sees his dead father in the company of angels, despite the church barriers between them. This "abrupt" reference to Donne's father, Stampfer believes, closes a "cluster" of sonnets. He writes that a "great process of integration is clearly under way" in the octave (272), while in the sestet Donne seems to be "strongly identifying with the Anglican position." The closing couplet is the most reserved of the four poems added in 1635 (*HSMade*, *HSLittle*, *HSSighs*, *HSSouls*), Stampfer argues, the content of the unnamed "true grief" shared only with God. Whatever the grief, however, Stampfer asserts that Donne's "mindes white truth" is not shaken (273).

Docherty (1986, 140–41) finds two competing hypotheses at the center of the sonnet: "(a) if faithful souls are glorified like angels, then they perceive truth immediately," and "(b) if, on the other hand, these souls have to interpret from duplicitous signs, how can they be assured of truth?" Donne, according to Docherty, situates these contrasting views within "the sphere of Donne's own betrayal of his father and of his father's religion" (140). Although the second hypothesis seems to be Donne's preference, Docherty notes, the emphasis here is upon "faith," and therefore the two hypotheses "collapse and resolve themselves into the advocated activity of 'faithful' interpretation." The poem itself, Docherty suggests, might imply "that Donne, despite outward appearances or signs, despite representations such as this one, has in fact retained the faith of Rome, and exists as a faithful representation of a father or God" (141).

Rollin (1986, 137), adopting a psychological reading of the Holy Sonnets, cites *HSSouls* as following a pattern "typical" of the poems, specifically in its broad mood swings. The sonnet begins, in Rollin's view, "with the speaker portraying himself as the Christian hero, triumphing over the world, the flesh, and the devil," but at line 5 "there arises the possibility of some discrepancy between the speaker's appearance of salvation and the reality of his inner insecurity," or what Rollin associates with the features of "bipolar disorders." The poem ends, according to Rollin, "ambivalently, with the same soul that was implied to be faithful in line 1 now being characterized as 'pensive' and requiring instruction."

Strier (1989, 370) finds "the same unacknowledged tensions" between Catholic self-reliance and Protestant dependency upon God in *HSSouls* that he finds elsewhere in the Holy Sonnets. Strier points to the sonnet's movement from "an assertive and positive sense of the self's status or agency" (e.g., "valiantly I hels wide mouth o'rstride"—l. 4) to a "surprising sense of the self's dependence on God for the genuineness of its own contrition."

Fish (1990, 242–45) finds in the sonnet the same desperation that he observes in *HSDue*, noting that it is, in fact, the "explicit subject" of *HSSouls*. When one begins to read the sonnet, according to Fish, "the question seems to be whether or not all faithful souls are glorified in the same way," but the words "As Angels" indicate that the "likeness" being questioned is between "all faithful souls" and "angels who are themselves glorified alike but perhaps not in the same manner (alike) as are faithful souls" (242). The question of whether or not his father's soul sees remains uncertain since, Fish points out, the construction is predicated on "If," and the fact of his father's Catholicism "reinvigorates the question that has been left behind in the turn of the second line: are faithful souls glorified alike even if they are faithful to papism." Furthermore, Fish observes, since "the question of whether his father is one who sees in that penetrating way has been left conspicuously open," the "suspicion" continues that "behind the sign of purity, behind the verbal report of spiritual valor, there is nothing," a "dreadful possibility" suggested by lines 5–8 (243). Lines 9–12 reinforce the possibility, Fish says, that "anyone can say they are faithful or sincere or 'white,'" but such claims remain "signs" and therefore continue to be "suspicious" when they "present the trappings of holiness." Fish argues that the poem, as a "structure of signs," is guilty of "all the things it itself identifies as strategies of dissembling: it has wept, mourned, dramatized devotion; and then, as if it were following its own script, the poem closes by performing the most reprehensible of these strategies; it calls on Jesus' name" at the end. In Fish's view, "there is no reason to believe that the turn to God is anything but one more instance of feigned devotion, one more *performance* of a piety for which the evidence remains circumstantial (that is, theatrical) and apparent, a matter of signs and show" (244). Thus, Fish concludes, here, as in the Elegies and Satyres, the "relentless assertion" of the "power of signs to bring their own referents into being—to counterfeit love and grief and piety— undermines the implicit claim of *this* producer of signs to be real, to be anything more than an effect of the resources he purports to control" (244–45). For Fish, the "large question" is whether or not Donne knows this, that is, "does he stand apart from the corrosive forces his speakers fail to escape?" Fish cites Rollin (1986) who answers in the affirmative, but Fish holds that Donne is "his poem's first reader, the desperate audience of its hoped-for effect," and "not only is he trying to convince readers of his ultimate sincerity—of his mind's white truth—he is trying to convince himself," which Fish claims is the case as well in HSWhat (245).

Language and Style

Ferry (1983, 234–36) reads HSSouls as another of Donne's sonnets, like HSShow, that draws from the conventions of love poetry and the poet-lover, "who borrows religious vocabulary to plead that his beloved recognize the true devotion in his heart" (234–35). Like the lover's complaint in traditional love poetry, according to Ferry, Donne's sonnet evokes "the sighs and tears inevitably used to express the lover's grief" as a vehicle for comparing this speaker's "true grief" (l. 14) (234). The speaker, in Ferry's view, "defends his sincerity because he is troubled by the separation of what is in his heart from its outward expression" (236). As a poet-lover, Ferry claims, the speaker "wrestles" throughout the poem with his "angry sense of discrepancy between what he knows with certainty of his inward state, and what imperfect representations of it appearances will make" (236).

Linville (1984a, 142–43) contends that closure in devotional poetry "depends upon epistemological, moral and theological attributes and truths which extend beyond what can be proven or demonstrated in the poem itself," and she finds HSSouls to be a clear illustration of this kind of closure. The poem, according to Linville, questions whether the soul of the speaker's father "shares the angels' mode of knowing—a mode which would enable him to perceive Donne's true spiritual state—only to remember at the end that what is important is God's knowledge" (142). Linville points out that no proof is expressed for the concluding statement despite the logical argument leading up to it (142–43). Rather, the sense of truth contained in the closure, in Linville's view, "derives from an extra-poetic truth and the persona's assent to it," along with the implication that "the persona's contrition and state of grace are real" (143).

Sloane (1985, 197–99) points out that for Donne "controversial modes of thought" were a "natural procedure," and then, when "controversy produced extremes that eventually collapsed in an a priori truth, it remained a function of rhetorical form to place the action in our imagination, and heart," to create an interiorized truth based on one's experience (197). In Sloane's view, HSSouls provides one example of "this habit of thought and motion of mind" (197). The sonnet begins confidently, but Sloane notes that as the speaker considers a second and contrasting alternative, "his initial confidence vanishes." According to Sloane, the sonnet functions as a "drama of emotion, one that shows the futility of rhetorical reasoning in facing this most urgent uncertainty," and hence, "the present emotion is the only true emotion," for "griefe" (l. 14) "displaces the initial confidence, as thoughts of God replace the initial thoughts of the dead father" (198). Sloane explains that "true griefe" is "the grief of knowing that the 'white truth' [l. 8] is not the whole truth, and that idolatry, blasphemy, and dissembling are also parts of the truth," so that "true griefe" occupies a "middle position," as a "mediator, and into that position the other distinctions collapse" (199). HSSouls appears "progressively antihumanist," Sloane suggests, "particularly in its final sorrowing dependence on the Creator of that dependence" (198).

Prosody

Esch (1955, 51) finds the sonnet Italian in form but at variance with the traditional structure. The first twelve lines, he observes, deal with the scholastic problem of the state of knowledge of the departed with the answer coming only in ll. 13–14, making for a dramatic resolution because of the delay and the brevity of the couplet. See also Holy Sonnets: Genre and Traditions.

Kiparsky (1977, 202) briefly cites the poetry of Donne, especially HSRound 8 and HSSouls 1, in his analysis of the rhythmic structure of English verse.

Themes

Grierson (1912, 2:232–33) argues that the sonnet turns on the "Scholastic doctrine of Angelic knowledge" and hence may be read: "If our minds or thoughts are known to the saints in heaven as to angels, not immediately, but by circumstances and signs (such as blushing or a quickened pulsation) which are apparent in us, how shall the sincerity of grief be known to them, since these signs are found in lovers, conjurors, and pharisees? 'Deo tantum sunt naturaliter cognitae cogitationes cordium.' 'God alone who put grief in my heart knows its sincerity.'"

Gardner (1952, 77) observes that the sonnet "rests on the distinction drawn by the Schoolmen between the mode of knowing of angels and the modes by which men know" and points to Aquinas, Summa, Iᵃ Pars, Qq. liv–lviii. She argues that angels "do not apprehend by means of images, nor do they need to reason from inferences; they know by immediate intuition." Donne, she suggests, "begins by wondering whether souls out of the body will know as angels do; but, at the close, by a characteristic twist he remembers 'Solus Deus cogitationes cordium cognoscere potest.'"

Reeves (1952, 101) paraphrases the poem: "How will the saints and angels be able to distinguish my sincere repentance from the feigned grief of hypocrites? Only God can judge of my sincerity."

Simon (1952, 122) argues that the poem is "on the whole less effective" than the other Holy Sonnets because it fails "to heighten feeling or stimulate thought." Donne, Simon contends, is still trying to intensify his confidence in God's love, but the comparison between his father and God is too "easy." As in other sonnets, she continues, he offers two hypotheses and introduces a conclusion, but "religious feeling" is lacking. As Simon puts it, "Donne can hardly expect to suggest his misery by saying that false devotion is often mistaken for true zeal"; hence, she concludes, the poem does not have the "note of true grief and sincere appeal for mercy" of the other Holy Sonnets. See also Holy Sonnets: Themes.

Peterson (1959, 514) finds in the poem the assurance that the progress of contrition, as outlined in the Anglican doctrine and followed in the previous fifteen sonnets (according to Gardner's [1952] arrangement—ed.), has been successful. The penitent, Peterson concludes, is now "in a state of grace." See also Holy Sonnets: Themes.

For Warnke (1967, 274), the "central question in this poem is whether the souls of the blessed have, like angels, intuitive knowledge, or whether, like the living, they are obliged to reason from appearances."

Lewalski and Sabol (1973, 159) summarize this sonnet as follows: "If blest souls know by immediate intuition as angels do, then my father knows of my repentance; if however they still must reason from sense impressions, then he will be misled by the similarity between my grief and zeal and other varieties of these emotions."

Lewalski (1979, 269) proposes that *HSSouls* (one of the new poems added in 1635—ed.) may have been placed after *HSRound* to demonstrate that the speaker has obtained "the true repentance" that he has been seeking. Lewalski finds that the sonnet "turns on scholastic distinctions of modes of knowing."

Sherwood (1984, 155–56) reads *HSSouls* as reflecting an ongoing concern of the Holy Sonnets, namely, "the ways in which reason is caught in the continuing tug of war between God and Satan" (155–56). Here "reason discovers," according to Sherwood, that even in times of "white truth" (l. 8), it "must bridle its wayward curiosity." Reason's "necessary task," Sherwood emphasizes, is "to discern the soul's true penitential grief as God's gift to his labouring soul" (156).

HSSouls and Other Works

Milward (1979 [1988, 96–98]) locates the primary source for *HSSouls* in St. Thomas Aquinas's *Summa* 1a 1ae (q. 57, a. 4), concerning "whether the angels know the thoughts of men's hearts" (96). Milward notes that in the second quatrain the speaker shifts to another opinion, that of St. Augustine, that "'the dispositions of men may easily be known not only when uttered in word, but even when conceived only in thought, through certain bodily signs that express the mind' (*De Divinatione* v)" (97). Milward notes other key allusions in the sestet: to "the Jewish 'Conjurers' of Ephesus" (Acts 19.13); Jesus's comparison of the Pharisees to "whited sepulchres" (Matt. 26.27–28), which may also contain "an echo" of a remark by Polonius in *Ham.* 3.1.46–49. In the closing couplet, Milward observes, the speaker turns to God and adopts Aquinas's conclusion that "only God can know the thoughts of men's hearts and the affections of their wills" (98).

Radzinowicz (1987, 52–55) includes *HSSouls* among the Holy Sonnets that reveal Donne's indebtedness to *anima mea* in the Psalms, or a dialogic relationship between speaker and soul. But Radzinowicz finds that whereas Donne uses the literary device in the other *anima mea* poems "to enable himself to write religious verse and to find the right kind of sanction for using his poetical skills and emotions in the service of religion," in *HSSouls* "the device doubts the propriety of using verse addresses to beg understanding from any audience whatsoever but God" (52). Radzinowicz adds, however, that "the habit of addressing truths to one's own soul, while anticipating the value to others of overhearing them, is both specific to the psalter and congregational in force" (55).

1–4 *If faythfull . . . hells wide mouth orestride.* **GUINEY** (1920) argues that in his devotional verse Donne was a child "of the old Church." Observes that his father "must have been a Catholic" and was a "living memory" for the poet in later years, as the lines reveal (15). **CAREY** (1981) finds reference in the opening four lines of the sonnet to Donne's thoughts "of his father's spirit watching his struggle," as Donne is about to abandon his father's Catholic religion (28). **CAREY** (1990b) notes that Donne's father died in 1576, when Donne was "barely four." Asserts that he was "almost certainly" a Roman Catholic, as was Donne's mother (455).

1–2 *If faythfull . . . As Angels,* **GROSART** (1872–73): "That is, if souls in heaven take the office of angels, or messengers and ministers of God's will" (2:291). **MARTZ** (1963): "'If faithfull souls in heaven are, like Angels, endowed with the power of intuitive knowledge' (as opposed to human modes of perception on earth)" (87).

1–2 *be alike glorified / As Angels,* **SMITH** (1971): "be blessed equally with angels, so that all have full angelic apprehension. Angels are said to apprehend by immediate intuition, whereas men reason by inference" (628). **BARAŃCZAK** (1984): angels were believed to differ from people in the ability of immediate intuitive understanding (161). **CAREY** (1990b) "Angelic knowledge was supposed to be intuitive not inferential" (455).

1 *be alike glorified* **STEIN** (1944): the phrase is an example of two unstressed followed by two stressed syllables (387).

2–4 *As Angels, . . . hells wide mouth orestride.* **PAYNE** (1926) says that images such as this "assure Donne of his place, in spite of much which is mere ingenuity" (149).

3 *even* **SHAWCROSS** (1967) glosses as "to the extent of" and cites Rev. 22.18: "For I testify unto every man that heareth the words of the prophecy of this book, If any man shall add unto these things, God shall add unto him the plagues that are written in this book" (348). Similarly, Booty (1990, 110).

4 *hells wide mouth* **LABRIOLA** (1990) cites this image in the context of his study of the use of iconographic details to interpret Donne's poetry on the Resurrection (66).

5 *discride* **GROSART** (1872–73): "'be descride to:' verb in causative sense = be made visible (by God's power) to" (2:291). **SHAWCROSS** (1967): "revealed" (348). **PATRIDES** (1985a): "known" (439). **BOOTY** (1990): "known; revealed" (110).

6–7 *By . . . not immediatlee* **RICHTER** (1902) cites the lines as an example of awkward enjambment (408–09).

6 *Circumstances, . . . Signes* **SMITH** (1971): "outward appearances, such as human reason has to go by" (628).

7 *Apparant in vs, not immediatlee* **GRIERSON** (1912): the comma after "vs" makes clear "the Scholastic doctrine of Angelic knowledge on which the sonnet turns" (2:232).

8–9 *How . . . weepe and mourne* **JONAS** (1940): Donne, having "broken the dam" of Petrarchan convention in his love poems, turned his ingenuity to the higher cause of religion (207–10).

8 *whight truthe* **SLOANE** (1985): "The truth is 'white' because it is, apparently, not the whole truth . . . . The 'white truth' is only the sort of truth perceptible to angels, a truth wherein action and resolve are matched, a kind of purity angels may see and approve" (199). **FISH** (1990): "A 'white truth' is a truth without color, without coverings, without commentary, but if colored, covered, and textualized truth are all anyone can see, then the white truth of his mind will continue to be an untried claim, and one moreover that is suspect, given the innumerable examples of those who feign commitments they do not have (ll. 9–12). Anyone can say they are faithful or sincere or 'white,' but such sayings, proffered as evidence of a truth beyond (or behind) signs, are themselves signs and never more suspicious than when they present the trappings of holiness" (243–44).

8 *tride* **MARTZ** (1963): "proven, tested" (87).

9–12 *They see . . . feigne devotion:* **TEAGUE** (1987): the lines reinforce the view that Donne's "vision of the world-as-it-is, attributed to on-looking souls, is grim" (32).

9 *Idolatrous Lovers* **SMITH** (1971): "lovers whose god is their mistress, or love itself" (628).

9 *Idolatrous* **RICHTER** (1902): in Donne's later poems there are fewer instances of a sequence of two unstressed syllables and they are frequently slurred to one syllable, as here (402). **PATRIDES** (1985a): "profane; self-regarding" (439).

10 *vile blasphemous Coniurers* **GARDNER** (1952) says that Donne used both "vile" and "vild" but finds the former better here "since 'vild' gives an awkward collocation of consonants." Notes that Donne, like Milton, "accents 'blasphemous' on the second syllable." Adds that conjurors "conjure spirits by employing words of power, such as the Sacred Name" (77). **ELLRODT** (1993): magicians call upon divine names in order to conjure up spirits (455).

10 *vile* **GROSART** (1872–73), reading "stile," says: "usually misprinted 'still'" (2:291).

10 *Coniurers* **SMITH** (1971): "magicians" (439). [So also, Patrides (1985a, 439), Booty (1990, 110), and Carey (1990b, 455).]

12–14 *Dissemblers . . . he put it in my brest.* **HAMER** (1930) comments on Donne's use of "overflow," his departure from the conventional breaks in the sonnet form, in this instance starting the sentence for the final couplet in the line before (201). **STEPHENSON** (1959): the lines put one in mind of Hopkins (304). **TEAGUE** (1987) finds that these lines show Donne's "divided view of himself," and the "solution." Believes that for Donne "suffering is inner, a 'vehement grief' not related to any other cause than itself," and cites *Lit* 89–90 ("Oh, to some/Not to be Martyrs, is a martyrdome") (33). **LINVILLE** (1984b): "the 'turn' in line cadence implies a movement of mind or soul, mirrored in the movement of enjambment" (76).

14 *griefe,* **SHAWCROSS** (1967): "suffering" (348). [So also, Booty (1990, 110).] **PATRIDES** (1985a) glosses as "pain, suffering" and notes God's "withholding of 'rest' in Herbert's *The Pulley*" (439).

 *HSSpit*

COMMENTARY

General Commentary

In an eighteenth-century Moravian Brethren's hymn-book (*A Collection of Hymns*) (1754 [1966, 19–20]), four Holy Sonnets—*HSMade*, *HSDue*, *HSSpit*, and *HSWhat*—are used, slightly altered, and combined to make up hymn number 383.

Herbold (1965, 279–81), reading *HSSpit* against the backdrop of a study of dialectics, refers to the poem as a "single dialectical syllogism" (279), holds that "the keynote of Donne's dialectics is his search for an equilibrium between balanced polarities" (280), and generalizes that Donne's dialectics in the Holy Sonnets is "chiefly between Faith and Doubt" (281).

Carey (1981, 48) interprets Donne's attempt at identification with Christ on the cross as a sign of his "hunger for pain." Even though Donne "flings himself on the nails and the sword," nothing happens, Carey says, for "he is not fit, he realizes, for those bloody joys." The poem reflects, in Carey's opinion, Donne's "spiritual paralysis, which signals God's desertion."

Grant (1983, 115–17, 166) analyzes the sonnet in the context of his view of the cross as that which "remains with us, as Thomas à Kempis says, calling for our constant self-correction and vigilant discrimination." In Grant's view, *HSSpit* "expresses the turbulence of a man coming to realise the paradox . . . of God's redemptive action, his 'strange love'" (115). Grant finds that the sonnet can be divided according to the Ignatian meditative model, "adapted by Donne for his Protestant purposes." Grant cites Lewalski's study of Protestant poetics (1979) in relation to Martz's study (1954, 1962) of what Grant describes as the "older 'Ignatian' view" (166n16). Grant divides the three quatrains according to the Ignatian process and the three faculties of the mind: "the first, evoking the scene of crucifixion," which "uses especially the power of memory," with Donne's speaker seeing himself "actually on the cross." The second quatrain, Grant observes, "brings understanding to bear on what memory has presented as phantasm," while the sestet "resolves the poem in a traditional colloquy or prayer, representing will," thus showing forth the Trinity (116). But at the end of the poem, according to Grant, the "strange love" is not available to the speaker and he is therefore "left waiting on it." For Grant, "the imagery rather presents the tension of faith that precedes contemplation" (117). Grant notes further that the poem "especially dramatises the 'I' in process of discovering, before the cross, the central importance of mortification, and its own radical impotence to overcome separation from God" (116).

Sherwood (1984, 117–18, 213) sees in the Holy Sonnets the soul's straining "toward conformity with the crucified Christ, while recognizing in its own spiritual tautness the measure of unlikeness," a dual perspective found in HSSpit. What Sherwood describes as the "self-idolatrous gesture to become Christ on the Cross" has the effect, he thinks, of aborting the "necessary humility of conformity" (117). Sherwood emphasizes Donne's "Augustinian disposition" here, that is, in "his notion of conformity [as] a matter of the will, turned away from God by sin, returned through love of the crucified Christ" (118). Sherwood notes that "Augustinian psychology, in emphasizing sin as a condition of the will, finds the basis of conformity in the turning of the will to God" (213n12).

Di Nola (1993, 113–14), stressing Donne's concept of sin as reflected in HSSpit, argues that the sincerity and straightforwardness of the poem confirm that Donne's mystical-metaphysical theology assumes the characteristics of an incarnational theology that finds the purity of its expression in a fluid, quiet and contemporary lyrical breath. Di Nola believes that Donne's theology is an authentic and genuine theology of the cross and of suffering.

Schoenfeldt (1994, 82–83) calls attention to the sonnet's distinction between "mortal monarchs [who] merely suspend sentence, [and] the speaker's heavenly monarch [who] actually condescended to suffer the punishment his subject deserves (l. 10)" (82–83). Similarly, Schoenfeldt observes, "mortal submission to God is revealed to be a kind of disguised aggression in comparison to Christ's submission to the flesh," as seen in lines 11–14. Schoenfeldt adds, therefore, that Christ, who disguises himself in "vile man's flesh" (l. 13), "descends the hierarchy not to receive an unwarranted blessing but to earn an unmerited blessing for his inferiors" (83).

The Poet/Persona

Praz (1925, 69) finds that Donne's need for expiation and purification elicits desperate appeals from the depths of his heart.

Payne (1926, 142) quotes the poem in full as a reflection of Donne's conviction that he has achieved genuine repentance rather than a fear of the consequences of sin.

Roy and Kapoor (1969, 121) remark that Donne's intense awareness of sin brings him to write HSSpit.

French (1970, 119–21) finds the "vehemence" of HSSpit "oddly disturbing" (119). He claims that the verse seems to be drawing sustenance from emotions of aggressive hostility, and the hostility, he says, plainly derives from self-hatred projected outwards onto the convenient Jewish scapegoat. The opening of the sonnet, according to French, is a "striking piece of sado-masochism" which has no grounds for justification in the poem (120). And the "disparaging implications," he suggests, of the words "supplant" and "gainfull intent," are "perhaps a way of working off against God some sense of resentment which cannot be overtly admitted" (121).

Stampfer (1970, 253–54) finds that in HSSpit Donne proceeds in the octave with "precipitous, futile action" in a premature attempt to identify with Christ (253). Stampfer remarks, furthermore, that the speaker reveals his presumption by desiring to take the place of Christ when he has neither the vision nor the grace. In the sestet, Stampfer says, the speaker seems to want to be in harmony with God, but he "hasn't the knack of participation." The speaker in this sonnet attempts to locate himself vis-à-vis the Jews as he does vis-à-vis the animal kingdom in HSWhy. But, Stampfer says, he is full of jealousies, grandiosities, and misgivings, and he chafes about having no clear sense of his place (254).

Altizer (1973, 85) argues that Donne's self-punishment occurs most often when the poet consciously attempts to identify himself with the suffering Christ, as in HSSpit. While Donne tries to envision Christ as both God and man, Altizer says, the final paradox of God's love is formulated so that, although God is brought down to human level, humanity is still cut off from the experience of his love. Donne can contemplate and identify with God, Altizer remarks, only when God appears as suffering man.

Blanch (1974, 481) writes that in HSSpit Donne "deflates his fears through contemplation of God's humility" and contrasts his sins with God's love, with "crucifixion images" emphasizing the poet's "desire to undergo the Passion of Christ." Blanch argues that the "allusion to 'vile man's flesh' [l. 13] is significant because God's adorning of this apparel suggests a distinct change in personality or nature—a lowering of self."

Brink (1977, 102) remarks that in HSSpit and HSWhy Donne "preaches to his soul in tones of hope newly vested in the Father, who holds the son in especial esteem, as though a reconciliation of natural father and son had taken place."

Low (1978, 66) remarks that halfway through HSSpit Donne moves from the purgative to the illuminative way, and that the speaker progresses from "personal fear of death and damnation to outward directed sorrow."

Smith (1984, 516–17) sees HSSpit as a poem in which the speaker in effect replaces Christ at its center "by drawing attention to his own sin and consequent suffering," a position that differs from those of St. Bernard and St. Bonaventure, for example (516). Smith alludes to Grant (1971), who contends that whereas Bonaventure's attitude is "self-effacing," Donne's is "self-aggrandizing and based on a misconception," but Smith adds that Donne ultimately must admit that "by my death can not be satisfied / My sinnes" (ll. 5–6), and therefore Donne "immediately assumes the other key role in the story, that of the crucifying Jews—except that he surpasses them in wickedness, for "I / Crucifie him daily, being now glorified" (ll. 7–8). Smith suggests that even though the notion that Christ is daily crucified by individual sins is a "commonplace," in HSSpit it "seems attributable to Donne's desire to be at the centre of his picture" (517).

Docherty (1986, 136–38) claims that in HSSpit there is "a clear and avowed impersonation of Christ on the part of the poet." But in Docherty's view, the impersonation (ll. 5–8) fails, yet this failure, "in its paradoxical turn, turns out to substantiate precisely the imitatio Christi," at least to the extent that Donne is "crossed [or crucified] figuratively, rhetorically" (136). Docherty contends that "the bearing of the cross requires the adoption of . . . the failed imitatio Christi from which the infidel can turn or deviate in order to come to a recognition of God in her or himself" (138). Docherty suggests that the poem could signify Donne's "position as 'representative' of Christ, in his role as Dean of Paul's" (137). This "manifestation" of

Donne as God—"however impure"—suggests throughout Donne's poetry, in Docherty's view, that "the Word, language, is based on a specific kind of 'flesh' or incarnation: the Word becoming flesh allows the construction of a phallogocentric ideology of language" (137).

Marotti (1986, 257) finds that in HSSpit, as in a number of other sonnets, Donne "creates the impression—at least in the octave—that the speaker is engaging as much in an act of shockingly witty self-assertion as in a gesture of repentance." He identifies "the problem of tone" in HSSpit, as the "self in performance and the self in devotion" appear here and in other Holy Sonnets "intractably, if creatively, at odds." Marotti explains Donne's attitude as reflective of "that self-conscious poetic performing in which he habitually engaged before his coterie readers."

Rollin (1986, 141–42) points to the unwavering position of the speaker in this sonnet: "for all the theatrics of its octet, [it] never wavers from the commonplaces of Christian dogma and, as a consequence, largely sustains a mood of spiritual confidence," in what Rollin describes as "an almost manic quality," evident, for example, in "the speaker's insistence that he is a more grievous sinner even than Christ's tormentors," which is a "variation on the strain of inverse narcissism" found elsewhere in the Holy Sonnets. Rollin concludes that "at the deepest levels of its psychological structure" HSSpit "provides its readers with materials not only for the evocation of unconscious narcissistic fantasies but also for sado-masochistic fantasies (torturers/victim) and for Oedipal fantasies (surrogate son supplanting surrogate father)" (142).

Strier (1989, 379) finds HSSpit "self-consciously and coherently Protestant." Donne "pretends," in Strier's view, "to invoke self-mortification in order to explicitly retreat from this pretense," since he recognizes that "taking Christ's place on the cross" would not be "efficacious." The sestet is nonetheless problematic, Strier thinks, in that it is "rather cool, quiet, and distant," but it is not "theologically or emotionally incoherent."

Coyle (1994, 141–43) contends that the opening lines "are spoken as if from the Cross, as if by Christ," to accomplish an identification of the speaker and Christ, but Coyle says that Christ was silent on the cross, so the words cannot be His. Soon, he observes, the poem signals the distance between the speaker and Christ by virtue of the speaker's consciousness of his sinfulness and the recognition that the speaker is "not Christ but an other," and then gradually the speaker is supplanted by a refocusing on Christ rather than on the speaker (142–43).

Genre and Traditions

Martz (1954, 50) analyzes the sonnet as one which includes all three steps in the Ignatian method of meditation, the "composition" (1–4), wherein "the speaker has made himself vividly present at the scene," the "analysis" (5–8), "as the understanding explores the theological significance of the scene," and the "colloquy" (9–14), a drawing forth of "affections" which suffuses "intellectual analysis with the emotions of love and wonder." See more under Holy Sonnets: Genre and Traditions. See also Grant (1983) under HSSpit: General Commentary.

Language and Style

Martz (1954, 83) observes that the senses "are strongly at work" in the poem.

Adams (1958, 111) comments that, as in this poem, Donne frequently tends to be self-consciously theatrical.

Patterson (1970, 105–08), tracing Renaissance satire to the Neoplatonic Ideas of Hermogenes, and in particular the three Ideas of Reproof (Asperity, Vehemence, and Vigor), argues that HSSpit is "obviously Vehement" (108).

In a detailed reading of the sonnet in the context of the "grammar of redemption," Asals (1979, 129) argues that HSSpit, beginning "by identifying the speaker's imperative voice with the voice of Christ as the speaker imitates Christ, modulates away from the union of speaker and Christ by the third line of the poem and exchanges the imperative for the less sanguine hortatory subjunctive ('O let mee then, his strange love still admire') by the start of the sestet of the poem." Asals adds that, "shifting mood once more," lines 11–14 are "spoken in the declarative third person and they explain what has transpired in the first ten lines of the poem." Asals concludes that, "by imitating God's language," whose mode is "command," the speaker is "restored by being transformed into Christ ('being now glorified')." And therefore, Asals states, "the poem documents its speaker's triumph over the common denominator of all sin: man's private and willful imperative impulse."

Elsky (1980, 76–79) distinguishes between religious poems that focus on the imitation of Christ and those that reenact salvation history, in which the meditator's soul is the site of the reenactment. Elsky shows that the latter approach is found primarily in Protestant rather than Roman Catholic verse (78–79). HSSpit, in Elsky's view, embodies this "subjectification of the remembrance of salvation history" such that the poet "begins by speaking in the voice of Christ from the cross," becoming "the sacrificial offering of Christ's Mystical Body" (76–77).

Yearwood (1982, 216) notes that the sonnet "is remarkable for its dramatic opening," for "only at line 7 does one realize that the speaker here is not Christ, but the persona—still trying to save himself, and still failing," in the conversion process recorded in the twelve sonnets of 1633, and creating overwhelming guilt.

Stanwood and Asals (1986, 125), in discussing Donne's use of voice and tense and their connection to "the revelation of self," locate its basis in the belief that "because Christ puts on manhood through His incarnation, we are able to put on the new man through the regeneration which He has thus made possible," and so in the human soul's ultimate destiny, "where human and divine can meet," we are able to "dress ourselves in Christ's garment." Stanwood and Asals find Donne describing "this 'rite of reclothing'" in HSSpit 11–14, "where the expectation is at once a hope and a fulfillment." In our "becoming a wholly new person," according to Stanwood and Asals, "we are also giving prophetic voice to the changes to come and which will have been made; for life is lived in the future perfect tense where whatever is looked for is accomplished."

Prosody

Esch (1955, 48–49) finds the poem somewhat at variance with the Italian structure, chiefly in the force of the final couplet. The octave, he observes, has a line of thought supported by an undercurrent of feeling in which the first two lines of each quatrain contain a demand or assertion for which the second two provide a basis. The focal point of the thought and rhythm, he continues, lies in the personal pronouns, especially in the sharp antithesis between the "I" and "hee" of line 3 and the "They" and "I" of line 7. Esch argues that the octave achieves its dynamic through the contrast between the speaker and the Jews, and in the sestet the full splendor and uniqueness of divine love is seen in the contrasting situations, one from the political (l. 10) and one from the biblical world (ll. 11–12), and in the clear sentiment of the final couplet.

Themes

Spörri-Sigel (1949, 87) observes that the tension in the poem is made visible in the sacrifice of Christ: the death of a sinless one for sinners, one whose love is such that he not only forgives but bears the punishment of the guilty, shows dramatically the difference between God and humankind. Donne's language, she notes, rises above dogma to a personal experience, a confidence that the love of God will be given him. The sonnet, she concludes, reflects the dualism between the sinless son of God and the sinful human being, but the dualism is canceled by love, with both natures manifest in the death of Christ, which overcomes the opposition between the two.

Reeves (1952, 101) calls the poem "an impassioned and self-reproachful assertion of the infinite love of God, who suffered in Christ's form the punishments due to man for his sins."

Peterson (1959, 506, 511), finding all nineteen Holy Sonnets exemplifying as a "controlling principle" the Anglican doctrine of contrition, notes that HSSpit is the first to express the second stage in the process of contrition, wherein sorrow becomes motivated not by fear, but by love of God. The octave, he says, contemplates that sorrow, the sestet divine mercy. See more under Holy Sonnets: Themes.

Roston (1974, 167–70) argues that in HSSpit Donne not only executes a "dramatic re-enactment" of the crucifixion of Christ, but also presents "a totally new picture of the event," contradicting the "normal assumptions brought to the poem" (167). He writes that in HSSpit Donne creates the "literary parallel" of the "mannerist scene" (168), arguing also that in HSSpit, as in the Songs and Sonets, Donne presents "an apparently impossible or absurdly exaggerated thesis" so as to "demonstrate by the subsequent validation of that extravagance the ultimate superiority of metaphor over literalism and hence of faith over the pragmatic" (169). Thus, according to Roston, in HSSpit the "distinction between the actual and the metaphorical crucifixion of Jesus dwindles away to irrelevancy" (170).

Lewalski (1979, 270–71) finds that HSSpit, HSWhy, and HSWhat focus upon Christ's crucifixion, but HSSpit "begins by attempting a false application" of the benefits of Christ's crucifixion, that is, by seeking "to arrogate to himself all the elements of Christ's passion, recognizing that his sins richly deserve them, but his faith reveals, of course, that the gesture is useless" (270). Nonetheless, according to Lewalski, "the sestet resolves the problem through faith in Christ's infinite mercy" (271).

Parker (1987, 75, 81), writing about the "powerful entanglement" in Donne's poetry of "the thread of death and the thread of life and love" (75), finds a particular concentration of these themes in HSSpit, citing it as a poem "which aspires to a peace beyond understanding, and which speaks to us with authority of a life which knows pain and sorrow" (81).

HSSpit and Other Works

Grant (1974, 41–42) writes that HSSpit is like St. Bonaventure's Laudisimus de Sancta Cruce in that it expresses a "desire for crucifixion" and uses "techniques of affective piety." Grant writes, however, that HSSpit, unlike St. Bonaventure's "self-effacing" hymn, is "highly personal because the poet records the experience of the individual in the act of meditation, in the act of arriving at understanding."

Hahn (1979, 69–78) calls attention to the "ingenious and audacious metaphysical reversal" of HSSpit: Donne, "as speaker, exchanges places with Christ, and impersonates the persecuted Savior on the cross." Hahn suggests that this impersonation by the speaker "dramatizes the speaker's participation in Christ's passion," and when the speaker later acknowledges "the pretentiousness of such an impersonation, it demonstrates man's sinful participation in Christ's Passion as one of the persecutors." Hahn emphasizes that Donne's reversal, and its effect, "depends also upon a long-standing devotional tradition" (69). Among those works that constitute that tradition, Hahn cites the "fervent meditations on the crucified Christ," which "originate in spiritual writings of the twelfth century, especially in the exercises of St. Bernard and St. Anselm"; "prayers, hymns and reflections encouraged the devout Christian to partake in Christ's sufferings through imaginative re-creation," for "impersonation would intensify the sinner's experience of Christ's pain and love" (70–71). These "re-creations" also were reflected in "the dramatic laments spoken by the Blessed Virgin at the Crucifixion," Hahn observes, such as that found in the twelfth century Planctus ante nescia, in which the Virgin Mary "excoriates the Jews" (71). Hahn notes that the drama in the lyrics, "especially the laments of Christ and the Virgin Mary," is incorporated into the medieval cycle plays (73). It is not surprising, according to Hahn, that, since much of the imagery "ultimately stems from earlier Latin originals that influenced the entire European tradition," Ignatius would bring them back together in his Spiritual Exercises (1548) (77). Hahn also cites Roston (1974) and his suggestion that HSSpit reveals Donne resorting to "mannerism and the metaphysical mode" (78).

Milward (1979 [1988, 67–69]) finds this seventh sonnet from 1633 (and Gardner's [1952] arrangement), which begins the second group of Holy Sonnets, moving from the "thought of the 'four last things' (without heaven) to that of the passion and death of Christ (by which the way to heaven has been opened to man)" (67). This movement and the colloquy before Christ crucified, according to Milward, follow the order of meditation in the First Week of the Ignatian Spiritual Exercises, and he also points to an "expanded form" of such a colloquy in Luis de la Puente's Meditations." In the first quatrain, Milward notes that the speaker feels that he deserves the punishment for his own sinfulness, and is the one who should be hanging on the cross. But with the movement to the sestet, Milward sees a transition "from lamentation over his sins, which have brought about the crucifixion of his Saviour, to admiration of that 'strange love' which Christ has shown for us on the cross" (69).

Here, according to Milward, the speaker "reflects on the typology of Jacob, in whom the early Christian Fathers found a figure of Christ to come" (69).

Davies (1994, 61–65) observes that the "traumatizing openings" of some Holy Sonnets grow out of the Ignatian meditative tradition, along with the "related visual analogues of Mannerist art, which portrayed the effects of the Passion or martyrs' deaths on forever-changed witnesses" (61). *HSSpit*, Davies notes, "transports us to a place we think we recognize as Calvary," with the "opening illusion" perhaps leading us to think that Christ is speaking, but readers recognize the mistake by line 3, when the "subversive 'I' of the poem detaches himself from the *imitatio Christi*," and when the speaker's indication of his "unworthiness" becomes an ironic admission of his complete incapacity to undertake the spiritual exercise of meditation" (62).

NOTES AND GLOSSES

1–8 *Spitt . . . beeing now glorifyde.* FRIEDERICH (1932) quotes the lines to illustrate the baroque tendency toward "self-flagellating exhibitionism" ("selbstquäler-ischem Exhibitionismus") and violent denunciation of self. Argues that baroque poets, like Donne, delight in tearing themselves to pieces publicly, actions which fanatics believe they owe to their "mutilated God" ("vergewaltigten Gott"), so that for them poetry becomes a form of confession (143). ESCH (1955) observes that the first two lines of each quatrain contain a demand or an assertion, the basis for which is supplied by the last two and notes that the focal point of both the thought and the rhythm of the octave lies in the personal pronouns, which achieve a dynamic in the contrast between the speaker and the Jews (48).

1–4 *Spitt . . . no iniquity hath dyde.* SPÖRRI-SIGEL (1949): Donne relates Christ's death to himself in an explosion of emotion that almost shatters the framework of language (73–74). LEVER (1974), noting the speaker's substitution of himself for the "humiliated Jesus," points to the heavy stresses on "my," "me," and "I" in the opening lines (181). SMITH (1991): the "drama brings home the enormity of the sinner's ingratitude, confronting him bodily with the irony of his obligation to Christ" (135). SMITH (1992): the speaker confronts the "irony of Christ's self-humiliation for us" and "wonders why the sinner should not suffer Christ's injuries in his own person" (90). WILCOX (1995): the "intensity" of the poetic meditation here may "push wit to the limit of its devotional usefulness," as the speaker's "initial demand challenges and maybe transgresses the boundary between self-humiliation and self-focus." Whether the intent is "to chastise or glorify, the poet puts himself center stage" in *HSSpit*, in effect "receiving the tortures of Calvary." The "potential for blasphemy," as the poet momentarily edges Christ "off the cross" and assumes "his place as redeemer of humankind," is "inherent in the activity of wit in wider terms" (11).

1–2 *Spitt . . . and crucify mee:* KORTEMME (1933): Donne displays his desire for repentance with the passion of a baroque spirit (45). MORRIS (1953): Donne expresses self-vilification, as does Hopkins in "Carrion Comfort" (l. 14) (74). **MARTZ** (1954): Donne's openings, as here, correspond to the "composition" or "proposing" step in the Ignatian method of meditation (31). [See also Holy Sonnets: Genre and Traditions.] **ESCH** (1955): the several stages of the Passion are emphasized by the rhythm and sound of the verbs (48). **LEVER** (1974) finds here the "anti-Jewish tradition of the established church," in spite of biblical references to Roman soldiers (Matt. 27.27–35, Mark 15.16–20, John 19.34) and to "women" and "people" in Luke 23.27, 48 (181). **ASALS** (1979): the opening lines are the "re-signing," i.e., the "rewriting and resigning" of the speaker to God that he "announced as his intention" in *HSDue* 1–2 (130).

1 *Spitt in my face ye Iewes, and pierce my side,* **HUNT** (1954), noting this line, says that there are times in the Holy Sonnets when Donne's opening lines have "superb dramatic power, bursting on the reader" as do those of his love poems (135). **ANONYMOUS** (1956): Donne's style here suggests Skelton's "rugged, passionate speech" (164). **COANDA** (1957): the line illustrates Donne's "morbidity" (181). [See also Holy Sonnets: Themes.] **PARINI** (1977) writes that *HSSpit* begins with a "traditional *compositio loci*" that moves to a "consideration of the meaning of Christ's sacrifice" (305).

1 *ye* **HAGSPIAN** (1957) questions Gardner's use (1952) of "yee" rather than "you," arguing that in tone the poem is a spontaneous outburst rather than a formal prayer, and that Donne seldom used "ye" in any form (501).

2 *scoffe,* **SMITH** (1971): "scoff at" (629). **CRAIK and CRAIK** (1986): "mock" (279).

3–6 *For I . . . the Iewes impietee:* **EVANS** (1982): Donne "despairs at his own helplessness" in the face of his sins, "and so his sin becomes a sin of pride" (21).

3–4 *For I . . . hath dyde.* **FAERBER** (1950): Christ's sacrificial death offends not only against reason but against our sense of justice as well (27). **SINFIELD** (1983): Donne "accepted the protestant view of his own unworthiness" and Christ's sacrifice as "witnesses to divine mercy" (11).

3 *For I haue sin'd, and sin'd: and humbly hee* **ESCH** (1955): the personal pronouns carry the theme of the octave (48).

3 *hee* **SHAWCROSS** (1967): "Jesus, who suffered all the cruelties mentioned in lines 1–2" (342). [So also, Booty (1990, 108).]

5 *satisfy'de* **GARDNER** (1952): "atoned for" (70). [So also Shaaber (1958, 103), Martz (1963, 89), Warnke (1967, 269), Smith (1971, 630), who also suggests "settled," Patrides (1985a, 441), Craik and Craik (1986, 279), and Booty (1990, 108).] **LEVER** (1974): "Requited" (181).

6 *passe* SHAABER (1958): "surpass" (103). [So also, Lever (1974, 181).]

7–8 *They . . . beeing now glorifyde.* FAERBER (1950): an example of "reaching back" ("Ausholen") by comparison, in which the killing in the first line intensifies the crucifying in the second (12). [See further under Holy Sonnets: Language and Style.] UL-HASAN (1958): Donne's struggle with sin produced in him a guilt complex, which caused him to feel "like an unholy murderer" (43). ROSTON (1990): Donne has here moved away from his initial identification with Christ, associating himself "reluctantly" with "the Judas figure as being more appropriate to the speaker's self," his "own grave impiety in moments of weakened faith" causing "greater anguish even than the sin of the original murderers" (384).

7 *They killd once an inglorious, but I* MELTON (1906): Donne's meter often stresses an insignificant word, here "an" (67). UL-HASAN (1958): the picture of Christ crucified haunted Donne's mind (35).

7 *inglorious,* SMITH (1971): "(a) an unknown wretched malefactor; (b) not yet ascended in glory" (630). CRAIK and CRAIK (1986): "of low rank; in antithesis to *glorified* (l. 8), ascended into heaven (see John 7:39)" (279).

8 *Crucify him dayly,* GARDNER (1952): cf. Heb. 6.6 ("They crucify to themselves the Son of God afresh, and put him to an open shame") (70). [So also, Smith (1971, 630), who adds that "every sin, knowingly indulged in, is a fresh crucifixion of Christ," Lewalski and Sabol (1973, 154), Craik and Craik (1986, 279), who explain, "by sinning," and Carey (1990b, 455).]

8 *beeing now glorifyde.* SMITH (1971): "now he is in his state of glory" (630). LEVER (1974): a reference to Christ, "whose divinity was made manifest by his church" (181).

8 *beeing* SHAABER (1958): "i.e., he being" (103).

9–14 *Oh let . . . to suffer wo.* PARINI (1977): the sestet is a "colloquy of adoration" (305). MILWARD and ISHII (1976): whereas Jacob used deceit for selfish gain, Christ came in human disguise to save humankind. What Donne especially admires is that *admirabile commercium* or "wonderful exchange" whereby the Creator of the human race has taken its humanity and given it his godhead in return. Donne may have had in mind a sermon of St. Augustine that speaks to this paradox (223–34).

9 *Oh let me then his strange love still admyre:* FAERBER (1950) argues that one of the functions of Donne's paradoxes is "self-stimulation" ("Selbststimulierung"). Claims that even when he keeps hammering at a contradiction to intensify his religious feeling, he grasps it and uses it as a stimulant for his spirit in order to transcend the assurance of intellect into the certainty of faith (33).

9 *admyre:* **SHAABER** (1958): "wonder at" (103). [So also, Smith (1971, 630) and Craik and Craik (1986, 279).] **PATRIDES** (1985a): "marvel at; gaze with pleasure" (441).

10 *Kings pardon, but he bore our punishment.* **SMITH** (1971): "at best kings pardon our crimes whereas Christ, the king of kings, bore the punishment of our sins for us" (630).

10 *Kings pardon,* **SHAWCROSS** (1967): "Kings show a kind of love by pardoning us for our sins" (342). **MAROTTI** (1994a) suggests that behind the image may be Donne's "wish that James would forgive him his past indiscretions and accept him into royal service" (79).

11–14 *And Iacob . . . weake inough to suffer wo.* **FAERBER** (1950): an example of "reaching back" ("Ausholen") by comparison, in which the subject and form of the first two lines intensify the experience of the final two (11). [See also Holy Sonnets: Language and Style.] **LABRIOLA** (1990) finds that these lines "can be explicated chiefly by reference to the iconography of the Annunciation," developing "an ironic contrast between Christ and Jacob." Extends his analysis by showing that "the etymology of Jacob's name (to deceive or supplant) highlights self-interest," for by wearing goatskins "to seem hirsute," he "gulls his blind father, Isaac, into conferring on him the blessing and the birthright intended to Esau." But observes that Christ, "against his self-interest, is attired in flesh to advance the cause of fallen humanity" (64). **DI NOLA** (1993): it is Christ's strange love that led him to become a man, making Himself weak enough to suffer, and thus human redemption is found in this strange love of God (114).

11–12 *And Iacob . . . with gainful intent:* **GROSART** (1872–73) points to Gen. 25 (2:291). **LEVER** (1974): dependent on a "[t]raditional exegesis of the Old Testament in terms of the New," Jacob's action is taken to "refigure Christ's assumption of human form" (181). **VICARI** (1989) finds here an "echo" of a commonplace emblem that was often applied to Christ, characteristic of the love of paradox and contradiction during the period (174).

11 *And Iacob . . . harsh attyre* **GARDNER** (1952) cites the account in Gen. 27.36 of Jacob covering his neck and hands with the skin of goats so as to receive his father's blessing (70). [Similarly, Shaaber (1958, 103), Martz (1963, 89), Shawcross (1967, 342), who adds that in Hebrew "Jacob" means "one who supplants," Warnke (1967, 269), Smith (1971, 630), Lewalski and Sabol (1973, 154), Cain (1981, 312), Barańczak (1984, 162), Patrides (1985a, 441), Booty (1990, 108), Carey (1990b, 455), and Ellrodt (1993, 456).] **ARCHER** (1977): "Christ is contrasted with one of the Old Testament types" (185).

11 *clothd* **MELTON** (1906): Donne on occasion would repeat a word in a stressed and an unstressed syllable, as here and in l. 13 (164).

11 *vile harsh attyre* **LEVER** (1974): according to the biblical account Jacob's garb is "[g]oodly raiment," but it is changed here "to suit the identification of Jacob with Christ" (181).

12 *supplant* **GARDNER** (1952) points to Esau's comment after Jacob's deception in Gen. 27.36 ("Is he not rightly named Jacob? for he hath supplanted me these two times") and notes the Vulgate ("supplantavit") and Geneva ("hath deceived") versions (70).

12 *gainfull* **SULLENS** (1964) says that Donne's use of the word in this sense is earlier than the first such use recorded in the *OED* (217).

13–14 *God cloth'd himselfe . . . suffer wo.* **SMITH** (1971): "whereas Jacob put on a vile harsh garb wholly for his own gain, Christ put on our vile flesh so as to be weak enough to suffer pain for us" (630).

 *HSVex*

COMMENTARY

General Commentary

An anonymous author in *Ath* (1899, 645–46) cites and prints *HSVex* as "a not uncharacteristic example of Donne's love for tearing an analogy to shreds" (646).

Herbold (1965, 280–81) defines dialectics as "a critical example of hypotheses and principles, an examination by discussion, at least by tacit discussion," and he holds that "the keynote of Donne's dialectics is his search for an equilibrium between balanced polarities" (280). Citing *HSVex*, Herbold says that Donne "accepted the dialectician's conviction" that "contraries meet in one" (l. 1), and he notes that Donne's dialectics in the Holy Sonnets is "chiefly between Faith and Doubt" (281).

Nye (1972, 356) calls *HSVex* the "most moving" of the Holy Sonnets and a "mercilessly scrupulous" poem.

Roston (1974, 91) argues that in *HSVex* Donne uses the same paradox of "consistent inconsistency" that he had used in *WomCon*, but he has applied it differently. He writes that instead of displaying his "mastery of labyrinthine reasoning," the paradox in *HSVex* "expresses the weary admission of the complexity of human fickleness and the deviousness of satanic temptation."

Aers and Kress (1981, 66) point to the imaging of the self "as an unpredictable succession of emotions which replace one another at random, giving no sense of an organic identity immersed in a temporal process" and being absent of a specific religious or ideological orientation. They contend that the first line of *HSVex* evokes this process as the speaker imagines himself as "a *place* where a-historical 'contraryes' suddenly happen to appear and 'meet,'" but nowhere in the poem does Donne assume "an ideologically coherent diagnosis of his states." Donne acknowledges, they observe, that although these emotions traditionally have been regarded positively (e.g., fear of God), they are also "experienced as quite arbitrary 'fitts,' as the product of 'a fantastique Ague.'"

Sherwood (1984, 103) argues that "in his middle years," Donne shows a "growing religious conviction" that "suffering and affliction rightly understood are the means to embrace God," such as we find in *HSVex*, where "'humorous' contrition . . . reveals that later joy was hard won."

Veith (1985, 123) claims that, for Donne, "an individual is assured of salvation only 'as long as he continues in faith' and repents of his sins, only as long as his will is aligned with God's." But the problem, Veith notes, is that Donne views himself as being "inconstant" to God much as he was "to his mistresses."

Rossi (1987, 71–72) comments that from the poem emerges the portrait of a man tormented, divided between love of God and a fascination with material and worldly things and between a conviction of not being worthy of pardon and a hope of winning the favor of a compassionate divinity.

Sessions (1987, 16–17) frames his analysis of *HSVex* in terms of the way it dramatizes what Sessions sees elsewhere in religious lyrics of the period, namely, "dangerous voices conscious of abandonment, even of suicide if the dialectic breaks down, as with Dido" (16). Sessions finds that readers of poems such as *HSVex* "encounter, at its deepest and simplest, a text whose dialectic represents the embrace of Eros but not at the price of truth," for "the text includes the look into the abyss of Thanatos opening at every moment of human existence" (16). According to Sessions, "contingency is everywhere" (17). The poem, Sessions claims, "opens with "the agony of division of self—'Oh, to vex me contraryes meete in one'—and ends in a moral stance and resolution, a unity of action that springs from honest self-recognition: 'Those are my best dayes, when I shake with feare'" (16). This "ongoing dialectic between lover and beloved," always "threatened by abandonment," produces, in Sessions's view, a "threatening dialectic of existence" (16–17).

Gill (1990, 107) finds *HSVex* to be different from other Holy Sonnets in that there is "no attempt to imagine the Last Judgment or the figure of Death or the crucified Christ"; rather, Donne is "entirely preoccupied with the puzzling and morally distressing changes in his own spiritual state." Gill sees two problems raised by the poem's focus on the self: "whether the narrowness of subject matter makes the sonnet more or less impressive than the others" and "whether the concern for the self and the concern for the poem as a poem" are in conflict with the "religious anguish of a man who is appalled at his own spiritual instability." Gill notes that "contraries" meeting in "one" is a "good description of the tensions of the poem itself" and points to "the rapid changes of tone, pace and cadence" of *HSVex*.

Guibbory (1993, 124) notes first that the sonnet is "undatable" and says that "the "contraryes" that "meete" in the speaker "define his identity," but she argues that they "create a sense not of wholeness but of conflict and dis-ease." Guibbory finds it appropriate that Donne expresses his conflicted state by paradox, "since paradox is self-contradictory, asserting that mutually contradictory statements are simultaneously true."

Low (1993, 69) states that the view of God in *HSVex* is that of one who "bears the 'rod' or scepter of authority [l. 11], the sign of his ability to punish his subjects." Low sees the "anxious speaker" as "assiduously" courting God, "In prayers, and flattering speaches [l. 10]."

Schoenfeldt (1994, 81–82) finds that despite Donne's belief in God's immanence, he is simultaneously conscious of God being "far more distant than even the most exalted monarch" (81). It is only in the sonnet's closing, Schoenfeldt points out, that Donne's speaker "explicitly hierarchize[s] the differences between courting [God] and true fear," that is, "an aggressive act of courtly submission is supplanted by a superficially similar but intrinsically different acknowledgment of God's terrifying power" (82).

Date and Circumstances

Novarr (1980, 120–21) considers the sonnet in light of the debate about its dating and placement in the Westmoreland manuscript, and in particular its concern with "inconstancy in vows, in devotion, and in contrition, a concern not limited to a man of the cloth." But if the poem is dated after 1617, Novarr notes, it is "closely related" to Donne's subject in *Tilman*: "the nature of Tilman's change, or lack of it, after he had committed himself to orders" (120). Novarr points out that the paradox at the center of the sonnet is "the old idea of immutable-in-mutability," and thus Donne's sense that he "has not fundamentally changed" has heightened importance "if we think that he wrote this sonnet after his ordination" (120–21). Moreover, Novarr adds, "the vexation he expresses at the contraries he finds in himself perhaps lends credence to a late date for the sonnet" (121).

The Poet/Persona

Aronstein (1920, 83) finds the poem an expression of the speaker's humility.

Simpson (1924, 113–14) cites the poem as a reflection of "the many agonies of heart and soul" Donne went through in his conversion from his early life. She observes that purgation caused the "keenest suffering" for one like Donne with his "strong passions and vivid memories of his earlier sins." She claims that the Holy Sonnets "give a vivid picture of his agony of mind," a phrase she later revised (1948, 83) to say less sweepingly only that the sonnet "describes the fluctuations of his spiritual life." Simpson then quotes HSMade and HSVex in full. In the second edition (1948) she omits HSMade.

Payne (1926, 143–44) quotes the poem in full to illustrate that Donne had not yet achieved stability in his faith, the permanent "ecstatic adoration" that he desired.

White (1936, 123–24) quotes HSVex in full as an example of Donne's "extraordinary capacity for self-observation," commenting that "the parting of the text, so dear to the heart of the seventeenth-century preacher, may be found at length" in the poem, "so amazing in its candor when it is recalled that the main burden of his self-censure falls not upon his unconverted past but upon his treacherous present."

Faerber (1950, 21) cites the poem to illustrate Donne's inability to achieve the certitude of faith, the central element of which is a torturous struggle, expressed in transient passages of devout fits and only sporadic instances of a more relaxed attitude.

Leishman (1951, 261–62), quoting the whole of HSVex, says that Donne, "watching himself with a kind of sad humour as he plays his difficult part" in the poem, recognizes the "continuity between Jack Donne and Dr. Donne."

Umbach (1951, 14–15) quotes the poem in full as an expression of Donne's "feeling of personal insufficiency." Umbach compares the sentiment to that expressed in Donne's letter to Sir Henry Goodyer written in September 1608 (*Letters*, p. 49), in which he complains that even God's gifts of thirst for the next life and prayer in this "are often envenomed, and putrified, and stray into corrupt disease."

Umbach (1954, 17) finds that the poem expresses Donne's agitation about the tension between flesh and spirit.

Stein (1962, 41) claims that the sonnet "confirms Donne's conviction that the contraries are not part of his individual bad luck or just punishment," but are rather a "settled part of God's law for man, which it is man's good luck to endure." In *HSVex*, Stein notes the presence of "witty inversions" and "explicit or implicit oppositions" that put the speaker, "as religious man," in a position of "struggling to reconcile his immediate experience with his detached and abstract understanding of that experience," and finding himself "directly trusting the wisdom potential in the extreme and preferring it above the established wisdom of mean ways."

Martz (1969b, 26–29) writes that Donne's "own deep knowledge of himself, gained by relentless self-scrutiny," is evident in the "analysis of his varied moods" in *HSVex*, "so personal and private that it exists in only one manuscript and remained unpublished until the year 1899" (26–27). Martz says that the sonnet shows us "the image of a man who is attempting to hold within his consciousness an almost unbearable range of interests," and he goes on to suggest that Donne, both in his life and in his writings, "represents every aspect of the European Renaissance" (29).

Stampfer (1970, 277) asserts that *HSVex* defines Donne's temperament in religious experience as a bundle of unpredictable contraries. The "thrust" of the poem, Stampfer writes, is a "flamboyant elaboration of the metaphysical shudder in his unpredictable presence."

Thomas (1972, 349–50) argues that for all of Donne's inability to make profession and practice one, he had, "in rare degree," the virtue of honesty. It "shines through all his work," Thomas states, "not least in his self-portrait" in *HSVex* (349). The first line of the poem, Thomas argues, provides the key to Donne's basic thought. Because he recognized his "erring nature," Thomas says, Donne acknowledged that "contraries met in one to 'vex' him." At the same time, Thomas notes, his "very plight" enabled him to see where to find the "harmony his deepest self desired" (350).

Parfitt (1972, 383) states that *HSVex* shows Donne aware of his changefulness and of himself as playing or trying out roles.

Waswo (1972, 131–32) remarks that Donne "presumably" doubted his salvation much of the time, as suggested in the spiritual vacillations of *HSVex* (131). However, he continues, it is at least possible that what some have identified as Donne's "neurotic, obsessive-compulsive concern for his own salvation" is in fact a "limitation of his style—a defect not in his character but in his literary equipment and its use" (132).

Blanch (1974, 483–84) argues that *HSVex* is significant because Donne's "attitude toward fear is disclosed for the first time" and because the poem "seems to explicate the entire sequence." He suggests that "begott" (l. 2) is an "oblique allusion to the Trinity" (483) and argues that Donne's "depiction of his shifting devotional attitudes" may lie behind the "lack of thematic order and the disjointed imagery" in the Holy Sonnets. He adds that in *HSVex* Donne "experiences a return of fear through his awareness of doubt" and says that what seems to be "a lack of artistic balance in thematic order" may in fact be attributable to Donne's "realistic depiction of his attempts to find God and spiritual peace." The "varied imagery," Blanch asserts, "reflects Donne's effort to draw upon every source available to him in his search for God's 'spouse'" (484). Donne, he concludes, welcomed fear.

Cathcart (1975, 158) says that *HSVex* is illustrative of Donne the casuist who writes of a world where "opposites attract and give each other value," but rational understanding gives way to inconstancy.

McCanles (1975, 70–71) finds that in *HSVex* the speaker of the poem is caught between the choices of flattering God or fearing Him. He states that the "oscillating paradoxes" of *HSVex* recount the "manic-depressive cycle of a soul too eager for resolution and certainty." Because the speaker "tries too hard to attain resolution" (70), McCanles notes, he fails to attain it. McCanles argues that because there is no resolution in *HSVex*, "the reader can only assent to the poem's dialectic" (71).

Rollin (1986, 145) calls attention to the fact that this sonnet, the last in Donne's sequence, may provide the Holy Sonnets with, "if not exactly a happy ending, at least an ending that is ego-reinforcing and thus therapeutic." According to Rollin, Donne's speaker may here come "closest to an accurate diagnosis of his own religious melancholy, his mind diseased, and thus he becomes more capable of ministering unto himself." The speaker "acknowledges his mood swings" and appears "to recognize that his condition is a chronic one." The speaker also seems to be aware, Rollin adds, "that the remedy may lie in his understanding that, though his 'fitts come and go away,' they are 'devout fitts,' due to an 'excess' rather than a 'defect of piety.'"

McNees (1992, 64) says that *HSVex* "precisely" captures the dilemma of the speaker who "lacks the faith in himself" to make the necessary commitment to the Anglican Confession. McNees thinks that Donne's renunciation of Roman Catholicism in favor of Anglicanism may have made him "wary of overpromising himself" and that, as well, his "struggle toward active repentance involves a personal battle with the speaker's individual will."

Gorbunov (1993, 125) finds *HSVex* consistent with the whole sonnet cycle in its atmosphere of fear and terror, corresponding to the contradictory nature of the poet's character, where inconstancy became a deeply rooted habit of mind. In Gorbunov's view, the lyrical hero is as separate from God as he was in the sonnets that came before. Separated from God by an abyss, Gorbunov concludes, the speaker finds that loneliness strengthens his faith, but amplifies his fear.

Young (1994, 173) finds that even in a late sonnet like *HSVex* Donne "manifests a vivid awareness of the inconsistency and insubstantiality, not only of the poetic persona, but also of the role of churchman and Christian" (ll. 1–4). Donne's "efforts at devotion," according to Young, "are no more than symptoms of the disease of sin, sporadic 'devout fitts' of a 'fantastique Ague.'"

Gabrieli (1995, 256) says that the sonnet reveals the feverish alternating and jousting of contradictory attitudes and movements in Donne's soul, which point to the opposing impulses and urges he possessed.

Structure

Esch (1955, 51) observes that *HSVex*, though Italian in form, varies from the customary structure. He contends that the theme of tension in the spiritual life, the struggle between the fallen and reborn "I," continues to line 11 and the conclusion comes only in lines 12–14, thereby enhancing the shock effect through the reduction in the final section. See more under Holy Sonnets: Genre and Traditions.

Miles (1972, 35–39) claims that an artist carries cognitive meanings into sensory meanings by the processes of patterning, processes that suggest not only surface design, but the possibilities of design from depth. Miles asserts that to look at such poems as Donne's sonnets "with a sense of the articulatable parts of language—not merely of simple sound at one extreme and sonnet-tradition on the other, but also of the central working grammar in its relation to the poem's logic and rhetoric," is to see, hear, and "to feel more of the poem's entity" (38). In HSVex, she says, surface design is a "steady tool": "line-ends enforced by rhymes; the rhymes parallel in meaning as in *would not, soone forgott, cold and hott*; a structure shifted between octave and sestet" (39). There are many kinds of parallels in the sonnet, she remarks; they are "persistently, structurally contrastive, and they are not resolved" (39). For Donne, Miles says, "a tight design is part of the air he breathes, the art he works in" (39).

Bellette (1975, 331) argues that HSVex "represents the most complete upsetting of the sonnet form" among the Holy Sonnets, writing that it conveys "a fruitless opposition of forces reflected in a highly antithetical structure and grammar, an opposition which serves not to resolve the sonnet, but only to 'vex' it." He states that the poem lacks an "initial framework" and is "wholly taken up with unguided and purposeless activity."

Gill (1990, 108) observes that unlike some of the other Holy Sonnets there is not in HSVex a "sharp break between the octave and the sestet," and he wonders if this feature makes HSVex "an impressively concentrated poem" or if, on the other hand, a reader misses "the drama of a change from one mood to another."

Language and Style

Williamson (1961, 35) says that HSVex includes a "tissue of paradoxes" that culminate in "an analogy with ague," reaching a "climax in Christian fear and paradox" at the end of the poem.

Evans (1982, 8, 11) claims that "nothing troubled Donne so persistently as the problem of sin and the problem of evil which lies behind it" (8). For Donne, in Evans's view, "evil is full of chance and unpredictability, and in its very contrariness it begets paradoxes," such as we find in the opening lines of HSVex (11).

Linville (1984b, 67) calls attention to Donne's "effective use in general of long Latinate words for their capacity to lighten stress" in a sonnet that expresses Donne's "dejected lament on his ephemeral devotion."

Rieke (1984, 4–6) discusses Donne's purposeful use of literary riddles (or "enigmas") and paradoxes, citing Donne's two most direct references to riddles in LovInf and HSVex, both of which include "complex paradoxes," suggesting that "paradox and riddling belong together" (6). In HSVex, Rieke observes, the speaker, "riddlingly distempered" (l. 7), alludes to his "rapid fluctuations between paradoxical extremes of 'cold and hot, / As praying, as mute, as infinite, as none' [ll. 7–8]" (6).

Sloane (1985, 292n4) notes that the view that "contraries can meet in one [l. 1] is a vivid expression of a rhetorical principle, however vexatious, which pervades Donne's mode of argumentation," offering a "view of epistemology that changes little in his lifetime" (cf. Sat3 98–99).

Mazzaro (1987, 245–46) points to HSVex as an example of the "density" of Donne's "verbal interplay," or the abandonment of "narrative" as a strategy to make sonnets "part of a false or fictive realm, words reacting with other words and being thrown back upon themselves" so as to "condense into the self-contained, individually characteristic" (245). According to Mazzaro, the end toward which the language of the poem has been building is the "fantastique Ague" of line 13 rather than "life." Mazzaro holds that critics have led readers to accept the "excessiveness or oddity of Donne's responses as tests of his individuality and sincerity," judging such responses "as 'probably right' in such a context," while forgetting "that it is Donne who is establishing the context," and that instead of challenging rhetorical form, the sonnet "presents a further realization of that form" (246).

Fish (1990, 247–51) contends that the "realization of radical instability" is "given full expression" in HSVex, a poem that "desires to face the specter down, but in the end is overwhelmed by it" (247–48). Fish holds that the problem is stated succinctly in the first line, that is, "if contraries meet in one, then one is not one—an entity that survives the passing of time—but two or many." According to Fish, the speaker's retrospective glance over his past reveals "only a succession of poses—contrition, devotion, fear—no one of which is sufficiently sustained to serve as the center he would like to be able to claim" (cf. ll. 9–10). Fish notes that Donne attempts a resolution in the final couplet ("my life may be characterized by changeful humors, but among those humors one speaks the genuine me") (248), but he finds little evidence within the poem to confirm the resolution; indeed, "one cannot rule out a reading in which the best days are the days when he best simulates the appropriate emotion." Fish cites Ferry (1983) but disagrees with Ferry's conclusion: Ferry assumes that the "'inward experience' or 'real self' is in fact there and the deficiency lies with the medium [i.e., language] that cannot faithfully translate it," but Fish argues not that language is weak but that "it is so strong that it does everything, exercising its power to such an extent that nothing, including the agent of that exercise, is left outside its sphere." For Fish this is not so much Donne's "insight" as the "problematic in which he remains caught even when he (or especially when he) is able to name it," as is suggested in one of Donne's sermons (Sermons, 2:282–83) (249). Fish holds that "the lesson of masculine persuasive force is that it can only be deployed at the cost of everything it purports to incarnate—domination, independence, assertion, masculinity itself," and thus Donne is "always folded back into the dilemmas he articulates, and indeed it is the very articulation of those dilemmas—the supposed bringing of them to self-consciousness—that gives them renewed and devouring life" (250–51).

Ellrodt (1993, 24–25) observes that for Donne the serious paradox is the intellectual "translation" ("traduction") of a fully lived, individual, unique experience, displaying itself, as it does in LovInf and HSVex, as an enigma.

Sacred and Profane

Leishman (1934, 89) finds Donne's religious poetry "intensely personal" in that he recognizes "with a kind of sad humour" the continuity between his early and later years, declaring in HSVex that he is "as 'humorous' in his repentance as formerly in his profane love."

Nye (1972, 356) says that in HSVex Donne "defines the temper of his sacred love"

and finds in that love the "same faults" that had "plagued his perception of the pro-
fane."

Ferry (1983, 242) notes that this sonnet, like other sonnets of "complaint" by
Donne, presents a "catalogue of 'contraryes,'" which have been "arranged as a com-
parison between 'prophane love' in the speaker's past and his present 'devout' state,
a comparison which again actually makes them one." Even though "the speaker now
courts God, rather than a mistress or many mistresses, his inward state is identical
with that of his past." Ferry observes, however, that the speaker does not seem to be
"fully satisfied" with the comparison, when he "makes an exception to it" in the
closing lines: "save that here/Those are my best dayes, when I shake with feare."
Ferry interprets these lines as indicating that "physical signs are not adequate repre-
sentations of inward states: 'true feare' cannot be distinguished by outward expres-
sion, such as the speaker has used in his complaint." The closing couplet, in Ferry's
view, "dismantles its own metaphor," thereby challenging the "comparison of an ague
to devout fits by pointing to the limits of its application."

Martz (1985, 10) contends that no English poet "lived more frequently or more
painfully in [the] mode of the conditional *if*," citing HSVex as a poem in which
the "oscillations" of Donne's being are "fully recognized." Whereas in his profane
love, he "shook with fear that his mistress was unfaithful to him or that she did
not love him," now, Martz states, after having taken religious vows, Donne's best days
are those that follow the words of Ps. 2.11 ("Serve the Lord with fear: and rejoice
with trembling") and Ps. 111.10 ("The fear of the Lord is the beginning of wisdom").

Ellrodt (1993, 456) comments that HSVex transposes onto the plan of divine love
the sensations and conditions of the soul inconsistent with the Petrarchan lover,
and thus confers a truthfulness onto these paradoxes.

Themes

Wiley (1950, 167–68) observes that Donne uses paradox to express the inadequacy
of human perception, in HSVex complaining of his own inconstant devotion.

Reeves (1952, 103) paraphrases the poem: "Donne frankly confesses that he is
inconstant in his devotion to God as he had been as a young man in love. His wa-
vering devotion is like a fever; except that his best (*i.e.*, most religious) moments
are those when he trembles most with the fear of God."

Peterson (1959, 516–17) argues that the poem rounds out the sequence of the
Holy Sonnets devoted to the Anglican experience of contrition. As such, he ex-
plains, it warns of excessive "scrupulosity" in spiritual life, in this case Donne's con-
cern about the inconstancy of his devotion brought about by his confusion regarding
"a deity who is at once absolutely just and infinitely merciful," a conflict which cre-
ates in the poet a "spiritual dryness." See more under Holy Sonnets: Themes.

Cruttwell (1966, 28–29) says that the theme of HSVex is "rage and disgust" at
what the speaker sees as the "inadequacy of his own devoutness" (28), an idea also
found in HSBatter. For some, Cruttwell acknowledges, both poems would be "too
obviously egoistic" for religious verse.

Lewalski (1979, 274) comments that HSVex "could relate to virtually any stage
of the Christian saga of regeneration," but she finds that it is "a fitting summary of

the vacillations and vicissitudes of the speaker's spiritual life." The speaker's variations in mood accord with the varying moods of the Holy Sonnets generally, and are, in Lewalski's view, a "personal version of that perpetual internal warfare Paul describes, between the old man and the new, the body and the spirit."

Milward (1979 [1988, 99, 109–10]), noting that HSVex appeared in neither 1633 nor 1635 but in NY3, calls it both the "last" of the Holy Sonnets and the "least holy among them, being in the form less of a meditation (looking to God in prayer) than of a confession (centred on himself)." The sonnet begins, Milward explains, with the speaker professing "to be vexed" by the fact that in him "contraryes meete in one," or more specifically, that "he finds that his past 'Inconstancy' has developed into 'A constant habit'" (109). The sestet, however, as Milward further explains, gives "examples of his changes in devotion." For "yesterday," in Milward's words, "he was afraid to 'view heaven' in his penitential sonnets, based on the *First Week* of the *Spiritual Exercises*" [presumably, HSMade, HSLittle, HSSighs, HSSouls—ed.], but "today, he turns 'in prayers, and flattering speaches' from fear to the love of God." But, Milward emphasizes, the speaker "expects a time when he will rely no longer on fixed meditations but 'quake with true feare' of God's punishments as his death approaches." These last sentiments, according to Milward, seem to capture Donne's "religious spirit" in that "for all his emphasis on love and mercy, he is most deeply obsessed by the fear of past sins and coming death" (110).

Shaw (1981, 63) observes that if we accept the late date of the sonnet given by Gardner (1952), HSVex confirms that Donne still was beset by "feares" even after he had "entered the Church."

Raspa (1983, 17) claims that HSVex underscores a theme evident elsewhere in Donne's poetry, namely, that "nothing else, not even the Creator, shared in one nature man's two sets of faculties," which "enabled man to taste separately and yet simultaneously temporal emotions and their eternal counterparts," and only humankind "possessed this powerful privilege." Donne speaks in the sonnet of the "exclusive character" of humankind "in terms of the 'contraryes' of mythic emotive force and personal experience meeting 'in one' and not of body and soul (ll. 1–3)."

Docherty (1986, 141–42) describes HSVex, as well as HSMade, as one of Donne's "crossing" poems, one in which a renewal or rebirth occurs. The sonnet is "seemingly about the paradox that fidelity to God depends upon betrayal or infidelity, promiscuity or ecclesia" (141). But as the last three lines of the sonnet state, Docherty notes, the "'devout fitts,' though in appearance like a disease, turn out to be therapeutic: disease and instability are a condition of health, of Donne's 'best dayes.'" Docherty concludes that "the paradox arises because the genuinely felt faith is one which demands constant renewal and restatement or reiteration," that is, "it has always to be on the point of beginning" (142).

HSVex and Other Works

Hemmerich (1965, 18–23) compares Gryphius and Donne and offers brief quotations from HSVex and HSMade to illustrate that fear and love are the object of both poets. In Donne, Hemmerich says, contrition always provokes passion.

D'Amico (1979, 24), in his comparison of the Petrarchan sonnet form to the sonnets of Donne, points out that Donne, "like Sidney, builds a final couplet into the Petrarchan sestet," thus "befitting a condition ["Ague"] which is by definition cold and hot." D'Amico adds that in Donne the "leaps of association are more acrobatic, as we move from the familiar oxymoron of heat and cold, to the high and low temperatures of a distemper and, finally, to the shaking with fear that is a healthful spiritual sign."

Ferry (1983, 220, 241) cites Cruttwell (1966), who finds an "introspectiveness" in both HSVex and Shakespeare's Sonnet 62, reinforcing Ferry's view that Donne's sonnets are part of a longer sonnet tradition that includes Sidney and Shakespeare (220). Ferry contends that HSVex presents itself as being "built on the model of a catalogue of 'contraryes' which, with sighs and tears," has been viewed as "one of the commonest modes in which sixteenth-century lovers complain." Ferry states that the speaker descends "from Troilus and from Petrarch's poet-lover," resembling particularly Petrarch's Sonnet 134 (*Pace non trovo*), and "also recalling complaints in the native tradition, of which Gascoigne's 'The passion of a Lover' contains a representative stanza" (241).

Raspa (1983, 139), within a larger comparison of Southwell and Donne, observes that the octaves of both Cor7 and HSVex consist of two quatrains, while the sestet of Cor7 has three couplets, that of HSVex two tercets. In Raspa's view, "these subdivisions were conventional to the sonnet genre," although "instead of these traditional subdivisions supporting the genre's conventional arguments, they repeated concepts epigrammatically." Raspa notes that neither HSVex nor Cor7 follows the traditional form of "an octet elaborating on a problem in a relationship which the sestet resolves." He adds that Southwell's "Upon the Image of Death" contains "structural elements" of Ignatius's *Spiritual Excercises* but HSVex does not.

Gaston (1986, 209) sees the musical setting of HSVex by Benjamin Britten as an occasion for the "high spirits of Donne's supplicant to break through." According to Gaston, the setting "provides suggestions of frivolity both to convey the inconstancy of the supplicant's spirit and to underscore his resulting anxiety," as in lines 12–13.

Gergye (1986, 172–78) compares the sonnets of Spenser and Donne to illustrate new trends in the poetry of Donne, including characteristics associated with Mannerist art. Spenser's poetry, in Gergye's view, continues to reflect Renaissance art in pure form, whereas Donne's sonnets, though still linked to their Petrarchan predecessor, do not simply mirror the Italian model (172). Gergye's comparison of Spenser's Sonnet XXX ("My loue is lyke to yse and I to Fyre") with a schematic figure of HSVex (174–75) draws out features that signal a completely different artistic trend (173). For example, Gergye finds both Spenser and Donne employing antithesis, but in Donne we see the disintegration of the symmetric organization of Spenser's sonnet-structure, and the line of thought becomes restlessly zigzagged and unbalanced (173). Gergye goes on to provide a detailed analysis of HSVex, illustrating, for example, the extent to which antitheses and tension are not so much resolved as situated in paradoxes. Gergye finds the growth of paradox in the structure and semantics of Donne's sonnets, but in Spenser's poetry the logical contradictions are resolved in the couplet (176). He further observes that in the Holy Sonnets, one of the basic propositions of Neoplatonic philosophy, namely, the idea that Woman and God are substantially the same, already disintegrates completely, for whereas in Donne's earlier works, the motif of Woman and earthly Love is an always returning element, in his later works the figure of Woman hardly appears, and the attributes of Love (courting, unreachableness, sexual movements) completely turn into descriptions of God's existence (177).

Rollin (1986, 145–46) refers to Robert Burton, who, in *The Anatomy of Melancholy*, according to Rollin, points out that being "vexed by contraries" may be a "sign of divine intervention in one's case: 'God often works by contrarieties, he first kills, and then makes alive, he woundeth first, and then healeth, he makes man sow in teares, that he may reap in joy; 'tis God's method'" [Burton, 1927 edition, p. 967]. Rollin adds that "it may be no delusion" therefore when Donne concludes that "Those are my best dayes, when I shake with feare" (145). Rollin thus proposes that *HSVex*, as the "traditional conclusion" of the Holy Sonnets, "may be seen as pointing readers of Donne toward his *Devotions*," wherein nothing seems "capable of undermining the ego of a human being wholly bent upon holy dying" (145–46).

Schoenfeldt (1994, 91–92) points out that whereas in *HSVex* Donne "contrasts the disingenuous spirituality of 'court[ing] God' to the authentic quaking of 'true fear,' Herbert explores throughout *The Temple* the explosive interaction of courtly supplication and religious fear."

NOTES AND GLOSSES

1–4 *Oh, . . . and in devotione.* WOOLF (1932) quotes the lines to illustrate Donne's inability to be "wholly set on one thing." Questions whether a man like Donne, so inquisitive and sceptical, so curious about "the flow and change of human life," could ever achieve the "wholeness and certainty" of "poets of purer life" (35–36). CRUTTWELL (1954) quotes the lines and comments that Donne is "aware of his own incurable multiplicity" and is powerless to change it, unable in his later years "*not* to write dramatically" (48). CHOI (1990) cites the opening lines to illustrate that the Holy Sonnets give us a glimpse into the nature of Donne's inner struggle, a consciousness that one does not know oneself (33).

1 *Oh, to vex me, contraryes meete in one:* WELLS (1940), citing this opening, notes that Donne often "passionately soliloquizes" (186). LEVER (1974) describes this as a "major theme of Renaissance thought, and the philosophic aspect of the age's (and Donne's) love of paradox" (183).

1 *vex* SMITH (1971): "trouble; agitate or shake" (636). GILL (1990): "the word had a much stronger meaning in the seventeenth century than it has today, being closer to shaken with anguish" (107).

1 *contraryes meete in one:* CRUTTWELL (1954) describes Donne's character and poetry as comparable to Shakespeare's characterization of figures in *Hamlet* and *Lear* as "compounds strange" (48).

2–6 *Inconstancy . . . and as soone forgott:* **HAMBURGER** (1944): Donne regrets his early "exercises in sophistry" (154).

2–3 *Inconstancy . . . when I would not* **CRUTTWELL** (1954): the paradox of constancy-inconstancy, referring here to Donne's sense of the insufficiency of his faith in God, is the reverse of his complaint about the inconstancy of the lovers of his secular poems (91).

2–3 *Inconstancy . . . constant* **GILL** (1990) wonders if the "verbal play upon this paradox" heightens or diminishes the "sense of the poet's distress" (107–08).

2 *vnnaturally* **SHAWCROSS** (1967): "both 'contrary to its nature' and 'cruelly'" (350).

3–4 *A constant . . . and in devotione.* **GRANSDEN** (1954): these lines and ll. 9–14 reflect Donne's sense of "the appalling difficulties of faith" (133).

3 *A constant habit;* **LEVER** (1974): the "discrepancy between a desire for consistency and constant changes of belief" (183).

4 *vowes,* **GILL** (1990) sees in this word, among others, an example of "the relationship between religious poetry and love poetry" that is evident in some of the Holy Sonnets (108).

4–5 *devotione. . . . contritione* **SMITH** (1971): "Both pronounced as four syllables" (636). [So also, Campbell (1989, 233).]

5–8 *As humorous . . . as infinite, as none.* **WHITE** (1951): in these lines, and in ll. 12–13, Donne expresses "a certain almost savage self-contempt" for his spiritual inadequacies, while at the same time demonstrating the strength and resolve to face them (365).

5 *humorous* **REEVES** (1952): "moody, changeable" (103). [Similarly, Shawcross (1967, 350), Booty (1990, 110), and Gill (1990, 108).] **WILLEY** (1954): "fickle, subject to changing 'humors'" (387). [Similarly, Craik and Craik (1986, 281) and Campbell (1989, 233).] **WARNKE** (1967): "capricious" (275). **SMITH** (1971): "changeable, subject to whim" (636). **PATRIDES** (1985a) glosses as "appertaining to one's 'humours' or dispositions . . . mercurial, changeable" and "any of the four 'humours' (blood, phlegm, black bile, yellow bile) which, according to the old physiology, determined one's health and disposition," and further points to Carey (1981) (447, 336).

5 *contritione* **GILL** (1990): "being sorry for one's sins" (108).

6 *my prophane love,* **LEVER** (1974): cf. *HSWhat* 9: "my idolatry" (183).

7–8 *As ridlingly . . . as infinite, as none.* **KORTEMME** (1933): the paradoxical effect is intensified by the piling up of opposites, sharpening the contrast (48).

CARLSON (1973) says that these lines should be read as an amplification of lines 5–6 and offers this paraphrase: "My contrition is as riddlingly distempered, as cold or as hot, as my profane love was, and it [contrition, again] is as praying, sometimes, and as mute, other times, as my profane love was, and it [my contrition] is as infinite sometimes, and as none [which is to say, non-existent] other times, as my profane love was." Finds in the language of these lines "an ironic series of possible allusions" to Donne's earlier poetry, making *HSVex* "a more interesting poem than critics have apparently considered it to be" (item 19).

7 *ridingly distemperd,* SHAWCROSS (1967): "As cryptically diluted or deranged, whether my contrition comes from melancholy or passion" (350). MARTZ (1969b): "disordered, in a state of puzzling instability" (27). SMITH (1971): "enigmatically disproportioned or unbalanced, now one extreme, now the other" (636). [Similarly, Campbell (1989, 233).] LEVER (1974): "Unbalanced" (183). [So also, Fowler (1991, 120).] GILL (1990): "his contrition wildly swings from one extreme to another as if he were unbalanced by disease" (108).

7 *cold and hott,* LEVER (1974): "From the 'elements' which made up the body's humours" (183).

8 *As praying, as mute; as infinite, as none.* ANONYMOUS ATH (1899) notes that he emended Gosse's line (1899) "As praying as mute; as infinite as none" to "As praying, as mute, as infinite, as none" (646).

8 *As praying, as mute;* SHAWCROSS (1967): "as praying is when it is unpronounced" (350). SMITH (1971): "as full of rapid alternations of petition and dumbness as the customary behaviour of a lover" (636).

8 *as infinite, as none.* SHAWCROSS (1967): "or it is as infinite as nothing else is" (350). SMITH (1971): "now infinitely contrite, now not contrite at all" (636).

8 *As . . . as* LEVER (1974): "Now . . . now" (183).

8 *none.* CRAIK and CRAIK (1986): "non-existent" (281). [So also, Fowler (1991, 120).]

9–14 *I durst . . . when I shake with feare.* FAERBER (1950) views the lines as evidence that Donne is constantly engaged in conquering his faith and can never surrender to a moment of tranquility (12). MARTZ (1954): an example of "the agony, the turbulence, the strenuosity" found in Donne (144).

9–11 *I durst . . . with true feare of his rod.* EVANS (1955): Donne "delights in the play of his own emotions and the sudden vagaries of his own ideas," here "the vacillations of his faith" (170–71). MAROTTI (1994a) observes that "courtiership, like amatory courtship, provided Donne with a scheme for his relationship with God" (79).

10 *In prayers, and flattering Speaches I court God:* **RUGOFF** (1939): the line is an example of religious devotion as a "sexual relationship" (86–87).

10 *flattering* **LEVER** (1974): "Intended to please" (183).

11 *To morrow . . . his rod.* **SHAWCROSS** (1967) points to Job 9.34–35: "Let him take his rod away from me, and let not his fear terrify me: Then would I speak, and not fear him; but it is not so with me" (350). [So also, Booty (1990, 110).] **GILL** (1990): "God's justice and punishment are frequently spoken of as a rod" (108).

11 *To morrow* **STEIN** (1944): the final syllable, with a "light vowel," is elided (390).

11 *true feare* **LEWALSKI** (1979): the speaker's "true feare" may imply the quality valued in Job 28.28 ("The feare of the Lord, that is wisdome"), confirming a "sound theological basis" for the concluding paradox: "Those are my best dayes, when I shake with feare" (274–75). **SCHOENFELDT** (1994) believes that the adjective "true" suggests that "not only the courting but also the fear to which it is contrasted can become strategic" (82).

12–13 *So my . . . a fantastique Ague:* **BENNETT** (1934), citing Donne's images of disease, notes that the "coming and going of his religious fervor is an ague" (37). **THOMPSON** (1935): virtue and repentance are not enough because the human being is too weak to conquer sin and death (13–14).

13–14 *Like a . . . shake with feare.* **BELLETTE** (1975): the couplet "is a particularly bleak paradox, speaking of a state of spiritual exhaustion" (332). **GILL** (1990) wonders if the paradoxical claim that his "best days" (a "phrase often used when talking about health") are those when he "shake[s] with fear" effectively sums up "the contraries of the poem" or is "just an example of the poet's love of verbal play" (108).

13 *fantastique Ague:* **LEVER** (1974): "Fever in the 'fancy,' one of the faculties of the mind, with 'understanding' and 'memory'" (183).

13 *fantastique* **SHAWCROSS** (1967): "imaginary, fantasy-inducing" (351). [Similarly, Booty (1990, 110).] **SMITH** (1971): "capricious, extravagant" (636). **GILL** (1990): "uncertain, extreme, unpredictable" (108).

13 *Ague:* **SMITH** (1971): "a fever, with paroxysms of hot and cold and fits of trembling" (636). [Similarly, Patrides (1985a, 447), Campbell (1989, 233), Booty (1990, 110), and Gill (1990, 108).] **CRAIK and CRAIK** (1986) gloss as "fever, with bouts of heat and cold" and point to ll. 7 and 14 (281). **FOWLER** (1991): "irregular fever" (120).

13 *here* **LEVER** (1974): "In this respect" (183).

14 *Those are my best dayes, when I shake with feare.* **WAGNER** (1947): Donne here acknowledges the power of bodily suffering (254). **PETERSON** (1959): the irony of the line arises from the Anglican belief that fear alone is not enough for salvation, and further that unless it is transcended by love, fear can be damning (517). **LEVER** (1974) says that the "shaking" is regarded as a "kind of quotidian fever" and points to the name "Quakers" applied to Fox's Christian sect (183).

HSWhat

COMMENTARY

General Commentary

In an eighteenth-century Moravian Brethren's hymn-book (*A Collection of Hymns*) (1754 [1966, 19–20]), four Holy Sonnets—*HSMade, HSDue, HSSpit,* and *HSWhat*—are used, slightly altered, and combined to make up hymn number 383.

Gosse (1899, 2:109) cites *HSWhat* as "[o]ne of the most remarkable" of the Holy Sonnets and finds in it a "memorable instance" of Donne's "clairvoyance" in reviewing his "profane past" after his conversion. To Gosse, Donne's reference to his earlier erotic poetry is "singularly characteristic" and "helps to explain why he preserved so carefully, to the very last, though he never would publish, the evidences of his early enslavement to the flesh." Gosse identifies the sonnet as Donne's "dialogue with his soul."

French (1970, 112–13), recalling Empson (1930—see *HSWhat*: Themes), says that there is in *HSWhat* a fallacy, for "a person who is being executed by slow torture is not really very beautiful" (112). The Christ presented in the poem is not a "beauteous forme," he maintains, but "something more like a 'horrid shape.'" Possibly, French continues, there is "an element of bargaining in Donne's logic"—that is, he may be saying, "I've given the reader every opportunity to conclude that You are a wicked spirit, so You can only prove Your beauty by <u>not</u> adjudging me to hell" (113). Donne is making Christ appear wicked so that he has to prove his beauty by not adjudging Donne to hell (113).

Altizer (1973, 85) suggests that *HSWhat* presents clearly the split between Christ as Judge and Christ as suffering, all-merciful Redeemer. The poem's central question, she contends, is "can the Christ who agonized on the cross and yet forgave his murderers condemn someone who loves Him 'unto hell?'" The answer is presented in a conceit based on paradox, she notes, but since the terms of the conceit are drawn from secular love poetry, the concluding paradox of God's mercy seems "somewhat contrived and banal."

Bellette (1975, 339) argues that in *HSWhat* "no possibility of divine indifference" is expressed. This sonnet, according to Bellette, is "carefully controlled" and "demonstrates a like congruence between thought and form."

Raspa (1983, 91) associates *HSWhat* with a "meditation directly on the self," noting that it is intended "to separate the poet from the world and force him to consider it correctly in terms of the spiritual universe." Donne accomplishes this, in Raspa's view, by portraying the darkness of the world in order "to bring into relief the inherent moral realities of the poet's and reader's lives," so that in the end, Donne's "black world was a provocative imitation of a desired inner state rather than its fair copy."

To Ray (1990b, 356–58), the speaker of *HSWhat* is asking his soul "to ponder intently the image of the crucified Christ who, through love, sacrificed himself for humanity," thus denoting a "loving God, not one that is wrathful, angry, and frightening" (356). Ray argues that the sestet reinforces this view of God by drawing a comparison of Christ to a lover. The worship of profane mistresses was motivated by his desire to get a woman "to yield to him," but now, Ray notes, the speaker "has turned away from his frivolous period of idolizing secular lovers and has chosen God as his true lover," yet he "strangely applies the same argument to convince his soul of the compassion of Christ and the consequent salvation of the soul that is the recipient of Christ's pity" (357). The speaker concludes, according to Ray, that the "'beauteous form' of the crucified Christ" just visualized is the "external manifestation of that internal goodness in Christ's pitying nature" (357–58).

The Poet/Persona

Fausset (1924, 243) finds that the poem reveals a Donne "more conscious as yet of sin than of grace," one who anticipates that the sight of Christ will "affright" him. The beauty of his mistresses, Fausset continues, was for Donne a sign of pity, hence he consoles himself that the beauty of Christ will show it the more.

Praz (1925, 68–69) interprets the poem as Donne's admission that no flattering image of fancy can attenuate the gravity of his own sin and the necessity for retribution and, however late, remorse.

Cohen (1963, 166–67) says that in *HSWhat* Donne "identifies himself with the suffering Christ" (166). Citing in particular *HSWhat* 1–4, he observes that the crucifixion occurs "on the Golgotha of his own soul" (167).

Parish (1963a, item 19) maintains that Donne deliberately offers "an example of a meditation inadequately devout." He sees the poem as a dramatic monologue, "unique among the Holy Sonnets in being intentionally an example of unwarranted assurance of salvation," and finds Donne employing trickery of words in this meditation, the kind of fallacious argument that he has used before in his Songs and Sonnets. But, concludes Parish, he may be "seducing his own soul," or else he is cajoling "a justly angry God."

Stampfer (1970, 256–57) finds in *HSWhat* "a host of voices in disarray" (256), with the speaker, his soul, his heart, and the image of Christ all appearing as presences in the poem. The "No, no" beginning the sestet, which answers the questions put by the octave, Stampfer says, "shrinks back" from possibly the vision of Christ, or the speaker's own sinfulness, or his "free panic," but the sestet strongly suggests a repentant courtly lover. Anticipating *HSBatter*, the speaker in the sestet of *HSWhat*, Stampfer believes, speaks to his soul as "a mistress presumably to Christ" (257).

Parfitt (1972, 384) remarks that the practice of meditation may have encouraged the habit of self-dramatization which seems innate in Donne, but the effect of his poems is best typified in *HSWhat*. In this sonnet, Parfitt writes, there is a strong sense of a part being acted out.

White and Rosen (1972, 54) claim that the "terrifying question" with which

HSWhat opens and the power of its portrait of the crucified Christ "tend to obscure the impact of the central analogy." They contend that just as the Petrarchan poet had "implored his mistresses" (in his "idolatry" [l. 9]) "to grant him sexual love by using the argument that beauty implies and is a sign of 'pity,'" so now he uses that same argument to implore Christ's love.

Stachniewski (1981, 693) observes the way the sonnet manifests Donne's spiritual state through its negative expressions, arguing that the poet's "conception of the state of grace as not going to hell is not a sign of spiritual health" and pointing to line 7 ("And can that tongue adjudge thee unto hell?"), a question the poem answers "ambiguously."

Smith (1984, 517) finds that Donne here, as in *HSSpit*, centers on his own needs rather than on the suffering of Christ, for Donne "evokes a picture of Christ on the Cross" (l. 5) not so much "to inspire pity and love for Christ but to test whether or not Christ will feel pity for Donne at the Last Judgement."

Gilman (1986, 90–91) interprets the poem as one of the Holy Sonnets situated in the midst of the Reformation iconoclastic tensions, observing that it "seems to pivot on the contrast between 'this present . . . night' [l. 1] of holy meditation and these past nights full of 'all my profane mistresses' [l. 10]; between the 'picture of Christ' [l. 3] and the 'idolatrie' [l. 9] now forsworn; between what Donne says to his soul now and what he said to his lovers then" (90). But for Gilman the poem moves toward blasphemy when the speaker "attempt[s] to seduce Christ into granting mercy" in the same way he earlier had seduced his "profane mistresses" (90–91). Gilman agrees with Carey (1981) that "this strange collapse of Donne's grave meditation into the rubble of amatory rhetoric" results from, in Carey's terms, "the incompetence of the polluted mind." Thus, Gilman says, "the horrid shape Donne would *not* see reasserts itself as the image rightly 'assign'd' to him, as a reflection of the idolatry that continues to dwell in his heart, and as a judgment upon it" (91). See also *HSBatter*: Themes and *HSShow*: General Commentary.

Rollin (1986, 142) finds *HSWhat* to be one of Donne's "less reflexive" sonnets, and therefore exhibiting less mood swing than other Holy Sonnets. Rollin contends that the poem's "shift of subject" from the "re-creation of the Crucifixion in its composition-of-place stage" to the "analysis of love's philosophy" does not result in a "radical shift in mood." Rollin notes that Robert Burton distinguishes between "love melancholy and religious melancholy," but that he "tentatively classifies the latter as a subdivision of the former" (see *The Anatomy of Melancholy*, ed. Floyd Dell and Paul Jordan Smith [New York: Tudor Publishing Co., 1927], p. 886).

Shawcross (1986b, 53–54, 63–64), urging the study of literature first as literature, rather than as biography or philosophy, illustrates his thesis by looking at *HSWhat*, a sonnet he labels "personal" (54). Dating the group of sonnets of which this sonnet is a part around 1609 (i.e., "after Donne's serious illness, during his patronage by the Countess of Bedford, and before his association with Sir Robert Drury" [63]), Shawcross finds that the sonnet "seems to reflect" a "contemplation of death, associated with the siege of illness" (63). Shawcross notes that the speaker "meditates that Judgment Day may come unannounced," but that the "concept of the crucified Christ" offers reassurance that the "Judgment of the Son on him will not doom him to hell but will forgive him his sins" (63–64). Shawcross concludes that "the poet is not yet on a unitive path, for he has not asserted positive action that he will undertake," but, according to Shawcross, "he has prepared for such action by renunciation of the past." And "while the sonnet is undoubtedly applicable to any Christian," Shawcross adds, "it seems to represent a personal meditation and resolution, which, when reviewed in chronological pattern with other data, will develop a perspective view of Donne at a period of crisis" (64).

Young (1987, 34–38) locates a Calvinist subtext in HSWhat (34). What the "anguished meditator" sees when he looks into his heart, according to Young, is "a graphic, Spanish baroque crucifix." With the sestet, in Young's view, the speaker attempts to strengthen his "assurance of salvation" by encouraging an "emotional and aesthetic response to the interior image of Christ that he has evoked" (35). The sonnet, "resonant with echoes of Sidney," and in particular *Astrophil and Stella*, Sonnet 1, is, in Young's words, "at best questionable, and a dubious means of assuring oneself of salvation" (36), a view reinforced by the "manipulative insincerity of the erotic analogy," which "infects" the speaker's "expression of desire for Christ" (36–37). Young concludes that it is not surprising that Donne's Holy Sonnets reveal a "certain diffidence and trepidation," for at the time Donne composed those poems, he was "neither still Catholic nor yet Protestant in a settled way that gave his conscience peace" (38).

To Strier (1989, 380–81), HSWhat "most clearly reveals Donne's inability in this period to conceive of divine love in terms of a loving relationship." Similar to HSWilt, he thinks, the sonnet "has very much the feeling of an exercise," for it "begins by stating its project and then attempts . . . to argue itself into love and comfort." In Strier's view, "the image of Christ as a savior is meant to eliminate that of Christ as judge," but in fact the image of the judge "seems to absorb that of the savior rather than being displaced by it" (380). Strier finds that the voice in the sestet does suddenly take on "some confidence, wit, and freedom of movement," but the force of the argument here "relies on the crucified Christ being immediately recognized as a 'beauteous forme,'" and that, in Strier's view, is "precisely what the octet has failed to establish." For Strier, Christ's "beauteous forme" is not evident enough in the sonnet "to bear the weight it must have" (381).

Fish (1990, 244–47) considers this sonnet as theatrical as HSDue, noting particularly the opening line inviting a reader "to imagine (or to be) an audience before whom this proposition will be elaborated," like Donne's sermons, "in the service of some homiletic point." But with the second line, Fish emphasizes, "everything changes abruptly," although the theatricalism continues, in that "the stage has shrunk from one on which Donne speaks to many of a (literally) cosmic question to a wholly interior setting populated only by versions of Donne" (245). As a meditation, Fish notes, HSWhat is "curious" in that Donne does not direct the meditation to his beloved, but instead "to another part of himself." Fish describes this focus as "prideful and perhaps worse, for it recharacterizes the Last Judgment as a moment staged and performed entirely by himself." This contraction of space, in Fish's view, is part of Donne's attempt to control the sonnet's development and the answer to the "urgent question" of HSWhat 7–8. Fish observes that the answer is "inevitable" and it arrives "immediately" in the "No, no" of line 9, but the intensity of the response betrays the uncertainty, so that "uncertainty and instability return with a vengeance" in lines 9–14. Fish cites approvingly Stachniewski's observation (1981) that "the argument of Donne's poems is often so strained that it alerts us to its opposite, the emotion or mental state in defiance of which the argumentative process was set to work" (246), noting that the argument is "part of a seductive strategy" in which "the soul is asked to read from the signifying surface of Christ's picture to his intention," but since Donne himself creates that surface, the "confident assertion of the last line has no support other than itself." Fish notes that line 14 has two textual variants ("assures" or "assumes"), holding that in either of the two variants, "This beauteous forme" points "not only to the form Donne has assigned to Christ's picture, but to the form of the poem itself." Fish finds that *HSWhat* "ends in the bravado" characteristic of some other Holy Sonnets, but that the "triumph of the rhetorical flourish" in this instance reminds us of its "insubstantiality" (247).

Genre and Traditions
Martz (1954, 83–84) finds in the sonnet "a fusion of passion and thought" typical of Ignatian meditation on the life of Christ, especially in its evocation of the senses, predominantly sight. Martz argues that in the first quatrain the memory sets up a picture of Christ crucified and in the second the picture is analyzed in details which keep the image before the eyes. He finds the sestet, where "mercy dominates," "unworthy" of the opening, for the reference to "profane mistresses" exhibits the "worst of taste," having "almost a tone of bragging." In his revised edition, Martz (1962, 84) changes his estimate, acknowledging the reference to be appropriate and explaining that the meditative mind "finds the answer to the soul's problem" by adopting an aspect of his former "idolatrie" to assure it of God's "pitious minde."

Low (1978, 67) finds that *HSWhat* uses a "double composition of place," the sestet being more personal than the octave.

Language and Style
Wild (1935, 421) finds in this sonnet about the Crucifixion evidence of a baroque sensibility in English poetry of the era.

Faerber (1950, 15) finds the poem a paradoxical contemplation of the consequences of death.

Adams (1958, 130) detects in the sonnet Donne's admission that he consciously uses hyperbole, exaggeration, and "poetic" language.

Sloane (1985, 204–06) points out that Donne could situate the picture of Christ in his memory, as he does in *Goodf*, but here Christ is placed in the "most volatile part of man's being," namely the heart, "a location warranted by man's role as lover, a role the speaker plays throughout the poem." Sloane states that, initially, the tortured picture of Christ is "horrifying," but later the picture is called "beautiful," creating an apparent contradiction a reader must reconcile. The first beauty, according to Sloane is in "Christ's selfless action of dying upon the cross for our sins and of praying forgiveness for his foes," which, Sloane argues, is the "true 'forme' of the beloved" (204). Sloane finds another beauty in the poem, namely, "the beauty of the argument itself." As is usual in Donne's poetry, Sloane contends, "the controversial habit of thought provokes corrections and reconciliations," as here the "profane" argument once used for "flattery and seduction" is, in this sacred context, used "to seduce the soul into consolation." Sloane claims that the speaker's "comforting realization" (ll. 11–12) is offered as a *zeugma*: a "parallel syntactical construction in which one element (in this case 'A signe') is meant to be used for both parts of the construction." Thus, Sloane adds, the figure is both a "'signe' of the speaker's conscious control of his formerly terrified emotions and thought" and a figure that "imposes that control, that disposition, on the audience." The audience in the poem, according to Sloane, is both the speaker's soul and the reader's. Furthermore, Sloane contends, the ambiguity does not stop there: "'this beauteous forme' is Christ, *and* the *zeugma, and* the disposition of the poem itself, rightly understood" (205). Sloane concludes that "Christ gives us one form, Donne another," for "the *zeugma* is itself transformed into the harmony of the final couplet, with its confidently regular rhythms, echoing sounds and balanced concepts . . . and perfect rhymes." Therefore, Sloane contends, "this process of making, the parodying of God, is unquestionably meant to include creating the reader by *in*forming him with the text—any text, poem or sermon, spoken or written." Sloane emphasizes that the poem's "true 'forme,' when we know how to interpret it (and Donne himself shows us how), is designed emotionally to place us within the text and the text within us" (206).

Shawcross (1987, 21–22) explores the effect of multiple manuscripts of Donne's poetry on how one ultimately should read the poems, theorizing, as an example, on the "sound effect and pattern" of the Westmoreland (NY3) version of *HSWhat* (22). Noting the generally high regard for NY3, Shawcross compares it to another ms., finding in NY3 that perhaps "liquidity is to be stressed and contrasted with the harshness of a 'k' sound," while in the second ms. alliteration perhaps "predominate[s]" (22). Readers should be aware, suggests Shawcross, that the text of a poem is not "unproblematical, etched indestructibly, somehow sacrosanct" (22).

Guibbory (1993, 127–28) sees here a continuation of Donne's "use of logic and witty argument, sometimes verging on blasphemy." In the sestet, in Guibbory's view, Donne addresses Christ, "drawing a startling analogy between his flattering, persuasive addresses to his prophane mistresses and his present address to God" (127). Guibbory concludes that many of the Holy Sonnets show that for Donne "reason and intellect are as essential to the poem's very existence as Donne believed they were to human nature." But in Guibbory's view, Donne's employment of reason and wit is "crossed by a profound distrust of reason" (128).

Prosody

Esch (1955, 47) observes that the sonnet is in the Italian form, with the question of the octave answered in the sestet in almost frivolous comparisons with the profane. See more under Holy Sonnets: Genre and Traditions.

Sacred and Profane

Gransden (1954, 130, 132) cites the poem as one in which Donne puts "secular passion to divine use" (130), paraphrasing it as, "If Christ appeared to me now, would he send me to hell? No, for surely his beauty is a sign that he will be merciful, an argument I used to use to women," that is, "beautiful women have been kind to me, so will not Christ also be kind?" (132).

Carey (1981, 47) finds the sestet blasphemous. In fact, for Carey, the sestet, unlike "the octave's resplendent serenity," is "grotesque erotic argument, which tilts it toward hysteria." According to Carey, the poem renders Donne's desperation as he "searches for some argument that will assure him of salvation."

Ferry (1983, 227, 229) claims that Donne's sonnet "consciously" follows the convention—as old as Dante's poetry—of turning religious language "back to sacred subjects by reassimilating the conventions of love sonnets." Donne's speakers in the Holy Sonnets are closer to "poet-lovers" than they are to "liturgical petitioners," according to Ferry, with specific associations made to "the history of love poetry." Ferry notes the speaker's comparison of a line of argument he previously used with his "profane mistresses" with that he now uses to his soul, and which "must be overheard by Christ" (227). Ferry feels that this similar manipulation of language is intended "to raise questions about the nature of what is in the speaker's heart, and its relation to his language," particularly in a sonnet beginning with a meditation on Christ (229).

Sherwood (1984, 150–51) describes the sonnet as a "problematic attempt to follow the right pattern of suffering and divine love in order to control the impulse to idolatrous love," but he finds that the "old patterns of sinful idolatry compulsively struggle to emerge," as "the question raised in the octave ('And can that tongue adjudge thee unto hell,/Which pray'd forgivenesse for his foes fierce spight?') is answered negatively in the sestet by the soul's regard for Christ's beauty ('This beauteous forme assures a pitious minde')" (150). But to Sherwood the "too obvious distinction" between the spiritual beauty of Christ and the physical beauty of the mistresses "blunts the argument that both, by analogy, assure pity and suggests instead the tenacity of old, sinful patterns in describing new realities" (151).

Zunder (1988, 88–90) contends that when Donne left Pyrford in 1606 and moved closer to London, at Mitcham, and began to apply once again for a government position, he was beginning to experience doubts about the "sufficiency" of the "individual love-relationship" (88–89). Zunder finds this change expressed in the Songs and Sonets, but also in HSWhat. This sonnet, which Zunder believes was most likely written in 1609, reveals a movement from the "individual human relationship to an individual religious relationship: from Ann Donne to God," a "transference," according to Zunder, "in a virtually Freudian sense." The speaker, meditating on the end of the world, "with the prospect of heaven or hell immediately before him," thus "generates a sense of crisis." In Zunder's view, the transference from Ann to God is "made initially through the Petrarchan conceit of the woman's image in the lover's heart" in lines 2–8 (89), but in the sestet "human love is rejected," for it is seen, Zunder notes, as "idolatry" or "false worship," and "it is superseded by divine love" (89–90).

Gill (1990, 104) finds that "the tension in so many Donne poems between divine and earthly love is vividly present here." Gill adds that whereas "the octave is intensely and vividly detailed in its presentation of the crucified Christ," the sestet "is more relaxed and even casual," to the extent that one can see the poet of line 9 "confidently shaking his head": "No, no; but as in my idolatry."

Hester (1992, xvii) points to the sonnet's allusions to Donne's private love experiences in lines 9–12 and further contends that, even more generally, the creation of Donne's "private devotion" in the Holy Sonnets "rests on its similarity to his private love life." According to Hester, "the religious devotion stirred by his vision of the 'picture of Christ crucified' in his heart (another Catholic baroque image recalled probably from his Catholic heritage and education) is finally defined in terms of its inversion of the code of Petrarchan frustration."

Low (1993, 77–78), commenting on the marriage trope in several Holy Sonnets, notes that it is "reversed" in HSWhat, as the "bloody face of the crucified Christ becomes a potential rival of 'all my profane mistresses'" (l. 10) (78).

Harland (1995, 162–63, 167–68) cites Cross, HSWhat, and Goodf to challenge the claim that Donne's "self-absorption" hinders his ability "to sympathize, to pity, to understand with tenderness those who are truly other and not merely versions of his multifaceted self." These poems, Harland asserts, "enact the drama of the ego breaking out of the prison of destructive self-preoccupation into a liberated state of true self-love which best expresses itself as willing and disinterested giving" (162). According to Harland, love of the crucified and suffering Christ "allows the self to transform itself into its best nature, to reflect Christ, and thereby to love itself fully" (163). For example, Harland says, the speaker in HSWhat contemplates the "face of the Judge who has been judged by the world and finds it horrifying," but the second half of the poem "records the regenerate response of one who has looked upon Christ" and has been converted to love. Because the speaker can see "the divine intent of redemption behind the ugly crucifixion, the event becomes beautiful," and thus the "seemingly cruel" crucifixion reveals, "ironically," a God who "takes pity on humankind" (167). Harland thinks, contra Carey (1981), that the speaker's "idolatrie" may refer to other than "imagined personal liaisons" but, for example, to the "false mistresses" of "Fame, Wit, Hope" (Christ 24–25) or the "strange gods" of Exod. 34.15–16 and Deut. 31.16. For Harland, the "mark of the regenerate soul" in HSWhat is that of a speaker who sees "beyond defacement to the true nature of Christ," for, as Christ "pierces through the deformity of sin to recognize his own image in the speaker," the speaker, in parallel fashion, "pierces through the ugliness of the crucified Christ to see Christ's essential beauty" (168).

Themes

Simpson (1924, 233) points to the "note of devotion to the Person of Christ" that appears in HSWhat and that echoes "again and again" in Donne's Sermons, and she cites in particular Sermons, 3:nos. 14 and 15.

Empson (1930, 168, 183–84) includes HSWhat in his study of a type of ambiguity in which "two or more meanings of a statement do not agree among themselves, but combine to make clear a more complicated state of mind in the author." It is a type, further, in which "the mixture of modes of judgment" may be puzzling, he says, "but they are not in the main focus of consciousness because the stress of the situation absorbs them, and they are felt to be natural under the circumstances" (168).

Empson quotes *HSWhat* in full, observing that in the opening lines the speaker, engaged perhaps in "the very act of sin," is struck by a "black unexpected terror" at the thought of the world's end. Empson senses, however, that the end of the poem gives a "general impression of security" in Christ's forgiveness (183–84), but he is displeased that in order to resolve the ambiguity of the poem Donne "shuffles up an old sophistry from Plato" that beauty is a sign of pity (184). In a later edition (1947, 146) Empson confirms his "distaste for the poem."

Leishman (1934, 90) observes that Donne "believed, or pretended to believe, that beauty was a sign of pity."

Bush (1945, 134) cites the poem to illustrate Donne's preoccupation with "the lurid shadow of death."

Spörri-Sigel (1949, 85) observes that Donne considers the possibility that he may be damned but concludes that if Christ will forgive his worst enemies, he will forgive him. This comfort, she contends, he derives from the beauty of Christ, thematically combining the Platonic concept of beauty with the Christian concept of love. She finds no tension between damnation and salvation in the poem, for Christ rules over Heaven and Hell, and so assures Donne of salvation.

Louthan (1951, 120–23), in explicating the poem, argues that Empson's distaste for *HSWhat* (1930) arises from his misunderstanding of the secular-sacred figure. Donne's conceit is not simply a Platonic commonplace that beauty is an index of benevolence but a complex paradox: Donne's old "idolatrie" is thus fully acceptable when employed in worship (121). Louthan asserts, further, that the ethical beauty of Christ's countenance "*outweighs* the esthetic ugliness," indeed "transforms it into esthetic beauty" (122). Christ's blood, he continues, obliterates his frowns, resulting in relative beauty, and it is in the end mercy that "causes us to identify ethical with esthetic beauty" (123).

Umbach (1951, 40–41) quotes the poem in full, comparing it to Donne's evocation of Christ's last day in *Death's Duel* (*Sermons*, 10:245–48).

Reeves (1952, 101) summarizes the poem: "The beauty of Christ's face on the cross is a guarantee of his mercy and forgiveness."

Simon (1952, 115) observes that Donne "cannot argue away fear" but that he believes the picture of Christ can do so, since it "assures a piteous mind."

Peterson (1959, 512) compares the sonnet to *HSScene*, earlier in the sequence of Holy Sonnets, finding that the process of contrition has progressed from "considering reason as a source of culpability to reason as a source of nobility." He finds that in *HSScene* God is feared as a judge, but that *HSWhat* is a meditation on his love and mercy. The assurance of the final line, Peterson notes, prepares for the next step in the progression, finding a way to return God's love. See also Holy Sonnets: Themes.

Lewalski (1979, 271) claims that *HSWhat*, the last of three consecutive sonnets on Christ's crucifixion in 1635 (along with *HSSpit* and *HSWhy*), "briefly recalls the Apocalypse, but now it is devoid of terror." But, Lewalski adds, the sestet "plays an almost scandalous variation upon the serious affirmation of faith in the octave," for the speaker "begs Christ for reassurance of his mercy, arguing the Platonic connection between Beauty and Goodness which he used to cite in wooing his 'profane mistresses,'" thus reflecting the speaker's ongoing need of Christ's reassurance in the matter of faith.

Guibbory (1986, 96) points out that even though Donne emphasizes the "efficacy of memory" in his writings and sermons, some Holy Sonnets, among them *HSWhat*, "imply that memory's ability to reunite man and God is limited." She points out that in this poem, though Donne's memory of Christ's Crucifixion leads him to feel that Christ will not "adjudge" him "unto hell," this confidence is "punctured" by the "fear, evident throughout this disturbing sonnet, that he can indeed be damned."

Sabine (1992, 2) argues that Donne "saw the possibilities of becoming 'A something else' [*Relic* 18], a "Christ who was at once other than him, and his other self" and cites *HSWhat* 3, where Donne superimposes "the picture of Christ crucified" on "the travesty of the Saviour's inner torment which was his soul."

Creswell (1995, 184–87), perceiving in the Holy Sonnets Donne's "rejection of truth as vision" and a move "toward 'hearing' the Word or turning to the 'voyce'" (184), argues that in *HSWhat* Christ's face "resists presentation altogether," the face becoming a "trope for the 'voyce' that imitates and lies prior to all speech and vision." To Creswell, the speaker, "contemplating the picture of Christ crucified," views "not the Light but the divine performative decree figured in the 'tongue' whose speech enacts its judgment" (ll. 7–8). Thus, Creswell claims, the "picture of Christ" that the speaker must "Marke in [his] heart" hints at "both a picture set before the eye and the act of inscription, an image of the Word as the originary decree, '*Dixit, & facta sunt*'" (186). For Donne, according to Creswell, "positing the Word as 'voyce' or 'visage' locates a materiality within the very heart of language," and thus, "the presentation of the Word both entails a return to the figurative and is marked as such" (187).

HSWhat and Other Works

Satterthwaite (1960, 211, 213) comments on Donne's use of conflict and of violent feeling, particularly in the Holy Sonnets (211), and discovers similarities between the final line of DuBellay's Sonnet 109 and Donne's final two lines in *HSWhat* (213).

Milward (1979 [1988, 74–76]) finds that although the sonnet's "composition of time" anticipates a parallel with *HSRound* "on the last day," it thwarts that expectation, and rather than "a meditation on the last judgment," turns instead to "the colloquy which St. Ignatius gives for the first exercise of the *First Week* on the three sins (of the angels, of Adam and Eve, and of one who dies in mortal sin)" (74). Milward adds that the colloquy "is not with Christ crucified, nor with his picture, but with his own soul," as in *HSBlack*. Milward identifies biblical references as well, noting that "the tongue that should sentence sinners to hell is stayed by Christ's own prayer for 'forgiveness for his foes fierce spight'" (see Luke 23.34), with the word "fierce" drawn from "the description of the Jews before Pilate" in Luke 23.15 (75).

Milward also cites echoing phrases in *HSSighs* 5 ("my idolatry"), *HSSouls* 9 ("idolatrous lovers"), and *HSVex* 6 ("my prophane love"), and he calls attention to the paradox "in the attribution of a 'beauteous forme' to Christ on the cross," given that in Isa. 53.2 the suffering Messiah has "no form nor comeliness . . . no beauty that we should desire him." Milward concludes that Donne looks beyond the "outward disfigurement" of Christ and to his "native appearance" as anticipated in Ps. 45: "Thou art fairer than the children of men" (cf. *Douai*: "beautiful above the sons of men") and as described by Ignatius in the *Meditation on the Two Standards*: "beautiful and attractive." Milward suggests that Donne also may be mindful of the words expressed by Antonio in *TN* 3.4.403–06: "In nature there's no blemish but the mind; / None can be call'd deform'd but the unkind: / Virtue is beauty, but the beauteous evil / Are empty trunks o'er flourish'd by the devil" (76).

Bennett (1982, 152–53) associates the sonnet with the practice of meditating on the Crucified Christ, but here, the soul is addressed rather than God, given that the poem "presents the picture of the Crucifixion as imprinted on [the speaker's] heart." Bennett also notes that the figure of Christ "is not of a tortured frame but of a body divinely beautiful: *optime complexionis*, in the medieval phrase" (152). He further notes that much as the medieval poet often "presented Christ as a knight in love with Mansoul," so in *HSWhat* Donne "presents him as loving his soul, addressed here as the poet would formerly ('in my idolatrie') have addressed a profane mistress" (153).

Briggs (1983, 169) finds that Donne "redeployed" the "imagery of Catholic religious experience" used in the Songs and Sonnets as "part of a Platonic religion of love, in which the doctrinal debates that had set faith against works, 'remembrance' against 'real presence,' and interrogated the relation of body to soul and mind" offered instead "ways of exploring the interaction of sexual desire and idealizing love." In this way, Briggs says, the "theological contexts of the love poetry are balanced by the erotic imagery of religious sonnets" such as *HSWhat*, which creates a "scandalous analogy between Christ's mercy and the sexual generosity of the poet's 'profane mistresses.'"

Gaston (1986, 209–10) observes about the fifth sonnet (*HSWhat*) of Benjamin Britten's musical sequence that Britten's setting "emphasizes the gradual shift from terror to confidence" (210). He points out that the "trills in the right hand persist for a time; the trembling does not stop at once, but diminishes slowly" (209). The "crucial moment," according to Gaston, "is the soul's contemplation of the crucified Christ," which in turn produces an anguish that is the source of "the strength that makes possible the final recognition" (210).

Radzinowicz (1987, 45, 49) draws a comparison between the sonnet and Ps. 143, both of which employ the poetical device of *anima mea*, the dialogue of a man with his soul (45). The sonnet's speaker, in Radzinowicz's view, though "convinced of his guilt," assures himself "that Christ will be compassionate, his physical beauty guaranteeing his mercy." Radzinowicz explains Donne's affirmation of the beauty of the body on the cross as "baroquely Christian." According to Radzinowicz, both Ps. 143 and *HSWhat* employ the *anima mea* device to emphasize that "the suffering speaker contains an even more suffering soul" (49).

Davies (1994, 23, 25) argues that Donne's work can be better understood by situating it within the traditions of Baroque and Mannerist art and architecture (23), citing as an example *HSWhat* 5. In Davies's view, Donne's version of "Jesus wept" has a "traumatizing beauty" as it contracts the "conflict of the Passion" into that one line. Davies notes that, as in Tintoretto's painting of *The Presentation of the Virgin*, "emphasis falls on the galvanized emotion of the ordinary human witnesses who guide our attention to the inset subject, so 'amasing' is the authenticating word in the sonnet which gives the scene its frisson of Eternity" (25).

Notes and Glosses

1–6 *What . . . from his pierc'd head fell.* **GRIERSON** (1912): the lines are the equal of the "magnificent openings" of Donne's love poems (2:lii–liii).

1–4 *What . . . can thee affright?* **BENNETT** (1934) finds here and in ll. 9–14 that Donne "trusts and mistrusts God's pity as the lover vacillates between the secure sense of being loved and the recurrent fear that love may yet be withdrawn" (27).

1 *What yf this present were the worlds last night?* **WHITE** (1936): for Donne (and "for most men of his time") God is "defined in terms of power and will"; He is the "Judge who fills the sinner's heart with terror" when the speaker poses the question here (133). **STAUFFER** (1946) cites the line as an example of the poet's ability to gain intensity through ellipsis, postponing meaning until the last syllable (73). **HUNT** (1954) finds that occasionally, as here, Donne's opening lines have "superb dramatic power, bursting on the reader" in a "coup de théâtre" (135). **MARTZ** (1954): the opening line corresponds to the "composition" or "proposing" stage of the Ignatian meditation (31). **CRAIK and CRAIK** (1986): "What if this present night were to bring the end of the world?" (279). **SMITH** (1992), citing this line, says that the Holy Sonnets characteristically "make a universal drama of religious life, in which every moment may confront us with the final annulment of time" (88).

1 *last night* **PATRIDES** (1985a): "the end of history at the Last Judgement" (442).

2–6 *Looke . . . from his pierc'd head fell.* **RAMSAY** (1917), citing these lines, notes that scripture is the source of Donne's knowledge of God (182).

2–4 *Looke . . . can thee affright?* **SMITH** (1991) (reading "Marke in my heart") notes that the "prospect of a present entry upon eternity" necessitates a "final showdown with ourselves, and with the exemplary events which bring time and the timeless together in one order." Points out that Christ's "double nature assures his power to transform events in time," as well as "our power to outbrave death" (133).

2–3 *Looke in my Hart, O Soule, . . . The picture of Christ crucifyde* **LEVER** (1974) says that the image is "[a]dapted from the common romance conceit that the poet has the picture of his mistress engraved upon his heart" (181). **NOVARR** (1980) (reading "Marke in my heart"), citing Donne's references to the Stations of the Cross in *Devotions*, Expostulation 16, says that Donne may have had in mind one of the "historical pictures" of the Stations when he wrote these lines (167n). SMITH (1992): "the prospect of a present entry upon eternity also calls for a showdown with ourselves and with the exemplary events that bring time and the timeless together in our order" (88).

2 *Looke in my Hart, O Soule, where thou dost dwell* HUNT (1954) notes that in some of Donne's poems the seat of the soul is the brain, in others the heart (223). SMITH (1971): some "scholastic metaphysicians thought that the heart is the seat of the soul" (631).

2 *Looke* GARDNER (1952) (reading "Marke") says that "Looke" could at the time "be used transitively" and cites the *OED* (71). GILL (1990) (reading "Mark"): "the word had contemplative and meditative connotations" (104).

2 *Soule,* LOUTHAN (1951): the poem is addressed to the speaker's soul (121).

3–5 *tell . . . the amazing Light,* BARRETT (1838) includes these lines as the epigraph for her poem "The Weeping Savior. Hymn III" (342).

3 *The picture of Christ crucifyde,* SMITH (1971) says that the "crucifix replaces the image of a mistress that secular lovers found in their hearts" and points to *Image* 1–5 (631).

4–6 *Whether . . . from his pierc'd head fell.* GRIERSON (1912) prefers a comma after "affright" and a full stop after "fell." Concludes that the lines can then be read: "Mark the picture of Christ in thy heart and ask, can that countenance affright thee in whose eyes the light of anger is quenched in tears, the furrows of whose frowns are filled with blood" (2:234).

4 *countenance* GILL (1990) notes that in the Bible "countenance" is frequently associated with God's face and cites Num. 6.26 (104).

4 *affright?* LOUTHAN (1951): the poem turns on the implications of the word: Christ took on his "hideous appearance" for the sake of the human soul, hence it could never frighten one that is contrite (122).

5–6 *Teares . . . from his pierc'd head fell.* UL-HASAN (1958): the visual, rather than symbolic, picture of Christ haunted Donne's mind (35). A. SMITH (1987), contending that Donne's wit is "never an irresponsible ingenuity for the sake of the performance itself," points to these lines as having "dramatic substance" and a "point." Notes that "the little play of figure vividly enacts the issue of the crucifixion itself, the tempering of Christ's justice by His mercy" (163–64). SMITH (1991): "The figurative action catches the complexity of final judgment, graphically setting the evidence of Christ's love to temper God's justice yet leaving the outcome perilously within the scope of the sinner's will. The wit is the means of realising the many-sidedness of religious experience, and of cutting right across the supposedly exclusive categories of Reformation theology" (136).

5 *Teares in his eyes quench the amazing Light,* **PATMORE [?]** (1846) cites this line as an example of "splendid thoughts and splendid words" in the Divine Poems (236). **GROSART** (1872–73) cites the line as one of several examples of "beauty and strength" in Donne (2:35–37). **DAVIES** (1994): "amasing" is the "stunned word which covers for all that cannot be said by the human witness: acknowledging only awe and wonder, it also conveys a visual afterglow of the unearthly intensity of a light to which the human eye is maladaptive and which can be conducted to us only through an impression of its staggering effect on the witness." Yet "the narrative order of the sentence conspires to delay the revelation until it is already over: 'amasing light' is in the accusative and does not reach us until it has been put out"; indeed, the "amasing light" is present only to be "quenched." Thus the "light from Jesus's eyes is all the more amazing for its absence; its destructibility, its conversion to darkness." "'Quench' puts it out like a fire, the agent being the paradox of those tokens of Divine humanity, Christ's tears. God can cry" (25).

5 *amazing Light,* **LOUTHAN** (1951): the light comes from Christ's eyes shining through tears and blood to show compassion (122).

5 *amazing* **GARDNER** (1952): "terrifying or dreadful. Donne speaks of Christ's tears on the cross in his sermon on the text 'Jesus wept'" (*Sermons,* 4:324) (71). **SHAABER** (1958): "dazzling" (104). **MARTZ** (1963): "terrifying, stupefying" (90). **SHAWCROSS** (1967): "fearful" (343). **KERMODE** (1968): "terrifying" (181). [So also, Lever (1974, 181), Patrides (1985a, 442), and Craik and Craik (1986, 280).] **SMITH** (1971): "overwhelming, terrifying" (631). **GILL** (1990): "frightening or even horrifying" (104). **BOOTY** (1990): "fearful, terrifying" (108). **FOWLER** (1991): "dreadful" (118). **FOWLER** (1995): "bewildering, dreadful" (261).

6 *pierc'd head* **GILL** (1990): see Mark 15.17: "and platted a crown of thorns and put it about his head" (104).

7–9 *And . . . as in myne idolatree* **MORRIS** (1953): the note of deep remorse, personal sinfulness, and repentance is to be found also in Hopkins's "Thee, God, I come from" (13–16) (77). Further, Donne's constant questioning of God, his tortured doubt, keeps him from attaining the kind of humility Eliot expresses in "Ash Wednesday" (III, 23–26; V, 13–14) (99–100).

7 *toung* **SHAWCROSS** (1967): "not only Christ's but that of those who turn the other cheek" (343).

7 *adiudge* **FOWLER** (1991): "sentence" (118).

8 *Which prayed . . . ranck spight?* **LEVER** (1974) (reading "fierce spite") points to Luke 23.5 and 34 (181). Similarly, Gill (1990, 104) and Fowler (1995, 261).

8 *ranck* GARDNER (1952) (reading "fierce") says that "ranck" is "more idiomatic" but that "fierce" is closer to Luke's account (23.5) of the trial of Jesus in almost all English versions (71).

8 *spight?* PATRIDES (1985a): "spite, malice" (443). [Similarly, Booty (1990, 108).]

9–14 *No, . . . assures a piteous mind.* DOGGETT (1934) observes that there is little evidence of Neoplatonic doctrine in Donne's poetry, an exception being these lines, which reflect a "belief in the aesthetic basis of Morality" (281). MARTZ (1954) finds the reference to "profane mistresses" to be "in the worst of taste," with "almost a tone of bragging" (84). Drops his criticism in the revised edition (1962), calling the reference to Donne's early "idolatree" a means of assuring the soul of God's "piteous mind" (84). CRUTTWELL (1954): the argument that "cruelty goes ill with beauty, which ought to be merciful" may be found in these lines and in Spenser's *Amoretti* 53 (13–14), both with divine parallels (66). GILL (1990) asks: "Does the gulf between the intense religious thinking of lines 1–8 and the (boastful?) recollections of *my profane mistresses* (10) point to the deeply divided state of the poet's soul, or is the whole poem trivialized by the comparison between divine and earthly love?" (104). Further notes the "difficulty" that the poem "depends upon the link, in both mistresses and Christ, between beauty and pity," and asks: "Is Christ presented in lines 1–8 as beautiful?" (108).

9–12 *No, . . . I say to thee* ANONYMOUS (1938) remarks on the "curious honesty" with which Donne harkens back "to memories of amorous torment and worldly satisfaction" (814). SMITH (1970) notes Donne's "effrontery" in applying to Christ the "casuistry he had once used to seduce women" (166).

9–10 *No, . . . my prophane Mistressis* FAUSSET (1938): Donne woos God as he "had in his 'idolatrie' wooed his 'profane mistresses'" (x). RUGOFF (1939): the lines are evidence that "at least once" Donne refers openly to the "transference" of imagery from erotic to religious verse (87). REEVES (1952) thinks that Donne's reference to the "prophane Mistressis" of his "Idolatree" is in bad taste (101).

9 *in myne Idolatree* GARDNER (1952) reads as "my idolatrie" but notes that "myne" is consistent with Donne's later tendency "to avoid *hiatus*" (71). GRANSDEN (1954): the phrase appears as well in *HSSighs*, in reference to Donne's profane mistresses (132). SMITH (1971): "amorous devotion to women, and worship of love" (631). [Similarly, Lever (1974, 181).] PATRIDES (1985a): "profane love" (443). CRAIK and CRAIK (1986): "worship of women" (280).

10 *prophane* SMITH (1971): "secular; blasphemous (because he worshipped women as goddesses)" (631). LEVER (1974): "Secular, unhallowed" (181). CRAIK and CRAIK (1986): "secular (as contrasted with spiritual)"; compare *HSVex* 6 (280).

11–12 *Bewty . . . rigor;* WILLEY (1954): "Beauty betokens a compassionate heart; ugliness betokens severity" (387). SHAWCROSS (1967): "Beauty is only a sign of pity; foulness is only a sign of rigor. That is, beauty arises from tenderness or kindness of love (mercy); ugliness arises from severity, cruelty, or mercilessness" (344). SMITH (1971): "beauty is a sign of compassion, and it is only ugly women who never relent towards their lovers" (631). CAIN (1981): "beauty is a sign of compassion, ugliness of unbending rigour" (312). PATRIDES (1985a): "Beauty is a sign of pity; ugliness, only a sign of strictness" (443). CRAIK and CRAIK (1986): "Beauty is a sign of pity, only ugliness is a sign of rigour" (280). HIEATT (1987): "Beauty is a sign of pity; only ugliness is unforgiving" (240).

11 *Bewty of pity,* GROSART (1872–73): "Beauty [is a sign] of pity" (2:291). [So also, Shaaber (1958, 104) and Lever (1974, 181), who adds that this is "an extension of the Renaissance Platonist view that physical beauty was a manifestation of ideal virtue."]

11 *foulnes* SHAABER (1958): "ugliness" (104). [So also, Lever (1974, 181).]

12 *to thee* SMITH (1971): "to his soul (reassuring it)" (631). [Similarly, Lever (1974, 181) and Craik and Craik (1986, 280).]

13–14 *To wicked . . . assures a piteous mind.* SPÖRRI-SIGEL (1949): in a combination of Christian and Platonic concepts, Christ's love is assured through his beauty (85). CAREY (1981) says that *HSWhat* ends with an "argumentative collapse," offering a "glimpse of a mind humiliatingly aware of its limits, when faced with the divine." Concludes that we witness a speaker, whose thoughts have been dominated by licentiousness, now only able to take recourse in "the hideous piffle about pity and pretty faces" (47). SMITH (1991): there is a bold explicitness in the concern about the "proper object of love" when the speaker "assures himself that the casuistry he had once used to seduce women—'all my profane mistresses'—becomes a true praise when it is used of Christ. Beauty is a sign of pity; only foulness signals rigour" (138). SMITH (1992), finding that Donne's religious verse "turn[s] upon a paradox that is central to the hope for eternal life" (i.e., "Christ's sacrificing himself to save mankind") and that "God's regimen is paradoxical," notes that in *HSWhat* Donne sees "no impropriety in entreating Christ with the casuistry he had used on his 'profane mistresses' when he assured them that only the ugly lack compassion" (90). ELLRODT (1993) states that the final argument sounds false: given that he draws a weak analogy between the beauty of a mistress and the beauty of the Crucified Christ with the bleeding brow, one would say that Donne tries desperately to conceive what he does not yet know: divine love (456).

13 *To wicked Sprights . . . Shapes assignd,* LEVER (1974) (reading "wicked spirits") points to the "folk tradition" suggested by the word "assigned" but also notes 2 Cor. 11.14 ("Satan himself is transformed into an angel of light"), indicating that "wicked spirits" might "assume beautiful shapes" (181).

14 *This bewteous forme assures a piteous mind.* PETERSON (1959): the "final

declaration of assurance" prepares for the next step in the process of contrition, finding a way to return God's love (512). [See also Holy Sonnets: Themes.] **LEWALSKI and SABOL** (1973): "Christ's beautiful form is a Platonic guarantee of a noble and generous mind" (155). **SLOANE** (1985): "piteous" suggests "both full of pity, or compassionate (in which case the 'minde' is Christ's), and pitiful, or moving to compassion (in which case the 'minde' is the speaker's, and ours)." The phrase can thus mean "at least three things: that the picture of Christ crucified gives clear evidence of divine compassion, that the evidence assures or gives comfort to the speaker's own pitiful mind," and that the "source of the comfort"—in part for the speaker but especially for the reader joining with the speaker in seeking assuring for "piteous minds"—is a "'forme' in the sense of emotion, rhetoric, poem" (206).

14 *This bewtcous forme* **SHAWCROSS** (1967): "the cross; since he asks that the cross be depicted in his heart, he seeks a mind given to pity (forgiveness) and piety" (344). **BOOTY** (1990): "Christ crucified" (108).

14 *assures* **GRIERSON** (1912), in rejecting "assumes," corrects "an obvious error of *all* the printed editions" (2:234). **LOUTHAN** (1951) prefers "assumes" because it "supplies all the relevant implications . . . in addition to implications of its own": since the "beauteous forme" assumes the presence of "a piteous minde," the soul is reassured (122–23). **GARDNER** (1952), in arguing for "assures" rather than the "assumes" of 1633, paraphrases the line: "the beauty of Christ is the guarantee of a compassionate mind." On the debate about Christ's physical beauty, remarks that some commentaries prefer Isa. 53.2 ("He hath no form nor comeliness; . . . there is no beauty that we should desire him") while others argue "that Christ's humanity was perfect and must therefore have included physical perfection" (71). **SHAABER** (1958): "assures" implies the unstated "(me that Christ has)" (104). **WILLIAMSON** (1960) takes issue with Grierson's substitution of "assures" for what he thinks should be "assumes," noting that "assumes" is the "commoner word" in Donne and that elsewhere "assure" appears only in "inter-assured" (106). Argues that for "any answer to the question with which the sonnet opens, the "significance of Christ" is paramount. Asserts that Donne's "'picture of Christ crucified' represents a figure of mingled pity and rigour," the significance of which becomes clear when one knows "whether that countenance can thee affright." Objects to "assures" because it makes "beauteous" more important than it actually is—"piteous minde" then "depends upon the less positive element in the proof" (107). Suggests that *HSWhat* "seems to develop primarily by the exclusion of 'rigour' through the exclusion of 'foulnesse,'" and finds that "'assures' makes the resolution turn on the less emphasized and less supported factor," while "assumes" points to the poet's logic in asserting that "this beautiful form supposes or takes for granted a piteous mind, and by his religious symbolism (crucifixion) that this beautiful form takes upon itself the character of pity." Concludes that "'assumes' carries the full weight of the sonnet" (106–07). **BALD** (1970a), suggesting a preference for "assures," says that "assumes" "gives the poem the flatness of a geometrical demonstration" (albeit one might argue "that the word would come naturally enough from one so soaked as Donne in the dialectic of scho-

lastic philosophy"), while "assures" "alters the whole effect of the poem and brings it to the triumphant climax which Donne surely intended" (38). **SMITH** (1971): "assures one of, guarantees" (632). [Similarly, Fowler (1991, 118).] **PATRIDES** (1985a) (reading "assumes") notes that the reading is "assures" in "the MSS and all modern editors" but points to Williamson (1960) (443). **PATRIDES** (1985b): the elimination of "'defective' or 'clumsy' readings from Donne's poetry is often based on principles that tend to shift as the occasion may happen to demand." Thus in HSWhat "the word 'assumes' in the last line is supported by all seventeenth-century editions but is displaced by 'assures' in all the reported manuscripts as well as in every modern edition" (370). **FISH** (1990) argues that in either of the variants, "This beauteous forme" points "not only to the form Donne has assigned to Christ's picture, but to the form of the poem itself, for the poem's "verbal felicity" alone is "doing either the assuring (which thus is no more than whistling in the dark) or the assuming (which as a word at least has the grace to name the weakness of the action it performs)" (247).

 *HSWhy*

COMMENTARY

General Commentary

Korninger (1956, 210) observes that Donne finds it inexplicable that God should place sinful humanity in charge of his Creation, a mystery surpassed only by the sacrificial death of Christ.

Raspa (1983, 46–47, 107) reads *HSWhy* through the lenses of "the ideal Renaissance man" in Ignatius of Loyola's *Spiritual Exercises*. Humankind, Raspa argues, is viewed as a "meditator on the self" and dominates over other creatures because of the capacity for meditation, not because of "his place as an actor in a worldly ladder of being" (46). In *HSWhy*, Raspa says, all creatures are subject to humankind, not because they rule, but because they meditate (46–47). Moreover, according to Raspa, "the subjection of all things to man's dominion was of a startling indifference," and nature, once imitated in verse, was a picture of the ultimate significance of time. Therefore, in Raspa's view, "Christ was not 'tied' to nature but followed its course to give it meaning elsewhere than in time (ll. 12–13)," so that in Donne's effort to order nature in verse, "the imitation of things in verse expressed this meaning momentarily" (107).

The Poet/Persona

Miner (1969, 19–20), noting that the audience in *HSWhy* shifts from the reader and speaker in the first four lines to the animals in lines 5 to 10 and back to the reader and speaker in the final lines, says that this movement demonstrates the "fluidity" or "kinesis" of the audience in Donne's poems (19). The two crucial terms of the "poetic relationship," Miner states, are the poet and the reader, and he suggests that in *HSWhy* (and also *Ind*) Donne achieves "private poetry" by establishing the terms upon which poet and reader are to meet. They are, he points out, joined by the "we" of line 1 and the "us" of line 11, but they are kept apart by the dramatic audience of the poem, the animals whose fictional character "sets the reader at a distance." The dramatic audience assures the privacy of the poet, Miner argues, because it distances the reader and it brings the poet closer to his speaker (20).

Brink (1977, 102) remarks that in *HSSpit* and *HSWhy* Donne "preaches to his soul in tones of hope newly vested in the Father, who holds the son in especial esteem, as though a reconciliation of natural father and son had taken place."

Strier (1989, 379) finds *HSWhy* similar to *HSSpit* in its "oddly thin" expression of feeling. In the middle of the sestet, according to Strier, Donne "exhorts himself

543

to 'wonder at a greater wonder' [l. 11] than the subservience of the animals, namely the crucifixion, but again little *sense* of wonder is evoked."

Genre and Traditions

Martz (1954, 43–44) observes that the sonnet has a "very close resemblance" to the conclusion of the second of the *Spiritual Exercises* of St. Ignatius Loyola for the first week of meditation (43). The parallels lie, he says, in "a single, scientific instance in the first quatrain," through "a shift to direct questioning of the animals" in the next six lines, to the "colloquy of mercy" with which the poem concludes (44). See also Holy Sonnets: Genre and Traditions.

Language and Style

Kortemme (1933, 48) observes that an antithesis between opposites extends over the entire poem, in which two parallels are developed with the second an elevation of the first, as when nature, sinless itself, is subservient to sinful and weak humankind and God the creator makes Himself subservient to his own creation.

Mahood (1950, 124) finds that the "violent *contemptus mundi*" that characterized the works of Donne's "middle years" has disappeared, and that his "new humanism has lost the intellectual arrogance of the old." In HSWhy, for example, Mahood claims that Donne describes the weakness of its fallen condition as heightening the dignity humankind gained by the Redemption.

Stampfer (1970, 255–56) argues that HSWhy comprises "impersonal meditations" that "go against the grain" in Donne. The accents in the first quatrain, he says, are metrically blurred and clumsy, without a tough, biting intellect to shape them. "Prodigall elements" (l. 2), for example, is too abstract to grip the imagination. The second quatrain, he contends, expands on the first somewhat more persuasively. However, the speaker "falls back on old sermons to express a dull, schooled conviction of weakness, a perfunctory disturbance" of the inferiority of humankind (255). By contrast, Stampfer observes, the antithesis in the sestet "catches fire," repeating and reinforcing the octave, but it is also "the shock of grasp, the startled crystallization of [the speaker's] impossible abasement" (256). Stampfer contends that the accent, which was badly muffled in the octave, grows suddenly intuitive; for example, he says, the word "weaker" weakens, violating the metrical accent. Likewise, Stampfer remarks, the "I" grows weak, almost obliterated by the contraction to "Weaker I am" (255–56). The synthesis in the concluding couplet contemplates God's ways in prayerful wonder. The turning toward God "intensifies a notch" in this sonnet, Stampfer says, as "shocked discovery settles to accepted instruction" (256).

Clark (1982, 76) finds that the most interesting typological references in Donne's "sacred lyrics" are those "based on movement from the Old Testament to the New." Clark explains, for example, that in HSWhy the octave asks, "Why are wee by all creatures waited on?" The sestet answers, according to Clark, "that Christ's sacrificial death saves his special creatures, humanity," an answer that develops from the "perfecting atonement of Christ" superceding "insufficient Mosaic sacrifices of the types, bulls and goats," as in Heb. 10.

Fenner (1982, 15) finds *HSWhy* achieving "its power entirely by a structure of explicit argument," for the sonnet "has no detailed imagery, absolutely no metaphors, scarcely anything that can be called 'figurative.'" The first ten lines, in Fenner's view, "manipulate" three words to create the paradox that "superior beings are in subjection to inferior," namely, "Elements," "Animals," and "Man" ("we"). Line twelve adds a fourth term ("Created Nature") which, according to Fenner, "must be even the highest place on the scale of value," since it "subdues" all else to "Man." And line thirteen introduces the last term, God, which creates the most extreme paradox of all, that is, "the Higher-than-the-highest makes Himself go below the lower-than-the-lowest." But for Fenner, the word "foes" in the final line is "the most impressive moment," in that it introduces a "new relationship of enmity," for "hate is confronted with love."

Structure

Esch (1955, 50–51) argues that the sonnet departs from the Italian structure in that lines 9–10 draw their meaning from the octave, and hence the turn comes in the final quatrain introduced by "But." The poem, Esch continues, forms a bridge to the metrical structure of sonnets where the turn is delayed and the antithesis between octave and sestet reduced. See more under Holy Sonnets: Genre and Traditions.

Simpson (1969, item 75) argues that the use of biblical allusions in *HSWhy* is a "subtle principle of structure" operative in the poem. This structural unity relates basic elements of mood and tone (that is, awe and wonder) to the central theme and paradox of the Atonement.

Themes

Reeves (1952, 101) paraphrases the poem: "It is a wonder that nature should be subject to man, who is more sinful and corrupt; it is an even greater wonder that the creator himself should have died for men."

Grenander (1955) explicates the sonnet, drawing attention to Donne's treatment of the paradoxical image of the "chain of being" and the sense of wonder it evokes, first minerals, then animals, then humans, and finally the "Creator." The wonder, Grenander continues, is that all nature is subservient to sinful and weaker humankind, and that the "Creator" of all died for the human "Creatures" he made.

Peterson (1959, 511–12) compares Donne's attitude toward reason here to that in *HSMin*, earlier in the sequence of Holy Sonnets. There, he observes, reason is the faculty that makes humankind responsible for their sins; here it is the gift of God's love that enables humankind to rule the natural world. See also Holy Sonnets: Themes.

Parini (1977, 305) writes that *HSWhy* "continues an exploration of the theme of redemption in spite of man's overwhelming sin," which prepares the way for the "*dies irae*" imagined in *HSWhat*.

To Low (1978, 67), *HSWhy* "reverts to the creatures, not to complain" as in *HSMin*, but "to wonder at their subjection to sinful man."

Lewalski (1979, 271) finds that *HSWhy* focuses upon the "wonderful circumstance"

that "purer elements" or a "whole creation untarnished by sin" serve sinful human-
ity, a focus that provides "a means to understand more fully the wonderful benefits
of Christ's crucifixion."

Shaw (1981, 45–46) views the speaker as one who "contemplates the 'catalogue'
of God's creatures and continues to feel," as in *HSDue*, "that he is odd man out in
God's world." The sonnet's "main note," according to Shaw, "is one of 'wonder' at
our Lord's condescension" (45). And therefore, Shaw notes, "redemption is perceived
in the last lines as a gracious consummation of the first act of Creation," suffering in
the flesh, as Christ did, "the full consequences of sin" (46).

HSWhy and other Works

Grant (1973, 39–41) argues that, between 1608 and 1615, Donne was demon-
strably interested in the *Heptaphus* of Pico (1489), especially book 5, chapters 6–7,
which might be a direct source for *HSWhy* (39). Grant asserts that there is identical
development and resolution of the argument in the two works, together with sig-
nificant verbal parallels (41).

Milward (1979 [1988, 71–73]) associates this sonnet with the *First Week* of the
Ignatian *Spiritual Exercises* in its attention to such wonders as why it is "that all crea-
tures not only leave us in life but even wait upon us" (71). Milward notes that the
speaker's voicing of wonder intensifies in the second quatrain, addressing his ques-
tions specifically to the animals. In the sestet, according to Milward, the speaker
establishes a "general contrast" between himself and other creatures by acknowledg-
ing that he is "weaker in nature and worse by reason of his sins" (72–73). The speaker's
greatest wonder, then, Milward points out, is that the Creator has "subdued" all
creatures to humankind, as in Ps. 8, and that He has died for all humanity (73).

Sherwood (1984, 155) finds in *HSWhy* a development grounded in Ignatian de-
votional exercises, a development similar to that in *HSWilt*. The "reasoning pro-
cess," he notes, assumes the form of "prolonged questioning that opposes man's dignity
as fulfilment of the created world to his sinful guilt," questions that in turn "preface
the 'wonder at a greater wonder' that the Creator died for his enemies."

Notes and Glosses

1–8 *Why . . . you might swallow and feed vpon?* **MATSUURA** (1953): Donne
questions why the elements and lower creatures wait upon man (13).

1–4 *Why . . . farther from corruption?* **MORRIS** (1953): the reference to man's
vileness is echoed in Hopkins's "God's Grandeur" (ll. 6–8) and "In the Valley of
Elwy" (ll. 9–11) (77).

1 *Why ame I by all Creatures wayted on?* **MELTON** (1906): in Donne's meter an
insignificant word often carries the stress, here "by" (70). **GRENANDER** (1955)
draws attention to the words "creatures," "Created," "Creator," and "Creatures" here
and in ll. 12–14, noting that Donne distinguishes between all of nature in the first

line and humankind specifically in the last by capitalizing "Creatures" in the latter (item 42).

2–4 *Why do . . . from corruption?* **WARNKE** (1967): "the elements, unlike man, are not composed of a mixture" (269). **LEVER** (1974): the "elements were each of one kind, hence less corruptible than man who, compounded of all four, suffered from their frequent imbalance" (181). [Similarly, Hieatt (1987, 239).]

2 *the prodigall Elements* **LEVER** (1974): "Earth, air, fire (as sunlight), and water, all lavish in gifts" (181).

2 *prodigall* **PATRIDES** (1985a): "wasteful" (442). [So also, Booty (1990, 108).]

3–4 *beeing more pure . . . from corruption?* **GARDNER** (1952): "Man, being compounded of the four elements, is mixed, not simple, and therefore more liable to corruption, which arises from inequality of mixture. [Similarly, Smith (1971, 630), who notes that the elements and creatures were not the "prime agent in the Fall" but "partake of its consequences only through human action," and thus they are "nearer the original state of created innocence" than is humankind.] But although the elements are 'simple,' they have not absolute purity and incorruptibility, which are the properties of spirit alone" (70). [Similarly, Lewalski and Sabol (1973, 154).]

3 *Life and foode to mee, beeing more pure then I,* **RICHTER** (1902): an example of "irregular meter" ("doppelte Taktumstellung") (395).

3 *then* **PATRIDES** (1985a): "than" (442).

4–8 *Simple, . . . and feed vpon?* **SIMPSON** (1969): l. 4 may draw meaning from 2 Pet. 2.12 ("But these, as natural brute beasts, made to be taken and destroyed . . . shall utterly perish in their own corruption"). If the development from "corruption" in l. 4 to the "brute beasts" of ll. 5–8 was accomplished through 2 Pet. 2.12, then it is instructive to examine biblical references to those beasts to understand better the paradoxes in ll. 5–8. While it is paradoxical that the strength of the horse would be subjected to the weakness of a human being, Donne may also have in mind Ps. 32.9 ("Be ye not as the horse, or as the mule, which have no understanding"). Further, Ps. 22.12–13 and 80.13 depict human "fear and apprehension" in the "relationship with bulls and boars." The sonnet uses these figures to stress the paradox that in spite of the creatures' strength and their potential danger, humankind ultimately has dominion over them (item 75).

4 *Simple,* **GRIERSON** (1912) prefers "simple" to the "simpler" of other editions, since "the simplicity of the elements does not admit to comparison." Reads the line: "The elements are purer than we are, and (being simple) farther from corruption" (2:234). **SHAABER** (1958): "not compounded (and therefore more durable)" (104). **MARTZ** (1963): "of a single substance, not mixed" (89).

4 *farther from corruption?* CAIN (1981): "because not unevenly mixed" (312).

4 *corruption? . . . subiection?* SMITH (1971): "Both pronounced as four syllables" (630).

5 *Why brookst thou ignorant horse subiection?* SMITH (1971): "why do you put up with man's making a slave of you?" (631).

5 *brookst* LEVER (1974): "Bearest" (181).

6–8 *Why . . . you might swallow and feed vpon?* MORRIS (1953) finds that Donne's lines have the cadence of everyday speech, as here where long stressed monosyllables assume the same value as two or three-syllable feet. Observes that Hopkins's sprung rhythm has the same effect, as in "The Wreck of the Deutschland" (20:6) (43).

6 *bore,* WARNKE (1967): "boar" (269). [So also, Patrides (1985a, 442) and Booty (1990, 108).]

6 *selily* REEVES (1952): "foolishly" (101). [So also, Lever (1974, 181).] MARTZ (1963): "sillily, foolishly" (89). SHAWCROSS (1967): "weakly, foolishly" (343). WARNKE (1967): "sillily" (269). SIMPSON (1969): "Seely" had a "complex connotation" in the early seventeenth century, indicating a "condition of spiritual blessedness, piety, and holiness." In the sixteenth century the term was used "to indicate a condition of innocent, undeserved suffering, *especially of animals*," and "it indicated a state of being deserving of pity or sympathy." SMITH (1971): "Meekly, naively" (631). [Similarly, Patrides (1985a, 442) and Booty (1990, 108).]

7 *Dissemble* SHAWCROSS (1967): "feign" (343). [So also, Patrides (1985a, 442) and Booty (1990, 108).]

7 *by one Mans stroke* SMITH (1971): "(a) the slaughterman's blow; (b) Adam's sin, for which the whole creation suffers death" (631).

8 *kind* LEVER (1974): "Race" (181).

9 *I'ame weaker, wo'is me,* BARRETT (1838) uses an alternative reading ("Weaker I am, woe is me") as the epigraph for her poem "The Weakest Thing" (355).

9 *wo'is me,* LEVER (1974): "Pronounced with a slur; almost 'woe's me'" (181).

10 *timorous.* SMITH (1971): "fearful" (631). [So also, Patrides (1985a, 442) and Booty (1990, 108).]

11–14 *But . . . his foes hath dyed.* SPÖRRI-SIGEL (1949): Donne emphasizes God's righteousness in contrast with sinful humanity by asking why nature should serve humankind, but instead of answering, calls to mind an even greater wonder, God's sacrifice for our salvation (73–74). SMITH (1991) suggests that in "posing such a question to himself Donne puts our domestic decorum in a final perspective." Observes that humankind "could claim no authority in a natural order" which it has "deranged" except for the fact that order is "restored to us by the supreme solicitude of the Creator himself." Emphasizes that the wit of Donne's poems never removes them from "common experience" but rather "discovers a metaphysical presence in our daily lives" (138).

11 *But wonder at a greater wonder; for to vs* MELTON (1906): in Donne's meter an insignificant word often carries the stress, here "at" (69). LEVER (1974) observes that this is a line "of five stresses without regular feet" (181).

13–14 *But their Creator, . . . hath dyed.* SMITH (1971): the "paradoxical progression of the argument is that the creatures are less guilty than man but have to serve men, while the Creator himself, who is not guilty at all, abases himself to serve men infinitely more" (631).

13 *But their Creator, whom Sin nor Nature tyed,* STEIN (1944): Donne follows the practice of Elizabethan dramatists in sometimes adding an extra syllable to a line, "admitting an extra feminine ending in the foot preceding the cesura" (393–94).

13 *whom Sin nor Nature tyed,* SHAWCROSS (1967): "whom neither sin nor nature restricted" (343).

13 *tyed,* SHAABER (1958): "restricted, bound" (104). [Similarly, Booty (1990, 108).] SMITH (1971): "(a) constricted, as men are by their frailty and death; (b) assigned to a definite place in the natural order" (631). PATRIDES (1985a): "constricted" (442).

 *HSWilt*

Commentary

General Commentary

The editor ("H.E.M.") of *Dies Consecrati: or, A New Christian Year with the Old Poets* (1855, 146, 200, 294) prints *HSDeath* (294) and *HSWilt* (146), along with *Cross*, abbreviated and slightly altered. *HSWilt*, recommended as a reading for Whitsunday, is edited by omitting lines 9–10 and altering some words.

Garrod (1946, x) singles out *HSDeath* and *HSWilt* from among the Divine Poems as works "men will not willingly let die."

Martz (1966, 49), discussing the process of meditation and its relationship to various poems of Donne, notes that in *HSWilt* Donne himself uses the term "meditation" in the second line.

Jackson (1970, 109–10) describes *HSWilt* as a poem representing "the mythic story of God's entry into the world" (109). The whole poem and especially the final two lines, he says, rehearse humankind's longing for God and God's return of love in an endless begetting and mutual reflection (110).

Mackenzie (1990, 76) finds *HSWilt* to be the "least successful" of the Holy Sonnets, noting that the opening lines "say all that needs to be said about it." The opening, he contends, offers a "set meditation" that will be "worked through," with nothing being done to "energise this into a poem."

The Poet/Persona

Stampfer (1970, 265) observes that this sonnet is a "diastole" of formal instruction following the "systole" of agonized feeling in *HSBatter* and that *HSWilt* "settles into place" much of the material of the earlier sonnets. Stampfer says that "the phobia of 'gluttonous death'" in *HSScene* 5 "rises to a wholesome 'digest, / My Soule'" in *HSWilt* 1–2 and that Donne's "obsessive image of himself as a usurped city" in *HSBatter* is healed through the portrait of Christ who died for "Us whom he'had made, and Satan stolne, to unbinde" (*HSWilt* 12). *HSWilt*, he concludes, "closes on a note of serene self-transcendence; for the first time, God and man exchange images in the intimacy of self-surrender."

Brink (1977, 102, 107) believes that in *HSWilt* Donne uncovers the "partially conscious vestiges of his lost father" and that he builds a "theological system of hope far more ample than any belonging to his days of inconstancy in love idolatry" (102). At the center of Brink's analysis lies his concern for describing Donne's "psychological salvation" in the religious poetry, which he declares is "a merciful release from bondage to compulsions within" (107).

Strier (1989, 378–79) regards this sonnet as "transparently an act of will rather than of spontaneity" (378). Moreover, according to Strier, the poem generally reads "like a spiritual exercise," and as such may be understood as a "doctrinally coherent, incarnationally focused" reframing of the "inchoate, ontologically focused" octave of HSDue—although, he adds, HSWilt "retains throughout a sense of mere correctness, of dutiful explication and paraphrase" (378–79).

Genre and Traditions

Martz (1954, 45–46) quotes HSWilt in full as an example of a sonnet that reflects but one of the steps in the Ignatian method of meditation, the "analysis" or "understanding" stage of the exercise. Martz finds the poem to restate a meditation annexed to the fourth week of Ignatius Loyola's *Spiritual Exercises*. See more under Holy Sonnets: Genre and Traditions.

Milward (1979 [1988, 80–82]) also attributes the focus of this sonnet to the *Spiritual Exercises* of St. Ignatius, but here the poet "jumps" from his attention in the earlier sonnets on the beginning stages of the *Exercises* "to their concluding *Contemplation for Obtaining Divine Love*" (80). The concluding couplet of the sonnet, Milward notes, "sums up" this divine love: "dwelling first on the gift of creation, by which 'man was made like God'" (l. 13) or "in the image of God" (Gen. 1.27), and then focusing on the "still greater gift of redemption, by which God himself was 'made like man'" (l. 14) (82).

Sherwood (1984, 155) compares the sonnet to the Ignatian devotional exercises and their grounding in acts of memory, understanding, and colloquy, and the "renewing" of the tripartite image of God within man. Sherwood finds HSWilt "to be purely rational in form," that is, focusing on "understanding" only. We see this, in Sherwood's view, in the soul's invitation to "'digest' a series of paradoxes in this 'wholsome meditation'" (ll. 1–2): for example, "the Father who has 'begot a Sonne most blest'" (l. 5) is also, and "contradictorily," "still begetting" (l. 6), while the "'Sonne of glory,' who created man, was slain" (l. 11). The effect, in Sherwood's view, is to stimulate "the soul to love and wonder."

Language and Style

Faerber (1950, 30–31) quotes the poem in full to illustrate the totality of religious paradoxes, which should calm the irritation caused by the contradictions of Christian belief and thereby stimulate piety. See also Holy Sonnets: Language and Style.

Labriola (1990, 66) emphasizes the value of using iconographic details to interpret Donne's poetry on the Resurrection, noting specifically HSWilt in which Donne "describes how the 'Sonne of glory came downe, and was slaine' [l. 10] in order to 'unbinde' [l. 12] humanity from the power of Satan."

Prosody

Esch (1955, 52) finds the sonnet Italian in form but closer to the Surrey-Shakespeare structure in that it develops the theme of God's incomprehensible love for human beings in three quatrains and draws a conclusion in the brilliant flash of the final couplet, which marvels at the paradox of God's act of salvation. See more under Holy Sonnets: Genre and Traditions.

Themes

Reeves (1952, 102) summarizes the argument: "God made man in his own image, to be a sharer in his glory; having lost man through man's transgressions, he was forced to buy him back again, as a robbed man has to buy back his own goods or lose them. This he did by giving his son, Christ, the likeness of man."

Peterson (1959, 513) observes that HSWilt "reaffirms the tenet that grace will not be forthcoming until the penitent's love of God is sufficient."

Lewalski (1979, 272) finds that HSWilt and HSPart, the last two sonnets of the 1633 and 1635 sequences, "focus upon the further ramifications of justification and regeneration." HSWilt, she says, "invites the soul to meditate upon God's love shown especially in the matter of the speaker's adoption as a son of God," and she points out that, according to the Calvinist paradigm, "adoption is the result of justification."

Yearwood (1982, 210, 218–19) suggests that the conversion process in Donne's twelve Holy Sonnets of 1633 (and following Gardner's [1952] order) "begins in pride, proceeds to confession and despair, and culminates in a humble joy and confidence" (210). Following what Yearwood describes as the spiritual "crisis" of HSBatter, the "voice of grace" returns in HSWilt, "piercing through the self-generated and self-directed frenzy of the soul," a response informed by "superior wisdom" regarding the "spiritual needs of the speaker," promising "forgiveness" by "summarizing the Christian events" and "by reminding the seeker that Christ is within him" (218). According to Yearwood, the voice of grace "reminds the soul that he does not need to be remade; Christ has been remade for him" (219).

Guibbory (1986, 94) finds here and elsewhere in the Holy Sonnets that "all memory's paths ultimately lead to God." For, she observes, when a person "remembers that God made 'his Temple' in man's breast [l. 4], chose him to be 'Coheire to'his glory' [l. 8] and 'was slaine' in order to redeem him [l. 11], that person will come to 'love God, as he thee.'"

NOTES AND GLOSSES

1–2 *Wilt thou love God, . . . meditation:* **GUIBBORY** (1980) suggests that the speaker's "desire for his soul to 'digest' this 'wholsome meditation' may be based on the "metaphoric descriptions of memory as the stomach or belly of the soul" in Augustine and St. Bernard (271–72). Notes that Donne attributes to Bernard the phrase "the stomach of the soul," though it "actually derives from Augustine" (272n27).

1 *digest* **SMITH** (1971): "reflect on methodically" (632).

3–4 *How God . . . his temple in thy brest.* **FAERBER** (1950): a paradox that not only contradicts reason but injures the sense of justice (27). [See also Holy Sonnets:

Language and Style.] **KLINCK** (1981): this is one of several poems about redemption that also include the Trinity, reminding us that "God the Spirit" makes his Temple in the poet's "brest [l. 4]," that the Father "has adopted us, but finding us alienated from Him, who had made us, sends the 'Sonne of glory' [l. 11] to redeem us from Satan" (251).

4 *doth make his temple in thy brest.* **GARDNER** (1952): cf. 1 Cor. 6.19: "Know ye not that your body is the temple of the Holy Ghost" (72). [So also, Lewalski and Sabol (1973, 156), Booty (1990, 109), and Carey (1990b, 455).] **PATRIDES** (1985a): see 1 Cor. 3.16: "know not that ye are the temple of God, and that the Spirit of God dwelleth in you?" (444). [So also, Booty (1990, 109).]

5–6 *The father . . . (for he nere begonne)* **FAERBER** (1950): in describing the paradox of God's infinity measured in time, Donne uses the present perfect tense in the first line to indicate that the divine act is completed and fixed in time, but in the second he picks up the movement toward the future and the past (24). [See more under Holy Sonnets: Language and Style.] **FISCHLER** (1994): the lines invoke the image of "the dynamic divine circle, removed from the context of linear time" (172).

6 *And still begetting, (for he nere begonne)* **GARDNER** (1952): "The Son is eternally, not temporarily begotten" (72). **SHAWCROSS** (1967): "the Son. That is, He is eternal; His being did not have a beginning, for He always was" (345). **WARNKE** (1967): "The begetting of Christ is an eternal process since God exists outside time" (271). **SMITH** (1971): "God begets Christ eternally, not in time where things have a beginning and an end" (632). **CAIN** (1981): "because it was an event beyond time" (312). **PATRIDES** (1985a): "'never begun' yet *still begetting* since God is outside time, not bound to past, present, or future." Donne observes that the creation and the Last Judgment "are not a minute asunder in respect of eternity, which hath no minutes" (*Sermons*, 6:331) (444) **BOOTY** (1990): "the Son, who is outside time, eternal, without a beginning" (109). **CAREY** (1990b): "God's acts are eternal, without beginning or end" (455).

7–8 *Hath daignd . . . endles rest.* **GARDNER** (1952) finds the source of the image in Rom. 8.15–17: "'But ye have received the Spirit of adoption . . . . The Spirit itself beareth witness . . . that we are the children of God . . . heirs of God, and joint-heirs with Christ' ('coheredes,' Vulgate; 'co-heires,' Rheims; 'heyres anexed with,' Geneva)" (72). Similarly, Smith (1971, 632), who mistakenly cites Rom. 8.30, Lewalski and Sabol (1973, 156), and Barańczak (1984, 162).

7 *adoption* **SMITH** (1971): "Pronounced as four syllables" (632).

8 *Saboths* **SHAWCROSS** (1967): "from the Hebrew meaning 'day of rest'" (345).

8 *Saboths endles rest.* **PATRIDES** (1985a) points to the last extant lines of *The Faerie Queene*: "all shall rest eternally / With Him that is the God of Sabbaoth hight" (444).

9–12 *And as . . . and Satan stole, to'vnbind.* **FAERBER** (1950) finds in the lines one of the paradoxes of Christ in that his sacrificial death should not have been necessary. Notes that Christ is comparable to the man who buys again from the thief the goods that were stolen from him (27). [See also Holy Sonnets: Language and Style.] **ARCHER** (1977): "he compares the incarnation to a man who searches for his stolen goods" (185). **SMITH** (1991): "Such wit does not work to embellish received truths. It brings the traffic of the world under the general laws which govern our fallen state" (136–37).

9–10 *And as . . . must loose or buy'it againe;* **RUGOFF** (1939), in cataloging images from "Commerce and Coinage," observes that Donne reaches "a peak in his juxtaposition of the holy and the worldly" in his "comparison of Christ paying with his life to redeem mankind from Satan" (146–47). **SMITH** (1971): "As the law stood, a man whose property was stolen and then sold lost his right in it to the purchaser, and could only recover it by buying it back again if the purchaser was willing to sell. In the same way, Christ has to pay with his life to recover his own property — us — from Satan" (632). **BARAŃCZAK** (1984): this statement is in agreement with legal regulations in power during Donne's life (162).

11 *Sonne of glory* **GROSART** (1872–73), reading "Sunne of glory," says: "'Sunne of glory' = Sun of Righteousness" (2:291).

11 *Sonne* **PATRIDES** (1985a): "also in the sense of 'Sunne' (the actual reading of 1635–69)," a pun in wide use that "predates the seventeenth century." Cf. John Lydgate, *Lyf of our Lady,* especially ll. 479–85, Herbert's "Sunday," and Vaughan's "Son-days" (444).

12 *Vs, whome . . . Satan stole,* **WARNKE** (1967): "us whom Satan had stolen" (271). [Similarly, Patrides (1985a, 444).]

12 *vnbind.* **SHAWCROSS** (1967): "(from the ties which man had made with Satan)" (345). [Similarly, Booty (1990, 109).]

13–14 *'Twas . . . like Man much more.* **UL-HASAN** (1958): Donne humanizes the Son and equates himself with "the Supreme Martyr" (36). **SMITH** (1971): the "comparison in degree suggests that the Fall had its fortunate aspect in that it evoked this surpassing demonstration of God's love for us" (632).

14 *much more.* **PATRIDES** (1985a): "the redemption of man was commonly regarded as a divine activity far superior to the creation of the world" (444).

WORKS CITED

Adams, Robert M. 1958. *Strains of Discord: Studies in Literary Openness*. Ithaca, NY: Cornell University Press.

———, ed. 1962. "John Donne (1572–1631)." In *The Norton Anthology of English Literature*, gen. ed. M. H. Abrams, 1:755–59, 783–86. New York: W. W. Norton. Rev. 1968, 1974, 1979, 1986, 1993.

Addleshaw, S. 1931. "A Famous Dean: Dr. John Donne of St. Paul's." *Church Quarterly Review* 113:38–54.

Aers, David and Gunther Kress. 1981. "Vexatious Contraries: A Reading of Donne's Poetry." In *Literature, Language and Society in England, 1580–1680*. Dublin: Gill and Macmillan; Totowa: Barnes & Noble Books. 49–75.

Albrecht, Roberta J. 1992. "Montage, Mise en Scène, and Miserable Acting: Feminist Discourse in Donne's Holy Sonnet X." *ELN* 29 (4):23–32.

Allain, Mathe. 1980. "Christ's Cross and Adam's Tree." *New Laurel Review* 10:18–24.

Allen, M. C. 1995. "George Herbert's Pastoral Wit." In *The Wit of Seventeenth-Century Poetry*, ed. Claude J. Summers and Ted-Larry Pebworth, 119–34. Columbia and London: University of Missouri Press.

Allinson, Mark. 1991. "Re-Visioning the Death Wish: Donne and Suicide." *Mosaic* 24, no. 1:31–46.

Altizer, Alma B. 1973. *Self and Symbolism in the Poetry of Michelangelo, John Donne, and Agrippa D'Aubigné*. The Hague: Martinus Nijhoff.

Alvarez, A. 1966. "Donne: Holy Sonnets." In *Master Poems of the English Language*, ed. Oscar Williams, 131–35. New York: Trident Press.

Alves, Leonard, F. S. C. 1985. "Well Done, Ill Donne: The Relevance of John Donne 1571/2–1631." *Eibunagaku to Eigogaku* 22:21–41.

Anonymous. 1840. *Selections from the Works of John Donne D. D.* Oxford: Talboys.

———. 1862–63. "On the Elizabethan Age, and some of its less-known Poets." *QR* 19:43–90.

———. 1864. "Dr. Donne." *The Leisure Hour* 13:555–58.

———. 1899. "*The Life and Letters of John Donne, Dean of St Paul's*. By Edmund Gosse. 2 vols. (Heinemann)." *Ath* 2:645–46.

———. 1900. "The Poetry of John Donne." *Ac* 59:608–09.

———. 1938. "Devotional Poetry: Donne to Wesley: The Search for an Unknown — Eden." *TLS* 24 December:814, 816.

———. 1956. "Poetic Tradition in Donne." *TLS* 16 March:164.

Ansari, Asloob Ahmad. 1974. "Two Modes of Utterance in Donne's Divine Poems." In *Essays on John Donne: A Quarter Centenary Tribute*, ed. Asloob Ahmad Ansari, 139–56. Aligarh: Aligarh Muslim University.

Archer, Stanley. 1961. "Meditation and the Structure of Donne's 'Holy Sonnets.'" *ELH* 35:137–47.

———. 1971. "Donne's Holy Sonnet IX." *Expl* 30:Item 4.

———. 1977. "The Archetypal Journey Motif in Donne's Divine Poems." In *New Essays on Donne*, ed. Gary A. Stringer, 173–91. Salzburg: Universität Salzburg.

Arndt, Murray D. 1990. "Distance on the Look of Death." *L&M* 9:38–49.

Aronstein, Philip. 1920. *John Donne als Dichter: Ein Beitrag zur Kenntnis der Englischen Renaissance*. Halle: Niemeyer. Publ. as "John Donne" in *Anglia* 44 (1920):115–213.

Asals, Heather. 1979. "John Donne and the Grammar of Redemption." *English Studies in Canada* 5:125–39.

Atkinson, A. D. 1951. "Donne Quotations in Johnson's Dictionary." *N&Q* 196:387–88.

Austin, Frances. 1992. *The Language of the Metaphysical Poets*. Basingstoke: Macmillan; New York: St. Martin's Press.

Badenhausen, Richard. 1992. "Wilfred Owen on John Donne: 'You've got a hell of a breath.'" *The Midwest Quarterly* 33 (2):181–92.

Bagg, Robert. 1969. "The Electromagnet and the Shred of Platinum." *Arion* 8:407–29.

Baker, Herschel. 1952. *The Wars of Truth: Studies in the Decay of Christian Humanism in the Earlier Seventeenth Century*. Cambridge: Harvard University Press.

Bald, R. C. 1970a. "Editorial Problems: A Preliminary Survey." In *Art and Error: Modern Textual Editing*, ed. Ronald Gottesman and Scott Bennet, 37–61. Bloomington and London: Indiana University Press.

———. 1970b. *John Donne: A Life*, ed. Wesley Milgate. New York and Oxford: Oxford University Press.

Banzer, Judith. 1961. "'Compound Manner': Emily Dickinson and the Metaphysical Poets." *AL* 32:417–33.

Barańczak, Stanislaw, ed. 1984. *John Donne: Wiersze wybrane whybór, przeklad, postowie i opracowamie*. Krakow, Wrocklon: Wydawnictwo Literackie.

Barrett, Elizabeth. 1838. *The Seraphim, and Other Poems*. London: Saunders and Otley.

Bartine, David. 1979. "Rhetorical Dimensions of Primary Performatives." In *Rhetoric 78: Proceedings of Theory of Rhetoric: Interdisciplinary Conference*, ed. Robert L. Brown, Jr. and Martin Steinmann, Jr., 1–8. Minneapolis: Univ of Minnesota Press.

Battenhouse, Roy W. 1942. "The Grounds of Religious Toleration in the Thought of John Donne." *Church History* 11:217–48.

Baumgaertner, Jill Peláez. 1994. "Rereading John Donne: The Art of Trompe-L'Oeil." *The Cresset* 57.7:4–9.

Baumlin, James S. 1991. *John Donne and the Rhetorics of Renaissance Discourse*. Columbia: University of Missouri Press.

Beal, Peter, comp. 1980. "John Donne." In *Index of English Literary Manuscripts, Vol. I, 1450–1625, Part 1, Andrewes–Donne*, 243–564. London: Mansell; New York: R.R. Bowker.

Beaver, Joseph C. 1967. "A Grammar of Prosody." *College English* 29:310–21.

Bedford, R. D. 1982. "Donne's Holy Sonnet, 'Batter My Heart.'" *N&Q* n.s. 29:15–19. Rpt. in R. D. Bedford, *Dialogues With Convention: Readings in Renaissance Poetry*, New York: Harvester Wheatsheaf Press, 1989; and in *John Donne's Poetry: Authoritative Texts, Criticism*, A Norton Critical Edition, ed. Arthur L. Clements, 333–38. 2nd ed. New York and London: W. W. Norton and Company, 1992.

Beer, Patricia. 1972. *An Introduction to the Metaphysical Poets*. London: Macmillan Press.

Bell, Arthur Henry. 1969. "Donne's Atonement Conceit in the Holy Sonnets." *The Cresset* 22:15–17.

Bellette, Anthony F. 1975. "'Little Worlds Made Cunningly': Significant Form in Donne's *Holy Sonnets* and 'Goodfriday, 1613. Riding Westward.'" *SP* 72:322–47.

Benet, Diana. 1984. "The 'Blest Order.'" In *Secretary of Praise: The Poetic Vocation of George Herbert*. Columbia: University of Missouri Press.

Bennett, J. A.W. 1982. "Donne, Herbert, Herrick." In *Poetry of the Passion: Studies in Twelve Centuries of English Verse*, 145–67. Oxford: Clarendon Press.

Bennett, Joan. 1934. *Four Metaphysical Poets: Donne, Herbert, Vaughan, Crashaw*. Cambridge: Cambridge University Press.

Bennett, Roger E., ed. 1942. *The Complete Poems of John Donne*. Chicago: Packard and Co.

Bergman, David and Daniel Mark Epstein, eds. 1983. *The Heath Guide to Poetry*. Lexington, MA; Toronto: D. C. Heath and Company.

Berry, Boyd M. 1976. *Process of Speech: Puritan Religious Writing and Paradise Lost*. Baltimore: The Johns Hopkins University Press.

Bethell, S. L. 1948. *Essays on Literary Criticism and the English Tradition*. London: Dennis Dobson.

Bewley, Marius. 1952. "Religious Cynicism in Donne's Poetry." *KR* 14:619–46.

Blamires, Henry. 1974. *A Short History of English Literature*. London: Methuen.

Blanch, Robert J. 1974. "Fear and Despair in Donne's Holy Sonnets." *American Benedictine Review* 25:476–84.

Blanchard, Margaret M. 1964. "The Leap into Darkness: Donne, Herbert, and God." *Renascence* 17:38–50.

Bloom, Harold, ed. 1986. *John Donne and the Seventeenth-Century Metaphysical Poets*. New York: Chelsea House Publishers.

Boase, Alan M. 1949. "Poètes Anglais et Francais de l'Époque Baroque." *Revue des Sciences Humaines* 55–56:155–84.

Bond, Ronald B. 1981. "John Donne and the Problem of 'Knowing Faith.'" *Mosaic* 14:25–35.

Bonnefoy, Yves. 1990. "Traduction Inédite de Deux Poémes de John Donne." In *Traduire la poésie*, 2–5. Paris: La Sorbonne Nouvelle.

Boone, Colin C. 1980. *Praxis der Interpretation: Englische Lyrik*. Tübingen: Max Niemeyer Verlag.

Booty, John E. 1982. "Contrition in Anglican Spirituality: Hooker, Donne, and Herbert." In *Anglican Spirituality*, ed. William J. Wolf, 25–48. Wilton, CT: Morehouse-Barlow.

———. 1984. "Joseph Hall, *The Arte of Divine Meditation*, and Anglican Spirituality." In *The Roots of the Modern Christian Tradition*, ed. E. Rozanne Elder, 200–28. The Spirituality of Western Christendom, II. Kalamazoo: Cistercian Publications.

———, ed. 1990. *John Donne: Selections from Divine Poems, Sermons, Devotions, and Prayers*. Preface by P. G. Stanwood. Mahwah, NJ: Paulist Press.

Borkowska, Ewa. 1994. *From Donne to Celan: Logo(theo)logical Patterns in Poetry*. Katowice: Wydawn. Uniwersytet Slaskiego.

Bottrall, Margaret. 1958. *Every Man a Phoenix: Studies in Seventeenth-Century Autobiography*. London: John Murray.

Bowers, Fredson. 1972. "Mulitple Authority: New Problems and Concepts of Copy-Text." *Library* 5th ser. 27:81–115. Reprinted in *Essays in Bibliography, Text, and Editing*, 466–87. Charlottesville: University Press of Virginia, 1975.

Bradford, Gamaliel. 1892. "The Poetry of Donne." *AR* 18.106:350–67. Rev. for *A Naturalist of Souls*.

Bredvold, Louis I. 1925. "The Religious Thought of Donne in Relation to Medieval and Later Traditions." In *Studies in Shakespeare, Milton, and Donne*, 191–232. University of Michigan Publications, Language and Literature, I. New York: Macmillan.

Briggs, Julia. 1983. *This Stage-Play World: English Literature and Its Backgrounds, 1580–1625*. Oxford and New York: Oxford University Press.

Brink, Andrew. 1977. "John Donne and the Obsession with Woman." In *Loss and Symbolic Repair: A Psychological Study of Some English Poets*, 80–111. Hamilton, Ontario: Cromlech Press.

Broadbent, J[ohn]. B. 1964. *Poetic Love*. London: Chatto and Windus.

———, ed. 1974. *Signet Classic Poets of the 17th Century*. The Signet Classic Poetry Series, gen. ed. John Hollander, 1:75–135. New York and Scarborough, Ontario: New American Library; London: The New English Library.

Brooke, Tucker. 1948. "The Renaissance." In *A Literary History of England*, ed. Albert C. Baugh, 313–696. New York: Appleton-Century-Crofts.

Brooks, Cleanth. 1939. *Modern Poetry and the Tradition*. Chapel Hill: University of North Carolina Press.

———, and Robert Penn Warren. 1938. *Understanding Poetry: An Anthology for College Students*. New York: Henry Holt.

Brooks, Helen B. 1995. "Donne's 'Goodfriday, 1613. Riding Westward' and Augustine's Psychology of Time." In *John Donne's Religious Imagination: Essays in Honor of John T. Shawcross*, ed. Raymond-Jean Frontain and Frances M. Malpezzi, 141–61. Conway, AR: UCA Press.

Brower, Reuben Arthur. 1951. *The Fields of Light: An Experiment in Critical Reading*. New York: Oxford University Press.

Buckley, Vincent. 1965. "John Donne's Passion." CR 8:19–31. Rpt. and slightly rev. in *Poetry and the Sacred*. London: Chatto & Windus, 1968.

Burgon, Geoffrey. 1984. *At the Round Earth's Imagined Corners: For Soprano, Trumpet and Organ*. London: Chester Music.

Burke, Victoria. 1995. "John Donne and the True Church." ER 5.3:32–35.

Bush, Douglas. 1945. *English Literature in the Early Seventeenth Century, 1600–1660*. Oxford: Oxford University Press.

———. 1965. *Prefaces to Renaissance Literature*. Cambridge: Harvard University Press.

Cain, T. G. S., ed. 1981. *Jacobean and Caroline Poetry*. London and New York: Methuen.

Caine, T. Hall, ed. 1882. *Sonnets of Three Centuries: A Selection Including Many Examples Hitherto Unpublished*. London: Elliot Stock.

Cameron, Sharon. 1979. *Lyric Time: Dickinson and the Limits of Genre*. Baltimore and London: Johns Hopkins University Press.

Campbell, Gordon. 1989. "John Donne." In *The Renaissance (1550–1660)*. Macmillan Anthologies of English Literature, Vol. 2. Gen. eds. A. Norman Jeffares and Michael Alexander, 220–42. Houndmills, Basingstoke, Hampshire, and London: Macmillan Education Ltd.

Carey, John. 1981. *John Donne: Life, Mind and Art*. New York: Oxford University Press.

———. 1990a. "Afterword 1990." In *John Donne: Life, Mind and Art*, 266–80. 2nd ed. Oxford: Oxford University Press.

———, ed. 1990b. *John Donne*. Oxford Authors, gen. ed. Frank Kermode. Oxford and New York: Oxford University Press.

Carleton, Frances Bridges. 1977. *The Dramatic Monologue: Vox Humana*. Salzburg: Universität Salzburg.

Carlson, Norme E. 1973. "Donne's 'Holy Sonnets, XIX.'" *Expl* 32:Item 19.

Carpenter, Frederic Ives, ed. 1897. *English Lyric Poetry 1500–1700*. London: Blackie & Son.

Carpenter, Peter. 1993. "Taking Liberties: Eliot's Donne." *Critical Survey* 5.3:278–88.

Cathcart, Dwight. 1975. *Doubting Conscience: Donne and the Poetry of Moral Argument*. Ann Arbor: University of Michigan Press.

Cattermole, Richard, ed. 1841. *Gems of Sacred Poetry*, 2 vols. London: John W. Parker.

Cayward, Margaret. 1980. "Donne's 'Batter My Heart, Three-Personed God.'" *Expl* 38.3:5.

Chadwick, John White. 1900. "John Donne, Poet and Preacher." *NewW* 9:31–48.

Chambers, E. K., ed. 1896. *The Poems of John Donne*. With an Introduction by George Saintsbury. The Muses Library. 2 vols. London: Lawrence & Bullen; New York: Charles Scribner's Sons.

Chanoff, David. 1980. "Donne's Anglicanism." *Recusant History* 15:154–67.

———. 1981. "The Biographical Context of Donne's Sonnet on the Church." *ABR* 32.4: 378–86.

Chatman, Seymour. 1965. *A Theory of Meter*. The Hague: Mouton.

Chatterjie, Visvanath. 1980. *Mysticism in English Poetry*. Calcutta: Progressive Publishers.

Ching, Marvin K. 1978. "The Relationship Among the Diverse Senses of a Pun." *The SECOL Bulletin: Southeastern Conference on Linguistics* 2:1–8.

Choi, Ye-Jung. 1990. "John Donne eui Anniversaries: jashin eui segae reul chiyu haryeoneun noryeok" ["John Donne's Anniversaries: an attempt to heal the world and himself"]. *English Studies* (Seoul National University, Korea) 14:23–36.

Clark, Ira. 1982. "Explicating the Heart and Dramatizing the Poet: Seventeenth-Century Innovations by English Emblematists and Donne." In *Christ Revealed: The History of the Neotypological Lyric Paradigm*, 64–79 (University of Florida Monographs. Humanities, no. 51). Gainesville: University Presses of Florida.

Clements, Arthur L. 1961. "The Paradox of Three-in-One." *MLN* 76:484–89. Rpt. in *John Donne's Poetry: Authoritative Texts, Criticism*, ed. A. L. Clements. New York: Norton, 1966.

———. 1990. *Poetry of Contemplation: John Donne, George Herbert, Henry Vaughan, and the Modern Period*. State University of New York Press.

———, ed. 1992. *John Donne's Poetry: Authoritative Texts, Criticism*. New York and London: W. W. Norton and Company. A Norton Critical Edition. 2nd ed.

Coakley, Sarah. 1995. "'Batter my heart . . .'? On Sexuality, and the Christian Doctrine of the Trinity." *Graven Images: A Journal of Culture, Law, and the Sacred* 2:74–83.

Coanda, Richard. 1957. "Hopkins and Donne: 'Mystic' and Metaphysical." *Renascence* 9:180–87.

Coffin, Charles Monroe. 1937. *John Donne and the New Philosophy*. New York: Columbia University Press.

———, ed. 1952. *The Complete Poetry and Selected Prose of John Donne*. New York: Modern Library.

Coffin, Robert P. Tristram and Alexander M. Witherspoon, eds. 1946. *Seventeenth-Century Prose and Poetry*. New York: Harcourt, Brace, and Company. 2nd ed. by Alexander M. Witherspoon and Frank J. Warnke. 1963.

Cohen, J. M. 1963. *The Baroque Lyric*. London: Hutchinson University Library.

Coiro, Ann Baynes. 1990. "'New-found-land': Teaching Metaphysical Poetry from the Other Side." In *Approaches to Teaching the Metaphysical Poets*, ed. Sidney Gottlieb, 81–88. New York: The Modern Language Association of America.

Colie, Rosalie. 1959. "Constantijn Huygens and the Metaphysical Mode." *The Germanic Review* 34:59–73.

Collmer, Robert G. 1961. "The Meditation on Death and Its Appearance in Metaphysical Poetry." *Neophil* 45:323–33.

Conrad, Peter. 1985. *The Everyman History of English Literature*. London: J. M. Dent & Sons. Rpt. as *The History of English Literature: One Indivisible, Unending Book*. Philadelphia: University of Pennsylvania Press, 1987.

Conte, Giuseppe. 1977. "Mistica e retorica: a propositio di un sonetto di John Donne." *Rivista di Storia e Letteratura Religiosa* 13:127–33.

Cornelius, David K. 1965. "Donne's Holy Sonnet XIV." *Expl* 24:item 25.

Cox, R. G. 1956a. "The Poems of John Donne." In *From Donne to Marvell*, ed. Boris Ford, 98–115. The Pelican Guide to English Literature. Vol. 3. Harmondsworth, Eng., and Baltimore: Penguin Books.

———. 1956b. "A Survey of Literature from Donne to Marvell." In *From Donne to Marvell*, ed. Boris Ford, 43–85. The Pelican Guide to English Literature. Vol. 3. Harmondsworth, Eng., and Baltimore: Penguin Books.

Coyle, Martin. 1994. "The Subject and the Sonnet." *English: The Journal of the English Association* 43:139–50.

Craik, T. W. and R. J. Craik, eds. *John Donne: Selected Poetry and Prose*. 1986. London and New York: Methuen.

Crawshaw, Eluned. 1972. "Hermetic Elements in Donne's Poetic Vision." In *John Donne: Essays in Celebration*, ed. A. J. Smith, 324–48. London: Methuen & Co.

Crennan, M. J. 1979. *In Search of Donne*. Sydney: English Association.

Creswell, Catherine. 1995. "Turning to See the Sound: Reading the Face of God in Donne's Holy Sonnets." In *John Donne's Religious Imagination: Essays in Honor of John T. Shawcross*, ed. Raymond-Jean Frontain and Frances M. Malpezzi, 181–201. Conway, AR: UCA Press.

Cruttwell, Patrick. 1954. *The Shakespearean Moment and Its Place in the Poetry of the 17th Century*. London: Chatto and Windus.

———. 1966. *The English Sonnet*. London: Longmans, Green.

Daiches, David. 1960. "Poetry after Spenser: The Jonsonian and Metaphysical Traditions." In *A Critical History of English Literature*. New York: Ronald Press.

———, and William Charvat, eds. 1950. *Poems in English, 1530–1940*. New York: Ronald Press.

Daley, Koos. 1990a. "Donne and Huygens Travel Westward." *Dutch Crossing* 40 (Spring):23–30.

———. 1990b. *The Triple Fool: A Critical Evaluation of Constantijn Huygens' Translations of John Donne*. Nieuwkoop: De Graaf.

———. 1992. "'Good Friday': Donne, Huygens and the Protestant Paradigm of Salvation." In *The Emporium: The Low Countries as a Cultural Crossroads in the Renaissance and the Eighteenth Century*, ed. C. C. Barfoot and Richard Todd, 43–58. DQR Studies in Literature, 10. Amsterdam; Atlanta, GA: Rodopi.

Dalglish, Jack. 1961. *Eight Metaphysical Poets*. New York: Macmillan.

D'Amico, Jack. 1979. *Petrarch in England: An Anthology of Parallel Texts from Wyatt to Milton*. Ravenna: Longo Editore.

Daniells, Roy. 1945. "Baroque Form in English Literature." *UTQ* 14:393–408.

Daniels, Earl. 1941. *The Art of Reading Poetry*. New York: Rinehart.

Daniels, Edgar F. 1972. "Donne's Holy Sonnets VI." *Expl* 31:item 12.

Dasgupta, Debbir Bikram. 1981. "'Death Be Not Proud': An Explication." *Journal of the Department of English* (University of Calcutta) 17.1:84–92.

Davies, Stevie. 1994. *John Donne*. "Writers and Their Work - New Series." Plymouth (UK): Northcote House Publishers Ltd.

De la Mare, Walter. 1913. "An Elizabethan Poet and Modern Poetry." *EdRev* 217:372–86.

Delany, Paul. 1970. "Donne's Holy Sonnet V, Lines 13–14." *ANQ* 9:6–7.

Demaray, John G. 1965. "Donne's Three Steps to Death." *Person* 46:366–81.

Den Boer, M. G. L. 1982. *De Ridder Met de Witte Pluim: John Donne, Dichter-Prediker*. Gavenhage: Boekencentrum.

Dennis, John, ed. 1873. *English Sonnets: A Selection*. London: Henry S. King.

Denonain, Jean-Jacques. 1956. *Thèmes et Formes de la Poésie "Métaphysique": Étude d'un aspect de la Littérature Anglaise au Dix-Septième Siècle*. Paris: Presses Universitaires de France.

De Quincey, Thomas. 1818. Column on Donne in the *Westmorland Gazette*. Rpt. in Charles Pollitt, *De Quincey's Editorship of the* Westmorland Gazette. Kendal: Atkinson and Pollitt, 1890, 70–71.

Deshler, Charles D. 1879. *Afternoons with the Poets*. New York: Harper & Brothers.

De Silva, D. M. 1971. "John Donne—An Un-Metaphysical Perspective." *The Ceylon Journal of the Humanities* 2:3–14.

Dickinson, Leon T. 1967. *Suggestions for Teachers of "Introduction to Literature."* New York: Holt, Rinehart, Winston.

Dickson, Donald R. 1987. "The Complexities of Biblical Typology in the Seventeenth Century." *Ren&R* n.s. 11:253–72.

Di Nola, Gerardo. 1993. *Tommaso Campanella: Il Nuovo Prometeo. Da Poeta-Vate-Profeta a Restauratore della Politica e del Diritto*. Collana Lumen, 9. Bologna: Edizioni Studio Domenicano.

DiPasquale, Theresa. 1991. "Ambivalent Mourning: Sacramentality, Idolatry, and Gender in 'Since she whome I lovd hath payd her last debt.'" *JDJ* 10:45–56.

———. 1994. "Cunning Elements: Water, Fire, and Sacramental Poetics in 'I am a little world.'" *PQ* 73.4:403–15.

Dittmar, Wilfried. 1975. "Holy Sonnets" and "An Anatomie of the World." In *Hauptwerke der englischen Literatur: Einzeldarstellungen und Interpretationem*, ed. Manfred Pfister, 95–96, 99–100. Munich: Kindler.

Docherty, Barbara. 1988. "Sentence into Cadence: The Word-Setting of Tippett and Britten." *Tempo* 116:2–11.

Docherty, Thomas. 1986. *John Donne, Undone*. London and New York: Methuen & Company.

Doggett, Frank A. 1934. "Donne's Platonism." *SR* 42:274–92.

Dollimore, Jonathon. 1984. *Radical Tragedy: Religion, Ideology and Power in the Drama of Shakespeare and His Contemporaries*. Chicago: University of Chicago Press.

Donker, Marjorie, and George M. Muldrow. 1982. *Dictionary of Literary-Rhetorical Conventions of the English Renaissance*. Westport, CT; London: Greenwood Press.

Drew, Elizabeth. 1933. *Discovering Poetry*. New York: W. W. Norton.

Dubinski, Roman. 1986. "Donne's Holy Sonnets and the Seven Penitential Psalms." *Ren&R* 10:201–16.

Dubrow, Heather. 1990. *A Happier Eden: The Politics of Marriage in the Stuart Epithalamium*. Ithaca and London: Cornell University Press.

———. 1995. *Echoes of Desire: English Petrarchism and Its Counterdiscourses*. Ithaca and London: Cornell University Press.

Duncan, Joseph. 1959. *The Revival of Metaphysical Poetry: The History of Style, 1800 to the Present*. Minneapolis: University of Minnesota Press.

Dundas, Judith. 1994. "'All Things Are Bigge With Jest': Wit as a Means of Grace." In *New Perspectives on the Seventeenth-Century English Religious Lyric*, ed. John R. Roberts, 124–42. Columbia and London: University of Missouri Press.

Dyce, Alexander, ed. 1833. *Specimens of English Sonnets*. London: W. Pickering.

Egan, James. 1985. "Donne's Wit of Death: Some Notes toward a Definition." *SPWVSRA* 10:25–34.

Eliot, T. S. 1930. "The Devotional Poets of the Seventeenth Century: Donne, Herbert, Crashaw." *Lis* 3:552–53.

Ellrodt, Robert. 1960. *L'Inspiration Personnelle et l'Esprit du Temps chez Les Poètes Métaphysiques Anglais*. 2 vols. in 3. Paris: Jose Corti.

———. 1980. "Angels and the Poetic Imagination from Donne to Traherne." In *English Renaissance Studies Presented to Dame Helen Gardner in Honour of her Seventieth Birthday*, ed. John Carey, 164–79. Oxford: Oxford University Press.

────. 1983. "Présence et Permanence de John Donne." In *John Donne*, ed. Jean-Marie Benoist, 17–29. Herissey: L'Age D'Homme.

────. 1987. "Poésie et vérité chez John Donne." *EA* 40:1–14.

────, trans. 1993. *John Donne: Poésie*. Paris: Imprimerie Nationale Éditions.

────. 1995. "The Search for Identity: From Montaigne to Donne." In *Confluences: John Donne and Modernity*, ed. Armand Himy and Margaret Llasera, 7–23. Nanterre: Université Paris X.

Elsky, Martin. 1980. "History, Liturgy, and Point of View in Protestant Meditative Poetry." *SP* 77:67–83.

Elton, Oliver. 1933. *The English Muse: A Sketch*. London: G. Bell and Sons.

Empson, William. 1930. *Seven Types of Ambiguity*. London: Chatto and Windus. Rev. ed. 1947.

────. 1935. *Some Versions of Pastoral*. London: Chatto & Windus.

────. 1949. "Donne and the Rhetorical Tradition." *KR* 11:571–87.

────. 1957. "Donne the Space Man." *KR* 19:337–99.

────. 1981. "There is no Penance Due to Innocence." *NYRB* 3 December:42–50.

Esch, Arno. 1955. *Englische Religiöse Lyrik des 17. Jahrhunderts: Studien zu Donne, Herbert, Crashaw, Vaughan*. Tübingen: Max Niemeyer.

Evans, Gillian R. 1978. *The Age of the Metaphysicals*. Authors in Their Age. Glasgow and London: Blackie & Sons.

────. 1982. "John Donne and the Augustinian Paradox of Sin." *RES* 33:1–22.

Evans, Maurice. 1955. *English Poetry in the Sixteenth Century*. London: Hutchinson's University Library.

Evett, David. 1986. "Donne's Poems and the Five Styles of Renascence Art." In "Essays in Literature and the Visual Arts." [Special Double Issue] ed. Richard S. Peterson. *JDJ* 5: 101–31.

Faerber, Hansruedi. 1950. *Das Paradoxe in der Dichtung von John Donne*. Zürich: Buchdruckerei Baublatt AG.

Fallon, Robert Thomas. 1991. "'Artillerie': Herbert's Strange Warfare." In *Praise Disjoined: Changing Patterns of Salvation in 17th-Century English Literature*, ed. William P. Shaw, 221–36. New York: Peter Lang.

Farmer, Norman, Jr. 1984. *Poets and the Visual Arts in Renaissance England*. Austin: University of Texas Press.

Faulkner, Eleanor and Edgar F. Daniels. 1976. "Donne's 'Holy Sonnets XVII' ('Since she whome I lovd'), 1–2." *Expl* 34:item 68.

Fausset, Hugh I'Anson. 1923. *Studies in Idealism*. London and Toronto: J. M. Dent & Sons; New York: E. P. Dutton & Co.

────. 1924. *John Donne: A Study in Discord*. London: Jonathan Cape.

────, ed. 1931a. *The Poems of John Donne*. Everyman's Library 867. London: J. M. Dent & Sons.

────. 1931b. "The Poet and His Vision." *Bo* 79:341–42.

────, ed. 1938. *The Holy Sonnets of John Donne*. London: J. M. Dent & Sons for Hague and Gill. Introduction rpt. in *Poets and Pundits: Essays and Addresses*, 130–34. London: Jonathan Cape, 1947.

Feist, Hans. 1945. *Ewiges England: Dichtung aus sieben Jahrhunderten von Chaucer bis Eliot*. Zurich: Verlag Amstutz, Herdeg & Co.

Fenner, Arthur. 1982. "Donne's 'Holy Sonnet XII.'" *Expl* 40.4:14–15.

Ferrari, Ferruccio. 1979. "B. Jonson e 'The Tribe of Ben'—Donne e Burton." In *L'Influenza Classica Nell'Inghilterra Del Seicento E La Poesia Di Robert Herrick*, 33–48. Messina-Firenze: Casa Editrice G. D'Anna.

562 ❦ WORKS CITED

Ferry, Anne. 1983. *The Inward Language: Sonnets of Wyatt, Sidney, Shakespeare and Donne.* Chicago and London: The University of Chicago Press.

Fiore, Peter Amadeus. 1972. "John Donne Today." In *Just So Much Honor: Essays Commemorating the Four-Hundredth Anniversary of the Birth of John Donne,* ed. Peter Amadeus Fiore, 1–8. University Park and London: The Pennsylvania State University Press.

Fisch, Harold. 1964. *Jerusalem and Albion: The Hebraic Factor in Seventeenth-Century Literature.* London: Routledge and Kegan Paul.

Fischler, Alan. 1994. "'Lines Which Circles Do Contain': Circles, the Cross, and Donne's Dialectic Scheme of Salvation." *PLL* 30:169–86.

Fish, Stanley. 1990. "Masculine Persuasive Force: Donne and Verbal Power." In *Soliciting Interpretation: Literary Theory and Seventeenth-Century English Poetry,* ed. Elizabeth D. Harvey and Katharine Eisaman Maus, 223–52. Chicago and London: University of Chicago Press.

Fishelov, David. 1992. "Yehuda Amichai: A Modern Metaphysical Poet." *Orbis Litterarum* 47.3:178–91.

Flanigan, Beverly Olson. 1986. "Donne's 'Holy Sonnet VII' as Speech Act." *Language and Style* 19:49–57.

Fleck, Jade C. 1994. "A Grammar of Eschatology in Seventeenth-Century Theological Prose and Poetry." In *Reform and Counterreform: Dialectics of the Word in Western Christianity Since Luther,* ed. John C. Hawley, 59–76. Berlin and New York: Mouton de Gruyter.

Flynn, Dennis. 1976. "Donne's Catholicism: II." *Recusant History* 13:178–95.

———. 1988. "'Awry and Squint': The Dating of Donne's Holy Sonnets." *JDJ* 7.1:35–46.

Ford, Boris, ed. 1982. *The Age of Shakespeare.* Vol. 2. *From Donne to Marvell.* Vol. 3. The New Pelican Guide to English Literature. Harmondsworth, Eng.: Penguin.

Foster, Thomas. 1931. "The Tragedy of John Donne." *The Month* (London) 157:404–09.

Fowler, Alastair. 1975. *Conceitful Thought: The Interpretation of English Renaissance Poems.* Edinburgh: Edinburgh University Press.

———, ed. 1991. *The New Oxford Book of Seventeenth Century Verse.* Oxford: Oxford University Press.

———, ed. 1995. *Metaphysical Lyrics and Poems of the Seventeenth Century.* Orig. ed. H. J. C. Grierson (1921). New Edition, rev. Alastair Fowler. Oxford: Oxford University Press.

Frankenberg, Lloyd. 1956. *Invitation to Poetry: A Round of Poems From John Skelton to Dylan Thomas Arranged With Comments.* Garden City, New York: Doubleday & Co.

Fraser, G. S. 1981. *A Short History of English Poetry.* Somerset, England: Open Books Publishing Ltd.

French, A. L. 1970. "The Psychopathology of Donne's Holy Sonnets." *CR* 13:111–24.

Friederich, Werner P. 1932. *Spiritualismus und Sensualismus in der Englischen Barocklyrik. Wiener Beiträge zur Englischen Philologie.* Vienna and Leipzig: Wilhelm Braumüller.

Frontain, Raymond-Jean. 1987. "Redemption Typology in John Donne's 'Batter My Heart.'" *JRMMRA* 8:163–76. Rpt. in *John Donne's Poetry: Authoritative Texts, Criticism.* Norton Critical Edition, ed. Arthur L. Clements, 338–49. New York and London: W. W. Norton & Company. 2nd ed. 1992.

———. 1992. "'With Holy Importunitie, with a Pious Impudencie': John Donne's Attempts to Provoke Election." *JRMMRA* 13:85–102.

———. 1995. "Introduction: 'Make all this All': The Religious Operations of John Donne's Imagination." In *John Donne's Religious Imagination: Essays in Honor of John T. Shawcross,* ed. Raymond-Jean Frontain and Frances M. Malpezzi, 1–27. Conway, AR: UCA Press.

Frost, Kate Gartner. 1990. *Holy Delight: Typology, Numerology, and Autobiography in Donne's Devotions upon Emergent Occasions.* Princeton: Princeton University Press.

Fuller, John. 1972. *The Sonnet.* "The Critical Idiom" 26, ed. John D. Jump. London: Methuen.

Furst, Clyde Bowman. 1896. "The Life and Poetry of Dr. John Donne, Dean of St. Paul's." *Cit* 2:229–37.

Fuzier, Jean. 1976. "Donne sonnettiste: Les Holy Sonnets et la tradition européenne." In *De Shakespeare à T. S. Eliot: Mélanges offerts à Henri Fluchère*, ed. Marie-Jeanne Durry et al., 153–71. (Études Anglaises 63.) Paris: Didier.

———. 1983. "John Donne et la formalité de l'essence." In *John Donne*, ed. Jean-Marie Benoist, 39–49. Herissey: L'Age D'Homme.

——— and Yves Denis, trans. 1962. *Poèmes de John Donne.* Introduction by Jean-Roger Poisson. Paris: Gallimard. 2nd ed. 1980.

Gabrieli, Vittorio. 1995. "John Donne, Thomas More e Roma." *Rivista di Letterature moderne e comparate* 48:235–62.

Galdon, Joseph A. 1975. *Typology and Seventeenth-Century Literature.* De proprietatibus litterarum, Series Maior 8. The Hague: Mouton.

Gardner, Helen, ed. 1952. *John Donne, The Divine Poems.* Oxford: Clarendon Press. Rev. ed. 1978.

———. 1953. "Donne's 'Divine Poems.'" *TLS* 30 January:73.

———, ed. 1957a. *The Metaphysical Poets.* Hammondsworth, Eng.: Penguin. Rev. ed. 1961.

———. 1957b. "Another Note on Donne: 'Since she whome I lov'd.'" *MLR* 52:564–65.

———. 1966a. "Correspondence: John Donne." *Critical Quarterly* 8:374–77.

———. 1966b. "The Titles of Donne's Poems." In *Friendship's Garland: Essays Presented to Mario Praz on his Seventieth Birthday*, ed. Vittorio Gabrieli, 189–208. Rome: Edizioni di Storia e Letteratura.

———. 1971. *Religion and Literature.* London: Faber and Faber.

Garnett, R., and E. W. Gosse. 1903. *English Literature: An Illustrated Record in Four Volumes.* Vol. 2 (*From the Age of Henry VIII to the Age of Milton*). London: William Heinemann; New York: Macmillan.

Garrett, John. 1986. *British Poetry Since the Sixteenth Century: A Student's Guide.* London: Macmillan; Totowa, NJ: Barnes and Noble, 1987.

Garrod, H. W., ed. 1946. *John Donne: Poetry and Prose, with Izaac Walton's Life. Appreciations by Ben Jonson, Coleridge, and Others.* Oxford: Clarendon Press.

Gaster, Clare, ed. 1986. *Holy Sonnets: John Donne.* Illustrated with boxwood engravings by Jill Barker. Limited edition (100 copies). Winchester: The Alembic Press.

Gaston, Paul L. 1986. "Britten's Donne and the Promise of Twentieth-Century Settings." In *The Eagle and the Dove: Reassessing John Donne.* ed. Claude J. Summers and Ted-Larry Pebworth. Columbia: University of Missouri Press.

Gergye, László. 1986. "Az angol szonett-tipus reneszánsz és manierista változata: Edmund Spenser és John Donne" ["The Renaissance and Mannerist Varieties of the English Sonnet: Edmund Spenser and John Donne"] *Filológiai Közlöny* [*Philological Review*]. Budapest. 32–33.3–4) (1986–87):165–79.

Gilfillan, George. 1860. *Specimens with Memoirs of the Less-Known British Poets.* 3 vols. Edinburgh: James Nichol.

Gill, Richard, ed. 1990. *John Donne: Selected Poems.* Oxford and New York: Oxford University Press.

Gilman, Ernest B. 1986. "'To adore, or scorne an image': Donne and the Iconoclastic Controversy." In "Essays in Literature and the Visual Arts." [Special Double Issue] Ed. Richard S. Peterson. *JDJ* 5:63–100. Rev. as ch. 5 in *Iconoclasm and Poetry in the English Reformation: Down Went Dagon.* Chicago and London: University of Chicago Press.

Girri, Alberto. 1963. *Poemas de John Donne*. Selección, prólogo y notas. Buenos Aires: Ediciones Culturales Argentinas.

González, José Manuel and Fernández de Sevilla. 1991. "La Poesía Metafísica de John Donne y Francisco de Quevedo." *Neophil* 75.4:548–61.

Gorbunov, A. N. 1990. "The Category of Time and the Conception of Love in English Poetry at the Turn of the Seventeenth Century." In *Shakespeare Readings*, ed. A. Aniksta, 68–87. Moscow.

———. 1993. *John Donne and English Poetry of the Sixteenth-Seventeenth Centuries*. Moscow: Moscow University Press.

Gosse, Edmund. 1893. "The Poetry of John Donne." *LLA* 199:429–36. Also in *NewR* 9(1893): 236–47. Rpt. in *The Jacobean Poets*.

———. 1894. *The Jacobean Poets*. London: J. Murray.

———. 1899. *The Life and Letters of John Donne, Dean of St. Paul's*. 2 vols. London: W. Heinemann. Rpt. Gloucester, Massachusetts: Peter Smith, 1959.

Graham, Desmond. 1968. *Introduction to Poetry*. London: Oxford University Press.

Granqvist, Raoul. 1975. *The Reputation of John Donne 1779–1873*. Acta Universitatis Upsaliensis 24. Uppsala: Almqvist & Wiksell.

Gransden, K. W. 1954. *John Donne*. London: Longmans, Green. Rev. ed. 1969. Hamden, Connecticut: Archon Books.

Grant, Patrick. 1971. "Augustinian Spirituality and the Holy Sonnets of John Donne." *ELH* 38:542–61.

———. 1973. "Donne, Pico, and Holy Sonnet XII." *HAB* 24:39–42.

———. 1974. *The Transformation of Sin: Studies in Donne, Herbert, Vaughan, and Traherne*. Montreal and London: McGill-Queen's University Press; Amherst: University of Massachusetts Press.

———. 1979. *Images and Ideas in Literature in the English Renaissance*. Amherst: University of Massachusetts Press.

———. 1983. *Literature of Mysticism in the Western Tradition*. London and Basingstoke: Macmillan.

———. 1985. *Literature and the Discovery of Method in the English Renaissance*. Athens: University of Georgia Press.

Gray, J. C. 1975. "Bondage and Deliverance in the 'Faerie Queene': Varieties of a Moral Imperative." *MLR* 70:1–12.

Gregory, Michael. 1974. "A Theory for Stylistics—Exemplified: Donne's 'Holy Sonnet XIV.'" *Lang&S* 7:108–18.

Grenander, M. E. 1955. "Donne's 'Holy Sonnets,' XII." *Expl* 13:Item 42.

———. 1960. "Holy Sonnets VIII and XVII: John Donne." *Boston University Studies in English* 4:95–105.

Grey, Mary. 1990. "The Core of our Desire: Re-imaging the Trinity." *Th* 93:363–72.

Grierson, Herbert J. C. 1909. "John Donne." In *The Cambridge History of English Literature*, ed. A. W. Ward and A. R. Waller, 4:196–223. Cambridge: Cambridge University Press.

———, ed. 1912. *The Poems of John Donne*. 2 vols. Oxford: Clarendon Press.

———, ed. 1921. *Metaphysical Lyrics and Poems of the Seventeenth Century*. Oxford: Clarendon Press.

———, ed. 1929. *Donne: Poetical Works*. Oxford: Oxford University Press.

———. 1948. "John Donne and the 'Via Media.'" *MLR* 43:305–14.

Groom, Bernard. 1955. *The Diction of Poetry from Spenser to Bridges*. Toronto: University of Toronto Press.

Grosart, Alexander Ballock, ed. 1872–73. *The Complete Poems of John Donne, D. D.* 2 vols. The Fuller Worthies' Library. London: Robson and Sons.

Grove, Robin. 1984. "Nature Methodiz'd." CR 26:52–68.

Guibbory, Achsah. 1980. "John Donne and Memory as 'the Art of *Salvation*.'" HLQ 43:261–74.

———. 1986. "John Donne: The Idea of Decay." In *The Map of Time: Seventeenth-Century English Literature and Ideas of Pattern in History*, 69–104. Urbana and Chicago: University of Illinois Press.

———. 1993. "John Donne." In *The Cambridge Companion to English Poetry: Donne to Marvell*, ed. Thomas N. Corns, 123–47. Cambridge: Cambridge University Press.

Guiney, Louise I. 1920. "Donne as a Lost Catholic Poet." *The Month* 136:13–19.

"H.E.M.," ed. 1855. *Dies Consecrati: or, A New Christian Year with the Old Poets*. Chobham: T. Medhurst; London: Longman & Co.

Haffenden, John. 1985. "The Importance of Empson (I): The Poems." EIC 35:1–24.

———, ed. 1993. "Introduction": *William Empson: Essays on Renaissance Literature*. Vol. 1: "Donne and the New Philosophy," 1–61. Cambridge: Cambridge University Press.

Hagerdorn, Maria. 1934. *Reformation und spanische Andachsliteratur, Luis de Granada in England*. Leipzig: Tauchnitz.

Hagspian, John V. 1957. "Some Cruxes in Donne's Poetry." N&Q ns 4:500–02.

Hahn, Thomas. 1979. "The Antecedents of Donne's 'Holy Sonnet XI.'" ABR 30:69–79.

Halewood, William H. 1970. *The Poetry of Grace: Reformation Themes and Structures in English Seventeenth-Century Poetry*. New Haven: Yale University Press.

Halle, Morris and Samuel Jay Keyser. 1966. "Chaucer and the Study of Prosody." *College English* 28:187–219.

———. 1971. *English Stress: Its Form, Its Growth and Its Role in Verse*. New York: Harper and Row.

Hamburger, Maik, ed. 1985. *John Donne: Zwar ist auch Dichtung Sünde: Gedichte Englische und Deutsch*. Nachdichtungen von Maik Hamburger und Christa Schuenke. Rev. ed. Leipzig: Philipp Reclam.

Hamburger, Michael. 1944. "Some Aspects of Donne." In *Transformation Two*, ed. Stefan Schimanski and Henry Treece, 149–62. London: Lindsay Drummond, Ltd.

Hamer, Enid. 1930. *The Metres of English Poetry*. New York: Macmillan.

Hamilton, George Rostrevor. 1926. "Wit and Beauty: A Study of Metaphysical Poetry." LMer 14:606–20.

Handley, Graham. 1991. *Brodie's Notes on The Metaphysical Poets*. London, Sydney, and Auckland: Pan Books.

Handscombe, Richard. 1980. "Donne's Holy Sonnet VI: A Problem of Plainness." Lang&S 13:98–108.

Harding, D. W. 1951. "Coherence of Theme in Donne's Poetry." KR 13:427–44.

Hardy, Evelyn. 1942. *Donne: A Spirit in Conflict*. London: Constable & Co.

Harland, Paul W. 1995. "'A True Transubstantiation': Donne, Self-love, and the Passion." In *John Donne's Religious Imagination: Essays in Honor of John T. Shawcross*, ed. Raymond-Jean Frontain and Frances M. Malpezzi, 162–80. Conway, AR: UCA Press.

Harman, Barbara Leah. 1982. *Costly Monuments: Representations of the Self in George Herbert's Poetry*. Cambridge, MA and London: Harvard University Press.

Hart, Kingsley. 1958. *John Donne: Poems of Love*. Westerham: Westerham Press.

ul-Hasan, Masood. 1958. *Donne's Imagery*. Aligarh, India: Faculty of Arts, Muslim University.

Haskin, Dayton. 2002. "No Edition Is an Island: The Place of the Nineteenth-Century American Editions within the History of Editing Donne's Poems." TEXT 14:169–207.

Hauser, Arnold. 1965. *Mannerism: the Crisis of the Renaissance and the Origin of Modern Art*. 2 vols. London: Routledge and Kegan Paul.

Haydn, Hiram. 1950. *The Counter-Renaissance*. New York: Harcourt, Brace & World.

Hayward, John., ed. 1929. *John Donne, Dean of St. Paul's: Complete Poetry and Selected Prose*. Bloomsbury: Nonesuch.

———, ed. 1950. *John Donne: A Selection of his Poetry*. Harmondsworth, Eng.: Penguin.

Hebaisha, Hoda. 1971. *John Donne: The Man and His Poetry. With an Anthology of Representative Poems*. Cairo: Anglo-Egyptian Bookshop.

Heffernan, Thomas. 1991. "Donne: Imitating the Antitheses of the Divine Artist." In *Art and Emblem: Early Seventeenth Century English Poetry of Devotion*, 57–60. Renaissance Monographs 17. Tokyo: The Renaissance Institute; Sophia University.

Heist, William W. 1968. "Donne on Divine Grace: Holy Sonnet No. XIV." *Papers of the Michigan Academy of Science, Arts, and Letters* 53:311–20.

Hemmerich, Gerd. 1965. "Metaphysical Passion ['Metaphysische Leidenschaft'] in the Lyrics of Andreas Gryphius and John Donne." *Text und Kritik* 7/8:18–23.

Henricksen, Bruce. 1972. "Donne's Orthodoxy." *TSLL* 14:5–16.

Herbold, Anthony. 1965. "'Seeking Secrets or Poëtiquenesse': Donne's Dialectics in the Divine Poems." *Moderna Språk* 59:277–94.

Herman, George. 1953. "Donne's *Holy Sonnets*, XIV." *Expl* 12:Item 18.

Hester, M. Thomas. 1987. "Re-Signing the Text of the Self: Donne's 'As due by many titles.'" In *"Bright Shootes of Everlastingness": The Seventeenth-Century Religious Lyric*, ed. Claude J. Summers and Ted-Larry Pebworth, 59–71. Columbia: University of Missouri Press.

———. 1991a. "'Impute this idle talke': The 'Leaven' Body of Donne's 'Holy Sonnet III.'" In *Praise Disjoined: Changing Patterns of Salvation in 17th-Century English Literature*, ed. William P. Shaw, 175–90. New York: Peter Lang.

———. 1991b. "The *troubled wit* of John Donne's 'blacke Soule.'" *Cithara* 31.1:16–27.

———, ed. 1992. *Seventeenth-Century British Nondramatic Poets: First Series. Dictionary of Literary Biography*. Vol. 121. Detroit, London: Gale Research Inc.

———. 1993. "'let them sleepe': Donne's Personal Allusion in *Holy Sonnet IV*." *PLL* 29.3:346–50.

Hieatt, A. Kent. 1987. "John Donne." In *Poetry in English: An Anthology*, ed. M. L. Rosenthal, 220–44. New York, Oxford: Oxford University Press.

Hillyer, Robert Silliman. 1941. "Introduction." In *The Complete Poetry and Selected Prose of John Donne and the Complete Poetry of William Blake*. New York: Random House.

Hirsch, David A. Hedrich. 1991. "Donne's Atomies and Anatomies: Deconstructed Bodies and the Resurrection of Atomic Theory." *SEL* 31.1:69–94.

Holdsworth, R. V. 1990. "The Death of Death in Donne's Holy Sonnets 10." *N&Q* 37.2:183.

Hollander, John and Frank Kermode, eds. 1973. *The Oxford Anthology of English Literature*. Vol. 1. New York: Oxford University Press.

Holmes, Elizabeth. 1929. *Aspects of Elizabethan Imagery*. Oxford: Basil Blackwell.

Holmes, M. Morgan. 1992. "Out of Egypt: John Donne and the Quest for Apocalyptic Recreation." In *Christianity and Literature* 42.1:25–40.

Höltgen, Karl Josef. 1964. "Eine Emblemfolge in Donnes *Holy Sonnet XIV*." *Archiv für das Studium der neueren Sprachen und Literaturen* 200:347–52.

Honig, Edwin and Oscar Williams, eds. 1968. *The Major Metaphysical Poets of the Seventeenth Century: John Donne, George Herbert, Richard Crashaw and Andrew Marvell: An Anthology*. New York: Washington Square Press, and New York: Atheneum.

Hooper, A. G., and C. J. D. Harvey. 1958. *Poems for Discussion: With Commentaries and Questions*. Cape Town: Oxford University Press.

Hopkins, Kenneth. 1962. *English Poetry: A Short History*. Philadelphia and New York: J. B. Lippincott.

Huebert, Ronald. 1977. *John Ford: Baroque English Dramatist.* Montreal: McGill-Queen's University Press.

Hunt, Clay. 1954. *Donne's Poetry: Essays in Literary Analysis.* New Haven: Yale University Press; London: Oxford University Press.

Hunt, Leigh. 1867. "An Essay on the Sonnet." In *The Book of the Sonnet*, ed. Leigh Hunt and S. Adams Lee. Vol. 1. Boston: Roberts Brothers.

Hunter, William B. 1983. "Difficulties in Interpretation of John Donne's *Satyre 1*." *SCB* 43:109–111.

Hussey, Maurice, ed. 1981. *Poetry 1600 to 1660.* Harlow: Longman.

Hutton, W. H. 1924. "John Donne, Poet and Preacher." *Theology* (London) 9:149–65.

Hyman, Lawrence W. 1982. "Humanism and 'Religious' Art." In *The Humanist* 42.2:49–50.

Iser, Wolfgang. 1960. "Manieristische Metaphorik in der englischen Dichtung." *Germanisch-Romanische Monatsschrift* n.s. 10:266–87.

Jackson, Robert S. 1970. *John Donne's Christian Vocation.* Evanston: Northwestern University Press.

Jerome, Judson. 1968. *Poetry: Premeditated Art.* Boston: Houghton Mifflin.

Johnson, Jeffrey. 1995. "Wrestling with God: John Donne in Prayer." In *John Donne's Religious Imagination: Essays in Honor of John T. Shawcross*, ed. Raymond-Jean Frontain and Frances M. Malpezzi, 306–23. Conway, AR: UCA Press.

Jonas, Leah. 1940. *The Divine Science: The Aesthetic of Some Representative Seventeenth-Century English Poets.* New York: Columbia University Press.

Jones, R. T. 1978. "John Donne's 'Songs and Sonets': The Poetic Value of Argument." *Theoria* 51:33–42.

———. 1986. *Studying Poetry: An Introduction.* London: Edward Arnold.

Judson, Alexander Corbin, ed. 1927. *Seventeenth Century Lyrics.* Chicago: University of Chicago Press.

Kamholtz, Jonathan Z. 1982. "Imminence and Eminence in Donne." *JEGP* 81.4:480–91.

Kawada, Akira. 1985. "John Donne to George Herbert: Shi wo megutte" [On John Donne and George Herbert with Special Reference to Death]. In *John Donne to sono Shuhen* [John Donne and Other Poets of the Seventeenth Century], 129–48. The Japan Society of Seventeenth-Century English Literature. Tokyo: Kinseido

Kawamura, Jōichirō. 1972. "Christ no Hanayome wa Dare ka - Donne no Shūkyo-shi Ippen wo Ronzu" [Who is Christ's Spouse? - A Discussion of a Divine Poem of Donne]. *Gengo Bunka* [Language Culture, Hitotsubashi University] 9:49–66.

Kermode, Frank. 1957. *John Donne.* Writers and Their Works 86. London: Longmans, Green & Co.

———, ed. 1968. *The Poems of John Donne.* Cambridge: Printed at the University printing house for the members of the Limited Editions Club.

———. 1974. "Donne: Lecture Five." In Frank Kermode, Stephen Fender, and Kenneth Palmer, *English Renaissance Literature: Introductory Lectures*, 83–95. London: Gray-Mills.

Kerrigan, William. 1974. "The Fearful Accommodations of John Donne." *ELR* 4:337–63.

———. 1983. *The Sacred Complex: On the Psychogenesis of Paradise Lost.* Cambridge, MA and London: Harvard University Press.

Keynes, Geoffrey. 1958. *A Bibliography of Dr. John Donne, Dean of Saint Paul's.* 3d ed. Cambridge: Cambridge University Press. 1st ed. 1914, 2d ed. 1932, 4th. ed. 1973.

King, Bruce. 1982. *Seventeenth-Century English Literature.* London and Basingstoke: Macmillan.

King, John N. 1982. *English Reformation Literature: The Tudor Origins of the Protestant Tradition.* Princeton: Princeton University Press.

Kiparsky, Paul. 1977. "The Rhythmic Structure of English Verse." *Linguistic Inquiry* 8:202.

Klause, John. 1983. *The Unfortunate Fall: Theodicy and the Moral Imagination of Andrew Marvell*. Hamden, CT: Archon Books.

———. 1986. "The Montaigneity of Donne's *Metempsychosis*." In *Renaissance Genres: Essays on Theory, History, and Interpretation*, ed. Barbara K. Lewalski, 418–43. Cambridge, MA and London: Harvard University Press.

Klause, John L. 1987. "Donne and the Wonderful." *ELR* 17.1:41–66.

Klawitter, George. 1991. "John Donne and Salvation Through Grace." In *Praise Disjoined: Changing Patterns of Salvation in Seventeenth-Century English Literature*, ed. William P. Shaw, 137–49. New York: Peter Lang.

Klinck, Dennis R. 1981. "John Donne's 'knottie Trinitie.'" *Renascence* 33.4:240–55.

Knox, George. 1956. "Donne's 'Holy Sonnets,' XIV." *Expl* 15:Item 2.

Kok, A. S. 1863. *English Poetry: Being Selections from the Works of British Poets, from the Time of Chaucer to the Present Day*. Schoonhoven: S. E. Van Nooten.

Korninger, Siegfried. 1956. *Die Naturaufassung in der Englischen Dictung des 17. Jahrhunderts*. Wien-Stuttgart: Wilhelm Braumüller.

Kortemme, Joseph. 1933. *Das Verhältnis John Donnes zur Scholastik und zum Barock: Eine Untersuchung zu den Anfängen des Englischen Barock*. Munster: Westfälischen Vereins Druckerie.

Kremen, Kathryn R. 1972. *The Imagination of the Resurrection: The Poetic Continuity of a Religious Motif in Donne, Blake, and Yeats*. Lewisburg, PA: Bucknell University Press, and Cranbury, NJ: Associated University Presses.

Kullmann, Thomas. 1994. "Höfischkeit und Spiritualität: Dramatische Elemente in der 'Metaphysical Poetry.'" In *Literaturwissenschaftliches Jahrbuch im Auftrage der Görres-Gesellschaft* 35:121–37.

Labriola, Albert C. 1990. "Iconographic Perspectives on Seventeenth-Century Religious Poetry." In *Approaches to Teaching the Metaphysical Poets*, ed. Sidney Gottlieb, 61–67. New York: The Modern Langage Association of America.

———. 1995. "*Christus Patiens* and *Christus Victor*: John Donne's Ultimate Reality and Meaning." *Ultimate Reality and Meaning* 18 (June): 92–101.

Lang, Andrew. 1912. *History of English Literature from "Beowulf" to Swinburne*. London: Longmans, Green and Co.

Langley, T. R. 1993. "Having Donne." *Cambridge Quarterly* 22:188–210.

Larson, Deborah Aldrich. 1989. *John Donne and Twentieth-Century Criticism*. Cranbury, NJ: Associated University Presses.

Lawler, Justus George. 1979. *Celestial Pantomime: Poetic Structures of Transcendence*. New Haven and London: Yale University Press.

Lawrence, Karen. 1985. "John Donne." In Karen Lawrence, Betsy Seifter, and Lois Ratner, *The McGraw-Hill Guide to English Literature*. Vol. 1. New York: McGraw-Hill.

Leech, Geoffrey. 1969. *A Linguistic Guide to English Poetry*. London and Harlow: Longmans, Green.

Legouis, Pierre. 1958. "John Donne and William Cowper: A Note on *The Task*, III, 712–24." *Anglia* 76:536–38.

Leishman, J. B. 1934. *The Metaphysical Poets: Donne, Herbert, Vaughan, Traherne*. Oxford: Clarendon Press.

———. 1951. *The Monarch of Wit: An Analytical and Comparative Study of the Poetry of John Donne*. London: Hutchinson's University Library. Further eds. in 1954, 1957, 1959, 1962, 1965.

———. 1954. "John Donne. The Divine Poems." *RES* ns 5:74–83.

———. 1962. "Donne and Seventeenth Century Poetry." In *John Donne: A Collection of*

Critical Essays (1896–1960), ed. Dame Helen Gardner, 109–22. Englewood Cliffs, NJ: Prentice-Hall.

Lemon, Lee T. 1969. *Approaches to Literature.* New York: Oxford University Press.

Levenson, J. C. 1953. "Holy Sonnets, XIV." *Expl* 11:Item 31.

———. 1954. "Donne's 'Holy Sonnets,' XIV." *Expl* 12:Item 36.

Lever, J. W. 1974. *Sonnets of the English Renaissance.* London: Athlone Press.

Levi, Peter. 1991. *The Art of Poetry.* New Haven and London: Yale University Press.

Lewalski, Barbara Kiefer. 1973. *Donne's Anniversaries and the Poetry of Praise: The Creation of a Symbolic Mode.* Princeton, NJ: Princeton University Press.

———. 1979. *Protestant Poetics and the Seventeenth-Century Religious Lyric.* Princeton: Princeton University Press.

———. 1987. "Lucy, Countess of Bedford: Images of a Jacobean Courtier and Patroness." In *Politics of Discourse: The Literature and History of Seventeenth-Century England*, ed. Kevin Sharpe and Steven N. Zwicker, 52–77. Berkeley: University of California Press.

———. and Andrew J. Sabol, eds. 1973. *Major Poets of the Earlier Seventeenth Century: Donne, Herbert, Vaughan, Crashaw, Jonson, Herrick, Marvell.* Indianapolis, IN: Odyssey Press.

Lewes, George Henry. 1838. "Donne's Poetical Works." *NMMC* 9:373–78.

Lightfoot, Joseph Barber. 1877. "Donne, the Poet-Preacher." In *The Classic Preachers of the English Church*, ed. John Edward Kempe. London: John Murray.

Linguanti, E. 1979–80. "Il vsao di argilla." In *Strumenti per l'analisi del testo letterario*, ed. E. Linguanti, T. Benussi, and G. Dente, 25–47. 2nd ed. Pisa: Libreria Goliardica.

Linsley, Joy L. 1995. "A Holy Puzzle: John Donne's 'Holy Sonnet XVII.'" In *John Donne's Religious Imagination: Essays in Honor of John T. Shawcross*, ed. Raymond-Jean Frontain and Frances M. Malpezzi, 202–13. Conway, AR: UCA Press.

Linville, Susan. 1978. "Donne's 'Holy Sonnets IX.'" *Expl* 36.4:21–22.

———. 1984a. "Contrary Faith: Poetic Closure and the Devotional Lyric." In *PLL* 20:141–53.

———. 1984b. "Enjambment and the Dialectics of Line Form in Donne's *Holy Sonnets*." *Style* 18:64–82.

Llasera, Margaret. 1986. "'Howrely in Inconstancee': Transience and Transformation in the Poetry of John Donne." *Bulletin de la Société d'études anglo-américaines des XVII et XVIII siècles.* 23:39–56.

Lloyd, Charles E. 1969. "The Author of Peace and Donne's Holy Sonnet XIV." *JHI* 30:251–52.

Lloyd-Evans, Barbara, ed. 1989. "John Donne." In *The Batsford Book of English Poetry: Chaucer to Arnold*, 281–300. London: B. T. Batsford Ltd.

Loewenstein, David. 1993. "Politics and Religion." In *The Cambridge Companion to English Poetry: Donne to Marvell*, ed. Thomas N. Corns, 3–30. Cambridge: Cambridge University Press.

Lofft, Capel, ed. 1813. *Laura, or An Anthology of Sonnets.* Vol. 5. London: R. A. Taylor for B. and R. Crosby.

Louthan, Doniphan. 1951. *The Poetry of John Donne: A Study in Exposition.* New York: Bookman Associates.

Low, Anthony. 1978. *Love's Architecture: Devotional Modes in Seventeenth-Century English Poetry.* New York: New York University Press.

———. 1982. "The 'Turning Wheele': Carew, Jonson, Donne (and the First) Law of Motion." *JDJ* 1:69–80.

———. 1993. *The Reinvention of Love: Poetry, politics and culture from Sidney to Milton.* Cambridge: Cambridge University Press. Ch. 3 rpt. (with minor changes) as "John Donne: 'The Holy Ghost is Amorous in His Metaphors'" in *New Perspectives on the Seven-*

teenth-Century English Religious Lyric, ed. John R. Roberts, 201–21. Columbia and London: University of Missouri Press, 1994.

Low, Lisa and Anthony John Harding. 1994. "Reading the Past: Reflecting the Present." In *Milton, the Metaphysicals, and Romanticism*, ed. Lisa Low and Anthony John Harding, 1–19. Cambridge: Cambridge University Press.

Lyon, T. 1937. *The Theory of Religious Liberty in England, 1603–39*. Cambridge: Cambridge University Press.

MacCarthy, Desmond. 1932. "John Donne." In *Criticism*, 36–60. London: Putnam. Rev. version of "John Donne." *NewQ* (1907–08):267–92.

MacDonald, George. 1868. *England's Antiphon*. London: Macmillan.

Mackenzie, Donald. 1990. *The Metaphysical Poets*. London: Macmillan.

Mahood, M. M. 1950. *Poetry and Humanism*. New Haven: Yale University Press.

Main, David M., ed. 1880. *A Treasury of English Sonnets*. Manchester: Alexander Ireland.

Makurenkova, S. 1994. *John Donne: Poetics and Rhetoric*. Moscow: Russian Academy of Sciences; Institute of World Literature.

Mallett, Phillip, ed. 1983. *John Donne: Selected Poems: Notes*. York Notes on Selected Poems. Harlow: Longman; York Press.

Malpezzi, Frances M. 1987. "The Weight/Lessness of Sin: Donne's 'Thou Hast Made Me' and the Psychostatic Tradition." *SCRev*: "A Special Issue: John Donne": 4.2:71–77.

———. 1995. "Donne's Transcendent Imagination: The Divine Poems as Hierophantic Experience." In *John Donne's Religious Imagination: Essays in Honor of John T. Shawcross*, ed. Raymond-Jean Frontain and Frances M. Malpezzi, 141–61. Conway, AR: UCA Press.

Manlove, Colin N. 1978. *Literature and Reality, 1600–1800*. London and Basingstoke: Macmillan.

———. 1989. *Critical Thinking: A Guide to Interpreting Literary Texts*. New York: St. Martin's Press.

———. 1992. *Christian Fantasy: From 1200 to the Present*. Houndmills, Basingstoke, Hampshire and London: The Macmillan Press, Ltd.

Mann, Lindsay A. 1985–86. "Sacred and Profane Love in Donne." *DR* 65:534–50.

Mano, D. Keith. 1979. "Reflections of a Christian Pornographer." *Christianity and Literature* 28:5–11.

Marandon, Sylvaine, vol. ed. 1984. "Six Poemes de John Donne," trans. Groupe D'Etudes et de Recherches Britanniques (GERB). In *Cahiers sur la Poésie*: "La traduction de la poésie" 1.1:133–57.

Marotti, Arthur F. 1981. "John Donne and the Rewards of Patronage." In *Patronage in the Renaissance*, ed. Guy Fitch Lytle and Stephen Orgel, 207–34. Princeton: Princeton University Press.

———. 1986. *John Donne, Coterie Poet*. Madison and London: University of Wisconsin Press.

———. 1994a. "Donne as Social Exile and Jacobean Courtier: The Devotional Verse and Prose of the Secular Man." In *Critical Essays on John Donne*, ed. Arthur F. Marotti, 77–101. New York: G. K. Hall.

———. 1994b. "Introduction." In *Critical Essays on John Donne*, ed. Arthur F. Marotti, 1–16. New York: G. K. Hall.

Martin, Bernard. 1990. *The Poetry of John Donne*. Horizon Studies in Literature. South Melbourne: Sydney University Press.

Martinet, Marie-Madeleine. 1982. "Les Figures de Répétition: Images de la Mélancholie Poétique au Début du 17ème Siècle." *BSEAA* 14:23–41.

———. 1984. "La Fin et le Commencement dans *Silex Scintillans*: De la Vision sans Nom aux Symboles dévoilés." *EA* 37:1–13.

———. 1987. "Un-done." In *Le Continent Européen et le Monde Anglo-Américain aux XVIIe et XVIIIe Siècles*, 62–64. Reims: Presses Universitaires de Reims.

Martz, Louis L. 1954. *The Poetry of Meditation: A Study of English Religious Literature of the Seventeenth Century*. Yale Studies in English 125. New Haven: Yale University Press; London: Oxford University Press. Rev. ed. 1962.

———. 1959. "Donne and the Meditative Tradition." *Thought* 34:269–78. Rpt. in *The Poem of the Mind*.

———. 1960. "John Donne: The Meditative Voice." *MR* 1:326–42. Rpt. in *The Poem of the Mind*.

———, ed. 1963. *The Meditative Poem: An Anthology of Seventeenth-Century Verse*. Garden City, NY: Doubleday. Rev. as *The Anchor Anthology of Seventeenth-Century Verse*, vol. 1. New York: New York University Press, and Garden City, NY: Doubleday, 1969.

———, 1966. *The Poem of the Mind: Essays on Poetry English and American*. New York: Oxford University Press. 2nd ed. 1969.

———, ed. 1969a. *The Anchor Anthology of Seventeenth-Century Verse*. Vol. 1. New York: New York University Press, and Garden City, NY: Doubleday.

———. 1969b. *The Wit of Love: Donne, Carew, Crashaw, Marvell*. Notre Dame, IN, and London: University of Notre Dame Press.

———. 1970. "The Action of the Self: Devotional Poetry in the Seventeenth Century." In *Metaphysical Poetry*, ed. Malcolm Bradbury and David Palmer, 101–22. Stratford-Upon-Avon Studies 11. New York: St. Martin's Press.

———. 1982. "Meditation as Poetic Strategy." *MP* 80:168–74.

———. 1985. "English Religious Poetry, from Renaissance to Baroque." *EIRC* 11:1–28. Rev. in *From Renaissance to Baroque: Essays on Literature and Art*, 3–38.

———. 1988. "Donne and Herbert: Vehement Grief and Silent Tears." *JDJ* 7.1:21–34. Rpt. in *From Renaissance to Baroque: Essays on Literature and Art*.

———. 1989. "The Generous Ambiguity of Herbert's *Temple*." In *A Fine Tuning: Studies of the Religious Poetry of Herbert and Milton*, ed. Mary A Maleski, 31–56. Binghamton, NY: Medieval and Renaissance Texts and Studies. Vol. 64. Rpt. in *From Renaissance to Baroque: Essays on Literature and Art*.

———. 1991. *From Renaissance to Baroque: Essays on Literature and Art*. Columbia: University of Missouri Press.

Masselink, Noralyn. 1992. "A Matter of Interpretation: Example and Donne's Role as Preacher and as Poet." *JDJ* 11.1–2:85–98.

Masson, David. 1967. "Thematic Analysis of Sounds in Poetry." In *Essays on the Language of Literature*, ed. Seymour Chatman and Samuel R. Levin, 54–68. Boston: Houghton Mifflin.

Matsuura, Kaichi. 1949. "A Study of Donne's Imagery." *SELit* 26:125–84. Rpt. in *A Study of Donne's Imagery*.

———. 1953. *A Study of Donne's Imagery: A Revelation of His Outlook on the World and His Vision of a Universal Christian Monarchy*. Tokyo: Kenkyusha.

Mazzaro, Jerome. 1987. "Striking through the Mask: Donne and Herbert at Sonnets." In *Like Season'd Timber: New Essays on George Herbert*, ed. Edmund Miller and Robert DiYanni, 241–53. New York: Peter Lang.

McCanles, Michael. 1975. "The Dialectical Structure of the Metaphysical Lyric: Donne, Herbert, Marvell." In *Dialectical Criticism and Renaissance Literature*, 54–117. Berkeley: University of California Press.

McCormick, Frank. 1983. "Donne, The Pope, and 'Holy Sonnets XIV.'" *CEA Critic* 45.2:23–24.

McGuire, Philip C. 1974. "Private Prayer and English Poetry in the Early Seventeenth Century." *SEL* 14:63–77.

McNees, Eleanor. 1987. "John Donne and the Anglican Doctrine of the Eucharist." *TSLL* 29:94–114.

———. 1992. "The Eschatology of Real Presence: Donne's Struggle Toward Conformity with Christ." In *Eucharistic Poetry: The Search for Presence in the Writings of John Donne, Gerard Manley Hopkins, Dylan Thomas, and Geoffrey Hill*, 33–68. Lewisburg: Bucknell University Press.

Melton, Wrightman Fletcher. 1906. *The Rhetoric of John Donne's Verse*. Baltimore: J. H. Furst.

Miles, Josephine. 1951. "The Language of the Donne Tradition." *KR* 13:37–49. Rev. in *Eras and Modes in English Poetry*, 20–32. Berkeley: University of California Press, 1957.

———. 1972. "Forest and Trees: or, The Sense at the Surface." *New Literary History* 4:35–45.

Miller, David M. 1971. *The Net of Hephaestus: A Study of Modern Criticism and Metaphysical Metaphor*. The Hague: Mouton.

Miller, Edmund. 1982. "John Donne." In *Critical Survey of Poetry: English Language Series*, ed. Frank N. Magill, 2:821–38. Englewood Cliffs, NJ: Salem Press.

——— and Robert Di Yanni, eds. 1986. *Like Season'd Timber: New Essays on George Herbert*. New York: Peter Lang.

Milward, Peter, S. J. 1979. *John Donne no 'Seinaru Sonnet'* [A Commentary on John Donne's *Holy Sonnets*]. Trans. Shōnosuke Ishii. Tokyo: Aratke Shuppan. Publ. in English as *A Commentary on the Holy Sonnets of John Donne*. Renaissance Monographs. Tokyo: The Renaissance Institute, Sophia University, 1988.

———. 1983. "Elizabeth-cho Shinwa o Megutte." *Sophia* 32:94–103.

———. 1988. *A Commentary on the Holy Sonnets of John Donne*. Renaissance Monographs. Tokyo: The Renaissance Institute, Sophia University.

———, and Shōnosuke Ishii. 1976. "John Donne no 'Seinaru Sonnet' Hyōshaku" [Commentary on John Donne's *Holy Sonnets*]. *Eigo Seinen* [The Rising Generation] (Tokyo: Kenkyu-sha, 1976–78) 122:17–19, 138–40, 222–24, 413–15, 541–44; 123: 21–23.

———, eds. 1982. *Eikoku Renaissance-ki no Bungei Yōshiki*. Tokyo: Aratake.

Mims, Edwin. 1948. *The Christ of the Poets*. New York: Abingdon-Cokesbury Press.

Miner, Earl. 1969. *The Metaphysical Mode from Donne to Cowley*. Princeton: Princeton University Press.

Mohanty, Christine Ann. 1988. "Penitential Sonnets 2 and 3: Anomaly in the Gardner Arrangement of Donne's *Holy Sonnets*." *N&Q* 35: 61–62.

Mollenkott, Virginia Ramey. 1981. "John Donne and the Limitations of Androgyny." *JEGP* 80:22–38.

Moloney, Michael Francis. 1944. *John Donne: His Flight from Mediaevalism*. New York: Russell and Russell.

———. 1950. "Donne's Metrical Practice." *PMLA* 65:232–39.

Moorman, Charles. 1989. "One Hundred Years of Editing the Canterbury Tales." *ChauR* 24:99–114.

Moravian Brethren. 1754. *A Collection of Hymns of the Children of God in All Ages, from the Beginning Till Now*. London: Printed, and to be had at all the Brethren's Chapels.

Morris, Brian. 1972. "Not, Siren-like, to tempt: Donne and the Composers." In *John Donne: Essays in Celebration*, ed. A. J. Smith, 219–51. London: Methuen.

Morris, David. 1953. *The Poetry of Gerard Manley Hopkins and T. S. Eliot in the Light of the Donne Tradition*. Bern: A. Francke.

Morris, Harry. 1973. "John Donne's Terrifying Pun." *PLL* 9:128–37.

Moseley, C. W. R. D. 1980. "A Reading of Donne's Holy Sonnet XIV." *Archiv für das Studium der neueren Sprachen und Literaturen* 217:103–08.

Moseley, Charles. 1989. *A Century of Emblems: An Introductory Anthology*. Brookfield, VT: Gower Publishing Co.

Mroczkowski, Przemsyslaw. 1981. "Pioropusz i Kadzielnica." In *Historia Literatury Angielskiej* (History of English Literature), 213–224. Zaklad Narodowy Im. Ossolińskich Wydawnictwo (Publications). Wroclaw, Warszawa (Poland).

Mueller, Janel. 1989. "Women Among the Metaphysicals: A Case, Mostly, of Being Donne For." *MP* 87, no. 2:142–58. Rpt. in *Critical Essays on John Donne*, ed. Arthur F. Marotti, 37–48. New York: G. K. Hall. 1994.

Mueller, William R. 1961. "Donne's Adulterous Female Town." *MLN* 76:312–14.

Mulder, John R. 1969. *The Temple of the Mind: Education and Literary Taste in Seventeenth-Century England*. Pegasus Backgrounds in English Literature. New York: Pegasus.

Müller, Wolfgang G. 1986. "Liturgie und Lyrik: John Donnes 'The Litanie.'" In *Literaturwissenschaftliches Jahrbuch*, 65–80. Berlin: Duncker & Humblot.

———. 1992. "Das Paradoxon in der englischen Barocklyrik: John Donne, George Herbert, Richard Crashaw." In *Das Paradox: Eine Herausforderung des abendländischen Denkens*, ed. Paul Geyer and Roland Hagenbüchle, 355–84. Tübingen: Stauffenburg.

Muraoka, Isamu. 1970–71. "Donne no Holy Sonnet 'Death be not proud'" [Donne's *Holy Sonnet* 'Death be not proud']. *Eigo Seinen* [The Rising Generation] (Tokyo: Kenkyusha) 116:246–48.

Nagasawa, Junji. 1983. *Eibungeishicho no Nagare to Sugatta*. Tokyo: Hokuseido.

Nardo, Anna K. 1986. "John Donne at Play and in Between." In *The Eagle and the Dove: Reassessing John Donne*, ed. Claude J. Summers and Ted-Larry Pebworth, 157–65. Columbia: University of Missouri Press. Rpt. in *The Ludic Self in Seventeenth-Century English Literature*.

———. 1991. *The Ludic Self in Seventeenth-Century English Literature*. Albany: State University of New York Press.

Nash, Walter. 1989. *Rhetoric: The Wit of Persuasion*. Oxford and Cambridge: Basil Blackwell.

Nelly, Una. 1969. *The Poet Donne: A Study in His Dialectic Method*. Cork, Ireland: Cork University Press.

Nelson, T. G. A. 1979. "Death, Dung, the Devil, and Worldly Delights: A Metaphysical Conceit in Harington, Donne, and Herbert." *SP* 76:272–87.

Newbolt, Henry. 1926. *Studies in Green and Gray*. London: Thomas Nelson and Sons.

———, ed. 1929. *Devotional Poets of the XVII Century*. London: Thomas Nelson and Sons.

Newton, Willoughby. 1959. "A Study of John Donne's Sonnet XIV." *ATR* 41:10–12.

Nicolson, Majorie Hope. 1950. *The Breaking of the Circle: Studies in the Effect of the "New Science" upon Seventeenth Century Poetry*. Evanston: Northwestern University Press.

———. 1956. *Science and the Imagination*. London: Oxford University Press.

Noble, James Ashcroft. 1880. "The Sonnet in England." *Contemporary Review* 38:446–71.

Norbrook, David. 1990. "The Monarchy of Wit and the Republic of Letters: Donne's Politics. In *Soliciting Interpretation: Literary Theory and Seventeenth-Century English Poetry*, ed. Elizabeth D. Harvey and Katharine Eisaman Maus, 3–36. Chicago and London: The University of Chicago Press.

——— and H. R. Woudhuysen, eds. 1992. *The Penguin Book of Renaissance Verse: 1509–1659*. Harmondsworth, Eng.: Penguin.

Novarr, David. 1980. *The Disinterred Muse: Donne's Texts and Contexts*. Ithaca: Cornell University Press.

———. 1987. "*Amor Vincit Omnia*: Donne and the Limits of Ambiguity." *MLR* 82:286–92.

Nye, Robert. 1972. "The Body is his Book: The Poetry of John Donne." *CritQ* 14:345–60. Trans. and rpt. as "'The body is his book': la poésie de John Donne." In *John Donne*, ed. Jean-Marie Benoist, 141–55, Herissey: L'Age D'Homme.

[OED]. 1884–1928. *A New English Dictionary on Historical Principles*, ed. James A. H. Murray et al. 125 fascicles. Corrected and reissued as *The Oxford English Dictionary*. 12 vols. and supplement. Oxford: Clarendon Press, 1933.

O'Connell, Patrick F. 1981. "The Successive Arrangements of Donne's 'Holy Sonnets.'" *PQ* 60:323–42.

———. 1985. "'Restore Thine Image': Structure and Theme in Donne's 'Goodfriday.'" *JDJ* 4:157–80.

Oldisworth, Giles. c. 1650. Annotations on a copy of the 1639 Poems. See also Sampson, John.

Oliveros, Alejandro. 1992. *La mirada del desengaño: John Donne y la poesia del barroco*. Ediciones del Rectorado. Valencia, Venezuela: Universidad de Carabobo.

Oppel, Horst and Kurt Schlüter. 1973. *Englische Dichtung des 16. und 17. Jahrhunderts*. Athenaion Essays: Studienausgaben zum Neuen Handbuch der Literaturwissenschaft. Vol. 3. Frankfurt am Main: Akademische Verlagsgesellschaft Athenaion.

Oras, Ants. 1960. *Pause Patterns in Elizabethan and Jacobean Drama: An Experiment in Prosody*. University of Florida Monographs 3. Gainesville: University of Florida Press.

Osmond, Percy H. 1919. *The Mystical Poets of the English Church*. London: Society for Promotion of Christian Knowledge; New York: Macmillan Co.

Osmond, Rosalie. 1990. *Mutual Accusation: Seventeenth-Century Body and Soul Dialogues in Their Literary and Theological Context*. Toronto: University of Toronto Press.

Osterwalder, Hans. 1995. "'Nor ever chaste, except You ravish me': The Love Imagery in John Donne's Secular and Religious Poems." *AAA-Arbeiten aus Anglistik und Amerikanistik*. (Institut für Anglistik, University of Graz, Austria) (Tübingen) 20.1:199–210.

Ousby, Ian, ed. 1993. *The Cambridge Guide to Literature in English*. Foreword by Doris Lessing. Rev. ed. Cambridge: Cambridge University Press.

Palgrave, Francis Turner, ed. 1889. *The Treasury of Sacred Song*. Oxford: Clarendon Press.

Pallotti, Donatella. 1993. "*Periculosa Et Pestilens Quaestio*: Interrogative Discourse in Donne's Holy Sonnets." In *English Studies in Transition: Papers from the ESSE Inaugural Conference (1991)*, ed. Robert Clark and Piero Boitani, 167–84. London and New York: Routledge.

Palmer, Alan and Veronica Palmer. 1981. "John Donne." In *Who's Who in Shakespeare's England?*, 67–68. New York: St. Martin's Press.

Parfitt, George A. E. 1972. "Donne, Herbert and the Matter of Schools." *Essays in Criticism* 22:381–95.

———. 1985. *English Poetry of the Seventeenth Century*. London and New York: Longman.

———. 1989. *John Donne: A Literary Life*. London: Macmillan.

Parini, Jay. 1977. "The Progress of the Soul: Donne and Hopkins in Meditation." *Forum for Modern Language Studies* 13:303–12.

Parish, John E. 1963a. "Donne's Holy Sonnet XIII." *Expl* 22:Item 19.

———. 1963b. "No. 14 of Donne's Holy Sonnets." *College English* 24:299–302. Rpt. as "The Sonnet's Unity," in *John Donne's Poetry: Authoritative Texts, Criticism*, ed. A. L. Clements, 255–59. New York: Norton, 1966.

Parker, David. 1987. "Images of Life and Death in the Spirituality of John Donne." *Ormand Papers* (Ormond College, University of Melbourne) 4:75–81.

Parker, Derek. 1975. *John Donne and His World*. London: Thames and Hudson.

Parker, Patricia. 1984. "Dilation and Delay: Renaissance Matrices." *PoT* 5:519–35.

Parry, Graham. 1985. "John Donne: Patronage, Friendship and Love." In *Seventeenth-Century Poetry: The Social Context*, 42–74. London: Hutchinson.

Partridge, A. C. 1964. *Orthography in Shakespeare and Elizabethan Drama: A Study of Colloquial Contractions, Elision, Prosody and Punctuation*. London: Edward Arnold.

———. 1971. *The Language of Renaissance Poetry: Spenser, Shakespeare, Donne, Milton*. London: Andre Deutsch.

———. 1978. *John Donne: Language and Style*. The Language Library, ed. Eric Partridge and David Crystal. London: Andre Deutsch.

Patmore, Coventry [?]. 1846. "Gallery of Poets. No. 1—John Donne." *LEM*. 1:228–36.

Patrick, J. Max. 1972. "Donne's Holy sonnets VI." *Expl* 31:Item 12.

Patrides, C. A., ed. 1985a. *The Complete English Poems of John Donne*. London and Melbourne: J. M. Dent & Sons. Introduction rpt. as "John Donne: The Aesthetics of Morality." In *Figures in a Renaissance Context*, ed. Claude J. Summers and Ted-Larry Pebworth, 89–116. Ann Arbor: University of Michigan Press, 1989.

———. 1985b. "John Donne Methodized; or, How to Improve Donne's Impossible Text with the Assistance of His Several Editors." *MP* 82:365–73.

Patterson, Annabel M. 1970. *Hermogenes and the Renaissance: Seven Ideas of Style*. Princeton: Princeton University Press.

Paulissen, May Nelson. 1982. *The Love Sonnets of Lady Mary Wroth: A Critical Introduction*. Elizabethan and Renaissance Studies 104, ed. James Hogg. Salzburg: Institut für Anglistik und Amerikanistik.

Pawar, Malovika. 1987. "The Agony of Faith: A Comparative Study of the Holy Sonnets of Donne and the 'Terrible Sonnets' of G.M. Hopkins." *PURBA* 18.2:39–52.

Payne, Frank Walter. 1926. *John Donne and his Poetry*. Poetry and Life Series 35. London: George G. Harrap.

Peterson, Douglas L. 1959. "John Donne's *Holy Sonnets* and the Anglican Doctrine of Contrition." *SP* 56:504–18.

———. 1967. *The English Lyric from Wyatt to Donne: A History of the Plain and Eloquent Styles*. Princeton: Princeton University Press. 2nd ed. East Lansing, MI: Colleagues Press, 1990.

Pezzini, Domenico. 1990. "La poesia della passione nella tradizione letteraria inglese: Dal 'Sogno della Croce' a R. S. Thomas." *RSLR* 26:460–507

Pinnington, A. J. 1987. "Prayer and Praise in John Donne's *La Corona*." In *Poetry and Faith in the English Renaissance: Essays in Honour of Professor Toyohiko Tatsumi's Seventieth Birthday*, ed. Peter Milward, 133–42. Tokyo: Renaissance Institute, Sophia University.

Pitts, Arthur W., Jr. 1971. "Donne's Holy Sonnets VI." *Expl* 29:Item 39.

Poisson, J. R. 1962. "Introduction." In *Poèmes de John Donne*, trans. Jean Fuzier and Yves Denis. Paris: Éditions Gallimard.

Policardi, Silvio. 1948. *John Donne: e la poesia metafisica del XVII secolo in Inghilterra*. Padova: CEDAM.

Pollard, Arthur. 1973. "John Donne: 'Show me deare Christ, thy spouse, so bright and cleare.'" *The Critical Survey* 6:16–20.

Pollitt, Charles. 1890. *DeQuincey's Editorship of the Westmoreland Gazette, with selections from his work on that Journal from July 1818, to November 1819*. Kendall: Atkinson and Pollitt.

Pollock, John J. 1973. "Reply to Elizabeth Schneider's 'Prufrock and After: The Theme of Change.'" *PMLA* 88:524.

———. 1978. "Another Donne Pun." *ANQ* 16:83.

Pop-Cornis, Marcel. 1975. *Modern English Poetry: A Critical and Historical Reader*. Timişoara: Universitatea din Timişoara.

Porter, Peter. 1991. *The Illustrated Poets: John Donne*. Selected and with an introduction by Peter Porter. London: Aurum Press.

––––––– and Anthony Thwaite, compilers. 1974. "John Donne (1572–1631)." In *The English Poets from Chaucer to Edward Thomas*, 95–107. London: Secker and Warburg.

Potter, George Reuben. 1934. "John Donne's Discovery of Himself." *UCPE* 4:3–23.

Power, Helen W. 1972. "The Speaker as Creator: The Voice in Donne's Poems." *XUS* 11: 21–28.

Praz, Mario. 1925. *Secentismo e Marinismo in Inghilterra: John Donne—Richard Crashaw*. Firenze: Casa Editrice "La Voce." Rev. as *La Poesia Metafisica Inglese del Seicento: John Donne*. Roma: Edizioni Italiane, 1945; and as *John Donne*. Torino: S. A. I. E., 1958.

––––––. 1931. "Donne and the Poetry of His Time." In *A Garland for John Donne, 1631–1931*, ed. Theodore Spencer, 51–72. Cambridge: Harvard University Press; London: Humphrey Milford, Oxford University Press. Rpt. in *The Flaming Heart: Essays on Crashaw, Machiavelli, and Other Studies in the Relations between Italian and English Literature from Chaucer to T. S. Eliot*. Garden City, NY: Doubleday, 1958.

––––––. 1970. *Mnemosyne: The Parallel Between Literature and the Visual Arts*. Bollingen Series 35. Princeton: Princeton University Press.

Prescott, Anne Lake. 1978. *French Poets and the English Renaissance: Studies in Fame and Transformation*. New Haven: Yale University Press.

Pritchard, R. E. 1986. "Donne's Angels in the Corners." *N&Q* 33:348–49.

Radzinowicz, Mary Ann. 1987. "'Anima Mea' Psalms and John Donne's Religious Poetry." In *"Bright Shootes of Everlastingnesse": The Seventeenth-Century Religious Lyric*, ed. Claude J. Summers and Ted-Larry Pebworth, 40–58. Columbia: University of Missouri Press.

Raine, Kathleen. 1945. "John Donne and the Baroque Doubt." *Horizon* 11:371–95.

Raiziss, Sona. 1952. *The Metaphysical Passion: Seven Modern American Poets and the Seventeenth-Century Tradition*. Philadelphia: University of Pennsylvania Press.

Rambuss, Richard. 1994. "Pleasure and Devotion: The Body of Jesus and Seventeenth-Century Religious Lyric." In *Queering the Renaissance*, ed. Jonathan Goldberg, 253–79. Durham and London: Duke University Press.

Ramsaran, John A. 1973. "English Metrical Psalms, Donne's Holy Sonnets and Tulasī Dāsa's Vinaya Patrikā." In *English and Hindi Religious Poetry: An Analogical Study*, 141–63. Leiden: E. J. Brill.

Ramsay, Mary Paton. 1917. *Les doctrines médiévales chez Donne, le poète métaphysicien de l'Angleterre (1573–1631)*. London: Oxford University Press.

Raspa, Anthony. 1983. *The Emotive Image: Jesuit Poetics in the English Renaissance*. Fort Worth: Texas Christian University Press.

Rawlinson, D. H. 1968. "Contrasting Poems: Jonson's 'To Heaven' and Donne's 'Thou Hast Made Me.'" In *The Practice of Criticism*, 104–13. Cambridge: Cambridge University Press.

Ray, Robert H. 1990a. "Ben Jonson and the Metaphysical Poets: Continuity in a Survey Course." In *Approaches to Teaching the Metaphysical Poets*, ed. Sidney Gottlieb, 89–96. New York: The Modern Langage Association of America.

––––––. 1990b. *A John Donne Companion*. New York and London: Garland Publishing, Inc.

Read, Herbert. 1928. *Phases of English Poetry*. London: Hogarth Press.

Reeves, James. 1952. *Selected Poems of John Donne*. The Poetry Bookshelf, gen. ed. James Reeves. London: Heinemann.

Reynolds, Mark. 1990. "Teaching the Metaphysical Poets in a Two-Year College." In *Approaches to Teaching the Metaphysical Poets*, ed. Sidney Gottlieb, 109–13. New York: The Modern Langage Association of America.

Richards, I. A. 1929. *Practical Criticism: A Study of Literary Judgment*. New York: Harcourt, Brace.

Richmond, Hugh M. 1958. "Donne and Ronsard." *N&Q* ns 5:534–36.

———. 1970. "Ronsard and the English Renaissance." *Comparative Literature Studies* 7:141–60.

———. 1981. *Puritans and Libertines: Anglo-French Literary Relations in the Reformation*. Berkeley: University of California Press.

Richter, Rudolph. 1902. "Der Vers bei Dr. John Donne." In *Beiträge zur Neueren Philologie*, 391–415. Vienna & Leipzig: Wilhelm Braumüller.

Ricks, Don M. 1966. "The Westmoreland Manuscript and the Order of Donne's Holy Sonnets." *SP* 63:187–95.

Rieke, Alison R. 1984. "Donne's Riddles." *JEGP* 83:1–20.

Riemer, A. P. 1982. "The Poetry of Religious Paradox—T.S. Eliot and the Metaphysicals." *Sydney Studies in English* 8:80–88.

Rissanen, Paavo. 1983. *John Donne's Doctrine of the Church*. Helsinki: Finnish Society for Missiology and Ecumenics.

Roberts, John R. 1982a. *John Donne: An Annotated Bibliography of Modern Criticism, 1968–1978*. Columbia: University of Missouri Press.

———. 1982b. "John Donne's Poetry: An Assessment of Modern Criticism." *JDJ* 1:55–67.

——— and Gary A. Stringer, eds. 1987. *SCRev* ("A Special Issue: John Donne") 4.2.

Robson, W. W. 1986. *A Prologue to English Literature*. London: B. T. Batsford.

Rogers, Pat, ed. 1987. *The Oxford Illustrated History of English Literature*. Oxford and New York: Oxford University Press.

———. 1992. "The Seventeenth Century: John Donne." In *An Outline of English Literature*, 159–66. Oxford and New York: Oxford University Press.

Rogers, W. Harry. 1862. *Spiritual Conceits: Extracted from the Writings of the Fathers, the Old English Poets, etc*. Illustrated by W. Harry Rogers. London: Griffith and Farran.

Rollin, Roger B. 1986. "'Fantastique Ague': The Holy Sonnets and Religious Melancholy." In *The Eagle and the Dove: Reassessing John Donne*, ed. Claude J. Summers and Ted-Larry Pebworth, 131–46. Columbia: University of Missouri Press.

———. 1994. "John Donne's *Holy Sonnets*—The Sequel: *Devotions upon Emergent Occasions*." *JDJ* 13.1–2:51–59.

———. 1995. "Witty by Design: Robert Herrick's *Hesperides*." In *The Wit of Seventeenth-Century Poetry*, ed. Claude J. Summers and Ted-Larry Pebworth, 135–50. Columbia and London: University of Missouri Press.

Romein, Tunis. 1984. "Donne's 'Holy Sonnet XIV.'" *Expl* 42.4:12–14.

Rosenthal, M. L., W. C. Hummel, and V. E. Leichty. 1944. *Effective Reading: Methods and Models*. Boston: Houghton Mifflin.

Rossi, Tiziana. 1987. "John Donne: Mística y erotismo bajo el signo de la muerte." *Hora de Poesia* 49–50:71–77.

Roston, Murray. 1974. *The Soul of Wit: A Study of John Donne*. Oxford: Clarendon Press.

———. 1987. *Renaissance Perspectives in Literature and the Visual Arts*. Princeton: Princeton University Press.

———. 1990. *Changing Perspectives in Literature and the Visual Arts, 1650–1820*. Princeton: Princeton University Press.

Roth, Regina. 1947. "Donne and Sonnets IX and X." *Gifthorse: A Yearbook of Writing*, 15–

18. Columbus: Association of Graduate Students in English. The Ohio State University.

Roy, V.K. and R.C. Kapoor. 1969. *John Donne and Metaphysical Poetry*. Delhi: Doaba House.

Ruf, Frederick J. 1993. "Lyric Autobiography: John Donne's *Holy Sonnets*." *Harvard Theological Review* 86.3:293–307.

Rugoff, Milton Allan. 1939. *Donne's Imagery: A Study of Creative Sources*. New York: Corporate. Rpt. New York: Russell & Russell, 1962.

Ruoff, James E., ed. 1972. *Major Elizabethan Poetry & Prose*. New York: Thomas Y. Crowell.

Ruotolo, Lucio P. 1966. "The Trinitarian Framework of Donne's Holy Sonnet XIV." *JHI* 27:445–46.

Russo, John Paul. 1989. *I.A. Richards: His Life and Work*. Baltimore: The Johns Hopkins University Press.

Sabine, Maureen. 1992. *Feminine Engendered Faith: The Poetry of John Donne and Richard Crashaw*. Houndmills, Basingstoke, Hampshire, and London: Macmillan Press Ltd.

Samarin, R. M. 1973. "The Tragedy of John Donne." *Voprosy Literatury* 17:162–78.

Sampson, John. 1921. "A Contemporary Light upon John Donne." *E&S* 7:82–107.

Samson, Patricia. 1963. "Words for Music." *Southern Review: An Australian Journal of Literary Studies* 1:46–52.

Sanders, Thomas E. 1967. *The Discovery of Poetry*. Glenview, IL: Scott, Foresman.

Sanders, Wilbur. 1971. *John Donne's Poetry*. Cambridge: Cambridge University Press.

Santisteban Olmedo, Francisco. 1977. "John Donne y la idea del amor." *Estudios de filologia inglesa* 3:99–118.

Satterthwaite, Alfred W. 1960. *Spenser, Ronsard, and DuBellay: A Renaissance Comparison*. Port Washington, NY: Kennikat Press.

Schelling, Felix E., ed. 1895. *A Book of Elizabethan Lyrics*. Boston: Ginn.

———. 1910. *English Literature During the Lifetime of Shakespeare*. New York: Henry Holt.

Schirmer, Walter F. 1937. *Geschichte der englischen Literatur von den Anfängen bis zur Gegenwart*. Halle: Max Niemeyer Verlag. 2nd ed. 1954.

Schlüter, Kurt. 1984. "The Influence of the Greek Prayer Hymn on the English Renaissance Sonnet: Aspects of Genre in Relation to Form of Verse." *Anglia* 102:323–48.

Schmidt, Michael. 1980. "John Donne." In *A Reader's Guide to Fifty British Poets, 1300–1900*, 134–135. London: Heinemann; Totowa, NJ: Barnes and Noble.

Schoenfeldt, Michael C. 1990. "'That Ancient Heat': Sexuality and Spirituality in *The Temple*." In *Soliciting Interpretation: Literary Theory and Seventeenth-Century English Poetry*, ed. Elizabeth D. Harvey and Katharine Eisaman Maus, 273–306. Chicago and London: University of Chicago Press.

———. 1991. *Prayer and Power: George Herbert and Renaissance Courtship*. Chicago and London: University of Chicago Press.

———. 1994. "The Poetry of Supplication: Toward a Cultural Poetics of the Religious Lyric." In *New Perspectives on the Seventeenth-Century English Religious Lyric*, ed. John R. Roberts, 75–104. Columbia and London: University of Missouri Press.

Schwartz, Elias. 1967. "Donne's 'Holy Sonnets, XIV.'" *Expl* 26:item 27.

———. 1968. "*Mimesis* and the Theory of Signs." *College English* 29:343–54.

Scott, W. S. 1945. *The Fantasticks: Donne, Herbert, Crashaw, Vaughan*. London: John Westhouse.

Selden, Raman. 1983. "Experiencing Election." *TLS* 24 June: 681.

Selden, Ray. 1983. "L'incarnation, conviction de John Donne." In *John Donne*, ed. Jean-Marie Benoist, 163–79. Herissey: L'Age D'Homme.

Sellin, Paul R. 1974. "The Hidden God: Reformation Awe in Renaissance English Literature." In *The Darker Vision of the Renaissance: Beyond the Fields of Reason*, ed. Robert S. Kinsman, 147–96. Berkeley: University of California Press.

Sencourt, Robert [Robert Esmonde Gordon George]. 1925. *Outflying Philosophy*. London: Simpkin, Marshall.

Sessions, William A. 1987. "Abandonment and the English Religious Lyric in the Seventeenth Century." In *"Bright Shootes of Everlastingnesse": The Seventeenth-Century Religious Lyric*, ed. Claude J. Summers and Ted-Larry Pebworth, 1–19. Columbia: University of Missouri Press.

Shaaber, M. A., ed. 1958. *John Donne: Selected Poems*. Crofts Classics, gen. eds. Samuel H. Beer and O. B. Hardison, Jr. Arlington Heights, IL: Harlan Davidson.

Shami, Jeanne. 1987. "John Donne: Geography as Metaphor." In *Geography and Literature: A Meeting of the Disciplines*, ed. William E. Mallory and Paul Simpson-Housley, 161–67. Syracuse: Syracuse University Press.

Shaw, Robert B. 1981. *The Call of God: The Theme of Vocation in the Poetry of Donne and Herbert*. Cambridge: Cowley.

Shawcross, John T., ed. 1967. *The Complete Poetry of John Donne*. Anchor Seventeenth-Century Series. Garden City, NY: Doubleday.

Shawcross, John. 1980. "The Book Index: Plutarch's *Moralia* and John Donne." *JRMMRA* 1: 53–62.

———. 1982. "Annihilating the Poet in Donne." *Rev* 4: 265–73.

———. 1983. "A Consideration of Title-Names in the Poetry of Donne and Yeats." *Names* 31, no.3: 159–66.

———. 1986a. "The Arrangement and Order of John Donne's Poems." In *Poems in Their Place: The Intertextuality and Order of Poetic Collections*, ed. Neil Fraistat, 119–63. Chapel Hill: University of North Carolina Press.

———. 1986b. "Poetry, Personal and Impersonal." In *The Eagle and the Dove: Reassessing John Donne*, ed. Claude J. Summers and Ted-Larry Pebworth, 53–66. Columbia: University of Missouri Press.

———. 1987. "'What do you read?' 'Words'—Ah, But Are They Donne's?" In *The Donne Dalhousie Discovery: Proceedings of a Symposium on the Acquisition and Study of the John Donne and Joseph Conrad Collections at Texas Tech University*, ed. Ernest W. Sullivan, II and David J. Murrah, 21–31. Lubbock, TX: Friends of the University Library / Southwest Collection.

———. 1988. "Scholarly Editions: Composite Editorial Principles of Single Copy-Texts, Multiple Copy-Texts, Edited Copy-Texts." *TEXT* 4:297–317.

———. 1991. *Intentionality and the New Traditionalism: Some Liminal Means to Literary Revisionism*. University Park: Penn State University Press.

———. 1994. "Kidnapping the Poets: The Romantics and Henry Vaughan." In *Milton, the Metaphysicals, and Romanticism*, ed. Lisa Low and Anthony John Harding, 185–203. Cambridge: Cambridge University Press.

Sherwood, Terry G. 1984. *Fulfilling the Circle: A Study of John Donne's Thought*. Toronto: University of Toronto Press.

———. 1989. *Herbert's Prayerful Art*. Toronto: University of Toronto Press.

Shullenberger, William. 1993. "Love as a Spectator Sport in John Donne's Poetry." In *Renaissance Discourses of Desire*, ed. Claude J. Summers and Ted-Larry Pebworth, 46–62. Columbia and London: University of Missouri Press.

Sicherman, Carol M. 1970. "Donne's Timeless *Anniversaries*." *UTQ* 39:127–43.

———. 1971. "Donne's Discoveries." *SEL* 11:69–88.

Silhol, Robert. 1962. "Réflexions sur les sources et la structure de *A Litanie* de John Donne." *EA* 15:329–46.

Simon, Irène. 1952. "Some Problems of Donne Criticism." *RLV* 18:317–24, 393–414; 19:14–39, 114–32, 201–02. Rpt. as *Some Problems of Donne Criticism*. Langues Vivantes 40. Bruxelles: Marcel Didier, 1952.

Simpson, Arthur L., Jr. 1969. "Donne's Holy Sonnets, XII." *Expl* 27:item 75.

Simpson, Evelyn M. 1924. *A Study of the Prose Works of John Donne*. Oxford: Oxford University Press. 2nd ed. 1948.

———. 1965. "Two Notes on Donne." *RES* ns 16:140–50.

Sinclair, William Macdonald. 1909. "John Donne: Poet and Preacher." *Transactions of the Royal Society of Literature* ns 2.29:179–202.

Sinfield, Alan. 1983. *Literature in Protestant England, 1560–1660*. London and Canberra; Croom Helm; Totowa, NJ: Barnes & Noble.

———. 1992. *Faultlines: Cultural Materialism and the Politics of Dissident Reading*. Berkeley: University of California Press.

Singer, Irving. 1984. *The Nature of Love: Courtly and Romantic*. Vol. 2. Chicago and London: The University of Chicago Press.

Singh, Brijraj, ed. 1992. *Five Seventeenth-Century Poets: Donne, Herbert, Crashaw, Marvell, Vaughan*. Delhi: Oxford University Press.

Singleton, Marion White. 1987. *God's Courtier: Configuring a Different Grace in George Herbert's Temple*. Cambridge: Cambridge University Press.

Skelton, Robin. 1978. "Poetry and Relativity." In *Poetic Truth*, 56–75. London: Heinemann; New York: Barnes & Noble; Agincourt: Book Society of Canada.

Skulsky, Harold. 1992. *Language Recreated: Seventeenth-Century Metaphorists and the Act of Metaphor*. Athens, GA and London: University of Georgia Press.

Slights, Camille Wells. 1981. *The Casuistical Tradition in Shakespeare, Donne, Herbert, and Milton*. Princeton: Princeton University Press.

Sloane, Mary Cole. 1974. "Emblem and Meditation: Some Parallels in John Donne's Imagery." *SAB* 39.2:74–79.

———. 1981. *The Visual in Metaphysical Poetry*. Atlantic Highlands, NJ: Humanities Press.

Sloane, Thomas O. 1985. *Donne, Milton, and the End of Humanist Rhetoric*. Berkeley, Los Angeles, and London: University of California Press.

Smith, A. J. 1956. "'Since she whom I lov'd': A Note on Punctuation." *MLR* 51:406–07.

———. 1970. "The Poetry of John Donne." In *English Poetry and Prose: 1540–1674*, ed. Christopher Ricks, 2:137–72. London: Barrie & Jenkins.

———, ed. 1971. *John Donne: The Complete English Poems*. Harmondsworth, Eng.: Penguin. Rpt. with corrections 1973, 1975.

———, ed. 1975. *John Donne: The Critical Heritage*. The Critical Heritage Series, gen. ed. B. C. Southam. London and Boston: Routledge and Kegan Paul.

———. 1991. *Metaphysical Wit*. Cambridge: Cambridge University Press.

———. 1992. "John Donne." In *Seventeenth-Century British Nondramatic Poets: First Series*. Dictionary of Literary Biography, ed. M. Thomas Hester, 77–96. Vol. 121. Detroit, London: Gale Research Inc.

Smith, Gary. 1987. "Gwendolyn Brooks's 'Children of the Poor,' Metaphysical Poetry and the Inconditions of Love." In *A Life Distilled: Gwendolyn Brooks, Her Poetry and Fiction*, ed. Maria K. Mootry and Gary Smith, 165–76. Urbana and Chicago: University of Illinois Press.

Smith, Julia J. 1984. "Donne and the Crucifixion." *MLR* 79:513–25.

Sobosan, Jeffery G. 1977. "Call and Response—The Vision of God in John Donne and George Herbert." *Religious Studies* 13:395–407.

Sparrow, John. 1964. "George Herbert and John Donne among the Moravians." *Bulletin of the New York Public Library* 68:625–53.

Spencer, Hazelton. 1952. *British Literature. Vol. 1: From Beowulf to Sheridan.* Boston: D. C. Heath.

Spiller, Michael R. G. 1992. *The Development of the Sonnet: An Introduction.* London and New York: Routledge.

Spörri-Sigel, Erika. 1949. *Liebe und Tod in John Donnes Dichtung.* Siebnen: Druckerei-Kurzi.

Spurr, Barry. 1991. "Salvation and Damnation in the *Divine Meditations* of John Donne." In *Praise Disjointed: Changing Patterns of Salvation in Seventeenth-Century English Literature,* ed. William P. Shaw, 165–74. New York: Peter Lang.

———. 1992. *The Poetry of John Donne.* Glebe, Australia: Fast Books; A Division of Wild and Woolley Pty. Ltd.

Stachniewski, John. 1981. "John Donne: The Despair of the 'Holy Sonnets.'" *ELH* 48:677–705. Rev. as "John Donne: The Despair of the 'Holy Sonnets.'" In *The Persecutory Imagination: English Puritanism and the Literature of Religious Despair,* 254–291. Oxford: Clarendon Press, 1991.

Stampfer, Judah. 1970. *John Donne and the Metaphysical Gesture.* New York: Funk & Wagnalls.

Stanwood, P. G. 1992. *The Sempiternal Season: Studies in Seventeenth-Century Devotional Writing.* New York: Peter Lang.

———. 1994. "Liturgy, Worship, and the Sons of Light." In *New Perspectives on the Seventeenth-Century English Religious Lyric,* ed. John R. Roberts, 105–23. Columbia: University of Missouri Press.

——— and Heather Ross Asals, eds. 1986. *John Donne and the Theology of Language.* Columbia: University of Missouri Press.

Stauffer, Donald A. 1946. *The Nature of Poetry.* New York: W. W. Norton.

Stark, John O. 1979. *Almanac of British and American Literature.* Littleton, CO: Libraries Unlimited.

Steele, Thomas J., S.J. 1971. "Donne's Holy Sonnets, XIV." *Expl* 29.9:item 74.

Stein, Arnold. 1942. "Donne and the Couplet." *PMLA* 57:676–96.

———. 1944. "Donne's Prosody." *PMLA* 59:373–97.

———. 1962. *John Donne's Lyrics: The Eloquence of Action.* Minneapolis: University of Minnesota Press.

———. 1986. *The House of Death: Messages from the English Renaissance.* Baltimore and London: Johns Hopkins University Press.

Stephens, John and Ruth Waterhouse. 1990. *Literature, Language and Change: From Chaucer to the Present.* London: Routledge.

Stephenson, A. A. 1959. "G. M. Hopkins and John Donne." *DownR* 77:300–20.

Stevenson, David L. 1954. "Among His Private Friends, John Donne?" *SCN* 12:7.

Stewart, Stanley. 1966. *The Enclosed Garden: The Tradition and the Image in Seventeenth-Century Poetry.* Madison, Milwaukee, London: University of Wisconsin Press.

Strier, Richard. 1989. "John Donne Awry and Squint: The 'Holy Sonnets,' 1608–1610." *MP* 86:357–84.

———. 1990. "Songs and Sonnets Go to Church: Teaching George Herbert." In *Approaches to Teaching the Metaphysical Poets,* ed. Sidney Gottlieb, 127–31. New York: The Modern Language Association of America.

———. 1994. "Lyric Poetry from Donne to Philips." In *The Columbia History of British Poetry,* ed. Carl Woodring and James Shapiro, 229–53. New York: Columbia University Press.

Stringer, Gary A. 1976. "Donne's Religious *Personae*: A Response." *SoQ* 14:191–94.

———. 1987. "When It's Done, It Will Be Donne: The Variorum Edition of the Poetry of John Donne." In *The Donne Dalhousie Discovery: Proceedings of a Symposium on the*

Acquisition and Study of the John Donne and Joseph Conrad Collections at Texas Tech University, ed. Ernest W. Sullivan, II and David J. Murrah, 57–62. Lubbock, TX: Friends of the University Library / Southwest Collection.

———. 2003. "Discovering Authorial Intention in the Manuscript Sequences of Donne's Holy Sonnets." In *Renaissance Papers 2002*, 127–44. Southeastern Renaissance Conference: Camden House.

Strzetelski, Jerzy. 1968. *The English Sonnet: Syntax and Style*. Krakow, Poland: Jagellonian University.

Stull, William L. 1975. "Elizabethan Precursors of Donne's 'Divine Meditations.'" *Comitatus* 6:29–44.

———. 1982a. "Sacred Sonnets in Three Styles." *SP* 79:78–99.

———. 1982b. "'Why Are not Sonnets Made of Thee?': A New Context for the 'Holy Sonnets' of Donne, Herbert, and Milton." *MP* 80:129–35.

———. 1984. "Sonnets Courtly and Christian." *University of Hartford Studies in Literature* 15.3/16.1:1–15.

Sullens, Zay Rusk. 1964. "Neologisms in Donne's English Poems." *Annali Instituto Universitario Orientale di Napoli, Sezione Germanica* 7:175–271.

Sullivan, Ceri. 1995. "Donne's Sifted Soul." *N&Q* 42.3:345–46.

Sullivan, Ernest W., II. 1993. *The Influence of John Donne: His Uncollected Seventeenth-Century Printed Verse*. Columbia and London: University of Missouri Press.

Summers, Claude J. 1987. "The Bride of the Apocalypse and the Quest for True Religions: Donne, Herbert, and Spenser." In *"Bright Shootes of Everlastingnesse": The Seventeenth-Century Religious Lyric*, ed. Claude J. Summers and Ted-Larry Pebworth, 72–95. Columbia: University of Missouri Press.

———. 1994. "Herrick, Vaughan, and the Poetry of Anglican Survivalism." In *New Perspectives on the Seventeenth-Century English Religious Lyric*, ed. John R. Roberts, 46–74. Columbia and London: University of Missouri Press.

Swardson, H. R. 1962. *Conflict between Christian and Classical Traditions in Seventeenth-Century Poetry*. Columbia: University of Missouri Press.

Symons, Arthur. 1899. "John Donne." *FR* n.s. 66:734–45. Rpt. in *Figures of Several Centuries*.

———. 1916. *Figures of Several Centuries*. London: Constable and Company.

Sypher, Wylie. 1955. *Four Stages of Renaissance Style: Transformations in Art and Literature, 1400–1700*. Garden City, NY: Doubleday.

Teague, Anthony. 1987. "Suffering, Trust and Hope in English Renaissance Literature." *The Renaissance Bulletin* 14:13–44.

Thomas, Gilbert. 1972. "John Donne." *The Aryan Path* 43:347–51.

Thomas, Helen S. 1976. "The Concept of the Persona in John Donne's Religious Poetry." *SoQ* 14:183–89.

Thomas, John A. 1976. "The Circle: Donne's Underlying Unity." In *"The Need Beyond Reason" and other Essays: College of Humanities Centennial Lectures 1975–76*, 14:89–103. Provo, UT: Brigham Young University Press.

Thompson, W. Meredith. 1935. *Der Tod in der englischen Lyrik des siebzehnten Jahrhunderts*. Breslau: Priebatsch.

Thorpe, James. 1987. *The Sense of Style: Reading English Prose*. Hamden, CT: Archon Books.

Thota, Anand Rao. 1982. *Emily Dickinson: The Metaphysical Tradition*. New Delhi: Arnold-Heinemann.

Threadgold, Terry. 1986. "Subjectivity, Ideology and the Feminine in John Donne's Poetry." In *Semiotics, Ideology, Language*, ed. Terry Threadgold, E. A. Grosz, Gunther

Kress, and M. A. K. Halliday, 297–325. Sydney Studies in Society and Culture, No. 3. Sydney: Sydney Association for Studies in Society and Culture.

Tillyard, E. M. W. 1956. *The Metaphysicals and Milton.* London: Chatto & Windus.

Todd, Richard. 1991. "Carew's 'Crown of Bayes': Epideixis and the Performative Rendering of Donne's Poetic Voice." *JDJ* 10:111–27.

Tomkinson, Cyril. 1931. "A Note on the Personal Religion of Dr. Donne." *Bo* 79:345–46.

Tomlinson, T. B. 1990. "Donne's Poetry and Belief in 17th-Century England." *CR* 30:25–39.

Trench, Richard Chenevix, ed. 1868. *A Household Book of English Poetry.* London: Macmillan.

Tromly, Frederic B. 1983. "Milton Responds to Donne: 'On Time' and 'Death Be Not Proud.'" *MP* 80:390–93.

Trost, Wilhelm. 1904. *Beiträge zur Kentniss des Stils von John Donne in seinen "Poetical Works."* Marburg: R. Friedrich's Universitätsbuchdruckerei.

Tsur, Reuven. 1974. "Poem, Prayer and Meditation: An Exercise in Literary Semantics." *Style* 8:405–24.

Turnell, Martin. 1938. *Poetry and Crisis.* London: Sands, The Paladin Press.

———. 1950. "John Donne and the Quest for Unity." *Nineteenth Century and After* 147:262–74. A rev. section appears in *Commonweal* 57 (1952):15–18.

Tuve, Rosemond. 1947. *Elizabethan and Metaphysical Poetry: Renaissance Poetic and Twentieth-Century Critics.* Chicago: University of Chicago Press.

Umbach, Herbert H. 1951. *The Prayers of John Donne.* New York: Bookman Associates.

———. 1954. "When a Poet Prays." *Cresset* 17:15–23.

Unger, Leonard and William O'Connor. 1953. *Poems for Study.* New York: Rinehart.

Untermeyer, Louis. 1938. *Play in Poetry: The Henry Ward Beecher Lectures Delivered at Amherst College, October, 1937.* New York: Harcourt Brace.

Upham, Alfred Horatio. 1908. *The French Influence in English Literature: From the Accession of Elizabeth to the Restoration.* New York: Columbia University Press.

Urnov, Mikhail D. 1988. "Shakespeare's Epoch and the 'School' of John Donne: The Transition from One Epoch to the Other." *Neohelicon* 15.1:51–55.

V. M. 1923. *Love Poems of John Donne with some account of his life taken from the writings in 1639 of Izaac Walton.* Soho: Nonesuch Press.

Van Emden, Joan. 1986. *The Metaphysical Poets.* Houndmills, Basingstoke, Hampshire, London: Macmillan Education Ltd.

Veith, Gene Edward, Jr. 1985. *Reformation Spirituality: The Religion of George Herbert.* Lewisburg: Bucknell University Press.

Vernon, John. 1979. "Donne's Holy Sonnet XIV." In *Poetry and the Body.* Urbana: University of Illinois Press.

Vicari, E. Patricia. 1989. *The View from Minerva's Tower: Learning and Imagination in* The Anatomy of Melancholy. Toronto: University of Toronto Press.

Wada, Tetsuzo. 1989. *An Essay on the Metaphysical Poets.* Tokyo: Chusekisha.

Wagner, G. A. 1947. "John Donne and the Spiritual Life." *PoetryR* 38:253–58.

Wagner, Linda Welshimer. 1965. "Donne's Secular and Religious Poetry." *Lock Haven Review* 7:13–22.

Walker, Julia M. 1988. "Left/Write/Right: Of Lock-Jaw and Literary Criticism." *JDJ* 7:133–139.

Wall, John N., Jr. 1976. "Donne's Wit of Redemption: The Drama of Prayer in the Holy Sonnets." *SP* 73:189–203.

———. 1988. *Transformations of the Word: Spenser, Herbert, Vaughan.* Athens: University of Georgia Press.

Walls, Peter. 1984. "'Music and Sweet Poetry'? Verse for English Lute Song and Continuo Song." *Music and Letters* 65 (July): 237–54.

Walter, James. 1975. "Donne's 'Holy Sonnet XVIII' and the Bride of Christ." *Innisfree* 2:4–7.

Walton, Izaak. 1640. "The Life and Death of Dr. Donne, Late Deane of St Pauls London." In *LXXX Sermons*, ed. John Donne (the younger), A5a–C1a. London: Printed for Richard Royston and Richard Marriot. The "Life" was reissued, with some changes, in 1658, 1670, and 1675.

———. 1670. "The Life of Mr. George Herbert." In *The Lives of Dr. John Donne, Sir Henry Wotton, Mr. Richard Hooker, Mr. George Herbert*. London: Printed by Tho. Newcomb for Richard Marriott.

Wanning, Andrews, ed. 1962. *Donne*. The Laurel Poetry Series, ed. Richard Wilbur. New York: Dell.

Wanninger, Mary Tenney. 1969. "Donne's Holy Sonnets XIV." *Expl* 28.4:item 37.

Ward, Adolphus William, ed. 1869. *The Poetical Works of Alexander Pope*. London: Macmillan.

Ward, Elizabeth. 1949. "Holy Sonnet X." *English "A" Analyst* 12:1–2.

Warnke, Frank J. 1961. *European Metaphysical Poetry*. Elizabethan Club 2. New Haven: Yale University Press.

———, ed. 1967. *John Donne: Poetry and Prose*. New York: Modern Library.

———. 1972. *Versions of Baroque: European Literature in the Seventeenth Century*. New Haven and London: Yale University Press.

———. 1987. *John Donne*. Boston: G.K. Hall.

Waswo, Richard. 1972. *The Fatal Mirror: Themes and Techniques in the Poetry of Fulke Greville*. Charlottesville: University Press of Virginia.

Watson, Robert N. 1994. *The Rest is Silence: Death as Annihilation in the English Renaissance*. Berkeley: University of California Press.

Wedgwood, C. V. 1950. *Seventeenth-Century English Literature*. 2nd ed. 1970. Oxford University Paperbacks Series, gen. eds. D. R. Newth and Anthony Quinton. London, Oxford, New York: Oxford University Press.

Wellek, René. 1986. *English Criticism, 1900–1950. A History of Modern Criticism. 1750–1950*. Vol. 5. New Haven and London: Yale University Press.

Wells, Henry W. 1940. *New Poets From Old: A Study in Literary Genetics*. New York: Columbia University Press.

Wennerstorm, Mary H. 1978. "Sonnets and Sound: Benjamin Britten's Setting of Shakespeare, Donne, and Keats." *Yearbook of Comparative and General Literature* 27: 59–61.

Whitby, Charles. 1923. "The Genius of Donne." *PoetryR* 14:67–81.

White, Gertrude M. and Joan G. Rosen. 1972. *A Moment's Monument: The Development of the Sonnet*. New York: Charles Scribner's Sons.

White, Helen C. 1936. *The Metaphysical Poets: A Study in Religious Experience*. New York: Macmillan.

———. 1951. "John Donne and the Psychology of Spiritual Effort." In *The Seventeenth Century: Studies in the History of English Thought and Literature from Bacon to Pope. By Richard Foster Jones and Others Writing in his Honor*, 355–68. Stanford: Stanford University Press; London: Oxford University Press.

Wiggins, Elizabeth Lewis. 1945. "Logic in the Poetry of John Donne." *SP* 42:41–60.

Wilcox, Helen. 1995. "No More Wit than a Christian?" In *The Wit of Seventeenth-Century Poetry*, ed. Claude J. Summers and Ted-Larry Pebworth, 9–21. Columbia and London: University of Missouri Press.

Wild, Friedrich. 1935. "Zum Problem des Barocks in der englischen Dichtung." *Anglia* 59: 414–22.

Wiley, Margaret L. 1950. "John Donne and the Poetry of Scepticism." *Hibbert Journal* 48:163–72.

———. 1954. "The Poetry of Donne: Its Interest and Influence Today." *E&S* ns 7:78–104.

Willey, Basil, ed. 1954. "John Donne." In *Major British Writers*, I:357–99. Gen. ed. G. B. Harrison. New York: Harcourt, Brace and World.

Williamson, George. 1930. *The Donne Tradition: A Study in English Poetry from Donne to the Death of Cowley.* Cambridge: Harvard University Press.

———. 1931. "Donne and the Poetry of Today." In *A Garland for John Donne, 1631–1931*, ed. Theodore Spencer, 153–76. Cambridge: Harvard University Press; London: Humphrey Milford, Oxford University Press.

———. 1940. "Textual Difficulties in the Interpretation of Donne's Poetry." *MP* 38:37–72. Rpt. in *Seventeenth Century Contexts.*

———. 1960. *Seventeenth Century Contexts.* Chicago: University of Chicago Press; London: Faber and Faber. Rpt. 1969.

———. 1961. *The Proper Wit of Poetry.* Chicago: University of Chicago Press.

Willmott, Richard, ed. and intro. 1985. *Four Metaphysical Poets: An Anthology of Poetry by Donne, Herbert, Marvell, and Vaughan.* Cambridge: Cambridge University Press.

Willy, Margaret, ed. 1971. *The Metaphysical Poets.* Columbia, SC: University of South Carolina Press; London: Edward Arnold.

———. 1979. "John Donne." In *Great Writers of the English Language: Poets*, ed. James Vinson and D. L. Kirkpatrick, 308–12. New York: St. Martin's Press. Rpt. in *The Renaissance, Excluding Drama*, ed. James Vinson and D. L. Kirkpatrick, 69–72. Great Writers Student Library, Vol. 2. London: Macmillan, 1983.

Wilson, Edward M. 1958. "Spanish and English Religious Poetry of the Seventeenth Century." *Journal of Ecclesiastical History* 9:38–53.

Wiltenburg, Robert. 1992. "Donne's Dialogue of One: The Self and the Soul." In *Reconsidering the Renaissance: Papers from the Twenty-First Annual Conference (1987).* Binghamton, NY: Medieval & Renaissance Texts and Studies, 93:413–27.

Winny, James. 1970. *A Preface to Donne.* Preface Books, gen. ed. Maurice Hussey. London: Longmans.

Winters, Yvor. 1948. "The Poetry of Gerard Manley Hopkins." *Hudson Review* 1:449–76; 2:61–93.

———. 1967. *Forms of Discovery.* Chicago: Alan Swallow.

Wolfe, Ralph Haven and Edgar F. Daniels. 1967. "Rime and Idea in Donne's Holy Sonnet X." *ANQ* 5:116–17.

Wolny, Ryszard. 1991. "Image of Death in John Donne's Love and Religious Poetry." *Filologia Angielska* 5:179–89.

Woodhouse, A. S. P. 1965. *The Poet and His Faith: Religion and Poetry in England from Spenser to Eliot and Auden.* Chicago: University of Chicago Press.

Woolf, Virginia. 1932. *The Second Common Reader.* London: Leonard and Virginia Woolf at the Hogarth Press.

Wordsworth, Dorothy. 1799? In *Lyrical Ballads, and Other Poems, 1797–1800 by William Wordsworth*, ed. James Butler and Karen Green. Ithaca: Cornell University Press, 1992.

Wordsworth, William. 1833. Letter to Alexander Dyce. In *The Letters of William and Dorothy Wordsworth*, ed. Alan G. Hill. 2nd ed. 6 vols. Oxford: Clarendon Press.

Wyld, Henry Cecil. 1923. *Studies in English Rhymes from Surrey to Pope.* London: John Murray.

Yarrow, Ralph. 1981. "Admitting The Infinite: John Donne's Poem 'Batter My Heart.'" *Studies in Mystical Literature* 1:210–17.

Yearwood, Stephenie. 1982. "Donne's Holy Sonnets: The Theology of Conversion." *TSLL* 24:208–221.

Yen, Julie. 1995. "'What doth Physicke profit thee?': The Pharmakon of Praise in *Ignatius His Conclave* and the *Holy Sonnets*." In *John Donne's Religious Imagination: Essays in Honor of John T. Shawcross*, ed. Raymond-Jean Frontain and Frances M. Malpezzi, 214–30. Conway, AR: UCA Press.

Yepes Boscán, Guillermo. 1966. "Elevacíon metafísica y estructura teológica en Soneto Sacro XIV de John Donne." In *Poésia inglesa y testimonio cristiano*. Maracaibo, Venezuela: Universidad del Zulia.

Young, Bruce W. 1986. "Thomas Hobbes versus the Poets: Form, Expression, and Metaphor in Early Seventeenth-Century Poetry." *Encyclia* 63:151–62.

Young, R. V., Jr. 1984. "Christopher Dawson and the Baroque Culture: An Approach to Seventeenth-Century Religious Poetry." In *The Dynamic Character of Christian Culture: Essays on Dawsonian Themes*, ed. Peter J. Cataldo, 127–58. Lanham, MD, and London: University Press of America.

———. 1987. "Donne's Holy Sonnets and the Theology of Grace." In *"Bright Shootes of Ever-lastingnesse": The Seventeenth-Century Religious Lyric*, ed. Claude J. Summers and Ted-Larry Pebworth, 20–39. Columbia: University of Missouri Press.

———. 1994. "Donne, Herbert, and The Postmodern Muse" in *New Perspectives on the Seventeenth-Century English Religious Lyric*, ed. John R. Roberts, 168–87. Columbia and London: University of Missouri Press.

Zemplényi, Ferenc. 1986. "Orthodoxy and Irony. Donne's Holy Sonnet N. 7 (4): At the Round Earth's Imagin'd Corners, Blow . . . ." *Studies in English and American (Budapest)* 6:155–70.

Zimmerman, Donald E. 1960. "The Nature of Man: John Donne's *Songs and Holy Sonnets*." *Emporia State Research Studies* 8:4–33.

Zitner, S. P. 1979. "Rhetoric and Doctrine in Donne's Holy Sonnet IV." *Ren&R* 3:66–76.

Zunder, William. 1982. *The Poetry of John Donne: Literature and the Culture in the Elizabethan and Jacobean Period*. Sussex: The Harvester Press; Totowa, NJ: Barnes and Noble.

———. 1988. "The Poetry of John Donne: Literature, History and Ideology." In *Jacobean Poetry and Prose: Rhetoric, Representation and the Popular Imagination*, ed. Clive Bloom, 78–95. New York: St. Martin's Press.

———. 1991. "Batter my Heart (Holy Sonnet 14)." In *Reference Guide to English Literature*, ed. D. L. Kirkpatrick, 1483–84. Vol. 3. St. James Reference Guides. Chicago and London: St. James Press.

INDEX OF AUTHORS
CITED IN THE COMMENTARY

486, 488, 495, 497, 506, 508, 521, 523, 538–
39, 541, 547–49, 553–54
Borkowska, Ewa, 175, 290
Bottrall, Margaret, 341
Bradford, Gamaliel, (1892) 405
Bredvold, Louis I., 134, 458–59
Briggs, Julia, 308, 535
Brink, Andrew, 150, 319, 349, 481, 500, 543,
550
Broadbent, J[ohn] B., (1964) 180, 440, (1974)
264, 408–09, 472, 477, 479–80
Brooke, Tucker, 147, 294, 306, 388
Brooks, Cleanth, 272–73
Brooks, Cleanth and Robert Penn Warren, 302,
371, 373–74
Brooks, Helen B., 219
Brower, Reuben Arthur, 394–95, 399, 409, 411–
13, 464, 479
Buckley, Vincent, 120, 148, 221, 285–86, 294,
395
Burgon, Geoffrey, 404
Burke, Victoria, 456, 473–78
Bush, Douglas, (1945) 134, 188, 230, 334, 388,
460, 533, (1965) 294

Cain, T. G. S., 141, 381, 386, 407, 411, 508,
540, 548, 553
Caine, T. Hall, 157, 168, 294
Cameron, Sharon, 358
Campbell, Gordon, 274, 313, 316–17, 521–23
Carey, John, (1981) 127, 130, 151, 153, 164,
224, 269, 296, 314, 321, 331, 339, 343, 351–
52, 369, 377, 391–92, 396, 435–36, 448, 454,
463, 495, 498, 521, 527, 531–32, 540,
(1990a) 275, (1990b) 131, 136, 144, 318,
329, 345–46, 386–87, 365, 407, 409, 412,
427, 430, 446–47, 486, 488, 495, 497, 507–
08, 553
Carleton, Frances Bridges, 333, 341
Carlson, Norme E., 522
Carpenter, Peter, 217, 297
Cathcart, Dwight, 125–26, 223, 258, 513–14
Cattermole, Richard, 116
Cayward, Margaret, 268–69
Chadwick, John White, 168, 403
Chambers (1896) 297
Chambers, E. K., 133, 297
Chanoff, David, (1980) 163–64, (1981) 457
Chatman, Seymour, 372
Chatterjie, Visvanath, 194
Ching, Marvin K., 275
Choi, Ye-Jung, 520
Clark, Ira, 336, 347, 383, 544
Clements, A. L., (1961) 224, 236, 243, 245,
260, 263, (1990) 198, 235–36
Coakley, Sarah, 241–42

Coanda, Richard, 190, 202, 204, 231, 254–55,
273, 307, 340, 358, 376, 378, 403, 506
Coffin, Charles Monroe, (1937) 334, 343, 344,
406, 425, (1952) 434
Coffin, Robert P. Tristram and Alexander M.
Witherspoon, 342, 346–47, 365, 407, 411
Cohen, J. M., 120, 205, 221, 276, 440, 461, 526
Coiro, Ann Baynes, 225
Colie, Rosalie, 214–15
Collmer, Robert G., 421
Conrad, Peter, 335, 394, 420
Cornelius, David K., 243, 245–46
Cox, R. G., (1956a) 137, 147, 180, 395, 400,
(1956b) 147, 180, 262, 362–63
Coyle, Martin, 154–55, 229, 501
Craik, T. W. and R. J. Craik, 263, 268, 272,
275, 287–88, 291, 314–18, 328–29, 342, 344,
346–47, 362–64, 379–81, 407, 411–13, 426–
29, 446, 448–49, 451–52, 468, 472–76, 478–
79, 485–88, 506–07, 521–23, 536, 538–40
Crawshaw, Eluned, 289
Crennan, M. J., 342, 344, 401, 403, 407, 109–
10, 413, 471–72
Creswell, Catherine, 175–76, 254, 260–61,
267–68, 534
Cruttwell, Patrick, (1954) 204, 318, 419, 461,
481, 485, 520–21, 539, (1966) 160–61, 208,
227, 517, 519

Daiches, David, 119
Daiches, David and William Charvat, 230, 254,
300, 306
Daley, Koos, (1990b) 207, 214–15, (1992) 457,
466
Dalglish, Jack, 237, 313, 410
D'Amico, Jack, 256, 518–19
Daniells, Roy, 394, 406
Daniels, Earl, 302–03, 312–18
Daniels, Edgar F., 427–28
Dasgupta, Debbir Bikram, 299, 305, 307
Davies, Stevie, 145, 155, 186, 218, 241, 358,
437, 505, 535–36, 538
De La Mare, Walter, 353
Delany, Paul, 347
Demaray, John G., 180–81, 190
Den Boer, M. G. L., 127, 207, 307, 360, 404,
456, 464
Dennis, John, 324
Denonain, Jean-Jacques, 160, 189, 201, 244,
282, 304, 325, 337, 355
De Quincey, Thomas, 293
Deshler, Charles D., 117, 292
De Silva, D. M., 462–63
Dickinson, Leon T., 295, 314, 317
Dickson, Donald R., 336, 338–39, 346
Di Nola, Gerardo, 217, 318, 360, 499, 508

Girri, Alberto, 120, 134

González, José Manuel and Fernández de Sevilla, 297

Gorbunov, A. N., (1990) 198, 215, (1993) 132, 136, 145, 166–67, 185, 436, 470, 514

Gosse, Edmund, (1893) 133, 157, 431, (1894) 157, (1899) 117, 133–35, 137, 141, 157–58, 221, 306, 348, 376, 405, 430, 456, 472, 481, 522, 525

Graham, Desmond, 237, 247

Granqvist, Raoul, (1975) 126, 181, 295, 349

Gransden, K. W., 118–19, 136–37, 147, 187, 189, 268, 275–77, 286, 298, 330–31, 343, 348, 351, 360–61, 379, 388, 393, 406, 416–17, 425, 445, 448, 461, 479, 485–86, 489, 521, 530–31, 539, (1969) 239–40

Grant, Patrick, (1971) 191–92, 500, (1973) 139, 546, (1974) 125, 319, 504, (1979) 193, (1983) 498, 501, (1985) 182

Gray, J. C., 270

Gregory, Michael, 232–33, 237, 240, 249, 262

Grenander, M. E., (1955) 545–47, (1960) 434, 439–40, 446, 490

Grey, Mary, 241–42

Grierson, Herbert J. C., (1909) 134, 294, 297, 456, 472, (1912) 118, 133–34, 136–38, 141–42, 152, 168, 178–79, 190, 294, 297, 310, 312, 332, 347, 377, 379, 383, 387, 405, 411, 424, 426–27, 445–46, 450, 456–58, 460–61, 469, 474, 486–87, 493, 496, 536–37, 541, 547, (1921) 134, 361–62, 424, 429, 458, 481, 485, (1929) 134–35, 146, 459, (1948) 351, 460

Groom, Bernard, 147, 475, 487

Grosart, Alexander Ballock, 126, 269, 288, 344, 376–77, 387, 411, 415, 489, 495–96, 508, 538, 540, 554

Grove, Robin, 351, 363

Guibbory, Achsah, (1980) 552, (1986) 196, 251–52, 259, 326, 338, 374, 534, 552, (1993) 241, 441, 511, 530

Guiney (1920) 495

Guiney, Louise I., 134, 495

"H.E.M," 293, 550

Haffenden, John, (1993) 339

Hagerdorn, Maria, 158

Hagspian, John V., 506

Hahn, Thomas, 504

Halewood, William H., 161, 222, 276, 279

Halle, Morris, 231

Hamburger, Maik, 224, 316, 318, 482, 486

Hamburger, Michael, 261, 292, 521

Hamer, Enid, 168, 201, 263, 312, 392–93, 497

Hamilton, George Rostrevor, 239

Handley, Graham, 240, 265, 275, 287, 289, 297, 312–13, 315–16, 328–32, 377, 379, 381, 407, 410, 412–13, 424, 426–27, 430, 445, 448–49, 452

Handscombe, Richard, 301, 318

Harding, D. W., 346, 486

Hardy, Evelyn, 158, 179, 187–88, 226–27, 269, 286, 330–31, 381, 414, 444

Harland, Paul W., 532

Harman, Barbara Leah, 352

Hart, Kingsley, 180

ul-Hasan, Masood, 262, 267, 269, 274–75, 304, 330, 345, 365, 385, 406, 421, 425, 445, 453, 478, 507, 537, 554

Hauser, Arnold, 170

Haydn, Hiram, 448–49

Hayward, John, (1929) 134–35, 411, (1950) 135

Hebaisha, Hoda, 123, 136, 139, 161, 192, 201, 206, 331

Heffernan, Thomas, 278–79, 283, 290

Heist, William W., 243, 247

Hemmerich, Gerd, 205, 358, 518

Henricksen , Bruce, 454

Herbold, Anthony, 148, 191, 276, 401, 498, 510

Herman, George, 243–44, 265, 267

Hester, M. Thomas, (1987) 321–23, (1991a) 132, 278, 417–18, 427, (1991b) 280–81, 285, 287, 289–91, (1992) 532, (1993) 404–05

Hieatt, A. Kent, 317, 344, 346–47, 407, 412, 473, 476, 479, 540, 547

Hillyer, Robert Silliman, 158, 294

Hirsch, David A. Hedrich, 199

Holdsworth, R. V., 318

Hollander, John and Frank Kermode, 136, 139–40, 161–62, 268, 270, 274, 287, 289, 313–14, 377–80, 412, 415, 432, 456

Holmes, Elizabeth, 340–41

Holmes, M. Morgan, 469

Höltgen, Karl Josef, 233, 255, 258

Honig, Edwin and Oscar Williams, 121, 134, 206

Hooper, A. G. and C. J. D. Harvey, 221, 231, 237, 244, 254–55, 264–65, 267

Hopkins, Kenneth, 180

Huebert, Ronald, 126

Hunt, Clay, 147, 170, 187, 262, 390, 395, 406, 409, 506, 536–37

Hunt, Leigh, 116–17, 293

Hunter, William B., 476

Hussey, Maurice, 393

Hutton, W. H., 134

Hyman, Lawrence W., 296

Jackson, Robert S., 227, 320, 453–54, 457, 465, 550

Jerome, Judson, 243, 247–48

Johnson, Jeffrey, 176
Jonas, Leah, 496
Jones, R. T., (1978) 295, 313, (1986) 313
Judson, Alexander Corbin, 134–35, 187, 365, 407

Kamholtz, Jonathan Z., 356
Kawada, Akira, 307, 309
Kawamura, Jōichirō, 463, 472, 477, 480
Kermode, Frank, (1957) 231, 264, 273, 278, 478, (1968) 344, 365, 385, 387, 453, 456, 538, (1974) 136, 140, 162, 230, 393, 431
Kerrigan, William, (1974) 181, 185, 215, 223, 232, 463–64, (1983) 234
King, Bruce, 127–28
King, John N., 128, 454
Kiparsky, Paul, 395–96, 493
Klause, John, (1983) 195, (1986) 374
Klause, John L., 409
Klawitter, George, 283–84
Klinck, Dennis R., 257, 263, 328, 355, 373, 385, 553
Knox, George, 243–44, 263, 270, 274
Kok, A. S., 116
Korninger, Siegfried, 543
Kortemme, Joseph, 187, 264, 271, 318, 320, 331, 361, 377–78, 475, 486, 488–89, 505, 521, 544
Kremen, Kathryn R., 192, 391, 413, 467
Kullmann, Thomas, 372, 375

Labriola, Albert C., (1990) 131, 291, 495, 508, 551, (1995) 242, 265, 274, 281–82, 291, 399, 414
Lang, Andrew, 176
Langley, T. R., 436–37, 447
Larson, Deborah Aldrich, 130, 436, 457
Lawler, Justus George, (1979) 249–50
Lawrence, Karen, 243, 251
Leech, Geoffrey, 231
Legouis, Pierre, 479
Leishman, J. B., (1934) 226, 298, 351, 390, 417, 467, 482, 516, 533, (1951) 134–35, 227, 261, 390, 434, 444, 460–61, 512, (1954) 135–37, 177, 189, 456, 460–61
Lemon, Lee T., 399–400
Levenson, J. C., (1953) 243–44, 262, (1954) 243–44, 266, 270–71, 279, 303, 376
Lever, J. W., 262, 268–69, 287–88, 292, 307, 312–13, 315–18, 328–30, 332, 342, 344–47, 361–65, 376–79, 381, 407, 410–14, 424–26, 429–30, 446, 448–49, 451, 473–80, 505–09, 520–24, 536, 538–40, 547–49
Levi, Peter, 389
Lewalski, Barbara Kiefer, (1973) 162, 381, (1979) 140, 164, 167, 193, 210, 227, 250, 282–83, 304–05, 325, 337, 355, 359, 373, 384, 387, 404, 422, 432, 438, 467, 478, 494, 498, 503, 517–18, 523, 533–34, 545–46, 552, (1987) 309–10
Lewalski, Barbara Kiefer and Andrew J. Sabol, 136, 140, 264, 329, 344–46, 386–87, 409, 411, 414, 429, 472–73, 479, 487–88, 494, 507–08, 541, 547, 553
Lewes, George Henry, 341
Lightfoot, Joseph Barber, 319
Linguanti, E., 320
Linsley, Joy L., 442, 449, 451
Linville, Susan, (1978) 380–81, (1984a) 279, 322, 383, 492, (1984b), 178, 238–39, 263, 282, 343, 378, 400, 421, 445, 476, 497, 515
Llasera, Margaret, 151
Lloyd, Charles E., 255–56
Lloyd-Evans, Barbara, 268, 271, 318, 410, 412
Loewenstein, David, 253, 266, 274, 374
Lofft, Capel, 348–49
Louthan, Doniphan, 179, 230–31, 237, 239, 254, 261–62, 341, 376–77, 439, 460, 465, 472–73, 479, 533, 537–38, 541
Low, Anthony, (1978) 163, 233, 295, 319–20, 369, 384, 422, 500, 529, 545, (1982) 356, (1993) 136, 145, 154, 185, 200, 202, 217, 226, 277, 324, 334, 384, 441–42, 466, 483, 511, 532
Low, Lisa and Anthony John Harding, 218
Lyon, T., 467

MacCarthy, Desmond, 226
MacDonald, George, 117, 168, 293, 348, 490
Mackenzie, Donald, 131, 277, 350, 550
Mahood, M. M., 135, 202, 368, 434, 449, 544
Main, David M., 117, 313–14, 317–18
Makurenkova, S., (1994) 205, 218
Mallett, Phillip, 195, 251, 265–66, 268–69, 271–72, 274–75, 283, 286–88, 292, 305, 313, 316–18, 326, 328–31, 373, 376–80, 402, 407, 410–14, 422, 425–26, 429, 438, 446–50, 452
Malpezzi, Frances M., (1987) 357, (1995) 132
Manlove, Colin N., (1978) 296, 314–15, 317, (1989) 310, (1992) 236, 398
Mann, Lindsay A., 182, 440, 466
Mano, D. Keith, 207, 240
Marandon, Sylvaine, 311–13, 317
Marotti, Arthur F., (1981) 127, 151, 173, 183, 234, 272, 275, 285, 298, 326, 330–31, 392, 424, 431–32, 455, 501, (1994a) 155–56, 175, 186, 200–01, 315, 411, 508, 522, (1994b) 156
Martin, Bernard, 145, 225, 236, 265–66, 269–70, 275
Martinet, Marie-Madeleine, (1982) 172, (1984) 209, (1987) 234–35

INDEX OF WRITERS AND HISTORICAL
FIGURES CITED IN THE COMMENTARY

Denis the Carthusian, 194
de Quevedo, Francisco, 327
de Ronsard, Pierre, 180, 207, 255–57, 307
Derrida, Jacques, 156
de Sales, Saint Francis, 158, 164, 171, 204
de Selve, Lazare, 207
de Vega, Lope, 204–05, 259
Dickinson, Emily, 205, 358–59
Digges, Thomas, 343
Donne, Anne, see More, Anne
Donne, Elizabeth, 455
Donne, Henry, 455
Drayton, Michael, 117, 157–58, 180, 256
Drummond, William, 116, 157, 207, 313, 354, 489
Drury, Sir Robert 527
Dryden, John, 406
Du Bartas, Guillaume de Salluste, 264
DuBellay, Joachim, 205, 207, 534
Dürer, Albrecht 361

Eckhart, Meister, 234
Elector Palatine (Frederick V), 456, 458, 474
Eliade, Mircea, 132
Eliot, T. S., 203, 211, 217, 255, 274, 290, 308, 360, 425, 485, 538
Elizabeth I, 164
Elsky, Martin, 210
Erasmus, Desiderius, 397

Favre, Antoine, 209
Ficino, Marsilio 242
Fletcher, John, 168
Fox, George, 524
Freake, John, 408
Freud, Sigmund, 152, 211, 462
Fussell, Paul 310

Galileo, 158, 334, 338, 341, 343–45, 391
Gascoigne, George, 354, 519
Goodyer, Sir Henry, 132, 359, 468, 512
Greco, El, 210, 214
Grévin, Jacques, 255
Greene, Robert, 117
Gryphius, Andreas, 358, 518

Hall, Joseph, 164
Harington, Sir John, 423
Harvey, Christopher, 255
Hay, James, 359
Heninger, S. K., Jr., 408
Henry VIII, 271–72
Herbert, George, 117, 123, 128, 130, 155, 158, 171, 184–85, 191, 195, 200–02, 204, 206, 207, 209, 211–17, 224, 233, 250, 252–55, 257–58, 260, 285, 301, 307–11, 328, 340, 381, 405, 437, 470–71, 484, 497, 520, 554

Herbert, Magdalen, 127, 133, 160, 217
Herbert, Rembert Bryce, 404
Hermogenes, 300, 502
Herrick, Robert, 132, 422
Hobbes, Thomas 239
Hooker, Richard, 163, 195, 338, 475
Hopkins, Gerard Manley, 160–61, 165, 177, 200, 202–04, 211–12, 217, 254–55, 262, 264–66, 269, 273, 279, 307, 313, 328, 331, 340, 347, 358, 360–63, 365–66, 372, 378, 403, 413, 428, 464, 470, 478, 484, 486–88, 497, 506, 538, 546, 548
Hugo, Hermannus, 255, 260
Husserl, Edmund, 193
Huygens, Constantijn, 207, 214–15

Ignatius of Loyola, Saint, 128, 137, 140, 147, 158–59, 163–64, 167, 203, 207, 233, 256, 284, 286, 307, 343, 359, 375, 397, 408, 420, 423, 484, 504, 519, 534–35, 543–44, 551

James I, 164, 275, 455, 508
Job, 134, 217
Johnson, Samuel 311
Johnson, Samuel, 116, 311
Jonson, Ben, 119, 168, 177–78, 306
Jung, Carl, 199

Keats, John, 403
Kempis, Thomas à, 498
Kepler, Johannes, 343, 391

Laud, William, 163
LeGallienne, Dorian, 205
Leigh, David, 437
Lok, Henry, 162, 207, 209, 354
Lucian, 424
Luther, Martin, 182, 191, 224, 367, 473, 476
Lydgate, John, 554

Marlowe, Christopher, 202, 218, 288, 377, 424
Marvell, Andrew, 206
Mary Magdalen, 160
Michaelangelo Buonarroti, 202, 206, 261, 331, 358
Milton, John, 157, 161, 176–77, 201–03, 207, 209, 229, 262, 299, 301, 308–09, 315, 376, 391, 395, 405, 411, 429, 442, 470, 496
Molza, Francesco Maria, 158
More, Anne, 120, 129, 133, 135, 137, 139, 141, 145–46, 168, 172, 181, 433–38, 440–52, 465
More, Thomas, 194, 287

Nashe, Thomas, 422–23

Oppenheimer, J. Robert, 241
Owen, Wilfred, 310–11

Parr, Elnathan, 355
Paul, Saint, 191
Pembroke, Countess of, 207
Perkins, William, 290
Persons, Robert, 423
Petrarch, Francesco, 125, 157, 165–66, 180,
   206, 219–20, 378, 444, 519
Pico della Mirandola, Giovanni, 139, 546
Plato, 156, 307, 432, 533
Plotinus, 243
Plutarch, 307
Ptolemy, 344
Puttenham, George, 178, 315
Pythagoras, 424

Quarles, Francis, 166, 258, 304, 307

Rabelais, François, 423
Raleigh, Sir Walter, 117, 293, 306, 308
Reni, Guido 275
Ricoeur, Paul, 374
Roberts, Donald Ramsay, 199

Sackville, Richard, third Earl of Dorset, 127,
   131, 136, 142–43, 297
Scève, Maurice, 206
Scupoli, Lorenzo, 159, 204, 353, 370
Shakespeare, William, 154–55, 157–58, 164–65,
   168, 177, 204, 208, 229, 234, 267, 288, 306,
   308, 317–18, 338, 340, 359, 364, 403–04,
   418–19, 423, 443, 519–20, 551
Sidney, Sir Philip, 162, 164–65, 171, 180, 207–
   09, 212, 423, 518, 528
Skelton, John, 167, 506
Socrates, 307
Southey, Robert, 126
Southwell, Robert, 158, 209, 424, 427, 519
Spenser, Edmund, 119, 158, 177, 180, 229, 440,
   470, 519, 539
Stanley, Ferdinando, fifth Earl of Derby, 144
Stanley, William, sixth Earl of Derby, 144
Surrey, Henry Howard, Earl of, 418, 551

Tansillo, Luigi, 158
Tate, Allen, 408
Tennyson, Alfred, Lord, 229, 254
Teresa, Saint, 182
Thomas, Dylan 310
Thompson, Francis, 187, 254
Tillich, Paul, 244, 273
Tintoretto, 208, 210, 536
Tippett, Michael, 213
Titian, 182
Tyndale, William, 429
van Huet, G. H. M., 404

Vaughan, Henry, 117, 155, 187, 206, 209, 340,
   468, 554
Very, Jones, 116–17
Virgil, 403
Vondel, Joost van den, 459
Vriesland, Victor E., 307, 404

Wesley, John, 205
Wiericx, Antoon, 255
Woodward, Roland, 142, 144, 463
Wordsworth, William, 218, 312
Wroth, Lady Mary, 258–59
Wyatt, Thomas, 164, 306

INDEX OF OTHER POEMS AND WORKS
OF DONNE CITED IN THE COMMENTARY

INDEX OF TITLES

(Since the numerical headings on individual Holy Sonnets vary from sequence to sequence, the entries below are alphabetized according to the short forms of reference listed on page xxi of this volume. Specific headings for poems presented in variant versions are listed under these main entries.)

INDEX OF FIRST LINES

(For ease of reference and alphabeticization, the spelling here has been lightly modernized. For poems presented in multiple versions, the line listed is that of the poem's first appearance, and the multiple page numbers refer to the poem's various appearances.)

About the Editors

Helen B. Brooks currently holds a joint term appointment as professor of English and professor in Interdisciplinary Studies in Humanities at Stanford University, where she teaches courses on John Donne, Shakespeare, and Renaissance/Early Modern intellectual and cultural history. She also serves as Associate Director of Interdisciplinary Studies in Humanities. She earned a joint Ph.D. in English and Humanities at Stanford University in 1980. She has published on Donne, Shakespeare, and John Davies of Hereford and on seventeenth-century religious poetry and the *Spiritual Exercises* of St. Ignatius of Loyola.

Robert T. Fallon is an emeritus professor of English at LaSalle University. He has published three books on John Milton and has served as president of the Milton Society of America. Since retirement he has edited *The Christian Soldier* and *Tracts of the English Civil War* and has published four books on Shakespeare—three in the *Theatergoer's Guide to Shakespeare* series and *How to Enjoy Shakespeare*. He has served on the executive board of the John Donne Society and is a Contributing Editor to the Songs and Sonets volume of the *Donne Variorum*.

Dennis Flynn is professor of English at Bentley College, where he teaches freshman writing, Horace, Thomas More, and Shakespeare. He is author of *John Donne and the Ancient Catholic Nobility* and has published several essays on Donne. He is a member of the *Donne Variorum* advisory board, the editorial board of the *John Donne Journal*, and the editorial board of *English Literary Renaissance*.

Paul A. Parrish is Regents Professor and Head of the Department of English at Texas A&M University, where he teaches courses on Renaissance and seventeenth-century literature. He is the author of *Richard Crashaw* and the editor of *Celebration: Introduction to Literature*, and has published articles on Donne, Crashaw, George Gascoigne, Milton, Ralph Ellison, and other Renaissance and modern writers. Parrish is a former executive director and president of the South Central Modern Language Association; a former president of Phi Beta Delta, the Honor Society for International Scholars; and a past president of the John Donne Society.

Ted-Larry Pebworth is William E. Stirton Professor in the Humanities and professor emeritus of English at the University of Michigan-Dearborn. He is author of *Owen Felltham*; co-author of *Ben Jonson*; and co-editor of *The Poems of Owen Felltham* and *Selected Poems of Ben Jonson* and of collections of essays on Herbert, on Jonson and the Sons of Ben, on Donne, on the seventeenth-century religious lyric, on poetry and politics in the seventeenth century, on Marvell, on Renaissance discourses of desire, and on representing women in the Renaissance. He is a past president of the John Donne Society.

Theodore J. Sherman is professor of English at Middle Tennessee State University, where he teaches courses in Old English and *Beowulf*, seventeenth-century literature, and fantasy literature. He is editor of *Mythlore: A Journal of J. R. R. Tolkien, C. S. Lewis, Charles Williams, and Mythopoeic Literature*. He is currently working on a facsimile edition of the Westmoreland manuscript of the poetry and prose of John Donne.

P. G. Stanwood, who is professor emeritus of English at the University of British Columbia, has published widely on Renaissance and later English literature. Among his editions are the posthumous books of Richard Hooker's *Of the Lawes of Ecclesiastical Polity*, John Cosin's *A Collection of Private Devotions*, Jeremy Taylor's *Holy Living* and *Holy Dying* (2 vols.), and (as co-editor) *John Donne and the Theology of Language* and *Selected Prose of Christina Rossetti*. He is the author of a book-length study of Izaak Walton and also of *The Sempiternal Season: Studies in Seventeenth-Century Devotional Literature*. He is a past president of the John Donne Society and of the International Association of University Professors of English, and a recipient of the honorary degree of Doctor of Sacred Letters from the University of Trinity College, Toronto.

Gary A. Stringer is visiting professor of English at Texas A&M University. Editor of volumes 4–9 of *Explorations in Renaissance Culture*, he has published essays on Donne, Milton, Dryden, and others, and has edited *New Essays on Donne* and co-edited a special issue of the *South Central Review* on John Donne. He is a member of the editorial board of the *John Donne Journal* and a former chair of the Committee on Scholarly Editions of the Modern Language Association. He is also a past president of the South Central Modern Language Association and of the John Donne Society.

Ernest W. Sullivan, II, is Edward S. Diggs Professor of English at Virginia Tech. He is editor of *Biathanatos by John Donne*; of *The First and Second Dalhousie Manuscripts: Poems and Prose by John Donne and Others*; and of *The Harmony of the Muses*, as well as co-editor of *Puzzles in Paper*. He is author of *The Influence of John Donne: His Uncollected Seventeenth-Century Printed Verse*. Sullivan is also the general textual editor of the Collected Works of Abraham Cowley. He is a past president of the John Donne Society.

DESIGNER: Sharon L. Sklar
TYPESETTER: J. Syd Conner
PRINTER AND BINDER: Thomson-Shore
TYPEFACE: Goudy Old Style